AMERICAN LITERATURE

VOLUME 2

Edited by

William E. Cain
Wellesley College

Alice McDermott
Johns Hopkins University

Lance Newman
Westminster College, Salt Lake City

Hilary E. Wyss
Auburn University

PEARSON

Boston Columbus Indianapolis New York San Francisco Upper Saddle River
Amsterdam Cape Town Dubai London Madrid Milan Munich Paris Montréal Toronto
Delhi Mexico City São Paulo Sydney Hong Kong Seoul Singapore Taipei Tokyo

Vice President and Editor in Chief: Joseph Terry
Senior Development Editor: Anne Brunell Ehrenworth
Executive Marketing Manager: Joyce Nilsen
Production Manager: Savoula Amanatidis
Project Coordination, Text Design, and Electronic Page Makeup: PreMediaGlobal
Cover Design Manager: Wendy Ann Fredericks
Cover Art: © Shutterstock
Photo Research: Integra
Senior Manufacturing Buyer: Dennis J. Para
Printer and Binder: R. R. Donnelley and Sons Company–Crawfordsville
Cover Printer: Lehigh-Phoenix Color Corporation–Hagerstown

For permission to use copyrighted material, grateful acknowledgment is made to the copyright holders on p. 1430, which are hereby made part of this copyright page.

Library of Congress Cataloging-in-Publication Data
American literature / edited by William E. Cain, Wellesley College; Lance Newman, Westminster College; Hilary E. Wyss, Auburn University; Alice McDermott, John Hopkins University. — Second edition.
  volumes cm.
  Includes index.
  ISBN-13: 978-0-13-405332-5 (V. 1)
  ISBN-10: 0-13-405332-X (V. 1)
  ISBN-13: 978-0-13-405336-3 (V. 2)
  ISBN-10: 0-13-405336-2 (V. 2)
1. American literature. 2. United States—Literary collections. I. Cain, William E., 1952–
PS507.A5753 2013
810.8—dc23

2013005725

10 9 8 7 6 5 4 3 2—DOC—17 16 15

Student Edition
ISBN-10: 0-13-405336-2
ISBN-13: 978-0-13-405336-3

Instructor's Review Copy
ISBN-10: 0-321-94485-2
ISBN-13: 978-0-321-94485-6

CONTENTS

CONTEXT AND RESPONSE: The Poetry of Lisel Mueller   588

CONTEXT AND RESPONSE: Pío Baroja, From *The Chasm*   670

GALLERY: American Writers and the Great Depression   730

GALLERY: Postmodernism   1147

PART FOUR: American Poetry Since 1945   1177

The new edition of *American Literature* presents an exciting opportunity for readers. In keeping with the first edition, we have created a text that provides a wide variety of selections. You will find many of the pieces you would expect to see in an American literature text, but we've also taken some leaps and included selections that are just as read-worthy, but perhaps not as well known. You will recognize most, perhaps all, of the authors of these selections, and once you read these works, you'll understand why they have been chosen for inclusion here.

New to This Edition

The second edition of this volume has been completely revised, with:

- Several new primary texts, including:

  - Selections from Ambrose Bierce's *The Devil's Dictionary*
  - Kate Chopin's "Désirée Baby"
  - Stephen Crane's "An Experiment in Misery" and "War Is Kind"
  - "Davis Matlock," which now complements Edgar Lee Masters's "Lucinda Matlock"
  - T. S. Eliot's "Gerontion" and "The Hollow Men"
  - John Cheever's "The Sorrows of Gin"
  - Grace Paley's "The Loudest Voice"
  - Raymond Carver's "Cathedral"

- Fourteen additional authors and poets and their works, including:

  - William James's "What Pragmatism Means"
  - Sui Sin Far's "Leaves from the Mental Portfolio of an Eurasian"
  - James Weldon Johnson's "Lift Every Voice and Sing" and "O Black and Unknown Bards"
  - Alan Tate's "Ode to the Confederate Dead"
  - Jhumpa Lahiri's "Hell-Heaven"
  - Frank Bidart's "Self-Portrait"
  - Billy Collins's "Sonnet" and his tribute to 9/11, "The Names"
  - Dave Smith's "Tide Pools"
  - Kay Ryan's "A Certain Kind of Eden" and "Home to Roost"
  - C. D. Wright's "Tours" and "Personals"
  - Jorie Graham's "Sea-Blue Aubade"
  - Andrew Hudgins's "Death and Doom"
  - Mark Doty's "Golden Retrievals" and "At the Gym"
  - Edward P. Jones, "Blindsided"

- Two new key features:
  - **Context and Response:** Brief excerpts from related literary texts and historical documents have been added after selected primary texts. These materials allow students to engage in historically informed close reading. Specific topics include:
    - an excerpt from *Artemus Ward (His Travels) Among the Mormons,* in which Ward—who had a lasting influence on Mark Twain—details his often-comedic travels aboard a steamship heading West
    - a sampling of poems by Dorothy Parker, who shared a penchant for sharp-tongued and satirical writing with Ambrose Bierce
    - a passage from *Interesting Narrative of the Life of Olaudah Equiano; or, Gustavus Vassa, the African, Written by Himself*, the first slave narrative to capture the world's attention, contrasts with Booker T. Washington's narrative
    - a collection of poetry of Lisel Mueller, who was strongly influenced by Edna St. Vincent Millay's work
    - a selection entitled "The Chasm," from Pío Baroja, a master of understatement whose work was avidly read by Ernest Hemingway
    - an excerpt from *Member of the Wedding*, a novel by Carson McCullers, whose career as a writer was encouraged by her friend, Tennessee Williams
    - an excerpt from *Herzog* by Saul Bellow, predecessor to Philip Roth, who also considered life through the lens of the middle-class Jewish protagonist
  - Four thematic **Galleries,** clusters of excerpts from documents that illustrate key trends in American social and literary history:
    - The South Since Reconstruction
    - American Writers and the Great Depression
    - Post-Modernism
    - American Sings the Blues: A Collection of Songs and Poems
- A rich selection of **images**—including daguerrotypes and photographs—are keyed to individual texts and provide a visual frame of reference for readers.

In addition to providing readers with a wealth of new material, the second edition of *American Literature* has been completely redesigned with the student in mind:

- A larger trim size and a more open design allow for ease of reading.
- A two-color format better displays key information, contributing to a more effective reading experience.
- Marginal space on every page provides a convenient place for readers to annotate the selections by jotting down questions, ideas, and thoughts about the works they encounter.

Taken together, these changes transform Volume Two of *American Literature* into a rich resource for the kind of historicist interpretation that has become the primary feature of twenty-first-century literary studies.

A Note about Annotating

Annotating literary texts helps us to read deeply and learn actively. Instead of blindly accepting a text as great literature or authoritative truth, deep question-asking readers enter into dialogue with the author. They seek to understand and push back against the author's claims about reality, ask probing questions, look for evidence, and finally decide why they like or dislike a piece of writing and why they agree or disagree with the way that it represents the world.

We invite you to become deep readers of the following texts. You might want to survey a text briefly before beginning to read it, taking note of its title, section headings, and chapter titles. Next you can make basic observations about the genre and the broad topic of the text that you are preparing to read. Note the date and place that the text was published and consider the historical context. Next, read the text slowly and carefully, stopping frequently to think critically and respond.

As a deep reader you will want to write notes in the margin of every page. Mark important words and phrases with a highlighter, a line in the margin, stars, circles, or other symbols. Highlight key ideas and central concepts. Mark transitions between major sections and other structural and organizational features.

In addition to highlighting key features of the text, we invite you to record your own evaluations and responses, using plusses and minuses, exclamation points, smiley faces, or whatever other symbols best help you express your thoughts. Along with writing summaries of key passages, you can sketch interpretive and evaluative comments, and write down questions. Make sure to indicate unclear passages with question marks.

Eventually, every deep reader develops an individualized system for annotating texts. Regardless of the details of your particular system, the discipline of deep reading will improve your comprehension and your recall of the texts you read; it will help you to find key passages during discussion, study, and writing; it will help you to recall the unfiltered thoughts and feelings that you had during your first encounters with texts; it will sharpen your awareness of important textual patterns and features; and it will enable you to develop your own interpretations and evaluations of literary texts.

These suggestions will enrich and deepen your understanding and enjoyment of literature, resulting in greater pleasure in your experience of a wide variety of authors and their works. You will see both an improvement in your performance on tests, essays, and other measures of your learning, and an intensifying of your own emotional and intellectual engagement with, and investment in, the literary history of the United States.

The example that follows shows how one student marked up a page from the text using many of the "deep reader" strategies described above. We invite you to use these strategies, or even to adapt your own, as you encounter each new selection in your course.

Letter to Luis de Santangel[1]
Regarding the First Voyage

SIR:

As I know that you will be pleased at the great victory with which Our Lord has crowned my voyage, I write this to you, from which you will learn how in thirty-three days, I passed from the Canary Islands to the Indies with the fleet which the most illustrious king and queen, our sovereigns, gave to me. And there I found very many islands filled with people innumerable, and of them all I have taken possession for their Highnesses, by proclamation made and with the royal standard unfurled, and no opposition was offered to me.

To the first island which I found I gave the name "San Salvador," in remembrance of the Divine Majesty, Who had marvellously bestowed all this; the Indians call it "Guanahani." To the second, I gave the name "Isla de Santa Maria de Concepcion," to the third, "Fernandina," to the fourth, "Isabella," to the fifth, "Isla Juana," and so to each one I gave a new name.

When I reached Juana, I followed its coast to the westward, and I found it to be so extensive that I thought that it must be the mainland, the province of Cathay.[2] And since there were neither towns nor villages on the seashore, but small hamlets only, with the people of which I could not have speech, because they all fled immediately, I went forward on the same course, thinking that I could not fail to find great cities and towns. And, at the end of many leagues, seeing that there was no change and that the coast was bearing me northwards, which I wished to avoid, since winter was already beginning and I proposed to make from it to the south, and as moreover the wind was carrying me forward, I determined not to wait for a change in the weather and retraced my path as far as a certain harbour known to me. From that point, I sent two men inland to learn if there were a king or great cities. They travelled three days' journey, finding an infinity of small hamlets and people without number, but nothing of importance. For this reason, they returned

I understood sufficiently from other Indians, whom I had already taken, that this land was nothing but an island, and therefore I followed its coast eastwards for one hundred and seven leagues to the point where it ended. And from that cape, I saw another island, distant eighteen leagues from the former, to the east, to which I at once gave the name "Espaniola." And I went there and followed its northern coast, as I had in the case of Juana, to the eastward for one hundred and eighty-eight great leagues in a straight line. This island and all the others are very fertile to a limitless degree, and this island is extremely so. In it there are many harbours on the coast of the

[1]Santangel was the minister of finance for the Spanish Crown.
[2]A province of China.

Acknowledgments

We wish to thank those instructors who provided invaluable feedback to us on both content and design, including Susanna Ashton, Clemson University; Charles Bane, University of Central Arkansas; Tamara Brattoli, Joliet Junior College; Joshua Dickinson, SUNY Jefferson; Florence Dore, University of North Carolina at Chapel Hill; Peter Dorman, Central Virginia Community College; Heidi M. Hanrahan, Shepherd University; Rachel Key, Grayson College; Isiah Lavender III, University of Central Arkansas; Michael LeMahieu, Clemson University; Andrea Lerner, California State University-Chico; Linda Wagner-Martin, University of North Carolina at Chapel Hill; Matthew Newcomb, SUNY New Paltz; William Rossi, University of Oregon; James Sodon, St. Louis Community College-Florissant Valley; Scott Suter, Bridgewater College; Andrew Tomko, Bergen Community College; and Audrey Wick, Blinn College.

We also remain grateful to the reviewers of the first edition, including Mark Baggett, Samford University; Laura Behling, Gustavus Adolphus College; Derek Bowe, Oakwood University; Vivian Brown, Morehouse College; Mark Canada, University of North Carolina at Pembroke; Melvin Clark, South Texas College; Thomas Cooley, The Ohio State University; Jonathan S. Cullick, Northern Kentucky University; David Curtis, Belmont University; Dr. Bill Dynes, University of Indianapolis; David H. Evans, Dalhousie University; Betty Hart, University of Southern Illinois; Sylvia Henneberg, Morehead State University; Dr. David Lavery, Middle Tennessee State University; Paul Lehman, University of Central Oklahoma; Mary Magoulick, Georgia College and State University; Quentin Miller, Suffolk University; Kevin Morris, Greenville Technical College; Julie Nash, University of Massachusetts at Lowell; Anne G. Myles, University of Northern Iowa; Paul Petrie, Southern Connecticut State University; Teresa Purvis, Lansing Community College; James A. Sappenfield, University of Milwaukee; John Scott, Bluegrass Community and Technical College; Allison Singley, Gettysburg College; Debbie Stallings, Hinds Community College; and Teresa Trevathan, South Plains College.

Bill Cain thanks Lance Newman, Hilary Wyss, and Alice McDermott for their excellent work, and Paula Bonilla for her invaluable assistance. He also thanks his friend and expert coauthor on many books, Sylvan Barnet. In addition, Joe Terry and, especially, Anne Brunell Ehrenworth deserve thanks for their good advice and support of this project. The production team at Pearson, especially Savoula Amanatidis, has been dedicated and professional throughout the process. Professor Cain also would like to express his gratitude to his colleagues and friends at Wellesley College. Above all, he is grateful for the love and support he has received from his wife Barbara and his daughters Julia and Isabel.

Alice McDermott thanks Bill Cain for his initial invitation and for his infinite patience. She is grateful to her students, past and present, "for our ongoing exchange of the stories we love."

Lance Newman thanks Willow Sellin and Freya Newman for their patience, William Cain and Hilary Wyss for their collaborative spirit, Joe Terry and Anne Brunell Ehrenworth for their dedication to this project, Joel Pace (University of Wisconsin–Eau Claire) for contributing to the gallery of texts related to slavery and abolition, and many colleagues for formative discussions about the literature of the United States, including especially Roderick

Coover (Temple University), William Keach (Brown University), Chris Koenig-Woodyard (University of Toronto), Mark Wallace (CSU San Marcos), and Laura Dassow Walls (Notre Dame University). The following students at Westminster College provided important feedback on the contents of this volume: Tavish Bell, Paul Christian, Stacy Cottrell, Chera Fernelius, Shannon Flynn, Taylor Hoffman, Barbara Lindley, Cyndi Lloyd, Jameson Madsen, Mattie Matheson, Zach Moon, Valerie Moore, Sheena Nyann, Joanna Pham, Mikayla Williamson, and Jackie Wilson.

Hilary E. Wyss thanks James Truman and Anna and Cameron Truman-Wyss for their support. Special thanks to Kirsten Iden (Auburn University) for contributing entries on Sarah Kemble Knight and Eliza Lucas Pinckney. The entire team at Pearson has been wonderful, with special thanks to Anne Brunell Ehrenworth and Sneha Pant. Finally, thanks to Bill Cain and Lance Newman for inviting me onto this project and for their unwavering enthusiasm throughout the entire process.

American Literature at the End of the Nineteenth Century

Literary Realism in America

Realism and literary realism are essential terms for literary study and, especially, for the study of American literature from the mid-nineteenth century to the present. But our understanding of the meaning and significance of these terms in American literary history can be deepened if we first consider their interesting, and revealing, origin.

According to *The Oxford American Dictionary of Current English* (1999), "realism" means:

1. The practice of regarding things in their true nature and dealing with them as they are.
2. Fidelity to nature in representation; the showing of life, etc., as it is in fact.

There is more to the word's meaning and history than this. If you consult Noah Webster's first edition of *An American Dictionary of the English Language* (1828), the major dictionary of the pre–Civil War period, you will not find an entry for "realism." Real, realist, and reality are included, but not realism. *Real* derives from the Latin word *res*, which means "thing." Webster's *American Dictionary* defines *real* as "actually being or existing, not fictitious or imaginary; true, genuine, not artificial; relating to things, not to persons, not personal." A realist is a scholastic philosopher "who maintains that things and not words, are the object of dialectics" (i.e., the branch of logic that teaches the rules and modes of reasoning).

Eighty-five years later, *Webster's Revised Unabridged Dictionary* (1913) lists these definitions but adds:

Art & Literature: Fidelity to nature or to real life; representation without idealization, and making no appeal to the imagination; adherence to the actual fact. The practice of assessing facts and the probabilities of the consequences of actions in an objective manner; avoidance of unrealistic or impractical beliefs or efforts. Contrasted to idealism, self-deception, over-imaginativeness, or visionariness.

The *Oxford English Dictionary* (1884–1928, OED), which scrutinizes the history of words, helps to explain the transition in meanings from the first *Webster's* to the later one. The OED includes *realism*, noting a number of specialized meanings that arose during the early to mid-nineteenth century in philosophy and legal theory. Here is another of the OED's definitions:

Close resemblance to what is real; fidelity of representation, rendering the precise details of the real thing or scene.

   In reference to art and literature, sometimes used as a term of commendation, when precision and vividness of detail are regarded as a merit, and sometimes unfavorably contrasted with idealized description or representation. It has often been used with the implication that the details are of an unpleasant or sordid character.

The first author mentioned is the English critic and writer John Ruskin, in 1856, and later authors cited include the statesman William Ewart Gladstone and the poet A. C. Swinburne. "Realism" thus originated in the middle of the nineteenth century, and writers and political figures made use of it. As George Watson observes in *The Story of the Novel* (1979), the word *realism* in English, as in the discourse of Ruskin, Gladstone, and Swinburne, drew as well from the French *réalisme*, a literary term from the 1820s that signified "a down-to-earth, even brutal, account of modern reality, claiming to fidelity."

A student early in the twentieth century seeking an explanation of literary realism would find this in the 1911 edition of the *Encyclopedia Britannica*: "In literature and art 'realism' is opposed to 'idealism' in various senses. The realist is (1) he who deliberately declines to select his subjects from the beautiful or harmonious, and, more especially, describes ugly things and brings out details of an unsavory sort; (2) he who deals with individuals, not types; (3) most properly, he who strives to represent the facts exactly as they are." By this time, "realism" was also a common category in literary anthologies and histories, as when Carl Van Doren, literary editor of *The Nation* magazine and an associate professor at Columbia University, discussed William Dean Howells in a chapter of *The Cambridge History of American Literature* (1917): "Holding so firmly to his religion of reality, and with his varied powers, it is not perhaps to be wondered at that Howells produced in his fourscore books the most considerable transcript of American life yet made by one man."

My stress on the origins of the word *realism* is a little misleading, since the idea or concept, if not the word itself, has been a part of literary and artistic theory and practice for many centuries. Scholars have noted the realism of classical Greek and Roman sculpture, the realism of Dutch and Spanish painting, the realism of such nineteenth-century artists as Gustave Courbet, Winslow Homer, and Thomas Eakins, and, in literature, the realism of Petronius, Boccaccio, Chaucer, Shakespeare, the seventeenth-century poets John Donne and Ben Jonson, the eighteenth-century satirists Jonathan Swift and Alexander Pope, and the novelists Daniel Defoe (*Robinson Crusoe*, 1719) and Henry Fielding (*Tom Jones*, 1749).

In a broad sense, realism in literature and art implies careful, close, attentive observation, truthful and detailed description, not idealization. What the writer presents must be credible and convincing. As Henry James stated in his essay "The Art of Fiction" (1884), "the air of reality (solidity of specification) seems to me to be the supreme virtue of a novel—the merit on which all its other merits...helplessly and submissively depend. If it be not there they are all as nothing, and if these be there, they owe their effect to the success with which the author has produced the illusion of life."

Realism also suggests taking account of persons, places, and things that prior artists and writers have neglected—those of the middle and lower classes, workers, women and minorities, and the ordinary circumstances of such people's lives. The French writers Jules and Edmond Goncourt, authors of *Germinie Lacerteux* (1864), a depiction of a poor, middle-aged maid, made a version of this claim explicitly:

> Living in the 19th century, in a time of universal suffrage, democracy, liberalism, we asked ourselves whether what one calls "the lower classes" have no right to the Novel; whether this society, below society, the common people, had to remain under the weight of literary interdict and of the scorn of writers.

The realist's rendering of character must be honest and accurate, not falsifying or sentimentalizing, as the English critic and editor G. H. Lewes stressed in "Realism and Art" (1859); realism is

> the basis of all Art, and its antithesis is not Idealism, but *Falsism*. When our painters represent peasants with regular features and irreproachable linen...and children utter long speeches of religious and poetic enthusiasm...an attempt is made to idealize, but the result is simply falsification and bad art.

Realism amounts both to a true (as Lewes contends) and to a new way of seeing. It means seeing what others have not. The modern French author and filmmaker Jean Cocteau perhaps had this in mind when he remarked: "True realism consists in revealing the surprising things which habits keep covered and prevent us from seeing" (1928). Realism, then, is *seeing* and something more, of *adding* to what is seen. It is not enough simply to give accurate descriptions. In an essay on Balzac (1886), Howells said: "When realism becomes false to itself, when it heaps up facts merely, and maps life instead of picturing it, realism will perish too. Every true realist instinctively knows this, and it is perhaps the reason why he is careful of every fact, and feels himself bound to express or to indicate its meaning at the risk of over-moralizing." Realism hence implies interpretation and moral instruction, an effort to explain the meanings of the observations that the writer has recorded and presented.

It is therefore incorrect to equate realism with common sense, with the perception of bare facts. Common sense is just that—"common." It may conceal reality rather than represent it. In *A Week on the Concord and Merrimack Rivers* (1849), Henry David Thoreau touched on this: "A true account of the actual is the rarest poetry, for common sense always takes a hasty and superficial view." Relying on common sense sounds good, but, Thoreau says, it can mean not seeing at all, and not really thinking, either. Common sense is what we agree upon, what we take for granted as obvious. It can prevent us from perceiving what is *really* true because it confirms our habitual beliefs and assumptions. Thoreau suggests that realism, if it is serious, is demanding, challenging work. There is a lot that a literary realist must resist: he or she writes against prevailing views and values, in opposition to the kind of stories and characters that readers expect to find presented and reinforced in books.

Variation Among Realist Writers

The thrust of realism in literature, in Howells's writings in particular, is that the writer should teach moral lessons that will benefit readers in the conduct of their lives. In "False and Truthful Fiction" (1887), Howells warned against the damage that bad novels caused, full of "idle lies about human nature and the social fabric." He believed that he could detect the difference between good and bad literature, damaging and morally fortifying fiction: "The tests are very plain and simple, and they are perfectly infallible. If a novel flatters the passions, and exalts them above the principles, it is poisonous; it may not kill, but it will certainly injure."

The scholar Everett Carter, in *Howells and the Age of Realism* (1954), has called attention, however, to the tension in the literary principles that Howells and his realist contemporaries advocated: "The morality of the realists, then, was built upon what appears a paradox—morality with an abhorrence of moralizing." Howells did not want to preach or lecture, but he did want to offer moral guidance, using as his vehicle the realistic novel rather than the "romance," a term that connoted for him the fantastic, the incredible, the faraway and exotic. Sentimental, over-passionate, ornate literary works were, in Howells's estimation, all too likely to mislead the naïve reader, encouraging him or, especially, her (he thought women readers were especially gullible) to believe in relationships, events, and experiences that were not typical—that were not true. Howells and the other realists were propelled by the belief that, as Richard H. Brodhead (1988) has argued, "literary reading is the chief gauge and sustainer of a culture, and so debased writing must be driven out by superior work to preserve civilization from collapse."

How would "civilization," through literary realism, be preserved? Here again Everett Carter is informative:

> Howells always claimed for his works a deep moral purpose.... It was based upon three propositions: that life, social life as lived in the world Howells knew, was valuable, and was permeated with morality; that its continued health depended upon the use of human reason to overcome the anarchic selfishness of human passions; that an objective portrayal of human life by art will illustrate the superior value of social, civilized man, of human reason over animal passion and primitive ignorance.

Realism, for Howells, thus refers to the effort to give an accurate, morally informed, and enlightening depiction of life. Largely through Howells's labors, the movement in the United States took flight during the 1870s and reached its height in the 1890s and early 1900s. As it developed nationally, its proponents learned much from French writers such as Honoré de Balzac (e.g., *Lost Illusions*, 1837–43) and Gustave Flaubert (*Madame Bovary*, 1857), and from Russian masters such as Ivan Turgenev (*Fathers and Sons*, 1862) and Leo Tolstoy (*War and Peace*, 1865–69, and *Anna Karenina*, 1875–77). Among British authors, George Eliot, in *Adam Bede* (1859), *The Mill on the Floss* (1860), and *Middlemarch: A Study of Provincial Life* (1871–72), was a significant influence. American authors admired her technical prowess, rich feeling for historical detail, and depth of knowledge.

In an illuminating passage in *Adam Bede*, Eliot explained the nature of the realism she favored:

> It is for this rare, precious quality of truthfulness that I delight in many Dutch paintings, which lofty-minded people despise. I find a source of delicious sympathy in these faithful pictures of a monotonous homely existence, which has been the fate of so many more among my fellow-mortals than a life of pomp or of absolute indigence, of tragic suffering or of world-stirring actions.

Realism in America also benefited from the scientific study of social life that Charles Darwin (*The Origin of Species*, 1859) and the French philosopher Auguste Comte, author of many books and essays on social evolution, had fostered. Literary critics and historians have also pointed to the ever-widening impact of newspapers and journalism as forms of documentation, which encouraged vivid observation and commentary; Mark Twain, Ambrose Bierce, Theodore Dreiser, Stephen Crane, and Ernest Hemingway are just a few of the American authors who began as newspaper reporters. The new art form of photography, in its unsparing accuracy (as in the photographs of the dead on the Civil War battlefield of Gettysburg), impelled writers, too, to aspire to a greater honesty and directness.

Realism, it is said, takes issue with "romanticism," and perhaps it does, if romanticism is taken to mean escapism, fantasy, and the otherworldly. But realism has a kinship to romanticism, as the British poet William Wordsworth's "Preface to *Lyrical Ballads*" (1800) indicates: "The principal object, then, proposed in these Poems was to choose incidents and situations from common life, and to relate or describe them, throughout, as far as was possible in a selection of language really used by men." A related point can be made in reply to those who say that American literary realism is a reaction against American romanticism, and against the transcendentalism that Ralph Waldo Emerson and his circle in Concord, Boston, and Cambridge articulated. Emerson celebrated inspiration, intuition, and the higher "spiritual" laws, but his work shows a concrete detail and keen clarity of observation from which a literary realist could draw invigorating lessons. In "The Poet" (1844), for example, Emerson declared: "We have yet had no genius in America, with tyrannous eye, which knew the value of our incomparable materials.... America is a poem in our eyes; its ample geography dazzles the imagination, and it will not wait long for metres." In his preface to the first edition of *Leaves of Grass* (1855), Whitman, influenced by Emerson, presented a parallel argument when he urged American poets "to enter the essences of the real things and past and present events."

Howells offers this cogent definition: "Realism is nothing more and nothing less than the truthful treatment of material." This is valuable up to a point, but its limits become clear when we remember that both Henry James and Mark Twain are frequently included among the ranks of American realists. Howells was a friend to, and supporter of, both of them, in his correspondence and in his role as editor of *The Atlantic Monthly* (1866–81) and *Harper's* (1886–92), prestigious magazines that offered literary and cultural commentary and that regularly published novels in monthly installments. Like Howells, Twain and James profited from literary and cultural institutions that published and supported them. But Twain and James were hostile to each other's work and perceived realism in the novel in very different ways. "The truthful treatment of material" is a goal that Howells, Twain, and James shared, yet their conception of how to achieve it was markedly different, as readers' experiences of their novels amply attest.

For Howells, realism involved setting, situation, and typical or representative characters, as in *The Rise of Silas Lapham* (1885), dealing with a self-reliant businessman, a paint manufacturer, who strives through his newly made wealth to enter the exclusive circles of Boston society. For Twain, realism was a matter of voice and dialect (frequently of a humorous, even outrageous kind), as shown in *Adventures of Huckleberry Finn* (1884–85)— not the invented or artificial speech that appeared in sentimental romances, but, rather, the speech that Americans in various regions of the country actually used, the tones and idioms of their everyday lives. Realism, for James, was based on tracing the operations of the mind, complex and subtle turns and patterns of consciousness. In the work of his early and middle phases, particularly in *The Portrait of a Lady* (1881) and *The Bostonians* (1886), James renders scene and setting in sharp, evocative detail, but the essence of his realism lies in the characters' thoughts and feelings. James is a psychological realist, whose precursor is Nathaniel Hawthorne, the creator of *The Scarlet Letter* (1850), with its tormented adulterer Hester Prynne, the agonized minister Arthur Dimmesdale, and the bitterly vengeful Roger Chillingworth.

Later American writers maintained that literary realism had not gone far enough, criticizing Howells in particular for the inadequacies of his views and values. Frank Norris and Theodore Dreiser, and Stephen Crane and Jack London, objected that Howells was too narrow, too timid and restricted, in his notion of realism and had failed to penetrate to the core truths about life: the huge capacity of environment to overmaster human choice-making—the French author Émile Zola, in "The Experimental Novel" (1880), asserted that "determinism governs everything"; the role played by accident and chance; and the irresistible fact and force of sexual desire. Crane's *Maggie: A Girl of the Streets* (1893), Norris's *McTeague* (1899), Dreiser's *Sister Carrie* (1900), and London's *The Sea-Wolf* (1904) are usually cited as examples of literary "naturalism," but one could identify them as heightened forms of realism—bolder, more provocative and unrelentingly candid explorations of a reality that, these writers judged, Howells and others faithful to his principles had been unable or unwilling to confront.

Comparative claims and assessments like these arise often in discussions of literary realism: who is *more* realistic, Howells or Dreiser? Twain or James? Which mid-nineteenth-century novel is *more* realistic, *Moby-Dick* (1851) or *Uncle Tom's Cabin* (1852)? Scholars and critics of the past might have replied that the sentimental Stowe is surely less realistic than Melville, who describes whaling with such gusto and precision. But many now are less sure about this evaluation. What, after all, could be more real than Stowe's engagement with slavery, sexual exploitation, and racial violence? Readers by the millions in the 1850s were deeply moved by her book because her characters seemed so true to life to them. *Moby-Dick* is one of the masterpieces of American and world literature, but a crazed captain's remorseless pursuit of a white whale is not the most realistic premise for a book one could imagine.

Twain's African American character Jim in *Adventures of Huckleberry Finn* is another case in point. We could say that Jim is "unrealistic," a stereotype. But it could be replied that Jim is, nonetheless, *more* realistic than many African American characters common in the so called plantation fiction of the period, which extolled the pleasures of the lost days of slavery and the contentment of blacks living in the South. Twain challenges, even as he remains to an extent within, the literary conventions and social attitudes of his own day. His realism is not as complete as twenty-first-century readers would wish, yet it needs to be understood in relation to the period when he wrote.

Realism and American History

As the African American novelist and critic Ralph Ellison, author of *Invisible Man* (1952), has observed:

> Writing at a time when the blackfaced minstrel was still popular, and shortly after a war which left even the abolitionists weary of those problems associated with the Negro, Twain fitted Jim into the outlines of the minstrel tradition, and it is from behind this stereotype mask that we see Jim's dignity and human capacity—and Twain's complexity—emerge.

Realism is an evolving, dynamic term: a character or story admired for its realism decades ago might strike us as insufficiently realistic, as not realistic enough. This is a judgment, or, rather, part of a critical conversation, that occurs in the study of literature. But even as we are involved in *that*, we need also to return the literary work to its historical context in order to analyze and assess the advance, in its own day, that such a story or character represented.

The scholar Lilian R. Furst has made a related comment in her survey of literary realism in American women authors:

> The realists' emphasis on everyday life led to a far greater prominence for women both as writers and as central characters in fiction. In the portrayal of everyday life, domestic themes such as marriage, money, family and social relationships, and tensions and conflicts within a local community play a vital part, fostering the new importance of women characters. Instead of ending with marriage and "they lived happily ever after," as had been the romantic tradition, realist novels opened with marriage, and examined its strains and stresses, which were particularly acute for women.

Furst points out the connection between literary realism and social change and reform, and she reminds us of the sweep and span of American history within which literary realism as a movement developed. The concept and content of "realism" alters over time: a woman writer, for example, through her own novel writing may be presenting a critique of the limitations and inadequacies of the realism of authors of an earlier era, or of authors of her own era who were leaving too much out, who were not as capaciously realist as they could be.

The rise of literary realism, and its evolution into literary naturalism, coincided with an extraordinary phase of American history. In American literature and art, as the cultural historian David Lubin has noted, realism

> stretched from the Civil War to World War I and includes Reconstruction and its demise, race riots, the rise of the Ku Klux Klan, the birth of the New Negro movement, Indian wars, the Spanish-American War, a bloody counterinsurgency operation in the newly acquired Philippines, financial panics and depressions, labor revolts,

anarchist bombings, a march of the unemployed on Washington, feminist activism and suffrage campaigns, civil service reform, the spread of corporate monopoly and the concomitant swelling of citizens' groups opposed to it, and the tidal wave of immigration that forever altered the face of America.

American literature provides us with historical insight, with cultural and social knowledge, about these historical events and controversies. Karl Marx, speaking about English literature of roughly the same time period, stated more than once that anyone seeking to understand the real conditions of life in nineteenth-century England should look not to formal histories and economic treatises, but, rather, to the novels of Charles Dickens and Elizabeth Gaskell. The same holds true for the United States. Rebecca Harding Davis's "Life in the Iron Mills" (1861), Howells's *A Hazard of New Fortunes* (1890), Charlotte Perkins Gilman's "The Yellow Wall-Paper" (1892), Twain's *Pudd'nhead Wilson* (1894), Dreiser's *Sister Carrie* (1900), Upton Sinclair's *The Jungle* (1906), John Steinbeck's *The Grapes of Wrath* (1939), and Richard Wright's *Native Son* (1940): these novels and stories describe and dramatize the realities of American life, revealing and exploring the history of the times. That is why these books and others frequently appear on the reading lists of American history courses.

In its relationship to history, realism is a *critical* literary practice. As Dreiser professed in an essay published in 1903 titled "True Art Speaks Plainly," those who dismiss direct portrayals of life as it is are seeking to evade "the disturbing and destroying of their own little theories concerning life, which in some cases may be nothing more than a quiet acceptance of things as they are without any regard to the well-being of the future." Realism is a reformer's literature, inspiring change in "things as they are."

On one level, we value literary works that speak to us as immediately, as vitally, as they did for readers at the time of first publication. These works manage to reflect and transcend their historical contexts: they feel (as we like to say) as if they could have been written yesterday. Yet there are novels, stories, plays, and poems that remain essential reading, whatever their limitations, because they teach us so much about societies and cultures of the past. Through the turn-of-the-century African American authors Frances Ellen Watkins Harper's *Iola Leroy* (1892) and Pauline E. Hopkins's *Contending Forces* (1900), for instance, readers today can enter into the complications of racial and sexual identity as the twentieth century began. They can gain an understanding of the prospects for and barriers to social and political progress that African Americans faced.

It is tempting to propose that realism is best summarized in the advice to writers that Hemingway gave: "Write about what you know." American authors of the mid- to late nineteenth century, and into the twentieth, centered on the customs and traditions, and the speech and manners, of the people and the regions they knew best. They were part of a movement or tendency in American literature, yet they were also highly individual in their styles and strategies as they worked to express their specific understanding of American reality. "American literature must be faithful to American conditions," declared the novelist Hamlin Garland in the opening paragraph of "Productive Conditions of American Literature" (1894): "Granting the variations in the personal comment of each artist, the output must be in its general character creative, not imitative. It should rise out of our conditions as naturally as the corn grows. It must be distinctly and unmistakably American." There were many forms that such an American orientation could take, many regions, with their diverse cultures and customs, for realists to investigate and transform into literary art.

Garland portrayed Midwestern farm life in *Main-Travelled Roads* (1891 and later editions); Sarah Orne Jewett examined rural communities in Maine in *Deephaven* (1877) and *The Country of the Pointed Firs* (1896); Kate Chopin depicted Louisiana locales in *Bayou Folk* (1894), *A Night in Acadie* (1897), and *The Awakening* (1899); Charles Waddell Chesnutt delved into Southern race relations, racism, and miscegenation in *The House Behind the Cedars* (1900) and *The Marrow of Tradition* (1901); Edith Wharton treated upper-class society in New York City in *The House of Mirth* (1905) and *The Custom of the Country* (1913) and the stark landscapes of western New England in *Ethan Frome* (1911) and *Summer* (1917); and Willa Cather capitalized upon her Nebraska experiences and memories for the characters and plots of *O Pioneers!* (1913), *The Song of the Lark* (1915), and *My Antonia* (1918).

The greatest regional realist of the twentieth century, whose career began a decade later than Cather's, is William Faulkner, who devised his fictional county of "Yoknapatawpha" from towns in Mississippi, evoking it in *Sartoris* (1929), *The Sound and the Fury* (1929), *Light in August* (1932), *Absalom, Absalom!* (1936), and other novels and many short stories.

It is true that by the time we get to Faulkner, who uses language and manipulates point of view and chronology so complicatedly, we have moved very far from the realism of William Dean Howells. But there is a way to regard both Howells and Faulkner as realists, however at odds their vision of the novel might initially seem, and however extravagantly different our responses to their books doubtless are. Howells is not as difficult as Faulkner, but he is hardly transparent, either. Literary realism designates a movement in American literature, but it is also the term for an effect that through his or her language a writer seeks to create. The English playwright, critic, and wit Oscar Wilde remarked in *The Decay of Lying* (1899): "All bad art comes from returning to life and nature, and elevating them into ideals." This sounds like a deft critique of realism, and perhaps Wilde intended it to be. Yet it is also a reminder that neither life nor nature can be described directly. Whatever is real about them, whatever makes them real, we can only articulate through language, through art and artifice. Realism is as much about literary form, the writer's uses of language, as it is about content, the choices of subjects and settings.

This is the final twist to the story of literary realism. A *really* realistic artist or writer is one who does something to what he or she sees, probing beneath the surface. As Emerson says in *The Conduct of Life* (1860), "Let us replace sentimentalism by realism, and dare to uncover those simple and terrible laws, which, be they seen or unseen, pervade and govern." Here, nearly a century later, is the poet Wallace Stevens ("Three Academic Pieces," no. 1, 1947): "What our eyes behold may well be the text of life but one's meditations on the text and the disclosures of these meditations are no less a part of the structure of reality." Pablo Picasso (1950) gives this statement about his artistic aims: "Reality is more than the thing itself.... Reality lies in how you see things.... A painter who copies a tree blinds himself to the real tree. I see things otherwise." From this perspective, the artist is the ultimate realist because he or she *makes* reality in acts of transformative, visionary craft.

As you turn to Twain and Howells, and the others included in this volume, you will consider more deeply the nature of "realism" in literature. What does it mean for a writer, an American or any writer, to be "realistic"? What is the relationship between realism and imagination? Is there one form, or many forms, that literary realism can adopt? Perhaps reality is a lot or a little in the eye of the beholder, and even if it is not, it seems to come alive for us as readers only through the special verbal representations that each writer provides for it. Or maybe reality—the realist's quest—is something stubbornly *there* after all; as the American science-fiction writer Philip K. Dick put it, "reality is that which, when you stop believing in it, doesn't go away."

Bibliographical note: Everett Carter, *Howells and the Age of Realism* (1954); Harold H. Kolb, *The Illusion of Life: American Realism as a Literary Form* (1969); *American Literary Naturalism: A Reassessment*, eds. Yoshinobu Hakutani and Lewis Fried (1975); Warner Berthoff, *The Ferment of Realism: American Literature, 1884–1919* (1965; rev. 1981); Alfred Habegger, *Gender, Fantasy, and Realism in American Literature* (1982); *American Realism: New Essays*, ed. Eric J. Sundquist (1982); June Howard, *Form and History in American Literary Naturalism* (1985); Amy Kaplan, *The Social Construction of American Realism* (1988); Lee Clark Mitchell, *Determined Fictions: American Literary Naturalism* (1989); *Realism and Representation: Essays on the Problem of Realism in Relation to Science, Literature, and Culture*, ed. George Levine (1993); and Michael Davitt Bell, *The Problem of American Realism: Studies in the Cultural History of a Literary Idea* (1993).

See also Kenneth W. Warren, *Black and White Strangers: Race and American Literary Realism* (1993); *American Realism and the Canon*, eds. Tom Quirk and Gary Scharnhorst (1994); *The Cambridge Companion to American Realism and Naturalism: Howells to London*, ed. Donald Pizer (1995); David Shi, *Facing Facts: Realism in American Thought and Culture, 1850–1920* (1995); and Stanley Corkin, *Realism and the Birth of the Modern United States: Cinema, Literature, and Culture* (1996). For primary sources and backgrounds: *Documents of Modern Literary Realism*, ed. George Becker (1963); and *Documents of American Realism and Naturalism*, ed. Donald Pizer (1998).

Also helpful are Cathy Boeckmann, *A Question of Character: Scientific Racism and the Genres of American Fiction, 1892–1912* (2000); Sally L. Kitch, *Higher Ground: From Utopianism to Realism in American Feminist Thought and Theory* (2000); Phillip Barrish, *American Literary Realism, Critical Theory, and Intellectual Prestige, 1880–1995* (2001); Barbara Hochman, *Getting at the Author: Reimagining Books and Reading in the Age of American Realism* (2001); Eric Carl Link, *The Vast and Terrible Drama: American Literary Naturalism in the Late Nineteenth Century* (2004); Henry B. Wonham, *Playing the Races: Ethnic Caricature and American Literary Realism* (2004); Rob Davidson, *The Master and the Dean*: *The Literary Criticism of Henry James and William Dean Howells* (2005); Gene Andrew Jarrett, *Deans and Truants: Race and Realism in African American Literature* (2007); and Jane F. Thrailkill, *Affecting Fictions: Mind, Body, and Emotion in American Literary Realism* (2007).

Recent studies include Stuart Burrows, *A Familiar Strangeness: American Fiction and the Language of Photography, 1839–1945* (2008); Daniel A. Novak, *Realism, Photography, and Nineteenth-Century Fiction* (2008); Nancy Bentley, *Frantic Panoramas: American Literature and Mass Culture, 1870–1920* (2009); Jean Carol Griffith, *The Color of Democracy in Women's Regional Writing* (2009); and Gregory S. Jackson, *The Word and Its Witness: The Spiritualization of American Realism* (2009).

SAMUEL L. CLEMENS (MARK TWAIN) ■ (1835–1910)

Mark Twain, whom his fellow novelist William Dean Howells described as "the Lincoln of our literature," claimed that as a writer he had the common touch, reaching a wide range of readers. "My books are water," he said. "Those of the great geniuses are wine. Everybody drinks water."

Mark Twain (this pseudonym is a river term that means "two fathoms deep"—that is, safe water) was born Samuel Langhorne Clemens in Florida, Missouri, and raised in Hannibal, Missouri, a town in the northeast part of the state, on the Mississippi River. His schooling ended at age twelve, the year his father died, and he then worked as a printer's apprentice, a writer for newspapers, and a printer in both the East and Middle West. In the late 1850s, Twain became a riverboat apprentice, receiving his own license a year or so later. He briefly served in the Confederate Army and then settled in Nevada, working for a paper there.

Twain headed to San Francisco in 1864, taking a job as a reporter and gaining national notice in 1865 for his story "The Notorious Jumping Frog of Calaveras County," published in *The Saturday Press* (New York) and reprinted below. In 1867, Twain published his first book, *The Celebrated Jumping Frog of Calaveras County, and Other Sketches*. His books of the next few years include *The Innocents Abroad* (1869), based on his travels to the Holy Land; *Roughing It* (1872), drawing on his Nevada and frontier experiences; and *The Gilded Age* (coauthored with Charles Dudley Warner, 1873), a grand satire of political corruption and economic chicanery. He also launched a successful career as a lecturer and tale-teller.

Twain wrote a number of important books in the final decades of his career, in particular *A Connecticut Yankee in King Arthur's Court* (1889) and *Pudd'nhead Wilson* (1894). But his three most noteworthy and influential books appeared in midcareer: *Tom Sawyer* (1876), *Life on the Mississippi* (1883; published in a shorter form in 1875), and *Adventures of Huckleberry Finn* (1884). For many years, Twain was characterized as a writer of boys' books like these, or as a humorist, one whose use of dialect and scandalous satire landed him in trouble with librarians and censors. But while he is a brilliant satirist and humorist who offers many rewards for boys (and girls), he is also a central figure in American literary history. His innovations in style and speech helped to make possible the achievements of Ernest Hemingway, William Faulkner, and Ralph Ellison, among many others.

Twain is a master of voices; and, as the critic Stanley Crouch has noted, he, more than anyone, "democratized" American literature, introducing into it an array of voices, dialects, rhythms, tones, and vocabularies that had not been there before. "All modern American literature," Hemingway said in 1935, "comes from one book by Mark Twain called *Huckleberry*

Finn.... All American writing comes from that. There was nothing before. There has been nothing as good since."

As *Adventures of Huckleberry Finn* shows, role-players, performers, actors, con artists, fakes, charlatans, and tricksters fascinated Twain—which suggests something about his view of American society and concept of human nature. He had a keen sense of pleasure and possibility, which the wide-open America of the pioneering days and after made richly possible, but also a deep, disturbed perception of human folly, cruelty, and exploitation, which over the years developed into a darkly misanthropic, despairing vision. What he witnessed in the nation (racism, lynching, thievery large and small), in the world (imperialist war, colonial brutality), and also close to home (the painful illnesses and deaths of his wife and two daughters) burned into him a terrible pessimism, an angrily reiterated assertion in his late writings that reality is a nightmarish delusion, that everything we think is real is meaningless.

There is darkness in the early and middle writings as well, but also much joy and exuberance, and great resourcefulness with and affection for the language, which is perhaps better termed, in Twain's case, "American" rather than English. The British writer Rudyard Kipling expressed this dimension of Twain well: "I love to think of the great and godlike Clemens. He is the biggest man you have on your side of the water by a damn sight, and don't you forget it. Cervantes [Spanish novelist Miguel de Cervantes, 1547–1616, author of *Don Quixote*, 1605–15] was a relation of his." The dramatist George Bernard Shaw made a related point, with an ironic touch that Twain would have appreciated: "Mark Twain and I are in very much the same position. We have to put things in such a way as to make people, who would otherwise hang us, believe that we are joking."

"The Notorious Jumping Frog of Calaveras County"—originally titled "Jim Smiley and His Jumping Frog"—is an early work based on a popular and well-known western tale (scholars have found other versions dating from the 1850s). On its publication, the Boston critic and essayist James Russell Lowell commended it as "the finest piece of humorous literature yet produced in America."

Twain's comic gifts are also displayed in his satiric essay on James Fenimore Cooper (1789–1851), an American author whose novels include five *Leather-Stocking Tales* about the frontiersman Natty Bumppo. Twain's critique is more than a little unfair and misleading, but this is a virtuoso performance, hilarious and devastating, as Twain pummels a popular author and, by implication, mocks readers who foolishly esteem this author's books.

For an introduction to Twain's life and times: Geoffrey C. Ward, *Mark Twain* (2001). Biography: Justin Kaplan, *Mr. Clemens and Mark Twain: A Biography* (1966); and Everett Emerson, *Mark Twain: A Literary Life* (2000). Critical studies include Kenneth S. Lynn, *Mark Twain and Southwestern*

Humor (1959); Henry Nash Smith, *Mark Twain: The Development of a Writer* (1962); and James M. Cox, *Mark Twain: The Fate of Humor* (1966). See also Tom Quirk, *Mark Twain: A Study of the Short Fiction* (1997); and Peter Messent, *The Short Works of Mark Twain: A Critical Study* (2001).

Good recent biographical and critical studies include: Fred Kaplan, *The Singular Mark Twain: A Biography* (2003); Larzer Ziff, *Mark Twain* (2004); Ron Powers, *Mark Twain: A Life* (2005); Michael Shelden, *Mark Twain, Man in White: The Grand Adventure of His Final Years* (2010); and Jerome Loving, *Mark Twain: The Adventures of Samuel L. Clemens* (2010). See also *Autobiography of Mark Twain*, volume 1, ed. Harriet Elinor Smith (2010).

The Notorious Jumping Frog of Calaveras[1] County

In compliance with the request of a friend of mine, who wrote me from the East, I called on good-natured, garrulous old Simon Wheeler, and inquired after my friend's friend, Leonidas W. Smiley, as requested to do, and I hereunto append the result. I have a lurking suspicion that *Leonidas W.* Smiley is a myth; that my friend never knew such a personage; and that he only conjectured that, if I asked old Wheeler about him, it would remind him of his infamous *Jim* Smiley, and he would go to work and bore me nearly to death with some infernal reminiscence of him as long and tedious as it should be useless to me. If that was the design, it certainly succeeded.

I found Simon Wheeler dozing comfortably by the barroom stove of the dilapidated tavern in the ancient mining camp of Angel's, and I noticed that he was fat and bald-headed, and had an expression of winning gentleness and simplicity upon his tranquil countenance. He roused up, and gave me good-day. I told him a friend of mine had commissioned me to make some inquiries about a cherished companion of his boyhood named *Leonidas W.* Smiley—*Rev. Leonidas W.* Smiley—a young minister of the Gospel, who he had heard was at one time a resident of Angel's Camp. I added that if Mr. Wheeler could tell me anything about this Rev. Leonidas W. Smiley, I would feel under many obligations to him.

Simon Wheeler backed me into a corner and blockaded me there with his chair, and then sat down and reeled off the monotonous narrative which follows this paragraph. He never smiled, he never frowned, he never changed his voice from the gentle-flowing key to which he tuned his initial sentence, he never betrayed the slightest suspicion of enthusiasm; but all through the interminable narrative there ran a vein of impressive earnestness and sincerity, which showed me plainly that, so far from his imagining that there was anything ridiculous or funny about his story, he

---

[1]Twain alerted readers that Calaveras is pronounced *Cal-e-vá-ras.*

regarded it as a really important matter, and admired its two heroes as men of transcendent genius in *finesse*. I let him go on in his own way, and never interrupted him once.

Rev. Leonidas W. H'm, Reverend Le—well, there was a feller here once by the name of *Jim* Smiley, in the winter of '49—or maybe it was the spring of '50—I don't recollect exactly, somehow, though what makes me think it was one or the other is because I remember the big flume wasn't finished when he first came to the camp; but any way, he was the curious-est man about always betting on anything that turned up you ever see, if he could get anybody to bet on the other side; and if he couldn't he'd change sides. Any way that suited the other man would suit *him*—any way just so's he got a bet, *he* was satisfied. But still he was lucky, uncommon lucky, he most always come out winner. He was always ready and laying for a chance; there couldn't be no solit'ry thing mentioned but that feller'd offer to bet on it, and take any side you please, as I was just telling you. If there was a horse-race, you'd find him flush or you'd find him busted at the end of it; if there was a dog-fight, he'd bet on it; if there was a cat-fight, he'd bet on it; if there was a chicken-fight, he'd bet on it; why, if there was two birds setting on a fence, he would bet you which one would fly first; or if there was a camp-meeting, he would be there reg'lar to bet on Parson Walker, which he judged to be the best exhorter about here, and so he was, too, and a good man. If he even seen a straddle-bug[2] start to go anywheres, he would bet you how long it would take him to get wherever he was going to, and if you took him up, he would foller that straddle-bug to Mexico but what he would find out where he was bound for and how long he was on the road. Lots of the boys here has seen that Smiley, and can tell you about him. Why, it never made no difference to *him*—he'd bet on *any* thing—the dangdest feller. Parson Walker's wife laid very sick once, for a good while, and it seemed as if they warn't going to save her; but one morning he come in, and Smiley up and asked how she was, and he said she was considerable better—thank the Lord for his inf'nite mercy—and coming on so smart that with the blessing of Prov'dence she'd get well yet; and Smiley, before he thought says, "Well, I'll risk two-and-a-half she don't anyway."

Thish-yer Smiley had a mare—the boys called her the fifteen-minute nag, but that was only in fun, you know, because of course she was faster than that—and he used to win money on that horse, for all she was so slow and always had the asthma, or the distemper, or the consumption, or something of that kind. They used to give her two or three hundred yards start, and then pass her under way; but always at the fag end of the race she'd get excited and desperate-like, and come cavorting and strad-dling up, and scattering her legs around limber, sometimes in the air, and

[2]A long-legged beetle.

sometimes out to one side among the fences, and kicking up m-o-r-e dust, and raising m-o-r-e racket with her coughing and sneezing and blowing her nose—and *always* fetch up at the stand just about a neck ahead, as near as you could cipher it down.

And he had a little small bull-pup, that to look at him you'd think he warn't worth a cent but to set around and look ornery and lay for a chance to steal something. But as soon as money was up on him he was a different dog; his under-jaw'd begin to stick out like the fo'castle of a steamboat, and his teeth would uncover and shine like the furnaces. And a dog might tackle him and bully-rag him, and bite him, and throw him over his shoulder two or three times, and Andrew Jackson[3]—which was the name of the pup—Andrew Jackson would never let on but what *he* was satisfied, and hadn't expected nothing else—and the bets being doubled and doubled on the side all the time, till the money was all up; and then all of a sudden he would grab that other dog jest by the j'int of his hind leg and freeze to it—not chaw, you understand, but only jest grip and hang on till they throwed up the sponge, if it was a year. Smiley always come out winner on that pup, till he harnessed a dog once that didn't have no hind legs, because they'd been sawed off by a circular saw, and when the thing had gone along far enough, and the money was all up, and he come to make a snatch for his pet holt, he saw in a minute how he's been imposed on, and how the other dog had him in the door, so to speak, and he 'peared surprised, and then he looked sorter discouraged-like, and didn't try no more to win the fight, and so he got shucked out bad. He give Smiley a look, as much as to say his heart was broke, and it was *his* fault, for putting up a dog that hadn't no hind legs for him to take holt of, which was his main dependence in a fight, and then he limped off a piece and laid down and died. It was a good pup, was that Andrew Jackson, and would have made a name for hisself if he'd lived, for the stuff was in him and he had genius— I know it, because he hadn't had no opportunities to speak of, and it don't stand to reason that a dog could make such a fight as he could under them circumstances if he hadn't no talent. It always makes me feel sorry when I think of that last fight of his'n, and the way it turned out.

Well, thish-yer Smiley had rat-tarriers, and chicken cocks, and tomcats and all them kind of things, till you couldn't rest, and you couldn't fetch nothing for him to bet on but he'd match you. He ketched a frog one day, and took him home, and said he cal'lated to educate him; and so he never done nothing for three months but set in his back yard and learn that frog to jump. And you bet you he *did* learn him, too. He'd give him a little punch behind, and the next minute you'd see that frog whirling in the air like a doughnut—see him turn one summerset, or may be a couple, if got a

[3]Nicknamed "Old Hickory," Andrew Jackson (1767–1845), a general born in South Carolina, served as the seventh president of the United States from 1829 to 1837.

good start, and come down flat-footed and all right, like a cat. He got him up so in the matter of ketching flies, and kep' him in practice so constant, that he'd nail a fly every time as fur as he could see him. Smiley said all a frog wanted was education, and he could do 'most anything—and I believe him. Why, I've seen him set Dan'l Webster[4] down here on this floor—Dan'l Webster was the name of the frog—and sing out, "Flies, Dan'l, flies!" and quicker'n you could wink, he'd spring straight up and snake a fly off'n the counter there, and flop down on the floor again as solid as a gob of mud, and fall to scratching the side of his head with his hind foot as indifferent as if he hadn't no idea he'd been doin' any more'n any frog might do. You never see a frog so modest and straightfor'ard as he was, for all he was so gifted. And when it come to fair and square jumping on a dead level, he could get over more ground at one straddle than any animal of his breed you ever see. Jumping on a dead level was his strong suit, you understand; and when it come to that, Smiley would ante up money on him as long as he had a red. Smiley was monstrous proud of his frog, and well he might be, for fellers that had traveled and been everywheres all said he laid over any frog that ever *they* see.

Well, Smiley kep' the beast in a little lattice box, and he used to fetch him down town sometimes and lay for a bet. One day a feller—a stranger in the camp, he was—come acrost him with his box, and says:

"What might it be that you've got in the box?"

And Smiley says, sorter indifferent-like, "It might be a parrot, or it might be a canary, maybe, but it ain't—it's only just a frog."

And the feller took it, and looked at it careful, and turned it round this way and that, and says, "H'm—so 'tis. Well, what's *he* good for?"

"Well," Smiley says, easy and careless, "he's good enough for *one* thing, I should judge—he can outjump any frog in Calaveras county."

The feller took the box again, and took another long, particular look, and give it back to Smiley, and says, very deliberate, "Well," he says, "I don't see no p'ints about that frog that's any better'n any other frog."

"Maybe you don't," Smiley says. "Maybe you understand frogs and maybe you don't understand 'em; maybe you've had experience, and maybe you ain't only a amature, as it were. Anyways, I've got *my* opinion and I'll risk forty dollars that he can outjump any frog in Calaveras county."

And the feller studied a minute, and then says, kinder sad like, "Well, I'm only a stranger here, and I ain't got no frog; but if I had a frog, I'd bet you."

And then Smiley says, "That's all right—that's all right—if you'll hold my box a minute, I'll go and get you a frog." And so the feller took the box, and put up his forty dollars along with Smiley's, and set down to wait.

[4]A great orator, a Massachusetts senator, and a champion of nationalism, Daniel Webster (1782–1852) was a vocal opponent of Andrew Jackson, battling him on many political issues. In 1836, Webster ran for the presidency but carried Massachusetts only. For the remainder of his career he aspired in vain to the presidency.

"Mark Twain's Celebrated Jumping Frog," woodcut,
The Daily Graphic (New York), c. 1875.

So he set there a good while thinking and thinking to hisself, and then he got the frog out and prized his mouth open and took a teaspoon and filled him full of quail shot—filled him pretty near up to his chin—and set him on the floor. Smiley he went to the swamp and slopped around in the mud for a long time, and finally he ketched a frog, and fetched him in, and give him to this feller, and says:

"Now, if you're ready, set him alongside of Dan'l, with his forepaws just even with Dan'l's, and I'll give the word." Then he says, "One—two—three—git!" and him and the feller touched up the frogs from behind, and the new frog hopped off lively, but Dan'l give a heave, and hysted up his shoulders—so—like a Frenchman, but it warn't no use—he couldn't budge; he was planted as solid as a church, and he couldn't no more stir than if he was anchored out. Smiley was a good deal surprised, and he was disgusted too, but he didn't have no idea what the matter was, of course.

The feller took the money and started away; and when he was going out at the door, he sorter jerked his thumb over his shoulder—so—at

Dan'l, and says again, very deliberate, "Well," he says, "*I* don't see no p'ints about that frog that's any better'n any other frog."

Smiley he stood scratching his head and looking down at Dan'l a long time, and at last he says, "I do wonder what in the nation that frog throw'd off for—I wonder if there ain't something the matter with him—he 'pears to look mighty baggy, somehow." And he ketched Dan'l by the nap of the neck, and hefted him, and says, "Why blame my cats if he don't weigh five pound!" and turned him upside down and he belched out a double handful of shot. And then he see how it was, and he was the maddest man—he set the frog down and took out after that feller, but he never ketched him. And—"

[Here Simon Wheeler heard his name called from the front yard, and got up to see what was wanted.] And turning to me as he moved away, he said: "Just set where you are, stranger, and rest easy—I ain't going to be gone a second."

But, by your leave, I did not think that a continuation of the history of the enterprising vagabond *Jim* Smiley would be likely to afford me much information concerning the *Rev. Leonidas W.* Smiley, and so I started away.

At the door I met the sociable Wheeler returning, and he button-holed me and recommenced:

"Well, thish-yer Smiley had a yaller one-eyed cow that didn't have no tail, only jest a short stump like a bannanner, and—"

However, lacking both time and inclination, I did not wait to hear about the afflicted cow, but took my leave.

[1865, 1867]

Fenimore Cooper's Literary Offenses

The Pathfinder and *The Deerslayer* stand at the head of Cooper's novels as artistic creations. There are others of his works which contain parts as perfect as are to be found in these, and scenes even more thrilling. Not one can be compared with either of them as a finished whole.

The defects in both of these tales are comparatively slight. They were pure works of art.

Prof. Lounsbury

The five tales reveal an extraordinary fullness of invention....
   One of the very greatest characters in fiction, Natty Bumppo....
   The craft of the woodsman, the tricks of the trapper, all the delicate art of the forest, were familiar to Cooper from his youth up.

Prof. Brander Matthews

> Cooper is the greatest artist in the domain of romantic fiction yet produced by America.
>
> *Wilkie Collins*

It seems to me that it was far from right for the Professor of English Literature in Yale, the Professor of English Literature in Columbia, and Wilkie Collins[1] to deliver opinions on Cooper's literature without having read some of it. It would have been much more decorous to keep silent and let persons talk who have read Cooper.

Cooper's art has some defects. In one place in *Deerslayer*,[2] and in the restricted space of two-thirds of a page, Cooper has scored 114 offenses against literary art out of a possible 115. It breaks the record.

There are nineteen rules governing literary art in the domain of romantic fiction—some say twenty-two. In *Deerslayer* Cooper violated eighteen of them. These eighteen require:

1. That a tale shall accomplish something and arrive somewhere. But the *Deerslayer* tale accomplishes nothing and arrives in the air.

2. They require that the episodes of a tale shall be necessary parts of the tale, and shall help to develop it. But as the *Deerslayer* tale is not a tale, and accomplishes nothing and arrives nowhere, the episodes have no rightful place in the work, since there was nothing for them to develop.

3. They require that the personages in a tale shall be alive, except in the case of corpses, and that always the reader shall be able to tell the corpses from the others. But this detail has often been overlooked in the *Deerslayer* tale.

4. They require that the personages in a tale, both dead and alive, shall exhibit a sufficient excuse for being there. But this detail also has been overlooked in the *Deerslayer* tale.

5. They require that when the personages of a tale deal in conversation, the talk shall sound like human talk, and be talk such as human beings would be likely to talk in the given circumstances, and have a discoverable meaning, also a discoverable purpose, and a show of relevancy, and remain in the neighborhood of the subject in hand, and be interesting to the reader, and help out the tale, and stop when the people cannot think of anything more to say. But this requirement has been ignored from the beginning of the *Deerslayer* tale to the end of it.

6. They require that when the author describes the character of a personage in his tale, the conduct and conversation of that personage shall justify said description. But this law gets little or no attention in the *Deerslayer* tale, as Natty Bumppo's case will amply prove.

---

[1]Wilkie Collins (1824–89), English novelist, playwright, and author of short stories.
[2]Novel by Cooper (1841).

7. They require that when a personage talks like an illustrated, gilt-edged, tree-calf, hand-tooled, seven-dollar Friendship's Offering[3] in the beginning of a paragraph, he shall not talk like a negro minstrel in the end of it. But this rule is flung down and danced upon in the *Deerslayer* tale.

8. They require that crass stupidities shall not be played upon the reader as "the craft of the woodsman, the delicate art of the forest," by either the author or the people in the tale. But this rule is persistently violated in the *Deerslayer* tale.

9. They require that the personages of a tale shall confine themselves to possibilities and let miracles alone; or, if they venture a miracle, the author must so plausibly set it forth as to make it look possible or reasonable. But these rules are not respected in the *Deerslayer* tale.

10. They require that the author shall make the reader feel a deep interest in the personages of his tale and in their fate; and that he shall make the reader love the good people in the tale and hate the bad ones. But the reader of the *Deerslayer* tale dislikes the good people in it, is indifferent to the others, and wishes they would all get drowned together.

11. They require that the characters in a tale shall be so clearly defined that the reader can tell beforehand what each will do in a given emergency. But in the *Deerslayer* tale this rule is vacated.

In addition to these large rules there are some little ones. These require that the author shall

12. *Say* what he is proposing to say, not merely come near it.

13. Use the right word, not its second cousin.

14. Eschew surplusage.[4]

15. Not omit necessary details.

16. Avoid slovenliness of form.

17. Use good grammar.

18. Employ a simple and straightforward style.

Even these seven are coldly and persistently violated in the *Deerslayer* tale.

Cooper's gift in the way of invention was not a rich endowment; but such as it was he liked to work it, he was pleased with the effects, and indeed he did some quite sweet things with it. In his little box of stage-properties he kept six or eight cunning devices, tricks, artifices for his savages and woodsmen to deceive and circumvent each other with, and he was never so happy as when he was working these innocent things and

---

[3]Fancy, ornate gift book.
[4]Surplusage: irrelevant matter, excess of words.

seeing them go. A favorite one was to make a moccasined person tread in the tracks of the moccasined enemy, and thus hide his own trail. Cooper wore out barrels and barrels of moccasins in working that trick. Another stage-property that he pulled out of his box pretty frequently was his broken twig. He prized his broken twig above all the rest of his effects, and worked it the hardest. It is a restful chapter in any book of his when somebody doesn't step on a dry twig and alarm all the reds and whites for two hundred yards around. Every time a Cooper person is in peril, and absolute silence is worth four dollars a minute, he is sure to step on a dry twig. There may be a hundred handier things to step on, but that wouldn't satisfy Cooper. Cooper requires him to turn out and find a dry twig; and if he can't do it, go and borrow one. In fact, the Leatherstocking Series ought to have been called the Broken Twig Series.

I am sorry there is not room to put in a few dozen instances of the delicate art of the forest, as practised by Natty Bumppo and some of the other Cooperian experts. Perhaps we may venture two or three samples. Cooper was a sailor—a naval officer; yet he gravely tells us how a vessel, driving toward a lee shore in a gale, is steered for a particular spot by her skipper because he knows of an *undertow* there which will hold her back against the gale and save her. For just pure woodcraft, or sailorcraft, or whatever it is, isn't that neat? For several years Cooper was daily in the society of artillery, and he ought to have noticed that when a cannon-ball strikes the ground it either buries itself or skips a hundred feet or so; skips again a hundred feet or so—and so on, till finally it gets tired and rolls. Now in one place he loses some "females"—as he always calls women—in the edge of a wood near a plain at night in a fog, on purpose to give Bumppo a chance to show off the delicate art of the forest before the reader. These mislaid people are hunting for a fort. They hear a cannon-blast, and a cannon-ball presently comes rolling into the wood and stops at their feet. To the females this suggests nothing. The case is very different with the admirable Bumppo. I wish I may never know peace again if he doesn't strike out promptly and *follow the track* of that cannon-ball across the plain through the dense fog and find the fort. Isn't it a daisy? If Cooper had any real knowledge of Nature's way of doing things, he had a most delicate art in concealing the fact. For instance: one of his acute Indian experts, Chingachgook[5] (pronounced Chicago, I think), has lost the trail of a person he is tracking through the forest. Apparently the trail is hopelessly lost. Neither you or I could ever have guessed out the way to find it. It was very different with Chicago. Chicago was not stumped for long. He turned a running stream out of its course, and there, in the slush in its old bed, were that person's moccasin tracks. The current did not wash them away, as it would have done in all other like cases—no, even the eternal

[5]Natty Bumppo's Indian friend.

laws of Nature have to vacate when Cooper wants to put up a delicate job of woodcraft on the reader.

We must be a little wary when Brander Matthews tells us that Cooper's books "reveal an extraordinary fullness of invention." As a rule, I am quite willing to accept Brander Matthews's literary judgments and applaud his lucid and graceful phrasing of them; but that particular statement needs to be taken with a few tons of salt. Bless your heart, Cooper hadn't any more invention than a horse; and I don't mean a high-class horse, either; I mean a clothes-horse. It would be very difficult to find a really clever "situation" in Cooper's books, and still more difficult to find one of any kind in which he has failed to render absurd by his handling of it. Look at the episodes of "the caves"; and at the celebrated scuffle between Maqua and those others on the table-land a few days later; and at Hurry Harry's queer water-transit from the castle to the ark; and at Deerslayer's half-hour with his first corpse; the quarrel between Hurry Harry[6] and the Deerslayer later; and at—but choose for yourself; you can't go amiss.

If Cooper had been an observer his inventive faculty would have worked better; not more interestingly, but more rationally, more plausibly. Cooper's proudest creations in the way of "situations" suffer noticeably from the absence of the observer's protecting gift. Cooper's eye was splendidly inaccurate. Cooper seldom saw anything correctly. He saw nearly all things as through a glass eye, darkly.[7] Of course a man who cannot see the commonest little every-day matters accurately is working at a disadvantage when he is constructing a "situation." In the *Deerslayer* tale Cooper has a stream which is fifty feet wide where it flows out of a lake; it presently narrows to twenty as it meanders along for no given reason, and yet when a stream acts like that it ought to be required to explain itself. Fourteen pages later the width of the brook's outlet from the lake has suddenly shrunk thirty feet, and become "the narrowest part of the stream." This shrinkage is not accounted for. The stream has bends in it, a sure indication that it has alluvial banks and cuts them; yet these bends are only thirty and fifty feet long. If Cooper had been a nice and punctilious observer he would have noticed that the bends were oftener nine hundred feet long than short of it.

Cooper made the exit of that stream fifty feet wide, in the first place, for no particular reason; in the second place, he narrowed it to less than twenty to accommodate some Indians. He bends a "sapling" to the form of an arch over this narrow passage, and conceals six Indians in its foliage. They are "laying" for a settler's scow or ark which is coming up the stream on its way to the lake; it is being hauled against the stiff current by a rope whose stationary end is anchored in the lake; its rate of progress cannot be

---

[6]The name of a woodsman and a trapper in *The Deerslayer*.
[7]1 Corinthians 13:12. Twain's reference is a parody of the actual wording in Corinthians, which refers to a glass, not a glass eye.

more than a mile an hour. Cooper describes the ark, but pretty obscurely. In the matter of dimensions "it was little more than a modern canal-boat." Let us guess, then, that it was about one hundred and forty feet long. It was of "greater breadth than common." Let us guess, then, that it was about sixteen feet wide. This leviathan had been prowling down bends which were but a third as long as itself, and scraping between banks where it had only two feet of space to spare on each side. We cannot too much admire this miracle. A low-roofed dwelling occupies "two-thirds of the ark's length"—a dwelling ninety feet long and sixteen feet wide, let us say—a kind of vestibule train. The dwelling has two rooms—each forty-five feet long and sixteen feet wide, let us guess. One of them is the bedroom of the Hutter girls, Judith and Hetty; the other is the parlor in the daytime, at night it is papa's bedchamber. The ark is arriving at the stream's exit now, whose width has been reduced to less than twenty feet to accommodate the Indians—say to eighteen. There is a foot to spare on each side of the boat. Did the Indians notice that there was going to be a tight squeeze there? Did they notice that they could make money by climbing out of that arched sapling and just stepping aboard when the ark scraped by? No, other Indians would have noticed these things, but Cooper's Indians never notice anything. Cooper thinks they are marvelous creatures for noticing, but he was almost always in error about his Indians. There was seldom a sane one among them.

The ark is one hundred and forty-feet long; the dwelling is ninety feet long. The idea of the Indians is to drop softly and secretly from the arched sapling to the dwelling as the ark creeps along under it at the rate of a mile an hour, and butcher the family. It will take the ark a minute and a half to pass under. It will take the ninety-foot dwelling a minute to pass under. Now, then, what did the six Indians do? It would take you thirty years to guess, and even then you would have to give it up, I believe. Therefore, I will tell you what the Indians did. Their chief, a person of quite extraordinary intellect for a Cooper Indian, warily watched the canal-boat as it squeezed along under him, and when he had got his calculations fined down to exactly the right shade, as he judged, he let go and dropped. And *missed the house!* That is actually what he did. He missed the house, and landed in the stern of the scow. It was not much of a fall, yet it knocked him silly. He lay there unconscious. If the house had been ninety-seven feet long he would have made the trip. The fault was Cooper's, not his. The error lay in the construction of the house. Cooper was no architect.

There still remained in the roost five Indians. The boat has passed under and is now out of their reach. Let me explain what the five did—you would not be able to reason it out for yourself. No. 1 jumped for the boat, but fell in the water astern of it. Then No. 2 jumped for the boat, but fell in the water still farther astern of it. Then No. 3 jumped for the boat, and fell a good way astern of it. Then No. 4 jumped for the boat, and fell in

the water *away* astern. Then even No. 5 made a jump for the boat—for he
was a Cooper Indian. In the matter of intellect, the difference between a
Cooper Indian and the Indian that stands in front of the cigar-shop is not
spacious. The scow episode is really a sublime burst of invention; but it
does not thrill, because the inaccuracy of the details throws a sort of air
of fictitiousness and general improbability over it. This comes of Cooper's
inadequacy as an observer.

The reader will find some examples of Cooper's high talent for inaccurate observation in the account of the shooting-match in *The Pathfinder*.[8]

> A common wrought nail was driven lightly into the target, its head
> having first been touched with paint.

The color of the paint is not stated—an important omission, but Cooper deals freely in important omissions. No, after all, it was not an important omission; for this nail-head is *a hundred yards from* the marksmen,
and could not have been seen by them at that distance, no matter what
its color might be. How far can the best eye see a common house-fly? A
hundred yards? It is quite impossible. Very well; eyes that cannot see a
house-fly that is a hundred yards away cannot see an ordinary nail-head at
that distance, for the size of the two objects is the same. It takes a keen
eye to see a fly or a nail-head at fifty yards—one hundred and fifty feet.
Can the reader do it?

The nail was lightly driven, its head painted, and game called. Then
the Cooper miracles began. The bullet of the first marksman chipped an
edge of the nail-head; the next man's bullet drove the nail a little way
into the target—and removed all the paint. Haven't the miracles gone far
enough now? Not to suit Cooper; for the purpose of this whole scheme is
to show off his prodigy, Deerslayer-Hawkeye-Long-Rifle-Leatherstocking-
Pathfinder-Bumppo before the ladies.

> "Be all ready to clench it, boys!" cried out Pathfinder, stepping into
> his friend's tracks the instant they were vacant. "Never mind a new
> nail; I can see that, though the paint is gone, and what I can see I
> can hit at a hundred yards, though it were only a mosquito's eye. Be
> ready to clench!"
> The rifle cracked, the bullet sped its way, and the head of the
> nail was buried in the wood, covered by the piece of flattened lead.

There, you see, is a man who could hunt flies with a rifle, and command a ducal salary in a Wild West show to-day if we had him back with us.

The recorded feat is certainly surprising as it stands; but it is not surprising enough for Cooper. Cooper adds a touch. He has made Pathfinder
do this miracle with another man's rifle; and not only that, but Pathfinder

---

[8]Novel by Cooper (1840).

did not have even the advantage of loading it himself. He had everything against him, and yet he made that impossible shot; and not only made it, but did it with absolute confidence, saying, "Be ready to clench." Now a person like that would have undertaken the same feat with a brickbat, and with Cooper to help he would have achieved it, too.

Pathfinder showed off handsomely that day before the ladies. His very first feat was a thing which no Wild West show can touch. He was standing with the group of marksmen, observing—a hundred yards from the target, mind; one Jasper raised his rifle and drove the center of the bull's eye. Then the Quartermaster fired. The target exhibited no result this time. There was a laugh. "It's a dead miss," said Major Lundie. Pathfinder waited an impressive moment or two; then said, in that calm, indifferent, know-it-all way of his, "No Major, he has covered Japser's bullet, as will be seen if any one will take the trouble to examine the target."

Wasn't it remarkable! How *could* he see that little pellet fly through the air and enter that distant bullet-hole? Yet that is what he did; for nothing is impossible to a Cooper person. Did any of those people have any deep-seated doubts about this thing? No; for that would imply sanity, and these were all Cooper people.

The respect for Pathfinder's skill and for his *quickness and accuracy of sight* [the italics are mine] was so profound and general, that the instant he made this declaration the spectators began to distrust their own opinions, and a dozen rushed to the target in order to ascertain the fact. There, sure enough, it was found that the Quartermaster's bullet had gone through the hole made by Jasper's, and that, too, so accurately as to require a minute examination to be certain of the circumstance, which, however, was soon clearly established by discovering one bullet over the other in the stump against which the target was placed.

They made a "minute" examination; but never mind, how could they know that there were two bullets in that hole without digging the latest one out? For neither probe nor eyesight could prove the presence of any more than one bullet. Did they dig? No; as we shall see. It is the Pathfinder's turn now; he steps out before the ladies, takes aim, and fires.

But, alas! Here is a disappointment; an incredible, an unimaginable disappointment—for the target's aspect is unchanged; there is nothing there but the same old bullet-hole!

"If one dared to hint at such a thing," cried Major Duncan, "I should say that the Pathfinder has also missed the target."

As nobody had missed it yet, the "also" was not necessary; but never mind about that, for the Pathfinder is going to speak.

"No, no, Major," said he, confidently, "that *would* be a risky declaration. I didn't load the piece, and can't say what was in it; but if it

was lead, you will find the bullet driving down those of the Quartermaster and Jasper, else is not my name Pathfinder."
A shout from the target announced the truth of this assertion."

Is the miracle sufficient as it stands? Not for Cooper. The Pathfinder
speaks again, as he "now slowly advances toward the stage occupied by
the females":

> "That's not all, boys, that's not all; if you find the target touched
> at all, I'll own to a miss. The Quartermaster cut the wood, but you'll
> find no wood cut by that last messenger."

The miracle is at last complete. He knew—doubtless *saw*—at the distance of a hundred yards—that his bullet had passed into the hole *without
fraying the edges*. There were now three bullets in that one hole—three
bullets embedded processionally in the body of the stump back of the target. Everybody knew this—somehow or other—and yet nobody had dug
any of them out to make sure. Cooper is not a close observer, but he is
interesting. He is certainly always that, no matter what happens. And he
is more interesting when he is not noticing what he is about than when he
is. This is a considerable merit.

The conversations in the Cooper books have a curious sound in our
modern ears. To believe that such talk really ever came out of people's
mouths would be to believe that there was a time when time was of no
value to a person who thought he had something to say; when it was the
custom to spread a two-minute remark out to ten; when a man's mouth
was a rolling mill, and busied itself all day long in turning four-foot pigs[9]
of thought into thirty-foot bars of conversational railroad iron by attenua-
tion; when subjects were seldom faithfully stuck to, but the talk wandered
all around and arrived nowhere; when conversations consisted mainly of
irrelevancies, with here and there a relevancy, a relevancy with an embarrassed look, as not being able to explain how it got there.

Cooper was certainly not a master in the construction of dialogue. Inaccurate observation defeated him here as it defeated him in so many other
enterprises of his. He even failed to notice that the man who talks corrupt
English six days in the week must and will talk it on the seventh, and can't
help himself. In the *Deerslayer* story he lets Deerslayer talk the showiest
kind of book-talk sometimes, and at other times the basest of base dialects. For instance, when some one asks him if he has a sweetheart, and if
so, where she abides, this is his majestic answer:

> "She's in the forest—hanging from the boughs of the trees, in a
> soft rain—in the dew on the open grass—the clouds that float
> about in the blue heavens—the birds that sing in the woods—the

---

[9]Pig iron, crude iron cast in blocks.

sweet springs where I slake my thirst—and in all the other glorious gifts that come from God's Providence!"

And he preceded that, a little before, with this:

"It consarns me as all things that touches a fri'nd consarns a fri'nd."

And this is another of his remarks:

"If I was Injin born, now, I might tell of this, or carry in the scalp and boast of the expl'ite of the whole tribe; or if my inimy had only been a bear"—[and so on].

We cannot imagine such a thing as a veteran Scotch Commander-in-Chief comporting himself in the field like a windy melodramatic actor, but Cooper could. On one occasion Alice and Cora were being chased by the French through a fog in the neighborhood of their father's fort:

"Point de quartier aux coquins!"[10] cried an eager pursuer, who seemed to direct the operations of the enemy.

"Stand firm and be ready, my gallant 60ths!" suddenly exclaimed a voice above them; "wait to see the enemy; fire low, and sweep the glacis."

"Father, father!" exclaimed a piercing cry from out of the mist; "it is I! Alice! thy own Elsie! spare, O! save your daughters!"

"Hold!" shouted the former speaker, in the awful tones of parental agony, the sound reaching even to the woods, and rolling back in solemn echo.

" 'Tis she! God has restored my children! Throw open the sally-port; to the field, 60ths, to the field! pull not a trigger, lest ye kill my lambs! Drive off these dogs of France with your steel!"

Cooper's word-sense was singularly dull. When a person has a poor ear for music he will flat and sharp right along without knowing it. He keeps near the tune, but it is *not* the tune. When a person has a poor ear for words, the result is a literary flatting and sharping; you perceive what he is intending to say, but you also perceive that he doesn't say it. This is Cooper. He was not a word-musician. His ear was satisfied with the *approximate* word. I will furnish some circumstantial evidence in support of this charge. My instances are gathered from half a dozen pages of the tale called *Deerslayer*. He uses "verbal" for "oral"; "precision" for "facility"; "phenomena" for "marvels"; "necessary" for "predetermined"; "unsophisticated" for "primitive"; "preparation" for "expectancy"; "rebuked" for "subdued"; "dependent on" for "resulting from"; "fact" for "condition"; "fact" for "conjecture"; "precaution" for "caution"; "explain" for "determine";

---

[10]"Give the radicals no quarter!"(French).

"mortified" for "disappointed"; "meretricious" for "facetious"; "materially" for "considerably"; "decreasing" for "deepening"; "increasing" for "disappearing"; "embedded" for "inclosed"; "treacherous" for "hostile"; "stood" for "stooped"; "softened" for "replaced"; "rejoined" for "remarked"; "situation" for "condition"; "different" for "differing"; "insensible" for "unsentient"; "brevity" for "celerity"; "distrusted" for "suspicious"; "mental imbecility" for "imbecility"; "eyes" for "sight"; "counteracting" for "opposing"; "funeral obsequies" for "obsequies."

There have been daring people in the world who claimed that Cooper could write English, but they are all dead now—all dead but Lounsbury. I don't remember that Lounsbury makes the claim in so many words, still he makes it, for he says that *Deerslayer* is a "pure work of art." Pure, in that connection, means faultless—faultless in all details—and language is a detail. If Mr. Lounsbury had only compared Cooper's English with the English which he writes himself—but it is plain that he didn't; and so it is likely that he imagines until this day that Cooper's is as clean and compact as his own. Now I feel sure, deep down in my heart, that Cooper wrote about the poorest English that exists in our language, and that the English of *Deerslayer* is the very worst that even Cooper ever wrote.

I may be mistaken, but it does seem to me that *Deerslayer* is not a work of art in any sense; it does seem to me that it is destitute of every detail that goes to the making of a work of art; in truth, it seems to me that *Deerslayer* is just simply a literary *delirium tremens*.[11]

A work of art? It has no invention; it has no order, system, sequence, or result; it has no life-likeness, no thrill, no stir, no seeming of reality; its characters are confusedly drawn, and by their acts and words they prove that they are not the sort of people the author claims that they are; its humor is pathetic; its pathos is funny; its conversations are—oh! indescribable; its love-scenes odious; its English a crime against the language.

Counting these out, what is left is Art. I think we must all admit that.

[1895]

---

[11]A severe delirium caused by alcohol poisoning.

■■ CONTEXT AND RESPONSE ■■

Artemus Ward (1834–1867)

Before Mark Twain emerged as leading raconteur of American homespun humor, there was Artemus Ward. Born Charles Farrar Browne in Waterford, Maine, the popular nineteenth-century humorist and newspaper editor adopted the folksy persona of a fictitious sideshow manager whose satirical comments were notorious for puns and misspellings. Some of Ward's pithy sayings remain familiar today, including, "It ain't so much the things we don't know that get us in trouble. It's the things we know that ain't so." It was Ward who urged Twain to contribute a comical sketch to a volume of collected tales, inspiring Twain to write the famous jumping frog story that launched a celebrated writing career.

Ward, who remained a lasting influence on Twain, published several books, including *Artemus Ward (His Travels) Among the Mormons* (1865), notable for its sympathy for—as well as its irreverence toward—the Church of the Latter-day Saints. Twain's own impression of Salt Lake City's residents followed Ward's in 1872 with the publication of *Roughing It,* a semi-autobiographical travelogue that includes a visit to that city. In the following selection, Ward conjures up a scene of chaotic bumblings aboard the steamship *Ariel* as it embarks upon its westward misadventures.

From Artemus Ward (His Travels) Among the Mormons

ON THE STEAMER. New York, Oct. 13, 1863.

The steamer Ariel starts for California at noon.

Her decks are crowded with excited passengers, who insanely undertake to "look after" their trunks and things; and what with our smashing against each other, and the yells of the porters, and the wails over lost baggage, and the crash of boxes, and the roar of the boilers, we are for the time-being about as unhappy a lot of maniacs as were ever thrown together.

I am one of them. I am rushing round with a glaring eye in search of a box.

Great jam, in which I find a sweet young lady, with golden hair, clinging to me fondly, and saying, "Dear George, farewell!"—Discovers her mistake, and disappears.

I should like to be George some more.

Confusion so great that I seek refuge in a state room, which contains a single lady of forty-five summers, who says, "Base man!—leave me!" I leave her.

By-and-by we cool down, and become somewhat regulated.

Next Day. When the gong sounds for breakfast we are fairly out on the sea, which runs roughly, and the Ariel rocks wildly. Many of the passengers are sick, and a young naval officer establishes a reputation as a wit by carrying to one of the invalids a plate of raw salt pork, swimming in cheap molasses. I am not sick; so I roll round the deck in the most cheerful sea-dog manner.

The next day and the next pass by in a serene manner. The waves are smooth now, and we can all eat and sleep. We might have enjoyed ourselves very well, I fancy, if the Ariel, whose capacity was about three hundred and fifty passengers, had not on this occasion carried nearly nine hundred, a hundred at least of whom were children of an unpleasant age. Captain Semmes captured the Ariel once, and it is to be deeply regretted that that thrifty buccaneer hadn't made mincemeat of her, because she is a miserable tub at best, and hasn't much more right to be afloat than a second-hand coffin has. I do not know her proprietor, Mr. C. Vanderbilt [Cornelius Vanderbilt, 1794–1877, American industrialist and philanthropist]; but I know of several excellent mill privileges in the State of Maine, and not one of them is so thoroughly Dam'd as he was all the way from New York to Aspinwall.

I had far rather say a pleasant thing than a harsh one; but it is due to the large number of respectable ladies and gentlemen, who were on board the steamer Ariel with me, that I state here that the accommodations on that steamer were very vile. If I did not so state, my conscience would sting me through life, and I should have horrid dreams like Richard III., Esq.

The proprietor apparently thought we were under going transportation for life to some lonely island, and the very waiters who brought us meats that any warden of any penitentiary would blush to offer convicts, seemed to think it was a glaring error our not being in chains.

As a specimen of the liberal manner in which this steamer was managed, I will mention that the purser (a very pleasant person, by the way) was made to unite the positions of purser, baggage-clerk, and doctor: and I one day had a lurking suspicion that he was among the waiters in the dining-cabin, disguised in a white jacket and slipshod pumps.

I have spoken my piece about the Ariel, and I hope Mr. Vanderbilt will reform ere it is too late. Dr. Watts [Isaac Watts, 1674–1748, English hymnwriter and theologian] says the vilest sinner may return as long as the gas-meters work well, or words to that effect.

[1865]

BRET HARTE ■ (1836–1902)

Bret Harte was born in Albany, New York. His father, a schoolteacher, died in 1845, and in 1849 Harte withdrew from school. In 1854 he, his mother, sister, and brother settled in Oakland, California, and he began writing poems and short stories for a weekly, *The Golden Era*, based in San Francisco. In the following years he held a number of jobs in northern California, including coal miner, tutor, and printer.

Harte's career as a writer got underway in earnest after he returned to San Francisco. He became a typesetter for, and a regular contributor to, *The Golden Era*; and some of his stories, published under the byline "The Bohemian," were included in *The Luck of Roaring Camp and Other Sketches* (1870), the book for which he is best known. In the late 1860s, Harte was named the editor of a new magazine, *Overland Monthly*, and he published there the two stories that won him a national audience, "The Luck of Roaring Camp" and "The Outcasts of Poker Flat" (see the following text).

Harte combined realism and sentimentality in a form that many readers, especially in the East, found greatly appealing, even as he embedded in the stories a measure of wit, irony, and an angled humor that a minority of more knowing readers could appreciate. The critic Charles A. Fleming makes an apt point:

> As a writer, Harte was a talented humorist who could take fairly routine story formulas and give them new vigor and settings. His background as a journalist gave him a brisk style and a special skill for describing people, their mannerisms, and dialogue.

For a time Harte's colorfully styled stories, sketches, and novels about the West were much in demand, as were his lectures—though audiences back East were sometimes disappointed that he wore a gentleman's suit rather than the buckskin of a frontiersman or the outfit of a miner. Many newspapers, magazines, and journals sought his services, and the University of California offered him a professorship. But his final three decades of literary work, overall, were not impressive. He wrote many books, benefiting along the way from political appointments and the support of patrons. Ultimately, however, his artistic legacy amounts to a few good stories and poems, and in the annals of American literary history he has been overshadowed by another writer (whom Harte knew) active in the Far West during the 1860s, Mark Twain.

For further study: Richard O'Connor, *Bret Harte: A Biography* (1966); Patrick D. Morrow, *Bret Harte: Literary Critic* (1979); Gary Scharnhorst, *Bret Harte: Opening the American Literary West* (2000); and Axel Nissen, *Bret Harte: Prince and Pauper* (2000).

Other resources include: Gary Scharnhorst, *Bret Harte: A Bibliography* (1995); and Linda D. Barnett, *Bret Harte: A Reference Guide* (1980). See also the discussion of Harte in Chris Packard, *Queer Cowboys and other Erotic Male Friendships in Nineteenth-Century American Literature* (2005).

The Outcasts of Poker Flat

As Mr. John Oakhurst, gambler, stepped into the main street of Poker Flat on the morning of the twenty-third of November, 1850, he was conscious of a change in its moral atmosphere from the preceding night. Two or three men, conversing earnestly together, ceased as he approached, and exchanged significant glances. There was a Sabbath lull in the air, which, in a settlement unused to Sabbath influences, looked ominous.

Mr. Oakhurst's calm, handsome face betrayed small concern of these indications. Whether he was conscious of any predisposing cause, was another question. "I reckon they're after somebody," he reflected; " likely it's me." He returned to his pocket the handkerchief with which he had been whipping away the red dust of Poker Flat from his neat boots, and quietly discharged his mind of any further conjecture.

In point of fact, Poker Flat was "after somebody." It had lately suffered the loss of several thousand dollars, two valuable horses, and a prominent citizen. It was experiencing a spasm of virtuous reaction, quite as lawless and ungovernable as any of the acts that had provoked it. A secret committee had determined to rid the town of all improper persons. This was done permanently in regard of two men who were then hanging from the boughs of a sycamore in the gulch, and temporarily in the banishment of certain other objectionable characters. I regret to say that some of these were ladies. It is but due to the sex, however, to state that their impropriety was professional, and it was only in such easily established standards of evil that Poker Flat ventured to sit in judgment.

Mr. Oakhurst was right in supposing that he was included in this category. A few of the committee had urged hanging him as a possible example, and a sure method of reimbursing themselves from his pockets of the sums he had won from them. "It's agin justice," said Jim Wheeler, "to let this yer young man from Roaring Camp—an entire stranger—carry away our money." But a crude sentiment of equity residing in the breasts of those who had been fortunate enough to win from Mr. Oakhurst, overruled this narrower local prejudice.

Mr. Oakhurst received his sentence with philosophic calmness, none the less coolly, that he was aware of the hesitation of his judges. He was too much of a gambler not to accept Fate. With him life was at best an uncertain game, and he recognized the usual percentage in favor of the dealer.

A body of armed men accompanied the deported wickedness of Poker Flat to the outskirts of the settlement. Besides Mr. Oakhurst, who was known to be a coolly desperate man, and for whose intimidation the armed escort was intended, the expatriated party consisted of a young woman familiarly known as "The Duchess"; another, who had gained the infelicitous title of "Mother Shipton,"[1] and "Uncle Billy," a suspected sluice-robber[2] and confirmed drunkard. The cavalcade provoked no comments from the spectators, nor was any word uttered by the escort. Only when the gulch which marked the uttermost limit of Poker Flat was reached, the leader spoke briefly and to the point. The exiles were forbidden to return at the peril of their lives.

As the escort disappeared, their pent-up feelings found vent in a few hysterical tears from "The Duchess," some bad language from Mother Shipton, and a Partheian[3] volley of expletives from Uncle Billy. The philosophic Oakhurst alone remained silent. He listened calmly to Mother Shipton's desire to cut somebody's heart out, to the repeated statements of "The Duchess" that she would die in the road, and to the alarming oaths that seemed to be bumped out of Uncle Billy as he rode forward. With the easy good-humor characteristic of his class, he insisted upon exchanging his own riding-horse, "Five Spot," for the sorry mule which the Duchess rode. But even this act did not draw the party into any closer sympathy. The young woman readjusted her somewhat draggled plumes with a feeble, faded coquetry; Mother Shipton eyed the possessor of "Five Spot" with malevolence, and Uncle Billy included the whole party in one sweeping anathema.

The road to Sandy Bar—a camp that not having as yet experienced the regenerating influences of Poker Flat, consequently seemed to offer some invitation to the emigrants—lay over a steep mountain range. It was distant a day's severe journey. In that advanced season, the party soon passed out of the moist, temperate regions of the foot-hills, into the dry, cold, bracing air of the Sierras. The trail was narrow and difficult. At noon the Duchess, rolling out of her saddle upon the ground, declared her intention of going no further, and the party halted.

The spot was singularly wild and impressive. A wooded amphitheatre, surrounded on three sides by precipitous cliffs of naked granite, sloped gently toward the crest of another precipice that overlooked the valley. It was undoubtedly the most suitable spot for a camp, had camping been advisable. But Mr. Oakhurst knew that scarcely half the journey to Sandy Bar was accomplished, and the party were not equipped or provisioned for delay. This fact he pointed out to his companions curtly, with a philosophic commentary on the folly of "throwing up their hand before the game was

---

[1]Mother Shipton (1488–1561) (Ursula Sontheil) was an English prophetess, regarded by many as a witch, who lived during the time of Henry VIII and Elizabeth I.
[2]A long inclined trough designed to separate gold ore from sediment.
[3]The Parthians, an ancient people of the northeast region of present-day Iran, were famous for their use of the "Parthian shot" in warfare. They preferred to ride around their enemy, avoiding direct contact and shooting them with arrows. When forced into a frontal attack they would retreat, but turn in their saddles and fire unexpectedly at their enemies as they fled the battlefield.

played out." But they were furnished with liquor, which in this emergency stood them in place of food, fuel, rest and prescience. In spite of his remonstrances, it was not long before they were more or less under its influence. Uncle Billy passed rapidly from a bellicose state into one of stupor, the Duchess became maudlin, and Mother Shipton snored. Mr. Oakhurst alone remained erect, leaning against a rock, calmly surveying them.

Mr. Oakhurst did not drink. It interfered with a profession which required coolness, impassiveness and presence of mind, and, in his own language, he "couldn't afford it." As he gazed at his recumbent fellowexiles, the loneliness begotten of his pariah-trade, his habits of life, his very vices, for the first time seriously oppressed him. He bestirred himself in dusting his black clothes, washing his hands and face, and other acts characteristic of his studiously neat habits, and for a moment forgot his annoyance. The thought of deserting his weaker and more pitiable companions never perhaps occurred to him. Yet he could not help feeling the want of that excitement, which singularly enough was most conducive to that calm equanimity for which he was notorious. He looked at the gloomy walls that rose a thousand feet sheer above the circling pines around him; at the sky, ominously clouded; at the valley below, already deepening into shadow. And doing so, suddenly he heard his own name called.

A horseman slowly ascended the trail. In the fresh, open face of the newcomer, Mr. Oakhurst recognized Tom Simson, otherwise known as "The Innocent" of Sandy Bar. He had met him some months before over a "little game," and had, with perfect equanimity, won the entire fortune— amounting to some forty dollars—of that guileless youth. After the game was finished, Mr. Oakhurst drew the youthful speculator behind the door and thus addressed him: "Tommy, you're a good little man, but you can't gamble worth a cent. Don't try it ever again." He then handed him his money back, pushed him gently from the room, and so made a devoted slave of Tom Simson.

There was a remembrance of this in his boyish and enthusiastic greeting of Mr. Oakhurst. He had started, he said, to go to Poker Flat to seek his fortune. "Alone?" No, not exactly alone; in fact—a giggle—he had run away with Piney Woods. Didn't Mr. Oakhurst remember Piney? She that used to wait on the table at the Temperance House? They had been engaged a long time, but old Jake Woods had objected, and so they had run away, and were going to Poker Flat to be married, and here they were. And they were tired out, and how lucky it was they had found a place to camp and company. All this The Innocent delivered rapidly, while Piney— a stout, comely damsel of fifteen—emerged from behind the pine tree, where she had been blushing unseen, and rode to the side of her lover.

Mr. Oakhurst seldom troubled himself with sentiment. Still less with propriety. But he had a vague idea that the situation was not felicitous.

He retained, however, his presence of mind sufficiently to kick Uncle Billy, who was about to say something, and Uncle Billy was sober enough to recognize in Mr. Oakhurst's kick a superior power that would not bear trifling. He then endeavored to dissuade Tom Simson from delaying further, but in vain. He even pointed out the fact that there was no provision, nor means of making a camp. But, unluckily, "The Innocent" met this objection by assuring the party that he was provided with an extra mule loaded with provisions, and by the discovery of a rude attempt at a log-house near the trail. "Piney can stay with Mrs. Oakhurst," said The Innocent, pointing to the Duchess, "and I can shift for myself."

Nothing but Mr. Oakhurst's admonishing foot saved Uncle Billy from bursting into a roar of laughter. As it was, he felt compelled to retire up the canyon until he could recover his gravity. There he confided the joke to the tall pine trees, with many slaps of his leg, contortions of his face, and the usual profanity. But when he returned to the party, he found them seated by a fire—for the air had grown strangely chill and the sky overcast—in apparently amicable conversation. Piney was actually talking in an impulsive, girlish fashion to the Duchess, who was listening with an interest and animation she had not shown for many days. The Innocent was holding forth, apparently with equal effect, to Mr. Oakhurst and Mother Shipton, who was actually relaxing into amiability. "Is this yer a d—d picnic?" said Uncle Billy, with inward scorn, as he surveyed the sylvan group, the glancing fire-light and the tethered animals in the foreground. Suddenly an idea mingled with the alcoholic fumes that disturbed his brain. It was apparently of a jocular nature, for he felt impelled to slap his leg again and cram his fist into his mouth.

As the shadows crept slowly up the mountain, a slight breeze rocked the tops of the pine trees, and moaned through their long and gloomy aisles. The ruined cabin, patched and covered with pine boughs, was set apart for the ladies. As the lovers parted, they unaffectedly exchanged a parting kiss, so honest and sincere that it might have been heard above the swaying pines. The frail Duchess and the malevolent Mother Shipton were probably too stunned to remark upon this last evidence of simplicity, and so turned without a word to the hut. The fire was replenished, the men lay down before the door, and in a few minutes were asleep.

Mr. Oakhurst was a light sleeper. Toward morning he awoke benumbed and cold. As he stirred the dying fire, the wind, which was now blowing strongly, brought to his cheek that which caused the blood to leave it—snow!

He started to his feet with the intention of awakening the sleepers, for there was no time to lose. But turning to where Uncle Billy had been lying he found him gone. A suspicion leaped to his brain and a curse to his lips. He ran to the spot where the mules had been tethered; they were no longer there. The tracks were already rapidly disappearing in the snow.

The momentary excitement brought Mr. Oakhurst back to the fire with his usual calm. He did not waken the sleepers. The Innocent slumbered peacefully, with a smile on his good-humored, freckled face. The virgin Piney slept beside her frailer sisters as sweetly as though attended by celestial guardians, and Mr. Oakhurst, drawing his blanket over his shoulders, stroked his mustachios and waited for the dawn. It came slowly in a whirling mist of snowflakes, that dazzled and confused the eye. What could be seen of the landscape appeared magically changed. He looked over the valley, and summed up the present and future in two words— "Snowed in!"

A careful inventory of the provisions, which, fortunately for the party, had been stored within the hut, and so escaped the felonious fingers of Uncle Billy, disclosed the fact that with care and prudence they might last ten days longer. "That is," said Mr. Oakhurst, *sotto voce*[4] to The Innocent, "if you're willing to board us. If you ain't—and perhaps you'd better not— you can wait till Uncle Billy gets back with provisions." For some occult reason, Mr. Oakhurst could not bring himself to disclose Uncle Billy's rascality, and so offered the hypothesis that he had wandered from the camp and had accidentally stampeded the animals. He dropped a warning to the Duchess and Mother Shipton, who of course knew the facts of their associate's defection. "They'll find out the truth about us *all*, when they find out anything," he added, significantly, "and there's no good frightening them now."

Tom Simson not only put all his worldly store at the disposal of Mr. Oakhurst, but seemed to enjoy the prospect of their enforced seclusion. "We'll have a good camp for a week, and then the snow'll melt, and we'll all go back together." The cheerful gayety of the young man and Mr. Oakhurst's calm infected the others. The Innocent, with the aid of pine boughs, extemporized a thatch for the roofless cabin, and the Duchess directed Piney in the rearrangement of the interior with a taste and tact that opened the blue eyes of that provincial maiden to their fullest extent. "I reckon now you're used to fine things at Poker Flat," said Piney. The Duchess turned away sharply to conceal something that reddened her cheeks through its professional tint, and Mother Shipton requested Piney not to "chatter." But when Mr. Oakhurst returned from a weary search for the trail, he heard the sound of happy laughter echoed from the rocks. He stopped in some alarm, and his thoughts first naturally reverted to the whiskey—which he had prudently *cachéd*.[5] "And yet it don't somehow sound like whiskey," said the gambler. It was not until he caught sight of the blazing fire through the still blinding storm, and the group around it, that he settled to the conviction that it was "square fun."

---

[4]In a low voice or whisper (Italian).
[5]Stored goods or valuables concealed in a hiding place, usually in case of emergencies (French).

Whether Mr. Oakhurst had *cachéd* his cards with the whiskey as something debarred the free access of the community, I cannot say. It was certain that, in Mother Shipton's words, he "didn't say cards once" during that evening. Haply the time was beguiled by an accordion, produced somewhat ostentatiously by Tom Simson, from his pack. Notwithstanding some difficulties attending the manipulation of this instrument, Piney Woods managed to pluck several reluctant melodies from its keys, to an accompaniment by The Innocent on a pair of bone castinets. But the crowning festivity of the evening was reached in a rude camp-meeting hymn, which the lovers, joining hands, sang with great earnestness and vociferation. I fear that a certain defiant tone and Covenanter's swing[6] to its chorus, rather than any devotional quality, caused it to speedily infect the others, who at last joined in the refrain:

"I'm proud to live in the service of the Lord,
And I'm bound to die in His army."

The pines rocked, the storm eddied and whirled above the miserable group, and the flames of their altar leaped heavenward, as if in token of the vow.

At midnight the storm abated, the rolling clouds parted, and the stars glittered keenly above the sleeping camp. Mr. Oakhurst, whose professional habits had enabled him to live on the smallest possible amount of sleep, in dividing the watch with Tom Simson, somehow managed to take upon himself the greater part of that duty. He excused himself to The Innocent, by saying that he had "often been a week without sleep." "Doing what?" asked Tom. "Poker!" replied Oakhurst, sententiously; "when a man gets a streak of luck—nigger-luck[7]—he don't get tired. The luck gives in first. Luck," continued the gambler, reflectively, "is a mighty queer thing. All you know about it for certain is that it's bound to change. And it's finding out when it's going to change that makes you. We've had a streak of bad luck since we left Poker Flat—you come along and slap you get into it, too. If you can hold your cards right along you're all right. For," added the gambler, with cheerful irrelevance,

"I'm proud to live in the service of the Lord,
And I'm bound to die in His army."

The third day came, and the sun, looking through the white-curtained valley, saw the outcasts divide their slowly decreasing store of provisions for the morning meal. It was one of the peculiarities of that mountain

---

[6]Covenanters were Scottish Presbyterians who supported either of two agreements, the National Covenant of 1638 or the Solemn League and Covenant of 1643, intended to defend and extend Presbyterianism. Their songs had a militant, warlike beat ("swing"). The refrain is from an early American spiritual, "Service of the Lord."
[7]This racist phrase connoted unexpected good luck.

climate that its rays diffused a kindly warmth over the wintry landscape, as if in regretful commiseration of the past. But it revealed drift on drift of snow piled high around the hut; a hopeless, uncharted, trackless sea of white lying below the rocky shores to which the castaways still clung. Through the marvellously clear air, the smoke of the pastoral village of Poker Flat rose miles away. Mother Shipton saw it, and from a remote pinnacle of her rocky fastness, hurled in that direction a final malediction. It was her last vituperative attempt, and perhaps for that reason was invested with a certain degree of sublimity. It did her good, she privately informed the Duchess. "Just you go out there and cuss, and see." She then set herself to the task of amusing "the child," as she and the Duchess were pleased to call Piney. Piney was no chicken, but it was a soothing and ingenious theory of the pair to thus account for the fact that she didn't swear and wasn't improper.

When night crept up again through the gorges, the reedy notes of the accordion rose and fell in fitful spasms and long-drawn gasps by the flickering camp-fire. But music failed to fill entirely the aching void left by insufficient food, and a new diversion was proposed by Piney—storytelling. Neither Mr. Oakhurst nor his female companions caring to relate their personal experiences, this plan would have failed, too, but for The Innocent. Some months before he had chanced upon a stray copy of Mr. Pope's[8] ingenious translation of the Iliad. He now proposed to narrate the principal incidents of that poem—having thoroughly mastered the argument and fairly forgotten the words—in the current vernacular of Sandy Bar. And so for the rest of that night the Homeric demi-gods again walked the earth. Trojan bully and wily Greek wrestled in the winds, and the great pines in the canyon seemed to bow to the wrath of the son of Peleus.[9] Mr. Oakhurst listened with quiet satisfaction. Most especially was he interested in the fate of "Ash-heels," as The Innocent persisted in denominating the "swift-footed Achilles."

So with small food and much of Homer and the accordion, a week passed over the heads of the outcasts. The sun again forsook them, and again from leaden skies the snow-flakes were sifted over the land. Day by day closer around them drew the snowy circle, until at last they looked from their prison over drifted walls of dazzling white, that towered twenty feet above their heads. It became more and more difficult to replenish their fires, even from the fallen trees beside them, now half-hidden in the drifts. And yet no one complained. The lovers turned from the dreary prospect and looked into each other's eyes, and were happy. Mr. Oakhurst

---

[8]An English essayist, critic, satirist, and Enlightenment poet, Alexander Pope (1688–1744) translated Homer's The Iliad into heroic couplets.
[9]Peleus, the son of Aeacus, king of Aegina, married the sea nymph Thetis. Their son, Achilles, the Greek hero of the Trojan War, could be mortally wounded in the heel only.

settled himself coolly to the losing game before him. The Duchess, more cheerful than she had been, assumed the care of Piney. Only Mother Shipton—once the strongest of the party—seemed to sicken and fade. At midnight on the tenth day she called Oakhurst to her side. "I'm going," she said, in a voice of querulous weakness, "but don't say anything about it. Don't waken the kids. Take the bundle from under my head and open it." Mr. Oakhurst did so. It contained Mother Shipton's rations for the last week, untouched. "Give 'em to the child," she said, pointing to the sleeping Piney. "You've starved yourself," said the gambler. "That's what they call it," said the woman querulously, as she lay down again, and turning her face to the wall, passed quietly away.

The accordion and the bones were put aside that day, and Homer was forgotten. When the body of Mother Shipton had been committed to the snow, Mr. Oakhurst took The Innocent aside, and showed him a pair of snow-shoes, which he had fashioned from the old pack-saddle. "There's one chance in a hundred to save her yet," he said, pointing to Piney; "but it's there," he added, pointing toward Poker Flat. "If you can reach there in two days she's safe." "And you?" asked Tom Simson. "I'll stay here," was the curt reply.

The lovers parted with a long embrace. "You are not going, too," said the Duchess, as she saw Mr. Oakhurst apparently waiting to accompany him. "As far as the canyon," he replied. He turned suddenly, and kissed the Duchess, leaving her pallid face aflame, and her trembling limbs rigid with amazement.

Night came, but not Mr. Oakhurst. It brought the storm again and the whirling snow. Then the Duchess, feeding the fire, found that some one had quietly piled beside the hut enough fuel to last a few days longer. The tears rose to her eyes, but she hid them from Piney.

The women slept but little. In the morning, looking into each other's faces, they read their fate. Neither spoke; but Piney, accepting the position of the stronger, drew near and placed her arm around the Duchess's waist. They kept this attitude for the rest of the day. That night the storm reached its greatest fury, and rending asunder the protecting pines, invaded the very hut.

Toward morning they found themselves unable to feed the fire, which gradually died away. As the embers slowly blackened, the Duchess crept closer to Piney, and broke the silence of many hours: "Piney, can you pray?" "No, dear," said Piney, simply. The Duchess, without knowing exactly why, felt relieved, and putting her head upon Piney's shoulder, spoke no more. And so reclining, the younger and purer pillowing the head of her soiled sister upon her virgin breast, they fell asleep.

The wind lulled as if it feared to waken them. Feathery drifts of snow, shaken from the long pine boughs, flew like white-winged birds, and settled about them as they slept. The moon through the rifted clouds looked down upon what had been the camp. But all human stain, all trace of earthly travail, was hidden beneath the spotless mantle mercifully flung from above.

They slept all that day and the next, nor did they waken when voices and footsteps broke the silence of the camp. And when pitying fingers brushed the snow from their wan faces, you could scarcely have told from the equal peace that dwelt upon them, which was she that had sinned. Even the Law of Poker Flat recognized this, and turned away, leaving them still locked in each other's arms.

But at the head of the gulch, on one of the largest pine trees, they found the deuce of clubs pinned to the bark with a bowie knife. It bore the following, written in pencil, in a firm hand:

†

BENEATH THIS TREE

LIES THE BODY

OF

JOHN OAKHURST,

WHO STRUCK A STREAK OF BAD LUCK

ON THE 23D OF NOVEMBER, 1850,

AND

HANDED IN HIS CHECKS

ON THE 7TH DECEMBER, 1850

†

And pulseless and cold, with a Derringer[10] by his side and a bullet in his heart, though still calm as in life, beneath the snow, lay he who was at once the strongest and yet the weakest of the outcasts of Poker Flat.

[1869]

---

[10]A small, easily concealed pistol invented by the gunsmith Henry Derringer (1786–1868).

WILLIAM DEAN HOWELLS ■ (1837–1920)

The author of more than one hundred books, William Dean Howells was born in Martins Ferry, Ohio, the second of eight children. Though his formal schooling was intermittent, he developed an interest in literature and, as a teenager, began writing poems, essays, and short stories for newspapers in the state. His first books were *Poems of Two Friends* (1860) and a campaign biography of Abraham Lincoln (1860); this same year he traveled to Boston, where he met James Russell Lowell, Oliver Wendell Holmes, and other luminaries of the literary scene.

As a reward for his Lincoln biography, Howells was appointed U.S. consul in Venice. Thus he was abroad during the Civil War and had the opportunity to immerse himself in European languages, literatures, and cultures. Returning to the United States, he published *Venetian Life* (1866), based on travel letters he had written for a Boston paper. He became the assistant editor of the *Atlantic Monthly* (1866–71) and then its editor (1871–81).

Howells was an important, influential literary figure, connected both to the older generation of Boston and Cambridge authors and critics and to the new generation of writers, such as Henry James and Mark Twain, whose work he encouraged and published. In the mid-1880s, Howells left his post at the *Atlantic Monthly* and began to write a column for *Harper's Monthly*.

Through his own novels and many critical essays and reviews, Howells advanced the cause of literary realism, a serious, honest, reflective study of commonplace people and places and things, manners, social habits, and customs. Two of Howells's best novels of this period are *A Modern Instance* (1882), about the failure of a marriage, and *The Rise of Silas Lapham* (1885), about the financial fall and moral ascent of a businessman new to Boston society.

Later in the 1880s and into the 1890s, Howells became troubled by the economic and social unrest and violence he saw breaking out in the nation. "There's something in the air," he said, "that won't allow you to live in the old way if you've got a grain of conscience or of humanity." His reading of the Russian author Leo Tolstoy's essays and stories informed his idea of his mission as a novelist, which was to "make men know each other better, that they may all be humbled and strengthened by a sense of their fraternity."

For Howells, the novelist was obliged to teach all persons and thereby dispute the boundaries of class. "Disdain[ing] the office of the teacher is one of the last refuges of the aristocratic spirit," he argued. Howells's view was ethical, not political, and in this respect he was not wholly equipped to understand the social crises erupting around him. The poet and essayist James Russell Lowell perhaps was making a version of this point when he identified Howells as "the sweetest socialist that ever was."

Staunchly liberal in outlook, Howells articulated and explored the state of the nation in such novels as *A Hazard of New Fortunes* (1890), keyed to the launching of a new magazine and the outbreak of a labor riot, and *A Traveler from Altruria* (1894), about a visitor from the utopia of Altruria who recounts the wonders of his democratic commonwealth, which are contrasted to the inequality and injustice of social conditions in America.

Howells's reputation faded during the first decades of the twentieth century. Once a pioneering and controversial spokesman for realism, he was now seen as old-fashioned and fussy. To the boisterous critic and editor H. L. Mencken, for example, Howells was a "Victorian" with no robust lessons in style or content to offer to the present, a writer who "really had nothing to say."

Yet Howells was more complex and interesting than Mencken and others suggested. Like Henry James, Howells wrote as a critic about Turgenev, Zola, and other European realists and naturalists, but he also wrote about the African American writers Charles Chesnutt, Booker T. Washington, and Paul Laurence Dunbar and about the Jewish author and editor Abraham Cahan. He was the first major voice to declare the greatness of Emily Dickinson's poetry (1891), and he encouraged and criticized writers as different from one another as James and Twain, and Frank Norris and Sarah Orne Jewett.

"Off to War," photograph by Harry Mellon Rhoads (1880/81–1975) of a parade in Denver, Colorado, in 1898, to honor soldiers leaving for the Spanish-American War.

"Editha," published in *Harper's Monthly* in January 1905, is a powerful antiwar story whose backdrop is the Spanish-American War of 1898, which Howells, Twain, the philosopher William James, and other writers and intellectuals denounced as a brutal display of U.S. imperialism. Howells also delves into the gender wars and the disquieting, even deadly, forms that male and female identities and relationships are encouraged by social convention to take. The female protagonist is self-absorbed and self-deluded, not able to perceive her manipulations of the man whom she supposedly loves. He, in turn, weakly taking refuge in ironic byplay and his own engaging and agreeable personality, is carried off to his doom.

For biography, see Edwin H. Cady, *The Road to Realism: The Early Years, 1837–1885, of William Dean Howells* (1956) and *The Realist at War: The Mature Years, 1885–1920, of William Dean Howells* (1958); Kenneth S. Lynn, *William Dean Howells: An American Life* (1971); John W. Crowley, *The Black Heart's Truth: The Early Career of W. D. Howells* (1985) and *The Dean of American Letters: The Late Career of William Dean Howells* (1999). See also Michael Anesko, *Letters, Fictions, Lives: Henry James and William Dean Howells* (1997). Critical studies include Everett Carter, *Howells and the Age of Realism* (1954); Alfred Habegger, *Gender, Fantasy, and Realism in American Literature* (1982); and Elizabeth Stevens Prioleau, *The Circle of Eros: Sexuality in the Work of William Dean Howells* (1983). See also Paul Abeln, *William Dean Howells and the Ends of Realism* (2005); and Susan Goodman and Carl Dawson, *William Dean Howells: A Writer's life* (2005).

Editha

The air was thick with the war feeling,[1] like the electricity of a storm which has not yet burst. Editha sat looking out into the hot spring afternoon, with her lips parted, and panting with the intensity of the question whether she could let him go. She had decided that she could not let him stay, when she saw him at the end of the still leafless avenue, making slowly up toward the house, with his head down, and his figure relaxed. She ran impatiently out on the veranda, to the edge of the steps, and imperatively demanded greater haste of him with her will before she called aloud to him, "George!"

He had quickened his pace in mystical response to her mystical urgence, before he could have heard her; now he looked up and answered, "Well?"

"Oh, how united we are!" she exulted, and then she swooped down the steps to him. "What is it?" she cried.

"It's war," he said, and he pulled her up to him, and kissed her.

---

[1]The Spanish-American War (1898) is also called "The Newspaper War" because sensationalist press supposedly brought on the fighting. The question remains whether the press merely reflected the public's desire for war or, in fact, actually fed it.

She kissed him back intensely, but irrelevantly, as to their passion, and uttered from deep in her throat, "How glorious!"

"It's war," he repeated, without consenting to her sense of it; and she did not know just what to think at first. She never knew what to think of him; that made his mystery, his charm. All through their courtship, which was contemporaneous with the growth of the war feeling, she had been puzzled by his want of seriousness about it. He seemed to despise it even more than he abhorred it. She could have understood his abhorring any sort of bloodshed; that would have been a survival of his old life when he thought he would be a minister, and before he changed and took up the law. But making light of a cause so high and noble seemed to show a want of earnestness at the core of his being. Not but that she felt herself able to cope with a congenital defect of that sort, and make his love for her save him from himself. Now perhaps the miracle was already wrought in him. In the presence of the tremendous fact that he announced, all triviality seemed to have gone out of him; she began to feel that. He sank down on the top step, and wiped his forehead with her handkerchief, while she poured out upon him her question of the origin and authenticity of his news.

All the while, in her duplex emotioning, she was aware that now at the very beginning she must put a guard upon herself against urging him, by any word or act, to take the part that her whole soul willed him to take, for the completion of her ideal of him. He was very nearly perfect as he was, and he must be allowed to perfect himself. But he was peculiar, and he might very well be reasoned out of his peculiarity. Before her reasoning went her emotioning: her nature pulling upon his nature, her womanhood upon his manhood, without her knowing the means she was using to the end she was willing. She had always supposed that the man who won her would have done something to win her; she did not know what, but something. George Gearson had simply asked her for her love, on the way home from a concert, and she gave her love to him, without, as it were, thinking. But now, it flashed upon her, if he could do something worthy to *have* won her—be a hero, *her* hero—it would be even better than if he had done it before asking her; it would be grander. Besides, she had believed in the war from the beginning.

"But don't you see, dearest," she said, "that it wouldn't have come to this, if it hadn't been in the order of Providence? And I call any war glorious that is for the liberation of people who have been struggling for years against the cruelest oppression. Don't you think so too?"

"I suppose so," he returned, languidly. "But war! Is it glorious to break the peace of the world?"

"That ignoble peace! It was no peace at all, with that crime and shame at our very gates." She was conscious of parroting the current phrases of the newspapers, but it was no time to pick and choose her words. She must sacrifice anything to the high ideal she had for him, and after a good deal of rapid argument she ended with the climax: "But now it doesn't matter about the how or why. Since the war has come, all that is gone. There are no two sides, any more. There is nothing now but our country."

He sat with his eyes closed and his head leant back against the veranda, and he said with a vague smile, as if musing aloud, "Our country—right or wrong."[2]

"Yes, right or wrong!" she returned fervidly. "I'll go and get you some lemonade." She rose rustling, and whisked away; when she came back with two tall glasses of clouded liquid, on a tray, and the ice clucking in them, he still sat as she left him, and she said as if there had been no interruption: "But there is no question of wrong in this case. I call it a sacred war. A war for liberty, and humanity, if ever there was one. And I know you will see it just as I do, yet."

He took half the lemonade at a gulp, and he answered as he set the glass down: "I know you always have the highest ideal. When I differ from you, I ought to doubt myself."

A generous sob rose in Editha's throat for the humility of a man, so very nearly perfect, who was willing to put himself below her.

Besides, she felt, more subliminally, that he was never so near slipping through her fingers as when he took that meek way.

"You shall not say that! Only, for once I happen to be right." She seized his hand in her two hands, and poured her soul from her eyes into his. "Don't you think so?" she entreated him.

He released his hand and drank the rest of his lemonade, and she added, "Have mine, too," but he shook his head in answering, "I've no business to think so, unless I act so, too."

Her heart stopped a beat before it pulsed on with leaps that she felt in her neck. She had noticed that strange thing in men; they seemed to feel bound to do what they believed, and not think a thing was finished when they said it, as girls did. She knew what was in his mind, but she pretended not, and she said, "Oh, I am not sure," and then faltered.

He went on as if to himself without apparently heeding her, "There's only one way of proving one's faith in a thing like this."

She could not say that she understood, but she did understand.

He went on again. "If I believed—if I felt as you do about this war—Do you wish me to feel as you do?"

Now she was really not sure; so she said, "George, I don't know what you mean."

He seemed to muse away from her as before. "There is a sort of fascination in it. I suppose that at the bottom of his heart every man would like at times to have his courage tested; to see how he would act."

[2]Part of a famous toast given in 1816 by American naval officer Stephen Decatur (1779–1820): "To our Country! In her intercourse with foreign nations, may she always be in the right; but our country, right or wrong!"

"How can you talk in that ghastly way!"

"It *is* rather morbid. Still, that's what it comes to, unless you're swept away by ambition, or driven by conviction. I haven't the conviction or the ambition, and the other thing is what it comes to with me. I ought to have been a preacher, after all; then I couldn't have asked it of myself, as I must, now I'm a lawyer. And you believe it's a holy war, Editha?" he suddenly addressed her. "Or, I know you do! But you wish me to believe so, too?"

She hardly knew whether he was mocking or not, in the ironical way he always had with her plainer mind. But the only thing was to be outspoken with him.

"George, I wish you to believe whatever you think is true, at any and every cost. If I've tried to talk you into anything, I take it all back."

"Oh, I know that, Editha. I know how sincere you are, and how—I wish I had your undoubting spirit! I'll think it over; I'd like to believe as you do. But I don't, now; I don't; indeed. It isn't this war alone; though this seems peculiarly wanton and needless; but it's every war—so stupid; it makes me sick. Why shouldn't this thing have been settled reasonably?"

"Because," she said, very throatily again, "God meant it to be war."

"You think it was God? Yes, I suppose that is what people will say."

"Do you suppose it would have been war if God hadn't meant it?"

"I don't know. Sometimes it seems as if God had put this world into men's keeping to work it as they pleased."

"Now, George, that is blasphemy."

"Well, I won't blaspheme. I'll try to believe in your pocket Providence," he said, and then he rose to go.

"Why don't you stay to dinner?" Dinner at Balcom's Works was at one o'clock.

"I'll come back to supper, if you'll let me. Perhaps I shall bring you a convert."

"Well, you may come back, on that condition."

"All right. If I don't come, you'll understand."

He went away without kissing her, and she felt it a suspension of their engagement. It all interested her intensely; she was undergoing a tremendous experience, and she was being equal to it. While she stood looking after him, her mother came out through one of the long windows, on to the veranda, with a catlike softness and vagueness.

"Why didn't he stay to dinner?"

"Because—because—war has been declared," Editha pronounced, without turning.

Her mother said, "Oh, my!" and then said nothing more until she had sat down in one of the large Shaker chairs, and rocked herself for some time. Then she closed whatever tacit passage of thought there had been in her mind with the spoken words, "Well, I hope *he* won't go."

"And *I* hope he *will*," the girl said, and confronted her mother with a stormy exaltation that would have frightened any creature less unimpressionable than a cat.

Her mother rocked herself again for an interval of cogitation. What she arrived at in speech was, "Well, I guess you've done a wicked thing, Editha Balcom."

The girl said, as she passed indoors through the same window her mother had come out by, "I haven't done anything—yet."

In her room, she put together all her letters and gifts from Gearson, down to the withered petals of the first flower he had offered, with that timidity of his veiled in that irony of his. In the heart of the packet she enshrined her engagement ring which she had restored to the pretty box he had brought it to her in. Then she sat down, if not calmly yet strongly, and wrote:

> "George: I understood—when you left me. But I think we had better emphasize your meaning that if we cannot be one in everything we had better be one in nothing. So I am sending these things for your keeping till you have made up your mind.
>
> "I shall always love you, and therefore I shall never marry any one else. But the man I marry must love his country first of all, and be able to say to me,
>
> > 'I could not love thee, dear, so much,
> > Loved I not honor more,[3]
>
> "There is no honor above America with me. In this great hour there is no other honor.
>
> "Your heart will make my words clear to you. I had never expected to say so much, but it has come upon me that I must say the utmost.
>
> > Editha."

She thought she had worded her letter well, worded it in a way that could not be bettered; all had been implied and nothing expressed.

She had it ready to send with the packet she had tied with red, white, and blue ribbon, when it occurred to her that she was not just to him, that she was not giving him a fair chance. He had said he would go and think it over, and she was not waiting. She was pushing, threatening, compelling. That was not a woman's part. She must have him free, free, free. She could not accept for her country or herself a forced sacrifice.

In writing her letter she had satisfied the impulse from which it sprang; she could well afford to wait till he had thought it over. She put

[3]From "To Lucasta. Going to the Warres," by English poet Richard Lovelace (1618–58).

the packet and the letter by, and rested serene in the consciousness of having done what was laid upon her by her love itself to do, and yet used patience, mercy, justice.

She had her reward. Gearson did not come to tea, but she had given him till morning, when, late at night there came up from the village the sound of a fife and drum with a tumult of voices, in shouting, singing, and laughing. The noise drew nearer and nearer; it reached the street end of the avenue; there it silenced itself, and one voice, the voice she knew best, rose over the silence. It fell; the air was filled with cheers; the fife and drum struck up, with the shouting, singing, and laughing again, but now retreating; and a single figure came hurrying up the avenue.

She ran down to meet her lover and clung to him. He was very gay, and he put his arm round her with a boisterous laugh. "Well, you must call me Captain, now; or Cap, if you prefer; that's what the boys call me. Yes, we've had a meeting at the town hall, and everybody has volunteered; and they selected me for captain, and I'm going to the war, the big war, the glorious war, the holy war ordained by the pocket Providence that blesses butchery. Come along; let's tell the whole family about it. Call them from their downy beds, father, mother, Aunt Hitty, and all the folks!"

But when they mounted the veranda steps he did not wait for a larger audience; he poured the story out upon Editha alone.

"There was a lot of speaking, and then some of the fools set up a shout for me. It was all going one way, and I thought it would be a good joke to sprinkle a little cold water on them. But you can't do that with a crowd that adores you. The first thing I knew I was sprinkling hell-fire on them. 'Cry havoc, and let slip the dogs of war.'[4] That was the style. Now that it had come to the fight, there were no two parties; there was one country, and the thing was to fight the fight to a finish as quick as possible. I suggested volunteering then and there, and I wrote my name first of all on the roster. Then they elected me—that's all. I wish I had some ice-water!"

She left him walking up and down the veranda, while she ran for the ice-pitcher and a goblet, and when she came back he was still walking up and down, shouting the story he had told her to her father and mother, who had come out more sketchily dressed than they commonly were by day. He drank goblet after goblet of the ice-water without noticing who was giving it, and kept on talking, and laughing through his talk wildly. "It's astonishing," he said, "how well the worse reason looks when you try to make it appear the better. Why, I believe I was the first convert to the war in that crowd to-night! I never thought I should like to kill a man; but now, I shouldn't care; and the smokeless powder lets you see the man drop

---

[4]Part of Antony's speech following the murder of Caesar, in Shakespeare's *Julius Caesar* (3.1.274). "Cry 'havoc!' and let loose the dogs of war, / That this foul deed shall smell above the earth / With carrion men, groaning for burial."

that you kill. It's all for the country! What a thing it is to have a country that *can't* be wrong, but if it is, is right anyway!"

Editha had a great, vital thought, an inspiration. She set down the ice-pitcher on the veranda floor, and ran up-stairs and got the letter she had written him. When at last he noisily bade her father and mother, "Well, good night. I forgot I woke you up; I sha'n't want any sleep myself," she followed him down the avenue to the gate. There, after the whirling words that seemed to fly away from her thoughts and refuse to serve them, she made a last effort to solemnize the moment that seemed so crazy, and pressed the letter she had written upon him.

"What's this?" he said, "Want me to mail it?"

"No, no. It's for you. I wrote it after you went this morning. Keep it—keep it—and read it sometime—" She thought, and then her inspiration came: "Read it if ever you doubt what you've done, or fear that I regret your having done it. Read it after you've started."

They strained each other in embraces that seemed as ineffective as their words, and he kissed her face with quick, hot breaths that were so unlike him, that made her feel as if she had lost her old lover and found a stranger in his place. The stranger said, "What a gorgeous flower you are, with your red hair, and your blue eyes that look black now, and your face with the color painted out by the white moonshine! Let me hold you under my chin, to see whether I love blood, you tiger-lily!"[5] Then he laughed Gearson's laugh, and released her, scared and giddy. Within her willfulness she had been frightened by a sense of subtler force in him, and mystically mastered as she had never been before.

She ran all the way back to the house, and mounted the steps panting. Her mother and father were talking of the great affair. Her mother said: "Wa'n't Mr. Gearson in rather of an excited state of mind? Didn't you think he acted curious?"

"Well, not for a man who'd just been elected captain and had to set'em up for the whole of Company A," her father chuckled back.

"What in the world do you mean, Mr. Balcom? Oh! There's Editha!" She offered to follow the girl indoors.

"Don't come, mother!" Editha called, vanishing.

Mrs. Balcom remained to reproach her husband. "I don't see much of anything to laugh at."

"Well, it's catching. Caught it from Gearson. I guess it won't be much of a war, and I guess Gearson don't think so, either. The other fellows will back down as soon as they see we mean it. I wouldn't lose any sleep over it. I'm going back to bed, myself."

---

[5]George compares Editha's coloring to a wild flower. In the traditional language of flowers, the tiger lily symbolizes pride.

Gearson came again next afternoon, looking pale, and rather sick, but quite himself, even to his languid irony. "I guess I'd better tell you, Editha, that I consecrated myself to your god of battles last night by pouring too many libations to him down my own throat. But I'm all right, now. One has to carry off the excitement, somehow."

"Promise me," she commanded, "that you'll never touch it again!"

"What! Not let the cannikin clink? Not let the soldier drink?[6] Well, I promise."

"You don't belong to yourself now; you don't even belong to me. You belong to your country, and you have a sacred charge to keep yourself strong and well for your country's sake. I have been thinking, thinking all night and all day long."

"You look as if you had been crying a little, too," he said with his queer smile.

"That's all past. I've been thinking, and worshipping you. Don't you suppose I know all that you've been through, to come to this? I've followed you every step from your old theories and opinions."

"Well, you've had a long row to hoe."

"And I know you've done this from the highest motives—"

"Oh, there won't be much pettifogging[7] to do till this cruel war is—"

"And you haven't simply done it for my sake. I couldn't respect you if you had."

"Well, then we'll say I haven't. A man that hasn't got his own respect intact wants the respect of all the other people he can corner. But we won't go into that. I'm in for the thing now, and we've got to face our future. My idea is that this isn't going to be a very protracted struggle; we shall just scare the enemy to death before it comes to a fight at all. But we must provide for contingencies, Editha. If anything happens to me—"

"Oh, George!" She clung to him sobbing.

"I don't want you to feel foolishly bound to my memory. I should hate that, wherever I happened to be."

"I am yours, for time and eternity—time and eternity." She liked the words; they satisfied her famine for phrases.

"Well, say eternity; that's all right; but time's another thing; and I'm talking about time. But there is something! My mother! If anything happens—"

She winced, and he laughed. "You're not the bold soldier-girl of yesterday!" Then he sobered. "If anything happens, I want you to help my mother out. She won't like my doing this thing. She brought me up to think war a fool thing as well as a bad thing. My father was in the civil

---

[6]Allusion to words sung by Iago in Shakespeare's *Othello* (2.3.71). A cannikin is a small drinking vessel. "And let me the cannikin clink / A soldier's a man / A life's but a span / Why then let a soldier drink."
[7]Quibbling, chicanery, shifty or crafty pleading.

war; all through it; lost his arm in it." She thrilled with the sense of the arm round her; what if that should be lost? He laughed as if divining her: "Oh, it doesn't run in the family, as far as I know!" Then he added, gravely, "He came home with misgivings about war, and they grew on him. I guess he and mother agreed between them that I was to be brought up in his final mind about it; but that was before my time. I only knew him from my mother's report of him and his opinions; I don't know whether they were hers first; but they were hers last. This will be a blow to her. I shall have to write and tell her—"

He stopped, and she asked, "Would you like me to write too, George?"

"I don't believe that would do. No, I'll do the writing. She'll understand a little if I say that I thought the way to minimize it was to make war on the largest possible scale at once—that I felt I must have been helping on the war somehow if I hadn't helped keep it from coming, and I knew I hadn't; when it came, I had no right to stay out of it."

Whether his sophistries satisfied him or not, they satisfied her. She clung to his breast, and whispered, with closed eyes and quivering lips, "Yes, yes, yes!"

"But if anything should happen, you might go to her, and see what you could do for her. You know? It's rather far off; she can't leave her chair—"

"Oh, I'll go, if it's the ends of the earth! But nothing will happen! Nothing *can*! I—"

She felt herself lifted with his rising, and Gearson was saying, with his arm still round her, to her father: "Well, we're off at once, Mr. Balcom. We're to be formally accepted at the capital, and then bunched up with the rest somehow, and sent into camp somewhere, and got to the front as soon as possible. We all want to be in the van, of course; we're the first company to report to the Governor. I came to tell Editha, but I hadn't got round to it."

She saw him again for a moment at the capital, in the station, just before the train started southward with his regiment. He looked well, in his uniform, and very soldierly, but somehow girlish, too, with his clean-shaven face and slim figure. The manly eyes and the strong voice satisfied her, and his preoccupation with some unexpected details of duty flattered her. Other girls were weeping and bemoaning themselves, but she felt a sort of noble distinction in the abstraction, the almost unconsciousness, with which they parted. Only at the last moment he said, "Don't forget my mother. It mayn't be such a walk-over as I supposed," and he laughed at the notion.

He waved his hand to her, as the train moved off—she knew it among a score of hands that were waved to other girls from the platform of the car, for it held a letter which she knew was hers. Then he went inside the car to read it, doubtless, and she did not see him again. But she felt safe for him through the strength of what she called her love. What she called her God, always speaking the name in a deep voice and with the implication of a mutual understanding, would watch over him and keep him and bring him back to her. If with an empty sleeve, then he should have three arms instead of two, for both of hers should be his for life. She did not see, though, why she should always be thinking of the arm his father had lost.

There were not many letters from him, but they were such as she could have wished, and she put her whole strength into making hers such as she imagined he could have wished, glorifying and supporting him. She wrote to his mother glorifying him as their hero, but the brief answer she got was merely to the effect that Mrs. Gearson was not well enough to write herself, and thanking her for her letter by the hand of some one who called herself "Yrs truly, Mrs. W.J. Andrews."

Editha determined not to be hurt, but to write again quite as if the answer had been all she expected. But before it seemed as if she could have written, there came news of the first skirmish, and in the list of the killed which was telegraphed as a trifling loss on our side, was Gearson's name. There was a frantic time of trying to make out that it might be, must be, some other Gearson; but the name, and the company and the regiment, and the State were too definitely given.

Then there was a lapse into depths out of which it seemed as if she never could rise again; then a lift into clouds far above all grief, black clouds, that blotted out the sun, but where she soared with him, with George, George! She had the fever that she expected of herself, but she did not die in it; she was not even delirious, and it did not last long. When she was well enough to leave her bed, her one thought was of George's mother, of his strangely worded wish that she should go to her and see what she could do for her. In the exaltation of the duty laid upon her—it buoyed her up instead of burdening her—she rapidly recovered.

Her father went with her on the long railroad journey from northern New York to western Iowa; he had business out at Davenport, and he said he could just as well go then as any other time; and he went with her to the little country town where George's mother lived in a little house on the edge of illimitable corn-fields, under trees pushed to a top of the rolling prairie. George's father had settled there after the civil war, as so many other old soldiers had done; but they were Eastern people, and Editha fancied touches of the East in the June rose overhanging the front door, and the garden with early summer flowers stretching from the gate of the paling fence.

It was very low inside the house, and so dim, with the closed blinds, that they could scarcely see one another: Editha tall and black in her crapes which filled the air with the smell of their dyes; her father standing decorously apart with his hat on his forearm, as at funerals; a woman rested in a deep armchair, and the woman who had let the strangers in stood behind the chair.

The seated woman turned her head round and up, and asked the woman behind her chair, "*Who* did you say?"

Editha, if she had done what she expected of herself, would have gone down on her knees at the feet of the seated figure and said, "I am George's Editha," for answer.

But instead of her own voice she heard that other woman's voice, saying, "Well, I don't know as I *did* get the name just right. I guess I'll have to make a little more light in here," and she went and pushed two of the shutters ajar.

Then Editha's father said in his public will-now-address-a-few-remarks tone, "My name is Balcom, ma'am; Junius H. Balcom, of Balcom's Works, New York; my daughter—"

"Oh!" The seated woman broke in, with a powerful voice, the voice that always surprised Editha from Gearson's slender frame. "Let me see you! Stand round where the light can strike on your face," and Editha dumbly obeyed. "So, you're Editha Balcom," she sighed.

"Yes," Editha said, more like a culprit than a comforter.

"What did you come for?" Mrs. Gearson asked.

Editha's face quivered, and her knees shook. "I came—because—because George—" She could go no farther.

"Yes," the mother said, "he told me he had asked you to come if he got killed. You didn't expect that, I suppose, when you sent him."

"I would rather have died myself than done it!" Editha said with more truth in her deep voice than she ordinarily found in it. "I tried to leave him free—"

"Yes, that letter of yours, that came back with his other things, left him free."

Editha saw now where George's irony came from.

"It was not to be read before—unless—until—I told him so," she faltered.

"Of course, he wouldn't read a letter of yours, under the circumstances, till he thought you wanted him to. Been sick?" the woman abruptly demanded.

"Very sick," Editha said, with self-pity.

"Daughter's life," her father interposed, "was almost despaired of, at one time."

Mrs. Gearson gave him no heed. "I suppose you would have been glad to die, such a brave person as you! I don't believe *he* was glad to die. He was always a timid boy, that way; he was afraid of a good many things; but if he was afraid he did what he made up his mind to. I suppose he made up his mind to go, but I knew what it cost him, by what it cost me when I heard of it. I had been through *one* war before. When you sent him you didn't expect he would get killed?"

The voice seemed to compassionate Editha, and it was time. "No," she huskily murmured.

"No, girls don't; women don't, when they give their men up to their country. They think they'll come marching back, somehow, just as gay as they went, or if it's an empty sleeve, or even an empty pantaloon, it's all the more glory, and they're so much the prouder of them, poor things."

The tears began to run down Editha's face; she had not wept till then; but it was now such a relief to be understood that the tears came.

"No, you didn't expect him to get killed," Mrs. Gearson repeated in a voice which was startlingly like Gearson's again. "You just expected him to kill some one else, some of those foreigners, that weren't there because they had any say about it, but because they had to be there, poor wretches—conscripts, or whatever they call 'em. You thought it would be all right for my George, *your* George, to kill the sons of those miserable mothers and the husbands of those girls that you would never see the faces of." The woman lifted her powerful voice in a psalmlike note. "I thank my God he didn't live to do it! I thank my God they killed him first, and that he ain't livin' with their blood on his hands!" She dropped her eyes which she had raised with her voice, and glared at Editha. "What you got that black on for?" She lifted herself by her powerful arms so high that her helpless body seemed to hang limp its full length. "Take it off, take it off, before I tear it from your back!"

The lady who was passing the summer near Balcom's Works was sketching Editha's beauty, which lent itself wonderfully to the effects of a colorist. It had come to that confidence which is rather apt to grow between artist and sitter, and Editha had told her everything.

"To think of your having such a tragedy in your life!" the lady said. She added: "I suppose there are people who feel that way about war. But when you consider the good this war had done—how much it has done for the country! I can't understand such people, for my part. And when you had come all the way out there to console her—got up out of a sick bed! Well!"

"I think," Editha said, magnanimously, "she wasn't quite in her right mind; and so did papa."

"Yes," the lady said, looking at Editha's lips in nature and then at her lips in art, and giving an empirical touch to them in the picture. "But how dreadful of her! How perfectly—excuse me—how *vulgar*!"

A light broke upon Editha in the darkness which she felt had been without a gleam of brightness for weeks and months. The mystery that had bewildered her was solved by the word; and from that moment she rose from grovelling in shame and self-pity, and began to live again in the ideal.

[1905]

AMBROSE BIERCE ■ (1842–1914)

One of thirteen children, Ambrose Bierce was born in Meigs County, southern Ohio, in a religiously devout household, and raised on a farm in Indiana. He spent only a year in high school, worked for a newspaper, attended Kentucky Military Institute, and then held a job in a store.

Bierce was a private, a sergeant, and, eventually, an officer in the Union Army from 1861 to 1865, and his experiences in a number of battles—he suffered serious wounds himself—were the basis for his grim, ironic stories about the Civil War, including the violent, nightmarishly surreal "Chickamauga," a gem of lurid detail and grotesque humor.

Like Mark Twain and Bret Harte, both of whom he knew, Bierce headed west to launch his career as a writer. He was a journalist and editor in California and also worked on short stories, the first of which, "The Haunted Valley," was published in 1871.

Having married the daughter of a prosperous miner, Bierce relocated to London, where he lived from 1872 to 1875, publishing several books of epigrams and sketches. Upon his return to the United States, he worked as an associate editor of *The Wasp*, a weekly newspaper in San Francisco, attempted to make his fortune in mining, and, when that failed, resumed his career as a newspaper columnist.

In the mid-1890s, Bierce moved again, this time to Washington, D.C., continuing there his work for local and national papers and magazines. His marriage was rocky, he drank too much, and two of his sons had troubles as well. By 1904 he was divorced, his relationship with his family at an end. He worked as a writer and caroused a lot, mostly in Washington, D.C.

Toward the end of 1913, Bierce left for Mexico, intent on meeting with Pancho Villa, the revolutionary leader. The last that is known of Bierce is a letter from Mexico dated December 26, 1913. For the next decade, even two decades, rumors reported that he was seen here or there or somewhere else, but it is now widely believed that he died in Mexico, perhaps in a siege in January 1914.

Mordant, misanthropic, and wickedly entertaining, Bierce is a compelling writer whose ironies reflect the horrors he witnessed during the Civil War, the fast-and-loose deal making he observed in the wild days of California mining and prospecting, and the bitter breakup of his marriage and family. As the scholar Jay Martin has noted, Bierce "was a fierce and stern moralist living in what he believed to be an age of moral looseness. For three decades he exposed, with apparently perverse relish, the rottenness of American life, its political corruption, its moral debasement, its economic chicanery."

Bierce's best stories are collected in *Tales of Soldiers and Civilians* (1892). He also is the author of a satiric work, *The Cynic's Word Book* (1906), later published in a new edition with the title, *The Devil's Dictionary* (1911).

Bierce came up with the idea of sour, ironic dictionary entries perhaps as early as 1869 and developed it in the mid- to late 1870s. In 1881 he used the title, "The Devil's Dictionary" for the first time, while he was working for *The Wasp*. This feature was popular, and Bierce from 1881 to 1886 wrote eighty-eight installments, each of them giving fifteen to twenty entries. Later, using the title "The Cynic's Dictionary," Bierce published additional entries in the *Examiner*, a San Francisco newspaper. Iconoclastic and impious, he favored the title *The Devil's Dictionary*, saying it was irreverent. Bierce's book has been reprinted often, in selected and complete editions. As the following selections indicate, it is a pointed, comic, mocking portrait of human foolishness, self-deception, and absurdity. Bierce believed that life was futile and compromised, doomed with no exceptions to a bad ending. "Bierce would bury his best friend with a sigh of relief," concluded the novelist Jack London, "and express satisfaction that he was done with him."

For an overview: M. E. Grenander, *Ambrose Bierce* (1971). Critical discussion can be found in *Critical Essays on Ambrose Bierce*, ed. Cathy N. Davidson (1982); and Cathy N. Davidson, *The Experimental Fictions of Ambrose Bierce: Structuring the Ineffable* (1984). See also Lawrence I. Berkove, *A Prescription for Adversity: The Moral Art of Ambrose Bierce* (2002). Another good resource: Robert L. Gale, *An Ambrose Bierce Companion* (2001). A good biography is Roy Morris Jr., *Ambrose Bierce: Alone in Bad Company* (1996); and Donald T. Blume focuses on the Civil War writings in *Ambrose Bierce's Civilians and Soldiers in Context: A Critical Study* (2004).

Chickamauga[1]

One sunny autumn afternoon a child strayed away from its rude home in a small field and entered a forest unobserved. It was happy in a new sense of freedom from control, happy in the opportunity of exploration and adventure; for this child's spirit, in bodies of its ancestors, had for thousands of years been trained to memorable feats of discovery and conquest—victories in battles whose critical moments were centuries, whose victors' camps were cities of hewn stone. From the cradle of its race it had conquered its way through two continents and passing a great sea had penetrated a third, there to be born to war and dominion as a heritage.

The child was a boy aged about six years, the son of a poor planter. In his younger manhood the father had been a soldier, had fought against naked savages[2] and followed the flag of his country into the capital of a civilized race to the far South. In the peaceful life of a planter the warrior-fire

---

[1]Civil War battle fought on September 19, 1863, near Chickamauga Creek in northwestern Georgia. The battle resulted in over 40,000 casualties but had no clear winner.
[2]May refer to the forced expulsion of the Cherokee people, who were driven from Georgia in the 1830s by Andrew Jackson as part of his Indian Removal Bill. Over 4,000 Cherokee died during the westward journey known as the Trail of Tears.

survived; once kindled, it is never extinguished. The man loved military
books and pictures and the boy had understood enough to make himself
a wooden sword, though even the eye of his father would hardly have
known it for what it was. This weapon he now bore bravely, as became the
son of an heroic race, and pausing now and again in the sunny spaces of
the forest assumed, with some exaggeration, the postures of aggression
and defense that he had been taught by the engraver's art. Made reckless
by the ease with which he overcame invisible foes attempting to stay his
advance, he committed the common enough military error of pushing the
pursuit to a dangerous extreme, until he found himself upon the margin
of a wide but shallow brook, whose rapid waters barred his direct advance
against the flying foe that had crossed with illogical ease. But the intrepid
victor was not to be baffled; the spirit of the race which had passed the
great sea burned unconquerable in that small breast and would not be
denied. Finding a place where some boulders in the bed of the stream lay
but a step or a leap apart, he made his way across and fell again upon the
rear-guard of his imaginary foe, putting all to the sword.

Now that the battle had been won, prudence required that he withdraw
to his base of operations. Alas; like many a mightier conqueror, and like
one, the mightiest, he could not

> curb the lust for war,
> Nor learn that tempted Fate will leave the loftiest star.[3]

Advancing from the bank of the creek he suddenly found himself confronted with a new and more formidable enemy: in the path that he was
following, sat, bolt upright, with ears erect and paws suspended before
it, a rabbit. With a startled cry the child turned and fled, he knew not
in what direction, calling with inarticulate cries for his mother, weeping,
stumbling, his tender skin cruelly torn by brambles, his little heart beating
hard with terror—breathless, blind with tears—lost in the forest! Then,
for more than an hour, he wandered with erring feet through the tangled
undergrowth, till at last, overcome by fatigue, he lay down in a narrow
space between two rocks, within a few yards of the stream and still grasping his toy sword, no longer a weapon but a companion, sobbed himself to
sleep. The wood birds sang merrily above his head; the squirrels, whisking
their bravery of tail, ran barking from tree to tree, unconscious of the pity
of it, and somewhere far away was a strange, muffled thunder, as if the
partridges were drumming in celebration of nature's victory over the son of
her immemorial enslavers. And back at the little plantation, where white
men and black were hastily searching the fields and hedges in alarm, a
mother's heart was breaking for her missing child.

[3]Lines from *Childe Harold's Pilgrimage* (1812–18), Canto 3, stanza 38, by the English Romantic poet
Lord Byron (1788–1824).

Hours passed, and then the little sleeper rose to his feet. The chill of the evening was in his limbs, the fear of the gloom in his heart. But he had rested, and he no longer wept. With some blind instinct which impelled to action he struggled through the undergrowth about him and came to a more open ground—on his right the brook, to the left a gentle acclivity studded with infrequent trees; over all, the gathering gloom of twilight. A thin, ghostly mist rose along the water. It frightened and repelled him; instead of recrossing, in the direction whence he had come, he turned his back upon it, and went forward toward the dark inclosing wood. Suddenly he saw before him a strange moving object which he took to be some large animal—a dog, a pig—he could not name it; perhaps it was a bear. He had seen pictures of bears, but knew of nothing to their discredit and had vaguely wished to meet one. But something in form or movement of this object—something in the awkwardness of its approach—told him that it was not a bear, and curiosity was stayed by fear. He stood still and as it came slowly on gained courage every moment, for he saw that at least it had not the long, menacing ears of the rabbit. Possibly his impressionable mind was half conscious of something familiar in its shambling, awkward gait. Before it had approached near enough to resolve his doubts he saw that it was followed by another and another. To right and to left were many more; the whole open space about him was alive with them—all moving toward the brook.

They were men. They crept upon their hands and knees. They used their hands only, dragging their legs. They used their knees only, their arms hanging idle at their sides. They strove to rise to their feet, but fell prone in the attempt. They did nothing naturally, and nothing alike, save only to advance foot by foot in the same direction. Singly, in pairs and in little groups, they came on through the gloom, some halting now and again while others crept slowly past them, then resuming their movement. They came by dozens and by hundreds; as far on either hand as one could see in the deepening gloom they extended, and the black wood behind them appeared to be inexhaustible. The very ground seemed in motion toward the creek. Occasionally one who had paused did not again go on, but lay motionless. He was dead. Some, pausing, made strange gestures with their hands, erected their arms and lowered them again, clasped their heads; spread their palms upward, as men are sometimes seen to do in public prayer.

Not all of this did the child note; it is what would have been noted by an elder observer; he saw little but that these were men, yet crept like babes. Being men, they were not terrible, though unfamiliarly clad. He moved among them freely, going from one to another and peering into their faces with childish curiosity. All their faces were singularly white and many were streaked and gouted with red. Something in this—something too, perhaps, in their grotesque attitudes and movements—reminded him of the painted clown whom he had seen last summer in the circus, and he laughed as he watched them. But on and ever on they crept, these maimed and bleeding men, as heedless as he of the dramatic contrast between his laughter and their own ghastly gravity. To him it was a merry spectacle. He had seen his father's negroes creep upon their hands and knees for his amusement—had ridden them so, "making believe" they were his horses. He now approached one of these crawling figures from behind and with an agile movement mounted it astride. The man sank upon his breast, recovered, flung the small boy fiercely to the ground as an unbroken colt might have done, then turned upon him a face that lacked a lower jaw—from the upper teeth to the throat was a great red gap fringed with hanging shreds of flesh and splinters of bone. The unnatural prominence of nose, the absence of chin, the fierce eyes, gave this man the appearance of a great bird of prey crimsoned in throat and breast by the blood of its quarry. The man rose to his knees, the child to his feet. The man shook his fist at the child; the child, terrified at last, ran to a tree near by, got upon the farther side of it and took a more serious view of the situation. And so the clumsy multitude dragged itself slowly and painfully along in hideous pantomime— moved forward down the slope like a swarm of great black beetles, with never a sound of going—in silence profound, absolute.

Instead of darkening, the haunted landscape began to brighten. Through the belt of trees beyond the brook shone a strange red light, the trunks and branches of the trees making a black lacework against it. It struck the creeping figures and gave them monstrous shadows, which caricatured their movements on the lit grass. It fell upon their faces, touching their whiteness with a ruddy tinge, accentuating the stains with which so many of them were freaked and maculated.[4] It sparkled on buttons and bits of metal in their clothing. Instinctively the child turned toward the growing splendor and moved down the slope with his horrible companions; in a few moments had passed the foremost of the throng—not much of a feat, considering his advantages. He placed himself in the lead, his wooden sword still in hand, and solemnly directed the march, conforming his pace to theirs and occasionally turning as if to see that his forces did not straggle. Surely such a leader never before had such a following.

Scattered about upon the ground now slowly narrowing by the encroachment of this awful march to water, were certain articles to which, in the leader's mind, were coupled no significant associations: an occasional blanket, tightly rolled lengthwise, doubled and the ends bound together with a string; a heavy knapsack here, and there a broken rifle—such things, in short, as are found in the rear of retreating troops, the "spoor"[5] of men flying from their hunters. Everywhere near the creek, which here had a margin of lowland, the earth was trodden into mud by the feet of

[4]Flecked and spotted.
[5]The track or trail of a wild animal pursued as game.

men and horses. An observer of better experience in the use of his eyes would have noticed that these footprints pointed in both directions; the ground had been twice passed over—in advance and in retreat. A few hours before, these desperate, stricken men, with their more fortunate and now distant comrades, had penetrated the forest in thousands. Their successive battalions, breaking into swarms and reforming in lines, had passed the child on every side—had almost trodden on him as he slept. The rustle and murmur of their march had not awakened him. Almost within a stone's throw of where he lay they had fought a battle; but all unheard by him were the roar of the musketry, the shock of the cannon, "the thunder of the captains and the shouting."[6] He had slept through it all, grasping his little wooden sword with perhaps a tighter clutch in unconscious sympathy with his martial environment, but as heedless of the grandeur of the struggle as the dead who had died to make the glory.

The fire beyond the belt of woods on the farther side of the creek, reflected to earth from the canopy of its own smoke, was now suffusing the whole landscape. It transformed the sinuous line of mist to the vapor of gold. The water gleamed with dashes of red, and red, too, were many of the stones protruding above the surface. But that was blood; the less desperately wounded had stained them in crossing. On them, too, the child now crossed with eager steps; he was going to the fire. As he stood upon the farther bank he turned about to look at the companions of his march. The advance was arriving at the creek. The stronger had already drawn themselves to the brink and plunged their faces into the flood. Three or four who lay without motion appeared to have no heads. At this the child's eyes expanded with wonder; even his hospitable understanding could not accept a phenomenon implying such vitality as that. After slaking their thirst these men had not the strength to back away from the water, nor to keep their heads above it. They were drowned. In rear of these, the open spaces of the forest showed the leader as many formless figures of his grim command as at first; but not nearly so many were in motion. He waved his cap for their encouragement and smilingly pointed with his weapon in the direction of the guiding light—a pillar of fire to this strange exodus.[7]

Confident of the fidelity of his forces, he now entered the belt of woods, passed through it easily in the red illumination, climbed a fence, ran across a field, turning now and again to coquet with his responsive shadow, and so approached the blazing ruin of a dwelling. Desolation everywhere! In all the wide glare not a living thing was visible. He cared nothing for that; the spectacle pleased, and he danced with glee in imitation of the wavering flames. He ran about, collecting fuel, but every object

---

[6]Job 39:25: "He saith among the trumpets, Ha, ha; and he smelleth the battle afar off, the thunder of the captains, and the shouting."
[7]Referring to the flight of the Israelites from Egypt in Exodus 13:21, during which "The Lord went before them by day in a pillar of cloud to lead them along the way, and by night in a pillar of fire to give them light."

that he found was too heavy for him to cast in from the distance to which the heat limited his approach. In despair he flung in his sword—a surrender to the superior forces of nature. His military career was at an end.

Shifting his position, his eyes fell upon some outbuildings which had an oddly familiar appearance, as if he had dreamed of them. He stood considering them with wonder, when suddenly the entire plantation, with its inclosing forest, seemed to turn as if upon a pivot. His little world swung half around; the points of the compass were reversed. He recognized the blazing building as his own home!

For a moment he stood stupefied by the power of the revelation, then ran with stumbling feet, making a half-circuit of the ruin. There, conspicuous in the light of the conflagration,[8] lay the dead body of a woman—the white face turned upward, the hands thrown out and clutched full of grass, the clothing deranged, the long dark hair in tangles and full of clotted blood. The greater part of the forehead was torn away, and from the jagged hole the brain protruded, overflowing the temple, a frothy mass of gray, crowned with clusters of crimson bubbles—the work of a shell.

The child moved his little hands, making wild, uncertain gestures. He uttered a series of inarticulate and indescribable cries—something between the chattering of an ape and the gobbling of a turkey—a startling, soulless, unholy sound, the language of a devil. The child was a deaf mute.

Then he stood motionless, with quivering lips, looking down upon the wreck.

[1889]

From The Devil's Dictionary

Apologize, v.i., To lay the foundation for a future offense.

Bigot, n., One who is obstinately and zealously attached to an opinion that you do not entertain.

Bride, n., A women with a fine prospect of happiness behind her.

Consult, v.t., To seek another's approval of a course already decided on.

Corporation, n., An ingenious device for obtaining individual profit without individual responsibility.

Day, n., A period of twenty-four hours, mostly misspent.

Distance, n., The only thing that the rich are willing for the poor to call theirs, and keep.

Education, n., That which discloses to the wise and disguises from the foolish their lack of understanding.

Famous, adj., Conspicuously miserable.

Friendship, n., A ship big enough to carry two in fair weather, but only one in foul.

[8]A great and destructive fire.

Future, n., That period of time in which our affairs prosper, our friends are true and our happiness is assured.

Handkerchief, n., A small square of silk or linen, used in various ignoble offices about the face and especially serviceable at funerals to conceal the lack of tears.

History, n., An account mostly false, of events mostly unimportant, which are brought about by rulers mostly knaves, and soldiers mostly fools.

I is the first letter of the alphabet, the first word of the language, the first thought of the mind, the first object of affection.

Idiot, n., A member of a large and powerful tribe whose influence in human affairs has always been dominant and controlling.

Imagination, n., A warehouse of facts, with poet and liar in joint ownership.

Justice, n., A commodity which in a more or less adulterated condition the State sells to the citizen as a reward for his allegiance, taxes and personal service.

Liberty, n., One of imagination's most precious possessions.

Logic, n., The art of thinking and reasoning in strict accordance with the limitations and incapacities of the human misunderstanding.

Mine, adj., Belonging to me if I can hold or seize it.

Oblivion, n., The state of condition in which the wicked cease from struggling and the dreary are at rest. Fame's eternal dumping ground. Cold storage for high hopes. A place where ambitious authors meet their works without pride and their betters without envy.

Opportunity, n., A favorable occasion for grasping a disappointment.

Patience, n., A minor form of despair, disguised as a virtue.

Philosophy, n., A route of many roads leading from nowhere to nothing.

Religion, n., A daughter of Hope and Fear, explaining to Ignorance the nature of Unknowable.

Responsibility, n., A detachable burden easily shifted to the shoulders of God, Fate, Fortune, Luck or one's neighbor.

Robber, n., A candid man of affairs.

Self-esteem, n., An erroneous appraisement.

Story, n., A narrative, commonly untrue.

Twice, adv., Once too often.

Vote, n., The instrument and symbol of a freeman's power to make a fool of himself and a wreck of his country.

Wedding, n., A ceremony at which two persons undertake to become one, one undertakes to become nothing, and nothing undertakes to become supportable.

Year, n., A period of three hundred and sixty-five disappointments.

Youth, n., The period of possibility.

[1911]

▪▪ CONTEXT AND RESPONSE ▪▪

The Poetry of Dorothy Parker

Although a gap of more than fifty years splits their ages, the writings of Dorothy Parker (1893–1967) and her forerunner Ambrose Bierce display a markedly similar sensibility. Both authors are notorious for their irreverent, sharp-tongued humor and for their morbid, satirical takes on social topics. Dorothy Parker was an American writer of poetry, short fiction, and movie scripts who received two Academy Award nominations. She was a founding member of the Algonquin Round Table, a group of famous New York City critics, comedians, and authors. Little is known about Parker's writing process or influences in part because she refused to save her personal letters for posterity. However, some current critics argue that she has not received the respect for her literary merit that she deserves because she wrote humorously and from a woman's perspective.

Parker's first volume of collected poems, *Enough Rope* (1926), from which the selections below are taken, sold briskly and won rave reviews. The following selections from that volume suggest that Parker and Bierce shared a knowing outlook on human foolishness, self-deception, and imperfection. Merrily skewering solemn topics like love, marriage, and suicide, Dorothy Parker could hold her own with the ghost of the larger-than-life nineteenth-century satirist Bierce—perhaps because neither took themselves too seriously. Despite recurring bouts of depression, Parker—of whom a fellow writer said, "This bird only sings when she is unhappy,"—survived multiple suicide attempts as a young writer to become a legend in her lifetime.

A Certain Lady

Oh, I can smile for you, and tilt my head,
And drink your rushing words with eager lips,
And paint my mouth for you a fragrant red,
And trace your brows with tutored finger-tips.
When you rehearse your list of loves to me,   5
Oh, I can laugh and marvel, rapturous-eyed.
And you laugh back, nor can you ever see
The thousand little deaths my heart has died.
And you believe, so well I know my part,

That I am gay as morning, light as snow,   10
And all the straining things within my heart
You'll never know.

Oh, I can laugh and listen, when we meet,
And you bring tales of fresh adventurings, —
Of ladies delicately indiscreet,   15
Of lingering hands, and gently whispered things.
And you are pleased with me, and strive anew
To sing me sagas of your late delights.
Thus do you want me—marveling, gay, and true,
Nor do you see my staring eyes of nights.   20
And when, in search of novelty, you stray,
Oh, I can kiss you blithely as you go ....
And what goes on, my love, while you're away,
You'll never know.

Comment

Oh, life is a glorious cycle of song,
A medley of extemporanea;
And love is a thing that can never go wrong;
And I am Marie of Roumania.

Finis

Now it's over, and now it's done;
Why does everything look the same?
Just as bright, the unheeding sun, —
Can't it see that the parting came?
People hurry and work and swear,   5
Laugh and grumble and die and wed,
Ponder what they will eat and wear, —
Don't they know that our love is dead?

Just as busy, the crowded street;
Cars and wagons go rolling on,   10
Children chuckle, and lovers meet, —
Don't they know that our love is gone?
No one pauses to pay a tear;
None walks slow, for the love that's through, —

I might mention, my recent dear,   15
I've reverted to normal, too.

Interview

The ladies men admire, I've heard,
Would shudder at a wicked word.
Their candle gives a single light;
They'd rather stay at home at night.
They do not keep awake till three,   5
Nor read erotic poetry.
They never sanction the impure,
Nor recognize an overture.
They shrink from powders and from paints ...
So far, I've had no complaints.   10

Love Song

My own dear love, he is strong and bold
And he cares not what comes after.
His words ring sweet as a chime of gold,
And his eyes are lit with laughter.
He is jubilant as a flag unfurled —   5
Oh, a girl, she'd not forget him.
My own dear love, he is all my world, —
And I wish I'd never met him.

My love, he's mad, and my love, he's fleet,
And a wild young wood-thing bore him!   10
The ways are fair to his roaming feet,
And the skies are sunlit for him.
As sharply sweet to my heart he seems
As the fragrance of acacia.
My own dear love, he is all my dreams, —   15
And I wish he were in Asia.

My love runs by like a day in June,

And he makes no friends of sorrows.
He'll tread his galloping rigadoon[9]
In the pathway of the morrows.   20
He'll live his days where the sunbeams start,

[9]a lively dance for couples.

Nor could storm or wind uproot him.
My own dear love, he is all my heart, —
And I wish somebody'd shoot him.

Observation

If I don't drive around the park,
I'm pretty sure to make my mark.
If I'm in bed each night by ten,
I may get back my looks again,
If I abstain from fun and such,   5
I'll probably amount to much,
But I shall stay the way I am,
Because I do not give a damn.

One Perfect Rose

A single flow'r he sent me, since we met.
All tenderly his messenger he chose;
Deep-hearted, pure, with scented dew still w—
One perfect rose.

I knew the language of the floweret;   5
"My fragile leaves," it said, "his heart enclose."
Love long has taken for his amulet
One perfect rose.

Why is it no one ever sent me yet
One perfect limousine, do you suppose?   10
Ah no, it's always just my luck to get
One perfect rose.

Resumé

Razors pain you;
Rivers are damp;
Acids stain you;
And drugs cause cramp.
Guns aren't lawful;   5
Nooses give;
Gas smells awful;
You might as well live.

WILLIAM JAMES ■ (1842–1910)

William James, born in New York City in 1842, was the eldest son of Henry James Sr., an eccentric religious writer and intermittently profound philosopher. One of William's brothers was Henry James (1843–1916), who became one of America's foremost novelists; he and William had a close, though also competitive, relationship, and, in later years, William expressed irritation with the complex, dense style of his brother's literary work.

The education of William and Henry, and of their brothers Garth Wilkinson (1845–83) and Robertson (1846–1910) and their sister Alice (1848–92), was erratic. Sometimes William studied with tutors; sometimes he attended private schools. During much of his youth and teenage years, the family traveled abroad and resided in Europe for long periods. It was his father's belief that the best education consisted of learning foreign languages, visiting galleries and museums, and exploring moral and religious questions. William did not attend college, for his father believed that colleges were "hotbeds of corruption."

In the late 1850s, James studied painting, but by 1860–61, he had given up his aspiration and enrolled in the Lawrence Scientific School, associated with Harvard University. He studied chemistry, anatomy, and other subjects but did not finish the requirements for the degree. He next attended Harvard Medical School, completing the M.D. in 1869.

In 1872, James taught a course on physiology at Harvard, and in 1875 he offered a course on psychology—the first to be offered in the United States. By 1880, James also was teaching philosophy, and in the following years he published essays on scientific and philosophical topics. His major work of this period is *The Principles of Psychology* (1890), which includes his influential account of consciousness as a "stream" that moves in succession and is always changing.

James also was drawn to religion, spiritualism, and mysticism, and in this field he produced a masterpiece, *The Varieties of Religious Experience* (1902), packed with fascinating quotations from many sources and richly abounding in James's vigorous, incisive reflections on religious feeling, and on conversion and regeneration in particular. James's interest in religion manifests itself in other essays and lectures, where he delves into the meaning of God and the Absolute.

James is a superb writer who belongs in anthologies of both American literature and philosophy: he gives briskly engaging, stimulating, creative turns of phrase and structures of analysis and argument to a host of topics in philosophy, psychology, and religion. James wrote for the academic community, where he had many admirers and respectful critics of his positions, and for common readers as well. A gifted lecturer, James wrote as if he were simultaneously in the midst of a conversation with himself and with his readers—a person speaking, a person thinking, pondering, debating, and ruminating, inviting our responses, disagreements, and qualifications. James is eager to share the topic at hand with us and is as interested in us as we are in him; he conveys the sense of a bright, vivid mind at work.

The philosopher George Santayana (1863–1952), one of James's colleagues at Harvard, said that in his writing James comes across to us as "an impulsive poet: a master in the art of recording or divining the lyric quality of experience as it actually came to him or to me" (*Persons and Places*, 1944). James other important books, which display throughout his supple, invigorating style, include three collections of essays, *The Will to Believe* (1897), *Pragmatism* (1907), and *The Meaning of Truth* (1909). The most significant of these is *Pragmatism*, which emerged from lectures that James presented at the Lowell Institute in Boston in 1906 and at Columbia University in 1907. "What Pragmatism Means" is the centerpiece of his book.

In this essay, James identifies the American philosopher Charles Saunders Peirce (1839–1914) as the founder of pragmatism. But it was James, along with John Dewey (1859–1952), who developed it and showed its application for philosophy, education, and social policy. In James's view, if we want to know what an idea means, then we need to ask what are the consequences to which it leads. If there are no consequences, then there is no meaning to the idea. Or, if there is, it is a meaning that does not matter. How in turn does this pertain to the problem of truth? There is no truth that is intrinsic in things; truth is the result, in behavior, to which belief in a thing directs us.

Beginning his essay with an amusing anecdote about a squirrel, James moves quickly to his main point—the meaning of "the pragmatic method" as it is focused in the question, "What difference would it practically make to any one if this notion rather than that notion were true?" Our concern when we study one side and the other in a debate or a disagreement, and when we consider the merits of a position, should not be, Is it right? Is it true?—as though rightness and truth were inherent, embedded in the thing itself. Rather, according to James, what we should inquire into is the "practical difference" that would follow if a principle or position or thing were right, were true. We know—perhaps we feel more than we know— what is right when we succeed in showing what the difference made by it would be. Impatient with gross abstractions, and with metaphysical dilemmas that cannot be solved, James calls on his readers to stress "concrete facts"—how these are or are not made different by our ideas about the world.

We value James for the open, curious, exploratory attitude toward life that he embodies and describes and that affects us in his writing—hearty, healthy, ready to enjoy life and to take on new experience, intent on the good differences that vital, experimental, nondogmatic thinking can produce. James had many colleagues and students who warmly esteemed him, and countless friends who cherished their relationship with him. They found him at one with his writing. In *Characters and Events* (1929), Dewey says of James: "He was not a philosopher who by taking pains acquired a literary gift; he was an artist who gave philosophic expression to the artist's sense of the unique, and to his love of the individual."

This attitude, however, was not an easy one for James to discover, and it took resilience and courage to maintain it. In large measure he was a pragmatist because of (and in resistance to) his own experiences of melancholy, depression, and fear.

Image of William James taken in approximately 1910 from the Bain News Service, one of the first news picture agencies in the United States.

In his account of "The Sick Soul" in *The Varieties of Religious Experience*, James says:

> The normal process of life contains moments as bad as any of those which insane melancholy is filled with, moments in which radical evil gets its innings and takes its solid turn. The lunatic's visions of horror are all drawn from the material of daily fact. Our civilization is founded on the shambles, and every individual existence goes out in a lonely spasm of helpless agony. If you protest, my friend, wait till you arrive there yourself!

Pragmatists, James stresses, recognize pain, loss, and death—hard facts of human life. It is the pain of life—the perception and sensation of pain as it takes us to the brink of madness—which we must face and acknowledge. Life requires fight and resolve, James believes, for us to endure it and make our way tough-mindedly through it. Pragmatism is full of hope and affirmation—James highlights programs for work, for moving forward. Yet a tragic spirit seems often to touch it and on occasion may strike us as being close to its center. Life has no essence; there are no necessities or essentials or first principles. All we have is ourselves, and the truth of our ideas, which is, James says, "what we say about them."

The best biography is Robert D. Richardson, *William James: In the Maelstrom of American Modernism* (2006). A significant older study is Ralph Barton Perry, *The Thought and Character of William James*, 2 vols. (1935). Also helpful are: Jacques Barzun, *A Stroll with William James* (1983); Howard M. Feinstein, *Becoming William James* (1984); Gerald Myers, *William James: His Life and Thought* (1986); Ross Posnock, *The Trial of Curiosity: Henry James, William James, and the Challenge of Modernity* (1991); and Richard M. Gale, *The Dividend Self of William James* (2007). For biographical and historical contexts, see: F. O. Matthiessen, ed., *The James Family* (1947); R.W.B. Lewis, *The James: A Family Narrative* (1991); and Paul Fisher, *House of Wits: An Intimate Portrait of the James Family* (2009).

What Pragmatism Means

Some years ago, being with a camping party in the mountains, I returned from a solitary ramble to find every one engaged in a ferocious metaphysical dispute. The *corpus* of the dispute was a squirrel—a live squirrel supposed to be clinging to one side of a tree-trunk; while over against the tree's opposite side a human being was imagined to stand. This human witness tries to get sight of the squirrel by moving rapidly round the tree, but no matter how fast he goes, the squirrel moves as fast in the opposite direction, and always keeps the tree between himself and the man, so that never a glimpse of him is caught. The resultant metaphysical problem now is this: *Does the man go round the squirrel or not?* He goes round the tree, sure enough, and the squirrel is on the tree; but does he go round the squirrel? In the unlimited leisure of the wilderness, discussion had been worn threadbare. Everyone had taken sides, and was obstinate; and the numbers on both sides were even. Each side, when I appeared therefore appealed to me to make it a majority. Mindful of the scholastic adage that whenever you meet a contradiction you must make a distinction, I immediately sought and found one, as follows: "Which party is right," I said, "depends on what you *practically mean* by 'going round' the squirrel. If you mean passing from the north of him to the east, then to the south, then to the west, and then to the north of him again, obviously the man does go round him, for he occupies these successive positions. But if on the contrary you mean being first in front of him, then on the right of him, then behind him, then on his left, and finally in front again, it is quite as obvious that the man fails to go round him, for by the compensating movements the squirrel makes, he keeps his belly turned towards the man all the time, and his back turned away. Make the distinction, and there is no occasion for any farther dispute. You are both right and both wrong according as you conceive the verb 'to go round' in one practical fashion or the other."

Although one or two of the hotter disputants called my speech a shuffling evasion, saying they wanted no quibbling or scholastic hairsplitting, but meant just plain honest English 'round,' the majority seemed to think that the distinction had assuaged the dispute.

I tell this trivial anecdote because it is a peculiarly simple example of what I wish now to speak of *as the pragmatic method*. The pragmatic method is primarily a method of settling metaphysical disputes that otherwise might be interminable. Is the world one or many?—fated or free?—material or spiritual?—here are notions either of which may or may not hold good of the world; and disputes over such notions are unending. The pragmatic method in such cases is to try to interpret each notion by tracing its respective practical consequences. What difference would it practically make to any one if this notion rather than that notion were true? If no practical difference whatever can be traced, then the alternatives mean practically the same thing, and all dispute is idle. Whenever a dispute is serious, we ought to be able to show some practical difference that must follow from one side or the other's being right. A glance at the history of the idea will show you still better what pragmatism means. The term is derived from the same Greek word πράγμα, meaning action, from which our words 'practice' and 'practical' come. It was first introduced into philosophy by Mr. Charles Peirce[1] in 1878. In an article entitled 'How to Make Our Ideas Clear,' in the Popular Science Monthly' for January of that year[2]

[1]Charles Sanders Peirce (1839–1914), American philosopher, logician, scientist, and mathematician.
[2]Translated in the *Revue Philosophique* for January, 1870 (vol. vii).

Mr. Peirce, after pointing out that our beliefs are really rules for action, said that, to develop a thought's meaning, we need only determine what conduct it is fitted to produce: that conduct is for us its sole significance. And the tangible fact at the root of all our thought distinctions, however subtle, is that there is no one of them so fine as to consist in anything but a possible difference of practice. To attain perfect clearness in our thoughts of an object, then, we need only consider what conceivable effects of a practical kind the object may involve—what sensations we are to expect from it, and what reactions we must prepare. Our conceptions of these effects, whether immediate or remote, is then for us the whole of our conception of the object, so far as that conception has positive significance at all.

This is the principle of Peirce, the principle of pragmatism. It lay entirely unnoticed by any one for twenty years, until I, in an address before Professor Howison's[3] philosophical union at the university of California, brought it forward again and made a special application of it to religion. By that date (1898) the times seemed ripe for its reception. The word 'pragmatism' spread, and at present it fairly spots the pages of the philosophic journals. On all hands we find the 'pragmatic movement' spoken of, sometimes with respect, sometimes with contumely, seldom with clear understanding. It is evident that the term applies itself conveniently to a number of tendencies that hitherto have lacked a collective name, and that it has 'come to stay.'

To take in the importance of Peirce's principle, one must get accustomed to applying it to concrete cases. I found a few years ago that Ostwald,[4] the illustrious Leipzig chemist, had been making perfectly distinct use of the principle of pragmatism in his lectures on the philosophy of science, though he had not called it by that name.

"All realities influence our practice," he wrote me, "and that influence is their meaning for us. I am accustomed to put questions to my classes in this way: In what respects would the world be different if this alternative or that were true? If I can find nothing that would become different, then the alternative has no sense."

That is, the rival views mean practically the same thing, and meaning, other than practical, there is for us none. Ostwald in a published lecture give this example of what he means. Chemists have long wrangled over the inner constitution of certain bodies called 'tautomerous.'[5] Their properties seemed equally consistent with the notion that an instable hydrogen atom oscillates inside of them, or that they are instable mixtures of two bodies.

[3]George Holmes Howison (1834–1916), American philosopher who established the philosophy department at the University of California, Berkeley.
[4]Wilhelm Ostwald (1853–1932), German chemist, philosopher, and historian of science.
[5]Tautomerism is the phenomenon shown by a compound of behaving in chemical reactions as though the atoms in its molecule were arranged in more than one way, expressible by different structural formulas.

Controversy raged; but never was decided. "It would never have begun," says Ostwald, "if the combatants had asked themselves what particular experimental fact could have been made different by one or the other view being correct. For it would then have appeared that no difference of fact could possibly ensue; and the quarrel was as unreal as if, theorizing in primitive times about the raising of dough by yeast, one party should have invoked a 'brownie,' while another insisted on an 'elf' as the true cause of the phenomenon."

It is astonishing to see how many philosophical disputes collapse into insignificance the moment you subject them to this simple test of tracing a concrete consequence. There can BE no difference anywhere that doesn't MAKE a difference elsewhere—no difference in abstract truth that doesn't express itself in a difference in concrete fact and in conduct consequent upon that fact, imposed on somebody, somehow, somewhere and somewhen. The whole function of philosophy ought to be to find out what definite difference it will make to you and me, at definite instants of our life, if this world-formula or that world-formula be the true one.

There is absolutely nothing new in the pragmatic method. Socrates[6] was an adept at it. Aristotle[7] used it methodically. Locke, Berkeley and Hume[8] made momentous contributions to truth by its means. Shadworth Hodgson[9] keeps insisting that realities are only what they are 'known-as.' But these forerunners of pragmatism used it in fragments: they were preluders only. Not until in our time has it generalized itself, become conscious of a universal mission, pretended to a conquering destiny. I believe in that destiny, and I hope I may end by inspiring you with my belief.

Pragmatism represents a perfectly familiar attitude in philosophy, the empiricist attitude, but it represents it, as it seems to me, both in a more radical and in a less objectionable form than it has ever yet assumed. A pragmatist turns his back resolutely and once for all upon a lot of inveterate habits dear to professional philosophers. He turns away from abstraction and insufficiency, from verbal solutions, from bad *a priori* reasons, from fixed principles, closed systems, and pretended absolutes and origins. He turns towards concreteness and adequacy, towards facts, towards action, and towards power. That means the empiricist temper regnant and the rationalist temper sincerely given up. It means the open air and possibilities of nature, as against dogma, artificiality, and the pretence of finality in truth.

[6]Greek philosopher (469–399 BCE).
[7]Greek philosopher (384–322 BCE).
[8]John Locke (1632–1704), English philosopher, author of *An Essay on Human Understanding* (1690); George Berkeley (1685–1753), Irish philosopher; David Hume (1711–76), Scottish philosopher.
[9]Shadworth Hollway Hodgson (1832–1912), English philosopher.

At the same time it does not stand for any special results. It is a method only. But the general triumph of that method would mean an enormous change in what I called in my last lecture the 'temperament' of philosophy.

Teachers of the ultra-rationalistic type would be frozen out, much as the courtier type is frozen out in republics, as the ultramontane[10] type of priest is frozen out in protestant lands. Science and metaphysics would come much nearer together, would in fact work absolutely hand in hand.

Metaphysics has usually followed a very primitive kind of quest. You know how men have always hankered after unlawful magic, and you know what a great part in *magic words* have always played. If you have his name, or the formula of incantation that binds him, you can control the spirit, genie, afrite,[11] or whatever the power may be. Solomon[12] knew the names of all the spirits, and having their names, he held them subject to his will. So the universe has always appeared to the natural mind as a kind of enigma, of which the key must be sought in the shape of some illuminating or power-bringing word or name. That word names the universe's *principle*, and to possess it is after a fashion to possess the universe itself. 'God,' 'Matter,' 'Reason,' 'the Absolute,' 'Energy,' are so many solving names. You can rest when you have them. You are at the end of your metaphysical quest.

But if you follow the pragmatic method, you cannot look on any such word as closing your quest. You must bring out of each word its practical cash-value, set it at work within the stream of your experience. It appears less as a solution, then, than as a program for more work, and more particularly as an indication of the ways in which existing realities may be *changed*.

Theories thus become instruments, not answers to enigmas, in which we can rest. We don't lie back upon them, we move forward, and, on occasion, make nature over again by their aid. Pragmatism unstiffens all our theories, limbers them up and sets each one at work. Being nothing essentially new, it harmonizes with many ancient philosophic tendencies. It agrees with nominalism for instance, in always appealing to particulars; with utilitarianism in emphasizing practical aspects; with positivism in its disdain for verbal solutions, useless questions and metaphysical abstractions.

All these, you see, are *anti-intellectualist* tendencies. Against rationalism as a pretension and a method pragmatism is fully armed and militant. But, at the outset, at least, it stands for no particular results. It has no dogmas, and no doctrines save its method. As the young Italian pragmatist Papini[13] has well said, it lies in the midst of our theories, like a corridor in a hotel. Innumerable chambers open out of it. In one you may find a man

---

[10]Someone who advocates supreme papal authority in matters of faith and doctrine.
[11]A powerful evil jinni, demon, or monstrous giant in Arabic mythology.
[12]Ruler of Israel (died c. 933 BCE), who was famed for his wisdom as a judge.
[13]Giovanni Papini (1881–1956), Italian pragmatist philosopher.

writing an atheistic volume; in the next some one on his knees praying for faith and strength; in a third a chemist investigating a body's properties. In a fourth a system of idealistic metaphysics is being excogitated; in a fifth the impossibility of metaphysics is being shown. But they all own the corridor, and all must pass through it if they want a practicable way of getting into or out of their respective rooms.

No particular results then, so far, but only an attitude of orientation, is what the pragmatic method means. *The attitude of looking away from first things, principles, 'categories,' supposed necessities; and of looking towards last things, fruits, consequences, facts.*

So much for the pragmatic method! You may say that I have been praising it rather than explaining it to you, but I shall presently explain it abundantly enough by showing how it works on some familiar problems. Meanwhile the word pragmatism has come to be used in a still wider sense, as meaning also a certain *theory of truth*. I mean to give a whole lecture to the statement of that theory, after first paving the way, so I can be very brief now. But brevity is hard to follow, so I ask for your redoubled attention for a quarter of an hour. If much remains obscure, I hope to make it clearer in the later lectures.

One of the most successfully cultivated branches of philosophy in our time is what is called inductive logic, the study of the conditions under which our sciences have evolved. Writers on this subject have begun to show a singular unanimity as to what the laws of nature and elements of fact mean, when formulated by mathematicians, physicists and chemists. When the first mathematical, logical, and natural uniformities, the first *laws*, were discovered, men were so carried away by the clearness, beauty and simplification that resulted, that they believed themselves to have deciphered authentically the eternal thoughts of the Almighty. His mind also thundered and reverberated in syllogisms. He also thought in conic sections, squares and roots and ratios, and geometrized like Euclid.[14] He made Kepler's[15] laws for the planets to follow; he made velocity increase proportionally to the time in falling bodies; he made the law of the sines for light to obey when refracted; he established the classes, orders, families and genera of plants and animals, and fixed the distances between them. He thought the archetypes of all things, and devised their variations; and when we rediscover any one of these his wondrous institutions, we seize his mind in its very literal intention.

But as the sciences have developed farther, the notion has gained ground that most, perhaps all, of our laws are only approximations. The laws themselves, moreover, have grown so numerous that there is no counting them; and so many rival formulations are proposed in all the

[14]Greek mathematician (c. 300 BCE), known for his work on the principles of geometry.
[15]Johannes Kepler (1571–1630), German astronomer, described the laws of planetary motion.

branches of science that investigators have become accustomed to the notion that no theory is absolutely a transcript of reality, but that any one of them may from some point of view be useful. Their great use is to summarize old facts and to lead to new ones. They are only a man-made language, a conceptual shorthand, as some one calls them, in which we write our reports of nature; and languages, as is well known, tolerate much choice of expression and many dialects.

Thus human arbitrariness has driven divine necessity from scientific logic. If I mention the names of Sigwart,[16] Mach, Ostwald, Pearson, Milhaud, Poincaré, Duhem, Heymans, those of you who are students will easily identify the tendency I speak of, and will think of additional names.

Riding now on the front of this wave of scientific logic Messrs. Schiller and Dewey[17] appear with their pragmatistic account of what truth everywhere signifies. Everywhere, these teachers say, 'truth' in our ideas and beliefs means the same thing that it means in science. It means, they say, nothing but this, *that ideas (which themselves are but parts of our experience) become true just in so far as they help us to get into satisfactory relation with other parts of our experience*, to summarize them and get about among them by conceptual short-cuts instead of following the interminable succession of particular phenomena. Any idea upon which we can ride, so to speak; any idea that will carry us prosperously from any one part of our experience to any other part, linking things satisfactorily, working securely, simplifying, saving labor; is true for just so much, true in so far forth, true *instrumentally*. This is the 'instrumental' view of truth taught so successfully at Chicago, the view that truth in our ideas means their power to 'work,' promulgated so brilliantly at Oxford.

Messrs. Dewey, Schiller and their allies, in reaching this general conception of all truth, have only followed the example of geologists, biologists and philologists. In the establishment of these other sciences, the successful stroke was always to take some simple process actually observable in operation—as denudation by weather, say, or variation from parental type, or change of dialect by incorporation of new words and pronunciations—and then to generalize it, making it apply to all times, and produce great results by summating its effects through the ages.

The observable process which Schiller and Dewey particularly singled out for generalization is the familiar one by which any individual settles into *new opinions*. The process here is always the same. The individual has

[16]Christoph von Sigwart (1830–1904), German philosopher and logician; Ernst Mach (1838–1916), Austrian physicist and philosopher; Ostwald (see Note 4); Karl Pearson (1857–1936), English mathematician; Gaston Samuel Milhaud (1858–1918), French philosopher; Jules-Henri Poincaré (1854–1912), French mathematician; Pierre Duhem (1861–1916), French physicist and historian of science; Gerardus Heymans (1857–1930), Dutch philosopher and psychologist. Some printings of this essay omit Heyman and instead refer to Ruyssen: Théodore Eugène César Ruyssen (1868–1967), French historian of philosophy.
[17]Ferdinand Canning Scott Schiller (1864–1937), German-British philosopher; John Dewey (1859–1952), American philosopher, psychologist, and educational reformer.

a stock of old opinions already, but he meets a new experience that puts them to a strain. Somebody contradicts them; or in a reflective moment he discovers that they contradict each other; or he hears of facts with which they are incompatible; or desires arise in him which they cease to satisfy. The result is an inward trouble to which his mind till then had been a stranger, and from which he seeks to escape by modifying his previous mass of opinions. He saves as much of it as he can, for in this matter of belief we are all extreme conservatives. So he tries to change first this opinion, and then that (for they resist change very variously), until at last some new idea comes up which he can graft upon the ancient stock with a minimum of disturbance of the latter, some idea that mediates between the stock and the new experience and runs them into one another most felicitously and expediently.

This new idea is then adopted as the true one. It preserves the older stock of truths with a minimum of modification, stretching them just enough to make them admit the novelty, but conceiving that in ways as familiar as the case leaves possible. An *outrée*[18] explanation, violating all our preconceptions, would never pass for a true account of a novelty. We should scratch round industriously till we found something less excentric. The most violent revolutions in an individual's beliefs leave most of his old order standing. Time and space, cause and effect, nature and history, and one's own biography remain untouched. New truth is always a go-between, a smoother-over of transitions. It marries old opinion to new fact so as ever to show a minimum of jolt, a maximum of continuity. We hold a theory true just in proportion to its success in solving this 'problem of maxima and minima.' But success in solving this problem is eminently a matter of approximation. We say this theory solves it on the whole more satisfactorily than that theory; but that means more satisfactorily to ourselves, and individuals will emphasize their points of satisfaction differently. To a certain degree, therefore, everything here is plastic.

The point I now urge you to observe particularly is the part played by the older truth. Failure to take account of it is the source of much of the unjust criticism levelled against pragmatism. Their influence is absolutely controlling. Loyalty to them is the first principle—in most cases it is the only principle; for by far the most usual way of handling phenomena so novel that they would make for a serious rearrangement of our preconception is to ignore them altogether, or to abuse those who bear witness for them.

You doubtless wish examples of this process of truth's growth, and the only trouble is their superabundance. The simplest case of new truth is of course the mere numerical addition of new kinds of facts, or of new single facts of old kinds, to our experience—an addition that involves no alteration in the old beliefs. Day follows day, and its contents are simply

[18]Excessive, outrageous (French).

added. The new contents themselves are not true, they simply *come* and *are*. Truth is *what we say about* them, and when we say that they have come, truth is satisfied by the plain additive formula.

But often the day's contents oblige a rearrangement. If I should now utter piercing shrieks and act like a maniac on this platform, it would make many of you revise your ideas as to the probable worth of my philosophy. 'Radium' came the other day as part of the day's content, and seemed for a moment to contradict our ideas of the whole order of nature, that order having come to be identified with what is called the conservation of energy. The mere sight of radium paying heat away indefinitely out of its own pocket seemed to violate that conservation. What to think? If the radiations from it were nothing but an escape of unsuspected 'potential' energy, per-existent inside of the atoms, the principle conservation would be saved. The discovery of 'helium' as the radiation's outcome, opened a way to this belief. So Ramsay's[19] view is generally held to be true, because, although it extends our old ideas of energy, it causes a minimum of alteration in their nature.

I need not multiply instances. A new opinion counts as 'true' just in proportion as it gratifies the individual's desire to assimilate the novel in his experience to his beliefs in stock. It must both lean on old truth and grasp new fact; and its success (as I said a moment ago) in doing this, is a matter for the individual's appreciation. When old truth grows, then, by new truth's addition, it is for subjective reasons. We are in the process and obey the reasons. That new idea is truest which performs most felicitously its function of satisfying our double urgency. It makes itself true, gets itself classed as true, by the way it works; grafting itself then upon the ancient body of truth, which thus grows much as a tree grows by the activity of a new layer of cambium.

Now Dewey and Schiller proceed to generalize this observation and to apply it to the most ancient parts of truth. They also once were plastic. They also were called true for human reasons. They also mediated between still earlier truths and what in those days were novel observations. Purely objective truth, truth in whose establishment the function of giving human satisfaction in marrying previous parts of experience with newer parts played no rôle whatever, is nowhere to be found. The reasons why we call things true is the reason why they *are* true, for 'to be true' *means* only to perform this marriage-function.

The trial of the human serpent is thus over everything. Truth independent; truth that we *find* merely; truth no longer malleable to human need; truth incorrigible, in a word; such truth exists indeed superabundantly—or is supposed to exist by rationalistically minded thinkers; but then it means only the dead heart of the living tree, and its being there

---

[19]Sir William Ramsay (1852–1916), Scottish chemist, discovered helium in 1895.

means only that truth also has its paleontology, and its 'prescription,' and may grow stiff with years of veteran service and petrified in men's regard by sheer antiquity. But how plastic even the oldest truths nevertheless really are has been vividly shown in our day by the transformation of logical and mathematical ideas, a transformation which seems even to be invading physics. The ancient formulas are reinterpreted as special expressions of much wider principles, principles that our ancestors never got a glimpse of in their present shape and formulation.

Mr. Schiller still gives to all this view of truth the name of 'Humanism,' but, for this doctrine too, the name of pragmatism seems fairly to be in the ascendant, so I will treat it under the name of pragmatism in these lectures.

Such then would be the scope of pragmatism—first, a method; and second, a genetic theory of what is meant by truth. And these two things must be our future topics.

What I have said of the theory of truth will, I am sure, have appeared obscure and unsatisfactory to most of you by reason of its brevity. I shall make amends for that hereafter. In a lecture on 'common sense' I shall try to show what I mean by truths grown petrified by antiquity. In another lecture I shall expatiate on the idea that our thoughts become true in proportion as they successfully exert their go-between function. In a third I shall show how hard it is to discriminate subjective from objective factors in Truth's development. You may not follow me wholly in these lectures; and if you do, you may not wholly agree with me. But you will, I know, regard me at least as serious, and treat my effort with respectful consideration.

You will probably be surprised to learn, then, that Messrs. Schiller's and Dewey's theories have suffered a hailstorm of contempt and ridicule. All rationalism has risen against them. In influential quarters Mr. Schiller, in particular, has been treated like an impudent schoolboy who deserves a spanking. I should not mention this, but for the fact that it throws so much sidelight upon that rationalistic temper to which I have opposed the temper of pragmatism. Pragmatism is uncomfortable away from facts. Rationalism is comfortable only in the presence of abstractions. This pragmatist talk about truths in the plural, about their utility and satisfactoriness, about the success with which they 'work,' etc., suggests to the typical intellectualist mind a sort of coarse lame second-rate makeshift article of truth. Such truths are not real truth. Such tests are merely subjective. As against this, objective truth must be something non-utilitarian, haughty, refined, remote, august, exalted. It must be an absolute correspondence of our thoughts with an equally absolute reality. It must be what we *ought* to think unconditionally. The conditioned ways in which we *do* think are so much irrelevance and matter for psychology. Down with psychology, up with logic, in all this question!

See the exquisite contrast of the types of mind! The pragmatist clings to facts and concreteness, observes truth at its work in particular cases, and generalizes. Truth, for him, becomes a class-name for all sorts of definite working-values in experience. For the rationalist it remains a pure abstraction, to the bare name of which we must defer. When the pragmatist undertakes to show in detail just *why* we must defer, the rationalist is unable to recognize the concretes from which his own abstraction is taken. He accuses us of *denying* truth; whereas we have only sought to trace exactly why people follow it and always ought to follow it. Your typical ultra-abstractionist fairly shudders at concreteness: other things equal, he positively prefers the pale and spectral. If the two universes were offered, he would always choose the skinny outline rather than the rich thicket of reality. It is so much purer, clearer, nobler.

I hope that as these lectures go on, the concreteness and closeness to facts of the pragmatism which they advocate may be what approves itself to you as its most satisfactory peculiarity. It only follows here the example of the sister-sciences, interpreting the unobserved by the observed. It brings old and new harmoniously together. It converts the absolutely empty notion of a static relation of 'correspondence' (what that may mean we must ask later) between our minds and reality, into that of a rich and active commerce (that any one may follow in detail and understand) between particular thoughts of ours, and the great universe of other experiences in which they play their parts and have their uses.

But enough of this at present? The justification of what I say must be postponed. I wish now to add a word in further explanation of the claim I made at our last meeting, that pragmatism may be a happy harmonizer of empiricist ways of thinking with the more religious demands of human beings.

Men who are strongly of the fact-loving temperament, you may remember me to have said, are liable to be kept at a distance by the small sympathy with facts which that philosophy from the present-day fashion of idealism offers them. It is far too intellectualistic. Old fashioned theism was bad enough, with its notion of God as an exalted monarch, made up of a lot of unintelligible or preposterous 'attributes'; but, so long as it held strongly by the argument from design, it kept some touch with concrete realities. Since, however, darwinism[20] has once for all displaced design from the minds of the 'scientific,' theism has lost the foothold; and some kind of an immanent or pantheistic[21] deity working *in* things rather than above them is, if any, the kind recommended to our contemporary imagination. Aspirants to a philosophic religion turn, as a rule, more hopefully

---

[20]Charles Darwin (1809–82), English naturalist. Darwinism maintains that organisms tend to produce offspring varying slightly from their parents, and that the process of natural selection tends to favor the survival of individuals whose peculiarities render them best adapted to their environment.
[21]Pantheism is a doctrine that equates God with the forces and laws of the universe.

nowadays towards idealistic pantheism than towards the older dualistic theism, in spite of the fact that the latter still counts able defenders.

But, as I said in my first lecture, the brand of pantheism offered is hard for them to assimilate if they are lovers of facts, or empirically minded. It is the absolutistic brand, spurning the dust and reared upon pure logic. It keeps no connexion whatever with concreteness. Affirming the Absolute Mind, which is its substitute for God, to be the rational presupposition of all particulars of fact, whatever they may be, it remains supremely indifferent to what the particular facts in our world actually are. Be they what they may, the Absolute will father them. Like the sick lion in Esop's fable, all footprints lead into his den, but *nulla vestigia retrorsum*.[22] You cannot redescend into the world of particulars by the Absolute's aid, or deduce any necessary consequences of detail important for your life from your idea of his nature. He gives you indeed the assurance that all is well with *Him*, and for his eternal way of thinking; but thereupon he leaves you to be finitely saved by your own temporal devices.

Far be it from me to deny the majesty of this conception, or its capacity to yield religious comfort to a most respectable class of minds. But from the human point of view, no one can pretend that it doesn't suffer from the faults of remoteness and abstractness. It is eminently a product of what I have ventured to call the rationalistic temper. It disdains empiricism's needs. It substitutes a pallid outline for the real world's richness. It is dapper, it is noble in the bad sense, in the sense in which to be noble is to be inapt for humble service. In this real world of sweat and dirt, it seems to me that when a view of things is 'noble,' that ought to count as a presumption against its truth, and as a philosophic disqualification. The prince of darkness may be a gentleman, as we are told he is, but whatever the God of earth and heaven is, he can surely be no gentleman. His menial services are needed in the dust of our human trials, even more than his dignity is needed in the empyrean.

Now pragmatism, devoted though she be to facts, has no such materialistic bias as ordinary empiricism labors under. Moreover, she has no objection whatever to the realizing of abstractions, so long as you get about among particulars with their aid and they actually carry you somewhere. Interested in no conclusions but those which our minds and our experiences work out together, she has no *a priori* prejudices against theology. *If theological ideas prove to have a value for concrete life, they will be true, for pragmatism, in the sense of being good for so much. For how much more they are true, will depend entirely on their relations to the other truths that also have to be acknowledged.*

What I said just now about the Absolute, of transcendental idealism, is a case in point. First, I called it majestic and said it yielded religious

[22]No signs of returning, no stepping back (Latin).

comfort to a class of minds, and then I accused it of remoteness and sterility. But so far as it affords such comfort, it surely is not sterile; it has that amount of value; it performs a concrete function. As a good pragmatist, I myself ought to call the Absolute true 'in so far forth,' then; and I unhesitatingly now do so.

But what does *true in so forth* mean in this case? To answer, we need only apply the pragmatic method. What do believers in the Absolute mean by saying that their belief affords them comfort? They mean that since, in the Absolute finite evil is 'overruled' already, we may, therefore, whenever we wish, treat the temporal as if it were potentially the eternal, be sure that we can trust its outcome, and, without sin, dismiss our fear, and drop the worry of our finite responsibility. In short, they mean that we have a right ever and anon to take a moral holiday, to let the world wag in its own way, feeling that its issues are in better hands than ours and are none of our business.

The universe is a system of which the individual members may relax their anxieties occasionally, in which the don't-care mood is also right for men, and moral holidays in order,—that, if I mistake not, is part, at least, of what the Absolute is 'known-as,' that is the great difference in our particular experiences which his being true makes, for us, that is his cash-value when he is pragmatically interpreted. Farther than that the ordinary lay-reader in philosophy who thinks favorably of absolute idealism does not venture to sharpen his conceptions. He can use the Absolute for so much, and so much is very precious. He is pained at hearing you speak incredulously of the Absolute, therefore, and disregards your criticisms because they deal with aspects of the conception that he fails to follow.

If the Absolute means this, and means no more than this, who can possibly deny the truth of it? To deny it would be to insist that men should never relax, and that holidays are never in order.

I am well aware how odd it must seem to some of you to hear me say that an idea is 'true' so long as to believe it is profitable to our lives. That it is *good*, for as much as it profits, you will gladly admit. If what we do by its aid is good, you will allow the idea itself to be good in so far forth, for we are the better for possessing it. But is it not a strange misuse of the word 'truth,' you will say, to call ideas also 'true' for this reason?

To answer this difficulty fully is impossible at this stage of my account. You touch here upon the very central point of Messrs. Schiller's, Dewey's and my own doctrine of truth, which I can not discuss with detail until my sixth lecture. Let me now say only this, that truth is *one species of good*, and not, as is usually supposed, a category distinct from good, and co-ordinate with it. *The true is the name of whatever proves itself to be good in the way of belief, and good, too, for definite, assignable reasons.* Surely you must admit this, that if there were *no* good for life in true ideas, or if the knowledge of them were positively disadvantageous and false ideas the only useful ones, then the current notion that truth is divine and precious, and its pursuit a duty, could never have grown up or become a dogma. In a world like that, our duty would be to *shun* truth, rather. But in this world, just as certain foods are not only agreeable to our taste, but good for our teeth, our stomach, and our tissues; so certain ideas are not only agreeable to think about, or agreeable as supporting other ideas that we are fond of, but they are also helpful in life's practical struggles. If there be any life that it is really better we should lead, and if there be any idea which, if believed in, would help us to lead that life, then it would be really *better for us* to believe in that idea, *unless, indeed, belief in it incidentally clashed with other greater vital benefits*.

'What would be better for us to believe'! This sounds very like a definition of truth. It comes very near to saying 'what we *ought* to believe': and in *that* definition none of you would find any oddity. Ought we ever not to believe what it is *better for us* to believe? And can we then keep the notion of what is better for us, permanently apart?

Pragmatism says no, and I fully agree with her. Probably you also agree, so far as the abstract statement goes, but with a suspicion that if we practically did believe everything that made for good in our own personal lives, we should be found indulging all kinds of fancies about this world's affairs, and all kinds of sentimental superstitions about a world hereafter. Your suspicion here is undoubtedly well founded, and it is evident that something happens when you pass from the abstract to the concrete that complicates the situation.

I said just now that what is better for us to believe is true *unless the belief incidentally clashes with some other vital benefit*. Now in real life what vital benefits is any particular belief of ours most liable to clash with? What indeed except the vital benefits yielded by *other beliefs* when these prove incompatible with the first ones? In other words, the greatest enemy of any one of our truths may be the rest of our truths. Truths have once for all this desperate instinct of self-preservation and of desire to extinguish whatever contradicts them. My belief in the Absolute, based on the good it does me, must run the gauntlet of all my other beliefs. Grant that it may be true in giving me a moral holiday. Nevertheless, as I conceive it,—and let me speak now confidentially, as it were, and merely in my own private person,—it clashes with other truths of mine whose benefits I hate to give up on its account. It happens to be associated with a kind of logic of which I am the enemy, I find that it entangles me in metaphysical paradoxes that are inacceptable, etc., etc. But as I have enough trouble in life already without adding the trouble of carrying these intellectual inconsistencies, I personally just give up the Absolute. I just *take* my moral holidays; or else as a professional philosopher, I try to justify them by some other principle.

If I could restrict my notion of the Absolute to its bare holiday-giving value, it wouldn't clash with my other truths. But we can not easily thus restrict our hypotheses. They carry supernumerary features, and these it is that clash so. My disbelief in the Absolute means then disbelief in those other supernumerary features, for I fully believe in the legitimacy of taking moral holidays.

You see by this what I meant when I called pragmatism a mediator and reconciler and said, borrowing the word from Papini, that she 'unstiffens' our theories. She has in fact no prejudices whatever, no obstructive dogmas, no rigid canons of what shall count as proof. She is completely genial. She will entertain any hypothesis, she will consider any evidence. It follows that in the religious field she is at a great advantage both over positivistic empiricism, with its anti-theological bias, and over religious rationalism, with its exclusive interest in the remote, the noble, the simple, and the abstract in the way of conception.

In short, she widens the field of search for God. Rationalism sticks to logic and the empyrean. Empiricism sticks to the external senses. Pragmatism is willing to take anything, to follow either logic or the senses and to count the humblest and most personal experiences. She will count mystical experiences if they have practical consequences. She will take a God who lives in the very dirt of private fact—if that should seem a likely place to find him.

Her only test of probable truth is what works best in the way of leading us, what fits every part of life best and combines with the collectivity of experience's demands, nothing being omitted. If theological ideas should do this, if the notion of God, in particular, should prove to do it, how could pragmatism possibly deny God's existence? She could see no meaning in treating as 'not true' a notion that was pragmatically so successful. What other kind of truth could there be, for her, that all this agreement with concrete reality?

In my last lecture I shall return again to the relations of pragmatism with religion. But you see already how democratic she is. Her manners are as various and flexible, her resources as rich and endless, and her conclusions as friendly as those of mother nature.

[1907]

HENRY JAMES ■ (1843–1916)

Henry James's grandfather was a millionaire, and his father, Henry James Sr., received enough of the benefits of the family fortune to enable him to pursue a life of reading, reflection, and writing. James's father was a strange and abstruse intellectual, absorbed in the work of the Swedish scientist, religious teacher, and mystic Emmanuel Swedenborg (1688–1772), whose influence led James Sr., to give his children a "sensuous education"—which meant little formal schooling but, instead, private tutoring and travel to and study in Europe, with immersion in foreign languages and cultures. Born in New York City, Henry James was the brother of the eminent American philosopher William James; two other brothers, Garth and Robertson, fought in the Civil War; and a sister, Alice, with few career possibilities open to her, ended up a brilliant invalid.

Living with his family in Cambridge, Massachusetts, and, for a period, in Newport, Rhode Island, James at first considered a career as a painter and then, in 1862, spent a term at Harvard Law School, but by the 1860s he was already underway in the writing of short stories and literary reviews and essays. His first story, "A Tragedy of Error," was published in 1864, and his first novel, *Watch and Ward*, appeared in monthly installments in 1871 as a serial in *The Atlantic Monthly* (a revised version was published in book form in 1878).

While James respected the intellectual, literary, and cultural milieu of Boston/Cambridge/Concord, particularly as it was represented by such notable figures as Ralph Waldo Emerson and Nathaniel Hawthorne, he concluded that it was thin and provincial, without the rich and deep traditions of Europe. The relationships, similarities, and differences between Americans and Europeans formed for James a lifelong literary subject, which he explored in a critical study of Hawthorne (1879), many short stories (e. g., "A Passionate Pilgrim" and "Travelling Companions"), and in a number of novels, including *The American* (1877), *Daisy Miller* (1878), *The Europeans* (1878), *The Portrait of a Lady* (1881), and *The Ambassadors* (1903).

James left the United States in 1875 to reside in Paris, where he met the French realist Gustave Flaubert and the Russian master Ivan Turgenev. The following year he moved to London, and England became his homeland—so much so that in 1915, with World War I underway, he asked for and received British citizenship.

Readers sometimes protest that not much happens in a story or novel by Henry James. One of his own friends observed that the problem with James was not that he bit off more than he could chew but that he chewed more than he bit off. But for James, "what happens" is not primarily a series of actions or events but, rather, the complicated movement of consciousness, of thought and feeling. This is the area or field that James explores and dramatizes. He said of himself, "I am interminably supersubtle and analytic"; and his fellow-novelist Joseph Conrad remarked, "He feels deeply and vividly every delicate shade."

James was an extraordinary person, dedicated to literary art as a life in itself, perhaps the supreme life. He wrote many novels, and many short stories, plays, literary and art criticism, essays and books on travel, auto-biographies, and more—about one hundred volumes altogether; his note-books and letters, too, are works of art in their own right.

James never married—his first loyalty was always to his vocation as a writer. He formed many friendships, however, including, later in life, passionate attachments to several younger men to whom he wrote fervent letters, many of which have been published.

This point bears—though how much is a matter of debate—on "The Pupil," a story James wrote in the summer of 1890 and published in 1891. The "tale of a sensitive boy and his attachment to his tutor," it is, the biog-rapher Leon Edel has explained, "the first of a series of the 1890s in which children suffer from parental neglect and indifference, and little boys die asserting their claim to love." Another biographer, Fred Kaplan, has called attention to "homoerotic resonances" in "The Pupil," though conceding that the text itself "refrains" from any explicit "mention of sexuality."

Kaplan suggests that the ending may expose in the tutor a sexual crisis, a moment of "homosexual panic." But it might instead, or, at the same time, highlight the panic that for James often accompanies the prospect of any attachment that threatens to become permanent—and hence would imperil the need to maintain separateness, disconnection, emotional and sexual freedom. In James's view, passionate attachment is a powerful desire and, even more, a grave danger to be guarded against—and this detachment from desire leads to painful, tragic, even deathly results, as in the follwoing story.

For an introduction: F. W. Dupee, *Henry James* (1951). Biographies in-clude Leon Edel, *Henry James: A Life* (1985); Fred Kaplan, *Henry James: The Imagination of Genius: A Biography* (1992); Lyndall Gordon, *A Private Life of Henry James: Two Women and His Art* (1998); and Sheldon M. Novick, *Henry James: The Young Master* (1996) and *Henry James: The Mature Master* (2007). See also *Dearly Beloved Friends: Henry James's Letters to Young Men*, ed. Steven H. Jobe and Susan E. Gunter (2002). For critical discussion of James's short stories: Krishna Baldev Vaid, *Technique in the Tales of Henry James* (1964); and Christina E. Albers, *A Reader's Guide to the Short Stories of Henry James* (1997). Studies of gender in James's work include: Hugh Stevens, *Henry James and Sexuality* (1998); Eric Haralson, *Henry James and Queer Modernity* (2003); and Leland S. Person, *Henry James and the Suspense of Masculinity* (2003). See also Edgar F. Harden, *A Henry James Chronology* (2005); *A Companion to Henry James,* ed. Greg W. Zacharias (2008); *Critical Companion to Henry James: A Literary Reference to His Life and Work,* ed. Eric Haralson and Kendall Johnson (2009); and *Henry James in Context,* ed. David McWhirter (2010).

The Pupil

1

The poor young man hesitated and procrastinated: it cost him such an effort to broach the subject of terms, to speak of money to a person who spoke only of feelings and, as it were, of the aristocracy. Yet he was unwilling to take leave, treating his engagement as settled, without some more conventional glance in that direction than he could find an opening for in the manner of the large affable lady who sat there drawing a pair of soiled *gants de Suède*[1] through a fat jewelled hand and, at once pressing and gliding, repeated over and over everything but the thing he would have liked to hear. He would have liked to hear the figure of his salary; but just as he was nervously about to sound that note the little boy came back—the little boy Mrs. Moreen had sent out of the room to fetch her fan. He came back without the fan, only with the casual observation that he couldn't find it. As he dropped this cynical confession he looked straight and hard at the candidate for the honour of taking his education in hand. This personage reflected somewhat grimly that the first thing he should have to teach his little charge would be to appear to address himself to his mother when he spoke to her—especially not to make her such an improper answer as that.

When Mrs. Moreen bethought herself of this pretext for getting rid of their companion Pemberton supposed it was precisely to approach the delicate subject of his remuneration.[2] But it had been only to say some things about her son that it was better a boy of eleven should n't catch. They were extravagantly to his advantage save when she lowered her voice to sigh, tapping her left side familiarly, "And all overclouded by *this*, you know; all at the mercy of a weakness—!" Pemberton gathered that the weakness was in the region of the heart. He had known the poor child was not robust: this was the basis on which he had been invited to treat,[3] through an English lady, an Oxford acquaintance, then at Nice, who happened to know both his needs and those of the amiable American family looking out for something really superior in the way of a resident tutor.

The young man's impression of his prospective pupil, who had come into the room as if to see for himself the moment Pemberton was admitted, was not quite the soft solicitation the visitor had taken for granted. Morgan Moreen was somehow sickly without being "delicate," and that he looked intelligent—it is true Pemberton would n't have enjoyed his being stupid—only added to the suggestion that, as with his big mouth and big ears he really could n't be called pretty, he might too utterly fail to please.

---

[1]Gloves (French).
[2]Payment, salary.
[3]Apply for a position.

Pemberton was modest, was even timid; and the chance that his small scholar would prove cleverer than himself had quite figured, to his anxiety, among the dangers of an untried experiment. He reflected, however, that these were risks one had to run when one accepted a position, as it was called, in a private family; when as yet one's university honours had, pecuniarily speaking, remained barren.[4] At any rate when Mrs. Moreen got up as to intimate that, since it was understood he would enter upon his duties within the week she would let him off now, he succeeded, in spite of the presence of the child, in squeezing out a phrase about the rate of payment. It was not the fault of the conscious smile which seemed a reference to the lady's expensive identity, it was not the fault of this demonstration, which had, in a sort, both vagueness and point, if the allusion did n't sound rather vulgar. This was exactly because she became still more gracious to reply: "Oh I can assure you that all that will be quite regular."

Pemberton only wondered, while he took up his hat, what "all that" was to amount to—people had such different ideas. Mrs. Moreen's words, however, seemed to commit the family to a pledge definite enough to elicit from the child a strange little comment in the shape of the mocking foreign ejaculation "Oh la-la!"

Pemberton, in some confusion, glanced at him as he walked slowly to the window with his back turned, his hands in his pockets and the air in his elderly shoulders of a boy who did n't play. The young man wondered if he should be able to teach him to play, though his mother had said it would never do and that this was why school was impossible. Mrs. Moreen exhibited no discomfiture; she only continued blandly: "Mr. Moreen will be delighted to meet your wishes. As I told you, he has been called to London for a week. As soon as he comes back you shall have it out with him."

This was so frank and friendly that the young man could only reply, laughing as his hostess laughed: "Oh I don't imagine we shall have much of a battle."

"They'll give you anything you like," the boy remarked unexpectedly, returning from the window. "We don't mind what anything costs—we live awfully well."

"My darling, you're too quaint!" his mother exclaimed, putting out to caress him a practised but ineffectual hand. He slipped out of it, but looked with intelligent innocent eyes at Pemberton, who had already had time to notice that from one moment to the other his small satiric face seemed to change its time of life. At this moment it was infantine, yet it appeared also to be under the influence of curious intuitions and knowledges. Pemberton rather disliked precocity and was disappointed to find gleams of it in a disciple not yet in his teens. Nevertheless he divined on the spot that Morgan wouldn't prove a bore. He would prove on the contrary a source of agitation. This idea held the young man, in spite of a certain repulsion.

---

[4]His university degree had failed to pay off financially.

"You pompous little person! We're not extravagant!" Mrs. Moreen gaily protested, making another unsuccessful attempt to draw the boy to her side. "You must know what to expect," she went on to Pemberton.

"The less you expect the better!" her companion interposed. "But we *are* people of fashion."

"Only so far as *you* make us so!" Mrs. Moreen tenderly mocked. "Well then, on Friday—don't tell me you're superstitious—and mind you don't fail us. Then you'll see us all. I'm so sorry the girls are out. I guess you'll like the girls. And, you know, I've another son, quite different from this one."

"He tries to imitate me," Morgan said to their friend.

"He tries? Why he's twenty years old!" cried Mrs. Moreen.

"You're very witty," Pemberton remarked to the child—a proposition his mother echoed with enthusiasm, declaring Morgan's sallies to be the delight of the house.

The boy paid no heed to this; he only enquired abruptly of the visitor, who was surprised afterwards that he hadn't struck him as offensively forward: "Do you *want* very much to come?"

"Can you doubt it after such a description of what I shall hear?" Pemberton replied. Yet he didn't want to come at all; he was coming because he had to go somewhere, thanks to the collapse of his fortune at the end of a year abroad spent on the system of putting his scant patrimony[5] into a single full wave of experience. He had had his full wave but couldn't pay the score[6] at his inn. Moreover he had caught in the boy's eyes the glimpse of a far-off appeal.

"Well, I'll do the best I can for you," said Morgan; with which he turned away again. He passed out of one of the long windows; Pemberton saw him go and lean on the parapet of the terrace. He remained there while the young man took leave of his mother, who, on Pemberton's looking as if he expected a farewell from him, interposed with: "Leave him, leave him; he's so strange!" Pemberton supposed her to fear something he might say. "He's a genius—you'll love him," she added. "He's much the most interesting person in the family." And before he could invent some civility to oppose to this she wound up with: "But we're all good, you know!"

"He's a genius—you'll love him!" were words that recurred to our aspirant before the Friday, suggesting among many things that geniuses were not invariably loveable. However, it was all the better if there was an element that would make tutorship absorbing: he had perhaps taken too much for granted it would only disgust him. As he left the villa after his interview he looked up at the balcony and saw the child leaning over it. "We shall have great larks!"[7] he called up.

---

[5]Inheritance.
[6]Debt.
[7]Adventures, good times.

Morgan hung fire a moment and then gaily returned: "By the time you come back I shall have thought of something witty!"

This made Pemberton say to himself "After all he's rather nice."

2

On the Friday he saw them all, as Mrs. Moreen had promised, for her husband had come back and the girls and the other son were at home. Mr. Moreen had a white moustache, a confiding manner and, in his buttonhole, the ribbon of a foreign order—bestowed, as Pemberton eventually learned, for services. For what services he never clearly ascertained: this was a point—one of a large number—that Mr. Moreen's manner never confided. What it emphatically did confide was that he was even more a man of the world than you might first make out. Ulick, the firstborn, was in visible training for the same profession—under the disadvantage as yet, however, of a buttonhole but feebly floral and a moustache with no pretensions to type. The girls had hair and figures and manners and small fat feet, but had never been out alone. As for Mrs. Moreen, Pemberton saw on a nearer view that her elegance was intermittent and her parts didn't always match. Her husband, as she had promised, met with enthusiasm Pemberton's ideas in regard to a salary. The young man had endeavoured to keep these stammerings modest, and Mr. Moreen made it no secret that *he* found them wanting in "style." He further mentioned that he aspired to be intimate with his children, to be their best friend, and that he was always looking out for them. That was what he went off for, to London and other places—to look out; and this vigilance was the theory of life, as well as the real occupation, of the whole family. They all looked out, for they were very frank on the subject of its being necessary. They desired it to be understood that they were earnest people, and also that their fortune, though quite adequate for earnest people, required the most careful administration. Mr. Moreen, as the parent bird, sought sustenance for the nest. Ulick invoked support mainly at the club, where Pemberton guessed that it was usually served on green cloth. The girls used to do up their hair and their frocks themselves, and our young man felt appealed to be glad, in regard to Morgan's education, that, though it must naturally be of the best, it did n't cost too much. After a little he *was* glad, forgetting at times his own needs in the interest inspired by the child's character and culture and the pleasure of making easy terms for him.

During the first weeks of their acquaintance Morgan had been as puzzling as a page in an unknown language—altogether different from the obvious little Anglo-Saxons[8] who had misrepresented childhood to Pemberton. Indeed the whole mystic volume in which the boy had been amateurishly bound demanded some practice in translation. To-day, after a

[8]British.

considerable interval, there is something phantasmagoric, like a prismatic reflexion or a serial novel, in Pemberton's memory of the queerness of the Moreens. If it were not for a few tangible tokens—a lock of Morgan's hair cut by his own hand, and the half-dozen letters received from him when they were disjoined—the whole episode and the figures peopling it would seem too inconsequent for anything but dreamland. Their supreme quaintness was their success—as it appeared to him for a while at the time; since he had never seen a family so brilliantly equipped for failure. Wasn't it success to have kept him so hatefully long? Wasn't it success to have drawn him in that first morning at déjeuner,[9] the Friday he came—it was enough to *make* one superstitious—so that he utterly committed himself, and this not by calculation or on a signal, but from a happy instinct which made them, like a band of gipsies, work so neatly together? They amused him as much as if they had really been a band of gipsies. He was still young and had not seen much of the world—his English years had been properly arid; therefore the reversed conventions of the Moreens—for they had *their* desperate proprieties—struck him as topsy-turvy. He had encountered nothing like them at Oxford; still less had any such note been struck to his younger American ear during the four years at Yale in which he had richly supposed himself to be reacting against a Puritan[10] strain. The reaction of the Moreens, at any rate, went ever so much further. He had thought himself very sharp that first day in hitting them all off in his mind with the "cosmopolite"[11] label. Later it seemed feeble and colourless—confessedly helplessly provisional.

He yet when he first applied it felt a glow of joy—for an instructor he was still empirical—rise from the apprehension that living with them would really be to see life. Their sociable strangeness was an intimation of that—their chatter of tongues, their gaiety and good humour, their infinite dawdling (they were always getting themselves up, but it took for ever, and Pemberton had once found Mr. Moreen shaving in the drawing-room), their French, their Italian and, cropping up in the foreign fluencies, their cold tough slices of American. They lived on maccaroni and coffee—they had these articles prepared in perfection—but they knew recipes for a hundred other dishes. They overflowed with music and song, were always humming and catching each other up, and had a sort of professional acquaintance with Continental[12] cities. They talked of "good places" as if they had been pickpockets or strolling players. They had at Nice a villa, a carriage, a piano and a banjo, and they went to official parties. They were a perfect calendar of the "days" of their friends, which Pemberton knew

[9]Luncheon (French).
[10]Referring to the settlers of the American colonies and their strict and scrupulous religious observances. The Puritan ethic advocated strict individual moral values and the redemptive value of hard work.
[11]A citizen of the world. Treating the entire world as one's own country, with no national attachments or prejudices.
[12]European.

them, when they were indisposed, to get out of bed to go to, and which made the week larger than life when Mrs. Moreen talked of them with Paula and Amy. Their initiations gave their new inmate at first an almost dazzling sense of culture. Mrs. Moreen had translated something at some former period—an author whom it made Pemberton feel *borné*[13] never to have heard of. They could imitate Venetian and sing Neapolitan, and when they wanted to say something very particular communicated with each other in an ingenious dialect of their own, an elastic spoken cipher which Pemberton at first took for some *patois*[14] of one of their countries, but which he "caught on to" as he would not have grasped provincial development of Spanish or German.

"It's the family language—Ultramoreen," Morgan explained to him drolly enough; but the boy rarely condescended to use it himself, though he dealt in colloquial Latin as if he had been a little prelate.

Among all the "days" with which Mrs. Moreen's memory was taxed she managed to squeeze in one of her own, which her friends sometimes forgot. But the house drew a frequented air from the number of fine people who were freely named there and from several mysterious men with foreign titles and English clothes whom Morgan called the Princes and who, on sofas with the girls, talked French very loud—though sometimes with some oddity of accent—as if to show they were saying nothing improper. Pemberton wondered how the Princes could ever propose in that tone and so publicly: he took for granted cynically that this was what was desired of them. Then he recognised that even for the chance of such an advantage Mrs. Moreen would never allow Paula and Amy to receive alone. These young ladies were not at all timid, but it was just the safeguards that made them so candidly free. It was a houseful of Bohemians[15] who wanted tremendously to be Philistines.[16]

In one respect, however, certainly, they achieved no rigour—they were wonderfully amiable and ecstatic about Morgan. It was a genuine tenderness, an artless admiration, equally strong in each. They even praised his beauty, which was small, and were as afraid of him as if they felt him of finer clay. They spoke of him as a little angel and a prodigy—they touched on his want of health with long, vague faces. Pemberton feared at first an extravagance that might make him hate the boy, but before this happened he had become extravagant himself. Later, when he had grown rather to hate the others, it was a bribe to patience for him that they were at any rate nice about Morgan, going on tiptoe if they fancied he was showing symptoms, and even giving up somebody's "day" to procure him a pleasure. Mixed with this too was the oddest wish to make him independent, as if

---

[13]Limited in scope or experience (French).
[14]A spoken dialect that differs materially from the standard or literary language.
[15]Social gypsies. The term is used to describe artists, writers, or actors who lead a free lifestyle, often contrasting sharply with general social convention and mores.
[16]Persons whose interests are chiefly bounded by material and commonplace things.

they had felt themselves not good enough for him. They passed him over to the new members of their circle very much as if wishing to force some charity of adoption on so free an agent and get rid of their own charge. They were delighted when they saw Morgan take so to his kind playfellow, and could think of no higher praise for the young man. It was strange how they contrived to reconcile the appearance, and indeed the essential fact, of adoring the child with their eagerness to wash their hands of him. Did they want to get rid of him before he should find them out? Pemberton was finding them out month by month. The boy's fond family, however this might be, turned their backs with exaggerated delicacy, as if to avoid the reproach of interfering. Seeing in time how little he had in common with them—it was by *them* he first observed it; they proclaimed it with complete humility—his companion was moved to speculate on the mysteries of transmission, the far jumps of heredity. Where his detachment from most of the things they represented had come from was more than an observer could say—it certainly had burrowed under two or three generations.

As for Pemberton's own estimate of his pupil, it was a good while before he got the point of view, so little had he been prepared for it by the smug young barbarians to whom the tradition of tutorship, as hitherto revealed to him, had been adjusted. Morgan was scrappy and surprising, deficient in many properties supposed common to the *genus* and abounding in others that were the portion only of the supernaturally clever. One day his friend made a great stride: it cleared up the question to perceive that Morgan *was* supernaturally clever and that, though the formula was temporarily meagre, this would be the only assumption on which one could successfully deal with him. He had the general quality of a child for whom life had not been simplified by school, a kind of homebred sensibility which might have been bad for himself but was charming for others, and a whole range of refinement and perception—little musical vibrations as taking as picked-up airs—begotten by wandering about Europe at the tail of his migratory tribe. This might not have been an education to recommend in advance, but its results with so special a subject were as appreciable as the marks on a piece of fine porcelain. There was at the same time in him a small strain of stoicism, doubtless the fruit of having had to begin early to bear pain, which counted for pluck and made it of less consequence that he might have been thought at school rather a polyglot little beast. Pemberton indeed quickly found himself rejoicing that school was out of the question: in any million of boys it was probably good for all but one, and Morgan was that millionth. It would have made him comparative and superior—it might have made him really require kicking. Pemberton would try to be school himself—a bigger seminary than five hundred grazing donkeys, so that, winning no prizes, the boy would remain unconscious and irresponsible and amusing—amusing, because, though life was already intense in his childish nature, freshness still made there a strong draught for jokes. It turned out that even in the still air of Morgan's various disabilities jokes flourished greatly. He was a pale lean acute undeveloped little cosmopolite, who liked intellectual gymnastics and who also, as regards the behaviour of mankind, had noticed more things than you might suppose, but who nevertheless had his proper playroom of superstitions, where he smashed a dozen toys a day.

3

At Nice once, toward evening, as the pair rested in the open air after a walk, and looked over the sea at the pink western lights, he said suddenly to his comrade: "Do you like it, you know—being with us all in this intimate way?"

"My dear fellow, why should I stay if I didn't?"

"How do I know you'll stay? I'm almost sure you won't, very long."

"I hope you don't mean to dismiss me," said Pemberton.

Morgan debated, looking at the sunset. "I think if I did right I ought to."

"Well, I know I'm supposed to instruct you in virtue; but in that case don't do right."

"You're very young—fortunately," Morgan went on, turning to him again.

"Oh yes, compared with you!"

"Therefore it won't matter so much if you do lose a lot of time."

"That's the way to look at it," said Pemberton accommodatingly.

They were silent a minute; after which the boy asked: "Do you like my father and my mother very much?"

"Dear me, yes. Charming people."

Morgan received this with another silence; then unexpectedly, familiarly, but at the same time affectionately, he remarked: "You're a jolly old humbug!"[17]

For a particular reason the words made our young man change colour. The boy noticed in an instant that he had turned red, whereupon he turned red himself and pupil and master exchanged a longish glance in which there was a consciousness of many more things than are usually touched upon, even tacitly, in such a relation. It produced for Pemberton an embarrassment; it raised in a shadowy form a question—this was the first glimpse of it—destined to play a singular and, as he imagined, owing to the altogether peculiar conditions, an unprecedented part in his intercourse with his little companion. Later, when he found himself talking with the youngster in a way in which few youngsters could ever have been talked with, he thought of that clumsy moment on the bench at Nice as the dawn of an understanding that had broadened. What had added to the

[17]Imposter, fraud, deceiver.

clumsiness then was that he thought it his duty to declare to Morgan that he might abuse him, Pemberton, as much as he liked, but must never abuse his parents. To this Morgan had the easy retort that he hadn't dreamed of abusing them; which appeared to be true: it put Pemberton in the wrong.

"Then why am I a humbug for saying *I* think them charming?" the young man asked, conscious of a certain rashness.

"Well—they're not your parents."

"They love you better than anything in the world—never forget that," said Pemberton.

"Is that why you like them so much?"

"They're very kind to me," Pemberton replied evasively.

"You *are* a humbug!" laughed Morgan, passing an arm into his tutor's. He leaned against him looking off at the sea again and swinging his long thin legs.

"Don't kick my shins," said Pemberton while he reflected "Hang it, I can't complain of them to the child!"

"There's another reason too," Morgan went on, keeping his legs still.

"Another reason for what?"

"Besides their not being your parents."

"I don't understand you," said Pemberton.

"Well, you will before long. All right!"

He did understand fully before long, but he made a fight even with himself before he confessed it. He thought it the oddest thing to have a struggle with the child about. He wondered he didn't hate the hope of the Moreens for bringing the struggle on. But by the time it began any such sentiment for that scion was closed to him. Morgan was a special case, and to know him was to accept him on his own odd terms. Pemberton had spent his aversion to special cases before arriving at knowledge. When at last he did arrive his quandary was great. Against every interest he had attached himself. They would have to meet things together. Before they went home that evening at Nice the boy had said, clinging to his arm:

"Well, at any rate you'll hang on to the last."

"To the last?"

"Till you're fairly beaten."

"*You* ought to be fairly beaten!" cried the young man, drawing him closer.

4

A year after he had come to live with them Mr. and Mrs. Moreen suddenly gave up the villa at Nice. Pemberton had got used to suddenness, having seen it practised on a considerable scale during two jerky little tours—one in Switzerland the first summer, and the other late in the winter, when they all ran down to Florence and then, at the end of ten days, liking it much less than they had intended, straggled back in mysterious depression.

They had returned to Nice "forever," as they said; but this didn't prevent their squeezing, one rainy muggy May night, into a second-class railway-carriage—you could never tell by which class they would travel—where Pemberton helped them to stow away a wonderful collection of bundles and bags. The explanation of this manœuvre was that they had determined to spend the summer "in some bracing place"; but in Paris they dropped into a small furnished apartment—a fourth floor in a third-rate avenue, where there was a smell on the staircase and the *portier*[18] was hateful—and passed the next four months in blank indigence.

The better part of this baffled sojourn was for the preceptor and his pupil, who, visiting the Invalides and Notre Dame, the Conciergerie and all the museums, took a hundred remunerative rambles. They learned to know their Paris, which was useful, for they came back another year for a longer stay, the general character of which in Pemberton's memory to-day mixes pitiably and confusedly with that of the first. He sees Morgan's shabby knickerbockers—the everlasting pair that didn't match his blouse and that as he grew longer could only grow faded. Hè remembers the particular holes in his three or four pair of coloured stockings.

Morgan was dear to his mother, but he never was better dressed than was absolutely necessary—partly, no doubt, by his own fault, for he was as indifferent to his appearance as a German philosopher. "My dear fellow, you *are* coming to pieces," Pemberton would say to him in sceptical remonstrance; to which the child would reply, looking at him serenely up and down: "My dear fellow, so are you! I don't want to cast you in the shade." Pemberton could have no rejoinder for this—the assertion so closely represented the fact. If however the deficiencies of his own wardrobe were a chapter by themselves he didn't like his little charge to look too poor. Later he used to say "Well, if we're poor, why, after all, shouldn't we look it?" and he consoled himself with thinking there was something rather elderly and gentlemanly in Morgan's disrepair—it differed from the untidiness of the urchin who plays and spoils his things. He could trace perfectly the degrees by which, in proportion as her little son confined himself to his tutor for society, Mrs. Moreen shrewdly forbore to renew his garments. She did nothing that didn't show, neglected him because he escaped notice, and then, as he illustrated this clever policy, discouraged at home his public appearances. Her position was logical enough—those members of her family who did show had\to be showy.

During this period and several others Pemberton was quite aware of how he and his comrade might strike people; wandering languidly through the Jardin des Plantes as if they had nowhere to go, sitting on the winter days in the galleries of the Louvre, so splendidly ironical to the homeless, as if for

[18]Doorman (French).

the advantage of the *calorifère*.[19] They joked about it sometimes: it was the sort of joke that was perfectly within the boy's compass. They figured themselves as part of the vast vague hand-to-mouth multitude of the enormous city and pretended they were proud of their position in it—it showed them "such a lot of life" and made them conscious of a democratic brotherhood. If Pemberton couldn't feel a sympathy in destitution with his small companion—for after all Morgan's fond parents would never have let him really suffer—the boy would at least feel it with him, so it came to the same thing. He used sometimes to wonder what people would think they were—to fancy they were looked askance at, as if it might be a suspected case of kidnapping. Morgan wouldn't be taken for a young patrician with a preceptor—he wasn't smart enough; though he might pass for his companion's sickly little brother. Now and then he had a five-franc piece, and except once, when they bought a couple of lovely neckties, one of which he made Pemberton accept, they laid it out scientifically in old books. This was sure to be a great day, always spent on the quays, in a rummage of the dusty boxes that garnish the parapets. Such occasions helped them to live, for their books ran low very soon after the beginning of their acquaintance. Pemberton had a good many in England, but he was obliged to write to a friend and ask him kindly to get some fellow to give him something for them.

If they had to relinquish that summer the advantage of the bracing climate the young man couldn't but suspect this failure of the cup when at their very lips to have been the effect of a rude jostle of his own. This had represented his first blow-out, as he called it, with his patrons; his first successful attempt—though there was little other success about it—to bring them to a consideration of his impossible position. As the ostensible eve of a costly journey the moment had struck him as favourable to an earnest protest, the presentation of an ultimatum. Ridiculous as it sounded, he had never yet been able to compass an uninterrupted private interview with the elder pair or with either of them singly. They were always flanked by their elder children, and poor Pemberton usually had his own little charge at his side. He was conscious of its being a house in which the surface of one's delicacy got rather smudged; nevertheless he had preserved the bloom of his scruple against announcing to Mr. and Mrs. Moreen with publicity that he shouldn't be able to go on longer without a little money. He was still simple enough to suppose Ulick and Paula and Amy might not know that since his arrival he had only had a hundred and forty francs; and he was magnanimous enough to wish not to compromise their parents in their eyes. Mr. Moreen now listened to him, as he listened to every one and to every thing, like a man of the world, and seemed to appeal to him—though not of course too grossly—to try and be a little more of one himself. Pemberton recognised in fact the importance

---

[19]Heater (French).

of the character—from the advantage it gave Mr. Moreen. He was not even confused or embarrassed, whereas the young man in his service was more so than there was any reason for. Neither was he surprised—at least any more than a gentleman had to be who freely confessed himself a little shocked—though not perhaps strictly at Pemberton.

"We must go into this, mustn't we, dear?" he said to his wife. He assured his young friend that the matter should have his very best attention; and he melted into space as elusively as if, at the door, he were taking an inevitable but deprecatory precedence. When, the next moment, Pemberton found himself alone with Mrs. Moreen it was to hear her say "I see, I see"—stroking the roundness of her chin and looking as if she were only hesitating between a dozen easy remedies. If they didn't make their push Mr. Moreen could at least disappear for several days. During his absence his wife took up the subject again spontaneously, but her contribution to it was merely that she had thought all the while they were getting on so beautifully. Pemberton's reply to this revelation was that unless they immediately put down something on account he would leave them on the spot and forever. He knew she would wonder how he would get away, and for a moment expected her to enquire. She didn't, for which he was almost grateful to her, so little was he in a position to tell.

"You won't, you *know* you won't—you're too interested," she said. "You *are* interested, you know you are, you dear kind man!" She laughed with almost condemnatory archness, as if it were a reproach—though she wouldn't insist; and flirted a soiled pocket-handkerchief at him.

Pemberton's mind was fully made up to take his step the following week. This would give him time to get an answer to a letter he had dispatched to England. If he did in the event nothing of the sort—that is if he stayed another year and then went away only for three months—it was not merely because before the answer to his letter came (most unsatisfactory when it did arrive) Mr. Moreen generously counted out to him, and again with the sacrifice to "form" of a marked man of the world, three hundred francs in elegant ringing gold. He was irritated to find that Mrs. Moreen was right, that he couldn't at the pinch bear to leave the child. This stood out clearer for the very reason that, the night of his desperate appeal to his patrons, he had seen fully for the first time where he was. Wasn't it another proof of the success with which those patrons practised their arts that they had managed to avert for so long the illuminating flash? It descended on our friend with a breadth of effect which perhaps would have struck a spectator as comical, after he had returned to his little servile room, which looked into a close court where a bare dirty opposite wall took, with the sound of shrill clatter, the reflexion of lighted back windows. He had simply given himself away to a band of adventurers. The idea, the word itself, wore a romantic horror for him—he had always lived on such safe lines. Later it assumed a more interesting, almost a soothing, sense: it pointed a moral, and Pemberton could enjoy a moral. The Moreens were adventurers not merely because they did n't pay their debts, because they lived on society, but because their whole view of life, dim and confused and instinctive, like that of clever colour-blind animals, was speculative and rapacious and mean. Oh they were "respectable," and that only made them more *immondes*![20] The young man's analysis, while he brooded, put it at last very simply—they were adventurers because they were toadies and snobs. That was the completest account of them—it was the law of their being. Even when this truth became vivid to their ingenious inmate he remained unconscious of how much his mind had been prepared for it by the extraordinary little boy who had now become such a complication in his life. Much less could he then calculate on the information he was still to owe the extraordinary little boy.

5

But it was during the ensuing time that the real problem came up—the problem of how far it was excusable to discuss the turpitude of parents with a child of twelve, of thirteen, of fourteen. Absolutely inexcusable and quite impossible it of course at first appeared; and indeed the question did n't press for some time after Pemberton had received his three hundred francs. They produced a temporary lull, a relief from the sharpest pressure. The young man frugally amended his wardrobe and even had a few francs in his pocket. He thought the Moreens looked at him as if he were almost too smart, as if they ought to take care not to spoil him. If Mr. Moreen had n't been such a man of the world he would perhaps have spoken of the freedom of such neckties on the part of a subordinate. But Mr. Moreen was always enough a man of the world to let things pass—he had certainly shown that. It was singular how Pemberton guessed that Morgan, though saying nothing about it, knew something had happened. But three hundred francs, especially when one owed money, could n't last for ever; and when the treasure was gone—the boy knew when it had failed—Morgan did break ground. The party had returned to Nice at the beginning of the winter, but not to the charming villa. They went to an hotel, where they stayed three months, and then moved to another establishment, explaining that they had left the first because, after waiting and waiting, they could n't get the rooms they wanted. These apartments, the rooms they wanted, were generally very splendid; but fortunately they never *could* get them—fortunately, I mean, for Pemberton, who reflected always that if they had got them there would have been a still scanter educational fund. What Morgan said at last was said suddenly, irrelevantly, when the moment came, in the middle of a lesson, and consisted of the apparently unfeeling words: "You ought to *filer*, you know—you really ought."

[20]Squalid (French).

Pemberton stared. He had learnt enough French slang from Morgan to know that to *filer* meant to cut sticks. "Ah my dear fellow, don't turn me off!"

Morgan pulled a Greek lexicon toward him—he used a Greek-German—to look out a word, instead of asking it of Pemberton. "You can't go on like this, you know."

"Like what, my boy?"

"You know they don't pay you up," said Morgan, blushing and turning his leaves.

"Don't pay me?" Pemberton stared again and feigned amazement. "What on earth put that into your head?"

"It has been there a long time," the boy replied rummaging his book.

Pemberton was silent, then he went on: "I say, what are you hunting for? They pay me beautifully."

"I'm hunting for the Greek for awful whopper," Morgan dropped.

"Find that rather for gross impertinence and disabuse your mind. What do I want of money?"

"Oh that's another question!"

Pemberton wavered—he was drawn in different ways. The severely correct thing would have been to tell the boy that such a matter was none of his business and bid him go on with his lines. But they were really too intimate for that; it was not the way he was in the habit of treating him; there had been no reason it should be. On the other hand Morgan had quite lighted on the truth—he really should n't be able to keep it up much longer; therefore why not let him know one's real motive for forsaking him? At the same time it was n't decent to abuse to one's pupil the family of one's pupil; it was better to misrepresent than to do that. So in reply to his comrade's last exclamation he just declared, to dismiss the subject, that he had received several payments.

"I say—I say!" the boy ejaculated, laughing.

"That's all right," Pemberton insisted. "Give me your written rendering."

Morgan pushed a copybook across the table, and he began to read the page, but with something running in his head that made it no sense. Looking up after a minute or two he found the child's eyes fixed on him and felt in them something strange. Then Morgan said: "I'm not afraid of the stern reality."

"I haven't yet seen the thing you *are* afraid of—I'll do you that justice!"

This came out with a jump—it was perfectly true—and evidently gave Morgan pleasure. "I've thought of it a long time," he presently resumed.

"Well, don't think of it any more."

The boy appeared to comply, and they had a comfortable and even an amusing hour. They had a theory that they were very thorough, and yet they seemed always to be in the amusing part of lessons, the intervals between the dull dark tunnels, where there were waysides and jolly views.

Yet the morning was brought to a violent end by Morgan's suddenly leaning his arms on the table, burying his head in them and bursting into
tears: at which Pemberton was the more startled that, as it then came over
him, it was the first time he had ever seen the boy cry and that the impression was consequently quite awful.

The next day, after much thought, he took a decision and, believing it
to be just, immediately acted on it. He cornered Mr. and Mrs. Moreen again
and let them know that if on the spot they didn't pay him all they owed
him he wouldn't only leave their house but would tell Morgan exactly what
had brought him to it.

"Oh you *haven't* told him?" cried Mrs. Moreen with a pacifying hand on
her well-dressed bosom.

"Without warning you? For what do you take me?" the young man
returned.

Mr. and Mrs. Moreen looked at each other; he could see that they appreciated, as tending to their security, his superstition of delicacy, and yet
that there was a certain alarm in their relief. "My dear fellow," Mr. Moreen
demanded, "what use *can* you have, leading the quiet life we all do, for
such a lot of money?"—a question to which Pemberton made no answer,
occupied as he was in noting that what passed in the mind of his patrons
was something like: "Oh then, if we've felt that the child, dear little angel,
has judged us and how he regards us, and we haven't been betrayed, he
must have guessed—and in short it's *general!*" an inference that rather
stirred up Mr. and Mrs. Moreen, as Pemberton had desired it should. At
the same time, if he had supposed his threat would do something towards bringing them round, he was disappointed to find them taking for
granted—how vulgar their perception *had* been!—that he had already
given them away. There was a mystic uneasiness in their parental breasts,
and that had been the inferior sense of it. None the less, however, his
threat did touch them; for if they had escaped it was only to meet a new
danger. Mr. Moreen appealed to him, on every precedent, as a man of the
world; but his wife had recourse, for the first time since his domestication
with them, to a fine *hauteur*,[21] reminding him that a devoted mother, with
her child, had arts that protected her against gross misrepresentation.

"I should misrepresent you grossly if I accused you of common honesty!" our friend replied; but as he closed the door behind him sharply,
thinking he had not done himself much good, while Mr. Moreen lighted
another cigarette, he heard his hostess shout after him more touchingly:

"Oh you do, you *do*, put the knife to one's throat!"

The next morning, very early, she came to his room. He recognised
her knock, but had no hope she brought him money; as to which he was
wrong, for she had fifty francs in her hand. She squeezed forward in her

[21]Loftiness of manner or bearing (French).

dressing-gown, and he received her in his own, between his bath-tub and his bed. He had been tolerably schooled by this time to the "foreign ways" of his hosts. Mrs. Moreen was ardent, and when she was ardent she didn't care what she did; so she now sat down on his bed, his clothes being on the chairs, and, in her preoccupation, forgot, as she glanced round, to be ashamed of giving him such a horrid room. What Mrs. Moreen's ardour now bore upon was the design of persuading him that in the first place she was very good-natured to bring him fifty francs, and that in the second, if he would only see it, he was really too absurd to expect to be *paid*. Wasn't he paid enough without perpetual money—wasn't he paid by the comfortable luxurious home he enjoyed with them all, without a care, an anxiety, a solitary want? Wasn't he sure of his position, and wasn't that everything to a young man like him, quite unknown, with singularly little to show, the ground of whose exorbitant pretensions it had never been easy to discover? Wasn't he paid above all by the sweet relation he had established with Morgan—quite ideal as from master to pupil—and by the simple privilege of knowing and living with so amazingly gifted a child; than whom really (and she meant literally what she said) there was no better company in Europe? Mrs. Moreen herself took to appealing to him as a man of the world; she said "Voyons, mon cher," and "My dear man, look here now"; and urged him to be reasonable, putting it before him that it was truly a chance for him. She spoke as if, according as he *should* be reasonable, he would prove himself worthy to be her son's tutor and of the extraordinary confidence they had placed in him.

After all, Pemberton reflected, it was only a difference of theory and the theory didn't matter much. They had hitherto gone on that of remunerated, as now they would go on that of gratuitous, service; but why should they have so many words about it? Mrs. Moreen at all events continued to be convincing; sitting there with her fifty francs she talked and reiterated, as women reiterate, and bored and irritated him, while he leaned against the wall with his hands in the pockets of his wrapper, drawing it together round his legs and looking over the head of his visitor at the grey negations of his window. She wound up with saying: "You see I bring you a definite proposal."

"A definite proposal?"

"To make our relations regular, as it were—to put them on a comfortable footing."

"I see—it's a system," said Pemberton. "A kind of organised blackmail."

Mrs. Moreen bounded up, which was exactly what he wanted. "What do you mean by that?"

"You practise on one's fears—one's fears about the child if one should go away."

"And pray what would happen to him in that event?" she demanded with majesty.

"Why he'd be alone with *you*."

"And pray with whom *should* a child be but with those whom he loves most?"

"If you think that, why don't you dismiss me?"

"Do you pretend he loves you more than he loves *us?*" cried Mrs. Moreen.

"I think he ought to. I make sacrifices for him. Though I've heard of those *you* make I don't see them."

Mrs. Moreen stared a moment; then with emotion she grasped her inmate's hand.

"*Will* you make it—the sacrifice?"

He burst out laughing. "I'll see. I'll do what I can. I'll stay a little longer. Your calculation's just—I *do* hate intensely to give him up; I'm fond of him and he thoroughly interests me, in spite of the inconvenience I suffer. You know my situation perfectly. I have n't a penny in the world and, occupied as you see me with Morgan, am unable to earn money."

Mrs. Moreen tapped her undressed arm with her folded bank-note. "Can't you write articles? Can't you translate as *I* do?"

"I don't know about translating; it's wretchedly paid."

"I'm glad to earn what I can," said Mrs. Moreen with prodigious virtue.

"You ought to tell me who you do it for." Pemberton paused a moment, and she said nothing; so he added: "I've tried to turn off some little sketches, but the magazines won't have them—they're declined with thanks."

"You see then you're not such a phoenix," his visitor pointedly smiled—"to pretend to abilities you're sacrificing for our sake."

"I have n't time to do things properly," he ruefully went on. Then as it came over him that he was almost abjectly good-natured to give these explanations he added: "If I stay on longer it must be on one condition—that Morgan shall know distinctly on what footing I am."

Mrs. Moreen demurred. "Surely you don't want to show off to a child?"

"To show *you* off, do you mean?"

Again she cast about, but this time it was to produce a still finer flower. "And *you* talk of blackmail!"

"You can easily prevent it," said Pemberton.

"And *you* talk of practising on fears!" she bravely pushed on.

"Yes, there's no doubt I'm a great scoundrel."

His patroness met his eyes—it was clear she was in straits. Then she thrust out her money at him. "Mr. Moreen desired me to give you this on account."

"I'm much obliged to Mr. Moreen, but we *have* no account."

"You won't take it?"

"That leaves me more free," said Pemberton.

"To poison my darling's mind?" groaned Mrs. Moreen.

"Oh your darling's mind—!" the young man laughed.

She fixed him a moment, and he thought she was going to break out tormentedly, pleadingly: "For God's sake, tell me what *is* in it!" But she checked this impulse—another was stronger. She pocketed the money— the crudity of the alternative was comical—and swept out of the room with the desperate concession: "You may tell him any horror you like!"

6

A couple of days after this, during which he had failed to profit by so free a permission, he had been for a quarter of an hour walking with his charge in silence when the boy became sociable again with the remark: "I'll tell you how I know it; I know it through Zénobie."

"Zénobie? Who in the world is *she?*"

"A nurse I used to have—ever so many years ago. A charming woman. I liked her awfully, and she liked me."

"There's no accounting for tastes. What is it you know through her?"

"Why what their idea is. She went away because they did n't fork out. She did like me awfully, and she stayed two years. She told me all about it—that at last she could never get her wages. As soon as they saw how much she liked me they stopped giving her anything. They thought she'd stay for nothing—just *because*, don't you know?" And Morgan had a queer little conscious lucid look. "She did stay ever so long—as long as she could. She was only a poor girl. She used to send money to her mother. At last she could n't afford it any longer, and went away in a fearful rage one night—I mean of course in a rage against *them*. She cried over me tremendously, she hugged me nearly to death. She told me all about it," the boy repeated. "She told me it was their idea. So I guessed, ever so long ago, that they have had the same idea with you."

"Zénobie was very sharp," said Pemberton. "And she made you so."

"Oh that was n't Zénobie; that was nature. And experience!" Morgan laughed.

"Well, Zénobie was a part of your experience."

"Certainly I was a part of hers, poor dear!" the boy wisely sighed. "And I'm part of yours."

"A very important part. But I don't see how you know I've been treated like Zénobie."

"Do you take me for the biggest dunce you've known?" Morgan asked. "Haven't I been conscious of what we've been through together?"

"What we've been through?"

"Our privations—our dark days."

"Oh our days have been bright enough."

Morgan went on in silence for a moment. Then he said: "My dear chap, you're a hero!"

"Well, you're another!" Pemberton retorted.

"No I'm not, but I ain't a baby. I won't stand it any longer. You must get some occupation that pays. I'm ashamed, I'm ashamed!" quavered the boy with a ring of passion, like some high silver note from a small cathedral chorister, that deeply touched his friend.

"We ought to go off and live somewhere together," the young man said.

"I'll go like a shot if you'll take me."

"I'd get some work that would keep us both afloat," Pemberton continued.

"So would I. Why should n't *I* work? I ain't such a beastly little muff as *that* comes to."

"The difficulty is that your parents would n't hear of it. They'd never part with you; they worship the ground you tread on. Don't you see the proof of it?" Pemberton developed. "They don't dislike me; they wish me no harm; they're very amiable people; but they're perfectly ready to expose me to any awkwardness in life for your sake."

The silence in which Morgan received his fond sophistry struck Pemberton somehow as expressive. After a moment the child repeated: "You *are* a hero!" Then he added: "They leave me with you altogether. You've all the responsibility. They put me off on you from morning till night. Why then should they object to my taking up with you completely? I'd help you."

"They're not particularly keen about my being helped, and they delight in thinking of you as *theirs*. They're tremendously proud of you."

"I'm not proud of *them*. But you know that," Morgan returned.

"Except for the little matter we speak of they're charming people," said Pemberton, not taking up the point made for his intelligence, but wondering greatly at the boy's own, and especially at this fresh reminder of something he had been conscious of from the first—the strangest thing in his friend's large little composition, a temper, a sensibility, even a private ideal, which made him as privately disown the stuff his people were made of. Morgan had in secret a small loftiness which made him acute about betrayed meanness; as well as a critical sense for the manners immediately surrounding him that was quite without precedent in a juvenile nature, especially when one noted that it had not made this nature "old-fashioned," as the word is of children—quaint or wizened or offensive. It was as if he had been a little gentleman and had paid the penalty by discovering that he was the only such person in his family. This comparison did n't make him vain, but it could make him melancholy and a trifle austere. While Pemberton guessed at these dim young things, shadows of shadows, he was partly drawn on and partly checked, as for a scruple, by the charm of attempting to sound the little cool shallows that were so quickly growing deeper. When he tried to figure to himself the morning twilight of childhood, so as to deal with it safely, he saw it was never fixed, never arrested, that ignorance, at the instant he touched it, was already flushing faintly into knowledge, that there was nothing that at a given moment you could say an intelligent child did n't know. It seemed to him that he himself knew too much to imagine Morgan's simplicity and too little to disembroil his tangle.

The boy paid no heed to his last remark; he only went on: "I'd have spoken to them about their idea, as I call it, long ago, if I had n't been sure what, they'd say."

"And what would they say?"

"Just what they said about what poor Zénobie told me—that it was a horrid dreadful story, that they had paid her every penny they owed her."

"Well, perhaps they had," said Pemberton.

"Perhaps they've paid you!"

"Let us pretend they have, and *n'en parlons plus*."[22]

"They accused her of lying and cheating"—

Morgan stuck to historic truth. "That's why I don't want to speak to them."

"Lest they should accuse me too?" To this Morgan made no answer, and his companion, looking down at him—the boy turned away his eyes, which had filled—saw that he could n't have trusted himself to utter. "You're right. Don't worry them," Pemberton pursued. "Except for that, they *are* charming people."

"Except for *their* lying and *their* cheating?"

"I say—I say!" cried Pemberton, imitating a little tone of the lad's which was itself an imitation.

"We must be frank, at the last; we *must* come to an understanding," said Morgan with the importance of the small boy who lets himself think he is arranging great affairs—almost playing at shipwreck or at Indians. "I know all about everything."

"I dare say your father has his reasons," Pemberton replied, but too vaguely, as he was aware.

"For lying and cheating?"

"For saving and managing and turning his means to the best account. He has plenty to do with his money. You're an expensive family."

"Yes, I'm very expensive," Morgan concurred in a manner that made his preceptor burst out laughing.

"He's saving for *you*," said Pemberton. "They think of you in everything they do."

"He might, while he's about it, save a little—" The boy paused, and his friend waited to hear what. Then Morgan brought out oddly: "A little reputation."

"Oh there's plenty of that. That's all right!"

"Enough of it for the people they know, no doubt. The people they know are awful."

"Do you mean the princes? We must n't abuse the princes."

---

[22]"Let us not speak about it any more" (French).

"Why not? They have n't married Paula—they have n't married Amy. They only clean out Ulick."

"You *do* know everything!" Pemberton declared.

"No I don't after all. I don't know what they live on, or how they live, or *why* they live! What have they got and how did they get it? Are they rich, are they poor, or have they a *modeste aisance*?[23] Why are they always chiveying me about—living one year like ambassadors and the next like paupers? Who are they, anyway, and what are they? I've thought of all that—I've thought of a lot of things. They're so beastly worldly. That's what I hate most—oh I've *seen* it! All they care about is to make an appearance and to pass for something or other. What the dickens do they want to pass for? What *do* they, Mr. Pemberton?"

"You pause for a reply," said Pemberton, treating the question as a joke, yet wondering too and greatly struck with his mate's intense if imperfect vision. "I have n't the least idea."

"And what good does it do? Have n't I seen the way people treat them—the 'nice' people, the ones they want to know? They'll take anything from them—they'll lie down and be trampled on. The nice ones hate that—they just sicken them. You're the only really nice person we know."

"Are you sure? They don't lie down for me!"

"Well, you shan't lie down for them. You've got to go—that's what you've got to do," said Morgan.

"And what will become of you?"

"Oh I'm growing up. I shall get off before long. I'll see you later."

"You had better let me finish you," Pemberton urged, lending himself to the child's strange superiority.

Morgan stopped in their walk, looking up at him. He had to look up much less than a couple of years before—he had grown, in his loose leanness, so long and high. "Finish me?" he echoed.

"There are such a lot of jolly things we can do together yet. I want to turn you out—I want you to do me credit."

Morgan continued to look at him. "To give you credit—do you mean?"

"My dear fellow, you're too clever to live."

"That's just what I'm afraid you think. No, no; it is n't fair—I can't endure it. We'll separate next week. The sooner it's over the sooner to sleep."

"If I hear of anything—any other chance—I promise to go," Pemberton said.

Morgan consented to consider this. "But you'll be honest," he demanded; "you won't pretend you have n't heard?"

"I'm much more likely to pretend I have."

"But what can you hear of, this way, stuck in a hole with us? You ought to be on the spot, to go to England—you ought to go to America."

[23]Literally, modest ease; financial comfort (French).

"One would think you were *my* tutor!" said Pemberton.

Morgan walked on and after a little had begun again: "Well, now that you know I know and that we look at the facts and keep nothing back—it's much more comfortable, is n't it?"

"My dear boy, it's so amusing, so interesting, that it will surely be quite impossible for me to forego such hours as these."

This made Morgan stop once more. "You *do* keep something back. Oh you're not straight—*I* am!"

"How am I not straight?"

"Oh you've got your idea!"

"My idea?"

"Why that I probably shan't make old—make older—bones, and that you can stick it out till I'm removed."

"You *are* too clever to live!" Pemberton repeated.

"I call it a mean idea," Morgan pursued. "But I shall punish you by the way I hang on."

"Look out or I'll poison you!" Pemberton laughed.

"I'm stronger and better every year. Have n't you noticed that there has n't been a doctor near me since you came?"

"*I'm* your doctor," said the young man, taking his arm and drawing him tenderly on again.

Morgan proceeded and after a few steps gave a sigh of mingled weariness and relief. "Ah now that we look at the facts it's all right!"

7

They looked at the facts a good deal after this; and one of the first consequences of their doing so was that Pemberton stuck it out, in his friend's parlance, for the purpose. Morgan made the facts so vivid and so droll, and at the same time so bald and so ugly, that there was fascination in talking them over with him, just as there would have been heartlessness in leaving him alone with them. Now that the pair had such perceptions in common it was useless for them to pretend they did n't judge such people; but the very judgement and the exchange of perceptions created another tie. Morgan had never been so interesting as now that he himself was made plainer by the side-light of these confidences. What came out in it most was the small fine passion of his pride. He had plenty of that, Pemberton felt—so much that one might perhaps wisely wish for it some early bruises. He would have liked his people to have a spirit and had waked up to the sense of their perpetually eating humble-pie. His mother would consume any amount, and his father would consume even more than his mother. He had a theory that Ulick had wriggled out of an "affair" at Nice: there had once been a flurry at home, a regular panic, after which they all went to bed and took medicine, not to be accounted for on any other supposition. Morgan had a romantic imagination, fed by poetry and history, and he would have liked those who "bore his name"—as he used to say to Pemberton with the humour that made his queer delicacies manly—to carry themselves with an air. But their one idea was to get in with people who did n't want them and to take snubs as if they were honourable scars. Why people did n't want them more he did n't know—that was people's own affair; after all they were n't superficially repulsive, they were a hundred times cleverer than most of the dreary grandees, the "poor swells" they rushed about Europe to catch up with. "After all they *are* amusing—they are!" he used to pronounce with the wisdom of the ages. To which Pemberton always replied: "Amusing—the great Moreen troupe? Why they're altogether delightful; and if it were n't for the hitch that you and I (feeble performers!) make in the *ensemble* they'd carry everything before them."

What the boy could n't get over was the fact that this particular blight seemed, in a tradition of self-respect, so undeserved and so arbitrary. No doubt people had a right to take the line they liked; but why should *his* people have liked the line of pushing and toadying and lying and cheating? What had their forefathers—all decent folk, so far as he knew—done to them, or what had *he* done to them? Who had poisoned their blood with the fifth-rate social ideal, the fixed idea of making smart acquaintances and getting into the *monde chic*,[24] especially when it was foredoomed to failure and exposure? They showed so what they were after; that was what made the people they wanted not want *them*. And never a wince for dignity, never a throb of shame at looking each other in the face, never any independence or resentment or disgust. If his father or his brother would only knock some one down once or twice a year! Clever as they were they never guessed the impression they made. They were good-natured, yes—as good-natured as Jews at the doors of clothing-shops! But was that the model one wanted one's family to follow? Morgan had dim memories of an old grandfather, the maternal, in New York, whom he had been taken across the ocean at the age of five to see: a gentleman with a high neck-cloth and a good deal of pronunciation, who wore a dress-coat in the morning, which made one wonder what he wore in the evening, and had, or was supposed to have, "property" and something to do with the Bible Society. It couldn't have been but that *he* was a good type. Pemberton himself remembered Mrs. Clancy, a widowed sister of Mr. Moreen's, who was as irritating as a moral tale and had paid a fortnight's visit to the family at Nice shortly after he came to live with them. She was "pure and refined," as Amy said over the banjo, and had the air of not knowing what they meant when they talked, and of keeping something rather important back. Pemberton judged that what she kept back was an approval of many of their ways; therefore it was to be supposed that she too was of a good type, and that Mr. and Mrs. Moreen and Ulick and Paula and Amy might easily have been of a better one if they would.

[24]Literally, "smart world" (French). The social world of fashionable or aristocratic people.

But that they wouldn't was more and more perceptible from day to day. They continued to "chivey," as Morgan called it, and in due time became aware of a variety of reasons for proceeding to Venice. They mentioned a great many of them—they were always strikingly frank and had the brightest friendly chatter, at the late foreign breakfast in especial, before the ladies had made up their faces, when they leaned their arms on the table, had something to follow the *demi-tasse*,[25] and, in the heat of familiar discussion as to what they "really ought" to do, fell inevitably into the languages in which they could *tutoyer*.[26] Even Pemberton liked them then; he could endure even Ulick when he heard him give his little flat voice for the "sweet sea-city." That was what made him have a sneaking kindness for them—that they were so out of the workaday world and kept him so out of it. The summer had waned when, with cries of ecstasy, they all passed out on the balcony that overhung the Grand Canal. The sunsets then were splendid and the Dorringtons had arrived. The Dorringtons were the only reason they hadn't talked of at breakfast; but the reasons they didn't talk of at breakfast always came out in the end. The Dorringtons on the other hand came out very little; or else when they did they stayed—as was natural—for hours, during which periods Mrs. Moreen and the girls sometimes called at their hotel (to see if they had returned) as many as three times running. The gondola was for the ladies, as in Venice too there were "days," which Mrs. Moreen knew in their order an hour after she arrived. She immediately took one herself, to which the Dorringtons never came, though on a certain occasion when Pemberton and his pupil were together at Saint Mark's—where, taking the best walks they had ever had and haunting a hundred churches, they spent a great deal of time—they saw the old lord turn up with Mr. Moreen and Ulick, who showed him the dim basilica as if it belonged to them. Pemberton noted how much less, among its curiosities, Lord Dorrington carried himself as a man of the world; wondering too whether, for such services, his companions took a fee from him. The autumn at any rate waned, the Dorringtons departed, and Lord Verschoyle, the eldest son, had proposed neither for Amy nor for Paula.

One sad November day, while the wind roared round the old palace and the rain lashed the lagoon, Pemberton, for exercise and even somewhat for warmth—the Moreens were horribly frugal about fires; it was a cause of suffering to their inmate—walked up and down the big bare sala with his pupil. The scagliola floor was cold, the high battered casements shook in the storm, and the stately decay of the place was unrelieved by a particle of furniture. Pemberton's spirits were low, and it came over him that the fortune of the Moreens was now even lower. A blast of desolation, a portent of disgrace and disaster, seemed to draw through the comfortless

---

[25]Literally, "half-cup" (French). Coffee.
[26]Literally, "to address as *tu*," or to know familiarly (French).

hall. Mr. Moreen and Ulick were in the Piazza, looking out for something, strolling drearily, in mackintoshes, under the arcades; but still, in spite of mackintoshes, unmistakeable men of the world. Paula and Amy were in bed—it might have been thought they were staying there to keep warm. Pemberton looked askance at the boy at his side, to see to what extent he was conscious of these dark omens. But Morgan, luckily for him, was now mainly conscious of growing taller and stronger and indeed of being in his fifteenth year. This fact was intensely interesting to him and the basis of a private theory—which, however, he had imparted to his tutor—that in a little while he should stand on his own feet. He considered that the situation would change—that in short he should be "finished," grown up, producible in the world of affairs and ready to prove himself of sterling ability. Sharply as he was capable at times of analysing, as he called it, his life, there were happy hours when he remained, as he also called it— and as the name, really, of their right ideal—"jolly" superficial; the proof of which was his fundamental assumption that he should presently go to Oxford, to Pemberton's college, and aided and abetted by Pemberton, do the most wonderful things. It depressed the young man to see how little in such a project he took account of ways and means: in other connexions he mostly kept to the measure. Pemberton tried to imagine the Moreens at Oxford and fortunately failed; yet unless they were to adopt it as a residence there would be no *modus vivendi*[27] for Morgan. How could he live without an allowance, and where was the allowance to come from? He, Pemberton, might live on Morgan; but how could Morgan live on *him?* What was to become of him anyhow? Somehow the fact that he was a big boy now, with better prospects of health, made the question of his future more difficult. So long as he was markedly frail the great consideration he inspired seemed enough of an answer to it. But at the bottom of Pemberton's heart was the recognition of his probably being strong enough to live and not yet strong enough to struggle or to thrive. Morgan himself at any rate was in the first flush of the rosiest consciousness of adolescence, so that the beating of the tempest seemed to him after all but the voice of life and the challenge of fate. He had on his shabby little overcoat, with the collar up, but was enjoying his walk.

It was interrupted at last by the appearance of his mother at the end of the sala. She beckoned him to come to her, and while Pemberton saw him, complaisant, pass down the long vista and over the damp false marble, he wondered what was in the air. Mrs. Moreen said a word to the boy and made him go into the room she had quitted. Then, having closed the door after him, she directed her steps swiftly to Pemberton. There *was* something in the air, but his wildest flight of fancy would n't have suggested

[27]A working arrangement (Latin). An agreement between two parties in dispute that enables them to live peacefully until the matter can be settled.

what it proved to be. She signified that she had made a pretext to get Morgan out of the way, and then she enquired—without hesitation—if the young man could favour her with the loan of three louis.[28] While, before bursting into a laugh, he stared at her with surprise, she declared that she was awfully pressed for the money; she was desperate for it—it would save her life.

"Dear lady, *c'est trop fort!*"[29] Pemberton laughed in the manner and with the borrowed grace of idiom that marked the best colloquial, the best anecdotic, moments of his friends themselves. "Where in the world do you suppose I should get three louis, *du train dont vous allez?*"[30]

"I thought you worked—wrote things. Don't they pay you?"

"Not a penny."

"Are you such a fool as to work for nothing?"

"You ought surely to know that."

Mrs. Moreen stared, then she coloured a little. Pemberton saw she had quite forgotten the terms—if "terms" they could be called—that he had ended by accepting from herself; they had burdened her memory as little as her conscience. "Oh yes, I see what you mean—you've been very nice about that; but why drag it in so often?" She had been perfectly urbane with him ever since the rough scene of explanation in his room the morning he made her accept *his* "terms"—the necessity of his making his case known to Morgan. She had felt no resentment after seeing there was no danger Morgan would take the matter up with her. Indeed, attributing this immunity to the good taste of his influence with the boy, she had once said to Pemberton "My dear fellow, it's an immense comfort you're a gentleman." She repeated this in substance now. "Of course you're a gentleman—that's a bother the less!" Pemberton reminded her that he had not "dragged in" anything that wasn't already in as much as his foot was in his shoe; and she also repeated her prayer that, somewhere and some-how, he would find her sixty francs. He took the liberty of hinting that if he could find them it wouldn't be to lend them to *her*—as to which he consciously did himself injustice, knowing that if he had them he would certainly put them at her disposal. He accused himself, at bottom and not unveraciously, of a fantastic, a demoralised sympathy with her. If misery made strange bedfellows it also made strange sympathies. It was moreover a part of the abasement of living with such people that one had to make vulgar retorts, quite out of one's own tradition of good manners. "Morgan, Morgan, to what pass have I come for you?" he groaned while Mrs. Moreen floated voluminously down the sala again to liberate the boy, wailing as she went that everything was too odious.

---

[28]A gold coin issued during the reign of Louis XIII (1601–43). In the nineteenth century, the name was transferred to the 20-franc piece. Mrs. Moreen is asking for a loan of about 60 francs.
[29]"It's too much!" (French).
[30]"At the rate you are going?" (French).

Before their young friend was liberated there came a thump at the door communicating with the stair-case, followed by the apparition of a dripping youth who poked in his head. Pemberton recognised him as the bearer of a telegram and recognised the telegram as addressed to himself. Morgan came back as, after glancing at the signature—that of a relative in London—he was reading the words: "Found jolly job for you, engagement to coach opulent youth on own terms. Come at once." The answer happily was paid and the messenger waited. Morgan, who had drawn near, waited too and looked hard at Pemberton; and Pemberton, after a moment, having met his look, handed him the telegram. It was really by wise looks—they knew each other so well now—that, while the telegraph-boy, in his waterproof cape, made a great puddle on the floor, the thing was settled between them. Pemberton wrote the answer with a pencil against the frescoed wall, and the messenger departed. When he had gone the young man explained himself.

"I'll make a tremendous charge; I'll earn a lot of money in a short time, and we'll live on it."

"Well, I hope the opulent youth will be a dismal dunce—he probably will," Morgan parenthesised—"and keep you a long time a-hammering of it in."

"Of course the longer he keeps me the more we shall have for our old age."

"But suppose *they* don't pay you!" Morgan awfully suggested.

"Oh there are not two such—!" But Pemberton pulled up; he had been on the point of using too invidious a term. Instead of this he said "Two such fatalities."

Morgan flushed—the tears came to his eyes. *"Dites toujours*[31] two such rascally crews!" Then in a different tone he added: "Happy opulent youth!"

"Not if he's a dismal dunce."

"Oh they're happier then. But you can't have everything, can you?" the boy smiled.

Pemberton held him fast, hands on his shoulders—he had never loved him so. "What will become of *you*, what will you do?" He thought of Mrs. Moreen, desperate for sixty francs.

"I shall become an *homme fait*."[32] And then as if he recognised all the bearings of Pemberton's allusion: "I shall get on with them better when you're not here."

"Ah don't say that—it sounds as if I set you against them!"

"You do—the sight of you. It's all right; you know what I mean. I shall be beautiful. I'll take their affairs in hand; I'll marry my sisters."

"You'll marry yourself!" joked Pemberton; as high, rather tense pleasantry would evidently be the right, or the safest, tone for their separation.

[31]"Go ahead and say it" (French).
[32]Literally, "made man" (French).

It was, however, not purely in this strain that Morgan suddenly asked: "But I say—how will you get to your jolly job? You'll have to telegraph to the opulent youth for money to come on."

Pemberton bethought himself. "They won't like that, will they?"

"Oh look out for them!"

Then Pemberton brought out his remedy. "I'll go to the American Consul; I'll borrow some money of him—just for the few days, on the strength of the telegram."

Morgan was hilarious. "Show him the telegram—then collar the money and stay!"

Pemberton entered into the joke sufficiently to reply that for Morgan he was really capable of that; but the boy, growing more serious, and to prove he had n't meant what he said, not only hurried him off to the Consulate—since he was to start that evening, as he had wired to his friend—but made sure of their affair by going with him. They splashed through the tortuous perforations and over the humpbacked bridges, and they passed through the Piazza, where they saw Mr. Moreen and Ulick go into a jeweller's shop. The Consul proved accommodating—Pemberton said it was n't the letter, but Morgan's grand air—and on their way back they went into Saint Mark's for a hushed ten minutes. Later they took up and kept up the fun of it to the very end; and it seemed to Pemberton a part of that fun that Mrs. Moreen, who was very angry when he had announced her his intention, should charge him, grotesquely and vulgarly and in reference to the loan she had vainly endeavoured to effect, with bolting lest they should "get something out" of him. On the other hand he had to do Mr. Moreen and Ulick the justice to recognise that when on coming in *they* heard the cruel news they took it like perfect men of the world.

8

When he got at work with the opulent youth, who was to be taken in hand for Balliol, he found himself unable to say if this aspirant had really such poor parts or if the appearance were only begotten of his own long association with an intensely living little mind. From Morgan he heard half a dozen times: the boy wrote charming young letters, a patchwork of tongues, with indulgent postscripts in the family Volapuk and, in little squares and rounds and crannies of the text, the drollest illustrations— letters that he was divided between the impulse to show his present charge as a vain, a wasted incentive, and the sense of something in them that publicity would profane. The opulent youth went up in due course and failed to pass; but it seemed to add to the presumption that brilliancy was not expected of him all at once that his parents, condoning the lapse, which they good-naturedly treated as little as possible as if it were Pemberton's, should have sounded the rally again, begged the young coach to renew the siege.

The young coach was now in a position to lend Mrs. Moreen three louis, and he sent her a post-office order even for a larger amount. In return for this favour he received a frantic scribbled line from her: "Implore you to come back instantly—Morgan dreadfully ill." They were on the rebound, once more in Paris—often as Pemberton had seen them depressed he had never seen them crushed—and communication was therefore rapid. He wrote to the boy to ascertain the state of his health, but awaited the answer in vain. He accordingly, after three days, took an abrupt leave of the opulent youth and, crossing the Channel, alighted at the small hotel, in the quarter of the Champs Elysées, of which Mrs. Moreen had given him the address. A deep if dumb dissatisfaction with this lady and her companions bore him company: they could n't be vulgarly honest, but they could live at hotels, in velvety entresols,[33] amid a smell of burnt pastilles, surrounded by the most expensive city in Europe. When he had left them in Venice it was with an irrepressible suspicion that something was going to happen; but the only thing that could have taken place was again their masterly retreat. "How is he? where is he?" he asked of Mrs. Moreen; but before she could speak these questions were answered by the pressure round his neck of a pair of arms, in shrunken sleeves, which still were perfectly capable of an effusive young foreign squeeze.

"Dreadfully ill—I don't see it!" the young man cried. And then to Morgan: "Why on earth did n't you relieve me? Why did n't you answer my letter?"

Mrs. Moreen declared that when she wrote he was very bad, and Pemberton learned at the same time from the boy that he had answered every letter he had received. This led to the clear inference that Pemberton's note had been kept from him so that the game to be practised should not be interfered with. Mrs. Moreen was prepared to see the fact exposed, as Pemberton saw the moment he faced her that she was prepared for a good many other things. She was prepared above all to maintain that she had acted from a sense of duty, that she was enchanted she had got him over, whatever they might say, and that it was useless of him to pretend he did n't know in all his bones that his place at such a time was with Morgan. He had taken the boy away from them and now had no right to abandon him. He had created for himself the gravest responsibilities and must at least abide by what he had done.

"Taken him away from you?" Pemberton exclaimed indignantly.

"Do it—do it for pity's sake; that's just what I want. I can't stand *this*— and such scenes. They're awful frauds—poor dears!" These words broke from Morgan, who had intermitted his embrace, in a key which made Pemberton turn quickly to him and see that he had suddenly seated himself, was breathing in great pain and was very pale.

---

[33]The floor just above the ground floor (French).

"*Now* do you say he's not in a state, my precious pet?" shouted his mother, dropping on her knees before him with clasped hands, but touching him no more than if he had been a gilded idol. "It will pass—it's only for an instant; but don't say such dreadful things!"

"I'm all right—all right," Morgan panted to Pemberton, whom he sat looking up at with a strange smile, his hands resting on either side on the sofa.

"Now do you pretend I've been dishonest, that I've deceived?" Mrs. Moreen flashed at Pemberton as she got up.

"It is n't *he* says it, it's I!" the boy returned, apparently easier but sinking back against the wall; while his restored friend, who had sat down beside him, took his hand and bent over him.

"Darling child, one does what one can; there are so many things to consider," urged Mrs. Moreen. "It's his *place*—his only place. You see *you* think it is now."

"Take me away—take me away," Morgan went on, smiling to Pemberton with his white face.

"Where shall I take you, and how—oh *how*, my boy?" the young man stammered, thinking of the rude way in which his friends in London held that, for his convenience, with no assurance of prompt return, he had thrown them over; of the just resentment with which they would already have called in a successor, and of the scant help to finding fresh employment that resided for him in the grossness of his having failed to pass his pupil.

"Oh we'll settle that. You used to talk about it," said Morgan. "If we can only go all the rest's a detail."

"Talk about it as much as you like, but don't think you can attempt it. Mr. Moreen would never consent—it would be so *very* hand-to-mouth," Pemberton's hostess beautifully explained to him. Then to Morgan she made it clearer: "It would destroy our peace, it would break our hearts. Now that he's back it will be all the same again. You'll have your life, your work and your freedom, and we'll all be happy as we used to be. You'll bloom and grow perfectly well, and we won't have any more silly experiments, will we? They're too absurd. It's Mr. Pemberton's place—everyone in his place. You in yours, your papa in his, me in mine—*n'est-ce pas, chéri?*[34] We'll all forget how foolish we've been and have lovely times."

She continued to talk and to surge vaguely about the little draped stuffy salon while Pemberton sat with the boy, whose colour gradually came back; and she mixed up her reasons, hinting that there were going to be changes, that the other children might scatter (who knew?—Paula had her ideas) and that then it might be fancied how much the poor old parent-birds would want the little nestling. Morgan looked at Pemberton, who would n't let him move; and Pemberton knew exactly how he felt at hearing himself called a little nestling. He admitted that he had had one

[34]"Is it not, darling?" (French).

or two bad days, but he protested afresh against the wrong of his mother's having made them the ground of an appeal to poor Pemberton. Poor Pemberton could laugh now, apart from the comicality of Mrs. Moreen's mustering so much philosophy for her defence—she seemed to shake it out of her agitated petticoats, which knocked over the light gilt chairs—so little did their young companion, *marked*, unmistakeably marked at the best, strike him as qualified to repudiate any advantage.

He himself was in for it at any rate. He should have Morgan on his hands again indefinitely; though indeed he saw the lad had a private theory to produce which would be intended to smooth this down. He was obliged to him for it in advance; but the suggested amendment didn't keep his heart rather from sinking, any more than it prevented him from accepting the prospect on the spot, with some confidence moreover that he should do so even better if he could have a little supper. Mrs. Moreen threw out more hints about the changes that were to be looked for, but she was such a mixture of smiles and shudders—she confessed she was very nervous—that he couldn't tell if she were in high feather or only in hysterics. If the family was really at last going to pieces why should n't she recognise the necessity of pitching Morgan into some sort of lifeboat? This presumption was fostered by the fact that they were established in luxurious quarters in the capital of pleasure; that was exactly where they naturally *would* be established in view of going to pieces. Moreover did n't she mention that Mr. Moreen and the others were enjoying themselves at the opera with Mr. Granger, and was n't *that* also precisely where one would look for them on the eve of a smash? Pemberton gathered that Mr. Granger was a rich vacant American—a big bill with a flourishy heading and no items; so that one of Paula's "ideas" was probably that this time she had n't missed fire—by which straight shot indeed she would have shattered the general cohesion. And if the cohesion was to crumble what would become of poor Pemberton? He felt quite enough bound up with them to figure to his alarm as a dislodged block in the edifice.

It was Morgan who eventually asked if no supper had been ordered for him; sitting with him below, later, at the dim delayed meal, in the presence of a great deal of corded green plush, a plate of ornamental biscuit and an aloofness marked on the part of the waiter. Mrs. Moreen had explained that they had been obliged to secure a room for the visitor out of the house; and Morgan's consolation—he offered it while Pemberton reflected on the nastiness of lukewarm sauces—proved to be, largely, that this circumstance would facilitate their escape. He talked of their escape—recurring to it often afterwards—as if they were making up a "boy's book" together. But he likewise expressed his sense that there was something in the air, that the Moreens could n't keep it up much longer. In point of fact, as Pemberton was to see, they kept it up for five or six months. All the while, however, Morgan's contention was designed to cheer him.

Mr. Moreen and Ulick, whom he had met the day after his return, accepted that return like perfect men of the world. If Paula and Amy treated it even with less formality an allowance was to be made for them, inasmuch as Mr. Granger had n't come to the opera after all. He had only placed his box at their service, with a bouquet for each of the party; there was even one apiece, embittering the thought of his profusion, for Mr. Moreen and Ulick. "They're all like that," was Morgan's comment; "at the very last, just when we think we've landed them they're back in the deep sea!"

Morgan's comments in these days were more and more free; they even included a large recognition of the extraordinary tenderness with which he had been treated while Pemberton was away. Oh yes, they could n't do enough to be nice to him, to show him they had him on their mind and make up for his loss. That was just what made the whole thing so sad and caused him to rejoice after all in Pemberton's return—he had to keep thinking of their affection less, had less sense of obligation. Pemberton laughed out at this last reason, and Morgan blushed and said "Well, dash it, you know what I mean." Pemberton knew perfectly what he meant; but there were a good many things that—dash it too!—it did n't make any clearer. This episode of his second sojourn in Paris stretched itself out wearily, with their resumed readings and wanderings and maunderings, their potterings on the quays, their hauntings of the museums, their occasional lingerings in the Palais Royal when the first sharp weather came on and there was a comfort in warm emanations, before Chevet's wonderful succulent window. Morgan wanted to hear all about the opulent youth—he took an immense interest in him. Some of the details of his opulence— Pemberton could spare him none of them—evidently fed the boy's appreciation of all his friend had given up to come back to him; but in addition to the greater reciprocity established by that heroism he had always his little brooding theory, in which there was a frivolous gaiety too, that their long probation was drawing to a close. Morgan's conviction that the Moreens could n't go on much longer kept pace with the unexpended impetus with which, from month to month, they did go on. Three weeks after Pemberton had rejoined them they went on to another hotel, a dingier one than the first; but Morgan rejoiced that his tutor had at least still not sacrificed the advantage of a room outside. He clung to the romantic utility of this when the day, or rather the night, should arrive for their escape.

For the first time, in this complicated connexion, our friend felt his collar gall him. It was, as he had said to Mrs. Moreen in Venice, *trop fort*[35]— everything was *trop fort*. He could neither really throw off his blighting burden nor find in it the benefit of a pacified conscience or of a rewarded affection. He had spent all the money accruing to him in England, and he saw his youth going and that he was getting nothing back for it. It was all

[35]Too much (French).

very well of Morgan to count it for reparation that he should now settle on him permanently—there was an irritating flaw in such a view. He saw what the boy had in his mind; the conception that as his friend had had the generosity to come back he must show his gratitude by giving him his life. But the poor friend did n't desire the gift—what could he do with Morgan's dreadful little life? Of course at the same time that Pemberton was irritated he remembered the reason, which was very honourable to Morgan and which dwelt simply in his making one so forget that he was no more than a patched urchin. If one dealt with him on a different basis one's misadventures were one's own fault. So Pemberton waited in a queer confusion of yearning and alarm for the catastrophe which was held to hang over the house of Moreen, of which he certainly at moments felt the symptoms brush his cheek and as to which he wondered much in what form it would find its liveliest effect.

Perhaps it would take the form of sudden dispersal—a frightened *sauve qui peut*,[36] a scuttling into selfish corners. Certainly they were less elastic than of yore; they were evidently looking for something they did n't find. The Dorringtons had n't re-appeared, the princes had scattered; was n't that the beginning of the end? Mrs. Moreen had lost her reckoning of the famous "days"; her social calendar was blurred—it had turned its face to the wall. Pemberton suspected that the great, the cruel discomfiture had been the unspeakable behaviour of Mr. Granger, who seemed not to know what he wanted, or, what was much worse, what *they* wanted. He kept sending flowers, as if to bestrew the path of his retreat, which was never the path of a return. Flowers were all very well, but—Pemberton could complete the proposition. It was now positively conspicuous that in the long run the Moreens were a social failure; so that the young man was almost grateful the run had not been short. Mr. Moreen indeed was still occasionally able to get away on business and, what was more surprising, was likewise able to get back. Ulick had no club, but you could n't have discovered it from his appearance, which was as much as ever that of a person looking at life from the window of such an institution; therefore Pemberton was doubly surprised at an answer he once heard him make his mother in the desperate tone of a man familiar with the worst privations. Her question Pemberton had not quite caught; it appeared to be an appeal for a suggestion as to whom they might get to take Amy. "Let the Devil take her!" Ulick snapped; so that Pemberton could see that they had not only lost their amiability but had ceased to believe in themselves. He could also see that if Mrs. Moreen was trying to get people to take her children she might be regarded as closing the hatches for the storm. But Morgan would be the last she would part with.

One winter afternoon—it was a Sunday—he and the boy walked far together in the Bois de Boulogne. The evening was so splendid, the cold

[36]Everyone for himself (French).

lemon-coloured sunset so clear, the stream of carriages and pedestrians so amusing and the fascination of Paris so great, that they stayed out later than usual and became aware that they should have to hurry home to arrive in time for dinner. They hurried accordingly, arm-in-arm, good-humoured and hungry, agreeing that there was nothing like Paris after all and that after everything too that had come and gone they were not yet sated with innocent pleasures. When they reached the hotel they found that, though scandalously late, they were in time for all the dinner they were likely to sit down to. Confusion reigned in the apartments of the Moreens—very shabby ones this time, but the best in the house—and before the inter-rupted service of the table, with objects displaced almost as if there had been a scuffle and a great wine-stain from an overturned bottle, Pemberton could n't blink the fact that there had been a scene of the last proprietary firmness. The storm had come—they were all seeking refuge. The hatches were down, Paula and Amy were invisible—they had never tried the most casual art upon Pemberton, but he felt they had enough of an eye to him not to wish to meet him as young ladies whose frocks had been confis-cated—and Ulick appeared to have jumped overboard. The host and his staff, in a word, had ceased to "go on" at the pace of their guests, and the air of embarrassed detention, thanks to a pile of gaping trunks in the pas-sage, was strangely commingled with the air of indignant withdrawal.

When Morgan took all this in—and he took it in very quickly—he co-loured to the roots of his hair. He had walked from his infancy among dif-ficulties and dangers, but he had never seen a public exposure. Pemberton noticed in a second glance at him that the tears had rushed into his eyes and that they were tears of a new and untasted bitterness. He wondered an instant, for the boy's sake, whether he might successfully pretend not to understand. Not successfully, he felt, as Mr. and Mrs. Moreen, dinnerless by their extinguished hearth, rose before him in their little dishonoured salon, casting about with glassy eyes for the nearest port in such a storm. They were not prostrate but were horribly white, and Mrs. Moreen had evi-dently been crying. Pemberton quickly learned however that her grief was not for the loss of her dinner, much as she usually enjoyed it, but the fruit of a blow that struck even deeper, as she made all haste to explain. He would see for himself, so far as that went, how the great change had come, the dreadful bolt had fallen, and how they would now all have to turn themselves about. Therefore cruel as it was to them to part with their darling she must look to him to carry a little further the influence he had so fortunately acquired with the boy—to induce his young charge to follow him into some modest retreat. They depended on him—that was the fact— to take their delightful child temporarily under his protection: it would leave Mr. Moreen and herself so much more free to give the proper atten-tion (too little, alas! had been given) to the readjustment of their affairs.

"We trust you—we feel we *can*," said Mrs. Moreen, slowly rubbing her plump white hands and looking with compunction hard at Morgan, whose chin, not to take liberties, her husband stroked with a tentative paternal forefinger.

"Oh yes—we feel that we *can*. We trust Mr. Pemberton fully, Morgan," Mr. Moreen pursued.

Pemberton wondered again if he might pretend not to understand; but everything good gave way to the intensity of Morgan's understanding. "Do you mean he may take me to live with him for ever and ever?" cried the boy. "May take me away, away, anywhere he likes?"

"For ever and ever? *Comme vous-y-allez!*"[37] Mr. Moreen laughed indulgently. "For as long as Mr. Pemberton may be so good."

"We've struggled, we've suffered," his wife went on; "but you've made him so your own that we've already been through the worst of the sacrifice."

Morgan had turned away from his father—he stood looking at Pemberton with a light in his face. His sense of shame for their common humiliated state had dropped; the case had another side—the thing was to clutch at *that*. He had a moment of boyish joy, scarcely mitigated by the reflexion that with this unexpected consecration of his hope—too sudden and too violent; the turn taken was away from a *good* boy's book—the "escape" was left on their hands. The boyish joy was there an instant, and Pemberton was almost scared at the rush of gratitude and affection that broke through his first abasement. When he stammered "My dear fellow, what do you say to *that*?" how could one not say something enthusiastic? But there was more need for courage at something else that immediately followed and that made the lad sit down quickly on the nearest chair. He had turned quite livid and had raised his hand to his left side. They were all three looking at him, but Mrs. Moreen suddenly bounded forward. "Ah his darling little heart!" she broke out; and this time, on her knees before him and without respect for the idol, she caught him ardently in her arms. "You walked him too far, you hurried him too fast!" she hurled over her shoulder at Pemberton. Her son made no protest, and the next instant, still holding him, she sprang up with her face convulsed and with the terrified cry "Help, help! he's going, he's gone!" Pemberton saw with equal horror, by Morgan's own stricken face, that he was beyond their wildest recall. He pulled him half out of his mother's hands, and for a moment, while they held him together, they looked all their dismay into each other's eyes. "He could n't stand it with his weak organ," said Pemberton—"the shock, the whole scene, the violent emotion."

"But I thought he *wanted* to go to you!" wailed Mrs. Moreen.

"I *told* you he did n't, my dear," her husband made answer. Mr. Moreen was trembling all over and was in his way as deeply affected as his wife. But after the very first he took his bereavement as a man of the world.

[1891]

---

[37]"How you go on!" (French).

JOEL CHANDLER HARRIS ■ (1848–1908)

Born in Eatonton, Georgia, the illegitimate son of an itinerant Irish day laborer who deserted the boy's mother, Joel Chandler Harris at age thirteen began working on a local newspaper published by Joseph Addison Turner, the owner of a 1,000-acre plantation in mid-Georgia and a strong supporter of slavery and the Confederacy. Here Harris began learning about African American slave laborers and their patterns and rhythms of speech and folklore. Turner encouraged Harris's literary ambitions and interests and gave him access to the plantation's well-stocked home library.

Harris then took jobs at a number of papers in the South, building a reputation as a comic writer, before accepting a position in 1876 with the *Atlanta Constitution*, where he worked for the next quarter-century. Among his first pieces, printed in October–December 1876, were sketches about African Americans that Harris centered on the character of Uncle Remus, a wise elderly black man. In July 1879, through Uncle Remus, Harris presented the first of his animal tales under the title "Negro Folklore: The Story of Mr. Rabbit and Mr. Fox, as Told by Uncle Remus." It later served as the opening to Harris's book, *Uncle Remus, His Songs and His Sayings* (1880).

Nights with Uncle Remus, an effort to capitalize on the success of the first set of tales, soon followed (1883), and Harris published still other *Uncle Remus* collections in later years, as well as books of children's stories, novels, and collections of short stories. He was often urged to give readings of his work, but he was shy and self-conscious and rarely did so—unlike his contemporary, Mark Twain, whose proposal for a joint tour Harris turned down.

Harris downplayed his own talents, saying, "As for myself—though you could hardly call me a real, sure enough author—I never have anything but the vaguest ideas of what I am going to write; but when I take my pen in hand, the dust clears away and the 'other fellow' takes charge." In a letter (1900) to the eminent novelist and literary realist William Dean Howells, he noted, "You know, of course, as far as literary art is concerned, I am poverty-stricken; and you know too, that my style and methods will cause you to pull your hair."

Yet in his own way Harris was a master of regional speech and dialect, crafting and organizing his tales around the warm manner and shrewd perception of Uncle Remus, who recounts each tale to a boy, the seven-year-old son of a plantation owner. Readers today may balk at the sentimentalized rendering of slavery and plantation life that Harris offers in his work and resist his use of dialect as condescending, if not demeaning. But in his own era Harris was a progressive, a believer in reconciliation between North and South and restoration of peaceful relations between whites and blacks (though, to be sure, with whites retaining the upper hand in social and political power). Harris's entertaining, satiric, ironic stories and their cast of characters, with their sly exploits, trickeries, and gaffes, and above all their brisk, vigorous forms of speech, remain engaging—and they have been influential not only on the development of characters in twentieth-century cartoons (for example, Road Runner and Wile E. Coyote), but also on the literary work of Ralph Ellison, Toni Morrison, and others.

For biography: Julia Collier Harris, *The Life and Letters of Joel Chandler Harris* (1918); and Paul M. Cousins, *Joel Chandler Harris: A Biography* (1968). For interpretation: *Critical Essays on Joel Chandler Harris*, ed. R. Bruce Bickley Jr. (1981); and Paul Mercer Cousins, *Joel Chandler Harris: A Study in the Culture of the South, 1848–1908* (1969). See also R. Bruce Bickley Jr., *Joel Chandler Harris* (1978; rev. ed. 1987). For literary and cultural contexts: *Tricksterism in Turn-of-the-Century American Literature: A Multicultural Perspective,* eds. Elizabeth Ammons and Annette White-Parks (1994); and *Trickster Lives: Culture and Myth in American Fiction,* ed. Jeanne Campbell Reesman (2001).

The Tar-Baby

[PART ONE]
The Wonderful Tar-Baby Story

"Didn't the fox *never* catch the rabbit, Uncle Remus?" asked the little boy the next evening.

"He come might nigh it, honey, sho's you born—Brer Fox did. One day atter Brer Rabbit fool 'im wid dat calamus root, Brer Fox went ter wuk en got 'im some tar, en mix it wid some turkentime, en fix up a contrapshun wat he call a Tar-Baby, en he tuck dish yer Tar-Baby en he sot 'er in de big road, en den he lay off in de bushes fer to see wat de news wuz gwineter be. En he didn't hatter wait long, nudder, kaze bimeby here come Brer Rabbit pacin' down de road—lippity-clippity, clippity-lippity—dez ez sassy ez a jay-bird. Brer Fox, he lay low. Brer Rabbit come prancin' 'long twel he spy de Tar-Baby, en den he fotch up on his behime legs like he wuz 'stonished. De Tar-Baby, she sot dar, she did, en Brer Fox, he lay low.

"'Mawnin'!' sez Brer Rabbit, sezee,—'nice wedder dis mawnin',' sezee.

"Tar-Baby ain't sayin' nothin', en Brer Fox, he lay low.

"'How duz yo' sym'tums seem ter segashuate?' sez Brer Rabbit, sezee.

"Brer Fox, he wink his eye slow, en lay low, en de Tar-Baby, she ain't sayin' nothin.'

"'How you come on den,? Is you deaf?' sez Brer Rabbit, sezee. "Kaze if you is, I kin holler louder,' sezee.

"Tar-Baby stay still, en Brer Fox, he lay low.

"'Youer stuck up, dat's w'at you is,' says Brer Rabbit, sezee, 'en I'm gwineter kyore you, dat's w'at I'm a gwineter do,' sezee.

"Brer Fox, he sorter chuckle in his stummuck, he did, but Tar-Baby ain't sayin' nothin'.

"'I'm gwineter larn you howter talk ter 'specttubble fokes ef hit's de las' ack,' sez Brer Rabbit, sezee. "Ef you don't take off dat hat en tell me howdy, I'm gwineter bus' you wide open,' sezee.

"Tar-Baby stay still, en Brer Fox, he lay low.

"Brer Rabbit keep on axin' 'im, en de Tar-Baby, she keep on sayin' nothin', twel present'y Brer Rabbit draw back wid his fis', he did, en blip he tuck 'er side er de head. Right dar's whar he broke his merlasses jug. His fis' stuck, en he can't pull loose. De tar hilt 'im. But Tar-Baby, she stay still, en Brer Fox, he lay low.

"'Ef you don't lemme loose, I'll knock you agin,' sez Brer Rabbit, sezee, en wid dat he fotch 'er a wipe wid de udder han', en dat stuck. Tar-Baby, she ain't sayin' nothin', en Brer Fox, he lay low.

"'Tu'n me loose, fo' I kick de natal stuffin' outen you,' sez Brer Rabbit, sezee, but de Tar-Baby, she ain't sayin' nothin'. She des hilt on, en den Brer Rabbit lose de use er his feet in de same way. Brer Fox, he lay low. Den Brer Rabbit squall out dat ef de Tar-Baby don't tu'n 'im loose he butt 'er cranksided. En den he butted, en his head got stuck. Den Brer Fox, he sa'ntered fort', lookin' des ez innercent ez one er yo' mammy's mockin'-birds.

"'Howdy, Brer Rabbit,' sez Brer Fox, sezee. 'You look sorter stuck up dis mawnin',' sezee, en den he rolled on de groun', en laughed en laughed twel he couldn't laugh no mo'. 'I speck you'll take dinner wid me dis time, Brer Rabbit, I done laid in some calamus root, en I ain't gwineter take no skuse,' sez Brer Fox, sezee.

Here Uncle Remus paused, and drew a two-pound yam out of the ashes.

"Did the fox eat the rabbit?" asked the little boy to whom the story had been told.

"Dat's all de fur de tale goes," replied the old man. "He mout, en den agin he moutent. Some say Jedge B'ar come 'long en loosed 'im—some say he didn't. I hear Miss Sally callin'. You better run 'long."

. . .

[PART TWO]
How Mr. Rabbit Was Too Sharp for Mr. Fox

"Uncle Remus," said the little boy one evening, when he had found the old man with little or nothing to do, "did the fox kill and eat the rabbit when he caught him with the Tar-Baby?"

"Law, honey, ain't I tell you 'bout dat?" replied the old darkey, chuckling slyly. "I 'clar ter grashus I ought er tole you dat, but old man Nod wuz ridin' on my eyeleds 'twel a leetle mo'n I'd a dis'member'd my own name, en den on to dat here come yo' mammy hollerin' atter you.

"W'at I tell you w'en I fus' begin? I tole you Brer Rabbit wuz a monstus soon creetur; leas'ways dat's w'at I laid out fer ter tell you. Well, den, honey, don't you go en make no udder calkalashuns, kaze in dem days

Brer Rabbit en his fambly wuz at de head er de gang w'en enny racket wuz on han', en dar dey stayed. 'Fo' you begins fer ter wipe yo' eyes 'bout Brer Rabbit, you wait en see whar'bouts Brer Rabbit gwineter fetch up at. But dat's needer yer ner dar.

"W'en Brer Fox fine Brer Rabbit mixt up wid de Tar-Baby, he feel might good, en he roll on de groun' en laff. Bimeby he up'n say, sezee:

"'Well, I speck I got you dis time, Brer Rabbit', sezee; 'maybe I ain't, but I speck I is. You been runnin' roun' here sassin' atter me a mighty long time, but I speck you done come ter de een' er de row. You bin cuttin' up yo' capers en bouncin' 'roun' in dis neighberhood ontwel you come ter b'leeve yo'se'f de boss er de whole gang. En den youer allers some'rs whar you got no bizness,' sez Brer Fox, sezee. 'Who ax you fer ter come en strike up a'quaintance wid dish yer Tar-Baby? En who stuck you up dar whar you iz? Nobody in de roun' worril. You des tuck en jam yo'se'f on dat Tar-Baby widout waitin' fer enny invite,' sez Brer Fox, sezee, 'en dar you is, en dar you'll stay twel I fixes up a bresh-pile and fires her up, kaze I'm gwineter bobby-cue you dis day, sho,' sez Brer Fox, sezee.

"Den Brer Rabbit talk mighty 'umble.

"'I don't keer w'at you do wid me, Brer Fox,' sezee, 'so you don't fling me in dat brier-patch. Roas' me, Brer Fox,' sezee, 'but don't fling me in dat brier-patch,' sezee.

"'Hit's so much trouble fer ter kindle a fier,' sez Brer Fox, sezee, 'dat I speck I'll hatter hang you,' sezee.

"'Hang me des ez high as you please, Brer Fox,' sez Brer Rabbit, sezee, 'but do fer de Lord's sake don't fling me in dat brier-patch,' sezee.

"'I ain't got no string,' sez Brer Fox, sezee, 'en now I speck I'll hatter drown you,' sezee.

"'Drown me des ez deep ez you please, Brer Fox,' sez Brer Rabbit, sezee, 'but do don't fling me in dat brier-patch,' sezee.

"'Dey ain't no water nigh,' sez Brer Fox, sezee, 'en now I speck I'll hatter skin you,' sezee.

"'Skin me, Brer Fox,' sez Brer Rabbit, sezee, 'snatch out my eyeballs, t'ar out my years by de roots, en cut off my legs,' sezee, 'but do please, Brer Fox, don't fling me in dat brier-patch,' sezee.

"Co'se Brer Fox wanter hut Brer Rabbit bad ez he kin, so he cotch 'im by de behime legs en slung 'im right in de middle er de brier-patch. Dar wuz a considerbul flutter whar Brer Rabbit struck de bushes, en Brer Fox sorter hang 'roun' fer ter see w'at wuz gwineter happen. Bimeby he hear somebody call 'im, en way up de hill he see Brer Rabbit settin' cross-legged on a chinkapin log koamin' de pitch outen his har wid a chip. Den Brer Fox know dat he bin swop off mighty bad. Brer Rabbit wuz bleedzed fer ter fling back some er his sass, en he holler out:

"'Bred en bawn in a brier-patch, Brer Fox—bred en bawn in a brier-patch!' en wid dat he skip out des ez lively ez a cricket in de embers."

[1880, 1895]

EMMA LAZARUS ■ (1849–1887)

Born in New York City, educated by private tutors, author of a book of poems when she was in her teens, befriended by the renowned men of letters Ralph Waldo Emerson and Henry Wadsworth Longfellow, Emma Lazarus secured a place in literary and cultural history through her poem "The New Colossus," published in 1883.

Lazarus's family was a prosperous and prominent one, and her upbringing as a Jewish American thus stood in sharp contrast to the far more difficult, burdensome, and anxiety-ridden conditions of life faced by the vast majority of Jewish and other immigrants to New York City and beyond in the latter half of the nineteenth century.

Between 1865 and 1915, twenty-five million immigrants arrived in the United States, nine million of them in the single decade from 1900 to 1910. Some estimates suggest that 80 percent of New York City's population and nearly 90 percent of Chicago's population were immigrants or the children of immigrants. By 1905, the population density of some sections of New York City had reached one thousand persons per acre, greater than that of Bombay, India.

Deeply responsive to the needs and challenges of Jewish immigrants in particular, Lazarus translated the work of Jewish poets and wrote essays on a range of subjects including literature, music, history, and art; these were published in important journals and magazines, such as *The Century* and *The Critic*, as well as in Jewish periodicals. She also established the Society for the Improvement and Colonization of East European Jews, part of her effort to promote the settlement of Jews in a national homeland in Palestine, and part, too, of her general commitment to a national and international Jewish revival.

"The New Colossus" was written for a fund-raising campaign for the pedestal of the Statue of Liberty, a gift, "Liberty Enlightening the World," from France to the United States. The title and opening lines allude to the Colossus (Latin for "giant statue") of Rhodes, one of the seven wonders of the ancient world; completed about the year 280 BCE, this representation of the sun god Helios stood about 100 feet high. (A few decades later, it was destroyed by an earthquake.) Lazarus honors the Statue of Liberty by means of this connection to the ancient Colossus even as she emphasizes the differences between the two. The Statue of Liberty, while powerful and forthright, is, more importantly, maternal, welcoming, nurturing; it offers refuge for the lowly.

The Statue of Liberty was formally dedicated in New York Harbor in 1886, and Lazarus died of cancer the following year at age thirty-eight. In 1903, "The New Colossus" was inscribed on a bronze plaque at the base of the statue.

For further study: Heinrich Eduard Jacob, *The World of Emma Lazarus* (1949); Dan Vogel, *Emma Lazarus* (1980); and Bette Roth Young, *Emma Lazarus in Her World: Life and Letters* (1995). Also stimulating: Ranen Omer-Sherman, *Diaspora and Zionism in Jewish American literature: Lazarus, Syrkin, Reznikoff, and Roth* (2002); and Esther Schor, *Emma Lazarus* (2006). See also two books by Barry Moreno: *The Statue of Liberty Encyclopedia* (2000); and *The Statue of Liberty: Images of America* (2004).

The Statue of Liberty, New York City. Photograph, early twentieth century.

The New Colossus[1]

Not like the brazen giant of Greek fame,
With conquering limbs astride from land to land;
Here at our sea-washed, sunset gates shall stand
A mighty woman with a torch, whose flame
Is the imprisoned lightning, and her name   5
Mother of Exiles. From her beacon-hand
Glows world-wide welcome; her mild eyes command
The air-bridged harbor that twin cities frame.
"Keep, ancient lands, your storied pomp!" cries she
With silent lips. "Give me your tired, your poor,   10
Your huddled masses yearning to breathe free,
The wretched refuse of your teeming shore.
Send these, the homeless, tempest-tost to me,
I lift my lamp beside the golden door!"

[1883]

[1]The Colossus of Rhodes, one of the wonders of the ancient world, was a 100-foot-high statue of the Greek god Helios that is reputed to have stood at the entrance of the harbor on the Island of Rhodes, located at the southwestern tip of Asia Minor where the Aegean Sea meets the Mediterranean.

SARAH ORNE JEWETT ■ (1849–1909)

Sarah Orne Jewett was born in the Jewett family home in South Berwick, on the coast of Maine, and died there at age sixty, and this community was the setting for her literary work. Jewett's father was a doctor, and she accompanied him on his visits to patients. Jewett graduated from Berwick Academy in 1865, which marked the end of her schooling. But she had already developed a passion for literature and published her first short story when she was eighteen. Soon, encouraged by the editor and novelist William Dean Howells, her work began to appear in *The Atlantic Monthly*, one of the foremost literary and cultural magazines.

Jewett's first book was a collection of sketches, *Deephaven* (1877), keyed to the relationship between two women spending their summer in Maine. Next came *A Country Doctor* (1884), a novel with a female protagonist who chooses a career in medicine over marriage. Jewett at one time had considered becoming a doctor herself.

A White Heron and Other Stories (1886), subtle, witty, and keenly observant, is perhaps Jewett's best book. Readers were drawn to her sense of detail, her feeling for local color and regional speech, idiom, pace of life, and manners. During this period Jewett formed a loving companionship with Annie Fields (1834–1915), whose deceased husband, James T. Fields, had been a publisher and an important figure in the literary society of Boston and Cambridge. Jewett and Fields spent a part of each year living together in Boston, and they also made trips to England and Europe.

Understated, highly intelligent, *The Country of the Pointed Firs* (1896), a series of interconnected stories with a Maine coastal village setting, exemplifies Jewett's sensitive and sharp artistry. It demonstrates, and embodies in its scenes and situations, the interplay between the telling of stories and the creating of friendships and communities.

Willa Cather, Kate Chopin, and other women writers found inspiration in Jewett's craft. In Jewett's nine collections of stories and five novels we find, said Cather, "the perfection that endures," and she ranked *The Country of the Pointed Firs* with Hawthorne's *The Scarlet Letter* and Twain's *Adventures of Huckleberry Finn* as the great works of American literature.

To some readers, Jewett's stories, like "The White Heron," might seem slight or thin and even somewhat strange, but for the attentive, appreciative reader, they are deep and profound, with symbolic richness and mythic power. "The White Heron," poised and lyrical, lingers in the mind, a poignant celebration of nature and spiritual transcendence.

For biography: Elizabeth Silverthorne, *Sarah Orne Jewett: A Writer's Life* (1993); and Paula Blanchard, *Sarah Orne Jewett: Her World and Her Work* (1994). For a range of critical responses: *Critical Essays on Sarah Orne Jewett*, ed. Gwen L. Nagel (1984); *Jewett and Her Contemporaries: Reshaping the Canon*, eds. Karen L. Kilcup and Thomas S. Edwards (1999). See also Sarah Way Sherman, *Sarah Orne Jewett: An American Persephone* (1989); and Margaret Roman, *Sarah Orne Jewett: Reconstructing Gender* (1992). See also Louis A. Renza, *"A White Heron" and The Question of Minor Literature* (1984); and *A Sarah Orne Jewett Companion*, ed. Robert L. Gale (1999).

A White Heron

1

The woods were already filled with shadows one June evening, just before eight o'clock, though a bright sunset still glimmered faintly among the trunks of the trees. A little girl was driving home her cow, a plodding, dilatory, provoking creature in her behavior, but a valued companion for all that. They were going away from whatever light there was, and striking deep into the woods, but their feet were familiar with the path, and it was no matter whether their eyes could see it or not.

There was hardly a night the summer through when the old cow could be found waiting at the pasture bars; on the contrary, it was her greatest pleasure to hide herself away among the huckleberry bushes, and though she wore a loud bell she had made the discovery that if one stood perfectly still it would not ring. So Sylvia had to hunt for her until she found her, and call Co'! Co'! with never an answering Moo, until her childish patience was quite spent. If the creature had not given good milk and plenty of it, the case would have seemed very different to her owners. Besides, Sylvia had all the time there was, and very little use to make of it. Sometimes in pleasant weather it was a consolation to look upon the cow's pranks as an intelligent attempt to play hide and seek, and as the child had no playmates she lent herself to this amusement with a good deal of zest. Though this chase had been so long that the wary animal herself had given an unusual signal of her whereabouts, Sylvia had only laughed when she came upon Mistress Moolly at the swampside, and urged her affectionately homeward with a twig of birch leaves. The old cow was not inclined to wander farther, she even turned in the right direction for once as they left the pasture, and stepped along the road at a good pace. She was quite ready to be milked now, and seldom stopped to browse. Sylvia wondered what her grandmother would say because they were so late. It was a great while since she had left home at half-past five o'clock, but everybody knew the difficulty of making this errand a short one. Mrs. Tilley had chased the hornéd torment too many summer evenings herself to blame any one else for lingering, and was only thankful as she waited that she had Sylvia, nowadays, to give such valuable assistance. The good woman suspected that Sylvia loitered occasionally on her own account; there never was such a child for straying about out-of-doors since the world was made! Everybody said that it was a good change for a little maid who had tried to grow for eight years in a crowded manufacturing town, but, as for Sylvia herself, it seemed as if she never had been alive at all before she came to live at the farm. She thought often with wistful compassion of a wretched geranium that belonged to a town neighbor.

"'Afraid of folks,'" old Mrs. Tilley said to herself, with a smile, after she had made the unlikely choice of Sylvia from her daughter's houseful of children, and was returning to the farm. "'Afraid of folks,' they said! I guess she won't be troubled no great with 'em up to the old place!" When they reached the door of the lonely house and stopped to unlock it, and the cat came to purr loudly, and rub against them, a deserted pussy, indeed, but fat with young robins, Sylvia whispered that this was a beautiful place to live in, and she never should wish to go home.

The companions followed the shady woodroad, the cow taking slow steps and the child very fast ones. The cow stopped long at the brook to drink, as if the pasture were not half a swamp, and Sylvia stood still and waited, letting her bare feet cool themselves in the shoal water, while the great twilight moths struck softly against her. She waded on through the brook as the cow moved away, and listened to the thrushes with a heart that beat fast with pleasure. There was a stirring in the great boughs overhead. They were full of little birds and beasts that seemed to be wide awake, and going about their world, or else saying good-night to each other in sleepy twitters. Sylvia herself felt sleepy as she walked along. However, it was not much farther to the house, and the air was soft and sweet. She was not often in the woods so late as this, and it made her feel as if she were a part of the gray shadows and the moving leaves. She was just thinking how long it seemed since she first came to the farm a year ago, and wondering if everything went on in the noisy town just the same as when she was there; the thought of the great red-faced boy who used to chase and frighten her made her hurry along the path to escape from the shadow of the trees.

Suddenly this little woods-girl is horror-stricken to hear a clear whistle not very far away. Not a bird's-whistle, which would have a sort of friendliness, but a boy's whistle, determined, and somewhat aggressive. Sylvia left the cow to whatever sad fate might await her, and stepped discreetly aside into the bushes, but she was just too late. The enemy had discovered her, and called out in a very cheerful and persuasive tone, "Halloa, little girl, how far is it to the road?" and trembling Sylvia answered almost inaudibly, "A good ways."

She did not dare to look boldly at the tall young man, who carried a gun over his shoulder, but she came out of her bush and again followed the cow, while he walked alongside.

"I have been hunting for some birds," the stranger said kindly, "and I have lost my way, and need a friend very much. Don't be afraid," he added gallantly. "Speak up and tell me what your name is, and whether you think I can spend the night at your house, and go out gunning early in the morning."

Sylvia was more alarmed than before. Would not her grandmother consider her much to blame? But who could have foreseen such an accident as this? It did not seem to be her fault, and she hung her head as if the stem of it were broken, but managed to answer "Sylvy," with much effort when her companion again asked her name.

Mrs. Tilley was standing in the doorway when the trio came into view. The cow gave a loud moo by way of explanation.

"Yes, you'd better speak up for yourself, you old trial! Where'd she tucked herself away this time, Sylvy?" But Sylvia kept an awed silence; she knew by instinct that her grandmother did not comprehend the gravity of the situation. She must be mistaking the stranger for one of the farmer-lads of the region.

The young man stood his gun beside the door, and dropped a lumpy game-bag beside it; then he bade Mrs. Tilley good-evening, and repeated his wayfarer's story, and asked if he could have a night's lodging.

"Put me anywhere you like," he said. "I must be off early in the morning, before day; but I am very hungry, indeed. You can give me some milk at any rate, that's plain."

"Dear sakes, yes," responded the hostess, whose long slumbering hospitality seemed to be easily awakened. "You might fare better if you went out to the main road a mile or so, but you're welcome to what we've got. I'll milk right off, and you make yourself at home. You can sleep on husks or feathers," she proffered graciously. "I raised them all myself. There's good pasturing for geese just below here towards the ma'sh. Now step round and set a plate for the gentleman, Sylvy!" And Sylvia promptly stepped. She was glad to have something to do, and she was hungry herself.

It was a surprise to find so clean and comfortable a little dwelling in this New England wilderness. The young man had known the horrors of its most primitive housekeeping, and the dreary squalor of that level of society which does not rebel at the companionship of hens. This was the best thrift of an old-fashioned farmstead, though on such a small scale that it seemed like a hermitage. He listened eagerly to the old woman's quaint talk, he watched Sylvia's pale face and shining gray eyes with ever growing enthusiasm, and insisted that this was the best supper he had eaten for a month, and afterward the new-made friends sat down in the door-way together while the moon came up.

Soon it would be berry-time, and Sylvia was a great help at picking. The cow was a good milker, though a plaguy[1] thing to keep track of, the

---

[1]Annoying or troublesome.

hostess gossiped frankly, adding presently that she had buried four children, so Sylvia's mother, and a son (who might be dead) in California were all the children she had left. "Dan, my boy, was a great hand to go gunning," she explained sadly. "I never wanted for pa'tridges or gray squer'ls while he was to home. He's been a great wand'rer, I expect, and he's no hand to write letters. There, I don't blame him, I'd ha' seen the world myself if it had been so I could."

"Sylvy takes after him," the grandmother continued affectionately, after a minute's pause. "There ain't a foot o' ground she don't know her way over, and the wild creaturs counts her one o' themselves. Squer'ls she'll tame to come an' feed right out o' her hands, and all sorts o' birds. Last winter she got the jaybirds to bangeing[2] here, and I believe she'd 'a' scanted herself of her own meals to have plenty to throw out amongst 'em, if I had n't kep' watch. Anything but crows, I tell her, I'm willin' to help support—though Dan he had a tamed one o' them that did seem to have reason same as folks. It was round here a good spell after he went away. Dan an' his father they did n't hitch,—but he never held up his head ag'in after Dan had dared him an' gone off."

The guest did not notice this hint of family sorrows in his eager interest in something else.

"So Sylvy knows all about birds, does she?" he exclaimed, as he looked round at the little girl who sat, very demure but increasingly sleepy, in the moonlight. "I am making a collection of birds myself. I have been at it ever since I was a boy." (Mrs. Tilley smiled.) "There are two or three very rare ones I have been hunting for these five years. I mean to get them on my own ground if they can be found."

"Do you cage 'em up?" asked Mrs. Tilley doubtfully, in response to this enthusiastic announcement.

"Oh no, they're stuffed and preserved, dozens and dozens of them," said the ornithologist, "and I have shot or snared every one myself. I caught a glimpse of a white heron a few miles from here on Saturday, and I have followed it in this direction. They have never been found in this district at all. The little white heron, it is," and he turned again to look at Sylvia with the hope of discovering that the rare bird was one of her acquaintances.

But Sylvia was watching a hop-toad in the narrow footpath.

"You would know the heron if you saw it," the stranger continued eagerly. "A queer tall white bird with soft feathers and long thin legs. And it would have a nest perhaps in the top of a high tree, made of sticks, something like a hawk's nest."

Sylvia's heart gave a wild beat; she knew that strange white bird, and had once stolen softly near where it stood in some bright green swamp

[2]Gathering.

grass, away over at the other side of the woods. There was an open place where the sunshine always seemed strangely yellow and hot, where tall, nodding rushes grew, and her grandmother had warned her that she might sink in the soft black mud underneath and never be heard of more. Not far beyond were the salt marshes just this side the sea itself, which Sylvia wondered and dreamed much about, but never had seen, whose great voice could sometimes be heard above the noise of the woods on stormy nights.

"I can't think of anything I should like so much as to find that heron's nest," the handsome stranger was saying. "I would give ten dollars to anybody who could show it to me," he added desperately, "and I mean to spend my whole vacation hunting for it if need be. Perhaps it was only migrating, or had been chased out of its own region by some bird of prey."

Mrs. Tilley gave amazed attention to all this, but Sylvia still watched the toad, not divining, as she might have done at some calmer time, that the creature wished to get to its hole under the door-step, and was much hindered by the unusual spectators at that hour of the evening. No amount of thought, that night, could decide how many wished-for treasures the ten dollars, so lightly spoken of, would buy.

The next day the young sportsman hovered about the woods, and Sylvia kept him company, having lost her first fear of the friendly lad, who proved to be most kind and sympathetic. He told her many things about the birds and what they knew and where they lived and what they did with themselves. And he gave her a jackknife, which she thought as great a treasure as if she were a desert-islander. All day long he did not once make her troubled or afraid except when he brought down some unsuspecting singing creature from its bough. Sylvia would have liked him vastly better without his gun; she could not understand why he killed the very birds he seemed to like so much. But as the day waned, Sylvia still watched the young man with loving admiration. She had never seen anybody so charming and delightful; the woman's heart, asleep in the child, was vaguely thrilled by a dream of love. Some premonition of that great power stirred and swayed these young creatures who traversed the solemn woodlands with soft-footed silent care. They stopped to listen to a bird's song; they pressed forward again eagerly, parting the branches—speaking to each other rarely and in whispers; the young man going first and Sylvia following, fascinated, a few steps behind, with her gray eyes dark with excitement.

She grieved because the longed-for white heron was elusive, but she did not lead the guest, she only followed, and there was no such thing as speaking first. The sound of her own unquestioned voice would have terrified her—it was hard enough to answer yes or no when there was need of that. At last evening began to fall, and they drove the cow home together, and Sylvia smiled with pleasure when they came to the place where she heard the whistle and was afraid only the night before.

2

Half a mile from home, at the farther edge of the woods, where the land was highest, a great pine-tree stood, the last of its generation. Whether it was left for a boundary mark, or for what reason, no one could say; the wood-choppers who had felled its mates were dead and gone long ago, and a whole forest of sturdy trees, pines and oaks and maples, had grown again. But the stately head of this old pine towered above them all and made a landmark for sea and shore miles and miles away. Sylvia knew it well. She had always believed that whoever climbed to the top of it could see the ocean; and the little girl had often laid her hand on the great rough trunk and looked up wistfully at those dark boughs that the wind always stirred, no matter how hot and still the air might be below. Now she thought of the tree with a new excitement, for why, if one climbed it at break of day could not one see all the world, and easily discover from whence the white heron flew, and mark the place, and find the hidden nest?

What a spirit of adventure, what wild ambition! What fancied triumph and delight and glory for the later morning when she could make known the secret! It was almost too real and too great for the childish heart to bear.

All night the door of the little house stood open and the whippoorwills came and sang upon the very step. The young sportsman and his old hostess were sound asleep, but Sylvia's great design kept her broad awake and watching. She forgot to think of sleep. The short summer night seemed as long as the winter darkness, and at last when the whippoorwills ceased, and she was afraid the morning would after all come too soon, she stole out of the house and followed the pasture path through the woods, hastening toward the open ground beyond, listening with a sense of comfort and companionship to the drowsy twitter of a half-awakened bird, whose perch she had jarred in passing. Alas, if the great wave of human interest which flooded for the first time this dull little life should sweep away the satisfactions of an existence heart to heart with nature and the dumb life of the forest!

There was the huge tree asleep yet in the paling moonlight, and small and silly Sylvia began with utmost bravery to mount to the top of it, with tingling, eager blood coursing the channels of her whole frame, with her bare feet and fingers, that pinched and held like bird's claws to the monstrous ladder reaching up, up, almost to the sky itself. First she must mount the white oak tree that grew alongside, where she was almost lost among the dark branches and the green leaves heavy and wet with dew; a bird fluttered off its nest, and a red squirrel ran to and fro and scolded pettishly at the harmless housebreaker. Sylvia felt her way easily. She had often climbed there, and knew that higher still one of the oak's upper branches chafed against the pine trunk, just where its lower boughs were set close together. There, when she made the dangerous pass from one tree to the other, the great enterprise would really begin.

She crept out along the swaying oak limb at last, and took the daring step across into the old pine-tree. The way was harder than she thought; she must reach far and hold fast, the sharp dry twigs caught and held her and scratched her like angry talons, the pitch made her thin little fingers clumsy and stiff as she went round and round the tree's great stem, higher and higher upward. The sparrows and robins in the woods below were beginning to wake and twitter to the dawn, yet it seemed much lighter there aloft in the pine-tree, and the child knew she must hurry if her project were to be of any use.

The tree seemed to lengthen itself out as she went up, and to reach farther and farther upward. It was like a great main-mast to the voyaging earth; it must truly have been amazed that morning through all its ponderous frame as it felt this determined spark of human spirit wending its way from higher branch to branch. Who knows how steadily the least twigs held themselves to advantage this light, weak creature on her way! The old pine must have loved his new dependent. More than all the hawks, and bats, and moths, and even the sweet voiced thrushes, was the brave, beating heart of the solitary gray-eyed child. And the tree stood still and frowned away the winds that June morning while the dawn grew bright in the east.

Sylvia's face was like a pale star, if one had seen it from the ground, when the last thorny bough was past, and she stood trembling and tired but wholly triumphant, high in the treetop. Yes, there was the sea with the dawning sun making a golden dazzle over it, and toward that glorious east flew two hawks with slow-moving pinions. How low they looked in the air from that height when one had only seen them before far up, and dark against the blue sky. Their gray feathers were as soft as moths; they seemed only a little way from the tree, and Sylvia felt as if she too could go flying away among the clouds. Westward, the woodlands and farms reached miles and miles into the distance; here and there were church steeples, and white villages, truly it was a vast and awesome world!

The birds sang louder and louder. At last the sun came up bewilderingly bright. Sylvia could see the white sails of ships out at sea, and the clouds that were purple and rose-colored and yellow at first began to fade away. Where was the white heron's nest in the sea of green branches, and was this wonderful sight and pageant of the world the only reward for having climbed to such a giddy height? Now look down again, Sylvia, where the green marsh is set among the shining birches and dark hemlocks; there where you saw the white heron once you will see him again; look, look! a white spot of him like a single floating feather comes up from the dead hemlock and grows larger, and rises, and comes close at last, and goes by the landmark pine with steady sweep of wing and outstretched slender neck and crested head. And wait! wait! do not move a foot or a finger, little girl, do not send an arrow of light and consciousness from your two eager eyes, for the heron has perched on a pine bough not far beyond yours, and cries back to his mate on the nest and plumes his feathers for the new day!

The child gives a long sigh a minute later when a company of shout-ing cat-birds comes also to the tree, and vexed by their fluttering and lawlessness the solemn heron goes away. She knows his secret now, the wild, light, slender bird that floats and wavers, and goes back like an ar-row presently to his home in the green world beneath. Then Sylvia, well satisfied, makes her perilous way down again, not daring to look far below the branch she stands on, ready to cry sometimes because her fingers ache and her lamed feet slip. Wondering over and over again what the stranger would say to her, and what he would think when she told him how to find his way straight to the heron's nest.

"Sylvy, Sylvy!" called the busy old grandmother again and again, but nobody answered, and the small husk bed was empty and Sylvia had disappeared.

The guest waked from a dream, and remembering his day's pleasure hurried to dress himself that might it sooner begin. He was sure from the way the shy little girl looked once or twice yesterday that she had at least seen the white heron, and now she must really be made to tell. Here she comes now, paler than ever, and her worn old frock is torn and tattered, and smeared with pine pitch. The grandmother and the sportsman stand in the door together and question her, and the splendid moment has come to speak of the dead hemlock-tree by the green marsh.

But Sylvia does not speak after all, though the old grandmother fret-fully rebukes her, and the young man's kind, appealing eyes are looking straight in her own. He can make them rich with money; he has promised it, and they are poor now. He is so well worth making happy, and he waits to hear the story she can tell.

No, she must keep silence! What is it that suddenly forbids her and makes her dumb? Has she been nine years growing and now, when the great world for the first time puts out a hand to her, must she thrust it aside for a bird's sake? The murmur of the pine's green branches is in her ears, she remembers how the white heron came flying through the golden air and how they watched the sea and the morning together, and Sylvia cannot speak; she cannot tell the heron's secret and give its life away.

Dear loyalty, that suffered a sharp pang as the guest went away disap-pointed later in the day, that could have served and followed him and loved him as a dog loves! Many a night Sylvia heard the echo of his whistle haunting the pasture path as she came home with the loitering cow. She forgot even her sorrow at the sharp report of his gun and the sight of thrushes and sparrows dropping silent to the ground, their songs hushed and their pretty feathers stained and wet with blood. Were the birds better friends than their hunter might have been,—who can tell? Whatever trea-sures were lost to her, woodlands and summer-time, remember! Bring your gifts and graces and tell your secrets to this lonely country child!

[1886]

KATE CHOPIN ■ (1850–1904)

Kate Chopin was born Kate O'Flaherty—her mother, Eliza Faris, at age six-teen had married Thomas O'Flaherty, age thirty-nine—in St. Louis, Missouri. She received a good education, supported by the women in the family and reinforced by a high school teacher (a nun at the Sacred Heart Academy) who encouraged Chopin's work as a writer. After her father's death in a rail-way accident, the household became even more woman-oriented—though a good deal of the work was performed by four slaves, which led the family to embrace the cause of the Confederacy during the Civil War.

In 1870, Chopin married Oscar Chopin, a cotton trader and the son of a wealthy planter from Louisiana. The two spent a three-month honeymoon in Europe. Residing in New Orleans upon their return, the Chopins had five sons during the 1870s, and Chopin was busy with motherhood and childrearing, with little time (except for letters and diaries) for writing. Her husband's financial troubles obliged the family to move to a village of about 650 people in northwest Louisiana, where, in 1879, Chopin's daugh-ter (her last child) was born.

When Chopin's husband died of malaria in December 1882, he left his wife and children in debt. But Chopin reorganized the family's holdings and managed to set the situation in order. In the aftermath of the loss of her husband, Chopin had a torrid affair with a married local planter named Albert Sampite, whom scholars have suggested is the model for the passionate male characters in a number of Chopin's stories, including, perhaps, "The Storm." Chopin broke off the affair in 1884 and returned to St. Louis, where she began to focus on the writing of fiction with a Louisiana setting and cast of characters.

Chopin was familiar with such American authors as Mary Wilkins Freeman and Sarah Orne Jewett, but she took inspiration from the subtle, penetrating short stories (some of which she translated into English) of the French writer Guy de Maupassant (1850–93), a master of irony and psychological realism. In her diary, she observed:

> Here was life, not fiction.... Here was a man who escaped from
> tradition and authority, who had entered into himself and looked
> out upon life through his own being and with his own eyes; and
> who, in a direct and simple way, told us what he saw.

Chopin published a novel, *At Fault* (1890), about a widow's love for a married man, followed by two collections of short stories, *Bayou Folk* (1894) and *A Night in Acadie* (1897). During this period, Chopin held a literary salon each Thursday in her home, and it became a gathering place in the city for literature and art.

Chopin's best-known novel, *The Awakening*, was published in 1899, and it was admired by women readers who responded positively to the yearning for freedom of her female protagonist, Edna Pontellier. It was harshly criticized by other readers and critics who were disturbed by Edna's adultery and abandonment of her children. Libraries in St. Louis refused to carry the book, and some of Chopin's friends shunned her. One reviewer concluded that *The Awakening* "leaves one sick of human nature," and another stated that it "should be labeled poison." The controversy that *The Awakening* triggered led to a dramatic slowing of Chopin's literary production, and she wrote only a few more stories.

Chopin wrote "Désirée's Baby," the first of the two following stories, in late 1892, and she published it in the January 1893 issue of *Vogue*. The setting is plantation Louisiana, in the pre–Civil War South. Chopin tells of the ironic, tragic intersections of race and gender, marriage and miscegenation, in the life of the wife and mother Désirée: we hear of her husband Armand's cruelty toward his slaves, and witness his cruel possessiveness and anger toward her and their child.

Yet it could be argued that Armand is the central character—it is noteworthy that when this story was first published, it was titled "The Father of Désirée's Baby." In the end he learns the truth about who he is: he at last sees something he might have suspected all along—something he could not believe ever could be possible. Through Désirée and Armand, Chopin thus shows that racial distinctions both are and are not based on appearances. Even more, she suggests that when the truth about race is at last revealed, it may turn out to be misleading, even false: in this story there is a truer truth beneath or behind the apparent one.

Written in July 1898, "The Storm" did not appear in print in Chopin's lifetime; it was published in 1969. No doubt it would have shocked her contemporaries, for not only does it depict a married woman who commits adultery but also it suggests that this act of adultery strengthens and enriches her marriage. As the critic Barbara C. Ewell noted, "The Storm" is "remarkable for its positive and frank portrayal of sexuality, presenting even adulterous passion as a natural and satisfying encounter, refreshing the lives of everyone involved."

For an overview: Peggy Skaggs, *Kate Chopin* (1985); and Barbara C. Ewell, *Kate Chopin* (1986). Biographies include Per Seyersted, *Kate Chopin: A Critical Biography* (1969); Emily Toth, *Kate Chopin* (1990); and Nancy A. Walker, *Kate Chopin: A Literary Life* (2001). For critical interpretation: *Kate Chopin Reconsidered: Beyond the Bayou*, eds. Lynda S. Boren and Sara deSaussure Davis (1992); and *Critical Essays on Kate Chopin*, ed. Alice Hall Petry (1996). See also Robert C. Evans, *Kate Chopin's Short Fiction: A Critical Companion* (2001); and Janet Beer, *Kate Chopin, Edith Wharton and Charlotte Perkins Gilman: Studies in Short Fiction* (2005). In *Kate Chopin: An Annotated Bibliography of Critical Works* (1999), Susan Disheroon Green, David Caudle, and Emily Toth list and annotate secondary sources and provide essays on the author's life and literary career. Another good resource is *The Cambridge Companion to Kate Chopin* (2008), ed. Janet Beer.

Désirée's Baby

As the day was pleasant, Madame Valmondé drove over to L'Abri to see Désirée and the baby.

It made her laugh to think of Désirée with a baby. Why, it seemed but yesterday that Désirée was little more than a baby herself; when Monsieur in riding through the gateway of Valmondé had found her lying asleep in the shadow of the big stone pillar.

The little one awoke in his arms and began to cry for "Dada." That was as much as she could do or say. Some people thought she might have strayed there of her own accord, for she was of the toddling age. The prevailing belief was that she had been purposely left by a party of Texans, whose canvas-covered wagon, late in the day, had crossed the ferry that Coton Maïs kept, just below the plantation. In time Madame Valmondé abandoned every speculation but the one that Désirée had been sent to her by a beneficent Providence to be the child of her affection, seeing that she was without child of the flesh. For the girl grew to be beautiful and gentle, affectionate and sincere,—the idol of Valmondé.

It was no wonder, when she stood one day against the stone pillar in whose shadow she had lain asleep, eighteen years before, that Armand Aubigny riding by and seeing her there, had fallen in love with her. That was the way all the Aubignys fell in love, as if struck by a pistol shot. The wonder was that he had not loved her before; for he had known her since his father brought him home from Paris, a boy of eight, after his mother died there. The passion that awoke in him that day, when he saw her at the gate, swept along like an avalanche, or like a prairie fire, or like anything that drives headlong over all obstacles.

Monsieur Valmondé grew practical and wanted things well considered: that is, the girl's obscure origin. Armand looked into her eyes and did not care. He was reminded that she was nameless. What did it matter about a name when he could give her one of the oldest and proudest in Louisiana? He ordered the *corbeille*[1] from Paris, and contained himself with what patience he could until it arrived; then they were married.

Madame Valmondé had not seen Désirée and the baby for four weeks. When she reached L'Abri she shuddered at the first sight of it, as she always did. It was a sad looking place, which for many years had not known the gentle presence of a mistress, old Monsieur Aubigny having married and buried his wife in France, and she having loved her own land too well ever to leave it. The roof came down steep and black like a cowl, reaching out beyond the wide galleries that encircled the yellow stuccoed house. Big, solemn oaks grew close to it, and their thick-leaved, far-reaching branches shadowed it like a pall. Young Aubigny's rule was a strict one, too, and

---

[1]Wedding gifts from the groom to the bride (French).

under it his negroes had forgotten how to be gay, as they had been during the old master's easy-going and indulgent lifetime.

The young mother was recovering slowly, and lay full length, in her soft white muslins and laces, upon a couch. The baby was beside her, upon her arm, where he had fallen asleep, at her breast. The yellow nurse woman[2] sat beside a window fanning herself.

Madame Valmondé bent her portly figure over Désirée and kissed her, holding her an instant tenderly in her arms. Then she turned to the child.

"This is not the baby!" she exclaimed, in startled tones. French was the language spoken at Valmondé in those days.

"I knew you would be astonished," laughed Désirée, "at the way he was grown. The little *cochon de lait!*[3] Look at his legs, mamma, and his hands and finger-nails,—real finger-nails. Zandrine had to cut them this morning. Isn't it true, Zandrine?"

The woman bowed her turbaned head majestically, "Mais si,[4] Madame."

"And the way he cries," went on Désirée, "is deafening. Armand heard him the other day as far away as La Blanche's cabin."

Madame Valmondé had never removed her eyes from the child. She lifted it and walked with it over to the window that was lightest. She scanned the baby narrowly, then looked as searchingly at Zandrine, whose face was turned to gaze across the fields.

"Yes, the child has grown, has changed;" said Madame Valmondé, slowly, as she replaced it beside its mother. "What does Armand say?"

Désirée's face became suffused with a glow that was happiness itself.

"Oh, Armand is the proudest father in the parish,[5] I believe, chiefly because it is a boy, to bear his name; though he says not,—that he would have loved a girl as well. But I know it isn't true. I know he says that to please me. And mamma," she added, drawing Madame Valmondé's head down to her, and speaking in a whisper, "he has n't punished one of them—not one of them—since baby is born. Even Négrillon, who pretended to have burnt his leg that he might rest from work—he only laughed, and said Négrillon was a great scamp. Oh, mamma, I'm so happy; it frightens me."

What Désirée said was true. Marriage, and later the birth of his son, had softened Armand Aubigny's imperious and exacting nature greatly. This was what made the gentle Désirée so happy, for she loved him desperately. When he frowned she trembled, but loved him. When he smiled, she asked no greater blessing of God. But Armand's dark, handsome face had not often been disfigured by frowns since the day he fell in love with her.

---

[2]Yellow nurse woman: she is of mixed racial heritage.
[3]Cochon de lait: suckling pig (French).
[4]Certainly (French).
[5]Louisiana is divided into parishes in the same way that other states of the United States are divided into counties.

When the baby was about three months old, Désirée awoke one day to the conviction that there was something in the air menacing her peace. It was at first too subtle to grasp. It had only been a disquieting suggestion; an air of mystery among the blacks; unexpected visits from far-off neighbors who could hardly account for their coming. Then a strange, an awful change in her husband's manner, which she dared not ask him to explain. When he spoke to her, it was with averted eyes, from which the old love-light seemed to have gone out. He absented himself from home; and when there, avoided her presence and that of her child, without excuse. And the very spirit of Satan seemed suddenly to take hold of him in his dealings with the slaves. Désirée was miserable enough to die.

She sat in her room, one hot afternoon, in her *peignoir*,[6] listlessly drawing through her fingers the strands of her long, silky brown hair that hung about her shoulders. The baby, half naked, lay asleep upon her own great mahogany bed, that was like a sumptuous throne, with its satin-lined half-canopy. One of La Blanche's little quadroon boys—half naked too—stood fanning the child slowly with a fan of peacock feathers. Désirée's eyes had been fixed absently and sadly upon the baby, while she was striving to penetrate the threatening mist that she felt closing about her. She looked from her child to the boy who stood beside him, and back again; over and over. "Ah!" It was a cry that she could not help; which she was not conscious of having uttered. The blood turned like ice in her veins, and a clammy moisture gathered upon her face.

She tried to speak to the little quadroon boy; but no sound would come, at first. When he heard his name uttered, he looked up, and his mistress was pointing to the door. He laid aside the great, soft fan, and obediently stole away, over the polished floor, on his bare tiptoes.

She stayed motionless, with gaze riveted upon her child, and her face the picture of fright.

Presently her husband entered the room, and without noticing her, went to a table and began to search among some papers which covered it.

"Armand," she called to him, in a voice which must have stabbed him, if he was human. But he did not notice. "Armand," she said again. Then she rose and tottered towards him. "Armand," she panted once more, clutching his arm, "look at our child. What does it mean? tell me."

He coldly but gently loosened her fingers from about his arm and thrust the hand away from him. "Tell me what it means!" she cried despairingly.

"It means," he answered lightly, "that the child is not white; it means that you are not white."

A quick conception of all that this accusation meant for her nerved her with unwonted courage to deny it. "It is a lie; it is not true, I am white! Look at my hair, it is brown; and my eyes are gray, Armand, you know

---

[6]Long outer garment (French).

they are gray. And my skin is fair," seizing his wrist. "Look at my hand; whiter than yours, Armand," she laughed hysterically.

"As white as La Blanche's," he returned cruelly; and went away leaving her alone with their child.

When she could hold a pen in her hand, she sent a despairing letter to Madame Valmondé.

"My mother, they tell me I am not white. Armand has told me I am not white. For God's sake tell them it is not true. You must know it is not true. I shall die. I must die. I cannot be so unhappy, and live."

The answer that came was as brief:

"My own Désirée: Come home to Valmondé; back to your mother who loves you. Come with your child."

When the letter reached Désirée she went with it to her husband's study, and laid it open upon the desk before which he sat. She was like a stone image: silent, white, motionless after she placed it there.

In silence he ran his cold eyes over the written words. He said nothing. "Shall I go, Armand?" she asked in tones sharp with agonized suspense.

"Yes, go."

"Do you want me to go?"

"Yes, I want you to go."

He thought Almighty God had dealt cruelly and unjustly with him; and felt, somehow, that he was paying Him back in kind when he stabbed thus into his wife's soul. Moreover he no longer loved her, because of the unconscious injury she had brought upon his home and his name.

She turned away like one stunned by a blow, and walked slowly towards the door, hoping he would call her back.

"Good-by, Armand," she moaned.

He did not answer her. That was his last blow at fate.

Désirée went in search of her child. Zandrine was pacing the sombre gallery with it. She took the little one from the nurse's arms with no word of explanation, and descending the steps, walked away, under the live-oak branches.

It was an October afternoon; the sun was just sinking. Out in the still fields the negroes were picking cotton.

Désirée had not changed the thin white garment nor the slippers which she wore. Her hair was uncovered and the sun's rays brought a golden gleam from its brown meshes. She did not take the broad, beaten road which led to the far-off plantation of Valmondé. She walked across a deserted field, where the stubble bruised her tender feet, so delicately shod, and tore her thin gown to shreds.

She disappeared among the reeds and willows that grew thick along the banks of the deep, sluggish bayou; and she did not come back again.

Some weeks later there was a curious scene enacted at L'Abri. In the centre of the smoothly swept back yard was a great bonfire. Armand

Aubigny sat in the wide hallway that commanded a view of the spectacle; and it was he who dealt out to a half dozen negroes the material which kept this fire ablaze.

A graceful cradle of willow, with all its dainty furbishings, was laid upon the pyre, which had already been fed with the richness of a priceless *layette*.[7] Then there were silk gowns, and velvet and satin ones added to these; laces, too, and embroideries; bonnets and gloves; for the *corbeille* had been of rare quality.

The last thing to go was a tiny bundle of letters; innocent little scribblings that Désirée had sent to him during the days of their espousal. There was the remnant of one back in the drawer from which he took them. But it was not Désirée's; it was part of an old letter from his mother to his father. He read it. She was thanking God for the blessing of her husband's love:—

"But, above all," she wrote, "night and day, I thank the good God for having so arranged our lives that our dear Armand will never know that his mother, who adores him, belongs to the race that is cursed with the brand of slavery."

[1893]

The Storm

1

The leaves were so still that even Bibi thought it was going to rain. Bobinôt, who was accustomed to converse on terms of perfect equality with his little son, called the child's attention to certain sombre clouds that were rolling with sinister intention from the west, accompanied by a sullen, threatening roar. They were at Friedheimer's store and decided to remain there till the storm had passed. They sat within the door on two empty kegs. Bibi was four years old and looked very wise.

"Mama'll be 'fraid, yes," he suggested with blinking eyes.

"She'll shut the house. Maybe she got Sylvie helpin' her this evenin'," Bobinôt responded reassuringly.

"No; she ent got Sylvie. Sylvie was helpin' her yistiday," piped Bibi.

Bobinôt arose and going across to the counter purchased a can of shrimps, of which Calixta was very fond. Then he returned to his perch on the keg and sat stolidly holding the can of shrimps while the storm burst. It shook the wooden store and seemed to be ripping great furrows in the distant field. Bibi laid his little hand on his father's knee and was not afraid.

[7] Collection of clothing for a newborn child.

2

Calixta, at home, felt no uneasiness for their safety. She sat at a side window sewing furiously on a sewing machine. She was greatly occupied and did not notice the approaching storm. But she felt very warm and often stopped to mop her face on which the perspiration gathered in beads. She unfastened her white sacque[1] at the throat. It began to grow dark, and suddenly realizing the situation she got up hurriedly and went about closing windows and doors.

Out on the small front gallery she had hung Bobinôt's Sunday clothes to air and she hastened out to gather them before the rain fell. As she stepped outside, Alcée Laballière rode in at the gate. She had not seen him very often since her marriage, and never alone. She stood there with Bobinôt's coat in her hands, and the big rain drops began to fall. Alcée rode his horse under the shelter of a side projection where the chickens had huddled and there were plows and a harrow piled up in the corner.

"May I come and wait on your gallery till the storm is over, Calixta?" he asked.

"Come 'long in, M'sieur Alcée."

His voice and her own startled her as if from a trance, and she seized Bobinôt's vest. Alcée, mounting to the porch, grabbed the trousers and snatched Bibi's braided jacket that was about to be carried away by a sudden gust of wind. He expressed an intention to remain outside, but it was soon apparent that he might as well have been out in the open: the water beat in upon the boards in driving sheets, and he went inside, closing the door after him. It was even necessary to put something beneath the door to keep the water out.

"My! what a rain! It's good two years sence it rain' like that," exclaimed Calixta as she rolled up a piece of bagging and Alcée helped her to thrust it beneath the crack.

She was a little fuller of figure than five years before when she married; but she had lost nothing of her vivacity. Her blue eyes still retained their melting quality; and her yellow hair, dishevelled by the wind and rain, kinked more stubbornly than ever about her ears and temples.

The rain beat upon the low, shingled roof with a force and clatter that threatened to break an entrance and deluge them there. They were in the dining room—the sitting room—the general utility room. Adjoining was her bed room, with Bibi's couch along side her own. The door stood open, and the room with its white, monumental bed, its closed shutters, looked dim and mysterious.

Alcée flung himself into a rocker and Calixta nervously began to gather up from the floor the lengths of a cotton sheet which she had been sewing.

"If this keeps up, *Dieu sait*[2] if the levees goin' to stan' it!" she exclaimed.

[1]A loose-fitting dress.
[2]"God knows" (French).

"What have you got to do with the levees?"

"I got enough to do! An' there's Bobinôt with Bibi out in that storm—if he only didn' left Friedheimer's!"

"Let us hope, Calixta, that Bobinôt's got sense enough to come in out of a cyclone."

She went and stood at the window with a greatly disturbed look on her face. She wiped the frame that was clouded with moisture. It was stiflingly hot. Alcée got up and joined her at the window, looking over her shoulder. The rain was coming down in sheets obscuring the view of far-off cabins and enveloping the distant wood in a gray mist. The playing of the lightning was incessant. A bolt struck a tall chinaberry tree at the edge of the field. It filled all visible space with a blinding glare and the crash seemed to invade the very boards they stood upon.

Calixta put her hands to her eyes, and with a cry, staggered backward. Alcée's arm encircled her, and for an instant he drew her close and spasmodically to him.

"*Bonté!*"[3] she cried, releasing herself from his encircling arm and retreating from the window, "the house'll go next! If I only knew w'ere Bibi was!" She would not compose herself; she would not be seated. Alcée clasped her shoulders and looked into her face. The contact of her warm, palpitating body when he had unthinkingly drawn her into his arms, had aroused all the old-time infatuation and desire for her flesh.

"Calixta," he said, "don't be frightened. Nothing can happen. The house is too low to be struck, with so many tall trees standing about. There! aren't you going to be quiet? say, aren't you?" He pushed her hair back from her face that was warm and steaming. Her lips were as red and moist as pomegranate seed. Her white neck and a glimpse of her full, firm bosom disturbed him powerfully. As she glanced up at him the fear in her liquid blue eyes had given place to a drowsy gleam that unconsciously betrayed a sensuous desire. He looked down into her eyes and there was nothing for him to do but to gather her lips in a kiss. It reminded him of Assumption.[4]

"Do you remember—in Assumption, Calixta?" he asked in a low voice broken by passion. Oh! she remembered; for in Assumption he had kissed her and kissed and kissed her; until his senses would well nigh fail, and to save her he would resort to a desperate flight. If she was not an immaculate dove in those days, she was still inviolate; a passionate creature whose very defenselessness had made her defense, against which his honor forbade him to prevail. Now—well, now—her lips seemed in a manner free to be tasted, as well as her round, white throat and her whiter breasts.

They did not heed the crashing torrents, and the roar of the elements made her laugh as she lay in his arms. She was a revelation in that dim, mysterious chamber; as white as the couch she lay upon. Her firm, elastic

[3]"Heavens!" (French).
[4]A town named for a church feast on August 15 celebrating the Virgin Mary's bodily ascent into heaven.

flesh that was knowing for the first time its birthright, was like a creamy lily that the sun invites to contribute its breath and perfume to the undying life of the world.

The generous abundance of her passion, without guile or trickery, was like a white flame which penetrated and found response in depths of his own sensuous nature that had never yet been reached.

When he touched her breasts they gave themselves up in quivering ecstasy, inviting his lips. Her mouth was a fountain of delight. And when he possessed her, they seemed to swoon together at the very borderland of life's mystery.

He stayed cushioned upon her, breathless, dazed, enervated, with his heart beating like a hammer upon her. With one hand she clasped his head, her lips lightly touching his forehead. The other hand stroked with a soothing rhythm his muscular shoulders.

The growl of the thunder was distant and passing away. The rain beat softly upon the shingles, inviting them to drowsiness and sleep. But they dared not yield.

The rain was over; and the sun was turning the glistening green world into a palace of gems. Calixta, on the gallery, watched Alcée ride away. He turned and smiled at her with a beaming face; and she lifted her pretty chin in the air and laughed aloud.

3

Bobinôt and Bibi, trudging home, stopped without at the cistern to make themselves presentable.

"My! Bibi, w'at will yo' mama say! You ought to be ashame'. You oughtn' put on those good pants. Look at 'em! An' that mud on yo' collar! How you got that mud on yo' collar, Bibi? I never saw such a boy!" Bibi was the picture of pathetic resignation. Bobinôt was the embodiment of serious solicitude as he strove to remove from his own person and his son's the signs of their tramp over heavy roads and through wet fields. He scraped the mud off Bibi's bare legs and feet with a stick and carefully removed all traces from his heavy brogans. Then, prepared for the worst—the meeting with an over-scrupulous housewife, they entered cautiously at the back door.

Calixta was preparing supper. She had set the table and was dripping coffee at the hearth. She sprang up as they came in.

"Oh, Bobinôt! You back! My! but I was uneasy. W'ere you been during the rain? An' Bibi? he ain't wet? he ain't hurt?" She had clasped Bibi and was kissing him effusively. Bobinôt's explanations and apologies which he had been composing all along the way, died on his lips as Calixta felt him to see if he were dry, and seemed to express nothing but satisfaction at their safe return.

"I brought you some shrimps, Calixta," offered Bobinôt, hauling the can from his ample side pocket and laying it on the table.

"Shrimps! Oh, Bobinôt! you too good fo' anything! and she gave him a smacking kiss on the cheek that resounded. *"J'vous réponds,*[5] we'll have a feas' to night! umph-umph!"

Bobinôt and Bibi began to relax and enjoy themselves, and when the three seated themselves at table they laughed much and so loud that anyone might have heard them as far away as Laballière's.

4

Alcée Laballière wrote to his wife, Clarisse, that night. It was a loving letter, full of tender solicitude. He told her not to hurry back, but if she and the babies liked it at Biloxi, to stay a month longer. He was getting on nicely; and though he missed them, he was willing to bear the separation a while longer—realizing that their health and pleasure were the first things to be considered.

5

As for Clarisse, she was charmed upon receiving her husband's letter. She and the babies were doing well. The society was agreeable; many of her old friends and acquaintances were at the bay. And the first free breath since her marriage seemed to restore the pleasant liberty of her maiden days. Devoted as she was to her husband, their intimate conjugal life was something which she was more than willing to forego for a while.

So the storm passed and every one was happy.

[1898]

---

[5]"Take my word; let me tell you" (French).

MARY WILKINS FREEMAN ▪ (1852–1930)

Mary Wilkins Freeman was born in Randolph, Massachusetts, about twenty miles south of Boston, of strict, religiously devout parents, Warren and Eleanor Wilkins, whose roots reached back to the settlement of Massachusetts in the 1630s and 1640s. Her family moved to Brattleboro, Vermont, when she was fifteen, but her father, a Civil War veteran, had trouble providing for the family. Freeman's father, mother, and sister died during the years in Brattleboro, and in 1884 she returned to Randolph, where for the next two decades she lived with a friend from childhood, Mary Wales, who was a source of comfort and support.

Freeman had begun to write and publish poems and stories in the early 1880s, hoping at the time to earn money to help her family's finances. She now focused on short-story writing in earnest, and her stories were published in journals and magazines and were collected in *A Humble Romance and Other Stories* (1887) and *A New England Nun and Other Stories* (1891). Many deal with the challenges faced by unmarried and, sometimes, married women in a New England village setting. Often poor or aged or both, these women struggle and strive to maintain or achieve independence.

Freeman married in 1902 after a long and troubled courtship. Her husband (they had met in 1892) was Charles Manning Freeman, seven years younger than she, who had earned a medical degree at Columbia University but who did not practice medicine. They moved to Metuchen, New Jersey, about twenty-five miles south of New York City, and were contented at first, but the marriage proved unhappy. He suffered from alcoholism and in 1920 was institutionalized, after which Freeman filed for a separation.

Freeman's regional stories—her best work—have a New England setting and atmosphere that evoke a faded but still formative context of Puritan beliefs and customs. As she explained in the preface to *A Humble Romance*, "these little stories are studies of the descendants of the Massachusetts Bay colonists, in whom can still be seen traces of those features of will and conscience, so strong as to be almost exaggerations and deformities, which characterized their ancestors." Freeman also wrote novels, ghost stories, poems, books for children, and a play. Esteemed for her sense of place, her handling of dialect, and psychological and emotional insight (especially about adversity and endurance, repression and resistance), Freeman's literary friends included Mark Twain, Sarah Orne Jewett, William Dean Howells, and Hamlin Garland.

"The Revolt of 'Mother'" depicts the rebellion of a long-faithful and obedient wife who finally asserts herself when she realizes her husband is not planning to build the home he had promised her. Freeman's own

Photograph of Mary Wilkins Freeman, taken by Bain News Service.

father, plagued by financial difficulties, had failed to give his wife the new house she had wanted, and this episode may be in the story's background—though Freeman emphasized that the "The Revolt of 'Mother'" was entirely a work of fiction and that the kind of revolt she described would have been, for a woman in real life, difficult, if not impossible.

For an introduction: Perry D. Westbrook, *Mary Wilkins Freeman* (1967). See also Leah Blatt Glasser, *In a Closet Hidden: The Life and Work of Mary E. Wilkins Freeman* (1996). Also helpful: *Critical Essays on Mary Wilkins Freeman*, ed. Shirley Marchalonis (1991). On the short stories: Mary R. Reichardt, *A Web of Relationship: Women in the Short Stories of Mary Wilkins Freeman* (1992) and *Mary Wilkins Freeman: A Study of the Short Fiction* (1997). See also *A Mary Wilkins Freeman Reader*, eds. Mary Eleanor Wilkins Freeman and Mary R. Reichardt (1997).

The Revolt of "Mother"

"Father!"

"What is it?"

"What are them men diggin' over there in the field for?"

There was a sudden dropping and enlarging of the lower part of the old man's face, as if some heavy weight had settled therein; he shut his mouth tight, and went on harnessing the great bay mare. He hustled the collar on to her neck with a jerk.

"Father!"

The old man slapped the saddle upon the mare's back.

"Look here, father, I want to know what them men are diggin' over in the field for, an' I'm goin' to know."

"I wish you'd go into the house, mother, an' 'tend to your own affairs," the old man said then. He ran his words together, and his speech was almost as inarticulate as a growl.

But the woman understood; it was her most native tongue. "I ain't goin' into the house till you tell me what them men are doin' over there in the field," said she.

Then she stood waiting. She was a small woman, short and straight-waisted like a child in her brown cotton gown. Her forehead was mild and benevolent between the smooth curves of gray hair; there were meek downward lines about her nose and mouth; but her eyes, fixed upon the old man, looked as if the meekness had been the result of her own will, never of the will of another.

They were in the barn, standing before the wide open doors. The spring air, full of the smell of growing grass and unseen blossoms, came in their faces. The deep yard in front was littered with farm wagons and piles of wood; on the edges, close to the fence and the house, the grass was a vivid green, and there were some dandelions.

The old man glanced doggedly at his wife as he tightened the last buckles on the harness. She looked as immovable to him as one of the rocks in his pasture-land, bound to the earth with generations of black-berry vines. He slapped the reins over the horse, and started forth from the barn.

"*Father!*" said she.

The old man pulled up. "What is it?"

"I want to know what them men are diggin' over there in that field for."

"They're diggin' a cellar, I s'pose, if you've got to know."

"A cellar for what?"

"A barn."

"A barn? You ain't goin' to build a barn over there where we was goin' to have a house, father?"

The old man said not another word. He hurried the horse into the farm wagon, and clattered out of the yard, jouncing as sturdily on his seat as a boy.

The woman stood a moment looking after him, then she went out of the barn across a corner of the yard to the house. The house, standing at right angles with the great barn and a long reach of sheds and out-buildings, was infinitesimal compared with them. It was scarcely as commodious for people as the little boxes under the barn eaves were for doves.

A pretty girl's face, pink and delicate as a flower, was looking out of one of the house windows. She was watching three men who were digging over in the field which bounded the yard near the road line. She turned quietly when the woman entered.

"What are they digging for, mother?" said she. "Did he tell you?"

"They're diggin' for—a cellar for a new barn."

"Oh, mother, he ain't going to build another barn?"

"That's what he says."

A boy stood before the kitchen glass combing his hair. He combed slowly and painstakingly, arranging his brown hair in a smooth hillock over his forehead. He did not seem to pay any attention to the conversation.

"Sammy, did you know father was going to build a new barn?" asked the girl.

The boy combed assiduously.

"Sammy!"

He turned, and showed a face like his father's under his smooth crest of hair. "Yes, I s'pose I did," he said, reluctantly.

"How long have you known it?" asked his mother.

"'Bout three months, I guess."

"Why didn't you tell of it?"

"Didn't think 'twould do no good."

"I don't see what father wants another barn for," said the girl, in her sweet, slow voice. She turned again to the window, and stared out at the digging men in the field. Her tender, sweet face was full of a gentle distress. Her forehead was as bald and innocent as a baby's, with the light hair strained back from it in a row of curl-papers. She was quite large, but her soft curves did not look as if they covered muscles.

Her mother looked sternly at the boy. "Is he goin' to buy more cows?" said she.

The boy did not reply; he was tying his shoes.

"Sammy, I want you to tell me if he's goin' to buy more cows."

"I s'pose he is."

"How many?"

"Four, I guess."

His mother said nothing more. She went into the pantry, and there was a clatter of dishes. The boy got his cap from a nail behind the door, took an old arithmetic from the shelf, and started for school. He was lightly built, but clumsy. He went out of the yard with a curious spring in the hips, that made his loose homemade jacket tilt up in the rear.

The girl went to the sink, and began to wash the dishes that were piled up there. Her mother came promptly out of the pantry, and shoved her aside. "You wipe 'em," said she; "I'll wash. There's a good many this mornin'."

The mother plunged her hands vigorously into the water, the girl wiped the plates slowly and dreamily. "Mother," said she, "don't you think it's too bad father's going to build that new barn, much as we need a decent house to live in?"

Her mother scrubbed a dish fiercely. "You ain't found out yet we're women-folks, Nanny Penn," said she. "You ain't seen enough of men-folks yet to. One of these days you'll find it out, an' then you'll know that we know only what men-folks think we do, so far as any use of it goes, an' how we'd ought to reckon men-folks in with Providence, an' not complain of what they do any more than we do of the weather."

"I don't care; I don't believe George is anything like that, anyhow," said Nanny. Her delicate face flushed pink, her lips pouted softly, as if she were going to cry.

"You wait an' see. I guess George Eastman ain't no better than other men. You hadn't ought to judge father, though. He can't help it, 'cause he don't look at things jest the way we do. An' we've been pretty comfortable here, after all. The roof don't leak—ain't never but once—that's one thing. Father's kept it shingled right up."

"I do wish we had a parlor."

"I guess it won't hurt George Eastman any to come to see you in a nice clean kitchen. I guess a good many girls don't have as good a place as this. Nobody's ever heard me complain."

"I ain't complained either, mother."

"Well, I don't think you'd better, a good father an' a good home as you've got. S'pose your father made you go out an' work for your livin'? Lots of girls have to that ain't no stronger an' better able to than you be."

Sarah Penn washed the frying-pan with a conclusive air. She scrubbed the outside of it as faithfully as the inside. She was a masterly keeper of her box of a house. Her one living-room never seemed to have in it any of the dust which the friction of life with inanimate matter produces. She swept, and there seemed to be no dirt to go before the broom; she cleaned, and one could see no difference. She was like an artist so perfect that he has apparently no art. To-day she got out a mixing bowl and a board, and rolled some pies, and there was no more flour upon her than upon her daughter who was doing finer work. Nanny was to be married in the fall, and she was sewing on some white cambric and embroidery. She sewed industriously while her mother cooked, her soft milk-white hands and wrists showed whiter than her delicate work.

"We must have the stove moved out in the shed before long," said Mrs. Penn. "Talk about not havin' things, it's been a real blessin' to be able to put a stove up in that shed in hot weather. Father did one good thing when he fixed that stove-pipe out there."

Sarah Penn's face as she rolled her pies had that expression of meek vigor which might have characterized one of the New Testament saints. She was making mince-pies. Her husband, Adoniram Penn, liked them better than any other kind. She baked twice a week. Adoniram often liked a piece of pie between meals. She hurried this morning. It had been later than usual when she began, and she wanted to have a pie baked for dinner. However deep a resentment she might be forced to hold against her husband, she would never fail in sedulous attention to his wants.

Nobility of character manifests itself at loop-holes when it is not provided with large doors. Sarah Penn's showed itself to-day in flaky dishes of pastry. So she made the pies faithfully, while across the table she could see, when she glanced up from her work, the sight that rankled in her patient and steadfast soul—the digging of the cellar of the new barn in the place where Adoniram forty years ago had promised her their new house should stand.

The pies were done for dinner. Adoniram and Sammy were home a few minutes after twelve o'clock. The dinner was eaten with serious haste. There was never much conversation at the table in the Penn family. Adoniram asked a blessing, and they ate promptly, then rose up and went about their work.

Sammy went back to school, taking soft sly lopes out of the yard like a rabbit. He wanted a game of marbles before school, and feared his father would give him some chores to do. Adoniram hastened to the door and called after him, but he was out of sight.

"I don't see what you let him go for, mother," said he. "I wanted him to help me unload that wood."

Adoniram went to work out in the yard unloading wood from the wagon. Sarah put away the dinner dishes, while Nanny took down her curl-papers and changed her dress. She was going down to the store to buy some more embroidery and thread.

When Nanny was gone, Mrs. Penn went to the door. "Father!" she called.

"Well, what is it!"

"I want to see you jest a minute, father."

"I can't leave this wood nohow. I've got to git it unloaded an' go for a load of gravel afore two o'clock. Sammy had ought to helped me. You hadn't ought to let him go to school so early."

"I want to see you jest a minute."

"I tell ye I can't, nohow, mother."

"Father, you come here." Sarah Penn stood in the door like a queen; she held her head as if it bore a crown; there was the patience which makes authority royal in her voice. Adoniram went.

Mrs. Penn led the way into the kitchen, and pointed to a chair. "Sit down, father," said she; "I've got somethin' I want to say to you."

He sat down heavily; his face was quite stolid, but he looked at her with restive eyes.

"Well, what is it, mother?"

"I want to know what you're buildin' that new barn for, father?"

"I ain't got nothin' to say about it."

"It can't be you think you need another barn?"

"I tell ye I ain't got nothin' to say about it, mother; an' I ain't goin' to say nothin'."

"Be you goin' to buy more cows?"

Adoniram did not reply; he shut his mouth tight.

"I know you be, as well as I want to. Now, father, look here"—Sarah Penn had not sat down; she stood before her husband in the humble fashion of a Scripture woman[1]—"I'm goin' to talk real plain to you; I never have sence I married you, but I'm goin' to now. I ain't never complained, an' I ain't goin' to complain now, but I'm goin' to talk plain. You see this room here, father; you look at it well. You see there ain't no carpet on the floor, an' you see the paper is all dirty, an' droppin' off the walls. We ain't had no new paper on it for ten year, an' then I put it on myself, an' it didn't cost but ninepence a roll. You see this room, father; it's all the one I've had to work in an' eat in an' sit in sence we was married. There ain't another woman in the whole town whose husband ain't got half the means you have but what's got better. It's all the room Nanny's got to have her company in; an' there ain't one of her mates but what's got better, an' their fathers not so able as hers is. It's all the room she'll have to be married in. What would you have thought, father, if we had had our weddin' in a room no better than this? I was married in my mother's parlor, with a carpet on the floor, an' stuffed furniture, an' a mahogany card-table. An' this is all the room my daughter will have to be married in. Look here, father!"

Sarah Penn went across the room as though it were a tragic stage. She flung open a door and disclosed a tiny bedroom, only large enough for a bed and bureau, with a path between. "There, father," said she—"there's all the room I've had to sleep in forty year. All my children were born there—the two that died, an' the two that's livin'. I was sick with a fever there."

She stepped to another door and opened it. It led into the small, ill-lighted pantry. "Here," said she, "is all the buttery[2] I've got—every place I've got for my dishes, to set away my victuals in, an' to keep my milk-pans in.

[1] Like an obedient wife in the Old Testament.
[2] Pantry.

Father, I've been takin' care of the milk of six cows in this place, an' now you're goin' to build a new barn, an' keep more cows, an' give me more to do in it."

She threw open another door. A narrow crooked flight of stairs wound upward from it. "There, father," said she, "I want you to look at the stairs that go up to them two unfinished chambers that are all the places our son an' daughter have had to sleep in all their lives. There ain't a prettier girl in town nor a more ladylike one than Nanny, an' that's the place she has to sleep in. It ain't so good as your horse's stall; it ain't so warm an' tight."

Sarah Penn went back and stood before her husband. "Now, father," said she, "I want to know if you think you're doin' right an' accordin' to what you profess. Here, when we was married, forty year ago, you promised me faithful that we should have a new house built in that lot over in the field before the year was out. You said you had money enough, an' you wouldn't ask me to live in no such place as this. It is forty year now, an' you've been makin' more money, an' I've been savin' of it for you ever since, an' you ain't built no house yet. You've built sheds an' cow-houses an' one new barn, an' now you're goin' to build another. Father, I want to know if you think it's right. You're lodgin' your dumb beasts better than you are your own flesh an' blood. I want to know if you think it's right."

"I ain't got nothin' to say."

"You can't say nothin' without ownin' it ain't right, father. An' there's another thing—I ain't complained; I've got along forty year, an' I s'pose I should forty more, if it wan't for that—if we don't have another house. Nanny she can't live with us after she's married. She'll have to go somewheres else to live away from us, an' it don't seem as if I could have it so, noways, father. She wa'n't ever strong. She's got considerable color, but there wa'n't ever any backbone to her. I've always took the heft of everything off her, an' she ain't fit to keep house an' do everything herself. She'll be all worn out inside of a year. Think of her doin' all the washin' an' ironin' an' bakin' with them soft white hands an' arms, an' sweepin'! I can't have it so, noways, father."

Mrs. Penn's face was burning; her mild eyes gleamed. She had pleaded her little cause like a Webster,[3] she had ranged from severity to pathos; but her opponent employed that obstinate silence which makes eloquence futile with mocking echoes. Adoniram arose clumsily.

"Father, ain't you got nothin' to say?" said Mrs. Penn.

"I've got to go off after that load of gravel. I can't stan' here talkin' all day."

"Father, won't you think it over, an' have a house built there instead of a barn?"

"I ain't got nothin' to say."

---

[3] Daniel Webster (1782–1852), American orator, statesman, and senator.

Adoniram shuffled out. Mrs. Penn went into her bedroom. When she came out, her eyes were red. She had a roll of unbleached cotton cloth. She spread it out on the kitchen table, and began cutting out some shirts for her husband. The men over in the field had a team to help them this afternoon; she could hear their halloos. She had a scanty pattern for the shirts; she had to plan and piece the sleeves.

Nanny came home with her embroidery, and sat down with her needle-work. She had taken down her curl-papers, and there was a soft roll of fair hair like an aureole over her forehead; her face was as delicately fine and clear as porcelain. Suddenly she looked up, and the tender red flamed all over her face and neck. "Mother," said she.

"What say?"

"I've been thinking—I don't see how we're goin' to have any—wedding in this room. I'd be ashamed to have his folks come if we didn't have any-body else."

"Mebbe we can have some new paper before then; I can put it on. I guess you won't have no call to be ashamed of your belongin's."

"We might have the wedding in the new barn," said Nanny, with gentle pettishness. "Why, mother, what makes you look so?"

Mrs. Penn had started, and was staring at her with a curious expres-sion. She turned again to her work, and spread out a pattern carefully on the cloth. "Nothin'," said she.

Presently Adoniram clattered out of the yard in his two-wheeled dump cart, standing as proudly upright as a Roman charioteer. Mrs. Penn opened the door and stood there a minute looking out; the halloos of the men sounded louder.

It seemed to her all through the spring months that she heard nothing but the halloos and the noises of saws and hammers. The new barn grew fast. It was a fine edifice for this little village. Men came on pleasant Sun-days, in their meeting suits and clean shirt bosoms, and stood around it admiringly. Mrs. Penn did not speak of it, and Adoniram did not mention it to her, although sometimes, upon a return from inspecting it, he bore himself with injured dignity.

"It's a strange thing how your mother feels about the new barn," he said, confidentially, to Sammy one day.

Sammy only grunted after an odd fashion for a boy; he had learned it from his father.

The barn was all completed ready for use by the third week in July. Adoniram had planned to move his stock in on Wednesday; on Tuesday he received a letter which changed his plans. He came in with it early in the morning. "Sammy's been to the post-office," said he, "an' I've got a letter from Hiram." Hiram was Mrs. Penn's brother, who lived in Vermont.

"Well," said Mrs. Penn, "what does he say about the folks?"

"I guess they're all right. He says he thinks if I come up country right off there's a chance to buy jest the kind of a horse I want." He stared reflectively out of the window at the new barn.

Mrs. Penn was making pies. She went on clapping the rolling-pin into the crust, although she was very pale, and her heart beat loudly.

"I dun' know but what I'd better go," said Adoniram. "I hate to go off jest now, right in the midst of hayin', but the ten-acre lot's cut, an' I guess Rufus an' the others can git along without me three or four days. I can't get a horse round here to suit me, nohow, an' I've got to have another for all that wood-haulin' in the fall. I told Hiram to watch out, an' if he got wind of a good horse to let me know. I guess I'd better go."

"I'll get out your clean shirt an' collar," said Mrs. Penn calmly.

She laid out Adoniram's Sunday suit and his clean clothes on the bed in the little bedroom. She got his shaving-water and razor ready. At last she buttoned on his collar and fastened his black cravat.

Adoniram never wore his collar and cravat except on extra occasions. He held his head high, with a rasped dignity. When he was all ready, with his coat and hat brushed, and a lunch of pie and cheese in a paper bag, he hesitated on the threshold of the door. He looked at his wife, and his manner was defiantly apologetic. "*If* them cows come to-day, Sammy can drive 'em into the new barn," said he; "an' when they bring the hay up, they can pitch it in there."

"Well," replied Mrs. Penn.

Adoniram set his shaven face ahead and started. When he had cleared the doorstep, he turned and looked back with a kind of nervous solemnity. "I shall be back by Saturday if nothin' happens," said he.

"Do be careful, father," returned his wife.

She stood in the door with Nanny at her elbow and watched him out of sight. Her eyes had a strange, doubtful expression in them; her peaceful forehead was contracted. She went in, and about her baking again. Nanny sat sewing. Her wedding-day was drawing nearer, and she was getting pale and thin with her steady sewing. Her mother kept glancing at her.

"Have you got that pain in your side this mornin'?" she asked.

"A little."

Mrs. Penn's face, as she worked, changed, her perplexed forehead smoothed, her eyes were steady, her lips firmly set. She formed a maxim for herself, although incoherently with her unlettered thoughts. "Unsolicited opportunities are the guideposts of the Lord to the new roads of life," she repeated in effect, and she made up her mind to her course of action.

"S'posin' I *had* wrote to Hiram," she muttered once, when she was in the pantry—"s'posin' I had wrote, an' asked him if he knew of any horse? But I didn't, an' father's goin' wa'n't none of my doin'. It looks like a providence." Her voice rang out quite loud at the last.

"What you talkin' about, mother?" called Nanny.

"Nothin'."

Mrs. Penn hurried her baking; at eleven o'clock it was all done. The load of hay from the west field came slowly down the cart track, and drew up at the new barn. Mrs. Penn ran out. "Stop!" she screamed—"stop!"

The men stopped and looked; Sammy upreared from the top of the load, and stared at his mother.

"Stop!" she cried out again. "Don't you put the hay in that barn; put it in the old one."

"Why, he said to put it in here," returned one of the hay-makers, wonderingly. He was a young man, a neighbor's son, whom Adoniram hired by the year to help on the farm.

"Don't you put the hay in the new barn; there's room enough in the old one, ain't there?" said Mrs. Penn.

"Room enough," returned the hired man, in his thick, rustic tones. "Didn't need the new barn, nohow, far as room's concerned. Well, I s'pose he changed his mind." He took hold of the horses' bridles.

Mrs. Penn went back to the house. Soon the kitchen windows were darkened, and a fragrance like warm honey came into the room.

Nanny laid down her work. "I thought father wanted them to put the hay into the new barn?" she said, wonderingly.

"It's all right," replied her mother.

Sammy slid down from the load of hay, and came in to see if dinner was ready.

"I ain't goin' to get a regular dinner to-day, as long as father's gone," said his mother. "I've let the fire go out. You can have some bread an' milk an' pie. I thought we could get along." She set out some bowls of milk, some bread and a pie on the kitchen table. "You'd better eat your dinner now," said she. "You might jest as well get through with it. I want you to help me afterward."

Nanny and Sammy stared at each other. There was something strange in their mother's manner. Mrs. Penn did not eat anything herself. She went into the pantry, and they heard her moving dishes while they ate. Presently she came out with a pile of plates. She got the clothes-basket out of the shed, and packed them in it. Nanny and Sammy watched. She brought out cups and saucers, and put them in with the plates.

"What you goin' to do, mother?" inquired Nanny, in a timid voice. A sense of something unusual made her tremble, as if it were a ghost. Sammy rolled his eyes over his pie.

"You'll see what I'm goin' to do," replied Mrs. Penn. "If you're through, Nanny, I want you to go up-stairs an' pack up your things; an' I want you, Sammy, to help me take down the bed in the bedroom."

"Oh, mother, what for?" gasped Nanny.

"You'll see."

During the next few hours a feat was performed by this simple, pious New England mother which was equal in its way to Wolfe's storming of the Heights of Abraham.[4] It took no more genius and audacity of bravery for Wolfe to cheer his wondering soldiers up those steep precipices, under the sleeping eyes of the enemy, than for Sarah Penn, at the head of her children, to move all their little household goods into the new barn while her husband was away.

Nanny and Sammy followed their mother's instructions without a murmur; indeed, they were overawed. There is a certain uncanny and superhuman quality about all such purely original undertakings as their mother's was to them. Nanny went back and forth with her light loads, and Sammy tugged with sober energy.

At five o'clock in the afternoon the little house in which the Penns had lived for forty years had emptied itself into the new barn.

Every builder builds somewhat for unknown purposes, and is in a measure a prophet. The architect of Adoniram Penn's barn, while he designed it for the comfort of four-footed animals, had planned better than he knew for the comfort of humans. Sarah Penn saw at a glance its possibilities. These great box-stalls, with quilts hung before them, would make better bedrooms than the one she had occupied for forty years, and there was a tight carriage-room. The harness-room, with its chimney and shelves, would make a kitchen of her dreams. The great middle space would make a parlor, by-and-by, fit for a palace. Up-stairs there was as much room as down. With partitions and windows, what a house would there be! Sarah looked at the row of stanchions before the allotted space for cows, and reflected that she would have her front entry there.

At six o'clock the stove was up in the harness-room, the kettle was boiling, and the table set for tea. It looked almost as home-like as the abandoned house across the yard had ever done. The young hired man milked, and Sarah directed him calmly to bring the milk to the new barn. He came gaping, dropping little blots of foam from the brimming pails on the grass. Before the next morning he had spread the story of Adoniram Penn's wife moving into the new barn all over the little village. Men assembled in the store and talked it over, women with shawls over their heads scuttled into each other's houses before their work was done. Any deviation from the ordinary course of life in this quiet town was enough to stop all progress in it. Everybody paused to look at the staid, independent figure on the side track. There was a difference of opinion with regard to her. Some held her to be insane; some, of a lawless and rebellious spirit.

Friday the minister went to see her. It was in the forenoon, and she was at the barn door shelling pease for dinner. She looked up and returned

---

[4]James Wolfe, a British general, scaled the Heights of Abraham, fought on the Plains of Abraham, and led his forces to victory over the French at Quebec in September 1759, but he died in the battle.

his salutation with dignity, then she went on with her work. She did not invite him in. The saintly expression of her face remained fixed, but there was an angry flush over it.

The minister stood awkwardly before her, and talked. She handled the pease as if they were bullets. At last she looked up, and her eyes showed the spirit that her meek front had covered for a lifetime.

"There ain't no use talkin', Mr. Hersey," said she. "I've thought it all over an' over, an' I believe I'm doin' what's right. I've made it the subject of prayer, an' it's betwixt me an' the Lord an' Adoniram. There ain't no call for nobody else to worry about it."

"Well, of course, if you have brought it to the Lord in prayer, and feel satisfied that you are doing right, Mrs. Penn," said the minister, help-lessly. His thin gray-bearded face was pathetic. He was a sickly man; his youthful confidence had cooled; he had to scourge himself up to some of his pastoral duties as relentlessly as a Catholic ascetic, and then he was prostrated by the smart.

"I think it's right jest as much as I think it was right for our fore-fathers to come over from the old country 'cause they didn't have what belonged to 'em," said Mrs. Penn. She arose. The barn threshold might have been Plymouth Rock from her bearing. "I don't doubt you mean well, Mr. Hersey," said she, "but there are things people hadn't ought to inter-fere with. I've been a member of the church for over forty year. I've got my own mind an' my own feet, an' I'm goin' to think my own thoughts an' go my own ways, an' nobody but the Lord is goin' to dictate to me unless I've a mind to have him. Won't you come in an' set down? How is Mis' Hersey?"

"She is well, I thank you," replied the minister. He added some more perplexed apologetic remarks; then he retreated.

He could expound the intricacies of every character study in the Scrip-tures, he was competent to grasp the Pilgrim Fathers and all historical innovators, but Sarah Penn was beyond him. He could deal with primal cases, but parallel ones worsted him. But, after all, although it was aside from his province, he wondered more how Adoniram Penn would deal with his wife than how the Lord would. Everybody shared the wonder. When Adoniram's four new cows arrived, Sarah ordered three to be put in the old barn, the other in the house shed where the cooking-stove had stood. That added to the excitement. It was whispered that all four cows were domiciled in the house.

Towards sunset on Saturday, when Adoniram was expected home, there was a knot of men in the road near the new barn. The hired man had milked, but he still hung around the premises. Sarah Penn had supper all ready. There were brown-bread and baked beans and a custard pie; it was the supper Adoniram loved on a Saturday night. She had a clean calico, and she bore herself imperturbably. Nanny and Sammy kept close at her heels. Their eyes were large, and Nanny was full of nervous tremors. Still there was to them more pleasant excitement than anything else. An inborn confidence in their mother over their father asserted itself.

Sammy looked out of the harness-room window. "There he is," he announced, in an awed whisper. He and Nanny peeped around the casing. Mrs. Penn kept on about her work. The children watched Adoniram leave the new horse standing in the drive while he went to the house door. It was fastened. Then he went around to the shed. That door was seldom locked, even when the family was away. The thought how her father would be confronted by the cow flashed upon Nanny. There was a hysterical sob in her throat. Adoniram emerged from the shed and stood looking about in a dazed fashion. His lips moved; he was saying something, but they could not hear what it was. The hired man was peeping around a corner of the old barn, but nobody saw him.

Adoniram took the new horse by the bridle and led him across the yard to the new barn. Nanny and Sammy slunk close to their mother. The barn doors rolled back, and there stood Adoniram, with the long mild face of the great Canadian farm horse looking over his shoulder.

Nanny kept behind her mother, but Sammy stepped suddenly forward, and stood in front of her.

Adoniram stared at the group. "What on airth you all down here for?" said he. "What's the matter over to the house?"

"We've come here to live, father," said Sammy. His shrill voice quavered out bravely.

"What"—Adoniram sniffed—"what is it smells like cookin'?" said he. He stepped forward and looked in the open door of the harness-room. Then he turned to his wife. His old bristling face was pale and frightened. "What on airth does this mean, mother?" he gasped.

"You come in here, father," said Sarah. She led the way into the harness-room and shut the door. "Now, father," said she, "you needn't be scared. I ain't crazy. There ain't nothin' to be upset over. But we've come here to live, an' we're goin' to live here. We've got jest as good a right here as new horses an' cows. The house wa'n't fit for us to live in any longer, an' I made up my mind I wa'n't goin' to stay there. I've done my duty by you forty year, an' I'm goin' to do it now; but I'm goin' to live here. You've got to put in some windows and partitions; an' you'll have to buy some furniture."

"Why, mother!" the old man gasped.

"You'd better take your coat off an' get washed—there's the washbasin—an' then we'll have supper."

"Why, mother!"

Sammy went past the window, leading the new horse to the old barn. The old man saw him, and shook his head speechlessly. He tried to take off his coat, but his arms seemed to lack the power. His wife helped him. She poured some water into the tin basin, and put in a piece of soap. She got the comb and brush, and smoothed his thin gray hair after he had washed. Then she put the beans, hot bread, and tea on the table. Sammy came in, and the family drew up. Adoniram sat looking dazedly at his plate, and they waited.

"Ain't you goin' to ask a blessin', father?" said Sarah.

And the old man bent his head and mumbled.

All through the meal he stopped eating at intervals, and stared furtively at his wife; but he ate well. The home food tasted good to him, and his old frame was too sturdily healthy to be affected by his mind. But after supper he went out, and sat down on the step of the smaller door at the right of the barn, through which he had meant his Jerseys to pass in stately file, but which Sarah designed for her front house door, and he leaned his head on his hands.

After the supper dishes were cleared away and the milk-pans washed, Sarah went out to him. The twilight was deepening. There was a clear green glow in the sky. Before them stretched the smooth level of field; in the distance was a cluster of haystacks like the huts of a village; the air was very cool and calm and sweet. The landscape might have been an ideal one of peace.

Sarah bent over and touched her husband on one of his thin, sinewy shoulders. "Father!"

The old man's shoulders heaved: he was weeping.

"Why, don't do so, father," said Sarah.

"I'll—put up the—partitions, an'—everything you—want, mother."

Sarah put her apron up to her face; she was overcome by her own triumph.

Adoniram was like a fortress whose walls had no active resistance, and went down the instant the right besieging tools were used. "Why, mother," he said, hoarsely, "I hadn't no idee you was so set on't as all this comes to."

[1890]

BOOKER T. WASHINGTON ▪ (1856–1915)

The leading African American educator and spokesman for his race from the 1880s until his death, Booker T. Washington remains a controversial figure, criticized by many for his "accommodation" to racism and segregation, admired by others for his achievements during a period of brutal hostility toward America's black population.

Washington was born a slave in Virginia in 1856, the son of a black mother and a white father whose identity Washington never knew. He grew up poor and labored as a boy in the coal and salt mines of West Virginia. Admitted to Hampton Institute in southeast Virginia in 1872, Washington showed the commitment to hard work and self-discipline that characterized his entire career and educational philosophy. After graduation, he taught in West Virginia for two years before returning to Hampton, where he helped to establish an educational program for Native American students.

In 1881, Samuel Chapman Armstrong, the head of Hampton Institute and Washington's friend and mentor, recommended to the Alabama state legislature that Washington be appointed the principal of a new school there for African Americans. Washington accepted the offer, and he made Tuskegee Normal and Industrial Institute into one of the foremost schools in the South and the embodiment of his vision of black uplift and self-help.

In speeches, essays, and books, such as *The Story of My Life and Work* (1900) and *Up from Slavery* (1901), Washington preached that African Americans should dedicate themselves to learning industrial trades and crafts and cease agitation for full social and political rights. This led to significant gains for African Americans in business and education, and the message appealed very much to white Americans in the South and in the North as well. Wealthy businessmen in particular, including Andrew Carnegie and John D. Rockefeller, responded favorably, funding Washington's school generously.

The historian and educator W. E. B. Du Bois, the journalist Monroe Trotter, and other African American writers, reformers, and intellectuals, however, attacked Washington's ideas. To them, he appeared to be accepting (that is, surrendering to) the South's discriminatory practices and hence was refusing to battle for the right of African Americans to reach their full potential. Washington's foes argued, in addition, that he stifled dissenting opinions and proposals, aiming always to advance himself and undermine any and all threats to his leadership and connections to white politicians and philanthropists.

On one level, these were fair and accurate criticisms. As a number of passages in *Up from Slavery* indicate—including the following chapter, which is keyed to an important speech Washington gave in Atlanta, Georgia, in 1895—Washington refused to challenge segregation and racial violence directly. "In all things that are purely social we can be as separate as the fingers," Washington declared. As the biographer Louis R. Harlan has observed, "Washington offered black acquiescence in disfranchisement and social segregation if whites would encourage black progress in economic and educational opportunity."

But on another level, the Du Bois/Trotter critique is misleading. Washington never said that African Americans were undeserving of full equality; he said, rather, that African Americans, starting from the bottom up, needed to demonstrate to the white majority that they merited, and should be granted, equal treatment in all areas of life. By law, this was their due, but they would have to earn it, for implicit in Washington's program was an acknowledgment of the depth and intensity of the racism that African Americans faced. There was much for black people in America to overcome, and their struggle for equality would be slow and difficult.

Agitation, confrontation, and direct action: these were not the strategies that, in Washington's judgment, would succeed during a period of extreme racial animosity and white supremacy. He saw himself as a realist, a pragmatist, a leader who was making improvements in the lives of African Americans at a time when most white Americans were either indifferent

Photograph of Booker T. Washington taken by Frances Benjamin Johnston around 1895. Johnston was one of the first female journalists and portrait photographers.

or hostile to black advancement. More complex and ambiguous than at first he might appear, shrewd and savvy in his understanding of his audiences (white and black, northern and southern), and cannily sensitive to the views they wanted to hear expressed, Washington was a masterful, if flawed, leader and writer whose legacy even now remains the focus of vigorous debate and discussion.

For biographical context, see *The Booker T. Washington Papers*, 13 vols., ed. Louis R. Harlan (1972–84); and Harlan, *Booker T. Washington: The Making of a Black Leader, 1856–1901* (1972) and *Booker T. Washington: The Wizard of Tuskegee, 1901–1915* (1983). For historical and literary interpretation: August Meier, *Negro Thought in America, 1880–1915: Racial Ideologies in the Age of Booker T. Washington* (1963); Stephen Butterfield, *Black Autobiography in America* (1974); and Houston A. Baker Jr., *Turning South Again: Re-thinking Modernism/Re-reading Booker T.* (2001). Also valuable are: Michael Rudolph West, *The Education of Booker T. Washington: American Democracy and the Idea of Race Relations* (2006); David H. Jackson Jr., *Booker T. Washington and the Struggle against White Supremacy: The Southern Educational Tours, 1908–1912* (2008); and Robert J. Norrell, *Up from History: The Life of Booker T. Washington* (2009). See also the essays in *Uncle Tom or New Negro? African Americans Reflect on Booker T. Washington and Up from Slavery One Hundred Years Later*, ed. Rebecca Carroll (2006).

From Up from Slavery

Chapter XIV

The Atlanta Exposition Address

The Atlanta Exposition, at which I had been asked to make an address as a representative of the Negro race, as stated in the last chapter, was opened with a short address from Governor Bullock.[1] After other interesting exercises, including an invocation from Bishop Nelson, of Georgia, a dedicatory ode by Albert Howell Jr., and addresses by the President of the Exposition, and Mrs. Joseph Thompson, the President of the Woman's Board, Governor Bullock introduced me with the words, "We have with us to-day a representative of Negro enterprise and Negro civilization."

When I arose to speak, there was considerable cheering, especially from the coloured people. As I remember it now, the thing that was uppermost in my mind was the desire to say something that would cement the friendship of the races and bring about hearty coöperation between them. So far as my outward surroundings were concerned, the only thing that I recall

---

[1]Rufus Bullock (1834–1907) was the first Republican to be elected to Georgia's highest political office, serving as governor from 1868 to 1871.

distinctly now is that when I got up, I saw thousands of eyes looking intently into my face. The following is the address which I delivered:—

Mr. President and Gentlemen of the Board of Directors and Citizens:

One-third of the population of the South is of the Negro race. No enterprise seeking the material, civil, or moral welfare of this section can disregard this element of our population and reach the highest success. I but convey to you, Mr. President and Directors, the sentiment of the masses of my race when I say that in no way have the value and manhood of the American Negro been more fittingly and generously recognized than by the managers of this magnificent Exposition at every stage of its progress. It is a recognition that will do more to cement the friendship of the two races than any occurrence since the dawn of our freedom.

Not only this, but the opportunity here afforded will awaken among us a new era of industrial progress. Ignorant and inexperienced, it is not strange that in the first years of our new life we began at the top instead of at the bottom; that a seat in Congress or the state legislature was more sought than real estate or industrial skill; that the political convention or stump speaking had more attractions than starting a dairy farm or truck garden.

A ship lost at sea for many days suddenly sighted a friendly vessel. From the mast of the unfortunate vessel was seen a signal, "Water, water; we die of thirst!" The answer from the friendly vessel at once came back, "Cast down your bucket where you are." A second time the signal, "Water, water; send us water!" ran up from the distressed vessel, and was answered, "Cast down your bucket where you are." And a third and fourth signal for water was answered, "Cast down your bucket where you are." The captain of the distressed vessel, at last heeding the injunction, cast down his bucket, and it came up full of fresh, sparkling water from the mouth of the Amazon River. To those of my race who depend on bettering their condition in a foreign land or who underestimate the importance of cultivating friendly relations with the Southern white man, who is their next-door neighbour, I would say: "Cast down your bucket where you are"—cast it down in making friends in every manly way of the people of all races by whom we are surrounded.

Cast it down in agriculture, mechanics, in commerce, in domestic service, and in the professions. And in this connection it is well to bear in mind that whatever other sins the South may be called to bear, when it comes to business, pure and simple, it is in the South that the Negro is given a man's chance in the commercial world, and in nothing is this Exposition more eloquent than in emphasizing this chance. Our greatest danger is that in the great leap from slavery to freedom we may overlook the fact that the masses of us are to live by the productions of our hands, and fail to keep in mind that we shall prosper in proportion as we learn to dignify and glorify common labour and put brains and skill into the common occupations of life; shall prosper in proportion as we learn to draw the line between the superficial and the substantial, the ornamental gewgaws[2] of life and the useful. No race can prosper till it learns that there is as much dignity in tilling a field as in writing a poem. It is at the bottom of life we must begin, and not at the top. Nor should we permit our grievances to overshadow our opportunities.

To those of the white race who look to the incoming of those of foreign birth and strange tongue and habits for the prosperity of the South, were I permitted I would repeat what I say to my own race, "Cast down your bucket where you are." Cast it down among the eight millions of Negroes whose habits you know, whose fidelity and love you have tested in days when to have proved treacherous meant the ruin of your firesides. Cast down your bucket among these people who have, without strikes and labour wars, tilled your fields, cleared your forests, builded your railroads and cities, and brought forth treasures from the bowels of the earth, and helped make possible this magnificent representation of the progress of the South. Casting down your bucket among my people, helping and encouraging them as you are doing on these grounds, and to education of head, hand, and heart, and you will find that they will buy your surplus land, make blossom the waste places in your fields, and run your factories. While doing this, you can be sure in the future, as in the past, that you and your families will be surrounded by the most patient, faithful, law-abiding, and unresentful people that the world has seen. As we have proved our loyalty to you in the past, in nursing your children, watching by the sick-bed of your mothers and fathers, and often following them with tear-dimmed eyes to their graves, so in the future, in our humble way, we shall stand by you with a devotion that no foreigner can approach, ready to lay down our lives, if need be, in defence of yours, interlacing our industrial, commercial, civil, and religious life with yours in a way that shall make the interests of both races one. In all things that are purely social we can be as separate as the fingers, yet one as the hand in all things essential to mutual progress.

There is no defence or security for any of us except in the highest intelligence and development of all. If anywhere there are efforts tending to curtail the fullest growth of the Negro, let these efforts be turned into stimulating, encouraging, and making him the most useful and intelligent citizen. Effort or means so invested

---

[2]Gewgaw: a showy thing, especially one that is useless or worthless.

will pay a thousand per cent interest. These efforts will be twice blessed—"blessing him that gives and him that takes."[3]

There is no escape through law of man or God from the inevitable:—

"The laws of changeless justice bind
    Oppressor with oppressed;
And close as sin and suffering joined
    We march to fate abreast."[4]

Nearly sixteen millions of hands will aid you in pulling the load upward, or they will pull against you the load downward. We shall constitute one-third and more of the ignorance and crime of the South, or one-third its intelligence and progress; we shall contribute one-third to the business and industrial prosperity of the South, or we shall prove a veritable body of death, stagnating, depressing, retarding every effort to advance the body politic.

Gentlemen of the Exposition, as we present to you our humble effort at an exhibition of our progress, you must not expect overmuch. Starting thirty years ago with ownership here and there in a few quilts and pumpkins and chickens (gathered from miscellaneous sources), remember the path that has led from these to the inventions and production of agricultural implements, buggies, steam-engines, newspapers, books, statuary, carving, paintings, the management of drug-stores and banks, has not been trodden without contact with thorns and thistles. While we take pride in what we exhibit as a result of our independent efforts, we do not for a moment forget that our part in this exhibition would fall far short of your expectations but for the constant help that has come to our educational life, not only from the Southern states, but especially from Northern philanthropists, who have made their gifts a constant stream of blessing and encouragement.

The wisest among my race understand that the agitation of questions of social equality is the extremest folly, and that progress in the enjoyment of all the privileges that will come to us must be the result of severe and constant struggle rather than of artificial forcing. No race that has anything to contribute to the markets of the world is long in any degree ostracized. It is important and right that all privileges of the law be ours, but it is vastly more important that we be prepared for the exercises of these privileges. The opportunity to earn a dollar in a factory just now is worth infinitely more than the opportunity to spend a dollar in an opera-house.

---

[3]From Shakespeare's *The Merchant of Venice*, 3.1.167: "It blesseth him that gives and him that takes."
[4]From "Song of the Negro Boatman," by the American poet John Greenleaf Whittier (1807–92).

In conclusion, may I repeat that nothing in thirty years has given us more hope and encouragement, and drawn us so near to you of the white race, as this opportunity offered by the Exposition; and here bending, as it were, over the altar that represents the results of the struggles of your race and mine, both starting practically empty-handed three decades ago, I pledge that in your effort to work out the great and intricate problem which God has laid at the doors of the South, you shall have at all times the patient, sympathetic help of my race; only let this be constantly in mind, that, while from representations in these buildings of the product of field, of forest, of mine, of factory, letters, and art, much good will come, yet far above and beyond material benefits will be that higher good, that, let us pray God, will come, in a blotting out of sectional differences and racial animosities and suspicions, in a determination to administer absolute justice, in a willing obedience among all classes to the mandates of law. This, this, coupled with our material prosperity, will bring into our beloved South a new heaven and a new earth.

The first thing that I remember, after I had finished speaking, was that Governor Bullock rushed across the platform and took me by the hand, and that others did the same. I received so many and such hearty congratulations that I found it difficult to get out of the building. I did not appreciate to any degree, however, the impression which my address seemed to have made, until the next morning, when I went into the business part of the city. As soon as I was recognized, I was surprised to find myself pointed out and surrounded by a crowd of men who wished to shake hands with me. This was kept up on every street on to which I went, to an extent which embarrassed me so much that I went back to my boarding-place. The next morning I returned to Tuskegee. At the station in Atlanta, and at almost all of the stations at which the train stopped between the city and Tuskegee, I found a crowd of people anxious to shake hands with me.

The papers in all the parts of the United States published the address in full, and for months afterward there were complimentary editorial references to it. Mr. Clark Howell, the editor of the Atlanta *Constitution,* telegraphed to a New York paper, among other words, the following, "I do not exaggerate when I say that Professor Booker T. Washington's address yesterday was one of the most notable speeches, both as to character and as to the warmth of its reception, ever delivered to a Southern audience. The address was a revelation. The whole speech is a platform upon which blacks and whites can stand with full justice to each other."

The Boston *Transcript* said editorially: "The speech of Booker T. Washington at the Atlanta Exposition, this week, seems to have dwarfed all the other proceedings and the Exposition itself. The sensation that it has caused in the press has never been equalled."

I very soon began receiving all kinds of propositions from lecture bureaus and editors of magazines and papers, to take the lecture platform, and to write articles. One lecture bureau offered me fifty thousand dollars, or two hundred dollars a night and expenses, if I would place my services at its disposal for a given period. To all these communications I replied that my life-work was at Tuskegee; and that whenever I spoke it must be in the interests of the Tuskegee school and my race, and that I would enter into no arrangements that seemed to place a mere commercial value upon my services.

Some days after its delivery I sent a copy of my address to the President of the United States, the Hon. Grover Cleveland.[5] I received from him the following autograph reply:—

Gray Gables
Buzzard's Bay, Mass., October 6, 1895

Booker T. Washington, Esq.:
My Dear Sir: I thank you for sending me a copy of your address delivered at the Atlanta Exposition.

I thank you with much enthusiasm for making the address. I have read it with intense interest, and I think the Exposition would be fully justified if it did not do more than furnish the opportunity for its delivery. Your words cannot fail to delight and encourage all who wish well for your race; and if our coloured fellow-citizens do not from your utterances gather new hope and form new determinations to gain every valuable advantage offered them by their citizenship, it will be strange indeed. Yours very truly,

Grover Cleveland

Later I met Mr. Cleveland, for the first time, when, as President, he visited the Atlanta Exposition. At the request of myself and others he consented to spend an hour in the Negro Building, for the purpose of inspecting the Negro exhibit and of giving the coloured people in attendance an opportunity to shake hands with him. As soon as I met Mr. Cleveland I became impressed with his simplicity, greatness, and rugged honesty. I have met him many times since then, both at public functions and at his private residence in Princeton, and the more I see of him the more I admire him. When he visited the Negro Building in Atlanta he seemed to give himself up wholly, for that hour, to the coloured people. He seemed to be as careful to shake hands with some old coloured "auntie" clad partially in rags, and to take as much pleasure in doing so, as if he were greeting some millionaire. Many of the coloured people took advantage of the occasion to get him to write his name in a book or on a slip of paper. He was as careful and patient in doing this as if he were putting his signature to some great state document.

[5]Grover Cleveland (1837–1908) served two terms as president of the United States (1885–89 and 1893–97).

Mr. Cleveland has not only shown his friendship for me in many personal ways, but has always consented to do anything I have asked of him for our school. This he has done, whether it was to make a personal donation or to use his influence in securing the donations of others. Judging from my personal acquaintance with Mr. Cleveland, I do not believe that he is conscious of possessing any colour prejudice. He is too great for that. In my contact with people I find that, as a rule, it is only the little, narrow people who live for themselves, who never read good books, who do not travel, who never open up their souls in a way to permit them to come into contact with other souls—with the great outside world. No man whose vision is bounded by colour can come into contact with what is highest and best in the world. In meeting men, in many places, I have found that the happiest people are those who do the most for others; the most miserable are those who do the least. I have also found that few things, if any, are capable of making one so blind and narrow as race prejudice. I often say to our students, in the course of my talks to them on Sunday evenings in the chapel, that the longer I live and the more experience I have of the world, the more I am convinced that, after all, the one thing that is most worth living for—and dying for, if need be—is the opportunity of making some one else more happy and more useful.

The coloured people and the coloured newspapers at first seemed to be greatly pleased with the character of my Atlanta address, as well as with its reception. But after the first burst of enthusiasm began to die away, and the coloured people began reading the speech in cold type, some of them seemed to feel that they had been hypnotized. They seemed to feel that I had been too liberal in my remarks toward the Southern whites, and that I had not spoken out strongly enough for what they termed the "rights" of the race. For a while there was a reaction, so far as a certain element of my own race was concerned, but later these reactionary ones seemed to have been won over to my way of believing and acting.

While speaking of changes in public sentiment, I recall that about ten years after the school at Tuskegee was established, I had an experience that I shall never forget. Dr. Lyman Abbott,[6] then the pastor of Plymouth Church, and also editor of the *Outlook* (then the *Christian Union*), asked me to write a letter for his paper giving my opinion of the exact condition, mental and moral of the coloured ministers in the South, as based upon my observations. I wrote the letter, giving the exact facts as I conceived them to be. The picture painted was a rather black one—or, since I am black, shall I say "white"? It could not be otherwise with a race but a few years out of slavery, a race which had not had time or opportunity to produce a competent ministry.

What I said soon reached every Negro minister in the country, I think, and the letters of condemnation which I received from them were not few.

---

[6]Lyman Abbott (1835–1922) was an American Congregationalist theologian, editor, and author.

I think that for a year after the publication of this article every association and every conference or religious body of any kind, of my race, that met, did not fail before adjourning to pass a resolution condemning me, or calling upon me to retract or modify what I had said. Many of these organizations went so far in their resolutions as to advise parents to cease sending their children to Tuskegee. One association even appointed a "missionary" whose duty it was to warn the people against sending their children to Tuskegee. This missionary had a son in the school, and I noticed that, whatever the "missionary" might have said or done with regard to others, he was careful not to take his son away from the institution. Many of the coloured papers, especially those that were the organs of religious bodies, joined in the general chorus of condemnation or demands for retraction.

During the whole time of the excitement, and through all the criticism, I did not utter a word of explanation or retraction. I knew that I was right, and that time and the sober second thought of the people would vindicate me. It was not long before the bishops and other church leaders began to make a careful investigation of the conditions of the ministry, and they found out that I was right. In fact, the oldest and most influential bishop in one branch of the Methodist Church said that my words were far too mild. Very soon public sentiment began making itself felt, in demanding a purifying of the ministry. While this is not yet complete by any means, I think I may say, without egotism, and I have been told by many of our most influential ministers, that my words had much to do with starting a demand for the placing of a higher type of men in the pulpit. I have had the satisfaction of having many who once condemned me thank me heartily for my frank words.

The change of the attitude of the Negro ministry, so far as regards myself, is so complete that at the present time I have no warmer friends among any class than I have among the clergymen. The improvement in the character and life of the Negro ministers is one of the most gratifying evidences of the progress of the race. My experience with them, as well as other events in my life, convince me that the thing to do, when one feels sure that he has said or done the right thing, and is condemned, is to stand still and keep quiet. If he is right, time will show it.

In the midst of the discussion which was going on concerning my Atlanta speech, I received a letter which I give below, from Dr. Gilman,[7] the President of Johns Hopkins University, who had been made chairman of the judges of award in connection with the Atlanta Exposition:—

Johns Hopkins University, Baltimore
President's Office, September 30, 1895

Dear Mr. Washington: Would it be agreeable to you to be one of the judges of Award in the Department of Education at Atlanta? If so, I shall be glad

[7]Daniel Coit Gilman (1831–1908) was an American educator and academician and president of the Johns Hopkins University from 1875 to 1901.

to place your name upon the list. A line by telegraph will be welcomed.
Yours very truly,

D. C. Gilman

I think I was even more surprised to receive this invitation than I had
been to receive the invitation to speak at the opening of the Exposition. It
was to be a part of my duty, as one of the jurors, to pass not only upon the
exhibits of the coloured schools, but also upon those of the white schools.
I accepted the position, and spent a month in Atlanta in performance of
the duties which it entailed. The board of jurors was a large one, consisting in all of sixty members. It was about equally divided between Southern white people and Northern white people. Among them were college
presidents, leading scientists and men of letters, and specialists in many
subjects. When the group of jurors to which I was assigned met for organization, Mr. Thomas Nelson Page,[8] who was one of the number, moved
that I be made secretary of that division, and the motion was unanimously
adopted. Nearly half of our division were Southern people. In performing
my duties in the inspection of the exhibits of white schools I was in every
case treated with respect, and at the close of our labours I parted from my
associates with regret.

I am often asked to express myself more freely than I do upon the political condition and the political future of my race. These recollections of my
experience in Atlanta give me the opportunity to do so briefly. My own belief is, although I have never before said so in so many words, that the time
will come when the Negro in the South will be accorded all the political
rights which his ability, character, and material possessions entitle him to.
I think, though, that the opportunity to freely exercise such political rights
will not come in any large degree through outside or artificial forcing, but
will be accorded to the Negro by the Southern white people themselves,
and that they will protect him in the exercise of those rights. Just as soon
as the South gets over the old feeling that it is being forced by "foreigners," or "aliens," to do something which it does not want to do, I believe
that the change in the direction that I have indicated is going to begin. In
fact, there are indications that it is already beginning in a slight degree.

Let me illustrate my meaning. Suppose that some months before the
opening of the Atlanta Exposition there had been a general demand from
the press and public platform outside the South that a Negro be given a
place on the opening programme, and that a Negro be placed upon the
board of jurors of award. Would any such recognition of the race have
taken place? I do not think so. The Atlanta officials went as far as they did
because they felt it to be a pleasure, as well as a duty, to reward what they
considered merit in the Negro race. Say what we will, there is something

[8]Thomas Nelson Page (1853–1922) of Virginia was a writer, historian, and diplomat.

in human nature which we cannot blot out, which makes one man, in the end, recognize and reward merit in another, regardless of colour or race.

I believe it is the duty of the Negro—as the greater part of the race is already doing—to deport himself modestly in regard to political claims, depending upon the slow but sure influences that proceed from the possession of property, intelligence, and high character for the full recognition of his political rights. I think that the according of the full exercise of political rights is going to be a matter of natural, slow growth, not an overnight, gourd-vine affair. I do not believe that the Negro should cease voting, for a man cannot learn the exercise of self-government by ceasing to vote, any more than a boy can learn to swim by keeping out of the water, but I do believe that in his voting he should more and more be influenced by those of intelligence and character who are his next-door neighbours.

I know coloured men who, through the encouragement, help, and advice of Southern white people, have accumulated thousands of dollars' worth of property, but who, at the same time, would never think of going to those same persons for advice concerning the casting of their ballots. This, it seems to me, is unwise and unreasonable, and should cease. In saying this I do not mean that the Negro should truckle, or not vote from principle, for the instant he ceases to vote from principle he loses the confidence and respect of the Southern white man even.

I do not believe that any state should make a law that permits an ignorant and poverty-stricken white man to vote, and prevents a black man in the same condition from voting. Such a law is not only unjust, but it will react, as all unjust laws do, in time; for the effect of such a law is to encourage the Negro to secure education and property, and at the same time it encourages the white man to remain in ignorance and poverty. I believe that in time, through the operation of intelligence and friendly race relations, all cheating at the ballot-box in the South will cease. It will become apparent that the white man who begins by cheating a Negro out of his ballot soon learns to cheat a white man out of his, and that the man who does this ends his career of dishonesty by the theft of property or by some equally serious crime. In my opinion, the time will come when the South will encourage all of its citizens to vote. It will see that it pays better, from every standpoint, to have healthy vigorous life than to have that political stagnation which always results when one-half of the population has no share and no interest in the Government.

As a rule, I believe in universal, free suffrage, but I believe that in the South we are confronted with peculiar conditions that justify the protection of the ballot in many of the states, for a while at least, either by an educational test, property test, or by both combined; but whatever tests are required, they should be made to apply with equal and exact justice to both races.

[1901]

▪▪ CONTEXT AND RESPONSE ▪▪

Olaudah Equiano (1745–1797)

The slave narrative, an account of a slave's endurance of harsh treatment and deprivation that typically concludes with freedom and good fortune, is an influential genre in American literature. Modern autobiographies and novels, including Richard Wright's *Black Boy* (1945) and Toni Morrison's *Beloved* (1987), that celebrate the individual's triumph over oppression form the enduring legacy of this genre. A significant addition to the slave narrative tradition, Booker T. Washington's twentieth-century autobiography *Up from Slavery* chronicles the influential African American's journey from illiterate slave to educated spokesperson for his race.

More than 100 freed or escaped slaves published their life stories between the mid-eighteenth century and the end of the Civil War; published in 1789, the autobiography of Olaudah Equiano was the first slave narrative to capture the world's imagination. As a privileged West African youth, Equiano survived a traumatic rite of passage aboard a slave ship only to labor in servitude once ashore, but he ultimately became a free and well-off British citizen. A recent controversy over whether Equiano was actually born in West Africa or North America raises the question of whether his famous account is legitimate or fabricated. However, the debate does not lessen the impact of his narrative. In this excerpt, a young Equiano realizes the full horror of his loss of liberty.

From Interesting Narrative of the Life of Olaudah Equiano; or, Gustavus Vassa, the African, Written by Himself

The first object which saluted my eyes when I arrived on the coast was the sea, and a slave ship, which was then riding at anchor, and waiting for its cargo. These filled me with astonishment, which was soon converted into terror when I was carried on board. I was immediately handled and tossed up to see if I were sound by some of the crew; and I was now persuaded that I had gotten into a world of bad spirits, and that they were going to kill me. Their complexions too differing so much from ours, their long hair, and the language they spoke, which was very different from any I had ever heard, united to confirm me in this belief. Indeed, such were the horrors of my views and fears at the moment, that, if ten thousand worlds had been my own, I would have freely parted with them all to have exchanged my condition with that of the meanest slave in my own country. When I looked around the ship too and saw a large furnace or copper boiling, and a multitude of black people of every description chained together, every one of their countenances express-ing dejection and sorrow, I no longer doubted of my fate; and, quite overpowered with horror and anguish, I fell motionless on the deck and fainted. When I recovered a little I found some black people about me, who I believed were some of those who brought me on board, and had been receiving their pay; they talked to me in order to cheer me, but all in vain. I asked them if we were not to be eaten by those white men with horrible looks, red faces, and long hair? They told me I was not; and one of the crew brought me a small portion of spirituous liquor in a wine glass; but being afraid of him, I would not take it out of his hand. One of the blacks therefore took it from him and gave it to me, and I took a little down my palate, which, instead of reviving me, as they thought it would, threw me into the greatest consternation at the strange feeling it produced having never tasted any such liquor before. Soon after this, the blacks who brought me on board went off, and left me abandoned to de-spair. I now saw myself deprived of all chance of returning to my native country, or even the least glimpse of hope of gaining the shore, which I now considered as friendly: and even wished for my former slavery, in preference for my present situation, which was filled with horrors of every kind, still heightened by my ignorance of what I was to undergo.

I was not long suffered to indulge my grief; I was soon put down under the decks, and there I received such a salutation in my nostrils as I had never experienced in my life; so that with the loathsomeness of the stench, and crying together, I became so sick and low that I was not able to eat, nor had I the least desire to taste anything. I now wished for the last friend, Death, to relieve me; but soon, to my grief, two of the white men offered me eatables; and, on my refusing to eat, one of them held me fast by the hands, and laid me across, I think, the wind-lass, and tied my feet, while the other flogged me severely. I had never experienced any thing of this kind before; and although not being used to the water, I naturally feared that element the first time I saw it; yet nevertheless, could I have got over the nettings, I would have jumped over the side; but I could not; and, besides, the crew used to watch us very closely who were not chained down to the decks, lest we should leap into the water; and I have seen some of these poor African prison-ers most severely cut for attempting to do so, and hourly whipped for not eating. This indeed was often the case with myself. In a little time after, amongst the poor chained men, I found some of my own nation, which in a small degree gave ease to my mind. I inquired of them what was to be done with us? they give me to understand we were to be carried to these white people's country to work for them.

CHARLES CHESNUTT ▩ (1858–1932)

Charles Chesnutt was born in Cleveland, Ohio, but he was raised in Fayetteville, North Carolina (his parents' home state), during the post–Civil War decades, a period of social and political upheaval and heightened racial tension in the South. Chesnutt taught in a local school and then, after a year in New York City, in 1884 he moved with his wife and family to Cleveland, where he passed the state bar exam and launched a career as a lawyer and legal stenographer.

Chesnutt published his first short story, "The Goophered Grapevine," in *The Atlantic Monthly* in August 1887, making use in it of African American storytelling traditions and techniques and aspects of black folk culture that few white readers had encountered. The notable Boston publisher Houghton Mifflin brought out a collection of Chesnutt's stories, titled *The Conjure Woman*, early in 1899, and later in the same year a second collection, *The Wife of His Youth and Other Stories of the Color Line*, was published as well.

Setting aside his legal career, Chesnutt devoted himself full-time to literature, delving into the topics of racial violence, racism, black-white sexual relationship, and intermarriage in three novels: *The House Behind the Cedars* (1900), *The Marrow of Tradition* (1901), and *The Colonel's Dream* (1905). These books are now praised, studied, and taught, especially *The Marrow of Tradition*, which is based on a horrific race riot that occurred in Wilmington, North Carolina, in 1898. But at the time of publication, they proved too disturbing and provocative to gain for Chesnutt the wide readership and economic security for his family that he desired.

So discouraged was Chesnutt about the poor sales of *The Marrow of Tradition* that he wondered whether he should examine the subject of race at all, observing in a letter (December 1901) to his publisher:

> I am beginning to suspect that the public as a rule does not care for books in which the principal characters are colored people.... I find a number of my friends advise me to break away from this theme for a while and write something which is entirely disassociated from it.... I am beginning to think somewhat the same way. If a novel which is generally acknowledged to be interesting, dramatic, well constructed, well written...cannot sell 5,000 copies within three months after its publication, there is something radically wrong somewhere, and I do not know where it is unless it be in the subject.

After 1905, often suffering from poor health, Chesnutt wrote only a few short stories.

"The Sheriff's Children" was originally published in *The Independent*, November 7, 1889, and was included in *The Wife of His Youth*; it was the first nondialect story by Chesnutt to appear in print. An emotionally charged, tragic narrative of race, miscegenation, and social authority and power, "The Sheriff's Children," like many of Chesnutt's best works, looks forward to the explorations of racial identity that William Faulkner, Richard Wright, and other writers undertook in their novels and stories decades later.

The issues of racial identity and intermixture that Chesnutt explored in "The Sheriff's Children" and other writings were immediate and personal for him. His parents were free African Americans. Both of his grandfathers were white (one of them was a slaveholder), and his grandmothers were mixed race. Chesnutt said that he was seven-eighths white, and he easily could have passed as white, though he never did. In an early journal entry, May 1880, he stated that his intention as a writer was not "so much the elevation of the colored people as the elevation of the whites" beyond "the unjust spirit of caste," a caste system that whites sought to implement and secure through intimidation and violence and strict, if misleading and falsifying, racial classification.

For biographical context and background, see Frances Richardson Keller, *An American Crusade: The Life of Charles Waddell Chesnutt* (1978); *The Journals of Charles W. Chesnutt*, ed. Richard H. Brodhead (1993); *To Be an Author: Letters of Charles W. Chesnutt, 1889–1905*, eds. Joseph R. McElrath Jr. and Robert C. Leitz III (1997); and *An Exemplary Citizen: Letters of Charles W. Chesnutt, 1906–1932*, eds. Jesse S. Crisler, Robert C. Leitz III, and Joseph R. McElrath Jr. (2002). See also William L. Andrews, *The Literary Career of Charles W. Chesnutt* (1980); and *Critical Essays on Charles W. Chesnutt*, ed. Joseph R. McElrath Jr. (1999). See also Sylvia L. Render, *Charles W. Chesnutt* (1980); Charles Duncan, *The Absent Man: The Narrative Craft of Charles W. Chesnutt* (1998); Matthew Wilson, *Whiteness in the Novels of Charles W. Chesnutt* (2004); and *Passing in the Works of Charles W. Chesnutt*, eds. Susan Prothro Wright and Ernestine Pickens Glass (2010). The *Library of America* series includes volumes of Chesnutt's essays and speeches (1999) and stories, novels, and essays (2002).

The Sheriff's Children

Branson County, North Carolina, is in a sequestered district of one of the staidest and most conservative States of the Union. Society in Branson County is almost primitive in its simplicity. Most of the white people own the farms they till, and even before the war there were no very wealthy families to force their neighbors, by comparison, into the category of "poor whites."

To Branson County, as to most rural communities in the South, the war is the one historical event that overshadows all others. It is the era from which all local chronicles are dated,—births, deaths, marriages, storms, freshets. No description of the life of any Southern community would be perfect that failed to emphasize the all pervading influence of the great conflict.

Yet the fierce tide of war that had rushed through the cities and along the great highways of the country had comparatively speaking but slightly disturbed the sluggish current of life in this region, remote from railroads and navigable streams. To the north in Virginia, to the west in Tennessee, and all along the seaboard the war had raged; but the thunder of its cannon had not disturbed the echoes of Branson County, where the loudest sounds heard were the crack of some hunter's rifle, the baying of some deep-mouthed hound, or the yodel of some tuneful negro on his way through the pine forest. To the east, Sherman's army[1] had passed on its march to the sea; but no straggling band of "bummers"[2] had penetrated the confines of Branson County. The war, it is true, had robbed the county of the flower of its young manhood; but the burden of taxation, the doubt and uncertainty of the conflict, and the sting of ultimate defeat, had been borne by the people with an apathy that robbed misfortune of half its sharpness.

The nearest approach to town life afforded by Branson County is found in the little village of Troy, the county scat, a hamlet with a population of four or five hundred.

Ten years make little difference in the appearance of these remote Southern towns. If a railroad is built through one of them, it infuses some enterprise; the social corpse is galvanized by fresh blood of civilization that pulses along the farthest ramifications of our great system of commercial highways. At the period of which I write, no railroad had come to Troy. If a traveler, accustomed to the bustling life of cities, could have ridden through Troy on a summer day, he might easily have fancied himself in a deserted village. Around him he would have seen weather-beaten houses, innocent of paint, the shingled roofs in many instances covered with a rich growth of moss. Here and there he would have met a razor-backed hog lazily rooting his way along the principal thoroughfare; and more than once he would probably have had to disturb the slumbers of some yellow dog, dozing away the hours in the ardent sunshine, and reluctantly yielding up his place in the middle of the dusty road.

On Saturdays the village presented a somewhat livelier appearance, and the shade trees around the court house square and along Front Street served as hitching-posts for a goodly number of horses and mules and stunted oxen, belonging to the farmer-folk who had come in to trade at the two or three local stores.

---

[1]William Tecumseh Sherman (1820–91). Civil War general best known for his infamous sixty-mile "March to the Sea" from Atlanta to Savannah at the end of 1864.
[2]Idle loafers, beggars.

A murder was a rare event in Branson County. Every well-informed citizen could tell the number of homicides committed in the county for fifty years back, and whether the slayer, in any given instance, had escaped, either by flight or acquittal, or had suffered the penalty of the law. So, when it became known in Troy early one Friday morning in summer, about ten years after the war, that old Captain Walker, who had served in Mexico under Scott,[3] and had left an arm on the field of Gettysburg, had been foully murdered during the night, there was intense excitement in the village. Business was practically suspended, and the citizens gathered in little groups to discuss the murder, and speculate upon the identity of the murderer. It transpired from testimony at the coroner's inquest, held during the morning, that a strange mulatto[4] had been seen going in the direction of Captain Walker's house the night before, and had been met going away from Troy early Friday morning, by a farmer on his way to town. Other circumstances seemed to connect the stranger with the crime. The sheriff organized a posse to search for him, and early in the evening, when most of the citizens of Troy were at supper, the suspected man was brought in and lodged in the county jail.

By the following morning the news of the capture had spread to the farthest limits of the county. A much larger number of people than usual came to town that Saturday,—bearded men in straw hats and blue homespun shirts, and butternut trousers of great amplitude of material and vagueness of outline; women in homespun frocks and slat-bonnets, with faces as expressionless as the dreary sandhills which gave them a meagre sustenance.

The murder was almost the sole topic of conversation. A steady stream of curious observers visited the house of mourning, and gazed upon the rugged face of the old veteran, now stiff and cold in death; and more than one eye dropped a tear at the remembrance of the cheery smile, and the joke—sometimes superannuated, generally feeble, but always good-natured—with which the captain had been wont to greet his acquaintances. There was a growing sentiment of anger among these stern men, toward the murderer who had thus cut down their friend, and a strong feeling that ordinary justice was too slight a punishment for such a crime.

Toward noon there was an informal gathering of citizens in Dan Tyson's store.

"I hear it 'lowed that Square Kyahtah's too sick ter hol' co'te this evenin'," said one, "an' that the purlim'nary hearin' 'll haf ter go over 'tel nex' week."

[3]General Winfield Scott (1786–1866). Known as Old Fuss and Feathers because of his attention to detail and penchant for gaudy uniforms, Scott's record included the War of 1812, the Mexican-American War, and the American Civil War (Union).
[4]A person having one white and one black parent, or a person of mixed race.

A look of disappointment went round the crowd.

"Hit's the durndes', meanes' murder ever committed in this caounty," said another, with moody emphasis.

"I s'pose the nigger 'lowed the Cap'n had some greenbacks,"[5] observed a third speaker.

"The Cap'n," said another, with an air of superior information, "has left two hairls of Confedrit money, which he 'spected 'ud be good some day er nuther."

This statement gave rise to a discussion of the speculative value of Confederate money[6]; but in a little while the conversation returned to the murder.

"Hangin' air too good fer the murderer," said one; "he oughter be burnt, stidier bein' hung."

There was an impressive pause at this point, during which a jug of moonlight whiskey went the round of the crowd.

"Well," said a round-shouldered farmer, who, in spite of his peaceable expression and faded gray eye, was known to have been one of the most daring followers of a rebel guerrilla chieftain, "what air yer gwine ter do about it? Ef you fellers air gwine ter set down an' let a wuthless nigger kill the bes' white man in Branson, an' not say nuthin' ner do nuthin', *I'll* move outen the caounty."

This speech gave tone and direction to the rest of the conversation. Whether the fear of losing the round-shouldered farmer operated to bring about the result or not is immaterial to this narrative; but, at all events, the crowd decided to lynch the negro. They agreed that this was the least that could be done to avenge the death of their murdered friend, and that it was a becoming way in which to honor his memory. They had some vague notions of the majesty of the law and the rights of the citizen, but in the passion of the moment these sunk into oblivion; a white man had been killed by a negro.

"The Cap'n was an ole sodger," said one of his friends solemnly. "He'll sleep better when he knows that a co'te-martial has be'n hilt an' jestice done."

By agreement the lynchers were to meet at Tyson's store at five o'clock in the afternoon, and proceed thence to the jail, which was situated down the Lumberton Dirt Road (as the old turnpike antedating the plank-road was called), about half a mile south of the court-house. When the preliminaries of the lynching had been arranged, and a committee appointed to manage the affair, the crowd dispersed, some to go to their dinners, and some to secure recruits for the lynching party.

---

[5]Slang for a U.S. legal-tender note first issued in 1862, named for the images printed in green ink on the back.
[6]Between 1861 and 1865, gambling on victory, the Confederacy issued currency to millions of Southerners. By the end of the war, Confederate notes were worthless.

It was twenty minutes to five o'clock, when an excited negro, panting and perspiring, rushed up to the back door of Sheriff Campbell's dwelling, which stood at a little distance from the jail and somewhat farther than the latter building from the court-house. A turbaned colored woman came to the door in response to the negro's knock.

"Hoddy, Sis' Nance."

"Hoddy, Brer Sam."

"Is de shurff in," inquired the negro.

"Yas, Brer Sam, he's eatin' his dinner," was the answer.

"Will yer ax 'im ter step ter de do' a minute, Sis' Nance?"

The woman went into the dining-room, and a moment later the sheriff came to the door. He was a tall, muscular man, of a ruddier complexion than is usual among Southerners. A pair of keen, deep-set gray eyes looked out from under bushy eyebrows, and about his mouth was a masterful expression, which a full beard, once sandy in color, but now profusely sprinkled with gray, could not entirely conceal. The day was hot; the sheriff had discarded his coat and vest, and had his white shirt open at the throat.

"What do you want, Sam?" he inquired of the negro, who stood hat in hand, wiping the moisture from his face with a ragged shirt-sleeve.

"Shurff, dey gwine ter hang de pris'ner w'at's lock' up in de jail. Dey're comin' dis a-way now. I wux layin' down on a sack er corn down at de sto', behine a pile er flour-bairls, w'en I hearn Doc' Cain en Kunnel Wright talkin' erbout it. I slip' outen de back do', en run here as fas' as I could. I hearn you say down ter de sto' once't dat you would n't let nobody take a pris'ner 'way fum you widout walkin' over yo' dead body, en I thought I'd let you know 'fo' dey come, so yer could pertec' de pris'ner."

The sheriff listened calmly, but his face grew firmer, and a determined gleam lit up his gray eyes. His frame grew more erect, and he unconsciously assumed the attitude of a soldier who momentarily expects to meet the enemy face to face.

"Much obliged, Sam," he answered. "I'll protect the prisoner. Who's coming?"

"I dunno who-all *is* comin'," replied the negro. "Dere's Mistah MeSwayne, en Doc' Cain, en Maje' McDonal', en Kunnel Wright, en a heap er yuthers. I wuz so skeered I done furgot mo'd'n half un em. I spec' dey mus' be mos' here by dis time, so I'll git outen de way, fer I don' want nobody fer ter think I wuz mix' up in dis business." The negro glanced nervously down the road toward the town, and made a movement as if to go away.

"Won't you have some dinner first?" asked the sheriff.

The negro looked longingly in at the open door, and sniffed the appetizing odor of boiled pork and collards.

"I ain't got no time fer ter tarry, Shurff," he said, "but Sis' Nance mought gin me sump'n I could kyar in my han' en eat on de way."

A moment later Nancy brought him a huge sandwich of split corn-pone, with a thick slice of fat bacon inserted between the halves, and a couple of baked yams. The negro hastily replaced his ragged hat on his head, dropped the yams in the pocket of his capacious trousers, and, taking the sandwich in his hand, hurried across the road and disappeared in the woods beyond.

The sheriff reentered the house, and put on his coat and hat. He then took down a double-barreled shotgun and loaded it with buckshot. Filling the chambers of a revolver with fresh cartridges, he slipped it into the pocket of the sack-coat which he wore.

A comely young woman in a calico dress watched these proceedings with anxious surprise.

"Where are you going, father?" she asked. She had not heard the conversation with the negro.

"I am goin' over to the jail," responded the sheriff. "There's a mob comin' this way to lynch the nigger we've got locked up. But they won't do it," he added, with emphasis.

"Oh, father! don't go!" pleaded the girl, clinging to his arm; "they'll shoot you if you don't give him up."

"You never mind me, Polly," said her father, reassuringly, as he gently unclasped her hands from his arm. "I'll take care of myself and the prisoner, too. There ain't a man in Branson County that would shoot me. Besides, I have faced fire too often to be scared away from my duty. You keep close in the house," he continued, "and if any one disturbs you just use the old horse-pistol in the top bureau drawer. It's a little old-fashioned, but it did good work a few years ago."

The young girl shuddered at this sanguinary[7] allusion, but made no further objection to her father's departure.

The sheriff of Branson was a man far above the average of the community in wealth, education, and social position. His had been one of the few families in the county that before the war had owned large estates and numerous slaves. He had graduated at the State University at Chapel Hill, and had kept up some acquaintance with current literature and advanced thought. He had traveled some in his youth, and was looked up to in the county as an authority on all subjects connected with the outer world. At first an ardent supporter of the Union, he had opposed the secession movement in his native State as long as opposition availed to stem the tide of public opinion. Yielding at last to the force of circumstances, he had entered the Confederate service rather late in the war, and served with distinction through several campaigns, rising in time to the rank of colonel. After the war he had taken the oath of allegiance, and had been chosen by the people as the most available candidate for the office of sheriff,

---

[7]Bloody.

to which he had been elected without opposition. He had filled the office for several terms, and was universally popular with his constituents.

Colonel or Sheriff Campbell, as he was indifferently called, as the military or civil title happened to be most important in the opinion of the person addressing him, had a high sense of the responsibility attaching to his office. He had sworn to do his duty faithfully, and he knew what his duty was, as sheriff, perhaps more clearly than he had apprehended it in other passages of his life. It was, therefore, with no uncertainty in regard to his course that he prepared his weapons and went over to the jail. He had no fears for Polly's safety.

The sheriff had just locked the heavy front door of the jail behind him when a half dozen horsemen, followed by a crowd of men on foot, came round a bend in the road and drew near the jail. They halted in front of the picket fence that surrounded the building, while several of the committee of arrangements rode on a few rods farther to the sheriff's house. One of them dismounted and rapped on the door with his riding-whip.

"Is the sheriff at home?" he inquired.

"No, he has just gone out," replied Polly, who had come to the door.

"We want the jail keys," he continued.

"They are not here," said Polly. "The sheriff has them himself." Then she added, with assumed indifference, "He is at the jail now."

The man turned away, and Polly went into the front room, from which she peered anxiously between the slats of the green blinds of a window that looked toward the jail. Meanwhile the messenger returned to his companions and announced his discovery. It looked as though the sheriff had learned of their design and was preparing to resist it.

One of them stepped forward and rapped on the jail door.

"Well, what is it?" said the sheriff, from within.

"We want to talk to you, Sheriff," replied the spokesman.

There was a little wicket in the door; this the sheriff opened, and answered through it.

"All right, boys, talk away. You are all strangers to me, and I don't know what business you can have." The sheriff did not think it necessary to recognize anybody in particular on such an occasion; the question of identity sometimes comes up in the investigation of these extra-judicial executions.

"We're a committee of citizens and we want to get into the jail."

"What for? It ain't much trouble to get into jail. Most people want to keep out."

The mob was in no humor to appreciate a joke, and the sheriff's witticism fell dead upon an unresponsive audience.

"We want to have a talk with the nigger that killed Cap'n Walker."

"You can talk to that nigger in the court-house, when he's brought out for trial. Court will be in session here next week. I know what you fellows want, but you can't get my prisoner to-day. Do you want to take the bread out of a poor man's mouth? I get seventy-five cents a day for keeping this prisoner, and he's the only one in jail. I can't have my family suffer just to please you fellows."

One or two young men in the crowd laughed at the idea of Sheriff Campbell's suffering for want of seventy-five cents a day; but they were frowned into silence by those who stood near them.

"Ef yer don't let us in," cried a voice, "we'll bu's' the do' open."

"Bust away," answered the sheriff, raising his voice so that all could hear. "But I give you fair warning. The first man that tries it will be filled with buckshot. I'm sheriff of this county; I know my duty, and I mean to do it."

"What's the use of kicking, Sheriff?" argued one of the leaders of the mob. "The nigger is sure to hang anyhow; he richly deserves it; and we've got to do something to teach the niggers their places, or white people won't be able to live in the county."

"There's no use talking, boys," responded the sheriff. "I'm a white man outside, but in this jail I'm sheriff; and if this nigger's to be hung in this county, I propose to do the hanging. So you fellows might as well right-about-face, and march back to Troy. You've had a pleasant trip, and the exercise will be good for you. You know *me*. I've got powder and ball, and I've faced fire before now, with nothing between me and the enemy, and I don't mean to surrender this jail while I'm able to shoot." Having thus announced his determination, the sheriff closed and fastened the wicket, and looked around for the best position from which to defend the building.

The crowd drew off a little, and the leaders conversed together in low tones.

The Branson County jail was a small, two-story brick building, strongly constructed, with no attempt at architectural ornamentation. Each story was divided into two large cells by a passage running from front to rear.

A grated iron door gave entrance from the passage to each of the four cells. The jail seldom had many prisoners in it, and the lower windows had been boarded up. When the sheriff had closed the wicket, he ascended the steep wooden stairs to the upper floor. There was no window at the front of the upper passage, and the most available position from which to watch the movements of the crowd below was the front window of the cell occupied by the solitary prisoner.

The sheriff unlocked the door and entered the cell. The prisoner was crouched in a corner, his yellow face, blanched with terror, looking ghastly in the semi-darkness of the room. A cold perspiration had gathered on his forehead, and his teeth were chattering with affright.

"For God's sake, Sheriff," he murmured hoarsely, "don't let 'em lynch me; I didn't kill the old man."

The sheriff glanced at the cowering wretch with a look of mingled contempt and loathing.

"Get up," he said sharply. "You will probably be hung sooner or later, but it shall not be to-day, if I can help it. I'll unlock your fetters, and if I can't hold the jail, you'll have to make the best fight you can. If I'm shot, I'll consider my responsibility at an end."

There were iron fetters on the prisoner's ankles, and handcuffs on his wrists. These the sheriff unlocked, and they fell clanking to the floor.

"Keep back from the window," said the sheriff. "They might shoot if they saw you."

The sheriff drew toward the window a pine bench which formed a part of the scanty furniture of the cell, and laid his revolver upon it. Then he took his gun in hand, and took his stand at the side of the window where he could with least exposure of himself watch the movements of the crowd below.

The lynchers had not anticipated any determined resistance. Of course they had looked for a formal protest, and perhaps a sufficient show of opposition to excuse the sheriff in the eye of any stickler for legal formalities. They had not however come prepared to fight a battle, and no one of them seemed willing to lead an attack upon the jail. The leaders of the party conferred together with a good deal of animated gesticulation, which was visible to the sheriff from his outlook, though the distance was too great for him to hear what was said. At length one of them broke away from the group, and rode back to the main body of the lynchers, who were restlessly awaiting orders.

"Well, boys," said the messenger, "we'll have to let it go for the present. The sheriff says he'll shoot, and he's got the drop on us this time. There ain't any of us that want to follow Cap'n Walker jest yet. Besides, the sheriff is a good fellow, and we don't want to hurt 'im. But," he added, as if to reassure the crowd, which began to show signs of disappointment, "the nigger might as well say his prayers, for he ain't got long to live."

There was a murmur of dissent from the mob, and several voices insisted that an attack be made on the jail. But pacific counsels finally prevailed, and the mob sullenly withdrew.

The sheriff stood at the window until they had disappeared around the bend in the road. He did not relax his watchfulness when the last one was out of sight. Their withdrawal might be a mere feint, to be followed by a further attempt. So closely, indeed, was his attention drawn to the outside, that he neither saw nor heard the prisoner creep stealthily across the floor, reach out his hand and secure the revolver which lay on the bench behind the sheriff, and creep as noiselessly back to his place in the corner of the room.

A moment after the last of the lynching party had disappeared there was a shot fired from the woods across the road; a bullet whistled by the window and buried itself in the wooden casing a few inches from where the sheriff was standing. Quick as thought, with the instinct born of a semi-guerrilla army experience, he raised his gun and fired twice at the point from which a faint puff of smoke showed the hostile bullet to have been sent. He stood a moment watching, and then rested his gun against the window, and reached behind him mechanically for the other weapon. It was not on the bench. As the sheriff realized this fact, he turned his head and looked into the muzzle of the revolver.

"Stay where you are, Sheriff," said the prisoner, his eyes glistening, his face almost ruddy with excitement.

The sheriff mentally cursed his own carelessness for allowing him to be caught in such a predicament. He had not expected anything of the kind. He had relied on the negro's cowardice and subordination in the presence of an armed white man as a matter of course. The sheriff was a brave man, but realized that the prisoner had him at an immense disadvantage. The two men stood thus for a moment, fighting a harmless duel with their eyes.

"Well, what do you mean to do?" asked the sheriff with apparent calmness.

"To get away, of course," said the prisoner, in a tone which caused the sheriff to look at him more closely, and with an involuntary feeling of apprehension; if the man was not mad, he was in a state of mind akin to madness, and quite as dangerous. The sheriff felt that he must speak the prisoner fair, and watch for a chance to turn the tables on him. The keen-eyed, desperate man before him was a different being altogether from the groveling wretch who had begged so piteously for life a few minutes before.

At length the sheriff spoke:—

"Is this your gratitude to me for saving your life at the risk of my own? If I had not done so, you would now be swinging from the limb of some neighboring tree."

"True," said the prisoner, "you saved my life, but for how long? When you came in, you said Court would sit next week. When the crowd went away they said I had not long to live. It is merely a choice of two ropes."

"While there's life there's hope," replied the sheriff. He uttered this commonplace mechanically, while his brain was busy in trying to think out some way of escape. "If you are innocent you can prove it."

The mulatto kept his eye upon the sheriff. "I did n't kill the old man," he replied; "but I shall never be able to clear myself. I was at his house at nine o'clock. I stole from it the coat that was on my back when I was taken. I would be convicted, even with a fair trial, unless the real murderer were discovered beforehand."

The sheriff knew this only too well. While he was thinking what argument next to use, the prisoner continued:—

"Throw me the keys—no, unlock the door."

The sheriff stood a moment irresolute. The mulatto's eye glittered ominously. The sheriff crossed the room and unlocked the door leading into the passage.

"Now go down and unlock the outside door."

The heart of the sheriff leaped within him. Perhaps he might make a dash for liberty, and gain the outside. He descended the narrow stairs, the prisoner keeping close behind him.

The sheriff inserted the huge iron key into the lock. The rusty bolt yielded slowly. It still remained for him to pull the door open.

"Stop!" thundered the mulatto, who seemed to divine the sheriff's purpose. "Move a muscle, and I'll blow your brains out."

The sheriff obeyed; he realized that his chance had not yet come.

"Now keep on that side of the passage, and go back upstairs."

Keeping the sheriff under cover of the revolver, the mulatto followed him up the stairs. The sheriff expected the prisoner to lock him into the cell and make his own escape. He had about come to the conclusion that the best thing he could do under the circumstances was to submit quietly, and take his chances of recapturing the prisoner after the alarm had been given. The sheriff had faced death more than once upon the battlefield. A few minutes before, well armed, and with a brick wall between him and them he had dared a hundred men to fight; but he felt instinctively that the desperate man confronting him was not to be trifled with, and he was too prudent a man to risk his life against such heavy odds. He had Polly to look after, and there was a limit beyond which devotion to duty would be quixotic and even foolish.

"I want to get away," said the prisoner, "and I don't want to be captured; for if I am I know I will be hung on the spot. I am afraid," he added somewhat reflectively, "that in order to save myself I shall have to kill you."

"Good God!" exclaimed the sheriff in involuntary terror; "you would not kill the man to whom you owe your own life."

"You speak more truly than you know," replied the mulatto. "I indeed owe my life to you."

The sheriff started. He was capable of surprise, even in that moment of extreme peril. "Who are you?" he asked in amazement.

"Tom, Cicely's son," returned the other. He had closed the door and stood talking to the sheriff through the grated opening. "Don't you remember Cicely—Cicely whom you sold, with her child, to the speculator on his way to Alabama?"

The sheriff did remember. He had been sorry for it many a time since. It had been the old story of debts, mortgages, and bad crops. He had quarreled with the mother. The price offered for her and her child had been unusually large, and he had yielded to the combination of anger and pecuniary stress.

"Good God!" he gasped, "you would not murder your own father?"

"My father?" replied the mulatto. "It were well enough for me to claim the relationship, but it comes with poor grace from you to ask anything by reason of it. What father's duty have you ever performed for me? Did you give me your name, or even your protection? Other white men gave their colored sons freedom and money, and sent them to the free States. *You* sold *me* to the rice swamps."

"I at least gave you the life you cling to," murmured the sheriff.

"Life?" said the prisoner, with a sarcastic laugh. "What kind of a life? You gave me your own blood, your own features,—no man need look at us together twice to see that,—and you gave me a black mother. Poor wretch! She died under the lash, because she had enough womanhood to call her soul her own. You gave me a white man's spirit, and you made me a slave, and crushed it out."

"But you are free now," said the sheriff. He had not doubted, could not doubt, the mulatto's word. He knew whose passions coursed beneath that swarthy skin and burned in the black eyes opposite his own. He saw in this mulatto what he himself might have become had not the safeguards of parental restraint and public opinion been thrown around him.

"Free to do what?" replied the mulatto. "Free in name, but despised and scorned and set aside by the people to whose race I belong far more than to my mother's."

"There are schools," said the sheriff. "You have been to school." He had noticed that the mulatto spoke more eloquently and used better language than most Branson County people.

"I have been to school, and dreamed when I went that it would work some marvelous change in my condition. But what did I learn? I learned to feel that no degree of learning or wisdom will change the color of my skin and that I shall always wear what in my own country is a badge of degradation. When I think about it seriously I do not care particularly for such a life. It is the animal in me, not the man, that flees the gallows. I owe you nothing," he went on, "and expect nothing of you; and it would be no more than justice if I should avenge upon you my mother's wrongs and my own. But still I hate to shoot you; I have never yet taken human life—for I did *not* kill the old captain. Will you promise to give no alarm and make no attempt to capture me until morning, if I do not shoot?"

So absorbed were the two men in their colloquy and their own tumultuous thoughts that neither of them had heard the door below move upon its hinges. Neither of them had heard a light step come stealthily up the stairs, nor seen a slender form creep along the darkening passage toward the mulatto.

The sheriff hesitated. The struggle between his love of life and his sense of duty was a terrific one. It may seem strange that a man who could sell his own child into slavery should hesitate at such a moment, when his life was trembling in the balance. But the baleful influence of human slavery poisoned the very fountains of life, and created new standards of right. The sheriff was conscientious; his conscience had merely been warped by his environment. Let no one ask what his answer would have been; he was spared the necessity of a decision.

"Stop," said the mulatto, "you need not promise. I could not trust you if you did. It is your life for mine; there is but one safe way for me; you must die."

He raised his arm to fire, when there was a flash—a report from the passage behind him. His arm fell heavily at his side, and the pistol dropped at his feet.

The sheriff recovered first from his surprise, and throwing open the door secured the fallen weapon. Then seizing the prisoner he thrust him into the cell and locked the door upon him; after which he turned to Polly, who leaned half-fainting against the wall, her hands clasped over her heart.

"Oh, father, I was just in time!" she cried hysterically, and, wildly sobbing, threw herself into her father's arms.

"I watched until they all went away," she said. "I heard the shot from the woods and I saw you shoot. Then when you did not come out I feared something had happened, that perhaps you had been wounded. I got out the other pistol and ran over here. When I found the door open, I knew something was wrong, and when I heard voices I crept upstairs, and reached the top just in time to hear him say he would kill you. Oh, it was a narrow escape!"

When she had grown somewhat calmer, the sheriff left her standing there and went back into the cell. The prisoner's arm was bleeding from a flesh wound. His bravado had given place to a stony apathy. There was no sign in his face of fear or disappointment or feeling of any kind. The sheriff sent Polly to the house for cloth, and bound up the prisoner's wound with a rude skill acquired during his army life.

"I'll have a doctor come and dress the wound in the morning," he said to the prisoner. "It will do very well until then, if you will keep quiet. If the doctor asks you how the wound was caused, you can say that you were struck by the bullet fired from the woods. It would do you no good to have it known that you were shot while attempting to escape."

The prisoner uttered no word of thanks or apology, but sat in sullen silence. When the wounded arm had been bandaged, Polly and her father returned to the house.

The sheriff was in an unusually thoughtful mood that evening. He put salt in his coffee at supper, and poured vinegar over his pancakes. To many of Polly's questions he returned random answers. When he had gone to bed he lay awake for several hours.

In the silent watches of the night, when he was alone with God, there came into his mind a flood of unaccustomed thoughts. An hour or two before, standing face to face with death, he had experienced a sensation similar to that which drowning men are said to feel—a kind of clarifying of the moral faculty, in which the veil of the flesh, with its obscuring passions and prejudices, is pushed aside for a moment, and all the acts of one's life stand out, in the clear light of truth, in their correct proportions and relations,—a state of mind in which one sees himself as God may be supposed to see him. In the reaction following his rescue, this feeling had given place for a time to far different emotions. But now, in the silence of midnight, something of this clearness of spirit returned to the sheriff. He saw that he had owed some duty to this son of his,—that neither law nor custom could destroy a responsibility inherent in the nature of mankind. He could not thus, in the eyes of God at least, shake off the consequences of his sin. Had he never sinned, this wayward spirit would never have come back from the vanished past to haunt him. As these thoughts came, his anger against the mulatto died away, and in its place there sprang up a great pity. The hand of parental authority might have restrained the passions he had seen burning in the prisoner's eyes when the desperate man spoke the words which had seemed to doom his father to death. The sheriff felt that he might have saved this fiery spirit from the slough of slavery; that he might have sent him to the free North, and given him there, or in some other land, an opportunity to turn to usefulness and honorable pursuits the talents that had run to crime, perhaps to madness; he might, still less, have given this son of his the poor simulacrum[8] of liberty which men of his caste could possess in a slave-holding community; or least of all, but still something, he might have kept the boy on the plantation, where the burdens of slavery would have fallen lightly upon him.

The sheriff recalled his own youth. He had inherited an honored name to keep untarnished; he had had a future to make; the picture of a fair young bride had beckoned him on to happiness. The poor wretch now stretched upon a pallet of straw between the brick walls of the jail had had none of these things,—no name, no father, no mother—in the true meaning of motherhood,—and until the past few years no possible future, and then one vague and shadowy in its outline, and dependent for form and substance upon the slow solution of a problem in which there were many unknown quantities.

From what he might have done to what he might yet do was an easy transition for the awakened conscience of the sheriff. It occurred to him,

---

[8]Having merely the appearance of a certain thing without possessing its substance or proper qualities.

purely as a hypothesis, that he might permit his prisoner to escape; but his oath of office, his duty as sheriff, stood in the way of such a course, and the sheriff dismissed the idea from his mind. He could, however, investigate the circumstances of the murder, and move Heaven and earth to discover the real criminal, for he no longer doubted the prisoner's innocence; he could employ counsel for the accused, and perhaps influence public opinion in his favor. An acquittal once secured, some plan could be devised by which the sheriff might in some degree atone for his crime against this son of his—against society—against God.

When the sheriff had reached this conclusion he fell into an unquiet slumber, from which he awoke late the next morning.

He went over to the jail before breakfast and found the prisoner lying on his pallet, his face turned to the wall; he did not move when the sheriff rattled the door.

"Good-morning," said the latter, in a tone intended to waken the prisoner.

There was no response. The sheriff looked more keenly at the recumbent figure; there was an unnatural rigidity about its attitude.

He hastily unlocked the door and, entering the cell, bent over the prostrate form. There was no sound of breathing; he turned the body over—it was cold and stiff. The prisoner had torn the bandage from his wound and bled to death during the night. He had evidently been dead several hours.

[1899]

HAMLIN GARLAND ■ (1860–1940)

Hamlin Garland based much of his fiction on his experiences as a poor boy and hardworking young man on farms in Wisconsin, Illinois, Iowa, and the Dakota territory. Influenced by the realist theory and practice of William Dean Howells and encouraged by Howells himself, Oliver Wendell Holmes, and other authors whom he had met while living in Boston, Garland began writing short stories, which were published in 1891 in *Main-Travelled Roads*, his most important book. He published several more collections of stories as well as a work of literary criticism, *Crumbling Idols* (1894), and a number of novels, the best of which is *Rose of Dutcher's Coolly* (1895), about a farm girl from Wisconsin who moves to Chicago and struggles to acquire a college education and become a writer. The prolific Garland (the author of some forty books) also wrote autobiographies, including *A Son of the Middle Border* "(1917) and *A Daughter of the Middle Border*" (1921).

Bleak, desolate, and bitter, Garland's most enduring work dramatizes the harsh but heroic lives led by Midwestern and Plains farmers. These stories exemplify Garland's theory of "veritism," which for him meant an accurate, unsentimental depiction of the outer circumstances and inner truths of the people he took as his subject. "Write of those things of which you know most," Garland professed, "and for which you care most. By so doing you will be true to yourself, true to your locality, and true to your time."

Garland's dedication page of *Main-Travelled Roads*, stories of "sorrow, resignation, and a sort of dumb despair," located this belief close to home:

> To my father and mother, whose half-century pilgrimage on the main-travelled road of life has brought them only toil and deprivation, this book of stories is dedicated by a son to whom every day brings a deepening sense of his parents' silent heroism.

A reformer as well as a writer, Garland maintained that to "raise the standard of art in America you must raise the standard of living." The story "Under the Lion's Paw," Garland's best, expresses his commitment to social and economic justice, and he often read it at meetings of tax-reform groups.

For an overview: Joseph B. McCullough, *Hamlin Garland* (1978). For biography, consult Donald Pizer, *Hamlin Garland's Early Work and Career* (1960); and *Selected Letters of Hamlin Garland*, eds. Keith Newlin and Joseph B. McCullough. (1998). Also valuable: *Critical Essays on Hamlin Garland*, eds. James Nagel (1982); and *The Critical Reception of Hamlin Garland, 1891–1978*, eds. Charles L. P. Silet, Robert E. Welch, and Richard Boudreau (1985). See also Keith Newlin, *Hamlin Garland: A Life* (2008); and *Hamlin Garland, Prairie Radical: Writings from the 1890s*, ed. Donald Pizer (2010).

Under the Lion's Paw

1

It was the last of autumn and first day of winter coming together. All day long the ploughmen on their prairie farms had moved to and fro on their wide level fields through the falling snow, which melted as it fell, wetting them to the skin—all day, notwithstanding the frequent squalls of snow, the dripping, desolate clouds, and the muck of the furrows, black and tenacious as tar.

Under their dripping harnesses the horses swung to and fro silently, with that marvelous uncomplaining patience which marks the horse. All day the wild-geese, honking wildly, as they sprawled sidewise down the wind, seemed to be fleeing from an enemy behind, and with neck out-thrust and wings extended, sailed down the wind, soon lost to sight.

Yet the ploughman behind his plough, though the snow lay on his ragged great-coat, and the cold clinging mud rose on his heavy boots, fettering him like gyves,[1] whistled in the very beard of the gale. As day passed, the snow, ceasing to melt, lay along the ploughed land, and lodged in the depth of the stubble, till on each slow round the last furrow stood out black and shining as jet between the ploughed land and the gray stubble.

When night began to fall, and the geese, flying low, began to alight invisibly in the near corn field, Stephen Council was still at work "finishing a land." He rode on his sulky-plough,[2] when going with the wind, but walked when facing it. Sitting bent and cold but cheery under his slouch hat, he talked encouragingly to his weary four-in-hand.[3]

"Come round there, boys!—round agin! We got t' finish this land. Come in there, Dan! *Stiddy*, Kate!—stiddy! None o' y'r tantrums, Kittie. It's purty tuff, but got a be did. *Tchk! tchk!* Step along, Pete! Don't let Kate git y'r single-tree[4] on the wheel. *Once* more!"

They seemed to know what he meant, and that this was the last round, for they worked with greater vigor than before.

"Once more, boys, an' sez I, oats an' a nice warm stall, an' sleep f'r all."

By the time the last furrow was turned on the land it was too dark to see the house, and the snow was changing to rain again. The tired and hungry man could see the light from the kitchen shining through the leafless hedge, and lifting a great shout, he yelled, "*Supper* f'r a half a dozen!"

It was nearly eight o'clock by the time he had finished his chores and started for supper. He was picking his way carefully through the mud, when the tall form of a man loomed up before him with a premonitory cough.

[1]Irons, shackles.
[2]A horse-drawn plow with wheels and a seat for a driver.
[3]A vehicle with four horses driven by one person.
[4]A crosspiece used to fasten a harness.

"Waddy ye want?" was the rather startled question of the farmer.

"Well, ye see," began the stranger, in a deprecating tone, "we'd like t' git in f'r the night. We've tried every house f'r the last two miles, but they hadn't any room f'r us. My wife's jest about sick, 'n' the children are cold and hungry—"

"Oh, y'want a stay all night, eh?"

"Yes, sir; it 'ud be a great accom—"

"Waal, I don't make it a practice t' turn anybuddy away hungry, not on sech nights as this. Drive right in. We 'ain't got much, but sech as it is—"

But the stranger had disappeared. And soon his steaming, weary team, with drooping heads and swinging single-trees, moved past the well on to the block beside the path. Council stood at the side of the "schooner"[5] and helped the children out—two little half-sleeping children—and then a small woman with a babe in her arms.

"There ye go!" he shouted, jovially, to the children. "*Now* we're all right. Run right along to the house there, an' tell Mam' Council you wants sumpthin' t' eat. Right this way, Mis'—Keep right off t' the right there. I'll go an' git a lantern. Come," he said to the dazed and silent group at his side.

"Mother," he shouted, as he neared the fragrant and warmly lighted kitchen, "here are some wayfarers an' folks who need sumpthin' t' eat an' a place t' snooze," he ended, pushing them all in.

Mrs. Council, a large, jolly, rather coarse-looking woman, took the children in her arms. "Come right in, you little rabbits. 'Most asleep, hay? Now here's a drink o' milk f'r each o'ye. I'll have s'm' tea in a minute. Take off y'r things and set up t' the fire."

While she set the children to drinking milk, Council got out his lantern and went out to the barn to help the stranger about his team, where his loud, hearty voice could be heard as it came and went between the hay-mow and the stalls.

The woman came to light as a small, timid, and discouraged-looking woman, but still pretty, in a thin and sorrowful way.

"Land sakes! An' you've travelled all the way from Clear Lake t'day in this mud! Waal! waal! No wunder you're all tired out. Don't wait f'r the men, Mis'—" She hesitated, waiting for the name. "Haskins."

"Mis' Haskins, set right up to the table an' take a good swig o' that tea, whilst I make y' s'm' toast. It's green tea, an' it's good. I tell Council as I git older I don't seem t' enjoy Young Hyson n'r gunpowder. I want the reel green tea, jest as it comes off'n the vines. Seems t' have more heart in it some way. Don't s'pose it has. Council says it's all in m' eye."

Going on in this easy way, she soon had the children filled with bread and milk and the woman thoroughly at home, eating some toast and sweet melon pickles, and sipping the tea.

[5]A covered wagon used by the 19th-century pioneers in crossing the North American prairies.

"*See* the little rats!" she laughed at the children. "They're full as they can stick now, and they want to go to bed. Now don't git up, Mis' Haskins; set right where you are, an' let me look after 'em. I know all about young ones, though I *am* all alone now. Jane went an' married last fall. But, as I tell Council, it's lucky we keep our health. Set right *there*, Mis' Haskins; I won't have you stir a finger."

It was an unmeasured pleasure to sit there in the warm, homely kitchen, the jovial chatter of the housewife driving out and holding at bay the growl of the impotent, cheated wind.

The little woman's eyes filled with tears, which fell down upon the sleeping baby in her arms. The world was not so desolate and cold and hopeless, after all.

"Now I hope Council won't stop out there and talk politics all night. He's the greatest man to talk politics an' read the *Tribune*. How old is it?"

She broke off and peered down at the face of the babe.

"Two months 'n' five days," said the mother, with a mother's exactness.

"Ye don't say! I want t' know! The dear little pudzy-wudzy," she went on, stirring it up in the neighborhood of the ribs with her fat forefinger.

"Pooty tough on 'oo to go gallavant'n' 'cross lots this way."

"Yes, that's so; a man can't lift a mountain," said Council, entering the door. "Sarah, this is Mr. Haskins, from Kansas. He's been eat up 'n' drove out by grasshoppers."

"Glad t' see yeh! Pa, empty that wash-basin, 'n' give him a chance t' wash."

Haskins was a tall man, with a thin, gloomy face. His hair was a reddish brown, like his coat, and seemed equally faded by the wind and sun. And his sallow face, though hard and set, was pathetic somehow. You would have felt that he had suffered much by the line of his mouth showing under his thin yellow mustache.

"Hain't Ike got home yet, Sairy?"

"Hain't seen 'im."

"W-a-a-l, set right up, Mr. Haskins; wade right into what we've got; 'tain't much, but we manage t' live on it—least I do; *she* gits fat on it," laughed Council, pointing his thumb at his wife.

After supper, while the women put the children to bed, Haskins and Council talked on, seated near the huge cooking stove, the steam rising from their wet clothing. In the Western fashion Council told as much of his own life as he drew from his guest. He asked but few questions; but by-and-by the story of Haskins's struggles and defeat came out. The story was a terrible one, but he told it quietly, seated with his elbows on his knees, gazing most of the time at the hearth.

"I didn't like the looks of the country, anyhow," Haskins said, partly rising and glancing at his wife. "I was ust t' northern Ingyannie,[6] where we hav' lots of timber 'n' lots of rain, 'n' I didn't like the looks o' that dry

[6]Indiana.

prairie. What galled me the worst was goin' s' far away acrosst so much fine land layin' all through here vacant."

"And the 'hoppers eat ye four years hand running, did they?"

"Eat! They wiped us out. They chawed everything that was green. They jest set around waitin' f'r us to die t' eat us too. My God! I ust t' dream of 'em sitt'n' 'round on the bedpost, six feet long, workin' their jaws. They eet the fork handles. They got worse 'n' worse, till they jest rolled on one another, piled up like snow in winter. Well, it ain't no use; if I was t' talk all winter I couldn't tell nawthin'. But all the while I couldn't help thinkin' of all that land back here that nobuddy was usin, that I ought a had 'stead o' bein' out there in that cussed country."

"Waal, why didn't ye stop an' settle here?" asked Ike, who had come in and was eating his supper.

"Fer the simple reason that you fellers wantid ten 'r fifteen dollars an acre fer the bare land, and I hadn't no money fer that kind o' thing."

"Yes, I do my own work," Mrs. Council was heard to say in the pause which followed. "I'm a-gettin' purty heavy t' be on m' laigs all day, but we can't afford t' hire, so I keep rackin' around somehow, like a foundered horse. S'lame—I tell Council he can't tell *how* lame I am, f'r I'm jest as lame in one laig as t'other." And the good soul laughed at the joke on herself as she took a handful of flour and dusted the biscuit board to keep the dough from sticking.

"Well, I hain't *never* been very strong," said Mrs. Haskins. "Our folks was Canadians an' small-boned, and then since my last child I hain't got up again fairly. I don't like t'complain—Tim has about all he can bear now— but they was days this week when I jest wanted to lay right down an' die."

"Waal, now, I'll tell ye," said Council, from his side of the stove, silencing everybody with his good-natured roar, "I'd go down and *see* Butler *anyway*, if I was you. I guess he'd let you have his place purty cheap; the farm's all run down. He's ben anxious t' let t' somebuddy next year. It 'ud be a good chance fer you. Anyhow, you go to bed, and sleep like a babe. I've got some ploughin' t' do anyhow, an' we'll see if somethin' can't be done about your case. Ike, you go out an' see if the horses is all right, an' I'll show the folks t' bed."

When the tired husband and wife were lying under the generous quilts of the spare bed, Haskins listened a moment to the wind in the eaves, and then said, with a slow and solemn tone,

"There are people in this world who are good enough t' be angels, an' only haff t' die to *be* angels."

2

Jim Butler was one of those men called in the West "land poor." Early in the history of Rock River he had come into the town and started in the grocery business in a small way, occupying a small building in a mean part of the town. At this period of his life he earned all he got, and was up early and late, sorting beans, working over butter, and carting his goods to and from the station. But a change came over him at the end of the second year, when he sold a lot of land for four times what he paid for it. From that time forward he believed in land speculation as the surest way of getting rich. Every cent he could save or spare from his trade he put into land at forced sale, or mortgages on land, which were "just as good as the wheat," he was accustomed to say.

Farm after farm fell into his hands, until he was recognized as one of the leading land-owners of the county. His mortgages were scattered all over Cedar County, and as they slowly but surely fell in, he sought usually to retain the former owner as tenant.

He was not ready to foreclose; indeed, he had the name of being one of the "easiest" men in the town. He let the debtor off again and again, extending the time whenever possible.

"I don't want y'r land," he said. "All I'm after is the int'rest on my money—that's all. Now if y' want 'o stay on the farm, why, I'll give y' a good chance. I can't have the land layin' vacant." And in many cases the owner remained as tenant.

In the mean time he had sold his store; he couldn't spend time in it; he was mainly occupied now with sitting around town on rainy days, smoking and "gassin' with the boys," or in riding to and from his farms. In fishing-time he fished a good deal. Doc Grimes, Ben Ashley, and Cal Cheatham were his cronies on these fishing excursions or hunting trips in the time of chickens or partridges. In winter they went to northern Wisconsin to shoot deer.

In spite of all these signs of easy life, Butler persisted in saying he "hadn't money enough to pay taxes on his land," and was careful to convey the impression that he was poor in spite of his twenty farms. At one time he was said to be worth fifty thousand dollars, but land had been a little slow of sale of late, so that he was not worth so much. A fine farm, known as the Higley place, had fallen into his hands in the usual way the previous year, and he had not been able to find a tenant for it. Poor Higley, after working himself nearly to death on it, in the attempt to lift the mortgage, had gone off to Dakota, leaving the farm and his curse to Butler.

This was the farm that Council advised Haskins to apply for, and the next day Council hitched up his team and drove down-town to see Butler.

"You jest lem *me* do the talkin'," he said. "We'll find him wearin' out his pants on some salt barrel somewears; and if he thought you *wanted* a place, he'd sock it to you hot and heavy. You jest keep quiet; I'll fix 'im."

Butler was seated in Ben Ashley's store, telling "fish yarns," when Council sauntered in casually.

"Hello, But! lyin' agin, hay?"

"Hello, Steve! how goes it?"

"Oh, so-so. Too dang much rain these days. I thought it was goin' t' freeze up f'r good last night. Tight squeak if I git m' ploughin' done. How's farmin' with *you* these days?"

"Bad. Ploughin' ain't half done."

"It 'ud be a religious idee f'r you t' go out and take a hand y'rself."

"I don't haff to," said Butler, with a wink.

"Got anybody on the Higley place?"

"No. Know of anybody?"

"Waal, no; not eggsackly. I've got a relation back t' Michigan who's ben hot an' cold on the idee o' comin' West f'r some time. *Might* come if he could git a good lay-out. What do you talk on the farm?"

"Well, I d' know. I'll rent it on shares, or I'll rent it money rent."

"Waal, how much money, say?"

"Well, say ten per cent on the price—$250."

"Waal, that ain't bad. Wait on 'im till 'e thrashes?"

Haskins listened eagerly to this important question, but Council was coolly eating a dried apple which he had speared out of a barrel with his knife. Butler studied him carefully.

"Well, knocks me out o' twenty-five dollars interest."

"My relation 'll need all he's got t' git his crops in," said Council, in the same indifferent way.

"Well, all right; *say* wait," concluded Butler.

"All right; this is the man. Haskins, this is Mr. Butler—no relation to Ben—the hardest-working man in Cedar County."

On the way home, Haskins said: "I ain't much better off. I'd like that farm; it's a good farm, but it's all run down, an' so 'm I. I could make a good farm of it if I had half a show. But I can't stock it n'r seed it."

"Waal, now, don't you worry," roared Council, in his ear. "We'll pull y' through somehow till next harvest. He's agreed t' hire it ploughed, an' you can earn a hundred dollars ploughin', an' y' c'n git the seed o' me, an' pay me back when y' can."

Haskins was silent with emotion, but at last he said, "I 'ain't got nothin' t' live on."

"Now don't you worry 'bout that. You jest make your head-quarters at ol' Steve Council's. Mother 'll take a pile o' comfort in havin' y'r wife an' children 'round. Y'see Jane's married off lately, an' Ike's away a good 'eal, so we'll be darn glad t' have ye stop with us this winter. Nex' spring we'll see if y' can't git a start agin;" and he chirruped to the team, which sprang forward with the rumbling, clattering wagon.

"Say, looky here, Council, you can't do this. I never saw—" shouted Haskins in his neighbor's ear.

Council moved about uneasily in his seat, and stopped his stammering gratitude by saying: "Hold on now; don't make such a fuss over a little thing. When I see a man down, an' things all on top of 'im, I jest like t' kick 'em off an' help 'im up. That's the kind of religion I got, an' it's about the *only* kind."

They rode the rest of the way home in silence. And when the red light of the lamp shone out into the darkness of the cold and windy night, and he thought of this refuge for his children and wife, Haskins could have put his arm around the neck of his burly companion and squeezed him like a lover; but he contented himself with saying, "Steve Council, you'll git y'r pay f'r this some day."

"Don't want any pay. My religion ain't run on such business principles."

The wind was growing colder, and the ground was covered with a white frost, as they turned into the gate of the Council farm, and the children came rushing out, shouting, "Papa's come!" They hardly looked like the same children who had sat at the table the night before. Their torpidity under the influence of sunshine and Mother Council had given way to a sort of spasmodic cheerfulness, as insects in winter revive when laid on the hearth.

3

Haskins worked like a fiend, and his wife, like the heroic little woman that she was, bore also uncomplainingly the most terrible burdens. They rose early and toiled without intermission till the darkness fell on the plain, then tumbled into bed, every bone and muscle aching with fatigue, to rise with the sun the next morning to the same round of the same ferocity of labor.

The eldest boy, now nine years old, drove a team all through the spring, ploughing and seeding, milked the cows, and did chores innumerable, in most ways taking the place of a man; an infinitely pathetic but common figure—this boy—on the American farm, where there is no law against child labor. To see him in his coarse clothing, his huge boots, and his ragged cap, as he stogged with a pail of water from the well, or trudged in the cold and cheerless dawn out into the frosty field behind his team, gave the city-bred visitor a sharp pang of sympathetic pain. Yet Haskins loved his boy, and would have saved him from this if he could, but he could not.

By June the first year the result of such Herculean[7] toil began to show on the farm. The yard was cleaned up and sown to grass, the garden ploughed and planted, and the house mended. Council had given them four of his cows.

"Take 'em an' run 'em on shares. I don't want a milk s' many. Ike's away s' much now, Sat'd'ys an' Sund'ys, I can't stand the bother anyhow."

---

[7]Of an effort similar in strength, courage, or labor to Hercules, the popular Greek hero known for his great strength.

Other men, seeing the confidence of Council in the new-comer, had sold him tools on time; and as he was really an able farmer, he soon had round him many evidences of his care and thrift. At the advice of Council he had taken the farm for three years, with the privilege of rerenting or buying at the end of the term.

"It's a good bargain, an' y' want 'o nail it," said Council. "If you have any kind ov a crop, you can pay half y'r debts, an' keep seed an' bread."

The new hope which now sprang up in the heart of Haskins and his wife grew great almost as a pain by the time the wide field of wheat began to wave and rustle and swirl in the winds of July. Day after day he would snatch a few moments after supper to go and look at it.

"Have ye seen the wheat t'-day, Nettie?" he asked one night as he rose from supper.

"No, Tim, I 'ain't had time."

"Well, take time now. Le's go look at it."

She threw an old hat on her head—Tommy's hat—and looking almost pretty in her thin sad way, went out with her husband to the hedge.

"Ain't it grand, Nettie? Just look at it."

It was grand. Level, russet here and there, heavy-headed, wide as a lake, and full of multitudinous whispers and gleams of health, it stretched away before the gazers like the fabled field of the cloth of gold.

"Oh, I think—I *hope* we'll have a good crop, Tim; and oh, how good the people have been to us!"

"Yes; I don't know where we'd be t'-day if it hadn't a ben f'r Council and his wife."

"They're the best people in the world," said the little woman, with a great sob of gratitude.

"We'll be into that field on Monday, sure," said Haskins, gripping the rail on the fence as if already at the work of the harvest.

The harvest came bounteous, glorious, but the winds came and blew it into tangles, and the rain matted it here and there close to the ground, increasing the work of gathering it threefold.

Oh, how they toiled in those glorious days! Clothing dripping with sweat, arms aching, filled with briars, fingers raw and bleeding, backs broken with the weight of heavy bundles, Haskins and his man toiled on. Tommy drove the harvester while his father and a hired man bound on the machine. In this way they cut ten acres every day, and almost every night after supper, when the hand went to bed, Haskins returned to the field, shocking the bound grain in the light of the moon. Many a night he worked till he staggered with utter fatigue; worked till his anxious wife came out to call him in to rest and lunch.

At the same time she cooked for the men, took care of the children, washed and ironed, milked the cows at night, made the butter, and sometimes fed the horses and watered them while her husband kept at the shocking. No slave in the Roman galleys[8] could have toiled so frightfully and lived, for this man *thought* himself a freeman, and that he was working for his wife and babes.

When he sank into his bed with a deep groan of relief, too tired to change his grimy, dripping clothing, he felt that he was getting nearer and nearer to a home of his own, and pushing the wolf of want a little further from his door.

There is no despair so deep as the despair of a homeless man or woman. To roam the roads of the country or the streets of the city, to feel there is no rood of ground on which the feet can rest, to halt weary and hungry outside lighted windows and hear laughter and song within—these are the hungers and rebellions that drive men to crime and women to shame.

It was the memory of this homelessness, and the fear of its coming again, that spurred Timothy Haskins and Nettie, his wife, to such ferocious labor during that first year.

4

"'M, yes; 'm, yes; first-rate," said Butler, as his eye took in the neat garden, the pigpen, and the well-filled barn-yard. "You're git'n' quite a stock around yer. Done well, eh?"

Haskins was showing Butler around the place. He had not seen it for a year, having spent the year in Washington and Boston with Ashley, his brother-in-law, who had been elected to Congress.

"Yes, I've laid out a good deal of money during the last three years. I've paid out three hundred dollars f'r fencin'."

"Um—h'm! I see, I see," said Butler, while Haskins went on.

"The kitchen there cost two hundred; the barn 'ain't cost much in money, but I've put a lot o' time on it. I've dug a new well, and I—"

"Yes, yes. I see! You've done well. Stalk worth a thousand dollars," said Butler, picking his teeth with a straw.

"About that," said Haskins, modestly. "We begin to feel 's if we wuz git'n' a home f'r ourselves; but we've worked hard. I tell ye we begin to feel it, Mr. Butler, and we're goin' t' begin t' ease up purty soon. We've been kind o' plannin' a trip back t' *her* folks after the fall ploughin's done."

"*Eggs*-actly!" said Butler, who was evidently thinking of something else. "I suppose you've kind o' kalklated on stayin' here three years more?"

"Well, yes. Fact is, I think I c'n buy the farm this fall, if you'll give me a reasonable show."

"Um—m! What do you call a reasonable show?"

"Waal; say a quarter down and three years' time."

---

[8]Ancient Roman galleys (ships) were often powered by slaves and convicts.

Butler looked at the huge stacks of wheat which filled the yard, over which the chickens were fluttering and crawling, catching grasshoppers, and out of which the crickets were singing innumerably. He smiled in a peculiar way as he said, "Oh, I won't be hard on yeh. But what did you expect to pay f'r the place?"

"Why, about what you offered it for before, twenty-five hundred dollars, or *possibly* three thousand," he added, quickly, as he saw the owner shake his head.

"This farm is worth five thousand and five hundred dollars," said Butler, in a careless but decided voice.

"*What!*" almost shrieked the astounded Haskins. 'What's that? Five thousand? Why, that's double what you offered it for three years ago."

"Of course; and it's worth it. It was all run down then; now it's in good shape. You've laid out fifteen hundred dollars in improvements, according to your own story."

"But *you* had nothin' t'do about that. It's my work an' my money."

"You bet it was; but it's my land."

"But what's to pay me for all?"

"'Ain't you had the use of 'em?" replied Butler, smiling calmly into his face.

Haskins was like a man struck on the head with a sand-bag; he couldn't think, he stammered as he tried to say: "But—I never 'd git the use. You'd rob me. More'n that: you agreed—you promised that I could buy or rent at the end of three years at—"

"That's all right. But I didn't say I'd let you carry off the improvements, nor that I'd go on renting the farm at two-fifty. The land is doubled in value, it don't matter how; it don't enter into the question; an' now you can pay me five hundred dollars a year rent, or take it on your own terms at fifty-five hundred, or—git out."

He was turning away, when Haskins, the sweat pouring from his face, fronted him, saying again:

"But *you've* done nothing to make it so. You hain't added a cent. I put it all there myself, expectin' to buy. I worked an' sweat to improve it. I was workin' f'r myself an' babes."

"Well, why didn't you buy when I offered to sell? What y' kickin' about?"

"I'm kickin' about payin' you twice f'r my own things—my own fences, my own kitchen, my own garden."

Butler laughed. "You're too green t'eat, young feller. *Your* improvements! The law will sing another tune."

"But I trusted your word."

"Never trust anybody, my friend. Besides, I didn't promise not to do this thing. Why, man, don't look at me like that. Don't take me for a thief. It's the law. The reg'lar thing. Everybody does it."

"I don't care if they do. It's stealin' jest the same. You take three thousand dollars of my money. The work o' my hands and my wife's." He broke down at this point. He was not a strong man mentally. He could face hardship, ceaseless toil, but he could not face the cold and sneering face of Butler.

"But I don't take it," said Butler, coolly. "All you've got to do is to go on jest as you've been a-doin', or give me a thousand dollars down, and a mortgage at ten percent on the rest."

Haskins sat down blindly on a bundle of oats near by, and with staring eyes and drooping head went over the situation. He was under the lion's paw. He felt a horrible numbness in his heart and limbs. He was hid in a mist, and there was no path out.

Butler walked about, looking at the huge stacks of grain, and pulling now and again a few handfuls out, shelling the heads in his hands and blowing the chaff away. He hummed a little tune as he did so. He had an accommodating air of waiting.

Haskins was in the midst of the terrible toil of the last year. He was walking again in the rain and the mud behind his plough, he felt the dust and dirt of the threshing. The ferocious husking-time, with its cutting wind and biting, clinging snows, lay hard upon him. Then he thought of his wife, how she had cheerfully cooked and baked, without holiday and without rest.

"Well, what do you think of it?" inquired the cool, mocking, insinuating voice of Butler.

"I think you're a thief and a liar," shouted Haskins, leaping up. "A black-hearted houn'!" Butler's smile maddened him; with a sudden leap he caught a fork in his hands, and whirled it in the air. "You'll never rob another man, damn ye!" he grated through his teeth, a look of pitiless ferocity in his accusing eyes.

Butler shrank and quivered, expecting the blow; stood, held hypnotized by the eyes of the man he had a moment before despised—a man transformed into an avenging demon. But in the deadly hush between the lift of the weapon and its fall there came a gush of faint, childish laughter, and then across the range of his vision, far away and dim, he saw the sun-bright head of his baby girl, as, with the pretty tottering run of a two-year-old, she moved across the grass of the door-yard. His hands relaxed; the fork fell to the ground; his head lowered.

"Make out y'r deed an' morgige, an' git off'n my land, an' don't ye never cross my line again; if y' do, I'll kill ye."

Butler backed away from the man in wild haste, and climbing into his buggy with trembling limbs, drove off down the road, leaving Haskins seated dumbly on the sunny pile of sheaves, his head sunk into his hands.

[1889]

CHARLOTTE PERKINS GILMAN ■ (1860–1935)

An influential feminist, reformer, intellectual, writer, and activist, Charlotte Perkins Gilman, born (her family name was Perkins) in Hartford, Connecticut, moved many times with her family when she was a child and in her teens. Her father had deserted his wife and children, and Gilman's mother and older brother struggled to find work.

Gilman studied for a short time at the Rhode Island School of Design, in Providence, and then she taught art and designed greeting cards. Despite her unease about becoming a wife and mother, Gilman married Charles Stetson, an artist, in 1884, and in 1885 gave birth to a daughter, an event that threw Gilman into a deep depression. She was treated by the eminent physician Dr. S. Weir Mitchell, who diagnosed her as suffering from "hysteria" and who for a remedy prescribed complete bed rest, no intellectual activity, and a return to domesticity. Gilman's experiences formed the basis for her famous story, "The Yellow Wall-Paper," written in 1890 and published in 1892.

Gilman then separated from her husband on mutually agreeable terms and moved to California; once the divorce was finalized, she allowed her daughter to be raised by her former husband and his second wife—a decision for which Gilman was publicly criticized. In 1900 Gilman remarried, to her cousin George Houghton Gilman, a lawyer, and they lived together contentedly, in New York and Connecticut, until his death in 1934. Suffering from breast cancer, Gilman took her own life the following year.

Gilman lectured extensively in the United States and Europe, and she wrote on many subjects and in many genres. Among her books are *Women and Economics* (1898), a wide-ranging study of past and present subordination of women, and *Herland* (1915), an utopian fiction describing an all-female society in which children are raised collectively and in which peace, prosperity, and harmony are achieved. Gilman also wrote nearly a thousand articles for magazines, journals, and newspapers.

From 1909 to 1916, Gilman served as editor of and chief contributor to *The Forerunner*, a monthly magazine that focused on social reform and economics but that included poems and stories (and two novels, written by Gilman) as well; she estimated that the amount of writing she did for it was equal to twenty-eight books. Shortly after she died her autobiography, *The Living of Charlotte Perkins Gilman*, was published, and it further consolidated her place among America's most significant feminist writers and reformers. "The one predominant duty," she concluded, "is to find one's work and do it, and I have striven mightily at that."

Harrowing, profound, and complex, "The Yellow Wall-Paper" examines and indicts both marriage and medicine—institutions that, in Gilman's view, seek to control and coerce women, driving them perilously close to or (as in the case of the narrator of this story) nightmarishly into madness.

"The Yellow Wall-Paper" gains much of its power from Gilman's own investment in the frightening plight and predicament of her protagonist. In a 1913 essay looking back in on the story's origins, she noted the nature of her own response to the treatment Dr. Mitchell had recommended:

> I went home and obeyed those directions for some three months, and came so near the borderline of utter mental ruin that I could see over.

"The feminine of Jekyll and Hyde" political cartoon, created by Udo Keppler and published in 1913. The cartoon shows a woman at two extremes, much like Gilman's short story.

Then, using the remnants of intelligence that remained, and helped by a wise friend, I cast the noted specialist's advice to the winds and went to work again—work, the normal life of every human being; work, in which is joy and growth and service, without which one is a pauper and a parasite—ultimately recovering some measure of power.

"The Yellow Wallpaper," she added, "was not intended to drive people crazy, but to save people from being driven crazy, and it worked."

For a good overview: Gary Scharnhorst, *Charlotte Perkins Gilman* (1985). Biographies include Mary A. Hill, *Charlotte Perkins Gilman: The Making of a Radical Feminist, 1860–1896* (1980); and Ann J. Lane, *To* Herland *and Beyond: The Life and Work of Charlotte Perkins Gilman* (1990). See also *The Captive Imagination: A Casebook on "The Yellow Wallpaper,"* ed. Catherine Golden (1992); *Critical Essays on Charlotte Perkins Gilman*, ed. Joanne B. Karpinski (1992); and *The Mixed Legacy of Charlotte Perkins Gilman*, eds. Catherine J. Golden and Joanna Schneider Zangrando (2000). Also helpful are: *Charlotte Perkins Gilman and Her Contemporaries: Literary and Intellectual Contexts*, ed. Denise D. Knight (2004); Helen Lefkowitz Horowitz, *Wild Unrest: Charlotte Perkins Gilman and the Making of "The Yellow Wallpaper"* (2010); and *Charlotte Perkins Gilman: New Texts, New Contexts*, eds. Jennifer S. Tuttle and Carol Farley Kessler (2011).

The Yellow Wall-Paper

It is very seldom that mere ordinary people like John and myself secure ancestral halls for the summer.

A colonial mansion, a hereditary estate, I would say a haunted house, and reach the height of romantic felicity—but that would be asking too much of fate!

Still I will proudly declare that there is something queer about it.

Else, why should it be let so cheaply? And why have stood so long untenanted?

John laughs at me, of course, but one expects that in marriage.

John is practical in the extreme. He has no patience with faith, an intense horror of superstition, and he scoffs openly at any talk of things not to be felt and seen and put down in figures.

John is a physician, and *perhaps*—(I would not say it to a living soul, of course, but this is dead paper and a great relief to my mind—) *perhaps* that is one reason I do not get well faster.

You see he does not believe I am sick!

And what can one do?

If a physician of high standing, and one's own husband, assures friends and relatives that there is really nothing the matter with one but temporary nervous depression—a slight hysterical tendency—what is one to do?

My brother is also a physician, and also of high standing, and he says the same thing.

So I take phosphates[1] or phosphites—whichever it is, and tonics, and journeys, and air, and exercise, and am absolutely forbidden to "work" until I am well again.

Personally, I disagree with their ideas.

Personally, I believe that congenial work, with excitement and change, would do me good.

But what is one to do?

I did write for a while in spite of them; but it *does* exhaust me a good deal—having to be so sly about it, or else meet with heavy opposition.

I sometimes fancy that in my condition if I had less opposition and more society and stimulus—but John says the very worst thing I can do is to think about my condition, and I confess it always makes me feel bad.

So I will let it alone and talk about the house.

The most beautiful place! It is quite alone, standing well back from the road, quite three miles from the village. It makes me think of English places that you read about, for there are hedges and walls and gates that lock, and lots of separate little houses for the gardeners and people.

There is a *delicious* garden! I never saw such a garden—large and shady, full of box-bordered paths, and lined with long grape-covered arbors with seats under them.

There were greenhouses, too, but they are all broken now.

There was some legal trouble, I believe, something about the heirs and coheirs; anyhow, the place has been empty for years.

That spoils my ghostliness, I am afraid, but I don't care—there is something strange about the house—I can feel it.

I even said so to John one moonlight evening, but he said what I felt was a *draught,* and shut the window.

I get unreasonably angry with John sometimes. I'm sure I never used to be so sensitive. I think it is due to this nervous condition.

But John says if I feel so, I shall neglect proper self-control; so I take pains to control myself—before him, at least, and that makes me very tired.

I don't like our room a bit. I wanted one downstairs that opened on the piazza and had roses all over the window, and such pretty old-fashioned chintz hangings! but John would not hear of it.

He said there was only one window and not room for two beds, and no near room for him if he took another.

---

[1] An effervescent soft drink containing phosphoric acid, soda water, and flavoring.

He is very careful and loving, and hardly lets me stir without special direction.

I have a schedule prescription for each hour in the day; he takes all care from me, and so I feel basely ungrateful not to value it more.

He said we came here solely on my account, that I was to have perfect rest and all the air I could get. "Your exercise depends on your strength, my dear," said he, "and your food somewhat on your appetite; but air you can absorb all the time." So we took the nursery at the top of the house.

It is a big, airy room, the whole floor nearly, with windows that look all ways, and air and sunshine galore. It was nursery first and then play-room and gymnasium, I should judge; for the windows are barred for little children, and there are rings and things in the walls.

The paint and paper look as if a boys' school had used it. It is stripped off—the paper—in great patches all around the head of my bed, about as far as I can reach, and in a great place on the other side of the room low down. I never saw a worse paper in my life.

One of those sprawling flamboyant patterns committing every artistic sin.

It is dull enough to confuse the eye in following, pronounced enough to constantly irritate and provoke study, and when you follow the lame un-certain curves for a little distance they suddenly commit suicide—plunge off at outrageous angles, destroy themselves in unheard of contradictions.

The color is repellent, almost revolting; a smoldering unclean yellow, strangely faded by the slow-turning sunlight.

It is a dull yet lurid orange in some places, a sickly sulphur tint in others.

No wonder the children hated it! I should hate it myself if I had to live in this room long.

There comes John, and I must put this away,—he hates to have me write a word.

We have been here two weeks, and I haven't felt like writing before, since that first day.

I am sitting by the window now, up in this atrocious nursery, and there is nothing to hinder my writing as much as I please, save lack of strength.

John is away all day, and even some nights when his cases are serious.

I am glad my case is not serious!

But these nervous troubles are dreadfully depressing.

John does not know how much I really suffer. He knows there is no *reason* to suffer, and that satisfies him.

Of course it is only nervousness. It does weigh on me so not to do my duty in any way!

I meant to be such a help to John, such a real rest and comfort, and here I am a comparative burden already!

Nobody would believe what an effort it is to do what little I am able,—to dress and entertain, and order things.

It is fortunate Mary is so good with the baby. Such a dear baby!

And yet I *cannot* be with him, it makes me so nervous.

I suppose John never was nervous in his life. He laughs at me so about this wall-paper!

At first he meant to repaper the room, but afterwards he said that I was letting it get the better of me, and that nothing was worse for a nervous patient than to give way to such fancies.

He said that after the wall-paper was changed it would be the heavy bedstead, and then the barred windows, and then that gate at the head of the stairs, and so on.

"You know the place is doing you good," he said, "and really, dear, I don't care to renovate the house just for a three months' rental."

"Then do let us go downstairs," I said, "there are such pretty rooms there."

Then he took me in his arms and called me a blessed little goose, and said he would go down cellar, if I wished, and have it whitewashed into the bargain.

But he is right enough about the beds and windows and things.

It is an airy and comfortable room as any one need wish, and, of course, I would not be so silly as to make him uncomfortable just for a whim.

I'm really getting quite fond of the big room, all but that horrid paper.

Out of one window I can see the garden, those mysterious deep-shaded arbors, the riotous old-fashioned flowers, and bushes and gnarly trees.

Out of another I get a lovely view of the bay and a little private wharf belonging to the estate. There is a beautiful shaded lane that runs down there from the house. I always fancy I see people walking in these numerous paths and arbors, but John has cautioned me not to give way to fancy in the least. He says that with my imaginative power and habit of story-making, a nervous weakness like mine is sure to lead to all manner of excited fancies, and that I ought to use my will and good sense to check the tendency. So I try.

I think sometimes that if I were only well enough to write a little it would relieve the press of ideas and rest me.

But I find I get pretty tired when I try.

It is so discouraging not to have any advice and companionship about my work. When I get really well, John says we will ask cousin Henry and Julia down for a long visit; but he says he would as soon put fireworks in my pillow-case as to let me have those stimulating people about now.

I wish I could get well faster.

But I must not think about that. This paper looks to me as if it *knew* what a vicious influence it had!

There is a recurrent spot where the pattern lolls like a broken neck and two bulbous eyes stare at you upside down.

I get positively angry with the impertinence of it and the everlasting-ness. Up and down and sideways they crawl, and those absurd, unblinking eyes are everywhere. There is one place where two breadths didn't match, and the eyes go all up and down the line, one a little higher than the other.

I never saw so much expression in an inanimate thing before, and we all know how much expression they have! I used to lie awake as a child and get more entertainment and terror out of blank walls and plain furni-ture than most children could find in a toy-store.

I remember what a kindly wink the knobs of our big, old bureau used to have, and there was one chair that always seemed like a strong friend.

I used to feel that if any of the other things looked too fierce I could always hop into that chair and be safe.

The furniture in this room is no worse than inharmonious, however, for we had to bring it all from downstairs. I suppose when this was used as a playroom they had to take the nursery things out, and no wonder! I never saw such ravages as the children have made here.

The wall-paper, as I said before, is torn off in spots, and it sticketh closer than a brother—they must have had perseverance as well as hatred.

Then the floor is scratched and gouged and splintered, the plaster it-self is dug out here and there, and this great heavy bed which is all we found in the room, looks as if it had been through the wars.

But I don't mind it a bit—only the paper.

There comes John's sister. Such a dear girl as she is, and so careful of me! I must not let her find me writing.

She is a perfect and enthusiastic housekeeper, and hopes for no better profession. I verily believe she thinks it is the writing which made me sick!

But I can write when she is out, and see her a long way off from these windows.

There is one that commands the road, a lovely shaded winding road, and one that just looks off over the country. A lovely country, too, full of great elms and velvet meadows.

This wall-paper has a kind of subpattern in a different shade, a particu-larly irritating one, for you can only see it in certain lights, and not clearly then.

But in the places where it isn't faded and where the sun is just so—I can see a strange, provoking, formless sort of figure, that seems to skulk about behind that silly and conspicuous front design.

There's sister on the stairs!

Well, the Fourth of July is over! The people are all gone and I am tired out. John thought it might do me good to see a little company, so we just had mother and Nellie and the children down for a week.

Of course I didn't do a thing. Jennie sees to everything now.

But it tired me all the same.

John says if I don't pick up faster he shall send me to Weir Mitchell[2] in the fall.

But I don't want to go there at all. I had a friend who was in his hands once, and she says he is just like John and my brother, only more so!

Besides, it is such an undertaking to go so far.

I don't feel as if it was worth while to turn my hand over for anything, and I'm getting dreadfully fretful and querulous.

I cry at nothing, and cry most of the time.

Of course I don't when John is here, or anybody else, but when I am alone.

And I am alone a good deal just now. John is kept in town very often by serious cases, and Jennie is good and lets me alone when I want her to.

So I walk a little in the garden or down that lovely lane, sit on the porch under the roses, and lie down up here a good deal.

I'm getting really fond of the room in spite of the wall-paper. Perhaps *because* of the wall-paper.

It dwells in my mind so!

I lie here on this great immovable bed—it is nailed down, I believe—and follow that pattern about by the hour. It is as good as gymnastics, I assure you. I start, we'll say, at the bottom, down in the corner over there where it has not been touched, and I determine for the thousandth time that I *will* follow that pointless pattern to some sort of a conclusion.

I know a little of the principle of design, and I know this thing was not arranged on any laws of radiation, or alternation, or repetition, or symmetry, or anything else that I ever heard of.

It is repeated, of course, by the breadths, but not otherwise.

Looked at in one way each breadth stands alone, the bloated curves and flourishes—a kind of "debased Romanesque" with *delirium tremens*[3]—go waddling up and down in isolated columns of fatuity.

But, on the other hand, they connect diagonally, and the sprawling outlines run off in great slanting waves of optic horror, like a lot of wallowing seaweeds in full chase.

The whole thing goes horizontally, too, at least it seems so, and I exhaust myself in trying to distinguish the order of its going in that direction.

They have used a horizontal breadth for a frieze, and that adds wonderfully to the confusion.

There is one end of the room where it is almost intact, and there, when the crosslights fade and the low sun shines directly upon it, I can almost fancy radiation after all,—the interminable grotesques seem to form around a common centre and rush off in headlong plunges of equal distraction.

It makes me tired to follow it. I will take a nap I guess.

[2]Dr. S. Weir Mitchell (1829–1914), an eminent physician who treated Gilman.
[3]A severe delirium caused by alcohol poisoning.

I don't know why I should write this.

I don't want to.

I don't feel able.

And I know John would think it absurd. But I *must* say what I feel and think in some way—it is such a relief!

But the effort is getting to be greater than the relief.

Half the time now I am awfully lazy, and lie down ever so much.

John says I mustn't lose my strength, and has me take cod liver oil and lots of tonics and things, to say nothing of ale and wine and rare meat.

Dear John! He loves me very dearly, and hates to have me sick. I tried to have a real earnest reasonable talk with him the other day, and tell him how I wish he would let me go and make a visit to Cousin Henry and Julia.

But he said I wasn't able to go, nor able to stand it after I got there; and I did not make out a very good case for myself, for I was crying before I had finished.

It is getting to be a great effort for me to think straight. Just this nervous weakness I suppose.

And dear John gathered me up in his arms, and just carried me upstairs and laid me on the bed, and sat by me and read to me till it tired my head.

He said I was his darling and his comfort and all he had, and that I must take care of myself for his sake, and keep well.

He says no one but myself can help me out of it, that I must use my will and self-control and not let any silly fancies run away with me.

There's one comfort, the baby is well and happy, and does not have to occupy this nursery with the horrid wall-paper.

If we had not used it, that blessed child would have! What a fortunate escape! Why, I wouldn't have a child of mine, an impressionable little thing, live in such a room for worlds.

I never thought of it before, but it is lucky that John kept me here after all, I can stand it so much easier than a baby, you see.

Of course I never mention it to them any more—I am too wise,—but I keep watch of it all the same.

There are things in that paper that nobody knows but me, or ever will.

Behind that outside pattern the dim shapes get clearer every day.

It is always the same shape, only very numerous.

And it is like a woman stooping down and creeping about behind that pattern. I don't like it a bit. I wonder—I begin to think—I wish John would take me away from here!

It is so hard to talk with John about my case, because he is so wise, and because he loves me so.

But I tried it last night.

It was moonlight. The moon shines in all around just as the sun does.

I hate to see it sometimes, it creeps so slowly, and always comes in by one window or another.

John was asleep and I hated to waken him, so I kept still and watched the moonlight on that undulating wall-paper till I felt creepy.

The faint figure behind seemed to shake the pattern, just as if she wanted to get out.

I got up softly and went to feel and see if the paper *did* move, and when I came back John was awake.

"What is it, little girl?" he said. "Don't go walking about like that—you'll get cold."

I thought it was a good time to talk, so I told him that I really was not gaining here, and that I wished he would take me away.

"Why, darling!" said he, "our lease will be up in three weeks, and I can't see how to leave before.

"The repairs are not done at home, and I cannot possibly leave town just now. Of course if you were in any danger, I could and would, but you really are better, dear, whether you can see it or not. I am a doctor, dear, and I know. You are gaining flesh and color, your appetite is better, I feel really much easier about you."

"I don't weigh a bit more," said I, "nor as much; and my appetite may be better in the evening when you are here, but it is worse in the morning when you are away!"

"Bless her little heart!" said he with a big hug, "she shall be as sick as she pleases! But now let's improve the shining hours by going to sleep, and talk about it in the morning!"

"And you won't go away?" I asked gloomily.

"Why, how can I, dear? It is only three weeks more and then we will take a nice little trip of a few days while Jennie is getting the house ready. Really dear you are better!"

"Better in body perhaps—" I began, and stopped short, for he sat up straight and looked at me with such a stern, reproachful look that I could not say another word.

"My darling," said he, "I beg of you, for my sake and for our child's sake, as well as for your own, that you will never for one instant let that idea enter your mind! There is nothing so dangerous, so fascinating, to a temperament like yours. It is a false and foolish fancy. Can you not trust me as a physician when I tell you so?"

So of course I said no more on that score, and we went to sleep before long. He thought I was asleep first, but I wasn't, and lay there for hours trying to decide whether that front pattern and the back pattern really did move together or separately.

On a pattern like this, by daylight, there is a lack of sequence, a defiance of law, that is a constant irritant to a normal mind.

The color is hideous enough, and unreliable enough, and infuriating enough, but the pattern is torturing.

You think you have mastered it, but just as you get well underway in following, it turns a back-somersault and there you are. It slaps you in the face, knocks you down, and tramples upon you. It is like a bad dream.

The outside pattern is a florid arabesque, reminding one of a fungus. If you can imagine a toadstool in joints, an interminable string of toadstools, budding and sprouting in endless convolutions—why, that is something like it.

That is, sometimes!

There is one marked peculiarity about this paper, a thing nobody seems to notice but myself, and that is that it changes as the light changes.

When the sun shoots in through the east window—I always watch for that first long, straight ray—it changes so quickly that I never can quite believe it.

That is why I watch it always.

By moonlight—the moon shines in all night when there is a moon—I wouldn't know it was the same paper.

At night in any kind of light, in twilight, candlelight, lamplight, and worst of all by moonlight, it becomes bars! The outside pattern I mean, and the woman behind it is as plain as can be.

I didn't realize for a long time what the thing was that showed behind, that dim sub-pattern, but now I am quite sure it is a woman.

By daylight she is subdued, quiet. I fancy it is the pattern that keeps her so still. It is so puzzling. It keeps me quiet by the hour.

I lie down ever so much now. John says it is good for me, and to sleep all I can.

Indeed he started the habit by making me lie down for an hour after each meal.

It is a very bad habit I am convinced, for you see I don't sleep.

And that cultivates deceit, for I don't tell them I'm awake—O no!

The fact is I am getting a little afraid of John.

He seems very queer sometimes, and even Jennie has an inexplicable look.

It strikes me occasionally, just as a scientific hypothesis,—that perhaps it is the paper!

I have watched John when he did not know I was looking, and come into the room suddenly on the most innocent excuses, and I've caught him several times *looking at the paper*! And Jennie too. I caught Jennie with her hand on it once.

She didn't know I was in the room, and when I asked her in a quiet, a very quiet voice, with the most restrained manner possible, what she was doing with the paper—she turned around as if she had been caught stealing, and looked quite angry—asked me why I should frighten her so!

Then she said that the paper stained everything it touched, that she had found yellow smooches on all my clothes and John's, and she wished we would be more careful!

Did not that sound innocent? But I know she was studying that pattern, and I am determined that nobody shall find it out but myself!

Life is very much more exciting now than it used to be. You see I have something more to expect, to look forward to, to watch. I really do eat better, and am more quiet than I was.

John is so pleased to see me improve! He laughed a little the other day, and said I seemed to be flourishing in spite of my wall-paper.

I turned it off with a laugh. I had no intention of telling him it was *because* of the wall-paper—he would make fun of me. He might even want to take me away.

I don't want to leave now until I have found it out. There is a week more, and I think that will be enough.

I'm feeling ever so much better! I don't sleep much at night, for it is so interesting to watch developments; but I sleep a good deal in the daytime.

In the daytime it is tiresome and perplexing.

There are always new shoots on the fungus, and new shades of yellow all over it. I cannot keep count of them, though I have tried conscientiously.

It is the strangest yellow, that wall-paper! It makes me think of all the yellow things I ever saw—not beautiful ones like buttercups, but old foul, bad yellow things.

But there is something else about that paper—the smell! I noticed it the moment we came into the room, but with so much air and sun it was not bad. Now we have had a week of fog and rain, and whether the windows are open or not, the smell is here.

It creeps all over the house.

I find it hovering in the dining-room, skulking in the parlor, hiding in the hall, lying in wait for me on the stairs.

It gets into my hair.

Even when I go to ride, if I turn my head suddenly and surprise it—there is that smell!

Such a peculiar odor, too! I have spent hours in trying to analyze it, to find what it smelled like.

It is not bad—at first, and very gentle, but quite the subtlest, most enduring odor I ever met.

In this damp weather it is awful, I wake up in the night and find it hanging over me.

It used to disturb me at first. I thought seriously of burning the house—to reach the smell.

But now I am used to it. The only thing I can think of that it is like is the *color* of the paper! A yellow smell.

There is a very funny mark on this wall, low down, near the mopboard. A streak that runs round the room. It goes behind every piece of furniture, except the bed, a long, straight, even *smooch,* as if it had been rubbed over and over.

I wonder how it was done and who did it, and what they did it for. Round and round and round—round and round and round—it makes me dizzy!

I really have discovered something at last.

Through watching so much at night, when it changes so, I have finally found out.

The front pattern *does* move—and no wonder! The woman behind shakes it!

Sometimes I think there are a great many women behind, and sometimes only one, and she crawls around fast, and her crawling shakes it all over.

Then in the very bright spots she keeps still, and in the very shady spots she just takes hold of the bars and shakes them hard.

And she is all the time trying to climb through. But nobody could climb through that pattern—it strangles so; I think that is why it has so many heads.

They get through, and then the pattern strangles them off and turns them upside down, and makes their eyes white!

If those heads were covered or taken off it would not be half so bad.

I think that woman gets out in the daytime!

And I'll tell you why—privately—I've seen her!

I can see her out of every one of my windows!

It is the same woman, I know, for she is always creeping, and most women do not creep by daylight.

I see her in that long shaded lane, creeping up and down. I see her in those dark grape arbors, creeping all around the garden.

I see her on that long road under the trees, creeping along, and when a carriage comes she hides under the blackberry vines.

I don't blame her a bit. It must be very humiliating to be caught creeping by daylight!

I always lock the door when I creep by daylight. I can't do it at night, for I know John would suspect something at once.

And John is so queer now, that I don't want to irritate him. I wish he would take another room! Besides, I don't want anybody to get that woman out at night but myself.

I often wonder if I could see her out of all the windows at once.

But, turn as fast as I can, I can only see out of one at one time.

And though I always see her, she *may* be able to creep faster than I can turn!

I have watched her sometimes away off in the open country, creeping as fast as a cloud shadow in a high wind.

If only that top pattern could be gotten off from the under one! I mean to try it, little by little.

I have found out another funny thing, but I shan't tell it this time! It does not do to trust people too much.

There are only two more days to get this paper off, and I believe John is beginning to notice. I don't like the look in his eyes.

And I heard him ask Jennie a lot of professional questions about me. She had a very good report to give.

She said I slept a good deal in the daytime.

John knows I don't sleep very well at night, for all I'm so quiet!

He asked me all sorts of questions, too, and pretended to be very loving and kind.

As if I couldn't see through him!

Still, I don't wonder he acts so, sleeping under this paper for three months.

It only interests me, but I feel sure John and Jennie are secretly affected by it.

Hurrah! This is the last day, but it is enough. John is to stay in town over night, and won't be out until this evening.

Jennie wanted to sleep with me—the sly thing! but I told her I should undoubtedly rest better for a night all alone.

That was clever, for really I wasn't alone a bit! As soon as it was moonlight and that poor thing began to crawl and shake the pattern, I got up and ran to help her.

I pulled and she shook, I shook and she pulled, and before morning we had peeled off yards of that paper.

A strip about as high as my head and half around the room.

And then when the sun came and that awful pattern began to laugh at me, I declared I would finish it to-day!

We go away to-morrow, and they are moving all my furniture down again to leave things as they were before.

Jennie looked at the wall in amazement, but I told her merrily that I did it out of pure spite at the vicious thing.

She laughed and said she wouldn't mind doing it herself, but I must not get tired.

How she betrayed herself that time!

But I am here, and no person touches this paper but me,—not *alive*!

She tried to get me out of the room—it was too patent! But I said it was so quiet and empty and clean now that I believed I would lie down again and sleep all I could; and not to wake me even for dinner—I would call when I woke.

So now she is gone, and the servants are gone, and the things are gone, and there is nothing left but that great bedstead nailed down, with the canvas mattress we found on it.

We shall sleep downstairs to-night, and take the boat home to-morrow.

I quite enjoy the room, now it is bare again.

How those children did tear about here!

This bedstead is fairly gnawed!

But I must get to work.

I have locked the door and thrown the key down into the front path.

I don't want to go out, and I don't want to have anybody come in, till John comes.

I want to astonish him.

I've got a rope up here that even Jennie did not find. If that woman does get out, and tries to get away, I can tie her!

But I forgot I could not reach far without anything to stand on!

This bed will *not* move!

I tried to lift and push it until I was lame, and then I got so angry I bit off a little piece at one corner—but it hurt my teeth.

Then I peeled off all the paper I could reach standing on the floor. It sticks horribly and the pattern just enjoys it! All those strangled heads and bulbous eyes and waddling fungus growths just shriek with derision!

I am getting angry enough to do something desperate. To jump out of the window would be admirable exercise, but the bars are too strong even to try.

Besides I wouldn't do it. Of course not. I know well enough that a step like that is improper and might be misconstrued.

I don't like to *look* out of the windows even—there are so many of those creeping women, and they creep so fast.

I wonder if they all come out of that wall-paper as I did?

But I am securely fastened now by my well-hidden rope—you don't get *me* out in the road there!

I suppose I shall have to get back behind the pattern when it comes night, and that is hard!

It is so pleasant to be out in this great room and creep around as I please!

I don't want to go outside. I won't, even if Jennie asks me to.

For outside you have to creep on the ground, and everything is green instead of yellow.

But here I can creep smoothly on the floor, and my shoulder just fits in that long smooch around the wall, so I cannot lose my way.

Why there's John at the door!

It is no use, young man, you can't open it!

How he does call and pound!

Now he's crying for an axe.

It would be a shame to break down that beautiful door!

"John dear!" said I in the gentlest voice, "the key is down by the front steps, under a plantain leaf!"

That silenced him for a few moments.

Then he said—very quietly indeed, "Open the door, my darling!"

"I can't," said I. "The key is down by the front door under a plantain leaf!"

And then I said it again, several times, very gently and slowly, and said it so often that he had to go and see, and he got it of course, and came in. He stopped short by the door.

"What is the matter?" he cried. "For God's sake, what are you doing!"

I kept on creeping just the same, but I looked at him over my shoulder.

"I've got out at last," said I, "in spite of you and Jane. And I've pulled off most of the paper, so you can't put me back!"

Now why should that man have fainted? But he did, and right across my path by the wall, so that I had to creep over him every time!

[1892]

EDITH WHARTON ■ (1862–1937)

Born to wealth and privilege, a member of upper-class New York society, with its moneyed distinctions and conservative codes of behavior, Edith Wharton, born Edith Newbold Jones, became a highly successful professional author—a rare achievement for women of her background and circle. She was amazingly hardworking and prolific, producing over the span of her career some forty books, including twenty-two novellas and novels and eleven collections of short stories.

Wharton was privately educated at home and spent much of her childhood in Italy, France, Germany, and Spain, learning foreign languages and being exposed to European cultures and traditions. Later in life, she said these experiences made her feel always "in exile in America," and in her fiction she often treats the complex interactions between America and Europe.

Wharton's parents, especially her mother, believed their daughter's literary interests and aspirations were inappropriate—indecorous and vulgar for a refined woman to pursue—and they did their best to discourage them. They hurried Edith into making her social debut, and in 1885 she married Teddy Wharton, a gregarious Bostonian, age thirty-six, of a fine family. The marriage soon proved an unhappy one, and Wharton, bored and suffocated, began actively to undertake the literary work her parents had sought to deny her.

In the early 1890s Wharton published a few poems and a story, and by the end of the decade she had published a book on architecture and interior decoration and a collection of short fiction. Her first novel, *The Valley of Decision*, with an eighteenth-century Italian setting, appeared in 1902, but it mattered less for itself than it did for clarifying to Wharton (as her friend and fellow writer Henry James pointed out to her) that her real subject, the subject she knew most about, from the inside, was high-society New York.

Sexual passion, marriage (and its frustrations and disappointments), separation, and divorce are the themes that Wharton explores not only in such New York novels as *The House of Mirth* (1905), *The Custom of the Country* (1913), and *The Age of Innocence* (1920) but also in her stark, grim novels set in western Massachusetts, *Ethan Frome* (1911) and *Summer* (1917). She probes the sexual hurt, emotional pain, confusion, perplexity, and despair of men and women trapped in loveless relationships or in strange, skewed marriages that require unpleasant or sometimes wry and odd adjustments of feeling, as the story "The Other Two" suggests. As the critic Irving Howe observed, "The arena of Wharton's imagination is the forefront of social life, where manners reveal moral stress or bias, and accepted forms of conduct may break under the weight of personal desire."

   Much of the tension in Wharton's work derives from her rejection of the rigid and repressive social outlook her parents represented, even as she satirizes and scorns the flashy, vulgar, uncultured, and morally fast and loose new groups of people who were dismantling the social, sexual, and moral conventions her parents had believed in and tried to protect. Divorce in Wharton's world was frowned upon; it was considered a disgrace. She thus chose to remain married—unhappily—to her husband (they had no children), though during 1907–08 she engaged in a secret passionate affair (which she described in a "love diary" discovered by scholars decades after her death) with Morton Fullerton (1865–1952), a writer and journalist. Finally, in 1913, after a two-year separation, she secured a divorce, an act that ratified and reaffirmed the independence that as a woman and as an admired and widely read author she had already achieved.

   For biographical and critical discussion: R. W. B. Lewis, *Edith Wharton: A Biography* (1975); Cynthia Griffin Wolff, *A Feast of Words: The*

Edith Wharton, 1905.

Triumph of Edith Wharton (1977; rev. ed., 1995); Elizabeth Ammons, *Edith Wharton's Argument with America* (1980); Shari Benstock, *No Gifts from Chance: A Biography of Edith Wharton* (1994); and Carol J. Singley, *Edith Wharton: Matters of Mind and Spirit* (1995). See also Barbara A. White, *Edith Wharton: A Study of the Short Fiction* (1991). Edgar F. Harden, *An Edith Wharton Chronology* (2005), is a good resource. For an excellent recent biography: Hermione Lee, *Edith Wharton* (2007). Also stimulating are: Jennifer Anne Haystock, *Edith Wharton and the Conversations of Literary Modernism* (2008); Dianne L. Chambers, *Feminist Readings of Edith Wharton: From Silence to Speech* (2009); and Katherine Joslin, *Edith Wharton and the Making of Fashion* (2009).

The Other Two

1

Waythorn, on the drawing-room hearth, waited for his wife to come down to dinner.

It was their first night under his own roof, and he was surprised at his thrill of boyish agitation. He was not so old, to be sure—his glass gave him little more than the five-and-thirty years to which his wife confessed—but he had fancied himself already in the temperate zone; yet here he was listening for her step with a tender sense of all it symbolised, with some old trail of verse about the garlanded nuptial door-posts floating through his enjoyment of the pleasant room and the good dinner just beyond it.

They had been hastily recalled from their honeymoon by the illness of Lily Haskett, the child of Mrs. Waythorn's first marriage. The little girl, at Waythorn's desire, had been transferred to his house on the day of her mother's wedding, and the doctor, on their arrival, broke the news that she was ill with typhoid,[1] but declared that all the symptoms were favourable. Lily could show twelve years of unblemished health, and the case promised to be a light one. The nurse spoke as reassuringly, and after a moment of alarm Mrs. Waythorn had adjusted herself to the situation. She was very fond of Lily—her affection for the child had perhaps been her decisive charm in Waythorn's eyes—but she had the perfectly balanced nerves which her little girl had inherited, and no woman ever wasted less tissue in unproductive worry. Waythorn was therefore quite prepared to see her come in presently, a little late because of a last look at Lily, but as serene and well-appointed as if her good-night kiss had been laid on the brow of health. Her composure was restful to him; it acted as ballast to

[1]Life-threatening illness caused by the bacteria *Salmonella typhi*, passed by ingesting contaminated food or water and causing fever, headache, malaise, abdominal distress, diarrhea, and cough.

his somewhat unstable sensibilities. As he pictured her bending over the child's bed he thought how soothing her presence must be in illness: her very step would prognosticate recovery.

His own life had been a gray one, from temperament rather than circumstance, and he had been drawn to her by the unperturbed gaiety which kept her fresh and elastic at an age when most women's activities are growing either slack or febrile. He knew what was said about her; for, popular as she was, there had always been a faint undercurrent of detraction. When she had appeared in New York, nine or ten years earlier, as the pretty Mrs. Haskett whom Gus Varick had unearthed somewhere—was it in Pittsburgh or Utica?—society, while promptly accepting her, had reserved the right to cast a doubt on its own indiscrimination. Enquiry, however, established her undoubted connection with a socially reigning family, and explained her recent divorce as the natural result of a runaway match at seventeen; and as nothing was known of Mr. Haskett it was easy to believe the worst of him.

Alice Haskett's remarriage with Gus Varick was a passport to the set whose recognition she coveted, and for a few years the Varicks were the most popular couple in town. Unfortunately, the alliance was brief and stormy, and this time the husband had his champions. Still, even Varick's stanchest[2] supporters admitted that he was not meant for matrimony, and Mrs. Varick's grievances were of a nature to bear the inspection of the New York courts. A New York divorce is in itself a diploma of virtue, and in the semi-widowhood of this second separation Mrs. Varick took on an air of sanctity, and was allowed to confide her wrongs to some of the most scrupulous ears in town. But when it was known that she was to marry Waythorn there was a momentary reaction. Her best friends would have preferred to see her remain in the role of the injured wife, which was as becoming to her as crape to a rosy complexion. True, a decent time had elapsed, and it was not even suggested that Waythorn had supplanted his predecessor. People shook their heads over him, however, and one grudging friend, to whom he affirmed that he took the step with his eyes open, replied oracularly: "Yes—and with your ears shut."

Waythorn could afford to smile at these innuendoes. In the Wall Street phrase, he had "discounted" them. He knew that society has not yet adapted itself to the consequences of divorce, and that till the adaptation takes place every woman who uses the freedom the law accords her must be her own social justification. Waythorn had an amused confidence in his wife's ability to justify herself. His expectations were fulfilled, and before the wedding took place Alice Varick's group had rallied openly to her support. She took it all imperturbably: she had a way of surmounting obstacles without seeming to be aware of them, and Waythorn looked back

[2]Staunch, loyal, and committed in attitude.

with wonder at the trivialities over which he had worn his nerves thin. He had the sense of having found refuge in a richer, warmer nature than his own, and his satisfaction, at the moment, was humourously summed up in the thought that his wife, when she had done all she could for Lily, would not be ashamed to come down and enjoy a good dinner.

The anticipation of such enjoyment was not, however, the sentiment expressed by Mrs. Waythorn's charming face when she presently joined him. Though she had put on her most engaging teagown she had neglected to assume the smile that went with it, and Waythorn thought he had never seen her look so nearly worried.

"What is it?" he asked. "Is anything wrong with Lily?"

"No; I've just been in and she's still sleeping." Mrs. Waythorn hesitated. "But something tiresome has happened."

He had taken her two hands, and now perceived that he was crushing a paper between them.

"This letter?"

"Yes—Mr. Haskett has written—I mean his lawyer has written."

Waythorn felt himself flush uncomfortably. He dropped his wife's hands.

"What about?"

"About seeing Lily. You know the courts—"

"Yes, yes," he interrupted nervously.

Nothing was known about Haskett in New York. He was vaguely supposed to have remained in the outer darkness from which his wife had been rescued, and Waythorn was one of the few who were aware that he had given up his business in Utica and followed her to New York in order to be near his little girl. In the days of his wooing, Waythorn had often met Lily on the doorstep, rosy and smiling, on her way "to see papa."

"I am so sorry," Mrs. Waythorn murmured.

He roused himself. "What does he want?"

"He wants to see her. You know she goes to him once a week."

"Well—he doesn't expect her to go to him now, does he?"

"No—he has heard of her illness; but he expects to come here."

"*Here?*"

Mrs. Waythorn reddened under his gaze. They looked away from each other.

"I'm afraid he has the right....You'll see....She made a proffer of the letter.

Waythorn moved away with a gesture of refusal. He stood staring about the softly lighted room, which a moment before had seemed so full of bridal intimacy.

"I'm so sorry," she repeated. "If Lily could have been moved—"

"That's out of the question," he returned impatiently.

"I suppose so."

Her lip was beginning to tremble, and he felt himself a brute.

"He must come, of course," he said. "When is—his day?"

"I'm afraid—to-morrow."

"Very well. Send a note in the morning."

The butler entered to announce dinner.

Waythorn turned to his wife. "Come—you must be tired. It's beastly, but try to forget about it," he said, drawing her hand through his arm.

"You're so good, dear. I'll try," she whispered back.

Her face cleared at once, and as she looked at him across the flowers, between the rosy candle-shades, he saw her lips waver back into a smile.

"How pretty everything is!" she sighed luxuriously.

He turned to the butler. "The champagne at once, please. Mrs. Waythorn is tired."

In a moment or two their eyes met above the sparkling glasses. Her own were quite clear and untroubled: he saw that she had obeyed his injunction and forgotten.

2

Waythorn, the next morning, went down town earlier than usual. Haskett was not likely to come till the afternoon, but the instinct of flight drove him forth. He meant to stay away all day—he had thoughts of dining at his club. As his door closed behind him he reflected that before he opened it again it would have admitted another man who had as much right to enter it as himself, and the thought filled him with a physical repugnance.

He caught the "elevated"[3] at the employees' hour, and found himself crushed between two layers of pendulous humanity. At Eighth Street the man facing him wriggled out, and another took his place. Waythorn glanced up and saw that it was Gus Varick. The men were so close together that it was impossible to ignore the smile of recognition on Varick's handsome overblown face. And after all—why not? They had always been on good terms, and Varick had been divorced before Waythorn's attentions to his wife began. The two exchanged a word on the perennial grievance of the congested trains, and when a seat at their side was miraculously left empty the instinct of self-preservation made Waythorn slip into it after Varick.

The latter drew the stout man's breath of relief. "Lord—I was beginning to feel like a pressed flower." He leaned back, looking unconcernedly at Waythorn. "Sorry to hear that Sellers is knocked out again."

"Sellers?" echoed Waythorn, starting at his partner's name.

Varick looked surprised. "You didn't know he was laid up with the gout?"[4]

---

[3]An elevated railroad.
[4]Painful form of arthritis caused by an excess of uric acid in the body, characterized by inflammation of the smaller joints and often spreading to the larger joints and the internal organs.

"No. I've been away—I only got back last night." Waythorn felt himself reddening in anticipation of the other's smile.

"Ah—yes; to be sure. And Sellers's attack came on two days ago. I'm afraid he's pretty bad. Very awkward for me, as it happens, because he was just putting through a rather important thing for me."

"Ah?" Waythorn wondered vaguely since when Varick had been dealing in "important things." Hitherto he had dabbled only in the shallow pools of speculation, with which Waythorn's office did not usually concern itself.

It occurred to him that Varick might be talking at random, to relieve the strain of their propinquity. That strain was becoming momentarily more apparent to Waythorn, and when, at Cortlandt Street, he caught sight of an acquaintance and had a sudden vision of the picture he and Varick must present to an initiated eye, he jumped up with a muttered excuse.

"I hope you'll find Sellers better," said Varick civilly, and he stammered back: "If I can be of any use to you—" and let the departing crowd sweep him to the platform.

At his office he heard that Sellers was in fact ill with the gout, and would probably not be able to leave the house for some weeks.

"I'm sorry it should have happened so, Mr. Waythorn," the senior clerk said with affable significance. "Mr. Sellers was very much upset at the idea of giving you such a lot of extra work just now."

"Oh, that's no matter," said Waythorn hastily. He secretly welcomed the pressure of additional business, and was glad to think that, when the day's work was over, he would have to call at his partner's on the way home.

He was late for luncheon, and turned in at the nearest restaurant instead of going to his club. The place was full, and the waiter hurried him to the back of the room to capture the only vacant table. In the cloud of cigar-smoke Waythorn did not at once distinguish his neighbours; but presently, looking about him, he saw Varick seated a few feet off. This time, luckily, they were too far apart for conversation, and Varick, who faced another way, had probably not even seen him; but there was an irony in their renewed nearness.

Varick was said to be fond of good living, and as Waythorn sat despatching his hurried luncheon he looked across half enviously at the other's leisurely degustation of his meal. When Waythorn first saw him he had been helping himself with critical deliberation to a bit of Camembert[5] at the ideal point of liquefaction, and now, the cheese removed, he was just pouring his *café double* from its little two-storied earthen pot. He poured slowly, his ruddy profile bent above the task, and one beringed white hand steadying the lid of the coffee-pot; then he stretched his other hand to

---

[5]A rich, soft French cheese.

the decanter of cognac at his elbow, filled a liqueur-glass, took a tentative sip, and poured the brandy into his coffee-cup.

Waythorn watched him in a kind of fascination. What was he thinking of—only of the flavour of the coffee and the liqueur? Had the morning's meeting left no more trace in his thoughts than on his face? Had his wife so completely passed out of his life that even this odd encounter with her present husband, within a week after her remarriage, was no more than an incident in his day? And as Waythorn mused, another idea struck him: had Haskett ever met Varick as Varick and he had just met? The recollection of Haskett perturbed him, and he rose and left the restaurant, taking a circuitous way out to escape the placid irony of Varick's nod.

It was after seven when Waythorn reached home. He thought the footman who opened the door looked at him oddly.

"How is Miss Lily?" he asked in haste.

"Doing very well, sir. A gentleman—"

"Tell Barlow to put off dinner for half an hour," Waythorn cut him off, hurrying upstairs.

He went straight to his room and dressed without seeing his wife. When he reached the drawing-room she was there, fresh and radiant. Lily's day had been good; the doctor was not coming back that evening.

At dinner Waythorn told her of Sellers's illness and of the resulting complications. She listened sympathetically, adjuring him not to let himself be overworked, and asking vague feminine questions about the routine of the office. Then she gave him the chronicle of Lily's day; quoted the nurse and doctor, and told him who had called to inquire. He had never seen her more serene and unruffled. It struck him, with a curious pang, that she was very happy in being with him, so happy that she found a childish pleasure in rehearsing the trivial incidents of her day.

After dinner they went to the library, and the servant put the coffee and liqueurs on a low table before her and left the room. She looked singularly soft and girlish in her rosy pale dress, against the dark leather of one of his bachelor armchairs. A day earlier the contrast would have charmed him.

He turned away now, choosing a cigar with affected deliberation.

"Did Haskett come?" he asked, with his back to her.

"Oh, yes—he came."

"You didn't see him, of course?"

She hesitated a moment. "I let the nurse see him."

That was all. There was nothing more to ask. He swung round toward her, applying a match to his cigar. Well, the thing was over for a week, at any rate. He would try not to think of it. She looked up at him, a trifle rosier than usual, with a smile in her eyes.

"Ready for your coffee, dear?"

He leaned against the mantelpiece, watching her as she lifted the coffee-pot. The lamplight struck a gleam from her bracelets and tipped her soft hair with brightness. How light and slender she was, and how each gesture flowed into the next! She seemed a creature all compact of harmonies. As the thought of Haskett receded, Waythorn felt himself yielding again to the joy of possessorship. They were his, those white hands with their flitting motions, his the light haze of hair, the lips and eyes....

She set down the coffee-pot, and reaching for the decanter of cognac, measured off a liqueur-glass and poured it into his cup.

Waythorn uttered a sudden exclamation.

"What is the matter?" she said, startled.

"Nothing; only—I don't take cognac in my coffee."

"Oh, how stupid of me," she cried.

Their eyes met, and she blushed a sudden agonised red.

3

Ten days later, Mr. Sellers, still house-bound, asked Waythorn to call on his way down town.

The senior partner, with his swaddled foot propped up by the fire, greeted his associate with an air of embarrassment.

"I'm sorry, my dear fellow; I've got to ask you to do an awkward thing for me."

Waythorn waited, and the other went on, after a pause apparently given to the arrangement of his phrases: "The fact is, when I was knocked out I had just gone into a rather complicated piece of business for—Gus Varick."

"Well?" said Waythorn, with an attempt to put him at his ease.

"Well—it's this way: Varick came to me the day before my attack. He had evidently had an inside tip from somebody, and had made about a hundred thousand. He came to me for advice, and I suggested his going in with Vanderlyn."

"Oh, the deuce!" Waythorn exclaimed. He saw in a flash what had happened. The investment was an alluring one, but required negotiation. He listened quietly while Sellers put the case before him, and, the statement ended, he said: "You think I ought to see Varick?"

"I'm afraid I can't as yet. The doctor is obdurate. And this thing can't wait. I hate to ask you, but no one else in the office knows the ins and outs of it."

Waythorn stood silent. He did not care a farthing for the success of Varick's venture, but the honour of the office was to be considered, and he could hardly refuse to oblige his partner.

"Very well," he said, "I'll do it."

That afternoon, apprised by telephone, Varick called at the office. Waythorn, waiting in his private room, wondered what the others thought of it. The newspapers, at the time of Mrs. Waythorn's marriage, had acquainted their readers with every detail of her previous matrimonial ventures, and

Waythorn could fancy the clerks smiling behind Varick's back as he was ushered in.

Varick bore himself admirably. He was easy without being undignified, and Waythorn was conscious of cutting a much less impressive figure. Varick had no experience of business, and the talk prolonged itself for nearly an hour while Waythorn set forth with scrupulous precision the details of the proposed transaction.

"I'm awfully obliged to you," Varick said as he rose. "The fact is I'm not used to having much money to look after, and I don't want to make an ass of myself—" He smiled, and Waythorn could not help noticing that there was something pleasant about his smile. "It feels uncommonly queer to have enough cash to pay one's bills. I'd have sold my soul for it a few years ago!"

Waythorn winced at the allusion. He had heard it rumoured that a lack of funds had been one of the determining causes of the Varick separation, but it did not occur to him that Varick's words were intentional. It seemed more likely that the desire to keep clear of embarrassing topics had fatally drawn him into one. Waythorn did not wish to be outdone in civility.

"We'll do the best we can for you," he said. "I think this is a good thing you're in."

"Oh, I'm sure it's immense. It's awfully good of you—" Varick broke off, embarrassed. "I suppose the thing's settled now—but if—"

"If anything happens before Sellers is about, I'll see you again," said Waythorn quietly. He was glad, in the end, to appear the more self-possessed of the two.

The course of Lily's illness ran smooth, and as the days passed Waythorn grew used to the idea of Haskett's weekly visit. The first time the day came round, he stayed out late, and questioned his wife as to the visit on his return. She replied at once that Haskett had merely seen the nurse downstairs, as the doctor did not wish any one in the child's sick-room till after the crisis.

The following week Waythorn was again conscious of the recurrence of the day, but had forgotten it by the time he came home to dinner. The crisis of the disease came a few days later, with a rapid decline of fever, and the little girl was pronounced out of danger. In the rejoicing which ensued the thought of Haskett passed out of Waythorn's mind, and one afternoon, letting himself into the house with a latchkey, he went straight to his library without noticing a shabby hat and umbrella in the hall.

In the library he found a small effaced-looking man with a thinnish gray beard sitting on the edge of a chair. The stranger might have been a piano-tuner, or one of those mysteriously efficient persons who are summoned in emergencies to adjust some detail of the domestic machinery. He blinked at Waythorn through a pair of gold-rimmed spectacles and said mildly: "Mr. Waythorn, I presume? I am Lily's father."

Waythorn flushed. "Oh—" he stammered uncomfortably. He broke off, disliking to appear rude. Inwardly he was trying to adjust the actual Haskett to the image of him projected by his wife's reminiscences. Waythorn had been allowed to infer that Alice's first husband was a brute.

"I am sorry to intrude," said Haskett, with his over-the-counter politeness.

"Don't mention it," returned Waythorn, collecting himself. "I suppose the nurse has been told?"

"I presume so. I can wait," said Haskett. He had a resigned way of speaking, as though life had worn down his natural powers of resistance.

Waythorn stood on the threshold, nervously pulling off his gloves.

"I'm sorry you've been detained. I will send for the nurse," he said; and as he opened the door he added with an effort: "I'm glad we can give you a good report of Lily." He winced as the *we* slipped out, but Haskett seemed not to notice it.

"Thank you, Mr. Waythorn. It's been an anxious time for me."

"Ah, well, that's past. Soon she'll be able to go to you." Waythorn nodded and passed out.

In his own room he flung himself down with a groan. He hated the womanish sensibility which made him suffer so acutely from the grotesque chances of life. He had known when he married that his wife's former husbands were both living, and that amid the multiplied contacts of modern existence there were a thousand chances to one that he would run against one or the other, yet he found himself as much disturbed by his brief encounter with Haskett as though the law had not obligingly removed all difficulties in the way of their meeting.

Waythorn sprang up and began to pace the room nervously. He had not suffered half as much from his two meetings with Varick. It was Haskett's presence in his own house that made the situation so intolerable. He stood still, hearing steps in the passage.

"This way, please," he heard the nurse say. Haskett was being taken upstairs, then: not a corner of the house but was open to him. Waythorn dropped into another chair, staring vaguely ahead of him. On his dressing-table stood a photograph of Alice, taken when he had first known her. She was Alice Varick then—how fine and exquisite he had thought her! Those were Varick's pearls about her neck. At Waythorn's instance they had been returned before her marriage. Had Haskett ever given her any trinkets—and what had become of them, Waythorn wondered? He realised suddenly that he knew very little of Haskett's past or present situation; but from the man's appearance and manner of speech he could reconstruct with curious precision the surroundings of Alice's first marriage. And it startled him to think that she had, in the background of her life, a phase of existence so different from anything with which he had connected her. Varick, whatever his faults, was a gentleman, in the conventional, traditional sense of the term: the sense which at that moment seemed, oddly enough, to have most meaning to Waythorn. He and Varick had the same social habits, spoke the same language, understood the same allusions. But this other man...it was grotesquely uppermost in Waythorn's mind that Haskett had worn a made-up tie attached with an elastic. Why should that ridiculous detail symbolise the whole man? Waythorn was exasperated by his own paltriness, but the fact of the tie expanded, forced itself on him, became as it were the key to Alice's past. He could see her, as Mrs. Haskett, sitting in a "front parlour" furnished in plush, with a pianola, and a copy of "Ben Hur"[6] on the centre-table. He could see her going to the theatre with Haskett—or perhaps even to a "Church Sociable"—she in a "picture hat" and Haskett in a black frock-coat, a little creased, with the made-up tie on an elastic. On the way home they would stop and look at the illuminated shop-windows, lingering over the photographs of New York actresses. On Sunday afternoons Haskett would take her for a walk, pushing Lily ahead of them in a white enamelled perambulator,[7] and Waythorn had a vision of the people they would stop and talk to. He could fancy how pretty Alice must have looked, in a dress adroitly constructed from the hints of a New York fashion-paper, and how she must have looked down on the other women, chafing at her life, and secretly feeling that she belonged in a bigger place.

For the moment his foremost thought was one of wonder at the way in which she had shed the phase of existence which her marriage with Haskett implied. It was as if her whole aspect, every gesture, every inflection, every allusion, were a studied negation of that period of her life. If she had denied being married to Haskett she could hardly have stood more convicted of duplicity than in this obliteration of the self which had been his wife.

Waythorn started up; checking himself in the analysis of her motives. What right had he to create a fantastic effigy of her and then pass judgment on it? She had spoken vaguely of her first marriage as unhappy, had hinted, with becoming reticence, that Haskett had wrought havoc among her young illusions....It was a pity for Waythorn's peace of mind that Haskett's very inoffensiveness shed a new light on the nature of those illusions. A man would rather think that his wife has been brutalised by her first husband than that the process has been reversed.

4

"Mr. Waythorn, I don't like that French governess of Lily's."

Haskett, subdued and apologetic, stood before Waythorn in the library, revolving his shabby hat in his hand.

---

[6]*Ben-Hur: A Tale of the Christ*, published in 1880 by Civil War general Lew Wallace (1827–1905), was the best-selling novel of the nineteenth century. It became a Broadway play in 1899.
[7]Baby carriage.

Waythorn, surprised in his armchair over the evening paper, stared back perplexedly at his visitor.

"You'll excuse my asking to see you," Haskett continued. "But this is my last visit, and I thought if I could have a word with you it would be a better way than writing to Mrs. Waythorn's lawyer."

Waythorn rose uneasily. He did not like the French governess either; but that was irrelevant.

"I am not so sure of that," he returned stiffly; "but since you wish it I will give your message to—my wife." He always hesitated over the possessive pronoun in addressing Haskett.

The latter sighed. "I don't know as that will help much. She didn't like it when I spoke to her."

Waythorn turned red. "When did you see her?" he asked.

"Not since the first day I came to see Lily—right after she was taken sick. I remarked to her then that I didn't like the governess."

Waythorn made no answer. He remembered distinctly that, after that first visit, he had asked his wife if she had seen Haskett. She had lied to him then, but she had respected his wishes since; and the incident cast a curious light on her character. He was sure she would not have seen Haskett that first day if she had divined that Waythorn would object, and the fact that she did not divine it was almost as disagreeable to the latter as the discovery that she had lied to him.

"I don't like the woman," Haskett was repeating with mild persistency. "She ain't straight, Mr. Waythorn—she'll teach the child to be underhand. I've noticed a change in Lily—she's too anxious to please—and she don't always tell the truth. She used to be the straightest child, Mr. Waythorn—" He broke off, his voice a little thick. "Not but what I want her to have a stylish education," he ended.

Waythorn was touched. "I'm sorry, Mr. Haskett; but frankly, I don't quite see what I can do."

Haskett hesitated. Then he laid his hat on the table, and advanced to the hearth-rug, on which Waythorn was standing. There was nothing aggressive in his manner, but he had the solemnity of a timid man resolved on a decisive measure.

"There's just one thing you can do, Mr. Waythorn," he said. "You can remind Mrs. Waythorn that, by the decree of the courts, I am entitled to have a voice in Lily's bringing up." He paused, and went on more deprecatingly: "I'm not the kind to talk about enforcing my rights, Mr. Waythorn. I don't know as I think a man is entitled to rights he hasn't known how to hold on to; but this business of the child is different. I've never let go there—and I never mean to."

The scene left Waythorn deeply shaken. Shamefacedly, in indirect ways, he had been finding out about Haskett; and all that he had learned was favourable. The little man, in order to be near his daughter, had sold out his share in a profitable business in Utica, and accepted a modest clerkship in a New York manufacturing house. He boarded in a shabby street and had few acquaintances. His passion for Lily filled his life. Waythorn felt that this exploration of Haskett was like groping about with a dark-lantern in his wife's past; but he saw now that there were recesses his lantern had not explored. He had never enquired into the exact circumstances of his wife's first matrimonial rupture. On the surface all had been fair. It was she who had obtained the divorce, and the court had given her the child. But Waythorn knew how many ambiguities such a verdict might cover. The mere fact that Haskett retained a right over his daughter implied an unsuspected compromise. Waythorn was an idealist. He always refused to recognise unpleasant contingencies till he found himself confronted with them, and then he saw them followed by a spectral train of consequences. His next days were thus haunted, and he determined to try to lay the ghosts by conjuring them up in his wife's presence.

When he repeated Haskett's request a flame of anger passed over her face; but she subdued it instantly and spoke with a slight quiver of outraged motherhood.

"It is very ungentlemanly of him," she said.

The word grated on Waythorn. "That is neither here nor there. It's a bare question of rights."

She murmured: "It's not as if he could ever be a help to Lily—"

Waythorn flushed. This was even less to his taste. "The question is," he repeated, "what authority has he over her?"

She looked downward, twisting herself a little in her seat. "I am willing to see him—I thought you objected," she faltered.

In a flash he understood that she knew the extent of Haskett's claims. Perhaps it was not the first time she had resisted them.

"My objecting has nothing to do with it," he said coldly; "if Haskett has a right to be consulted you must consult him."

She burst into tears, and he saw that she expected him to regard her as a victim.

Haskett did not abuse his rights. Waythorn had felt miserably sure that he would not. But the governess was dismissed, and from time to time the little man demanded an interview with Alice. After the first outburst she accepted the situation with her usual adaptability. Haskett had once reminded Waythorn of the piano-tuner, and Mrs. Waythorn, after a month or two, appeared to class him with that domestic familiar. Waythorn could not but respect the father's tenacity. At first he had tried to cultivate the suspicion that Haskett might be "up to" something, that he had an object in securing a foothold in the house. But in his heart Waythorn was sure of Haskett's single-mindedness; he even guessed in the latter a mild contempt for such advantages as his relation with the Waythorns might offer.

Haskett's sincerity of purpose made him invulnerable, and his successor had to accept him as a lien on the property.

Mr. Sellers was sent to Europe to recover from his gout, and Varick's affairs hung on Waythorn's hands. The negotiations were prolonged and complicated; they necessitated frequent conferences between the two men, and the interests of the firm forbade Waythorn's suggesting that his client should transfer his business to another office.

Varick appeared well in the transaction. In moments of relaxation his coarse streak appeared, and Waythorn dreaded his geniality; but in the office he was concise and clear-headed, with a flattering deference to Waythorn's judgment. Their business relations being so affably established, it would have been absurd for the two men to ignore each other in society. The first time they met in a drawing-room, Varick took up their intercourse in the same easy key, and his hostess's grateful glance obliged Waythorn to respond to it. After that they ran across each other frequently, and one evening at a ball Waythorn, wandering through the remoter rooms, came upon Varick seated beside his wife. She coloured a little, and faltered in what she was saying; but Varick nodded to Waythorn without rising, and the latter strolled on.

In the carriage, on the way home, he broke out nervously: "I didn't know you spoke to Varick."

Her voice trembled a little. "It's the first time—he happened to be standing near me; I didn't know what to do. It's so awkward, meeting everywhere—and he said you had been very kind about some business."

"That's different," said Waythorn.

She paused a moment. "I'll do just as you wish," she returned pliantly. "I thought it would be less awkward to speak to him when we meet."

Her pliancy was beginning to sicken him. Had she really no will of her own—no theory about her relation to these men? She had accepted Haskett—did she mean to accept Varick? It was "less awkward," as she had said, and her instinct was to evade difficulties or to circumvent them. With sudden vividness Waythorn saw how the instinct had developed. She was "as easy as an old shoe"—a shoe that too many feet had worn. Her elasticity was the result of tension in too many different directions. Alice Haskett—Alice Varick—Alice Waythorn—she had been each in turn, and had left hanging to each name a little of her privacy, a little of her personality, a little of the inmost self where the unknown god abides.

"Yes—it's better to speak to Varick," said Waythorn wearily.

5

The winter wore on, and society took advantage of the Waythorns' acceptance of Varick. Harassed hostesses were grateful to them for bridging over a social difficulty, and Mrs. Waythorn was held up as a miracle of good taste. Some experimental spirits could not resist the diversion of throwing Varick and his former wife together, and there were those who thought he found a zest in the propinquity. But Mrs. Waythorn's conduct remained irreproachable. She neither avoided Varick nor sought him out. Even Waythorn could not but admit that she had discovered the solution of the newest social problem.

He had married her without giving much thought to that problem. He had fancied that a woman can shed her past like a man. But now he saw that Alice was bound to hers both by the circumstances which forced her into continued relation with it, and by the traces it had left on her nature. With grim irony Waythorn compared himself to a member of a syndicate. He held so many shares in his wife's personality and his predecessors were his partners in the business. If there had been any element of passion in the transaction he would have felt less deteriorated by it. The fact that Alice took her change of husbands like a change of weather reduced the situation to mediocrity. He could have forgiven her for blunders, for excesses; for resisting Haskett, for yielding to Varick; for anything but her acquiescence and her tact. She reminded him of a juggler tossing knives; but the knives were blunt and she knew they would never cut her.

And then, gradually, habit formed a protecting surface for his sensibilities. If he paid for each day's comfort with the small change of his illusions, he grew daily to value the comfort more and set less store upon the coin. He had drifted into a dulling propinquity with Haskett and Varick and he took refuge in the cheap revenge of satirising the situation. He even began to reckon up the advantages which accrued from it, to ask himself if it were not better to own a third of a wife who knew how to make a man happy than a whole one who had lacked opportunity to acquire the art. For it *was* an art, and made up, like all others, of concessions, eliminations and embellishments; of lights judiciously thrown and shadows skilfully softened. His wife knew exactly how to manage the lights, and he knew exactly to what training she owed her skill. He even tried to trace the source of his obligations, to discriminate between the influences which had combined to produce his domestic happiness: he perceived that Haskett's commonness had made Alice worship good breeding, while Varick's liberal construction of the marriage bond had taught her to value the conjugal virtues; so that he was directly indebted to his predecessors for the devotion which made his life easy if not inspiring.

From this phase he passed into that of complete acceptance. He ceased to satirise himself because time dulled the irony of the situation and the joke lost its humour with its sting. Even the sight of Haskett's hat on the hall table had ceased to touch the springs of epigram. The hat was often seen there now, for it had been decided that it was better for Lily's father to visit her than for the little girl to go to his boarding-house. Waythorn, having acquiesced in this arrangement, had been surprised to find how little difference it made. Haskett was never obtrusive, and the few visitors who met him on the stairs were unaware of his identity. Waythorn did not know how often he saw Alice, but with himself Haskett was seldom in contact.

One afternoon, however, he learned on entering that Lily's father was waiting to see him. In the library he found Haskett occupying a chair in his usual provisional way. Waythorn always felt grateful to him for not leaning back.

"I hope you'll excuse me, Mr. Waythorn," he said rising. "I wanted to see Mrs. Waythorn about Lily, and your man asked me to wait here till she came in."

"Of course," said Waythorn, remembering that a sudden leak had that morning given over the drawing-room to the plumbers.

He opened his cigar-case and held it out to his visitor, and Haskett's acceptance seemed to mark a fresh stage in their intercourse. The spring evening was chilly, and Waythorn invited his guest to draw up his chair to the fire. He meant to find an excuse to leave Haskett in a moment; but he was tired and cold, and after all the little man no longer jarred on him.

The two were enclosed in the intimacy of their blended cigar-smoke when the door opened and Varick walked into the room. Waythorn rose abruptly. It was the first time that Varick had come to the house, and the surprise of seeing him, combined with the singular inopportuneness of his arrival, gave a new edge to Waythorn's blunted sensibilities. He stared at his visitor without speaking.

Varick seemed too preoccupied to notice his host's embarrassment.

"My dear fellow," he exclaimed in his most expansive tone, "I must apologize for tumbling in on you in this way, but I was too late to catch you down town, and so I thought—"

He stopped short, catching sight of Haskett, and his sanguine colour deepened to a flush which spread vividly under his scant blond hair. But in a moment he recovered himself and nodded slightly. Haskett returned the bow in silence, and Waythorn was still groping for speech when the footman came in carrying a tea-table.

The intrusion offered a welcome vent to Waythorn's nerves. "What the deuce are you bringing this here for?" he said sharply.

"I beg your pardon, sir, but the plumbers are still in the drawing-room, and Mrs. Waythorn said she would have tea in the library." The footman's perfectly respectful tone implied a reflection on Waythorn's reasonableness.

"Oh, very well," said the latter resignedly, and the footman proceeded to open the folding tea-table and set out its complicated appointments. While this interminable process continued the three men stood motionless, watching it with a fascinated stare, till Waythorn, to break the silence, said to Varick: "Won't you have a cigar?"

He held out the case he had just tendered to Haskett, and Varick helped himself with a smile. Waythorn looked about for a match, and finding none, proffered a light from his own cigar. Haskett, in the background, held his ground mildly, examining his cigar-tip now and then, and stepping forward at the right moment to knock its ashes into the fire.

The footman at last withdrew, and Varick immediately began: "If I could just say half a word to you about this business—"

"Certainly," stammered Waythorn; "in the dining-room—"

But as he placed his hand on the door it opened from without, and his wife appeared on the threshold.

She came in fresh and smiling, in her street dress and hat, shedding a fragrance from the boa which she loosened in advancing.

"Shall we have tea in here, dear?" she began; and then she caught sight of Varick. Her smile deepened, veiling a slight tremor of surprise.

"Why, how do you do?" she said with a distinct note of pleasure.

As she shook hands with Varick she saw Haskett standing behind him. Her smile faded for a moment, but she recalled it quickly, with a scarcely perceptible side-glance at Waythorn.

"How do you do, Mr. Haskett?" she said, and shook hands with him a shade less cordially.

The three men stood awkwardly before her, till Varick, always the most self-possessed, dashed into an explanatory phrase.

"We—I had to see Waythorn a moment on business," he stammered, brick-red from chin to nape.

Haskett stepped forward with his air of mild obstinacy. "I am sorry to intrude; but you appointed five o'clock—" he directed his resigned glance to the time-piece on the mantel.

She swept aside their embarrassment with a charming gesture of hospitality.

"I'm so sorry—I'm always late; but the afternoon was so lovely." She stood drawing off her gloves, propitiatory and graceful, diffusing about her a sense of ease and familiarity in which the situation lost its grotesqueness. "But before talking business," she added brightly, "I'm sure every one wants a cup of tea."

She dropped into her low chair by the tea-table, and the two visitors, as if drawn by her smile, advanced to receive the cups she held out.

She glanced about for Waythorn, and he took the third cup with a laugh.

[1904]

SUI SIN FAR (EDITH MAUDE EATON) ▪ (1865–1914)

Edith Maude Eaton, known by her pseudonym Sui Sin Far ("water fragrant flower," "narcissus," or "lily" in Chinese), is one of the leading early voices of Asian American literature and multicultural writing in the United States. Biracial, bicultural, and unmarried, she wrote with eloquence and insight in short stories and journalistic pieces about the challenges she faced and the struggles she endured. In 1912, she published her only book, *Mrs. Spring Fragrance*—it went out of print two years later. It was reprinted in 1995 and now is taught frequently in women's studies and Asian American and American literature courses.

Eaton was born in Macclesfield, England, the eldest daughter of a Chinese mother, who was a missionary, and a British father, a merchant. At an early age she journeyed with her family to Hudson City, New York (120 miles north of Manhattan), and then to Canada, settling in Montreal, where she helped to care for her many siblings and sold her father's paintings and her own lace door to door. Neither she nor her siblings learned to speak Chinese. One of them, Winnifred (1875–1954), also became an author, writing popular romantic novels with exotic settings, under the pseudonym Onoto Watanna.

In her late teens Eaton began newspaper work and, soon thereafter, short-story writing, using the name Sui Sin Far. Eaton is especially poignant and illuminating in her portraits of immigrant families and depictions of the lives of women. She travelled widely from coast to coast in the United States, and spent time in Jamaica as well, but, in ill health, she returned to Canada in 1913 and died in Montreal (which she viewed as her true home) the following year.

"Leaves from the Mental Portfolio of an Eurasian" (1909) is perhaps Eaton's best piece of writing. She touches on moments in her childhood and adulthood, from age four to forty, calling attention to racial prejudice—shown by whites and Chinese—and pointing to "Eurasian" as the best term, for her identity. The scholar Amy Ling has said: "If we set Sui Sin Far into the context of her time and place, in late nineteenth-century sinophobic and imperialistic Euro-American nations, then we admit that for her, a Eurasian woman who could pass as white, to choose to champion the Chinese and working-class women and to identify herself as such, publicly and in print, an act of great determination and courage."

Eaton's output, while limited, was significant: she is one of the pioneers of Asian American studies. As Elizabeth Ammons has noted: "That Sui Sin Far invented herself—created her own voice—out of such deep silencing and systemic racist repression was one of the triumphs of American literature at the turn of the century." Critics, teachers, and students esteem and celebrate Eaton for affirming her Chinese ancestry and heritage in her work during a period of intense anti-Asian feeling in the United States.

For further study: Annette White-Parks, *Sui Sin Far/Edith Maude Eaton: A Literary Biography* (1995); and Dominika Ferens, *Edith and Winnifred Eaton: Chinatown Missions and Japanese Romances* (2002). An important source is Mrs. Spring Fragrance *and Other Writings*, eds. Amy Ling and Annette White-Parks (1995). See also the discussions of Sui Sin Far in: Amy Ling, *Between Worlds: Women Writers of Chinese Ancestry* (1990); Elizabeth Ammons, *Conflicting Stories: American Women Writers at the Turn of the Twentieth Century* (1992); and *Ethnicity and the American Short Story*, ed. Julie Brown (1997). For context: *Reading the Literatures of Asian America*, eds. Shirley Geok-lin Lim and Amy Ling (1992); *Form and Transformation in Asian American Literature*, eds. Zhou Xiaojing and Samina Najmi (2005); *Asian American Literary Studies*, ed. Guiyou Huang (2005); and *Literary Gestures: The Aesthetic in Asian American Writing*, eds. Rocío G. Davis and Sue-Im Lee (2006).

Leaves from the Mental Portfolio of an Eurasian

When I look back over the years I see myself, a little child of scarcely four years of age, walking in front of my nurse, in a green English lane, and listening to her tell another of her kind that my mother is Chinese. "Oh, Lord!" exclaims the informed. She turns around and scans me curiously from head to foot. Then the two women whisper together. Tho the word "Chinese" conveys very little meaning to my mind, I feel that they are talking about my father and mother and my heart swells with indignation. When we reach home I rush to my mother and try to tell her what I have heard. I am a young child. I fail to make myself intelligible. My mother does not understand, and when the nurse declares to her, "Little Miss Sui is a story-teller," my mother slaps me.

Many a long year has past over my head since that day—the day on which I first learned that I was something different and apart from other children, but tho my mother has forgotten it, I have not.

I see myself again, a few years older. I am playing with another child in a garden. A girl passes by outside the gate. "Mamie," she cries to my companion. "I wouldn't speak to Sui if I were you. Her mamma is Chinese."

"I don't care," answers the little one beside me. And then to me, "Even if your mamma is Chinese, I like you better than I like Annie."

"But I don't like you," I answer, turning my back on her. It is my first conscious lie.

I am at a children's party, given by the wife of an Indian officer whose children were schoolfellows of mine. I am only six years of age, but have attended a private school for over a year, and have already learned that China is a heathen country, being civilized by England. However, for the time being, I am a merry romping child. There are quite a number of grown people present. One, a white haired old man, has his attention called to me by the hostess. He adjusts his eyeglasses and surveys me critically. "Ah, indeed!" her exclaims. "Who would have thought it at first glance. Yet now I see the difference between her and other children. What a peculiar coloring! Her mother's eyes and hair and her father's features, I presume. Very interesting little creature!"

I had been called from my play for the purpose of inspection. I do not return to it. For the rest of the evening I hide myself behind a hall door and refuse to show myself until it is time to go home.

My parents have come to America. We are in Hudson City, N.Y., and we are very poor. I am out with my brother, who is ten months older than myself. We pass a Chinese store, the door of which is open. "Look!" says Charlie. "Those men in there are Chinese!" Eagerly I gaze into the long low room. With the exception of my mother, who is English bred with English ways and manner of dress, I have never seen a Chinese person. The two men within the store are uncouth specimens of their race, drest in working blouses and pantaloons with queues hanging down their backs. I recoil with a sense of shock.

"Oh, Charlie," I cry. "Are we like that?"

"Well, we're Chinese, and they're Chinese, too, so we must be!" returns my seven-year-old brother.

"Of course you are," puts in a boy who has followed us down the street, and who lives near us and has seen my mother: "Chinky, Chinky, Chinaman, yellow-face, pig-tail, rat-eater." A number of other boys and several little girls join in with him.

"Better than you," shouts my brothers, facing the crowd. He is younger and smaller than any there, and I am even more insignificant than he; but my spirit revives.

"I'd rather be Chinese than anything else in the world," I scream.

They pull my hair, they tear my clothes, they scratch my face, and all but lame my brother; but the white blood in our veins fights valiantly for the Chinese half of us. When it is all over, exhausted and bedraggled, we crawl home, and report to our mother that we have "won the battle."

"Are you sure?" asks my mother doubtfully.

"Of course. They ran from us. They were frightened," returns my brother.

My mother smiles with satisfaction.

"Do you hear?" she asks my father.

"Umm," he observes, raising his eyes from his paper for an instant. My childish instinct, however, tells me that he is more interested than he appears, to be.

It is tea time, but I cannot eat. Unobserved I crawl away. I do not sleep that night. I am too excited and I ache all over. Our opponents had been so very much stronger and bigger than we. Toward morning, however, I fall into a doze from which I awake myself, shouting:

"Sound the battle cry;
    See the foe is nigh."

My mother believes in sending us to Sunday school. She has been brought up in a Presbyterian college.

The scene of my life shifts to Eastern Canada. The sleigh which has carried us from the station stops in front of a little French Canadian hotel. Immediately we are surrounded by a number of villagers, who stare curiously at my mother as my father assists her to alight from the sleigh. Their curiosity, however, is tempered with kindness, as they watch, one after another, the little black heads of my brothers and sisters and myself emerge out of the buffalo robe, which is part of the sleigh's outfit. There are six of us, four girls and two boys; the eldest, my brother, being only seven years of age. My father and mother are still in their twenties. "Les pauvres enfants,"[1] the inhabitants murmur, as they help to carry us into the hotel. Then in lower tones: "Chinoise, Chinoise."

For some time after our arrival, whenever we children are sent for a walk, our footsteps are dogged by a number of young French and English Canadians, who amuse themselves with speculations as to whether, we being Chinese, are susceptible to pinches and hair pulling, while older persons pause and gaze upon us, very much in the same way that I have seen people gaze upon strange animals in a menagerie. Now and then we are stopt and plied with questions as to what we eat and drink, how we go to sleep, if my mother understands what my father says to her, if we sit on chairs or squat on floors, etc., etc., etc.

There are many pitched battles, of course, and we seldom leave the house without being armed for conflict. My mother takes a great interest in our battles, and usually cheers us on, tho I doubt whether she understands the depth of the troubled waters thru which her little children wade. As to my father, peace is his motto, and he deems it wisest to be blind and deaf to many things.

School days are short, but memorable. I am in the same class with my brother, my sister next to me in the class below. The little girl whose desk my sister shares shrinks close against the wall as my sister takes her place. In a little while she raises her hand.

"Please, teacher!"
"Yes, Annie."
"May I change my seat?"
"No, you may not!"

[1]The poor children (French).

The little girl sobs. "Why should she have to sit beside a —"

Happily my sister does not seem to hear, and before long the two little girls become great friends. I have many such experiences.

My brother is remarkably bright; my sister next to me has a wonderful head for figures, and when only eight years of age helps my father with his night work accounts. My parents compare her with me. She is of sturdier build than I, and, as my father says, "Always has her wits about her." He thinks her more like my mother, who is very bright and interested in every little detail of practical life. My father tells me that I will never make half the woman that my mother is or that my sister will be. I am not as strong as my sisters, which makes me feel somewhat ashamed, for I am the eldest little girl, and more is expected of me. I have no organic disease, but the strength of my feelings seems to take from me the strength of my body. I am prostrated at times with attacks of nervous sickness. The doctor says that my heart is unusually large; but in the light of the present I know that the cross of the Eurasian bore too heavily upon my childish shoulders. I usually hide my weakness from the family until I cannot stand. I do not understand myself, and I have an idea that the others will despise me for not being as strong as they. Therefore, I like to wander away alone, either by the river or in the bush. The green fields and flowing water have a charm for me. At the age of seven, as it is today, a bird on the wing is my emblem of happiness.

I have come from a race on my mother's side which is said to be the most stolid and insensible to feeling of all races, yet I look back over the years and see myself so keenly alive to every shade of sorrow and suffering that it is almost a pain to live.

If there is any trouble in the house in the way of a difference between my father and mother, or if any child is punished, how I suffer! And when harmony is restored, heaven seems to be around me. I can be sad, but I can also be glad. My mother's screams of agony when a baby is born almost drive me wild, and long after her pangs have subsided I feel them in my own body. Sometimes it is a week before I can get to sleep after such an experience.

A debt owing by my father fills me with shame. I feel like a criminal when I pass the creditor's door. I am only ten years old. And all the while the question of nationality perplexes my little brain. Why are we what we are? I and my brothers and sisters. Why did God make us to be hooted and stared at? Papa is English, mamma is Chinese. Why couldn't we have been either one thing or the other? Why is my mother's race despised? I look into the faces of my father and mother. Is she not every bit as dear and good as he? Why? Why? She sings us the songs she learned at her English school. She tells us tales of China. Tho a child when she left her native land she remembers it well, and I am never tired of listening to the story of how she was stolen from her home. She tells us over and over again of her meeting with my father in Shanghai and the romance of their marriage. Why? Why?

I do not confide in my father and mother. They would not understand. How could they? He is English, she is Chinese. I am different to both of them—a stranger, tho their own child. "What are we?" I ask my brother. "It doesn't matter, sissy," he responds. But it does. I love poetry, particularly heroic pieces. I also love fairy tales. Stories of everyday life do not appeal to me. I dream dreams of being great and noble; my sisters and brothers also. I glory in the idea of dying at the stake and a great genie arising from the flames and declaring to those who have scorned us: "Behold, how great and glorious and noble are the Chinese people!"

My sisters are apprenticed to a dressmaker; my brother is entered in an office. I tramp around and sell my father's pictures, also some lace which I make myself. My nationality, if I had only known it at that time, helps to make sales. The ladies who are my customers call me "The Little Chinese Lace Girl." But it is a dangerous life for a very young girl. I come near to "mysteriously disappearing" many a time. The greatest temptation was in the thought of getting far away from where I was known, to where no mocking cries of "Chinese!" "Chinese!" could reach.

Whenever I have the opportunity I steal away to the library and read every book I can find on China and the Chinese. I learn that China is the oldest civilized nation on the face of the earth and a few other things. At eighteen years of age what troubles me is not that I am what I am, but that others are ignorant of my superiority. I am small, but my feelings are big—and great is my vanity.

My sisters attended dancing classes, for which they pay their own fees. In spite of covert smiles and sneers, they are glad to meet and mingle with other young folk. They are not sensitive in the sense that I am. And yet they understand. One of them tells me that she overhead a young many say to another that he would rather marry a pig than a girl with Chinese blood in her veins.

In course of time I too learn shorthand and take a position in an office. Like my sister, I teach myself, but, unlike my sister, I have neither the perseverance nor the ability to perfect myself. Besides, to a temperament like mine, it is torture to spend the hours in transcribing other people's thoughts. Therefore, altho I can always earn a moderately good salary, I do not distinguish myself in the business world as does she.

When I have been working for some years I open an office of my own. The local papers patronize me and give me a number of assignments, including most of the local Chinese reporting. I meet many Chinese persons, and when they get into trouble am often called upon to fight their battles in the papers. This I enjoy. My heart leaps for joy when I read one day an article by a New York Chinese in which he declares, "The Chinese in America owe an everlasting debt of gratitude to Sui Sin Far for the bold stand she has taken in their defense."

The Chinaman who wrote the article seeks me out and calls upon me. He is a clever and witty man, a graduate of one of the American colleges and as well a Chinese scholar. I learn that he has an American wife and several children. I am very much interested in these children, and when I meet them my heart throbs in sympathetic tune with the tales they relate of their experiences as Eurasians. "Why did papa and mamma born us?" asks one. Why?

I also meet other Chinese men who compare favorably with the white men of my acquaintance in mind and heart qualities. Some of them are quite handsome. They have not as finely cut noses and as well developed chins as the white men, but they have smoother skins and their expression is more serene; their hands are better shaped and their voices softer.

Some little Chinese women whom I interview are very anxious to known whether I would marry a Chinaman. I do not answer No. They clap their hands delightedly, and assure me that the Chinese are much the finest and best of all men. They are, however, a little doubtful as to whether one could be persuaded to care for me, full-blooded Chinese people having a prejudice against the half white.

Fundamentally, I muse, all people are the same. My mother's race is as prejudiced as my father's. Only when the whole world becomes as one family will human beings be able to see clearly and hear distinctly. I believe that some day a great part of the world will be Eurasian. I cheer myself with the thought that I am but a pioneer. A pioneer should glory in suffering.

"You were walking with a Chinaman yesterday," accuses an acquaintance.

"Yes, what of it?"

"You ought not to. It isn't right."

"Not right to walk with one of my mother's people? Oh, indeed!"

I cannot reconcile his notion of righteousness with my own.

I am living in a little town away off on the north shore of a big lake. Next to me at the dinner table is the man for whom I work as a stenographer. There are also a couple of business men, a young girl and her mother.

Some one makes a remark about the cars full of Chinamen that past that morning. A transcontinental railway runs thru the town.

My employer shakes his rugged head. "Somehow or other," says he, "I cannot reconcile myself to the thought that the Chinese are humans like ourselves. They may have immortal souls, but their faces seem to be so utterly devoid of expression that I cannot help but doubt."

"Souls," echoes the town clerk. "Their bodies are enough for me. A Chinaman is, in my eyes, more repulsive than a nigger."

"They always give me such a creepy feeling," puts in the young girl with a laugh.

"I wouldn't have one in my house," declares my landlady.

"Now, the Japanese are different altogether. There is something bright and likeable about those men," continues Mr. K.

A miserable, cowardly feeling keeps me silent. I am in a Middle West town. If I declare what I am, every person in the place will hear about it the next day. The population is in the main made up of working folks with strong prejudices against my mother's countrymen. The prospect before me is not an enviable one—if I speak. I have no longer an ambition to die at the stake for the sake of demonstrating the greatness and nobleness of the Chinese people.

Mr. K. turns to me with a kindly smile.

"What makes Miss Far so quiet?" he asks.

"I don't suppose she finds the 'washee washee men' particularly interesting subjects of conversation," volunteers the young manager of the local bank.

With a great effort I raise my eyes from my plate. "Mr. K.," I say, addressing my employer, "the Chinese people may have no souls, no expression on their faces, be altogether beyond the pale of civilization, but whatever they are, I want you to understand that I am—I am a Chinese."

There is silence in the rooms for a few minutes. Then Mr. K. pushes back his plate and standing up beside me, says:

"I should not have spoken as I did. I know nothing whatever about the Chinese. It was pure prejudice. Forgive me!"

I admire Mr. K.'s moral courage in apologizing to me; he is a conscientious Christian man, but I do not remain much longer in the little town.

I am under a tropic sky, meeting frequently and conversing with persons who are almost as high upon in the world as birth, education and money can set them. The environment is peculiar, for I am also surrounded by a race of people, the reputed descendants of Ham,[1] the son of Noah, whose offspring, it was prophesied, should be the servants of the songs of Shem and Japheth. As I am a descendant, according to the Bible, of both Shem and Japheth, I have a perfect right to set my heel upon the Ham people; but tho I see others around me following out the Bible suggestion, it is not in my nature to be arrogant to any but those who seek to impress me with their superiority, which the poor black maid who has been assigned to me by the hotel certainly does not. My employer's wife takes me to task for this. "It is unnecessary," she says, "to thank a black person for service."

---

[1]According to Genesis 10, Noah had three sons: Ham, forefather of the southern peoples (Hamitic); Shem, forefather of the middle peoples (Semitic); and Japheth, forefather of the northern peoples (Japhetic Eurasia). Many supporters of slavery and racial discrimination referred to the "curse of Ham" to justify the mistreatment of people of Black African ancestry, who were believed to be descendants of Ham.

The novelty of life in the West Indian island is not without its charm. The surroundings, people, manner of living, are so entirely different from what I have been accustomed to up North that I feel as if I were "born again." Mixing with people of fashion, and yet not of them, I am not of sufficient importance to create comment or curiosity. I am busy nearly all day and often well into the night. It is not monotonous work, but it is certainly strenuous. The planters and business men of the island take me as a matter of course and treat me with kindly courtesy. Occasionally an Englishman will warn me against the "brown boys" of the island, little dreaming that I too am of the "brown people" of the earth.

When it begins to be whispered about the place that I am not all white, some of the "sporty" people seek my acquaintance. I am small and look much younger than my years. When, however, they discover that I am a very serious and sober-minded spinster indeed, they retire quite gracefully, leaving me a few amusing reflections.

One evening a card is brought to my room. It bears the name of some naval officer. I go down to my visitor, thinking he is probably some one who, having been told that I am a reporter for the local paper, has brought me an item of news. I find him lounging in an easy chair on the veranda of the hotel–a big, blond, handsome fellow, several years younger than I.

"You are Lieutenant —?" I inquire.

He bows and laughs a little. The laugh doesn't suit him somehow– and it doesn't suit me, either.

"If you have anything to tell me, please tell it quickly, because I'm very busy."

"Oh, you don't really mean that," he answers, with another silly and offensive laugh. "There's always plenty of time for good times. That's what I am here for. I saw you at the races the other day and twice at King's House. My ship will be here for—weeks."

"Do you wish that noted?" I ask.

"Oh, no! Why–I came just because I had an idea that you might like to know me. I would like to know you. You look such a nice little body. Say, wouldn't you like to go for a sail this lovely night? I will tell you all about the sweet little Chinese girls I met when we were at Hong Kong. They're not so shy!"

I leave Eastern Canada for the Far West, so reduced by another attack of rheumatic fever that I only weigh eighty-four pounds. I travel on an advertising contract. It is presumed by the railway company that in some way or other I will give them full value for their transportation across the continent. I have been ordered beyond the Rockies by the doctor, who declares that I will never regain my strength in the East. Nevertheless, I am but two days in San Francisco when I start out in search of work. It is the first time that I have sought work as a stranger in a strange town. Both of the other positions away from home were secured for me by home influence. I am quite surprised to find that there is no demand for my services in San Francisco and that no one is particularly interested in me. The best I can do is to accept an offer from a railway agency to typewrite their correspondence for $5 a month. I stipulate, however, that I shall have the privilege of taking in outside work and that my hours shall be light. I am hopeful that the sale of a story or newspaper article may add to my income, and I console myself with the reflection that, considering that I still limp and bear traces of sickness, I am fortunate to secure any work at all.

The proprietor of one of the San Francisco papers, to whom I have a letter of introduction, suggests that I obtain some subscriptions from the people of China town, that district of the city having never been canvassed. This suggestion I carry out with enthusiasm, tho I find that the Chinese merchants and people generally are inclined to regard me with suspicion. They have been imposed upon so many times by unscrupulous white people. Another drawback—save for a few phrases, I am unacquainted with my mother tongue. How, then, can I expect these people to accept me as their own countrywoman? The Americanized Chinamen actually laugh in my face when I tell them that I am of their race. However, they are not all "doubting Thomases."[2] Some little women discover that I have Chinese hair, color of eyes and complexion, also that I love rice and tea. This settles the matter for them—and for their husbands.

My Chinese instincts develop. I am no longer the little girl who shrunk against my brother at the first sight of a Chinaman. Many and many a time, when alone in a strange place, has the appearance of even a humble laundryman given me a sense of protection and made me feel quite at home. This fact of itself proves to me that prejudice can be eradicated by association.

I meet a half Chinese, half white girl. Her face is plastered with a thick white coat of paint and her eyelids and eyebrows are blackened so that the shape of her eyes and the whole expression of her face is changed. She was born in the East, and at the age of eighteen came West in answer to an advertisement. Living for many years among the working class, she had heard little but abuse of the Chinese. It is not difficult, in a land like California, for a half Chinese, half white girl to pass as one of Spanish or Mexican origin. This poor child does, tho she lives in nervous dread of being "discovered." She becomes engaged to a young man, but fears to tell him what she is, and only does so when compelled by a fearless American girl friend. This girl, who knows her origin, realizing that the truth sooner or later must be told, and better soon than late, advises the Eurasian to confide in the young man, assuring her that he loves her well enough not

[2]Refers to the apostle Thomas, who did not believe that Jesus had been resurrected until he had proof. See John 20: 24–29.

to allow her nationality to stand, a bar sinister, between them. But the Eurasian prefers to keep her secret, and only reveals it to the man who is to be her husband when driven to bay by the American girl, who declares that if the halfbreed will not tell the truth she will. When the young man hears that the girl he is engaged to has Chinese blood in her veins, he exclaims: "Oh, what will my folks say?" But that is all. Love is stronger than prejudice with him, and neither he nor she deems it necessary to inform his "folks."

The Americans, having for many years manifested a much higher regard for the Japanese than for the Chinese, several half Chinese young men and women, thinking to advance themselves, both in a social and business sense, pass as Japanese. They continue to be known as Eurasians; but a Japanese Eurasian does not appear in the same light as a Chinese Eurasian. The unfortunate Chinese Eurasians! Are not those who compel them to thus cringe more to be blamed than they?

People, however, are not all alike. I meet white men, and women, too, who are proud to mate with those who have Chinese blood in their veins, and think it a great honor to be distinguished by the friendship of such. There are also Eurasians and Eurasians. I know of one who allowed herself to become engaged to a white man after refusing him nine times. She had discouraged him in every way possible, had warned him that she was half Chinese; that her people were poor, that every week or month she sent home a certain amount of her earnings, and that the man she married would have to do as much, if not more; also, most uncompromising truth of all, that she did not love him and never would. But the resolute and undaunted lover swore that it was a matter of indifference to him whether she was a Chinese or a Hottentot,[3] that it would be his pleasure and privilege to allow her relations double what it was in her power to bestow, and as to not loving him—that did not matter at all. He loved her. So, because the young woman had a married mother and married sisters, who were always picking at her and gossiping over her independent manner of living, she finally consented to marry him, recording the agreement in her diary thus:

"I have promised to become the wife of — — on — —, 189—, because the world is so cruel and sneering to a single woman—and for no other reason."

Everything went smoothly until one day. The young man was driving a pair of beautiful horses and she was seated by his side, trying very hard to imagine herself in love with him, when a Chinese vegetable gardener's cart came rumbling along. The Chinaman was a jolly-looking individual in

---

[3]A member of a native South African race, first met by the Dutch. Hottentot, "stutterer or stammerer," was applied to these people because of the frequency of clicks in their speech.

blue cotton blouse and pantaloons, his rakish looking hat being kept in place by a long queue which was pulled upward from his neck and wound around it. The young woman was suddenly possest with the spirit of mischief. "Look!" she cried, indicating the Chinaman, "there's my brother. Why don't you salute him?"

The man's face fell a little. He sank into a pensive mood. The wicked one by his side read him like an open book.

"When we are married," said she, "I intend to give a Chinese party every month."

No answer.

"As there are very few aristocratic Chinese in this city, I shall fill up with the laundrymen and vegetable farmers. I don't believe in being exclusive in democratic America, do you?"

He hadn't a grain of humor in his composition, but a sickly smile contorted his features as he replied:

"You shall do just as you please, my darling. But—but—consider a moment. Wouldn't it be just a little pleasanter for us if, after we are married, we allowed it to be presumed that you were—er—Japanese? So many of my friends have inquired of me if that is not your nationality. They would be so charmed to meet a little Japanese lady."

"Hadn't you better oblige them by finding one?"

"Why—er—what do you mean?"

"Nothing much in particular. Only—I am getting a little tired of this," taking off his ring.

"You don't mean what you say! Oh, put it back, dearest! You know I would not hurt your feelings for the world!"

"You haven't. I'm more than pleased. But I do mean what I say."

That evening the "ungrateful" Chinese Eurasian diaried, among other things, the following:

"Joy, oh, joy! I'm free once more. Never again shall I be untrue to my own heart. Never again will I allow any one to 'hound' or 'sneer' me into matrimony."

I secure transportation to many California points. I meet some literary people, chief among whom is the editor of the magazine who took my first Chinese stories. He and his wife give me a warm welcome to their ranch. They are broadminded people, whose interest in me is sincere and intelligent, not affected and vulgar. I also meet some funny people who advise me to "trade" upon my nationality. They tell me that if I wish to succeed in literature in America I should dress in Chinese costume, carry a fan in my hand, wear a pair of scarlet beaded slippers, live in New York, and come of high birth. Instead of making myself familiar with the Chinese Americans around me, I should discourse on my spirit acquaintance with Chinese ancestors and quote in between the "Good mornings" and "How d'ye dos" of editors.

"Confucius, Confucius, how great is Confucius, Before Confucius, there never was Confucius.[4] After Confucius, there never came Confucius," etc., etc., etc.,

or something like that, both illuminating and obscuring, don't you know. They forget, or perhaps they are not aware that the old Chinese sage taught "The way of sincerity is the way of heaven."

My experiences as an Eurasian never cease; but people are not now as prejudiced as they have been. In the West, too, my friends are more advanced in all lines of thought than those whom I knew in Eastern Canada—more genuine, more sincere, with less of the form of religion, but more of its spirit.

So I roam backward and forward across the continent. When I am East, my heart is West. When I am West, my heart is East. Before long I hope to be in China. As my life began in my father's country it may end in my mother's.

After all I have no nationality and am not anxious to claim any. Individuality is more than nationality. "You are you and I am I," says Confucius. I give my right hand to the Occidentals and my left to the Orientals, hoping that between them they will not utterly destroy the insignificant "connecting link." And that's all.

[1909]

[4]Chinese thinker and social philosopher (551 BCE–479 BCE).

W. E. B. DU BOIS ■ (1868–1963)

W. E. B. Du Bois led an extraordinary life that spanned ninety-five years, from the presidency of Andrew Johnson and the period of Reconstruction that followed the Civil War to the presidency of John F. Kennedy and the political tensions of the Cold War. He was born in Great Barrington, western Massachusetts, a town of five thousand residents that included an African American community numbering about fifty. He was raised by his mother and her relatives after his father deserted the family when Du Bois was an infant. In his youth he became a lover of books, graduating with honors from the local high school in 1885.

As Du Bois explained in his *Autobiography* (posthumously published in 1968), he then "went South," to "the South of slavery, rebellion, and black folk," spending four years (1885–88) at Fisk University in Nashville, Tennessee. Du Bois next attended Harvard, where he received a second bachelor's degree, cum laude, in 1890. He pursued graduate study in history at Harvard (MA, 1891; PhD, 1895) and at the University of Berlin (1892–94), where he noted in his journal that his goal was "to make a name in science, to make a name in art, and thus to raise my race."

In the 1890s, few professional careers were open to African Americans. Du Bois taught English and classical and foreign languages at Wilberforce University in central Ohio (1894–96) and undertook research (1896–97) in Philadelphia as an "assistant instructor" of sociology at the University of Pennsylvania. He then joined the faculty of Atlanta University in Georgia, which had been founded in 1865 to provide black youths with a "liberal and Christian education," and there he taught economics, history, and sociology.

Du Bois's first book, based on his dissertation, was *The Suppression of the African Slave Trade to the United States of America, 1638–1870* (1896); it was the first volume in the *Harvard Historical Studies* series. His next was *The Philadelphia Negro* (1899), a study of African Americans in Philadelphia, for which he conducted hundreds of interviews in order to gather information about the people, their backgrounds, and the environment in which they lived.

Du Bois's later books include the epic historical study *Black Reconstruction in America, 1860–1880* (1935); *Dusk of Dawn* (1940), which he described as "not so much my autobiography as the autobiography of a concept of race"; and *Color and Democracy: Colonies and Peace* (1945), one of many writings of the 1940s and 1950s that challenged imperialism and made the case for African independence.

Politically radical and sympathetic to the Soviet Union and the People's Republic of China, Du Bois was carefully watched, harassed, and persecuted by the U.S. government. Embittered by this treatment, Du Bois applied on October 1, 1961, for membership in the Communist Party of the USA. He renounced his U.S. citizenship and took up residence in Ghana, where he died.

In his major work, *The Souls of Black Folk* (1903), excerpted in the following text, Du Bois examines the history of slavery and segregation in the United States and emphasizes, more generally, that "the problem of the Twentieth Century is the problem of the color line." He speaks of "the Veil" that separates blacks from whites and describes the "double consciousness" that defines the dual American and African identities of his people. In one of the book's sharpest chapters, Du Bois criticizes as timid and compromising the policies of Booker T. Washington (1856–1915), the founder of Tuskegee Institute in Alabama and the leading spokesman for African Americans on the national scene.

In 1909 Du Bois helped to establish the National Association for the Advancement of Colored People (NAACP), for which he served as director of publications and research; in 1910 he became the editor of the NAACP's monthly magazine, *The Crisis,* a position he held until 1934. He was a crucial figure for the writers and artists of the Harlem Renaissance and the "New Negro" movement of the 1920s, repeatedly affirming in the pages of *The Crisis* the "Beauty of Black." It was this vision that the poets Claude McKay, Countee Cullen, and Langston Hughes, and the novelists and short-story writers Jean Toomer, Nella Larsen, and Zora Neale Hurston, in their different but related ways, expressed and explored.

Image of William Edward Burghardt Dubois, taken by Bain News Service.

For an excellent overview: Arnold Rampersad, *The Art and Imagination of W. E. B. Du Bois* (1976). A good brief biography: Manning Marable, *W. E. B. Du Bois: Black Radical Democrat* (1986). A major two-volume study: David Levering Lewis, *W. E. B. Du Bois: Biography of a Race, 1868–1919* (1993) and *W. E. B. Du Bois: The Fight for Equality and the American Century, 1919–1963* (2000). See also *Critical Essays on W. E. B. Du Bois*, ed. William L. Andrews (1985); Shamoon Zamir, *Dark Voices: W. E. B. Du Bois and American Thought, 1888–1903* (1995); Raymond Wolters, *Du Bois and His Rivals* (2002); and Edward J. Blum, *W. E. B. Du Bois: American Prophet* (2007).

From The Souls of Black Folk

Of Mr. Booker T. Washington[1] and Others

From birth till death enslaved; in word, in deed, unmanned!

Hereditary bondsmen! Know yet not
Who would be free themselves must strike the blow?

—BYRON[2]

Easily the most striking thing in the history of the American Negro since 1876[3] is the ascendancy of Mr. Booker T. Washington. It began at the time when war memories and ideals were rapidly passing; a day of astonishing commercial development was dawning; a sense of doubt and

[1]The educator and black leader Booker T. Washington (1856–1915) was the first president of Tuskegee Institute, a college in Alabama, founded for African Americans, which he helped to build with his own hands. A former slave, he was liberated at the end of the Civil War and educated at Hampton Institute in Virginia, where he later taught before assuming leadership of Tuskegee. In 1895 Washington gave his famous but controversial "Atlanta Compromise" speech at the Atlanta Exposition, in which he urged blacks to improve job skills and usefulness rather than pursue equal rights. "The opportunity to earn a dollar in a factory just now is worth infinitely more than the opportunity to spend a dollar in an opera-house." This "compromise" of political and social rights, he hoped, would reduce racial tensions in the South and provide the African American labor force with a means to support themselves and their families.
[2]Lord Byron (1812–18), from *Childe Harold's Pilgrimage* (1812), Canto 2, 74.710, 76.720–21. The music is from a Negro spiritual, "A Great Camp Meeting in the Promised Land," which includes the words, "Going to mourn and never tire / Mourn and never tire, mourn and never tire."
[3]In 1876 federal troops withdrew from the South, ending the period known as Reconstruction. Without the support of the federal government, what little power African Americans had gained after the Civil War was essentially lost.

hesitation overtook the freedmen's sons,—then it was that his leading began. Mr. Washington came, with a simple definite programme, at the psychological moment when the nation was a little ashamed of having bestowed so much sentiment on Negroes, and was concentrating its energies on Dollars. His programme of industrial education, conciliation of the South, and submission and silence as to civil and political rights, was not wholly original; the Free Negroes from 1830 up to war-time had striven to build industrial schools, and the American Missionary Association had from the first taught various trades; and Price[4] and others had sought a way of honorable alliance with the best of the Southerners. But Mr. Washington first indissolubly linked these things; he put enthusiasm, unlimited energy, and perfect faith into his programme, and changed it from a by-path into a veritable Way of Life. And the tale of the methods by which he did this is a fascinating study of human life.

It startled the nation to hear a Negro advocating such a programme after many decades of bitter complaint; it startled and won the applause of the South, it interested and won the admiration of the North; and after a confused murmur of protest, it silenced if it did not convert the Negroes themselves.

To gain the sympathy and coöperation of the various elements comprising the white South was Mr. Washington's first task; and this, at the time Tuskegee was founded, seemed, for a black man, well-nigh impossible. And yet ten years later it was done in the word spoken at Atlanta: "In all things purely social we can be as separate as the five fingers, and yet one as the hand in all things essential to mutual progress." This "Atlanta Compromise"[5] is by all odds the most notable thing in Mr. Washington's career. The South interpreted it in different ways: the radicals received it as a complete surrender of the demand for civil and political equality; the conservatives, as a generously conceived working basis for mutual understanding. So both approved it, and to-day its author is certainly the most distinguished Southerner since Jefferson Davis,[6] and the one with the largest personal following.

Next to this achievement comes Mr. Washington's work in gaining place and consideration in the North. Others less shrewd and tactful had formerly essayed to sit on these two stools and had fallen between them; but as Mr. Washington knew the heart of the South from birth and training, so by singular insight he intuitively grasped the spirit of the age which was dominating the North. And so thoroughly did he learn the speech and thought of triumphant commercialism, and the ideals of material

---

[4]Thomas Frederick Price (1860–1919) was a Catholic missionary from North Carolina who founded the Maryknoll Foreign Mission Society in 1911.
[5]See note 1.
[6]Born in Kentucky and raised in Louisiana, Jefferson Davis (1808–89) served as president of the Confederate States of America during the Civil War.

prosperity, that the picture of a lone black boy poring over a French grammar[7] amid the weeds and dirt of a neglected home soon seemed to him the acme of absurdities. One wonders what Socrates[8] and St. Francis of Assisi[9] would say to this.

And yet this very singleness of vision and thorough oneness with his age is a mark of the successful man. It is as though Nature must needs make men narrow in order to give them force. So Mr. Washington's cult has gained unquestioning followers, his work has wonderfully prospered, his friends are legion, and his enemies are confounded. To-day he stands as the one recognized spokesman of his ten million fellows, and one of the most notable figures in a nation of seventy millions. One hesitates, therefore, to criticise a life which, beginning with so little, has done so much. And yet the time is come when one may speak in all sincerity and utter courtesy of the mistakes and shortcomings of Mr. Washington's career, as well as of his triumphs, without being thought captious or envious, and without forgetting that it is easier to do ill than well in the world.

The criticism that has hitherto met Mr. Washington has not always been of this broad character. In the South especially has he had to walk warily to avoid the harshest judgments,—and naturally so, for he is dealing with the one subject of deepest sensitiveness to that section. Twice— once when at the Chicago celebration of the Spanish-American War[10] he alluded to the color-prejudice that is "eating away the vitals of the South," and once when he dined with President Roosevelt[11]—has the resulting Southern criticism been violent enough to threaten seriously his popularity. In the North the feeling has several times forced itself into words, that Mr. Washington's counsels of submission overlooked certain elements of true manhood, and that his educational programme was unnecessarily narrow. Usually, however, such criticism has not found open expression, although, too, the spiritual sons of the Abolitionists have not been

---

[7] A reference to Booker T. Washington's autobiography, *Up from Slavery* (1901), in which he expounds on the absurdity of useless knowledge: "...one of the saddest things I ever saw...was a young man... sitting down in a one-room cabin, with grease on his clothing, filth all around him, and weeds in the yard and garden, engaged in studying French grammar."

[8] Greek philosopher (469–399 BCE) who lived in ancient Athens. His technique of philosophic inquiry, the Socratic method, often included questioning the definitions of social mores, political justice, or religion in order to elicit contradictions from the responses, encouraging deeper inquiry into the concepts.

[9] Francis of Assisi (1181–1226) was the founder of the Franciscan Order. In 1205 he left his worldly life behind and devoted himself to caring for poor.

[10] See note 11.

[11] Theodore Roosevelt (1858–1919), twenty-sixth president of the United States. In 1897 Roosevelt was appointed Assistant Secretary of the Navy by the then newly elected President William McKinley. In 1898 Roosevelt made a concerted and successful effort to initiate war with Spain over Cuba. While motivated partly by humanitarian reasons, many feel Roosevelt was driven mainly by an exaggerated conception of the glory of war. "No qualities called out by a purely peaceful life stand on a level with those stern and virile virtues which move the men of stout heart and strong hand who uphold the honor of their flag in battle," he wrote. He distinguished himself during the Spanish American War in 1898, and later became McKinley's vice president. When McKinley was assassinated in 1901, Roosevelt assumed the presidency.

prepared to acknowledge that the schools founded before Tuskegee, by men of broad ideals and self-sacrificing spirit, were wholly failures or worthy of ridicule. While, then, criticism has not failed to follow Mr. Washington, yet the prevailing public opinion of the land has been but too willing to deliver the solution of a wearisome problem into his hands, and say, "If that is all you and your race ask, take it."

Among his own people, however, Mr. Washington has encountered the strongest and most lasting opposition, amounting at times to bitterness, and even today continuing strong and insistent even though largely silenced in outward expression by the public opinion of the nation. Some of this opposition is, of course, mere envy; the disappointment of displaced demagogues and the spite of narrow minds. But aside from this, there is among educated and thoughtful colored men in all parts of the land a feeling of deep regret, sorrow, and apprehension at the wide currency and ascendancy which some of Mr. Washington's theories have gained. These same men admire his sincerity of purpose, and are willing to forgive much to honest endeavor which is doing something worth the doing. They cooperate with Mr. Washington as far as they conscientiously can; and, indeed, it is no ordinary tribute to this man's tact and power that, steering as he must between so many diverse interests and opinions, he so largely retains the respect of all.

But the hushing of the criticism of honest opponents is a dangerous thing. It leads some of the best of the critics to unfortunate silence and paralysis of effort, and others to burst into speech so passionately and intemperately as to lose listeners. Honest and earnest criticism from those whose interests are most nearly touched,—criticism of writers by readers, of government by those governed, of leaders by those led,—this is the soul of democracy and the safeguard of modern society. If the best of the American Negroes receive by outer pressure a leader whom they had not recognized before, manifestly there is here a certain palpable gain. Yet there is also irreparable loss,—a loss of that peculiarly valuable education which a group receives when by search and criticism it finds and commissions its own leaders. The way in which this is done is at once the most elementary and the nicest problem of social growth. History is but the record of such group-leadership; and yet how infinitely changeful is its type and character! And of all types and kinds, what can be more instructive than the leadership of a group within a group?—that curious double movement where real progress may be negative and actual advance be relative retrogression. All this is the social student's inspiration and despair.

Now in the past the American Negro has had instructive experience in the choosing of group leaders, founding thus a peculiar dynasty which in the light of present conditions is worth while studying. When sticks and stones and beasts form the sole environment of a people, their attitude is largely one of determined opposition to and conquest of natural forces. But when to earth and brute is added an environment of men and ideas, then the attitude of the imprisoned group may take three main forms,—a feeling of revolt and revenge; an attempt to adjust all thought and action to the will of the greater group; or, finally, a determined effort at self-realization and self-development despite environing opinion. The influence of all of these attitudes at various times can be traced in the history of the American Negro, and in the evolution of his successive leaders.

Before 1750, while the fire of African freedom still burned in the veins of the slaves, there was in all leadership or attempted leadership but the one motive of revolt and revenge,—typified in the terrible Maroons,[12] the Danish blacks,[13] and Cato of Stono,[14] and veiling all the Americas in fear of insurrection. The liberalizing tendencies of the latter half of the eighteenth century brought, along with kindlier relations between black and white, thoughts of ultimate adjustment and assimilation. Such aspiration was especially voiced in the earnest songs of Phyllis,[15] in the martyrdom of Attucks,[16] the fighting of Salem and Poor,[17] the intellectual accomplishments of Banneker and Derham,[18] and the political demands of the Cuffes.[19]

Stern financial and social stress after the war cooled much of the previous humanitarian ardor. The disappointment and impatience of the Negroes at the persistence of slavery and serfdom voiced itself in two movements.

---

[12]The maroons were fugitive black slaves or their descendants who settled in the mountains and forests of Guiana and the West Indies.

[13]Slaves from the Danish West Indies who revolted in 1733 because of poor living conditions and lack of food.

[14]Cato of Stono was the leader of "Cato's Conspiracy" or the "Stono Rebellion," a slave revolt in 1739 in Stono, South Carolina, during which approximately eighty slaves armed themselves and attempted to march toward Florida (then owned by Spain). Forty-four blacks and twenty-one whites died before the rebellion was put down.

[15]Poet Phillis Wheatley (c.1753–84) was born in Africa. When she was about eight years old, she was kidnapped and sold into slavery. She was purchased by the Wheatley family who taught her to read and write. She wrote her first verses when she was thirteen years old. The first bound volume of her poems was *Poems on Various Subjects, Religious and Moral* (1773).

[16]Crispus Attucks (c.1723–70) was either an escaped or freed slave who had the distinction of being one of the first people killed as a result of the political unrest that led to the American Revolutionary War. On March 5, 1770, he joined a mob of Boston citizens who, angry over new taxes, began a fight with a small British unit of soldiers on the steps of the State House. The soldiers fired upon the mob, killing five colonists, including Attucks. He was quickly made a hero and a martyr of the Boston Massacre. In 1888, a statue of Attucks was dedicated on Boston Common.

[17]Peter Salem (c. 1750–1816) and Salem Poor (1747–80) were black soldiers who fought at the Battle of Bunker Hill during the Revolutionary War.

[18]Benjamin Banneker (1731–1806) was a black mathematician. James Derham (1762–1805) was a former slave from Philadelphia who learned medicine from his master. After buying his freedom, he distinguished himself as the first recognized black physician in America, becoming a prominent physician in New Orleans.

[19]Paul Cuffe (1759–1817) was a seaman and political reformer from Cuttyhunk, Massachusetts. His father was of African descent, and his mother was a Native American. In 1780, he and his brother John made an unsuccessful appeal to the courts of Massachusetts to challenge the charge of taxes to individuals who were denied the right to vote. However, in 1783, an act was passed giving African Americans legal rights and privileges in Massachusetts. In 1815, he led a voyage of thirty-eight freed African Americans emigrating to Sierra Leone.

The slaves in the South, aroused undoubtedly by vague rumors of the Haytian revolt, made three fierce attempts at insurrection,—in 1800 under Gabriel in Virginia,[20] in 1822 under Vesey in Carolina,[21] and in 1831 again in Virginia under the terrible Nat Turner.[22] In the Free States, on the other hand, a new and curious attempt at self-development was made. In Philadelphia and New York color-prescription led to a withdrawal of Negro communicants from white churches and the formation of a peculiar socio-religious institution among the Negroes known as the African Church,— an organization still living and controlling in its various branches over a million of men.

Walker's wild appeal[23] against the trend of the times showed how the world was changing after the coming of the cotton-gin. By 1830 slavery seemed hopelessly fastened on the South, and the slaves thoroughly cowed into submission. The free Negroes of the North, inspired by the mulatto immigrants from the West Indies, began to change the basis of their demands; they recognized the slavery of slaves, but insisted that they themselves were freemen, and sought assimilation and amalgamation with the nation on the same terms with other men. Thus, Forten and Purvis[24] of Philadelphia, Shad of Wilmington,[25] Du Bois of New Haven,[26] Barbadoes of Boston,[27] and others, strove singly and together as men, they said, not as slaves; as "people of color," not as "Negroes." The trend of the times, however, refused them recognition save in individual and exceptional cases, considered them as one with all the despised blacks, and they soon found themselves striving to keep even the rights they formerly had of voting and working and moving as freemen. Schemes of migration and colonization arose among them; but these they refused to entertain, and they eventually turned to the Abolition movement as a final refuge.

---

[20]A Virginia slave who conspired to attack Richmond with a thousand other slaves in 1800. The revolt was revealed by two slaves before it could occur, and Gabriel and two other leaders of uprising were executed for their part in the conspiracy.

[21]Denmark Vesey (c. 1767–1822) was a former slave who purchased his freedom in 1800. He led an unsuccessful uprising in South Carolina. He was hanged for his role in the uprising.

[22]A slave (1800–31) who led a revolt in 1831, later called "Nat Turner's Rebellion," in Southampton, Virginia, during which over sixty whites and more than one hundred slaves were killed or executed.

[23]Referring to a pamphlet written and distributed by the militant abolitionist David Walker (1785–1830).

[24]James Forten (1766–1842) was a free African American civic leader from Philadelphia. He promoted temperance and peace, and he devoted money and personal time to the abolitionist effort. Robert Purvis (1810–98) was an abolitionist who helped found the American Anti-Slavery Society in 1833 and also served as president of the Underground Railroad.

[25]Abraham Shadd (1801–82) was an abolitionist who served on the first board of managers of the American Anti-Slavery Society, and was a delegate from Delaware for the first Negro National Convention in 1830.

[26]Alexander Du Bois (1803–87), grandfather of the author who helped found the Negro Episcopal Parish of St. Luke in New Haven, Connecticut.

[27]James G. Barbadoes (1796–1841), a free African American barber from Boston, Massachusetts, and a delegate at the first National Negro Convention along with Forten, Purvis, and Shadd (see notes 24 and 25).

Here, led by Remond,[28] Nell,[29] Wells-Brown,[30] and Douglass,[31] a new period of self-assertion and self-development dawned. To be sure, ultimate freedom and assimilation was the ideal before the leaders, but the assertion of the manhood rights of the Negro by himself was the main reliance, and John Brown's raid[32] was the extreme of its logic. After the war and emancipation, the great form of Frederick Douglass, the greatest of American Negro leaders, still led the host. Self-assertion, especially in political lines, was the main programme, and behind Douglass came Elliot,[33] Bruce,[34] and Langston,[35] and the Reconstruction politicians, and, less conspicuous but of greater social significance, Alexander Crummell[36] and Bishop Daniel Payne.[37]

Then came the Revolution of 1876, the suppression of the Negro votes, the changing and shifting of ideals, and the seeking of new lights in the great night. Douglass, in his old age, still bravely stood for the ideals of his early manhood,—ultimate assimilation *through* self-assertion, and on no other terms. For a time Price arose as a new leader, destined, it seemed, not to give up, but to re-state the old ideals in a form less repugnant to the white South. But he passed away in his prime. Then came the new leader. Nearly all the former ones had become leaders by the silent suffrage of their fellows, had sought to lead their own people alone, and were usually, save Douglass, little known outside their race. But Booker T. Washington arose as essentially the leader not of one race but of two,—a compromiser between the South, the North, and the Negro. Naturally the Negroes resented, at first bitterly, signs of compromise which surrendered their civil and political rights, even though this was to be exchanged

[28]Charles Lenox Remond (1810–73) was a free African American from Salem, Massachusetts. The Massachusetts Anti-Slavery Society chose him as one of its delegates for the World Anti-Slavery Convention in London in 1840.
[29]William Cooper Nell (1816–74) was an abolitionist and writer who was the first African American to hold an official public office (clerk in the U.S. Post Office). He lobbied to secure school privileges for black children in Boston.
[30]William Wells-Brown (c. 1816–84) was a writer and dramatist noted for his novel, *Clotel* (1853).
[31]Frederick Douglass (1818–95) is considered the foremost African American abolitionist. A former slave, he advised President Abraham Lincoln during the Civil War, and continued to serve in politics until his death in Washington, D.C.
[32]John Brown (1800–59), abolitionist who, after proslavery forces attacked and burned the town of Lawrence, Kansas, led a small abolitionist force to nearby Pottawatomie Creek, where they killed five proslavery men on the night of May 24, 1856. Taken with the idea of abolition through violence, he launched a raid on Harpers Ferry, Virginia, in October 1859, but was captured, tried for treason, and hanged, becoming a legend in the North and a martyr of the antislavery movement.
[33]Robert Brown Elliot (1842–84), African American politician from South Carolina who served in the U.S. House of Representatives.
[34]Blanche K. Bruce (1841–98), former slave who became the first African American to serve a full term in the U.S. Senate from 1875 to 1881.
[35]John Mercer Langston (1829–97), former slave who later became a lawyer and politician.
[36]Alexander Crummell (1819–98) was an African American clergyman and missionary for the Episcopal Church.
[37]Daniel Alexander Payne (1811–98) was a bishop of the African Methodist Episcopal church and president of Wilberforce University in Ohio, the nation's oldest private African American university.

for larger chances of economic development. The rich and dominating North, however, was not only weary of the race problem, but was investing largely in Southern enterprises, and welcomed any method of peaceful coöperation. Thus, by national opinion, the Negroes began to recognize Mr. Washington's leadership; and the voice of criticism was hushed.

Mr. Washington represents in Negro thought the old attitude of adjustment and submission; but adjustment at such a peculiar time as to make his programme unique. This is an age of unusual economic development, and Mr. Washington's programme naturally takes an economic cast, becoming a gospel of Work and Money to such an extent as apparently almost completely to overshadow the higher aims of life. Moreover, this is an age when the more advanced races are coming in closer contact with the less developed races, and the race-feeling is therefore intensified; and Mr. Washington's programme practically accepts the alleged inferiority of the Negro races. Again, in our own land, the reaction from the sentiment of war time has given impetus to race-prejudice against Negroes, and Mr. Washington withdraws many of the high demands of Negroes as men and American citizens. In other periods of intensified prejudice all the Negro's tendency to self-assertion has been called forth; at this period a policy of submission is advocated. In the history of nearly all other races and peoples the doctrine preached at such crises has been that manly self-respect is worth more than lands and houses, and that a people who voluntarily surrender such respect, or cease striving for it, are not worth civilizing.

In answer to this, it has been claimed that the Negro can survive only through submission. Mr. Washington distinctly asks that black people give up, at least for the present, three things,—

First, political power,
Second, insistence on civil rights,
Third, higher education of Negro youth,—

and concentrate all their energies on industrial education, and accumulation of wealth, and the conciliation of the South. This policy has been courageously and insistently advocated for over fifteen years, and has been triumphant for perhaps ten years. As a result of this tender of the palm-branch, what has been the return? In these years there have occurred:

1. The disfranchisement of the Negro.
2. The legal creation of a distinct status of civil inferiority for the Negro.
3. The steady withdrawal of aid from institutions for the higher training of the Negro.

These movements are not, to be sure, direct results of Mr. Washington's teachings; but his propaganda has, without a shadow of doubt, helped their speedier accomplishment. The question then comes: Is it possible, and probable, that nine millions of men can make effective progress in economic lines if they are deprived of political rights, made a servile caste, and allowed only the most meagre chance for developing their exceptional men? If history and reason give any distinct answer to these questions, it is an emphatic *No*. And Mr. Washington thus faces the triple paradox of his career:

1. He is striving nobly to make Negro artisans business men and property-owners; but it is utterly impossible, under modern competitive methods, for workingmen and property-owners to defend their rights and exist without the right of suffrage.

2. He insists on thrift and self-respect, but at the same time counsels a silent submission to civic inferiority such as is bound to sap the manhood of any race in the long run.

3. He advocates common-school[38] and industrial training, and depreciates institutions of higher learning; but neither the Negro common-schools, nor Tuskegee itself, could remain open a day were it not for teachers trained in Negro colleges, or trained by their graduates.

This triple paradox in Mr. Washington's position is the object of criticism by two classes of colored Americans. One class is spiritually descended from Toussaint the Savior,[39] through Gabriel, Vesey, and Turner, and they represent the attitude of revolt and revenge; they hate the white South blindly and distrust the white race generally, and so far as they agree on definite action, think that the Negro's only hope lies in emigration beyond the borders of the United States. And yet, by the irony of fate, nothing has more effectually made this programme seem hopeless than the recent course of the United States toward weaker and darker peoples in the West Indies, Hawaii, and the Philippines,—for where in the world may we go and be safe from lying and brute force?

The other class of Negroes who cannot agree with Mr. Washington has hitherto said little aloud. They deprecate the sight of scattered counsels, of internal disagreement; and especially they dislike making their just criticism of a useful and earnest man an excuse for a general discharge of venom from small-minded opponents. Nevertheless, the questions involved are so fundamental and serious that it is difficult to see how men like the Grimkes,[40] Kelly Miller,[41] J. W. E. Bowen[42] and other representatives of

[38]Public school.
[39]François Dominique Toussaint L'Ouverture (1743–1803), a former Haitian slave and martyr for the liberation of Haiti from the French.
[40]Archibald Grimké (1849–1930) and Francis Grimké (1850–1937); brothers who were sons of a white father and a slave mother, they became civil rights leaders.
[41]Kelly Miller (1863–1939), was the dean of Howard University who was also the first African American student admitted to Johns Hopkins University.
[42]John Wesley Edward Bowen (1855–1933), clergyman and educator who became president of Gammon Theological Seminary of Atlanta.

this group, can much longer be silent. Such men feel in conscience bound to ask of this nation three things:

1. The right to vote.
2. Civic equality.
3. The education of youth according to ability.

They acknowledge Mr. Washington's invaluable service in counselling patience and courtesy in such demands; they do not ask that ignorant black men vote when ignorant whites are debarred, or that any reasonable restrictions in the suffrage should not be applied; they know that the low social level of the mass of the race is responsible for much discrimination against it, but they also know, and the nation knows, that relentless color-prejudice is more often a cause than a result of the Negro's degradation; they seek the abatement of this relic of barbarism, and not its systematic encouragement and pampering by all agencies of social power from the Associated Press to the Church of Christ. They advocate, with Mr. Washington, a broad system of Negro common schools supplemented by thorough industrial training; but they are surprised that a man of Mr. Washington's insight cannot see that no such educational system ever has rested or can rest on any other basis than that of the well-equipped college and university, and they insist that there is a demand for a few such institutions throughout the South to train the best of the Negro youth as teachers, professional men, and leaders.

This group of men honor Mr. Washington for his attitude of conciliation toward the white South; they accept the "Atlanta Compromise" in its broadest interpretation; they recognize, with him, many signs of promise, many men of high purpose and fair judgment, in this section; they know that no easy task has been laid upon a region already tottering under heavy burdens. But, nevertheless, they insist that the way to truth and right lies in straightforward honesty, not in indiscriminate flattery; in praising those of the South who do well and criticising uncompromisingly those who do ill; in taking advantage of the opportunities at hand and urging their fellows to do the same, but at the same time in remembering that only a firm adherence to their higher ideals and aspirations will ever keep those ideals within the realm of possibility. They do not expect that the free right to vote, to enjoy civic rights, and to be educated, will come in a moment; they do not expect to see the bias and prejudices of years disappear at the blast of a trumpet; but they are absolutely certain that the way for a people to gain their reasonable rights is not by voluntarily throwing them away and insisting that they do not want them; that the way for a people to gain respect is not by continually belittling and ridiculing themselves; that, on the contrary, Negroes must insist continually, in season and out of season, that voting is necessary to modern manhood, that color discrimination is barbarism, and that black boys need education as well as white boys.

In failing thus to state plainly and unequivocally the legitimate demands of their people, even at the cost of opposing an honored leader, the thinking classes of American Negroes would shirk a heavy responsibility,—a responsibility to themselves, a responsibility to the struggling masses, a responsibility to the darker races of men whose future depends so largely on this American experiment, but especially a responsibility to this nation,—this common Fatherland. It is wrong to encourage a man or a people in evil-doing; it is wrong to aid and abet a national crime simply because it is unpopular not to do so. The growing spirit of kindliness and reconciliation between the North and South after the frightful difference of a generation ago ought to be a source of deep congratulation to all, and especially to those whose mistreatment caused the war; but if that reconciliation is to be marked by the industrial slavery and civic death of those same black men, with permanent legislation into a position of inferiority, then those black men, if they are really men, are called upon by every consideration of patriotism and loyalty to oppose such a course by all civilized methods, even though such opposition involves disagreement with Mr. Booker T. Washington. We have no right to sit silently by while the inevitable seeds are sown for a harvest of disaster to our children, black and white.

First, it is the duty of black men to judge the South discriminatingly. The present generation of Southerners are not responsible for the past, and they should not be blindly hated or blamed for it. Furthermore, to no class is the indiscriminate endorsement of the recent course of the South toward Negroes more nauseating than to the best thought of the South. The South is not "solid"; it is a land in the ferment of social change, wherein forces of all kinds are fighting for supremacy; and to praise the ill the South is today perpetrating is just as wrong as to condemn the good. Discriminating and broad-minded criticism is what the South needs,—needs it for the sake of her own white sons and daughters, and for the insurance of robust, healthy mental and moral development.

Today even the attitude of the Southern whites toward the blacks is not, as so many assume, in all cases the same; the ignorant Southerner hates the Negro, the workingmen fear his competition, the money-makers wish to use him as a laborer, some of the educated see a menace in his upward development, while others—usually the sons of the masters—wish to help him to rise. National opinion has enabled this last class to maintain the Negro common schools, and to protect the Negro partially in property, life, and limb. Through the pressure of the money-makers, the Negro is in danger of being reduced to semi-slavery, especially in the country districts; the workingmen, and those of the educated who fear the Negro, have united to disfranchise him, and some have urged his deportation; while the passions of the ignorant are easily aroused to lynch and abuse any black man. To praise this intricate whirl of thought and prejudice is nonsense; to inveigh indiscriminately against "the South" is unjust; but to use the same breath in praising Governor Aycock,[43] exposing Senator Morgan,[44] arguing with Mr. Thomas Nelson Page,[45] and denouncing Senator Bill Tillman,[46] is not only sane, but the imperative duty of thinking black men.

It would be unjust to Mr. Washington not to acknowledge that in several instances he has opposed movements in the South which were unjust to the Negro; he sent memorials to the Louisiana and Alabama constitutional conventions, he has spoken against lynching, and in other ways has openly or silently set his influence against sinister schemes and unfortunate happenings. Notwithstanding this, it is equally true to assert that on the whole the distinct impression left by Mr. Washington's propaganda is, first, that the South is justified in its present attitude toward the Negro because of the Negro's degradation; secondly, that the prime cause of the Negro's failure to rise more quickly is his wrong education in the past; and, thirdly, that his future rise depends primarily on his own efforts. Each of these propositions is a dangerous half-truth. The supplementary truths must never be lost sight of: first, slavery and race-prejudice are potent if not sufficient causes of the Negro's position; second, industrial and common-school training were necessarily slow in planting because they had to await the black teachers trained by higher institutions,—it being extremely doubtful if any essentially different development was possible, and certainly a Tuskegee was unthinkable before 1880; and, third, while it is a great truth to say that the Negro must strive and strive mightily to help himself, it is equally true that unless his striving be not simply seconded, but rather aroused and encouraged, by the initiative of the richer and wiser environing group, he cannot hope for great success.

In his failure to realize and impress this last point, Mr. Washington is especially to be criticised. His doctrine has tended to make the whites, North and South, shift the burden of the Negro problem to the Negro's shoulders and stand aside as critical and rather pessimistic spectators; when in fact the burden belongs to the nation, and the hands of none of us are clean if we bend not our energies to righting these great wrongs.

The South ought to be led, by candid and honest criticism, to assert her better self and do her full duty to the race she has cruelly wronged and is still wronging. The North—her co-partner in guilt—cannot salve

---

[43]Charles Brantley Aycock (1859–1912) was governor of North Carolina (1901–05) who established a literacy test to prevent African Americans from voting.

[44]Edwin D. Morgan (1811–83) governor of New York (1859–63) and U.S. Senator (1863–69) who voted in the minority in President Johnson's veto of the Freedman's Bureau Bill, which would have extended the life of the Freedman's Bureau, an organization that provided relief to destitute African Americans. His veto was later overturned.

[45]An American writer (1853–1922) from Virginia who romanticized the antebellum South in his novels.

[46]Benjamin R. Tillman (1847–1918), governor of South Carolina (1890–94) and U.S. Senator (1895–1918) who actively worked to frame an article in the South Carolina state constitution that practically denied African Americans the right to vote and who encouraged the use of force to prevent black civil rights.

her conscience by plastering it with gold. We cannot settle this problem by diplomacy and suaveness, by "policy" alone. If worse come to worst, can the moral fibre of this country survive the slow throttling and murder of nine millions of men?

The black men of America have a duty to perform, a duty stern and delicate,—a forward movement to oppose a part of the work of their greatest leader. So far as Mr. Washington preaches Thrift, Patience, and Industrial Training for the masses, we must hold up his hands and strive with him, rejoicing in his honors and glorying in the strength of this Joshua[47] called of God and of man to lead the headless host. But so far as Mr. Washington apologizes for injustice, North or South, does not rightly value the privilege and duty of voting, belittles the emasculating effects of caste distinctions, and opposes the higher training and ambition of our brighter minds,—so far as he, the South, or the Nation, does this,—we must unceasingly and firmly oppose them. By every civilized and peaceful method we must strive for the rights which the world accords to men, clinging unwaveringly to those great words which the sons of the Fathers would fain forget: "We hold these truths to be self-evident: That all men are created equal; that they are endowed by their Creator with certain unalienable rights; that among these are life, liberty, and the pursuit of happiness."

[1903]

---

[47]Israelite leader who succeeded Moses and led his people into the Promised Land.

THEODORE DREISER ■ (1871–1945)

Born into a large family, the son of German immigrants, Theodore Dreiser grew up poor in Indiana, moved five times as a child and teen, and felt oppressed by the strict Catholic upbringing he received. Dreiser's early experiences of hardship stayed with him and shaped his subjects and themes as a writer. After high school, he attended Indiana University for a year and then worked as a newspaper reporter and freelance writer for magazines. Lonely, often depressed, Dreiser tried to write fiction, spurred on by his brother Paul, a songwriter.

Dreiser's first novel, *Sister Carrie*, was published in 1900, but the publisher, Doubleday, Page, and Company, gave it little support, making many major and minor changes in the manuscript that Dreiser had submitted and refusing to advertise and promote the book. The protagonist of Dreiser's story has sex with men outside marriage, abandons her husband, and is not punished for her transgressions, all of which, Dreiser's publisher concluded, would disturb and anger far too many readers if the book were to be widely circulated.

Bitter and wounded by this treatment, Dreiser came close to committing suicide. Thanks to his brother Paul, he found a job with Butterick Publications, where he edited several women's magazines, and he was successful and well paid. *Sister Carrie* was reissued in 1907 and, along with Dreiser's second novel, *Jennie Gerhardt* (1911), won for him a more positive reception, though some reviewers continue to upbraid him for indecency. Throughout his career he frequently found himself in trouble with censors and guardians of public morality.

Dreiser's later novels include *The Financier* (1912), about the exploits of a wealthy, powerful businessman, Frank Cowperwood, whose strength of will and energy enable him to defeat his enemies and overcome obstacles that would have destroyed lesser men; and *An American Tragedy* (1925), a huge novel that tells of a young man, Clyde Griffiths, driven to murder by his ambition to gain social status and distinction.

Typically, Dreiser's books are identified as examples of literary naturalism, and it is true that in them he dramatizes the impact of biological drives and environmental forces. But Dreiser's form of naturalism is complicated and ambivalent because, as both Carrie and Cowperwood in their different ways show, he does not believe that all men and women are passive victims, unable to exercise any agency. Some of Dreiser's characters are broken and doomed by fate, caught in the terrible grip of circumstances they cannot control, while others prove more resourceful and shrewd, manipulating or transcending the situations they encounter.

During the 1930s, the Great Depression decade, Dreiser was active in the world of radical politics, skeptical about the capacity of capitalism to reform itself, and sympathetic to (if also critical of) Communism and the Soviet Union, as two works of reportage and analysis, *Dreiser Looks at Russia* (1928) and *Tragic America* (1931), indicate. By this point his best days as a writer of fiction were behind him. Neither *The Bulwark* (1946) nor the posthumously published *The Stoic* (1947) has much to recommend it. Shortly before his death, in a final gesture of social and political protest, Dreiser joined the Communist Party.

Dreiser has been criticized as an awkward, clumsy stylist, but his style is suited to the groping, questing, inarticulate but obsessed personalities he portrays. There is a dogged, implacable honesty to his vision that exerts a compelling appeal. As the writer Sherwood Anderson said in 1919, Dreiser "is very, very old. I do not know how many years he has lived, perhaps forty, perhaps fifty, but he is very old. Something gray and bleak and hurtful, that has been in the world perhaps forever, is personified in him." Few readers identify with Dreiser's characters, yet, at the same time, many readers nonetheless feel that he understands the nature of human— especially sexual—motivation; that he grasps the struggle for survival that the poor face (and that anyone, however rich and seemingly safe, to his or her shock one day might face as well); and that he expresses permanent truths about the hunger of persons for emotional and spiritual fulfillment and the glittery allure of fame and luxury.

The critic Philip L. Gerber cogently summarized Dreiser's importance:

> Dreiser was the first American to portray with truth and power our modern world of commerce and mechanization, the first to portray the dismal depersonalization of the individual which results from urbanization, and intensifying societal pressure to conform, the first to draw us frankly and grimly as a nation of status-seekers.

"Old Rogaum and His Theresa" (1901; rpt. 1918), is one of Dreiser's earliest and best stories. Set in New York, it deals with the pressures of life (especially social and sexual) in the big city, the challenges faced by immigrants in America as they struggle with the English language and authority figures (in this case, the police), and the bitter differences between the first and second generations of immigrants. Like *Sister Carrie*, this story shows the wayward desires of a young woman and the dangers of unconventional sexual behavior.

For biography: W. A. Swanberg, *Dreiser* (1965); and Richard Lingeman, *Theodore Dreiser*, 2 vols. (1986–90). For analyses of the works: Robert H. Elias, *Theodore Dreiser: Apostle of Nature* (1948); and Donald Pizer, *The*

A family living in a tenement in New York City, 1917, making patriotic flag pins for approximately $2 a week. Photograph by Lewis W. Hine.

Novels of Theodore Dreiser: A Critical Study (1976). See also *Critical Essays on Theodore Dreiser*, ed. Donald Pizer (1981); and *Theodore Dreiser and American Culture: New Readings*, ed. Yoshinobu Hakutani (2000). *A Theodore Dreiser Encyclopedia*, ed. Keith Newlin (2003), is helpful; and Jerome Loving, *The Last Titan: A Life of Theodore Dreiser* (2005) is a good recent biography.

Old Rogaum and His Theresa

In all Bleecker Street was no more comfortable doorway than that of the butcher Rogaum, even if the first floor was given over to meat market purposes. It was to one side of the main entrance, which gave ingress to the butcher shop, and from it led up a flight of steps, at least five feet wide, to the living rooms above. A little portico stood out in front of it, railed on either side, and within was a second or final door, forming, with the outer or storm door, a little area, where Mrs. Rogaum and her children frequently sat of a summer's evening. The outer door was never locked, owing to the inconvenience it would inflict on Mr. Rogaum, who had no other way of getting upstairs. In winter, when all had gone to bed, there had been cases in which belated travelers had taken refuge there from the snow or sleet. One or two newsboys occasionally slept there, until routed out by Officer Maguire, who, seeing it half open one morning at two o'clock, took occasion to look in. He jogged the newsboys sharply with his stick, and then, when they were gone, tried the inner door, which was locked.

"You ought to keep that outer door locked, Rogaum," he observed to the phlegmatic[1] butcher the next evening, as he was passing, "people might get in. A couple o' kids was sleepin' in there last night."

"Ach, dot iss no difference," answered Rogaum pleasantly. "I haf der inner door locked, yet. Let dem sleep. Dot iss no difference."

"Better lock it," said the officer, more to vindicate his authority than anything else. "Something will happen there yet."

The door was never locked, however, and now of a summer evening Mrs. Rogaum and the children made pleasant use of its recess, watching the rout of street cars and occasionally belated trucks go by. The children played on the sidewalk, all except the budding Theresa (eighteen just turning), who, with one companion of the neighborhood, the pretty Kenrihan girl, walked up and down the block, laughing, glancing, watching the boys. Old Mrs. Kenrihan lived in the next block, and there, sometimes, the two stopped. There, also, they most frequently pretended to be when talking with the boys in the intervening side street. Young "Connie" Almerting and George Goujon were the bright particular mashers[2] who held the attention of the maidens in this block. These two made their acquaintance in the customary bold, boyish way, and thereafter the girls had an urgent desire to be out in the street together after eight, and to linger where the boys could see and overtake them.

Old Mrs. Rogaum never knew. She was a particularly fat, old German lady, completely dominated by her liege and portly lord, and at nine o'clock regularly, as he had long ago deemed meet and fit, she was wont to betake her way upward and so to bed. Old Rogaum himself, at that hour, closed the market and went to his chamber.

Before that all the children were called sharply, once from the doorstep below and once from the window above, only Mrs. Rogaum did it first and Rogaum last. It had come, because of a shade of lenience, not wholly apparent in the father's nature, that the older of the children needed two callings and sometimes three. Theresa, now that she had "got in" with the Kenrihan maiden, needed that many calls and even more.

She was just at that age for which mere thoughtless, sensory life holds its greatest charm. She loved to walk up and down in the as yet bright street where were voices and laughter, and occasionally moonlight streaming down. What a nuisance it was to be called at nine, anyhow. Why should one have to go in then, anyhow. What old fogies her parents were, wishing to go to bed so early. Mrs. Kenrihan was not so strict with her

---

[1]Having a disposition supposed to result from the predominance of phlegm among the bodily humors; slow, sluggish, cold, dull.

[2]A womanizer or man who makes indecent public advances toward women.

daughter. It made her pettish when Rogaum insisted, calling as he often did, in German, "Come you now," in a very hoarse and belligerent voice.

She came, eventually, frowning and wretched, all the moonlight calling her, all the voices of the night urging her to come back. Her innate opposition due to her urgent youth made her coming later and later, however, until now, by August of this, her eighteenth year, it was nearly ten when she entered, and Rogaum was almost invariably angry.

"I vill lock you oudt," he declared, in strongly accented English, while she tried to slip by him each time. "I vill show you. Du sollst[3] come ven I say, yet. Hear now."

"I'll not," answered Theresa, but it was always under her breath.

Poor Mrs. Rogaum troubled at hearing the wrath in her husband's voice. It spoke of harder and fiercer times which had been with her. Still she was not powerful enough in the family councils to put in a weighty word. So Rogaum fumed unrestricted.

There were other nights, however, many of them, and now that the young sparks of the neighborhood had enlisted the girls' attention, it was a more trying time than ever. Never did a street seem more beautiful. Its shabby red walls, dusty pavements and protruding store steps and iron railings seemed bits of the ornamental paraphernalia of heaven itself. These lights, the cars, the moon, the street lamps! Theresa had a tender eye for the dashing Almerting, a young idler and loafer of the district, the son of a stationer farther up the street. What a fine fellow he was, indeed! What a handsome nose and chin! What eyes! What authority! His cigarette was always cocked at a high angle, in her presence, and his hat had the least suggestion of being set to one side. He had a shrewd way of winking one eye, taking her boldly by the arm, hailing her as, "Hey, Pretty!" and was strong and athletic and worked (when he worked) in a tobacco factory. His was a trade, indeed, nearly acquired, as he said, and his jingling pockets attested that he had money of his own. Altogether he was very captivating.

"Aw, whaddy ya want to go in for?" he used to say to her, tossing his head gayly on one side to listen and holding her by the arm, as old Rogaum called. "Tell him yuh didn't hear."

"No, I've got to go," said the girl, who was soft and plump and fair—a Rhine maiden type.

"Well, yuh don't have to go just yet. Stay another minute. George, what was that fellow's name that tried to sass us the other day?"

"Theresa!" roared old Rogaum forcefully. "If you do not now come! Ve vill see!"

"I've got to go," repeated Theresa with a faint effort at starting. "Can't you hear? Don't hold me. I haf to."

[3]You shall (German).

"Aw, whaddy ya want to be such a coward for? Y' don't have to go. He won't do nothin' tuh yuh. My old man was always hollerin' like that up tuh a coupla years ago. Let him holler! Say, kid, but yuh got sweet eyes! They're as blue! An' your mouth—"

"Now stop! You hear me!" Theresa would protest softly, as, swiftly, he would slip an arm about her waist and draw her to him, sometimes in a vain, sometimes in a successful effort to kiss her.

As a rule she managed to interpose an elbow between her face and his, but even then he would manage to touch an ear or a cheek or her neck— sometimes her mouth, full and warm—before she would develop sufficient energy to push him away and herself free. Then she would protest mock earnestly or sometimes run away.

"Now, I'll never speak to you any more, if that's the way you're going to do. My father don't allow me to kiss boys, anyhow," and then she would run, half ashamed, half smiling to herself as he would stare after her, or if she lingered, develop a kind of anger and even rage.

"Aw, cut it! Whaddy ya want to be so shy for? Dontcha like me? What's gettin' into yuh, anyhow? Hey?"

In the meantime George Goujon and Myrtle Kenrihan, their companions, might be sweeting and going through a similar contest, perhaps a hundred feet up the street or near at hand. The quality of old Rogaum's voice would by now have become so raucous, however, that Theresa would have lost all comfort in the scene and, becoming frightened, hurry away. Then it was often that both Almerting and Goujon as well as Myrtle Kenrihan would follow her to the corner, almost in sight of the irate old butcher.

"Let him call," young Almerting would insist, laying a final hold on her soft white fingers and causing her to quiver thereby.

"Oh, no," she would gasp nervously. "I can't."

"Well, go on, then," he would say, and with a flip of his heel would turn back, leaving Theresa to wonder whether she had alienated him forever or no. Then she would hurry to her father's door.

"Muss ich all my time spenden calling, mit you on de streeds oudt?" old Rogaum would roar wrathfully, the while his fat hand would descend on her back. "Take dot now. Vy don'd you come ven I call? In now. I vill show you. Und come you yussed vunce more at dis time—ve vill see if I am boss in my own house, aber! Komst du vun minute nach[4] ten to-morrow und you vill see vot you vill get. I vill der door lock. Du sollst not in kommen. Mark! Oudt sollst du stayen—oudt!" and he would glare wrathfully at her retreating figure.

Sometimes Theresa would whimper, sometimes cry or sulk. She almost hated her father for his cruelty, "the big, fat, rough thing," and just because she wanted to stay out in the bright streets, too! Because he was old

[4]After (German).

and stout and wanted to go to bed at ten, he thought every one else did. And outside was the dark sky with its stars, the street lamps, the cars, the tinkle and laughter of eternal life!

"Oh!" she would sigh as she undressed and crawled into her small neat bed. To think that she had to live like this all her days! At the same time old Rogaum was angry and equally determined. It was not so much that he imagined that his Theresa was in bad company as yet, but he wished to forefend against possible danger. This was not a good neighborhood by any means. The boys around here were tough. He wanted Theresa to pick some nice sober youth from among the other Germans he and his wife knew here and there—at the Lutheran Church, for instance. Otherwise she shouldn't marry. He knew she only walked from his shop to the door of the Kenrihans and back again. Had not his wife told him so? If he had thought upon what far pilgrimage her feet had already ventured, or had even seen the dashing Almerting hanging near, then had there been wrath indeed. As it was, his mind was more or less at ease.

On many, many evenings it was much the same. Sometimes she got in on time, sometimes not, but more and more "Connie" Almerting claimed her for his "steady," and bought her ice-cream. In the range of the short block and its confining corners it was all done, lingering by the curbstone and strolling a half block either way in the side streets, until she had offended seriously at home, and the threat was repeated anew. He often tried to persuade her to go on picnics or outings of various kinds, but this, somehow, was not to be thought of at her age—at least with him. She knew her father would never endure the thought, and never even had the courage to mention it, let alone run away. Mere lingering with him at the adjacent street corners brought stronger and stronger admonishments—even more blows and the threat that she should not get in at all.

Well enough she meant to obey, but on one radiant night late in June the time fled too fast. The moon was so bright, the air so soft. The feel of far summer things was in the wind and even in this dusty street. Theresa, in a newly starched white summer dress, had been loitering up and down with Myrtle when as usual they encountered Almerting and Goujon. Now it was ten, and the regular calls were beginning.

"Aw, wait a minute," said "Connie." "Stand still. He won't lock yuh out."

"But he will, though," said Theresa. "You don't know him."

"Well, if he does, come on back to me. I'll take care of yuh. I'll be here. But he won't though. If you stayed out a little while he'd letcha in all right. That's the way my old man used to try to do me but it didn't work with me. I stayed out an' he let me in, just the same. Don'tcha let him kidja." He jingled some loose change in his pocket.

Never in his life had he had a girl on his hands at any unseasonable hour, but it was nice to talk big, and there was a club to which he belonged, The Varick Street Roosters, and to which he had a key. It would be closed and empty at this hour, and she could stay there until morning, if need be or with Myrtle Kenrihan. He would take her there if she insisted. There was a sinister grin on the youth's face.

By now Theresa's affections had carried her far. This youth with his slim body, his delicate strong hands, his fine chin, straight mouth and hard dark eyes—how wonderful he seemed! He was but nineteen to her eighteen but cold, shrewd, daring. Yet how tender he seemed to her, how well worth having! Always, when he kissed her now, she trembled in the balance. There was something in the iron grasp of his fingers that went through her like fire. His glance held hers at times when she could scarcely endure it.

"I'll wait, anyhow," he insisted.

Longer and longer she lingered, but now for once no voice came.

She began to feel that something was wrong—a greater strain than if old Rogaum's voice had been filling the whole neighborhood.

"I've got to go," she said.

"Gee, but you're a coward, yuh are!" said he derisively. "What'r yuh always so scared about? He always says he'll lock yuh out, but he never does."

"Yes, but he will," she insisted nervously. "I think he has this time. You don't know him. He's something awful when he gets real mad. Oh, Connie, I must go!" For the sixth or seventh time she moved, and once more he caught her arm and waist and tried to kiss her, but she slipped away from him.

"Ah, yuh!" he exclaimed. "I wish he would lock yuh out!"

At her own doorstep she paused momentarily, more to soften her progress than anything. The outer door was open as usual, but not the inner. She tried it, but it would not give. It was locked! For a moment she paused, cold fear racing over her body, and then knocked.

No answer.

Again she rattled the door, this time nervously, and was about to cry out.

Still no answer.

At last she heard her father's voice, hoarse and indifferent, not addressed to her at all, but to her mother.

"Let her go, now," it said savagely, from the front room where he supposed she could not hear. "I vill her a lesson teach."

"Hadn't you better let her in now, yet?" pleaded Mrs. Rogaum faintly.

"No," insisted Mr. Rogaum. "Nefer! Let her go now. If she vill alvays stay oudt, let her stay now. Ve vill see how she likes dot."

His voice was rich in wrath, and he was saving up a good beating for her into the bargain, that she knew. She would have to wait and wait and plead, and when she was thoroughly wretched and subdued he would let her in and beat her—such a beating as she had never received in all her born days.

Again the door rattled, and still she got no answer. Not even her call brought a sound.

Now, strangely, a new element, not heretofore apparent in her nature but nevertheless wholly there, was called into life, springing in action as Diana,[5] full formed. Why should he always be so harsh? She hadn't done anything but stay out a little later than usual. He was always so anxious to keep her in and subdue her. For once the cold chill of her girlish fears left her, and she wavered angrily.

"All right," she said, some old German stubbornness springing up, "I won't knock. You don't need to let me in, then."

A suggestion of tears was in her eyes, but she backed firmly out onto the stoop and sat down, hesitating. Old Rogaum saw her, lowering down from the lattice, but said nothing. He would teach her for once what were proper hours!

At the corner, standing, Almerting also saw her. He recognized the simple white dress, and paused steadily, a strange thrill racing over him. Really they had locked her out! Gee, this was new. It was great, in a way. There she was, white, quiet, shut out, waiting at her father's doorstep.

Sitting thus, Theresa pondered a moment, her girlish rashness and anger dominating her. Her pride was hurt and she felt revengeful. They would shut her out, would they? All right, she would go out and they should look to it how they would get her back—the old curmudgeons. For the moment the home of Myrtle Kenrihan came to her as a possible refuge, but she decided that she need not go there yet. She had better wait about awhile and see—or walk and frighten them. He would beat her, would he? Well, maybe he would and maybe he wouldn't. She might come back, but still that was a thing afar off. Just now it didn't matter so much. "Connie" was still there on the corner. He loved her dearly. She felt it.

Getting up, she stepped to the now quieting sidewalk and strolled up the street. It was a rather nervous procedure, however. There were street cars still, and stores lighted and people passing, but soon these would not be, and she was locked out. The side streets were already little more than long silent walks and gleaming rows of lamps.

At the corner her youthful lover almost pounced upon her.

"Locked out, are yuh?" he asked, his eyes shining.

For the moment she was delighted to see him, for a nameless dread had already laid hold of her. Home meant so much. Up to now it had been her whole life.

"Yes," she answered feebly.

"Well, let's stroll on a little," said the boy. He had not as yet quite made up his mind what to do, but the night was young. It was so fine to have her with him—his.

At the farther corner they passed Officers Maguire and Delahanty, idly swinging their clubs and discussing politics.

[5]The Roman goddess of the moon, hunting, and women in childbirth. Her Greek counterpart, Artemis, was reputed to be born fully grown.

"'Tis a shame," Officer Delahanty was saying, "the way things are run now," but he paused to add, "Ain't that old Rogaum's girl over there with young Almerting?"

"It is," replied Maguire, looking after.

"Well, I'm thinkin' he'd better be keepin' an eye on her," said the former. "She's too young to be runnin' around with the likes o' him."

Maguire agreed. "He's a young tough," he observed. "I never liked him. He's too fresh. He works over here in Myer's tobacco factory, and belongs to The Roosters. He's up to no good, I'll warrant that."

"Teach 'em a lesson, I would," Almerting was saying to Theresa as they strolled on. "We'll walk around a while an' make 'em think yuh mean business. They won't lock yuh out any more. If they don't let yuh in when we come back. I'll find yuh a place, all right."

His sharp eyes were gleaming as he looked around into her own. Already he had made up his mind that she should not go back if he could help it. He knew a better place than home for this night, anyhow—the club room of the Roosters, if nowhere else. They could stay there for a time, anyhow.

By now old Rogaum, who had seen her walking up the street alone, was marveling at her audacity, but thought she would soon come back. It was amazing that she should exhibit such temerity, but he would teach her! Such a whipping! At half-past ten, however, he stuck his head out of the open window and saw nothing of her. At eleven, the same. Then he walked the floor.

At first wrathful, then nervous, then nervous and wrathful, he finally ended all nervous, without a scintilla of wrath. His stout wife sat up in bed and began to wring her hands.

"Lie down!" he commanded. "You make me sick. I know vot I am doing!"

"Is she still at der door?" pleaded the mother.

"No," he said. "I don't tink so. She should come ven I call."

His nerves were weakening, however, and now they finally collapsed.

"She vent de stread up," he said anxiously after a time. "I vill go after."

Slipping on his coat, he went down the stairs and out into the night. It was growing late, and the stillness and gloom of midnight were nearing. Nowhere in sight was his Theresa. First one way and then another he went, looking here, there, everywhere, finally groaning.

"Ach, Gott!" he said, the sweat bursting out on his brow, "vot in Teufel's[6] name iss dis?"

He thought he would seek a policeman, but there was none. Officer Maguire had long since gone for a quiet game in one of the neighboring saloons. His partner had temporarily returned to his own beat. Still old Rogaum hunted on, worrying more and more.

Finally he bethought him to hasten home again, for she must have got back. Mrs. Rogaum, too, would be frantic if she had not. If she were not

[6]Devil (German).

there he must go to the police. Such a night! And his Theresa—This thing could not go on.

As he turned into his own corner he almost ran, coming up to the little portico wet and panting. At a puffing step he turned, and almost fell over a white body at his feet, a prone and writhing woman.

"Ach, Gott!" he cried aloud, almost shouting in his distress and excitement. "Theresa, vot iss dis? Wilhelmina, a light now. Bring a light now, I say, for himmel's sake! Theresa hat sich *umgebracht*.[7] Help!"

He had fallen to his knees and was turning over the writhing, groaning figure. By the pale light of the street, however, he could make out that it was not his Theresa, fortunately, as he had at first feared, but another and yet there was something very like her in the figure.

"Um!" said the stranger weakly. "Ah!"

The dress was gray, not white as was his Theresa's, but the body was round and plump. It cut the fiercest cords of his intensity, this thought of death to a young woman, but there was something else about the situation which made him forget his own troubles.

Mrs. Rogaum, loudly admonished, almost tumbled down the stairs. At the foot she held the light she had brought—a small glass oil-lamp—and then nearly dropped it. A fairly attractive figure, more girl than woman, rich in all the physical charms that characterize a certain type, lay near to dying. Her soft hair had fallen back over a good forehead, now quite white. Her pretty hands, well docked with rings, were clutched tightly in an agonized grip. At her neck a blue silk shirtwaist and light lace collar were torn away where she had clutched herself, and on the white flesh was a yellow stain as of one who had been burned. A strange odor reeked in the area, and in one corner was a spilled bottle.

"Ach, Gott!" exclaimed Mrs. Rogaum. "It iss a vooman! She haf herself gekilt. Run for der police! Oh, my! oh, my!"

Rogaum did not kneel for more than a moment. Somehow, this creature's fate seemed in some psychic way identified with that of his own daughter. He bounded up, and jumping out his front door, began to call lustily for the police. Officer Maguire, at his social game nearby, heard the very first cry and came running.

"What's the matter here, now?" he exclaimed, rushing up full and ready for murder, robbery, fire, or, indeed, anything in the whole roster of human calamities.

"A vooman!" said Rogaum excitedly. "She haf herself *umgebracht*. She iss dying. Ach, Gott! in my own doorstep, yet!"

"Vere iss der hospital?" put in Mrs. Rogaum, thinking clearly of an ambulance, but not being able to express it. "She iss gekilt, sure. Oh! Oh!" and bending over her the poor old motherly soul stroked the tightened

[7]Theresa has killed herself (German).

hands, and trickled tears upon the blue shirtwaist. "Ach, vy did you do dot?" she said. "Ach, for vy?"

Officer Maguire was essentially a man of action. He jumped to the sidewalk, amid the gathering company, and beat loudly with his club upon the stone flagging. Then he ran to the nearest police phone, returning to aid in any other way he might. A milk wagon passing on its way from the Jersey ferry with a few tons of fresh milk aboard, he held it up and demanded a helping.

"Give us a quart there, will you?" he said authoritatively. "A woman's swallowed acid in here."

"Sure," said the driver, anxious to learn the cause of the excitement. "Got a glass, anybody?"

Maguire ran back and returned, bearing a measure. Mrs. Rogaum stood looking nervously on, while the stocky officer raised the golden head and poured the milk.

"Here, now, drink this," he said. "Come on. Try an' swallow it."

The girl, a blonde of the type the world too well knows, opened her eyes, and looked, groaning a little.

"Drink it," shouted the officer fiercely. "Do you want to die? Open your mouth!"

Used to a fear of the law in all her days, she obeyed now, even in death. The lips parted, the fresh milk was drained to the end, some spilling on neck and cheek.

While they were working old Rogaum came back and stood looking on, by the side of his wife. Also Officer Delahanty, having heard the peculiar wooden ring of the stick upon the stone in the night, had come up.

"Ach, ach," exclaimed Rogaum rather distractedly, "und she iss oudt yet. I could not find her. Oh, oh!"

There was a clang of a gong up the street as the racing ambulance turned rapidly in. A young hospital surgeon dismounted, and seeing the woman's condition, ordered immediate removal. Both officers and Rogaum, as well as the surgeon, helped place her in the ambulance. After a moment the lone bell, ringing wildly in the night, was all the evidence remaining that a tragedy had been here.

"Do you know how she came here?" asked Officer Delahanty, coming back to get Rogaum's testimony for the police.

"No, no," answered Rogaum wretchedly. "She vass here alretty. I vass for my daughter loog. Ach, himmel,[8] I haf my daughter lost. She iss avay."

Mrs. Rogaum also chattered, the significance of Theresa's absence all the more painfully emphasized by this.

The officer did not at first get the import of this. He was only interested in the facts of the present case.

"You say she was here when you come? Where was you?"

[8]Heavens (German).

"I say I vass for my daughter loog. I come here, and der vooman vass here now alretty."

"Yes. What time was this?"

"Only now yet. Yussed a half-hour."

Officer Maguire had strolled up, after chasing away a small crowd that had gathered with fierce and unholy threats. For the first time now he noticed the peculiar perturbation of the usually placid German couple.

"What about your daughter?" he asked, catching a word as to that.

Both old people raised their voices at once.

"She haf gone. She haf run avay. Ach, himmel, ve must for her loog. Quick—she could not get in. Ve had der door shut."

"Locked her out, eh?" inquired Maguire after a time, hearing much of the rest of the story.

"Yes," explained Rogaum. "It was to schkare her a liddle. She vould not come ven I called."

"Sure, that's the girl we saw walkin' with young Almerting, do ye mind? The one in the white dress," said Delahanty to Maguire.

"White dress, yah!" echoed Rogaum, and then the fact of her walking with some one came home like a blow.

"Did you hear dot?" he exclaimed even as Mrs. Rogaum did likewise. *"Mein Gott, hast du gehoert?"*[9]

He fairly jumped as he said it. His hands flew on to his stout and ruddy head.

"Whaddy ya want to let her out for nights?" asked Maguire roughly, catching the drift of the situation "That's no time for young girls to be out, anybody and with these toughs around here. Sure, I saw her nearly two hours ago."

"Ach," groaned Rogaum. "Two hours yet. Ho, ho, ho!" His voice was quite hysteric.

"Well, go on in," said Officer Delahanty. "There's no use yellin' out here. Give us a description of her an' we'll send out an alarm. You won't be able to find her walkin' around."

Her parents described her exactly. The two men turned to the nearest police box and then disappeared, leaving the old German couple in the throes of distress. A time-worn old church-clock nearby now chimed out one and then two. The notes cut like knives. Mrs. Rogaum began fearfully to cry. Rogaum walked and blustered to himself.

"It's a queer case, that," said Officer Delahanty to Maguire after having reported the matter of Theresa, but referring solely to the outcast of the doorway so recently sent away and in whose fate they were much more interested. She being a part of the commercialized vice of the city, they were curious as to the cause of her suicide. "I think I know that woman. I think I know where she came from. You do, too—Adele's, around the corner, eh?

[9]"My God, did you hear that?" (German).

She didn't come into that doorway by herself, either. She was put there. You know how they do."

"You're right," said Maguire. "She was put there, all right, and that's just where she come from, too."

The two of them now tipped up their noses and cocked their eyes significantly.

"Let's go around," added Maguire.

They went, the significant red light over the transom at 68 telling its own story. Strolling leisurely up, they knocked. At the very first sound a painted denizen of the half-world opened the door.

"Where's Adele?" asked Maguire as the two, hats on as usual, stepped in.

"She's gone to bed."

"Tell her to come down."

They seated themselves deliberately in the gaudy mirrored parlor and waited, conversing between themselves in whispers. Presently a sleepy-looking woman of forty in a gaudy robe of heavy texture, and slippered in red, appeared.

"We're here about that suicide case you had tonight. What about it? Who was she? How'd she come to be in that doorway around the corner? Come, now," Maguire added, as the madam assumed an air of mingled injured and ignorant innocence, "you know. Can that stuff! How did she come to take poison?"

"I don't know what you're talking about," said the woman with the utmost air of innocence. "I never heard of any suicide."

"Aw, come now," insisted Delahanty, "the girl around the corner. You know. We know you've got a pull, but we've got to know about this case, just the same. Come across now. It won't be published. What made her take the poison?"

Under the steady eyes of the officers the woman hesitated, but finally weakened.

"Why—why—her lover went back on her—that's all. She got so blue we just couldn't do anything with her. I tried to, but she wouldn't listen."

"Lover, eh?" put in Maguire as though that were the most unheard-of thing in the world. "What was his name?"

"I don't know. You never can tell that."

"What was her name—Annie?" asked Delahanty wisely, as though he knew but was merely inquiring for form's sake.

"No—Emily."

"Well, how did she come to get over there, anyhow?" inquired Maguire most pleasantly.

"George took her," she replied, referring to a man-of-all-work about the place.

Then little by little as they sat there the whole miserable story came out, miserable as all the wilfulness and error and suffering of the world.

"How old was she?"

"Oh, twenty-one."

"Well, where'd she come from?"

"Oh, here in New York. Her family locked her out one night, I think."

Something in the way the woman said this last brought old Rogaum and his daughter back to the policemen's minds. They had forgotten all about her by now, although they had turned in an alarm. Fearing to interfere too much with this well-known and politically controlled institution, the two men left, but outside they fell to talking of the other case.

"We ought to tell old Rogaum about her some time," said Maguire to Delahanty cynically. "He locked his kid out to-night."

"Yes, it might be a good thing for him to hear that," replied the other. "We'd better go round there an' see if his girl's back yet. She may be back by now," and so they returned but little disturbed by the joint miseries.

At Rogaum's door they once more knocked loudly.

"Is your daughter back again?" asked Maguire when a reply was had.

"Ach, no," replied the hysterical Mrs. Rogaum, who was quite alone now. "My husband he haf gone oudt again to loog vunce more. Oh, my! Oh, my!"

"Well, that's what you get for lockin' her out," returned Maguire loftily, the other story fresh in his mind. "That other girl downstairs here tonight was locked out too, once." He chanced to have a girl-child of his own and somehow he was in the mood for pointing a moral. "You oughtn't to do anything like that. Where d'yuh expect she's goin' to if you lock her out?"

Mrs. Rogaum groaned. She explained that it was not her fault, but anyhow it was carrying coals to Newcastle[10] to talk to her so. The advice was better for her husband.

The pair finally returned to the station to see if the call had been attended to.

"Sure," said the sergeant, "certainly. Whaddy ya think?" and he read from the blotter before him:

"'Look out for girl, Theresa Rogaum. Aged 18; height, about 5, 3; light hair, blue eyes, white cotton dress, trimmed with blue ribbon. Last seen with lad named Almerting, about 19 years of age, about 5, 9; weight 135 pounds.'"

There were other details even more pointed and conclusive. For over an hour now, supposedly, policemen from the Battery to Harlem, and far beyond, had been scanning long streets and dim shadows for a girl in a white dress with a youth of nineteen,—supposedly.

Officer Halsey, another of this region, which took in a portion of Washington Square, had seen a good many couples this pleasant summer evening since the description of Theresa and Almerting had been read to him over the telephone, but none that answered to these. Like Maguire and

---

[10]A pointless exercise. Newcastle, England, was famous for its export of coal by sea.

Delahanty, he was more or less indifferent to all such cases, but idling on a corner near the park at about three a.m., a brother officer, one Paisly by name, came up and casually mentioned the missing pair also.

"I bet I saw that couple, not over an hour ago. She was dressed in white, and looked to me as if she didn't want to be out. I didn't happen to think at the time, but now I remember. They acted sort o' funny. She did, anyhow. They went in this park down at the Fourth Street end there."

"Supposing we beat it, then," suggested Halsey, weary for something to do.

"Sure," said the other quickly, and together they began a careful search, kicking around in the moonlight under the trees. The moon was leaning moderately toward the west, and all the branches were silvered with light and dew. Among the flowers, past clumps of bushes, near the fountain, they searched, each one going his way alone. At last, the wandering Halsey paused beside a thick clump of flaming bushes, ruddy, slightly, even in the light. A murmur of voices greeted him, and something very much like the sound of a sob.

"What's that?" he said mentally, drawing near and listening.

"Why don't you come on now?" said the first of the voices heard. "They won't let you in any more. You're with me, ain't you? What's the use cryin'?"

No answer to this, but no sobs. She must have been crying silently.

"Come on. I can take care of yuh. We can live in Hoboken. I know a place where we can go to-night. That's all right."

There was a movement as if the speaker were patting her on the shoulder.

"What's the use cryin'? Don't you believe I love yuh?"

The officer who had stolen quietly around to get a better view now came closer. He wanted to see for himself. In the moonlight, from a comfortable distance, he could see them seated. The tall bushes were almost all about the bench. In the arms of the youth was the girl in white, held very close. Leaning over to get a better view, he saw him kiss her and hold her—hold her in such a way that she could but yield to him, whatever her slight disinclination.

It was a common affair at earlier hours, but rather interesting now. The officer was interested. He crept nearer.

"What are you two doin' here?" he suddenly inquired, rising before them, as though he had not seen.

The girl tumbled out of her compromising position, speechless and blushing violently. The young man stood up, nervous, but still defiant.

"Aw, we were just sittin' here," he replied.

"Yes? Well, say, what's your name? I think we're lookin' for you two, anyhow. Almerting?"

"That's me," said the youth.

"And yours?" he added, addressing Theresa.

"Theresa Rogaum," replied the latter brokenly, beginning to cry.

"Well, you two'll have to come along with me," be added laconically. "The Captain wants to see both of you," and he marched them solemnly away.

"What for?" young Almerting ventured to inquire after a time, blanched with fright.

"Never mind," replied the policeman irritably.

"Come along, you'll find out at the station house. We want you both. That's enough."

At the other end of the park Paisly joined them, and, at the station-house, the girl was given a chair. She was all tears and melancholy with a modicum possibly of relief at being thus rescued from the world. Her companion, for all his youth, was defiant if circumspect, a natural animal defeated of its aim.

"Better go for her father," commented the sergeant, and by four in the morning old Rogaum, who had still been up and walking the floor, was rushing station-ward. From an earlier rage he had passed to an almost killing grief, but now at the thought that he might possibly see his daughter alive and well once more he was overflowing with a mingled emotion which contained rage, fear, sorrow, and a number of other things. What should he do to her if she were alive? Beat her? Kiss her? Or what? Arrived at the station, however, and seeing his fair Theresa in the hands of the police, and this young stranger lingering near, also detained, he was beside himself with fear, rage, affection.

"You! You!" he exclaimed at once, glaring at the imperturbable Almerting, when told that this was the young man who was found with his girl. Then, seized with a sudden horror, he added, turning to Theresa, "Vot haf you done? Oh, oh! You! You!" he repeated again to Almerting angrily, now that he felt that his daughter was safe. "Come not near my tochter any more! I vill preak your effery pone, du teufel, du!"

He made a move toward the incarcerated lover, but here the sergeant interfered.

"Stop that, now," he said calmly. "Take your daughter out of here and go home, or I'll lock you both up. We don't want any fighting in here. D'ye hear? Keep your daughter off the streets hereafter, then she won't get into trouble. Don't let her run around with such young toughs as this." Almerting winced. "Then there won't anything happen to her. We'll do whatever punishing's to be done."

"Aw, what's eatin' him!" commented Almerting dourly, now that he felt himself reasonably safe from a personal encounter. "What have I done? He locked her out, didn't he? I was just keepin' her company till morning."

"Yes, we know all about that," said the sergeant, "and about you, too. You shut up, or you'll go down-town to Special Sessions[11]. I want no guff out o' you." Still he ordered the butcher angrily to be gone.

[11]Courts with jurisdiction over minor crimes and misdemeanors.

Old Rogaum heard nothing. He had his daughter. He was taking her home. She was not dead—not even morally injured in so far as he could learn. He was a compound of wondrous feelings. What to do was beyond him.

At the corner near the butcher shop they encountered the wakeful Maguire, still idling, as they passed. He was pleased to see that Rogaum had his Theresa once more. It raised him to a high, moralizing height.

"Don't lock her out any more," he called significantly. "That's what brought the other girl to your door, you know!"

"Vot iss dot?" said Rogaum.

"I say the other girl was locked out. That's why she committed suicide."

"Ach, I know," said the husky German under his breath, but he had no intention of locking her out. He did not know what he would do until they were in the presence of his crying wife, who fell upon Theresa, weeping. Then he decided to be reasonably lenient.

"She vass like you," said the old mother to the wandering Theresa, ignorant of the seeming lesson brought to their very door. "She vass loog like you."

"I vill not vip you now," said the old butcher solemnly, too delighted to think of punishment after having feared every horror under the sun, "aber, go not oudt any more. Keep off de streads so late. I von't haf it. Dot loafer, aber—let him yussed come here some more! I fix him!"

"No, no," said the fat mother tearfully, smoothing her daughter's hair. "She vouldn't run avay no more yet, no, no." Old Mrs. Rogaum was all mother.

"Well, you wouldn't let me in," insisted Theresa, "and I didn't have any place to go. What do you want me to do? I'm not going to stay in the house all the time."

"I fix him!" roared Rogaum, unloading all his rage now on the recreant lover freely. "Yussed let him come some more! Der penitentiary he should haf!"

"Oh, he's not so bad," Theresa told her mother, almost a heroine now that she was home and safe. "He's Mr. Almerting, the stationer's boy. They live here in the next block."

"Don't you ever bother that girl again," the sergeant was saying to young Almerting as he turned him loose an hour later. "If you do, we'll get you, and you won't get off under six months. Y' hear me, do you?"

"Aw, I don't want 'er," replied the boy truculently and cynically. "Let him have his old daughter. What'd he want to lock 'er out for? They'd better not lock 'er out again though, that's all I say. I don't want 'er."

"Beat it!" replied the sergeant, and away he went.

[1901, 1918]

STEPHEN CRANE ■ (1871–1900)

Best known for his Civil War novel, *The Red Badge of Courage* (1895), Stephen Crane was born in Newark, New Jersey, the fourteenth and youngest child (nine survived) in the family. His father, a graduate of the College of New Jersey (now Princeton University), was the presiding elder of Methodist churches in the Newark district and an author whose books and articles decried the use of alcohol and tobacco, card playing, and other ungodly diversions, all of which his son Stephen later embraced. Mrs. Crane, the daughter of a Methodist minister and the niece of a Methodist bishop, wrote essays for Methodist journals and New York and Philadelphia papers, gave lectures, and was a member of the Women's Christian Temperance Union.

Crane attended Pennington Seminary, a coeducational Methodist boarding school in New Jersey, and then entered Claverack College and Hudson River Institute, a junior college and military school in Columbia County, New York. During the fall 1890 semester, Crane was a student at Lafayette College in Pennsylvania. He was asked to leave because of "scholastic delinquencies," having failed nearly all of his courses. He spent the spring 1891 semester at Syracuse University in upstate New York but was no more successful as a student there. He did not return to Syracuse in the fall of 1891 but chose instead to explore the slums, brothels, and saloons of the Bowery on the lower east side of Manhattan, New York City.

By early the following year, Crane had completed and revised the draft of *Maggie*, his first major work of fiction, the story of a mistreated but innocent girl and her harsh life in a New York City slum. Crane affirmed he had written with a purpose, noting in an inscription in gift copies that he sought in *Maggie* "to show that environment is a tremendous thing in the world and frequently shapes lives regardless. If one proves that theory, one makes room in Heaven for all sorts of souls (notably an occasional street girl) who are not confidently expected to be there by many excellent people." Though sometimes rebuking Crane's realism as overdone, as too brutal and sordid, reviewers commended *Maggie* for its depiction of the horrors of slum life. The novelist Hamlin Garland (whom Crane had heard lecture in August 1891) and William Dean Howells, dean of American letters, especially admired it.

The Red Badge of Courage was first published in a much-shortened form (18,000 of the manuscript's 55,000 words) in the *Philadelphia Press* in December 1894, and, through syndication, in a number of other newspapers. From late January to mid-May 1895, Crane worked as a correspondent in the American West and in Mexico, but by early fall he had prepared a revised version of the manuscript, and it was published—Crane called it "a psychological portrayal of fear"—by D. Appleton and Company in October. While not a moneymaker for Crane, it was a critical success, and he wrote five more Civil War stories between September 1895 and February 1896, including "The Veteran" and "An Episode of War."

During the remainder of his tragically short life—he suffered for years from tuberculosis and eventually succumbed to it—Crane lived in America and England with Cora Taylor, the proprietor of a high-class bawdy house in Jacksonville, Florida. He traveled extensively as a war correspondent, wrote stories and essays at a frantic pace to pay his ever-mounting debts, and enjoyed the friendship and admiration of Henry James, Joseph Conrad, and other writers.

"An Experiment in Misery," published in 1894, reflects Crane's own experiences living and moving among the downtrodden in the grim Bowery environment. Keyed to a walk through the city of "a youth," the story—perhaps one should term it a sketch of slum-life initiation and disorientation—shows Crane's mastery of mood and point of view. Its power comes from the interplay of vivid, strange, surreal description, harsh and beaten-down existence, and coarse, desperate dialogue.

"An Episode of War," published in 1899, is striking for the vivid focus of Crane's descriptions, for its unnerving psychological insight, and for the eerie tone of the narrator's observations and reflections. Crane depicts the pain and puzzlement of the wounded (and unnamed) lieutenant and the cruel deception practiced by the surgeon without wasting a word. His haunting clarity and unusual piercing economy as a writer (he was also a poet of surreal, visionary, condensed lyrics) is one of his greatest strengths—one that Ernest Hemingway, Ralph Ellison, and other later writers adapted and developed in their work.

For a brief biography: James B. Colvert, *Stephen Crane* (1984). For fuller accounts, see: Christopher Benfey, *The Double Life of Stephen Crane* (1992); and Linda H. Davis, *Badge of Courage: The Life of Stephen Crane* (1998). Also valuable: *The Crane Log: A Documentary Life of Stephen Crane, 1871–1900*, eds. Stanley Wertheim and Paul M. Sorrentino (1994); and Stanley Wertheim, *A Stephen Crane Encyclopedia* (1997); and *Stephen Crane Remembered*, ed. Paul Sorrentino (2006), which collects descriptions of Crane by those who knew him. For commentary on the novels and stories: Chester L. Wolford, *Stephen Crane: A Study of the Short Fiction* (1989); and Micheal W. Schaefer, *A Reader's Guide to the Short Stories of Stephen Crane* (1996); and Perry Lentz, *Private Fleming at Chancellorsville:* The Red Badge of Courage *and the Civil War* (2006). The novelist Edmund White recreates the final days of Crane's life in *Hotel De Dream: A New York Novel* (2007).

An Experiment in Misery

IT was late at night, and a fine rain was swirling softly down, causing the pavements to glisten with hue of steel and blue and yellow in the rays of the innumerable lights. A youth was trudging slowly, without enthusiasm, with his hands buried deep in his trouser's pockets, towards the down-town places where beds can be hired for coppers.[1] He was clothed in an aged and tattered suit, and his derby was a marvel of dust-covered crown and torn rim. He was going forth to eat as the wanderer may eat, and sleep as the homeless sleep. By the time he had reached City Hall Park he was so completely plastered with yells of "bum" and "hobo," and with various unholy epithets that small boys had applied to him at intervals, that he was in a state of the most profound dejection. The sifting rain saturated the old velvet collar of his overcoat, and as the wet cloth pressed against his neck, he felt that there no longer could be pleasure in life. He looked about him searching for an outcast of highest degree that they too might share miseries, but the lights threw a quivering glare over rows and circles of deserted benches that glistened damply, showing patches of wet sod behind them. It seemed that their usual freights had fled on this night to better things. There were only squads of well-dressed Brooklyn people who swarmed towards the bridge.

The young man loitered about for a time and then went shuffling off down Park Row. In the sudden descent in style of the dress of the crowd he felt relief, and as if he were at last in his own country. He began to see tatters that matched his tatters. In Chatham Square there were aimless men strewn in front of saloons and lodging-houses, standing sadly, patiently, reminding one vaguely of the attitudes of chickens in a storm. He aligned himself with these men, and turned slowly to occupy himself with the flowing life of the great street.

Through the mists of the cold and storming night, the cable cars went in silent procession, great affairs shining with red and brass, moving with formidable power, calm and irresistible, dangerful and gloomy, breaking silence only by the loud fierce cry of the gong. Two rivers of people swarmed along the side walks, spattered with black mud, which made each shoe leave a scar-like impression. Overhead elevated trains with a shrill grinding of the wheels stopped at the station, which upon its leg-like pillars seemed to resemble some monstrous kind of crab squatting over the street. The quick fat puffings of the engines could be heard. Down an alley there were sombre curtains of purple and black, on which street lamps dully glittered like embroidered flowers.

A saloon stood with a voracious air on a corner. A sign leaning against the front of the door-post announced "Free hot soup to-night!" The swing doors, snapping to and fro like ravenous lips, made gratified smacks as the saloon gorged itself with plump men, eating with astounding and endless appetite, smiling in some indescribable manner as the men came from all directions like sacrifices to a heathenish superstition.

[1]Pennies.

Caught by the delectable sign the young man allowed himself to be swallowed. A bar-tender placed a schooner[2] of dark and portentous beer on the bar. Its monumental form up-reared until the froth a-top was above the crown of the young man's brown derby.

"Soup over there, gents," said the bar-tender affably. A little yellow man in rags and the youth grasped their schooners and went with speed toward a lunch counter, where a man with oily but imposing whiskers ladled genially from a kettle until he had furnished his two mendicants with a soup that was steaming hot, and in which there were little floating suggestions of chicken. The young man, sipping his broth, felt the cordiality expressed by the warmth of the mixture, and he beamed at the man with oily but imposing whiskers, who was presiding like a priest behind an altar. "Have some more, gents?" he inquired of the two sorry figures before him. The little yellow man accepted with a swift gesture, but the youth shook his head and went out, following a man whose wondrous seediness promised that he would have a knowledge of cheap lodging-houses.

On the side-walk he accosted the seedy man. "Say, do you know a cheap place to sleep?"

The other hesitated for a time gazing sideways. Finally he nodded in the direction of the street, "I sleep up there," he said, "when I've got the price."

"How much?"

"Ten cents."

The young man shook his head dolefully. "That's too rich for me."

At that moment there approached the two a reeling man in strange garments. His head was a fuddle of bushy hair and whiskers, from which his eyes peered with a guilty slant. In a close scrutiny it was possible to distinguish the cruel lines of a mouth which looked as if its lips had just closed with satisfaction over some tender and piteous morsel. He appeared like an assassin steeped in crimes performed awkwardly.

But at this time his voice was tuned to the coaxing key of an affectionate puppy. He looked at the men with wheedling eyes, and began to sing a little melody for charity.

"Say, gents, can't yeh give a poor feller a couple of cents t' git a bed. I got five, and I gits anudder two I gits me a bed. Now, on th' square, gents, can't yeh jest gimme two cents t' git a bed? Now, yeh know how a respecter'ble gentlem'n feels when he's down on his luck, an' I_____"

The seedy man, staring with imperturbable countenance at a train which clattered overhead, interrupted in an expressionless voice—"Ah, go t' h—!"

But the youth spoke to the prayerful assassin in tones of astonishment and inquiry. "Say, you must be crazy! Why don't yeh strike somebody that looks as if they had money?"

---

[2]A large, tall drinking glass.

The assassin, tottering about on his uncertain legs, and at intervals brushing imaginary obstacles from before his nose, entered into a long explanation of the psychology of the situation. It was so profound that it was unintelligible.

When he had exhausted the subject, the young man said to him—

"Let's see th' five cents."

The assassin wore an expression of drunken woe at this sentence, filled with suspicion of him. With a deeply pained air he began to fumble in his clothing, his red hands trembling. Presently he announced in a voice of bitter grief, as if he had been betrayed— "There's on'y four."

"Four," said the young man thoughtfully. "Well, look-a-here, I'm a stranger here, an' if ye'll steer me to your cheap joint I'll find the other three."

The assassin's countenance became instantly radiant with joy. His whiskers quivered with the wealth of his alleged emotions. He seized the young man's hand in a transport of delight and friendliness.

"B' Gawd," he cried, "if ye'll do that, b' Gawd, I'd say yeh was a damned good fellow, I would, an' I'd remember yeh all m' life, I would b' Gawd, an' if I ever got a chance I'd return the compliment"—he spoke with drunken dignity,—"b' Gawd, I'd treat yeh white, I would, an' I'd allus remember yeh."

The young man drew back, looking at the assassin coldly. "Oh, that's all right," he said. "You show me th' joint—that's all you've got t' do."

The assassin, gesticulating gratitude, led the young man along a dark street. Finally he stopped before a little dusty door. He raised his hand impressively. "Look-a-here," he said, and there was a thrill of deep and ancient wisdom upon his face, "I've brought yeh here, an' that's my part, ain't it? If th' place don't suit yeh, yeh needn't git mad at me, need yeh? There won't be no bad feelin', will there?"

"No," said the young man.

The assassin waved his arm tragically, and led the march up the steep stairway. On the way the young man furnished the assassin with three pennies. At the top a man with benevolent spectacles looked at them through a hole in a board. He collected their money, wrote some names on a register, and speedily was leading the two men along a gloom-shrouded corridor.

Shortly after the beginning of this journey the young man felt his liver turn white, for from the dark and secret places of the building there suddenly came to his nostrils strange and unspeakable odours, that assailed him like malignant diseases with wings. They seemed to be from human bodies closely packed in dens; the exhalations from a hundred pairs of reeking lips; the fumes from a thousand bygone debauches; the expression of a thousand present miseries.

A man, naked save for a little snuff-coloured undershirt, was parading sleepily along the corridor. He rubbed his eyes, and, giving vent to a prodigious yawn, demanded to be told the time.

"Half-past one."

The man yawned again. He opened a door, and for a moment his form was outlined against a black, opaque interior. To this door came the three men, and as it was again opened the unholy odours rushed out like fiends, so that the young man was obliged to struggle as against an overpowering wind.

It was some time before the youth's eyes were good in the intense gloom within, but the man with benevolent spectacles led him skilfully, pausing but a moment to deposit the limp assassin upon a cot. He took the youth to a cot that lay tranquilly by the window, and showing him a tall locker for clothes that stood near the head with the ominous air of a tombstone, left him.

The youth sat on his cot and peered about him. There was a gas-jet in a distant part of the room, that burned a small flickering orange-hued flame. It caused vast masses of tumbled shadows in all parts of the place, save where, immediately about it, there was a little grey haze. As the young man's eyes became used to the darkness, he could see upon the cots that thickly littered the floor the forms of men sprawled out, lying in death-like silence, or heaving and snoring with tremendous effort, like stabbed fish.

The youth locked his derby and his shoes in the mummy case near him, and then lay down with an old and familiar coat around his shoulders. A blanket he handed gingerly, drawing it over part of the coat. The cot was covered with leather, and as cold as melting snow. The youth was obliged to shiver for some time on this affair, which was like a slab. Presently, however, his chill gave him peace, and during this period of leisure from it he turned his head to stare at his friend the assassin, whom he could dimly discern where he lay sprawled on a cot in the abandon of a man filled with drink. He was snoring with incredible vigour. His wet hair and beard dimly glistened, and his inflamed nose shone with subdued lustre like a red light in a fog.

Within reach of the youth's hand was one who lay with yellow breast and shoulders bare to the cold drafts. One arm hung over the side of the cot, and the fingers lay full length upon the wet cement floor of the room. Beneath the inky brows could be seen the eyes of the man exposed by the partly opened lids. To the youth it seemed that he and this corpselike being were exchanging a prolonged stare, and that the other threatened with his eyes. He drew back watching his neighbour from the shadows of his blanket edge. The man did not move once through the night, but lay in this stillness as of death like a body stretched out expectant of the surgeon's knife.

And all through the room could be seen the tawny hues of naked flesh, limbs thrust into the darkness, projecting beyond the cots; upreared knees, arms hanging long and thin over the cot edges. For the most part they were statuesque, carven, dead. With the curious lockers standing all about like tombstones, there was a strange effect of a graveyard where bodies were merely flung.

Yet occasionally could be seen limbs wildly tossing in fantastic night-mare gestures, accompanied by guttural cries, grunts, oaths. And there was one fellow off in a gloomy corner, who in his dreams was oppressed by some frightful calamity, for of a sudden he began to utter long wails that went almost like yells from a hound, echoing wailfully and weird through this chill place of tombstones where men lay like the dead.

The sound in its high piercing beginnings, that dwindled to final melancholy moans, expressed a red and grim tragedy of the unfathomable possibilities of the man's dreams. But to the youth these were not merely the shrieks of a vision-pierced man: they were an utterance of the meaning of the room and its occupants. It was to him the protest of the wretch who feels the touch of the imperturbable granite wheels, and who then cries with an impersonal eloquence, with a strength not from him, giving voice to the wail of a whole section, a class, a people. This, weaving into the young man's brain, and mingling with his views of the vast and sombre shadows that, like mighty black fingers, curled around the naked bodies, made the young man so that he did not sleep, but lay carving the biographies for these men from his meagre experience. At times the fellow in the corner howled in a writhing agony of his imaginations.

Finally a long lance-point of grey light shot through the dusty panes of the window. Without, the young man could see roofs drearily white in the dawning. The point of light yellowed and grew brighter, until the golden rays of the morning sun came in bravely and strong. They touched with radiant colour the form of a small fat man, who snored in stuttering fashion. His round and shiny bald head glowed suddenly with the valour of a decoration. He sat up, blinked at the sun, swore fretfully, and pulled his blanket over the ornamental splendours of his head.

The youth contentedly watched this rout of the shadows before the bright spears of the sun, and presently he slumbered. When he awoke he heard the voice of the assassin raised in valiant curses. Putting up his head, he perceived his comrade seated on the side of the cot engaged in scratching his neck with long finger-nails that rasped like files.

"Hully Jee, dis is a new breed. They've got can-openers on their feet." He continued in a violent tirade.

The young man hastily unlocked his closet and took out his shoes and hat. As he sat on the side of the cot lacing his shoes, he glanced about and saw that daylight had made the room comparatively commonplace and uninteresting. The men, whose faces seemed stolid, serene or absent, were engaged in dressing, while a great crackle of bantering conversation arose.

A few were parading in unconcerned nakedness. Here and there were men of brawn, whose skins shone clear and ruddy. They took splendid poses, standing massively like chiefs. When they had dressed in their ungainly garments there was an extraordinary change. They then showed bumps and deficiencies of all kinds.

There were others who exhibited many deformities. Shoulders were slanting, humped, pulled this way and pulled that way. And notable among these latter men was the little fat man, who had refused to allow his head to be glorified. His pudgy form, builded like a pear, bustled to and fro, while he swore in fishwife fashion. It appeared that some article of his apparel had vanished.

The young man attired speedily, and went to his friend the assassin. At first the latter looked dazed at the sight of the youth. This face seemed to be appealing to him through the cloud wastes of his memory. He scratched his neck and reflected. At last he grinned, a broad smile gradually spreading until his countenance was a round illumination. "Hello, Willie," he cried cheerily.

"Hello," said the young man. "Are yeh ready t' fly?"

"Sure." The assassin tied his shoe carefully with some twine and came ambling.

When he reached the street the young man experienced no sudden relief from unholy atmospheres. He had forgotten all about them, and had been breathing naturally, and with no sensation of discomfort or distress.

He was thinking of these things as he walked along the street, when he was suddenly startled by feeling the assassin's hand, trembling with excitement, clutching his arm, and when the assassin spoke, his voice went into quavers from a supreme agitation.

"I'll be hully, bloomin' blowed if there wasn't a feller with a nightshirt on up there in that joint."

The youth was bewildered for a moment, but presently he turned to smile indulgently at the assassin's humour.

"Oh, you're a d——d liar," he merely said.

Whereupon the assassin began to gesture extravagantly, and take oath by strange gods. He frantically placed himself at the mercy of remarkable fates if his tale were not true.

"Yes, he did! I cross m'heart thousan' times!" he protested, and at the moment his eyes were large with amazement, his mouth wrinkled in unnatural glee.

"Yessir! A nightshirt! A hully white nightshirt!"

"You lie!"

"No, sir! I hope ter die b'fore I kin git anudder ball if there wasn't a jay wid a hully, bloomin' white nightshirt!"

His face was filled with the infinite wonder of it.

"A hully white nightshirt," he continually repeated.

The young man saw the dark entrance to a basement restaurant. There was a sign which read "No mystery about our hash!" and there were other age-stained and world-battered legends which told him that the place was within his means. He stopped before it and spoke to the assassin. "I guess I'll git somethin' t' eat."

At this the assassin, for some reason, appeared to be quite embarrassed. He gazed at the seductive front of the eating place for a moment. Then he started slowly up the street. "Well, good-bye, Willie," he said bravely.

For an instant the youth studied the departing figure. Then he called out, "Hol' on a minnet." As they came together he spoke in a certain fierce way, as if he feared that the other would think him to be charitable. "Look-a-here, if yeh wanta git some breakfas' I'll lend yeh three cents t' do it with. But say, look-a-here, you've gota git out an' hustle. I ain't goin' t' support yeh, or I'll go broke b'fore night. I ain't no millionaire."

"I take me oath, Willie," said the assassin earnestly, "th' on'y thing I really needs is a ball. Me t'roat feels like a fryin'-pan. But as I can't get a ball, why, th' next bes' thing is breakfast, an' if yeh do that for me, b' Gawd, I say yeh was th' whitest lad I ever see."

They spent a few moments in dexterous exchanges of phrases, in which they each protested that the other was, as the assassin had originally said, "a respecter'ble gentlem'n." And they concluded with mutual assurances that they were the souls of intelligence and virtue. Then they went into the restaurant.

There was a long counter, dimly lighted from hidden sources. Two or three men in soiled white aprons rushed here and there.

The youth bought a bowl of coffee for two cents and a roll for one cent. The assassin purchased the same. The bowls were webbed with brown seams, and the tin spoons wore an air of having emerged from the first pyramid. Upon them were black moss-like encrustations of age, and they were bent and scarred from the attacks of long-forgotten teeth. But over their repast the wanderers waxed warm and mellow. The assassin grew affable as the hot mixture went soothingly down his parched throat, and the young man felt courage flow in his veins.

Memories began to throng in on the assassin, and he brought forth long tales, intricate, incoherent, delivered with a chattering swiftness as from an old woman. "——great job out'n Orange. Boss keep yeh hustlin' though all time. I was there three days, and then I went an' ask 'im t' lend me a dollar. 'G-g-go ter the devil,' he ses, an' I lose me job."

"South no good. Damn niggers work for twenty-five an' thirty cents a day. Run white man out. Good grub though. Easy livin'."

"Yas; useter work little in Toledo, raftin' logs. Make two or three dollars er day in the spring. Lived high. Cold as ice though in the winter."

"I was raised in northern N'York. O-o-oh, yeh jest oughto live there. No beer ner whisky though, way off in the woods. But all th' good hot grub yeh can eat. B' Gawd, I hung around there long as I could till th' ol' man fired me. 'Git t' hell outa here, yeh wuthless skunk, git t' hell outa here, an' go die,' he ses. 'You're a hell of a father,' I ses, 'you are,' an' I quit 'im."

As they were passing from the dim eating place, they encountered an old man who was trying to steal forth with a tiny package of food, but a tall man with an indomitable moustache stood dragon fashion, barring the way of escape. They heard the old man raise a plaintive protest. "Ah, you always want to know what I take out, and you never see that I usually bring a package in here from my place of business."

As the wanderers trudged slowly along Park Row, the assassin began to expand and grow blithe. "B' Gawd, we've been livin' like kings," he said, smacking appreciative lips.

"Look out, or we'll have t' pay fer it t'night," said the youth with gloomy warning.

But the assassin refused to turn his gaze toward the future. He went with a limping step, into which he injected a suggestion of lamblike gambols. His mouth was wreathed in a red grin.

In the City Hall Park the two wanderers sat down in the little circle of benches sanctified by traditions of their class. They huddled in their old garments, slumbrously conscious of the march of the hours which for them had no meaning.

The people of the street hurrying hither and thither made a blend of black figures changing yet frieze-like. They walked in their good clothes as upon important missions, giving no gaze to the two wanderers seated upon the benches. They expressed to the young man his infinite distance from all that he valued. Social position, comfort, the pleasures of living, were unconquerable kingdoms. He felt a sudden awe.

And in the background a multitude of buildings, of pitiless hues and sternly high, were to him emblematic of a nation forcing its regal head into the clouds, throwing no downward glances; in the sublimity of its aspirations ignoring the wretches who may flounder at its feet. The roar of the city in his ear was to him the confusion of strange tongues, babbling heedlessly; it was the clink of coin, the voice of the city's hopes which were to him no hopes.

He confessed himself an outcast, and his eyes from under the lowered rim of his hat began to glance guiltily, wearing the criminal expression that comes with certain convictions.

[1894]

An Episode of War

The lieutenant's rubber blanket lay on the ground, and upon it he had poured the company's supply of coffee. Corporals and other representatives of the grimy and hot-throated men who lined the breast-work[1] had come for each squad's portion.

---

[1] A rough and temporary fortification, about chesthigh, used as defense against an enemy; a parapet.

The lieutenant was frowning and serious at this task of division. His lips pursed as he drew with his sword various crevices in the heap, until brown squares of coffee, astoundingly equal in size, appeared on the blanket. He was on the verge of a great triumph in mathematics, and the corporals were thronging forward, each to reap a little square, when suddenly the lieutenant cried out and looked quickly at a man near him as if he suspected it was a case of personal assault. The others cried out also when they saw blood upon the lieutenant's sleeve.

He had winced like a man stung, swayed dangerously, and then straightened. The sound of his hoarse breathing was plainly audible. He looked sadly, mystically, over the breast-work at the green face of a wood, where now were many little puffs of white smoke. During this moment the men about him gazed statue-like and silent, astonished and awed by this catastrophe which happened when catastrophes were not expected—when they had leisure to observe it.

As the lieutenant stared at the wood, they too swung their heads, so that for another instant all hands, still silent, contemplated the distant forest as if their minds were fixed upon the mystery of a bullet's journey.

The officer had, of course, been compelled to take his sword into his left hand. He did not hold it by the hilt. He gripped it at the middle of the blade, awkwardly. Turning his eyes from the hostile wood, he looked at the sword as he held it there, and seemed puzzled as to what to do with it, where to put it. In short, this weapon had of a sudden become a strange thing to him. He looked at it in a kind of stupefaction, as if he had been endowed with a trident, a sceptre, or a spade.

Finally he tried to sheathe it. To sheathe a sword held by the left hand, at the middle of the blade, in a scabbard hung at the left hip, is a feat worthy of a sawdust ring.[2] This wounded officer engaged in a desperate struggle with the sword and the wobbling scabbard, and during the time of it he breathed like a wrestler.

But at this instant the men, the spectators, awoke from their stone-like poses and crowded forward sympathetically. The orderly-sergeant took the sword and tenderly placed it in the scabbard. At the time, he leaned nervously backward, and did not allow even his finger to brush the body of the lieutenant. A wound gives strange dignity to him who bears it. Well men shy from this new and terrible majesty. It is as if the wounded man's hand is upon the curtain which hangs before the revelations of all existence—the meaning of ants, potentates, wars, cities, sunshine, snow, a feather dropped from a bird's wing; and the power of it sheds radiance upon a bloody form, and makes the other men understand sometimes that they are little. His comrades look at him with large eyes thoughtfully. Moreover, they fear vaguely that the weight of a finger upon him might

[2]A circus act; that which is performed in the ring of a circus.

send him headlong, precipitate the tragedy, hurl him at once into the dim, grey unknown. And so the orderly-sergeant, while sheathing the sword, leaned nervously backward.

There were others who proffered assistance. One timidly presented his shoulder and asked the lieutenant if he cared to lean upon it, but the latter waved him away mournfully. He wore the look of one who knows he is the victim of a terrible disease and understands his helplessness. He again stared over the breast-work at the forest, and then, turning, went slowly rearward. He held his right wrist tenderly in his left hand as if the wounded arm was made of very brittle glass.

And the men in silence stared at the wood, then at the departing lieutenant; then at the wood, then at the lieutenant.

As the wounded officer passed from the line of battle, he was enabled to see many things which as a participant in the fight were unknown to him. He saw a general on a black horse gazing over the lines of blue infantry at the green woods which veiled his problems. An aide galloped furiously, dragged his horse suddenly to a halt, saluted, and presented a paper. It was, for a wonder, precisely like a historical painting.

To the rear of the general and his staff a group, composed of a bugler, two or three orderlies, and the bearer of the corps standard, all upon maniacal horses, were working like slaves to hold their ground, preserve their respectful interval, while the shells boomed in the air about them, and caused their chargers to make furious quivering leaps.

A battery, a tumultuous and shining mass, was swirling toward the right. The wild thud of hoofs, the cries of the riders shouting blame and praise, menace and encouragement, and, last, the roar of the wheels, the slant of the glistening guns, brought the lieutenant to an intent pause. The battery swept in curves that stirred the heart; it made halts as dramatic as the crash of a wave on the rocks, and when it fled onward this aggregation of wheels, levers, motors had a beautiful unity, as if it were a missile. The sound of it was a war-chorus that reached into the depths of man's emotion.

The lieutenant, still holding his arm as if it were of glass, stood watching this battery until all detail of it was lost, save the figures of the riders, which rose and fell and waved lashes over the black mass.

Later, he turned his eyes toward the battle, where the shooting sometimes crackled like bush-fires, sometimes sputtered with exasperating irregularity, and sometimes reverberated like the thunder. He saw the smoke rolling upward and saw crowds of men who ran and cheered, or stood and blazed away at the inscrutable distance.

He came upon some stragglers, and they told him how to find the field hospital. They described its exact location. In fact, these men, no longer having part in the battle, knew more of it than others. They told the performance of every corps, every division, the opinion of every general. The lieutenant, carrying his wounded arm rearward, looked upon them with wonder.

At the roadside a brigade was making coffee and buzzing with talk like a girls' boarding-school. Several officers came out to him and inquired concerning things of which he knew nothing. One, seeing his arm, began to scold. "Why, man, that's no way to do. You want to fix that thing." He appropriated the lieutenant and the lieutenant's wound. He cut the sleeve and laid bare the arm, every nerve of which softly fluttered under his touch. He bound his handkerchief over the wound, scolding away in the meantime. His tone allowed one to think that he was in the habit of being wounded every day. The lieutenant hung his head, feeling, in this presence, that he did not know how to be correctly wounded.

The low white tents of the hospital were grouped around an old schoolhouse. There was here a singular commotion. In the foreground two ambulances interlocked wheels in the deep mud. The drivers were tossing the blame of it back and forth, gesticulating and berating, while from the ambulances, both crammed with wounded, there came an occasional groan. An interminable crowd of bandaged men were coming and going. Great numbers sat under the trees nursing heads or arms or legs. There was a dispute of some kind raging on the steps of the schoolhouse. Sitting with his back against a tree a man with a face as grey as a new army blanket was serenely smoking a corncob pipe. The lieutenant wished to rush forward and inform him that he was dying.

A busy surgeon was passing near the lieutenant. "Good-morning," he said, with a friendly smile. Then he caught sight of the lieutenant's arm, and his face at once changed. "Well, let's have a look at it." He seemed possessed suddenly of a great contempt for the lieutenant. This wound evidently placed the latter on a very low social plane. The doctor cried out impatiently: "What mutton-head had tied it up that way anyhow?" The lieutenant answered, "Oh, a man."

When the wound was disclosed the doctor fingered it disdainfully. "Humph," he said. "You come along with me and I'll 'tend to you." His voice contained the same scorn as if he were saying: "You will have to go to jail."

The lieutenant had been very meek, but now his face flushed, and he looked into the doctor's eyes. "I guess I won't have it amputated," he said.

"Nonsense, man! Nonsense! Nonsense!" cried the doctor. "Come along, now. I won't amputate it. Come along. Don't be a baby."

"Let go of me," said the lieutenant, holding back wrathfully, his glance fixed upon the door of the old schoolhouse, as sinister to him as the portals of death.

And this is the story of how the lieutenant lost his arm. When he reached home, his sisters, his mother, his wife, sobbed for a long time at the sight of the flat sleeve. "Oh, well," he said, standing shamefaced amid these tears, "I don't suppose it matters so much as all that."

[1899]

Wounded soldiers outside a hospital in Fredericksburg, VA, photographed between 1861 and 1865.

War Is Kind

Do not weep, maiden, for war is kind.
Because your lover threw wild hands toward the sky
And the affrighted steed ran on alone,
Do not weep.
War is kind.   5

Hoarse, booming drums of the regiment,
Little souls who thirst for fight,
These men were born to drill and die.
The unexplained glory flies above them,
Great is the Battle-God, great, and his Kingdom—   10
A field where a thousand corpses lie.

Do not weep, babe, for war is kind.
Because your father tumbled in the yellow trenches,
Raged at his breast, gulped and died,
Do not weep.   15
War is kind.

Swift blazing flag of the regiment,
Eagle with crest of red and gold,
These men were born to drill and die.
Point for them the virtue of slaughter,   20

Make plain to them the excellence of killing
And a field where a thousand corpses lie.

Mother whose heart hung humble as a button
On the bright splendid shroud of your son,
Do not weep.   25
War is kind.

[1899]

Jack London's parents were unmarried, and he was born John Griffith Chaney, becoming Jack London after his mother married a man named John London, nine months after the boy's birth. When he was barely in his teens, London, using a sloop he had purchased, turned himself into an oyster pirate in San Francisco Bay. Eager for adventure ("My body and soul were starved," he recalled), by the end of 1893 London had served an eight-month stint as a seaman, and the following year he spent as a laborer and a tramp.

London attended high school in Oakland in 1895 and was enrolled for a semester in 1897 at the University of California at Berkeley. This was the extent of his formal education. He became a member of the Socialist Labor Party and an aspiring writer; his first published story for a fee appeared in May 1899. Soon London was writing stories for a number of periodicals, and in 1900 his first book, *The Son of the Wolf*, a collection of stories, was published.

Though married and the father of two daughters, London traveled to England in 1902 and spent nearly two months among the poor in the East End of London, experiences that formed the basis for *The People of the Abyss* (1903).

London was a writing machine, producing countless short pieces and one book after another in very short order. His other important works (in addition to much that was hurried and superficial) include: *The Call of the Wild* (1903; it has been translated into eighty languages), about a tame dog transformed through its adventures into the leader of a pack of wolves; *The Sea-Wolf* (1904), the tale of a ruthless, brilliant sea captain; *White Fang* (1906), about the domestication of a savage dog; *The Iron Heel* (1908), which the scholar Robert E. Spiller termed "a terrifying forecast of Fascism and its evils"; and *Martin Eden* (1909), the partly autobiographical story of a seaman who becomes a famous author, a success that dooms him.

Living at peak intensity, London traveled widely (taking, for example, a trip through the South Seas, 1907–09), was a war correspondent around the world, divorced and remarried, and began acquiring property in 1905 for a ranch in the Sonoma Valley, churning out publications the entire time and making vast sums of money. Altogether he wrote twenty novels, two hundred stories, and four hundred essays and other nonfiction pieces on all sorts of subjects—socialism, hoboing, alcoholism, prizefighting, and much more.

London lacked the patience that would have made him a keener critic of his own prose and that would have prevented him from publishing so much mediocre stuff. But his talent was remarkable, and he was effective, as in the story "To Build a Fire," reprinted here, at describing the impact of nature, in all of its raw power, on human beings and creatures. Storms at sea, savage battles, titanic personalities—these were the passionate, shocking, elemental dimensions of life and larger-than-life that London grippingly depicted and dramatized. At its best, his work draws the reader into a world that is supercharged and superhuman, akin to Greek epics, Norse sagas, and Icelandic legends.

"Every atom of organic life is plastic," London maintained:

> The finest specimens now in existence were once all pulpy infants capable of being moulded this way or that. Let the pressure be one way and we have atavism—the reversion to the wild; the other—domestication, civilization. I have always been impressed by the awful plasticity of life and I feel that I can never lay enough stress upon the marvelous power and influence of environment.

Biographies: Andrew Sinclair, *Jack: A Biography of Jack London* (1977); and Alex Kershaw, *Jack London: A Life* (1998). Also illuminating: Joan D. Hedrick, *Solitary Comrade: Jack London and His Work* (1982); Jonathan Auerbach, *Male Call: Becoming Jack London* (1996); and Jeanne Campbell Reesman, *Jack London: A Study of the Short Fiction* (1999). Collections of criticism include *Critical Essays on Jack London*, ed. Jacqueline Tavernier-Courbin (1983); *The Critical Response to Jack London*, ed. Susan M. Nuernberg (1995); and *Jack London: One Hundred Years a Writer*, eds. Sara S. Hodson and Jeanne Campbell Reesman (2002). See also James L. Haley, *Wolf: The Lives of Jack London* (2010).

To Build a Fire

Day had broken cold and gray, exceedingly cold and gray, when the man turned aside from the main Yukon trail and climbed the high earth-bank, where a dim and little-travelled trail led eastward through the fat spruce timberland. It was a steep bank, and he paused for breath at the top, excusing the act to himself by looking at his watch. It was nine o'clock. There was no sun nor hint of sun, though there was not a cloud in the sky. It was a clear day, and yet there seemed an intangible pall over the face of things, a subtle gloom that made the day dark, and that was due to the absence of sun. This fact did not worry the man. He was used to the lack of sun. It had been days since he had seen the sun, and he knew that a few more days must pass before that cheerful orb, due south, would just peep above the sky-line and dip immediately from view.

The man flung a look back along the way he had come. The Yukon lay a mile wide and hidden under three feet of ice. On top of this ice were as many feet of snow. It was all pure white, rolling in gentle undulations where the ice-jams of the freeze-up had formed. North and south, as far as his eye could see, it was unbroken white, save for a dark hair-line that curved and twisted from around the spruce-covered island to the south, and that curved and twisted away into the north, where it disappeared behind another spruce-covered island. This dark hair-line was the trail—the main trail—that led south five hundred miles to the Chilcoot Pass, Dyea, and salt water; and that led north seventy miles to Dawson, and still on to the north a thousand miles to Nulato, and finally to St. Michael on Bering Sea, a thousand miles and half a thousand more.

But all this—the mysterious, far-reaching hair-line trail, the absence of sun from the sky, the tremendous cold, and the strangeness and weirdness of it all—made no impression on the man. It was not because he was long used to it. He was a newcomer in the land, a *chechaquo*,[1] and this was his first winter. The trouble with him was that he was without imagination. He was quick and alert in the things of life, but only in the things, and not in the significances. Fifty degrees below zero meant eighty-odd degrees of frost. Such fact impressed him as being cold and uncomfortable, and that was all. It did not lead him to meditate upon his frailty as a creature of temperature, and upon man's frailty in general, able only to live within certain narrow limits of heat and cold; and from there on it did not lead him to the conjectural field of immortality and man's place in the universe. Fifty degrees below zero stood for a bite of frost that hurt and that must be guarded against by the use of mittens, ear-flaps, warm moccasins, and thick socks. Fifty degrees below zero was to him just precisely fifty degrees below zero. That there should be anything more to it than that was a thought that never entered his head.

As he turned to go on, he spat speculatively. There was a sharp, explosive crackle that startled him. He spat again. And again, in the air, before it could fall to the snow, the spittle crackled. He knew that at fifty below spittle crackled on the snow, but this spittle had crackled in the air. Undoubtedly it was colder than fifty below—how much colder he did not know. But the temperature did not matter. He was bound for the old claim on the left fork of Henderson Creek, where the boys were already. They had come over across the divide from the Indian Creek country, while he had come the roundabout way to take a look at the possibilities of getting out logs in the spring from the islands in the Yukon. He would be in to camp by six o'clock; a bit after dark, it was true, but the boys would be there, a fire would be going, and a hot supper would be ready. As for lunch, he pressed his hand against the protruding bundle under his jacket. It was also under his shirt, wrapped up in a handkerchief and lying against the naked skin. It was the only way to keep the biscuits from freezing. He smiled agreeably to himself; as he thought of those biscuits, each cut open and sopped in bacon grease, and each enclosing a generous slice of fried bacon.

He plunged in among the big spruce trees. The trail was faint. A foot of snow had fallen since the last sled had passed over, and he was glad

[1]A tenderfoot, a newcomer or novice.

he was without a sled, travelling light. In fact, he carried nothing but the lunch wrapped in the handkerchief. He was surprised, however, at the cold. It certainly was cold, he concluded, as he rubbed his numb nose and cheekbones with his mittened hand. He was a warm-whiskered man, but the hair on his face did not protect the high cheek-bones and the eager nose that thrust itself aggressively into the frosty air.

At the man's heels trotted a dog, a big native husky, the proper wolf-dog, gray-coated and without any visible or temperamental difference from its brother, the wild wolf. The animal was depressed by the tremendous cold. It knew that it was no time for travelling. Its instinct told it a truer tale than was told to the man by the man's judgment. In reality, it was not merely colder than fifty below zero; it was colder than sixty below, than seventy below. It was seventy-five below zero. Since the freezing-point is thirty two above zero, it meant that one hundred and seven degrees of frost obtained. The dog did not know anything about thermometers. Possibly in its brain there was no sharp consciousness of a condition of very cold such as was in the man's brain. But the brute had its instinct. It experienced a vague but menacing apprehension that subdued it and made it slink along at the man's heels, and that made it question eagerly every unwonted movement of the man as if expecting him to go into camp or to seek shelter somewhere and build a fire. The dog had learned fire, and it wanted fire, or else to burrow under the snow and cuddle its warmth away from the air.

The frozen moisture of its breathing had settled on its fur in a fine powder of frost, and especially were its jowls, muzzle, and eyelashes whitened by its crystalled breath. The man's red beard and mustache were likewise frosted, but more solidly, the deposit taking the form of ice and increasing with every warm, moist breath he exhaled. Also, the man was chewing tobacco, and the muzzle of ice held his lips so rigidly that he was unable to clear his chin when he expelled the juice. The result was that a crystal beard of the color and solidity of amber was increasing its length on his chin. If he fell down it would shatter itself, like glass, into brittle fragments. But he did not mind the appendage. It was the penalty all tobacco-chewers paid in that country, and he had been out before in two cold snaps. They had not been so cold as this, he knew, but by the spirit thermometer at Sixty Mile he knew they had been registered at fifty below and at fifty-five.

He held on through the level stretch of woods for several miles, crossed a wide flat of niggerheads,[2] and dropped down a bank to the frozen bed of a small stream. This was Henderson Creek, and he knew he was ten miles from the forks. He looked at his watch. It was ten o'clock. He was making four miles an hour, and he calculated that he would arrive at the forks at half-past twelve. He decided to celebrate that event by eating his lunch there.

[2]Tangled vegetation that makes walking difficult.

The dog dropped in again at his heels, with a tail drooping discouragement, as the man swung along the creek-bed. The furrow of the old sled-trail was plainly visible, but a dozen inches of snow covered the marks of the last runners. In a month no man had come up or down that silent creek. The man held steadily on. He was not much given to thinking, and just then particularly he had nothing to think about save that he would eat lunch at the forks and that at six o'clock he would be in camp with the boys. There was nobody to talk to; and, had there been, speech would have been impossible because of the ice-muzzle on his mouth. So he continued monotonously to chew tobacco and to increase the length of his amber beard.

Once in a while the thought reiterated itself that it was very cold and that he had never experienced such cold. As he walked along he rubbed his cheek-bones and nose with the back of his mittened hand. He did this automatically, now and again changing hands. But rub as he would, the instant he stopped his cheek-bones went numb, and the following instant the end of his nose went numb. He was sure to frost his cheeks; he knew that, and experienced a pang of regret that he had not devised a nose-strap of the sort Bud wore in cold snaps. Such a strap passed across the cheeks, as well, and saved them. But it didn't matter much, after all. What were frosted cheeks? A bit painful, that was all; they were never serious.

Empty as the man's mind was of thoughts, he was keenly observant, and he noticed the changes in the creek, the curves and bends and timber-jams, and always he sharply noted where he placed his feet. Once, coming around a bend, he shied abruptly, like a startled horse, curved away from the place where he had been walking, and retreated several paces back along the trail. The creek he knew was frozen clear to the bottom,—no creek could contain water in that arctic winter,—but he knew also that there were springs that bubbled out from the hillsides and ran along under the snow and on top the ice of the creek. He knew that the coldest snaps never froze these springs, and he knew likewise their danger. They were traps. They hid pools of water under the snow that might be three inches deep, or three feet. Sometimes a skin of ice half an inch thick covered them, and in turn was covered by the snow. Sometimes there were alternate layers of water and ice-skin, so that when one broke through he kept on breaking through for a while, sometimes wetting himself to the waist.

That was why he had shied in such panic. He had felt the give under his feet and heard the crackle of snow-hidden ice-skin. And to get his feet wet in such a temperature meant trouble and danger. At the very least it meant delay, for he would be forced to stop and build a fire, and under its protection to bare his feet while he dried his socks and moccasins. He stood and studied the creek-bed and its banks, and decided that the flow of water came from the right. He reflected awhile, rubbing his nose and cheeks, then skirted to the left, stepping gingerly and testing the footing for each step. Once clear of the danger, he took a fresh chew of tobacco and swung along at his four-mile gait.

In the course of the next two hours he came upon several similar traps. Usually the snow above the hidden pools had a sunken, candied appearance that advertised the danger. Once again, however, he had a close call; and once, suspecting danger, he compelled the dog to go on in front. The dog did not want to go. It hung back until the man shoved it forward, and then it went quickly across the white, unbroken surface. Suddenly it broke through, floundered to one side, and got away to firmer footing. It had wet its forefeet and legs, and almost immediately the water that clung to it turned to ice. It made quick efforts to lick the ice off its legs, then dropped down in the snow and began to bite out the ice that had formed between the toes. This was a matter of instinct. To permit the ice to remain would mean sore feet. It did not know this. It merely obeyed the mysterious prompting that arose from the deep crypts of its being. But the man knew, having achieved a judgment on the subject, and he removed the mitten from his right hand and helped tear out the ice-particles. He did not expose his fingers more than a minute, and was astonished at the swift numbness that smote them. It certainly was cold. He pulled on the mitten hastily, and beat the hand savagely across his chest.

At twelve o'clock the day was at its brightest. Yet the sun was too far south on its winter journey to clear the horizon. The bulge of the earth intervened between it and Henderson Creek, where the man walked under a clear sky at noon and cast no shadow. At half-past twelve, to the minute, he arrived at the forks of the creek. He was pleased at the speed he had made. If he kept it up, he would certainly be with the boys by six. He unbuttoned his jacket and shirt and drew forth his lunch. The action consumed no more than a quarter of a minute, yet in that brief moment the numbness laid hold of the exposed fingers. He did not put the mitten on, but, instead, struck the fingers a dozen sharp smashes against his leg. Then he sat down on a snow-covered log to eat. The sting that followed upon the striking of his fingers against his leg ceased so quickly that he was startled. He had had no chance to take a bite of biscuit. He struck the fingers repeatedly and returned them to the mitten, baring the other hand for the purpose of eating. He tried to take a mouthful, but the ice-muzzle prevented. He had forgotten to build a fire and thaw out. He chuckled at his foolishness, and as he chuckled he noted the numbness creeping into the exposed fingers. Also, he noted that the stinging which had first come to his toes when he sat down was already passing away. He wondered whether the toes were warm or numb. He moved them inside the moccasins and decided that they were numb.

He pulled the mitten on hurriedly and stood up. He was a bit frightened. He stamped up and down until the stinging returned into the feet. It certainly was cold, was his thought. That man from Sulphur Creek had spoken the truth when telling how cold it sometimes got in the country. And he had laughed at him at the time! That showed one must not be too sure of things. There was no mistake about it, it *was* cold. He strode up and down, stamping his feet and threshing his arms, until reassured by the returning warmth. Then he got out matches and proceeded to make a fire. From the undergrowth, where high water of the previous spring had lodged a supply of seasoned twigs, he got his fire-wood. Working carefully from a small beginning, he soon had a roaring fire, over which he thawed the ice from his face and in the protection of which he ate his biscuits. For the moment the cold of space was outwitted. The dog took satisfaction in the fire, stretching out close enough for warmth and far enough away to escape being singed.

When the man had finished, he filled his pipe and took his comfortable time over a smoke. Then he pulled on his mittens, settled the ear-flaps of his cap firmly about his ears, and took the creek trail up the left fork. The dog was disappointed and yearned back toward the fire. This man did not know cold. Possibly all the generations of his ancestry had been ignorant of cold, of real cold, of cold one hundred and seven degrees below freezing point. But the dog knew; all its ancestry knew, and it had inherited the knowledge. And it knew that it was not good to walk abroad in such fearful cold. It was the time to lie snug in a hole in the snow and wait for a curtain of cloud to be drawn across the face of outer space whence this cold came. On the other hand, there was no keen intimacy between the dog and the man. The one was the toil-slave of the other, and the only caresses it had ever received were the caresses of the whip-lash and of harsh and menacing throat-sounds that threatened the whip-lash. So the dog made no effort to communicate its apprehension to the man. It was not concerned in the welfare of the man; it was for its own sake that it yearned back toward the fire. But the man whistled, and spoke to it with the sound of whip-lashes, and the dog swung in at the man's heels and followed after.

The man took a chew of tobacco and proceeded to start a new amber beard. Also, his moist breath quickly powdered with white his mustache, eyebrows, and lashes. There did not seem to be so many springs on the left fork of the Henderson, and for half an hour the man saw no signs of any. And then it happened. At a place where there were no signs, where the soft, unbroken snow seemed to advertise solidity beneath, the man broke through. It was not deep. He wet himself halfway to the knees before he floundered out to the firm crust.

He was angry, and cursed his luck aloud. He had hoped to get into camp with the boys at six o'clock, and this would delay him an hour, for he would have to build a fire and dry out his foot-gear. This was imperative at that low temperature—he knew that much; and he turned aside to the bank, which he climbed. On top, tangled in the underbrush about the trunks of several small spruce trees, was a high-water deposit of dry fire-wood—sticks and twigs, principally, but also larger portions of seasoned branches and fine, dry, last-year's grasses. He threw down several large pieces on top of the snow. This served for a foundation and prevented the young flame from drowning itself in the snow it otherwise would melt. The flame he got by touching a match to a small shred of birch-bark that he took from his pocket. This burned even more readily than paper. Placing it on the foundation, he fed the young flame with wisps of dry grass and with the tiniest dry twigs.

He worked slowly and carefully, keenly aware of his danger. Gradually, as the flame grew stronger, he increased the size of the twigs with which he fed it. He squatted in the snow, pulling the twigs out from their entanglement in the brush and feeding directly to the flame. He knew there must be no failure. When it is seventy-five below zero, a man must not fail in his first attempt to build a fire—that is, if his feet are wet. If his feet are dry, and he fails, he can run along the trail for half a mile and restore his circulation, But the circulation of wet and freezing feet cannot be restored by running when it is seventy-five below. No matter how fast he runs, the wet feet will freeze the harder.

All this the man knew. The old-timer on Sulphur Creek had told him about it the previous fall, and now he was appreciating the advice. Already all sensation had gone out of his feet. To build the fire he had been forced to remove his mittens, and the fingers had quickly gone numb. His pace of four miles an hour had kept his heart pumping blood to the surface of his body and to all the extremities. But the instant he stopped, the action of the pump eased down. The cold of space smote the unprotected tip of the planet, and he, being on that unprotected tip, received the full force of the blow. The blood of his body recoiled before it. The blood was alive, like the dog, and like the dog it wanted to hide away and cover itself up from the fearful cold. So long as he walked four miles an hour, he pumped that blood, willy-nilly, to the surface; but now it ebbed away and sank down into the recesses of his body. The extremities were the first to feel its absence. His wet feet froze the faster, and his exposed fingers numbed the faster, though they had not yet begun to freeze. Nose and cheeks were already freezing, while the skin of all his body chilled as it lost its blood.

But he was safe. Toes and nose and cheeks would be only touched by the frost, for the fire was beginning to burn with strength. He was feeding it with twigs the size of his finger. In another minute he would be able to feed it with branches the size of his wrist, and then he could remove his wet footgear, and, while it dried, he could keep his naked feet warm by the fire, rubbing them at first, of course, with snow. The fire was a success. He was safe. He remembered the advice of the old-timer on Sulphur Creek, and smiled. The old-timer had been very serious in laying down the law that no man must travel alone in the Klondike after fifty below. Well, here he was; he had had the accident; he was alone; and he had saved him-self. Those old-timers were rather womanish, some of them, he thought. All a man had to do was to keep his head, and he was all right. Any man who was a man could travel alone. But it was surprising, the rapidity with which his cheeks and nose were freezing. And he had not thought his fingers could go lifeless in so short a time. Lifeless they were, for he could scarcely make them move together to grip a twig, and they seemed remote from his body and from him. When he touched a twig, he had to look and see whether or not he had hold of it. The wires were pretty well down between him and his finger-ends.

All of which counted for little. There was the fire, snapping and crack-ling and promising life with every dancing flame. He started to untie his moccasins. They were coated with ice; the thick German socks were like sheaths of iron halfway to the knees; and the moccasin strings were like rods of steel all twisted and knotted as by some conflagration. For a mo-ment he tugged with his numb fingers, then, realizing the folly of it, he drew his sheath-knife.

But before he could cut the strings, it happened. It was his own fault or, rather, his mistake. He should not have built the fire under the spruce tree. He should have built it in the open. But it had been easier to pull the twigs from the brush and drop them directly on the fire. Now the tree under which he had done this carried a weight of snow on its boughs. No wind had blown for weeks, and each bough was fully freighted. Each time he had pulled a twig he had communicated a slight agitation to the tree—an imperceptible agitation, so far as he was concerned, but an agita-tion sufficient to bring about the disaster. High up in the tree one bough capsized its load of snow. This fell on the boughs beneath, capsizing them. This process continued, spreading out and involving the whole tree. It grew like an avalanche, and it descended without warning upon the man and the fire, and the fire was blotted out! Where it had burned was a mantle of fresh and disordered snow.

The man was shocked. It was as though he had just heard his own sentence of death. For a moment he sat and stared at the spot where the fire had been. Then he grew very calm. Perhaps the old-timer on Sulphur Creek was right. If he had only had a trail-mate he would have been in no danger now. The trail-mate could have built the fire. Well, it was up to him to build the fire over again, and this second time there must be no failure. Even if he succeeded, he would most likely lose some toes. His feet must be badly frozen by now, and there would be some time before the second fire was ready.

Such were his thoughts, but he did not sit and think them. He was busy all the time they were passing through his mind. He made a new foundation for a fire, this time in the open, where no treacherous tree could blot it out. Next, he gathered dry grasses and tiny twigs from the high-water flotsam. He could not bring his fingers together to pull them out, but he was able to gather them by the handful. In this way he got many rotten twigs and bits of green moss that were undesirable, but it was the best he could do. He worked methodically, even collecting an armful of the larger branches to be used later when the fire gathered strength. And all the while the dog sat and watched him, a certain yearning wistfulness in its eyes, for it looked upon him as the fire-provider, and the fire was slow in coming.

When all was ready, the man reached in his pocket for a second piece of birch-bark. He knew the bark was there, and, though he could not feel it with his fingers, he could hear its crisp rustling as he fumbled for it. Try as he would, he could not clutch hold of it. And all the time, in his consciousness, was the knowledge that each instant his feet were freezing. This thought tended to put him in a panic, but he fought against it and kept calm. He pulled on his mittens with his teeth, and threshed his arms back and forth, beating his hands with all his might against his sides. He did this sitting down, and he stood up to do it; and all the while the dog sat in the snow, its wolf-brush of a tail curled around warmly over its fore-feet, its sharp wolf-ears pricked forward intently as it watched the man. And the man, as he beat and threshed with his arms and hands, he felt a great surge of envy as he regarded the creature that was warm and secure in its natural covering.

After a time he was aware of the first faraway signals of sensation in his beaten fingers. The faint tingling grew stronger till it evolved into a stinging ache that was excruciating, but which the man hailed with sat-isfaction. He stripped the mitten from his right hand and fetched forth the birch-bark. The exposed fingers were quickly going numb again. Next he brought out his bunch of sulphur matches. But the tremendous cold had already driven the life out of his fingers. In his effort to separate one match from the others, the whole bunch fell in the snow. He tried to pick it out of the snow, but failed. The dead fingers could neither touch nor clutch. He was very careful. He drove the thought of his freezing feet, and nose, and cheeks, out of his mind, devoting his whole soul to the matches. He watched, using the sense of vision in place of that of touch, and when he saw his fingers on each side the bunch, he closed them—that is, he willed to close them, for the wires were down, and the fingers did not obey. He pulled the mitten on the right hand, and beat it fiercely against his knee. Then, with both mittened hands, he scooped the bunch of matches, along with much snow, into his lap. Yet he was no better off.

After some manipulation he managed to get the bunch between the heels of his mittened hands. In this fashion he carried it to his mouth. The ice crackled and snapped when by a violent effort he opened his mouth. He drew the lower jaw in, curled the upper lip out of the way, and scraped the bunch with his upper teeth in order to separate a match. He succeeded in getting one, which he dropped on his lap. He was no better off. He could not pick it up. Then he devised a way. He picked it up in his teeth and scratched it on his leg. Twenty times he scratched before he succeeded in lighting it. As it flamed he held it with his teeth to the birch-bark. But the burning brimstone went up his nostrils and into his lungs, causing him to cough spasmodically. The match fell into the snow and went out.

The old-timer on Sulphur Creek was right, he thought in the moment of controlled despair that ensued: after fifty below, a man should travel with a partner. He beat his hands, but failed in exciting any sensation. Suddenly he bared both hands, removing the mittens with his teeth. He caught the whole bunch between the heels of his hands. His arm-muscles not being frozen enabled him to press the hand-heels tightly against the matches. Then he scratched the bunch along his leg. It flared into flame, seventy sulphur matches at once! There was no wind to blow them out. He kept his head to one side to escape the strangling fumes, and held the blazing bunch to the birch-bark. As he so held it, he became aware of sensation in his hand. His flesh was burning. He could smell it. Deep down below the surface he could feel it. The sensation developed into pain that grew acute. And still he endured it, holding the flame of the matches clumsily to the bark that would not light readily because his own burning hands were in the way, absorbing most of the flame.

At last, when he could endure no more, he jerked his hands apart. The blazing matches fell sizzling into the snow, but the birch-bark was alight. He began laying dry grasses and the tiniest twigs on the flame. He could not pick and choose, for he had to lift the fuel between the heels of his hands. Small pieces of rotten wood and green moss clung to the twigs, and he bit them off as well as he could with his teeth. He cherished the flame carefully and awkwardly. It meant life, and it must not perish. The withdrawal of blood from the surface of his body now made him begin to shiver, and he grew more awkward. A large piece of green moss fell squarely on the little fire. He tried to poke it out with his fingers, but his shivering frame made him poke too far, and he disrupted the nucleus of the little fire, the burning grasses and tiny twigs separating and scattering. He tried to poke them together again, but in spite of the tenseness of the effort, his shivering got away with him, and the twigs were hopelessly scattered. Each twig gushed a puff of smoke and went out. The fire-provider had failed. As he looked apathetically about him, his eyes chanced on the dog, sitting across the ruins of the fire from him, in the snow, making restless, hunching movements, slightly lifting one forefoot and then the other, shifting its weight back and forth on them with wistful eagerness.

The sight of the dog put a wild idea into his head. He remembered the tale of the man, caught in a blizzard, who killed a steer and crawled inside the carcass, and so was saved. He would kill the dog and bury his hands in the warm body until the numbness went out of them. Then he could build another fire. He spoke to the dog, calling it to him; but in his voice was a strange note of fear that frightened the animal, who had never known the man to speak in such way before. Something was the matter, and its suspicious nature sensed danger—it knew not what danger, but somewhere, somehow, in its brain arose an apprehension of the man. It flattened its ears down at the sound of the man's voice, and its restless, hunching movements and the liftings and shiftings of its forefeet became more pronounced; but it would not come to the man. He got on his hands and knees and crawled toward the dog. This unusual posture again excited suspicion, and the animal sidled mincingly away.

The man sat up in the snow for a moment and struggled for calmness. Then he pulled on his mittens, by means of his teeth, and got upon his feet. He glanced down at first in order to assure himself that he was really standing up, for the absence of sensation in his feet left him unrelated to the earth. His erect position in itself started to drive the webs of suspicion from the dog's mind; and when he spoke peremptorily, with the sound of whiplashes in his voice, the dog rendered its customary allegiance and came to him. As it came within reaching distance, the man lost his control. His arms flashed out to the dog, and he experienced genuine surprise when he discovered that his hands could not clutch, that there was neither bend nor feeling in the fingers. He had forgotten for the moment that they were frozen and that they were freezing more and more. All this happened quickly, and before the animal could get away, he encircled its body with his arms. He sat down in the snow, and in this fashion held the dog, while it snarled and whined and struggled.

But it was all he could do, hold its body encircled in his arms and sit there. He realized that he could not kill the dog. There was no way to do it. With his helpless hands he could neither draw nor hold his sheath-knife nor throttle the animal. He released it, and it plunged wildly away, with tail between its legs, and still snarling. It halted forty feet away and surveyed him curiously, with ears sharply pricked forward. The man looked down at his hands in order to locate them, and found them hanging on the ends of his arms. It struck him as curious that one should have to use his eyes in order to find out where his hands were. He began threshing his arms back and forth, beating the mittened hands against his sides. He did this for five minutes, violently, and his heart pumped enough blood up to the surface to put a stop to his shivering. But no sensation was aroused in the hands. He had an impression that they hung like weights on the ends of his arms, but when he tried to run the impression down, he could not find it.

A certain fear of death, dull and oppressive, came to him. This fear quickly became poignant as he realized that it was no longer a mere matter of freezing his fingers and toes, or of losing his hands and feet, but that it was a matter of life and death with the chances against him. This threw him into a panic, and he turned and ran up the creek-bed along the old, dim trail. The dog joined in behind and kept up with him. He ran blindly, without intention, in fear such as he had never known in his life. Slowly, as he ploughed and floundered through the snow, he began to see things again—the banks of the creek, the old timber-jams, the leafless aspens, and the sky. The running made him feel better. He did not shiver. Maybe, if he ran on, his feet would thaw out; and, anyway, if he ran far enough, he would reach camp and the boys. Without doubt he would lose some fingers and toes and some of his face; but the boys would take care of him, and save the rest of him when he got there. And at the same time there was another thought in his mind that said he would never get to the camp and the boys; that it was too many miles away, that the freezing had too great a start on him, and that he would soon be stiff and dead. This thought he kept in the background and refused to consider. Sometimes it pushed itself forward and demanded to be heard, but he thrust it back and strove to think of other things.

It struck him as curious that he could run at all on feet so frozen that he could not feel them when they struck the earth and took the weight of his body. He seemed to himself to skim along above the surface, and to have no connection with the earth. Somewhere he had once seen a winged Mercury[3], and he wondered if Mercury felt as he felt when skimming over the earth.

His theory of running until he reached camp and the boys had one flaw in it: he lacked the endurance. Several times he stumbled, and finally he tottered, crumpled up, and fell. When he tried to rise, he failed. He must sit and rest, he decided, and next time he would merely walk and keep on going. As he sat and regained his breath, he noted that he was feeling quite warm and comfortable. He was not shivering, and it even seemed that a warm glow had come to his chest and trunk. And yet, when he touched his nose or cheeks, there was no sensation. Running would not thaw them out. Nor would it thaw out his hands and feet. Then the thought came to him that the frozen portions of his body must be extending. He tried to keep this thought down, to forget it, to think of something else; he was aware of the panicky feeling that it caused, and he was afraid of the panic. But the thought asserted itself, and persisted, until it produced a vision of his body totally frozen. This was too much, and he made another wild run along the trail. Once he slowed down to a walk, but the thought of the freezing extending itself made him run again.

And all the time the dog ran with him, at his heels. When he fell down a second time, it curled its tail over its forefeet and sat in front of him, facing him, curiously eager and intent. The warmth and security of the animal angered him, and he cursed it till it flattened down its ears appeasingly. This time the shivering came more quickly upon the man. He was losing in his battle with the frost. It was creeping into his body from all

---

[3]The Roman god of eloquence, skill, trading, and thieving; the herald and messenger of the gods.

sides. The thought of it drove him on, but he ran no more than a hundred feet, when he staggered and pitched headlong. It was his last panic. When he had recovered his breath and control, he sat up and entertained in his mind the conception of meeting death with dignity. However, the conception did not come to him in such terms. His idea of it was that he had been making a fool of himself, running around like a chicken with its head cut off—such was the simile that occurred to him. Well, he was bound to freeze anyway, and he might as well take it decently. With this new-found peace of mind came the first glimmerings of drowsiness. A good idea, he thought, to sleep off to death. It was like taking an anaesthetic. Freezing was not so bad as people thought. There were lots worse ways to die.

He pictured the boys finding his body next day. Suddenly he found himself with them, coming along the trail and looking for himself. And, still with them, he came around a turn in the trail and found himself lying in the snow. He did not belong with himself any more, for even then he was out of himself, standing with the boys and looking at himself in the snow. It certainly was cold, was his thought. When he got back to the States he could tell the folks what real cold was. He drifted on from this to a vision of the old-timer on Sulphur Creek. He could see him quite clearly, warm and comfortable, and smoking a pipe.

"You were right, old hoss[4]; you were right," the man mumbled to the old-timer of Sulphur Creek.

Then the man drowsed off into what seemed to him the most comfortable and satisfying sleep he had ever known. The dog sat facing him and waiting. The brief day drew to a close in a long, slow twilight. There were no signs of a fire to be made, and, besides, never in the dog's experience had it known a man to sit like that in the snow and make no fire. As the twilight drew on, its eager yearning for the fire mastered it, and with a great lifting and shifting of forefeet, it whined softly, then flattened its ears down in anticipation of being chidden by the man. But the man remained silent. Later, the dog whined loudly. And still later it crept close to the man and caught the scent of death. This made the animal bristle and back away. A little longer it delayed, howling under the stars that leaped and danced and shone brightly in the cold sky. Then it turned and trotted up the trail in the direction of the camp it knew, where were the other food-providers and fire-providers.

[1902]

[4]Horse.

▪▪ GALLERY ▪▪

The South Since Reconstruction

When we speak of Reconstruction, we are referring to the processes and procedures through which the eleven Confederate states, once the Civil War ended in April 1865, were restored to the Union and rebuilt in political, social, and economic terms with loyal governments and emancipated slaves. Determined to establish and maintain civil rights for African Americans— four million slaves had been liberated—radical Republican members of Congress pushed forward with a sweeping agenda for change that President Andrew Johnson, who took office after Lincoln's assassination, resisted. This led to his impeachment by Republicans who were frustrated with (as they viewed it) his pro-South sympathies—he had been a slaveholder himself. In the subsequent trial in the Senate, Johnson retained his office as president by a single vote.

Reconstruction came to an end in 1877 when the Republican Rutherford B. Hayes became president after a highly controversial and contested election. He withdrew federal troops from the South, with the white North and South reaching an accord that the race issue would be left to the authority of the Southern states where the vast majority of African Americans lived. The Supreme Court ruled that the civil rights acts of 1866 and 1875, designed to guarantee equal rights to all citizens in transportation and public accommodations, were unconstitutional; other Court decisions further eroded the gains that African Americans had made.

The result by 1900, propelled by the Supreme Court's decision in Plessy v. Ferguson (1896), was a widespread system of racial segregation. Separate but equal, so the Court declared, but while the system was separate— in jobs, transportation, housing, and so on—it was not equal. Slavery was gone, yet for the white South the distinctions between black and white had to remain and to be enforced.

Black men were granted the right to vote by the Fifteenth Amendment, ratified in 1870, and many African Americans were elected (nearly all of them as Republicans) to state legislatures and other positions and offices during Reconstruction. A number were elected to the U.S. House of Representatives and the Senate. But even with federal support, it proved difficult for African Americans to make significant economic progress; they desperately needed money, land, education, and much else, and on a massive scale. Whites in the South confronted newly freed African Americans with violence: sexual assaults, beatings, and murders.

Meanwhile in the North, racism was less overtly vicious, but it was entrenched there as well. Life for Black citizens in the North was better but still bad: few whites in the North advocated and fought for integration.

Nor did voting rights, so essential for the preservation of freedoms, endure. As Elizabeth Anderson and Jeffrey Jones have noted: "Between 1890 and 1908, every state in the Deep South adopted a new state constitution, explicitly for the purpose of disenfranchising blacks. Various devices were used—poll taxes, literacy tests, arbitrary registration practices, felony disenfranchisement (for only those crimes that blacks disproportionately committed)." By 1920, African Americans had been almost completely disenfranchised.

The forms of segregation in the South, legal and traditional and customary, which were put securely into place in the late nineteenth century and early twentieth century, intensified as the modern age in America moved forward. The scholar Drew D. Hansen has observed that in 1963 "not single child in South Carolina, Alabama, or Mississippi attended an integrated public school." In county after county with large numbers of African American residents, very few of them, and in some cases none of them at all, were registered to vote; those who could vote encountered threat and intimidation if they tried to.

Conditions for African American men and women were cruel and harsh—we might say, un-American—but again we need to remember how grievous were the conditions for them in the North. This was the painful reality that African American families found when they sought, for example, to move into white neighborhoods or mix with whites or seek fair and equal treatment. The novelists Richard Wright in *Native Son* (1940) and Ann Petry in *The Street* (1946) shockingly demonstrated the pervasiveness of Northern bigotry. So separated were African Americans from white neighborhoods that they were invisible; as the title of Ralph Ellison's *Invisible Man* (1952) emphasized, in both public and private settings whites typically did not and could not see the black bodies next to them.

Among the many turn-of-the-century novels depicting Reconstruction and its aftermath in the late 1800s and early 1900s are Albion Tourgée's *A Fool's Errand* (1879) and *Bricks without Straw* (1880), George Washington Cable's *John March, Southerner* (1894), and Thomas Dixon's virulently racist but hugely popular *The Leopard's Spots* (1902), *The Clansman* (1905), and *The Traitor* (1907). Other significant works are Frances Harper's *Iola Leroy* (1892), one of the first novels by an African American woman, and Mark Twain's *Adventures of Huckleberry Finn* (1885) and *Pudd'nhead Wilson* (1894), both of which are set in the days of slavery, yet which are illuminating about racial attitudes in the post-Reconstruction period when Twain wrote them.

The following materials could be supplemented many times over, and they intersect with selections by Charles Chesnutt, William Faulkner, and others included in this anthology. The relationship between blacks and whites in America, the relationship of black and white Americas, is one of the abiding themes in American history and literature, and it has seized the attention of many of this nation's most gifted writers, artists, and photographers. It could be said that now, in the early decades of the twentieth century, we have made progress into or toward a post-racial America. Then again, though the progress is real, the hope for equality and justice still exceeds the reality, and the insights, arguments, and claims in the selections here will linger and continue to bear on and burden America's future.

FREDERICK DOUGLASS ■ (1818–1895)

With vividness and power, Frederick Douglass described his escape in September 1838 from slavery in Maryland in his *Narrative of the Life of Frederick Douglass* (1845); he wrote and lectured extensively for the abolitionist cause; he launched and edited his own newspapers; and he recruited African Americans for the Union army. His career before and during the Civil War decades was extraordinary.

We associate Douglass so much with the fight against slavery that often we forget that he lived three decades beyond the surrender in 1865 of the Confederacy. For him, the war for the African American people and the soul of the United States included more than abolition. Freedom as Douglass conceived of it, and as he affirmed in many essays and speeches, meant not only freedom from bondage but also civil and political rights. In the following selection, Douglass states that the "colored population" is here to stay, and that the American future must unify rather than divide the races from one another.

Douglass was not naïve or hesitant: he forthrightly attacked racism, segregation, and violence meted out to African Americans. He also possessed pride in his people and confidence in their potential: he was certain that in the long run liberty for both black and white was essential—and interdependent. His final book was *The Life and Times of Frederick Douglass*, published in 1881 and revised and expanded in 1892.

The Future of the Negro

It would require the ken[1] of a statesman and the vision of a prophet combined to tell with certainty what will be the ultimate future of the colored people of the United States, and to neither of these qualifications can I lay

---

[1]One's range of knowledge or sight.

claim. We have known the colored man long as a slave, but we have not known him long as a freeman and as an American citizen. What he was as a slave we know; what he will be in his new relation to his fellow-men, time and events will make clear. One thing, however, may safely be laid down as probable, and that is, that the negro, in one form and complexion or another, may be counted upon as a permanent element of the population of the United States. He is now seven millions, has doubled his number in thirty years, and is increasing more rapidly than the more favored population of the South. The idea of his becoming extinct finds no support in this fact. But will he emigrate? No! Individuals may, but the masses will not. Dust will fly, but the earth will remain. The expense of removal to a foreign land, the difficulty of finding a country where the conditions of existence are more favorable than here, attachment to native land, gradual improvement in moral surroundings, increasing hope of a better future, improvement in character and value by education, impossibility of finding any part of the globe free from the presence of white men,—all conspire to keep the negro here, and compel him to adjust himself to American civilization.

In the face of history I do not deny that a darker future than I have indicated may await the black man. Contact of weak races with strong has not always been beneficent. The weak have been oppressed, persecuted, driven out, and destroyed. The Hebrews in Egypt, the Moors in Spain, the Caribs in the West Indies, the Picts in Scotland, the Indians and Chinese in our own country, show what may happen to the negro. But happily he has a moral and political hold upon this country, deep and firm, one which in some measure destroys the analogy between him and other weak peoples and classes. His religion and civilization are in harmony with those of the people among whom he lives. He worships with them in a common temple and at a common altar, and to drag him away is to destroy the temple and tear down the altar. Drive out the negro and you drive out Christ, the Bible, and American liberty with him. The thought of setting apart a State or Territory and confining the negro within its borders is a delusion. If the North and South could not live separately in peace, and without bloody and barbarous border wars, the white and black cannot. If the negro could be bottled up, who could or would bottle up the irrepressible white man? What barrier has been strong enough to confine him? Plainly enough, migration is no policy for the negro. He would invite the fate of the Indian, and be pushed away before the white man's bayonet.

Nor do I think that the negro will become more distinct as a class. Ignorant, degraded, and repulsive as he was during his two hundred years of slavery, he was sufficiently attractive to make possible an intermediate race of a million, more or less. If this has taken place in the face of those odious barriers, what is likely to occur when the colored man puts away his ignorance and degradation and becomes educated and prosperous? The tendency of the age is unification, not isolation; not to clans and classes, but to human brotherhood. It was once degradation intensified for a Norman to associate with a Saxon; but time and events have swept down the barriers between them, and Norman and Saxon have become Englishmen. The Jew was once despised and hated in Europe, and is so still in some parts of that continent; but he has risen, and is rising to higher consideration, and no man is now degraded by association with him anywhere. In like manner the negro will rise in the social scale. For a time the social and political privileges of the colored people may decrease. This, however, will be apparent rather than real. An abnormal condition, born of war, carried him to an altitude unsuited to his attainments. He could not sustain himself there. He will now rise naturally and gradually, and hold on to what he gets, and will not drop from dizziness. He will gain both by concession and by self-assertion. Shrinking cowardice wins nothing from either meanness or magnanimity. Manly self-assertion and eternal vigilance are essential to negro liberty, not less than to that of the white man.

[1884]

GEORGE WASHINGTON CABLE ■ (1844–1925)

Born in New Orleans, and a wounded veteran of the Confederate army, George Washington Cable began his career as a writer with stories and sketches about life in Louisiana. His first books were a collection of stories, *Old Creole Days* (1879), and a novel, *The Grandissimes* (1880), about a Creole family in New Orleans in the early 1800s, and other novels and collections of stories followed these two. But Cable also was known for his controversial and, for his period, progressive essays in the 1880s about slavery and emancipation, race relations, and the past, present, and future of the South.

"The Freedman's Case in Equity," excerpted in the following text, was published in *Century Magazine* in 1885—in the same issue with the second installment of Mark Twain's *Adventures of Huckleberry Finn*. The hostile reaction to these essays, in which Cable criticized discrimination and prejudice, impelled him to leave the South—he said it was not a "free country." From 1885 until his death he and his family lived in Northampton, in western Massachusetts, exiled from the South.

From The Freedman's Case in Equity

As between master and slave, the "feelings engendered by the war" are too trivial, or at least were too short-lived, to demand our present notice. One relation and feeling the war destroyed: the patriarchal tie and its often really tender and benevolent sentiment of dependence and protection. When the slave became a freedman the sentiment of alienism became for the first time complete. The abandonment of this relation was not one-sided; the slave, even before the master, renounced it. Countless times, since reconstruction began, the master has tried, in what he believed to be everybody's interest, to play on that old sentiment. But he found it a harp without strings. The freedman could not formulate, but he could see, all our old ideas of autocracy and subserviency, of master and menial, of an arbitrarily fixed class to guide and rule, and another to be guided and ruled. He rejected the overture. The old master, his well-meant condescensions slighted, turned away estranged, and justified himself in passively withholding that simpler protection without patronage which any one American citizen, however exalted, owes to any other, however humble.

Could the freedman in the bitterest of those days have consented to throw himself upon just that one old relation, he could have found a physical security for himself and his house such as could not, after years of effort, be given him by constitutional amendments, Congress, United States marshals, regiments of regulars, and ships of war. But he could not; the very nobility of the civilization that had held him in slavery had made him too much a man to go back to that shelter; and by his manly neglect to do so he has proved to us who once ruled over him that, be his relative standing among the races of men what it may, he is worthy to be free.

To be a free man is his still distant goal. Twice he has been a freedman. In the days of compulsory reconstruction he was freed in the presence of his master by that master's victorious foe. In these days of voluntary reconstruction he is virtually freed by the consent of his master, but the master retaining the exclusive right to define the bounds of his freedom. Many everywhere have taken up the idea that this state of affairs is the end to be desired and the end actually sought in reconstruction as handed over to the States. I do not charge such folly to the best intelligence of any American community; but I cannot ignore my own knowledge that the average thought of some regions rises to no better idea of the issue.

The belief is all too common that the nation, having aimed at a wrong result and missed, has left us of the Southern States to get now such other result as we think best. I say this belief is not universal. There are those among us who see that America has no room for a state of society which makes its lower classes harmless by abridging their liberties, or, as one of the favored class lately said to me, has "got 'em so they don't give no trouble." There is a growing number who see that the one thing we cannot afford to tolerate at large is a class of people less than citizens; and that every interest in the land demands that the freedman be free to become in all things, as far as his own personal gifts will lift and sustain him, the same sort of American citizen he would be if, with the same intellectual and moral caliber, he were white.

Thus we reach the ultimate question of fact. Are the freedman's liberties suffering any real abridgment? The answer is easy. The letter of the laws, with but few exceptions, recognizes him as entitled to every right of an American citizen; and to some it may seem unimportant that there is scarcely one public relation of life in the South where he is not arbitrarily and unlawfully compelled to hold toward the white man the attitude of an alien, a menial, and a probable reprobate, by reason of his race and color. One of the marvels of future history will be that it was counted a small matter, by a majority of our nation, for six millions of people within it, made by its own decree a component part of it, to be subjected to a system of oppression so rank that nothing could make it seem small except the fact that they had already been ground under it for a century and a half.

Examine it. It proffers to the freedman a certain security of life and property, and then holds the respect of the community, that dearest of earthly boons, beyond his attainment. It gives him certain guarantees against thieves and robbers, and then holds him under the unearned contumely of the mass of good men and women. It acknowledges in constitutions and statutes his title to an American's freedom and aspirations, and then in daily practice heaps upon him in every public place the most odious distinctions, without giving ear to the humblest plea concerning mental or moral character. It spurns his ambition, tramples upon his languishing self-respect, and indignantly refuses to let him either buy with money, or earn by any excellence of inner life or outward behavior, the most momentary immunity from these public indignities even for his wife and daughters. Need we cram these pages with facts in evidence, as if these were charges denied and requiring to be proven? They are simply the present avowed and defended state of affairs peeled of its exteriors.

Nothing but the habit, generations old, of enduring it could make it endurable by men not in actual slavery. Were we whites of the South to remain every way as we are, and our six million blacks to give place to any sort of whites exactly their equals, man for man, in mind, morals, and wealth, provided only that they had tasted two years of American freedom, and were this same system of tyrannies attempted upon them, there would be as bloody an uprising as this continent has ever seen. We can say this quietly. There is not a scruple's weight of present danger. These six million freedmen are dominated by nine million whites immeasurably stronger than they, backed by the virtual consent of thirty-odd millions more.

Indeed, nothing but the habit of oppression could make such oppression possible to a people of the intelligence and virtue of our Southern whites, and the invitation to practice it on millions of any other than the children of their former slaves would be spurned with a noble indignation.

Suppose, for a moment, the tables turned. Suppose the courts of our Southern States, while changing no laws requiring the impaneling of jurymen without distinction as to race, etc., should suddenly begin to draw their thousands of jurymen all black, and well-nigh every one of them counting not only himself, but all his race, better than any white man. Assuming that their average of intelligence and morals should be not below that of jurymen as now drawn, would a white man, for all that, choose to be tried in one of those courts? Would he suspect nothing? Could one persuade him that his chances of even justice were all they should be, or all they would be were the court not evading the law in order to sustain an outrageous distinction against him because of the accidents of his birth? Yet only read white man for black man, and black man for white man, and that—I speak as an eye-witness—has been the practice for years, and is still so to-day; an actual emasculation, in the case of six million people both as plaintiff and defendant, of the right of trial by jury.

In this and other practices the outrage falls upon the freedman. Does it stop there? Far from it. It is the first premise of American principles that whatever elevates the lower stratum of the people lifts all the rest, and whatever holds it down holds all down. For twenty years, therefore, the nation has been working to elevate the freedman. It counts this one of the great necessities of the hour. It has poured out its wealth publicly and privately for this purpose. It is confidently expected that it will soon bestow a royal gift of millions for the reduction of the illiteracy so largely shared by the blacks. Our Southern States are, and for twenty years have been, taxing themselves for the same end. The private charities alone of the other States have given twenty millions in the same good cause. Their colored seminaries, colleges, and normal schools dot our whole Southern country, and furnish our public colored schools with a large part of their teachers.

All this and much more has been or is being done in order that, for the good of himself and everybody else in the land, the colored man may be elevated as quickly as possible from all the debasements of slavery and semi-slavery to the full stature and integrity of citizenship. And it is in the face of all this that the adherent of the old regime stands in the way to every public privilege and place—steamer landing, railway platform, theater, concert-hall, art display, public library, public school, court-house, church, everything—flourishing the hot branding-iron of ignominious distinctions. He forbids the freedman to go into the water until he is satisfied that he knows how to swim, and for fear he should learn hangs mill-stones about his neck.

[1885]

HENRY W. GRADY ■ (1850–1889)

The popular Georgia editor, journalist, and orator Henry W. Grady spoke and wrote on behalf of the "New South," the South that was taking shape, growing, and developing in the aftermath of its defeat in the Civil War. His audience was in the South but as much or more in the North as well: Grady sought to convince northerners that the southern states offered good opportunities for investment, business, and industry.

The following speech, as the excerpts from it show, presents Grady's view of the relationship between the South's white and black populations. He delivered it late in 1886, before the New England Society of New York City, a prestigious organization, founded in 1885, devoted to charity, philanthropy, and education.

One of those in attendance was William Tecumseh Sherman, the Union general who in November 1864 had burned Atlanta to the ground. To all in the audience, Grady declared that the bitter divisions of the Civil War were two decades in the past and that North and South now were truly one nation. He stressed that the South's dependence on plantation agriculture had faded away, and that whites and African Americans there were working together as partners to achieve prosperity.

From The New South

I want to say to General Sherman—who is considered an able man in our hearts, though some people think he is a kind of careless man about fire—that from the ashes he left us in 1864 we have raised a brave and beautiful city; that somehow or other we have caught the sunshine in the bricks and mortar of our homes, and have builded therein not one ignoble prejudice or memory. [Applause.]

But in all this what have we accomplished? What is the sum of our work? We have found out that in the general summary the free Negro counts more than he did as a slave. We have planted the schoolhouse on the hilltop and made it free to white and black. We have sowed towns and cities in the place of theories and put business above politics. [Applause.] We have challenged your spinners in Massachusetts and your iron-makers in Pennsylvania. We have learned that the $400,000,000 annually received from our cotton crop will make us rich, when the supplies that make it are home-raised. We have reduced the commercial rate of interest from twenty-four to six percent, and are floating four per cent bonds. We have learned that one Northern immigrant is worth fifty foreigners, and have smoothed the path to southward, wiped out the place where Mason and Dixon's line[1] used to be, and hung our latch-string out to you and yours. [Prolonged cheers.]

We have reached the point that marks perfect harmony in every household, when the husband confesses that the pies which his wife cooks are as good as those his mother used to bake; and we admit that the sun shines as brightly and the moon as softly as it did "before the war." [Laughter.] We have established thrift in city and country. We have fallen in love with work. We have restored comfort to homes from which culture and elegance never departed. We have let economy take root and spread among us as rank as the crabgrass which sprang from Sherman's cavalry camps, until we are ready to lay odds on the Georgia Yankee, as he manufactures relics of the battlefield in a one-story shanty and squeezes pure olive oil out of his cotton-seed, against any downeaster that ever swapped wooden nutmegs for flannel sausages in the valleys of Vermont. [Loud and continuous laughter.]

Above all, we know that we have achieved in these "piping times of peace"[2] a fuller independence for the South than that which our fathers sought to win in the forum by their eloquence or compel on the field by their swords. [Loud applause.]

It is a rare privilege, sir, to have had part, however humble, in this work. Never was nobler duty confided to human hands than the uplifting and upbuilding of the prostrate and bleeding South, misguided perhaps, but beautiful in her suffering, and honest, brave and generous always. [Applause.] In the record of her social, industrial, and political illustrations we await with confidence the verdict of the world.

But what of the Negro? Have we solved the problem he presents or progressed in honor and equity towards the solution? Let the record speak to the point. No section shows a more prosperous laboring population than the Negroes of the South; none in fuller sympathy with the employing and land-owning class. He shares our school fund, has the fullest protection of our laws and the friendship of our people. Self-interest, as well as honor, demand that he should have this. Our future, our very existence depend upon our working out this problem in full and exact justice.

We understand that when Lincoln signed the Emancipation Proclamation, your victory was assured; for he then committed you to the cause of human liberty, against which the arms of man cannot prevail [Applause]; while those of our statesmen who trusted to make slavery the cornerstone

---

[1]The Mason–Dixon line was surveyed in the mid-eighteenth century by Charles Mason and Jeremiah Dixon. It forms a line of demarcation among four states, forming part of the borders of Pennsylvania, Maryland, Delaware, and West Virginia (which in this period was part of the state of Virginia). In popular usage, the Mason–Dixon Line highlights a social, cultural, and political boundary between the northeastern United States and the southern United States—a boundary also between free states and slave states.
[2]A phrase from the Roman poet Ovid (c. 43 BCE–c. AD 18), Elegy VI.

of the Confederacy doomed us to defeat as far as they could, committing us to a cause that reason could not defend or the sword maintain in the sight of advancing civilization.... [Renewed applause.]

The relations of the Southern people with the Negro are close and cordial. We remember with what fidelity for four years he guarded our defenceless women and children, whose husbands and fathers were fighting against his freedom. To his eternal credit be it said that whenever he struck a blow for his own liberty he fought in open battle, and when at last he raised his black and humble hands that the shackles might be struck off, those hands were innocent of wrong against his helpless charges, and worthy to be taken in loving grasp by every man who honors loyalty and devotion. [Applause.]

Ruffians have maltreated him, rascals have misled him, philanthropists established a bank for him, but the South, with the North, protects against injustice to this simple and sincere people. To liberty and enfranchisement is as far as law can carry the Negro. The rest must be left to conscience and common sense. It should be left to those among whom his lot is cast, with whom he is indissolubly connected and whose prosperity depends upon their possessing his intelligent sympathy and confidence. Faith has been kept with him in spite of calumnious assertions to the contrary by those who assume to speak for us or by frank opponents. Faith will be kept with him in the future, if the South holds her reason and integrity.... [Applause.]

Under the old regime the Negroes were slaves to the South, the South was a slave to the system. The old plantation, with its simple police regulation and its feudal habit, was the only type possible under slavery. Thus we gathered in the hands of a splendid and chivalric oligarchy the substance that should have been diffused among the people, as the rich blood, under certain artificial conditions, is gathered at the heart, filling that with affluent rapture, but leaving the body chill and colorless. [Applause.]

The Old South rested everything on slavery and agriculture, unconscious that these could neither give nor maintain healthy growth. The new South presents a perfect democracy, the oligarchs leading in the popular movement—a social system compact and closely knitted, less splendid on the surface but stronger at the core—a hundred farms for every plantation, fifty homes for every palace, and a diversified industry that meets the complex needs of this complex age.

The New South is enamored of her new work. Her soul is stirred with the breath of a new life. The light of a grander day is falling fair on her face. She is thrilling with the consciousness of growing power and prosperity. As she stands upright, full-statured and equal among the people of the earth, breathing the keen air and looking out upon the expanding horizon, she understands that her emancipation came because in the inscrutable wisdom of God her honest purpose was crossed and her brave armies were beaten. [Applause.]

This is said in no spirit of time-serving or apology. The South has nothing for which to apologize. She believes that the late struggle between the States was war and not rebellion, revolution and not conspiracy, and that her convictions were as honest as yours. I should be unjust to the dauntless spirit of the South and to my own convictions if I did not make this plain in this presence. The South has nothing to take back.

In my native town of Athens is a monument that crowns its central hills—a plain, white shaft. Deep cut into its shining side is a name dear to me above the names of men, that of a brave and simple man who died in brave and simple faith. Not for all the glories of New England—from Plymouth Rock all the way—would I exchange the heritage he left me in his soldier's death. To the foot of that shaft I shall send my children's children to reverence him who ennobled their name with his heroic blood. But, sir, speaking from the shadow of that memory, which I honor as I do nothing else on earth, I say that the cause in which he suffered and for which he gave his life was adjudged by higher and fuller wisdom than his or mine, and I am glad that the omniscient God held the balance of battle in His Almighty hand, and that human slavery was swept forever from American soil—the American Union saved from the wreck of war. [Loud applause.]

This message comes to you from consecrated ground. Every foot of the soil about the city in which I live is sacred as a battleground of the Republic. Every hill that invests it is hallowed to you by the blood of your brothers, who died for your victory, and doubly hallowed to us by the blood of those who died hopeless, but undaunted, in defeat—sacred soil to all of us rich with memories that make us purer and stronger and better, silent but stanch witnesses in its red desolation of the matchless valor of American hearts and the deathless glory of American arms—speaking an eloquent witness in its white peace and prosperity to the indissoluble union of American States and the imperishable brotherhood of the American people.... [Immense cheering.]

[1886]

U.S. SUPREME COURT

On June 7, 1892, in a carefully planned action, Homer Plessy, a New Orleans man of mixed race (he was 7/8 white), ignored the sign "colored only" and took a seat in the whites-only compartment of a Louisiana railroad car. He was arrested, and his lawyer, Albion Tourgée, responded by maintaining that the state law requiring "separate but equal accommodations" was unconstitutional.

A New Orleans judge, John H. Ferguson, ruled against Plessy, and eventually his appeal of Ferguson's decision made its way to the United States Supreme Court. The Court's decision against Plessy gave support to the many laws and ordinances in the Southern states that established and preserved segregation for many decades. It at last was successfully challenged in the 1950s and 1960s through the efforts of Martin Luther King Jr. and countless others in the civil rights movement, buttressed by Supreme Court decisions, (especially, Brown v. Board Education of Topeka, Kansas, 1954) and federal civil-rights acts.

In 1896 the forceful opinion expressed by the majority on the Court was that the Louisiana law did not imply any superiority of white over black: thus, the majority explained, African Americans should not feel they are any less, in any way diminished, because a railroad segregates its passengers. After all, no white person, said the Court, would conclude that such a law would make him or her any less: whites would view themselves as superior whatever a law might state. The excerpt below indicates the majority's line of reasoning, its argument. In a dissent from the majority's decision, Justice John M. Harlan wrote: "Our Constitution is color-blind and neither knows nor tolerates classes among citizens." His was the sole dissenting vote.

From Plessy v. Ferguson, 1896

We consider the underlying fallacy of the plaintiff's argument to consist in the assumption that the enforced separation of the two races stamps the colored race with a badge of inferiority. If this be so, it is not by reason of anything found in the act, but solely because the colored race chooses to put that construction upon it. The argument necessarily assumes that if, as has been more than once the case, and is not unlikely to be so again, the colored race should become the dominant power in the state legislature, and should enact a law in precisely similar terms, it would thereby relegate the white race to an inferior position. We imagine that the white race, at least, would not acquiesce in this assumption. The argument also assumes that social prejudices may be overcome by legislation, and that equal rights cannot be secured to the negro except by an enforced commingling of the two races. We cannot accept this proposition. If the two races are to meet upon terms of social equality, it must be the result of natural affinities, a mutual appreciation of each other's merits and a voluntary consent of individuals. As was said by the Court of Appeals of New York in *People v. Gallagher*, 93 N.Y. 438, 448, "this end can neither be accomplished nor promoted by laws which conflict with the general sentiment of the community upon whom they are designed to operate. When the government, therefore, has secured to each of its citizens equal rights before the law and equal opportunities for improvement and progress, it has accomplished the end for which it was organized and performed all of the functions respecting social advantages with which it is endowed." Legislation is powerless to eradicate racial instincts or to abolish distinctions based upon physical differences, and the attempt to do so can only result in accentuating the difficulties of the present situation. If the civil and political rights of both races be equal one cannot be inferior to the other civilly or politically. If one race be inferior to the other socially, the Constitution of the United States cannot put them upon the same plane.

It is true that question of the proportion of colored blood necessary to constitute a colored person, as distinguished from a white person, is one upon which there is a difference of opinion in the different States, some holding that any visible admixture of black blood stamps the person as belonging to the colored race, others that it depends upon the preponderance of blood, and still others that the predominance of white blood must only be in the proportion of three fourths. But these are questions to be determined under the laws of each State and are not properly put in issue in this case. Under the allegations of his petition it may undoubtedly become a question of importance whether, under the laws of Louisiana, the petitioner belongs to the white or colored race.

The judgment of the court below is, therefore,
Affirmed.

MARION POST WOLCOTT ■ (1910–1990)

Marion Post Wolcott was born in Montclair, New Jersey, and after suffering through her parent's bitter divorce, she was trained as a teacher and took a position in a school in the mill town of Whitinsville, Massachusetts. Increasingly, however, she became interested in photography, and she received encouragement from the noted photographer Paul Strand and others. With her sister Helen, Wolcott lived and studied in Vienna in the early 1930s, where she witnessed the rise of Nazism and the brutalities it inflicted. During the 1930s she worked for the Farm Security Administration (FSA) as a member of its documentary photography unit.

"As an FSA documentary photographer," Wolcott said, "I was committed to changing the attitudes of people by familiarizing America with the plight of the underprivileged, especially in rural America." For nearly four years, beginning in September 1938, she travelled, usually alone, throughout New England and the Southern states on assignments. In 1986, summing up her career, Wolcott stated that her goal always had been to show and record "our present quality of life, the causes of the present malaise in our society— and the world—the evidences of it. History, which will affect this and many generations, is being made, is right out there."

Movie House Entrance, Mississippi Delta, 1939. Photograph by Marion Post Wolcott.

H. L. MENCKEN ■ (1880–1956)

Born in Baltimore, Maryland, the American journalist, critic, and lexi-
cographer H. L. Mencken was a force on the literary, cultural, and
political scenes during the first half of the twentieth century. The
author of many reviews, essays, and books, Mencken also was the editor (with George Jean Nathan) of *The Smart Set* and of *The American
Mercury*, important periodicals. He was, in addition, a vigorous supporter of American authors, most notably Theodore Dreiser, acting as
an advocate for them in his journalism and publishing their work.

Highly opinionated and flamboyant, Mencken enjoyed stirring up
a fuss and furor; he was a performer in his writing and took exuberant delight in condemning hypocrisy, sham, and puritanism. In
the essay excerpted here—"Bozart" is a satiric pun on the Southern pronunciation of "beaux-arts"—Mencken takes aim at the South,
mocking it as a cultural wasteland, intellectually barren—a desert.
This essay enraged many in the South, including John Crowe Ransom, Donald Davidson, and other poets, critics, and fiction writers
who were part of the Fugitive and Agrarian movements, defenders of
Southern values and traditions and advocates of Southern identity
and uniqueness.

From The Sahara of the Bozart

Virginia is the best of south to-day, and Georgia is perhaps the worst. The one is simply senile; the other is crass, gross, vulgar and obnoxious. Between lies a vast plain of mediocrity, stupidity, lethargy, almost of dead silence. In the north, of course, there is also grossness, crassness, vulgarity. The north, in its way, is also stupid and obnoxious. But nowhere in the north is there such complete sterility, so depressing a lack of all civilized gesture and aspiration.

One would find it difficult to unearth a second-rate city between the Ohio and the Pacific that isn't struggling to establish an orchestra, or setting up a little theater, or going in for an art gallery, or making some other effort to get into touch with civilization. These efforts often fail, and sometimes they succeed rather absurdly, but under them there is at least an impulse that deserves respect, and that is the impulse to seek beauty and to experiment with ideas, and so to give the life of every day a certain dignity and purpose. You will find no such impulse in the south.

There are no committees down there cadging subscriptions for orchestras; if a string quartet is ever heard there, the news of it has never come out; an opera troupe, when it roves the land, is a nine days' wonder. The little theater movement has swept the whole country, enormously augmenting the public interest in sound plays, giving new dramatists their chance, forcing reforms upon the commercial theater. Everywhere else the wave rolls high—but along the line of the Potomac it breaks upon a rock-bound shore. There is no little theater beyond. There is no gallery of pictures. No artist ever gives exhibitions. No one talks of such things. No one seems to be interested in such things.

LIZETTE WOODWORTH REESE ■ (1856–1935)

Like H. L. Mencken, who became an admirer of her verse, Lizette Woodworth Reese was Maryland-born, in the small town of Waverly. Though not widely known today, she was a significant figure in the 1920s and 1930s, the author of more than a dozen books of poetry and prose.

It has been said of Reese, who was not only a writer but for many years a schoolteacher, that while she is nostalgic, she is not sentimental. Her concise, pointed style won her the respect of William Dean Howells and other critics and writers of the late nineteenth century and early twentieth century. Some even have been led to compare her with Emily Dickinson and Edna St. Vincent Millay. Reese's body of work lacks their depth and intensity, and ultimately she is a very good minor poet, not a major one. But she knew the virtues of restraint, under statement, and tactful omission, and both what to say, and what to leave unsaid and implied, as the haunting sonnet "A War Memory (1865)," attests. It is included in Reese's volume *Spicewood* (1920).

A War Memory

God bless this house and keep us all from hurt.
She led us gravely up the straight long stair;
We were afraid; two held her by the skirt,
One by the hand, and so to bed and prayer.
How frail a thing the little candle shone!   5
Beneath its flame looked dim and soft and high
The chair, the drawers; she like a tall flower blown
In a great space under a shadowy sky.
God bless us all and Lee and Beauregard.[1]—
Without, a soldier paced, in hated blue,   10
The road betwixt the tents in pale array
And our gnarled gate. But in the windy yard
White tulips raced along the drip of dew;—
Our mother with her candle went away.

[1920]

DONALD DAVIDSON ■ (1893–1968)

Donald Davidson was a poet, essayist, and a professor for four decades at Vanderbilt University in Nashville, Tennessee. A stalwart spokesman for the region, history, and tradition of the South and a critic of industrialism, Davidson along with John Crowe Ransom, Allen Tate, Robert Penn Warren, and others was a member of both the Fugitive and Southern Agrarian groups in the 1920s and 1930s. These Southern men of letters opposed both capitalism and socialism and pledged fidelity to the customs, virtues, and values of farm life—a life maintained through intimate contact with the land, a life that would not fall victim to the modern ideology of fast-paced, relentless social and industrial progress.

The scholar F. Eugene Heath has noted: "Although their version of agrarianism derived from their experience as southerners, they maintained

---

[1]The Confederate generals Robert E. Lee (1807–70), who commanded the Army of Northern Virginia, and P. G. T. Beauregard (1818–93), who ordered the bombardment of Fort Sumter, April 1861, which began the Civil War.

that they were expressing universal ideals. In their estimation, a society dominated by science, technology, and industry, and a nation inclined to favor the urban over the rural population, would suffer an impoverishment of manners, art, education, community, and spirit."

An eloquent partisan and patriot of the Southern cause, Davidson's books include *The Tall Men* (1927), a blank-verse poem; *The Attack on Leviathan: Essays on Regionalism and Nationalism* (1938), essays on politics, culture, and economics; *Lee in the Mountains and Other Poems* (1938), short narrative poems on Robert E. Lee and other Southern heroes; *Still Rebels, Still Yankees* (1957), a collection of conservative (some would say, reactionary) essays; and *The Long Street* (1961), perhaps his best collection of poems.

The following excerpt is taken from Davidson's contribution to the Agrarians' main volume of social and cultural criticism and commentary, *I'll Take My Stand*, published in 1930. Here he criticizes Henry W. Grady and other proponents of the New South; bears witness to the importance of an agrarian economy—as opposed to one based on industry; celebrates the culture and civilization of the South before the Civil War; honors the contributions that the South has made to art and literature; and briefly comments on (and raises questions about) the literary success and achievement of a host of Southern writers.

From A Mirror for Artists

For a century and a half the South has preserved its agrarian economy. On one occasion, it fought to the death for principles now clearly defined, in the light of history, as representing fundamentally the cause of agrarianism against industrialism. The South lost its battle. What was worse for the nation, it lost the peace—first in the Reconstruction, second by temporarily conforming, under the leadership of men like Walter H. Page and Henry W. Grady, to "new South" doctrines subversive of its native genius. Yet the agrarian South did not vanish. Only at this late day has it given any general promise of following the industrial program with much real consent. The danger of such consent is real. So far as industrialism triumphs and is able to construct a really "new" South, the South will have nothing to contribute to modern issues. It will merely imitate and repeat the mistakes of other sections. The larger promise of the South is in another direction. Its historic and social contribution should be utilized.

It offers the possibility of an integrated life, American in the older rather than the newer sense. Its population is homogeneous. Its people share a common past, which they are not likely to forget; for aside from having Civil War battlefields at their doorsteps, the Southern people have long cultivated a historical consciousness that permeates manners, localities, institutions, the very words and cadence of social intercourse. This consciousness, too often misdescribed as merely romantic and gallant, really signifies a close connection with the eighteenth-century European America that is elsewhere forgotten.

In the South the eighteenth-century social inheritance flowered into a gracious civilization that, despite its defects, was actually, civilization, true and indigenous, well diffused, well established.

Its culture was sound and realistic in that it was not at war with its own economic foundations. It did not need to be paraded loudly; it was not thought about particularly. The manners of planters and countrymen did not require them to change their beliefs and temper in going from cornfield to drawing-room, from cotton rows to church or frolic. They were the same persons everywhere.

There was also a fair balance of aristocratic and democratic elements. Plantation affected frontier; frontier affected plantation. The balance might be illustrated by pairings; it was no purely aristocratic or purely democratic South that produced Thomas Jefferson and Andrew Jackson, Robert E. Lee and Stonewall Jackson, John C. Calhoun and Andrew Johnson, Poe and Simms. There was diversity with unity. There was also leisureliness, devotion to family and neighborhood, local self-sufficiency and self-government, and a capacity, up through the 'sixties, for developing leaders.

Above all, the South was agrarian, and agrarian it still remains very largely. Whether it still retains its native, inborn ways is a question open to argument in the minds of those who know the South mainly from hearsay. In the South itself, especially in its scattering and deluded industrial centres, there is much lip-service to progress—the more because industrialism make a very loud noise, with all its extravagant proclamations of better times; and the South has known hard times only too well. Yet probably the secret ambition of most Southern city-dwellers, especially those in apartment houses, is to retire to the farm and live like gentlemen. There are still plenty of people who find the brassy methods of tradesmen a little uncouth. The Southern tradition is probably more vital than its recent epitaphists have announced. If it were not alive, even in the younger generations, this book would never be written. But these are considerations which are touched upon elsewhere. My business is to consider to what extent if offers the kind of society we are looking for.

One must allow that the South of the past, for all its ways of life, did not produce much "great" art. An obvious retort to such a criticism would be, "Neither did the rest of America." Also I might say, as it is frequently said, that the long quarrel between Southern agrarianism and Northern industrialism drove the genius of the South largely into the political rather than the artistic field. A good case might be made out, indeed, for political writing itself as a kind of art in which the South excelled, as in forensic art.

Yet this is not the whole story. So far as the arts have flourished in the South, they have been, up to a very recent period, in excellent harmony with their milieu. The South has always had a native architecture, adapted from classic models into something distinctly Southern; and nothing more clearly and satisfactorily belongs where it is, or better expresses the beauty and stability of an ordered life, than its old country homes, with their pillared porches, their simplicity of design, their sheltering groves, their walks bordered with boxwood shrubs. The South has been rich in the folk-arts, and is still rich in them—in ballads, country songs and dances, in hymns and spirituals, in folk tales, in the folk crafts of weaving, quilting, furniture-making. Though these are best preserved in mountain fastness and remote rural localities, they were not originally so limited. They were widespread; and though now they merely survive, they are certainly indicative of a society that could not be termed inartistic. As for the more sophisticated arts, the South has always practiced them as a matter of course. I shall not attempt to estimate the Southern contribution to literature with some special array of names; the impassioned scholars who are busily resurrecting Chivers, Kennedy, Byrd, Longstreet, Sut Lovingood, and such minor persons, in their rediscovery of American literature, will presently also get around again to Cooke, Page, Cable, Allen, and the like. What I should particularly like to note is that the specious theory that an "independent" country ought to originate an independent art, worthy of its national greatness, did not originate in the South. Emerson fostered such a theory, Whitman tried to practice it, and the call for the "great American novel" has only lately died of its own futility. Since the day when Southerners read Mr. Addison or got Mr. Stuart[1] to paint grandfather's portrait; they have not, on the whole, been greatly excited over the idea that America is obliged to demonstrate its originality by some sharp divorce from the European tradition.

What might have happened, had not the Civil War disrupted the natural course of affairs, I cannot venture to say. Certainly an indigenous art would have had a good chance to spring up in the South, as the inevitable expression of modes of life rather favorable to the arts. What kind of art it might have been, or whether it would have been "great," I do not know. We should, however, recognize that the appearance or non-appearance of a "great" art or a "great" artist can hardly be accepted as a final criterion for judging a society. That is a typically modern view, implying that society merely exists to produce the artist, and it is wrong. Certainly the "great" art cannot be made by fiat; it probably hates compulsion. But an artistic life, in the social sense, is achievable under right conditions; and then, probably when we least expect it, the unpredictable great art arrives. If art has any real importance in life, it is as a significant and beautiful way

[1]Joseph Addison (1672–1719), English essayist, poet, and dramatist; Gilbert Charles Stuart (1755–1828), U.S. artist, sometimes termed "the father of American portraiture."

of shaping whatever there is to be shaped in life, secular and religious, private and public, Let me go back to my thesis. I do not suggest that the South itself is about to become the seat of some grand revival of the arts—though some might happen. I do suggest that the South, as a distinct, provincial region, offers terms of life favorable to the arts, which in the last analysis are a by-product anyway and will not bear too much self-conscious solicitude.

Our megalopolitan agglomerations, which make great ado about art, are actually sterile on the creative side; they patronize art, they merchandise it, but do not produce it. The despised hinterland, which is rather carefree about the matter, somehow manages to beget the great majority of American artists. True, they often migrate to New York, at considerable risk to their growth; they as often move away again, to Europe or some treasured local retreat. Our large cities affect a cosmopolitan air but have little of the artistic cosmopolitanism that once made Paris a Mecca. They do not breed literary groups; the groups appear in the hinterland. We have only to examine the biographies of our artists to learn how provincial are the sources of our arts. The Mid-Western excitement of some years ago was a provincial movement, as is today the Southern outburst. Zona Gale, Robert Frost, James Branch Cabell, Julia Peterkin, Sherwood Anderson, Willa Cather, and many others are provincialists. The Little Theater movement is provincial; it has decentralized dramatic art and broken the grip of Broadway.

And certainly the provincial artist ought to enjoy special blessings. More nearly than his big-city colleague, he should be able to approximate a harmonious relation between artist and environment. Especially to his advantage is his nearness to nature in the physical sense—which ought to mean, not that he becomes in the narrow sense an artist "of the soil," dealing in the picturesque, but that nature is an eternal balancing factor in his art, a presence neither wholly benign nor wholly hostile, continually reminding him that art is not a substitute for nature. Likewise he is far from the commercial fury and the extreme knowingness of the merchandizing centers. He works unaware of critical politics; he is ignorant of how this or that career was "put over," he does not have to truckle and wear himself out at drinking bouts and literary teas, he is not obliged to predict cleverly the swings of the artistic pendulum before they fairly begin to swing.

Even so, he cannot escape the infection of the cities by mere geographical remoteness. The skepticism and malaise of the industrial mind reach him anyway, though somewhat subdued, and attack his art in the very process of creation. Unself-conscious expression cannot fully be attained. It is conditioned by the general state of society, which he cannot escape. It is inhibited by the ideals of the market place, which are, after all, very powerful.

In the South today we have artists whose work reveals richness, repose, brilliance, continuity. The performance of James Branch Cabell has a consistency that might have been more flickering and unstable if it had originated in some less quiet region than Virginia. The novels of Ellen Glasgow have a strength that may come from long, slow prosecution by a mind far from nervous. Yet these and others have not gone untainted. Why does Mr. Cabell seem so much nearer to Paris than to Richmond, to Anatole France than to Lee and Jefferson? Why does Miss Glasgow, self-styled the "social historian" of Virginia, propagate ideas that would be more quickly approved by Oswald Garrison Villard[2] than by the descendants of first families? Why are DuBose Heyward's and Paul Green's studies of negro life so palpably tinged with latter-day abolitionism? Why does T. S. Stribling write like a spiritual companion of Harriet Beecher Stowe and Clarence Darrow?[3]

The answer is in every case the same. The Southern tradition in which these writers would share has been discredited and made artistically inaccessible; and the ideas, modes, attitudes that discredited it, largely not Southern, have been current and could be used. One has to look closely at the provincial Southern artists to discover traces of the indigenous Southern. Some would argue that this is as it should be. Perhaps they should not be expected to perform like Southerners, but like artists, and in that case we could do no better than to admonish them to be artists without regard to geography. Still it remains astonishing that they should adopt somebody else's geography and contrarily write like Northerners—at that, like Northerners made sick by an overdose of their own industrialism.

We should not here fall into the typically American mistake of imagining that admonition will succeed in getting the Southern artist to perform more like a Southerner and a provincial. For many reasons the Southern tradition deserves rehabilitation, but not among them is the reason that it would thus enable Southern artists to be strictly Southern artists. If the Southern tradition were an industrial tradition, it would deserve to be cast out rather than cherished. It happens, however, to be an agrarian tradition. And so it needs it to be defined for the present age, as a mode of life congenial to the arts which are among the things we esteem as more than material blessings. In the emergency it needs, in fact, to be consciously studied and maintained by artists, Southern or not, as affording a last stand in America against the industrial devourer—a stand that might prove to be a turning-point.

The artist should not forget that in those times he is called on to play the part both of a person and of an artist. Of the two, that of person is more immediately important. As an artist he will do best to flee the infection of our times, to stand for decentralization in the arts, to resist with

[2]American journalist (1872–1949); his grandfather on his mother's side was the fiery abolitionist William Lloyd Garrison (1805–79).
[3]Clarence Seward Darrow (1857–1938), American lawyer; he was the defense counsel for John T. Scopes, a teacher in Dayton, Tennessee, who was charged with violating state law for teaching the theory of evolution in a public school in 1925.

every atom of his strength the false gospels of art as a luxury which can be sold in commercial quantities or which can be hallowed by segregation in discreet shrines. But he cannot wage this fight by remaining on his perch as artist. He must be a person first of all, even though for the time being he may become less of an artist. He must enter the common arena and become a citizen. Whether he chooses, as citizen-person, to be a farmer or to run for Congress is a matter of individual choice; but in that general direction his duty lies.

[1930]

ARTHUR ROTHSTEIN ■ (1915–1985)

Born in New York City, the son of immigrants, Arthur Rothstein, soon after graduation from Columbia University in 1935, began work under the direction of Roy Stryker for the photography project of the Resettlement Administration, later the Farm Security Administration. As a member of this project for five years, Rothstein was a colleague of Walker Evans, Ben Shahn, and Dorothea Lange. He travelled widely in the United States, documenting the conditions of life faced by the poor, lowly, and downtrodden, focusing on their suffering and deprivation but also on their endurance and dignity.

About his work, Rothstein said: "Because powerful images are fixed in the mind more readily than words, the photographer needs no interpreter. A photograph means the same thing all over the world and no translator is required. Photography is truly a universal language, transcending all boundaries of race, politics and nationality." The author of many books, Rothstein was a member of the staff of *Look* magazine from the early 1940s to 1971, and is considered one of the foremost photojournalists of the mid-twentieth century.

Here Rothstein has photographed, in February 1940, a Confederate flag outside a movie theater, in Winchester, Virginia, which is showing *Gone With the Wind*, the popular film (nearly four hours long) based on Margaret Mitchell's romantic novel (1936) about the South and the Civil War. In both the novel and the film, slaves are portrayed as dutiful and content, faithful to their white masters.

Southern Movie Theater, 1940. Photograph by Arthur Rothstein.

Modern American Literature

America at the Turn of the Century: The Modern Age Begins

James Fenimore Cooper, Nathaniel Hawthorne, and Henry James are just a few of the many nineteenth-century authors who expressed deep concern about the past, present, and future of "American" literature. The nation seemed to them so youthful, so limited, even impoverished, in its cultural and literary accomplishments and traditions: What was there for an American to write about? Would there ever be a reason for writers in this new nation to produce rich, timely, complex works of literary art?

These concerns, urgent then, now seem quaint in relation not only to the America we experience today but also to the America that was rushing dynamically into existence during the decades when Cooper and the others issued their fateful warnings. By the latter decades of the nineteenth century, the United States was a huge, powerful nation and society. How could it *not* be a vast and beckoning subject for writers? By the beginning of the twentieth century, there was an extraordinary range of "American" issues for American writers to examine and explore, and they did so in a variety of literary forms, including the essay, novel, poem, play, and autobiography.

The Rise of Big Business and Industrial Production

This period witnessed, for example, the rise and consolidation of big business, monopolies, and trusts. By the 1880s John D. Rockefeller's Standard Oil Company controlled 90 percent of the nation's oil. The U.S. Steel Corporation, the first billion-dollar enterprise, formed in 1901 and, based on the steel empire Andrew Carnegie had built, employed nearly 170,000 workers and controlled 60 to 70 percent of the nation's steel business; its annual gross income was greater than that of the U.S. Treasury. "The gospel left behind by [the railroad magnate] Jay Gould," said Mark Twain, "is doing giant work in our days. Its message is 'Get money. Get it quickly. Get it in abundance. Get it dishonestly, if you can, honestly if you must.'" By 1900, 1 percent of the corporations exercised control over one-third of the nation's manufacturing. This was at a time when the average income of workers was somewhere between $400 and $500 per year; the minimum for a decent standard of living was $600.

In 1900 there were 20 million industrial workers, of whom 1.7 million were children—double the number in 1870. By 1900 as well, accidents killed about 35,000 workers each year and injured half a million more. Critics, reformers, and progressive journalists turned their attention to these facts of modern American life in a host of significant books of reportage and analysis:

Henry Demarest Lloyd, *Wealth Against Commonwealth* (1894)
Jacob Riis, *How the Other Half Lives* (1890)
Frances Kellor, *Out of Work: A Study of Employment Agencies* (1904; rev. 1915)
John Moody, *The Truth About the Trusts* (1904)
Lincoln Steffens, *The Shame of the Cities* (1904)
Robert Hunter, *Poverty* (1904)
Ida M. Tarbell, *History of Standard Oil Company* (1904)
David Graham Phillips, *The Treason of the Senate* (1906)
Ray Stannard Baker, *Following the Color Line* (1908)

By the mid-1890s the United States was the world's leader in industrial production, with an output greater than that of England, France, and Germany combined. In the mid-nineteenth century, in the era of Ralph Waldo Emerson and Henry David Thoreau, few factories employed more than 500 workers. By 1900 there were 1,500 factories that employed 500 or more workers; some were much larger, including the General Electric plants in Lynn, Massachusetts (11,000 workers), and Schenectady, New York (15,000), and the Cambria Steel factory in Johnstown, Pennsylvania, which employed 20,000 persons by 1910. The United States was now the leading industrial power in the world—an exhilarating, fearful reality that American writers would engage.

The landscape, too, was being radically transformed. In 1900, the year the Automobile Club of America held its first meeting and automobile show (in Madison Square Garden, New York City, November 3–10), there were only 4,000 registered automobiles in the entire country, with about 10 miles of paved roads for them. By 1910 nearly 200,000 automobiles were built annually. In 1913 Henry Ford organized the first automobile assembly line, and soon 1,000 Model-T cars were being produced each workday. Before the assembly line came into operation, the manufacture of a car took Ford's workers nearly 13 hours; the assembly line cut the time to an hour and a half. In the following year the Ford Motor Company produced 250,000 cars. By 1915 there were 3.5 million cars in the nation, and by 1923, 15 million.

Ford alarmed many business owners by providing a high wage of $5 per day, but his revolutionary goal was to pay his workers well enough to enable them to buy the cars they made—and because of the assembly-line system, the price of a Model-T was slashed from $950 in 1909 to $290 in 1924. As Ford explained in an entry for the *Encyclopedia Britannica* (1926), "The experience of Ford Motor Co. has been that mass production precedes mass consumption and makes it possible, by reducing costs and thus permitting both greater use-convenience and price-convenience." (The success of assembly-line and mass-production techniques in automobile manufacturing led to the same process for the manufacture of farm equipment, typewriters, machine tools, sewing machines, and other items.) Many Americans still could not afford, or else did not want to own, a car; for them there was public transportation, and beginning in 1915, the taxicab (a driver was called a "cabbie" in the Midwest, a "hacker" or "hackie" in the East). But installment buying—another innovation—allowed many who could not afford the full price to purchase cars.

By 1929 the auto industry employed more than 375,000 workers, and hundreds of thousands of others held jobs related to it—for instance, making tires and building highways. The center of the industry, Detroit, grew in population from 285,000 in 1900 to 1.5 million in 1930. The romance and the horror of the automobile are best evoked in F. Scott Fitzgerald's *The Great Gatsby*, with its sleek cars coming and going from Gatsby's estate, but it figures in much cultural criticism of the period, as when Paul Rosenfeld, writing about the literary critic and essayist Van Wyck Brooks in *Port of New York* (1924), described the drift of America: "The spectacle of the youth of a land concentrating its mind entirely in the carburetors of motor cars; the vision of a population traveling about Sunday afternoons in automobiles, and swallowing the scenery through their open mouths, seemed to him a collapse of very life."

By the mid-1920s, 25,000 people each year were being killed in traffic accidents, more than two-thirds of them pedestrians. But cars offered too many advantages for Americans to feel they could be given up. Robert and Helen Lynd, in *Middletown* (1929), concluded: "As, at the turn of the century, business-class people began to feel apologetic if they did not have a telephone, so ownership of an automobile has now reached the point of being an accepted essential of normal living." By 1930, more than 45 million Americans, which was one-third of the total population, took "automobile vacations," traveling to tourist camps and cabins. As the Lynds noted, the automobile had "revolutionized leisure."

The automobile industry was powerful evidence of the transformations of the American scene and of the changes taking place throughout the culture that both would equip American writers with dramatic material to write about and would threaten them. Could a book compete with the thrilling practicality of a car and, as automobile design became more dashing with its colors and curves, its aesthetic appeal? For that matter, why write at all, when the allure of business was so great? As Andrew Carnegie observed in *The Empire of Business* (1902), becoming a financial success in twentieth-century America required visionary power and energy:

> The young man who begins in a financial firm and deals with capital invested in a hundred different ways—in bonds upon our railway systems, in money lent to the merchant, and to the manufacturer to enable them to work their wonders—soon finds romance in business and unlimited room for the imagination.

For the worker without access to capital, the situation was less glamorous. In *My Philosophy of Industry* (1929), Henry Ford tried to claim that all was well:

> It has been asserted that machine production kills the creative ability of the craftsman. This is not true. The machine demands that man be its master; it compels mastery more than the old methods did. The number of skilled craftsman in proportion to the working population has greatly increased under the conditions brought

about by the machine. They get better wages and more leisure in which to exercise their creative faculties.

But as the engineer Frederick Winslow Taylor's words in *The Principles of Scientific Management* (1911) unintentionally revealed, the "science" of work, with its emphasis on machines and productivity, had made the situation of the laborer a grim one:

> One of the very first requirements for a man who is fit to handle pig iron as a regular occupation is that he shall be so stupid and so phlegmatic that he more nearly resembles in his mental make-up the ox than any other type....He is so stupid that the word "percentage" has no meaning to him, and he must consequently be trained by a man more intelligent than himself into the habit of working in accordance with the laws of this science before he can be successful.

Thorstein Veblen, in *The Theory of Business Enterprise* (1904), caught accurately this dehumanization of the American worker: "The machine...compels the adaptation of the workman to his work, rather than the adaptation of the work to the workman. The machine technology rests on a knowledge of impersonal, material cause and effect, not on the dexterity, diligence, or personal force of the workman." In this environment, who would be the writers, and who would be the readers? Jurgis, the protagonist of Upton Sinclair's *The Jungle* (1906), saw how workers killed and carved cattle on the line: "They worked with furious intensity, literally upon the run—at a pace with which there is nothing to be compared except a football game. It was all highly specialized labor, each man having his task to do." A man's consciousness was his task.

At the time of Sinclair's novel, the U.S. Steel Works in Homestead, Pennsylvania, was running two grueling shifts, one of 10½ hours during the day, and the other of 13½ hours through the night. According to one study, a steelworker on either of these shifts could not make enough money to support a family of five even if he worked every day of the year.

Corporations and monopolies meant power and control of wealth, resources, workers, and, eventually, authors. As the financier J. P. Morgan explained: "I like a little competition, but I like combination better." By 1910, 40 percent of the clerical workers and wage earners in the nation were living in poverty; and this figure did not take into account tenant farmers, sharecroppers, and others living in rural areas.

"Extremes of wealth and poverty are threatening the existence of the government," wrote the labor leader George McNeill in *The Labor Movement: The Problem of Today* (1887): "In the light of these facts, we declare that there is an inevitable and irresistible conflict between the wage-system of labor and the republican system of government—the wage laborer attempting to save the government, and the capitalist class ignorantly attempting to subvert it." The social reformer and economist Henry George, campaigning in 1886 for mayor of New York, stated: "All men who work for a living, whether by hand or head, are underpaid. Labor nowhere has its full and fair reward. Everywhere the struggle for existence, the difficulty of making a living, is far greater than it ought to be." Speaking in Kansas in the 1890s, the Populist orator and agitator Mary K. Lease declared, "Wall Street owns the country. It is no longer a government of the people, and for the people, but a government of Wall Street, by Wall Street, and for Wall Street." "I am for Socialism," affirmed Eugene V. Debs, "because I am for humanity. We have been cursed with the reign of gold long enough. Money constitutes no proper basis of civilization."

Workers resisted and massed their forces in response to new industrial conditions, and their struggle was rendered in novels by writers as different as William Dean Howells (*Annie Kilburn*, 1889; *A Hazard of New Fortunes*, 1890), John Hay (*The Bread-Winners*, 1884), Mary Wilkins Freeman (*The Portion of Labor*, 1901), and Edith Wharton (*The Fruit of the Tree*, 1907). The National Labor Union (1866–72) and the Knights of Labor (1878–93) opposed the wage system and organized both skilled and unskilled workers. The American Federation of Labor (AFL), formed in 1886 with 150,000 members, by 1897 had achieved a membership of 500,000 (60 percent of the union members in the nation).

By 1914 the AFL, led by Samuel Gompers, had two million members. It concentrated on skilled craftsmen, not unskilled and immigrant workers, and its goals were the improvement of working conditions and the increase of wages. The Industrial Workers of the World, formed in Chicago in 1905, welcomed all workers, including women, immigrants, minorities, and even the unemployed. From 1916 to 1920, more than one million workers went on strike every year. In 1919 alone, four million workers—20 percent of the workforce—went on strike. In the two-year span from 1916 to 1918, membership in the AFL rose from 2 million to 2.7 million. By 1920, membership stood at almost 3.3 million.

Labor unrest during the first decades of the century was widespread. In early 1919, for example, tens of thousands of workers went on strike in Seattle, bringing the city to a halt. In the same year 50,000 clothing workers went on strike in New York City; 120,000 textile workers struck in New Jersey and New England; and 400,000 coal miners and 350,000 striking steelworkers closed down industry in 10 states and sparked violent protests and brutal crackdowns by the company and police.

Women were working in increasing numbers too. By 1900 nearly 20 percent of the workforce was female, and in such industries as shoe- and garment-making, women comprised between 40 and 60 percent. By the first decade of the twentieth century, 60 percent of New York City's young immigrant women worked for wages. The women who toiled in the garment industry were between the ages of sixteen and twenty-five; they worked six days a week, about fifty-five to sixty hours per week, and were paid six dollars weekly. Between 1920 and 1930 the number of employed women increased from eight to eleven million, and by 1915 women were responsible for 80 percent of consumer purchasing. More money in the hands of women led to a new measure of freedom for them—evident in, for instance, the change in the divorce rate, which increased from one in every twenty-one marriages in 1880 to one in every nine by 1915–16. For Edith Wharton, caught in an unhappy marriage, divorce was unthinkable at the turn of the century, but it became possible for her—something she could imagine doing without social shame—in 1913.

Many women remained at home, yet their lives were made easier because of developments in food processing and preparation, such as prepackaged flour and soups and sauces in cans. Those in the upper class and upper middle class, like Wharton, enjoyed the advantages, too, of indoor plumbing, central heating, and electricity. By the 1920s and into the 1930s these changes improved the lives of even more women and their families; they had oil furnaces, electric stoves, vacuum cleaners, washing machines, and toasters—and radios to listen to while the work was being done.

Women also at last won the right to vote. The suffrage movement was led by Carrie Chapman Catt (1859–1947) and Anna Howard Shaw (1847–1919); its membership grew from 13,000 in the early 1890s to two million by the late 1910s. Congress passed the

Nineteenth Amendment in June 1919, and it was ratified by the states in August 1920, enabling women to vote in the fall presidential election. As Catt noted:

> To get that word, male, out of the Constitution, cost the women of the country 52 years of pauseless campaign; 56 state referendum campaigns; 480 legislative campaigns to get state suffrage amendments submitted; 47 state constitutional convention campaigns; 277 state party convention campaigns; 30 national party convention campaigns to get suffrage planks in the party platforms; 19 campaigns with 19 successive Congresses to get the federal amendment submitted; and the final ratification campaign.

The impact of the movement on literature can be seen in all the literary genres—in, for example, such suffragist plays as Charlotte Perkins Gilman's *Something to Vote For* (1911) and Emily Sargent Lewis's *Election Day: A Suffrage Play* (1912), and in Gilman's speeches, stories, poems, and cultural criticism.

Immigration and Population Increase

The latter decades of the nineteenth century and early decades of the twentieth also were periods of mass immigration to the United States, and the voices and idioms of the new Americans would enrich American literature—though some writers and critics at the time said that the immigrants' dissonant "alien" languages would imperil the nation's language and literature, as Henry James fretted in *The American Scene* (1907).

Between 1865 and 1915, 25 million immigrants arrived, 9 million of them in the single decade from 1900 to 1910. Some estimates have suggested that 80 percent of New York City's population and nearly 90 percent of Chicago's were immigrants or the children of immigrants. By 1905 the population density of some sections of New York City had reached 1,000 persons an acre, greater than that of Bombay [since 1995, Mumbai], India. As the Christian sociologist Josiah Strong said, "We must face the inevitable. The new civilization is certain to be urban; and the problem of the twentieth century will be the city," where the majority of immigrants and workers congregated (*The Twentieth Century City*, 1898). Jane Addams made a related point in *The Spirit of Youth and the City Streets* (1909): "Let us know the modern city in its weakness and wickedness, and then seek to rectify and purify it until it shall be free at least from the grosser temptations which now beset the young people who are living in its tenement houses and working in its factories."

Addams and others criticized, and sought to improve, the conditions that immigrants faced in the cities and workers endured in factories and plants. But they proposed their reforms in the face of a general belief in the rightness of America's development as an industrial power and, by the turn of the century, as an imperialist power that Providence blessed and directed. In his second annual message to Congress, December 5, 1898, reviewing the United States' triumph in the war against Spain, which occurred from mid-April to mid-August, President William McKinley declared, "In tracing these events we are constantly reminded of our obligations to the Divine Master for His watchful care over us and His safe guidance, for which the nation makes reverent acknowledgment and offers humble prayer for the continuance of His favor."

Senator Albert J. Beveridge, also in 1898, gave this claim an even more extravagant rendering, reaching back to the rhetoric of Puritan settlement:

> Fellow-Americans, we are God's chosen people. Yonder at Bunker Hill and Yorktown His providence was above us. At New Orleans and on ensanguined seas His hand sustained us. Abraham Lincoln was His minister and His was the altar of freedom the boys in blue set up on a hundred smoking battlefields. His power directed Dewey in the east, and He delivered the Spanish fleet into our hands on Liberty's natal day as he delivered the elder Armada into the hands of our English sires two centuries ago.[1]

A number of the country's foremost writers and intellectuals spoke and wrote fervently against imperial expansion, against this massing of power as it surged during and in the aftermath of the Spanish-American War. The critic and man of letters Charles Eliot Norton in April 1898 told his students at Harvard they should not serve in "this wretched, needless and, consequently, iniquitous war." The war was, he later wrote, "a bitter disappointment to the lover of his country," a "turning-back from the path of civilization to that of barbarism." The philosopher William James, in "The Philippine Tangle," *Boston Evening Transcript* (March 1, 1899), stated: "We are destroying down to the root every germ of a healthy national life in these unfortunate people, and we are surely helping to destroy for one generation at least their faith in God and man. No life shall you have, we say, except as a gift from our philanthropy after your unconditional submission to our will." The African American educator Kelly Miller made an even broader point in "The Effect of Imperialism Upon the Negro Race" (1900), linking imperialism and racism: "The whole trend of imperial aggression is antagonistic to the feebler races. It is a revival of racial arrogance....Will the Negro stultify himself and become a part of the movement which must end in his own humiliation?"

These moral, social, and cultural arguments were, however, made in the midst of America's relentless industrial development and ever-growing economic might worldwide and thus had little influence. As Frank Vanderlip, a top executive for the National City Bank of New York, explained in "The American 'Commercial Invasion' of Europe" (1902), America was acquiring "supremacy in the world's markets." Further, "So many industries have been sending rapidly increasing contributions to swell the rising tide of our foreign commerce that it is difficult to tell any detailed story of American commercial expansion without making it read like a trade catalogue."

The United States thus was extending its power outward and attracting millions of workers and their families from abroad. Many immigrants came to America intending to stay only for a short time. In some years, 70 percent of the immigrants were men who came alone; and studies have suggested that during periods of slow or declining economic growth in the United States, more immigrants left the country than entered it. Still, between 1890 and 1920, more than 18 million immigrants arrived in the United States, including nearly 4 million from Italy, 3.6 million from Austria-Hungary, and 3 million from Russia. Most of them settled in cities, and these became even more of a source of alarm

---

[1]George Dewey (1837–1917), U.S. naval officer. Appointed commodore of the navy in 1896, he was the hero of the battle of Manila Bay in the Philippines in 1898 during the Spanish-American War. The elder Armada: a Spanish naval invasion force sent against England by Philip II of Spain in 1588. It was defeated by the English fleet and almost completely destroyed by storms near the Hebrides, off the northwestern coast of Scotland.

and fascination for observers of the social and cultural scene. In 1860 there were nine cities with populations of 100,000 or higher; by 1910 that figure had grown to fifty.

By 1900 the nation's five largest cities—New York, Chicago, Philadelphia, St. Louis, and Boston—contained 10 percent of its population. New York City grew from 1.2 million in 1880 to 5.6 million in 1920. Chicago grew from 100,000 in 1860 to 2 million in 1910 to 2.7 million in 1920, and, as many black men and women left the South and headed North, its African American population rose from 44,000 in 1910 to 234,000 in 1930. "Here," wrote the novelist Frank Norris about Chicago in *The Pit* (1903),

> of all her cities, throbbed the true life—the true power and spirit of America; gigantic, crude with the crudity of youth, disdaining rivalry; sane and healthy and vigorous; brutal in its ambition; arrogant in the new-found knowledge of its giant strength; prodigal of its wealth, infinite in its desires.

Many writers, cultural conservatives, and reformers were troubled by the high numbers of immigrants. In *How the Other Half Lives* (1890), Jacob Riis reported of the Lower East Side in New York City that the native-born "are not here. In their place has come this queer conglomerate mass of heterogeneous elements, ever striving and working like whiskey and beer in one glass, and with the like result: final union and a prevailing taint of whiskey." In the city, said Riis, "One may find for the asking an Italian, a German, a French, African, Spanish, Bohemian, Russian, Scandinavian, Jewish, and Chinese colony....The one thing you shall vainly ask for in the chief city of America is a distinctly American community." To Josiah Strong, "the city is the nerve center of our civilization. It is also the storm center....The city has become a serious menace to our civilization." The editor and reformer Henry George observed, "This life of great cities is not the natural life of man. He must under such conditions deteriorate, physically, mentally, morally." Immigration was sharply cut back in the 1920s with the passage of the Immigration Restriction Act (1921; as part of this measure, Asian immigration was banned) and the National Origins Act (1924).

As American literature was being defined and debated, so on another level was the status of *American* itself. It was undergoing a new articulation, with inclusions and exclusions. Who has the right to be an American? Who belongs; who does not?

A Rise in Literacy

The population figures of the nation's largest cities suggest the ever-increasing market that existed for books, journals, and magazines. In this respect, conditions for American writers improved because there were more, and more diverse kinds, of American readers, who read not only in English but also many other languages. By 1900, 50 percent of African Americans were literate, as were 85 percent of the immigrant population and 90 percent of the native-born white population. By 1930, 95 percent of the population was literate.

The rise in literacy was connected to the expansion of educational opportunities, which for American literature meant an expanding number of readers, courses, and required and recommended texts. In 1860 there were only 100 public high schools; by 1914 there were 12,000. By 1910 the number of students attending public grammar and high schools had tripled from what it had been at the time of the Civil War, reaching a total of almost 18 million. Students spent more days in school, and funding increased substantially—though unevenly (not at all in rural areas; less for African Americans than for whites). In 1900, on average a child attended school 100 days annually, an increase from 80 in 1880.

On the other hand, in 1900 only 50 percent of the white population, ages five to twenty, was enrolled in school, with the figure falling to 30 percent for nonwhites. The figures for subsequent decades were encouraging but always showed much need for improvement. By 1930, 60 percent of high school–age children were in school—which meant that 40 percent were not, and one in seven college-age men and women was in college (a jump from one in 33 in 1900)—which meant that six out of seven were not. Between 1920 and 1930 college enrollment jumped from 600,000 to 1.1 million, though this still meant only 5 percent of college-age Americans was enrolled.

Beginning in 1893 with the Committee of Ten, chaired by Harvard's president Charles William Eliot, educators, scholars, and administrators reformed the curriculum for those attending college, deemphasizing classical languages and increasing the attention paid to science and foreign languages. In 1910, 5,000 students were enrolled at the University of Chicago, making it the largest in the country. The state universities of Minnesota and Michigan and the private universities Harvard and Columbia each enrolled about 4,000 students. All of these were soon outpaced by the University of California, where the enrollment in 1920 reached 13,000.

For college-educated and non–college-educated readers alike there were many newspapers, journals, and magazines presenting articles on all sorts of subjects. In addition to the respected, well-established *Atlantic Monthly*, *Harper's*, *The Century*, and *Scribner's*, new general-audience periodicals appeared: *McCall's* (1870), *Popular Science* (1872), *Woman's Home Companion* (1873), *Ladies' Home Journal* (1883, reaching a circulation of 1 million by 1900), *Cosmopolitan* (1886), *Collier's* (1888), and *Vogue* (1892). By the early 1920s ten magazines, including *Ladies' Home Journal* and the *Saturday Evening Post* (which had begun in 1821), had circulations of 2.5 million or more.

The author, editor, and classicist Harry Thurston Peck, who launched *The Bookman* in February 1895, included as one of his regular features a list of "Books in Demand" in the bookstores of a number of U.S. cities; the heading was changed in 1903 to "The Six Best Sellers," the origin of the best-seller list. Such lists brought books to the attention of reader-consumers, making them feel under pressure to stay current by reading what others were reading. The Book-of-the-Month Club, another means of promoting and selling books and turning them into best-sellers, began in 1926.

Many popular American books showed little literary distinction, but they treated subjects and themes that readers found compelling. The rags-to-riches Horatio Alger books sold extremely well, as did books by the industrialist and philanthropist Andrew Carnegie, such as *The Gospel of Wealth* (1900). The novelist Emily Post, at the request of her publisher, wrote *Etiquette* (1922), which promptly sold 500,000 copies. The Ohio-born Zane Grey published his first Western novel, *The Spirit of the Border*, in 1906; others soon followed, including *Riders of the Purple Sage* (1912), *Wanderer of the Wasteland* (1923), and *West of the Pecos* (1937), with total sales of more than 13 million by 1939. The New York clergyman Charles Monroe Sheldon's *In His Steps*, which told the story of a life lived as Jesus would have led it, sold more than 8 million copies in the decades after its publication in 1897.

Jesus was also enlisted in books, articles, and speeches in the cause of money-making and business, as in the Baptist preacher Russell H. Conwell's "Acres of Diamonds" lecture, which he delivered 6,000 times; as Conwell stressed, "You ought to get rich, and it is your duty to get rich....To make money honestly is to preach the gospel" (1915). Bruce Barton, an advertising executive, achieved the greatest religious-literary success of all during the period with *The Man Nobody Knows*, which portrayed Jesus as the first major businessman (1924); Jesus Christ "picked up twelve men from the bottom ranks of business and forged them into an organization that conquered the world."

Periodicals and books abounded for America's diverse religious and ethnic populations. By 1900 nearly 600,000 Jews were living in New York City, well over a million by 1910, and by 1930 the number exceeded 2 million, and Jewish writers, editors, and publishers produced a thriving Yiddish literature that in its daily press reached hundreds of thousands of readers. In addition to the Yiddish newspapers in New York City, others were published in Chicago, Cleveland, and Philadelphia; these included such material as important national and local news, advice columns, serialized novels (e.g., by the Polish-born Yiddish writer Sholem Asch), and advertisements for Ivory Soap and Vaseline. (By 1940 New York City had nearly 250 foreign-language newspapers, magazines, and journals.) This is the context from which emerged the stories of assimilation told in Mary Antin's *The Promised Land* (1912) and Marcus Ravage's *An American in the Making* (1917), and also the fictional exploration of the necessity for and cost of assimilation and Americanization in Abraham Cahan's *The Rise of David Levinsky* (1917) and Anzia Yezierska's *Hungry Hearts and Other Stories* (1920) and *Bread Givers* (1925). "The very clothes I wore and the very food I ate had a fatal effect on my religious habits," Cahan's protagonist says. "If you attempt to bend your religion to the spirit of your surroundings, it breaks. It falls to pieces."

Leisure Time and Entertainment

There were limits to how much Americans read or could read at the turn of the century. Many worked long hours and had little time for reading, leisure, and recreation. In the 1890s a steelworker on average worked sixty-six hours per six-day workweek, and a baker sixty-five. A housewife devoted six or more hours per day to cleaning the home and preparing meals.

However, by 1920 housewives were spending less time on housework, and for working men, the hours of the workweek had declined to about fifty hours. Saturday work had either been reduced to a half-day or eliminated entirely, a reform pushed at first by Jewish workers in the clothing industry who wanted Saturday off in order to observe the Sabbath. In 1926 Henry Ford instituted the five-day week for workers in his automobile plant. To him, this was a good business move; working people needed leisure time to use the automobiles they bought with the wages he paid them, so they then would want to buy and enjoy another, better one.

Less time at work thus meant much more than an increase in time for reading, and the expansion of opportunities for leisure and entertainment complicated and challenged the efforts of American writers and critics to exercise the impact on the culture they desired and give American literature a vivid presence. Americans had plenty of diversions, and more of them all the time. National mail-order houses, for example, were established by Montgomery Ward and by Sears, Roebuck, enabling people across the country to enjoy access to the same goods. By 1900 each of these companies was selling well over 20,000 items. There were also large department stores, such as that begun by John Wanamaker in Philadelphia (the first in the nation, 1875) and the Strauses in New York City. Americans could shop at home or travel to grand retail stores to shop for goods in person, as Theodore Dreiser described in *Sister Carrie* (1900).

Within cities, moving from place to place was becoming much easier. The horse car was gradually replaced by the electric trolley car, which by 1900 was the main mode of public transportation in most cities. Major cities, in addition, built elevated railway lines and underground subway systems. In 1904 the subway in New York City made it possible to travel underground the entire length of Manhattan. Electricity illuminated the city at night, and the telephone enabled quick communication.

For their entertainment at home, Americans could listen to phonograph records (2 million phonographs were produced in 1919, and by 1921 sales of records reached 100 million), and outside the home, many people began to attend classical concerts. A pressing concern among music critics, teachers, and patrons of the arts in fact was how to make it possible for more Americans to hear the music of the European masters. Carnegie Hall in New York City (1891), Symphony Hall in Boston (1900), and Orchestral Hall in Chicago (1904) were built so that audiences could attend performances of compositions by Beethoven, Handel, and others. Musicians began to receive appointments in classical music at colleges and universities to provide training in the European tradition for young American composers, and the teachers at conservatories—for example, the New England Conservatory in Boston, established in 1867—pursued similar aims to good effect. In 1915 there were seventeen symphony orchestras in the United States; by 1939 there were 270. One of the great musical triumphs of the first decade of the century was the Austrian composer Gustav Mahler's presentation in 1909 of Wagner's *Tristan und Isolde* at the Metropolitan Opera in New York City. Featuring Olive Fremstad (1871-1951) in the role of Isolde—Fremstad was the model for the Wagner enthusiast Willa Cather's opera-singer protagonist Thea Kronborg in *The Song of the Lark* (1915)—this production was an overpowering experience. Mahler said he had "never known a performance of *Tristan* to equal this."

Classical music, compared to other forms of entertainment, was a minority taste. Vaudeville and minstrel shows were far more popular. In the 1880s the theater owner and vaudeville manager B. F. Keith began the practice of "continuous performances" running twelve hours at a time. In "The Vogue of Vaudeville" (*National Magazine*, November 1898), Keith said, "As to the sort of entertainment which seems to please most, light, frothy acts, with no particular plot, but abounding in songs, dances, bright dialogues and clean repartee, seem to appeal most." By 1915 Keith's company controlled 1,500 theaters, and as many as 20,000 acts were competing for bookings. Vaudeville shows outdrew other forms of entertainment by ten to one.

Spectator sports (especially boxing, baseball, and college football) were popular, as were traveling shows, perhaps the most famous of which was Buffalo Bill's Wild West, begun by and starring William F. Cody (1846-1917), an Indian fighter and scout nicknamed Buffalo Bill for his buffalo-hunting exploits in the 1860s. In July 1869 he was featured as the hero of a dime novel written by the journalist Ned Buntline (1821-86)—the first of 1,700 books devoted to his adventures. Cody himself was soon the star of a hit play (hated by the critics) on Broadway in 1872, and after taking part in the Sioux Wars of 1875-76, he became an even more legendary figure. He capitalized on his renown in 1883 with the first of his Wild West shows, featuring expert marksmanship by "Little Sure Shot" Annie Oakley (1860–26), reenactments of stagecoach robberies and Pony Express rides, and recreations of such historical events as Custer's Last Stand.[2] The Indian chief and warrior Sitting Bull (1831–90) was the star attraction in 1885.

Buffalo Bill's Wild West traveled the country every year until 1916 (Cody himself retired in 1912); in 1893, six million people saw the show. It was also popular in Europe, touring there in 1887, 1889, and 1891. In 1913 Cody started a film company, intending to produce films that would give accurate depictions (with as many of the original participants as possible) of episodes in his own life and in Western history. He made eight films (little footage survives), one of which took as its subject the massacre at Wounded Knee, South Dakota, where in 1890 the U.S. Army killed 300 Sioux Indians. By the 1890s Indian tribes were scattered in reservations across the country and were a minority population in territory undergoing settlement by whites; in 1900 there were only 20,000 Sioux in South Dakota's total population of 400,000, and 70,000 in Oklahoma's total population of 1 million in 1907.

By the 1910s and 1920s the film industry too was vigorously underway. The first movie with a plot was *The Great Train Robbery* (1903); the first movie with sound was *The Jazz Singer* (1927); and the first movie in color was *Becky Sharp* (1935). By the mid-1920s there were 20,000 movie theaters, and 50 million Americans attended them each week. As early as 1910, 300,000 New Yorkers (in a city with a total population of 4.8 million) attended the movies every day. In 1939 the major studios produced nearly 400 films, which brought in $673 million in revenue ($11 billion in 2013 dollars). Every week of that year, 50 million people attended at least one movie, seeing such films as *Gone with the Wind*; *The Wizard of Oz*; *Goodbye Mr. Chips*; *Mr. Smith Goes to Washington*; *Stagecoach*; *Wuthering Heights*; *The Hunchback of Notre Dame*; *Ninotchka*; *The Rules of the Game*; *The Roaring Twenties*; *Gunga Din*; and *Pinocchio*. By the mid-1940s weekly attendance at movies was 90 million.

There was radio as well. The first professional broadcast occurred on November 2, 1920, when station KDKA in Pittsburgh presented the results of the 1920 presidential election. The first World Series game was broadcast locally from the Polo Grounds in New York City in October 1922; the first broadcast of a political convention was that of the Democrats in New York City in July 1924; and the first radio broadcast of a presidential speech in December 1924, by President Coolidge. In September 1927, 50 million people listened to the heavyweight championship fight between Jack Dempsey and Gene Tunney, held in Chicago before a crowd of 104,000 people. This was also the year of the first national broadcast of the World Series, as Babe Ruth's New York Yankees swept the Pittsburgh Pirates in four straight games.

In 1930–31, the Columbia Broadcasting System (CBS) began live Sunday broadcasts of performances by the New York Philharmonic Orchestra, conducted by Arturo Toscanini. Listeners could also enjoy the jazz musicians Duke Ellington and Benny Goodman. By the late 1920s there were 500 radio stations and 6 million radios. By 1935, 70 percent of homes in the United States had radios; according to surveys, radio was America's favorite pastime—well ahead of, for example, reading. By 1940 nearly every family owned a radio.

---

[2]George Armstrong Custer (1839–76), U.S. cavalry officer. In 1876, he was killed, along with all of his men (266) in a battle (popularly known as Custer's Last Stand) with the Sioux Indians at Little Bighorn, Montana.

Television began in April 1939 with the National Broadcasting Company's airing of President Franklin D. Roosevelt's opening of the New York World's Fair. The first televised sporting event also took place in 1939, as 400 TV sets tuned in to a baseball game between Columbia and Princeton at Baker Field in upper Manhattan. Only 0.4 percent of the population owned TV sets in 1948; by the end of the decade the percentage was only a point or two higher—but by the late 1950s the figure had soared to nearly 90 percent. By the 1990s the average American spent one-quarter of his or her life watching television.

As the twentieth century approached, many writers, intellectuals, and cultural critics were already commenting on the astounding social, technological, and cultural transformations that had occurred in the United States and that would accelerate during the first decades of the new century. The historian Henry Adams observed, "My country in 1900 is something totally different from my own country in 1860. I am wholly a stranger in it. Neither I, nor anyone else, understands it." The novelist Jack London wrote, "Never in the history of the world was society in so terrific flux as it is right now....The swift changes in our industrial system are causing equally swift changes in our religious, political, and social structures. An unseen and fearful evolution is taking place in the fiber and structure of society. One can only dimly feel these things, but they are in the air, now, today." An English observer, James Bryce, author of *The American Commonwealth* (1888), stated in an essay in 1905:

> That which most strikes the visitor to America today is its prodigious material development. Industrial growth, swift thirty or forty years ago, advances more swiftly now....With this extraordinary material development it is natural that in the United States, business, that is to say, industry, commerce, and finance, should have more and more come to overshadow and dwarf all other interests, all other occupations....Business is king.

At the same time, as America's newness as an industrial and commercial power was noted, the oldness, the datedness, of its literary ideas and cultural practices was targeted for change by progressive and liberal writers and intellectuals. The radical journalist John Reed, in a manifesto for *The Masses* (1912), announced: "The broad purpose of *The Masses* is a social one; to everlastingly attack old systems, old morals, old prejudices—the whole weight of outworn thought that dead men have settled upon us." The journalist and biographer Hutchins Hapgood, in the *New York Globe* (January 27, 1913), made a related point: "There seems a vague but real relationship between all the real workers of our day. Whether in literature, plastic art, the labor movement...we find an instinct to blow up the old forms and traditions, to dynamite the baked and hardened earth so that fresh flowers can grow." "Those who are young to-day," wrote Walter Lippmann in *Drift and Mastery* (1914), "are born into a world in which the foundations of the older order survive only as habits or by default.... There isn't a human relation, whether of parent and child, husband and wife, worker and employer, that doesn't move in a strange situation. There are no precedents to guide us, no wisdom that wasn't made for a simpler age."

This claim was voiced repeatedly. The economist, author, and writer for *The New Republic*, Walter E. Weyl, in *The New Democracy* (1912), maintained:

> Every day new projects are launched for political, industrial, and social amelioration, and below the level of the present lies the greater project of the future. Reform is piecemeal and yet rapid. It is carried along divergent lines by people

holding separate interests, and yet it moves toward a common end. It combines into a general movement toward a new democracy.

The Baptist clergyman and educator Walter Rauschenbusch, in *Christianizing the Social Order* (1913), set the agenda for the coming years:

> Our business is to make over an antiquated and immoral social system; to get rid of laws, customs, maxims, and philosophies inherited from an evil and despotic past; to create just and brotherly relations between great groups and classes of society; and thus to lay a social foundation on which modern men individually can live and work in a fashion that will not outrage all the better elements in them. Our inherited Christian faith dealt with individuals; our present task deals with society.

Looking back from the vantage point of the mid-1930s, the critic and urban historian Lewis Mumford, in "The Metropolitan Milieu," included in a volume (1934) devoted to the photographer Alfred Stieglitz, outlined the challenges that writers and artists faced at the turn of the century, when old ideas about art and culture reigned:

> The problem for the creative mind in the 'nineties, whether he was a young writer like Stephen Crane or a young man with a passion for photography like Alfred Stieglitz, was to face this New York of boundless misdirected energy and to capture a portion of that wasteful flow for his own purposes, using its force without accepting its habitual channels and its habitual destinations. But there was still another problem: and that was to conquer, with equal resolution, the gentility, the tepid over refinement, the academic inertness and lack of passionate faith, masquerading as sound judgment, which were characteristic of the stale fugitive culture of the bourgeoisie. The genteel standards that prevailed were worse than no standards at all: dead objects, dead techniques, dead forms of worship, cast a morbid shadow on every enterprise of the mind, making mind itself a sham, causing vitality to seem somehow shameful.

In an interview (March 1913) published in *Arts and Decoration*, the painter William Glackens also focused on the impact of inhibiting social conventions on artistic work: "Our own art is arid and bloodless. It is like nothing so much as dry bones. It shows that we are afraid to be impulsive, afraid to forget restraint, afraid above everything to appear ridiculous."

But for many, such as the poet Edwin Arlington Robinson, the obstacles to art and literature posed by a powerful society, highly developed in business and technology, yet underdeveloped culturally, amounted to an exciting opportunity:

> I am just beginning to fully realize that America is the hopper [container] through which the whole civilization of the world is to be ground—consciously or otherwise. I am not much of an American, either—in a popular way; but I am glad to feel an inkling as to what the western continent was made for.

The dynamism of American society seemed at first a terrible barrier to literature and art, yet it presented to aspiring writers and artists something prodigious and energizing they were inspired to take on, describe, work with, celebrate, denounce, and overcome.

The cubist painter Max Weber, for example, born in Russia in 1881, wrote in late 1912 while living in New York: "This is a wonderful age we are living in now. Everyone has more creative liberty. The creative mind finds new ways and stops at no law laid down by, or piled upon us by lesser or non-creative minds....It is great to live now! It is harder, but what of that? The hunger we have now! The embrace!" Also in 1912, the painter John Butler Yeats exclaimed, "The fiddles are tuning as it were all over America." To the artist Marcel Duchamp, in the *New York Tribune* (September 12, 1915), the problem if anything was that Americans themselves were slow in perceiving that the future was with them, not with the English and Europeans: "If only America would realize that the art of Europe is finished—dead—and that America is the country of the art of the future." During the first decades of the century, recalled the critic Malcolm Cowley (1898–1989), "Everywhere new institutions were being founded—magazines, clubs, little theaters, art or free-love or single-tax colonies, experimental schools, picture galleries....Everywhere was a sense of comradeship and immense possibilities for change."

By the 1900s, then, the problem of little or nothing to write about that had troubled Cooper, Hawthorne, James, and others had disappeared. There was plenty to write about—maybe too much, more than any writer could encompass. The vastness of the American scene and its complexities of class, gender, race, ethnicity, and much more did not deter the nation's writers but rather fueled their ambition, inspiring, motivating, and energizing their art.

Bibliography: Robert H. Wiebe, *The Search for Order, 1877–1920* (1967); Howard Mumford Jones, *The Age of Energy: Varieties of American Experience, 1865–1915* (1971); T. J. Jackson Lears, *No Place of Grace: Antimodernism and the Transformation of American Culture, 1880–1920* (1981); Alan Trachtenberg, *The Incorporation of America: Culture and Society in the Gilded Age* (1982); Peter Conn, *The Divided Mind: Ideology and Imagination in America, 1898–1917* (1983); and Miles Orvell, *The Real Thing: Imitation and Authenticity in American Culture, 1880–1940* (1989).

For texts and contexts, see Laurence Rainey, *Modernism: An Anthology* (2005); *Gender in Modernism: New Geographies, Complex Intersections*, ed. Bonnie Kime Scott (2007); and Lawrence P. Jackson, *The Indignant Generation: A Narrative History of African American Writers and Critics, 1937–1960* (2011).

See also Rita Keresztesi, *Strangers at Home: American Ethnic Modernism Between the World Wars* (2005); Charles Altieri, *The Art of Twentieth-Century American Poetry: Modernism and After* (2006); Seth Moglen, *Mourning Modernity: Literary Modernism and the Injuries of American Capitalism* (2007); Patricia Bradley, *Making American Culture: A Social History, 1900–1920* (2009); Gordon Hutner, *What America Read: Taste, Class, and the Novel, 1920–1960* (2009); Richard Lehan, *Literary Modernism and Beyond: The Extended Vision and the Realm of the Text* (2009); Nick Salvato, *Uncloseting Drama: American Modernism and Queer Performance* (2010); and Sarah Wilson, *Melting-Pot Modernism* (2010).

Also insightful are Sara Blair, *Harlem Crossroads: Black Writers and the Photograph in the Twentieth Century* (2007); James Goodwin, *Modern American Grotesque: Literature and Photography* (2009); and Jeff Allred, *American Modernism and Depression Documentary* (2010).

EDGAR LEE MASTERS ■ (1868–1950)

Born in Garnett, Kansas, Edgar Lee Masters was raised in Lewistown in west central Illinois. He attended college for a year, studied law on his own, was admitted to the bar, and established a successful legal practice. At the same time, he wrote poetry; his first collection, *A Book of Verses*, was published in 1898.

Encouraged by a publisher he knew and stimulated by his reading of J. W. Mackail's *Selected Epigrams from the Greek Anthology* (1890), a collection of 4,000 brief poems composed between 1000 and 700 BCE, Masters transformed an idea for a novel he had been considering, a novel that would explore the lives of people in a small town, into a collection of poems. Given the title *Spoon River Anthology*, published in 1915, and published again the following year in an expanded edition, the book consists of 244 poems, monologues delivered by the dead in an Illinois graveyard. It sold briskly and soon became one of the most widely read books of poetry in American literature.

Its success, in a way, is surprising. Masters did not use rhyme or most other conventions of verse. Sometimes the writing seems like a flat, bare kind of prose. But the tone and point of view struck a chord—the honesty about sexual desire and frustration, the forthright complaint about and criticism of the values of a small town, the lack of love, and the frayed spirit of community. Though many of the poems are absorbing on their own, taken together they become even richer and more moving, a collective wistful heartache, through their interconnections and the comparisons and contrasts that Masters sets up among them. Masters understands the inner lives of his speakers, exposes their mistakes and blindnesses, yet shows compassion for their all-too-human frailties and unrealized dreams.

Many of the poems in Masters's book are stark, grim expressions of regret and disappointment. "Lucinda Matlock" takes account of these views but counters them, affirming the vital appreciation of life that makes life meaningful.

The next poem in the sequence, "Davis Matlock," is spoken by Lucinda's husband, and in its related but different form of affirmation of life, it makes a fitting (and revealing) companion piece to the poem that precedes it. Masters illuminates for us how each person thought and felt and leads us to imagine and reflect upon their relationship as a couple.

A prolific author who wrote poems, novels, plays, and biographies— some fifty books altogether—Masters never reached in these other works the level of literary distinction he achieved in *Spoon River Anthology*. But this one work as endures as an American classic.

The best point of departure is *Spoon River Anthology: An Annotated Edition*, ed. John E. Hallwas (1992). For further study, see John Theodore Flanagan, *Edgar Lee Masters: The Spoon River Poet and His Critics* (1974);

and Herbert K. Russell, *Edgar Lee Masters: A Biography* (2001). A good critical study is Ronald Primeau, *Beyond Spoon River: The Legacy of Edgar Lee Masters* (2011).

Lucinda Matlock

I went to the dances at Chandlerville,
And played snap-out[1] at Winchester.
One time we changed partners,
Driving home in the moonlight of middle June,
And then I found Davis.   5
We were married and lived together for seventy years,
Enjoying, working, raising the twelve children,
Eight of whom we lost
Ere I had reached the age of sixty.
I spun, I wove, I kept the house, I nursed the sick,   10
I made the garden, and for holiday
Rambled over the fields where sang the larks,
And by Spoon River gathering many a shell,
And many a flower and medicinal weed—
Shouting to the wooded hills, singing to the green valleys.   15
At ninety-six I had lived enough, that is all,
And passed to a sweet repose.
What is this I hear of sorrow and weariness,
Anger, discontent and drooping hopes?
Degenerate sons and daughters,   20
Life is too strong for you—
It takes life to love Life.

[1915]

Davis Matlock

Suppose it is nothing but the hive:
That there are drones and workers
And queens, and nothing but storing honey—
(Material things as well as culture and wisdom)—
For the next generation, this generation never living,   5
Except as it swarms in the sun-light of youth,
Strengthening its wings on what has been gathered,
And tasting, on the way to the hive

---

[1] An American party game, also called *snap*, played at country dances, in which one player chases another outside a circle made of the other players.

From the clover field, the delicate spoil.
Suppose all this, and suppose the truth: 10
That the nature of man is greater
Than nature's need in the hive;
And you must bear the burden of life,
As well as the urge from your spirit's excess—
Well, I say to live it out like a god   15
Sure of immortal life, though you are in doubt,
Is the way to live it.
If that doesn't make God proud of you
Then God is nothing but gravitation,
Or sleep is the golden goal.   20

[1915]

EDWIN ARLINGTON ROBINSON ■ (1869–1935)

Edwin Arlington Robinson based Tilbury Town, the setting for many of his poems, on Gardner, Maine, where his family moved the year after he was born. Unhappy as a child and teenager, Robinson studied at Harvard from 1891 to 1893, but he was forced to leave because of financial setbacks suffered by his family and because of the ill health of both his mother (his father had died in 1892) and a brother.

Robinson's work was included in *The Harvard Advocate*, a literary magazine. *The Torrent and the Night Before*, his first book of verse, appeared in 1896, published at his own expense; in a revised form, it was reissued the following year, retitled *The Children of the Night*.

Robinson took a job in the New York City subway system, having failed to establish a paying career as a writer. But he received a lucky break with the publication of *Captain Craig and Other Poems* (1902). President Theodore Roosevelt came across a copy and praised it in a magazine article, and he offered Robinson a position in the U.S. Customs House in New York City. Robinson held this job from 1905 to 1910. It required little; as one biographer noted, Robinson's tasks "consisted of opening his roll-top desk, reading the paper, closing the desk, leaving the paper in his chair to show he had been there, and going home." Robinson returned the favor by dedicating *The Town Down the River* (1910) to Roosevelt.

Determined and solitary, Robinson was not unhappy when his time at the Customs House ended. He felt that even this kind of work interfered with his poetry writing, his main interest in life and one that, through the support of friends, he was able to pursue. The winter months he spent in New York City living with friends, while during the summer months he stayed at the McDowell Colony in Peterborough, New Hampshire, where musicians, artists, and writers were in residence.

The Man Against the Sky (1916) was Robinson's first major success. The poet-critic Amy Lowell called attention to its "great power...dynamic with experience and knowledge of life," and she featured him in a section of her important book *Tendencies in Modern American Poetry* (1917). His later work includes a trilogy based on the Arthurian legends: *Merlin* (1917), *Lancelot* (1920), and *Tristram* (1927), a best-seller.

Robinson believed that human existence was full of tragedies, failures, and disappointments. As one contemporary critic observed, "Always defeat—always failure: surely the theme of human failure, with all its variations and nuances, has been treated so exhaustively by no other poet as by Robinson. One would not have believed there were so many ways to fail."

His poems usually make a direct impression, but he is subtle and sensitive, sharply aware of the complexity of emotions and relationships. As the poems here, "Richard Cory," "Miniver Cheevy," and "Eros Turannos," reveal, Robinson is a master at presenting balked, suppressed, frustrated feeling and its maddening impact on the mind and punishment of the heart.

Yet Robinson had a tough-minded admiration for the lost and lonely and defeated characters he describes, for the measure of courage they display in their sexual, emotional, and spiritual struggles. He was not an innovator; he operated within poetry's common forms and conventions. Yet he was dedicated to his craft, and in his early poems, before he embarked on the long verse narratives that seem tedious today, he offered a distinctive voice and an anguished but unflinching vision. "No poet ever understood loneliness or separateness better than Robinson," the poet James Dickey said,

> or knew the self-consuming furnace that the brain can become in isolation, the suicidal hellishness of it, doomed as it is to feed on itself in answerless frustration, fated to this condition by the accident of birth, which carries with it the hunger for certainty and the intolerable load of personal recollection.

The following older studies are helpful: Hermann Hagedorn, *Edwin Arlington Robinson: A Biography* (1938); Ellsworth Barnard, *Edwin Arlington Robinson: A Critical Study* (1952); Edwin S. Fussell, *Edwin Arlington Robinson: The Literary Background of a Traditional Poet* (1954); Wallace Ludwig Anderson, *Edwin Arlington Robinson: A Critical Introduction* (1967); and Louis Coxe, *Edwin Arlington Robinson: The Life of Poetry* (1969). See also Richard Hoffpair, *The Contemplative Poetry of Edwin Arlington Robinson, Robert Frost, and Yvor Winters* (2002); and Scott Donaldson, *Edwin Arlington Robinson: A Poet's Life* (2007).

Richard Cory

Whenever Richard Cory went down town,
We people on the pavement looked at him:
He was a gentleman from sole to crown,
Clean favored, and imperially slim.

And he was always quietly arrayed,   5
And he was always human when he talked;
But still he fluttered pulses when he said,
"Good-morning," and he glittered when he walked.

And he was rich,—yes, richer than a king,—
And admirably schooled in every grace: 10
In fine, we thought that he was everything
To make us wish that we were in his place.

So on we worked, and waited for the light,
And went without the meat, and cursed the bread;
And Richard Cory, one calm summer night,   15
Went home and put a bullet through his head.

[1896]

Miniver Cheevy

Miniver Cheevy, child of scorn,
    Grew lean while he assailed the seasons;
He wept that he was ever born,
    And he had reasons.

Miniver loved the days of old 5
    When swords were bright and steeds were prancing;
The vision of a warrior bold
    Would set him dancing.

Miniver sighed for what was not,
    And dreamed, and rested from his labors; 10
He dreamed of Thebes[1] and Camelot,[2]
    And Priam's[3] neighbors.

Miniver mourned the ripe renown
    That made so many a name so fragrant;
He mourned Romance, now on the town, 15
    And Art, a vagrant.

Miniver loved the Medici,[4]
    Albeit he had never seen one;
He would have sinned incessantly
    Could he have been one. 20

Miniver cursed the commonplace
    And eyed a khaki suit with loathing;
He missed the mediæval grace
    Of iron clothing.

Miniver scorned the gold he sought, 25
    But sore annoyed was he without it;
Miniver thought, and thought, and thought,
    And thought about it.

Miniver Cheevy, born too late,
    Scratched his head and kept on thinking; 30
Miniver coughed, and called it fate,
    And kept on drinking.

[1910]

[1] An ancient city in Boeotia, Greece, and the setting of Sophocles's tragedies about Oedipus.
[2] The legendary English court of King Arthur and his Knights of the Round Table.
[3] The king of the doomed city of Troy in Homer's epic *The Iliad*.
[4] A wealthy family of Florence, Italy, who were great patrons of the arts during the Renaissance.

Eros Turannos[1]

She fears him, and will always ask
    What fated her to choose him;
She meets in his engaging mask
    All reasons to refuse him;
But what she meets and what she fears   5
Are less than are the downward years,
Drawn slowly to the foamless weirs[2]
    Of age, were she to lose him.

Between a blurred sagacity
    That once had power to sound him,   10
And Love, that will not let him be
    The Judas[3] that she found him,
Her pride assuages her almost,
As if it were alone the cost.—
He sees that he will not be lost,   15
    And waits and looks around him.

A sense of ocean and old trees
    Envelops and allures him;
Tradition, touching all he sees,
    Beguiles and reassures him;   20
And all her doubts of what he says
Are dimmed with what she knows of days—
Till even prejudice delays
    And fades, and she secures him.

The falling leaf inaugurates   25
    The reign of her confusion;
The pounding wave reverberates
    The dirge of her illusion;
And home, where passion lived and died,
Becomes a place where she can hide,   30
While all the town and harbor side
    Vibrate with her seclusion.

We tell you, tapping on our brows,
    The story as it should be,—
As if the story of a house   35
    Were told, or ever could be;

[1]Love the king. (Greek)
[2]A low dam, or an enclosure of stakes set in a stream to trap fish.
[3]Judas Iscariot is the disciple who betrayed Christ. The name is synonymous with one who betrays under the guise of friendship.

We'll have no kindly veil between
Her visions and those we have seen,—
As if we guessed what hers have been,
Or what they are or would be.   40

Meanwhile we do no harm; for they
That with a god have striven,
Not hearing much of what we say,
Take what the god has given;
Though like waves breaking it may be,   45
Or like a changed familiar tree,
Or like a stairway to the sea
Where down the blind are driven.

[1916]

JAMES WELDON JOHNSON ■ (1871–1938)

The multitalented African American novelist, poet, journalist, critic, editor composer, civil rights leader, diplomat, and educator James Weldon Johnson was born in Jacksonville, Florida, and educated at Stanton School there. He attended Atlanta University, graduating in 1894, and then returned to Jacksonville, where he became principal of the Stanton School. The following year, Johnson launched the *Daily American*, a newspaper devoted to the African American community. It lasted only a year, but it was a significant step for Johnson as a writer and editor, and it brought him to the attention of Booker T. Washington and W. E. B. Du Bois.

Johnson then studied law; he became, in 1897, the first African American to be admitted to the Florida bar. But he quickly tired of the practice of law, and, after moving to New York City, he collaborated with his brother John Rosamond Johnson (1873–1954) on song-and-dance acts and musicals.

Johnson's major books include *The Autobiography of an Ex-Colored Man* (1912), a novel about racial "passing"; *God's Trombones* (1927), sermons by an African American preacher in verse paragraphs; *Black Manhattan* (1930), a study of New York City; and *Along This Way* (1933), his autobiography. Through his diverse array of work, Johnson prepared the way for, and contributed to, the Harlem Renaissance.

Dedicated to preserving, commemorating, and making widely available the achievements of African Americans in poetry, Johnson also was an important editor. He compiled *The Book of American Negro Poetry* (1922; rev. ed., 1931), a landmark anthology, and, with his brother, he edited two collections of American Negro Spirituals (1925, 1926).

Johnson also served as U.S. consul in Nicaragua and Venezuela, and from 1916 to 1930 he was field secretary for the National Association for the Advancement of Colored People (NAACP) and later its general secretary. In 1930, Johnson resigned from the NAACP to take a position on the faculty of Fisk University, in Nashville, Tennessee. He was killed in a car accident while vacationing in Maine; his funeral was held in Harlem, and more than 2,000 came to honor his life and achievements.

The first poem, "Lift Every Voice and Sing" is a collaboration, words and music, by the Johnson brothers, which they wrote in 1900 for the celebration of Abraham Lincoln's birthday at the Stanton School. It became popular throughout the South and eventually in the North, and two decades after its composition the NAACP adopted it as the "Negro National Hymn." Johnson was fond of hearing the song performed by the young: "The lines of this song repay me in elation, almost of exquisite anguish, whenever I hear them sung by Negro children," he said in 1935.

James Weldon Johnson, December 3, 1932. Photograph by Carl Van Vechten (1880–1964), an American writer and photographer and a patron of the Harlem Renaissance.

"O Black and Unknown Bards," from 1908, is Johnson's tribute to the composers—whose names we do not know—of African American spirituals. Quoting a number of spirituals in his poem, Johnson, though an agnostic himself, honors the significance of religion in the lives of the African American people and the extraordinary contribution to the community made by these anonymous authors.

For surveys of Johnson's life and literary and political career, see Eugene D. Levy, *James Weldon Johnson: Black Leader, Black Voice* (1973); Robert E. Fleming, *James Weldon Johnson* (1987); and *Critical Essays on James Weldon Johnson*, eds. Kenneth M. Price and Lawrence J. Oliver (1997). See also *In Search of Democracy: The NAACP Writings of James Weldon Johnson, Walter White, and Roy Wilkins*, ed. Sondra Kathryn Wilson (1999); and *The Essential Writings of James Weldon Johnson*, ed. Rudolph P. Byrd (2008). Sondra K. Wilson has edited a two-volume collection, *The Selected Writings of James Weldon Johnson* (1995), which brings together much of his newspaper and magazine work.

Lift Every [or Ev'ry] Voice and Sing

Lift every voice and sing
Till earth and heaven ring,
Ring with the harmonies of Liberty;
Let our rejoicing rise
High as the listening skies,   5
Let it resound loud as the rolling sea.
Sing a song full of the faith that the dark past has taught us,
Sing a song full of the hope that the present has brought us,
Facing the rising sun of our new day begun
Let us march on till victory is won.   10

Stony the road we trod,
Bitter the chastening rod,
Felt in the days when hope unborn had died;
Yet with a steady beat,
Have not our weary feet   15
Come to the place for which our fathers sighed?
We have come over a way that with tears has been watered,
We have come, treading our path through the blood of the slaughtered,
Out from the gloomy past,
Till now we stand at last   20
Where the white gleam of our bright star is cast.

God of our weary years,
God of our silent tears,
Thou who has brought us thus far on the way;
Thou who has by Thy might   25
Led us into the light,
Keep us forever in the path, we pray.
Lest our feet stray from the places, our God, where we met Thee,
Lest, our hearts drunk with the wine of the world, we forget Thee;
Shadowed beneath Thy hand,   30
May we forever stand.
True to our God,
True to our native land.

[1900]

O Black and Unknown Bards

O black and unknown bards of long ago,
How came your lips to touch the sacred fire?
How, in your darkness, did you come to know
The power and beauty of the minstrel's lyre?
Who first from midst his bonds lifted his eyes?   5
Who first from out the still watch, lone and long,

Feeling the ancient faith of prophets rise
Within his dark-kept soul, burst into song?

Heart of what slave poured out such melody
As "Steal away to Jesus"? On its strains   10
His spirit must have nightly floated free,
Though still about his hands he felt his chains.
Who heard great "Jordan roll"? Whose starward eye
Saw chariot "swing low"? And who was he
That breathed that comforting, melodic sigh,   15
"Nobody knows de trouble I see"?

What merely living clod, what captive thing,
Could up toward God through all its darkness grope,
And find within its deadened heart to sing
These songs of sorrow, love and faith, and hope?   20
How did it catch that subtle undertone,
That note in music heard not with the ears?
How sound the elusive reed so seldom blown,
Which stirs the soul or melts the heart to tears.

Not that great German master in his dream   25
Of harmonies that thundered amongst the stars
At the creation, every heard a theme
Nobler than "Go down, Moses." Mark its bars
How like a mighty trumpet-call they stir
The blood. Such are the notes that men have sung   30
Going to valorous deeds; such tones there were
That helped make history when Time was young.

There is a wide, wide wonder in it all,
That from degraded rest and servile toil
The fiery spirit of the seer should call   35
These simple children of the sun and soil.
O black slave singers, gone, forgot, unfamed,
You—you alone, of all the long, long line
Of those who've sung untaught, unknown, unnamed,
Have stretched out upward, seeking the divine.   40

You sang not deeds of heroes or of kings;
No chant of bloody war, no exulting pean[1]
Of arms-won triumphs; but your humble strings
You touched in chord with music empyrean.
You sting far better than you knew; the songs   45
That for your listeners' hungry hearts sufficed
Still live,—but more than this to you belongs:
You sang a race from wood and stone to Christ.

[1]Also paean, a song of joyful praise, thanksgiving, or exultation.

[1908]

PAUL LAURENCE DUNBAR ■ (1872–1906)

Though his literary career was tragically brief—he died of tuberculosis at age thirty-three—Paul Laurence Dunbar produced an impressive body of work. He was the author of short stories, novels, and, above all, poems, many of which were written in dialect but many others of which were in standard English, drawing on and extending his wide reading in English Romantic poets (Keats and Wordsworth) and in popular nineteenth-century American poets, including Henry Wadsworth Longfellow and James Whitcomb Riley.

Born in Dayton, Ohio, Dunbar was the son of former slaves from Kentucky. He grew up poor, but his mother encouraged his enjoyment of literature—poetry and songs in particular—and urged him to excel in grammar and high school. The only African American in his high school class, he compiled an excellent record, editing the school paper and serving as president of the literary society. Soon he began to give readings of his verse (he had written his first poem when he was six), and in 1893 his first book, *Oak and Ivy*, appeared.

The following year, the eminent African American writer and orator Frederick Douglass said that Dunbar was "the most promising young colored man in America." Unfortunately, as a young African American his prospects for work were so few that he was obliged to accept a menial job as an elevator operator in a Dayton hotel.

Known by some as "the elevator poet," Dunbar published a second book, *Majors and Minors* (1895), and it secured for him an even wider audience and national recognition. His first two books were then reissued under the title *Lyrics of Lowly Life* (1896), with an introduction by the important novelist and critic William Dean Howells, who praised the dialect poems highly: "These are divinations and reports of what passes in the hearts and minds of a lowly people whose poetry had hitherto been inarticulately expressed in music, but now finds, for the first time in our tongue, literary interpretation of a very artistic completeness." But he spoke less glowingly about the poems not written in dialect, and, in Dunbar's opinion, this contributed to the neglect of his more serious verse.

Sometimes Dunbar is criticized for conceding too much, especially in his dialect poems, to the racist stereotypes and attitudes of his era. But in much of his work, Dunbar is passionately critical of the conditions of life imposed on African Americans in the 1890s and 1900s, and is militant, bitter, and angry in his cries of protest. A number of his best poems are sheer expressions of pain, such as the two printed here—"Sympathy," which is keyed to the confinement and isolation of an African American speaker, and "We Wear the Mask," which gives a wounded reflection on the role-playing that African Americans were obliged to practice, pretending to experience a happiness that they did not feel. Both of these poems bear witness to the limitations on his artistic endeavors that Dunbar faced, an African American writer in a literary world that whites dominated and controlled.

For further study, begin with *The Paul Laurence Dunbar Reader: A Selection of the Best of Paul Laurence Dunbar's Poetry and Prose*, eds. Jay Martin and Gossie H. Hudson (1975); and *The Collected Poetry of Paul Laurence Dunbar*, ed. Joanne M. Braxton (1993). See also Addison Gayle, *Oak and Ivy: A Biography of Paul Laurence Dunbar* (1971); Peter Revell, *Paul Laurence Dunbar* (1979); and *We Wear the Mask: Paul Laurence Dunbar and the Politics of Representative Reality*, ed. Willie J. Harrell Jr. (2010).

Sympathy

I know what the caged bird feels, alas!
   When the sun is bright on the upland slopes;
When the wind stirs soft through the springing grass,
And the river flows like a stream of glass;
   When the first bird sings and the first bud opes,   5
And the faint perfume from its chalice steals—
I know what the caged bird feels!

I know why the caged bird beats his wing
   Till its blood is red on the cruel bars;
For he must fly back to his perch and cling   10
When he fain would be on the bough a-swing;
   And a pain still throbs in the old, old scars
And they pulse again with a keener sting—
   I know why he beats his wing!

I know why the caged bird sings, ah me,   15
   When his wing is bruised and his bosom sore,—
When he beats his bars and he would be free;
It is not a carol of joy or glee,
   But a prayer that he sends from his heart's deep core,
But a plea, that upward to Heaven he flings—   20
I know why the caged bird sings!

                    [1899]

We Wear the Mask

We wear the mask that grins and lies,
It hides our cheeks and shades our eyes,—
This debt we pay to human guile;
With torn and bleeding hearts we smile,
And mouth with myriad subtleties.   5

Why should the world be over-wise,
In counting all our tears and sighs?
Nay, let them only see us, while
   We wear the mask.

We smile, but, O great Christ, our cries   10
To thee from tortured souls arise.
We sing, but oh the clay is vile
Beneath our feet, and long the mile;
But let the world dream otherwise,
   We wear the mask!   15

[1896]

Willa Cather was born in Virginia in a farming community of the Shenandoah Valley. When she was a child her family relocated to Nebraska, a harsh and challenging environment (the land, she recalled, was "naked as the back of your hand"), still in the early stages of settlement, populated by German, French, Russian, and other immigrants. These early experiences, and her rich trove of memories about Nebraska's people and places, became the basis for many of her novels and stories.

Living in the southern section of the state, in Red Cloud (population about 2,500), Cather took part in dramatic productions, studied Latin and Greek, and, through neighbors, made her first discoveries of European literature. She was an undergraduate at the University of Nebraska, and during these years published her first stories as well as reviews and essays in local newspapers.

For ten years, beginning in 1896, Cather worked for a women's magazine and taught high school in Pittsburgh, Pennsylvania. She composed essays and reviews on art, literature, and music and worked on her own fiction. A collection of poems, *April Twilights*, appeared in 1903, followed by her first collection of stories, *The Troll Garden*, in 1905. "Paul's Case," here, Cather's only story with a Pittsburgh setting, was first published in May 1905; it later was included in her second collection of stories, *Youth and the Bright Medusa* (1920).

Cather's publisher, S. S. McClure, offered her a job as a staff writer for his magazine, *McClure's*; she moved to New York City and, by 1908, held the position of managing editor. She struggled with her writing, troubled by time-consuming editorial demands that interfered with and blocked her creativity. While on a leave of absence from *McClure's*, Cather completed the revisions of *Alexander's Bridge,* her first novel, published in 1912, and began work on the manuscript that would become *O Pioneers!*, published in 1913 and dedicated to Sarah Orne Jewett, the author of *The Country of the Pointed Firs*, whose artistry and friendship Cather highly valued. She decided to resign from *McClure's*, and in the coming years she enjoyed much success among readers and critics, producing such sharp, sensitive, and evocative novels, with richly absorbing characters and grand, mysterious landscapes, as *The Song of the Lark* (1915), *My Antonia* (1918), *The Professor's House* (1925), and *Death Comes for the Archbishop* (1927).

Recently, critics have begun to explore the possibility of gay and lesbian themes in Cather's fiction, including "Paul's Case." There is disagreement about whether or not Cather herself was a lesbian; there is no way to know for certain how much or how little sexual experience she had. But it is clear that the loves of Cather's life were women, two in particular: Isabelle McClung, the daughter of a Pittsburgh judge, whom Cather loved deeply and with whose family she lived for a number of years; and Edith

Lewis, with whom Cather shared an apartment while she worked in New York City and who became Cather's lifelong companion. With these biographical details in mind, some have proposed about "Paul's Case" that its introverted, alienated, and embittered protagonist, rebelling against the dreary commonplace and seeking escape and refuge in the arts, may be struggling with (i.e., trying to understand and articulate) the nature of his sexual identity. Others, skeptical of such an interpretation, have maintained that "Paul's Case" focuses instead on the painful predicament of an aspiring lover of art, suffering in a community hostile to his desires and dreams.

The sexual tensions, pressures, and afflictions that Cather touches on and explores in "Paul's Case" make the story all the more compelling. One recalls, in this context, her observation in 1922 that literary art achieves its power from "the inexplicable presence of the thing not named," from "whatever is felt upon the page without being specifically named there." Near the end of her life, Cather destroyed all of the personal letters in her possession, and she instructed her friends to do the same, and many did as she asked. We know Cather above all through her subtle, highly expressive art.

The range of biographical and critical commentary is suggested by the following: James Woodress, *Willa Cather: Her Life and Art* (1970); Sharon O'Brien, *Willa Cather: The Emerging Voice* (1987); Hermione Lee, *Willa Cather: Double Lives* (1989); Marilee Lindemann, *Willa Cather: Queering America* (1999); Janis P. Stout, *Willa Cather: The Writer and Her World* (2000); and Joan Acocella, *Willa Cather and the Politics of Criticism* (2000). See also Marilyn Arnold, *Willa Cather's Short Fiction* (1984). Also stimulating on the biography is David Porter, *On The Divide: The Many Lives of Willa Cather* (2008). For good surveys of recent interpretations, see *Willa Cather and the Culture of Belief: A Collection of Essays*, ed. John J. Murphy, with Linda Hunter Adams, Jesse S. Crisler (2002); and *Willa Cather: A Writer's Worlds*, eds. John J. Murphy, Françoise Palleau-Papin, and Robert Thacker (2010). The correspondence that survived is included in *The Letters of Willa Cather*, ed. Andrew Jewell and Janis Stout (2013).

Paul's Case

A Study in Temperament

It was Paul's afternoon to appear before the faculty of the Pittsburgh High School to account for his various misdemeanours. He had been suspended a week ago, and his father had called at the Principal's office and confessed his perplexity about his son. Paul entered the faculty room suave and smiling. His clothes were a trifle outgrown and the tan velvet on the collar of his open overcoat was frayed and worn; but for all that there was something of the dandy about him, and he wore an opal pin in his neatly knotted black four-in-hand,[1] and a red carnation in his button-hole. This

---

[1]A necktie tied in a loose knot with two hanging ends, popular in the late 19th and early 20th centuries.

latter adornment the faculty somehow felt was not properly significant of the contrite spirit befitting a boy under the ban of suspension.

Paul was tall for his age and very thin, with high, cramped shoulders and a narrow chest. His eyes were remarkable for a certain hysterical brilliancy and he continually used them in a conscious, theatrical sort of way, peculiarly offensive in a boy. The pupils were abnormally large, as though he were addicted to belladonna,[2] but there was a glassy glitter about them which that drug does not produce.

When questioned by the Principal as to why he was there, Paul stated, politely enough, that he wanted to come back to school. This was a lie, but Paul was quite accustomed to lying; found it, indeed, indispensable for overcoming friction. His teachers were asked to state their respective charges against him, which they did with such a rancour and aggrievedness as evinced that this was not a usual case. Disorder and impertinence were among the offences named, yet each of his instructors felt that it was scarcely possible to put into words the real cause of the trouble, which lay in a sort of hysterically defiant manner of the boy's; in the contempt which they all knew he felt for them, and which he seemingly made not the least effort to conceal. Once, when he had been making a synopsis of a paragraph at the blackboard, his English teacher had stepped to his side and attempted to guide his hand. Paul had started back with a shudder and thrust his hands violently behind him. The astonished woman could scarcely have been more hurt and embarrassed had he struck at her. The insult was so involuntary and definitely personal as to be unforgettable. In one way and another, he had made all his teachers, men and women alike, conscious of the same feeling of physical aversion. In one class he habitually sat with his hand shading his eyes; in another he always looked out of the window during the recitation; in another he made a running commentary on the lecture, with humorous intention.

His teachers felt this afternoon that his whole attitude was symbolized by his shrug and his flippantly red carnation flower, and they fell upon him without mercy, his English teacher leading the pack. He stood through it smiling, his pale lips parted over his white teeth. (His lips were continually twitching, and he had a habit of raising his eyebrows that was contemptuous and irritating to the last degree.) Older boys than Paul had broken down and shed tears under that baptism of fire, but his set smile did not once desert him, and his only sign of discomfort was the nervous trembling of the fingers that toyed with the buttons of his overcoat, and an occasional jerking of the other hand that held his hat. Paul was always smiling, always glancing about him, seeming to feel that people might be watching him and trying to detect something. This conscious expression,

---

[2]Also called *deadly nightshade*, the extract from belladonna is used medicinally to dilate the pupil of the eye or to relieve muscle spasms.

since it was as far as possible from boyish mirthfulness, was usually attributed to insolence or "smartness."

As the inquisition proceeded, one of his instructors repeated an im-
pertinent remark of the boy's, and the Principal asked him whether he
thought that a courteous speech to have made a woman. Paul shrugged his
shoulders slightly and his eyebrows twitched.

"I don't know," he replied. "I didn't mean to be polite or impolite, either. I guess it's a sort of way I have of saying things regardless."

The Principal, who was a sympathetic man, asked him whether he
didn't think that a way it would be well to get rid of. Paul grinned and said
he guessed so. When he was told that he could go, he bowed gracefully and
went out. His bow was but a repetition of the scandalous red carnation.

His teachers were in despair, and his drawing master voiced the feeling
of them all when he declared there was something about the boy which
none of them understood. He added: "I don't really believe that smile of
his comes altogether from insolence; there's something sort of haunted
about it. The boy is not strong, for one thing. I happen to know that he
was born in Colorado, only a few months before his mother died out there
of a long illness. There is something wrong about the fellow."

The drawing master had come to realize that, in looking at Paul, one
saw only his white teeth and the forced animation of his eyes. One warm afternoon the boy had gone to sleep at his drawing-board, and his master had
noted with amazement what a white, blue-veined face it was; drawn and
wrinkled like an old man's about the eyes, the lips twitching even in his
sleep, and stiff with a nervous tension that drew them back from his teeth.

His teachers left the building dissatisfied and unhappy; humiliated to
have felt so vindictive toward a mere boy, to have uttered this feeling in
cutting terms, and to have set each other on, as it were, in the gruesome
game of intemperate reproach. Some of them remembered having seen a
miserable street cat set at bay by a ring of tormentors.

As for Paul, he ran down the hill whistling the Soldiers' Chorus from
Faust[3] looking wildly behind him now and then to see whether some of his
teachers were not there to writhe under his light-heartedness. As it was
now late in the afternoon and Paul was on duty that evening as usher at
Carnegie Hall,[4] he decided that he would not go home to supper. When he
reached the concert hall the doors were not yet open and, as it was chilly
outside, he decided to go up into the picture gallery—always deserted at
this hour—where there were some of Rafelli's[5] gay studies of Paris streets

[3]An opera by the French composer Charles Gounod (1818–93) based on the legend of Johann Faust, a
medieval German astrologer and necromancer reputed to have sold his soul to the devil. In Gounod's
opera, Faust makes his damning bargain in exchange for youth and beauty in order to beguile the
maiden Marguerite, whose brother, Valentin, is away at war. Faust seduces and abandons her. The
"Soldier's Chorus, 'Gloire immortelle,'" featured in Act III, heralds Valentin's return. Valentin later dies
in a duel with Faust.
[4]The Carnegie Music Hall in Pittsburgh.
[5]Jean-François Raffaëlli (1850–1924), French painter.

and an airy blue Venetian scene or two that always exhilarated him. He was delighted to find no one in the gallery but the old guard, who sat in one corner, a newspaper on his knee, a black patch over one eye and the other closed. Paul possessed himself of the place and walked confidently up and down, whistling under his breath. After a while he sat down before a blue Rico[6] and lost himself. When he bethought him to look at his watch, it was after seven o'clock, and he rose with a start and ran downstairs, making a face at Augustus,[7] peering out from the cast-room, and an evil gesture at the Venus of Milo[8] as he passed her on the stairway.

When Paul reached the ushers' dressing-room half-a-dozen boys were there already, and he began excitedly to tumble into his uniform. It was one of the few that at all approached fitting, and Paul thought it very becoming—though he knew that the tight, straight coat accentuated his narrow chest, about which he was exceedingly sensitive. He was always considerably excited while he dressed, twanging all over to the tuning of the strings and the preliminary flourishes of the horns in the music-room; but to-night he seemed quite beside himself, and he teased and plagued the boys until, telling him that he was crazy, they put him down on the floor and sat on him.

Somewhat calmed by his suppression, Paul dashed out to the front of the house to seat the early comers. He was a model usher; gracious and smiling he ran up and down the aisles; nothing was too much trouble for him; he carried messages and brought programmes as though it were his greatest pleasure in life, and all the people in his section thought him a charming boy, feeling that he remembered and admired them. As the house filled, he grew more and more vivacious and animated, and the colour came to his cheeks and lips. It was very much as though this were a great reception and Paul were the host. Just as the musicians came out to take their places, his English teacher arrived with checks for the seats which a prominent manufacturer had taken for the season. She betrayed some embarrassment when she handed Paul the tickets, and a *hauteur*[9] which subsequently made her feel very foolish. Paul was startled for a moment, and had the feeling of wanting to put her out; what business had she here among all these fine people and gay colours? He looked her over and decided that she was not appropriately dressed and must be a fool to sit downstairs in such togs. The tickets had probably been sent her out of kindness, he reflected as he put down a seat for her, and she had about as much right to sit there as he had.

When the symphony began Paul sank into one of the rear seats with a long sigh of relief, and lost himself as he had done before the Rico. It

[6]Refers to a painting by the Spanish artist Martin Rico y Ortega (1833–1908).
[7]A copy of the statue of Augustus Caesar, located at the royal villa at Prima Porta.
[8]A copy of the famous armless torso of Venus, the goddess of beauty, now located at the Louvre in Paris.
[9]Arrogance (French).

was not that symphonies, as such, meant anything in particular to Paul, but the first sigh of the instruments seemed to free some hilarious and potent spirit within him; something that struggled there like the Genius in the bottle found by the Arab fisherman. He felt a sudden zest of life; the lights danced before his eyes and the concert hall blazed into unimaginable splendour. When the soprano soloist came on, Paul forgot even the nastiness of his teacher's being there and gave himself up to the peculiar stimulus such personages always had for him. The soloist chanced to be a German woman, by no means in her first youth, and the mother of many children; but she wore an elaborate gown and a tiara, and above all she had that indefinable air of achievement, that world-shine upon her, which, in Paul's eyes, made her a veritable queen of Romance.

After a concert was over Paul was always irritable and wretched until he got to sleep, and to-night he was even more than usually restless. He had the feeling of not being able to let down, of its being impossible to give up this delicious excitement which was the only thing that could be called living at all. During the last number he withdrew and, after hastily changing his clothes in the dressing-room, slipped out to the side door where the soprano's carriage stood. Here he began pacing rapidly up and down the walk, waiting to see her come out.

Over yonder the Schenley, in its vacant stretch, loomed big and square through the fine rain, the windows of its twelve stories glowing like those of a lighted card-board house under a Christmas tree. All the actors and singers of the better class stayed there when they were in the city, and a number of the big manufacturers of the place lived there in the winter. Paul had often hung about the hotel, watching the people go in and out, longing to enter and leave school-masters and dull care behind him forever.

At last the singer came out, accompanied by the conductor, who helped her into her carriage and closed the door with a cordial *auf wiedersehen*[10] which set Paul to wondering whether she were not an old sweetheart of his. Paul followed the carriage over to the hotel, walking so rapidly as not to be far from the entrance when the singer alighted and disappeared behind the swinging glass doors that were opened by a negro in a tall hat and a long coat. In the moment that the door was ajar, it seemed to Paul that he, too, entered. He seemed to feel himself go after her up the steps, into the warm, lighted building, into an exotic, a tropical world of shiny, glistening surfaces and basking ease. He reflected upon the mysterious dishes that were brought into the dining-room, the green bottles in buckets of ice, as he had seen them in the supper party pictures of the *Sunday World* supplement. A quick gust of wind brought the rain down with sudden vehemence, and Paul was startled to find that he was still outside in

[10]Farewell (German).

the slush of the gravel driveway; that his boots were letting in the water and his scanty overcoat was clinging wet about him; that the lights in front of the concert hall were out, and that the rain was driving in sheets between him and the orange glow of the windows above him. There it was, what he wanted—tangibly before him, like the fairy world of a Christmas pantomime, but mocking spirits stood guard at the doors, and, as the rain beat in his face, Paul wondered whether he were destined always to shiver in the black night outside, looking up at it.

He turned and walked reluctantly toward the car tracks. The end had to come sometime; his father in his night-clothes at the top of the stairs, explanations that did not explain, hastily improvised fictions that were forever tripping him up, his upstairs room and its horrible yellow wall-paper, the creaking bureau with the greasy plush collar-box, and over his painted wooden bed the pictures of George Washington and John Calvin,[11] and the framed motto, "Feed my Lambs," which had been worked in red worsted by his mother.

Half an hour later, Paul alighted from his car and went slowly down one of the side streets off the main thoroughfare. It was a highly respect-able street, where all the houses were exactly alike, and where business men of moderate means begot and reared large families of children, all of whom went to Sabbath-school and learned the shorter catechism, and were interested in arithmetic; all of whom were as exactly alike as their homes, and of a piece with the monotony in which they lived. Paul never went up Cordelia Street without a shudder of loathing. His home was next the house of the Cumberland minister. He approached it to-night with the nerveless sense of defeat, the hopeless feeling of sinking back forever into ugliness and commonness that he had always had when he came home. The moment he turned into Cordelia Street he felt the waters close above his head. After each of these orgies of living, he experienced all the phys-ical depression which follows a debauch; the loathing of respectable beds, of common food, of a house penetrated by kitchen odours; a shuddering repulsion for the flavourless, colourless mass of every-day existence; a morbid desire for cool things and soft lights and fresh flowers.

The nearer he approached the house, the more absolutely unequal Paul felt to the sight of it all; his ugly sleeping chamber; the cold bath-room with the grimy zinc tub, the cracked mirror, the dripping spiggots; his father, at the top of the stairs, his hairy legs sticking out from his night-shirt, his feet thrust into carpet slippers. He was so much later than usual that there would certainly be inquiries and reproaches. Paul stopped short before the door. He felt that he could not be accosted by his father to-night; that he could not toss again on that miserable bed. He would not go

---

[11]French theologian and a key leader of the sixteenth-century Protestant Reformation. He preached a popular, systematic presentation of Christian doctrine, arguing that salvation comes from God's grace and that faith is a divine gift resulting from God's unconditional decree of election.

in. He would tell his father that he had no car fare, and it was raining so hard he had gone home with one of the boys and stayed all night.

Meanwhile, he was wet and cold. He went around to the back of the house and tried one of the basement windows, found it open, raised it cautiously, and scrambled down the cellar wall to the floor. There he stood, holding his breath, terrified by the noise he had made, but the floor above him was silent, and there was no creak on the stairs. He found a soap-box, and carried it over to the soft ring of light that streamed from the furnace door, and sat down. He was horribly afraid of rats, so he did not try to sleep, but sat looking distrustfully at the dark, still terrified least he might have awakened his father. In such reactions, after one of the experiences which made days and nights out of the dreary blanks of the calendar, when his senses were deadened, Paul's head was always singularly clear. Suppose his father had heard him getting in at the window and had come down and shot him for a burglar? Then, again, suppose his father had come down, pistol in hand, and he had cried out in time to save himself, and his father had been horrified to think how nearly he had killed him? Then, again, suppose a day should come when his father would remember that night, and wish there had been no warning cry to stay his hand? With this last supposition Paul entertained himself until daybreak.

The following Sunday was fine; the sodden November chill was broken by the last flash of autumnal summer. In the morning Paul had to go to church and Sabbath-school, as always. On seasonable Sunday afternoons the burghers of Cordelia Street always sat out on their front "stoops," and talked to their neighbours on the next stoop, or called to those across the street in neighbourly fashion. The men usually sat on gay cushions placed upon the steps that led down to the sidewalk, while the women, in their Sunday "waists," sat in rockers on the cramped porches, pretending to be greatly at their ease. The children played in the streets; there were so many of them that the place resembled the recreation grounds of a kindergarten. The men on the steps—all in their shirt sleeves, their vests unbuttoned—sat with their legs well apart, their stomachs comfortably protruding, and talked of the prices of things, or told anecdotes of the sagacity of their various chiefs and overlords. They occasionally looked over the multitude of squabbling children, listened affectionately to their high-pitched, nasal voices, smiling to see their own proclivities reproduced in their offspring, and interspersed their legends of the iron kings with remarks about their sons' progress at school, their grades in arithmetic, and the amounts they had saved in their toy banks.

On this last Sunday of November, Paul sat all the afternoon on the lowest step of his "stoop," staring into the street, while his sisters, in their rockers, were talking to the minister's daughters next door about how many shirt-waists they had made in the last week, and how many waffles some one had eaten at the last church supper. When the weather was warm, and

his father was in a particularly jovial frame of mind, the girls made lemonade, which was always brought out in a red-glass pitcher, ornamented with
forget-me-nots in blue enamel. This the girls thought very fine, and the
neighbours always joked about the suspicious colour of the pitcher.

To-day Paul's father sat on the top step, talking to a young man who
shifted a restless baby from knee to knee. He happened to be the young
man who was daily held up to Paul as a model, and after whom it was his
father's dearest hope that he would pattern. This young man was of a
ruddy complexion, with a compressed, red mouth, and faded, near-sighted
eyes, over which he wore thick spectacles, with gold bows that curved
about his ears. He was clerk to one of the magnates of a great steel corporation, and was looked upon in Cordelia Street as a young man with a
future. There was a story that, some five years ago—he was now barely
twenty-six—he had been a trifle dissipated, but in order to curb his ap-
petites and save the loss of time and strength that a sowing of wild oats
might have entailed, he had taken his chief's advice, oft reiterated to his
employees, and at twenty-one had married the first woman whom he could
persuade to share his fortunes. She happened to be an angular school-
mistress, much older than he, who also wore thick glasses, and who had
now borne him four children, all near-sighted, like herself.

The young man was relating how his chief, now cruising in the
Mediterranean, kept in touch with all the details of the business, arranging his office hours on his yacht just as though he were at home, and
"knocking off work enough to keep two stenographers busy." His father
told, in turn, the plan his corporation was considering, of putting in an
electric railway plant at Cairo. Paul snapped his teeth; he had an awful
apprehension that they might spoil it all before he got there. Yet he rather
liked to hear these legends of the iron kings, that were told and retold on
Sundays and holidays; these stories of palaces in Venice, yachts on the
Mediterranean, and high play at Monte Carlo appealed to his fancy, and he
was interested in the triumphs of these cash boys who had become famous,
though he had no mind for the cash-boy stage.

After supper was over, and he had helped to dry the dishes, Paul nervously asked his father whether he could go to George's to get some help
in his geometry, and still more nervously asked for car fare. This latter request he had to repeat, as his father, on principle, did not like to hear requests for money, whether much or little. He asked Paul whether he could
not go to some boy who lived nearer, and told him that he ought not to
leave his school work until Sunday; but he gave him the dime. He was not
a poor man, but he had a worthy ambition to come up in the world. His
only reason for allowing Paul to usher was, that he thought a boy ought to
be earning a little.

Paul bounded upstairs, scrubbed the greasy odour of the dish-water
from his hands with the ill-smelling soap he hated, and then shook over

his fingers a few drops of violet water from the bottle he kept hidden in his drawer. He left the house with his geometry conspicuously under his arm, and the moment he got out of Cordelia Street and boarded a downtown car, he shook off the lethargy of two deadening days, and began to live again.

The leading juvenile of the permanent stock company which played at one of the downtown theatres was an acquaintance of Paul's, and the boy had been invited to drop in at the Sunday-night rehearsals whenever he could. For more than a year Paul had spent every available moment loitering about Charley Edwards's dressing-room. He had won a place among Edwards's following not only because the young actor, who could not afford to employ a dresser, often found him useful, but because he recognized in Paul something akin to what churchmen term "vocation."

It was at the theatre and at Carnegie Hall that Paul really lived; the rest was but a sleep and a forgetting. This was Paul's fairy tale, and it had for him all the allurement of a secret love. The moment he inhaled the gassy, painty, dusty odour behind the scenes, he breathed like a prisoner set free, and felt within him the possibility of doing or saying splendid, brilliant, poetic things. The moment the cracked orchestra beat out the overture from Martha,[12] or jerked at the serenade from Rigoletto,[13] all stupid and ugly things slid from him, and his senses were deliciously, yet delicately fired.

Perhaps it was because, in Paul's world, the natural nearly always wore the guise of ugliness, that a certain element of artificiality seemed to him necessary in beauty. Perhaps it was because his experience of life elsewhere was so full of Sabbath-school picnics, petty economics, wholesome advice as to how to succeed in life, and the unescapable odours of cooking, that he found this existence so alluring, these smartly-clad men and women so attractive, that he was so moved by these starry apple orchards that bloomed perennially under the lime-light.

It would be difficult to put it strongly enough how convincingly the stage entrance of that theatre was for Paul the actual portal of Romance. Certainly none of the company ever suspected it, least of all Charley Edwards. It was very like the old stories that used to float about London of fabulously rich Jews, who had subterranean halls there, with palms, and fountains, and soft lamps and richly apparelled women who never saw the disenchanting light of London day. So, in the midst of that smoke-palled city, enamoured of figures and grimy toil, Paul had his secret temple, his wishing carpet, his bit of blue-and-white Mediterranean shore bathed in perpetual sunshine.

Several of Paul's teachers had a theory that his imagination had been perverted by garish fiction, but the truth was that he scarcely ever read

---

[12]Opera by Friedrich von Flotow (1812–83).
[13]Opera by Giuseppe Verdi (1813–1901).

at all. The books at home were not such as would either tempt or corrupt a youthful mind, and as for reading the novels that some of his friends urged upon him—well, he got what he wanted much more quickly from music; any sort of music, from an orchestra to a barrel organ. He needed only the spark, the indescribable thrill that made his imagination master of his senses, and he could make plots and pictures enough of his own. It was equally true that he was not stage struck—not, at any rate, in the usual acceptation of that expression. He had no desire to become an actor, any more than he had to become a musician. He felt no necessity to do any of these things; what he wanted was to see, to be in the atmosphere, float on the wave of it, to be carried out, blue league after blue league, away from everything.

After a night behind the scenes, Paul found the school-room more than ever repulsive; the bare floors and naked walls; the prosy men who never wore frock coats, or violets in their button-holes; the women with their dull gowns, shrill voices, and pitiful seriousness about prepositions that govern the dative. He could not bear to have the other pupils think, for a moment, that he took these people seriously; he must convey to them that he considered it all trivial, and was there only by way of a jest, anyway. He had autograph pictures of all the members of the stock company which he showed his classmates, telling them the most incredible stories of his familiarity with these people, of his acquaintance with the soloists who came to Carnegie Hall, his suppers with them and the flowers he sent them. When these stories lost their effect, and his audience grew listless, he became desperate and would bid all the boys good-bye, announcing that he was going to travel for awhile; going to Naples, to Venice, to Egypt. Then, next Monday, he would slip back, conscious and nervously smiling; his sister was ill, and he should have to defer his voyage until spring.

Matters went steadily worse with Paul at school. In the itch to let his instructors know how heartily he despised them and their homilies, and how thoroughly he was appreciated elsewhere, he mentioned once or twice that he had no time to fool with theorems; adding—with a twitch of the eyebrows and a touch of that nervous bravado which so perplexed them— that he was helping the people down at the stock company; they were old friends of his.

The upshot of the matter was, that the Principal went to Paul's father, and Paul was taken out of school and put to work. The manager at Carnegie Hall was told to get another usher in his stead; the doorkeeper at the theatre was warned not to admit him to the house; and Charley Edwards remorsefully promised the boy's father not to see him again.

The members of the stock company were vastly amused when some of Paul's stories reached them—especially the women. They were hard-working women, most of them supporting indigent husbands or brothers, and they laughed rather bitterly at having stirred the boy to such fervid and florid inventions. They agreed with the faculty and with his father that Paul's was a bad case.

The east-bound train was ploughing through a January snow-storm; the dull dawn was beginning to show grey when the engine whistled a mile out of Newark. Paul started up from the seat where he had lain curled in uneasy slumber, rubbed the breath-misted window glass with his hand, and peered out. The snow was whirling in curling eddies above the white bottom lands, and the drifts lay already deep in the fields and along the fences, while here and there the long dead grass and dried weed stalks protruded black above it. Lights shone from the scattered houses, and a gang of labourers who stood beside the track waved their lanterns.

Paul had slept very little, and he felt grimy and uncomfortable. He had made the all-night journey in a day coach, partly because he was ashamed, dressed as he was, to go into a Pullman, and partly because he was afraid of being seen there by some Pittsburgh business man, who might have noticed him in Denny & Carson's office. When the whistle awoke him, he clutched quickly at his breast pocket, glancing about him with an uncertain smile. But the little, clay-bespattered Italians were still sleeping, the slatternly women across the aisle were in open-mouthed oblivion, and even the crumby, crying babies were for the nonce stilled. Paul settled back to struggle with his impatience as best he could.

When he arrived at the Jersey City station, he hurried through his breakfast, manifestly ill at ease and keeping a sharp eye about him. After he reached the Twenty-third Street station, he consulted a cabman, and had himself driven to a men's furnishing establishment that was just opening for the day. He spent upward of two hours there, buying with endless reconsidering and great care. His new street suit he put on in the fitting-room; the frock coat and dress clothes he had bundled into the cab with his linen. Then he drove to a hatter's and a shoe house. His next errand was at Tiffany's, where he selected his silver and a new scarfpin. He would not wait to have his silver marked, he said. Lastly, he stopped at a trunk shop on Broadway, and had his purchases packed into various travelling bags.

It was a little after one o'clock when he drove up to the Waldorf, and after settling with the cabman, went into the office. He registered from Washington; said his mother and father had been abroad, and that he had come down to await the arrival of their steamer. He told his story plausibly and had no trouble, since he volunteered to pay for them in advance, in engaging his rooms; a sleeping-room, sitting-room and bath.

Not once, but a hundred times Paul had planned this entry into New York. He had gone over every detail of it with Charley Edwards, and in his scrap book at home there were pages of description about New York hotels, cut from the Sunday papers. When he was shown to his sitting-room on the eighth floor, he saw at a glance that everything was as it should be;

there was but one detail in his mental picture that the place did not realize, so he rang for the bell boy and sent him down for flowers. He moved
about nervously until the boy returned, putting away his new linen and
fingering it delightedly as he did so. When the flowers came, he put them
hastily into water, and then tumbled into a hot bath. Presently he came
out of his white bath-room, resplendent in his new silk underwear, and
playing with the tassels of his red robe. The snow was whirling so fiercely
outside his windows that he could scarcely see across the street, but within
the air was deliciously soft and fragrant. He put the violets and jonquils
on the taboret[14] beside the couch, and threw himself down, with a long
sigh, covering himself with a Roman blanket. He was thoroughly tired; he
had been in such haste, he had stood up to such a strain, covered so much
ground in the last twenty-four hours, that he wanted to think how it had
all come about. Lulled by the sound of the wind, the warm air, and the
cool fragrance of the flowers, he sank into deep, drowsy retrospection.

It had been wonderfully simple; when they had shut him out of the
theatre and concert hall, when they had taken away his bone, the whole
thing was virtually determined. The rest was a mere matter of opportunity.
The only thing that at all surprised him was his own courage—for he realized well enough that he had always been tormented by fear, a sort of
apprehensive dread that, of late years, as the meshes of the lies he had
told closed about him, had been pulling the muscles of his body tighter
and tighter. Until now, he could not remember the time when he had not
been dreading something. Even when he was a little boy, it was always
there—behind him, or before, or on either side. There had always been the
shadowed corner, the dark place into which he dared not look, but from
which something seemed always to be watching him—and Paul had done
things that were not pretty to watch, he knew.

But now he had a curious sense of relief, as though he had at last
thrown down the gauntlet to the thing in the corner.

Yet it was but a day since he had been sulking in the traces;[15] but yesterday afternoon that he had been sent to the bank with Denny & Carson's
deposit, as usual—but this time he was instructed to leave the book to be
balanced. There was above two thousand dollars in checks, and nearly a
thousand in the bank notes which he had taken from the book and quietly
transferred to his pocket. At the bank he had made out a new deposit slip.
His nerves had been steady enough to permit of his returning to the office, where he had finished his work and asked for a full day's holiday tomorrow, Saturday, giving a perfectly reasonable pretext. The bank book,
he knew, would not be returned before Monday or Tuesday, and his father
would be out of town for the next week. From the time he slipped the
bank notes into his pocket until he boarded the night train for New York,

[14]A small table, often used as a stand for houseplants or flowers.
[15]That is, back at work; traces are the straps connecting an animal to the load being pulled.

he had not known a moment's hesitation. It was not the first time Paul had steered through treacherous waters.

How astonishingly easy it had all been; here he was, the thing done; and this time there would be no awakening, no figure at the top of the stairs. He watched the snow flakes whirling by his window until he fell asleep.

When he awoke, it was three o'clock in the afternoon. He bounded up with a start; half of one of his precious days gone already! He spent more than an hour in dressing, watching every stage of his toilet carefully in the mirror. Everything was quite perfect; he was exactly the kind of boy he had always wanted to be.

When he went downstairs, Paul took a carriage and drove up Fifth Avenue toward the Park. The snow had somewhat abated; carriages and tradesmen's wagons were hurrying soundlessly to and fro in the winter twilight; boys in woollen mufflers were shovelling off the doorsteps; the avenue stages made fine spots of colour against the white street. Here and there on the corners were stands, with whole flower gardens blooming under glass cases, against the sides of which the snow flakes stuck and melted; violets, roses, carnations, lilies of the valley—somehow vastly more lovely and alluring that they blossomed thus unnaturally in the snow. The Park itself was a wonderful stage winter-piece.

When he returned, the pause of the twilight had ceased, and the tune of the streets had changed. The snow was falling faster, lights streamed from the hotels that reared their dozen stories fearlessly up into the storm, defying the raging Atlantic winds. A long, black stream of carriages poured down the avenue, intersected here and there by other streams, tending horizontally. There were a score of cabs about the entrance of his hotel, and his driver had to wait. Boys in livery were running in and out of the awning stretched across the sidewalk, up and down the red velvet carpet laid from the door to the street. Above, about, within it all was the rumble and roar, the hurry and toss of thousands of human beings as hot for pleasure as himself, and on every side of him towered the glaring affirmation of the omnipotence of wealth.

The boy set his teeth and drew his shoulders together in a spasm of realization; the plot of all dramas, the text of all romances, the nerve-stuff of all sensations was whirling about him like the snow flakes. He burnt like a faggot[16] in a tempest.

When Paul went down to dinner, the music of the orchestra came floating up the elevator shaft to greet him. His head whirled as he stepped into the thronged corridor, and he sank back into one of the chairs against the wall to get his breath. The lights, the chatter, the perfumes, the bewildering medley of colour—he had, for a moment, the feeling of not being able

---

[16]A bundle of sticks or twigs used for fuel.

to stand it. But only for a moment; these were his own people, he told himself. He went slowly about the corridors, through the writing-rooms, smoking-rooms, reception-rooms, as though he were exploring the chambers of an enchanted palace, built and peopled for him alone.

When he reached the dining-room he sat down at a table near a window. The flowers, the white linen, the many-coloured wine glasses, the gay toilettes of the women, the low popping of corks, the undulating repetitions of the *Blue Danube*[17] from the orchestra, all flooded Paul's dream with bewildering radiance. When the roseate tinge of his champagne was added—that cold, precious, bubbling stuff that creamed and foamed in his glass—Paul wondered that there were honest men in the world at all. This was what all the world was fighting for, he reflected; this was what all the struggle was about. He doubted the reality of his past. Had he ever known a place called Cordelia Street, a place where fagged-looking business men got on the early car; mere rivets in a machine they seemed to Paul,—sickening men, with combings of children's hair always hanging to their coats, and the smell of cooking in their clothes. Cordelia Street—Ah! that belonged to another time and country; had he not always been thus, had he not sat here night after night, from as far back as he could remember, looking pensively over just such shimmering textures, and slowly twirling the stem of a glass like this one between his thumb and middle finger? He rather thought he had.

He was not in the least abashed or lonely. He had no especial desire to meet or to know any of these people; all he demanded was the right to look on and conjecture, to watch the pageant. The mere stage properties were all he contended for. Nor was he lonely later in the evening, in his lodge at the Metropolitan. He was now entirely rid of his nervous misgivings, of his forced aggressiveness, of the imperative desire to show himself different from his surroundings. He felt now that his surroundings explained him. Nobody questioned the purple; he had only to wear it passively. He had only to glance down at his attire to reassure himself that here it would be impossible for any one to humiliate him.

He found it hard to leave his beautiful sitting-room to go to bed that night, and sat long watching the raging storm from his turret window. When he went to sleep it was with the lights turned on in his bedroom; partly because of his old timidity, and partly so that, if he should wake in the night, there would be no wretched moment of doubt, no horrible suspicion of yellow wall-paper, or of Washington and Calvin above his bed.

Sunday morning the city was practically snow-bound. Paul breakfasted late, and in the afternoon he fell in with a wild San Francisco boy, a freshman at Yale, who said he had run down for a "little flyer" over Sunday. The young man offered to show Paul the night side of the town, and the two boys went out together after dinner, not returning to the hotel until seven o'clock the next morning. They had started out in the confiding warmth

[17]English title of a waltz by the Austrian composer Johann Strauss II, composed in 1866.

of a champagne friendship, but their parting in the elevator was singularly cool. The freshman pulled himself together to make his train, and Paul went to bed. He awoke at two o'clock in the afternoon, very thirsty and dizzy, and rang for ice-water, coffee, and the Pittsburgh papers.

On the part of the hotel management, Paul excited no suspicion. There was this to be said for him, that he wore his spoils with dignity and in no way made himself conspicuous. Even under the glow of his wine he was never boisterous, though he found the stuff like a magician's wand for wonder-building. His chief greediness lay in his ears and eyes, and his excesses were not offensive ones. His dearest pleasures were the grey winter twilights in his sitting-room; his quiet enjoyment of his flowers, his clothes, his wide divan, his cigarette and his sense of power. He could not remember a time when he had felt so at peace with himself. The mere release from the necessity of petty lying, lying every day and every day, restored his self-respect. He had never lied for pleasure, even at school; but to be noticed and admired, to assert his difference from other Cordelia Street boys; and he felt a good deal more manly, more honest, even, now that he had no need for boastful pretensions, now that he could, as his actor friends used to say, "dress the part." It was characteristic that remorse did not occur to him. His golden days went by without a shadow, and he made each as perfect as he could.

On the eighth day after his arrival in New York, he found the whole affair exploited in the Pittsburgh papers, exploited with a wealth of detail which indicated that local news of a sensational nature was at a low ebb. The firm of Denny & Carson announced that the boy's father had refunded the full amount of the theft, and that they had no intention of prosecuting. The Cumberland minister had been interviewed, and expressed his hope of yet reclaiming the motherless lad, and his Sabbath-school teacher declared that she would spare no effort to that end. The rumor had reached Pittsburgh that the boy had been seen in a New York hotel, and his father had gone East to find him and bring him home.

Paul had just come in to dress for dinner; he sank into a chair, weak to the knees, and clasped his head in his hands. It was to be worse than jail, even; the tepid waters of Cordelia Street were to close over him finally and forever. The grey monotony stretched before him in hopeless, unrelieved years; Sabbath-school, Young People's Meeting, the yellow-papered room, the damp dish-towels; it all rushed back upon him with a sickening vividness. He had the old feeling that the orchestra had suddenly stopped, the sinking sensation that the play was over. The sweat broke out on his face, and he sprang to his feet, looked about him with his white, conscious smile, and winked at himself in the mirror. With something of the old childish belief in miracles with which he had so often gone to class, all his lessons unlearned, Paul dressed and dashed whistling down the corridor to the elevator.

He had no sooner entered the dining-room and caught the measure of the music than his remembrance was lightened by his old elastic power of claiming the moment, mounting with it, and finding it all sufficient. The glare and glitter about him, the mere scenic accessories had again, and for the last time, their old potency. He would show himself that he was game, he would finish the thing splendidly. He doubted, more than ever, the existence of Cordelia Street, and for the first time he drank his wine recklessly. Was he not, after all, one of those fortunate beings born to the purple, was he not still himself and in his own place? He drummed a nervous accompaniment to the Pagliacci[18] music and looked about him, telling himself over and over that it had paid.

He reflected drowsily, to the swell of the music and the chill sweetness of his wine, that he might have done it more wisely. He might have caught an outbound steamer and been well out of their clutches before now. But the other side of the world had seemed too far away and too uncertain then; he could not have waited for it, his need had been too sharp. If he had to choose over again, he would do the same thing to-morrow. He looked affectionately about the dining-room, now gilded with a soft mist. Ah, it had paid indeed!

Paul was awakened next morning by a painful throbbing in his head and feet. He had thrown himself across the bed without undressing, and had slept with his shoes on. His limbs and hands were lead heavy, and his tongue and throat were parched and burnt. There came upon him one of those fateful attacks of clear-headedness that never occurred except when he was physically exhausted and his nerves hung loose. He lay still and closed his eyes and let the tide of things wash over him.

His father was in New York; "stopping at some joint or other," he told himself. The memory of successive summers on the front stoop fell upon him like a weight of black water. He had not a hundred dollars left; and he knew now, more than ever, that money was everything, the wall that stood between all he loathed and all he wanted. The thing was winding itself up; he had thought of that on his first glorious day in New York, and had even provided a way to snap the thread. It lay on his dressing-table now; he had got it out last night when he came blindly up from dinner, but the shiny metal hurt his eyes, and he disliked the looks of it.

He rose and moved about with a painful effort, succumbing now and again to attacks of nausea. It was the old depression exaggerated; all the world had become Cordelia Street. Yet somehow he was not afraid of anything, was absolutely calm; perhaps because he had looked into the dark corner at last and knew. It was bad enough, what he saw there, but somehow not so bad as his long fear of it had been. He saw everything clearly now. He had a feeling that he had made the best of it, that he had lived

[18]Opera by Ruggero Leoncavallo (1857–1919).

the sort of life he was meant to live, and for half an hour he sat staring at the revolver. But he told himself that was not the way, so he went downstairs and took a cab to the ferry.

When Paul arrived at Newark, he got off the train and took another cab, directing the driver to follow the Pennsylvania tracks out of the town. The snow lay heavy on the roadways and had drifted deep in the open fields. Only here and there the dead grass or dried weed stalks projected, singularly black, above it. Once well into the country, Paul dismissed the carriage and walked, floundering along the tracks, his mind a medley of irrelevant things. He seemed to hold in his brain an actual picture of everything he had seen that morning. He remembered every feature of both his drivers, of the toothless old woman from whom he had bought the red flowers in his coat, the agent from whom he had got his ticket, and all of his fellow-passengers on the ferry. His mind, unable to cope with vital matters near at hand, worked feverishly and deftly at sorting and grouping these images. They made for him a part of the ugliness of the world, of the ache in his head, and the bitter burning on his tongue. He stooped and put a handful of snow into his mouth as he walked, but that, too, seemed hot. When he reached a little hillside, where the tracks ran through a cut some twenty feet below him, he stopped and sat down.

The carnations in his coat were drooping with the cold, he noticed; their red glory all over. It occurred to him that all the flowers he had seen in the glass cases that first night must have gone the same way, long before this. It was only one splendid breath they had, in spite of their brave mockery at the winter outside the glass; and it was a losing game in the end, it seemed, this revolt against the homilies by which the world is run. Paul took one of the blossoms carefully from his coat and scooped a little hole in the snow, where he covered it up. Then he dozed a while, from his weak condition, seeming insensible to the cold.

The sound of an approaching train awoke him, and he started to his feet, remembering only his resolution, and afraid least he should be too late. He stood watching the approaching locomotive, his teeth chattering, his lips drawn away from them in a frightened smile; once or twice he glanced nervously sidewise, as though he were being watched. When the right moment came, he jumped. As he fell, the folly of his haste occurred to him with merciless clearness, the vastness of what he had left undone. There flashed through his brain, clearer than ever before, the blue of Adriatic water, the yellow of Algerian sands.

He felt something strike his chest, and that his body was being thrown swiftly through the air, on and on, immeasurably far and fast, while his limbs were gently relaxed. Then, because the picture-making mechanism was crushed, the disturbing visions flashed into black, and Paul dropped back into the immense design of things.

[1905]

GERTRUDE STEIN ■ (1874–1946)

The quirky, self-absorbed, brilliant Gertrude Stein, one of the pioneering figures of literary and cultural modernism and an author convinced of her unprecedented genius ("Einstein was the creative philosophic mind of the century and I have been the creative literary mind of the century"), was born in Allegheny, Pennsylvania, of an upper-middle-class family. She lived next in Vienna and Paris, returning with her family to the United States in 1878. She was raised in Oakland, California, and later in San Francisco, and, beginning in 1892, after the death of her father, in Baltimore, Maryland. Already Stein was a vigorous reader of literature, fascinated by the shapes and sounds of words, phrases, and sentences, recalling later in life, "I suppose other things may be more exciting to others.... I like the feeling the everlasting feeling of sentences as they diagram themselves."

Stein attended Radcliffe College, where she studied with the eminent American philosopher William James. For her final exam in James's course, she wrote at the top of the page, "Dear Professor James, I am sorry but really I do not feel a bit like an examination paper in philosophy today." He sent her a card the next day: "I understand perfectly how you feel, I often feel like that myself," and he then awarded her the highest grade in the course.

After Radcliffe, Stein enrolled in medical school at Johns Hopkins University in Baltimore. But she grew disenchanted with her preparations for a career as a doctor, and in 1904, leaving her medical studies behind, she traveled to Paris to live with her brother Leo in an apartment, 27 Rue de Fleurus, which became a salon for avant-garde art and literature. "Paris," she said, "was the place that suited those of us that were to create the twentieth century art and literature." It would be thirty years before she visited the United States again.

Gertrude and Leo Stein were among the first collectors of paintings by Henri Matisse, George Braque, and Pablo Picasso; Cezanne especially, Renoir, and Gauguin were represented in their collection as well. Through her advice and encouragement, Stein supported the cause of modern art and crucially influenced such visiting and expatriate American writers as Sherwood Anderson and Ernest Hemingway.

Stein was a great innovator, highly experimental in much of her work, and the result is that many readers find her novels (e.g., *The Making of Americans*, 1,000 pages, written 1906–08, published 1925), essays, lectures, and poems too abstract, extremely strange, obscure, even unfathomable. Her statements about language suggest the operations of her determined yet profound, idiosyncratically angled mind:

> The composition is the thing seen by everyone living in the living
> they are doing, they are the composing of the composition that at

the time they are living is the composition of the time in which they are living.

A noun is a name of anything, why after a thing is named write about it. A name is adequate or it is not...things once they are named does not go on doing anything to them and so why write in nouns. Nouns are the name of anything and just naming names is alright when you want to call a roll but is it good for anything else.

The Autobiography of Alice B. Toklas (1933), however, written by Stein but presented as the autobiography of her companion (Toklas had moved in with Stein and her brother in 1909), is accessible and engaging, irresistible for both its revelations and its evasions, and wickedly witty in its comments on Hemingway and others. Her earlier book *Three Lives* (1909), from which the story here, "The Gentle Lena," is taken, while perhaps peculiar and baffling at first, also is a mesmerizing literary performance.

"The Gentle Lena" is one of the three stories (the other two are "The Good Anna" and "Melanctha") that focus on lower-class women and their aspirations, struggles, and disappointments. The style is rhythmic, repetitive, ironic, and evocative as the reader adjusts to it. In all three of the stories, Stein brings patiently to light the depth and complexity of her characters' psychological and emotional experience. On one level, that of the plot, not much happens; but on another, deeper level, each story is intense and compelling. "The Gentle Lena," the best known, delineates meticulously the consciousness of a passive, quiet, feeble, victimized protagonist, accustomed to unhappiness.

Surveys of the life and works include Janet Hobhouse, *Everybody Who Was Anybody: A Biography of Gertrude Stein* (1975); and Bettina L. Knapp, *Gertrude Stein* (1990). For more detail, see James R. Mellow, *Charmed Circle: Gertrude Stein and Company* (1974). See also Linda Simon, *Gertrude Stein Remembered* (1994); and *The Critical Response to Gertrude Stein*, ed. Kirk Curnutt (2000). For critical studies, see Randa Dubnick, *The Structure of Obscurity: Gertrude Stein, Language, and Cubism* (1984); Jayne L. Walker, *The Making of a Modernist: Gertrude Stein from Three Lives to Tender Buttons* (1984); Harriet Scott Chessman, *The Public Is Invited to Dance: Representation, the Body, and Dialogue in Gertrude Stein* (1989); and Barbara Will, *Gertrude Stein, Modernism, and the Problem of "Genius"* (2000).

Recent scholarship includes Steven Meyer, *Irresistible Dictation: Gertrude Stein and the Correlations of Writing and Science* (2001); Anna Linzie, *The True Story of Alice B. Toklas: A Study of Three Autobiographies* (2006); Janet Malcolm, *Two Lives: Gertrude and Alice* (2007); Wanda M. Corn and Tirza True Latimer, *Seeing Gertrude Stein: Five Stories* (2011); and Timothy W. Gallow, *Writing Celebrity: Stein, Fitzgerald, and the Modern(ist) Art of Self-Fashioning* (2011).

Gertrude Stein, January 4, 1935. Photograph by Carl Van Vechten (1880–1964), an American writer and photographer, as well as Stein's friend and literary executor.

The Gentle Lena

Lena was patient, gentle, sweet and german. She had been a servant for four years and had liked it very well.

Lena had been brought from Germany to Bridgepoint by a cousin and had been in the same place there for four years.

This place Lena had found very good. There was a pleasant, unexacting mistress and her children, and they all liked Lena very well.

There was a cook there who scolded Lena a great deal but Lena's german patience held no suffering and the good incessant woman really only scolded so for Lena's good.

Lena's german voice when she knocked and called the family in the morning was as awakening, as soothing, and as appealing, as a delicate soft breeze in midday, summer. She stood in the hallway every morning a long time in her unexpectant and unsuffering german patience calling to the young ones to get up. She would call and wait a long time and then call again, always even, gentle, patient, while the young ones fell back often into that precious, tense, last bit of sleeping that gives a strength of joyous vigor in the young, over them that have come to the readiness of middle age, in their awakening.

Lena had good hard work all morning, and on the pleasant, sunny afternoons she was sent out into the park to sit and watch the little two year old girl baby of the family.

The other girls, all them that make the pleasant, lazy crowd, that watch the children in the sunny afternoons out in the park, all liked the simple, gentle, german Lena very well. They all, too, liked very well to tease her, for it was so easy to make her mixed and troubled, and all help-less, for she could never learn to know just what the other quicker girls meant by the queer things they said.

The two or three of these girls, the ones that Lena always sat with, always worked together to confuse her. Still it was pleasant, all this life for Lena.

The little girl fell down sometimes and cried, and then Lena had to soothe her. When the little girl would drop her hat, Lena had to pick it up and hold it. When the little girl was bad and threw away her playthings, Lena told her she could not have them and took them from her to hold until the little girl should need them.

It was all a peaceful life for Lena, almost as peaceful as a pleasant lei-sure. The other girls, of course, did tease her, but then that only made a gentle stir within her.

Lena was a brown and pleasant creature, brown as blonde races often have them brown, brown, not with the yellow or the red or the chocolate brown of sun burned countries, but brown with the clear color laid flat on the light toned skin beneath, the plain, spare brown that makes it right to have been made with hazel eyes, and not too abundant straight, brown hair, hair that only later deepens itself into brown from the straw yellow of a german childhood.

Lena had the flat chest, straight back and forward falling shoulders of the patient and enduring working woman, though her body was now still in its milder girlhood and work had not yet made these lines too clear.

The rarer feeling that there was with Lena, showed in all the even quiet of her body movements, but in all it was the strongest in the patient, old-world ignorance, and earth made pureness of her brown, flat, soft fea-tured face. Lena had eyebrows that were a wondrous thickness. They were black, and spread, and very cool, with their dark color and their beauty, and beneath them were her hazel eyes, simple and human, with the earth patience of the working, gentle, german woman.

Yes it was all a peaceful life for Lena. The other girls, of course, did tease her, but then that only made a gentle stir within her.

"What you got on your finger Lena," Mary, one of the girls she always sat with, one day asked her. Mary was good natured, quick, intelligent and Irish.

Lena had just picked up the fancy paper made accordion that the little girl had dropped beside her, and was making it squeak sadly as she pulled it with her brown, strong, awkward finger.

"Why, what is it, Mary, paint?" said Lena, putting her finger to her mouth to taste the dirt spot.

"That's awful poison Lena, don't you know?" said Mary, "that green paint that you just tasted."

Lena had sucked a good deal of the green paint from her finger. She stopped and looked hard at the finger. She did not know just how much Mary meant by what she said.

"Ain't it poison, Nellie, that green paint, that Lena sucked just now," said Mary. "Sure it is Lena, it's real poison, I ain't foolin' this time anyhow."

Lena was a little troubled. She looked hard at her finger where the paint was, and she wondered if she had really sucked it.

It was still a little wet on the edges and she rubbed it off a long time on the inside of her dress, and in between she wondered and looked at the finger and thought, was it really poison that she had just tasted.

"Ain't it too bad, Nellie, Lena should have sucked that," Mary said.

Nellie smiled and did not answer. Nellie was dark and thin, and looked Italian. She had a big mass of black hair that she wore high up on her head and that made her face look very fine.

Nellie always smiled and did not say much, and then she would look at Lena to perplex her.

And so they all three sat with their little charges in the pleasant sunshine a long time. And Lena would often look at her finger and wonder if it was really poison that she had just tasted and then she would rub her finger on her dress a little harder.

Mary laughed at her and teased her and Nellie smiled a little and looked queerly at her.

Then it came time, for it was growing cooler, for them to drag together the little ones, who had begun to wander, and to take each one back to its own mother. And Lena never knew for certain whether it was really poison, that green stuff that she had tasted.

During these four years of service, Lena always spent her Sundays out at the house of her aunt, who had brought her four years before to Bridgepoint.

This aunt, who had brought Lena, four years before, to Bridgepoint, was a hard, ambitious, well meaning, german woman. Her husband was a grocer in the town, and they were very well to do. Mrs. Haydon, Lena's aunt, had two daughters who were just beginning as young ladies, and she had a little boy who was not honest and who was very hard to manage.

Mrs. Haydon was a short, stout, hard built, german woman. She always hit the ground very firmly and compactly as she walked. Mrs. Haydon was all a compact and well hardened mass, even to her face, reddish and darkened from its early blonde, with its hearty, shiny, checks, and doubled chin well covered over with the uproll from her short, square neck.

The two daughters, who were fourteen and fifteen, looked like un-kneaded, unformed mounds of flesh beside her.

The elder girl, Mathilda, was blonde, and slow, and simple, and quite fat. The younger, Bertha, who was almost as tall as her sister, was dark, and quicker, and she was heavy, too, but not really fat.

These two girls the mother had brought up very firmly. They were well taught for their position. They were always both well dressed, in the same kinds of hats and dresses, as is becoming in two german sisters. The mother liked to have them dressed in red. Their best clothes were red dresses, made of good heavy cloth, and strongly trimmed with braid of a glistening black. They had stiff, red felt hats, trimmed with black velvet ribbon, and a bird. The mother dressed matronly, in a bonnet and in black, always sat between her two big daughters, firm, directing, and repressed.

The only weak spot in this good german woman's conduct was the way she spoiled her boy, who was not honest and who was very hard to manage.

The father of this family was a decent, quiet, heavy, and uninterfering german man. He tried to cure the boy of his bad ways, and make him honest, but the mother could not make herself let the father manage, and so the boy was brought up very badly.

Mrs. Haydon's girls were now only just beginning as young ladies, and so to get her niece, Lena, married, was just then the most important thing that Mrs. Haydon had to do.

Mrs. Haydon had four years before gone to Germany to see her parents, and had taken the girls with her. This visit had been for Mrs. Haydon most successful, though her children had not liked it very well.

Mrs. Haydon was a good and generous woman, and she patronized her parents grandly, and all the cousins who came from all about to see her. Mrs. Haydon's people were of the middling class of farmers. They were not peasants, and they lived in a town of some pretension, but it all seemed very poor and smelly to Mrs. Haydon's american born daughters.

Mrs. Haydon liked it all. It was familiar, and then here she was so wealthy and important. She listened and decided, and advised all of her relations how to do things better. She arranged their present and their future for them, and showed them how in the past they had been wrong in all their methods.

Mrs. Haydon's only trouble was with her two daughters, whom she could not make behave well to her parents. The two girls were very nasty to all their numerous relations. Their mother could hardly make them kiss their grandparents, and every day the girls would get a scolding. But then Mrs. Haydon was so very busy that she did not have time to really manage her stubborn daughters.

These hard working, earth-rough german cousins were to these american born children, ugly and dirty, and as far below them as were italian or negro workmen, and they could not see how their mother could ever bear to touch them, and then all the women dressed so funny, and were worked all rough and different.

The two girls stuck up their noses at them all, and always talked in English to each other about how they hated all these people and how they wished their mother would not do so. The girls could talk some German, but they never chose to use it.

It was her eldest brother's family that most interested Mrs. Haydon. Here there were eight children, and out of the eight, five of them were girls.

Mrs. Haydon thought it would be a fine thing to take one of these girls back with her to Bridgepoint and get her well started. Everybody liked that she should do so, and they were all willing that it should be Lena.

Lena was the second girl in her large family. She was at this time just seventeen years old. Lena was not an important daughter in the family. She was always sort of dreamy and not there. She worked hard and went very regularly at it, but even good work never seemed to bring her near.

Lena's age just suited Mrs. Haydon's purpose. Lena could first go out to service, and learn how to do things, and then, when she was a little older, Mrs. Haydon could get her a good husband. And then Lena was so still and docile, she would never want to do things her own way. And then, too, Mrs. Haydon, with all her hardness had wisdom, and she could feel the rarer strain there was in Lena.

Lena was willing to go with Mrs. Haydon. Lena did not like her german life very well. It was not the hard work but the roughness that disturbed her. The people were not gentle, and the men when they were glad were very boisterous, and would lay hold of her and roughly tease her. They were good people enough around her, but it was all harsh and dreary for her.

Lena did not really know that she did not like it. She did not know that she was always dreamy and not there. She did not think whether it would be different for her away off there in Bridgepoint. Mrs. Haydon took her and got her different kinds of dresses, and then took her with them to the steamer. Lena did not really know what it was that had happened to her.

Mrs. Haydon, and her daughters, and Lena traveled second class on the steamer. Mrs. Haydon's daughters hated that their mother should take Lena. They hated to have a cousin, who was to them, little better than a nigger, and then everybody on the steamer there would see her. Mrs. Haydon's daughters said things like this to their mother, but she never stopped to hear them, and the girls did not dare to make their meaning very clear. And so they could only go on hating Lena hard, together. They could not stop her from going back with them to Bridgepoint.

Lena was very sick on the voyage. She thought, surely before it was over that she would die. She was so sick she could not even wish that she had not started. She could not eat, she could not moan, she was just blank and scared, and sure that every minute she would die. She could not hold herself in, nor help herself in her trouble. She just staid where she had been put, pale, and scared, and weak, and sick, and sure that she was going to die.

Mathilda and Bertha Haydon had no trouble from having Lena for a cousin on the voyage, until the last day that they were on the ship, and by that time they had made their friends and could explain.

Mrs. Haydon went down every day to Lena, gave her things to make her better, held her head when it was needful, and generally was good and did her duty by her.

Poor Lena had no power to be strong in such trouble. She did not know how to yield to her sickness nor endure. She lost all her little sense of being in her suffering. She was so scared, and then at her best, Lena, who was patient, sweet and quiet, had not self-control, nor any active courage.

Poor Lena was so scared and weak, and every minute she was sure that she would die.

After Lena was on land again a little while, she forgot all her bad suffering. Mrs. Haydon got her the good place, with the pleasant unexacting mistress, and her children, and Lena began to learn some English and soon was very happy and content.

All her Sundays out Lena spent at Mrs. Haydon's house. Lena would have liked much better to spend her Sundays with the girls she always sat with, and who often asked her, and who teased her and made a gentle stir within her, but it never came to Lena's unexpectant and unsuffering german nature to do something different from what was expected of her, just because she would like it that way better. Mrs. Haydon had said that Lena was to come to her house every other Sunday, and so Lena always went there.

Mrs. Haydon was the only one of her family who took any interest in Lena. Mr. Haydon did not think much of her. She was his wife's cousin and he was good to her, but she was for him stupid, and a little simple, and very dull, and sure some day to need help and to be in trouble. All young poor relations, who were brought from Germany to Bridgepoint were sure, before long, to need help and to be in trouble.

The little Haydon boy was always very nasty to her. He was a hard child for any one to manage, and his mother spoiled him very badly. Mrs. Haydon's daughters as they grew older did not learn to like Lena any better. Lena never knew that she did not like them either. She did not know that she was only happy with the other quicker girls, she always sat with in the park, and who laughed at her and always teased her.

Mathilda Haydon, the simple, fat, blonde, older daughter felt very badly that she had to say that this was her cousin Lena, this Lena who was little better for her than a nigger. Mathilda was an overgrown, slow, flabby, blonde, stupid, fat girl, just beginning as a woman; thick in her speech and dull and simple in her mind, and very jealous of all her family and of other girls, and proud that she could have good dresses and new hats and learn music, and hating very badly to have a cousin who was a common servant. And then Mathilda remembered very strongly that dirty nasty place that Lena came from and that Mathilda had so turned up her nose at, and where she had been made so angry because her mother scolded her and liked all those rough cow-smelly people.

Then, too, Mathilda would get very mad when her mother had Lena at their parties, and when she talked about how good Lena was, to certain german mothers in whose sons, perhaps, Mrs. Haydon might find Lena a good husband. All this would make the dull, blonde, fat Mathilda very angry. Sometimes she would get so angry that she would, in her thick, slow way, and with jealous anger blazing in her light blue eyes, tell her mother that she did not see how she could like that nasty Lena; and then her mother would scold Mathilda, and tell her that she knew her cousin Lena was poor and Mathilda must be good to poor people.

Mathilda Haydon did not like relations to be poor. She told all her girl friends what she thought of Lena, and so the girls would never talk to Lena at Mrs. Haydon's parties. But Lena in her unsuffering and unexpectant patience never really knew that she was slighted. When Mathilda was with her girls in the street or in the park and would see Lena, she always turned up her nose and barely nodded to her, and then she would tell her friends how funny her mother was to take care of people like that Lena, and how, back in Germany, all Lena's people lived just like pigs.

The younger daughter, the dark, large, but not fat, Bertha Haydon, who was very quick in her mind, and in her ways, and who was the favorite with her father, did not like Lena, either. She did not like her because for her Lena was a fool and so stupid, and she would let those Irish and Italian girls laugh at her and tease her, and everybody always made fun of Lena, and Lena never got mad, or even had sense enough to know that they were all making an awful fool of her.

Bertha Haydon hated people to be fools. Her father, too, thought Lena was a fool, and so neither the father nor the daughter ever paid any attention to Lena, although she came to their house every other Sunday.

Lena did not know how all the Haydons felt. She came to her aunt's house all her Sunday afternoons that she had out, because Mrs. Haydon had told her she must do so. In the same way Lena always saved all of her wages. She never thought of any way to spend it. The german cook, the good woman who always scolded Lena, helped her to put it in the bank each month, as soon as she got it. Sometimes before it got into the bank to be taken care of, somebody would ask Lena for it. The little Haydon boy sometimes asked and would get it, and sometimes some of the girls, the ones Lena always sat with, needed some more money; but the german cook, who always scolded Lena, saw to it that this did not happen very often. When it did happen she would scold Lena very sharply, and for the next few months she would not let Lena touch her wages, but put it in the bank for her on the same day that Lena got it.

So Lena always saved her wages, for she never thought to spend them, and she always went to her aunt's house for her Sundays because she did not know that she could do anything different.

Mrs. Haydon felt more and more every year that she had done right to bring Lena back with her, for it was all coming out just as she had expected. Lena was good and never wanted her own way, she was learning English, and saving all her wages, and soon Mrs. Haydon would get her a good husband.

All these four years Mrs. Haydon was busy looking around among all the german people that she knew for the right man to be Lena's husband, and now at last she was quite decided.

The man Mrs. Haydon wanted for Lena was a young german-american tailor, who worked with his father. He was good and all the family were very saving, and Mrs. Haydon was sure that this would be just right for Lena, and then too, this young tailor always did whatever his father and his mother wanted.

This old german tailor and his wife, the father and the mother of Herman Kreder, who was to marry Lena Mainz, were very thrifty, careful people. Herman was the only child they had left with them, and he always did everything they wanted. Herman was now twenty-eight years old, but he had never stopped being scolded and directed by his father and his mother. And now they wanted to see him married.

Herman Kreder did not care much to get married. He was a gentle soul and a little fearful. He had a sullen temper, too. He was obedient to his father and his mother. He always did his work well. He often went out on Saturday nights and on Sundays, with other men. He liked it with them but he never became really joyous. He liked to be with men and he hated to have women with them. He was obedient to his mother, but he did not care much to get married.

Mrs. Haydon and the elder Kreders had often talked the marriage over. They all three liked it very well. Lena would do anything that Mrs. Haydon wanted, and Herman was always obedient in everything to his father and his mother. Both Lena and Herman were saving and good workers and neither of them ever wanted their own way.

The elder Kreders, everybody knew, had saved up all their money, and they were hard, good german people, and Mrs. Haydon was sure that with these people Lena would never be in any trouble. Mr. Haydon would not say anything about it. He knew old Kreder had a lot of money and owned some good houses, and he did not care what his wife did with that simple, stupid Lena, so long as she would be sure never to need help or to be in trouble.

Lena did not care much to get married. She liked her life very well where she was working. She did not think much about Herman Kreder. She thought he was a good man and she always found him very quiet. Neither of them ever spoke much to the other. Lena did not care much just then about getting married.

Mrs. Haydon spoke to Lena about it very often. Lena never answered anything at all. Mrs. Haydon thought, perhaps Lena did not like Herman Kreder. Mrs. Haydon could not believe that any girl not even Lena, really had no feeling about getting married.

Mrs. Haydon spoke to Lena very often about Herman. Mrs. Haydon sometimes got very angry with Lena. She was afraid that Lena, for once, was going to be stubborn, now when it was all fixed right for her to be married.

"Why you stand there so stupid, why don't you answer, Lena," said Mrs. Haydon one Sunday, at the end of a long talking that she was giving Lena about Herman Kreder, and about Lena's getting married to him.

"Yes ma'am," said Lena, and then Mrs. Haydon was furious with this stupid Lena. "Why don't you answer with some sense, Lena, when I ask you if you don't like Herman Kreder. You stand there so stupid and don't answer just like you ain't heard a word what I been saying to you. I never see anybody like you, Lena. If you going to burst out at all, why don't you burst out sudden instead of standing there so silly and don't answer. And here I am so good to you, and find you a good husband so you can have a place to live in all your own. Answer me, Lena, don't you like Herman Kreder? He is a fine young fellow, almost too good for you, Lena, when you stand there so stupid and don't make no answer. There ain't many poor girls that get the chance you got now to get married."

"Why, I do anything you say, Aunt Mathilda. Yes, I like him. He don't say much to me, but I guess he is a good man, and I do anything you say for me to do."

"Well then Lena, why you stand there so silly all the time and not answer when I asked you."

"I didn't hear you say you wanted I should say anything to you. I didn't know you wanted me to say nothing. I do whatever you tell me it's right for me to do. I marry Herman Kreder, if you want me."

And so for Lena Mainz the match was made.

Old Mrs. Kreder did not discuss the matter with her Herman. She never thought that she needed to talk such things over with him. She just told him about getting married to Lena Mainz who was a good worker and very saving and never wanted her own way, and Herman made his usual little grunt in answer to her.

Mrs. Kreder and Mrs. Haydon fixed the day and made all the arrangements for the wedding and invited everybody who ought to be there to see them married.

In three months Lena Mainz and Herman Kreder were to be married.

Mrs. Haydon attended to Lena's getting all the things that she needed. Lena had to help a good deal with the sewing. Lena did not sew very well. Mrs. Haydon scolded because Lena did not do it better, but then she was very good to Lena, and she hired a girl to come and help her. Lena still stayed on with her pleasant mistress, but she spent all her evenings and Sundays with her aunt and all the sewing.

Mrs. Haydon got Lena some nice dresses. Lena liked that very well. Lena liked having new hats even better, and Mrs. Haydon had some made for her by a real milliner who made them very pretty.

Lena was nervous these days, but she did not think much about getting married. She did not know really what it was, that, which was always coming nearer.

Lena liked the place where she was with the pleasant mistress and the good cook, who always scolded, and she liked the girls she always sat with. She did not ask if she would like being married any better. She always did whatever her aunt said and expected, but she was always nervous when she saw the Kreders with their Herman. She was excited and she liked her new hats, and everybody teased her and every day her marrying was coming nearer, and yet she did not really know what it was, this that was about to happen to her.

Herman Kreder knew more what it meant to be married and he did not like it very well. He did not like to see girls and he did not want to have to have one always near him. Herman always did everything that his father and his mother wanted and now they wanted that he should be married.

Herman had a sullen temper; he was gentle and he never said much. He liked to go out with other men, but he never wanted that there should be any women with them. The men all teased him about getting married. Herman did not mind the teasing but he did not like very well the getting married and having a girl always with him.

Three days before the wedding day, Herman went away to the country to be gone over Sunday. He and Lena were to be married Tuesday afternoon. When the day came Herman had not been seen or heard from.

The old Kreder couple had not worried much about it. Herman always did everything they wanted and he would surely come back in time to get married. But when Monday night came, and there was no Herman, they went to Mrs. Haydon to tell her what had happened.

Mrs. Haydon got very much excited. It was hard enough to work so as to get everything all ready, and then to have that silly Herman go off that way, so no one could tell what was going to happen. Here was Lena and everything all ready, and now they would have to make the wedding later so that they would know that Herman would be sure to be there.

Mrs. Haydon was very much excited, and then she could not say much to the old Kreder couple. She did not want to make them angry, for she wanted very badly now that Lena should be married to their Herman.

At last it was decided that the wedding should be put off a week longer. Old Mr. Kreder would go to New York to find Herman, for it was very likely that Herman had gone there to his married sister.

Mrs. Haydon sent word around, about waiting until a week from that Tuesday, to everybody that had been invited, and then Tuesday morning she sent for Lena to come down to see her.

Mrs. Haydon was very angry with poor Lena when she saw her. She scolded her hard because she was so foolish, and now Herman had gone off and nobody could tell where he had gone to, and all because Lena always was so dumb and silly. And Mrs. Haydon was just like a mother to her, and Lena always stood there so stupid and did not answer what anybody asked her, and Herman was so silly too, and now his father had to go and find him. Mrs. Haydon did not think that any old people should be good to their children. Their children always were so thankless, and never paid any attention, and older people were always doing things for their good. Did Lena think it gave Mrs. Haydon any pleasure, to work so hard to make Lena happy, and get her a good husband, and then Lena was so thankless and never did anything that anybody wanted. It was a lesson to poor Mrs. Haydon not to do things any more for anybody. Let everybody take care of themselves and never come to her with any troubles; she knew better now than to meddle to make other people happy. It just made trouble for her and her husband did not like it. He always said she was too good, and nobody ever thanked her for it, and there Lena was always standing stupid and not answering anything anybody wanted. Lena could always talk enough to those silly girls she liked so much, and always sat with, but who never did anything for her except to take away her money, and here was her aunt who tried so hard and was so good to her and treated her just like one of her own children and Lena stood there, and never made any answer and never tried to please her aunt, or to do anything that her aunt wanted. "No, it ain't no use your standin' there and cryin', now, Lena. It's too late now to care about that Herman. You should have cared some before, and then you wouldn't have to stand there and cry now, and be a disappointment to me, and then I get scolded by my husband for taking care of everybody, and nobody ever thankful. I am glad you got the sense to feel sorry now, Lena, anyway, and I try to do what I can to help you out in your trouble, only you don't deserve to have anybody take any trouble for you. But perhaps you know better next time. You go home now and take care you don't spoil your clothes and that new hat, you had no business to be wearin' that this morning, but you ain't got no sense at all, Lena, I never in my life see anybody be so stupid."

Mrs. Haydon stopped and poor Lena stood there in her hat, all trimmed with pretty flowers, and the tears coming out of her eyes, and Lena did not know what it was that she had done, only she was not going to be married and it was a disgrace for a girl to be left by a man on the very day she was to be married.

Lena went home all alone, and cried in the street car.

Poor Lena cried very hard all alone in the street car. She almost spoiled her new hat with her hitting it against the window in her crying. Then she remembered that she must not do so.

The conductor was a kind man and he was very sorry when he saw her crying. "Don't feel so bad, you get another feller, you are such a nice girl," he said to make her cheerful. "But Aunt Mathilda said now, I never get married," poor Lena sobbed out for her answer. "Why you really got trouble like that," said the conductor. "I just said that now to josh you. I didn't ever think you really was left by a feller. He must be a stupid feller. But don't you worry, he wasn't much good if he could go away and leave you, lookin' to be such a nice girl. You just tell all your trouble to me, and I help you." The car was empty and the conductor sat down beside her to put his arm around her, and to be a comfort to her. Lena suddenly remembered where she was, and if she did things like that her aunt would scold her. She moved away from the man into the corner. He laughed, "Don't be scared," he said, "I wasn't going to hurt you. But you just keep up your spirit. You are a real nice girl, and you'll be sure to get a real good husband. Don't you let nobody fool you. You're all right and I don't want to scare you."

The conductor went back to his platform to help a passenger get on the car. All the time Lena stayed in the street car, he would come in every little while and reassure her, about her not to feel so bad about a man who hadn't no more sense than to go away and leave her. She'd be sure yet to get a good man, she needn't be so worried, he frequently reassured her.

He chatted with the other passenger who had just come in, a very well dressed old man, and then with another who came in later, a good sort of a working man, and then another who came in, a nice lady, and he told them all about Lena's having trouble, and it was too bad there were men who treated a poor girl so badly. And everybody in the car was sorry for poor Lena and the workman tried to cheer her, and the old man looked sharply at her, and said she looked like a good girl, but she ought to be more careful and not to be so careless, and things like that would not happen to her, and the nice lady went and sat beside her and Lena liked it, though she shrank away from being near her.

So Lena was feeling a little better when she got off the car, and the conductor helped her, and he called out to her, "You be sure you keep up a good heart now. He wasn't no good that feller and you were lucky for to lose him. You'll get a real man yet, one that will be better for you. Don't you be worried, you're a real nice girl as I ever see in such trouble," and the conductor shook his head and went back into his car to talk it over with the other passengers he had there.

The german cook, who always scolded Lena, was very angry when she heard the story. She never did think Mrs. Haydon would do so much for

Lena, though she was always talking so grand about what she could do for everybody. The good german cook always had been a little distrustful of her. People who always thought they were so much never did really do things right for anybody. Not that Mrs. Haydon wasn't a good woman. Mrs. Haydon was a real, good, german woman, and she did really mean to do well by her niece Lena. The cook knew that very well, and she had always said so, and she always had liked and respected Mrs. Haydon, who always acted very proper to her, and Lena was so backward, when there was a man to talk to, Mrs. Haydon did have hard work when she tried to marry Lena. Mrs. Haydon was a good woman, only she did talk sometimes too grand. Perhaps this trouble would make her see it wasn't always so easy to do, to make everybody do everything just like she wanted. The cook was very sorry now for Mrs. Haydon. All this must be such a disappointment, and such a worry to her, and she really had always been very good to Lena. But Lena had better go and put on her other clothes and stop with all that crying. That wouldn't do nothing now to help her, and if Lena would be a good girl, and just be real patient, her aunt would make it all come out right yet for her. "I just tell Mrs. Aldrich, Lena, you stay here yet a little longer. You know she is always so good to you, Lena, and I know she let you, and I tell her all about that stupid Herman Kreder. I got no patience, Lena, with anybody who can be so stupid. You just stop now with your crying, Lena, and take off them good clothes and put them away so you don't spoil them when you need them, and you can help me with the dishes and everything will come off better for you. You see if I ain't right by what I tell you. You just stop crying now Lena quick, or else I scold you."

Lena still choked a little and was very miserable inside her but she did everything just as the cook told her.

The girls Lena always sat with were very sorry to see her look so sad with her trouble. Mary the Irish girl sometimes got very angry with her. Mary was always very hot when she talked of Lena's aunt Mathilda, who thought she was so grand, and had such stupid, stuck up daughters. Mary wouldn't be a fat fool like that ugly tempered Mathilda Haydon, not for anything anybody could ever give her. How Lena could keep on going there so much when they all always acted as if she was just dirt to them, Mary never could see. But Lena never had any sense of how she should make people stand round for her, and that was always all the trouble with her. And poor Lena, she was so stupid to be sorry for losing that gawky fool who didn't ever know what he wanted and just said "ja" to his mamma and his papa, like a baby, and was scared to look at a girl straight, and then sneaked away the last day like as if somebody was going to do something to him. Disgrace, Lena talking about disgrace! It was a disgrace for a girl to be seen with the likes of him, let alone to be married to him. But that poor Lena, she never did know how to show herself off for what she was really. Disgrace to have him go away and leave her. Mary would just like to get a chance to show him. If Lena wasn't worth fifteen like Herman Kreder, Mary would just eat her own head all up. It was a good riddance Lena had of that Herman Kreder and his stingy, dirty parents, and if Lena didn't stop crying about it,—Mary would just naturally despise her.

Poor Lena, she knew very well how Mary meant it all, this she was always saying to her. But Lena was very miserable inside her. She felt the disgrace it was for a decent german girl that a man should go away and leave her. Lena knew very well that her aunt was right when she said the way Herman had acted to her was a disgrace to everyone that knew her. Mary and Nellie and the other girls she always sat with were always very good to Lena but that did not make her trouble any better. It was a disgrace the way Lena had been left, to any decent family, and that could never be made any different to her.

And so the slow days wore on, and Lena never saw her Aunt Mathilda. At last on Sunday she got word by a boy to go and see her aunt Mathilda. Lena's heart beat quick for she was very nervous now with all this that had happened to her. She went just as quickly as she could to see her Aunt Mathilda.

Mrs. Haydon quick, as soon as she saw Lena, began to scold her for keeping her aunt waiting so long for her, and for not coming in all the week to see her, to see if her aunt should need her, and so her aunt had to send a boy to tell her. But it was easy, even for Lena, to see that her aunt was not really angry with her. It wasn't Lena's fault, went on Mrs. Haydon, that everything was going to happen all right for her. Mrs. Haydon was very tired taking all this trouble for her, and when Lena couldn't even take trouble to come and see her aunt, to see if she needed anything to tell her. But Mrs. Haydon really never minded things like that when she could do things for anybody. She was tired now, all the trouble she had been taking to make things right for Lena, but perhaps now Lena heard it she would learn a little to be thankful to her. "You get all ready to be married Tuesday, Lena, you hear me," said Mrs. Haydon to her. "You come here Tuesday morning and I have everything all ready for you. You wear your new dress I got you, and your hat with all them flowers on it, and you be very careful coming you don't get your things all dirty, you so careless all the time, Lena, and not thinking, and you act sometimes you never got no head at all on you. You go home now, and you tell your Mrs. Aldrich that you leave her Tuesday. Don't you go forgetting now, Lena, anything I ever told you what you should do to be careful. You be a good girl, now Lena. You get married Tuesday to Herman Kreder." And that was all Lena ever knew of what had happened all this week to Herman Kreder. Lena forgot there was anything to know about it. She was really to be married Tuesday, and her Aunt Mathilda said she was a good girl, and now there was no disgrace left upon her.

Lena now fell back into the way she always had of being always dreamy and not there, the way she always had been, except for the few days she was so excited, because she had been left by a man the very day she was to have been married. Lena was a little nervous all these last days, but she did not think much about what it meant for her to be married.

Herman Kreder was not so content about it. He was quiet and was sullen and he knew he could not help it. He knew now he just had to let himself get married. It was not that Herman did not like Lena Mainz. She was so good as any other girl could be for him. She was a little better perhaps than other girls he saw, she was so very quiet, but Herman did not like to always have to have a girl around him. Herman had always done everything that his mother and his father wanted. His father had found him in New York, where Herman had gone to be with his married sister.

Herman's father when he had found him coaxed Herman a long time and went on whole days with his complaining to him, always troubled but gentle and quite patient with him, and always he was worrying to Herman about what was the right way his boy Herman should always do, always whatever it was his mother ever wanted from him, and always Herman never made him any answer.

Old Mr. Kreder kept on saying to him, he did not see how Herman could think now, it could be any different. When you make a bargain you just got to stick right to it, that was the only way old Mr. Kreder could ever see it, and saying you would get married to a girl and she got everything all ready, that was a bargain just like one you make in business and Herman he had made it, and now Herman he would just have to do it, old Mr. Kreder didn't see there was any other way a good boy like his Herman had, to do it. And then too that Lena Mainz was such a nice girl and Herman hadn't ought to really give his father so much trouble and make him pay out all that money, to come all the way to New York just to find him, and they both lose all that time from their working, when all Herman had to do was just to stand up, for an hour, and then he would be all right married, and it would be all over for him, and then everything at home would never be any different to him.

And his father went on; there was his poor mother saying always how her Herman always did everything before she ever wanted, and now just because he got notions in him, and wanted to show people how he could be stubborn, he was making all this trouble for her, and making them pay all that money just to run around and find him. "You got no idea Herman, how bad mama is feeling about the way you been acting Herman," said old Mr. Kreder to him. "She says she never can understand how you can be so thankless Herman. It hurts her very much you been so stubborn, and she find you such a nice girl for you, like Lena Mainz who is always just so quiet and always saves up all her wages, and she never wanting her own way at all like some girls are always all the time to have it, and your mama trying so hard, just so you could be comfortable Herman to be married, and then you act so stubborn Herman. You like all young people

Herman, you think only about yourself, and what you are just wanting, and your mama she is thinking only what is good for you to have, for you in the future. Do you think your mama wants to have a girl around to be a bother, for herself, Herman. Its just for you Herman she is always thinking, and she talks always about how happy she will be, when she sees her Herman married to a nice girl, and then when she fixed it all up so good for you, so it never would be any bother to you, just the way she wanted you should like it, and you say yes all right, I do it, and then you go away like this and act stubborn, and make all this trouble everybody to take for you, and we spend money, and I got to travel all round to find you. You come home now with me Herman and get married, and I tell your mama she better not say anything to you about how much it cost me to come all the way to look for you—Hey Herman," said his father coaxing, "Hey, you come home now and get married. All you got to do Herman is just to stand up for an hour Herman, and then you don't never to have any more bother to it—Hey Herman!—you come home with me to-morrow and get married. Hey Herman."

Herman's married sister liked her brother Herman, and she had always tried to help him, when there was anything she knew he wanted. She liked it that he was so good and always did everything that their father and their mother wanted, but still she wished it could be that he could have more his own way, if there was anything he ever wanted.

But now she thought Herman with his girl was very funny. She wanted that Herman should be married. She thought it would do him lots of good to get married. She laughed at Herman when she heard the story. Until his father came to find him, she did not know why it was Herman had come just then to New York to see her. When she heard the story she laughed a good deal at her brother Herman and teased him a good deal about his running away, because he didn't want to have a girl to be all the time around him.

Herman's married sister liked her brother Herman, and she did not want him not to like to be with women. He was good, her brother Herman, and it would surely do him good to get married. It would make him stand up for himself stronger. Herman's sister always laughed at him and always she would try to reassure him. "Such a nice man as my brother Herman acting like as if he was afraid of women. Why the girls all like a man like you Herman, if you didn't always run away when you saw them. It do you good really Herman to get married, and then you got somebody you can boss around when you want to. It do you good Herman to get married, you see if you don't like it, when you really done it. You go along home now with papa, Herman and get married to that Lena. You don't know how nice you like it Herman when you try once how you can do it. You just don't be afraid of nothing, Herman. You good enough for any girl to marry, Herman. Any girl be glad to have a man like you to be always with them Herman. You just go along home with papa and try it what I say, Herman. Oh you so funny Herman, when you sit there, and then run away and leave your girl behind you. I know she is crying like anything Herman for to lose you. Don't be bad to her Herman. You go along home with papa now and get married Herman. I'd be awful ashamed Herman, to really have a brother didn't have spirit enough to get married, when a girl is just dying for to have him. You always like me to be with you Herman. I don't see why you say you don't want a girl to be all the time around you. You always been good to me Herman, and I know you always be good to that Lena, and you soon feel just like as if she had always been there with you. Don't act like as if you wasn't a nice strong man, Herman. Really I laugh at you Herman, but you know I like awful well to see you real happy. You go home and get married to that Lena, Herman. She is a real pretty girl and real nice and good and quiet and she make my brother Herman very happy. You just stop your fussing now with Herman, papa. He go with you to-morrow papa, and you see he like it so much to be married, he make everybody laugh just to see him be so happy. Really truly, that's the way it will be with you Herman. You just listen to me what I tell you Herman." And so his sister laughed at him and reassured him, and his father kept on telling what the mother always said about her Herman, and he coaxed him and Herman never said anything in answer, and his sister packed his things up and was very cheerful with him, and she kissed him, and then she laughed and then she kissed him, and his father went and bought the tickets for the train, and at last late on Sunday he brought Herman back to Bridgepoint with him.

It was always very hard to keep Mrs. Kreder from saying what she thought, to her Herman, but her daughter had written her a letter, so as to warn her not to say anything about what he had been doing, to him, and her husband came in with Herman and said, "Here we are come home mama, Herman and me, and we are very tired it was so crowded coming," and then he whispered to her. "You be good to Herman, mama, he didn't mean to make us so much trouble," and so old Mrs. Kreder, held in what she felt was so strong in her to say to her Herman. She just said very stiffly to him, "I'm glad to see you come home to-day, Herman." Then she went to arrange it all with Mrs. Haydon.

Herman was now again just like he always had been, sullen and very good, and very quiet, and always ready to do whatever his mother and his father wanted. Tuesday morning came, Herman got his new clothes on and went with his father and his mother to stand up for an hour and get married. Lena was there in her new dress, and her hat with all the pretty flowers, and she was very nervous for now she knew she was really very soon to be married. Mrs. Haydon had everything all ready. Everybody was there just as they should be and very soon Herman Kreder and Lena Mainz were married.

When everything was really over, they went back to the Kreder house together. They were all now to live together, Lena and Herman and the old father and the old mother, in the house where Mr. Kreder had worked so many years as a tailor, with his son Herman always there to help him.

Irish Mary had often said to Lena she never did see how Lena could ever want to have anything to do with Herman Kreder and his dirty stingy parents. The old Kreders were to an Irish nature, a stingy, dirty couple. They had not the free-hearted, thoughtless, fighting, mud bespattered, ragged, peat-smoked cabin dirt that irish Mary knew and could forgive and love. Theirs was the german dirt of saving, of being dowdy and loose and foul in your clothes so as to save them and yourself in washing, having your hair greasy to save it in the soap and drying, having your clothes dirty, not in freedom, but because so it was cheaper, keeping the house close and smelly because so it cost less to get it heated, living so poorly not only so as to save money but so they should never even know themselves that they had it, working all the time not only because from their nature they just had to and because it made them money but also that they never could be put in any way to make them spend their money.

This was the place Lena now had for her home and to her it was very different than it could be for an irish Mary. She too was german and was thrifty, though she was always so dreamy and not there. Lena was always careful with things and she always saved her money, for that was the only way she knew how to do it. She never had taken care of her own money and she never had thought how to use it.

Lena Mainz had been, before she was Mrs. Herman Kreder, always clean and decent in her clothes and in her person, but it was not because she ever thought about it or really needed so to have it, it was the way her people did in the german country where she came from, and her Aunt Mathilda and the good german cook who always scolded, had kept her on and made her, with their scoldings, always more careful to keep clean and to wash real often. But there was no deep need in all this for Lena and so, though Lena did not like the old Kreders, though she really did not know that, she did not think about their being stingy dirty people.

Herman Kreder was cleaner than the old people, just because it was his nature to keep cleaner, but he was used to his mother and his father, and he never thought that they should keep things cleaner. And Herman too always saved all his money, except for that little beer he drank when he went out with other men of an evening the way he always liked to do it, and he never thought of any other way to spend it. His father had always kept all the money for them and he always was doing business with it. And then too Herman really had no money, for he always had worked for his father, and his father had never thought to pay him.

And so they began all four to live in the Kreder house together, and Lena began soon with it to look careless and a little dirty, and to be more lifeless with it, and nobody ever noticed much what Lena wanted, and she never really knew herself what she needed.

The only real trouble that came to Lena with their living all four there together, was the way old Mrs. Kreder scolded. Lena had always been used to being scolded, but this scolding of old Mrs. Kreder was very different from the way she ever before had had to endure it.

Herman, now he was married to her, really liked Lena very well. He did not care very much about her but she never was a bother to him being there around him, only when his mother worried and was nasty to them because Lena was so careless, and did not know how to save things right for them with their eating, and all the other ways with money, that the old woman had to save it.

Herman Kreder had always done everything his mother and his father wanted but he did not really love his parents very deeply. With Herman it was always only that he hated to have any struggle. It was all always all right with him when he could just go along and do the same thing over every day with his working, and not to hear things, and not to have people make him listen to their anger. And now his marriage, and he just knew it would, was making trouble for him. It made him hear more what his mother was always saying, with her scolding. He had to really hear it now because Lena was there, and she was so scared and dull always when she heard it. Herman knew very well with his mother, it was all right if one ate very little and worked hard all day and did not hear her when she scolded, the way Herman always had done before they were so foolish about his getting married and having a girl there to be all the time around him, and now he had to help her so the girl could learn too, not to hear it when his mother scolded, and not to look so scared, and not to eat much, and always to be sure to save it.

Herman really did not know very well what he could do to help Lena to understand it. He could never answer his mother back to help Lena, that never would make things any better for her, and he never could feel in himself any way to comfort Lena, to make her strong not to hear his mother, in all the awful ways she always scolded. It just worried Herman to have it like that all the time around him. Herman did not know much about how a man could make a struggle with a mother, to do much to keep her quiet, and indeed Herman never knew much how to make a struggle against anyone who really wanted to have anything very badly. Herman all his life never wanted anything so badly, that he would really make a struggle against any one to get it. Herman all his life only wanted to live regular and quiet, and not talk much and to do the same way every day like every other with his working. And now his mother had made him get married to this Lena and now with his mother making all that scolding, he had all this trouble and this worry always on him.

Mrs. Haydon did not see Lena now very often. She had not lost her interest in her niece Lena, but Lena could not come much to her house to see her, it would not be right, now Lena was a married woman. And then too Mrs. Haydon had her hands full just then with her two daughters, for she was getting them ready to find them good husbands, and then too her own husband now worried her very often about her always spoiling that boy of hers, so he would be sure to turn out no good and be a disgrace to a german family, and all because his mother always spoiled him. All these things were very worrying now to Mrs. Haydon, but still she wanted to be good to Lena, though she could not see her very often. She only saw her when Mrs. Haydon went to call on Mrs. Kreder or when Mrs. Kreder came to see Mrs. Haydon, and that never could be very often. Then too these days Mrs. Haydon could not scold Lena, Mrs. Kreder was always there with her, and it would not be right to scold Lena when Mrs. Kreder was there, who had now the real right to do it. And so her aunt always said nice things now to Lena, and though Mrs. Haydon sometimes was a little worried when she saw Lena looking sad and not careful, she did not have time just then to really worry much about it.

Lena now never any more saw the girls she always used to sit with. She had no way now to see them and it was not in Lena's nature to search out ways to see them, nor did she now ever think much of the days when she had been used to see them. They never any of them had come to the Kreder house to see her. Not even Irish Mary had ever thought to come to see her. Lena had been soon forgotten by them. They had soon passed away from Lena and now Lena never thought any more that she had ever known them.

The only one of her old friends who tried to know what Lena liked and what she needed, and who always made Lena come to see her, was the good german cook who had always scolded. She now scolded Lena hard for letting herself go so, and going out when she was looking so untidy. "I know you going to have a baby Lena, but that's no way for you to be looking. I am ashamed most to see you come and sit here in my kitchen, looking so sloppy and like you never used to Lena. I never see anybody like you Lena. Herman is very good to you, you always say so, and he don't treat you bad even though you don't deserve to have anybody good to you, you so careless all the time, Lena, letting yourself go like you never had anybody tell you what was the right way you should know how to be looking. No, Lena, I don't see no reason you should let yourself go so and look so untidy Lena, so I am ashamed to see you sit there looking so ugly, Lena. No Lena that ain't no way ever I see a woman make things come out better, letting yourself go so every way and crying all the time like as if you had real trouble. I never wanted to see you marry Herman Kreder, Lena, I knew what you got to stand with that old woman always, and that old man, he is so stingy too and he don't say things out but he ain't any better in his heart than his wife with her bad ways, I know that Lena, I know they don't hardly give you enough to eat, Lena, I am real sorry for

you Lena, you know that Lena, but that ain't any way to be going round
so untidy Lena, even if you have got all that trouble. You never see me do
like that Lena, though sometimes I got a headache so I can't see to stand
to be working hardly, and nothing comes right with all my cooking, but I
always see Lena, I look decent. That's the only way a german girl can make
things come out right Lena. You hear me what I am saying to you Lena.
Now you eat something nice Lena, I got it all ready for you, and you wash
up and be careful Lena and the baby will come all right to you, and then I
make your Aunt Mathilda see that you live in a house soon all alone with
Herman and your baby, and then everything go better for you. You hear
me what I say to you Lena. Now don't let me ever see you come looking
like this any more Lena, and you just stop with that always crying. You
ain't got no reason to be sitting there now with all that crying, I never see
anybody have trouble it did them any good to do the way you are doing,
Lena. You hear me Lena. You go home now and you be good the way I tell
you Lena, and I see what I can do. I make your Aunt Mathilda make old
Mrs. Kreder let you be till you get your baby all right. Now don't you be
scared and so silly Lena. I don't like to see you act so Lena when really you
got a nice man and so many things really any girl should be grateful to be
having. Now you go home Lena to-day and you do the way I say, to you,
and I see what I can do to help you."

"Yes Mrs. Aldrich" said the good german woman to her mistress later,
"Yes Mrs. Aldrich that's the way it is with them girls when they want so
to get married. They don't know when they got it good Mrs. Aldrich. They
never know what it is they're really wanting when they got it, Mrs. Aldrich.
There's that poor Lena, she just been here crying and looking so careless so I scold her, but that was no good that marrying for that poor
Lena, Mrs. Aldrich. She do look so pale and sad now Mrs. Aldrich, it just
break my heart to see her. She was a good girl was Lena, Mrs. Aldrich, and
I never had no trouble with her like I got with so many young girls nowadays, Mrs. Aldrich, and I never see any girl any better to work right than
our Lena, and now she got to stand it all the time with that old woman
Mrs. Kreder. My! Mrs. Aldrich, she is a bad old woman to her. I never see
Mrs. Aldrich how old people can be so bad to young girls and not have no
kind of patience with them. If Lena could only live with her Herman, he
ain't so bad the way men are, Mrs. Aldrich, but he is just the way always
his mother wants him, he ain't got no spirit in him, and so I don't really
see no help for that poor Lena. I know her aunt, Mrs. Haydon, meant it all
right for her Mrs. Aldrich, but poor Lena, it would be better for her if her
Herman had stayed there in New York that time he went away to leave her.
I don't like it the way Lena is looking now, Mrs. Aldrich. She looks like
as if she don't have no life left in her hardly, Mrs. Aldrich, she just drags
around and looks so dirty and after all the pains I always took to teach her
and to keep her nice in her ways and looking. It don't do no good to them,

for them girls to get married Mrs. Aldrich, they are much better when they only know it, to stay in a good place when they got it, and keep on regular with their working. I don't like it the way Lena looks now Mrs. Aldrich. I wish I knew some way to help that poor Lena, Mrs. Aldrich, but she is a bad old woman, that old Mrs. Kreder, Herman's mother. I speak to Mrs. Haydon real soon, Mrs. Aldrich, I see what we can do now to help that poor Lena."

These were really bad days for poor Lena. Herman always was real good to her and now he even sometimes tried to stop his mother from scolding Lena. "She ain't well now mama, you let her be now you hear me. You tell me what it is you want she should be doing, I tell her. I see she does it right just the way you want it mama. You let be, I say now mama, with that always scolding Lena. You let be, I say now, you wait till she is feeling better." Herman was getting really strong to struggle, for he could see that Lena with that baby working hard inside her, really could not stand it any longer with his mother and the awful ways she always scolded.

It was a new feeling Herman now had inside him that made him feel he was strong to make a struggle. It was new for Herman Kreder really to be wanting something, but Herman wanted strongly now to be a father, and he wanted badly that his baby should be a boy and healthy. Herman never had cared really very much about his father and his mother, though always, all his life, he had done everything just as they wanted, and he had never really cared much about his wife, Lena, though he always had been very good to her, and had always tried to keep his mother off her, with the awful way she always scolded, but to be really a father of a little baby, that feeling took hold of Herman very deeply. He was almost ready, so as to save his baby from all trouble, to really make a strong struggle with his mother and with his father, too, if he would not help him to control his mother.

Sometimes Herman even went to Mrs. Haydon to talk all this trouble over. They decided then together, it was better to wait there all four together for the baby, and Herman could make Mrs. Kreder stop a little with her scolding, and then when Lena was a little stronger, Herman should have his own house for her, next door to his father, so he could always be there to help him in his working, but so they could eat and sleep in a house where the old woman could not control them and they could not hear her awful scolding.

And so things went on, the same way, a little longer. Poor Lena was not feeling any joy to have a baby. She was scared the way she had been when she was so sick on the water. She was scared now every time when anything would hurt her. She was scared and still and lifeless, and sure that every minute she would die. Lena had no power to be strong in this kind of trouble, she could only sit still and be scared, and dull, and lifeless, and sure that every minute she would die.

Before very long, Lena had her baby. He was a good, healthy little boy, the baby. Herman cared very much to have the baby. When Lena was a little stronger he took a house next door to the old couple, so he and his own family could eat and sleep and do the way they wanted. This did not seem to make much change now for Lena. She was just the same as when she was waiting with her baby. She just dragged around and was careless with her clothes and all lifeless, and she acted always and lived on just as if she had no feeling. She always did everything regular with the work, the way she always had had to do it, but she never got back any spirit in her. Herman was always good and kind, and always helped her with her working. He did everything he knew to help her. He always did all the active new things in the house and for the baby. Lena did what she had to do the way she always had been taught it. She always just kept going now with her working, and she was always careless, and dirty, and a little dazed, and lifeless. Lena never got any better in herself of this way of being that she had had ever since she had been married.

Mrs. Haydon never saw any more of her niece, Lena. Mrs. Haydon had now so much trouble with her own house, and her daughters getting married, and her boy, who was growing up, and who always was getting so much worse to manage. She knew she had done right by Lena. Herman Kreder was a good man, she would be glad to get one so good, sometimes, for her own daughters, and now they had a home to live in together, separate from the old people, who had made their trouble for them. Mrs. Haydon felt she had done very well by her niece, Lena, and she never thought now she needed any more to go and see her. Lena would do very well now without her aunt to trouble herself any more about her.

The good german cook who had always scolded, still tried to do her duty like a mother to poor Lena. It was very hard now to do right by Lena. Lena never seemed to hear now what anyone was saying to her. Herman was always doing everything he could to help her. Herman always, when he was home, took good care of the baby. Herman loved to take care of his baby. Lena never thought to take him out or to do anything she didn't have to.

The good cook sometimes made Lena come to see her. Lena would come with her baby and sit there in the kitchen, and watch the good woman cooking, and listen to her sometimes a little, the way she used to, while the good german woman scolded her for going around looking so careless when now she had no trouble, and sitting there so dull, and always being just so thankless. Sometimes Lena would wake up a little and get back into her face her old, gentle, patient, and unsuffering sweetness, but mostly Lena did not seem to hear much when the good german woman scolded. Lena always liked it when Mrs. Aldrich her good mistress spoke to her kindly, and then Lena would seem to go back and feel herself to be like she was when she had been in service. But mostly Lena just lived along and was careless in her clothes, and dull, and lifeless.

By and by Lena had two more little babies. Lena was not so much scared now when she had the babies. She did not seem to notice very much when they hurt her, and she never seemed to feel very much now about anything that happened to her.

They were very nice babies, all these three that Lena had, and Herman took good care of them always. Herman never really cared much about his wife, Lena. The only things Herman ever really cared for were his babies. Herman always was very good to his children. He always had a gentle, tender way when he held them. He learned to be very handy with them. He spent all the time he was not working, with them. By and by he began to work all day in his own home so that he could have his children always in the same room with him.

Lena always was more and more lifeless and Herman now mostly never thought about her. He more and more took all the care of their three children. He saw to their eating right and their washing, and he dressed them every morning, and he taught them the right way to do things, and he put them to their sleeping, and he was now always every minute with them. Then there was to come to them, a fourth baby. Lena went to the hospital near by to have the baby. Lena seemed to be going to have much trouble with it. When the baby was come out at last, it was like its mother lifeless. While it was coming, Lena had grown very pale and sicker. When it was all over Lena had died, too, and nobody knew just how it had happened to her.

The good german cook who had always scolded Lena, and had always to the last day tried to help her, was the only one who ever missed her. She remembered how nice Lena had looked all the time she was in service with her, and how her voice had been so gentle and sweet-sounding, and how she always was a good girl, and how she never had to have any trouble with her, the way she always had with all the other girls who had been taken into the house to help her. The good cook sometimes spoke so of Lena when she had time to have a talk with Mrs. Aldrich, and this was all the remembering there now ever was of Lena.

Herman Kreder now always lived very happy, very gentle, very quiet, very well content alone with his three children. He never had a woman any more to be all the time around him. He always did all his own work in his house, when he was through every day with the work he was always doing for his father. Herman always was alone, and he always worked alone, until his little ones were big enough to help him. Herman Kreder was very well content now and he always lived very regular and peaceful, and with every day just like the next one, always alone now with his three good, gentle children.

[1909]

AMY LOWELL ■ (1874–1925)

Amy Lowell was born on an estate in Brookline, Massachusetts, the youngest of five children and a member of a wealthy and distinguished Boston family. One of her distant cousins was the noteworthy nineteenth-century poet and essayist James Russell Lowell; Abbott Lawrence Lowell, one of her brothers, was the president of Harvard University from 1909 to 1933; and Robert Lowell, a major mid-twentieth-century poet, was another of her cousins.

Educated at home and in private schools in the Boston area, Lowell traveled several times with her family to Europe, gaining knowledge of foreign languages and cultures. Drawn to literature, a wide-ranging reader amid the thousands of books in the family library, she published in 1910 a poem, "Fixed Ideas," in *The Atlantic Monthly*, and her first book of poems, *A Dome of Many-Coloured Glass*, appeared two years later.

Lowell is best known for her involvement in the Imagist movement, whose members included Ezra Pound and H. D., both of whom Lowell met in London in the summer of 1913. She was drawn to their emphasis on clarity and precision. "Concentration," she affirmed, "is the very essence of poetry"; she said she wanted to "produce poetry that is hard and clear, never blurred nor indefinite." She promoted these principles through lectures and three volumes of the anthology *Some Imagist Poets* (1915–17), which she funded. Her key role as a patroness of and spokeswoman for Imagism angered the jealous and competitive Pound, who mocked her and derided her work.

Lowell was flamboyant and eccentric. She slept during the day and wrote at night and enjoyed smoking cigars; on a trip to England, she sent over by ship her maroon automobile—which was driven by a chauffeur in a maroon coat. Lowell suffered from a number of health problems and was overweight—which led some male poets and critics to make cruel jokes about her (Pound, for instance, referred to her as a "hippopoetess").

Developing her Imagist methods, Lowell attempted a "polyphonic" style, combining elements of loose, free forms and conventional verse techniques and patterns. Like others of the period, she read, explored, and experimented with Japanese and Chinese poetry. Her significant critical work, *Tendencies in Modern American Poetry* (1917), was based on a well-attended series of lectures she presented. Lowell was deeply attached as well to the poems and letters of the English Romantic poet John Keats, whom she viewed as the great precursor of Imagism and whose biography she wrote (1925).

Lowell was unmarried. She lived with an actress, Ada Dwyer Russell, eleven years her senior, who was her secretary and companion until Lowell's death. It is not known whether their relationship was sexual—and at Lowell's instruction, after her death Russell burned all of her personal papers and correspondence. It is clear that Lowell loved Russell passionately, as her many erotic, intense love poems, several of which are printed here, suggest.

The feelings in Lowell's poems are carefully articulated—powerfully expressive, yet often veiled, their true nature and object concealed. Lowell is, paradoxically, both open and closed, free and restricted, finding in poetry a form that both does and does not enable her to say what she feels. The relationship of her views, values, and feelings to the prevailing social and cultural attitudes of her era is one of the sources of her work's fascination and significance.

For a brief survey of the life and work, see Richard Benvenuto, *Amy Lowell* (1985). See also Horace Gregory, *Amy Lowell: Portrait of the Poet in Her Time* (1958); Jean Gould, *Amy: The World of Amy Lowell and the Imagist Movement* (1975); Glenn Richard Ruihley, *The Thorn of a Rose: Amy Lowell Reconsidered* (1975); and C. David Heymann, *American Aristocracy: The Lives and Times of James Russell, Amy, and Robert Lowell* (1980). See also the stimulating collection *Amy Lowell: American Modern*, eds. Adrienne Munich and Melissa Bradshaw (2004).

The Captured Goddess

Over the housetops,
Above the rotating chimney-pots,
I have seen a shiver of amethyst,
And blue and cinnamon have flickered
A moment,   5
At the far end of a dusty street.

Through sheeted rain
Has come a lustre of crimson,
And I have watched moonbeams
Hushed by a film of palest green.   10

It was her wings,
Goddess!
Who stepped over the clouds,
And laid her rainbow feathers
Aslant on the currents of the air.   15

I followed her for long,
With gazing eyes and stumbling feet.
I cared not where she led me,
My eyes were full of colours:
Saffrons, rubies, the yellows of beryls,   20
And the indigo-blue of quartz;
Flights of rose, layers of chrysoprase,

Points of orange, spirals of vermilion,
The spotted gold of tiger-lily petals,
The loud pink of bursting hydrangeas.   25
I followed,
And watched for the flashing of her wings.

In the city I found her,
The narrow-streeted city.
In the market-place I came upon her,   30
Bound and trembling.
Her fluted wings were fastened to her sides with cords,
She was naked and cold,
For that day the wind blew
Without sunshine.   35

Men chaffered for her,
They bargained in silver and gold,
In copper, in wheat,
And called their bids across the marketplace.

The Goddess wept.   40

Hiding my face I fled,
And the grey wind hissed behind me,
Along the narrow streets.

                                                   [1914]

Venus Transiens[1]

Tell me,
Was Venus more beautiful
Than you are,
When she topped
The crinkled waves,   5
Drifting shoreward
On her plaited shell?
Was Botticelli's[2] vision
Fairer than mine;
And were the painted rosebuds   10
He tossed his lady,
Of better worth
Than the words I blow about you
To cover your too great loveliness

---

[1]Venus is the Roman goddess of beauty. The Latin expression *Venus transiens* may be interpreted as "Venus passing over," "Venus changing over," or "Venus in transition."
[2]One of the more famous paintings of Sandro Botticelli (1446–1510) is *The Birth of Venus* (c. 1486), in which the goddess is depicted emerging from the sea. She stands on a scallop shell and is gently blown toward the shore by the gods.

As with a gauze   15
Of misted silver?
For me,
You stand poised
In the blue and buoyant air,
Cinctured by bright winds,   20
Treading the sunlight.
And the waves which precede you
Ripple and stir
The sands at my feet.

[1919]

Madonna of the Evening Flowers

All day long I have been working,
Now I am tired.
I call: "Where are you?"
But there is only the oak tree rustling in the wind.
The house is very quiet,   5
The sun shines in on your books,
On your scissors and thimble just put down,
But you are not there.
Suddenly I am lonely:
Where are you?   10
I go about searching.

Then I see you,
Standing under a spire a pale blue larkspur,
With a basket of roses on your arm.
You are cool, like silver,   15
And you smile.
I think the Canterbury bells[1] are playing little tunes.

You tell me that the peonies need spraying,
That the columbines have overrun all bounds,
That the pyrus japonica should be cut back and rounded.   20
You tell me these things.
But I look at you, heart of silver,
White heart-flame of polished silver,
Burning beneath the blue steeples of the larkspur,
And I long to kneel instantly at your feet,   25
While all about us peal the loud, sweet *Te Deums*[2] of the Canterbury
    bells.

[1919]

---

[1]Bell-shaped blue flowers that bloom in spring; also called *bellflowers*. Also a pun on the famous bells of
Canterbury Cathedral, the seat of the Church of England.
[2]Christian hymns in praise of God.

September, 1918

This afternoon was the colour of water falling through sunlight;
The trees glittered with the tumbling of leaves;
The sidewalks shone like alleys of dropped maple leaves,
And the houses ran along them laughing out of square, open windows.
Under a tree in the park,   5
Two little boys, lying flat on their faces,
Were carefully gathering red berries
To put in a pasteboard box.
Some day there will be no war,
then I shall take out this afternoon   10
And turn it in my fingers,
And remark the sweet taste of it upon my palate,
And note the crisp variety of its flights of leaves.
To-day I can only gather it
And put it into my lunch-box,   15
For I have time for nothing
But the endeavour to balance myself
Upon a broken world.

[1919]

New Heavens for Old

I am useless.
What I do is nothing.
What I think has no savour.
There is an almanac between the windows:
It is of the year when I was born.   5

My fellows call to me to join them,
They shout for me,
Passing the house in a great wind of vermilion banners.
They are fresh and fulminant.
They are indecent and strut with the thought of it,   10
They laugh, and curse, and brawl,
And cheer a holocaust of "Who comes firsts!" at the iron fronts of the
    houses at the two edges of the street.
Young men with naked hearts jeering between iron house-fronts,
Young men with naked bodies beneath their clothes
Passionately conscious of them,   15
Ready to strip off their clothes,
Ready to strip off their customs, their usual routine,
Clamouring for the rawness of life,
In love with appetite,

Proclaiming it as a creed,   20
Worshipping youth,
Worshipping themselves.
They call for women and the women come,
They bare the whiteness of their lusts to the dead gaze of the old
     housefronts,
They roar down the street like flame,   25
They explode upon the dead houses like new, sharp fire.

But I—
I arrange three roses in a Chinese vase:
A pink one,
A red one,
A yellow one.   30
I fuss over their arrangement.
Then I sit in a South window
And sip pale wine with a touch of hemlock[1] in it,
And think of Winter nights,   35
And field-mice crossing and re-crossing
The spot which will be my grave.

                                  [1927]

The Taxi

When I go away from you
The world beats dead
Like a slackened drum.
I call out for you against the jutted stars
And shout into the ridges of the wind.   5
Streets coming fast,
One after the other,
Wedge you away from me,
And the lamps of the city prick my eyes
So that I can no longer see your face.   10
Why should I leave you,
To wound myself upon the sharp edges of the night?

                                  [1914]

[1]A poisonous weed.

Though̶ ̶̶d with pastoral scenes in New England, Robert Frost was born i̶ ̶̶cisco, California. His family moved to Massachusetts in 1885, ̶ ̶̶ath of Frost's father. He attended high school in Lawrence, Massac̶.̶.̶.̶.̶, ̶nd proceeded in 1892 to Dartmouth College in Hanover, New Hampshire, but spent less than a semester there. Frost then taught school in Massachusetts and in 1895 married Elinor White, who had been valedictorian with him in his senior year in high school. Their long relationship (she died in 1938) was tense and difficult and filled with terrible anguish (two of their children died young; two older daughters suffered amid troubled marriages; another daughter died giving birth; and a son committed suicide). But Elinor was a major source of inspiration for Frost, and the trials and rewards of their marriage are in the background of many of his poems.

During the next few years, Frost took courses at Harvard (1897–99), continued with the poetry-writing he had begun in high school, farmed in Derry, New Hampshire, and taught at Pinkerton's Academy, located in Derry.

In 1912, Frost took a dramatic step: He sold the farm and traveled with his family to England, where he intended to focus on a career as a writer. His first book, *A Boy's Will*, was published in England in 1913 (and a year later in the United States), and two more followed: *North of Boston* (1914) and *Mountain Interval* (1916).

Frost benefited at this time from the friendship and support of Ezra Pound, who published an essay on him in Harriet Monroe's influential magazine, *Poetry*. Another friend was the English writer Edward Thomas, whom Frost influenced, and whose only book of poetry, published before his death in World War I, was dedicated to Frost.

Frost and his family returned to the United States in February 1915. He purchased a farm in Franconia, New Hampshire, wrote and published extensively, and won critical notice as a writer, teacher, lecturer, and reader of his verse. Frost became one of the most widely honored and popular American poets of the twentieth century, more than succeeding in his ambition to compose "a few poems it will be hard to get rid of."

Frost was not a fan of free verse. "I'd just as soon," he remarked, "play tennis with the net down." The key for Frost was to integrate rhyme, meter, and stanza with the tones, pitches, and effects of the speaking voice. "For Frost there must always be in poetry the reconciliation between the cadence, the rhythm, of the spoken sentence and the cadence, the rhythm, of the meter," his biographer Lawrance Thompson has said.

Frost is a poet of the ear as well as of the eye: his organizations of words, sly and suggestive, must be heard. He commented in an interview (1915):

What we do get in life and miss so often in literature is the sentence sounds that underlie the words. Words in themselves do not convey meaning, and to [...prove] this, which may seem entirely unreasonable to any one who does not understand the psychology of sound, let us take the example of two people who are talking on the other side of a closed door, whose voices can be heard but whose words cannot be distinguished. Even though the words do not carry, the sound of them does, and the listener can catch the meaning of the conversation....Art is the amplification and sophistication of the proverbial turns of speech.

Frost seems and sounds simple: compared to much modern poetry, which is overtly difficult and dense, his poems are congenial, lingering in the mind and memorable. But on close inspection, Frost's complexity, depth, and subtle irony (laced with comic, dry wit) resonate in the lines, in the tones of the voice that speaks in the poems, a voice that is direct yet elusive, haunting, profound. Perhaps this explains why one critic described Frost as the "hardest" of modern poets and why another—perhaps thinking of such poems as "The Road Not Taken," "Fire and Ice," "Nothing Gold Can Stay," "Desert Places," and "Design," here—termed him America's "most philosophical" poet.

There is much pain in Frost—in, for example, "Home Burial"—and terror and fear, even horror, as in "'Out, Out'—." Mysteries abound about the self and its relationships with other persons and about the self and its efforts to gauge its relationship to nature and the universe. Frost has a strong sense of disorder, chaos, entropy, decay. Life is dark, deep, hard to fathom. It is a challenge to find meaning in existence; it is a challenge simply to be alive. In this tough struggle, poetry functions, for Frost, as a "momentary stay against confusion."

On Frost's tombstone is the inscription: "I had a lover's quarrel with the world."

For an overview, see William H. Pritchard, *Frost: A Literary Life Reconsidered* (1984; new ed., 1993). Biographies include Jeffrey Meyers, *Robert Frost: A Biography* (1996); and Jay Parini, *Robert Frost: A Life* (2000). For more details, see Lawrance Thompson, *Robert Frost*, 3 vols. (1966–76). For critical interpretation, see Reuben Brower, *The Poetry of Robert Frost: Constellations of Intention* (1963); Richard Poirier, *Robert Frost: The Work of Knowing* (1977); and Mark Richardson, *The Ordeal of Robert Frost: The Poet and His Poetics* (1997). Also illuminating are *Robert Frost on Writing*, ed. Elaine Barry (1973); and *Frost: Centennial Essays*, compiled by the Committee on the Frost Centennial of the University of Southern Mississippi, 3 vols. (1974–78; vols. 2 & 3, ed. Jac Tharpe). See also Robert Pack, *Belief and Uncertainty in the Poetry of Robert Frost* (2003); Robert Faggen, *The Cambridge Introduction to Robert Frost* (2008); and Marit J. MacArthur,

Robert Frost, photographed by Walter Albertin, on Frost's 85th birthday (1959).

The American Landscape in the Poetry of Frost, Bishop, and Ashbery (2010). Also recommended is Tim Kendall, *The Art of Robert Frost* (2012), which combines a selection of poems with a critical study.

The Pasture

I'm going out to clean the pasture spring;
I'll only stop to rake the leaves away
(And wait to watch the water clear, I may):
I sha'n't be gone long.—You come too.

I'm going out to fetch the little calf   5
That's standing by the mother. It's so young,
It totters when she licks it with her tongue.
I sha'n't be gone long.—You come too.

[1914]

Mending Wall

Something there is that doesn't love a wall,
That sends the frozen-ground-swell under it,
And spills the upper boulders in the sun;
And makes gaps even two can pass abreast.
The work of hunters is another thing: 5
I have come after them and made repair
Where they have left not one stone on a stone,
But they would have the rabbit out of hiding,
To please the yelping dogs. The gaps I mean,
No one has seen them made or heard them made,   10
But at spring mending-time we find them there.
I let my neighbor know beyond the hill;
And on a day we meet to walk the line
And set the wall between us once again.
We keep the wall between us as we go.   15
To each the boulders that have fallen to each.
And some are loaves and some so nearly balls
We have to use a spell to make them balance:
'Stay where you are until our backs are turned!'
We wear our fingers rough with handling them.   20
Oh, just another kind of outdoor game,
One on a side. It comes to little more:
There where it is we do not need the wall:
He is all pine and I am apple orchard.
My apple trees will never get across   25
And eat the cones under his pines, I tell him.
He only says, 'Good fences make good neighbors.'
Spring is the mischief in me, and I wonder
If I could put a notion in his head:
'Why do they make good neighbors? Isn't it   30
Where there are cows? But here there are no cows.
Before I built a wall I'd ask to know
What I was walling in or walling out,
And to whom I was like to give offense.
Something there is that doesn't love a wall,   35
That wants it down. I could say 'Elves' to him,
But it's not elves exactly, and I'd rather
He said it for himself. I see him there
Bringing a stone grasped firmly by the top
In each hand, like an old-stone savage armed.   40
He moves in darkness as it seems to me,
Not of woods only and the shade of trees.

He will not go behind his father's saying,
And he likes having thought of it so well
He says again, 'Good fences make good neighbors.'   45

[1914]

Home Burial

He saw her from the bottom of the stairs
Before she saw him. She was starting down,
Looking back over her shoulder at some fear.
She took a doubtful step and then undid it
To raise herself and look again. He spoke   5
Advancing toward her: 'What is it you see
From up there always—for I want to know.'
She turned and sank upon her skirts at that,
And her face changed from terrified to dull.
He said to gain time: 'What is it you see,'   10
Mounting until she cowered under him.
'I will find out now—you must tell me, dear.'
She, in her place, refused him any help
With the least stiffening of her neck and silence.
She let him look, sure that he wouldn't see,   15
Blind creature; and a while he didn't see.
But at last he murmured, 'Oh,' and again, 'Oh.'

'What is it—what?' she said.
                    'Just that I see.'
'You don't,' she challenged. 'Tell me what it is.'   20

'The wonder is I didn't see at once.
I never noticed it from here before.
I must be wonted to it—that's the reason.
The little graveyard where my people are!
So small the window frames the whole of it.   25
Not so much larger than a bedroom, is it?
There are three stones of slate and one of marble,
Broad-shouldered little slabs there in the sunlight
On the sidehill. We haven't to mind *those*.
But I understand: it is not the stones,   30
But the child's mound——'

                    'Don't, don't, don't, don't,' she cried.

She withdrew shrinking from beneath his arm
That rested on the banister, and slid downstairs;
And turned on him with such a daunting look,   35
He said twice over before he knew himself:
'Can't a man speak of his own child he's lost?'

'Not you! Oh, where's my hat? Oh, I don't need it!
I must get out of here. I must get air.
I don't know rightly whether any man can.'   40

'Amy! Don't go to someone else this time.
Listen to me. I won't come down the stairs.'
He sat and fixed his chin between his fists.
'There's something I should like to ask you, dear.'

'You don't know how to ask it.'   45
                          'Help me, then.'

Her fingers moved the latch for all reply.

'My words are nearly always an offense.
I don't know how to speak of anything
So as to please you. But I might be taught,   50
I should suppose. I can't say I see how.
A man must partly give up being a man
With women-folk. We could have some arrangement
By which I'd bind myself to keep hands off
Anything special you're a-mind to name.   55
Though I don't like such things 'twixt those that love.
Two that don't love can't live together without them.
But two that do can't live together with them.'
She moved the latch a little. 'Don't—don't go.
Don't carry it to someone else this time.   60
Tell me about it if it's something human.
Let me into your grief. I'm not so much
Unlike other folks as your standing there
Apart would make me out. Give me my chance.
I do think, though, you overdo it a little.   65
What was it brought you up to think it the thing
To take your mother-loss of a first child
So inconsolably—in the face of love.
You'd think his memory might be satisfied———'

'There you go sneering now!'   70
                    'I'm not, I'm not!
You make me angry. I'll come down to you.
God, what a woman! And it's come to this,
A man can't speak of his own child that's dead.'

'You can't because you don't know how to speak.   75
If you had any feelings, you that dug
With your own hand—how could you?—his little grave;
I saw you from that very window there,

Making the gravel leap and leap in air,
Leap up, like that, like that, and land so lightly   80
And roll back down the mound beside the hole.
I thought, Who is that man? I didn't know you.
And I crept down the stairs and up the stairs
To look again, and still your spade kept lifting.
Then you came in. I heard your rumbling voice   85
Out in the kitchen, and I don't know why,
But I went near to see with my own eyes.
You could sit there with the stains on your shoes
Of the fresh earth from your own baby's grave
And talk about your everyday concerns.   90
You had stood the spade up against the wall
Outside there in the entry, for I saw it.'

'I shall laugh the worst laugh I ever laughed.
I'm cursed. God, if I don't believe I'm cursed.'

'I can repeat the very words you were saying.   95
"Three foggy mornings and one rainy day
Will rot the best birch fence a man can build."
Think of it, talk like that at such a time!
What had how long it takes a birch to rot
To do with what was in the darkened parlor?   100
You *couldn't* care! The nearest friends can go
With anyone to death, comes so far short
They might as well not try to go at all.
No, from the time when one is sick to death,
One is alone, and he dies more alone.   105
Friends make pretense of following to the grave,
But before one is in it, their minds are turned
And making the best of their way back to life
And living people, and things they understand.
But the world's evil. I won't have grief so   110
If I can change it. Oh, I won't, I won't!'

'There, you have said it all and you feel better.
You won't go now. You're crying. Close the door.
The heart's gone out of it: why keep it up?
Amy! There's someone coming down the road!'   115

'*You*—oh, you think the talk is all. I must go—
Somewhere out of this house. How can I make you——'

'If—you—do!' She was opening the door wider.
'Where do you mean to go? First tell me that.
I'll follow and bring you back by force. I *will*!—'   120

[1914]

After Apple-Picking

My long two-pointed ladder's sticking through a tree
Toward heaven still,
And there's a barrel that I didn't fill
Beside it, and there may be two or three
Apples I didn't pick upon some bough.   5
But I am done with apple-picking now.
Essence of winter sleep is on the night,
The scent of apples: I am drowsing off.
I cannot rub the strangeness from my sight
I got from looking through a pane of glass   10
I skimmed this morning from the drinking trough
And held against the world of hoary grass.
It melted, and I let it fall and break.
But I was well
Upon my way to sleep before it fell,   15
And I could tell
What form my dreaming was about to take.
Magnified apples appear and disappear,
Stem end and blossom end,
And every fleck of russet showing clear.   20
My instep arch not only keeps the ache,
It keeps the pressure of a ladder-round.
I feel the ladder sway as the boughs bend.
And I keep hearing from the cellar bin
The rumbling sound   25
Of load on load of apples coming in.
For I have had too much
Of apple-picking: I am overtired
Of the great harvest I myself desired.
There were ten thousand thousand fruit to touch,   30
Cherish in hand, lift down, and not let fall.
For all
That struck the earth,
No matter if not bruised or spiked with stubble,
Went surely to the cider-apple heap   35
As of no worth.
One can see what will trouble
This sleep of mine, whatever sleep it is.
Were he not gone,
The woodchuck could say whether it's like his   40
Long sleep, as I describe its coming on,
Or just some human sleep.

[1914]

The Wood-Pile

Out walking in the frozen swamp one gray day,
I paused and said, 'I will turn back from here.
No, I will go on farther—and we shall see.'
The hard snow held me, save where now and then
One foot went through. The view was all in lines   5
Straight up and down of tall slim trees
Too much alike to mark or name a place by
So as to say for certain I was here
Or somewhere else: I was just far from home.
A small bird flew before me. He was careful   10
To put a tree between us when he lighted,
And say no word to tell me who he was
Who was so foolish as to think what *he* thought.
He thought that I was after him for a feather—
The white one in his tail; like one who takes   15
Everything said as personal to himself.
One flight out sideways would have undeceived him.
And then there was a pile of wood for which
I forgot him and let his little fear
Carry him off the way I might have gone,   20
Without so much as wishing him good-night.
He went behind it to make his last stand.
It was a cord of maple, cut and split
And piled—and measured, four by four by eight.
And not another like it could I see.   25
No runner tracks in this year's snow looped near it.
And it was older sure than this year's cutting,
Or even last year's or the year's before.
The wood was gray and the bark warping off it
And the pile somewhat sunken. Clematis   30
Had wound strings round and round it like a bundle.
What held it though on one side was a tree
Still growing, and on one a stake and prop,
These latter about to fall. I thought that only
Someone who lived in turning to fresh tasks   35
Could so forget his handiwork on which
He spent himself, the labor of his ax,
And leave it there far from a useful fireplace
To warm the frozen swamp as best it could
With the slow smokeless burning of decay.   40

[1914]

The Road Not Taken

Two roads diverged in a yellow wood,
And sorry I could not travel both
And be one traveler, long I stood
And looked down one as far as I could
To where it bent in the undergrowth;   5

Then took the other, as just as fair,
And having perhaps the better claim,
Because it was grassy and wanted wear;
Though as for that the passing there
Had worn them really about the same,   10

And both that morning equally lay
In leaves no step had trodden black.
Oh, I kept the first for another day!
Yet knowing how way leads on to way,
I doubted if I should ever come back.   15

I shall be telling this with a sigh
Somewhere ages and ages hence:
Two roads diverged in a wood, and I—
I took the one less traveled by,
And that has made all the difference.   20

[1916]

Birches

When I see birches bend to left and right
Across the lines of straighter darker trees,
I like to think some boy's been swinging them.
But swinging doesn't bend them down to stay
As ice-storms do. Often you must have seen them   5
Loaded with ice a sunny winter morning
After a rain. They click upon themselves
As the breeze rises, and turn many-colored
As the stir cracks and crazes their enamel.
Soon the sun's warmth makes them shed crystal shells   10
Shattering and avalanching on the snow-crust—
Such heaps of broken glass to sweep away
You'd think the inner dome of heaven had fallen.
They are dragged to the withered bracken[1] by the load,
And they seem not to break; though once they are bowed   15

---

[1]Large coarse ferns or thicket of such plants.

So low for long, they never right themselves:
You may see their trunks arching in the woods
Years afterwards, trailing their leaves on the ground
Like girls on hands and knees that throw their hair
Before them over their heads to dry in the sun.   20
But I was going to say when Truth broke in
With all her matter-of-fact about the ice-storm
I should prefer to have some boy bend them
As he went out and in to fetch the cows—   25
Some boy too far from town to learn baseball,
Whose only play was what he found himself,
Summer or winter, and could play alone.
One by one he subdued his father's trees
By riding them down over and over again   30
Until he took the stiffness out of them,
And not one but hung limp, not one was left
For him to conquer. He learned all there was
To learn about not launching out too soon
And so not carrying the tree away   35
Clear to the ground. He always kept his poise
To the top branches, climbing carefully
With the same pains you use to fill a cup
Up to the brim, and even above the brim.
Then he flung outward, feet first, with a swish,   40
Kicking his way down through the air to the ground.
So was I once myself a swinger of birches.
And so I dream of going back to be.
It's when I'm weary of considerations,
And life is too much like a pathless wood   45
Where your face burns and tickles with the cobwebs
Broken across it, and one eye is weeping
From a twig's having lashed across it open.
I'd like to get away from earth awhile
And then come back to it and begin over.   50
May no fate willfully misunderstand me
And half grant what I wish and snatch me away
Not to return. Earth's the right place for love:
I don't know where it's likely to go better.
I'd like to go by climbing a birch tree,   55
And climb black branches up a snow-white trunk
Toward heaven, till the tree could bear no more,
But dipped its top and set me down again.
That would be good both going and coming back.
One could do worse than be a swinger of birches.   60

[1916]

'Out, Out—'[1]

The buzz saw snarled and rattled in the yard
And made dust and dropped stove-length sticks of wood,
Sweet-scented stuff when the breeze drew across it.
And from there those that lifted eyes could count
Five mountain ranges one behind the other   5
Under the sunset far into Vermont.
And the saw snarled and rattled, snarled and rattled,
As it ran light, or had to bear a load.
And nothing happened: day was all but done.
Call it a day, I wish they might have said   10
To please the boy by giving him the half hour
That a boy counts so much when saved from work.
His sister stood beside them in her apron
To tell them 'Supper.' At that word, the saw,
As if to prove saws knew what supper meant,   15
Leaped out at the boy's hand, or seemed to leap—
He must have given the hand. However it was,
Neither refused the meeting. But the hand!
The boy's first outcry was a rueful laugh,
As he swung toward them holding up the hand   20
Half in appeal, but half as if to keep
The life from spilling. Then the boy saw all—
Since he was old enough to know, big boy
Doing a man's work, though a child at heart—
He saw all spoiled. 'Don't let him cut my hand off—   25
The doctor, when he comes. Don't let him, sister!'
So. But the hand was gone already.
The doctor put him in the dark of ether.
He lay and puffed his lips out with his breath.
And then—the watcher at his pulse took fright.   30
No one believed. They listened at his heart.
Little—less—nothing!—and that ended it.
No more to build on there. And they, since they
Were not the one dead, turned to their affairs.

[1916]

---

[1]A quotation from William Shakespeare's play *Macbeth* (5.5.23–26): "Out, out, brief candle! / Life's but a walking shadow, a poor player, / That struts and frets his hour upon the stage, / And then is heard no more."

Fire and Ice

Some say the world will end in fire,
Some say in ice.
From what I've tasted of desire
I hold with those who favor fire.
But if it had to perish twice,   5
I think I know enough of hate
To say that for destruction ice
Is also great
And would suffice.

[1923]

Nothing Gold Can Stay

Nature's first green is gold,
Her hardest hue to hold.
Her early leaf's a flower;
But only so an hour.
Then leaf subsides to leaf.   5
So Eden sank to grief,
So dawn goes down to day.
Nothing gold can stay.

[1923]

Stopping by Woods on a Snowy Evening

Whose woods these are I think I know.
His house is in the village though;
He will not see me stopping here
To watch his woods fill up with snow.

My little horse must think it queer   5
To stop without a farmhouse near
Between the woods and frozen lake
The darkest evening of the year.

He gives his harness bells a shake
To ask if there is some mistake.   10
The only other sound's the sweep
Of easy wind and downy flake.

The woods are lovely, dark and deep,
But I have promises to keep,
And miles to go before I sleep,   15
And miles to go before I sleep.

[1923]

Desert Places

Snow falling and night falling fast, oh, fast
In a field I looked into going past,
And the ground almost covered smooth in snow,
But a few weeds and stubble showing last.

The woods around it have it—it is theirs.   5
All animals are smothered in their lairs.
I am too absent-spirited to count;
The loneliness includes me unawares.

And lonely as it is, that loneliness
Will be more lonely ere it will be less—   10
A blanker whiteness of benighted snow
With no expression, nothing to express.

They cannot scare me with their empty spaces
Between stars—on stars where no human race is.
I have it in me so much nearer home   15
To scare myself with my own desert places.

[1936]

Design

I found a dimpled spider, fat and white,
On a white heal-all, holding up a moth
Like a white piece of rigid satin cloth—
Assorted characters of death and blight
Mixed ready to begin the morning right,   5
Like the ingredients of a witches' broth—
A snow-drop spider, a flower like a froth,
And dead wings carried like a paper kite.

What had that flower to do with being white,
The wayside blue and innocent heal-all?   10
What brought the kindred spider to that height,
Then steered the white moth thither in the night?
What but design of darkness to appall?—
If design govern in a thing so small.

[1936]

Neither Out Far Nor In Deep

The people along the sand
All turn and look one way.
They turn their back on the land.
They look at the sea all day.

As long as it takes to pass   5
A ship keeps raising its hull;
The wetter ground like glass
Reflects a standing gull.

The land may vary more;
But wherever the truth may be—   10
The water comes ashore,
And the people look at the sea.

They cannot look out far.
They cannot look in deep.
But when was that ever a bar   15
To any watch they keep?

[1936]

SHERWOOD ANDERSON ■ (1876–1941)

On November 28, 1912, Sherwood Anderson, the president of Anderson Manufacturing Company (known for its roofing and paint products) in Elyria, northern Ohio, walked out the door of his office and turned his back on his responsibilities as a businessman and as a husband and the father of three children. No longer would Anderson neglect his calling as a literary artist for the sake of commonplace prosperity and success—"money making" (as he phrased it) "as an end in itself."

Anderson's decision was a painful one for his family, but it made for a compelling story about the responsibility of an artist to pursue his or her vocation whatever the cost. This story gave Anderson a legendary status among American writers in the late 1910s and 1920s. His example, his commitment to his craft, and his friendship made Anderson a central figure in the life and literary career of such noteworthy authors as William Faulkner, Ernest Hemingway, John Steinbeck, and Thomas Wolfe.

Anderson was born in Camden in southwestern Ohio and raised in Clyde, farther north; he later made Clyde the setting for the stories in his best and most influential book, *Winesburg, Ohio* (1919). He worked in Chicago in the mid-1890s as a laborer, was in the military during the Spanish-American War (1898), studied at Wittenberg Academy in Ohio, and then returned to Chicago, where he enjoyed success as an advertising writer. Later he married, started a family, and did well as an Ohio businessman.

Leaving his business and family behind on that fateful day in 1912 and relocating to Chicago, Anderson published his first novel, *Windy McPherson's Son* in 1916, and he remarried in the same year (more marriages followed in later years). His significant books include the novels *Marching Men* (1917) and *Poor White* (1920), the story collections *The Triumph of the Egg* (1921) and *Horses and Men* (1923), and the autobiographical *A Story Teller's Story* (1924). Assessing these books, the pugnacious, respected critic H. L. Mencken said in the 1920s that Anderson was "America's Most Distinctive Novelist." His later work, undertaken while he published and edited newspapers in Virginia, is less successful, though he did produce an interesting book of essays, *Puzzled America* (1935), about his travels in the United States during the first years of the Great Depression. He died while on a trip to South America; his gravestone states (as he had instructed): "Life, Not Death, Is the Great Adventure."

"Hands," the second story in *Winesburg, Ohio*, may have been written during Anderson's years in Elyria, and he termed it "my first authentic tale." It describes a balding man of middle age, Wing Biddlebaum, whose hands seem to possess a life of their own, and his relationship with George Willard, a young man working as a reporter for the town newspaper. A fervent man, possibly homosexual, Wing is a former schoolteacher who displayed an affection for his students that made him suspicious and feared,

Sherwood Anderson, photographed by Carl Van Vechten in 1933, the same
year Anderson married Eleanor Copenhaver.

seen as a real or a potential molester of boys. Intimacy is no longer a possibility for Wing, for his gestures might be misinterpreted and bring perse-
cution down upon him. Like many of Anderson's characters in *Winesburg,
Ohio*, he leads a lonely, unfulfilled life, misunderstood, wandering, and
ostracized, defined by his always-in-motion hands.

A good point of departure: Irving Howe, *Sherwood Anderson* (1951). For
further biographical details, see Kim Townsend, *Sherwood Anderson* (1987).
Also useful are Robert Allen Papinchak, *Sherwood Anderson: A Study of the
Short Fiction* (1992); and Judy Jo Small, *A Reader's Guide to the Short Stories of Sherwood Anderson* (1994). The best recent biographical and critical study is Walter B. Rideout, *Sherwood Anderson: A Writer in America*, 2
volumes (2005, 2007).

Hands

Upon the half decayed veranda of a small frame house that stood near the
edge of a ravine near the town of Winesburg, Ohio, a fat little old man
walked nervously up and down. Across a long field that had been seeded for

clover but that had produced only a dense crop of yellow mustard weeds, he could see the public highway along which went a wagon filled with berry pickers returning from the fields. The berry pickers, youths and maidens, laughed and shouted boisterously. A boy clad in a blue shirt leaped from the wagon and attempted to drag after him one of the maidens, who screamed and protested shrilly. The feet of the boy in the road kicked up a cloud of dust that floated across the face of the departing sun. Over the long field came a thin girlish voice. "Oh, you Wing Biddlebaum, comb your hair, it's falling into your eyes," commanded the voice to the man, who was bald and whose nervous little hands fiddled about the bare white forehead as though arranging a mass of tangled locks.

Wing Biddlebaum, forever frightened and beset by a ghostly band of doubts, did not think of himself as in any way a part of the life of the town where he had lived for twenty years. Among all the people of Winesburg but one had come close to him. With George Willard, son of Tom Willard, the proprietor of the New Willard House, he had formed something like a friendship. George Willard was the reporter on the Winesburg Eagle and sometimes in the evenings he walked out along the highway to Wing Biddlebaum's house. Now as the old man walked up and down on the veranda, his hands moving nervously about, he was hoping that George Willard would come and spend the evening with him. After the wagon containing the berry pickers had passed, he went across the field through the tall mustard weeds and climbing a rail fence peered anxiously along the road to the town. For a moment he stood thus, rubbing his hands together and looking up and down the road, and then, fear overcoming him, ran back to walk again upon the porch on his own house.

In the presence of George Willard, Wing Biddlebaum, who for twenty years had been the town mystery, lost something of his timidity, and his shadowy personality, submerged in a sea of doubts, came forth to look at the world. With his young reporter at his side, he ventured in the light of day into Main Street or strode up and down on the rickety front porch of his own house, talking excitedly. The voice that had been low and trembling became shrill and loud. The bent figure straightened. With a kind of wriggle, like a fish returned to the brook by the fisherman, Biddlebaum the silent began to talk, striving to put into words the ideas that had been accumulated by his mind during long years of silence.

Wing Biddlebaum talked much with his hands. The slender expressive fingers, forever active, forever striving to conceal themselves in his pockets or behind his back, came forth and became the piston rods of his machinery of expression.

The story of Wing Biddlebaum is a story of hands. Their restless activity, like unto the beating of the wings of an imprisoned bird, had given him his name. Some obscure poet of the town had thought of it. The hands alarmed their owner. He wanted to keep them hidden away and looked with amazement at the quiet inexpressive hands of other men who worked beside him in the fields, or passed, driving sleepy teams on country roads.

When he talked to George Willard, Wing Biddlebaum closed his fists and beat with them upon a table or on the walls of his house. The action made him more comfortable. If the desire to talk came to him when the two were walking in the fields, he sought out a stump or the top board of a fence and with his hands pounding busily talked with renewed ease.

The story of Wing Biddlebaum's hands is worth a book in itself. Sympathetically set forth it would tap many strange, beautiful qualities in obscure men. It is a job for a poet. In Winesburg the hands had attracted attention merely because of their activity. With them Wing Biddlebaum had picked as high as a hundred and forty quarts of strawberries in a day. They became his distinguishing feature, the source of his fame. Also they made more grotesque an already grotesque and elusive individuality. Winesburg was proud of the hands of Wing Biddlebaum in the same spirit in which it was proud of Banker White's new stone house and Wesley Moyer's bay stallion, Tony Tip, that had won the two-fifteen trot at the fall races in Cleveland.

As for George Willard, he had many times wanted to ask about the hands. At times an almost overwhelming curiosity had taken hold of him. He felt that there must a reason for their strange activity and their inclination to keep hidden away and only a growing respect for Wing Biddlebaum kept him from blurting out the questions that were often in his mind.

Once he had been on the point of asking. The two were walking in the fields on a summer afternoon and had stopped to sit upon a grassy bank. All afternoon Wing Biddlebaum had talked as one inspired. By a fence he had stopped and beating like a giant woodpecker upon the top board had shouted at George Willard, condemning his tendency to be too much influenced by the people about him. "You are destroying yourself," he cried. "You have the inclination to be alone and to dream and you are afraid of dreams. You want to be like others in town here. You hear them talk and you try to imitate them."

On the grassy bank Wing Biddlebaum had tried again to drive his point home. His voice became soft and reminiscent, and with a sigh of contentment he launched into a long rambling talk, speaking as one lost in a dream.

Out of the dream Wing Biddlebaum made a picture for George Willard. In the picture men lived again in a kind of pastoral golden age. Across a green open country came clean-limbed young men, some afoot, some mounted upon horses. In crowds the young men came to gather about the feet of an old man who sat beneath a tree in a tiny garden and who talked to them.

Wing Biddlebaum became wholly inspired. For once he forgot the hands. Slowly they stole forth and lay upon George Willard's shoulders.

Something new and bold came into the voice that talked. "You must try to forget all you have learned," said the old man. "You must begin to dream. From this time on you must shut your ears to the roaring of the voices."

Pausing in his speech, Wing Biddlebaum looked long and earnestly at George Willard. His eyes glowed. Again he raised the hands to caress the boy and then a look of horror swept over his face.

With a convulsive movement of his body, Wing Biddlebaum sprang to his feet and thrust his hands deep into his trousers pockets. Tears came to his eyes. "I must be getting along home. I can talk no more with you," he said nervously.

Without looking back, the old man had hurried down the hillside and across a meadow, leaving George Willard perplexed and frightened upon the grassy slope. With a shiver of dread the boy arose and went along the road toward town. "I'll not ask him about his hands," he thought, touched by the memory of the terror he had seen in the man's eyes. "There's something wrong, but I don't want to know what it is. His hands have something to do with his fear of me and of everyone."

And George Willard was right. Let us look briefly into the story of his hands. Perhaps our talking of them will arouse the poet who will tell the hidden wonder story of the influence for which the hands were but fluttering pennants of promise.

In his youth Wing Biddlebaum had been a school teacher in a town in Pennsylvania. He was not then known as Wing Biddlebaum, but went by the less euphonic name of Adolph Myers. As Adolph Myers he was much loved by the boys of his school.

Adolph Myers was meant by nature to be a teacher of youth. He was one of those rare, little-understood men who rule by a power so gentle that it passes as a lovable weakness. In their feeling for the boys under their charge such men are not unlike the finer sort of women in their love of men.

And yet that is but crudely stated. It needs the poet there. With the boys of his school, Adolph Myers had walked in the evening or had sat talking until dusk upon the schoolhouse steps lost in a kind of dream. Here and there went his hands, caressing the shoulders of the boys, playing about the tousled heads. As he talked his voice became soft and musical. There was a caress in that also. In a way the voice and the hands, the stroking of the shoulders and the touching of the hair were a part of the schoolmaster's effort to carry a dream into the young minds. By the caress that was in his fingers he expressed himself. He was one of those men in whom the force that creates life is diffused, not centralized. Under the caress of his hands doubt and disbelief went out of the minds of the boys and they began also to dream.

And then the tragedy. A half-witted boy of the school became enamored of the young master. In his bed at night he imagined unspeakable things and in the morning went forth to tell his dreams as facts. Strange, hideous accusations fell from his loose-hung lips. Through the Pennsylvania town went a shiver. Hidden, shadowy doubts that had been in men's minds concerning Adolph Myers were galvanized into beliefs.

The tragedy did not linger. Trembling lads were jerked out of bed and questioned. "He put his arms about me," said one. His fingers were always playing in my hair," said another.

One afternoon a man of the town, Henry Bradford, who kept a saloon, came to the schoolhouse door. Calling Adolph Myers into the school yard he began to beat him with his fists. As his hard knuckles beat down into the frightened face of the school-master, his wrath became more and more terrible. Screaming with dismay, the children ran here and there like disturbed insects. "I'll teach you to put your hands on my boy, you beast," roared the saloon keeper, who, tired of beating the master, had begun to kick him about the yard.

Adolph Myers was driven from the Pennsylvania town in the night. With lanterns in their hands a dozen men came to the door of the house where he lived alone and commanded that he dress and come forth. It was raining and one of the men had a rope in his hands. They had intended to hang the school-master, but something in his figure, so small, white, and pitiful, touched their hearts and they let him escape. As he ran away into the darkness they repented of their weakness and ran after him, swearing and throwing sticks and great balls of soft mud at the figure that screamed and ran faster and faster into the darkness.

For twenty years Adolph Myers had lived alone in Winesburg. He was but forty but looked sixty-five. The name of Biddlebaum he got from a box of goods seen at a freight station as he hurried through an eastern Ohio town. He had an aunt in Winesburg, a black-toothed old woman who raised chickens, and with her he lived until she died. He had been ill for a year after the experience in Pennsylvania, and after his recovery worked as a day laborer in the fields, going timidly about and striving to conceal his hands. Although he did not understand what had happened he felt that the hands must be to blame. Again and again the fathers of the boys had talked of the hands. "Keep your hands to yourself," the saloon keeper had roared, dancing, with fury in the schoolhouse yard.

Upon the veranda of his house by the ravine, Wing Biddlebaum continued to walk up and down until the sun had disappeared and the road beyond the field was lost in the grey shadows. Going into his house he cut slices of bread and spread honey upon them. When the rumble of the evening train that took away the express cars loaded with the day's harvest of berries had passed and restored the silence of the summer night, he went again to walk upon the veranda. In the darkness he could not see the hands and they became quiet. Although he still hungered for the presence of the boy, who was the medium through which he expressed his love of man, the hunger became again a part of his loneliness and his waiting. Lighting a lamp, Wing Biddlebaum washed the few dishes soiled by his simple meal and, setting up a folding cot by the screen door that led to the porch, prepared to undress for the night. A few stray white bread crumbs lay on the cleanly washed floor by the table; putting the lamp upon a low stool he began to pick up the crumbs, carrying them to his mouth one by one with unbelievable rapidity. In the dense blotch of light beneath the table, the kneeling figure looked like a priest engaged in some service of his church. The nervous expressive fingers, flashing in and out of the light, might well have been mistaken for the fingers of the devotee going swiftly through decade after decade of his rosary.[1]

[1919]

---

[1] A string of beads used in a prayer of devotion to the Virgin Mary.

SUSAN GLASPELL ■ (1876–1948)

Born in Davenport, Iowa, Susan Glaspell graduated in 1899 from Drake University in Des Moines, Iowa, and took a job as a journalist for the *Des Moines Daily News*. But once her short stories, regional in setting and romantic in plot, began to appear in *The Ladies' Home Journal* and other popular magazines, she turned away from newspaper work.

Glaspell moved to New York City's Greenwich Village in 1911, and two years later she married George Cram Cook, a Davenport, Iowa-born Harvard graduate, writer, and stage director. Together in 1915 they established the Provincetown Players in Provincetown, Massachusetts, on the easternmost tip of Cape Cod.

A gifted group of directors, writers, actors, and actresses, formed in opposition to Broadway commercialism and drawn to experimental drama, the Provincetown Players included such talented figures as the playwright Eugene O'Neill, the poet and playwright (noted for her one-act satires) Edna St. Vincent Millay, and the radical journalist John Reed (later the author of *Ten Days That Shook the World*, 1919, an eyewitness account of the Russian Revolution). The Players first performed in The Wharf Theater in Provincetown, and, in 1916–17, in Greenwich Village at The Playwright's Theater. By the mid-1920s, they had produced nearly 100 plays.

Both an actress and a playwright, Glaspell wrote a number of dramatic works during this period, including *Women's Honor* (1918), *Bernice* (1919), *The Inheritors* (1921), and *The Verge* (1922). Often having a feminist slant, they show the impact on Glaspell of her experiences as a founding member of Heterodoxy, a group of women radicals active in New York City from 1910 to 1920. Her other works include a novel, *The Glory of the Conquered* (1909), which describes a scientist's blindness and death as he nears making a major discovery; and a later play, *Alison's House* (1930), based on the life of Emily Dickinson and dealing with the disagreements and tensions among members of a dead poet's family about whether or not to publish her work.

Cook died in 1924, while he and Glaspell were living in Greece. The following year she married Norman Matson, a playwright and novelist, but they divorced in 1932. Settling in Provincetown, no longer writing for the stage, Glaspell devoted the final phase of her career to the writing of novels.

The play, *Trifles*, is now recognized as a classic work of feminism and of women's literature. Based on a murder that Glaspell had covered while on the staff of the *Des Moines Daily News* and written in only ten days, *Trifles* was staged by the Provincetown Players in 1916; the next year, Glaspell rewrote it as a short story, titled "A Jury of Her Peers." The play focuses on the arrest of a woman suspected of murdering her husband, and its action is keyed to a character who never appears on stage—one of Glaspell's favorite devices. A shrewd, provocative treatment of gender roles and conflicts, *Trifles* explores the themes of public and private lives, law and justice, power and powerlessness, and male and female forms of perception.

For biography, see Barbara Ozieblo, *Susan Glaspell: A Critical Biography* (2000). For critical interpretation, see Veronica Makowsky, *Susan Glaspell's Century of American Women: A Critical Interpretation of Her Work* (1993); *Susan Glaspell: Essays on Her Theater and Fiction*, ed. Linda Ben-Zvi (1995); and J. Ellen Gainor, *Susan Glaspell in Context: American Theater, Culture, and Politics, 1915–1948* (2001). Also helpful are Mary E. Papke, *Susan Glaspell: A Research and Production Sourcebook* (1993); and *Susan Glaspell: Essays on Her Theater and Fiction*, ed. Linda Ben-Zvi (1995). The best recent study is Linda Ben-Zvi, *Susan Glaspell: Her Life and Times* (2005).

Trifles

George Henderson, *county attorney*
Henry Peters, *sheriff*
Lewis Hale, *a neighboring farmer*
Mrs. Peters
Mrs. Hale

Scene *The kitchen is the now abandoned farmhouse of John Wright, a gloomy kitchen, and left without having been put in order—unwashed pans under the sink, a loaf of bread outside the bread-box, a dish-towel on the table—other signs of incompleted work. At the rear the outer door opens and the Sheriff comes in followed by the County Attorney and Hale. The Sheriff and Hale are men in middle life, the County Attorney is a young man; all are much bundled up and go at once to the stove. They are followed by the two women—the Sheriff's wife first; she is a slight wiry woman, a thin nervous face. Mrs. Hale is larger and would ordinarily be called more comfortable looking, but she is disturbed now and looks fearfully about as she enters. The women have come in slowly, and stand close together near the door.*

County Attorney *(rubbing his hands):*   This feels good. Come up to the fire, ladies.
Mrs. Peters *(after taking a step forward):*   I'm not—cold.
Sheriff *(unbuttoning his overcoat and stepping away from the stove as if to mark the beginning of official business):*   Now, Mr. Hale, before we move things about, you explain to Mr. Henderson just what you saw when you came here yesterday morning.
County Attorney: By the way, has anything been moved? Are things just as you left them yesterday?
Sheriff *(looking about):*   It's just the same. When it dropped below zero last night I thought I'd better send Frank out this morning to make a

fire for us—no use getting pneumonia with a big case on, but I told him not to touch anything except the stove—and you know Frank.

County Attorney: Somebody should have been left here yesterday.

Sheriff: Oh—yesterday. When I had to send Frank to Morris Center for that man who went crazy—I want you to know I had my hands full yesterday. I knew you could get back from Omaha by today and as long as I went over everything here myself—

County Attorney: Well, Mr. Hale, tell just what happened when you came here yesterday morning.

Hale: Harry and I had started to town with a load of potatoes. We came along the road from my place and as I got here I said, 'I'm going to see if I can't get John Wright to go in with me on a party telephone.' I spoke to Wright about it once before and he put me off, saying folks talked too much anyway, and all he asked was peace and quiet—I guess you know about how much he talked himself; but I thought maybe if I went to the house and talked about it before his wife, though I said to Harry that I didn't know as what his wife wanted made much difference to John—

County Attorney: Let's talk about that later, Mr. Hale. I do want to talk about that, but tell now just what happened when you got to the house.

Hale: I didn't hear or see anything; I knocked at the door, and still it was all quiet inside. I knew they must be up, it was past eight o'clock. So I knocked again, and I thought I heard somebody say, 'Come in.' I wasn't sure, I'm not sure yet, but I opened the door—this door *(indicating the door by which the two women are still standing)* and there in that rocker—*(pointing to it)* sat Mrs. Wright.

(They all look at the rocker.)

County Attorney: What—was she doing?

Hale: She was rockin' back and forth. She had her apron in her hand and was kind of—pleating it.

County Attorney: And how did she—look?

Hale: Well, she looked queer.

County Attorney: How do you mean—queer?

Hale: Well, as if she didn't know what she was going to do next. And kind of done up.

County Attorney: How did she seem to feel about your coming?

Hale: Why, I don't think she minded—one way or other. She didn't pay much attention. I said, 'How do, Mrs. Wright it's cold, ain't it?' And she said, 'Is it?'—and went on kind of pleating at her apron. Well, I was surprised; she didn't ask me to come up to the stove, or to set down, but just sat there, not even looking at me, so I said, 'I want to see John.' And then she—laughed. I guess you would call it a laugh. I thought of

Harry and the team outside, so I said a little sharp: 'Can't I see John?' 'No', she says, kind o' dull like. 'Ain't he home?' says I. 'Yes', says she, 'he's home'. 'Then why can't I see him?' I asked her, out of patience. "Cause he's dead', says she. *'Dead?'* says I. She just nodded her head, not getting a bit excited, but rockin' back and forth. 'Why—where is he?' says I, not knowing what to say. She just pointed upstairs—like that *(himself pointing to the room above)* I got up, with the idea of going up there. I walked from there to here—then I says, 'Why, what did he die of?' 'He died of a rope round his neck', says she, and just went on pleatin' at her apron. Well, I went out and called Harry. I thought I might—need help. We went upstairs and there he was lyin'—

County Attorney: I think I'd rather have you go into that upstairs, where you can point it all out. Just go on now with the rest of the story.

Hale: Well, my first thought was to get that rope off. It looked...*(stops, his face twitches)*...but Harry, he went up to him, and he said, 'No, he's dead all right, and we'd better not touch anything.' So we went back down stairs. She was still sitting that same way. 'Has anybody been notified?' I asked. 'No', says she unconcerned. 'Who did this, Mrs. Wright?' said Harry. He said it business-like—and she stopped pleatin' of her apron. 'I don't know', she says. 'You don't *know*?' says Harry. 'No', says she. 'Weren't you sleepin' in the bed with him?' says Harry. 'Yes', says she, 'but I was on the inside'. 'Somebody slipped a rope round his neck and strangled him and you didn't wake up?' says Harry. 'I didn't wake up', she said after him. We must 'a looked as if we didn't see how that could be, for after a minute she said, 'I sleep sound'. Harry was going to ask her more questions but I said maybe we ought to let her tell her story first to the coroner, or the sheriff, so Harry went fast as he could to Rivers' place, where there's a telephone.

County Attorney: And what did Mrs. Wright do when she knew that you had gone for the coroner?

Hale: She moved from that chair to this one over here *(pointing to a small chair in the corner)* and just sat there with her hands held together and looking down. I got a feeling that I ought to make some conversation, so I said I had come in to see if John wanted to put in a telephone, and at that she started to laugh, and then she stopped and looked at me—scared. *(the County Attorney, who has had his notebook out, makes a note)* I dunno, maybe it wasn't scared. I wouldn't like to say it was. Soon Harry got back, and then Dr Lloyd came, and you, Mr Peters, and so I guess that's all I know that you don't.

County Attorney *(looking around)*:   I guess we'll go upstairs first—and then out to the barn and around there. *(to the Sheriff)* You're convinced that there was nothing important here—nothing that would point to any motive.

Sheriff: Nothing here but kitchen things.

(*The County Attorney, after again looking around the kitchen, opens the door of a cupboard closet. He gets up on a chair and looks on a shelf. Pulls his hand away, sticky.*)

County Attorney: Here's a nice mess.

(*The women draw nearer.*)

Mrs. Peters (*to the other woman*): Oh, her fruit; it did freeze. (*to the Lawyer*) She worried about that when it turned so cold. She said the fire'd go out and her jars would break.

Sheriff: Well, can you beat the women! Held for murder and worryin' about her preserves.

County Attorney: I guess before we're through she may have something more serious than preserves to worry about.

Hale: Well, women are used to worrying over trifles.

(*The two women move a little closer together.*)

County Attorney (*with the gallantry of a young politician*): And yet, for all their worries, what would we do without the ladies? (*the women do not unbend. He goes to the sink, takes a dipperful of water from the pail and pouring it into a basin, washes his hands. Starts to wipe them on the roller-towel, turns it for a cleaner place*) Dirty towels! (*kicks his foot against the pans under the sink*) Not much of a housekeeper, would you say, ladies?

Mrs. Hale (*stiffly*): There's a great deal of work to be done on a farm.

County Attorney: To be sure. And yet (*with a little bow to her*) I know there are some Dickson county farmhouses which do not have such roller towels.

(*He gives it a pull to expose its length again.*)

Mrs. Hale: Those towels get dirty awful quick. Men's hands aren't always as clean as they might be.

County Attorney: Ah, loyal to your sex, I see. But you and Mrs. Wright were neighbors. I suppose you were friends, too.

Mrs. Hale (*shaking her head*): I've not seen much of her of late years. I've not been in this house—it's more than a year.

County Attorney: And why was that? You didn't like her?

Mrs. Hale: I liked her all well enough. Farmers' wives have their hands full, Mr. Henderson. And then—

County Attorney: Yes—?

Mrs. Hale (*looking about*): It never seemed a very cheerful place.

County Attorney: No—it's not cheerful. I shouldn't say she had the homemaking instinct.

Mrs. Hale: Well, I don't know as Wright had, either.

County Attorney: You mean that they didn't get on very well?

Mrs. Hale: No, I don't mean anything. But I don't think a place'd be any cheerfuller for John Wright's being in it.

County Attorney: I'd like to talk more of that a little later. I want to get the lay of things upstairs now.

(He goes to the left, where three steps lead to a stair door.)

Sheriff: I suppose anything Mrs. Peters does'll be all right. She was to take in some clothes for her, you know, and a few little things. We left in such a hurry yesterday.

County Attorney: Yes, but I would like to see what you take, Mrs. Peters, and keep an eye out for anything that might be of use to us.

Mrs. Peters: Yes, Mr. Henderson.

(The women listen to the men's steps on the stairs, then look about the kitchen.)

Mrs. Hale: I'd hate to have men coming into my kitchen, snooping around and criticising.

(She arranges the pans under sink which the Lawyer had shoved out of place.)

Mrs. Peters: Of course it's no more than their duty.

Mrs. Hale: Duty's all right, but I guess that deputy sheriff that came out to make the fire might have got a little of this on. *(gives the roller towel a pull)* Wish I'd thought of that sooner. Seems mean to talk about her for not having things slicked up when she had to come away in such a hurry.

Mrs. Peters *(who has gone to a small table in the left rear corner of the room, and lifted one end of a towel that covers a pan):*   She had bread set.

(Stands still.)

Mrs. Hale *(eyes fixed on a loaf of bread beside the bread-box, which is on a low shelf at the other side of the room. Moves slowly toward it):*   She was going to put this in there. *(picks up loaf, then abruptly drops it. In a manner of returning to familiar things)* It's a shame about her fruit. I wonder if it's all gone. *(gets up on the chair and looks)* I think there's some here that's all right, Mrs. Peters. Yes—here; *(holding it toward the window)* this is cherries, too. *(looking again)* I declare I believe that's the only one. *(gets down, bottle in her hand. Goes to the sink and wipes it off on the outside)* She'll feel awful bad after all her hard work in the hot weather. I remember the afternoon I put up my cherries last summer.

(She puts the bottle on the big kitchen table, center of the room. With a sigh, is about to sit down in the rocking-chair. Before she is seated realizes what

chair it is; with a slow look at it, steps back. The chair which she has touched
rocks back and forth.)

Mrs. Peters: Well, I must get those things from the front room closet. *(she
goes to the door at the right, but after looking into the other room, steps
back)* You coming with me, Mrs. Hale? You could help me carry them.

*(They go in the other room; reappear, Mrs. Peters carrying a dress and skirt,
Mrs. Hale following with a pair of shoes.)*

Mrs. Peters: My, it's cold in there.

(She puts the clothes on the big table, and hurries to the stove.)

Mrs. Hale *(examining the skirt)*: Wright was close. I think maybe that's
why she kept so much to herself. She didn't even belong to the Ladies
Aid. I suppose she felt she couldn't do her part, and then you don't
enjoy things when you feel shabby. She used to wear pretty clothes
and be lively, when she was Minnie Foster, one of the town girls singing in the choir. But that—oh, that was thirty years ago. This all you
was to take in?

Mrs. Peters: She said she wanted an apron. Funny thing to want, for
there isn't much to get you dirty in jail, goodness knows. But I suppose
just to make her feel more natural. She said they was in the top drawer
in this cupboard. Yes, here. And then her little shawl that always hung
behind the door. *(opens stair door and looks)* Yes, here it is.

(Quickly shuts door leading upstairs.)

Mrs. Hale *(abruptly moving toward her)*: Mrs. Peters?
Mrs. Peters: Yes, Mrs. Hale?
Mrs. Hale: Do you think she did it?
Mrs. Peters *(in a frightened voice)*: Oh, I don't know.
Mrs. Hale: Well, I don't think she did. Asking for an apron and her little
shawl. Worrying about her fruit.
Mrs. Peters *(starts to speak, glances up, where footsteps are heard in the
room above. In a low voice)*: Mr. Peters says it looks bad for her. Mr.
Henderson is awful sarcastic in a speech and he'll make fun of her
sayin' she didn't wake up.
Mrs. Hale: Well, I guess John Wright didn't wake when they was slipping
that rope under his neck.
Mrs. Peters: No, it's strange. It must have been done awful crafty and
still. They say it was such a—funny way to kill a man, rigging it all
up like that.
Mrs. Hale: That's just what Mr. Hale said. There was a gun in the house.
He says that's what he can't understand.
Mrs. Peters: Mr. Henderson said coming out that what was needed for
the case was a motive; something to show anger, or—sudden feeling.

Mrs. Hale (*who is standing by the table*):   Well, I don't see any signs of anger around here. (*she puts her hand on the dish towel which lies on the table, stands looking down at table, one half of which is clean, the other half messy*) It's wiped to here. (*makes a move as if to finish work, then turns and looks at loaf of bread outside the breadbox. Drops towel. In that voice of coming back to familiar things.*) Wonder how they are finding things upstairs. I hope she had it a little more red-up up there. You know, it seems kind of*sneaking.* Locking her up in town and then coming out here and trying to get her own house to turn against her!

Mrs. Peters: But Mrs. Hale, the law is the law.

Mrs. Hale: I s'pose 'tis. (*unbuttoning her coat*) Better loosen up your things, Mrs. Peters. You won't feel them when you go out.

(*Mrs. Peters takes off her fur tippet, goes to hang it on hook at back of room, stands looking at the under part of the small corner table.*)

Mrs. Peters: She was piecing a quilt.

(*She brings the large sewing basket and they look at the bright pieces.*)

Mrs. Hale: It's log cabin pattern. Pretty, isn't it? I wonder if she was goin' to quilt it or just knot it?

(*Footsteps have been heard coming down the stairs. The Sheriff enters followed by Hale and the County Attorney.*)

Sheriff: They wonder if she was going to quilt it or just knot it!

(*The men laugh, the women look abashed.*)

County Attorney (*rubbing his hands over the stove*):   Frank's fire didn't do much up there, did it? Well, let's go out to the barn and get that cleared up.

(*The men go outside.*)

Mrs. Hale (*resentfully*):   I don't know as there's anything so strange, our takin' up our time with little things while we're waiting for them to get the evidence. (*she sits down at the big table smoothing out a block with decision*) I don't see as it's anything to laugh about.

Mrs. Peters (*apologetically*):   Of course they've got awful important things on their minds.

(*Pulls up a chair and joins Mrs. Hale at the table.*)

Mrs. Hale (*examining another block*):   Mrs. Peters, look at this one. Here, this is the one she was working on, and look at the sewing! All the rest of it has been so nice and even. And look at this! It's all over the place! Why, it looks as if she didn't know what she was about!

(*After she has said this they look at each other, then start to glance back at the door. After an instant Mrs. Hale has pulled at a knot and ripped the sewing.*)

Mrs. Peters: Oh, what are you doing, Mrs. Hale?

Mrs. Hale *(mildly):* Just pulling out a stitch or two that's not sewed very good. *(threading a needle)* Bad sewing always made me fidgety.

Mrs. Peters *(nervously):* I don't think we ought to touch things.

Mrs. Hale: I'll just finish up this end. *(suddenly stopping and leaning forward)* Mrs. Peters?

Mrs. Peters: Yes, Mrs. Hale?

Mrs. Hale: What do you suppose she was so nervous about?

Mrs. Peters: Oh—I don't know. I don't know as she was nervous. I sometimes sew awful queer when I'm just tired. *(Mrs. Hale starts to say something, looks at Mrs. Peters, then goes on sewing)* Well I must get these things wrapped up. They may be through sooner than we think. *(putting apron and other things together)* I wonder where I can find a piece of paper, and string.

Mrs. Hale: In that cupboard, maybe.

Mrs. Peters *(looking in cupboard):* Why, here's a bird-cage. *(holds it up)* Did she have a bird, Mrs. Hale?

Mrs. Hale: Why, I don't know whether she did or not—I've not been here for so long. There was a man around last year selling canaries cheap, but I don't know as she took one; maybe she did. She used to sing real pretty herself.

Mrs. Peters *(glancing around):* Seems funny to think of a bird here. But she must have had one, or why would she have a cage? I wonder what happened to it.

Mrs. Hale: I s'pose maybe the cat got it.

Mrs. Peters: No, she didn't have a cat. She's got that feeling some people have about cats—being afraid of them. My cat got in her room and she was real upset and asked me to take it out.

Mrs. Hale: My sister Bessie was like that. Queer, ain't it?

Mrs. Peters *(examining the cage):* Why, look at this door. It's broke. One hinge is pulled apart.

Mrs. Hale *(looking too):* Looks as if someone must have been rough with it.

Mrs. Peters: Why, yes.

(She brings the cage forward and puts it on the table.)

Mrs. Hale: I wish if they're going to find any evidence they'd be about it. I don't like this place.

Mrs. Peters: But I'm awful glad you came with me, Mrs. Hale. It would be lonesome for me sitting here alone.

Mrs. Hale: It would, wouldn't it? *(dropping her sewing)* But I tell you what I do wish, Mrs. Peters. I wish I had come over sometimes when she was here. I—*(looking around the room)*—wish I had.

Mrs. Peters: But of course you were awful busy, Mrs. Hale—your house and your children.

Mrs. Hale: I could've come. I stayed away because it weren't cheerful—and that's why I ought to have come. I—I've never liked this place. Maybe because it's down in a hollow and you don't see the road. I dunno what it is, but it's a lonesome place and always was. I wish I had come over to see Minnie Foster sometimes. I can see now—*(shakes her head)*

Mrs. Peters: Well, you mustn't reproach yourself, Mrs. Hale. Somehow we just don't see how it is with other folks until—something comes up.

Mrs. Hale: Not having children makes less work—but it makes a quiet house, and Wright out to work all day, and no company when he did come in. Did you know John Wright, Mrs. Peters?

Mrs. Peters: Not to know him; I've seen him in town. They say he was a good man.

Mrs. Hale: Yes—good; he didn't drink, and kept his word as well as most, I guess, and paid his debts. But he was a hard man, Mrs. Peters. Just to pass the time of day with him—*(shivers)* Like a raw wind that gets to the bone. *(pauses, her eye falling on the cage)* I should think she would 'a wanted a bird. But what do you suppose went with it?

Mrs. Peters: I don't know, unless it got sick and died.

(She reaches over and swings the broken door, swings it again, both women watch it.)

Mrs. Hale: You weren't raised round here, were you? *(Mrs. Peters shakes her head)* You didn't know—her?

Mrs. Peters: Not till they brought her yesterday.

Mrs. Hale: She—come to think of it, she was kind of like a bird herself—real sweet and pretty, but kind of timid and—fluttery. How—she—did—change. *(silence; then as if struck by a happy thought and relieved to get back to everyday things)* Tell you what, Mrs. Peters, why don't you take the quilt in with you? It might take up her mind.

Mrs. Peters: Why, I think that's a real nice idea, Mrs. Hale. There couldn't possibly be any objection to it, could there? Now, just what would I take? I wonder if her patches are in here—and her things.

(They look in the sewing basket.)

Mrs. Hale: Here's some red. I expect this has got sewing things in it. *(brings out a fancy box)* What a pretty box. Looks like something somebody would give you. Maybe her scissors are in here. *(Opens box. Suddenly puts her hand to her nose)* Why—*(Mrs. Peters bends nearer, then turns her face away)* There's something wrapped up in this piece of silk.

Mrs. Peters: Why, this isn't her scissors.

Mrs. Hale *(lifting the silk):*   Oh, Mrs. Peters—it's—

(Mrs. Peters bends closer.)

Mrs. Peters: It's the bird.

Mrs. Hale *(jumping up):*   But, Mrs. Peters—look at it! It's neck! Look at its neck! It's all—other side *to.*

Mrs. Peters: Somebody—wrung—its—neck.

(Their eyes meet. A look of growing comprehension, of horror. Steps are heard outside. Mrs. Hale slips box under quilt pieces, and sinks into her chair. Enter Sheriff and County Attorney. Mrs. Peters rises.)

County Attorney *(as one turning from serious things to little pleasantries):*   Well ladies, have you decided whether she was going to quilt it or knot it?

Mrs. Peters: We think she was going to—knot it.

County Attorney: Well, that's interesting, I'm sure. *(seeing the birdcage)* Has the bird flown?

Mrs. Hale *(putting more quilt pieces over the box):*   We think the—cat got it.

County Attorney *(preoccupied):*   Is there a cat?

(Mrs. Hale glances in a quick covert way at Mrs. Peters.)

Mrs. Peters: Well, not *now.* They're superstitious, you know. They leave.

County Attorney *(to Sheriff Peters, continuing an interrupted conversation):*   No sign at all of anyone having come from the outside. Their own rope. Now let's go up again and go over it piece by piece. *(they start upstairs)* It would have to have been someone who knew just the—

(Mrs. Peters sits down. The two women sit there not looking at one another, but as if peering into something and at the same time holding back. When they talk now it is in the manner of feeling their way over strange ground, as if afraid of what they are saying, but as if they can not help saying it.)

Mrs. Hale: She liked the bird. She was going to bury it in that pretty box.

Mrs. Peters *(in a whisper):*   When I was a girl—my kitten—there was a boy took a hatchet, and before my eyes—and before I could get there—*(covers her face an instant)* If they hadn't held me back I would have—*(catches herself, looks upstairs where steps are heard, falters weakly)*—hurt him.

Mrs. Hale *(with a slow look around her):*   I wonder how it would seem never to have had any children around. *(pause)* No, Wright wouldn't like the bird—a thing that sang. She used to sing. He killed that, too.

Mrs. Peters *(moving uneasily):*   We don't know who killed the bird.

Mrs. Hale: I knew John Wright.

Mrs. Peters: It was an awful thing was done in this house that night, Mrs. Hale. Killing a man while he slept, slipping a rope around his neck that choked the life out of him.

Mrs. Hale: His neck. Choked the life out of him.

(Her hand goes out and rests on the bird-cage.)

Mrs. Peters *(with rising voice)*:   We don't know who killed him. We don't know.

Mrs. Hale *(her own feeling not interrupted)*:   If there'd been years and years of nothing, then a bird to sing to you, it would be awful—still, after the bird was still.

Mrs. Peters *(something within her speaking)*:   I know what stillness is. When we homesteaded in Dakota, and my first baby died—after he was two years old, and me with no other then—

Mrs. Hale *(moving)*:   How soon do you suppose they'll be through, looking for the evidence?

Mrs. Peters: I know what stillness is. *(pulling herself back)*. The law has got to punish crime, Mrs. Hale.

Mrs. Hale *(not as if answering that)*:   I wish you'd seen Minnie Foster when she wore a white dress with blue ribbons and stood up there in the choir and sang. *(a look around the room)* Oh, I *wish* I'd come over here once in a while! That was a crime! That was a crime! Who's going to punish that?

Mrs. Peters *(looking upstairs)*:   We mustn't—take on.

Mrs. Hale: I might have known she needed help! I know how things can be—for women. I tell you, it's queer, Mrs. Peters. We live close together and we live far apart. We all go through the same things—it's all just a different kind of the same thing. *(brushes her eyes, noticing the bottle of fruit, reaches out for it)* If I was you, I wouldn't tell her her fruit was gone. Tell her it ain't. Tell her it's all right. Take this in to prove it to her. She—she may never know whether it was broke or not.

Mrs. Peters *(takes the bottle, looks about for something to wrap it in; takes petticoat from the clothes brought from the other room, very nervously begins winding this around the bottle. In a false voice)*:   My, it's a good thing the men couldn't hear us. Wouldn't they just laugh! Getting all stirred up over a little thing like a—dead canary. As if that could have anything to do with—with—wouldn't they laugh!

(The men are heard coming down stairs.)

Mrs. Hale *(under her breath)*:   Maybe they would—maybe they wouldn't.

County Attorney: No, Peters, it's all perfectly clear except a reason for doing it. But you know juries when it comes to women. If there was some definite thing. Something to show—something to make a story about—a thing that would connect up with this strange way of doing it—

(The women's eyes meet for an instant. Enter Hale from outer door.)

Hale: Well, I've got the team around. Pretty cold out there.

County Attorney: I'm going to stay here a while by myself. *(to the Sheriff)* You can send Frank out for me, can't you? I want to go over everything. I'm not satisfied that we can't do better.

Sheriff: Do you want to see what Mrs. Peters is going to take in?

(The Lawyer goes to the table, picks up the apron, laughs.)

County Attorney: Oh, I guess they're not very dangerous things the ladies have picked out. *(Moves a few things about, disturbing the quilt pieces which cover the box. Steps back)* No, Mrs. Peters doesn't need supervising. For that matter, a sheriff's wife is married to the law. Ever think of it that way, Mrs. Peters?

Mrs. Peters: Not—just that way.

Sheriff *(chuckling):*   Married to the law. *(moves toward the other room)* I just want you to come in here a minute, George. We ought to take a look at these windows.

County Attorney *(scoffingly):*   Oh, windows!

Sheriff: We'll be right out, Mr. Hale.

(Hale goes outside. The Sheriff follows the County Attorney into the other room. Then Mrs. Hale rises, hands tight together, looking intensely at Mrs. Peters, whose eyes make a slow turn, finally meeting Mrs. Hale's. A moment Mrs. Hale holds her, then her own eyes point the way to where the box is concealed. Suddenly Mrs. Peters throws back quilt pieces and tries to put the box in the bag she is wearing. It is too big. She opens box, starts to take bird out, cannot touch it, goes to pieces, stands there helpless. Sound of a knob turning in the other room. Mrs. Hale snatches the box and puts it in the pocket of her big coat. Enter County Attorney and Sheriff.)

County Attorney *(facetiously):*   Well, Henry, at least we found out that she was not going to quilt it. She was going to—what is it you call it, ladies?

Mrs. Hale *(her hand against her pocket):*   We call it—knot it, Mr. Henderson.

(CURTAIN)

[1916]

CARL SANDBURG ■ (1878–1967)

Born in Galesburg, Illinois, Carl Sandburg was the son of Swedish immigrants. His parents were poor, and Sandburg worked as a dishwasher, shoeshiner, milk delivery boy, and bricklayer to help the family. He did not attend high school. At age seventeen he left Illinois for Kansas, riding the freight trains and traveling as a hobo. He served in Puerto Rico during the Spanish-American War (1898), and there he met a young man who had attended Lombard College in Galesburg, who urged Sandburg to continue his education.

In 1898 Sandburg entered Lombard College, where he received advice and support for his literary ambitions from a teacher, Philip Green Wright. Sandburg's first book, a pamphlet of poems, *Reckless Ecstasy*, appeared in 1904; Wright provided the money for its publication.

After college, Sandburg moved to Milwaukee, making a living as a newspaper reporter and an advertising writer, marrying Lillian Steichen (sister of the noted photographer Edward Steichen), and becoming actively involved in left-wing politics; from 1910 to 1912, he was the secretary to the first Socialist mayor of Milwaukee.

Relocating to Chicago, Sandburg began to publish poems in *Poetry* magazine, which Harriet Monroe, a Chicago-born writer, had founded in 1912. Along with Theodore Dreiser, Edgar Lee Masters, Sherwood Anderson, and others, Sandburg was identified with the "Chicago Literary Renaissance," a movement that sought to call attention to the Midwest as America's heartland and a central location for new literary forms that would depict the contemporary urban scene, the impact of materialism and industrialization, and the decay and disappearance of rural values and traditions.

Sandburg's books of poetry, written in free verse, are akin in form to Walt Whitman's long lines in *Leaves of Grass* (1855); and they possess the spirit of earnestness and affirmation that Sandburg valued in Ralph Waldo Emerson, whose books, he claimed, he "wanted in every room" of his house. Sandburg's big-voiced, passionate early volumes include *Chicago Poems* (1916), *Cornhuskers* (1918), *Smoke and Steel* (1920), and *Slabs of the Sunburnt West* (1922). "Chicago," winner of a poetry competition in 1910 and later included in *Chicago Poems*, shows his vigorous, rugged realism and his tone of gritty uplift.

As the poet-critic Daniel Hoffman has pointed out, Sandburg was the first significant American poet raised in a home in which English was not the first language, and this shaped and enriched the rhythms and tones of his work. Sandburg's biographer Penelope Niven has made the related point that the early books, in particular, used "the living language of modern speech," as English was enhanced by the terms, phrases, and usages of the native languages of America's many immigrant groups.

Sandburg was the brawny, big-hearted poet of immigrants and labor-ers, of common men and women, an enemy of exploitation and injustice, a celebratory singer of the working people of America, its industries and factories, and its grand panoramas of mountains, rivers, and landscapes. "The great mid-West," observed the poet, critic, and anthologist Louis Untermeyer, "that vast region of steel mills and slaughterhouses, of corn-fields and prairies, of crowded cities and empty skies, spoke through Carl Sandburg." In the mid-nineteenth century, a network of railroad lines began to connect Chicago to the Midwest farmlands and to the major urban markets of the East, and by 1860s the city had become the center for the meatpacking industry. In 1870, three million hogs and cattle were shipped and slaughtered, processed and preserved, there; by 1890, the number had increased to twelve million. In 1900, 25,000 employees worked in Chicago stockyards, more than one-third of the total nationwide. Conditions often were horrid for these workers, as the novelist Upton Sinclair showed to sensational effect in his novel *The Jungle* (1906). By 1920/21, not long after the publication of Sandburg's book of Chicago poems, meatpacking in Chicago employed 40,000 people and was handling fifteen million hogs and cattle per year.

Sandburg remained a popular poet (he said he wrote "simple poems for simple people"), but during the 1920s he embarked on a biographical study of Abraham Lincoln—it required six volumes to complete (1926–39)—and today perhaps even more people are aware of him for the Lincoln biography than for his verse. Sandburg also wrote books of children's tales, including *Rootabaga Stories* (1922) and *Rootabaga Pigeons* (1923). In addition, he made important contributions to the study of American song, folklore, and oral tradition through his compilations *The American Songbag* (1927) and *The New American Songbag* (1950). Often he toured the country, reading his own poems and reciting the poems and singing the ballads (accompa-nying himself on the banjo or the guitar) included in these books.

For further study, see Joseph Haas and Gene Lovitz, *Carl Sandburg: A Pictorial Biography* (1967); Penelope Niven, *Carl Sandburg: A Biography* (1991); North Callahan, *Carl Sandburg: His Life and Works* (1987); and Philip R. Yannella, *The Other Carl Sandburg* (1996). Also interesting is Kenneth Dodson, *The Poet and the Sailor: The Story of My Friendship with Carl Sandburg* (2007).

Chicago

Hog Butcher for the World,
Tool Maker, Stacker of Wheat,
Player with Railroads and the Nation's Freight Handler;
Stormy, husky, brawling,
City of the Big Shoulders:

5

They tell me you are wicked and I believe them, for I have seen your
    painted women under the gas lamps luring the farm boys.
And they tell me you are crooked and I answer: Yes, it is true I have seen
    the gunman kill and go free to kill again.
And they tell me you are brutal and my reply is: On the faces of women
    and children I have seen the marks of wanton hunger.
And having answered so I turn once more to those who sneer at this my
    city, and I give them back the sneer and say to them:
Come and show me another city with lifted head singing so proud to be
    alive and coarse and strong and cunning.   10
Flinging magnetic curses amid the toil of piling job on job, here is a tall
    bold slugger set vivid against the little soft cities;
Fierce as a dog with tongue lapping for action, cunning as a savage
    pitted against the wilderness,
    Bareheaded,
    Shoveling,
    Wrecking,   15
    Planning,
    Building, breaking, rebuilding,
Under the smoke, dust all over his mouth, laughing with white teeth,
Under the terrible burden of destiny laughing as a young man laughs,
Laughing even as an ignorant fighter laughs who has never lost
    a battle,   20
Bragging and laughing that under his wrist is the pulse, and under his ribs
    the heart of the people,
Laughing!
Laughing, the stormy, husky, brawling laughter of Youth, half-naked,
    sweating, proud to be Hog Butcher, Tool Maker, Stacker of Wheat,
    Player with Railroads and Freight Handler to the Nation.

                                                       [1916]

WALLACE STEVENS ■ (1879–1955)

Praised by the critic Harold Bloom as "the best and most representative American poet of our time," Wallace Stevens was born in Reading, Pennsylvania. His family was prosperous, and he benefited from a fine home library and attended a good school, where he took lessons in Greek and Latin. He received a Harvard education (1897–1900), studying German and French, forming a friendship with the eminent philosopher George Santayana, and publishing poems in both of Harvard's literary journals, *The Advocate* and the *Harvard Monthly*.

Stevens worked for a short time as a journalist in New York City but, discontented, he entered (firmly encouraged by his father) the New York School of Law in 1901 and was admitted to the New York bar in 1904. He struggled as a lawyer, even as he wrote poetry and read widely in his off hours. Finally, his career took a turn for the better when he took a job as a lawyer for an insurance company and soon began to consider making a career change into the insurance field. He accepted a position in 1916 with the Hartford Accident and Indemnity Company in Hartford, Connecticut, and was successful there, becoming vice president in 1934.

Some might have seen such a commitment as time taken away from writing but, in Stevens's view, "it gives a man character to have this daily contact with a job." Married in 1908 and the father of a daughter in 1924, Stevens lived in Hartford, working at the insurance company, taking pleasure in food and wine, gardening, listening to music, pursuing his long-time interest in art galleries and museums, and writing extraordinary poems, including some of the best written by any poet during the twentieth century.

Not until Stevens was 44, however, did he publish his first book, *Harmonium*. Often playful, delighting in the music of words, this collection includes a number of strangely somber poems as well, such as "The Snow Man," and, in a more grandiose and extended mode, "Sunday Morning." Stevens had high hopes for the book, and the critical response to it disappointed him. Discouraged, he wrote little during the next few years. He noted too that his literary work slowed following the birth of his daughter; he wryly told one correspondent that being a parent was a "terrible blow to poor literature." *Ideas of Order*, his second book, finally appeared in 1935.

In a sense Stevens had only one subject, the relationship between the imagination and reality, but it was a complex subject, and he explored it often, above all in his richly moving work, "The Idea of Order at Key West," included here. Like the great Romantic writers William Wordsworth and Samuel Taylor Coleridge, Stevens affirms that the imagination transforms and alters reality—which is a celebratory and affirmative vision. But this vision is shadowed by Stevens's insights into its implications about the nature of reality itself. So much depends on the imagination, which is powerfully creative yet burdened, vulnerable because of the sheer immensity of the task assigned to it.

Something of the grandeur, mystery, and fragility of Stevens's work is implied in this passage from his book of essays, *The Necessary Angel: Essays on Reality and the Imagination* (1951):

> What makes the poet the potent figure that he is, or was, or ought to be, is that he creates the world to which we turn incessantly and without knowing it and that he gives to life the supreme fictions without which we are unable to conceive of it.

Sometimes Stevens looks at the world and sees it as lush, exotic, and extravagant. On other occasions he sees only emptiness, blankness, and godlessness. "In the absence of a belief in God," he said, "the mind turns to its own creations and examines them, not alone from the aesthetic point of view, but for what they reveal, for what they validate and invalidate."

Dandyish and comic in some poems, Stevens is also, especially in his later, more spare and meditative work, tough-minded and courageous, unsparing in his engagement with the world's absence of meaning.

Not all readers take pleasure in Stevens. To some he comes across as self-absorbed, too fond of writing poems about poetry and as peculiarly detached in his literary production from the pressures of the everyday life of family and work that in his own life he knew intimately. The poet-critic Louise Bogan commented that Stevens's "is a natural world strangely empty of human beings." Another critic, George F. Whicher, claimed, "Something of the talent of a Sherlock Holmes is needed to penetrate Stevens's oblique implications. His poetry is keyed to readers who delight in solving puzzles." Stevens himself observed, "Life is not people and scene but thought and feeling. The world is myself. Life is myself."

While it is true that Stevens appeals to some tastes more than others, his work can be appreciated for its craft and sublime ambition when it is approached in the right spirit, with pleasure in the array of images and patterns of language that Stevens has designed in tribute to the imagination's prowess. The poet Robert Pack gives this tip:

> The merging of the abstract and the mental with the concrete and the sensual is perhaps the most characteristic quality of Stevens's style. If a poem begins with a generalization, he will proceed to illustrate it, or, if a poem commences with a series of illustrations, it will end with a generalization.

Slow to achieve wide recognition, Stevens was honored with prizes and awards in his final years. *The Auroras of Autumn* (1950) was given the National Book Award in poetry, and his *Collected Poems* (1954) received the Pulitzer Prize for poetry and another National Book Award.

Good points of departure include Susan B. Weston, *Wallace Stevens: An Introduction to the Poetry* (1977) and Tony Sharpe, *Wallace Stevens: A*

Literary Life (2000). For biography, see Holly Stevens, *Souvenirs and Prophecies: The Young Wallace Stevens* (1977) and Joan Richardson, *Wallace Stevens*, 2 vols. (1986–88). See also Peter Brazeau, *Parts of a World: Wallace Stevens Remembered: An Oral Biography* (1983). For critical discussion, see Harold Bloom, *Wallace Stevens: The Poems of Our Climate* (1977); Milton J. Bates, *Wallace Stevens: A Mythology of Self* (1985); George S. Lensing, *Wallace Stevens: A Poet's Growth* (1986); Mark Halliday, *Stevens and the Interpersonal* (1991); and James Longenbach, *Wallace Stevens: The Plain Sense of Things* (1991).

Recent studies include Daniel Schwarz, *Narrative and Representation in the Poetry of Wallace Stevens* (1993); Alan Filreis, *Modernism from Left to Right* (1994); Janet McCann, *Wallace Stevens Revisited* (1995); Jacqueline Vaught Brogan, *The Violence Within/The Violence Without: Wallace Stevens and the Emergence of a Revolutionary Poetics* (2003); and Malcolm Woodland, *Wallace Stevens and the Apocalyptic Mode* (2005). A helpful resource is Eleanor Cook, *A Reader's Guide to Wallace Stevens* (2007).

The Snow Man

One must have a mind of winter
To regard the frost and the boughs
Of the pine-trees crusted with snow;

And have been cold a long time
To behold the junipers shagged with ice,   5
The spruces rough in the distant glitter

Of the January sun; and not to think
Of any misery in the sound of the wind,
In the sound of a few leaves,

Which is the sound of the land   10
Full of the same wind
That is blowing in the same bare place

For the listener, who listens in the snow,
And, nothing himself, beholds
Nothing that is not there and the nothing that is.   15

[1923]

Sunday Morning

I

Complacencies of the peignoir, and late
Coffee and oranges in a sunny chair,
And the green freedom of a cockatoo
Upon a rug mingle to dissipate

The holy hush of ancient sacrifice. 5
She dreams a little, and she feels the dark
Encroachment of that old catastrophe,
As a calm darkens among water-lights.
The pungent oranges and bright, green wings
Seem things in some procession of the dead, 10
Winding across wide water, without sound.
The day is like wide water, without sound,
Stilled for the passing of her dreaming feet
Over the seas, to silent Palestine,[1]
Dominion of the blood and sepulchre.[2] 15

II

Why should she give her bounty to the dead?
What is divinity if it can come
Only in silent shadows and in dreams?
Shall she not find in comforts of the sun,
In pungent fruit and bright, green wings, or else 20
In any balm or beauty of the earth,
Things to be cherished like the thought of heaven?
Divinity must live within herself:
Passions of rain, or moods in falling snow;
Grievings in loneliness, or unsubdued 25
Elations when the forest blooms; gusty
Emotions on wet roads on autumn nights;
All pleasures and all pains, remembering
The bough of summer and the winter branch.
These are the measures destined for her soul. 30

III

Jove[3] in the clouds had his inhuman birth.
No mother suckled him, no sweet land gave
Large-mannered motions to his mythy mind.
He moved among us, as a muttering king,
Magnificent, would move among his hinds,[4] 35
Until our blood, commingling, virginal,
With heaven, brought such requital to desire
The very hinds discerned it, in a star.

---

[1]The territory of present-day Israel, which includes Jerusalem, the site recorded in the New Testament as the location of Jesus's crucifixion and burial.
[2]A tomb or place of burial.
[3]The leading god of the Roman pantheon.
[4]Farmhands or servants, shepherds.

Shall our blood fail? Or shall it come to be
The blood of paradise? And shall the earth
Seem all the paradise that we shall know?
The sky will be much friendlier then than now,
A part of labor and a part of pain,
And next in glory to enduring love,
Not this dividing and indifferent blue.

40

45

IV

She says, "I am content when wakened birds,
Before they fly, test the reality
Of misty fields, by their sweet questionings;
But when the birds are gone, and their warm fields
Return no more, where, then, is paradise?"
There is not any haunt of prophecy,
Nor any old chimera[5] of the grave,
Neither the golden underground, nor isle
Melodious, where spirits gat them home,
Nor visionary south, nor cloudy palm
Remote on heaven's hill, that has endured
As April's green endures; or will endure
Like her remembrance of awakened birds,
Or her desire for June and evening, tipped
By the consummation of the swallow's wings.

50

55

60

V

She says, "But in contentment I still feel
The need for some imperishable bliss."
Death is the mother of beauty; hence from her,
Alone, shall come fulfilment to our dreams
And our desires. Although she strews the leaves
Of sure obliteration on our paths,
The path sick sorrow took, the many paths
Where triumph rang its brassy phrase, or love
Whispered a little out of tenderness,
She makes the willow shiver in the sun
For maidens who were wont to sit and gaze
Upon the grass, relinquished to their feet.
She causes boys to pile new plums and pears
On disregarded plate. The maidens taste
And stray impassioned in the littering leaves.

65

70

75

[5]Literally, a creature from Greek mythology possessing the head of a lion, the body of a goat, and the
tail of a serpent. Figuratively, an unreal creature or phantasm of the imagination.

VI

Is there no change of death in paradise?
Does ripe fruit never fall? Or do the boughs
Hang always heavy in that perfect sky,
Unchanging, yet so like our perishing earth,
With rivers like our own that seek for seas   80
They never find, the same receding shores
That never touch with inarticulate pang?
Why set the pear upon those river-banks
Or spice the shores with odors of the plum?
Alas, that they should wear our colors there,   85
The silken weavings of our afternoons,
And pick the strings of our insipid lutes!
Death is the mother of beauty, mystical,
Within whose burning bosom we devise
Our earthly mothers waiting, sleeplessly.   90

VII

Supple and turbulent, a ring of men
Shall chant in orgy on a summer morn
Their boisterous devotion to the sun,
Not as a god, but as a god might be,
Naked among them, like a savage source.   95
Their chant shall be a chant of paradise,
Out of their blood, returning to the sky;
And in their chant shall enter, voice by voice,
The windy lake wherein their lord delights,
The trees, like serafin,[6]—and echoing hills,   100
That choir among themselves long afterward.
They shall know well the heavenly fellowship
Of men that perish and of summer morn.
And whence they came and whither they shall go
The dew upon their feet shall manifest.   105

VIII

She hears, upon that water without sound,
A voice that cries, "The tomb in Palestine
Is not the porch of spirits lingering.
It is the grave of Jesus, where he lay."
We live in an old chaos of the sun,   110

---

[6]Seraphim, or angels. In the Bible, the prophet Isaiah (6:2) has a vision of seraphim as creatures with six wings hovering above the throne of God.

Or old dependency of day and night,
Or island solitude, unsponsored, free,
Of that wide water, inescapable.
Deer walk upon our mountains, and the quail
Whistle about us their spontaneous cries;   115
Sweet berries ripen in the wilderness;
And, in the isolation of the sky,
At evening, casual flocks of pigeons make
Ambiguous undulations as they sink,
Downward to darkness, on extended wings.   120

[1915, 1923]

Anecdote of the Jar

I placed a jar in Tennessee,
And round it was, upon a hill.
It made the slovenly wilderness
Surround that hill.

The wilderness rose up to it,   5
And sprawled around, no longer wild.
The jar was round upon the ground
And tall and of a port in air.

It took dominion everywhere.
The jar was gray and bare.   10
It did not give of bird or bush,
Like nothing else in Tennessee.

[1923]

Thirteen Ways of Looking at a Blackbird

I

Among twenty snowy mountains,
The only moving thing
Was the eye of the blackbird.

II

I was of three minds,
Like a tree   5
In which there are three blackbirds.

III

The blackbird whirled in the autumn winds.
It was a small part of the pantomime.

IV

A man and a woman
Are one.
A man and a woman and a blackbird
Are one.

V

I do not know which to prefer,
The beauty of inflections
Or the beauty of innuendoes,   15
The blackbird whistling
Or just after.

VI

Icicles filled the long window
With barbaric glass.
The shadow of the blackbird
Crossed it, to and fro.   20
The mood
Traced in the shadow
An indecipherable cause.

VII

O thin men of Haddam,[1]   25
Why do you imagine golden birds?
Do you not see how the blackbird
Walks around the feet
Of the women about you?

VIII

I know noble accents   30
And lucid, inescapable rhythms;
But I know, too,
That the blackbird is involved
In what I know.

10

---

[1] A town in Connecticut. Stevens stated that the reference to the "thin men" of this town is "entirely fanciful"; he said, too, that he liked the sound of the name.

IX

When the blackbird flew out of sight,   35
It marked the edge
Of one of many circles.

X

At the sight of blackbirds
Flying in a green light,
Even the bawds[2] of euphony[3]   40
Would cry out sharply.

XI

He rode over Connecticut
In a glass coach.
Once, a fear pierced him,
In that he mistook   45
The shadow of his equipage[4]
For blackbirds.

XII

The river is moving.
The blackbird must be flying.

XIII

It was evening all afternoon.   50
It was snowing
And it was going to snow.
The blackbird sat
In the cedar-limbs.

[1931]

[2]A prostitute or loose woman.
[3]A group of words with a pleasing sound.
[4]A carriage, usually with servants.

The Death of a Soldier

Life contracts and death is expected,
As in a season of autumn.
The soldier falls.

He does not become a three-days personage,
Imposing his separation,   5
Calling for pomp.

Death is absolute and without memorial,
As is a season of autumn,
When the wind stops,

When the wind stops and, over the heavens,   10
The clouds go, nevertheless,
In their direction.

[1931]

The Idea of Order at Key West

She sang beyond the genius of the sea.
The water never formed to mind or voice,
Like a body wholly body, fluttering
Its empty sleeves; and yet its mimic motion
Made constant cry, caused constantly a cry,   5
That was not ours although we understood,
Inhuman, of the veritable ocean.

The sea was not a mask. No more was she.
The song and water were not medleyed sound
Even if what she sang was what she heard,   10
Since what she sang was uttered word by word.
It may be that in all her phrases stirred
The grinding water and the gasping wind;
But it was she and not the sea we heard.

For she was the maker of the song she sang.   15
The ever-hooded, tragic-gestured sea
Was merely a place by which she walked to sing.
Whose spirit is this? we said, because we knew
It was the spirit that we sought and knew
That we should ask this often as she sang.   20

If it was only the dark voice of the sea
That rose, or even colored by many waves;
If it was only the outer voice of sky

And cloud, of the sunken coral water-walled,
However clear, it would have been deep air,   25
The heaving speech of air, a summer sound
Repeated in a summer without end
And sound alone. But it was more than that,
More even than her voice, and ours, among
The meaningless plungings of water and the wind,   30
Theatrical distances, bronze shadows heaped
On high horizons, mountainous atmospheres
Of sky and sea.

               It was her voice that made
The sky acutest at its vanishing.   35
She measured to the hour its solitude.
She was the single artificer of the world
In which she sang. And when she sang, the sea,
Whatever self it had, became the self
That was her song, for she was the maker. Then we,   40
As we beheld her striding there alone,
Knew that there never was a world for her
Except the one she sang and, singing, made.

Ramon Fernandez,[1] tell me, if you know,
Why, when the singing ended and we turned   45
Toward the town, tell why the glassy lights,
The lights in the fishing boats at anchor there,
As the night descended, tilting in the air,
Mastered the night and portioned out the sea,
Fixing emblazoned zones and fiery poles,   50
Arranging, deepening, enchanting night.

Oh! Blessed rage for order, pale Ramon,
The maker's rage to order words of the sea,
Words of the fragrant portals, dimly-starred,
And of ourselves and of our origins,   55
In ghostlier demarcations, keener sounds.

                                   [1936]

---

[1]While Stevens insisted that "Ramon Fernandez [was] not intended to be anyone at all," a literary
critic in the 1930s by that name would have been known to Stevens. Fernandez's work appeared in the
Partisan Review and the *Criterion*.

Of Modern Poetry

The poem of the mind in the act of finding
What will suffice. It has not always had
To find: the scene was set; it repeated what
Was in the script.
                    Then the theatre was changed   5
To something else. Its past was a souvenir.

It has to be living, to learn the speech of the place.
It has to face the men of the time and to meet
The women of the time. It has to think about war
And it has to find what will suffice. It has   10
To construct a new stage. It has to be on that stage
And, like as insatiable actor, slowly and
With meditation, speak words that in the ear,
In the delicatest ear of the mind, repeat,
Exactly, that which it wants to hear, at the sound   15
Of which, an invisible audience listens,
Not to the play, but to itself, expressed
In an emotion as of two people, as of two
Emotions becoming one. The actor is
A metaphysician in the dark, twanging   20
An instrument, twanging a wiry string that gives
Sounds passing through sudden rightnesses, wholly
Containing the mind, below which it cannot descend,
Beyond which it has no will to rise.
                          It must   25
Be the finding of a satisfaction, and may
Be of a man skating, a woman dancing, a woman
Combing. The poem of the act of the mind.

                                        [1942]

The Plain Sense of Things

After the leaves have fallen, we return
To a plain sense of things. It is as if
We had come to an end of the imagination,
Inanimate in an inert savoir.[1]

---

[1]Knowledge (French).

It is difficult even to choose the adjective   5
For this blank cold, this sadness without cause.
The great structure has become a minor house.
No turban walks across the lessened floors.

The greenhouse never so badly needed paint.
The chimney is fifty years old and slants to one side.   10
A fantastic effort has failed, a repetition
In a repetitiousness of men and flies.

Yet the absence of the imagination had
Itself to be imagined. The great pond,
The plain sense of it, without reflections, leaves,   15
Mud, water like dirty glass, expressing silence

Of a sort, silence of a rat come out to see,
The great pond and its waste of the lilies, all this
Had to be imagined as an inevitable knowledge,
Required, as a necessity requires.   20

[1954]

WILLIAM CARLOS WILLIAMS ■ (1883–1963)

Spanish, not English, was the primary language of the household in which William Carlos Williams, born in 1883 in Rutherford, New Jersey, was brought up. His father, of English birth, had been raised in the West Indies and was an Episcopalian and a businessman, and his mother, born in Puerto Rico of half-Basque, half-Jewish ancestry and baptized a Catholic, had studied painting for three years in Paris. After attending public school in Rutherford, Williams, along with his mother and brother, spent the next two years in Europe, and he was enrolled in schools near Geneva and in Paris.

Williams returned to the United States for high school and then attended medical school at the University of Pennsylvania, where he met the future poets Ezra Pound and H. D. and the painter Charles Demuth. After further study and travel in Europe, Williams returned to Rutherford, establishing his medical practice in 1910 and later becoming the chief pediatrician of a hospital in nearby Paterson. In 1912 he married Florence Herman, who, as "Flossie," figures in a number of his poems.

Williams was a prolific, original, and, as the years passed, increasingly influential writer—above all as a poet but also as an author of short stories and novels, an essayist, an autobiographer, and much more. Though something of a cosmopolitan himself through his family upbringing, education abroad, and travels, Williams came to differ with his friend Pound and with T. S. Eliot, both of whom, in Williams's view, had overdeveloped their relationship with European literary tradition and culture and strayed too far from the American scene and idiom. Eliot's *The Waste Land* he scorned as a poem for the classroom, artificial and pedantic.

Seeking to hone an American poetic, Williams keyed his verse to the concrete and commonplace things of this nation's life, history, and experience. He was keenly interested in photography (e.g., Alfred Stieglitz's work) and in advanced forms of modern painting—the cubism of Picasso and Braque, for example—and he possessed a sharp, strong visual sense ("no ideas but in things," he said), a precise and clear imagery, and a rich feeling for the turns and shifts and dynamics of American rhythms.

As Williams explained in his memoir, *I Wanted to Write a Poem:*

> Very early I began to question whether to rhyme and decided: No....I found I couldn't say what I had to say in rhyme. It got in my way. With Whitman, I decided rhyme belonged to another age; it didn't matter; it was not important at all....I began to begin lines with lower-case letters. I thought it pretentious to begin every line with a capital letter....When I came to the end of a rhythmic unit (not necessarily a sentence) I ended the line....I was trying for something. The rhythmic unit usually came to me in a lyrical outburst. I wanted it to look that way on the page. I didn't go in for

long lines because of my nervous nature. I couldn't. The rhythmic pace was the pace of speech, an excited pace because I was excited when I wrote.

Williams's major works include *Spring and All* (1923), his first important book, combining poetry and prose; *The Collected Poems*, 2 vols. (1986, 1988); his five-book epic, *Paterson* (1946–58; new ed., 1992), a verbal collage that includes letters, poems, and newspaper stories; *In the American Grain* (1925), a brilliant experimental study of American cultural history; *The Knife of the Times and Other Stories* (1932); *White Mule* (1937), a novel; the *Autobiography* (1951); and *Selected Essays* (1954).

On first encounter, some readers find Williams almost too accessible and even wonder if the poems are really poetry or prose arbitrarily broken up into lines and stanzas. Yet Williams is the opposite of arbitrary. As the critic George F. Whicher has pointed out, Williams "avoids any suspicion of emotional heightening, and cultivates a flat, matter-of-fact, conversational tone, which might easily become intolerable if not combined with an extreme rapidity of pace and a startling succession of sensations." He finely crafts each poem, however simple-seeming at a glance it might appear, and is extremely conscious of the arrangement of the words on the page and the relationship of words to white space. Williams presents the poem as a visual experience, an object, a "machine made of words," and also as an aural experience, with the words shaped by the breath, rhythm, and controlling beat of the poet's voice (Williams's phrase for this is the "variable foot," a new kind of poetic meter).

Allen Ginsberg and other Beat writers in the late 1940s and 1950s responded to Williams's poetry and prose with admiration and affection, and his work was also a source of inspiration for Charles Olson, Robert Creeley, Denise Levertov, and many others. Less well-known than Frost, Eliot, or Stevens during his lifetime, Williams now ranks with them as a major American poet of the twentieth century. His influence on other poets may be the greatest of all.

Biographies include Reed Whittemore, *William Carlos Williams, Poet from Jersey* (1975) and Paul Mariani, *William Carlos Williams: A New World Naked* (1981). See also *William Carlos Williams: Man and Poet*, ed. Carroll F. Terrell (1983) and *Pound/Williams: Selected Letters of Ezra Pound and William Carlos Williams*, ed. Hugh Witemeyer (1996). For a sampling of critical opinion, see *William Carlos Williams: The Critical Heritage*, ed. Charles Doyle (1980) and *Critical Essays on William Carlos Williams*, eds. Steven Gould Axelrod and Helen Deese (1995). For critical studies, see Charles Doyle, *William Carlos Williams and the American Poem* (1982); Carl Rapp, *William Carlos Williams and Romantic Idealism* (1984); Stephen Cushman, *William Carlos Williams and the Meanings of Measure* (1985); and Bernard Duffey, *A Poetry of Presence: The Writing of William Carlos Williams* (1986).

The diversity of approaches is indicated by Ron Callan, *William Carlos Williams and Transcendentalism* (1992); T. Hugh Crawford, *Modernism, Medicine, and William Carlos Williams* (1993); Peter Halter, *The Revolution in the Visual Arts and the Poetry of William Carlos Williams* (1994); Barry Ahearn, *William Carlos Williams and Celebrity* (1994); Julio Marzan, *The Spanish American Roots of William Carlos Williams* (1994); and Stanley Koehler, *Countries of the Mind: The Poetry of William Carlos Williams* (1998).

The most important recent book is Herbert A. Liebowitz, *Something Urgent I Have to Say to You: The Life and Works of William Carlos Williams* (2011).

William Carlos Williams, date unknown.

The Young Housewife

At ten A.M. the young housewife
moves about in negligee behind
the wooden walls of her husband's house.
I pass solitary in my car.

Then again she comes to the curb   5
to call the ice-man, fish-man, and stands
shy, uncorseted, tucking in
stray ends of hair, and I compare her
to a fallen leaf.

The noiseless wheels of my car   10
rush with a crackling sound over
dried leaves as I bow and pass smiling.

[1916]

Portrait of a Lady

Your thighs are appletrees
whose blossoms touch the sky.
Which sky? The sky
where Watteau[1] hung a lady's
slipper. Your knees   5
are a southern breeze—or
a gust of snow. Agh! what
sort of man was Fragonard?[2]
—as if that answered
anything. Ah, yes—below   10
the knees, since the tune
drops that way, it is
one of those white summer days,
the tall grass of your ankles
flickers upon the shore—   15
Which shore?—
the sand clings to my lips—
Which shore?

---

[1]Jean-Antoine Watteau (1684–1721), a French painter who often depicted lovers in idealized
landscapes.
[2]Jean-Honoré Fragonard (1732–1806), a French painter whose subject matter of young lovers was more
erotically charged than that of Watteau. It is Fragonard's *The Swing* that depicts a girl who has kicked
her slipper into the air, not Watteau's.

Agh, petals maybe. How
should I know?   20
Which shore? Which shore?
I said petals from an appletree.

                                                                 [1920]

Spring and All

I

By the road to the contagious hospital
under the surge of the blue
mottled clouds driven from the
northeast—a cold wind. Beyond, the
waste of broad, muddy fields   5
brown with dried weeds, standing and fallen

patches of standing water
the scattering of tall trees

All along the road the reddish
purplish, forked, upstanding, twiggy   10
stuff of bushes and small trees
with dead, brown leaves under them
leafless vines—

Lifeless in appearance, sluggish
dazed spring approaches—   15

They enter the new world naked,
cold, uncertain of all
save that they enter. All about them
the cold, familiar wind—

Now the grass, tomorrow   20
the stiff curl of wildcarrot leaf

One by one objects are defined—
It quickens: clarity, outline of leaf

But now the stark dignity of
entrance—Still, the profound change   25
has come upon them: rooted, they
grip down and begin to awaken

II

Pink confused with white
flowers and flowers reversed
take and spill the shaded flame   30
darting it back
into the lamp's horn

petals aslant darkened with mauve

red where in whorls
petal lays its glow upon petal   35
round flamegreen throats
petals radiant with transpiercing light
contending
        above

the leaves   40
reaching up their modest green
from the pot's rim

and there, wholly dark, the pot
gay with rough moss.
                [1923]

To Elsie

The pure products of America
go crazy—
mountain folk from Kentucky

or the ribbed north end of
Jersey   5
with its isolate lakes and

valleys, its deaf-mutes, thieves
old names
and promiscuity between

devil-may-care men who have taken   10
to railroading
out of sheer lust of adventure—

and young slatterns,[1] bathed
in filth
from Monday to Saturday   15

to be tricked out that night
with gauds[2]
from imaginations which have no

peasant traditions to give them
character   20
but flutter and flaunt

sheer rags—succumbing without
emotion
save numbed terror

under some hedge of choke-cherry   25
or viburnum[3]—
which they cannot express—

Unless it be that marriage
perhaps
with a dash of Indian blood   30

will throw up a girl so desolate
so hemmed round
with disease or murder

that she'll be rescued by an
agent—   35
reared by the state and

sent out at fifteen to work in
some hard-pressed
house in the suburbs—

some doctor's family, some Elsie—   40
voluptuous water
expressing with broken

brain the truth about us—
her great
ungainly hips and flopping breasts   45

[1] An untidy or slovenly woman or girl; a slut.
[2] Showy or flashy ornaments.
[3] A kind of shrub.

addressed to cheap
jewelry
and rich young men with fine eyes

as if the earth under our feet
were   50
an excrement of some sky

and we degraded prisoners
destined
to hunger until we eat filth

while the imagination strains   55
after deer
going by fields of goldenrod in

the stifling heat of September
Somehow
it seems to destroy us   60

It is only in isolate flecks that
something
is given off

No one
to witness   65
and adjust, no one to drive the car

[1923]

The Red Wheelbarrow

so much depends
upon

a red wheel
barrow

glazed with rain   5
water

beside the white
chickens

[1923]

Death

He's dead

the dog won't have to
sleep on his potatoes
any more to keep them
from freezing   5

he's dead
the old bastard—
He's a bastard because

there's nothing
legitimate in him any   10
more
      he's dead
He's sick-dead

          he's
a godforsaken curio   15
without
any breath in it

He's nothing at all
      he's dead
Shrunken up to skin   20

      Put his head on
one chair and his
feet on another and
he'll lie there
like an acrobat—   25

Love's beaten. He
beat it. That's why
he's insufferable—
      because
he's here needing a   30
shave and making love
an inside howl
of anguish and defeat—
He's come out of the man

and he's let
the man go—
                    the liar

Dead
        his eyes
rolled up out of
the light—a mockery   40

            which
love cannot touch—
just bury it
and hide its face—   45
for shame.

                                        [1930]

This Is Just to Say

I have eaten
the plums
that were in
the icebox

and which   5
you were probably
saving
for breakfast

Forgive me
they were delicious   10
so sweet
and so cold

                                        [1934]

The Dance

In Breughel's great picture, The Kermess,[1]
the dancers go round, they go round and
around, the squeal and the blare and the
tweedle of bagpipes, a bugle and fiddles

---

[1]Pieter Breughel (c. 1525–69), Flemish painter known for his paintings of peasant life, including the painting mentioned in this poem titled *The Kermess* or *The Carnival*.

tipping their bellies (round as the thick-sided 5
glasses whose wash they impound)
their hips and their bellies off balance
to turn them. Kicking and rolling about
the Fair Grounds, swinging their butts, those
shanks must be sound to bear up under such 10
rollicking measures, prance as they dance
in Breughel's great picture, The Kermess.

[1944]

Landscape with the Fall of Icarus

According to Breughel
when Icarus[1] fell
it was spring

a farmer was ploughing
his field 5
the whole pageantry

of the year was
awake tingling
near

the edge of the sea 10
concerned
with itself

sweating in the sun
that melted
the wings' wax 15

unsignificantly
off the coast
there was

a splash quite unnoticed
this was 20
Icarus drowning

[1960, 1962]

---

[1]Reference to Breughel's painting *The Fall of Icarus*. A character in Greek mythology, Icarus was the son
a master builder, Daedalus. Facing imprisonment, Daedalus creates wax wings for Icarus and himself
to fly from danger. Although warned by his father not to fly too close to the sun, Icarus, in his joy,
ignores his father's advice, his wings melt, and he falls into the sea.

Ezra Pound is a hard author to write about. A crucial adviser and friend
to T. S. Eliot, James Joyce, Robert Frost, Ernest Hemingway, and Marianne
Moore, among others, he was one of the most influential figures in twentieth-
century literature. In his social, cultural, and political views, however, he
was a fanatical anti-Semitic bigot and Fascist and Nazi sympathizer.

Pound's major literary project, occupying him for half a century, was the
Cantos, 116 of them in all. Admired by specialists, praised by some poets, the
Cantos, with the exception of a few passages and sections (e.g., *Canto I*, included here), appeal little to most readers. What endures in Pound's work are
the early poems, his translations, and the literary essays and reviews from
the first part of his career. His most significant books are *Personae* (1909), a
collection of short poems; *Cantos I–XVI* (1925); *How to Read* (1931), a work
of literary criticism; *The ABC of Reading* (1934), another lively critical book;
Literary Essays (1954); and *The Translations of Ezra Pound* (1953).

Pound was born in Hailey, Idaho, but raised in a suburb near Philadelphia,
where his father held a job at the U.S. mint. He was an undergraduate at the
University of Pennsylvania and at Hamilton College in central New York, and
then took a master's degree, focusing on foreign languages, at the University
of Pennsylvania in 1906. He taught at Wabash College in Indiana for two
years, but then left for Europe, where he traveled extensively, settling finally
in London and supporting himself through teaching and writing reviews and
essays—and also serving for a period as secretary to the Irish poet William
Butler Yeats.

Through wide-ranging reading and study, Pound developed an interest
in Japanese and Chinese poetry, which shaped his work as an Imagist poet,
wherein he stressed clarity and precision in language and avoided the conventions of rhyme and meter. As an Imagist (see "In a station...," included
here), Pound aimed to "compose in the sequence of the musical phrase, not
in the sequence of the metronome." Clean, crisp, clear presentation, imaging
the object directly, without elaborate diction and artifice, was Pound's creed.

In 1917 Pound accepted a position as the London editor of the *Little
Review*, a literary magazine launched in Chicago in 1914. He was a shrewd
and energizing critic, a mentor, a rabble-rouser on behalf of the avant-
garde in literature and art, and a cultural force. T. S. Eliot recalled, "Pound
did not create the poets: but he created a situation in which for the first
time, there was a 'modern movement in poetry' in which English and
American poets collaborated, knew each other's works, and influenced
each other....If it had not been for the work that Pound did...the isolation
of American poets might have continued for a long time."

Moving to Italy in the mid 1920s, Pound veered hard right in his politics, supporting the Italian dictator Benito Mussolini and, during World
War II, making radio broadcasts on behalf of the Fascist and Nazi causes

and lashing out at the United States, President Franklin D. Roosevelt, and Jews. At war's end Pound was denounced as a traitor, and in 1946 he was declared mentally ill and committed to a hospital in Washington, D.C. For the *Pisan Cantos LXXIV–LXXXIV*, he was awarded the Bollingen Prize for poetry—a decision that sparked angry discussion, debate, and protest, for the judges, separating poetry from politics, chose to overlook that Pound had been a traitor to his country and a propagandist for monstrous regimes. In 1958 Pound was released, and he lived in Venice until his death.

For biography, see Humphrey Carpenter, *A Serious Character: The Life of Ezra Pound* (1988). Resources include Peter Brooker, *A Student's Guide to the Selected Poems of Ezra Pound* (1979); Christine Froula, *A Guide to Ezra Pound's Selected Poems* (1983); and Ezra Pound, ed. *Harold Bloom* (1987). For critical analysis, see Donald Davie, *Ezra Pound: Poet as Sculptor* (1964); Hugh Kenner, *The Poetry of Ezra Pound* (1951; rpt. with a new preface by the author, 1985) and *The Pound Era* (1972); Michael J. Alexander, *The Poetic Achievement of Ezra Pound* (1979); Albert Gelpi, *A Coherent Splendor: The American Poetic Renaissance, 1910–1950* (1987); and Christopher Beach, *ABC of Influence: Ezra Pound and the Remaking of American Poetic Tradition* (1992). See also, among recent studies, Leon Surette, *Pound in Purgatory: From Economic Radicalism to Anti-Semitism* (1999); Ira B. Nadel, *Ezra Pound: A Literary Life* (2004); Rebecca Beasley, *Ezra Pound and the Visual Culture of Modernism* (2007); David Moody, *Ezra Pound, Poet: A Portrait of the Man and His Work* (2007); and *Ezra Pound in Context*, ed. Ira B. Nadel (2010).

Photograph of Ezra Pound by E.O. Hoppé, 1918.

Portrait d'une Femme[1]

Your mind and you are our Sargasso Sea,[2]
London has swept about you this score years
And bright ships left you this or that in fee:
Ideas, old gossip, oddments of all things,
Strange spars of knowledge and dimmed wares of price.   5
Great minds have sought you—lacking someone else.
You have been second always. Tragical?
No. You preferred it to the usual thing:
One dull man, dulling and uxorious,
One average mind—with one thought less, each year.   10
Oh, you are patient, I have seen you sit
Hours, where something might have floated up.
And now you pay one. Yes, you richly pay.
You are a person of some interest, one comes to you
And takes strange gain away: 15
Trophies fished up; some curious suggestion;
Fact that leads nowhere; and a tale or two,
Pregnant with mandrakes,[3] or with something else
That might prove useful and yet never proves,
That never fits a corner or shows use,   20
Or finds its hour upon the loom of days:
The tarnished, gaudy, wonderful old work;
Idols and ambergris[4] and rare inlays,
These are your riches, your great store; and yet
For all this sea-hoard of deciduous things,   25
Strange woods half sodden, and new brighter stuff:
In the slow float of differing light and deep,
No! there is nothing! In the whole and all,
Nothing that's quite your own.
                         Yet this is you.   30

                                        [1912]

[1]Portrait of a lady (French).
[2]An area of the North Atlantic Ocean between the Azores and the West Indies known for its warm currents and sluggish waters.
[3]The root of the mandrake plant, used to promote conception. It was credited with medicinal properties due to its shape's resemblance to the human body.
[4]A rare and odoriferous waxy substance found floating in tropical seas or in the intestines of the sperm whale, formerly used in perfumery.

A Pact

I make a pact with you, Walt Whitman[1]—
I have detested you long enough.
I come to you as a grown child
Who has had a pig-headed father;
I am old enough now to make friends.   5
It was you that broke the new wood,
Now is a time for carving.
We have one sap and one root—
Let there be commerce between us.

                                        [1913, 1916]

In a Station of the Metro[1]

The apparition of these faces in the crowd;
Petals on a wet, black bough.

                                        [1913, 1916]

The River-Merchant's Wife: A Letter

While my hair was still cut straight across my forehead
I played about the front gate, pulling flowers.
You came by on bamboo stilts, playing horse,
You walked about my seat, playing with blue plums.
And we went on living in the village of Chokan:[1]   5
Two small people, without dislike or suspicion.

At fourteen I married My Lord you.
I never laughed, being bashful.
Lowering my head, I looked at the wall.
Called to, a thousand times, I never looked back.   10

At fifteen I stopped scowling,
I desired my dust to be mingled with yours
Forever and forever and forever.
Why should I climb the look out?

At sixteen you departed,   15
You went into far Ku-to-yen,[2] by the river of swirling eddies,
And you have been gone five months.
The monkeys make sorrowful noise overhead.

---

[1]An American poet (1819–92) best known for his exuberant collection *Leaves of Grass* (1855).
Whitman's free verse and rhythmic innovation sharply contrasted with the rigid rhyming and structural
patterns of earlier poets and revolutionized poetry for future generations.
[1]The Paris subway.
[1]A suburb of the Chinese city of Nanking.
[2]A Chinese river.

You dragged your feet when you went out.
By the gate now, the moss is grown, the different mosses,   20
Too deep to clear them away!
The leaves fall early this autumn, in wind.
The paired butterflies are already yellow with August
Over the grass in the West garden;
They hurt me. I grow older.   25
If you are coming down through the narrows of the river Kiang,
Please let me know beforehand,
And I will come out to meet you

As far as Cho-fu-Sa.³

*By Rihaku*⁴

[1915]

Canto I¹

And then went down to the ship,
Set keel to breakers, forth on the godly sea, and
We set up mast and sail on that swart ship,
Bore sheep aboard her, and our bodies also
Heavy with weeping, and winds from sternward   5
Bore us out onward with bellying canvas,
Circe's² this craft, the trim-coifed goddess.
Then sat we amidships, wind jamming the tiller,
Thus with stretched sail, we went over sea till day's end.
Sun to his slumber, shadows o'er all the ocean,   10
Came we then to the bounds of deepest water,
To the Kimmerian lands,³ and peopled cities
Covered with close-webbed mist, unpierced ever
With glitter of sun-rays
Nor with stars stretched, nor looking back from heaven   15
Swartest night stretched over wretched men there.
The ocean flowing backward, came we then to the place
Aforesaid by Circe.
Here did they rites, Perimedes and Eurylochus,⁴
And drawing sword from my hip   20

---

³A beach several hundred miles from Nanking.
⁴The Japanese name for Li Po (701–762), from whose work Pound's poem was adapted.
¹The first sixty-seven lines of Canto I are a loose translation of section XI of Homer's *The Odyssey*, which describes Ulysses's journey to the underworld to consult with the blind Theban prophet, Tiresias.
²Odysseus lived for a year with Circe, an enchantress who dwelt in the island of Aea.
³A mythical place where the people dwell in eternal fog and darkness.
⁴Two members of Odysseus's crew.

I dug the ell-square pitkin;[5]
Poured we libations unto each the dead,
First mead and then sweet wine, water mixed with white flour.
Then prayed I many a prayer to the sickly death's-heads;
As set in Ithaca,[6] sterile bulls of the best   25
For sacrifice, heaping the pyre with goods,
A sheep to Tiresias[7] only, black and a bell-sheep.[8]
Dark blood flowed in the fosse,[9]
Souls out of Erebus,[10] cadaverous dead, of brides
Of youths and of the old who had borne much;   30
Souls stained with recent tears, girls tender,
Men many, mauled with bronze lance heads,
Battle spoil, bearing yet dreory[11] arms,
These many crowded about me; with shouting,
Pallor upon me, cried to my men for more beasts;   35
Slaughtered the herds, sheep slain of bronze;
Poured ointment, cried to the gods,
To Pluto[12] the strong, and praised Proserpine;[13]
Unsheathed the narrow sword,
I sat to keep off the impetuous impotent dead,   40
Till I should hear Tiresias.
But first Elpenor[14] came, our friend Elpenor,
Unburied, cast on the wide earth,
Limbs that we left in the house of Circe,
Unwept, unwrapped in sepulchre, since tolls urged other.   45
Pitiful spirit. And I cried in hurried speech:
"Elpenor, how art thou come to this dark coast?
"Cam'st thou afoot, outstripping seamen?"
          And he in heavy speech:
"Ill fate and abundant wine. I slept in Circe's ingle.   50
"Going down the long ladder unguarded,
"I fell against the buttress,
"Shattered the nape-nerve, the soul sought Avernus.[15]
"But thou, O King, I bid remember me, unwept, unburied,

[5]A small pit.
[6]One of the seven Ionian islands in Greece and Odysseus's home.
[7]Tiresias was a blind seer and soothsayer featured prominently in *Oedipus Rex*.
[8]A sheep that leads the herd.
[9]Ditch (Latin).
[10]Hades was split into two regions: Erebus, through which the dead must pass shortly after death, and Tartarus, the deeper region.
[11]Bloody.
[12]The Roman god of the underworld.
[13]The goddess of the underworld and wife of Pluto.
[14]Odysseus's youngest crewmember, who broke his neck when, drunk, he fell from Circe's roof.
[15]In Roman mythology, a crater near Naples that was believed to be the entrance to the underworld. Also a name for the underworld itself.

"Heap up mine arms, be tomb by sea-bord, and inscribed: 55
"*A man of no fortune, and with a name to come.*
"And set my oar up, that I swung mid fellows."

And Anticlea[16] came, whom I beat off, and then Tiresias Theban,
Holding his golden wand, knew me, and spoke first:
"A second time? why? man of ill star,   60
"Facing the sunless dead and this joyless region?
"Stand from the fosse, leave me my bloody bever[17]
"For soothsay."
          And I stepped back,
And he strong with the blood, said then: "Odysseus   65
Shalt return through spiteful Neptune,[18] over dark seas,
"Lose all companions." And then Anticlea came.
Lie quiet Divus. I mean, that is Andreas Divus,[19]
In officina Wecheli, 1538, out of Homer.
And he sailed, by Sirens and thence outward and away   70
And unto Circe.
          Venerandam,[20]
In the Cretan's phrase, with the golden crown, Aphrodite,[21]
Cypri munimenta sortita est,[22] mirthful, oricalchi,[23] with golden
Girdles and breast bands, thou with dark eyelids   75
Bearing the golden bough of Argicida.[24] So that:

[1925]

---

[16]Odysseus's mother. Odysseus has been told to speak to no one until he has first found Tiresias.

[17]Odysseus gives Tiresias a libation (drink) of blood that will enable the soothsayer to speak.

[18]The god and ruler of the sea, who created storms to delay Odysseus's return home.

[19]Pound refers to Renaissance scholar Andreas Divus's 1538 translation of Homer's *The Odyssey*, which he used as the foundation for the first sixty-seven lines of this Canto.

[20]To be worshipped (Latin). Pound refers to another (Latin) translation of Homeric hymns (*Hymni Deoru*') by Georgius Dartona Cretensis (the "Cretan").

[21]The Greek goddess of love.

[22]"The fortresses of Cyprus were her appointed realm" (Latin).

[23]Of copper (Latin).

[24]Pound associates the golden bough with the magic wand of the god Hermes, slayer of the many-eyed giant Argus ("Argicida").

H. D. (HILDA DOOLITTLE) ■ (1886–1961)

The best of the Imagist poets, H. D. was born in Bethlehem, Pennsylvania; her mother was a musician, her father was an astronomer, and she was raised according to the tenets of the Moravian Brethren, an evangelical branch of Protestantism. H. D. was educated at Bryn Mawr (1904–06), where one of her classmates was the future poet Marianne Moore, and at the University of Pennsylvania, where her friends included William Carlos Williams and Ezra Pound.

In 1911 H. D. traveled to Europe for the summer and soon made the decision to reside abroad permanently. Along with Pound (who gave H. D. her pen name), Amy Lowell, and others, H. D. advanced the theory and practice of Imagism, a small but significant movement of British and American poets from about 1912 to 1917. The Imagists, reacting to the sentimentality and ornate diction of late Victorian verse, aimed instead for clarity, precision, exactness, and intensity. They stressed, too, freedom in choice of subject matter and flexibility in rhythm.

Influenced by the Japanese haiku and by ancient Greek poetry, the Imagists' lyrics often were short, focused on a single sharp image. H. D.'s "Oread" (a mountain nymph), included here, was highlighted by Pound as an especially potent example of the Imagist form. Critics of Imagism objected to the absence of rhyme, meter, and narrative, and later in their careers the Imagists, including H. D., moved in new directions. The Imagists published their work in *Poetry* (Chicago), *The Egoist* (London), and other journals, in *Des Imagistes: An Anthology*, edited by Pound, and in three anthologies edited by Lowell and published 1915–17.

The love of H. D.'s life was Winifred Ellerman, who had taken the name Bryher. H. D. met her in England in July 1918, and they became intimate companions (though both were married), traveling together as cousins. With Bryher, H. D. was involved in avant-garde filmmaking in the 1920s, and during this decade and beyond she developed and deepened interests in Greek culture and civilization, mysticism, spiritualism, and Freudian psychology.

Perhaps because of her absorption in classical mythology (both "Leda" and "Helen," included here, show this), bisexuality, intense response to Freud, and feminist principles, H. D. did not in her lifetime receive the notice she deserved. But her work came increasingly to the attention of younger poets in the 1950s and 1960s, including Robert Duncan and Denise Levertov. Her central role in the making of modern literature and culture—her collaborations and friendships connected her to Pound, D. H. Lawrence, the African American actor Paul Robeson, and many others—is now acknowledged and esteemed.

Among H. D.'s important books of poetry are *Sea Garden* (1916), *Trilogy* (1946), and *Helen in Egypt* (1961). As the poem included here suggests, Helen of Troy was a compelling figure for H. D.; the critic Susan Stanford Friedman observes, "'Helen' takes as its subject the woman who has been the literary and mythic symbol of sexual beauty and illicit love in western culture. Much has been written about her, but H. D.'s poem does something new: it implicitly attacks the traditional imagery of Helen and implies that such perspectives have silenced Helen's own voice." A complex, passionate, myth-saturated, and boldly visionary writer, H. D. is today best approached through the *Collected Poems, 1912–1944*, ed. Louis L. Martz (1983).

Biographies include Janice S. Robinson, *H. D.: The Life and Work of an American Poet* (1982); and Barbara Guest, *Herself Defined: The Poet H. D. and Her World* (1984). For critical interpretation, see Susan Stanford Friedman, *Psyche Reborn: The Emergence of H. D.* (1981); and Rachel Blau DuPlessis, *H. D.: The Career of That Struggle* (1986). Two collections of essays are illuminating: *H. D., Woman and Poet*, ed. Michael King (1986); and *Signets: Reading H. D.*, eds. Susan Stanford Friedman and Rachel Blau DuPlessis (1990). See also Eileen Gregory, *H. D. and Hellenism* (1997); Diana Collecott, *H. D. and Sapphic Modernism, 1910–1950* (1999), Georgia Taylor, *H. D. and the Public Sphere of Modernist Women Writers 1913–1946* (2001); and Adalaide Morris, *How to Live/What to Do: H. D.'s Cultural Poetics* (2003).

Oread[1]

Whirl up, sea—
whirl your pointed pines,
splash your great pines
on our rocks,
hurl your green over us,   5
cover us with your pools of fir.

[1914, 1924]

[1] A nymph of hills and mountains.

Leda[1]

Where the slow river
meets the tide,
a red swan lifts red wings
and darker beak,
and underneath the purple down   5
of his soft breast
uncurls his coral feet.

Through the deep purple
of the dying heat
of sun and mist,   10
the level ray of sun-beam
has caressed
the lily with dark breast,
and flecked with richer gold
its golden crest.   15

Where the slow lifting
of the tide,
floats into the river
and slowly drifts
among the reeds,   20
and lifts the yellow flags,
he floats
where tide and river meet.

Ah kingly kiss—
no more regret   25
nor old deep memories
to mar the bliss;
where the low sedge is thick,
the gold day-lily
outspreads and rests   30
beneath soft fluttering
of red swan wings
and the warm quivering
of the red swan's breast.

[1919, 1921]

---

[1]In Greek mythology, Leda is a beautiful woman seduced by Zeus while he is disguised as a swan. She gave birth to an egg from which hatched the twins Castor and Pollux. Later she gave birth to Helen (of Troy), also fathered by Zeus.

Helen[1]

All Greece hates
the still eyes in the white face,
the lustre as of olives
where she stands,
and the white hands.　　　　　　　　5

All Greece reviles
the wan face when she smiles,
hating it deeper still
when it grows wan and white,
remembering past enchantments　　　10
and past ills.
Greece sees unmoved,
God's daughter, born of love,
the beauty of cool feet
and slenderest knees,　　　　　　　15
could love indeed the maid,
only if she were laid,
white ash amid funereal cypresses.

[1924]

---

[1]The daughter of Leda and Zeus was reputed to be the most beautiful woman in the world. She married Menelaus of Greece but was kidnapped by Paris and taken to Troy, which precipitated the Trojan War.

MARIANNE MOORE ■ (1887–1972)

Marianne Moore's poetry has been criticized as difficult and obscure, but the demands she places on readers result from her desire to achieve precision and exactness—which, for her, meant challenging and changing conventional forms of expression, phrase-making, and imagery Moore said in 1951:

Moore described her working habits in 1951:

> I work best in the morning, but usually keep on, afternoon and evening. I seldom use a desk, (write on a pad or portfolio). I seem to myself an observer, an interested hack rather than an author, but am an extremist with regard to exact statement; am quoted as having said, 'I write exercises in composition'; perhaps said, 'I look on my verse as exercises in composition.' When I have finished a thing it is, so far as I know, the last thing I shall write; but if taken unaware by what charms or stirs me up, I may write again.

Moore's commitment to her craft was reiterated in facts about herself she set out a decade later:

> Line of Work: Writing.
> But what would you really rather do? The same.
> ("Marianne Moore," *Esquire*, July 1962)

Moore's wit, poise, and playfulness are suggested in these excerpts. As the critic Randall Jarrell noted, she "is one of the most perceptive of writers, sees extraordinarily....What intelligence vibrates in the sounds, the rhythms, the pauses, in all of Miss Moore's poems, often, is enough to give the reader great pleasure, since it is a tone of much wit and precision and intelligence, the voice of a person of good taste and good sense and good will, of a genuinely human being."

Moore was born in Kirkwood, Missouri, a suburb of St. Louis, but she grew up in Carlisle, Pennsylvania, where her mother moved the family in 1896. She received her bachelor's degree from Bryn Mawr (H. D. was a student there at the same time), concentrating in her coursework on history, politics, law, and also biology—which, she claimed, sparked an interest in animals that carried over into her verse. She taught for several years at Carlisle Indian School, where her students included the extraordinary athlete (and later Olympic star) Jim Thorpe.

Moore and her mother relocated to Greenwich Village in New York City in 1915, and, in 1921, she took a job at the New York Public Library—the same year in which (through H. D.'s efforts) her first book, *Poems*, appeared. Moore enjoyed friendships with William Carlos Williams and other writers, and published in *The Dial*, a notable literary journal, eventually becoming first its acting editor (1925) and then its editor (1926–29). She and her mother moved to Brooklyn in 1929, where Moore remained (she was unmarried) for the rest of her life, taking pleasure in the exploits of the New York Yankees baseball team.

Like the Imagist poets (Ezra Pound and H. D., among others), Moore emphasized condensed imagery and statement, but her work was highly allusive as well, incorporating fragments and even quotations from other authors and texts. Moore received many honors, prizes, and awards, including the Pulitzer Prize for poetry, the National Book Award, and the Bollingen Prize for her *Collected Poems* (1951). Her *Complete Poems* was published in 1967 (rev. ed., 1981), her *Complete Prose* in 1986, and her *Selected Letters* in 1997.

As early as 1935, T. S. Eliot said of Moore:

My conviction, for what it is worth, has remained unchanged for the last fourteen years: that Miss Moore's poems form part of the small body of durable poetry written in our time; of that small body of writings, among what passes for poetry, in which an original sensibility and alert intelligence and deep feeling have been engaged in maintaining the life of the English language.

Marianne Moore, November 13, 1948. Photograph by Carl Van Vechten (1880–1964), American writer and photographer.

Whimsical, exploratory, intense, bookish (even pedantic), crisply detailed, experimental, and peculiarly brilliant; compressed, ambiguous, and elusive: as the following poems testify, Moore is one of modern literature's most intriguingly distinctive, and sometimes perplexing, voices.

For biography, see Charles Molesworth, *Marianne Moore: A Literary Life* (1990). For a range of critical opinion, see Marianne Moore: *Woman and Poet*, ed. Patricia Willis (1990). Helpful critical studies include Bonnie Costello, *Marianne Moore: Imaginary Possessions* (1981); Taffy Martin, *Marianne Moore: Subversive Modernist* (1986); Grace Schulman, *Marianne Moore: The Poetry of Engagement* (1986); John M. Slatin, *The Savage's Romance: The Poetry of Marianne Moore* (1986); and Cristanne Miller, *Marianne Moore: Questions of Authority* (1995). See also Linda Leavell, *Marianne Moore and the Visual Arts: Prismatic Color* (1995), and Elisabeth W. Joyce, *Cultural Critique and Abstraction: Marianne Moore and the Avant-Garde* (1998). *Marianne Moore: "A Right Good Salvo of Barks,"* eds. Linda Leavell, Cristanne Miller, and Robin G. Schulze (2005), includes scholarly essays and poems responding to Moore's work. For a study of the New York literary and art worlds: Ellen Levy, *Criminal Ingenuity: Moore, Cornell, Ashbery, and the Struggle Between the Arts* (2011).

Poetry

I too, dislike it: there are things that are important beyond all
    this fiddle.
  Reading it, however, with a perfect contempt for it, one
    discovers that there is in
it after all, a place for the genuine.
  Hands that can grasp, eyes
  that can dilate, hair that can rise   5
    if it must, these things are important not because a
high sounding interpretation can be put upon them but because
    they are
  useful; when they become so derivative as to become
    unintelligible,
  the same thing may be said for all of us, that we
    do not admire what   10
    we cannot understand: the bat,
      holding on upside down or in quest of something to

eat, elephants pushing, a wild horse taking a roll, a tireless wolf
    under
  a tree, the immovable critic twitching his skin like a horse
    that feels a flea, the base
  ball fan, the statistician—   15

nor is it valid
    to discriminate against "business documents and

school-books"[1]: all these phenomena are important. One must
        make a distinction
    however: when dragged into prominence by half poets, the
        result is not poetry,
    nor till the poets among us can be   20
"literalists of
the imagination"[2]—above
        insolence and triviality and can present

for inspection, imaginary gardens with real toads in them, shall
    we have
    it. In the meantime, if you demand on the one hand,   25
    the raw material of poetry in
        all its rawness and
        that which is on the other hand
            genuine, then you are interested in poetry.

                                                    [1921]

A Grave

Man looking into the sea,
taking the view from those who have as much right to it as you have
    yourself,
it is human nature to stand in the middle of a thing,
but you cannot stand in the middle of this;
the sea has nothing to give but a well excavated grave.   5
The firs stand in a procession, each with an emerald turkey-foot
    at the top,
reserved as their contours, saying nothing;
repression, however, is not the most obvious characteristic of the sea;
the sea is a collector, quick to return a rapacious look.
There are other besides you who have worn that look—   10
whose expression is no longer a protest; the fish no longer investigate
    them

---

[1] *Diary of Tolstoy* (Dutton), p. 84: "Where the boundary between prose and poetry lies, I shall never be able to understand. The question is raised in manuals of style, yet the answer to it lies beyond me. Poetry is verse: prose is not verse. Or else poetry is everything with the exception of business documents and school books." [Moore's note].

[2] Yeats, *Ideas of Good and Evil*. "The limitation of his view was from the very intensity of his vision; he was a too literal realist of imagination, as others are of nature; and because he believed that the figures seen by the mind's eye, when exalted by inspiration were 'eternal existences,' symbols of divine essences, he hated every grace of style that might obscure their lineaments." [Moore's note].

for their bones have not lasted:
men lower nets, unconscious of the fact that they are desecrating a grave,
and row quickly away—the blades of the oars
moving together like the feet of water-spiders as if there were no such
    thing as death.   15
The wrinkles progress upon themselves in a phalanx[1]—beautiful under
    networks of foam,
and fade breathlessly while the sea rustles in and out of the seaweed;
the birds swim through the air at top speed, emitting cat-calls as
    heretofore—
the tortoise-shell scourges about the feet of the cliffs, in motion beneath
    them
and the ocean, under the pulsation of lighthouses and noise of
    bell-buoys,   20
advances as usual, looking as if it were not that ocean in which dropped
    things are bound to sink—
in which if they turn and twist, it is neither with volition nor
    consciousness.

                                                 [1924]

To a Snail

If "compression is the first grace of style,"[1]
you have it. Contractility is a virtue
as modesty is a virtue.
It is not the acquisition of any one thing
that is able to adorn,   5
or the incidental quality that occurs
as a concomitant of something well said,
that we value in style,
but the principle that is hid:
in the absence of feet, "a method of conclusions";   10
"a knowledge of principles,"
in the curious phenomenon of your occipital[2] horn.

                                               [1924]

---

[1]A military formation of heavily armed infantry drawn up closely, with shields joined and long spears overlapping, employed by the ancient Greeks.
[1]Quote from *Demetrius on Style*, translated by W. Hamilton Fyfe, "The very first grace of style is that which comes from compression." [Moore's note].
[2]Pertaining to the back of the head.

JOHN CROWE RANSOM ■ (1888–1974)

Born in Pulaski, Tennessee, the son of a Methodist minister, John Crowe Ransom attended Vanderbilt University, graduating in 1909, and was the recipient of a Rhodes Scholarship at Oxford University in England. After serving in World War I, he taught at Vanderbilt, wrote essays, and began to make a name for himself as a poet through a series of highly crafted lyrics, many of which were composed in an intense period between 1923 and 1926.

Ransom's poems are easy to underestimate; they lack the conspicuous networks of allusion and imagery that much modernist poetry, inspired by T. S. Eliot and Ezra Pound, features. Witty, ironic, and subtle, such poems as "Bells for John Whiteside's Daughter" are, nonetheless, in their own way modern too, simple-seeming but complex in organization and exploration of theme. The terms "classical," "formalist," and even "archaic" have been applied to Ransom's verse, but these both illuminate and fail to do full justice to its intricacy.

Ransom was a gifted teacher and valued friend, and he was at the center of a group of poets, critics, and intellectuals at Vanderbilt that included Allen Tate, Donald Davidson, Robert Penn Warren, Cleanth Brooks, and Randall Jarrell. Beginning in the late 1920s, Ransom and others, first known as the Fugitive poets and then, moving more directly into cultural criticism, as the Agrarians, produced a solid, if controversial, body of conservative social thought; stalwart defenders of the traditional South, they attacked northern industrialism and urbanization. The key book of the Agrarian movement was *I'll Take My Stand* (1930), and to it Ransom contributed the introductory "Statement of Principles" and an essay, "Reconstructed but Unregenerate." A related work by Ransom, *God Without Thunder*, dealing with the need to restore orthodoxy and "a virile and concrete God," also was published in 1930.

By the mid- to late 1930s, Ransom's hopes for a transformation in southern life had waned; increasingly, he turned his attention to the state of literary criticism and the teaching of English in colleges and universities. In 1937 he accepted a position at Kenyon College and there became the editor in 1939 of *The Kenyon Review*, soon making it one of the most noteworthy journals of literature and criticism in the country. In two important books, *The World's Body* (1938) and *The New Criticism* (1941), he argued for a new theory and practice of literary criticism that focused on the text itself rather than on biographical, historical, political, and other backgrounds and contexts. Taking its name from Ransom's book, the New Criticism became the dominant form of literary criticism of the twentieth century, establishing itself through journals, programs, institutes, critical monographs, and first-rate anthologies and textbooks, which Warren, Brooks, and others prepared.

Ransom's example inspired teachers, critics, and students. At Kenyon he was a force in the young literary lives of the poets James Wright and Robert Lowell and the short-story writer Peter Taylor. But while he remained an important literary and critical mentor, influence, and authority, he wrote relatively few poems after the 1920s, preferring instead to revise his earlier work. The revisions, which not all readers admire, are included in *Selected Poems* (1963). His *Selected Essays* (1984) and *Selected Letters* (1985) are also important books in the history of modern poetry and literary criticism. In his poetry and prose, and in his correspondence as well, Ransom engages in "a celebration of life," as his friend Warren observed, "manifested in the virtues of charity and endurance, tenderness and gaiety."

For biography and critical discussion, see Thomas Daniel Young, *Gentleman in a Dustcoat: A Biography of John Crowe Ransom* (1976) and Kieran Quinlan, *John Crowe Ransom's Secular Faith* (1989). See also John L. Stewart, *The Burden of Time: The Fugitives and Agrarians; the Nashville Groups of the 1920's and 1930's; and the Writing of John Crowe Ransom, Allen Tate, and Robert Penn Warren* (1965). Paul K. Conkin, *The Southern Agrarians* (1988); Mark Jancovich, *The Cultural Politics of the New Criticism* (1993); Mark Malvasi, *The Unregenerate South: The Agrarian Thought of John Crowe Ransom, Allen Tate, and Donald Davidson* (1997); and Paul V. Murphy, *The Rebuke of History: The Southern Agrarians and American Conservative Thought* (2001).

Piazza Piece

—I am a gentleman in a dustcoat trying
To make you hear. Your ears are soft and small
And listen to an old man not at all,
They want the young men's whispering and sighing.
But see the roses on your trellis dying   5
And hear the spectral singing of the moon;
For I must have my lovely lady soon.
I am a gentleman in a dustcoat trying.

—I am a lady young in beauty waiting
Until my truelove comes, and then we kiss.   10
But what grey man among the vines is this
Whose words are dry and faint as in a dream?
Back from my trellis, Sir, before I scream!
I am a lady young in beauty waiting.

[1927]

T. S. ELIOT ■ (1888–1965)

Although T. S. Eliot's reputation as a poet and a critic has somewhat declined in the decades since his death, he remains the most important American (and English) poet and critic of the twentieth century. He was the author of the modern period's most influential (and controversial) poem, *The Waste Land* (1922), and its most authoritative literary essays and reviews. "A Great Man Gone" was the title of the obituary for Eliot in the *Times Literary Supplement* (January 7, 1965); "for many readers," its author concluded, "Mr. Eliot's death will be like the death of a part of themselves."

Born in St. Louis, Missouri, the seventh and youngest child of Henry Ware Eliot, a businessman, and Charlotte Stearns Eliot, an amateur poet and volunteer social worker, Eliot attended private schools and then entered Harvard University in 1906, receiving his bachelor's degree in 1909, his master's in 1911, and completing all of his doctoral work except the dissertation just before the outbreak of World War I in 1914.

At Harvard, Eliot became interested in philosophy and comparative literature; Dante's *Divine Comedy* was a sublime discovery for him. For his poetry and criticism, however, the crucial experience during his Harvard years was his reading in December 1908 of Arthur Symons's *The Symbolist Movement in Literature* (1899), a book by an English poet-critic that introduced French symbolist poetry to English and American readers. Eliot was already writing verse himself, publishing some of it in *The Harvard Advocate*; from 1909 to 1911 he worked on two of his best poems, "Portrait of a Lady" and "The Love Song of J. Alfred Prufrock," adeptly using the kind of irony and symbolism he had encountered in the French poets—Charles Baudelaire, Arthur Rimbaud, and Jules Laforgue—whom Symons quoted and discussed.

From October 1910 to September 1911 Eliot studied at the Sorbonne in Paris, and then, on his return to Harvard, he pursued graduate work and served as a teaching assistant for two years. For his dissertation topic he focused on the writings of the British idealist philosopher F. H. Bradley (1846–1924), author of *Appearance* and *Reality* (1893). His research led him to the University of Marburg in Germany in the summer of 1914, but then, as the threat of world war loomed, he relocated to Merton College, Oxford, England.

In London in September 1914 Eliot met Ezra Pound, who quickly became his adviser, editor, and literary agent. "The Love Song of J. Alfred Prufrock" was published in *Poetry* magazine in June 1915 and, in the following month, Eliot married Vivien (sometimes Vivienne) Haigh-Wood, a relationship that soon unraveled as Vivien's mental and physical illnesses deepened in the 1920s and 1930s.

Eliot's work is itself impersonal and objective; it is filled—especially the poetry—with masks, role-playing, and multiple voices. Yet it is saturated with personal pain, regret, sexual desire, and emotional and spiritual yearning.

This is one of the potent paradoxes of Eliot's art, in his prose as well as in his poetry, and a main reason why it has haunted and fascinated readers.

In March 1917, tired of the makeshift teaching he had undertaken, Eliot took a job in the colonial and foreign department of Lloyd's Bank, a position he held for the next eight years; at the same time, he labored on his poetry. His first volume, *Prufrock and Other Observations*, appeared in 1917. He also wrote literary criticism, publishing brilliant essays and book reviews in the *Times Literary Supplement* and other leading periodicals and including a number of them in *The Sacred Wood* (1920), a landmark collection of criticism and theory.

Worn down by the demands of caring for his wife, in October 1921 Eliot went to Margate, in southeast England, for rest and treatment of nervous disorder. A month later he left for a sanatorium in Lausanne, Switzerland, where he was a patient for six weeks and where he worked on the draft of a long poem he had started years earlier. In Paris, on his way back to London, he showed the draft to Pound, who edited it skillfully and turned it—in Eliot's words—from "a jumble of good and bad passages into a poem," the poem that became *The Waste Land*.

Allusive, collage-like, experimental, and technically daring, idiomatic, hallucinatory, showily learned, and archly witty, ominous to the point of being apocalyptic, *The Waste Land* was a primary text of literary modernism, rivaled in importance only by James Joyce's novel *Ulysses*. The poem was published in *The Criterion*, a new literary and cultural quarterly edited by Eliot, in October 1922, reprinted in *The Dial* in November, and included in Eliot's *Poems 1900–1925*. *The Waste Land* was, Pound declared, "the justification of the 'movement', of our modern experiment, since 1900."

"The Hollow Men," published in 1925, is another significant work from this period—Eliot told Pound that it was "post-Waste." It is a vivid, eerie account of death, despair, and emotional and spiritual exhaustion, a failed quest. Perhaps, as the scholar Ronald Bush has suggested, there is a slight measure of hope and affirmation, or at least a desire for fulfillment: "Psychologically, the drama moves downward from resistance to submission, but spiritually it moves upward from proud isolation through humility to a thirst for divine love." But for many readers the unforgettable final lines resonate with sorrow and fear, the low, broken, plaintive sounds of a "whimper."

In 1927 Eliot became a British citizen, and in the following year he identified himself as a "classicist in literature, royalist in politics, and Anglo-Catholic in religion." From 1932 to 1933 Eliot held the Charles Eliot Norton professorship of poetry at Harvard, where his duties consisted of delivering lectures that became *The Use of Poetry and the Use of Criticism* (1933). During the same period he presented the Page Barbour Lectures at the University of Virginia, later published as *After Strange Gods: A Primer of Modern Heresy* (1933), a book that displayed a censorious attitude toward much contemporary literature and that was marred by anti-Semitism.

Eliot's most noteworthy work in the final phase of his career was the four-part poem *Four Quartets* (1940–43); "Burnt Norton," here, is the first. It is a brooding, somber exploration of and quest for religious faith, and is striking in its continuities with and departures from the poetry with which Eliot made his mark in the 1910s and 1920s.

For biography, see Peter Ackroyd, *T. S. Eliot: A Life* (1984); and Lyndall Gordon, *T. S. Eliot: An Imperfect Life* (1999). For critical analysis and discussion, see Hugh Kenner, *The Invisible Poet: T. S. Eliot* (1959); *Eliot in His Time: Essays on the Occasion of the Fiftieth Anniversary of The Waste Land*, ed. A. Walton Litz (1973); Ronald Bush, *T. S. Eliot: A Study in Character and Style* (1984); and Louis Menand, *Discovering Modernism: T. S. Eliot and His Context* (1987).

Among many recent studies, see Christopher Ricks, *Decisions and Revisions in T. S. Eliot* (2003); *Gender, Desire, and Sexuality in T. S. Eliot*, eds. Cassandra Laity and Nancy K. Gish (2004); James E. Miller Jr., *T. S. Eliot: The Making of an American Poet, 1888–1922* (2005); Craig Raine, *T. S. Eliot* (2006); and *T. S. Eliot and the Concept of Tradition*, eds. Giovanni Cianci and Jason Harding (2007). Another good resource is *T. S. Eliot: The Contemporary Reviews*, ed. Jewel Spears Brooker (2004). See also: *T. S. Eliot in Context*, ed. Jason Harding (2011). An important resource, in progress: *The Letters of T. S. Eliot*, ed. Valerie Eliot (revised ed., 2011-).

Photograph of T.S. Eliot, taken around 1925-30.

The Love Song of J. Alfred Prufrock

S'io credessi che mia risposta fosse
a persona che mai tornasse al mondo,
questa fiamma staria senza più scosse.
Ma per ciò che giammai di questo fondo
non tornò vivo alcun, s'i'odo il vero,
senza tema d'infamia ti rispondo.[1]

Let us go then, you and I,
When the evening is spread out against the sky
Like a patient etherised[2] upon a table;
Let us go, through certain half-deserted streets,
The muttering retreats   5
Of restless nights in one-night cheap hotels
And sawdust restaurants with oyster-shells:
Streets that follow like a tedious argument
Of insidious intent
To lead you to an overwhelming question...   10
Oh, do not ask, 'What is it?'
Let us go and make our visit.

In the room the women come and go
Talking of Michelangelo.[3]

The yellow fog that rubs its back upon the window-panes,   15
The yellow smoke that rubs its muzzle on the window-panes,
Licked its tongue into the corners of the evening,
Lingered upon the pools that stand in drains,
Let fall upon its back the soot that falls from chimneys,
Slipped by the terrace, made a sudden leap,   20
And seeing that it was a soft October night,
Curled once about the house, and fell asleep.

For indeed there will be time
For the yellow smoke that slides along the street
Rubbing its back upon the window-panes;   25
There will be time, there will be time

---

[1]*S'io credessi che mia risposta fosse*: A quote from the *Inferno*, Canto 27, lines 61–66 by Dante Alighieri (1265–1321): "If I thought that my reply would be to one who would ever return to the world, this flame would stay without further movement; but since none has ever returned alive from this depth, if what I hear is true, I answer you without fear of infamy." (Italian). The lines are spoken by Count Guido da Montefeltro (1223–98), condemned to burn in hell for giving treacherous advice to Pope Boniface. Guido admits he tells Dante the truth of his crimes only because he believes the poet to be one of the dead who cannot return to tell others of his guilty admission.
[2]Sedated.
[3]Michelangelo Buonarroti (1475–1564), the famous Italian painter, sculptor, architect, and poet, best known for his sculpture *David* and his work on the ceiling of the Sistine Chapel.

To prepare a face to meet the faces that you meet;
There will be time to murder and create,
And time for all the works and days of hands
That lift and drop a question on your plate;   30
Time for you and time for me,
And time yet for a hundred indecisions,
And for a hundred visions and revisions,
Before the taking of a toast and tea.

In the room the women come and go   35
Talking of Michelangelo.

And indeed there will be time
To wonder, 'Do I dare?' and, 'Do I dare?'
Time to turn back and descend the stair,
With a bald spot in the middle of my hair—   40
(They will say: 'How his hair is growing thin!')
My morning coat, my collar mounting firmly to the chin,
My necktie rich and modest, but asserted by a simple pin—
(They will say: 'But how his arms and legs are thin!')
Do I dare   45
Disturb the universe?
In a minute there is time
For decisions and revisions which a minute will reverse.
For I have known them all already, known them all—
Have known the evenings, mornings, afternoons,   50
I have measured out my life with coffee spoons;
I know the voices dying with a dying fall
Beneath the music from a farther room.
      So how should I presume?

And I have known the eyes already, known them all—   55
The eyes that fix you in a formulated phrase,
And when I am formulated, sprawling on a pin,
When I am pinned and wriggling on the wall,
Then how should I begin
To spit out all the butt-ends of my days and ways?   60
      And how should I presume?

And I have known the arms already, known them all—
Arms that are braceleted and white and bare
(But in the lamplight, downed with light brown hair!)
Is it perfume from a dress   65
That makes me so digress?

Arms that lie along a table, or wrap about a shawl.
   And should I then presume?
   And how should I begin?

Shall I say, I have gone at dusk through narrow streets   70
And watched the smoke that rises from the pipes
Of lonely men in shirt-sleeves, leaning out of windows?...

I should have been a pair of ragged claws
Scuttling across the floors of silent seas.

And the afternoon, the evening, sleeps so peacefully!   75
Smoothed by long fingers,
Asleep...tired...or it malingers,
Stretched on the floor, here beside you and me.
Should I, after tea and cakes and ices,
Have the strength to force the moment to its crisis?   80
But though I have wept and fasted, wept and prayed,
Though I have seen my head (grown slightly bald) brought in
   upon a platter,[4]
I am no prophet—and here's no great matter;
I have seen the moment of my greatness flicker,
And I have seen the eternal Footman hold my coat, and snicker,   85
And in short, I was afraid.

And would it have been worth it, after all,
After the cups, the marmalade, the tea,
Among the porcelain, among some talk of you and me,
Would it have been worth while,   90
To have bitten off the matter with a smile,
To have squeezed the universe into a ball
To roll it towards some overwhelming question,
To say: 'I am Lazarus,[5] come from the dead,
Come back to tell you all, I shall tell you all'—   95
If one, settling a pillow by her head,
   Should say: 'That is not what I meant at all.
   That is not it, at all.'

[4]Referring to the biblical story of Salomé and John the Baptist (Mark 6:17–28). Princess Salomé was the daughter of Queen Herodias, who was married to King Herod. John the Baptist had publicly denounced the Queen's marriage to Herod and was imprisoned for his opposition. After watching Salomé dance, Herod promised to grant her anything she wished. At her mother's prompting, Salomé requested the head of John the Baptist be delivered to her on a platter.

[5]The Bible contains two stories involving a man named Lazarus. In Luke 16:19–31 Lazarus is a poor man who futilely begs crumbs from a rich man's table. Lazarus dies and goes to heaven while the rich man goes to hell. The rich man begs that Lazarus be returned to earth to warn the rich man's surviving brothers of their folly. Abraham, in heaven, denies the request, explaining that Lazarus's errand would be futile: "If they hear not Moses and the prophets, neither will they be persuaded, though one rose from the dead." Another story (John 11:1–44) recounts how Jesus raises his beloved friend Lazarus from the dead at the request of Lazarus's sisters, Martha and Mary of Bethany.

And would it have been worth it, after all,
Would it have been worth while,   100
After the sunsets and the dooryards and the sprinkled streets,
After the novels, after the teacups, after the skirts that trail along the
      floor—
And this, and so much more?—
It is impossible to say just what I mean!
But as if a magic lantern[6] threw the nerves in patterns on a screen: 105
Would it have been worth while
If one, settling a pillow or throwing off a shawl,
And turning toward the window, should say:
      'That is not it at all,
      That is not what I meant, at all.'   110

No! I am not Prince Hamlet,[7] nor was meant to be;
Am an attendant lord, one that will do
To swell a progress,[8] start a scene or two,
Advise the prince; no doubt, an easy tool,
Deferential, glad to be of use,   115
Politic, cautious, and meticulous;
Full of high sentence, but a bit obtuse;
At times, indeed, almost ridiculous—
Almost, at times, the Fool.[9]

I grow old...I grow old...   120
I shall wear the bottoms of my trousers rolled.

Shall I part my hair behind? Do I dare to eat a peach?
I shall wear white flannel trousers, and walk upon the beach.
I have heard the mermaids singing, each to each.

I do not think that they will sing to me.   125

I have seen them riding seaward on the waves
Combing the white hair of the waves blown back
When the wind blows the water white and black.

We have lingered in the chambers of the sea
By sea-girls wreathed with seaweed red and brown   130
Till human voices wake us, and we drown.

                                                            [1915, 1917]

[6]An early form of projector used to magnify still pictures on a screen.
[7]The title character in William Shakespeare's tragic play *Hamlet*.
[8]A state journey made by a royal or noble personage, often depicted on Elizabethan stages.
[9]A stock character of Elizabethan and Jacobean drama who utters truths while appearing incomprehensibly simpleminded.

The Waste Land

*'Nam Sibyllam quidem Cumis ego ipse oculis meis vidi in ampulla
pendere, et cum illi pueri dicerent: Σιβμλλα τι θέλειζ; respondebat
illa: άποθανεῖν θέλω.'*[1]

For Ezra Pound
il miglior fabbro.[2]

I. THE BURIAL OF THE DEAD[3]

April is the cruellest month, breeding
Lilacs out of the dead land, mixing
Memory and desire, stirring
Dull roots with spring rain.
Winter kept us warm, covering   5
Earth in forgetful snow, feeding
A little life with dried tubers.
Summer surprised us, coming over the Starnbergersee[4]
With a shower of rain; we stopped in the colonnade,
And went on in sunlight, into the Hofgarten,[5]   10
And drank coffee, and talked for an hour.
Bin gar keine Russin, stamm' aus Litauen, echt deutsch.[6]
And when we were children, staying at the arch-duke's,
My cousin's, he took me out on a sled,
And I was frightened. He said, Marie,   15
Marie, hold on tight. And down we went.
In the mountains, there you feel free.
I read, much of the night, and go south in the winter.
What are the roots that clutch, what branches grow
Out of this stony rubbish? Son of man,[7]   20
You cannot say, or guess, for you know only
A heap of broken images, where the sun beats,
And the dead tree gives no shelter, the cricket no relief,[8]

---

[1]From *The Satyricon,* by the Roman satirist Gaius Petronius (c. 27–66): "For I once saw with my own eyes
the Sibyl at Cumae hanging in a bottle, and when the boys asked her 'What do you want?' she responded:
'I wish to die.' Apollo promised the Sibyl of Cumae anything she wanted if she would spend a single
night with him. She asked for as many years of life as grains of sand she could fit into her hand. Once he
granted her wish, she refused to follow through with the bargain. He cursed her to eternal life without
eternal youth. She shriveled into a frail undying body, so tiny it fit into a jar hung from a tree."
[2]"The better craftsman." (Italian). A compliment Dante Alighieri (1265–1321) pays to the troubadour
poet Arnaut Daniel (fl. 1180–1200) in the *Purgatorio.* Eliot uses Dante's words to pay a similar compliment to his friend Ezra Pound (1885–1972), who helped him edit *The Waste Land.*
[3]The name of the burial service in the Anglican *Book of Common Prayer.*
[4]A lake in Munich, Germany.
[5]A park in Munich, Germany.
[6]"I am not Russian at all; I am Lithuanian, a genuine German." (German)
[7]From Ezekiel 2:1, in which God sends the prophet Ezekiel to warn the children of Israel. "Son of man,
stand upon thy feet, and I will speak unto thee."
[8]From Ecclesiastes 12:5, describing old age: "...and the almond tree shall flourish, and the grasshopper
shall be a burden, and desire shall fail."

And the dry stone no sound of water. Only
There is shadow under this red rock,[9]   25
(Come in under the shadow of this red rock),
And I will show you something different from either
Your shadow at morning striding behind you
Or your shadow at evening rising to meet you;
I will show you fear in a handful of dust.   30

> *Frisch weht der Wind*
> *Der Heimat zu*
> *Mein Irisch Kind,*
> *Wo weilist du?*[10]

'You gave me hyacinths[11] first a year ago;   35
'They called me the hyacinth girl.'
—Yet when we came back, late, from the hyacinth garden,
Your arms full, and your hair wet, I could not
Speak, and my eyes failed, I was neither
Living nor dead, and I knew nothing,   40
Looking into the heart of light, the silence
Oed' und leer das Meer.[12]

Madam Sosostris, famous clairvoyante,
Had a bad cold, nevertheless
Is known to be the wisest woman in Europe,   45
With a wicked pack of cards.[13] Here, said she,
Is your card, the drowned Phoenician Sailor,
(Those are pearls that were his eyes.[14] Look!)
Here is Belladonna,[15] the Lady of the Rocks,
The lady of situations.   50
Here is the man with three staves, and here the Wheel,

---

[9]From Isaiah 32:2, regarding the prophecy of the reign of the Messiah, which "shall be as an hiding place from the wind, and a covert from the tempest; as rivers of water in a dry place, as the shadow of a great rock in a weary land."

[10]From the opera *Tristan und Isolde*, Act I, verses 5–8, by Richard Wagner (1813–83). "Fresh the wind blows to the homeland; my Irish child, where are you waiting?" (German)

[11]Hyacinths are purple spring flowers named for Hyacinthus of Greek myth. Hyacinthus was accidentally killed by the god Apollo, who made a flower spring up from his blood. The return of spring revives the memory of his fate.

[12]From *Tristan und Isolde*, Act III, verse 24, spoken by shepherds to the dying Tristan as he waits for his love, Isolde. "Empty and barren is the sea." (German)

[13]Tarot cards used to predict the future. Not all of the cards Eliot cites are in the standard Tarot deck. The man with three staves, the hanged man, and the wheel of fortune are all tarot cards. The Phoenician sailor, Belladonna, and the one-eyed merchant are admitted products of Eliot's imagination.

[14]From Act I, Scene ii, line 398 of Shakespeare's *The Tempest*. "Full fathom five thy father lies / Of his bones are coral made: / Those are pearls that were his eyes: / Nothing of him that doth fade, / But doth suffer a sea-change / Into something rich and strange."

[15]Also called *deadly nightshade*, extract of belladonna is used medicinally to dilate the pupil of the eye or to relieve muscle spasms; a poison.

And here is the one-eyed merchant, and this card,
Which is blank, is something he carries on his back,
Which I am forbidden to see. I do not find
The Hanged Man. Fear death by water.   55
I see crowds of people, walking round in a ring.
Thank you. If you see dear Mrs. Equitone,
Tell her I bring the horoscope myself:
One must be so careful these days.

Unreal City,[16]   60
Under the brown fog of a winter dawn,
A crowd flowed over London Bridge, so many,
I had not thought death had undone so many.[17]
Sighs, short and infrequent, were exhaled,
And each man fixed his eyes before his feet.   65
Flowed up the hill and down King William Street,
To where Saint Mary Woolnoth[18] kept the hours
With a dead sound on the final stroke of nine.
There I saw one I knew, and stopped him, crying: 'Stetson!
'You who were with me in the ships at Mylae![19]   70
'That corpse you planted last year in your garden,
'Has it begun to sprout? Will it bloom this year?
'Or has the sudden frost disturbed its bed?
'O keep the Dog far hence, that's friend to men,
'Or with his nails he'll dig it up again![20]   75
'You! hypocrite lecteur!—mon semblable,—mon frère!'[21]

II. A GAME OF CHESS[22]

The Chair she sat in, like a burnished throne,[23]
Glowed on the marble, where the glass
Held up by standards wrought with fruited vines

[16]Eliot quotes a line from "Les Sept Vieillards" ("The Seven Old Men") by the French poet Charles Baudelaire (1821–67): "Swarming city, city full of dreams, / Where the specter in broad daylight accosts the passerby."
[17]From Dante's *Inferno*, Canto III, lines 55-57: "So long a train of people, / That I should never have believed / That death had undone so many." Dante refers to the souls he sees in the first circle of hell, containing the masses of those who have wasted their lives earning neither praise nor blame.
[18]A church on King William Street, located in London's financial district.
[19]The battle of Mylae, fought in 260 BCE, was a surprising naval victory of the Romans over the Carthaginians in the First Punic War.
[20]Eliot refers to the play *The White Devil* (1612), by John Webster (1578–1632). In Webster's bloody tragedy, one of the women, Cornelia, driven mad with grief, sings a dirge for her son: "But keep the wolf far thence, that's foe to men, / For with his nails he'll dig them up again." (Act V, Scene iv, lines 97–98).
[21]"Hypocrite reader!—my likeness—my brother!" (French) Eliot refers to the final line of a poem of Charles Baudelaire (1821–67), "Au Lecteur" ("To the Reader"), the preface to his book *Fleurs du Mal*.
[22]Eliot borrows the title of a play (1624) by the English playwright Thomas Middleton (1580–1627), an allegorical description of the political conflict between England and Spain. Another Middleton play, *Women Beware Women* (1627), also uses chess as a plot device; in it, a young woman is seduced while her mother-in-law is absorbed in a chess game.
[23]An allusion to Cleopatra's barge in Shakespeare's *Antony and Cleopatra* (Act II, scene ii, line 190). "The barge she sat in, like a burnish'd throne, / Burnt on the water."

From which a golden Cupidon peeped out 80
(Another hid his eyes behind his wing)
Doubled the flames of sevenbranched candelabra
Reflecting light upon the table as
The glitter of her jewels rose to meet it,
From satin cases poured in rich profusion. 85
In vials of ivory and coloured glass
Unstoppered, lurked her strange synthetic perfumes,
Unguent, powdered, or liquid—troubled, confused
And drowned the sense in odours; stirred by the air
That freshened from the window, these ascended 90
In fattening the prolonged candle-flames,[24]
Flung their smoke into the laquearia,[25]
Stirring the pattern on the coffered ceiling.
Huge sea-wood fed with copper
Burned green and orange, framed by the coloured stone, 95
In which sad light a carvèd dolphin swam.
Above the antique mantel was displayed
As though a window gave upon the sylvan scene[26]
The change of Philomel, by the barbarous king[27]
So rudely forced; yet there the nightingale 100
Filled all the desert with inviolable voice
And still she cried, and still the world pursues,
'Jug Jug'[28] to dirty ears.
And other withered stumps of time
Were told upon the walls; staring forms 105
Leaned out, leaning, hushing the room enclosed.
Footsteps shuffled on the stair.
Under the firelight, under the brush, her hair
Spread out in fiery points
Glowed into words, then would be savagely still. 110

'My nerves are bad to-night. Yes, bad. Stay with me.
'Speak to me. Why do you never speak. Speak.
   'What are you thinking of? What thinking? What?

[24]A reference to the Roman poet Virgil's (70–19 BCE) description of the banquet Dido gives for her Trojan lover, Aeneas, in *The Aeneid*.
[25]A paneled ceiling.
[26]A reference to the epic poem *Paradise Lost* by John Milton (1608–74), in which Milton describes Satan looking at the garden of Eden.
[27]From the *Metamorphoses*, VI, by the Roman poet Ovid (43 BCE–AD 18). King Tereus raped his wife's sister, Philomela, and cut out her tongue to hide his crime. Philomela revealed the assault by weaving it into a piece of embroidery she sent to her sister, Procne. When Procne discovered what her husband had done, she sought revenge by killing their son, Itys, and serving him to Tereus for dinner. The sisters fled and were turned into birds by the gods—Procne into a swallow and Philomela into a nightingale.
[28]A representation of the song of the nightingale in Elizabethan poetry.

'I never know what you are thinking. Think.'
I think we are in rats' alley[29]   115
Where the dead men lost their bones.

'What is that noise?'
                    The wind under the door.[30]
'What is that noise now? What is the wind doing?'
                    Nothing again nothing.   120
                                                  'Do
'You know nothing? Do you see nothing? Do you remember
'Nothing?'
      I remember
Those are pearls that were his eyes.   125
'Are you alive, or not? Is there nothing in your head?'
                                                  But

O O O O that Shakespeherian Rag[31]—
It's so elegant
So intelligent   130
'What shall I do now? What shall I do?'
'I shall rush out as I am, and walk the street
'With my hair down, so. What shall we do tomorrow?

'What shall we ever do?'

                    The hot water at ten.   135
And if it rains, a closed car at four.
And we shall play a game of chess,
Pressing lidless eyes and waiting for a knock upon the door.
When Lil's husband got demobbed,[32] I said—
I didn't mince my words, I said to her myself,   140
HURRY UP PLEASE ITS TIME[33]
Now Albert's coming back, make yourself a bit smart.
He'll want to know what you done with that money he gave you
To get yourself some teeth. He did, I was there.
You have them all out, Lil, and get a nice set,   145
He said, I swear, I can't bear to look at you.
And no more can't I, I said, and think of poor Albert,
He's been in the army four years, he wants a good time,

---

[29]Eliot's note refers readers to Part III, line 195.
[30]Reference to a play, *The Devil's Law Case* (1623), by John Webster, in which a duke is cured of an infection by the very wound intended to kill him. His doctor asks, "Is the wind in that door still?" meaning, "Is he still alive?"
[31]A music-hall song popular around 1912.
[32]Discharged from the army.
[33]Traditional warning of British bartenders that the pub is closing.

And if you don't give it him, there's other wills, I said.
Oh is there, she said. Something o' that, I said. 150
Then I'll know who to thank, she said, and give me a straight look.
HURRY UP PLEASE ITS TIME
If you don't like it you can get on with it, I said.
Others can pick and choose if you can't.
But if Albert makes off, it won't be for lack of telling. 155
You ought to be ashamed, I said, to look so antique.
(And her only thirty-one.)
I can't help it, she said, pulling a long face,
It's them pills I took, to bring it off, she said.
(She's had five already, and nearly died of young George.) 160
The chemist[34] said it would be all right, but I've never been the same.
You *are* a proper fool, I said.
Well, if Albert won't leave you alone, there it is, I said,
What you get married for it if you don't want children?
HURRY UP PLEASE ITS TIME 165
Well, that Sunday Albert was home, they had a hot gammon,[35]
And they asked me in to dinner, to get the beauty of it hot—
HURRY UP PLEASE ITS TIME
HURRY UP PLEASE ITS TIME
Goonight Bill. Goonight Lou. Goonight May. Goonight. 170
Ta ta. Goonight. Goonight.
Good night, ladies, good night, sweet ladies,[36] good night, good night.

III. THE FIRE SERMON[37]

The river's tent is broken; the last fingers of leaf
Clutch and sink into the wet bank. The wind
Crosses the brown land, unheard. The nymphs are departed. 175
Sweet Thames, run softly,[38] till I end my song.
The river bears no empty bottles, sandwich papers,
Silk handkerchiefs, cardboard boxes, cigarette ends
Or other testimony of summer nights. The nymphs are departed.
And their friends, the loitering heirs of City directors; 180
Departed, have left no addresses.

---

[34]Pharmacist.
[35]Ham or bacon.
[36]An allusion to the popular song "Good Night, Ladies" and to Shakespeare's tragedy *Hamlet*, in which Ophelia sings her mad song before drowning herself (Act IV, scene v, line 72).
[37]An allusion to Buddha's Fire Sermon, which urges humans to eliminate desire, for only in the absence of passion can they be free.
[38]A reference to the marriage poem "Prothalamion," by the English Renaissance poet Edmund Spencer (1552–99).

By the waters of Leman I sat down and wept...[39]
Sweet Thames, run softly till I end my song,
Sweet Thames, run softly, for I speak not loud or long.
But at my back in a cold blast I hear[40]   185
The rattle of the bones, and chuckle spread from ear to ear.
A rat crept softly through the vegetation
Dragging its slimy belly on the bank
While I was fishing in the dull canal
On a winter evening round behind the gashouse   190
Musing upon the king my brother's wreck
And on the king my father's death before him.[41]
White bodies naked on the low damp ground
And bones cast in a little low dry garret,
Rattled by the rat's foot only, year to year.   195
But at my back from time to time I hear
The sound of horns and motors, which shall bring
Sweeney to Mrs. Porter in the spring.[42]
O the moon shone bright on Mrs. Porter
And on her daughter   200
They wash their feet in soda water[43]
Et, O ces voix d'enfants, chantant dans la coupole![44]

Twit twit twit
Jug jug jug jug jug jug
So rudely forc'd.   205
Tereu[45]

Unreal City
Under the brown fog of a winter noon
Mr. Eugenides, the Smyrna[46] merchant
Unshaven, with a pocket full of currants   210

[39]Lac Léman is the French name for Lake Geneva, in Switzerland, where Eliot recovered from a nervous breakdown in 1921. Also a reference to Psalm 137: "By the waters of Babylon, there we sat down, yea, we wept, when we remembered Zion."
[40]A play on lines from the poem "To His Coy Mistress," by Andrew Marvell (1621–78): "But at my back I always hear / Time's winged chariot hurrying near; / And yonder all before us lie / Deserts of vast eternity."
[41]Another reference to Shakespeare's Tempest, Act I, scene ii.
[42]Eliot twists several stories in these lines. The allegorical masque A Parliament of Bees, by the English poet John Day (1574–c.1640), contains these lines: "When of the sudden, listening, you shall hear, / A noise of horns and hunting, which shall bring Actaeon to Diana in the Spring, / Where all shall see her naked skin." In Greek mythology, Actaeon was a hunter who spied on the goddess Artemis while she bathed. She turned him into a stag, and he was torn to shreds by his own hounds.
[43]Eliot's note: "I do not know the origin of the ballad from which these lines are taken. It was reported to me from Sydney, Australia." Mrs. Porter ran a brothel in Cairo, Egypt. She and her daughter were the inspiration for a risqué ragtime song. Kenneth Asher, in T. S. Eliot and Ideology (1995), supplies the following text of the song: "O the moon shone bright on Mrs. Porter / And on the daughter of Mrs. Porter. / They wash their feet in soda water / and so they oughter / To keep them clean."
[44]"And oh those children's voices singing in the dome!" (French). Eliot quotes the last line of the sonnet "Parsifal," by Paul Verlaine (1844–96).
[45]See note 27.
[46]A city in western Turkey that was a major port in the ancient world.

C.i.f. London: documents at sight,[47]
Asked me in demotic French
To luncheon at the Cannon Street Hotel[48]
Followed by a weekend at the Metropole.[49]
At the violet hour, when the eyes and back   215
Turn upward from the desk, when the human engine waits
Like a taxi throbbing waiting,
I Tiresias, though blind, throbbing between two lives,[50]
Old man with wrinkled female breasts, can see
At the violet hour, the evening hour that strives   220
Homeward, and brings the sailor home from sea,[51]
The typist home at teatime, clears her breakfast, lights
Her stove, and lays out food in tins.
Out of the window perilously spread
Her drying combinations touched by the sun's last rays,   225
On the divan are piled (at night her bed)
Stockings, slippers, camisoles, and stays.
I Tiresias, old man with wrinkled dugs
Perceived the scene, and foretold the rest—
I too awaited the expected guest.   230
He, the young man carbuncular, arrives,
A small house agent's clerk, with one bold stare,
One of the low on whom assurance sits
As a silk hat on a Bradford millionaire.[52]
The time is now propitious, as he guesses,   235
The meal is ended, she is bored and tired,
Endeavours to engage her in caresses
Which still are unreproved, if undesired.
Flushed and decided, he assaults at once;

[47]"The currants were quoted at a price 'cost insurance and freight to London'; and the Bill of Lading, etc., were to be handed to the buyer upon payment of sight draft" [Eliot's note].
[48]A hotel, attached to London's Cannon Street station, frequented by business travelers.
[49]A luxury hotel in the resort city of Brighton, England.
[50]In ancient Greek myth, Tiresias was a blind prophet. A popular account of the origin of his blindness and his prophetic talent recounts that he was walking in the woods when he came upon two serpents copulating; he struck them with his staff and was miraculously transformed into a woman for seven years. Later, Zeus and Hera argued over who experienced more sexual pleasure, men or women. Zeus said women, while Hera claimed it was men. To settle the argument, they consulted Tiresias, as he had been both, and Tiresias sided with Zeus. In her anger, Hera struck Tiresias blind. Because Zeus could not undo her punishment, he compensated Tiresias with the gift of prophecy, thus making him a blind "seer." In Sophocles's play *Oedipus Tyrannus*, Tiresias claims that Oedipus's marriage to his mother, Jocasta, is the source of the curse that has turned Thebes into a barren wasteland. Eliot's note: "Tiresias, although a mere spectator and not indeed a 'character,' is yet the most important personage in the poem, uniting all the rest. Just as the one-eyed merchant, seller of currants, melts into the Phoenician sailor, and the latter is not wholly distinct from Ferdinand, Prince of Naples, so all the women are one woman, and the two sexes meet in Tiresias. What Tiresias sees, in fact, is the substance of the poem. The whole passage from Ovid is of great anthropological interest."
[51]Eliot echoes both the Greek poet Sappho (c. 600 BCE) and the *Requiem* of the Scottish writer Robert Louis Stevenson (1850–94): "Home is the sailor, home from sea."
[52]Bradford, England, is an industrial city that experienced a manufacturing boom during World War I.

Exploring hands encounter no defence;   240
His vanity requires no response,
And makes a welcome of indifference.
(And I Tiresias have foresuffered all
Enacted on this same divan or bed;
I who have sat by Thebes below the wall   245
And walked among the lowest of the dead.)
Bestows one final patronising kiss,
And gropes his way, finding the stairs unlit...
She turns and looks a moment in the glass,
Hardly aware of her departed lover;   250
Her brain allows one half-formed thought to pass:
'Well now that's done: and I'm glad it's over.'
When lovely woman stoops to folly[53] and
Paces about her room again, alone,
She smoothes her hair with automatic hand,   255
And puts a record on the gramophone.

'This music crept by me upon the waters'[54]
And along the Strand, up Queen Victoria Street.[55]
O City city, I can sometimes hear
Beside a public bar in Lower Thames Street,   260
The pleasant whining of a mandoline
And a clatter and a chatter from within
Where fishmen lounge at noon: where the walls
Of Magnus Martyr[56] hold
Inexplicable splendour of Ionian white and gold.   265

      The river sweats[57]
      Oil and tar
The barges drift
With the turning tide
Red sails   270
Wide
To leeward, swing on the heavy spar.
The barges wash

[53]A quote from the novel The Vicar of Wakefield, by Oliver Goldsmith (1730–74), in which Olivia sings, "When lovely woman stoops to folly, / And finds too late that men betray, / What charm can sooth her melancholy, / What art can wash her guilt away? / The only art her guilt to cover, / To hide her shame from every eye, / To give repentance to her lover, / And wring his bosom—is to die."
[54]Another reference to Shakespeare's Tempest (Act I, scene ii, lines 391–33).
[55]Two streets in London adjacent to the Thames River.
[56]The church of St. Magnus Martyr, designed by Sir Christopher Wren (1632–1723) and a favorite of Eliot: "The interior of St. Magnus Martyr is to my mind one of the finest among Wren's interiors."
[57]"The Song of the (three) Thames-daughters begins here. From line 292–306 inclusive they speak in turn" [Eliot's note]. Lines 277–278 and 290–291 reflect the lament of the Rhine maidens for the lost splendor of the Rhine River in the opera Die Götterdämmerung [The Twilight of the Gods], by Richard Wagner (1812–83).

Drifting logs
Down Greenwich reach
Past the Isle of Dogs.[58]   275
    Weialala leia
    Wallala leialala

Elizabeth and Leicester[59]
Beating oars   280
The stern was formed
A gilded shell
Red and gold
The brisk swell
Rippled both shores   285
Southwest wind
Carried down stream
The peal of bells
White towers
    Weialala leia   290
    Wallala leialala

'Trams and dusty trees.
Highbury bore me. Richmond and Kew
Undid me.[60] By Richmond I raised my knees
Supine on the floor of a narrow canoe.'   295

'My feet are at Moorgate,[61] and my heart
Under my feet. After the event
He wept. He promised 'a new start.'
I made no comment. What should I resent?'
'On Margate Sands.[62]   300
I can connect
Nothing with nothing.
The broken fingernails of dirty hands.
My people humble people who expect
Nothing.'
    la la   305

[58]The Isle of Dogs is a peninsula in the Thames River opposite the London borough of Greenwich.
[59]A reference to the romance between Queen Elizabeth I (1553–1603) and Lord Robert Dudley, Earl of Leicester (1532–88).
[60]Eliot refers to lines from Dante's *Purgatorio*: "Remember me, who am La Pia. / Siena made me, Maremma undid me." Highbury is a neighborhood in London. Richmond and Kew are boating places along the Thames.
[61]A London slum.
[62]Margate is an English seaside resort.

To Carthage then I come[63]

Burning burning burning burning
O Lord Thou pluckest me out[64]
O Lord Thou pluckest   310

burning

IV. DEATH BY WATER

Phlebas the Phoenician, a fortnight dead,
Forgot the cry of gulls, and the deep sea swell
And the profit and loss.

                          A current under sea   315
Picked his bones in whispers. As he rose and fell
He passed the stages of his age and youth
Entering the whirlpool.

                          Gentile or Jew
O you who turn the wheel and look to windward,   320
Consider Phlebas, who was once handsome and tall as you.

V. WHAT THE THUNDER SAID[65]

After the torchlight red on sweaty faces[66]
After the frosty silence in the gardens
After the agony in stony places
The shouting and crying   325
Prison and palace and reverberation
Of thunder of spring over distant mountains
He who was living is now dead
We who were living are now dying
With a little patience   330

Here is no water but only rock
Rock and no water and the sandy road

---

[63]A quote from *The Confessions of St. Augustine,* in which St. Augustine (354–430) recounts his reckless and immoral youth. "To Carthage then I came, where a cauldron of unholy loves sang all about mine ears."
[64]Another allusion to St. Augustine's *Confessions.*
[65]Eliot's note on this section: "In the first part of Part V three themes are employed: the journey to Emmaus, the approach to the Chapel Perilous (See Miss Weston's book) and the present decay of eastern Europe." Eliot prefaces his notes on *The Waste Land* with a reference to Jessie L. Weston (1850–1928): "Not only the title, but the plan and a good deal of the incidental symbolism of the poem were suggested by Miss Jessie L. Weston's book on the Grail legend: *From Ritual to Romance.* Indeed, so deeply am I indebted, Miss Weston's book will elucidate the difficulties of the poem much better than my notes can do; and I recommend it (apart from the great interest of the book itself) to any who think such elucidation of the poem worth the trouble."
[66]An allusion to the agony of Christ in the garden and his arrest, crucifixion, and burial.

The road winding above among the mountains
Which are mountains of rock without water 335
If there were water we should stop and drink
Amongst the rock one cannot stop or think
Sweat is dry and feet are in the sand
If there were only water amongst the rock
Dead mountain mouth of carious[67] teeth that cannot spit
Here one can neither stand nor lie nor sit 340
There is not even silence in the mountains
But dry sterile thunder without rain
There is not even solitude in the mountains
But red sullen faces sneer and snarl
From doors of mudcracked houses 345

If there were water

    And no rock
    If there were rock
    And also water
    And water 350
    A spring
    A pool among the rock
    If there were the sound of water only
    Not the cicada[68]
    And dry grass singing
    But sound of water over a rock 355
    Where the hermit-thrush sings in the pine trees
    Drip drop drip drop drop drop drop
    But there is no water
Who is the third who walks always beside you?[69] 360
When I count, there are only you and I together
But when I look ahead up the white road
There is always another one walking beside you
Gliding wrapt in a brown mantle, hooded
I do not know whether a man or a woman 365
—But who is that on the other side of you?

---

[67]Decayed.
[68]An insect with large transparent wings, noted for its shrill chirping sound.
[69]"The following lines were stimulated by the account of one of the Antarctic expeditions (I forget which, but I think one of Shackleton's): it was related that the party of explorers, at the extremity of their strength, had the constant delusion that there was *one more member* than could actually be counted" [Eliot's note]. His reference is to the Antarctic explorer Ernest H. Shackleton (1874–1922). He also alludes to Luke 24:13–16, which describes Jesus's walk following his resurrection to the town of Emmaus with two of his disciples, who do not recognize him.

What is that sound high in the air[70]
Murmur of maternal lamentation
Who are those hooded hordes swarming
Over endless plains, stumbling in cracked earth   370
Ringed by the flat horizon only
What is the city over the mountains
Cracks and reforms and bursts in the violet air
Falling towers
Jerusalem Athens Alexandria   375
Vienna London
Unreal

A woman drew her long black hair out tight
And fiddled whisper music on those strings
And bats with baby faces in the violet light   380
Whistled, and beat their wings
And crawled head downward down a blackened wall
And upside down in air were towers
Tolling reminiscent bells, that kept the hours
And voices singing out of empty cisterns and exhausted wells.   385

In this decayed hole among the mountains
In the faint moonlight, the grass is singing
Over the tumbled graves, about the chapel
There is the empty chapel, only the wind's home.
It has no windows, and the door swings,   390
Dry bones can harm no one.
Only a cock stood on the rooftree
Co co rico co co rico
In a flash of lightning. Then a damp gust
Bringing rain   395

Ganga[71] was sunken, and the limp leaves
Waited for rain, while the black clouds
Gathered far distant, over Himavant.[72]
The jungle crouched, humped in silence.
Then spoke the thunder   400

---

[70]A quote from *Glimpse of Chaos* (*Blick ins Chaos*) by Hermann Hesse (1877–1962). In English translation: "Already half of Europe, already at least half of Eastern Europe is on the way to Chaos, drives drunkenly in sacred madness along the edge of the abyss, and moreover, sings, sings drunken hymns as Dmitri Karamasoff sang in [the novel] *The Brothers Karamazov* by Fyodor Dostoevsky [1821–81]. The offended bourgeois laughs at these songs, the saint and seer hear them with tears."
[71]The Ganges River in India.
[72]A sacred mountain in the Tibetan Himalayas.

DA[73]
Datta: what have we given?
My friend, blood shaking my heart
The awful daring of a moment's surrender
Which an age of prudence can never retract   405
By this, and this only, we have existed
Which is not to be found in our obituaries
Or in memories draped by the beneficent spider[74]
Or under seals broken by the lean solicitor
In our empty rooms   410
DA
Dayadhvam: I have heard the key[75]
Turn in the door once and turn once only
We think of the key, each in his prison
Thinking of the key, each confirms a prison   415
Only at nightfall, aethereal rumours
Revive for a moment a broken Coriolanus[76]
DA
Damyata: The boat responded
Gaily, to the hand expert with sail and oar   420
The sea was calm, your heart would have responded
Gaily, when invited, beating obedient
To controlling hands

                I sat upon the shore
Fishing, with the arid plain behind me[77]   425
Shall I at least set my lands in order?[78]
London Bridge is falling down falling down falling down
Poi s'ascose nel foco che gli affina[79]

---

[73]Eliot refers to an ancient Indian myth from the *Brihadaranyaka Upanishad*, in which three groups—lower gods, men, and demons—ask the creator god, Prajapati, for wisdom. Prajapati utters only the syllable "da." The lower gods interpret the syllable as *damyata,* meaning "control yourself." The men believe it to mean *datta,* "to give." And the demons interpret the syllable to mean *dayadhvam,* "to be compassionate." The myth explains that Prajapati repeats the lesson of the three virtues—self-control, generosity, and mercy—with each clap of thunder, "da, da, da."

[74]From John Webster's *The White Devil* (Act V, scene vi): "They'll remarry / Ere the worm pierce your winding sheet, ere the spider / Make a thin curtain for your epitaphs."

[75]"[In the Inferno,] Ugolino recalls his imprisonment with his children, where they starved to death: 'And I heard below the door of the horrible tower being locked up.'" (Canto XXXIII, 46) [Eliot's note].

[76]The tragic Roman general of Shakespeare's play *Coriolanus.* He leads an attack on Rome after he is banished from the city and later is killed by soldiers of the enemy army he had joined.

[77]Eliot refers to the myth of the Fisher King discussed in Weston's book *From Ritual to Romance* (1920). See note 65.

[78]From Isaiah 38:1, "Thus saith the Lord. Set thine house in order, for thou shalt die, and not live."

[79]From Dante's *Purgatorio,* Canto XXVI. "Then he hid himself in the fire that refines them." (Italian). Eliot refers to Dante's encounter with Arnaut Daniel (see note 2). Daniel is punished for lust, and he warns Dante to "be mindful in time of my suffering" before he returns to the fire that will cleanse him of his sins.

Quando fiam uti chelidon[80]—O swallow swallow
Le Prince d'Aquitaine à la tour abolie[81]   430
These fragments I have shored against my ruins
Why then Ile fit you. Hieronymo's mad againe.[82]
Datta. Dayadhvam. Damyata.
                         Shantih   shantih   shantih[83]

                                                                [1922]

Gerontion

> *Thou hast nor youth nor age*
> *But as it were an after dinner sleep*
> *Dreaming of both.*

HERE I am, an old man in a dry month,
Being read to by a boy, waiting for rain.
I was neither at the hot gates
Nor fought in the warm rain
Nor knee deep in the salt marsh, heaving a cutlass,   5
Bitten by flies, fought.
My house is a decayed house,
And the jew squats on the window sill, the owner,
Spawned in some estaminet of Antwerp,
Blistered in Brussels, patched and peeled in London.   10
The Goat coughs at night in the field overhead;
Rocks, moss, stonecrop, iron, merds.
The woman keeps the kitchen, makes tea.
Sneezes at evening, poking the peevish gutter.

                    I an old man,   15
A dull head among windy spaces.

Signs are taken for wonders. "We would see a sign"
The word within a word, unable to speak a word,

[80]"When shall I be as the swallow?" (Latin) From the anonymous poem "Pervigilium Veneris" ("The Vigil of Venus"). The last stanza of the poem includes a reference to Philomela, who longs to be as the swallow so she may have her voice back (see note 27).
[81]"The Prince of Aquitaine in the ruined tower." (French) Eliot cites the source for this line as the sonnet "El Desdichado" ("The Disinherited"), by Gerard de Nerval (1808–55). De Nerval (a pseudonym of Gerard Labrunie) begins his poem, "I move in darkness—widowed—beyond solace, / The Prince of Aquitaine in a ruined tower. / My one star is dead; the black sun of sadness / Eclipses the constellation of my guitar."
[82]A reference to the famous play *The Spanish Tragedy: Hieronymo Is Mad Again* (1594), by Thomas Kyd (1557–97). The play tells the story of Horatio, who falls in love with Bel-Imperia but is murdered by the Prince of Portugal and by Bel-Imperia's brother Lorenzo. Horatio's father, Hieronymo, sets out to avenge his son's death, feigning madness to avoid suspicion. Asked to write a play, he agrees, muttering, "Why then Ile [I will] fit you" with the double meaning of "accommodate" and "get even." He then writes a play in which he kills his son's murderers—who are acting in the play—during the performance.
[83]"The peace that passeth understanding" (Sanskrit). Eliot's note: "Repeated here as a formal ending to an Upanishad"—that is, a sacred Hindu text.

Swaddled with darkness. In the juvescence of the year
Came Christ the tiger   20

In depraved May, dogwood and chestnut, flowering judas,
To be eaten, to be divided, to be drunk
Among whispers; by Mr. Silvero
With caressing hands, at Limoges
Who walked all night in the next room;   25
By Hakagawa, bowing among the Titians;
By Madame de Tornqist, in the dark room
Shifting the candles; Fraulein von Kulp
Who turned in the hall, one hand on the door. Vacant shuttles
Weave the wind. I have no ghosts,   30
An old man in a draughty house
Under a windy knob.

After such knowledge, what forgiveness? Think now
History has many cunning passages, contrived corridors
And issues, deceives with whispering ambitions,   35
Guides us by vanities. Think now
She gives when our attention is distracted
And what she gives, gives with such supple confusions
That the giving famishes the craving. Gives too late
What's not believed in, or if still believed,   40
In memory only, reconsidered passion. Gives too soon
Into weak hands, what's thought can be dispensed with
Till the refusal propagates a fear. Think
Neither fear nor courage saves us. Unnatural vices
Are fathered by our heroism. Virtues   45
Are forced upon us by our impudent crimes.
These tears are shaken from the wrath-bearing tree.

The tiger springs in the new year. Us he devours. Think at last
We have not reached conclusion, when I
Stiffen in a rented house. Think at last   50
I have not made this show purposelessly
And it is not by any concitation
Of the backward devils
I would meet you upon this honestly.
I that was near your heart was removed therefrom   55
To lose beauty in terror, terror in inquisition.
I have lost my passion; why should I need to keep it
Since what is kept must be adulterated?
I have lost my sight, smell, hearing, taste and touch:
How should I used it for your closer contact?   60

These with a thousand small deliberations
Protract the profit of their chilled delirium.
Excite the membrane, when the sense has cooled,
With pungent sauces, multiply variety
In a wilderness of mirrors. What will the spider do,   65
Suspend its operations, will the weevil
Delay? De Bailhache, Fresca, Mrs. Cammel, whirled
Beyond the circuit of the suuddering Bear
In fractured atoms. Gull against the wind, in the windy straits
Of Belle Isle, or running on the Horn,   70
White feathers in the snow, the Gulf claims.
And an old man driven by the Trades
To a a sleepy corner.

              Tenants of the house,
Thoughts of a dry brain in a dry season.   75

The Hollow Men[1]

> *Mistah Kurtz—he dead.*[2]
>
> *A penny for the Old Guy*[3]

I

We are the hollow men
We are the stuffed men
Leaning together
Headpiece filled with straw. Alas!
Our dried voices, when   5
We whisper together
Are quiet and meaningless
As wind in dry grass
Or rats' feet over broken glass
In our dry cellar   10

    Shape without form, shade without colour,
Paralysed force, gesture without motion:

---

[1]The phrase comes from Shakespeare's *Julius Caesar* (1599), Brutus's description of his friend Cassius (4.2.23).
[2]A quotation from *Heart of Darkness* (1902), a novella about colonialism in Africa by Joseph Conrad (1857–1924). Kurtz is a trader and commander who becomes a kind of god among the Africans.
[3]British children use this phrase on Guy Fawkes Day (November 5) to ask for firecrackers. Guy Fawkes (1570–1606) was one of a group of Catholics who planned the failed Gunpowder plot of 1605—the plan was to blow up the House of Lords during the state opening of Parliament on November 5, 1605. Fawkes and others were executed. The Old Guy referred to here is an effigy burned on Guy Fawkes Day.

Those who have crossed[4]
With direct eyes, to death's other Kingdom
Remember us—if at all—not as lost   15
Violent souls, but only
As the hollow men
The stuffed men.

II

Eyes I dare not meet in dreams
In death's dream kingdom
These do not appear:
There, the eyes are
Sunlight on a broken column   5
There, is a tree swinging
And voices are
In the wind's singing
More distant and more solemn
Than a fading star.   10

    Let me be no nearer
In death's dream kingdom
Let me also wear
Such deliberate disguises
Rat's coat, crowskin, crossed staves[5]   15
In a field
Behaving as the wind behaves
No nearer—

    Not that final meeting
In the twilight kingdom   20

III

This is the dead land
This is cactus land
Here the stone images
Are raised, here they receive
The supplication of a dead man's hand   5
Under the twinkle of a fading star.

[4]In Greek myth, the souls of the dead must cross the River Styx, the river that forms the boundary between the earth and the underworld.
[5]Farmers use scarecrows and the hanging bodies of animals to frighten away animals that threaten crops.

Is it like this
In death's other kingdom
Waking alone
At the hour when we are
Trembling with tenderness
Lips that would kiss
Form prayers to broken stone.

IV

The eyes are not here
There are no eyes here
In this valley of dying stars
In this hollow valley
This broken jaw of our lost kingdoms   5

In this last of meeting places
We grope together
And avoid speech
Gathered on this beach of the tumid river

Sightless, unless   10
The eyes reappear
As the perpetual star
Multifoliate rose[6]
Of death's twilight kingdom
The hope only   15
Of empty men.

V

Here we go round the prickly pear[7]
Prickly pear prickly pear
Here we go round the prickly pear
At five o'clock in the morning.

Between the idea   5
And the reality
Between the motion
And the act
Falls the Shadow

                          For Thine is the Kingdom[8]   10

---

[6] A symbol of Paradise, in which the saints are the petals of the rose, in Dante's *Paradiso* (28.30), part of his epic poem *The Divine Comedy* (1308–21).

[7] A cactus that grows in the desert. Eliot is echoing here the popular children's song, "Here we go round the mulberry bush...."

[8] A phrase from the end of the Lord's Prayer, "For thine is the Kingdom, and the power, and the glory, for ever. Amen."

Between the conception
And the creation
Between the emotion
And the response
Falls the Shadow   15
                          Life is very long[9]

Between the desire
And the spasm
Between the potency
And the existence   20
Between the essence
And the descent
Falls the Shadow
            For Thine is the Kingdom

    For Thine is   25
Life is
For Thine is the

    This is the way the world ends[10]
This is the way the world ends
This is the way the world ends
Not with a bang but a whimper.   30

                                                        [1925]

Burnt Norton[1]

τοῦ λόγου δ'ἐόντος ξυνοῦ ζώουσιν οἱ πολλοὶ ὡς ἰδίαν ἔχοντες
φρόνησιν.

                                        1. p. 77. Fr. 2.[2]

ὁδὸς ἄνω κάτω μία καὶ ὡυτή

                                        1. p. 89. Fr. 60.

Diels: Die Fragmente der Vorsokratiker (Herakleitos).[3]

I

Time present and time past[4]
Are both perhaps present in time future,
And time future contained in time past.
If all time is eternally present

---

[9]From *An Outcast of the Islands* (1896), a novel by Joseph Conrad.
[10]Another echo from the "Mulberry Bush" song, "This is the way we clap our hands."
[1]A manor house in Gloucestershire, England, visited by Eliot. Its grounds inspired the poem's central image—the ethereal rose garden. The rose is a symbol of love and passion.
[2]A fragment from the Greek philosopher Heraclitus (c. 540–475 BCE). "Although the Word is common to all, the majority of people live as though they had a private wisdom of their own" (Greek).
[3]ὁδὸς ανω κατω μια και ωυτή: Also from Heraclitus: "The way upward and the way downward are one and the same."
[4]The opening lines allude to Ecclesiastes 3:15 "That which hath been is now; and that which is to be hath already been."

All time is unredeemable.   5
What might have been is an abstraction
Remaining a perpetual possibility
Only in a world of speculation.
What might have been and what has been
Point to one end, which is always present.   10
Footfalls echo in the memory
Down the passage which we did not take
Towards the door we never opened
Into the rose-garden. My words echo
Thus, in your mind.   15
                                    But to what purpose
Disturbing the dust on a bowl of rose-leaves
I do not know.
                                    Other echoes
Inhabit the garden. Shall we follow?   20
Quick, said the bird, find them, find them,
Round the corner. Through the first gate,
Into our first world, shall we follow
The deception of the thrush? Into our first world.
There they were, dignified, invisible,   25
Moving without pressure, over the dead leaves,
In the autumn heat, through the vibrant air,
And the bird called, in response to
The unheard music hidden in the shrubbery,
And the unseen eyebeam crossed, for the roses   30
Had the look of flowers that are looked at.
There they were as our guests, accepted and accepting.
So we moved, and they, in a formal pattern,
Along the empty alley, into the box circle,[5]
To look down into the drained pool.   35
Dry the pool, dry concrete, brown edged,
And the pool was filled with water out of sunlight,
And the lotos rose, quietly, quietly,
The surface glittered out of heart of light,
And they were behind us, reflected in the pool.   40
Then a cloud passed, and the pool was empty.
Go, said the bird, for the leaves were full of children,
Hidden excitedly, containing laughter.
Go, go, go, said the bird: human kind
Cannot bear very much reality.   45
Time past and time future

---

[5]Boxwood shrubs planted in a circle.

What might have been and what has been
Point to one end, which is always present.

II

Garlic and sapphires in the mud
Clot the bedded axle-tree.   50
The trilling wire in the blood
Sings below inveterate scars
And reconciles forgotten wars.
The dance along the artery
The circulation of the lymph   55
Are figured in the drift of stars
Ascend to summer in the tree
We move above the moving tree
In light upon the figured leaf[6]
And hear upon the sodden floor   60
Below, the boarhound and the boar
Pursue their pattern as before
But reconciled among the stars.

At the still point of the turning world. Neither flesh nor fleshless;
Neither from nor towards; at the still point, there the dance is,   65
But neither arrest nor movement. And do not call it fixity,
Where past and future are gathered. Neither movement from nor towards,
Neither ascent nor decline. Except for the point, the still point,
There would be no dance, and there is only the dance.
I can only say, *there* we have been: but I cannot say where.   70
And I cannot say, how long, for that is to place it in time.

The inner freedom from the practical desire,
The release from action and suffering, release from the inner
And the outer compulsion, yet surrounded
By a grace of sense, a white light still and moving,   75
Erhebung[7] without motion, concentration
Without elimination, both a new world
And the old made explicit, understood
In the completion of its partial ecstasy,
The resolution of its partial horror.   80
Yet the enchainment of past and future
Woven in the weakness of the changing body,
Protects mankind from heaven and damnation

---

[6]A reference to section 43 of the poem "In Memoriam" (1850), by Alfred, Lord Tennyson (1809–92):
"So that still garden of the souls / In many a figured leaf enrolls / The total world since life began."
[7]Elevation (German).

Which flesh cannot endure.

Time past and time future   85

Allow but a little consciousness.
To be conscious is not to be in time
But only in time can the moment in the rose-garden,
The moment in the arbour where the rain beat,
The moment in the draughty church at smokefall   90
Be remembered; involved with past and future.
Only through time time is conquered.

III

Here is a place of disaffection
Time before and time after
In a dim light: neither daylight   95
Investing form with lucid stillness
Turning shadow into transient beauty
With slow rotation suggesting permanence
Nor darkness to purify the soul
Emptying the sensual with deprivation   100
Cleansing affection from the temporal.
Neither plenitude nor vacancy. Only a flicker
Over the strained time-ridden faces
Distracted from distraction by distraction
Filled with fancies and empty of meaning   105
Tumid apathy with no concentration
Men and bits of paper, whirled by the cold wind
That blows before and after time,
Wind in and out of unwholesome lungs
Time before and time after.   110
Eructation of unhealthy souls
Into the faded air, the torpid
Driven on the wind that sweeps the gloomy hills of London,
Hampstead and Clerkenwell, Campden and Putney,
Highgate, Primrose and Ludgate.[8] Not here   115
Not here the darkness, in this twittering world.

Descend lower, descend only
Into the world of perpetual solitude,
World not world, but that which is not world,
Internal darkness, deprivation   120
And destitution of all property,
Desiccation of the world of sense,

[8]London neighborhoods.

Evacuation of the world of fancy,
Inoperancy of the world of spirit;
This is the one way, and the other   125
Is the same, not in movement
But abstention from movement; while the world moves
In appetency, on its metalled ways
Of time past and time future.

IV

Time and the bell have buried the day,   130
The black cloud carries the sun away.
Will the sunflower turn to us, will the clematis
Stray down, bend to us; tendril and spray
Clutch and cling?
Chill   135
Fingers of yew be curled
Down on us? After the kingfisher's wing
Has answered light to light, and is silent, the light is still
At the still point of the turning world.

V

Words move, music moves   140
Only in time; but that which is only living
Can only die. Words, after speech, reach
Into the silence. Only by the form, the pattern,
Can words or music reach
The stillness, as a Chinese jar still   145
Moves perpetually in its stillness.
Not the stillness of the violin, while the note lasts,
Not that only, but the co-existence,
Or say that the end precedes the beginning,
And the end and the beginning were always there   150
Before the beginning and after the end.
And all is always now. Words strain,
Crack and sometimes break, under the burden,
Under the tension, slip, slide, perish,
Decay with imprecision, will not stay in place,   155
Will not stay still. Shrieking voices
Scolding, mocking, or merely chattering,
Always assail them. The Word in the desert[9]
Is most attacked by voices of temptation,

[9]An allusion to the temptation of Christ in the wilderness (Mark 1:12; Matthew 4:1–8; Luke 4:1–13).

The crying shadow in the funeral dance,   160
The loud lament of the disconsolate chimera.[10]

    The detail of the pattern is movement,
As in the figure of the ten stairs.[11]
Desire itself is movement
Not in itself desirable;   165
Love is itself unmoving,
Only the cause and end of movement,
Timeless, and undesiring
Except in the aspect of time
Caught in the form of limitation   170
Between un-being and being.
Sudden in a shaft of sunlight
Even while the dust moves
There rises the hidden laughter
Of children in the foliage   175
Quick now, here, now, always—
Ridiculous the waste sad time
Stretching before and after.

                                                          [1936, 1943]

---

[10]A creature from Greek mythology possessing the head of a lion (sometimes several heads), the body of a goat, and the tail of a serpent.
[11]A reference to John of the Cross (1542–91), *The Dark Night of the Soul*, which describes "ten steps on the mystical ladder of divine love," or the soul's ascent to God.

EUGENE O'NEILL ■ (1888–1953)

Born in New York City, the son of the Catholic Irish-born actor James O'Neill, who was acclaimed for his leading role in *The Count of Monte Cristo*, Eugene O'Neill attended both Catholic and nonsectarian schools. He then began undergraduate study at Princeton University in 1906–07 but left at the end of the spring semester. In October 1909 O'Neill married and then immediately took a trip to Honduras in a quest for gold; stricken with malaria, he returned to the United States in April 1910. But soon he turned again to work as a seaman, voyaging to South America and England.

Back in New York City in 1911, O'Neill lived in a room in a saloon and suffered from alcoholism and tuberculosis. Late in 1912 he underwent treatment in a sanatorium in Connecticut; there he read Sophocles, Aeschylus, Euripides, Shakespeare, Henrik Ibsen, George Bernard Shaw, August Strindberg, and other dramatists. He also was an attentive reader of Joseph Conrad, Jack London, and other novelists. The father of a son, divorced from his wife (he married again in 1918, and after another divorce in 1929 he married for the third time), O'Neill composed a number of one-act plays. The best of these was *Bound East for Cardiff*, which explores the life of a sailor and the looming power of the sea.

In the fall of 1914 O'Neill studied playwriting at Harvard, and then the following year he settled in New York City's Greenwich Village. In June 1916 O'Neill became connected to a group of innovative actors, actresses, writers, and artists that gathered in Provincetown on the tip of Cape Cod, Massachusetts. Known as the Provincetown Players, they performed at The Wharf Theatre in Provincetown and later in theaters in Greenwich Village. O'Neill, Edna St. Vincent Millay, Sherwood Anderson, and Susan Glaspell were some of the authors whose plays were presented by the Provincetown Players. A production of *Bound East for Cardiff* in November 1916 marked O'Neill's debut with the Provincetown group.

O'Neill wrote more than fifty plays, and most scholars agree that he is the foremost American playwright. His many important plays include *Beyond the Horizon* (1918), about two brothers on a farm who are in love with the same girl; *The Hairy Ape* (1920), dealing with a brutish stoker (that is, a person tending the furnace on a steamship or steam locomotive) who is destroyed when he attempts to move outside his social class; *Anna Christie* (1921), about a girl from a farm who falls into prostitution, attracts a lover, but then loses him when she tells him about her past; *Desire Under the Elms* (1924), keyed to the sexual attraction between a son and his stepmother; *Strange Interlude* (1928), a nine-act drama covering twenty-five years in the life of a middle-class woman; *Mourning Becomes Electra*, a trilogy of sexuality, guilt, and suicide based on Aeschylus's *Oresteia* and portraying the lives of a New England family at the time of the Civil War (1931); *Ah, Wilderness!* (1933), O'Neill's only comedy; *The*

Iceman Cometh (1939), about the bitter, brooding interactions among derelicts and a salesman in a saloon; *Long Day's Journey into Night* (1940), which treats the four members of the Tyrone family—closely modeled on O'Neill's parents, himself, and his brother—during the year 1912; and *A Moon for the Misbegotten* (1943), based even more specifically on the painful life of O'Neill's alcoholic brother.

Many scholars consider the 1930s and the 1940s to mark O'Neill's major phase as a dramatist, but from 1934 to 1946 not one of his plays was produced on Broadway, which was in large measure the result of the failure of *Days Without End* (1934), perhaps his weakest, most unsatisfying work. His greatest Broadway triumphs did not take place until three years after his death, with major productions of both *The Iceman Cometh* and *Long Day's Journey into Night*.

Produced by the Provincetown Players in New York City in November 1920, *The Emperor Jones*, included here, is another of O'Neill's major plays, an expressionist drama in eight scenes punctuated by the sound of tom-tom drumming. Its action has three settings: Emperor Jones's palace, the edge of the Great Forest, and the Great Forest itself—which, as the drama critic Sylvan Barnet noted, in part suggests "the jungle of the human mind, the world of inarticulate elemental passions that seethe beneath the fragile surface of reason."

The Emperor Jones tells the story of an African American, formerly a Pullman porter, who in two years' time somehow has become the ruler of an island in the West Indies. Corrupt and oppressive, he faces the looming rebellion of his subjects. Desperately, he flees through the jungle to a French gunboat but, tormented by visions and demons, he suffers a terrible, tragic death.

Readers and theatergoers today may object to the frequent use of the n-word and to some aspects of O'Neill's depiction of Jones, as when he describes the main character's features as "typically Negroid" and when Jones speaks in dialect. But Charles W. Chesnutt, Zora Neale Hurston, and other African American writers of the late nineteenth and twentieth centuries employed dialect as well, using it to convey the speech patterns and rhythms of their characters—it was a common literary device. Henry Smithers, the Cockney trader in O'Neill's cast of characters, speaks in dialect as well.

As the critic John Henry Raleigh (1965) has said, "Brutus Jones is physical power and vitality...set off against the physical decadence of Smithers." At the time of its writing and initial performance, *The Emperor Jones* marked an important advance, presenting a black man who was neither a fool nor a clown but, rather, confident, strong-willed, and intelligent. He is brutal, as his first name, Brutus, implies; but Brutus is also the name of one of the heroic, doomed conspirators against Caesar—"the noblest Roman of them all," as Shakespeare refers to him in *Julius Caesar*.

The role of Jones was performed by Charles Gilpin (1878–1930), who thereby became the first black actor to take the lead role in an integrated cast; according to one reviewer of the 1920 production, Gilpin gave "the most thrilling performance" of the season. Another reviewer stated that O'Neill's play is "an extraordinarily striking and dramatic study of panic fear" that "reinforces the impression that for strength and originality he has no rival among the American writers for the stage."

Powerful and disturbing, *The Emperor Jones* is a landmark in the history of American theater. The world-renowned singer, actor, and political activist Paul Robeson (1898–1976) also performed the role of Emperor Jones in a stage revival in 1924, and then again nine years later in the film adaptation. Of the film, the *New York* Times review wrote, "It is a distinguished offering, resolute and firm, with a most compelling portrayal by Paul Robeson of the ambitious Negro Pullman Porter, Brutus Jones." (September 20, 1933) A recent critic, Kevin Hagopian, commenting on O'Neill's text and Robeson's performance, extends the point: "*The Emperor Jones* remains a remarkable refraction of the many lives the race led in the years of the Great Migration northward, and the terrible forced exile of African Americans from the soul of America."

For biography, see Arthur and Barbara Gelb, *O'Neill* (1962; rev. ed., 1973); and Louis Sheaffer, *O'Neill, Son and Playwright* (1968); and *O'Neill, Son and Artist* (1973). For critical studies, see Travis Bogard, *Contour in Time: The Plays of Eugene O'Neill* (1972; rev. ed., 1988); and Doris Alexander, *Eugene O'Neill's Creative Struggle: The Decisive Decade, 1924–1933* (1992). For a range of responses and interpretations, see *Critical Essays on Eugene O'Neill*, ed. James J. Martine (1984); and *Critical Approaches to O'Neill*, ed. John H. Stroupe (1988). Resources include Margaret Loftus Ranald, *The Eugene O'Neill Companion* (1984) and *The Cambridge Companion to Eugene O'Neill*, ed. Michael Manheim (1998). See also Stephen A. Black, *Eugene O'Neill: Beyond Mourning and Tragedy* (1999); *Performing O'Neill: Conversations with Actors and Directors*, ed. Yvonne Shafer; and John Patrick Diggins, *Eugene O'Neill's America: Desire under Democracy* (2007).

The Emperor Jones

CHARACTERS

BRUTUS JONES, *emperor*

HENRY SMITHERS, *a Cockney trader*

AN OLD NATIVE WOMAN

LEM, *a native chief*

SOLDIERS, *adherents of Lem*

THE LITTLE FORMLESS FEARS

JEFF

THE NEGRO CONVICTS
THE PRISON GUARD
THE PLANTERS
THE AUCTIONEER
THE SLAVES
THE CONGO WITCH-DOCTOR
THE CROCODILE GOD

The action of the play takes place on an island in the West Indies as yet not self-determined by white Marines. The form of native government is, for the time being, an empire.

Scene 1

SCENE: *The audience chamber in the palace of the Emperor—a spacious, high-ceilinged room with bare, white-washed walls. The floor is of white tiles. In the rear, to the left of center, a wide archway giving out on a portico with white pillars. The palace is evidently situated on high ground for beyond the portico nothing can be seen but a vista of distant hills, their summits crowned with thick groves of palm trees. In the right wall, center, a smaller arched doorway leading to the living quarters of the palace. The room is bare of furniture with the exception of one huge chair made of uncut wood which stands at center, its back to rear. This is very apparently the Emperor's throne. It is painted a dazzling, eye-smiting scarlet. There is a brilliant orange cushion on the seat and another smaller one is placed on the floor to serve as a footstool. Strips of matting, dyed scarlet, lead from the foot of the throne to the two entrances.*

It is late afternoon but the sunlight still blazes yellowly beyond the portico and there is an oppressive burden of exhausting heat in the air. As the curtain rises, a native Negro woman sneaks in cautiously from the entrance on the right. She is very old, dressed in cheap calico, bare-footed, a red bandana handkerchief covering all but a few stray wisps of white hair. A bundle bound in colored cloth is carried over her shoulder on the end of a stick. She hesitates beside the doorway, peering back as if in extreme dread of being discovered. Then she begins to glide noiselessly, a step at a time, toward the doorway in the rear. At this moment, Smithers appears beneath the portico.

Smithers is a tall, stoop-shouldered man about forty. His bald head, perched on a long neck with an enormous Adam's apple, looks like an egg. The tropics have tanned his naturally pasty face with its small, sharp features to a sickly yellow, and native rum has painted his pointed nose to a startling red. His little, washy-blue eyes are red-rimmed and dart about him like a ferret's. His expression is one of unscrupulous meanness, cowardly and dangerous. He is dressed in a worn riding suit of dirty white drill, puttees, spurs, and wears a white cork helmet. A cartridge belt with an automatic revolver is around his waist. He carries a riding whip in his hand. He sees the woman and stops to watch her suspiciously. Then, making up his mind, he steps quickly on tiptoe into the room. The woman, looking back over her shoulder continually, does not see him until it is too late. When she does Smithers springs forward and grabs her firmly by the shoulder. She struggles to get away, fiercely but silently.

Smithers (*tightening his grasp—roughly*):   Easy! None o' that, me birdie. You can't wriggle out now. I got me 'ooks on yer.

Woman (*seeing the uselessness of struggling, gives way to frantic terror, and sinks to the ground, embracing his knees supplicatingly*) No tell him! No tell him, Mister!

Smithers (*with great curiosity*):   Tell 'im? (*Then scornfully.*) Oh, you mean 'is bloomin' Majesty. What's the gaime, any 'ow? What are you sneakin' away for? Been stealin' a bit, I s'pose. (*He taps her bundle with his riding whip significantly.*)

Woman (*shaking her head vehemently*):   No, me no steal.

Smithers: Bloody liar! But tell me what's up. There's somethin' funny goin' on. I smelled it in the air first thing I got up this mornin'. You blacks are up to some devilment. This palace of 'is is like a bleedin' tomb. Where's all the 'ands?

(*The woman keeps sullenly silent. Smithers raises his whip threateningly.*)

Ow, yer won't, won't yer? I'll show yer what's what.

Woman (*coweringly*):   I tell, Mister. You no hit. They go—all go. (*She makes a sweeping gesture toward the hills in the distance.*)

Smithers: Run away—to the 'ills?

Woman: Yes, Mister. Him Emperor—Great Father. (*She touches her forehead to the floor with a quick mechanical jerk.*) Him sleep after eat. Then they go—all go. Me old woman. Me left only. Now me go too.

Smithers (*his astonishment giving way to an immense, mean satisfaction*):   Ow! So that's the ticket! Well, I know bloody well wot's in the air—when they runs orf to the 'ills. The tom-tom 'll be thumping out there bloomin' soon. (*With extreme vindictiveness.*) And I'm bloody glad of it, for one! Serve 'im right! Puttin' on airs, the stinkin' nigger! 'Is Majesty! Gawd blimey! I only 'opes I'm there when they takes 'im out to shoot 'im. (*Suddenly.*) 'E's still 'ere all right, ain't 'e?

Woman: Yes. Him sleep.

Smithers: 'E's bound to find out soon as 'e wakes up. 'E's cunnin' enough to know when 'is time's come.

(*He goes to the doorway on right and whistles shrilly with his fingers in his mouth. The old woman springs to her feet and runs out of the doorway, rear. Smithers goes after her, reaching for his revolver.*)

Stop or I'll shoot! (*Then stopping—indifferently.*) Pop orf then, if yer like, yer black cow. (*He stands in the doorway, looking after her.*)

(Jones enters from the right. He is a tall, powerfully-built, full-blooded Negro of middle age. His features are typically negroid, yet there is something decidedly distinctive about his face—an underlying strength of will, a hardy, self-reliant confidence in himself that inspires respect. His eyes are alive with a keen, cunning intelligence. In manner he is shrewd, suspicious, evasive. He wears a light blue uniform coat, sprayed with brass buttons, heavy gold chevrons on his shoulders, gold braid on the collar, cuffs, etc. His pants are bright red with a light blue stripe down the side. Patent-leather laced boots with brass spurs, and a belt with a long-barreled, pearl-handled revolver in a holster complete his make up. Yet there is something not altogether ridiculous about his grandeur. He has a way of carrying it off.)

Jones (*not seeing anyone—greatly irritated and blinking sleepily— shouts*):   Who dare whistle dat way in my palace? Who dare wake up de Emperor? I'll git de hide frayled off some o' you niggers sho'!

Smithers (*showing himself—in a manner half-afraid and half-defiant*):   It was me whistled to yer. (*As Jones frowns angrily.*) I got news for yer.

Jones (*putting on his suavest manner, which fails to cover up his contempt for the white man*):   Oh, it's you, Mister Smithers. (*He sits down on his throne with easy dignity.*) What news you got to tell me?

Smithers (*coming close to enjoy his discomfiture*):   Don't yer notice nothin' funny today?

Jones (*coldly*):   Funny? No. I ain't perceived nothin' of de kind!

Smithers: Then yer ain't so foxy as I thought yer was. Where's all your court? (*Sarcastically.*) The Generals and the Cabinet Ministers and all?

Jones (*imperturbably*):   Where dey mostly runs de minute I closes my eyes—drinkin' rum and talkin' big down in de town. (*Sarcastically.*) How come you don't know dat? Ain't you sousin' with 'em most every day?

Smithers (*stung but pretending indifference—with a wink*):   That's part of the day's work. I got ter—ain't I—in my business?

Jones (*contemptuously*):   Yo' business!

Smithers (*imprudently enraged*):   Gawd blimey, you was glad enough for me ter take yer in on it when you landed here first. You didn' 'ave no 'igh and mighty airs in them days!

Jones (*his hand going to his revolver like a flash—menacingly*):   Talk polite, white man! Talk polite, you heah me! I'm boss heah now, is you fergettin'? (*The Cockney seems about to challenge this last statement with the facts but something in the other's eyes holds and cows him.*)

Smithers (*in a cowardly whine*):   No 'arm meant, old top.

Jones (*condescendingly*):   I accepts yo' apology. (*Lets his hand fall from his revolver.*) No use'n you rakin' up ole times. What I was den is one thing. What I is now 's another. You didn't let me in on yo' crooked

work out o' no kind feelin's dat time. I done de dirty work fo' you—
and most o' de brain work, too, fo' dat matter—and I was wu'th money
to you, dat's de reason.

Smithers: Well, blimey, I give yer a start, didn't I—when no one else
would. I wasn't afraid to 'ire yer like the rest was—'count of the story
about your breakin' jail back in the States.

Jones: No, you didn't have no s'cuse to look down on me fo' dat. You
been in jail you'self more'n once.

Smithers (*furiously*):   It's a lie! (*Then trying to pass it off by an attempt at
scorn.*) Garn! Who told yer that fairy tale?

Jones: Dey's some tings I ain't got to be tole. I kin see 'em in folk's eyes.
(*Then after a pause—meditatively.*) Yes, you sho' give me a start. And
it didn't take long from dat time to git dese fool, woods' niggers right
where I wanted dem. (*With pride.*) From stowaway to Emperor in two
years! Dat's goin' some!

Smithers (*with curiosity*):   And I bet you got yer pile o' money 'id safe
some place.

Jones (*with satisfaction*):   I sho' has! And it's in a foreign bank where no
pusson don't ever git it out but me no matter what come. You didn't
s'pose I was holdin' down dis Emperor job for de glory in it, did you?
Sho'! De fuss and glory part of it, dat's only to turn de heads o' de
low-flung, bush niggers dat's here. Dey wants de big circus show for
deir money. I gives it to 'em an' I gits de money. (*With a grin.*) De long
green, dat's me every time! (*Then rebukingly.*) But you ain't got no
kick agin me, Smithers. I'se paid you back all you done for me many
times. Ain't I pertected you and winked at all de crooked tradin' you
been doin' right out in de broad day? Sho' I has—and me makin' laws
to stop it at de same time! (*He chuckles.*)

Smithers (*grinning*):   But, meanin' no 'arm, you been grabbin' right and
left yourself, ain't yer? Look at the taxes you've put on 'em! Blimey!
You've squeezed 'em dry!

Jones (*chuckling*):   No, dey ain't *all* dry yet. I'se still heah, ain't I?

Smithers (*smiling at his secret thought*):   They're dry right now, you'll
find out. (*Changing the subject abruptly.*) And as for me breakin' laws,
you've broke 'em all yerself just as fast as yer made 'em.

Jones: Ain't I de Emperor? De laws don't go for him. (*Judicially.*) You
heah what I tells you, Smithers. Dere's little stealin' like you does, and
dere's big stealin' like I does. For de little stealin' dey gits you in jail
soon or late. For de big stealin' dey makes you Emperor and puts you
in de Hall o' Fame when you croaks. (*Reminiscently.*) If dey's one thing
I learns in ten years on de Pullman ca's listenin' to de white quality
talk, it's dat same fact. And when I gits a chance to use it I winds up
Emperor in two years.

Smithers (*unable to repress the genuine admiration of the small fry for the large*): Yes, yer turned the bleedin' trick, all right. Blimey, I never seen a bloke 'as 'ad the bloomin' luck you 'as.

Jones (*severely*): Luck? What you mean—luck?

Smithers: I suppose you'll say as that swank about the silver bullet ain't luck—and that was what first got the fool blacks on yer side the time of the revolution, wasn't it?

Jones (*with a laugh*): Oh, dat silver bullet! Sho' was luck! But I makes dat luck, you heah? I loads de dice! Yessuh! When dat murderin' nigger ole Lem hired to kill me takes aim ten feet away and his gun misses fire and I shoots him dead, what you heah me say?

Smithers: You said yer'd got a charm so's no lead bullet'd kill yer. You was so strong only a silver bullet could kill yer, you told 'em. Blimey, wasn't that swank for yer—and plain, fat-'eaded luck?

Jones (*proudly*): I got brains and I uses 'em quick. Dat ain't luck.

Smithers: Yer know they wasn't 'ardly liable to get no silver bullets. And it was luck 'e didn't 'it you that time.

Jones (*laughing*): And dere all dem fool, bush niggers was kneelin' down and bumpin' deir heads on de ground like I was a miracle out o' de Bible. Oh Lawd, from dat time on I has dem all eatin' out of my hand. I cracks de whip and dey jumps through.

Smithers (*with a sniff*): Yankee bluff done it.

Jones: Ain't a man's talkin' big what makes him big—long as he makes folks believe it? Sho', I talks large when I ain't got nothin' to back it up, but I ain't talkin' wild just de same. I knows I kin fool 'em—I *knows* it—and dat's backin' enough of' my game. And ain't I got to learn deir lingo and teach some of dem English befo' I kin talk to 'em? Ain't dat wuk? You ain't never learned ary word er it, Smithers, in de ten years you been heah, dough yo' knows it's money in yo' pocket tradin' wid 'em if you does. But you'se too shiftless to take de trouble.

Smithers (*flushing*): Never mind about me. What's this I've 'eard about yer really 'avin' a silver bullet moulded for yourself?

Jones: It's playin' out my bluff. I has de silver bullet moulded and I tells 'em when de time comes I kills myself wid it. I tells 'em dat's 'cause I'm de on'y man in de world big enuff to git me. No use'n deir tryin'. And dey falls down and bumps deir heads. (*He laughs.*) I does dat so's I kin take a walk in peace widout no jealous nigger gunnin' at me from behind de trees.

Smithers (*astonished*): Then you 'ad it made—'onest?

Jones: Sho' did. Heah she be. (*He takes out his revolver, breaks it, and takes the silver bullet out of one chamber.*) Five lead an' dis silver baby at de last. Don't she shine pretty? (*He holds it in his hand, looking at it admiringly, as if strangely fascinated.*)

Smithers: Let me see. (*Reaches out his hand for it.*)

Jones (*harshly*):   Keep yo' hands whar dey b'long, white man. (*He replaces it in the chamber and puts the revolver back on his hip.*)

Smithers (*snarling*):   Gawd blimey! Think I'm a bleedin' thief, you would.

Jones: No, 'tain't dat. I knows you'se scared to steal from me. On'y I ain't 'lowin' nary body to touch dis baby. She's my rabbit's foot.

Smithers (*sneering*):   A bloomin' charm, wot? (*Venomously.*) Well, you'll need all the bloody charms you 'as before long, s' 'elp me!

Jones (*judicially*):   Oh, I'se good for six months yit 'fore dey gits sick o' my game. Den, when I sees trouble comin', I makes my getaway.

Smithers: Ho! You got it all planned, ain't yer?

Jones: I ain't no fool. I knows dis Emperor's time is sho't. Dat why I make hay when de sun shine. Was you thinkin' I'se aimin' to hold down dis job for life? No, suh! What good is gittin' money if you stays back in dis raggedy country? I wants action when I spends. And when I sees dese niggers gittin' up deir nerve to tu'n me out, and I'se got all de money in sight, I resigns on de spot and beats it quick.

Smithers: Where to?

Jones: None o' yo' business.

Smithers: Not back to the bloody States, I'll lay my oath.

Jones (*suspiciously*):   Why don't I? (*Then with an easy laugh.*) You mean 'count of dat story 'bout me breakin' from jail back dere? Dat's all talk.

Smithers (*skeptically*):   Ho, yes!

Jones (*sharply*):   You ain't 'sinuatin' I'se a liar, is you?

Smithers (*hastily*):   No, Gawd strike me! I was only thinkin' o' the bloody lies you told the blacks 'ere about killin' white men in the States.

Jones (*angered*):   How come dey're lies?

Smithers: You'd 'ave been in jail if you 'ad, wouldn't yer then? (*With venom.*) And from what I've 'eard, it ain't 'ealthy for a black to kill a white man in the States. They burns 'em in oil, don't they?

Jones (*with cool deadliness*):   You mean lynchin' 'd scare me? Well, I tells you, Smithers, maybe I does kill one white man back dere. Maybe I does. And maybe I kills another right heah 'fore long if he don't look out.

Smithers (*trying to force a laugh*):   I was on'y spoofin' yer. Can't yer take a joke? And you was just sayin' you'd never been in jail.

Jones (*in the same tone—slightly boastful*):   Maybe I goes to jail dere for gettin' in an argument wid razors ovah a crap game. Maybe I gits twenty years when dat colored man die. Maybe I gits in 'nother argument wid de prison guard was overseer ovah us when we're wukin' de roads. Maybe he hits me wid a whip and I splits his head wid a shovel and runs away and files de chain off my leg and gits away safe. Maybe I does all dat an' maybe I don't. It's a story I tells you so's you knows I'se de kind of man dat if you evah repeats one word of it, I ends yo' stealin' on dis yearth mighty damn quick!

Smithers (*terrified*):   Think I'd peach on yer? Not me! Ain't I always been yer friend?

Jones (*suddenly relaxing*):   Sho' you has—and you better be.

Smithers (*recovering his composure—and with it his malice*):   And just to show yer I'm yer friend, I'll tell yer that bit o' news I was goin' to.

Jones: Go ahead! Shoot de piece. Must be bad news from de happy way you look.

Smithers (*warningly*):   Maybe it's gettin' time for you to resign—with that bloomin' silver bullet, wot? (*He finishes with a mocking grin.*)

Jones (*puzzled*):   What's dat you say? Talk plain.

Smithers: Ain't noticed any of the guards or servants about the place today, I 'aven't.

Jones (*carelessly*):   Dey're all out in de garden sleepin' under de trees. When I sleeps, dey sneaks a sleep, too, and I pretends I never suspicions it. All I got to do is to ring de bell and dey come flyin', makin' a bluff dey was wukin' all de time.

Smithers (*in the same mocking tone*):   Ring the bell now an' you'll bloody well see what I means.

Jones (*startled to alertness, but preserving the same careless tone*):   Sho' I rings. (*He reaches below the throne and pulls out a big, common dinner bell which is painted the same vivid scarlet as the throne. He rings this vigorously—then stops to listen. Then he goes to both doors, rings again, and looks out.*)

Smithers (*watching him with malicious satisfaction, after a pause—mockingly*):   The bloody ship is sinkin' an' the bleedin' rats 'as slung their 'ooks.

Jones (*in a sudden fit of anger flings the bell clattering into a corner*):   Low-flung, woods' niggers! (*Then catching Smithers' eye on him, he controls himself and suddenly bursts into a low chuckling laugh.*) Reckon I overplays my hand dis once! A man can't take de pot on a bob-tailed flush all de time. Was I sayin' I'd sit in six months mo'? Well, I'se changed my mind den. I cashes in and resigns de job of Emperor right dis minute.

Smithers (*with real admiration*):   Blimey, but you're a cool bird, and no mistake.

Jones: No use'n fussin'. When I knows de game's up I kisses it good-bye widout no long waits. Dey've all run off to de hills, ain't dey?

Smithers: Yes—every bleedin' man jack of 'em.

Jones: Den de revolution is at de post. And de Emperor better git his feet smokin' up de trail. (*He starts for the door in rear.*)

Smithers: Goin' out to look for your 'orse? Yer won't find any. They steals the 'orses first thing. Mine was gone when I went for 'im this mornin'. That's wot first give me a suspicion of wot was up.

Jones (*alarmed for a second, scratches his head, then philosophically*):   Well, den I hoofs it. Feet, do yo' duty! (*He pulls out a gold watch and looks at it.*) Three-thuty. Sundown's at six-thuty or dere-abouts. (*Puts his watch back—with cool confidence.*) I got plenty o' time to make it easy.

Smithers: Don't be so bloomin' sure of it. They'll be after you 'ot and 'eavy. Ole Lem is at the bottom o' this business an' 'e 'ates you like 'ell. 'E'd rather do for you than eat 'is dinner, 'e would!

Jones (*scornfully*):   Dat fool no-count nigger! Does you think I'se scared o' him? I stands him on his thick head more'n once befo' dis, and I does it again if he come in my way...(*Fiercely.*) And dis time I leave him a dead nigger fo' sho'!

Smithers: You'll 'ave to cut through the big forest—an' these blacks 'ere can sniff and follow a trail in the dark like 'ounds. You'd 'ave to 'ustle to get through that forest in twelve hours even if you knew all the bloomin' trails like a native.

Jones (*with indignant scorn*):   Look-a-heah, white man! Does you think I'se a natural bo'n fool? Give me credit fo' havin' some sense, fo' Lawd's sake! Don't you s'pose I'se looked ahead and made sho' of de chances? I'se gone out in dat big forest, pretendin' to hunt, so many times dat I knows it high an' low like a book. I could go through on dem trails wid my eyes shut. (*With great contempt.*) Think dese ign'rent bush niggers dat ain't got brains enuff to know deir own names even can catch Brutus Jones? Huh, I s'pects not! Not on yo' life! Why, man, de white men went after me wid bloodhounds where I come from an' I jes' laughs at 'em. It's a shame to fool dese black trash around heah, dey're so easy. You watch me, man! I'll make dem look sick, I will. I'll be 'cross de plain to de edge of de forest by time dark comes. Once in de woods in de night, dey got a swell chance o' findin' dis baby! Dawn tomorrow I'll be out at de oder side and on de coast what dat French gunboat is stayin'. She picks me up, take me to Martinique when she go dar, and dere I is safe wid a mighty big bankroll in my jeans. It's easy as rollin' off a log.

Smithers (*maliciously*):   But s'posin' somethin' 'appens wrong an' they do nab yer?

Jones (*decisively*):   Dey don't—dat's de answer.

Smithers: But, just for argyment's sake—what'd you do?

Jones (*frowning*):   I'se got five lead bullets in dis gun good enuff fo' common bush niggers—and after dat I got de silver bullet left to cheat 'em out o' gittin' me.

Smithers (*jeeringly*):   Ho, I was fergettin' that silver bullet. You'll bump yourself orf in style, won't yer? Blimey!

Jones (*gloomily*):   You kin bet yo' whole roll on one thing, white man. Dis baby plays out his string to de end and when he quits, he quits wid a bang de way he ought. Silver bullet ain't none too good for him when he go, dat's a fac'! (*Then shaking off his nervousness—with a*

confident laugh.) Sho'! What is I talkin' about? Ain't come to dat yit
and I never will—not wid trash niggers like dese yere. (*Boastfully.*)
Silver bullet bring me luck anyway. I kin out-guess, outrun, outfight,
an' outplay de whole lot o' dem all ovah de board any time o' de day er
night! You watch me!

(*From the distant hills comes the faint, steady thump of a tom-tom, low and
vibrating. It starts at a rate exactly corresponding to normal pulse beat—72
to the minute—and continues at a gradually accelerating rate from this
point uninterruptedly to the very end of the play.*)

    *Jones starts at the sound. A strange look of apprehension creeps into
his face for a moment as he listens. Then he asks, with an attempt to regain
his most casual manner.*)

What's dat drum beatin' fo'?

Smithers (*with a mean grin*):   For you. That means the bleedin' ceremony
    'as started. I've 'eard it before and I knows.

Jones: Cer'mony? What cer'mony?

Smithers: The blacks is 'oldin' a bloody meetin', 'avin' a war dance, get-
    tin' their courage worked up b'fore they starts after you.

Jones: Let dem! Dey'll sho' need it!

Smithers: And they're there 'oldin' their 'eathen religious service—
    makin' no end of devil spells and charms to 'elp 'em against your silver
    bullet. (*He guffaws loudly.*) Blimey, but they're balmy as 'ell!

Jones (*a tiny bit awed and shaken in spite of himself*):   Huh! Takes more'n
    dat to scare dis chicken!

Smithers (*scenting the other's feeling—maliciously*):   Ternight when it's
    pitch black in the forest, they'll 'ave their pet devils and ghosts 'oun-
    din' after you. You'll find yer bloody 'air 'll be standin' on end before
    termorrow mornin'. (*Seriously.*) It's a bleedin' queer place, that stinkin'
    forest, even in daylight. Yer don't know what might 'appen in there,
    it's that rotten still. Always sends the cold shivers down my back min-
    ute I gets in it.

Jones (*with a contemptuous sniff*):   I an't no chicken-liver like you is. Trees
    an' me, we'se friends, and dar's a full moon comin' bring me light. And
    let dem po' niggers make all de fool spells dey'se a min' to. Does yo'
    s'pect I'se silly enuff to b'lieve in ghosts an' ha'nts an' all dat ole woman's
    talk? G'long, white man! You ain't talkin' to me. (*With a chuckle.*) Doesn't
    you know dey's got to do wid a man was member in good standin' o' de
    Baptist Church? Sho' I was dat when I was porter on de Pullmans, befo'
    I gits into my little trouble. Let dem try deir heathen tricks. De Baptist
    Church done pertect me and land dem all in hell. (*Then with more confi-
    dent satisfaction.*) And I'se got little silver bullet o' my own, don't forgit.

Smithers: Ho! You 'aven't give much 'eed to your Baptist Church since
    you been down 'ere. I've 'eard myself you 'ad turned yer coat an' was

takin' up with their blarsted witch-doctors, or whatever the 'ell yer calls the swine.

Jones (*vehemently*):   I pretends to! Sho' I pretends! Dat's part o' my game from de fust. If I finds out dem niggers believes dat black is white, den I yells it out louder 'n deir loudest. It don't git me nothin' to do missionary work for de Baptist Church. I'se after de coin, an' I lays my Jesus on de shelf for de time bein'. (*Stops abruptly to look at his watch—alertly.*) But I ain't got de time to waste no more fool talk wid you. I'se gwine away from heah dis secon'. (*He reaches in under the throne and pulls out an expensive Panama hat with a bright multi-colored band and sets it jauntily on his head.*) So long, white man! (*With a grin.*) See you in jail sometime, maybe!

Smithers: Not me, you won't. Well, I wouldn't be in yer bloody boots for no bloomin' money, but 'ere's wishin' yer luck just the same.

Jones (*contemptuously*):   Yo're de frightenedest man evah I see! I tells you I'se safe's 'f I was in New York City. It takes dem niggers from now to dark to git up de nerve to start somethin'. By dat time, I'se got a head start dey never kotch up wid.

Smithers (*maliciously*):   Give my regards to any ghosts yer meets up with.

Jones (*grinning*):   If dat ghost got money, I'll tell him never ha'nt you less'n he wants to lose it.

Smithers (*flattered*):   Garn! (*Then curiously.*) Ain't yer takin' no luggage with yer?

Jones: I travels light when I wants to move fast. And I got tinned grub buried on de edge o' de forest. (*Boastfully.*) Now say dat I don't look ahead an' use my brains! (*With a wide, liberal gesture.*) I will all dat's left in de palace to you—and you better grab all you kin sneak away wid befo' dey gits here.

Smithers (*gratefully*):   Righto—and thanks ter yer. (*As Jones walks toward the door in rear—cautioningly.*) Say! Look 'ere, you ain't goin' out that way, are yer?

Jones: Does you think I'd slink out de back door like a common nigger? I'se Emperor yit, ain't I? And de Emperor Jones leaves de way he comes, and dat black trash don't dare stop him—not yit, leastways. (*He stops for a moment in the doorway, listening to the far-off but insistent beat of the tom-tom.*) Listen to dat roll-call, will you? Must be mighty big drum carry dat far. (*Then with a laugh.*) Well, if dey ain't no whole brass band to see me off, I sho' got de drum part of it. So long, white man. (*He puts his hands in his pockets and with studied carelessness, whistling a tune, he saunters out of the doorway and off to the left.*)

Smithers (*looks after him with a puzzled admiration*):   'E's got 'is bloomin' nerve with 'im, s'elp me! (*Then angrily.*) Ho—the bleedin' nigger—puttin' on 'is bloody airs! I 'opes they nabs 'im an' gives 'im what's what! (*Then putting business before the pleasure of this thought,* looking around him with cupidity.) A bloke ought to find a 'ole lot in this palace that'd go for a bit of cash. Let's take a look, 'Arry, me lad. (*He starts for the doorway on right as*

THE CURTAIN FALLS

SCENE 2

SCENE: *Nightfall. The end of the plain where the Great Forest begins. The foreground is sandy, level ground dotted by a few stones and clumps of stunted bushes covering close against the earth to escape the buffeting of the trade wind. In the rear the forest is a wall of darkness dividing the world. Only when the eye becomes accustomed to the gloom can the outlines of separate trunks of the nearest trees be made out, enormous pillars of deeper blackness. A somber monotone of wind lost in the leaves moans in the air. Yet this sound serves but to intensify the impression of the forest's relentless immobility, to form a background throwing into relief its brooding, implacable silence.*

Jones enters from the left, walking rapidly. He stops as he nears the edge of the forest, looks around him quickly, peering into the dark as if searching for some familiar landmark. Then, apparently, satisfied that he is where he ought to be, he throws himself on the ground, dog-tired.

Well, heah I is. In de nick o' time, too! Little mo' an' it'd be blacker'n de ace of spades heahabouts. (*He pulls a bandana handkerchief from his hip pocket and mops off his perspiring face.*) Sho'! Gimme air! I'se tuckered out sho' nuff. Dat soft Emperor job ain't no trainin' fo' a long hike ovah dat plain in de brilin' sun. (*Then with a chuckle.*) Cheah up, nigger, de worst is yet to come. (*He lifts his head and stares at the forest. His chuckle peters out abruptly. In a tone of awe.*) My goodness, look at dem woods, will you? Dat no-count Smithers said dey'd be black an' he sho' called de turn. (*Turning away from them quickly and looking down at his feet, he snatches at a chance to change the subject—solicitously.*) Feet, you is holdin' up yo' end fine an' I sutinly hopes you ain't blisterin' none. It's time you git a rest. (*He takes off his shoes, his eyes studiously avoiding the forest. He feels of the soles of his feet gingerly.*) You is still in de pink—on'y a little mite feverish. Cool yo'selfs. Remember you done got a long journey yit befo' you. (*He sits in a weary-attitude, listening to the rhythmic beating of the tom-tom. He grumbles in a loud tone to cover up a growing uneasiness.*) Bush niggers! Wonder dey wouldn't get sick o' beatin' dat drum. Sound louder, seem like. I wonder if dey's startin' after me? (*He scrambles to his feet, looking back across the plain.*) Couldn't see dem now, nohow, if dey was hundred feet away. (*Then shaking himself like a wet dog to get rid of these depressing thoughts.*) Sho', dey's miles an' miles behind. What you gittin' fidgety about? (*But he sits down and begins to lace up his shoes in great haste, all the time muttering reassuringly.*) You know what? Yo' belly is empty, dat's what's de matter wid you. Come time to eat! Wid nothin' but wind on yo' stumach, o' course you feels jiggedy. Well, we eats right heah an' now soon's I gits dese pesky shoes laced up! (*He finishes lacing up his shoes.*) Dere! Now le's see. (*Gets on his hands and knees and searches the ground around him with his eyes.*) White stone, white stone, where is you? (*He sees the first white stone and crawls to it—with satisfaction.*) Heah you is! I knowed dis was de right place. Box of grub, come to me. (*He turns over the stone and feels in under it—in a tone of dismay.*) Ain't heah! Gorry, is I in de right place or isn't I? Dere's 'nother stone. Guess dat's it. (*He scrambles to the next stone and turns it over.*) Ain't heah, neither! Grub, what is you? Ain't heah. Gorry, has I got to go hungry into dem woods—all de night? (*While he is talking he scrambles from one stone to another, turning them over in frantic haste. Finally, he jumps to his feet excitedly.*) Is I lost de place? Must have! But how dat happen when I was followin' de trail across de plain in broad daylight? (*Almost plaintively.*) I'se hungry, I is! I gotta git my feed. Whar's my strength gonna come from if I doesn't? Gorry, I gotta find dat grub high an' low somehow! Why it come dark so quick like dat? Can't see nothin'. (*He scratches a match on his trousers and peers about him. The rate of the beat of the far-off tom-tom increases perceptibly as he does so. He mutters in a bewildered voice.*) How come all dese white stones come heah when I only remembers one? (*Suddenly, with a frightened gasp, he flings the match on the ground and stamps on it.*) Nigger, is you gone crazy mad? Is you lightin' matches to show dem whar you is? Fo' Lawd's sake, use yo' haid. Gorry, I'se got to be careful! (*He stares at the plain behind him apprehensively, his hand on his revolver.*) But how come all dese white stones? And whar's dat tin box o' grub I had all wrapped up in oil cloth?

(*While his back is turned, the Little Formless Fears creep out from the deeper blackness of the forest. They are black, shapeless, only their glittering little eyes can be seen. If they have any describable form at all it is that of a grubworm about the size of a creeping child. They move noiselessly, but with deliberate, painful effort, striving to raise themselves on end, failing and sinking prone again. Jones turns about to face the forest. He stares up at the tops of the trees, seeking vainly to discover his whereabouts by their conformation.*)

Can't tell nothin' from dem trees! Gorry, nothin' 'round heah look like I evah seed it befo'. I'se done lost de place sho' 'nuff! (*With mournful foreboding.*) It's mighty queer! It's mighty queer! (*With sudden forced defiance—in an angry tone.*) Woods, is you tryin' to put somethin' ovah on me?

(*From the formless creatures on the ground in front of him comes a tiny gale of low mocking laughter like a rustling of leaves. They squirm upward toward him in twisted attitudes. Jones looks down, leaps backward with a yell of terror, yanking out his revolver as he does so—in a quavering voice.*)

What's dat? Who's dar? What is you? Git away from me befo' I shoots you up! You don't?...

(*He fires. There is a flash, a loud report, then silence broken only by the far-off, quickened throb of the tom-tom. The formless creatures have scurried back into the forest. Jones remains fixed in his position, listening intently. The sound of the shot, the reassuring feel of the revolver in his hand, have somewhat restored his shaken nerve. He addresses himself with renewed confidence.*)

Dey're gone. Dat shot fix 'em. Dey was only little animals—little wild pigs, I reckon. Dey've maybe rooted out yo' grub an' eat it. Sho', you fool nigger, what you think dey is—ha'nts? (*Excitedly.*) Gorry, you give de game away when you fire dat shot. Dem niggers heah dat fo' su'tin! Time you beat it in de woods widout no long waits. (*He starts for the forest—hesitates before the plunge—then urging himself in with manful resolution.*) Git in, nigger! What you skeered at? Ain't nothin' dere but de trees! Git in! (*He plunges boldly into the forest.*)

SCENE 3

SCENE: *Nine o'clock. In the forest. The moon has just risen. Its beams, drifting through the canopy of leaves, make a barely perceptible, suffused, eerie glow. A dense low wall of underbrush and creepers is in the nearer foreground, fencing in a small triangular clearing. Beyond this is the massed blackness of the forest like an encompassing barrier. A path is dimly discerned leading down to the clearing from left, rear, and winding away from it again toward the right. As the scene opens nothing can be distinctly made out. Except for the beating of the tom-tom, which is a trifle louder and quicker than in the previous scene, there is silence, broken every few seconds by a queer, clicking sound. Then gradually the figure of the Negro, Jeff, can be discerned crouching on his haunches at the rear of the triangle. He is middle-aged, thin, brown in color, is dressed in a Pullman porter's uniform, cap, etc. He is throwing a pair of dice on the ground before him, picking them up, shaking them, casting them out with the regular, rigid, mechanical movements of an automaton. The heavy, plodding footsteps of someone approaching along the trail from the left are heard and Jones' voice, pitched in a slightly higher key and strained in a cheering effort to overcome its own tremors.*

De moon's rizen. Does you heah dat, nigger? You gits more light from dis out. No mo' buttin' yo' fool head agin' de trunks an' scratchin' de hide off yo' legs in de bushes. Now you sees whar yo'se gwine. So cheer up! From now on you has a snap. (*He steps just to the rear of the triangular clearing and mops off his face on his sleeve. He has lost his Panama hat. His face is scratched, his brilliant uniform shows several large rents.*) What time's it gittin' to be, I wonder? I dassent light no match to find out. Phoo'. It's wa'm an' dat's a fac'! (*Wearily.*) How long I been makin' tracks in dese woods? Must be hours an' hours. Seems like fo'evah! Yit can't be, when de moon's jes' riz. Dis am a long night fo' yo', yo' Majesty! (*With a mournful chuckle.*) Majesty! Der ain't much majesty 'bout dis baby now. (*With attempted cheerfulness.*) Never min'. It's all part o' de game. Dis night come to an end like everything else. And when you gits dar safe and has dat bankroll in yo' hands you laughs at all dis. (*He starts to whistle but checks himself abruptly.*) What yo' whistlin' for, you po' dope! Want all de worl' to heah you? (*He stops talking to listen.*) Heah dat ole drum! Sho' gits nearer from de sound. Dey're packin' it along wid 'em. Time fo' me to move. (*He takes a step forward, then stops—worriedly.*) What's dat odder queer clickety sound I heah? Dere it is! Sound close! Sound like—sound like—Fo' God sake, sound like some nigger was shootin' crap! (*Frightenedly.*) I better beat it quick when I gits dem notions. (*He walks quickly into the clear space—then stands transfixed as he sees Jeff—in a terrified gasp.*) Who dar? Who dat? Is dat you, Jeff? (*Starting toward the other, forgetful for a moment of his surroundings and really believing it is a living man that he sees—in a tone of happy relief.*) Jeff! I'se sho' mighty glad to see you! Dey tol' me you done died from dat razor cut I gives you. (*Stopping suddenly, bewilderedly.*) But how you come to be heah, nigger? (*He stares fascinatedly at the other who continues his mechanical play with the dice. Jones' eyes begin to roll wildly. He stutters.*) Ain't you gwine—look up—can't you speak to me? Is you—is you—a ha'nt? (*He jerks out his revolver in a frenzy of terrified rage.*) Nigger, I kills you dead once. Has I got to kill you again? You take it den. (*He fires. When the smoke clears away Jeff has disappeared. Jones stands trembling—then with a certain reassurance.*) He's gone, anyway. Ha'nt or no ha'nt, dat shot fix him. (*The beat of the far-off tom-tom is perceptibly louder and more rapid. Jones becomes conscious of it—with a start, looking back over his shoulder.*) Dey's gittin' near! Dey's comin' fast! And heah I is shootin' shots to let 'em know jes' whar I is. Oh, Gorry, I'se got to run. (*Forgetting the path he plunges wildly into the underbrush in the rear and disappears in the shadow.*)

SCENE 4

SCENE: *Eleven o'clock. In the forest. A wide dirt road runs diagonally from right, front, to left, rear. Rising sheer on both sides the forest walls it in. The moon is now up. Under its light the road glimmers ghastly and unreal. It is as if the forest had stood aside momentarily to let the road pass through and accomplish its veiled purpose. This done, the forest will fold in upon itself again and the road will be no more. Jones stumbles in from the forest on the right. His uniform is ragged and torn. He looks about him with numbed surprise when he sees the road, his eyes blinking in the bright moonlight. He flops down exhaustedly and pants heavily for a while. Then with sudden anger.*

I'm meltin' wid heat! Runnin' an' runnin' an' runnin'! Damn dis heah coat! Like a strait-jacket! (*He tears off his coat and flings it away from him, revealing himself stripped to the waist.*) Dere! Dat's better! Now I kin breathe! (*Looking down at his feet, the spurs catch his eye.*) And to hell wid dese high-fangled spurs. Dey're what's been a-trippin' me up an' breakin' my neck. (*He unstraps them and flings them away disgustedly.*) Dere! I gits rid o' dem frippety Emperor trappin's an' I travels lighter. Lawd! I'se tired! (*After a pause, listening to the insistent beat of the tom-tom in the distance.*) I must 'a put some distance between myself an' dem—runnin' like dat—and yit—dat damn drum sound jes' de same—nearer, even. Well, I guess I a'most holds my lead anyhow. Dey won't never catch up. (*With a sigh.*) If on'y my fool legs stands up. Oh, I'se sorry I evah went in for dis. Dat Emperor job is sho' hard to shake. (*He looks around him suspiciously.*) How'd dis road evah git heah? Good level road, too. I never remembers seein' it befo'. (*Shaking his head apprehensively.*) Dese woods is sho' full o' de queerest things at night. (*With a sudden terror.*) Lawd God, don't let me see no more o' dem ha'nts! Dey gits my goat! (*Then trying to talk himself into confidence.*) Ha'nts! You fool nigger, dey ain't no such things! Don't de Baptist parson tell you dat many time? Is you civilized, or is you like dese ign'rent black niggers heah? Sho'! Dat was all in yo' own head. Wasn't nothin' dere. Wasn't no Jeff! Know what? You jus' get seein' dem things 'cause yo' belly's empty and you's sick wid hunger inside. Hunger 'fects yo' head and yo' eyes. Any fool know dat. (*Then pleading fervently.*) But bless God, I don't come across no more o' dem, whatever dey is! (*Then cautiously.*) Rest! Don't talk! Rest! You needs it. Den you gits on yo' way again. (*Looking at the moon.*) Night's half gone a'most. You hits de coast in de mawning! Den you'se all safe.

(*From the right forward a small gang of Negroes enter. They are dressed in striped convict suits, their heads are shaven, one leg drags limpingly, shackled to a heavy ball and chain. Some carry picks, the others shovels. They are followed by a white man dressed in the uniform of a prison guard. A Winchester rifle is slung across his shoulders and he carries a heavy whip. At a signal from the Guard they stop on the road opposite where Jones*) is sitting. Jones, who has been staring up at the sky, unmindful of their noiseless approach, suddenly looks down and sees them. His eyes pop out, he tries to get to his feet and fly, but sinks back, too numbed by fright to move. His voice catches in a choking prayer.)

Lawd Jesus!

(The Prison Guard cracks his whip—noiselessly—and at that signal all the convicts start to work on the road. They swing their picks, they shovel, but not a sound comes from their labor. Their movements, like those of Jeff in the preceding scene, are those of automatons,—rigid, slow, and mechanical. The Prison Guard points sternly at Jones with his whip, motions him to take his place among the other shovelers. Jones gets to his feet in a hypnotized stupor. He mumbles subserviently.)

Yes, suh! Yes, suh! I'se comin'.

(As he shuffles, dragging one foot, over to his place, he curses under his breath with rage and hatred.)

God damn yo' soul, I gits even wid you yit, sometime.

(As if there were a shovel in his hands he goes through weary, mechanical gestures of digging up dirt, and throwing it to the roadside. Suddenly the Guard approaches him angrily, threateningly. He raises his whip and lashes Jones viciously across the shoulders with it. Jones winces with pain and cowers abjectly. The Guard turns his back on him and walks away contemptuously. Instantly Jones straightens up. With arms upraised as if his shovel were a club in his hands he springs murderously at the unsuspecting Guard. In the act of crashing down his shovel on the white man's skull, Jones suddenly becomes aware that his hands are empty. He cries despairingly.)

Whar's my shovel? Gimme my shovel till I splits his damn head! (Appealing to his fellow convicts.) Gimme a shovel, one o' you, fo' God's sake!

(They stand fixed in motionless attitudes, their eyes on the ground. The Guard seems to wait expectantly, his back turned to the attacker. Jones bellows with baffled, terrified rage, tugging frantically at his revolver.)

I kills you, you white debil, if it's de last thing I evah does! Ghost or debil, I kill you again!

(He frees the revolver and fires point blank at the Guard's back. Instantly the walls of the forest close in from both sides, the road and the figures of the convict gang are blotted out in an enshrouding darkness. The only sounds are a crashing in the underbrush as Jones leaps away in mad flight and the throbbing of the tom-tom, still far distant, but increased in volume of sound and rapidity of beat.)

SCENE 5

SCENE: *One o'clock. A large circular clearing, enclosed by the serried ranks of gigantic trunks of tall trees whose tops are lost to view. In the center is a big dead stump worn by time into a curious resemblance to an auction block. The moon floods the clearing with a clear light. Jones forces his way in through the forest on the left. He looks wildly about the clearing with hunted, fearful glances. His pants are in tatters, his shoes cut and misshapen, flapping about his feet. He slinks cautiously to the stump in the center and sits down in a tense position, ready for instant flight. Then he holds his head in his hands and rocks back and forth, moaning to himself miserably.*

Oh Lawd, Lawd! Oh Lawd, Lawd! (*Suddenly he throws himself on his knees and raises his clasped hands to the sky—in a voice of agonized pleading.*) Lawd Jesus, heah my prayer! I'se a po' sinner, a po' sinner! I knows I done wrong, I knows it! When I cotches Jeff cheatin' wid loaded dice my anger overcomes me and I kills him dead! Lawd, I done wrong! When dat guard hits me wid de whip, my anger overcomes me, and I kills him dead. Lawd, I done wrong! And down heah whar dese fool bush niggers raises me up to the seat o' de mighty, I steals all I could grab. Lawd, I done wrong! I knows it! I'se sorry! Forgive me, Lawd! Forgive dis po' sinner! (*Then beseeching terrifiedly.*) And keep dem away, Lawd! Keep dem away from me! And stop dat drum soundin' in my ears! Dat begin to sound ha'nted, too. (*He gets to his feet, evidently slightly reassured by his prayer—with attempted confidence.*) De Lawd'll preserve me from dem ha'nts after dis. (*Sits down on the stump again.*) I ain't skeered o' real men. Let dem come. But dem odders ... (*He shudders—then looks down at his feet, working his toes inside the shoes—with a groan.*) Oh, my po' feet! Dem shoes ain't no use no more 'ceptin' to hurt. I'se better off widout dem. (*He unlaces them and pulls them off—holds the wrecks of the shoes in his hands and regards them mournfully.*) You was real, A-one patin' leather, too. Look at you now. Emperor, you'se gittin' mighty low!

(*He sits dejectedly and remains with bowed shoulders, staring down at the shoes in his hands as if reluctant to throw them away. While his attention is thus occupied, a crowd of figures silently enter the clearing from all sides. All are dressed in Southern costumes of the period of the fifties of the last century. There are middle-aged men who are evidently well-to-do planters. There is one spruce, authoritative individual—the Auctioneer. There is a crowd of curious spectators, chiefly young belles and dandies who have come to the slave-market for diversion. All exchange courtly greetings in dumb show and chat silently together. There is something stiff, rigid, unreal, marionettish about their movements. They group themselves about the stump. Finally a batch of slaves are led in from the left by an attendant—three men*

*of different ages, two women, one with a baby in her arms, nursing. They
are placed to the left of the stump, beside Jones.*

*The white planters look them over appraisingly as if they were cattle, and
exchange judgments on each. The dandies point with their fingers and make
witty remarks. The belles titter bewitchingly. All this in silence save for the
ominous throb of the tom-tom. The Auctioneer holds up his hand, taking his
place at the stump. The group strain forward attentively. He touches Jones
on the shoulder peremptorily, motioning for him to stand on the stump—
the auction block.*

*Jones looks up, sees the figures on all sides, looks wildly for some opening
to escape, sees none, screams and leaps madly to the top of the stump to
get as far away from them as possible. He stands there, cowering, paralyzed
with horror. The Auctioneer begins his silent spiel. He points to Jones, appeals to the planters to see for themselves. Here is a good field hand, sound
in wind and limb as they can see. Very strong still in spite of his being middle-aged. Look at that back. Look at those shoulders. Look at the muscles
in his arms and his sturdy legs. Capable of any amount of hard labor. Moreover, of a good disposition, intelligent and tractable. Will any gentleman
start the bidding? The Planters raise their fingers, make their bids. They are
apparently all eager to possess Jones. The bidding is lively, the crowd interested. While this has been going on, Jones has been seized by the courage
of desperation. He dares to look down and around him. Over his face abject
terror gives way to mystification, to gradual realization—stutteringly.)*

> What you all doin', white folks? What's all dis? What you all lookin' at
> me fo'? What you doin' wid me, anyhow? (*Suddenly convulsed with rag-
> ing hatred and fear.*) Is dis a auction? Is you sellin' me like dey uster
> befo' de war? (*Jerking out his revolver just as the Auctioneer knocks
> him down to one of the planters—glaring from him to the purchaser.*)
> And *you* sells me? And *you* buys me? I shows you I'se a free nigger,
> damn yo' souls!

*(He fires at the Auctioneer and at the Planter with such rapidity that the two
shots are almost simultaneous. As if this were a signal the walls of the forest
fold in. Only blackness remains and silence broken by Jones as he rushes off,
crying with fear—and by the quickened, ever louder beat of the tom-tom.)*

Scene 6

*scene: Three o'clock. A cleared space in the forest. The limbs of the trees meet
over it forming a low ceiling about five feet from the ground. The interlocked
ropes of creepers reaching upward to entwine the tree trunks give an arched
appearance to the sides. The space thus enclosed is like the dark, noisome
hold of some ancient vessel. The moonlight is almost completely shut out*

and only a vague, wan light filters through. There is the noise of someone approaching from the left, stumbling and crawling through the undergrowth. Jones' voice is heard between chattering moans.

Oh, Lawd, what I gwine do now? Ain't got no bullet left on'y de silver one. If mo' o' dem ha'nts come after me, how I gwine skeer dem away? Oh, Lawd, on'y de silver one left—an' I gotta save dat fo' luck. If I shoots dat one I'm a goner sho'! Lawd, it's black heah! What's de moon? Oh, Lawd, don't dis night evah come to an end? (*By the sounds, he is feeling his way cautiously forward.*) Dere! Dis feels like a clear space. I gotta lie down an' rest. I don't care if dem niggers does cotch me. I gotta rest.

(*He is well forward now where his figure can be dimly made out. His pants have been so torn away that what is left of them is no better than a breech cloth. He flings himself full length, face downward on the ground, panting with exhaustion. Gradually it seems to grow lighter in the enclosed space and two rows of seated figures can be seen behind Jones. They are sitting in crumpled, despairing attitudes, hunched, facing one another with their backs touching the forest walls as if they were shackled to them. All are Negroes, naked save for loin cloths. At first they are silent and motionless. Then they begin to sway slowly forward toward each other and back again in unison, as if they were laxly letting themselves follow the long roll of a ship at sea. At the same time, a low, melancholy murmur rises among them, increasing gradually by rhythmic degrees which seem to be directed and controlled by the throb of the tom-tom in the distance, to a long, tremulous wail of despair that reaches a certain pitch, unbearably acute, then falls by slow gradations of tone into silence and is taken up again. Jones starts, looks up, sees the figures, and throws himself down again to shut out the sight. A shudder of terror shakes his whole body as the wail rises up about him again. But the next time, his voice, as if under some uncanny compulsion, starts with the others. As their chorus lifts he rises to a sitting posture similar to the others, swaying back and forth. His voice reaches the highest pitch of sorrow, of desolation. The light fades out, the other voices cease, and only darkness is left. Jones can be heard scrambling to his feet and running off, his voice sinking down the scale and receding as he moves farther and farther away in the forest. The tom-tom beats louder, quicker, with a more insistent, triumphant pulsation.*)

Scene 7

SCENE: *Five o'clock. The foot of a gigantic tree by the edge of a great river. A rough structure of boulders, like an altar, is by the tree. The raised river bank is in the nearer background. Beyond this the surface of the river spreads out, brilliant and unruffled in the moonlight, blotted out and merged into a veil of bluish mist in the distance. Jones' voice is heard from the left rising and falling in the long, despairing wail of the chained slaves, to the rhythmic beat of the tom-tom. As his voice sinks into silence, he enters the open space. The expression of his face is fixed and stony, his eyes have an obsessed glare, he moves with a strange deliberation like a sleepwalker or one in a trance. He looks around at the tree, the rough stone altar, the moonlit surface of the river beyond, and passes his hand over his head with a vague gesture of puzzled bewilderment. Then, as if in obedience to some obscure impulse, he sinks into a kneeling, devotional posture before the altar. Then he seems to come to himself partly, to have an uncertain realization of what he is doing, for he straightens up and stares about him horrifiedly—in an incoherent mumble.*

> What—what is I doin'? What is—dis place? Seems like—seems like I know dat tree—an' dem stones—an' de river. I remember—seems like I been heah befo'. (*Tremblingly.*) Oh, Gorry, I'se skeered in dis place! I'se skeered! Oh, Lawd, pertect dis sinner!

(Crawling away from the altar, he cowers close to the ground, his face hidden, his shoulders heaving with sobs of hysterical fright. From behind the trunk of the tree, as if he had sprung out of it, the figure of the Congo Witch-doctor appears. He is wizened and old, naked except for the fur of some small animal tied about his waist, its bushy tail hanging down in front. His body is stained all over a bright red. Antelope horns are on each side of his head, branching upward. In one hand he carries a bone rattle, in the other a charm stick with a bunch of white cockatoo feathers tied to the end. A great number of glass beads and bone ornaments are about his neck, ears, wrists, and ankles. He struts noiselessly with a queer prancing step to a position in the clear ground between Jones and the altar. Then with a preliminary, summoning stamp of his foot on the earth, he begins to dance and to chant. As if in response to his summons the beating of the tom-tom grows to a fierce, exultant boom whose throbs seem to fill the air with vibrating rhythm. Jones looks up, starts to spring to his feet, reaches a half-kneeling, half-squatting position and remains rigidly fixed there, paralyzed with awed fascination by this new apparition. The Witch-doctor sways, stamping with his foot, his bone rattle clicking the time. His voice rises and falls in a weird, monotonous croon, without articulate word divisions. Gradually his dance becomes clearly one of a narrative in pantomime, his croon is an incantation, a charm to allay the fierceness of some implacable deity demanding sacrifice. He flees, he is pursued by devils, he hides, he flees again. Ever wilder and wilder becomes his flight, nearer and nearer draws the pursuing evil, more and more the spirit of terror gains possession of him. His croon, rising to intensity, is punctuated by shrill cries. Jones has become completely hypnotized. His voice joins in the incantation, in the cries, he beats time with his hands and sways his body to and fro from the waist. The whole spirit and meaning of the dance has entered into him, has become his

spirit. Finally the theme of the pantomime halts on a howl of despair, and is taken up again in a note of savage hope. There is a salvation. The forces of evil demand sacrifice. They must be appeased. The Witch-doctor points with his wand to the sacred tree, to the river beyond, to the altar, and finally to Jones with a ferocious command. Jones seems to sense the meaning of this. It is he who must offer himself for sacrifice. He beats his forehead abjectly to the ground, moaning hysterically.)

Mercy, Oh Lawd! Mercy! Mercy on dis po' sinner.

(The Witch-doctor springs to the river bank. He stretches out his arms and calls to some god within its depths. Then he starts backward slowly, his arms remaining out. A huge head of a crocodile appears over the bank and its eyes, glittering greenly, fasten upon Jones. He stares into them fascinatedly. The Witch-doctor prances up to him, touches him with his wand, motions with hideous command toward the waiting monster. Jones squirms on his belly nearer and nearer, moaning continually.)

Mercy, Lawd! Mercy!

(The crocodile heaves more of his enormous bulk onto the land. Jones squirms toward him. The Witch-doctor voice shrills out in furious exulation, the tom-tom beats madly. Jones cries out in a fierce, exhausted spasm of anguished pleading.)

Lawd, save me! Lawd Jesus, heah my prayer!

(Immediately, in answer to his prayer, comes the thought of the one bullet left him. He snatches at his hip, shouting defiantly.)

De silver bullet! You don't git me yit!

(He fires at the green eyes in front of him. The head of the crocodile sinks back behind the river bank, the Witch-doctor springs behind the sacred tree and disappears. Jones lies with his face to the ground, his arms outstretched, whimpering with fear as the throb of the tom-tom fills the silence about him with a somber pulsation, a baffled but revengeful power.)

Scene 8

SCENE: *Dawn. Same as Scene 2, the dividing line of forest and plain. The nearest tree trunks are dimly revealed but the forest behind them is still a mass of glooming shadows. The tom-tom seems on the very spot, so loud and continuously vibrating are its beats. Lem enters from the left, followed by a small squad of his soldiers, and by the Cockney trader, Smithers. Lem is a heavy-set, ape-faced old savage of the extreme African type, dressed only in a loin cloth. A revolver and cartridge belt are about his waist. His soldiers are in different degrees of rag-concealed nakedness. All wear broad palm-leaf hats. Each one carries a rifle. Smithers is the same as in Scene 1. One of the soldiers, evidently a tracker, is peering about keenly on the ground. He grunts and points to the spot where Jones entered the forest. Lem and Smithers come to look.*

Smithers (*after a glance, turns away in disgust*):   That's where 'e went in right enough. Much good it'll do yer. 'E's miles orf by this an' safe to the Coast, damn 'is 'ide! I tole yer yer'd lose 'im, didn't I?—wastin' the 'ole bloomin' night beatin' yer bloody drum and castin' yer silly spells! Gawd blimey, wot a pack!

Lem (*gutturally*):   We cotch him. You see. (*He makes a motion to his soldiers who squat down on their haunches in a semi-circle.*)

Smithers (*exasperatedly*):   Well, ain't yer goin' in an' 'unt 'im in the woods? What the 'ell's the good of waitin'?

Lem (*imperturbably—squatting down himself*):   We cotch him.

Smithers (*turning away from him contemptuously*):   Aw! Garn! 'E's a better man than the lot o' you put together. I 'ates the sight o' 'im but I'll say that for 'im.

(*A sound of snapping twigs comes from the forest. The soldiers jump to their feet, cocking their rifles alertly. Lem remains sitting with an imperturbable expression, but listening intently. The sound from the woods is repeated. Lem makes a quick signal with his hand. His followers creep quickly but noiselessly into the forest, scattering so that each enters at a different spot.*)

Smithers (*in the silence that follows—in a contemptuous whisper*):   You ain't thinkin' that would be 'im, I 'ope?

Lem (*calmly*):   We cotch him.

Smithers: Blarsted fat 'eads! (*Then after a second's thought—wonderingly.*) Still an' all, it might 'appen. If 'e lost 'is bloody way in these stinkin' woods 'e'd likely turn in a circle without 'is knowin' it. They all does.

Lem (*peremptorily*):   Sssh!

(*The reports of several rifles sound from the forest, followed a second later by savage, exultant yells. The beating of the tom-tom abruptly ceases. Lem looks up at the white man with a grin of satisfaction.*)

We cotch him. Him dead.

Smithers (*with a snarl*):   'Ow d'yer know it's 'im an' 'ow d'yer know 'e's dead?

Lem. My mens dey got 'um silver bullets. Dey kill him shore.

Smithers (*astonished*):   They got silver bullets?

Lem. Lead bullet no kill him. He got um strong charm. I cook um money, make um silver bullet, make um strong charm, too.

Smithers (*light breaking upon him*):   So that's wot you was up to all night, wot? You was scared to put after 'im till you'd moulded silver bullets, eh?

Lem (*simply stating a fact*):   Yes. Him got strong charm. Lead no good.

Smithers (*slapping his thigh and guffawing*):   Haw-haw! If yer don't beat all 'ell! (*Then recovering himself—scornfully.*) I'll bet yer it ain't 'im they shot at all, yer bleedin' looney!

Lem (*calmly*):   Dey come bring him now.

(*The soldiers come out of the forest, carrying Jones' limp body. There is a little reddish-purple hole under his left breast. He is dead. They carry him to Lem, who examines his body with great satisfaction. Smithers over his shoulder—in a tone of frightened awe.*)

Well, they did for yer right enough, Jonsey, me lad! Dead as a 'erring! (*Mockingly.*) Where's yer 'igh an' mighty airs now, yer bloomin' Majesty? (*Then with a grin.*) Silver bullets! Gawd blimey, but yer died in the 'eighth o' style, any'ow!

(*Lem makes a motion to the soldiers to carry the body out left. Smithers speaks to him sneeringly.*)

Smithers: And I s'pose you think it's yer bleedin' charms and yer silly beatin' the drum that made 'im run in a circle when 'e'd lost 'imself, don't yer?

(*But Lem makes no reply, does not seem to hear the question, walks out left after his men. Smithers looks after him with contemptuous scorn.*)

Stupid as 'ogs, the lot of 'em! Blarsted niggers!

Curtain Falls

[1920]

CLAUDE MCKAY ▪ (1889–1948)

Born in central Jamaica, the son of a prosperous farmer, Claude McKay wrote his first poems in dialect, inspired by Walter Jekyll (1849–1929), an expatriate and folklorist from Great Britain. These were gathered in two books, *Songs of Jamaica*, which celebrates the Jamaican peasantry, and *Constab Ballads*, both published in 1912. In the same year McKay emigrated to the United States. He attended Tuskegee Institute in Alabama and then Kansas State College but, hoping to pursue a career as a writer, he moved to New York City, where he became connected to a group of left-wing intellectuals and writers, including the critic and novelist Waldo Frank, and Max Eastman, editor of *The Liberator*, a radical magazine. McKay traveled widely, making a trip to the Soviet Union in 1922–23 and settling for several years in France in the mid-1920s.

McKay's book of poems *Harlem Shadows* was published in 1922, and it placed him among the pioneering members of the Harlem Renaissance, an important movement in African American literature and the arts during the 1920s. Much of his most powerful verse is highly political, its radical content expressed within traditional forms, such as the sonnet. Two of his most memorable works, included here, are "If We Must Die"—which Winston Churchill later quoted to exhort the British during the Battle of Britain in World War II—and "America," which in its vision of "treasures sinking in the sand" echoes Shelley's "Ozymandias" (1818), with its "colossal Wreck" from which "the lone and level sands stretch far away." Both of these poems voice anger and bitterness at oppression yet declare a determination to resist, to fight back. In other poems, McKay eloquently recalls the life and landscape of Jamaica and his ambivalent feelings about New York City.

McKay's other writings include three novels: *Home to Harlem* (1928), *Banjo* (1929), and (the best of the group) *Banana Bottom* (1933). He is also the author of a collection of short stories, *Gingertown* (1932); an autobiography, *A Long Way from Home* (1937); and a book of essays, *Harlem: Negro Metropolis* (1940).

For biography, see Wayne F. Cooper, *Claude McKay: Rebel Sojourner in the Harlem Renaissance* (1987). Critical studies include Tyrone Tillery, *Claude McKay: A Black Poet's Struggle for Identity* (1992); and Winston James, *A Fierce Hatred of Injustice: Claude McKay's Jamaica and His Poetry of Rebellion* (2000). See also Heather Hathaway, *Caribbean Waves: Relocating Claude McKay and Paule Marshall* (1999); and Gary Edward Holcomb, *Claude McKay, Code Name Sasha: Queer Black Marxism and the Harlem Renaissance* (2007).

If We Must Die

If we must die, let it not be like hogs
Hunted and penned in an inglorious spot,
While round us bark the mad and hungry dogs,
Making their mock at our accursèd lot.
If we must die, O let us nobly die,   5
So that our precious blood may not be shed
In vain; then even the monsters we defy
Shall be constrained to honor us though dead!
O kinsmen! we must meet the common foe!
Though far outnumbered let us show us brave,   10
And for their thousand blows deal one deathblow!
What though before us lies the open grave?
Like men we'll face the murderous, cowardly pack,
Pressed to the wall, dying, but fighting back!

[1919]

America

Although she feeds me bread of bitterness,
And sinks into my throat her tiger's tooth,
Stealing my breath of life, I will confess
I love this cultured hell that tests my youth!
Her vigor flows like tides into my blood,   5
Giving me strength erect against her hate.
Her bigness sweeps my being like a flood.
Yet as a rebel fronts a king in state,
I stand within her walls with not a shred
Of terror, malice, not a word of jeer.   10
Darkly I gaze into the days ahead,
And see her might and granite wonders there,
Beneath the touch of Time's unerring hand,
Like priceless treasures sinking in the sand.

[1921]

KATHERINE ANNE PORTER ■ (1890–1980)

Her maternal grandmother raised Katherine Anne Porter, born in Indian Creek, Texas, after her mother's death, when Porter was only two. She left school at age fourteen and married two years later, converting to her husband's religion of Roman Catholicism. Separating from her husband not long after, she traveled and worked as a journalist in Mexico, becoming involved there in revolutionary politics. She began writing stories, though she did not publish her first collection, *Flowering Judas and Other Stories*, until 1930, when she was forty. This book gathered stories written during the 1920s, a number of which Porter placed in a Mexican setting, including "Flowering Judas."

During the 1930s, Porter lived mostly in Europe; when she returned to the United States, she published *Pale Horse, Pale Rider: Three Short Novels* (1939), which includes the title story, "Old Mortality," and "Noon Wine," and which recounts the experiences of a woman named Miranda, who has affinities with Porter herself. *The Leaning Tower and Other Stories* (1944) followed, consisting of six stories, and again Miranda figures in it. But Porter's career faltered as she struggled for two decades to complete a novel keyed to a journey aboard ship from Mexico to Germany in 1931. Finally published in 1962, *Ship of Fools* sold well but received a mixed response from critics. Porter also devoted much effort and energy to a book about the New England scholar-minister Cotton Mather and the Salem witch trials, but she did not manage to finish it.

Porter was a dedicated, meticulous writer; as she noted, "there is no describing what my life has been because of my one fixed desire: to be a good artist, responsible to the last comma for what I write." However, in her life and work, she is sometimes hard to get hold of; she once said, "I shall try to tell the truth, but the result will be fiction," and this observation implies the complex inwardness of Porter as well as of her most absorbing characters.

A significant influence on Eudora Welty and Flannery O'Connor, Porter summed up her achievement in *Collected Stories* (1965), and "Flowering Judas" is one of the volume's highlights. "It was written," Porter recalled, "between seven o'clock and midnight on a very cold December,1929, in Brooklyn. The experiences from which it was made occurred several years before in Mexico, just after the Obregon revolution." (Alvaro Obregon was a small farmer who eventually became president of Mexico.)

"Flowering Judas" is an alluring but elusive story, rich with symbolism and carefully rendered in point of view, in which Porter explores the themes of sexuality, political revolution, religion, and betrayal.

For biography: Joan Givner, *Katharine Anne Porter: A Life* (1982) and Darlene Harbour Unrue, *Katherine Anne Porter: The Life of an Artist* (2005). Critical interpretation is provided by Jane K. DeMouy, *Katherine Anne Porter's Women: The Eye of Her Fiction* (1983); Robert H. Brinkmeyer Jr., *Katherine Anne Porter's Artistic Development* (1993); and Janis P. Stout, *Katherine Anne Porter: A Sense of the Times* (1995). See also *Katherine Anne Porter Remembered*, ed. Darlene Harbour Unrue (2010).

Flowering Judas[1]

Braggioni sits heaped upon the edge of a straight-backed chair much too small for him, and sings to Laura in a furry, mournful voice. Laura has begun to find reasons for avoiding her own house until the latest possible moment, for Braggioni is there almost every night. No matter how late she is, he will be sitting there with a surly, waiting expression, pulling at his kinky yellow hair, thumbing the strings of his guitar, snarling a tune under his breath. Lupe the Indian maid meets Laura at the door, and says with a flicker of a glance towards the upper room, "He waits."

Laura wishes to lie down, she is tired of her hairpins and the feel of her long tight sleeves, but she says to him, "Have you a new song for me this evening?" If he says yes, she asks him to sing it. If he says no, she remembers his favorite one, and asks him to sing it again. Lupe brings her a cup of chocolate and a plate of rice, and Laura eats at the small table under the lamp, first inviting Braggioni, whose answer is always the same: "I have eaten, and besides, chocolate thickens the voice."

Laura says, "Sing, then," and Braggioni heaves himself into song. He scratches the guitar familiarly as though it were a pet animal, and sings passionately off key, taking the high notes in a prolonged painful squeal. Laura, who haunts the markets listening to the ballad singers, and stops every day to hear the blind boy playing his reed-flute in Sixteenth of September Street,[2] listens to Braggioni with pitiless courtesy, because she dares not smile at his miserable performance. Nobody dares to smile at him. Braggioni is cruel to everyone, with a kind of specialized insolence, but he is so vain of his talents, and so sensitive to slights, it would require a cruelty and vanity greater than his own to lay a finger on the vast cureless wound of his self-esteem. It would require courage, too, for it is dangerous to offend him, and nobody has this courage.

Braggioni loves himself with such tenderness and amplitude and eternal charity that his followers—for he is a leader of men, a skilled revolutionist, and his skin has been punctured in honorable warfare—warm

---

[1]A tree with purplish flowers, named for Judas Iscariot, the disciple who betrayed Christ. According to legend, Judas hanged himself from such a tree.
[2]A street in Morelia, Mexico, where the story takes place.

themselves in the reflected glow, and say to each other: "He has a real nobility, a love of humanity raised above mere personal affections." The excess of this self-love has flowed out, inconveniently for her, over Laura, who, with so many others, owes her comfortable situation and her salary to him. When he is in a very good humor, he tells her, "I am tempted to forgive you for being a *gringa. Gringita!*"[3] and Laura, burning, imagines herself leaning forward suddenly, and with a sound back-handed slap wiping the suety[4] smile from his face. If he notices her eyes at these moments he gives no sign.

She knows what Braggioni would offer her, and she must resist tenaciously without appearing to resist, and if she could avoid it she would not admit even to herself the slow drift of his intention. During these long evenings which have spoiled a long month for her, she sits in her deep chair with an open book on her knees, resting her eyes on the consoling rigidity of the printed page when the sight and sound of Braggioni singing threaten to identify themselves with all her remembered afflictions and to add their weight to her uneasy premonitions of the future. The gluttonous bulk of Braggioni has become a symbol of her many disillusions, for a revolutionist should be lean, animated by heroic faith, a vessel of abstract virtues. This is nonsense, she knows it now and is ashamed of it. Revolution must have leaders, and leadership is a career for energetic men. She is, her comrades tell her, full of romantic error, for what she defines as cynicism in them is merely "a developed sense of reality." She is almost too willing to say, "I am wrong, I suppose I don't really understand the principles," and afterward she makes a secret truce with herself, determined not to surrender her will to such expedient logic. But she cannot help feeling that she has been betrayed irreparably by the disunion between her way of living and her feeling of what life should be, and at times she is almost contented to rest in this sense of grievance as a private store of consolation. Sometimes she wishes to run away, but she stays. Now she longs to fly out of this room, down the narrow stairs, and into the street where the houses lean together like conspirators under a single mottled lamp, and leave Braggioni singing to himself.

Instead she looks at Braggioni, frankly and clearly, like a good child who understands the rules of behavior. Her knees cling together under sound blue serge,[5] and her round white collar is not purposely nun-like. She wears the uniform of an idea, and has renounced vanities. She was born Roman Catholic, and in spite of her fear of being seen by someone who might make a scandal of it, she slips now and again into some crumbling little church, kneels on the chilly stone, and says a Hail Mary on the

---

[3]A female foreigner (that is, non-Mexican). The term is usually used pejoratively to describe Americans in Mexico. *Gringita* is a diminutive variation of gringa that means "cute little foreign girl."
[4]Having the nature of suet or pasty fat.
[5]A durable twilled cloth.

gold rosary she bought in Tehuantepec.[6] It is no good and she ends by examining the altar with its tinsel flowers and ragged brocades, and feels tender about the battered doll-shape of some male saint whose white, lace-trimmed drawers hang limply around his ankles below the hieratic dignity of his velvet robe. She has encased herself in a set of principles derived from her early training, leaving no detail of gesture or of personal taste untouched, and for this reason she will not wear lace made on machines. This is her private heresy, for in her special group the machine is sacred, and will be the salvation of the workers. She loves fine lace, and there is a tiny edge of fluted cobweb on this collar, which is one of twenty precisely alike, folded in blue tissue paper in the upper drawer of her clothes chest.

Braggioni catches her glance solidly as if he had been waiting for it, leans forward, balancing his paunch between his spread knees, and sings with tremendous emphasis, weighing his words. He has, the song relates, no father and no mother, nor even a friend to console him; lonely as a wave of the sea he comes and goes, lonely as a wave. His mouth opens round and yearns sideways, his balloon cheeks grow oily with the labor of song. He bulges marvelously in his expensive garments. Over his lavender collar, crushed upon a purple necktie, held by a diamond hoop: over his ammunition belt of tooled leather worked in silver, buckled cruelly around his gasping middle: over the tops of his glossy yellow shoes Braggioni swells with ominous ripeness, his mauve silk hose stretched taut, his ankles bound with the stout leather thongs of his shoes.

When he stretches his eyelids at Laura she notes again that his eyes are the true tawny yellow cat's eyes. He is rich, not in money, he tells her, but in power, and this power brings with it the blameless ownership of things, and the right to indulge his love of small luxuries. "I have a taste for the elegant refinements," he said once, flourishing a yellow silk handkerchief before her nose. "Smell that? It is Jockey Club, imported from New York." Nonetheless he is wounded by life. He will say so presently. "It is true everything turns to dust in the hand, to gall on the tongue." He sighs and his leather belt creaks like a saddle girth. "I am disappointed in everything as it comes. Everything." He shakes his head. "You, poor thing, you will be disappointed too. You are born for it. We are more alike than you realize in some things. Wait and see. Some day you will remember what I have told you, you will know that Braggioni was your friend."

Laura feels a slow chill, a purely physical sense of danger, a warning in her blood that violence, mutilation, a shocking death, wait for her with lessening patience. She has translated this fear into something homely, immediate, and sometimes hesitates before crossing the street. "My personal fate is nothing, except as the testimony of a mental attitude," she reminds herself,

---

[6]A town on the Pacific coast of Mexico.

quoting from some forgotten philosophic primer, and is sensible enough to add, "Anyhow, I shall not be killed by an automobile if I can help it."

"It may be true I am as corrupt, in another way, as Braggioni," she thinks in spite of herself, "as callous, as incomplete," and if this is so, any kind of death seems preferable. Still she sits quietly, she does not run. Where could she go? Uninvited she has promised herself to this place; she can no longer imagine herself as living in another country, and there is no pleasure in remembering her life before she came here.

Precisely what is the nature of this devotion, its true motives, and what are its obligations? Laura cannot say. She spends part of her days in Xochimilco,[7] near by, teaching Indian children to say in English, "The cat is on the mat." When she appears in the classroom they crowd about her with smiles on their wise, innocent, clay-colored faces, crying, "Good morning, my titcher!" in immaculate voices, and they make of her desk a fresh garden of flowers every day.

During her leisure she goes to union meetings and listens to busy important voices quarreling over tactics, methods, internal politics. She visits the prisoners of her own political faith in their cells, where they entertain themselves with counting cockroaches, repenting of their indiscretions, composing their memoirs, writing out manifestoes and plans for their comrades who are still walking about free, hands in pockets, sniffing fresh air. Laura brings them food and cigarettes and a little money, and she brings messages disguised in equivocal phrases from the men outside who dare not set foot in the prison for fear of disappearing into the cells kept empty for them. If the prisoners confuse night and day, and complain, "Dear little Laura, time doesn't pass in this infernal hole, and I won't know when it is time to sleep unless I have a reminder," she brings them their favorite narcotics, and says in a tone that does not wound them with pity, "Tonight will really be night for you," and though her Spanish amuses them, they find her comforting, useful. If they lose patience and all faith, and curse the slowness of their friends in coming to their rescue with money and influence, they trust her not to repeat everything, and if she inquires, "Where do you think we can find money, or influence?" they are certain to answer, "Well, there is Braggioni, why doesn't he do something?"

She smuggles letters from headquarters to men hiding from firing squads in back streets in mildewed houses, where they sit in tumbled beds and talk bitterly as if all Mexico were at their heels, when Laura knows positively they might appear at the band concert in the Alameda[8] on Sunday morning, and no one would notice them. But Braggioni says, "Let them sweat a little. The next time they may be careful. It is very restful to have them out of the way for a while." She is not afraid to knock on any

---

[7]A suburb of Mexico City that still would have been a small town at the time Porter wrote the story.
[8]A public walkway, park.

door in any street after midnight, and enter in the darkness, and say to one of these men who is really in danger: "They will be looking for you—seriously—tomorrow morning after six. Here is some money from Vicente. Go to Vera Cruz and wait."

She borrows money from the Roumanian agitator to give to his bitter enemy the Polish agitator. The favor of Braggioni is their disputed territory, and Braggioni holds the balance nicely, for he can use them both. The Polish agitator talks love to her over café tables, hoping to exploit what he believes is her secret sentimental preference for him, and he gives her misinformation which he begs her to repeat as the solemn truth to certain persons. The Roumanian is more adroit. He is generous with his money in all good causes, and lies to her with an air of ingenuous candor, as if he were her good friend and confidant. She never repeats anything they may say. Braggioni never asks questions. He has other ways to discover all that he wishes to know about them.

Nobody touches her, but all praise her gray eyes, and the soft, round under lip which promises gayety, yet is always grave, nearly always firmly closed: and they cannot understand why she is in Mexico. She walks back and forth on her errands, with puzzled eyebrows, carrying her little folder of drawings and music and school papers. No dancer dances more beautifully than Laura walks, and she inspires some amusing, unexpected ardors, which cause little gossip, because nothing comes of them. A young captain who had been a soldier in Zapata's army[9] attempted, during a horseback ride near Cuernavaca,[10] to express his desire for her with the noble simplicity befitting a rude folk-hero: but gently, because he was gentle. This gentleness was his defeat, for when he alighted, and removed her foot from the stirrup, and essayed to draw her down into his arms, her horse, ordinarily a tame one, shied fiercely, reared and plunged away. The young hero's horse careered blindly after his stable-mate, and the hero did not return to the hotel until rather late that evening. At breakfast he came to her table in full charro[11] dress, gray buckskin jacket and trousers with strings of silver buttons down the leg, and he was in a humorous, careless mood. "May I sit with you?" and "You are a wonderful rider. I was terrified that you might be thrown and dragged. I should never have forgiven myself. But I cannot admire you enough for your riding!"

"I learned to ride in Arizona," said Laura.

"If you will ride with me again this morning, I promise you a horse that will not shy with you," he said. But Laura remembered that she must return to Mexico City at noon.

---

[9]Emiliano Zapata (1879–1919) was a Mexican revolutionary hero who led a peasant uprising in Morelos in 1911 against the dictator Porfirio Díaz (1830–1915). Zapata was murdered in 1919.
[10]A city about 75 miles south of Mexico City.
[11]The costume worn by accomplished Mexican horsemen of special status.

Next morning the children made a celebration and spent their playtime writing on the blackboard, "We lov ar ticher," and with tinted chalks they drew wreaths of flowers around the words. The young hero wrote her a letter: "I am a very foolish, wasteful, impulsive man. I should have first said I love you, and then you would not have run away. But you shall see me again." Laura thought, "I must send him a box of colored crayons," but she was trying to forgive herself for having spurred her horse at the wrong moment.

A brown, shock-haired youth came and stood in her patio one night and sang like a lost soul for two hours, but Laura could think of nothing to do about it. The moonlight spread a wash of gauzy silver over the clear spaces of the garden, and the shadows were cobalt blue. The scarlet blossoms of the Judas tree were dull purple, and the names of the colors repeated themselves automatically in her mind, while she watched not the boy, but his shadow, fallen like a dark garment across the fountain rim, trailing in the water. Lupe came silently and whispered expert counsel in her ear: "If you will throw him one little flower, he will sing another song or two and go away." Laura threw the flower, and he sang a last song and went away with the flower tucked in the band of his hat. Lupe said, "He is one of the organizers of the Typographers Union, and before that he sold corridos[12] in the Merced market, and before that, he came from Guanajuato,[13] where I was born. I would not trust any man, but I trust least those from Guanajuato."

She did not tell Laura that he would be back again the next night, and the next, nor that he would follow her at a certain fixed distance around the Merced market, through the Zócalo,[14] up Francisco I. Madero Avenue, and so along the Paseo de la Reforma to Chapultepec Park, and into the Philosopher's Footpath, still with that flower withering in his hat, and an indivisible attention in his eyes.

Now Laura is accustomed to him, it means nothing except that he is nineteen years old and is observing a convention with all propriety, as though it were founded on a law of nature, which in the end it might well prove to be. He is beginning to write poems which he prints on a wooden press, and he leaves them stuck like handbills in her door. She is pleasantly disturbed by the abstract, unhurried watchfulness of his black eyes which will in time turn easily towards another object. She tells herself that throwing the flower was a mistake, for she is twenty-two years old and knows better; but she refuses to regret it, and persuades herself that her negation of all external events as they occur is a sign that she is gradually perfecting herself in the stoicism she strives to cultivate against that disaster she fears, though she cannot name it.

[12]Ballads, a centuries-old form of narrative song.
[13]A large city in central Mexico.
[14]A great square in the heart of Mexico City. The locations that follow are other sites in Mexico City.

She is not at home in the world. Every day she teaches children who remain strangers to her, though she loves their tender round hands and their
charming opportunist savagery. She knocks at unfamiliar doors not knowing whether a friend or a stranger shall answer, and even if a known face
emerges from the sour gloom of that unknown interior, still it is the face of a
stranger. No matter what this stranger says to her, nor what her message to
him, the very cells of her flesh reject knowledge and kinship in one monotonous word. No. No. No. She draws her strength from this one holy talismanic
word which does not suffer her to be led into evil. Denying everything, she
may walk anywhere in safety, she looks at everything without amazement.

No, repeats this firm unchanging voice of her blood; and she looks at
Braggioni without amazement. He is a great man, he wishes to impress
this simple girl who covers her great round breasts with thick dark cloth,
and who hides long, invaluably beautiful legs under a heavy skirt. She is
almost thin except for the incomprehensible fullness of her breasts, like a
nursing mother's, and Braggioni, who considers himself a judge of women,
speculates again on the puzzle of her notorious virginity, and takes the
liberty of speech which she permits without a sign of modesty, indeed,
without any sort of sign, which is disconcerting.

"You think you are so cold, *gringita!* Wait and see. You will surprise yourself some day! May I be there to advise you!" He stretches his eyelids at her,
and his ill-humored cat's eyes waver in a separate glance for the two points of
light marking the opposite ends of a smoothly drawn path between the swollen curve of her breasts. He is not put off by that blue serge, nor by her resolutely fixed gaze. There is all the time in the world. His cheeks are bellying
with the wind of song. "O girl with the dark eyes," he sings, and reconsiders.
"But yours are not dark. I can change all that. O girl with the green eyes, you
have stolen my heart away!" then his mind wanders to the song, and Laura
feels the weight of his attention being shifted elsewhere. Singing thus, he
seems harmless, he is quite harmless, there is nothing to do but sit patiently
and say "No," when the moment comes. She draws a full breath, and her
mind wanders also, but not far. She dares not wander too far.

Not for nothing has Braggioni taken pains to be a good revolutionist and
a professional lover of humanity. He will never die of it. He has the malice,
the cleverness, the wickedness, the sharpness of wit, the hardness of heart,
stipulated for loving the world profitably. *He will never die of it.* He will live
to see himself kicked out from his feeding trough by other hungry world-
saviors. Traditionally he must sing in spite of his life which drives him to
bloodshed, he tells Laura, for his father was a Tuscany[15] peasant who drifted
to Yucatan and married a Maya woman: a woman of race, an aristocrat. They
gave him the love and knowledge of music, thus: and under the rip of his
thumbnail, the strings of the instrument complain like exposed nerves.

---

[15]A region of northern Italy.

Once he was called Delgadito by all the girls and married women who ran after him; he was so scrawny all his bones showed under his thin cotton clothing, and he could squeeze his emptiness to the very backbone with his two hands. He was a poet and the revolution was only a dream then; too many women loved him and sapped away his youth, and he could never find enough to eat anywhere, anywhere! Now he is a leader of men, crafty men who whisper in his ear, hungry men who wait for hours outside his office for a word with him, emaciated men with wild faces who waylay him at the street gate with a timid, "Comrade, let me tell you..." and they blow the foul breath from their empty stomachs in his face.

He is always sympathetic. He gives them handfuls of small coins from his own pocket, he promises them work, there will be demonstrations, they must join the unions and attend the meetings, above all they must be on the watch for spies. They are closer to him than his own brothers, without them he can do nothing—until tomorrow, comrade!

Until tomorrow. "They are stupid, they are lazy, they are treacherous, they would cut my throat for nothing," he says to Laura. He has good food and abundant drink, he hires an automobile and drives in the Paseo on Sunday morning, and enjoys plenty of sleep in a soft bed beside a wife who dares not disturb him; and he sits pampering his bones in easy billows of fat, singing to Laura, who knows and thinks these things about him. When he was fifteen, he tried to drown himself because he loved a girl, his first love, and she laughed at him. "A thousand women have paid for that," and his tight little mouth turns down at the corners. Now he perfumes his hair with Jockey Club, and confides to Laura: "One woman is really as good as another for me, in the dark. I prefer them all."

His wife organizes unions among the girls in the cigarette factories, and walks in picket lines, and even speaks at meetings in the evening. But she cannot be brought to acknowledge the benefits of true liberty. "I tell her I must have my freedom, net. She does not understand my point of view." Laura has heard this many times. Braggioni scratches the guitar and meditates. "She is an instinctively virtuous woman, pure gold, no doubt of that. If she were not, I should lock her up, and she knows it."

His wife, who works so hard for the good of the factory girls, employs part of her leisure lying on the floor weeping because there are so many women in the world, and only one husband for her, and she never knows where nor when to look for him. He told her: "Unless you can learn to cry when I am not here, I must go away for good." That day he went away and took a room at the Hotel Madrid.

It is this month of separation for the sake of higher principles that has been spoiled not only for Mrs. Braggioni, whose sense of reality is beyond criticism, but for Laura, who feels herself bogged in a nightmare. Tonight Laura envies Mrs. Braggioni, who is alone, and free to weep as much as she pleases about a concrete wrong. Laura has just come from a visit to the prison, and she is waiting for tomorrow with a bitter anxiety as if tomorrow may not come, but time may be caught immovably in this hour, with herself transfixed, Braggioni singing on forever, and Eugenio's body not yet discovered by the guard.

Braggioni says: "Are you going to sleep?" Almost before she can shake her head, he begins telling her about the May-day disturbances coming on in Morelia,[16] for the Catholics hold a festival in honor of the Blessed Virgin, and the Socialists celebrate their martyrs on that day. "There will be two independent processions, starting from either end of town, and they will march until they meet, and the rest depends..." He asks her to oil and load his pistols. Standing up, he unbuckles his ammunition belt, and spreads it laden across her knees. Laura sits with the shells slipping through the cleaning cloth dipped in oil, and he says again he cannot understand why she works so hard for the revolutionary idea unless she loves some man who is in it. "Are you not in love with someone?" "No," says Laura. "And no one is in love with you?" "No." "Then it is your own fault. No woman need go begging. Why, what is the matter with you? The legless beggar woman in the Alameda has a perfectly faithful lover. Did you know that?"

Laura peers down the pistol barrel and says nothing, but a long, slow faintness rises and subsides in her; Braggioni curves his swollen fingers around the throat of the guitar and softly smothers the music out of it, and when she hears him again he seems to have forgotten her, and is speaking in the hypnotic voice he uses when talking in small rooms to a listening, close-gathered crowd. Some day this world, now seemingly so composed and eternal, to the edges of every sea shall be merely a tangle of gaping trenches, of crashing walls and broken bodies. Everything must be torn from its accustomed place where it has rotted for centuries, hurled skyward and distributed, cast down again clean as rain, without separate identity. Nothing shall survive that the stiffened hands of poverty have created for the rich and no one shall be left alive except the elect spirits destined to procreate a new world cleansed of cruelty and injustice, ruled by benevolent anarchy: "Pistols are good, I love them, cannon are even better, but in the end I pin my faith to good dynamite," he concludes, and strokes the pistol lying in her hands. "Once I dreamed of destroying this city, in case it offered resistance to General Ortíz, but it fell into his hands like an overripe pear."

He is made restless by his own words, rises and stands waiting. Laura holds up the belt to him: "Put that on, and go kill somebody in Morelia, and you will be happier," she says softly. The presence of death in the room makes her bold. "Today, I found Eugenio going into a stupor. He refused to allow me to call the prison doctor. He had taken all the tablets I brought him yesterday. He said he took them because he was bored."

[16]A city 180 miles west of Mexico City.

"He is a fool, and his death is his own business," says Braggioni, fastening his belt carefully.

"I told him if he had waited only a little while longer, you would have got him set free," says Laura. "He said he did not want to wait."

"He is a fool and we are well rid of him," says Braggioni, reaching for his hat.

He goes away. Laura knows his mood has changed, she will not see him any more for a while. He will send word when he needs her to go on errands into strange streets, to speak to the strange faces that will appear, like clay masks with the power of human speech, to mutter their thanks to Braggioni for his help. Now she is free, and she thinks, I must run while there is time. But she does not go.

Braggioni enters his own house where for a month his wife has spent many hours every night weeping and tangling her hair upon her pillow. She is weeping now, and she weeps more at the sight of him, the cause of all her sorrows. He looks about the room. Nothing is changed, the smells are good and familiar, he is well acquainted with the woman who comes toward him with no reproach except grief on her face. He says to her tenderly: "You are so good, please don't cry any more, you dear good creature." She says, "Are you tired, my angel? Sit here and I will wash your feet." She brings a bowl of water, and kneeling, unlaces his shoes, and when from her knees she raises her sad eyes under her blackened lids, he is sorry for everything, and bursts into tears. "Ah, yes, I am hungry, I am tired, let us eat something together," he says, between sobs. His wife leans her head on his arm and says, "Forgive me!" and this time he is refreshed by the solemn, endless rain of her tears.

Laura takes off her serge dress and puts on a white linen nightgown and goes to bed. She turns her head a little to one side, and lying still, reminds herself that it is time to sleep. Numbers tick in her brain like little clocks, soundless doors close of themselves around her. If you would sleep, you must not remember anything, the children will say tomorrow, good morning, my teacher, the poor prisoners who come every day bringing flowers to their jailor. 1-2-3-4-5—it is monstrous to confuse love with revolution, night with day, life with death—ah, Eugenio!

The tolling of the midnight bell is a signal, but what does it mean? Get up, Laura, and follow me: come out of your sleep, out of your bed, out of this strange house. What are you doing in this house? Without a word, without fear she rose and reached for Eugenio's hand, but he eluded her with a sharp, sly smile and drifted away. This is not all, you shall see— Murderer, he said, follow me, I will show you a new country, but it is far away and we must hurry. No, said Laura, not unless you take my hand, no; and she clung first to the stair rail, and then to the topmost branch of the Judas tree that bent down slowly and set her upon the earth, and then to the rocky ledge of a cliff, and then to the jagged wave of a sea that was not water but a desert of crumbling stone. Where are you taking me, she asked in wonder but without fear. To death, and it is a long way off, and we must hurry, said Eugenio. No, said Laura, not unless you take my hand. Then eat these flowers, poor prisoner, said Eugenio in a voice of pity, take and eat: and from the Judas tree he stripped the warm bleeding flowers, and held them to her lips. She saw that his hand was fleshless, a cluster of small white petrified branches, and his eye sockets were without light, but she ate the flowers greedily for they satisfied both hunger and thirst. Murderer! said Eugenio, and Cannibal! This is my body and my blood. Laura cried No! and at the sound of her own voice, she awoke trembling, and was afraid to sleep again.

[1929, 1930]

ZORA NEALE HURSTON ■ (1891–1960)

Zora Neale Hurston was born a decade earlier than she claimed. Eatonville, Florida, the first African American township in the United States, was her place of birth and upbringing, and—her father was its first mayor—it figures prominently in her fiction and autobiography. Hurston's mother died when her daughter was only thirteen, and Zora and her father's second wife got along badly. She left school and took a number of odd jobs, including as a maid for a white woman in a theatrical company. But eventually Hurston returned to school, graduating from Morgan Academy in Baltimore, Maryland, in 1918, and then taking courses off and on at Howard University in Washington, D.C. during 1918–24. There she made the acquaintance of the African American scholar Alain Locke (1885–1954), who encouraged her literary aspirations.

Hurston's first story was published in the journal *Opportunity* in December 1924, and she was a key figure, in drama and fiction, on the Harlem literary scene in the 1920s. With the help of wealthy white patrons she attended Barnard College, advanced in her studies, and made connection with the eminent anthropologist Franz Boas. With his support, Hurston began graduate work at Columbia University, which led to research into folk stories and tales in the South. Her *Mules and Men* (1935) is the first collection by an African American of Negro folklore.

Already the author of one novel, *Jonah's Gourd Vine* (1934), Hurston traveled to the Caribbean to undertake further anthropological research. While she was there she completed her next novel, *Their Eyes Were Watching God* (1937). A passionate, if often painful, story of female development and of sexual and emotional awakening, it is one of the most influential novels in the African American literary tradition. It inspired Alice Walker and Toni Morrison as well as other notable African American women authors.

Hurston was active as a writer and widely published throughout the 1930s and 1940s; her work of these years included *Dust Tracks on a Road* (1942), an autobiography from which a number of passages were cut because Hurston's publisher deemed them too critical of whites. But her career came to a halt in September 1948, when she was accused of having sex with a ten-year-old boy. She was innocent, but after this public humiliation she wrote next to nothing, scraping by as a maid, a librarian, and a teacher in Florida.

"The Gilded Six-Bits," Hurston's most well-known story, is an exploration of the marital and sexual ups and downs of a poor African American couple. Hurston is skillful in her handling of point of view and, even more, of dialogue, which displays her sensitive feeling for the images and rhythms of African American speech. Hurston herself was married twice, and her relationships with men were troubled, as "The Gilded Six-Bits" reflects.

Zora Neale Hurston, 1938. Photograph by Carl Van Vechten (1880–1964).

For further reading, see *Dust Tracks on a Road: An Autobiography*, ed. Robert E. Hemenway (2nd ed., 1984) and *Zora Neale Hurston: A Life in Letters*, ed. Carla Kaplan (2002). Also recommended are Robert E. Hemenway, *Zora Neale Hurston: A Literary Biography* (1977); Lillie P. Howard, *Zora Neale Hurston* (1980); *Zora Neale Hurston: Critical Perspectives Past and Present*, eds. Henry Louis Gates Jr. and K. A. Appiah (1993); Susan Edwards Meisenhelder, *Hitting a Straight Lick with a Crooked Stick: Race and Gender in the Work of Zora Neale Hurston* (1999); and Valerie Boyd, *Wrapped in Rainbows: The Life of Zora Neale Hurston* (2002). Recent studies include Tiffany Ruby Patterson, *Zora Neale Hurston and a History of Southern Life* (2005); *"The Inside Light": New Critical Essays on Zora Neale Hurston*, ed. Deborah G. Plant (2010) and Virginia Lynn Moylan, *Zora Neale Hurston's Final Decade* (2011).

The Gilded Six-Bits[1]

It was a Negro yard around a Negro house in a Negro settlement that looked to the payroll of the G. and G. Fertilizer works for its support.

But there was something happy about the place. The front yard was parted in the middle by a sidewalk from gate to door-step, a sidewalk edged on either side by quart bottles driven neck down into the ground on a slant. A mess of homey flowers planted without a plan but blooming cheerily from their helter-skelter places. The fence and house were white-washed. The porch and steps scrubbed white.

The front door stood open to the sunshine so that the floor of the front room could finish drying after its weekly scouring. It was Saturday. Every-thing clean from the front gate to the privy house. Yard raked so that the strokes of the rake would make a pattern. Fresh newspaper cut in fancy edge on the kitchen shelves.

Missie May was bathing herself in the galvanized washtub in the bed-room. Her dark-brown skin glistened under the soapsuds that skittered down from her wash rag. Her stiff young breasts thrust forward aggres-sively like broad-based cones with the tips lacquered in black.

She heard men's voices in the distance and glanced at the dollar clock on the dresser.

"Humph! Ah'm way behind time t'day! Joe gointer be heah 'fore Ah git mah clothes on if Ah don't make haste."

She grabbed the clean meal sack at hand and dried herself hurriedly and began to dress. But before she could tie her slippers, there came the ring of singing metal on wood. Nine times.

Missie May grinned with delight. She had not seen the big tall man come stealing in the gate and creep up the walk grinning happily at the joyful mischief he was about to commit. But she knew that it was her hus-band throwing silver dollars in the door for her to pick up and pile beside her plate at dinner. It was this way every Saturday afternoon. The nine dollars hurled into the open door, he scurried to a hiding place behind the cape jasmine bush and waited.

Missie May promptly appeared at the door in mock alarm.

"Who dat chunkin' money in mah do'way?" she demanded.

No answer from the yard. She leaped off the porch and began to search the shrubbery. She peeped under the porch and hung over the gate to look up and down the road. While she did this, the man behind the jasmine darted to the china berry tree. She spied him and gave chase.

"Nobody ain't gointer be chunkin' money at me and Ah not do 'em nothin'," she shouted in mock anger. He ran around the house with Missie

[1]A bit is a unit of value equivalent to an eighth of a dollar; it is used in even multiples only, as two or four bits. Two bits equals a quarter; six bits is seventy-five cents. *Gilded* means "covered with gold-colored foil"—figuratively, "made to look more valuable than the object actually is."

May at his heels. She overtook him at the kitchen door. He ran inside but could not close it after him before she crowded in and locked with him in a rough and tumble. For several minutes the two were a furious mass of male and female energy. Shouting, laughing, twisting, turning, tussling, tickling each other in the ribs; Missie May clutching onto Joe and Joe trying, but not too hard, to get away.

"Missie May, take yo' hand out mah pocket!" Joe shouted out between laughs.

"Ah ain't, Joe, not lessen you gwine gimme whateve' it is good you got in yo' pocket. Turn it go, Joe, do Ah'll tear yo' clothes."

"Go on tear 'em. You de one dat pushes de needles round heah. Move yo' hand Missie May."

"Lemme git dat paper sack out yo' pocket. Ah bet it's candy kisses."

"Tain't. Move yo' hand. Woman ain't got no business in a man's clothes nohow. Go way."

Missie May gouged way down and gave an upward jerk and triumphed.

"Unhhunh! Ah got it. It 'tis so candy kisses. Ah knowed you had somethin' for me in yo' clothes. Now Ah got to see whut's in every pocket you got."

Joe smiled indulgently and let his wife go through all of his pockets and take out the things that he had hidden there for her to find. She bore off the chewing gum, the cake of sweet soap, the pocket handkerchief as if she had wrested them from him, as if they had not been bought for the sake of this friendly battle.

"Whew! dat play-fight done got me all warmed up," Joe exclaimed. "Got me some water in de kittle?"

"Yo' water is on de fire and yo' clean things is cross de bed. Hurry up and wash yo'self and git changed so we kin eat. Ah'm hongry." As Missie said this, she bore the steaming kettle into the bedroom.

"You ain't hongry, sugar," Joe contradicted her. "Youse jes' a little empty. Ah'm de one whut's hongry. Ah could eat up camp meetin', back off 'ssociation, and drink Jurdan[2] dry. Have it on de table when Ah git out de tub."

"Don't you mess wid mah business, man. You git in yo' clothes. Ah'm a real wife, not no dress and breath. Ah might not look lak one, but if you burn me, you won't git a thing but wife ashes."

Joe splashed in the bedroom and Missie May fanned around in the kitchen. A fresh red and white checked cloth on the table. Big pitcher of buttermilk beaded with pale drops of butter from the churn. Hot fried mullet,[3] crackling bread, ham hock atop a mound of string beans and new potatoes, and perched on the window-sill a pone of spicy potato pudding.

Very little talk during the meal but that little consisted of banter that pretended to deny affection but in reality flaunted it. Like when Missie

[2]The Jordan River in Israel, often cited in the Bible.
[3]A type of fish that is widely caught for food.

May reached for a second helping of the tater pone. Joe snatched it out of her reach.

After Missie May had made two or three unsuccessful grabs at the pan, she begged, "Aw, Joe gimme some mo' dat tater pone."[4]

"Nope, sweetenin' is for us men-folks. Y'all pritty lil frail eels don't need nothin' lak dis. You too sweet already."

"Please, Joe."

"Naw, naw. Ah don't want you to git no sweeter than whut you is already. We goin' down de road a lil piece t'night so you go put on yo' Sunday-go-to-meetin' things."

Missie May looked at her husband to see if he was playing some prank. "Sho nuff, Joe?"

"Yeah. We goin' to de ice cream parlor."

"Where de ice cream parlor at, Joe?"

"A new man done come heah from Chicago and he done got a place and took and opened it up for a ice cream parlor, and bein' as it's real swell, Ah wants you to be one de first ladies to walk in dere and have some set down."

"Do Jesus, Ah ain't knowed nothin' 'bout it. Who de man done it?"

"Mister Otis D. Slemmons, of spots and places—Memphis, Chicago, Jacksonville, Philadelphia and so on."

"Dat heavy-set man wid his mouth full of gold teethes?"

"Yeah. Where did you see 'im at?"

"Ah went down to de sto' tuh git a box of lye and Ah seen 'im standin' on de corner talkin' to some of de mens, and Ah come on back and went to scrubbin' de floor, and he passed and tipped his hat whilst Ah was scourin' de steps. Ah thought Ah never seen *him* befo'."

Joe smiled pleasantly. "Yeah, he's up to date. He got de finest clothes Ah ever seen on a colored man's back."

"Aw, he don't look no better in his clothes than you do in yourn. He got a puzzlegut[5] on 'im and he so chuckle-headed, he got a pone behind his neck."

Joe looked down at his own abdomen and said wistfully, "Wisht Ah had a build on me lak he got. He ain't puzzle-gutted, honey. He jes' got a corperation. Dat make 'm look lak a rich white man. All rich mens is got some belly on 'em."

"Ah seen de pitchers of Henry Ford[6] and he's a spare-built man and Rockefeller[7] look lak he ain't got but one gut. But Ford and Rockefeller and dis Slemmons and all de rest kin be as many-gutted as dey please,

---

[4]In the South, any bread made with corn meal, or a very fine light bread, enriched with milk, eggs, and so on and made in flat cakes.

[5]Potbelly.

[6]The successful and powerful business leader (1863–1947) who revolutionized the auto industry.

[7]John D. Rockefeller (1839–1937), the force behind the Standard Oil Company, which grew to dominate the oil industry and became one of the first big trusts in the United States.

Ah'm satisfied wid you jes lak you is, baby. God took pattern after a pine tree and built you noble. Youse a pritty man, and if Ah knowed any way to make you mo' pritty still Ah'd take and do it."

Joe reached over gently and toyed with Missie May's ear. "You jes' say dat cause you love me, but Ah know Ah can't hold no light to Otis D. Slemmons. Ah ain't never been nowhere and Ah ain't got nothin' but you."

Missie May got on his lap and kissed him and he kissed back in kind. Then he went on. "All de womens is crazy 'bout 'im everywhere he go."

"How you know dat, Joe?"

"He tole us so hisself."

"Dat don't make it so. His mouf is cut cross-ways, ain't it? Well, he kin lie jes' lak anybody else."

"Good Lawd, Missie! You womens sho is hard to sense into things. He's got a five-dollar gold piece for a stick-pin and he got a ten-dollar gold piece on his watch chain and his mouf is jes' crammed full of gold teethes. Sho wisht it wuz mine. And whut make it so cool, he got money 'cumu-lated. And womens give it all to 'im."

"Ah don't see whut de womens see on 'im. Ah wouldn't give 'im a wink if de sheriff wuz after 'im."

"Well, he tole us how de white womens in Chicago give 'im all dat gold money. So he don't 'low nobody to touch it at all. Not even put dey finger on it. Dey tole 'im not to. You kin make 'miration at it, but don't tetch it."

"Whyn't he stay up dere where dey so crazy 'bout 'im?"

"Ah reckon dey done made 'im vast-rich and he wants to travel some. He say dey wouldn't leave 'im hit a lick of work. He got mo' lady people crazy 'bout him than he kin shake a stick at."

"Joe, Ah hates to see you so dumb. Dat stray nigger jes' tell y'all any-thing and y'all b'lieve it."

"Go 'head on now, honey and put on yo' clothes. He talkin' 'bout his pritty womens—Ah want 'im to see *mine*."

Missie May went off to dress and Joe spent the time trying to make his stomach punch out like Slemmons' middle. He tried the rolling swagger of the stranger, but found that his tall bone-and-muscle stride fitted ill with it. He just had time to drop back into his seat before Missie May came in dressed to go.

On the way home that night Joe was exultant. "Didn't Ah say ole Otis was swell? Can't he talk Chicago talk? Wuzn't dat funny whut he said when great big fat ole Ida Armstrong come in? He asted me, 'Who is dat broad wid de forte shake?' Dat's a new word. Us always thought forty was a set of figgers but he showed us where it means a whole heap of things. Some-times he don't say forty, he jes' say thirty-eight and two and dat mean de same thing. Know whut he tole me when Ah wuz payin' for our ice cream? He say, 'Ah have to hand it to you, Joe. Dat wife of yours is jes' thirty-eight and two. Yessuh, she's forte!' Ain't he killin'?"

"He'll do in case of a rush. But he sho is got uh heap uh gold on 'im. Dat's de first time Ah ever seed gold money. It lookted good on him sho nuff, but it'd look a whole heap better on you."

"Who, me? Missie May youse crazy! Where would a po' man lak me git gold money from?"

Missie May was silent for a minute, then she said, "Us might find some goin' long de road some time. Us could."

"Who would be losin' gold money round heah? We ain't even seen none dese white folks wearin' no gold money on dey watch chain. You must be figgerin' Mister Packard or Mister Cadillac goin' pass through heah."

"You don't know whut been lost 'round heah. Maybe somebody way back in memorial times lost they gold money and went on off and it ain't never been found. And then if we wuz to find it, you could wear some 'thout havin' no gang of womens lak dat Slemmons say he got."

Joe laughed and hugged her. "Don't be so wishful 'bout me. Ah'm satisfied de way Ah is. So long as Ah be yo' husband, Ah don't keer 'bout nothin' else. Ah'd ruther all de other womens in de world to be dead than for you to have de toothache. Less we go to bed and git our night rest."

It was Saturday night once more before Joe could parade his wife in Slemmons' ice cream parlor again. He worked the night shift and Saturday was his only night off. Every other evening around six o'clock he left home, and dying dawn saw him hustling home around the lake where the challenging sun flung a flaming sword from east to west across the trembling water.

That was the best part of life—going home to Missie May. Their whitewashed house, the mock battle on Saturday, the dinner and ice cream parlor afterwards, church on Sunday nights when Missie out-dressed any woman in town—all, everything was right.

One night around eleven the acid[8] ran out at the G. and G. The foreman knocked off the crew and let the steam die down. As Joe rounded the lake on his way home, a lean moon rode the lake in a silver boat. If anybody had asked Joe about the moon on the lake, he would have said he hadn't paid it any attention. But he saw it with his feelings. It made him yearn painfully for Missie. Creation obsessed him. He thought about children. They had been married more than a year now. They had money put away. They ought to be making little feet for shoes. A little boy child would be about right.

He saw a dim light in the bedroom and decided to come in through the kitchen door. He could wash the fertilizer dust off himself before presenting himself to Missie May. It would be nice for her not to know that he was there until he slipped into his place in bed and hugged her back. She always liked that.

[8]Used in making fertilizer.

He eased the kitchen door open slowly and silently, but when he went to set his dinner bucket on the table he bumped it into a pile of dishes, and something crashed to the floor. He heard his wife gasp in fright and hurried to reassure her.

"Iss me, honey. Don't git skeered."

There was a quick, large movement in the bedroom. A rustle, a thud, and a stealthy silence. The light went out.

What? Robbers? Murderers? Some varmint attacking his helpless wife, perhaps. He struck a match, threw himself on guard and stepped over the door-sill into the bedroom.

The great belt on the wheel of Time slipped and eternity stood still. By the match light he could see the man's legs fighting with his breeches in his frantic desire to get them on. He had both chance and time to kill the intruder in his helpless condition—half in and half out of his pants—but he was too weak to take action. The shapeless enemies of humanity that live in the hours of Time had waylaid Joe. He was assaulted in his weakness. Like Samson awakening after his haircut.[9] So he just opened his mouth and laughed.

The match went out and he struck another and lit the lamp. A howling wind raced across his heart, but underneath its fury he heard his wife sobbing and Slemmons pleading for his life. Offering to buy it with all that he had. "Please, suh, don't kill me. Sixty-two dollars at de sto'. Gold money."

Joe just stood. Slemmons looked at the window, but it was screened. Joe stood out like a rough-backed mountain between him and the door. Barring him from escape, from sunrise, from life.

He considered a surprise attack upon the big clown that stood there laughing like a chessy cat.[10] But before his fist could travel an inch, Joe's own rushed out to crush him like a battering ram. Then Joe stood over him.

"Git into yo' damn rags, Slemmons, and dat quick."

Slemmons scrambled to his feet and into his vest and coat. As he grabbed his hat, Joe's fury overrode his intentions and he grabbed at Slemmons with his left hand and struck at him with his right. The right landed. The left grazed the front of his vest. Slemmons was knocked a somersault into the kitchen and fled through the open door. Joe found himself alone with Missie May, with the golden watch charm clutched in his left fist. A short bit of broken chain dangled between his fingers.

---

[9]A reference to the story of Samson and Delilah (Judges 13–16). Samson was a man of incredible strength who won many battles against the Philistines. His lover, Delilah, learned that the source of his strength was in his long hair, which she cut off while he slept as part of a financial bargain she struck with the Philistines. The Philistines attacked and overpowered Samson just as he awakened and discovered his strength was gone.

[10]Cheshire cat, an allusion to the grinning cat in *Alice's Adventures in Wonderland* (1865), by Lewis Carroll (1832–89).

Missie May was sobbing. Wails of weeping without words. Joe stood, and after awhile he found out that he had something in his hand. And then he stood and felt without thinking and without seeing with his natural eyes. Missie May kept on crying and Joe kept on feeling so much and not knowing what to do with all his feelings, he put Slemmons' watch charm in his pants pocket and took a good laugh and went to bed.

"Missie May, whut you cryin' for?"

"Cause Ah love you so hard and Ah know you don't love *me* no mo'."

Joe sank his face into the pillow for a spell then he said huskily, "You don't know de feelings of dat yet, Missie May."

"Oh Joe, honey, he said he wuz gointer give me dat gold money and he jes' kept on after me——"

Joe was very still and silent for a long time. Then he said, "Well, don't cry no mo', Missie May. Ah got yo' gold piece for you."

The hours went past on their rusty ankles. Joe still and quiet on one bed-rail and Missie May wrung dry of sobs on the other. Finally the sun's tide crept upon the shore of night and drowned all its hours. Missie May with her face stiff and streaked towards the window saw the dawn come into her yard. It was day. Nothing more. Joe wouldn't be coming home as usual. No need to fling open the front door and sweep off the porch, making it nice for Joe. Never no more breakfast to cook; no more washing and starching of Joe's jumper-jackets and pants. No more nothing. So why get up?

With this strange man in her bed, she felt embarrassed to get up and dress. She decided to wait till he had dressed and gone. Then she would get up, dress quickly and be gone forever beyond reach of Joe's looks and laughs. But he never moved. Red light turned to yellow, then white.

From beyond the no-man's land between them came a voice. A strange voice that yesterday had been Joe's.

"Missie May, ain't you gonna fix me no breakfus'?"

She sprang out of bed. "Yeah, Joe. Ah didn't reckon you wuz hongry."

No need to die today. Joe needed her for a few more minutes anyhow.

Soon there was a roaring fire in the cook stove. Water bucket full and two chickens killed. Joe loved fried chicken and rice. She didn't deserve a thing and good Joe was letting her cook him some breakfast. She rushed hot biscuits to the table as Joe took his seat.

He ate with his eyes in his plate. No laughter, no banter.

"Missie May, you ain't eatin' yo' breakfus'."

"Ah don't choose none, Ah thank yuh."

His coffee cup was empty. She sprang to refill it. When she turned from the stove and bent to set the cup beside Joe's plate, she saw the yellow coin on the table between them.

She slumped into her seat and wept into her arms.

Presently Joe said calmly, "Missie May, you cry too much. Don't look back lak Lot's wife and turn to salt."[11]

The sun, the hero of every day, the impersonal old man that beams as brightly on death as on birth, came up every morning and raced across the blue dome and dipped into the sea of fire every evening. Water ran down hill and birds nested.

Missie knew why she didn't leave Joe. She couldn't. She loved him too much, but she could not understand why Joe didn't leave her. He was polite, even kind at times, but aloof.

There were no more Saturday romps. No ringing silver dollars to stack beside her plate. No pockets to rifle. In fact the yellow coin in his trousers was like a monster hiding in the cave of his pockets to destroy her.

She often wondered if he still had it, but nothing could have induced her to ask nor yet to explore his pockets to see for herself. Its shadow was in the house whether or no.

One night Joe came home around midnight and complained of pains in the back. He asked Missie to rub him down with liniment. It had been three months since Missie had touched his body and it all seemed strange. But she rubbed him. Grateful for the chance. Before morning, youth triumphed and Missie exulted. But the next day, as she joyfully made up their bed, beneath her pillow she found the piece of money with the bit of chain attached.

Alone to herself, she looked at the thing with loathing, but look she must. She took it into her hands with trembling and saw first thing that it was no gold piece. It was a gilded half dollar. Then she knew why Slemmons had forbidden anyone to touch his gold. He trusted village eyes at a distance not to recognize his stick-pin as a gilded quarter, and his watch charm as a four-bit piece.

She was glad at first that Joe had left it there. Perhaps he was through with her punishment. They were man and wife again. Then another thought came clawing at her. He had come home to buy from her as if she were any woman in the long house.[12] Fifty cents for her love. As if to say that he could pay as well as Slemmons. She slid the coin into his Sunday pants pocket and dressed herself and left his house.

Half way between her house and the quarters she met her husband's mother, and after a short talk she turned and went back home. Never would she admit defeat to that woman who prayed for it nightly. If she had not the substance of marriage she had the outside show. Joe must leave *her*. She let him see she didn't want his old gold four-bits too.

[11]A reference to the tale of Lot in Genesis 19:17–26. God decided to destroy the immoral city of Sodom but allowed Lot to flee with his family, warning them not to look back. Lot's wife disobeyed and was turned into a pillar of salt.
[12]House of prostitution.

She saw no more of the coin for some time though she knew that Joe could not help finding it in his pocket. But his health kept poor, and he came home at least every ten days to be rubbed.

The sun swept around the horizon, trailing its robes of weeks and days. One morning as Joe came in from work, he found Missie May chopping wood. Without a word he took the ax and chopped a huge pile before he stopped.

"You ain't got no business choppin' wood, and you know it."

"How come? Ah been choppin' it for de last longest."

"Ah ain't blind. You makin' feet for shoes."[13]

"Won't you be glad to have a lil baby chile, Joe?"

"You know dat 'thout astin' me."

"Iss gointer be a boy chile and de very spit of you."

"You reckon, Missie May?"

"Who else could it look lak?"

Joe said nothing, but he thrust his hand deep into his pocket and fingered something there.

It was almost six months later Missie May took to bed and Joe went and got his mother to come wait on the house.

Missie May was delivered of a fine boy. Her travail was over when Joe came in from work one morning. His mother and the old women were drinking great bowls of coffee around the fire in the kitchen.

The minute Joe came into the room his mother called him aside.

"How did Missie May make out?" he asked quickly.

"Who, dat gal? She strong as a ox. She gointer have plenty mo'. We done fixed her wid de sugar and lard to sweeten her for de nex' one."

Joe stood silent awhile.

"You ain't ast 'bout de baby, Joe. You oughter be mighty proud cause he sho is de spittin' image of yuh, son. Dat's yourn all right, if you never git another one, dat un is yourn. And you know Ah'm mighty proud too, son, cause Ah never thought well of you marryin' Missie May cause her ma used tuh fan her foot round right smart and Ah been mighty skeered dat Missie May wuz gointer git misput on her road."

Joe said nothing. He fooled around the house till late in the day then just before he went to work, he went and stood at the foot of the bed and asked his wife how she felt. He did this every day during the week.

On Saturday he went to Orlando to make his market. It had been a long time since he had done that.

Meat and lard, meal and flour, soap and starch. Cans of corn and tomatoes. All the staples. He fooled around town for awhile and bought bananas and apples. Way after while he went around to the candy store.

"Hello, Joe," the clerk greeted him. "Ain't seen you in a long time."

---

[13]You're pregnant.

"Nope, Ah ain't been heah. Been round in spots and places."

"Want some of them molasses kisses you always buy?"

"Yessuh." He threw the gilded half dollar on the counter. "Will dat spend?"

"Whut is it, Joe? Well, I'll be doggone! A gold-plated four-bit piece. Where'd you git it, Joe?"

"Offen a stray nigger dat come through Eatonville. He had it on his watch chain for a charm—goin' round making out iss gold money. Ha ha! He had a quarter on his tie pin and it wuz all golded up too. Tryin' to fool people. Makin' out he so rich and everything. Ha! Ha! Tryin' to tole off folkses wives from home."

"How did you git it, Joe? Did he fool you, too?"

"Who, me? Naw suh! He ain't fooled me none. Know whut Ah done? He come round me wid his smart talk. Ah hauled off and knocked 'im down and took his old four-bits way from 'im. Gointer buy my wife some good ole lasses kisses wid it. Gimme fifty cents worth of dem candy kisses."

"Fifty cents buys a mighty lot of candy kisses, Joe. Why don't you split it up and take some chocolate bars, too. They eat good, too."

"Yessuh, dey do, but Ah wants all dat in kisses. Ah got a lil boy chile home now. Tain't a week old yet, but he kin suck a sugar tit[14] and maybe eat one them kisses hisself."

Joe got his candy and left the store. The clerk turned to the next customer. "Wisht I could be like these darkies. Laughin' all the time. Nothin' worries 'em."

Back in Eatonville, Joe reached his own front door. There was the ring of singing metal on wood. Fifteen times. Missie May couldn't run to the door, but she crept there as quickly as she could.

"Joe Banks, Ah hear you chunkin' money in mah do'way. You wait till Ah got mah strength back and Ah'm gointer fix you for dat."

[1933]

---

[14] A small amount of sugar wrapped in gauze and used to pacify infants.

EDNA ST. VINCENT MILLAY ■ (1892–1950)

Edna St. Vincent Millay was born in Rockland, Maine, and raised by her mother after her parents' divorce in 1900. She gained access to a college education through the help of a friend and patron who admired her literary talent, in particular her long poem "Renascence." After undertaking some course work at Barnard, Millay attended Vassar College in Poughkeepsie, New York, graduating in 1917. She then moved to Greenwich Village in New York City and became an active member of the cultural avant-garde.

Charismatic, passionate, sexually liberated—an early biographer termed her "the unrivaled embodiment of sex appeal" and "the Miss America of 1920"—Millay published many books of poetry, beginning with *Renascence and Other Poems* (1917), and she was acclaimed both as an author and as a highly dramatic reader of her verse. From the late 1920s through the 1930s and into the 1940s, Millay also was involved in a number of liberal and left-wing causes, including the controversial trial and execution of the anarchists Sacco and Vanzetti. Two of her pointed political poems, "Apostrophe to Man" and "I Forgot for a Moment," are included here.

Compared to the boldest, most innovative women poets of the post–World War II decades, such as Sylvia Plath and Anne Sexton, Millay can seem self-contained and conventional, and this may explain why her reputation began to fade after her death in 1950. But at their best, her lyrics possess a striking tone of wounded bitterness and piercing psychological and emotional intensity. Erotic, defiant, helpless, angry, despairing, vengeful, resilient, complex—Millay evokes and explores the meanings, and the consequences, of falling in and out of love. She can sound vulnerable and mournful in one line or stanza only to shift toward a tough cynicism in the next, as she enacts a variety of love-lost and love-torn roles.

Though Robert Frost is a greater poet, to an extent Millay's work resembles his: both favored traditional forms (e.g., the sonnet) and patterns of meter and rhyme, and both are more deeply interesting (and difficult) than they at first appear.

Two biographies complement one another well: Daniel Mark Epstein, *What Lips My Lips Have Kissed: The Loves and Love Poems of Edna St. Vincent Millay* (2001); and Nancy Milford, *Savage Beauty: The Life of Edna St. Vincent Millay* (2001). See also *Letters of Edna St. Vincent Millay*, ed. Allan Ross Macdougall (1952). Interpretive work can be found in *Critical Essays on Edna St. Vincent Millay*, ed. William B. Thesing (1993); and *Millay at 100: A Critical Reappraisal*, ed. Diane P. Freedman (1995). Catherine Cucinella, *Poetics of the Body: Edna St. Vincent Millay, Elizabeth Bishop, Marilyn Chin, and Marilyn Hacker* (2010).

Edna St. Vincent Millay, January 14, 1933. Photograph by Carl Van Vechten (1880–1964).

Recuerdo[1]

We were very tired, we were very merry—
We had gone back and forth all night on the ferry.
It was bare and bright, and smelled like a stable—
But we looked into a fire, we leaned across a table,
We lay on a hill-top underneath the moon;   5
And the whistles kept blowing, and the dawn came soon.

We were very tired, we were very merry—
We had gone back and forth all night on the ferry;
And you ate an apple, and I ate a pear,
From a dozen of each we had bought somewhere;   10
And the sky went wan, and the wind came cold,
And the sun rose dripping, a bucketful of gold.

---

[1]"I remember," "memory,", or "souvenir" (Spanish). A form of remembrance intended to memorialize
the dead and comfort the living that is usually presented as a written narrative or ballad.

We were very tired, we were very merry,
We had gone back and forth all night on the ferry.
We hailed, "Good morrow, mother!" to a shawl-covered head,   15
And bought a morning paper, which neither of us read;
And she wept, "God bless you!" for the apples and pears,
And we gave her all our money but our subway fares.

[1920]

[I think I should have loved you presently]

I think I should have loved you presently,
And given in earnest words I flung in jest;
And lifted honest eyes for you to see,
And caught your hand against my cheek and breast;
And all my pretty follies flung aside   5
That won you to me, and beneath your gaze,
Naked of reticence and shorn of pride,
Spread like a chart my little wicked ways.
I, that had been to you, had you remained,
But one more waking from a recurrent dream,   10
Cherish no less the certain stakes I gained,
And walk your memory's halls, austere, supreme,
A ghost in marble of a girl you knew
Who would have loved you in a day or two.

[1920]

[I, being born a woman and distressed]

I, being born a woman and distressed
By all the needs and notions of my kind,
Am urged by your propinquity to find
Your person fair, and feel a certain zest
To bear your body's weight upon my breast: 5
So subtly is the fume of life designed,
To clarify the pulse and cloud the mind,
And leave me once again undone, possessed.
Think not for this, however, the poor treason
Of my stout blood against my staggering brain,   10
I shall remember you with love, or season
My scorn with pity,—let me make it plain:
I find this frenzy insufficient reason
For conversation when we meet again.

[1923]

Apostrophe to Man *(on reflecting that the world is ready to go to war again)*

Detestable race, continue to expunge yourself, die out.
Breed faster, crowd, encroach, sing hymns, build bombing airplanes;
Make speeches, unveil statues, issue bonds, parade;
Convert again into explosives the bewildered ammonia and the distracted
    cellulose;
Convert again into putrescent matter drawing flies   5
The hopeful bodies of the young; exhort,
Pray, pull long faces, be earnest, be all but overcome, be photographed;
Confer, perfect your formulae, commercialize
Bacteria harmful to human tissue,
Put death on the market;   10
Breed, crowd, encroach, expand, expunge yourself, die out,
Homo called *sapiens*.

[1934]

[I too beneath your moon, almighty Sex]

I too beneath your moon, almighty Sex,
Go forth at nightfall crying like a cat,
Leaving the lofty tower I laboured at
For birds to foul and boys and girls to vex
With tittering chalk; and you, and the long necks   5
Of neighbours sitting where their mothers sat
Are well aware of shadowy this and that
In me, that's neither noble nor complex.
Such as I am, however, I have brought
To what it is, this tower; it is my own;   10
Though it was reared To Beauty, it was wrought
From what I had to build with: honest bone
Is there, and anguish; pride; and burning thought;
And lust is there, and nights not spent alone.

[1939]

Spring

To what purpose, April, do you return again?
Beauty is not enough.
You can no longer quiet me with the redness
Of little leaves opening stickily.
I know what I know.   5
The sun is hot on my neck as I observe
The spikes of the crocus.
The smell of the earth is good.

It is apparent that there is no death.
But what does that signify? 10
Not only under ground are the brains of men
Eaten by maggots.
Life in itself
Is nothing,
An empty cup, a flight of uncarpeted stairs. 15
It is not enough that yearly, down this hill,
April
Comes like an idiot, babbling and strewing flowers.

[1921]

I Forgot for a Moment

JULY 1940

I forgot for a moment France; I forgot England; I forgot
    my care:
I lived for a moment in a world where I was free to be
With the things and people that I love, and I was happy
    there.
I forgot for a moment Holland, I forgot my heavy care.
I lived for a moment in a world so lovely, so inept 5
At twisted words and crookèd deeds, it was as if I slept
    and dreamt.

It seemed that all was well with Holland—not a tank had
    crushed
The tulips there.
Mile after mile the level lowlands blossomed—yellow
    square, white square,
Scarlet strip and mauve strip bright beneath the
brightly clouded sky, the round clouds and the gentle air. 10
Along the straight canals between striped fields of tulips
    in the morning sailed
Broad ships, their hulls by tulip-beds concealed, only the sails
    showing.

It seemed that all was well with England—the harsh foreign
    voice hysterically vowing,
Once more, to keep its word, at length was disbelieved,
    and hushed.

It seemed that all was well with France, with her straight
    roads 15
Lined with slender poplars, and the peasants on the sky-
    line ploughing.

[1940]

■■ CONTEXT AND RESPONSE ■■

The Poetry of Lisel Mueller

Like Edna St. Vincent Millay's poetry, the poetry of Lisel Mueller stems
from the Modernists, a movement that searched for renewal amid
the sterile, industrialized landscape of a post–World War I world. An
American poet and translator, Mueller was born in Hamburg, Germany,
in 1924. To escape the Nazis, Mueller's family fled to the Midwestern
United States when she was 15. She won the National Book Award in
1981 for her volume of collected poems, *The Need to Hold Still* (1980).
In 1997, she won a Pulitzer Prize for *Alive Together: New and Selected
Poems*.

Mueller was strongly influenced by Millay, especially by Millay's
intensely personal later poems. Like Millay, Mueller's poetry is highly
lyrical, and like Millay, Mueller often wove together elements of myth
and fairy tale. In addition, Mueller's themes are deeply rooted in memory—both personal family memories and collective cultural memory,
especially the grim legacy of war. The following selections underscore
Mueller's respect for history and her fascination with the power of language to make meaning out of humanity's broken existence.

LISEL MUELLER ■ (1924–)

When I Am Asked

When I am asked
how I began writing poems,
I talk about the indifference of nature.

It was soon after my mother died,
a brilliant June day,   5
everything blooming.

I sat on a gray stone bench
In a lovingly planted garden,
but the day lilies were as deaf
as the ears of drunken sleepers   10
and the roses curved inward.
Nothing was black or broken
and not a leaf fell

and the sun blared endless commercials
for summer holidays.   15

I sat on a gray stone bench
ringed with the ingénue faces
of pink and white impatiens
and placed my grief
in the mouth of language,   20
the only thing that would grieve with me.

Names

A few names tell it all,
the whole incredible history
of one generation, mine;
names that we cannot manage
with a drum-roll, like Waterloo,   5
nor pitch to the eloquence
of tragic Gettysburg.

Hiroshima sticks in our throats'
we choke on the bones of Buchenwald,
spit out the stones of Berlin.   10
Who says Vietnam
burns his tongue,
and Mississippi, o Mississippi
scrubs out our mouths
till we cry mercy.   15

On Reading an Anthology of Postwar German Poetry

America saved me
and history played me false:
I was not crushed
under rubble, nor was I beaten
along a frozen highway;   5
my children are not dead
of postwar hunger;
my love is back with brain
intact, his toes accounted for;
I have coaxed no one into the chamber of death.   10

My mind is out of joint. For me
rock stands for dignity,
fire is an element, the moon
is not necessarily poisoned,
snow exists for its own sake.   15

I know enough to refuse to say
that life is good,
but I act as though it were.
And skeptical about love, I survive
by the witness of my own.   20

My habits have not been broken.
I am among these poets
a Briar Rose, a Rip Van Winkle,
a stranger to the beginnings
they make from the stench of evil,   25
the burial of Man:
I marvel, as The Word
rises from bedrock, lifts,
and splits, a living cell,
into its destinies.   30

ARCHIBALD MACLEISH ■ (1892–1982)

Archibald MacLeish was born and raised in Glencoe, Illinois. He attended Yale, graduating with a major in English in 1915, and then, after serving in the artillery in World War I, graduated first in his class from Harvard Law School.

He disliked his occupation as a lawyer in Boston, however, quit his firm in 1923, and traveled with his wife and children to Paris to focus on writing poetry. There he became part of the expatriate community that included F. Scott Fitzgerald and Ernest Hemingway.

MacLeish returned to the United States in 1928, and in the 1930s he worked for *Fortune* magazine. During World War II, he was an adviser to and a diplomat for the Roosevelt administration.

He was, in addition, Librarian of Congress from 1939 to 1944. From 1949 to 1962, MacLeish was Boylston Professor of Rhetoric and Oratory at Harvard.

MacLeish's first books, *Songs for a Summer Day (A Sonnet Cycle)* (1915) and *Tower of Ivory* (1917), comprise conventional lyrics shaped by A. C. Swinburne and other nineteenth-century poets. The poetry of the next phase of his career bears witness to the influence of T. S. Eliot and the French symbolists, such as Jules Laforgue and Stéphane Mallarmé, to whom Eliot had called attention to in his literary criticism. MacLeish's verse in the 1930s and 1940s grew patriotic and partisan (he believed that poetry should be "public speech"), championing democracy and liberalism. For this, he was criticized by modernist poets and critics, who quoted back to him his own words in "Ars Poetica" (included here): "a poem should not mean / but be."

MacLeish wrote a number of verse plays, the most notable of which, *J. B.* (1958), was a reworking of the Book of Job, and a book of critical essays, *Poetry and Experience* (1961). The highlight of his literary career was the publication of his *Collected Poems, 1915–1952* (1952), which was widely honored.

"Ars Poetica" ("The Art of Poetry") takes its Latin title from a first-century AD work by the Roman poet Horace.

For further reading and background, see *Letters of Archibald MacLeish, 1907–1982*, ed. R. H. Winnick (1983); *Archibald MacLeish: Reflections*, eds. Bernard A. Drabeck and Helen E. Ellis (1986); and Scott Donaldson, in collaboration with R. H. Winnick, *Archibald MacLeish: An American Life* (1992).

Ars Poetica

A poem should be palpable and mute
As a globed fruit,

Dumb
As old medallions to the thumb,

Silent as the sleeve-worn stone   5
Of casement ledges where the moss has grown—

A poem should be wordless
As the flight of birds.

A poem should be motionless in time
As the moon climbs,   10

Leaving, as the moon releases
Twig by twig the night-entangled trees,

Leaving, as the moon behind the winter leaves,
Memory by memory the mind—

A poem should be motionless in time   15
As the moon climbs.

A poem should be equal to:
Not true.

For all the history of grief
An empty doorway and a maple leaf.   20

For love
The leaning grasses and two lights above the sea—

A poem should not mean
But be.

[1926]

E. E. CUMMINGS ■ (1894–1962)

E. E. Cummings was born in Cambridge, Massachusetts, and received his undergraduate (1915) and master's (1916) degrees from Harvard. In 1917 he entered the ambulance corps in France, where he was mistakenly accused of treasonable activity by the French and confined for four months in a prison camp—an experience he drew upon for his first book, *The Enormous Room* (1922). The following year Cummings published his first book of poetry, *Tulips and Chimneys*, and soon followed *&* (1925), *XLI Poems* (1925), and *is 5* (1926). The author of many books of poetry, Cummings was also a playwright and an accomplished painter.

Cummings's attitude toward life is joyous and exhilarated, but he is also a stinging satirist, especially on politics and religion, celebrating (like Emerson and Thoreau) the individual and attacking oppressive doctrine and the demand for conformity. His poems are immediately recognizable because of the liberties he took, and the experiments he performed, with the conventions of line and stanza length and typography. Cummings wanted to be rebellious and energizing, sophisticated in his craft yet earnest, even naïve, and accessible and pleasure-giving as other modern poets—T. S. Eliot, for instance—were not.

Cummings delighted in the eccentricities and idiosyncrasies of his arrangements (and disarrangements) of words, grammar, and punctuation. He adopted and extended the typographical practices that the French poets Stéphane Mallarmé and Guillaume Apollinaire had displayed in some of their verse; and, even more, he learned from the cubist art of Georges Braque and Pablo Picasso, breaking up and reorganizing his verbal material on the page as the painters had reshaped and redesigned the surface of the canvas and explored the rich potential of the collage. "The day of the spoken lyric is past," Cummings asserted. "The poem which has at last taken its place does not sing itself; it builds itself, three dimensionally, gradually, subtly, in the consciousness of the experiencer."

At his best, Cummings's daring and self-delighting techniques are sprightly, witty, and stimulating, but they also led him to produce many poems that are mannered and trivial and in which he seems too clever for his own good and serenely complacent about his ideas and themes. He wrote less for the ear than for the eye; this defines both his strength—indeed, the nature of his originality—and his limitation.

Cummings is most effective when his formal innovations contend with the pressure of a real subject—a significant relationship with a parent or lover (e.g., "if there are any heavens..."), or a social or cultural issue he genuinely cares about (e.g., "Buffalo Bill's..."). Witty, affecting (if sometimes sentimental), exuberant, impudent, and entertaining, Cummings was, like Robert Frost, a favorite on college campuses during the 1950s,

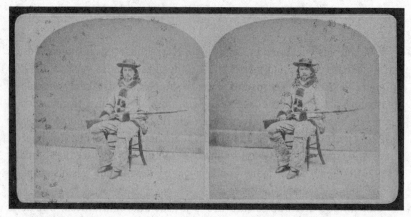

Stereograph of William Frederick "Buffalo Bill" Cody holding his rifle. Stereographs are two virtually identical images that, when viewed through a stereoscope, give a 3-D illusion. Taken by Edric L. Eaton.

and, like Frost and Langston Hughes, he remains one of the most popular American poets of the twentieth century.

For an overview, see Richard S. Kennedy, *E. E. Cummings Revisited* (1994). For biography, see Kennedy, *Dreams in the Mirror: A Biography of E. E. Cummings* (1980). For critical studies, see Norman Friedman, *E. E. Cummings: The Art of His Poetry* (1960) and *E. E. Cummings: The Growth of a Writer* (1964); and Rushworth Kidder, *E. E. Cummings: An Introduction to the Poetry* (1979). Christopher Sawyer-Lauçanno, *E. E. Cummings: A Biography* (2004); and Milton A. Cohen, *Beleaguered Poets and Leftist Critics: Stevens, Cummings, Frost, and Williams in the 1930s* (2010).

in Just-

/

in Just-
spring   when the world is mud-
luscious the little
lame balloonman

whistles   far   and wee   5

and eddieandbill come
running from marbles and
piracies and it's
spring

when the world is puddle-wonderful   10

the queer
old balloonman whistles

far   and   wee
and bettyandisbel come dancing

from hop-scotch and jump-rope and   15

it's
spring
and
 the

   goat-footed   20

balloonMan   whistles
far
and
wee
        [1920, 1923]

Buffalo Bill's

Buffalo Bill 's
defunct
  who used to
  ride a watersmooth-silver
      stallion   5
and break onetwothreefourfive pigeonsjustlikethat
        Jesus

he was a handsome man
    and what i want to know is
how do you like your blueeyed boy   10
Mister Death
        [1920, 1923]

the Cambridge ladies who live in furnished souls

the Cambridge ladies who live in furnished souls
are unbeautiful and have comfortable minds
(also,with the church's protestant blessings
daughters,unscented shapeless spirited)
they believe in Christ and Longfellow,[1] both dead,   5

[1]Henry Wadsworth Longfellow (1846–1917), American poet, educator, and linguist noted for using American themes in his poetry. Longfellow was a professor at Harvard University in Cambridge, Massachusetts.

are invariably interested in so many things—
at the present writing one still finds
delighted fingers knitting for the is it Poles?
perhaps. While permanent faces coyly bandy
scandal of Mrs. N and Professor D   10
.... the Cambridge ladies do not care, above
Cambridge if sometimes in its box of
sky lavender and cornerless, the
moon rattles like a fragment of angry candy

[1923]

next to of course god america i

"next to of course god america i
love you land of the pilgrims' and so forth oh
say can you see by the dawn's early my
country 'tis of centuries come and go
and are no more what of it we should worry   5
in every language even deafanddumb
thy sons acclaim your glorious name by gorry
by jingo by gee by gosh by gum
why talk of beauty what could be more beaut-
iful than these heroic happy dead   10
who rushed like lions to the roaring slaughter
they did not stop to think they died instead
then shall the voice of liberty be mute?"
He spoke. And drank rapidly a glass of water

[1925]

if there are any heavens my mother will
(all by herself) have

if there are any heavens my mother will (all by herself) have
one. It will not be a pansy heaven nor
a fragile heaven of lilies-of-the-valley but
it will be a heaven of blackred roses

my father will be (deep like a rose   5
tall like a rose)

standing near my

(swaying over her
silent)
with eyes which are really petals and see   10

nothing with the face of a poet really which
is a flower and not a face with
hands
which whisper
This is my beloved my   15

                     (suddenly in sunlight
he will bow,

& the whole garden will bow)

                                         [1931]

somewhere i have never travelled, gladly beyond

somewhere i have never travelled, gladly beyond
any experience, your eyes have their silence:
in your most frail gesture are things which enclose me,
or which i cannot touch because they are too near

your slightest look easily will unclose me   5
though i have closed myself as fingers,
you open always petal by petal myself as Spring opens
(touching skilfully, mysteriously) her first rose

or if your wish be to close me, i and
my life will shut very beautifully, suddenly,   10
as when the heart of this flower imagines
the snow carefully everywhere descending;

nothing which we are to perceive in this world equals
the power of your intense fragility: whose texture
compels me with the colour of its countries,   15
rendering death and forever with each breathing

(i do not know what it is about you that closes
and opens; only something in me understands
the voice of your eyes is deeper than all roses)
nobody, not even the rain, has such small hands   20

                                         [1931]

anyone lived in a pretty how town

anyone lived in a pretty how town
(with up so floating many bells down)
spring summer autumn winter
he sang his didn't he danced his did.

Women and men (both little and small)   5
cared for anyone not at all
they sowed their isn't they reaped their same
sun moon stars rain

children guessed (but only a few
and down they forgot as up they grew   10
autumn winter spring summer)
that noone loved him more by more

when by now and tree by leaf
she laughed his joy she cried his grief
bird by snow and stir by still   15
anyone's any was all to her

someones married their everyones
laughed their cryings and did their dance
(sleep wake hope and then) they
said their nevers they slept their dream   20

stars rain sun moon
(and only the snow can begin to explain
how children are apt to forget to remember
with up so floating many bells down)

one day anyone died i guess   25
(and noone stooped to kiss his face)
busy folk buried them side by side
little by little and was by was

all by all and deep by deep
and more by more they dream their sleep   30
noone and anyone earth by april
wish by spirit and if by yes.

Women and men (both dong and ding)
summer autumn winter spring
reaped their sowing and went their came   35
sun moon stars rain

[1940]

JEAN TOOMER ■ (1894–1967)

Jean Toomer's book *Cane*, which weaves together sketches, poetry, and drama, was not much of a success when it was published in 1923, selling only 500 copies. Many readers were disturbed by the work's depiction of racism, racial violence, eroticism, and miscegenation, and still others were perplexed and disoriented by the shifts in point of view and genre experimentation that reflected Toomer's attentive study of Gertrude Stein, Sherwood Anderson, and other modernists. But both at the time of publication and in subsequent decades, Toomer, through this book, exercised a significant influence on African American writers, critics, and intellectuals. Langston Hughes, Zora Neale Hurston, Sterling Brown, and, more recently, Alice Walker, Ernest Gaines, and Gloria Naylor are just a few of the significant figures in the African American tradition who learned from and adapted his style, exploration of identity, and heady blend of sexuality and spirituality.

Born in Washington, D.C., Toomer was the grandson of P. B. S. Pinchback, a noteworthy African American political leader in Louisiana during Reconstruction. After his graduation from high school, Toomer pursued college studies at a number of institutions from 1914 to 1917 while working to support himself, but he never managed to complete his degree. His potential as a writer in published poems and sketches was recognized early by the literary critic and novelist Waldo Frank and the cultural critic and literary intellectual Van Wyck Brooks. Their support and friendship were important for Toomer, but even more so was his experience as a superintendent of a school for African American children in Sparta, Georgia. His four months there, living in the community and getting to know its customs and values, inspired his book *Cane*. Its first section portrays the lives of black people in Georgia; its second turns to black urban life in Washington, D.C., and Chicago; and its third, in dramatic form, presents an educated black artist from the city living in a rural setting.

Toomer never again reached the level of artistry he displayed in *Cane*. He became absorbed in the teachings of George Ivanovich Gurdjieff (1872–1949), an Armenian spiritualist and author, then later broke with him and, having taken part for some years in the activities of the Quakers, in 1940 joined the Society of Friends.

Responding with impatience to those who urged him to return to the forms and themes of *Cane*, Toomer stated, "Why people have expected me to write a second and a third and a fourth book like *Cane* is one of the queer misunderstandings of my life." In part, the issue here is that Toomer claimed to have written *Cane* in order to settle his own racial unease and discontent, and he defined himself not as a Negro or as a "black" or as an African American but rather as an American of "Scotch, Welsh, German, English, French, Dutch, Spanish, and some dark blood." Fair-skinned himself, he thereby sought to criticize and distance himself from the aggressive inquiry into doubled racial and national identities that preoccupied such strong African American voices as W. E. B. Du Bois, Richard Wright, James Baldwin, and Ralph Ellison. The scholars Rudolph P. Byrd and Henry Louis Gates Jr., who have studied Toomer in detail, have developed the point further, calling attention to this light-skinned writer's conflicts and ambivalences about his racial identity. Byrd and Gates conclude that Toomer, "for all of his pioneering theorizing about what today we might call multicultural or mixed-raced ancestry, was a negro who decided to pass for white." On his marriage license in 1831, for example, both Toomer and Margery Latimer are identified as "white." Three years later, he stated that he was unwilling to contribute to the writer and activist Nancy Cunard's anthology *The Negro*: "though I am interested in and deeply value the Negro, I am not a Negro." In this same year, Toomer was quoted in the *Baltimore Afro-American* newspaper: "I would not consider it libelous for anyone to refer to me as a colored man, but I have not lived as one, nor do I really know whether there is colored blood in me or not." Toomer was inside and outside racial classifications; he sometimes referred to himself simply as "American," as "neither white nor black nor in-between."

"Georgia Dusk," included here, is a brooding, evocative poem, symbolic and mystical. "Fern," the story that follows it in *Cane*, tells of a beautiful, complex woman; it is also a revealing story about the point of view and feeling of the narrator, who is drawn to Fern's sensual presence. Is Fern black or white, Negro or Jewish, or something more, or different, than such categories imply? Elusive, unattainable, beyond category, Fern solicits and evades the perceptual powers of those who seek to know and contain her.

For biographical and critical contexts, see Nellie Y. McKay, *Jean Toomer, Artist: A Study of His Literary Life and Work, 1894–1936* (1984) and Cynthia Earl Kerman and Richard Eldridge, *The Lives of Jean Toomer: A Hunger for Wholeness* (1987). See also *Jean Toomer: A Critical Evaluation*, ed. Therman B. O'Daniel (1988); Charles Scruggs and Lee VanDemarr, *Jean Toomer and the Terrors of American History* (1998); and *Jean Toomer and the Harlem Renaissance*, eds. Geneviève Fabre and Michel Feith (2001). Recent studies include: Nathan Grant, *Masculinist Impulses: Toomer, Hurston, Black Writing, and Modernity* (2004); and Mark Whalan, *Race, Manhood, and Modernism in America: The Short Story Cycles of Sherwood Anderson and Jean Toomer* (2007). See also: *Jean Toomer: Selected Essays and Literary Criticism*, ed. Robert B. Jones (1996); and an important new edition of *Cane*, eds. Henry Louis Gates Jr. and Rudolph P. Byrd (2011).

Georgia Dusk

The sky, lazily disdaining to pursue
  The setting sun, too indolent to hold
  A lengthened tournament for flashing gold,
Passively darkens for night's barbecue,

A feast of moon and men and barking hounds,　　　　　5
　　An orgy for some genius of the South
　　With blood-hot eyes and cane-lipped scented mouth,
Surprised in making folk-songs from soul sounds.

The sawmill blows its whistle, buzz-saws stop,
　　And silence breaks the bud of knoll and hill,　　　10
　　Soft settling pollen where plowed lands fulfill
Their early promise of a bumper crop.

Smoke from the pyramidal sawdust pile
　　Curls up, blue ghosts of trees, tarrying low
　　Where only chips and stumps are left to show　　　15
The solid proof of former domicile.

Meanwhile, the men, with vestiges of pomp,
　　Race memories of king and caravan,
　　High-priests, an ostrich, and a juju-man,[1]
Go singing through the footpaths of the swamp.　　　20

Their voices rise . . the pine trees are guitars,
　　Strumming, pine-needles fall like sheets of rain . .
　　Their voices rise . . the chorus of the cane
Is caroling a vesper to the stars. .

O singers, resinous and soft your songs　　　　　25
　　Above the sacred whisper of the pines,
　　Give virgin lips to cornfield concubines,
Bring dreams of Christ to dusky cane-lipped throngs.

[1923]

Fern

Face flowed into her eyes. Flowed in soft cream foam and plaintive ripples, in such a way that wherever your glance may momentarily have rested, it immediately thereafter wavered in the direction of her eyes. The soft suggestion of down slightly darkened, like the shadow of a bird's wing might, the creamy brown color of her upper lip. Why, after noticing it, you sought her eyes, I cannot tell you. Her nose was aquiline, Semitic.[2] If you have heard a Jewish cantor[3] sing, if he has touched you and made your own sorrow seem trivial when compared with his, you will know my feeling when I follow the curves of her profile, like mobile rivers, to their common delta. They were

---

[1] A West African native tribesman who controls the magical charms and amulets (juju) of the tribe.
[2] Pertaining to the Semites; Jewish.
[3] Singer in religious services.

strange eyes. In this, that they sought nothing—that is, nothing that was obvious and tangible and that one could see, and they gave the impression that nothing was to be denied. When a woman seeks, you will have observed, her eyes deny. Fern's eyes desired nothing that you could give her; there was no reason why they should withhold. Men saw her eyes and fooled themselves. Fern's eyes said to them that she was easy. When she was young, a few men took her, but got no joy from it. And then, once done, they felt bound to her (quite unlike their hit and run with other girls), felt as though it would take them a lifetime to fulfill an obligation which they could find no name for. They became attached to her, and hungered after finding the barest trace of what she might desire. As she grew up, new men who came to town felt as almost everyone did who ever saw her: that they would not be denied. Men were everlastingly bringing her their bodies. Something inside of her got tired of them, I guess, for I am certain that for the life of her she could not tell why or how she began to turn them off. A man in fever is no trifling thing to send away. They began to leave her, baffled and ashamed, yet vowing to themselves that some day they would do some fine thing for her: send her candy every week and not let her know whom it came from, watch out for her wedding-day and give her a magnificent something with no name on it, buy a house and deed it to her, rescue her from some unworthy fellow who had tricked her into marrying him. As you know, men are apt to idolize or fear that which they cannot understand, especially if it be a woman. She did not deny them, yet the fact was that they were denied. A sort of superstition crept into their consciousness of her being somehow above them. Being above them meant that she was not to be approached by anyone. She became a virgin. Now a virgin in a small southern town is by no means the usual thing, if you will believe me. That the sexes were made to mate is the practice of the South. Particularly, black folks were made to mate. And it is black folks whom I have been talking about thus far. What white men thought of Fern I can arrive at only by analogy. They let her alone.

Anyone, of course, could see her, could see her eyes. If you walked up the Dixie Pike most any time of day, you'd be most like to see her resting listless-like on the railing of her porch, back propped against a post, head tilted a little forward because there was a nail in the porch post just where her head came which for some reason or other she never took the trouble to pull out. Her eyes, if it were sunset, rested idly where the sun, molten and glorious, was pouring down between the fringe of pines. Or maybe they gazed at the gray cabin on the knoll from which an evening folk-song was coming. Perhaps they followed a cow that had been turned loose to roam and feed on cotton-stalks and corn leaves. Like as not they'd settle on some vague spot above the horizon, though hardly a trace of wistfulness would come to them. If it were dusk, then they'd wait for the searchlight of the evening train which you could see miles up the track before it flared across the Dixie Pike, close to her home. Wherever they looked, you'd follow them and then waver back. Like her face, the whole country-side seemed to flow into her eyes. Flowed into them with the soft listless cadence of Georgia's South. A young Negro, once, was looking at her, spell-bound, from the road. A white man passing in a buggy had to flick him with his whip if he was to get by without running him over. I first saw her on her porch. I was passing with a fellow whose crusty numbness (I was from the North and suspected of being prejudiced and stuck-up) was melt-ing as he found me warm. I asked him who she was. "That's Fern," was all that I could get from him. Some folks already thought that I was given to nosing around; I let it go at that, so far as questions were concerned. But at first sight of her I felt as if I heard a Jewish cantor sing. As if his sing-ing rose above the unheard chorus of a folk-song. And I felt bound to her. I too had my dreams: something I would do for her. I have knocked about from town to town too much not to know the futility of mere change of place. Besides, picture if you can, this cream-colored solitary girl sitting at a tenement window looking down on the indifferent throngs of Harlem. Better that she listen to folk-songs at dusk in Georgia, you would say, and so would I. Or, suppose she came up North and married. Even a doctor or a lawyer, say, one who would be sure to get along—that is, make money. You and I know, who have had experience in such things, that love is not a thing like prejudice which can be bettered by changes of town. Could men in Washington, Chicago, or New York, more than the men of Georgia, bring her something left vacant by the bestowal of their bodies? You and I who know men in these cities will have to say, they could not. See her out and out a prostitute along State Street in Chicago. See her move into a south-ern town where white men are more aggressive. See her become a white man's concubine...Something I must do for her. There was myself. What could I do for her? Talk, of course. Push back the fringe of pines upon new horizons. To what purpose? and what for? Her? Myself? Men in her case seem to lose their selfishness. I lost mine before I touched her. I ask you, friend (it makes no difference if you sit in the Pullman[4] or the Jim Crow[5] as the train crosses her road), what thoughts would come to you—that is, after you'd finished with the thoughts that leap into men's minds at the sight of a pretty woman who will not deny them; what thoughts would come to you, had you seen her in a quick flash, keen and intuitively, as she sat there on her porch when your train thundered by? Would you have got off at the next station and come back for her to take her where? Would

---

[4]A railway car arranged as a lounge, usually with special arrangements for use as a sleeping-car.
[5]In the segregated South, African Americans were forced to sit in the Jim Crow section (the back) of railway cars and were not allowed to sit in the Pullman cars. *Jim Crow* refers to the practice of discrimi-nating against African Americans through a set of laws passed in the Southern states. The term origi-nally referred to a black character featured in nineteenth-century musical productions in which white performers wore blackface. In 1881, Tennessee passed the first Jim Crow law segregating railway cars. Other Southern states soon followed.

you have completely forgotten her as soon as you reached Macon, Atlanta, Augusta, Pasadena, Madison, Chicago, Boston, or New Orleans? Would you tell your wife or sweetheart about a girl you saw? Your thoughts can help me, and I would like to know. Something I would do for her...

One evening I walked up the Pike on purpose, and stopped to say hello. Some of her family were about, but they moved away to make room for me. Damn if I knew how to begin. Would you? Mr. and Miss So-and-So, people, the weather, the crops, the new preacher, the frolic, the church benefit, rabbit and possum hunting, the new soft drink they had at old Pap's store, the schedule of the trains, what kind of town Macon was, Negro's migration north, boll-weevils, syrup, the Bible—to all these things she gave a yassur or nassur, without further comment. I began to wonder if perhaps my own emotional sensibility had played one of its tricks on me. "Let's take a walk," I at last ventured. The suggestion, coming after so long an isolation, was novel enough, I guess, to surprise. But it wasn't that. Something told me that men before me had said just that as a prelude to the offering of their bodies. I tried to tell her with my eyes. I think she understood. The thing from her that made my throat catch, vanished. Its passing left her visible in a way I'd thought, but never seen. We walked down the Pike with people on all the porches gaping at us. "Doesn't it make you mad?" She meant the row of petty gossiping people. She meant the world. Through a cane-brake that was ripe for cutting, the branch was reached. Under a sweet-gum tree, and where reddish leaves had dammed the creek a little, we sat down. Dusk, suggesting the almost imperceptible procession of giant trees, settled with a purple haze about the cane. I felt strange, as I always do in Georgia, particularly at dusk. I felt that things unseen to men were tangibly immediate. It would not have surprised me had I had vision. People have them in Georgia more often than you would suppose. A black woman once saw the mother of Christ and drew her in charcoal on the court-house wall...When one is on the soil of one's ancestors, most anything can come to one...From force of habit, I suppose, I held Fern in my arms—that is, without at first noticing it. Then my mind came back to her. Her eyes, unusually weird and open, held me. Held God. He flowed in as I've seen the countryside flow in. Seen men. I must have done something—what, I don't know, in the confusion of my emotion. She sprang up. Rushed some distance from me. Fell to her knees, and began swaying, swaying. Her body was tortured with something it could not let out. Like boiling sap it flooded arms and fingers till she shook them as if they burned her. It found her throat, and spattered inarticulately in plaintive, convulsive sounds, mingled with calls to Christ Jesus. And then she sang, brokenly. A Jewish cantor singing with a broken voice. A child's voice, uncertain, or an old man's. Dusk hid her; I could hear only her song. It seemed to me as though she were pounding her head in anguish upon the ground. I rushed to her. She fainted in my arms.

There was talk about her fainting with me in the canefield. And I got one or two ugly looks from town men who'd set themselves up to protect her. In fact, there was talk of making me leave town. But they never did. They kept a watch-out for me, though. Shortly after, I came back North. From the train window I saw her as I crossed her road. Saw her on her porch, head tilted a little forward where the nail was, eyes vaguely focused on the sunset. Saw her face flow into them, the countryside and something that I call God, flowing into them...Nothing ever really happened. Nothing ever came to Fern, not even I. Something I would do for her. Some fine unnamed thing...And, friend, you? She is still living, I have reason to know. Her name, against the chance that you might happen down that way, is Fernie May Rosen.

[1923]

F. SCOTT FITZGERALD ■ (1896–1940)

Born in St. Paul, Minnesota, descended on his father's side from Francis Scott Key, who wrote the lyrics of "The Star-Spangled Banner," F. Scott Fitzgerald attended private and prep schools and then took an active part in literary and theatrical activities at Princeton University, where he was an undergraduate. However, he did poorly in his courses and failed to complete the requirements for his degree. He joined the army in 1917 and, while in training camp, wrote the draft of *This Side of Paradise* (originally titled "The Romantic Egotist"). The book was published in 1920 and sold 40,000 copies in six months. This novel, along with two collections of stories, *Flappers and Philosophers* (1920) and *Tales of the Jazz Age* (1922), made Fitzgerald a celebrity author. The captivating chronicler of the pleasures and perils of the 1920s compounded his image by marrying the glamorous, vivacious, and gifted Zelda Sayre (1900–48) of Montgomery, Alabama.

Fitzgerald is best known for his evocative study of the American dream of success in *The Great Gatsby* (1925), now a staple of high school and college curricula. His other books include *The Beautiful and the Damned* (1922), which treats the decline into dissipation of a self-indulgent young artist and his wife; *Tender Is the Night* (1934), a story of a psychiatrist and the wealthy patient to whom he is fatally attracted and whom he marries; *The Last Tycoon* (1941), an unfinished novel that explores the Hollywood film industry; and *The Crack-Up* (1945), a collection of notebook entries, letters, and essays assembled and edited after Fitzgerald's death by the literary critic (and his Princeton classmate) Edmund Wilson (1895–1972).

Fitzgerald's novels are uneven, and—here he differs from Hemingway and Faulkner—his work made no significant changes in the theory and practice of literary style, of the form of the novel and short story. He was highly talented, with a marvelous gift for metaphor and a disquietingly sharp feeling for decline, disappointment, despair, and psychological and emotional breakdown. But even *The Great Gatsby*, for all of its distinction, is flawed; as Fitzgerald acknowledged, Gatsby is less of a character than an idea, one that affirms and mocks, cherishes and derides, sentimentalizes and scorns the American capacity for extraordinary self-invention.

Fitzgerald wrote too much too fast, in desperate need of money to support his fast-paced lifestyle and to pay for the treatment of Zelda's mental illness, a type of schizophrenia that required her to spend many months in private sanatoriums in Europe and the United States. He knew he was abusing his talent, that he was producing a great deal that was mediocre or worse. Fascinated and repelled by his own self-absorption, he saw the limits of the illusions—about fame, wealth, status, New York, and Paris—that continued to mesmerize him.

The best of Fitzgerald's short stories is the center of his achievement; in them he pointedly portrays and examines themes he found harder to present fully and effectively in his longer works. Toward the end of his career, he said, "I have asked a lot of my emotions—one hundred and twenty stories. The price was high...because there was one little drop of something, not blood, not a tear, not my seed, but me more intimately than these, in every story, it was the extra I had."

"Babylon Revisited," here, written in December 1930 and published in the *Saturday Evening Post* in February 1931, is a compelling account of personal devastation, marital breakdown and its consequences for children, and the dire cost of narcissistic self-display and pleasure-loving excess. Charlie Wales is trying to remake himself after a period of wild parties and drunken sprees that ended in the death of his wife. Seeking to gain custody of his daughter, Charlie must convince his sister-in-law, who blames him for her sister's death, of his reform. He fails, the victim of bad timing and his own weakness.

Appearance and reality, illusion and truth—these are issues that Fitzgerald knows and describes searchingly, and in "Babylon Revisited" he succeeds in connecting the plight of his main character to the historical and cultural changes brought about when the Jazz Age broke apart amid the stock market crash of 1920 and the beginnings of the Great Depression. Wounded and ravaged in tone, "Babylon Revisited" is one of Fitzgerald's most enduring works.

Biographies include Scott Donaldson, *Fool for Love: F. Scott Fitzgerald* (1983); James R. Mellow, *Invented Lives: F. Scott and Zelda Fitzgerald* (1984); and Jeffrey Meyers, *Scott Fitzgerald: A Biography* (1994). For studies of the stories: see John Kuehl, *F. Scott Fitzgerald: A Study of the Short Fiction* (1991); *The Short Stories of F. Scott Fitzgerald: New Approaches in Criticism*, ed. Jackson R. Bryer (1982); and Alice Hall Petry, *Fitzgerald's Craft of Short Fiction: The Collected Stories, 1920–1935* (1989).

Among the many recent studies and reference works, see Mary Jo Tate, *F. Scott Fitzgerald A to Z: The Essential Reference to His Life and Work* (1998); Ronald Berman, *Fitzgerald, Hemingway, and the Twenties* (2001); Nathan Miller, *New World Coming: The 1920s and the Making of Modern America* (2003); *The Sons of Maxwell Perkins: Letters of F. Scott Fitzgerald, Ernest Hemingway, Thomas Wolfe, and Their Editor*, ed. Matthew J. Bruccoli, with Judith S. Baughman (2004); Keith Gandal, *The Gun and the Pen: Hemingway, Fitzgerald, Faulkner, and the Fiction of Mobilization* (2008); and Scott Donaldson, *Fitzgerald & Hemingway: Works and Days* (2009).

Babylon[1] Revisited

I

"And where's Mr. Campbell?" Charlie asked.

"Gone to Switzerland. Mr. Campbell's a pretty sick man, Mr. Wales."

"I'm sorry to hear that. And George Hardt?" Charlie inquired.

"Back in America, gone to work."

"And where is the Snow Bird?"

"He was in here last week. Anyway, his friend, Mr. Schaeffer, is in Paris."

Two familiar names from the long list of a year and a half ago. Charlie scribbled an address in his notebook and tore out the page.

"If you see Mr. Schaeffer, give him this," he said. "It's my brother-in-law's address. I haven't settled on a hotel yet."

He was not really disappointed to find Paris was so empty. But the stillness in the Ritz bar was strange and portentous. It was not an American bar any more—he felt polite in it, and not as if he owned it. It had gone back into France. He felt the stillness from the moment he got out of the taxi and saw the doorman, usually in a frenzy of activity at this hour, gossiping with a *chasseur*[2] by the servants' entrance.

Passing through the corridor, he heard only a single, bored voice in the once-clamorous women's room. When he turned into the bar he traveled the twenty feet of green carpet with his eyes fixed straight ahead by old habit; and then, with his foot firmly on the rail, he turned and surveyed the room, encountering only a single pair of eyes that fluttered up from a newspaper in the corner. Charlie asked for the head barman, Paul, who in the latter days of the bull market had come to work in his own custom-built car—disembarking, however, with due nicety at the nearest corner. But Paul was at his country house today and Alix giving him information.

"No, no more," Charlie said, "I'm going slow these days."

Alix congratulated him: "You were going pretty strong a couple of years ago."

"I'll stick to it all right," Charlie assured him. "I've stuck to it for over a year and a half now."

"How do you find conditions in America?"[3]

"I haven't been to America for months. I'm in business in Prague, representing a couple of concerns there. They don't know about me down there."

Alix smiled.

"Remember the night of George Hardt's bachelor dinner here?" said Charlie. "By the way, what's become of Claude Fessenden?"

[1] A magnificent city that was once the capital of the Chaldee Empire, described in the Bible as the city where the Jews were enslaved by King Nebuchadnezzar (the Babylonian Captivity). The name now refers rhetorically to any luxurious city or materialistic and sensual society.
[2] Hotel messenger, bellhop (French).
[3] The story takes place in the aftermath of the stock market crash of 1929. The men discuss the radical changes that occurred as a result of the severe financial shift of many people's fortunes.

Alix lowered his voice confidentially: "He's in Paris, but he doesn't come here any more. Paul doesn't allow it. He ran up a bill of thirty thousand francs, charging all his drinks and his lunches, and usually his dinner, for more than a year. And when Paul finally told him he had to pay, he gave him a bad check."

Alix shook his head sadly.

"I don't understand it, such a dandy fellow. Now he's all bloated up—" He made a plump apple of his hands.

Charlie watched a group of strident queens installing themselves in a corner.

"Nothing affects them," he thought. "Stocks rise and fall, people loaf or work, but they go on forever." The place oppressed him. He called for the dice and shook with Alix for the drink.

"Here for long, Mr. Wales?"

"I'm here for four or five days to see my little girl."

"Oh-h! You have a little girl?"

Outside, the fire-red, gas-blue, ghost-green signs shone smokily through the tranquil rain. It was late afternoon and the streets were in movement; the *bistros*[4] gleamed. At the corner of the Boulevard des Capucines he took a taxi. The Place de la Concorde moved by in pink majesty; they crossed the logical Seine, and Charlie felt the sudden provincial quality of the left bank.[5]

Charlie directed his taxi to the Avenue de l'Opera, which was out of his way. But he wanted to see the blue hour spread over the magnificent façade, and imagine that the cab horns, playing endlessly the first few bars of *Le Plus que Lent*,[6] were the trumpets of the Second Empire. They were closing the iron grill in front of Brentano's Book-store, and people were already at dinner behind the trim little bourgeois hedge of Duval's. He had never eaten at a really cheap restaurant in Paris. Five-course dinner, four francs fifty, eighteen cents, wine included. For some odd reason he wished that he had.

As they rolled on to the Left Bank and he felt its sudden provincialism, he thought, "I spoiled this city for myself. I didn't realize it, but the days came along one after another, and then two years were gone, and everything was gone, and I was gone."

He was thirty-five, and good to look at. The Irish mobility of his face was sobered by a deep wrinkle between his eyes. As he rang his brother-in-law's bell in the Rue Palatine, the wrinkle deepened till it pulled down his brows; he felt a cramping sensation in his belly. From behind the maid who opened the door darted a lovely little girl of nine who shrieked "Daddy!"

[4]Small restaurants.
[5]Paris is divided by the Seine River. The right bank is more cosmopolitan, while the left bank is more quiet and provincial.
[6]A slow piano waltz by the French composer Claude Debussy (1862–1918).

and flew up, struggling like a fish, into his arms. She pulled his head around by one ear and set her cheek against his.

"My old pie," he said.

"Oh, daddy, daddy, daddy, daddy, dads, dads, dads!"

She drew him into the salon, where the family waited, a boy and a girl his daughter's age, his sister-in-law and her husband. He greeted Marion with his voice pitched carefully to avoid either feigned enthusiasm or dislike, but her response was more frankly tepid, though she minimized her expression of unalterable distrust by directing her regard toward his child. The two men clasped hands in a friendly way and Lincoln Peters rested his for a moment on Charlie's shoulder.

The room was warm and comfortably American. The three children moved intimately about, playing through the yellow oblongs that led to other rooms; the cheer of six o'clock spoke in the eager smacks of the fire and the sounds of French activity in the kitchen. But Charlie did not relax; his heart sat up rigidly in his body and he drew confidence from his daughter, who from time to time came close to him, holding in her arms the doll he had brought.

"Really extremely well," he declared in answer to Lincoln's question. "There's a lot of business there that isn't moving at all, but we're doing even better than ever. In fact, damn well. I'm bringing my sister over from America next month to keep house for me. My income last year was bigger than it was when I had money. You see, the Czechs—"

His boasting was for a specific purpose; but after a moment, seeing a faint restiveness in Lincoln's eye, he changed the subject.

"Those are fine children of yours, well brought up, good manners."

"We think Honoria's a great little girl too."

Marion Peters came back from the kitchen. She was a tall woman with worried eyes, who had once possessed a fresh American loveliness. Charlie had never been sensitive to it and was always surprised when people spoke of how pretty she had been. From the first there had been an instinctive antipathy between them.

"Well, how do you find Honoria?" she asked.

"Wonderful. I was astonished how much she's grown in ten months. All the children are looking well."

'We haven't had a doctor for a year. How do you like being back in Paris?"

"It seems very funny to see so few Americans around."

"I'm delighted," Marion said vehemently. "Now at least you can go into a store without their assuming you're a millionaire. We've suffered like everybody, but on the whole it's a good deal pleasanter."

"But it was nice while it lasted," Charlie said. "We were a sort of royalty, almost infallible, with a sort of magic around us. In the bar this afternoon"— he stumbled, seeing his mistake—"there wasn't a man I knew."

She looked at him keenly. "I should think you'd have had enough of bars."

"I only stayed a minute. I take one drink every afternoon, and no more."

"Don't you want a cocktail before dinner?" Lincoln asked.

"I take only one drink every afternoon, and I've had that."

"I hope you keep to it," said Marion.

Her dislike was evident in the coldness with which she spoke, but Charlie only smiled; he had larger plans. Her very aggressiveness gave him an advantage, and he knew enough to wait. He wanted them to initiate the discussion of what they knew had brought him to Paris.

At dinner he couldn't decide whether Honoria was most like him or her mother. Fortunate if she didn't combine the traits of both that had brought them to disaster. A great wave of protectiveness went over him. He thought he knew what to do for her. He believed in character; he wanted to jump back a whole generation and trust in character again as the eternally valuable element. Everything else wore out.

He left soon after dinner, but not to go home. He was curious to see Paris by night with clearer and more judicious eyes than those of other days. He bought a *strapontin*[7] for the Casino and watched Josephine Baker[8] go through her chocolate arabesques.

After an hour he left and strolled toward Montmartre, up the Rue Pigalle into the Place Blanche. The rain had stopped and there were a few people in evening clothes disembarking from taxis in front of cabarets, and *cocottes*[9] prowling singly or in pairs, and many Negroes. He passed a lighted door from which issued music, and stopped with the sense of familiarity; it was Bricktop's, where he had parted with so many hours and so much money. A few doors farther on he found another ancient rendezvous and incautiously put his head inside. Immediately an eager orchestra burst into sound, a pair of professional dancers leaped to their feet and a maître d'hôtel swooped toward him, crying, "Crowd just arriving, sir!" But he withdrew quickly.

"You have to be damn drunk," he thought.

Zelli's was closed, the bleak and sinister cheap hotels surrounding it were dark; up in the Rue Blanche there was more light and a local, colloquial French crowd. The Poet's Cave had disappeared, but the two great mouths of the Café of Heaven and the Café of Hell still yawned— even devoured, as he watched, the meager contents of a tourist bus—a German, a Japanese, and an American couple who glanced at him with frightened eyes.

So much for the effort and ingenuity of Montmartre. All the catering to vice and waste was on an utterly childish scale, and he suddenly realized

---

[7]A folding chair (French).
[8]An African American jazz singer and dancer (1906–75) who starred in several Paris productions.
[9]Coquettes; prostitutes (French).

the meaning of the word "dissipate"—to dissipate into thin air; to make nothing out of something. In the little hours of the night every move from place to place was an enormous human jump, an increase of paying for the privilege of slower and slower motion.

He remembered thousand-franc notes given to an orchestra for playing a single number, hundred-franc notes tossed to a doorman for calling a cab.

But it hadn't been given for nothing.

It had been given, even the most wildly squandered sum, as an offering to destiny that he might not remember the things most worth remembering, the things that now he would always remember—his child taken from his control, his wife escaped to a grave in Vermont.

In the glare of a *brasserie*[10] a woman spoke to him. He bought her some eggs and coffee, and then, eluding her encouraging stare, gave her a twenty-franc note and took a taxi to his hotel.

II

He woke upon a fine fall day—football weather. The depression of yesterday was gone and he liked the people on the streets. At noon he sat opposite Honoria at Le Grand Vatel, the only restaurant he could think of not reminiscent of champagne dinners and long luncheons that began at two and ended in a blurred and vague twilight.

"Now, how about vegetables? Oughtn't you to have some vegetables?"

"Well, yes."

"Here's *épinards* and *chou-fleur* and carrots and *haricots*."[11]

"I'd like *chou-fleur*."

"Wouldn't you like to have two vegetables?"

"I usually only have one at lunch." The waiter was pretending to be inordinately fond of children. "*Qu'elle est mignonne la petite! Elle parle exactement comme une Française.*"[12]

"How about dessert? Shall we wait and see?"

The waiter disappeared. Honoria looked at her father expectantly.

"What are we going to do?"

"First, we're going to that toy store in the Rue Saint-Honoré and buy you anything you like. And then we're going to the vaudeville at the Empire."

She hesitated. "I like it about the vaudeville, but not the toy store."

"Why not?"

"Well, you brought me this doll." She had it with her. "And I've got lots of things. And we're not rich any more, are we?"

"We never were. But today you are to have anything you want."

"All right," she agreed resignedly.

---

[10]A restaurant and bar specializing in common cuisine.
[11]Spinach; *Chou-Fleur*: Cauliflower; *Haricots*: Green beans (French).
[12]How cute she is! She speaks just like a French girl! (French)

When there had been her mother and a French nurse he had been inclined to be strict; now he extended himself, reached out for a new tolerance; he must be both parents to her and not shut any of her out of communication.

"I want to get to know you," he said gravely. "First let me introduce myself. My name is Charles J. Wales, of Prague."

"Oh, daddy!" her voice cracked with laughter.

"And who are you, please?" he persisted, and she accepted a rôle immediately: "Honoria Wales, Rue Palatine, Paris."

"Married or single?"

"No, not married. Single."

He indicated the doll. "But I see you have a child, madame."

Unwilling to disinherit it, she took it to her heart and thought quickly: "Yes, I've been married, but I'm not married now. My husband is dead."

He went on quickly, "And the child's name?"

"Simone. That's after my best friend at school."

"I'm very pleased that you're doing so well at school."

"I'm third this month," she boasted. "Elsie"—that was her cousin—"is only about eighteenth, and Richard is about at the bottom."

"You like Richard and Elsie, don't you?"

"Oh, yes. I like Richard quite well and I like her all right."

Cautiously and casually he asked: "And Aunt Marion and Uncle Lincoln—which do you like best?"

"Oh, Uncle Lincoln, I guess."

He was increasingly aware of her presence. As they came in, a murmur of "...adorable" followed them, and now the people at the next table bent all their silences upon her, staring as if she were something no more conscious than a flower.

"Why don't I live with you?" she asked suddenly. "Because mamma's dead?"

"You must stay here and learn more French. It would have been hard for daddy to take care of you so well."

"I don't really need much taking care of any more. I do everything for myself."

Going out of the restaurant, a man and a woman unexpectedly hailed him.

"Well, the old Wales!"

"Hello there, Lorraine....Dunc."

Sudden ghosts out of the past: Duncan Schaeffer, a friend from college. Lorraine Quarrles, a lovely, pale blonde of thirty; one of a crowd who had helped them make months into days in the lavish times of three years ago.

"My husband couldn't come this year," she said, in answer to his question. "We're poor as hell. So he gave me two hundred a month and told me I could do my worst on that....This your little girl?"

"What about coming back and sitting down?" Duncan asked.

"Can't do it." He was glad for an excuse. As always, he felt Lorraine's passionate, provocative attraction, but his own rhythm was different now.

"Well, how about dinner?" she asked.

"I'm not free. Give me your address and let me call you."

"Charlie, I believe you're sober," she said judicially. "I honestly believe he's sober, Dunc. Pinch him and see if he's sober."

Charlie indicated Honoria with his head. They both laughed.

"What's your address?" said Duncan skeptically.

He hesitated, unwilling to give the name of his hotel.

"I'm not settled yet. I'd better call you. We're going to see the vaudeville at the Empire."

"There! That's what I want to do," Lorraine said. "I want to see some clowns and acrobats and jugglers. That's just what we'll do, Dunc."

"We've got to do an errand first," said Charlie. "Perhaps we'll see you there."

"All right, you snob....Good-by, beautiful little girl."

"Good-by."

Honoria bobbed politely.

Somehow, an unwelcome encounter. They liked him because he was functioning, because he was serious; they wanted to see him, because he was stronger than they were now, because they wanted to draw a certain sustenance from his strength.

At the Empire, Honoria proudly refused to sit upon her father's folded coat. She was already an individual with a code of her own, and Charlie was more and more absorbed by the desire of putting a little of himself into her before she crystallized utterly. It was hopeless to try to know her in so short a time.

Between the acts they came upon Duncan and Lorraine in the lobby where the band was playing.

"Have a drink?"

"All right, but not up at the bar. We'll take a table."

"The perfect father."

Listening abstractedly to Lorraine, Charlie watched Honoria's eyes leave their table, and he followed them wistfully about the room, wondering what they saw. He met her glance and she smiled.

"I liked that lemonade," she said.

What had she said? What had he expected? Going home in a taxi afterward, he pulled her over until her head rested against his chest.

"Darling, do you ever think about your mother?"

"Yes, sometimes," she answered vaguely.

"I don't want you to forget her. Have you got a picture of her?"

"Yes, I think so. Anyhow, Aunt Marion has. Why don't you want me to forget her?"

"She loved you very much."

"I loved her too."

They were silent for a moment.

"Daddy, I want to come and live with you," she said suddenly. His heart leaped; he had wanted it to come like this.

"Aren't you perfectly happy?"

"Yes, but I love you better than anybody. And you love me better than anybody, don't you, now that mummy's dead?"

"Of course I do. But you won't always like me best, honey. You'll grow up and meet somebody your own age and go marry him and forget you ever had a daddy."

"Yes, that's true," she agreed tranquilly.

He didn't go in. He was coming back at nine o'clock and he wanted to keep himself fresh and new for the thing he must say then.

"When you're safe inside, just show yourself in that window."

"All right. Good-by, dads, dads, dads, dads."

He waited in the dark street until she appeared, all warm and glowing, in the window above and kissed her fingers out into the night.

III

They were waiting. Marion sat behind the coffee service in a dignified black dinner dress that just faintly suggested mourning. Lincoln was walking up and down with the animation of one who had already been talking. They were as anxious as he was to get into the question. He opened it almost immediately:

"I suppose you know what I want to see you about—why I really came to Paris."

Marion played with the black stars on her necklace and frowned.

"I'm awfully anxious to have a home," he continued. "And I'm awfully anxious to have Honoria in it. I appreciate your taking in Honoria for her mother's sake, but things have changed now"—he hesitated and then continued more forcibly—"changed radically with me, and I want to ask you to reconsider the matter. It would be silly for me to deny that about three years ago I was acting badly—"

Marion looked up at him with hard eyes.

"—but all that's over. As I told you, I haven't had more than a drink a day for over a year, and I take that drink deliberately, so that the idea of alcohol won't get too big in my imagination. You see the idea?"

"No," said Marion succinctly.

"It's a sort of stunt I set myself. It keeps the matter in proportion."

"I get you," said Lincoln. "You don't want to admit it's got any attraction for you."

"Something like that. Sometimes I forget and don't take it. But I try to take it. Anyhow, I couldn't afford to drink in my position. The people I represent are more than satisfied with what I've done, and I'm bringing my sister over from Burlington to keep house for me, and I want awfully to have Honoria too. You know that even when her mother and I weren't getting along well we never let anything that happened touch Honoria. I know she's fond of me and I know I'm able to take care of her and—well, there you are. How do you feel about it?"

He knew that now he would have to take a beating. It would last an hour or two hours, and it would be difficult, but if he modulated his inevitable resentment to the chastened attitude of the reformed sinner, he might win his point in the end.

Keep your temper, he told himself. You don't want to be justified. You want Honoria.

Lincoln spoke first: "We've been talking it over ever since we got your letter last month. We're happy to have Honoria here. She's a dear little thing, and we're glad to be able to help her, but of course that isn't the question——"

Marion interrupted suddenly. "How long are you going to stay sober, Charlie?" she asked.

"Permanently, I hope."

"How can anybody count on that?"

"You know I never did drink heavily until I gave up business and came over here with nothing to do. Then Helen and I began to run around with——"

"Please leave Helen out of it. I can't bear to hear you talk about her like that."

He stared at her grimly; he had never been certain how fond of each other the sisters were in life.

"My drinking only lasted about a year and a half—from the time we came over until I—collapsed."

"It was time enough."

"It was time enough," he agreed.

"My duty is entirely to Helen," she said. "I try to think what she would have wanted me to do. Frankly, from the night you did that terrible thing you haven't really existed for me. I can't help that. She was my sister."

"Yes."

"When she was dying she asked me to look out for Honoria. If you hadn't been in a sanitarium then, it might have helped matters."

He had no answer.

"I'll never in my life be able to forget the morning when Helen knocked at my door, soaked to the skin and shivering, and said you'd locked her out."

Charlie gripped the sides of the chair. This was more difficult than he expected; he wanted to launch out into a long expostulation and explanation, but he only said: "The night I locked her out—" and she interrupted, "I don't feel up to going over that again."

After a moment's silence Lincoln said: "We're getting off the subject. You want Marion to set aside her legal guardianship and give you Honoria. I think the main point for her is whether she has confidence in you or not."

"I don't blame Marion," Charlie said slowly, "but I think she can have entire confidence in me. I had a good record up to three years ago. Of course, it's within human possibilities I might go wrong any time. But if we wait much longer I'll lose Honoria's childhood and my chance for a home." He shook his head, "I'll simply lose her, don't you see?"

"Yes, I see," said Lincoln.

"Why didn't you think of all this before?" Marion asked.

"I suppose I did, from time to time, but Helen and I were getting along badly. When I consented to the guardianship, I was flat on my back in a sanitarium and the market had cleaned me out. I knew I'd acted badly, and I thought if it would bring any peace to Helen, I'd agree to anything. But now it's different. I'm functioning, I'm behaving damn well, so far as——"

"Please don't swear at me," Marion said.

He looked at her, startled. With each remark the force of her dislike became more and more apparent. She had built up all her fear of life into one wall and faced it toward him. This trivial reproof was possibly the result of some trouble with the cook several hours before. Charlie became increasingly alarmed at leaving Honoria in this atmosphere of hostility against himself; sooner or later it would come out, in a word here, a shake of the head there, and some of that distrust would be irrevocably implanted in Honoria. But he pulled his temper down out of his face and shut it up inside him; he had won a point, for Lincoln realized the absurdity of Marion's remark and asked her lightly since when she had objected to the word "damn."

"Another thing," Charlie said: "I'm able to give her certain advantages now. I'm going to take a French governess to Prague with me. I've got a lease on a new apartment——"

He stopped, realizing that he was blundering. They couldn't be expected to accept with equanimity the fact that his income was again twice as large as their own.

"I suppose you can give her more luxuries than we can," said Marion. "When you were throwing away money we were living along watching every ten francs....I suppose you'll start doing it again."

"Oh, no," he said. "I've learned. I worked hard for ten years, you know—until I got lucky in the market, like so many people. Terribly lucky. It didn't seem any use working any more, so I quit."

There was a long silence. All of them felt their nerves straining, and for the first time in a year Charlie wanted a drink. He was sure now that Lincoln Peters wanted him to have his child.

Marion shuddered suddenly; part of her saw that Charlie's feet were planted on the earth now, and her own maternal feeling recognized the naturalness of his desire; but she had lived for a long time with a prejudice— a prejudice founded on a curious disbelief in her sister's happiness, and which, in the shock of one terrible night, had turned to hatred for him.

It had all happened at a point in her life where the discouragement of ill health and adverse circumstances made it necessary for her to believe in tangible villainy and a tangible villain.

"I can't help what I think!" she cried out suddenly. "How much you were responsible for Helen's death, I don't know. It's something you'll have to square with your own conscience."

An electric current of agony surged through him; for a moment he was almost on his feet, an unuttered sound echoing in his throat. He hung on to himself for a moment, another moment.

"Hold on there," said Lincoln uncomfortably. "I never thought you were responsible for that."

"Helen died of heart trouble," Charlie said dully.

"Yes, heart trouble." Marion spoke as if the phrase had another meaning for her.

Then, in the flatness that followed her outburst, she saw him plainly and she knew he had somehow arrived at control over the situation. Glancing at her husband, she found no help from him, and as abruptly as if it were a matter of no importance, she threw up the sponge.

"Do what you like!" she cried, springing up from her chair. "She's your child. I'm not the person to stand in your way. I think if it were my child I'd rather see her—"She managed to check herself. "You two decide it. I can't stand this. I'm sick. I'm going to bed."

She hurried from the room; after a moment Lincoln said:

"This has been a hard day for her. You know how strongly she feels—" His voice was almost apologetic: "When a woman gets an idea in her head."

"Of course."

"It's going to be all right. I think she sees now that you—can provide for the child, and so we can't very well stand in your way or Honoria's way."

"Thank you, Lincoln."

"I'd better go along and see how she is."

"I'm going."

He was still trembling when he reached the street, but a walk down the Rue Bonaparte to the *quais*[13] set him up, and as he crossed the Seine, fresh and new by the *quai* lamps, he felt exultant. But back in his room he couldn't sleep. The image of Helen haunted him. Helen whom he had loved so until they had senselessly begun to abuse each other's love, tear it into shreds. On that terrible February night that Marion remembered so vividly, a slow quarrel had gone on for hours. There was a scene at the Florida, and then he attempted to take her home, and then she kissed young Webb at a table; after that there was what she had hysterically said. When he arrived home alone he turned the key in the lock in wild anger. How could he know she would arrive an hour later alone, that there would be a snowstorm in

---

[13]Quay; a paved bank by a waterway (French).

which she wandered about in slippers, too confused to find a taxi? Then the aftermath, her escaping pneumonia by a miracle, and all the attendant horror. They were "reconciled," but that was the beginning of the end, and Marion, who had seen with her own eyes and who imagined it to be one of many scenes from her sister's martyrdom, never forgot.

Going over it again brought Helen nearer, and in the white, soft light that steals upon half sleep near morning he found himself talking to her again. She said that he was perfectly right about Honoria and that she wanted Honoria to be with him. She said she was glad he was being good and doing better. She said a lot of other things—very friendly things—but she was in a swing in a white dress, and swinging faster and faster all the time, so that at the end he could not hear clearly all that she said.

IV

He woke up feeling happy. The door of the world was open again. He made plans, vistas, futures for Honoria and himself, but suddenly he grew sad, remembering all the plans he and Helen had made. She had not planned to die. The present was the thing—work to do and someone to love. But not to love too much, for he knew the injury that a father can do to a daughter or a mother to a son by attaching them too closely: afterward, out in the world, the child would seek in the marriage partner the same blind tenderness and, failing probably to find it, turn against love and life.

It was another bright, crisp day. He called Lincoln Peters at the bank where he worked and asked if he could count on taking Honoria when he left for Prague. Lincoln agreed that there was no reason for delay. One thing—the legal guardianship. Marion wanted to retain that a while longer. She was upset by the whole matter, and it would oil things if she felt that the situation was still in her control for another year. Charlie agreed, wanting only the tangible, visible child.

Then the question of a governess. Charles sat in a gloomy agency and talked to a cross Béarnaise and to a buxom Breton[14] peasant, neither of whom he could have endured. There were others whom he would see tomorrow.

He lunched with Lincoln Peters at Griffons, trying to keep down his exultation.

"There's nothing quite like your own child," Lincoln said. "But you understand how Marion feels too."

"She's forgotten how hard I worked for seven years there," Charlie said. "She just remembers one night."

"There's another thing." Lincoln hesitated. "While you and Helen were tearing around Europe throwing money away, we were just getting along. I didn't touch any of the prosperity because I never got ahead enough

[14]Natives of Béarn and Breton, two regions of the rustic French countryside.

to carry anything but my insurance. I think Marion felt there was some kind of injustice in it—you not even working toward the end, and getting richer and richer."

"It went just as quick as it came," said Charlie.

"Yes, a lot of it stayed in the hands of *chasseurs* and saxophone players and maîtres d'hôtel—well, the big party's over now. I just said that to explain Marion's feeling about those crazy years. If you drop in about six o'clock tonight before Marion's too tired, we'll settle the details on the spot."

Back at his hotel, Charlie found a *pneumatique*[15] that had been redirected from the Ritz bar where Charlie had left his address for the purpose of finding a certain man.

> "DEAR CHARLIE: You were so strange when we saw you the other day that I wondered if I did something to offend you. If so, I'm not conscious of it. In fact, I have thought about you too much for the last year, and it's always been in the back of my mind that I might see you if I came over here. We *did* have such good times that crazy spring, like the night you and I stole the butcher's tricycle, and the time we tried to call on the president and you had the old derby rim and the wire cane. Everybody seems so old lately, but I don't feel old a bit. Couldn't we get together some time today for old time's sake? I've got a vile hang-over for the moment, but will be feeling better this afternoon and will look for you about five in the sweatshop at the Ritz.
>
> > Always devotedly,
> > LORRAINE."

His first feeling was one of awe that he had actually, in his mature years, stolen a tricycle and pedaled Lorraine all over the étoile between the small hours and dawn. In retrospect it was a nightmare. Locking out Helen didn't fit in with any other act of his life, but the tricycle incident did—it was one of many. How many weeks or months of dissipation to arrive at that condition of utter irresponsibility?

He tried to picture how Lorraine had appeared to him then—very attractive; Helen was unhappy about it, though she said nothing. Yesterday, in the restaurant, Lorraine had seemed trite, blurred, worn away. He emphatically did not want to see her, and he was glad Alix had not given away his hotel address. It was a relief to think, instead, of Honoria, to think of Sundays spent with her and of saying good morning to her and of knowing she was there in his house at night, drawing her breath in the darkness.

At five he took a taxi and bought presents for all the Peters—a piquant cloth doll, a box of Roman soldiers, flowers for Marion, big linen handkerchiefs for Lincoln.

---

[15] A message sent via the pneumatic dispatch system in Paris, which sent letters or messages by means of compressed air tubes.

He saw, when he arrived in the apartment, that Marion had accepted the inevitable. She greeted him now as though he were a recalcitrant member of the family, rather than a menacing outsider. Honoria had been told she was going; Charlie was glad to see that her tact made her conceal her excessive happiness. Only on his lap did she whisper her delight and the question "When?" before she slipped away with the other children.

He and Marion were alone for a minute in the room, and on an impulse he spoke out boldly:

"Family quarrels are bitter things. They don't go according to any rules. They're not like aches or wounds; they're more like splits in the skin that won't heal because there's not enough material. I wish you and I could be on better terms."

"Some things are hard to forget," she answered. "It's a question of confidence." There was no answer to this and presently she asked, "When do you propose to take her?"

"As soon as I can get a governess. I hoped the day after tomorrow."

"That's impossible. I've got to get her things in shape. Not before Saturday."

He yielded. Coming back into the room, Lincoln offered him a drink.

"I'll take my daily whisky," he said.

It was warm here, it was a home, people together by a fire. The children felt very safe and important; the mother and father were serious, watchful. They had things to do for the children more important than his visit here. A spoonful of medicine was, after all, more important than the strained relations between Marion and himself. They were not dull people, but they were very much in the grip of life and circumstances. He wondered if he couldn't do something to get Lincoln out of his rut at the bank.

A long peal at the door-bell; the *bonne à tout faire*[16] passed through and went down the corridor. The door opened upon another long ring, and then voices, and the three in the salon looked up expectantly; Richard moved to bring the corridor within his range of vision, and Marion rose. Then the maid came back along the corridor, closely followed by the voices, which developed under the light into Duncan Schaeffer and Lorraine Quarrles.

They were gay, they were hilarious, they were roaring with laughter. For a moment Charlie was astounded; unable to understand how they ferreted out the Peters' address.

"Ah-h-h!" Duncan wagged his finger roguishly at Charlie. "Ah-h-h!"

They both slid down another cascade of laughter. Anxious and at a loss, Charlie shook hands with them quickly and presented them to Lincoln and Marion. Marion nodded, scarcely speaking. She had drawn back a step

[16]A maid of all work (French).

toward the fire; her little girl stood beside her, and Marion put an arm about her shoulder.

With growing annoyance at the intrusion, Charlie waited for them to explain themselves. After some concentration Duncan said:

"We came to invite you out to dinner. Lorraine and I insist that all this chi-chi, cagy business 'bout your address got to stop."

Charlie came closer to them, as if to force them backward down the corridor.

"Sorry, but I can't. Tell me where you'll be and I'll phone you in half an hour."

This made no impression. Lorraine sat down suddenly on the side of a chair, and focusing her eyes on Richard, cried, "Oh, what a nice little boy! Come here, little boy." Richard glanced at his mother, but did not move. With a perceptible shrug of her shoulders, Lorraine turned back to Charlie:

"Come and dine. Sure your cousins won' mine. See you so sel'om. Or solemn."

"I can't," said Charlie sharply. "You two have dinner and I'll phone you."

Her voice became suddenly unpleasant. "All right, we'll go. But I remember once when you hammered on my door at four A.M. I was enough of a good sport to give you a drink. Come on, Dunc."

Still in slow motion, with blurred, angry faces, with uncertain feet, they retired along the corridor.

"Good night," Charlie said.

"Good night!" responded Lorraine emphatically.

When he went back into the salon Marion had not moved, only now her son was standing in the circle of her other arm. Lincoln was still swinging Honoria back and forth like a pendulum from side to side.

"What an outrage!" Charlie broke out. "What an absolute outrage!"

Neither of them answered. Charlie dropped into an armchair, picked up his drink, set it down again and said:

"People I haven't seen for two years having the colossal nerve——"

He broke off. Marion had made the sound "Oh!" in one swift, furious breath, turned her body from him with a jerk and left the room.

Lincoln set down Honoria carefully.

"You children go in and start your soup," he said, and when they obeyed, he said to Charlie:

"Marion's not well and she can't stand shocks. That kind of people make her really physically sick."

"I didn't tell them to come here. They wormed your name out of somebody. They deliberately——"

"Well, it's too bad. It doesn't help matters. Excuse me a minute."

Left alone, Charlie sat tense in his chair. In the next room he could hear the children eating, talking in monosyllables, already oblivious to the scene between their elders. He heard a murmur of conversation from a farther room and then the ticking bell of a telephone receiver picked up, and in a panic he moved to the other side of the room and out of earshot.

In a minute Lincoln came back. "Look here, Charlie. I think we'd better call off dinner for tonight. Marion's in bad shape."

"Is she angry with me?"

"Sort of," he said, almost roughly. "She's not strong and—"

"You mean she's changed her mind about Honoria?"

"She's pretty bitter right now. I don't know. You phone me at the bank tomorrow."

"I wish you'd explain to her I never dreamed these people would come here. I'm just as sore as you are."

"I couldn't explain anything to her now."

Charlie got up. He took his coat and hat and started down the corridor. Then he opened the door of the dining room and said in a strange voice, "Good night, children."

Honoria rose and ran around the table to hug him.

"Good night, sweetheart," he said vaguely, and then trying to make his voice more tender, trying to conciliate something, "Good night, dear children."

V

Charlie went directly to the Ritz bar with the furious idea of finding Lorraine and Duncan, but they were not there, and he realized that in any case there was nothing he could do. He had not touched his drink at the Peters', and now he ordered a whisky-and-soda. Paul came over to say hello.

"It's a great change," he said sadly. "We do about half the business we did. So many fellows I hear about back in the States lost everything, maybe not in the first crash, but then in the second. Your friend George Hardt lost every cent, I hear. Are you back in the States?"

"No, I'm in business in Prague."

"I heard that you lost a lot in the crash."

"I did," and he added grimly, "but I lost everything I wanted in the boom."

"Selling short."

"Something like that."

Again the memory of those days swept over him like a nightmare—the people they had met travelling; then people who couldn't add a row of figures or speak a coherent sentence. The little man Helen had consented to dance with at the ship's party, who had insulted her ten feet from the table; the women and girls carried screaming with drink or drugs out of public places——

—The men who locked their wives out in the snow, because the snow of twenty-nine wasn't real snow. If you didn't want it to be snow, you just paid some money.

He went to the phone and called the Peters' apartment; Lincoln answered.

"I called up because this thing is on my mind. Has Marion said anything definite?"

"Marion's sick," Lincoln answered shortly. "I know this thing isn't altogether your fault, but I can't have her go to pieces about it. I'm afraid we'll have to let it slide for six months; I can't take the chance of working her up to this state again."

"I see."

"I'm sorry, Charlie."

He went back to his table. His whisky glass was empty, but he shook his head when Alix looked at it questioningly. There wasn't much he could do now except send Honoria some things; he would send her a lot of things tomorrow. He thought rather angrily that this was just money—he had given so many people money....

"No, no more," he said to another waiter. "What do I owe you?"

He would come back some day; they couldn't make him pay forever. But he wanted his child, and nothing was much good now, beside that fact. He wasn't young any more, with a lot of nice thoughts and dreams to have by himself. He was absolutely sure Helen wouldn't have wanted him to be so alone.

[1931]

LOUISE BOGAN ■ (1897–1970)

Born in Livermore Falls, Maine, Louise Bogan was raised in New England mill towns and suffered from the animosity between her parents. One of her brothers was killed in World War I, and her other brother later died from the effects of alcoholism. Her first poems were composed when she was a high school student in Boston; by then she was already an avid, attentive reader of literature old and new, and her early poems show the influence of the Victorian poets A. C. Swinburne and Christina Rossetti.

In 1919, separating from the husband she had married in 1916, Bogan moved to New York City to focus on a career as a writer. She became friends with a number of aspiring poets and critics, including the man of letters Edmund Wilson, who encouraged her efforts as a book reviewer. Bogan remarried in 1925, but this marriage, too, was difficult and troubled (it ended in 1937), and it made worse the periods of depression that afflicted her throughout her life.

Bogan has been undervalued as a poet, and perhaps she contributed somewhat to this herself; "minor art," she noted with an eye toward her own work, "needs to be hard, condensed, and durable." Omit the term "minor," however, and one has a characterization of Bogan's poetry at its best. Her poetry is finely wrought and focused, structured with a discipline and concentrated force that recalls John Donne and the metaphysical poets of the seventeenth century. Her first book of poems, *Body of This Death*, was published in 1923; even better were the next two, *Dark Summer* (1929) and *The Sleeping Fury* (1937).

Of the poems given below, "Medusa" displays Bogan's skill in her craft, as she expresses her intense visions of female identity and the strengths and limits of a woman's power, and of her freedom. Beneath the controlled surface, Bogan's feelings about love, loss, sorrow, and pain are charged and provocative; as the poet Adrienne Rich noted, there is often a " 'sleeping fury' beneath "the severe, lyrical mode."

Bogan reviewed poetry for *The New Yorker* from the 1930s through the 1960s, and her excellent literary criticism merits attention. Her *Achievement in American Poetry, 1900–1950* (1951) is rewarding, as are the pieces gathered in *A Poet's Alphabet: Reflections on the Literary Art and Vocation*, eds. Robert Phelps and Ruth Limmer (1970). The poet-critic W. H. Auden remarked that Bogan was the best poetry critic in the United States.

The Blue Estuaries: Poems, 1923–1968 (1968; rpt. 1977), containing 103 poems, is Bogan's final complete edition. See also *What the Woman Lived: Selected Letters of Louise Bogan, 1920–1970*, ed. Ruth Limmer (1973). *A Poet's Prose: Selected Writings Of Louise Bogan*, ed. Mary Kinzie (2005), includes fiction, journal entries, literary criticism, uncollected poems, and unpublished poems and drafts.

For biography, see Elizabeth Frank, *Louise Bogan: A Portrait* (1985). Critical interpretation can be found in Jaqueline Ridgeway, *Louise Bogan* (1984); Martha Collins, *Critical Essays on Louise Bogan* (1984); Gloria Bowles, *Louise Bogan's Aesthetic of Limitation* (1987); and Lee Upton, *Obsession and Release: Rereading the Poetry of Louise Bogan* (1996). Also stimulating, on the contending forces of modernism and anti-modernism, is Alan Filreis, *Counter-revolution of the Word: The Conservative Attack on Modern Poetry, 1945–1960* (2007).

Medusa[1]

I had come to the house, in a cave of trees,
Facing a sheer sky.
Everything moved,—a bell hung ready to strike,
Sun and reflection wheeled by.

When the bare eyes were before me   5
And the hissing hair,
Held up at a window, seen through a door.
The stiff bald eyes, the serpents on the forehead
Formed in the air.

This is a dead scene forever now.   10
Nothing will ever stir.
The end will never brighten it more than this,
Nor the rain blur.

The water will always fall, and will not fall,
And the tipped bell make no sound.   15
The grass will always be growing for hay
Deep on the ground.

And I shall stand here like a shadow
Under the great balanced day,
My eyes on the yellow dust, that was lifting in the wind,   20
And does not drift away.

                                                                   [1923]

---

[1]Medusa, a figure in Greek myth, had snakes for hair. She was one of the Gorgons, hideous female monsters whose appearance turned to stone anyone who looked at them. Perseus, using his shield as a mirror, was able to kill Medusa by looking at her reflection rather than directly at her. He then cut off her head and gave it to Athena.

WILLIAM FAULKNER ■ (1897–1962)

Born in New Albany, Mississippi, William Faulkner, when he was five, moved with his family to Oxford in Lafayette County, in the northern part of the state. As early as grade school, Faulkner told people, "I want to be a writer," modeling himself on his great-grandfather, William C. Falkner, who was a plantation owner, an officer in the Confederate army, and a novelist.

Faulkner was a high school dropout, but he managed to gain admission as a "special student" to the University of Mississippi. He lasted, however, only a year. During World War I he served in the Royal Canadian Air Force; he had been rejected by the American Air Force because he was not tall enough. Faulkner then held a number of jobs in the Oxford area, wrote poetry, traveled in 1923 to New York City, but soon returned to Oxford.

In 1925, in New Orleans, Faulkner became friends with the short-story writer and novelist Sherwood Anderson, who helped Faulkner to publish his first novel, *Soldier's Pay* (1926). Anderson gave Faulkner some condescending but crucial advice: "You're a country boy; all you know is that little patch up there in Mississippi where you started from. But that's all right too." Soon, with the publication of *Sartoris* and—a greater novel— *The Sound and the Fury*, both in 1929, Faulkner was under way in transforming his native grounds into the fictional locale "Yoknapatawpha County." "I like to think of the world I created," he reflected, "as being a kind of keystone in the universe; that, small as the keystone is, if it were ever taken away the universe itself would collapse."

The Sound and the Fury, and the novels that followed in the next few years—*As I Lay Dying* (1930), *Light in August* (1932), and *Absalom, Absalom!* (1936)—are extraordinary feats of the imagination, dazzling, challenging, and inspiring in their style, multiple points of view, and structure. Faulkner is challenging for many readers because his language is so often daring in its leaps and transitions, and passionately complex. But the critic Malcolm Cowley offers an insight that suggests the connections in form and theme that Faulkner shares with other writers in the American tradition:

> Faulkner unites in his work two of the dominant trends in American literature from the beginning: that of the psychological horror story as developed by Hawthorne, Poe, and Stephen Crane, among others; and that of realistic frontier humor, with Mark Twain as its best example. If you imagine Huckleberry Finn living in the House of Usher and telling uproarious stories while the walls crumble about him, that will give you the double quality of Faulkner's work at its best.

Faulkner's exploration of American and southern history, race and racism, and the family is penetrating, sometimes extreme, and disturbing, in the novels above all but in the short stories, too, as in "That Evening Sun," here, a story tense with menace, terror, racial hostility, sexuality, and violence. "Faulkner's 'special world,' his great subject," the critic Irving Howe noted, "is the South: the Southern memory, the Southern reality, the Southern myth." His influence on many southern writers, including Flannery O'Connor, Carson McCullers, and Robert Penn Warren, was immense.

Faulkner's other important books include *The Hamlet* (1940); *Go Down, Moses and Other Stories* (1942); *Intruder in the Dust* (1948); *Collected Stories* (1950); and *Uncollected Stories* (1979).

"That Evening Sun" was first published in March 1931 in *American Mercury* magazine with the title "That Evening Sun Go Down"; a revised version, as given in *Collected Stories*, is printed here. The uses of the n-word, disturbing to our ears, tell us much about the period and setting of the story and about the era in which it was written.

For biography, see Joseph Blotner, *Faulkner: A Biography* (1984); and Frederick R. Karl, *William Faulkner, American Writer: A Biography* (1989). Among the many critical and historical studies, good points of departure include Cleanth Brooks, *William Faulkner: The Yoknapatawpha Country* (1963); and *William Faulkner: Toward Yoknapatawpha and Beyond* (1978); Eric J. Sundquist, *Faulkner: The House Divided* (1983); Joel Williamson, *William Faulkner and Southern History* (1993); and Daniel J. Singal, *William Faulkner: The Making of a Modernist* (1997). See also Diane Brown Jones, *A Reader's Guide to the Short Stories of William Faulkner* (1994).

William Faulkner, 1954. Photograph by Carl Van Vechten.

Recent scholarship includes Jay Parini, *One Matchless Time: A Life of William Faulkner* (2005); Carolyn Porter, *William Faulkner* (2007); John T. Matthews, *William Faulkner: Seeing through the South* (2009); and Philip M. Weinstein, *Becoming Faulkner: The Art and Life of William Faulkner* (2010).

That Evening Sun

I

Monday is no different from any other weekday in Jefferson now. The streets are paved now, and the telephone and electric companies are cutting down more and more of the shade trees—the water oaks, the maples and locusts and elms—to make room for iron poles bearing clusters of bloated and ghostly and bloodless grapes, and we have a city laundry which makes the rounds on Monday morning, gathering the bundles of clothes into bright-colored, specially-made motor cars: the soiled wearing of a whole week now flees apparitionlike behind alert and irritable electric horns, with a long diminishing noise of rubber and asphalt like tearing silk, and even the Negro women who still take in white people's washing after the old custom, fetch and deliver it in automobiles.

But fifteen years ago, on Monday morning the quiet, dusty, shady streets would be full of Negro women with, balanced on their steady, turbaned heads, bundles of clothes tied up in sheets, almost as large as cotton bales, carried so without touch of hand between the kitchen door of the white house and the blackened washpot beside a cabin door in Negro Hollow.

Nancy would set her bundle on the top of her head, then upon the bundle in turn she would set the black straw sailor hat which she wore winter and summer. She was tall, with a high, sad face sunken a little where her teeth were missing. Sometimes we would go a part of the way down the lane and across the pasture with her, to watch the balanced bundle and the hat that never bobbed nor wavered, even when she walked down into the ditch and up the other side and stooped through the fence. She would go down on her hands and knees and crawl through the gap, her head rigid, uptilted, the bundle steady as a rock or a balloon, and rise to her feet again and go on.

Sometimes the husbands of the washing women would fetch and deliver the clothes, but Jesus never did that for Nancy, even before father told him to stay away from our house, even when Dilsey was sick and Nancy would come to cook for us.

And then about half the time we'd have to go down the lane to Nancy's cabin and tell her to come on and cook breakfast. We would stop at the ditch, because father told us to not have anything to do with Jesus—he was a short black man, with a razor scar down his face—and we would throw rocks at Nancy's house until she came to the door, leaning her head around it without any clothes on.

"What yawl mean, chunking my house?" Nancy said. "What you little devils mean?"

"Father says for you to come on and get breakfast," Caddy said. "Father says it's over a half an hour now, and you've got to come this minute."

"I aint studying no breakfast," Nancy said. "I going to get my sleep out."

"I bet you're drunk," Jason said. "Father says you're drunk. Are you drunk, Nancy?"

"Who says I is?" Nancy said. "I got to get my sleep out. I aint studying no breakfast."

So after a while we quit chunking the cabin and went back home. When she finally came, it was too late for me to go to school. So we thought it was whisky until that day they arrested her again and they were taking her to jail and they passed Mr. Stovall. He was the cashier in the bank and a deacon in the Baptist church, and Nancy began to say:

"When you going to pay me, white man? When you going to pay me, white man? It's been three times now since you paid me a cent—" Mr. Stovall knocked her down, but she kept on saying, "When you going to pay me, white man? It's been three times now since—" until Mr. Stovall kicked her in the mouth with his heel and the marshal caught Mr. Stovall back, and Nancy lying in the street, laughing. She turned her head and spat out some blood and teeth and said, "It's been three times now since he paid me a cent."

That was how she lost her teeth, and all that day they told about Nancy and Mr. Stovall, and all that night the ones that passed the jail could hear Nancy singing and yelling. They could see her hands holding to the window bars, and a lot of them stopped along the fence, listening to her and to the jailer trying to make her stop. She didn't shut up until almost daylight, when the jailer began to hear a bumping and scraping upstairs and he went up there and found Nancy hanging from the window bar. He said that it was cocaine and not whisky, because no nigger would try to commit suicide unless he was full of cocaine, because a nigger full of cocaine wasn't a nigger any longer.

The jailer cut her down and revived her; then he beat her, whipped her. She had hung herself with her dress. She had fixed it all right, but when they arrested her she didn't have on anything except a dress and so she didn't have anything to tie her hands with and she couldn't make her hands let go of the window ledge. So the jailer heard the noise and ran up there and found Nancy hanging from the window, stark naked, her belly already swelling out a little, like a little balloon.

When Dilsey was sick in her cabin and Nancy was cooking for us, we could see her apron swelling out; that was before father told Jesus to stay away from the house. Jesus was in the kitchen, sitting behind the stove, with his razor scar on his black face like a piece of dirty string. He said it was a watermelon that Nancy had under her dress.

"It never come off of your vine, though," Nancy said.

"Off of what vine?" Caddy said.

"I can cut down the vine it did come off of," Jesus said.

"What makes you want to talk like that before these chillen?" Nancy said. "Whyn't you go on to work? You done et. You want Mr. Jason to catch you hanging around his kitchen, talking that way before these chillen?"

"Talking what way?" Caddy said. "What vine?"

"I cant hang around white man's kitchen," Jesus said. "But white man can hang around mine. White man can come in my house, but I cant stop him. When white man want to come in my house, I aint got no house. I cant stop him, but he cant kick me outen it. He cant do that."

Dilsey was still sick in her cabin. Father told Jesus to stay off our place. Dilsey was still sick. It was a long time. We were in the library after supper.

"Isn't Nancy through in the kitchen yet?" mother said. "It seems to me that she has had plenty of time to have finished the dishes."

"Let Quentin go and see," father said. "Go and see if Nancy is through, Quentin. Tell her she can go on home."

I went to the kitchen. Nancy was through. The dishes were put away and the fire was out. Nancy was sitting in a chair, close to the cold stove. She looked at me.

"Mother wants to know if you are through," I said.

"Yes," Nancy said. She looked at me. "I done finished." She looked at me.

"What is it?" I said. "What is it?"

"I aint nothing but a nigger," Nancy said. "It aint none of my fault."

She looked at me, sitting in the chair before the cold stove, the sailor hat on her head. I went back to the library. It was the cold stove and all, when you think of a kitchen being warm and busy and cheerful. And with a cold stove and the dishes all put away, and nobody wanting to eat at that hour.

"Is she through?" mother said.

"Yessum," I said.

"What is she doing?" mother said.

"She's not doing anything. She's through."

"I'll go and see," father said.

"Maybe she's waiting for Jesus to come and take her home," Caddy said.

"Jesus is gone," I said. Nancy told us how one morning she woke up and Jesus was gone.

"He quit me," Nancy said. "Done gone to Memphis, I reckon. Dodging them city *po*-lice for a while, I reckon."

"And a good riddance," father said. "I hope he stays there."

"Nancy's scaired of the dark," Jason said.

"So are you," Caddy said.

"I'm not," Jason said.

"Scairy cat," Caddy said.

"I'm not," Jason said.

"You, Candace!" mother said. Father came back.

"I am going to walk down the lane with Nancy," he said. "She says that Jesus is back."

"Has she seen him?" mother said.

"No. Some Negro sent her word that he was back in town. I wont be long."

"You'll leave me alone, to take Nancy home?" mother said. "Is her safety more precious to you than mine?"

"I wont be long," father said.

"You'll leave these children unprotected, with that Negro about?"

"I'm going too," Caddy said. "Let me go, Father."

"What would he do with them, if he were unfortunate enough to have them?" father said.

"I want to go, too," Jason said.

"Jason!" mother said. She was speaking to father. You could tell that by the way she said the name. Like she believed that all day father had been trying to think of doing the thing she wouldn't like the most, and that she knew all the time that after a while he would think of it. I stayed quiet, because father and I both knew that mother would want him to make me stay with her if she just thought of it in time. So father didn't look at me. I was the oldest. I was nine and Caddy was seven and Jason was five.

"Nonsense," father said. "We wont be long."

Nancy had her hat on. We came to the lane. "Jesus always been good to me," Nancy said. "Whenever he had two dollars, one of them was mine." We walked in the lane. "If I can just get through the lane," Nancy said, "I be all right then."

The lane was always dark. "This is where Jason got scared on Hallowe'en," Caddy said.

"I didn't," Jason said.

"Cant Aunt Rachel do anything with him?" father said. Aunt Rachel was old. She lived in a cabin beyond Nancy's, by herself. She had white hair and she smoked a pipe in the door, all day long; she didn't work any more. They said she was Jesus' mother. Sometimes she said she was and sometimes she said she wasn't any kin to Jesus.

"Yes, you did," Caddy said. "You were scairder than Frony. You were scairder than T.P. even. Scairder than niggers."

"Cant nobody do nothing with him," Nancy said. "He say I done woke up the devil in him and aint but one thing going to lay it down again."

"Well, he's gone now," father said. "There's nothing for you to be afraid of now. And if you'd just let white men alone."

"Let what white men alone?" Caddy said. "How let them alone?"

"He aint gone nowhere," Nancy said. "I can feel him. I can feel him now, in this lane. He hearing us talk, every word, hid somewhere, waiting. I aint seen him, and I aint going to see him again but once more, with that razor in his mouth. That razor on that string down his back, inside his shirt. And then I aint going to be even surprised."

"I wasn't scaired," Jason said.

"If you'd behave yourself, you'd have kept out of this," father said. "But it's all right now. He's probably in St. Louis now. Probably got another wife by now and forgot all about you."

"If he has, I better not find out about it," Nancy said. "I'd stand there right over them, and every time he wropped her, I'd cut that arm off. I'd cut his head off and I'd slit her belly and I'd shove—"

"Hush," father said.

"Slit whose belly, Nancy?" Caddy said.

"I wasn't scaired," Jason said. "I'd walk right down this lane by myself."

"Yah," Caddy said. "You wouldn't dare to put your foot down in it if we were not here too."

II

Dilsey was still sick, so we took Nancy home every night until mother said, "How much longer is this going on? I to be left alone in this big house while you take home a frightened Negro?"

We fixed a pallet[1] in the kitchen for Nancy. One night we waked up, hearing the sound. It was not singing and it was not crying, coming up the dark stairs. There was a light in mother's room and we heard father going down the hall, down the back stairs, and Caddy and I went into the hall. The floor was cold. Our toes curled away from it while we listened to the sound. It was like singing and it wasn't like singing, like the sounds that Negroes make.

Then it stopped and we heard father going down the back stairs, and we went to the head of the stairs. Then the sound began again, in the stairway, not loud, and we could see Nancy's eyes halfway up the stairs, against the wall. They looked like cat's eyes do, like a big cat against the wall, watching us. When we came down the steps to where she was, she quit making the sound again, and we stood there until father came back up from the kitchen, with his pistol in his hand. He went back down with Nancy and they came back with Nancy's pallet.

We spread the pallet in our room. After the light in mother's room went off, we could see Nancy's eyes again. "Nancy," Caddy whispered, "are you asleep, Nancy?"

---

[1] A straw bed or mattress.

Nancy whispered something. It was oh or no, I dont know which. Like nobody had made it, like it came from nowhere and went nowhere, until it was like Nancy was not there at all; that I had looked so hard at her eyes on the stairs that they had got printed on my eyeballs, like the sun does when you have closed your eyes and there is no sun. "Jesus," Nancy whispered. "Jesus."

"Was it Jesus?" Caddy said. "Did he try to come into the kitchen?"

"Jesus," Nancy said. Like this: Jeeeeeeeeeeeeeeeesus, until the sound went out, like a match or a candle does.

"It's the other Jesus she means," I said.

"Can you see us, Nancy?" Caddy whispered. "Can you see our eyes too?"

"I aint nothing but a nigger," Nancy said. "God knows. God knows."

"What did you see down there in the kitchen?" Caddy whispered. "What tried to get in?"

"God knows," Nancy said. We could see her eyes. "God knows."

Dilsey got well. She cooked dinner. "You'd better stay in bed a day or two longer," father said.

"What for?" Dilsey said. "If I had been a day later, this place would be to rack and ruin. Get on out of here now, and let me get my kitchen straight again."

Dilsey cooked supper too. And that night, just before dark, Nancy came into the kitchen.

"How do you know he's back?" Dilsey said. "You aint seen him."

"Jesus is a nigger," Jason said.

"I can feel him," Nancy said. "I can feel him laying yonder in the ditch."

"Tonight?" Dilsey said. "Is he there tonight?"

"Dilsey's a nigger too," Jason said.

"You try to eat something," Dilsey said.

"I dont want nothing," Nancy said.

"I aint a nigger," Jason said.

"Drink some coffee," Dilsey said. She poured a cup of coffee for Nancy. "Do you know he's out there tonight? How come you know it's tonight?"

"I know," Nancy said. "He's there, waiting. I know. I done lived with him too long. I know what he is fixing to do fore he know it himself."

"Drink some coffee," Dilsey said. Nancy held the cup to her mouth and blew into the cup. Her mouth pursed out like a spreading adder's,[2] like a rubber mouth, like she had blown all the color out of her lips with blowing the coffee.

"I aint a nigger," Jason said. "Are you a nigger, Nancy?"

"I hellborn, child," Nancy said. "I wont be nothing soon. I going back where I come from soon."

---

[2] Another name for the Eastern hognose snake.

III

She began to drink the coffee. While she was drinking, holding the cup in both hands, she began to make the sound again. She made the sound into the cup and the coffee sploshed out onto her hands and her dress. Her eyes looked at us and she sat there, her elbows on her knees, holding the cup in both hands, looking at us across the wet cup, making the sound. "Look at Nancy," Jason said. "Nancy cant cook for us now. Dilsey's got well now."

"You hush up," Dilsey said. Nancy held the cup in both hands, looking at us, making the sound, like there were two of them: one looking at us and the other making the sound. "Whyn't you let Mr. Jason telefoam the marshal?" Dilsey said. Nancy stopped then, holding the cup in her long brown hands. She tried to drink some coffee again, but it sploshed out of the cup, onto her hands and her dress, and she put the cup down. Jason watched her.

"I cant swallow it," Nancy said. "I swallows but it wont go down me."

"You go down to the cabin," Dilsey said. "Frony will fix you a pallet and I'll be there soon."

"Wont no nigger stop him," Nancy said.

"I aint a nigger," Jason said. "Am I, Dilsey?"

"I reckon not," Dilsey said. She looked at Nancy. "I dont reckon so. What you going to do, then?"

Nancy looked at us. Her eyes went fast, like she was afraid there wasn't time to look, without hardly moving at all. She looked at us, at all three of us at one time. "You member that night I stayed in yawls' room?" she said. She told about how we waked up early the next morning, and played. We had to play quiet, on her pallet, until father woke up and it was time to get breakfast. "Go and ask your maw to let me stay here tonight," Nancy said. "I wont need no pallet. We can play some more."

Caddy asked mother. Jason went too. "I cant have Negroes sleeping in the bedrooms," mother said. Jason cried. He cried until mother said he couldn't have any dessert for three days if he didn't stop. Then Jason said he would stop if Dilsey would make a chocolate cake. Father was there.

"Why dont you do something about it?" mother said. "What do we have officers for?"

"Why is Nancy afraid of Jesus?" Caddy said. "Are you afraid of father, mother?"

"What could the officers do?" father said. "If Nancy hasn't seen him, how could the officers find him?"

"Then why is she afraid?" mother said.

"She says he is there. She says she knows he is there tonight."

"Yet we pay taxes," mother said. "I must wait here alone in this big house while you take a Negro woman home."

"You know that I am not lying outside with a razor," father said.

"I'll stop if Dilsey will make a chocolate cake," Jason said. Mother told us to go out and father said he didn't know if Jason would get a chocolate cake or not, but he knew what Jason was going to get in about a minute. We went back to the kitchen and told Nancy.

"Father said for you to go home and lock the door, and you'll be all right," Caddy said. "All right from what, Nancy? Is Jesus mad at you?" Nancy was holding the coffee cup in her hands again, her elbows on her knees and her hands holding the cup between her knees. She was looking into the cup. "What have you done that made Jesus mad?" Caddy said. Nancy let the cup go. It didn't break on the floor, but the coffee spilled out, and Nancy sat there with her hands still making the shape of the cup. She began to make the sound again, not loud. Not singing and not unsinging. We watched her.

"Here," Dilsey said. "You quit that, now. You get aholt of yourself. You wait here. I going to get Versh to walk home with you." Dilsey went out.

We looked at Nancy. Her shoulders kept shaking, but she quit making the sound. We watched her. "What's Jesus going to do to you?" Caddy said. "He went away."

Nancy looked at us. "We had fun that night I stayed in yawls' room, didn't we?"

"I didn't," Jason said. "I didn't have any fun."

"You were asleep in mother's room," Caddy said. "You were not there."

"Let's go down to my house and have some more fun," Nancy said.

"Mother wont let us," I said. "It's too late now."

"Dont bother her," Nancy said. "We can tell her in the morning. She wont mind."

"She wouldn't let us," I said.

"Dont ask her now," Nancy said. "Dont bother her now."

"She didn't say we couldn't go," Caddy said.

"We didn't ask," I said.

"If you go, I'll tell," Jason said.

"We'll have fun," Nancy said. "They won't mind, just to my house. I been working for yawl a long time. They won't mind."

"I'm not afraid to go," Caddy said. "Jason is the one that's afraid. He'll tell."

"I'm not," Jason said.

"Yes, you are," Caddy said. "You'll tell."

"I won't tell," Jason said. "I'm not afraid."

"Jason ain't afraid to go with me," Nancy said. "Is you, Jason?"

"Jason is going to tell," Caddy said. The lane was dark.

We passed the pasture gate. "I bet if something was to jump out from behind that gate, Jason would holler."

"I wouldn't," Jason said. We walked down the lane. Nancy was talking loud.

"What are you talking so loud for, Nancy?" Caddy said.

"Who; me?" Nancy said. "Listen at Quentin and Caddy and Jason saying I'm talking loud."

"You talk like there was five of us here," Caddy said. "You talk like father was here too."

"Who; me talking loud, Mr. Jason?" Nancy said.

"Nancy called Jason 'Mister,' " Caddy said.

"Listen how Caddy and Quentin and Jason talk," Nancy said.

"We're not talking loud," Caddy said. "You're the one that's talking like father—"

"Hush," Nancy said; "hush, Mr. Jason."

"Nancy called Jason 'Mister' aguh—"

"Hush," Nancy said. She was talking loud when we crossed the ditch and stooped through the fence where she used to stoop through with the clothes on her head. Then we came to her house. We were going fast then. She opened the door. The smell of the house was like the lamp and the smell of Nancy was like the wick, like they were waiting for one another to begin to smell. She lit the lamp and closed the door and put the bar up. Then she quit talking loud, looking at us.

"What're we going to do?" Caddy said.

"What do yawl want to do?" Nancy said.

"You said we would have some fun," Caddy said.

There was something about Nancy's house; something you could smell besides Nancy and the house. Jason smelled it, even. "I don't want to stay here," he said. "I want to go home."

"Go home, then," Caddy said.

"I don't want to go by myself," Jason said.

"We're going to have some fun," Nancy said.

"How?" Caddy said.

Nancy stood by the door. She was looking at us, only it was like she had emptied her eyes, like she had quit using them. "What do you want to do?" she said.

"Tell us a story," Caddy said. "Can you tell a story?"

"Yes," Nancy said.

"Tell it," Caddy said. We looked at Nancy. "You don't know any stories."

"Yes," Nancy said. "Yes, I do."

She came and sat in a chair before the hearth. There was a little fire there. Nancy built it up, when it was already hot inside. She built a good blaze. She told a story. She talked like her eyes looked, like her eyes watching us and her voice talking to us did not belong to her. Like she was living somewhere else, waiting somewhere else. She was outside the cabin. Her voice was inside and the shape of her, the Nancy that could stoop under a barbed wire fence with a bundle of clothes balanced on her head as though without weight, like a balloon, was there. But that was all. "And so this here queen come walking up to the ditch, where that bad man was hiding. She was walking up to the ditch, and she say, 'If I can just get past this here ditch,' was what she say...."

"What ditch?" Caddy said. "A ditch like that one out there? Why did a queen want to go into a ditch?"

"To get to her house," Nancy said. She looked at us. "She had to cross the ditch to get into her house quick and bar the door."

"Why did she want to go home and bar the door?" Caddy said.

IV

Nancy looked at us. She quit talking. She looked at us. Jason's legs stuck straight out of his pants where he sat on Nancy's lap. "I don't think that's a good story," he said. "I want to go home."

"Maybe we had better," Caddy said. She got up from the floor. "I bet they are looking for us right now." She went toward the door.

"No," Nancy said. "Don't open it." She got up quick and passed Caddy. She didn't touch the door, the wooden bar.

"Why not?" Caddy said.

"Come back to the lamp," Nancy said. "We'll have fun. You don't have to go."

"We ought to go," Caddy said. "Unless we have a lot of fun." She and Nancy came back to the fire, the lamp.

"I want to go home," Jason said. "I'm going to tell."

"I know another story," Nancy said. She stood close to the lamp. She looked at Caddy, like when your eyes look up at a stick balanced on your nose. She had to look down to see Caddy, but her eyes looked like that, like when you are balancing a stick.

"I won't listen to it," Jason said. "I'll bang on the floor."

"It's a good one," Nancy said. "It's better than the other one."

"What's it about?" Caddy said. Nancy was standing by the lamp. Her hand was on the lamp, against the light, long and brown.

"Your hand is on that hot globe," Caddy said. "Don't it feel hot to your hand?"

Nancy looked at her hand on the lamp chimney. She took her hand away, slow. She stood there, looking at Caddy, wringing her long hand as though it were tied to her wrist with a string.

"Let's do something else," Caddy said.

"I want to go home," Jason said.

"I got some popcorn," Nancy said. She looked at Caddy and then at Jason and then at me and then at Caddy again. "I got some popcorn."

"I don't like popcorn," Jason said. "I'd rather have candy."

Nancy looked at Jason. "You can hold the popper." She was still wringing her hand; it was long and limp and brown.

"All right," Jason said. "I'll stay a while if I can do that. Caddy can't hold it. I'll want to go home again if Caddy holds the popper."

Nancy built up the fire. "Look at Nancy putting her hands in the fire," Caddy said. "What's the matter with you, Nancy?"

"I got popcorn," Nancy said. "I got some." She took the popper from under the bed. It was broken. Jason began to cry.

"Now we can't have any popcorn," he said.

"We ought to go home, anyway," Caddy said. "Come on, Quentin."

"Wait," Nancy said; "wait. I can fix it. Don't you want to help me fix it?"

"I don't think I want any," Caddy said. "It's too late now."

"You help me, Jason," Nancy said. "Don't you want to help me?"

"No," Jason said. "I want to go home."

"Hush," Nancy said; "hush. Watch. Watch me. I can fix it so Jason can hold it and pop the corn." She got a piece of wire and fixed the popper.

"It won't hold good," Caddy said.

"Yes, it will," Nancy said. "Yawl watch. Yawl help me shell some corn."

The popcorn was under the bed too. We shelled it into the popper and Nancy helped Jason hold the popper over the fire.

"It's not popping," Jason said. "I want to go home."

"You wait," Nancy said. "It'll begin to pop. We'll have fun then." She was sitting close to the fire. The lamp was turned up so high it was beginning to smoke.

"Why don't you turn it down some?" I said.

"It's all right," Nancy said. "I'll clean it. Yawl wait. The popcorn will start in a minute."

"I don't believe it's going to start,"Caddy said. "We ought to start home, anyway. They'll be worried."

"No," Nancy said. "It's going to pop. Dilsey will tell um yawl with me. I been working for yawl long time. They won't mind if yawl at my house. You wait, now. It'll start popping any minute now."

Then Jason got some smoke in his eyes and he began to cry. He dropped the popper into the fire. Nancy got a wet rag and wiped Jason's face, but he didn't stop crying.

"Hush," she said. "Hush." But he didn't hush. Caddy took the popper out of the fire.

"It's burned up," she said. "You'll have to get some more popcorn, Nancy."

"Did you put all of it in?" Nancy said.

"Yes," Caddy said. Nancy looked at Caddy. Then she took the popper and opened it and poured the cinders into her apron and began to sort the grains, her hands long and brown, and we watching her.

"Haven't you got any more?" Caddy said.

"Yes," Nancy said; "yes. Look. This here ain't burnt. All we need to do is—"

"I want to go home," Jason said. "I'm going to tell."

"Hush," Caddy said. We all listened. Nancy's head was already turned toward the barred door, her eyes filled with red lamplight. "Somebody is coming," Caddy said.

Then Nancy began to make that sound again, not loud, sitting there above the fire, her long hands dangling between her knees; all of a sudden water began to come out on her face in big drops, running down her face, carrying in each one a little turning ball of firelight like a spark until it dropped off her chin. "She's not crying," I said.

"I ain't crying," Nancy said. Her eyes were closed. "I ain't crying. Who is it?"

"I don't know," Caddy said. She went to the door and looked out. "We've got to go now," she said. "Here comes father."

"I'm going to tell," Jason said. "Yawl made me come."

The water still ran down Nancy's face. She turned in her chair. "Listen. Tell him. Tell him we going to have fun. Tell him I take good care of yawl until in the morning. Tell him to let me come home with yawl and sleep on the floor. Tell him I won't need no pallet. We'll have fun. You member last time how we had so much fun?"

"I didn't have fun," Jason said. "You hurt me. You put smoke in my eyes. I'm going to tell."

V

Father came in. He looked at us. Nancy did not get up.

"Tell him," she said.

"Caddy made us come down here," Jason said. "I didn't want to."

Father came to the fire. Nancy looked up at him. "Can't you go to Aunt Rachel's and stay?" he said. Nancy looked up at father, her hands between her knees. "He's not here," father said. "I would have seen him. There's not a soul in sight."

"He in the ditch," Nancy said. "He waiting in the ditch yonder."

"Nonsense," father said. He looked at Nancy. "Do you know he's there?"

"I got the sign," Nancy said.

"What sign?"

"I got it. It was on the table when I come in. It was a hog-bone, with blood meat still on it, laying by the lamp. He's out there. When yawl walk out that door, I gone."

"Gone where, Nancy?" Caddy said.

"I'm not a tattletale," Jason said.

"Nonsense," father said.

"He out there," Nancy said. "He looking through that window this minute, waiting for yawl to go. Then I gone."

"Nonsense," father said. "Lock up your house and we'll take you on to Aunt Rachel's."

"'Twont do no good," Nancy said. She didn't look at father now, but he looked down at her, at her long, limp, moving hands. "Putting it off wont do no good."

"Then what do you want to do?" father said.

"I don't know," Nancy said. "I can't do nothing. Just put it off. And that don't do no good. I reckon it belong to me. I reckon what I going to get ain't no more than mine."

"Get what?" Caddy said. "What's yours?"

"Nothing," father said. "You all must get to bed."

"Caddy made me come," Jason said.

"Go on to Aunt Rachel's," father said.

"It won't do no good," Nancy said. She sat before the fire, her elbows on her knees, her long hands between her knees. "When even your own kitchen wouldn't do no good. When even if I was sleeping on the floor in the room with your chillen, and the next morning there I am, and blood—"

"Hush," father said. "Lock the door and put out the lamp and go to bed."

"I scared of the dark," Nancy said. "I scared for it to happen in the dark."

"You mean you're going to sit right here with the lamp lighted?" father said. Then Nancy began to make the sound again, sitting before the fire, her long hands between her knees. "Ah, damnation," father said. "Come along, chillen. It's past bedtime."

"When yawl go home, I gone," Nancy said. She talked quieter now, and her face looked quiet, like her hands. "Anyway, I got my coffin money saved up with Mr. Lovelady." Mr. Lovelady was a short, dirty man who collected the Negro insurance, coming around to the cabins or the kitchens every Saturday morning, to collect fifteen cents. He and his wife lived at the hotel. One morning his wife committed suicide. They had a child, a little girl. He and the child went away. After a week or two he came back alone. We would see him going along the lanes and the back streets on Saturday mornings.

"Nonsense," father said. "You'll be the first thing I'll see in the kitchen tomorrow morning."

"You'll see what you'll see, I reckon," Nancy said. "But it will take the Lord to say what that will be."

VI

We left her sitting before the fire.

"Come and put the bar up," father said. But she didn't move. She didn't look at us again, sitting quietly there between the lamp and the fire. From some distance down the lane we could look back and see her through the open door.

"What, Father?" Caddy said. "What's going to happen?"

"Nothing," father said. Jason was on father's back, so Jason was the tallest of all of us. We went down into the ditch. I looked at it, quiet. I couldn't see much where the moonlight and the shadows tangled.

"If Jesus is hid here, he can see us, cant he?" Caddy said.

"He's not there," father said. "He went away a long time ago."

"You made me come," Jason said, high; against the sky it looked like father had two heads, a little one and a big one. "I didn't want to."

We went up out of the ditch. We could still see Nancy's house and the open door, but we couldn't see Nancy now, sitting before the fire with the door open, because she was tired. "I just done got tired," she said. "I just a nigger. It ain't no fault of mine."

But we could hear her, because she began just after we came up out of the ditch, the sound that was not singing and not unsinging. "Who will do our washing now, Father?" I said.

"I'm not a nigger," Jason said, high and close above father's head.

"You're worse," Caddy said, "you are a tattletale. If something was to jump out, you'd be scairder than a nigger."

"I wouldn't," Jason said.

"You'd cry," Caddy said.

"Caddy," father said.

"I wouldn't!" Jason said.

"Scairy cat," Caddy said.

"Candace!" father said.

[1931]

ERNEST HEMINGWAY ■ (1899–1961)

Ernest Hemingway was the first, and the greatest, literary celebrity of the twentieth century, and on an international scale. He was known throughout the world for his exploits and adventures as a hunter, fisherman, soldier, and aficionado of the bullfight. He was also one of the finest and most influential writers of the modern era, the master of a style that many have imitated (and sometimes parodied) but that none has rivaled.

Hemingway was born in Oak Park, Illinois. His father was a doctor, and his mother was a pious woman highly accomplished in music. Hemingway played sports in high school and also showed some interest in writing. Not much of a student, he enjoyed spending the summer months hunting and fishing in northern Michigan. Hemingway did not attend college but instead took a job with the *Kansas City Star* newspaper. At age nineteen he took part in World War I as an ambulance driver, suffering serious wounds in Italy.

After his return to the United States, and after a period of work in Toronto, Canada, Hemingway settled in Paris, where he met and learned from Gertrude Stein, Ezra Pound, and other writers, intellectuals, and artists who championed advanced forms of art and literature. Hemingway's first important book was a collection of short stories, *In Our Time*, published in 1925; this was followed by two highly accomplished novels, *The Sun Also Rises* (1926), about the lives of expatriates in Paris and Spain, and *A Farewell to Arms* (1929), which draws on Hemingway's own experiences in World War I.

Hemingway remained an active and widely published author throughout the 1930s. His best work of this decade includes *The Fifth Column and the First Forty-Nine Stories* (1938) and *For Whom the Bell Tolls* (1940), which takes as its setting the Spanish Civil War. But a period of decline then began to weaken and limit Hemingway's literary production. He labored on a number of manuscripts, several of which have been published (and their reliability is questionable) since his death. But only *The Old Man and the Sea* (1952) recaptured the magic that distinguished Hemingway's best writing of earlier decades. Suffering from a host of ailments and the lingering effects of many injuries and accidents, dependent on drugs and liquor, and in anguish about his inability to write as well as he once did, Hemingway committed suicide in July 1961.

Hemingway's vision of life is elementary but powerful, and it is suggested by the title of one of his collections of stories, *Winner Take Nothing*. Hemingway always felt shadowed by death, and for him this made essential the cultivation of a code of disciplined appreciation of the good things that life offers—fine food, drink, women, the thrill of action, the excitement of sports, the splendor of nature. Experiences of life at its most intense, rich, and beautiful could stave off, though they could never, of course, defeat, the looming fact of death, and Hemingway writes about them time and again, as in the bitter, violent, and tragic story about sexual conflict, "The Short Happy Life of Francis Macomber," printed here.

Yet it sometimes seems that Hemingway believed death might be beaten after all, and that this would transpire through the creation of works of art, great stories, and novels, eternal monuments of literary craftsman-ship. He made this point memorably: "From things that have happened and from things as they exist and from all things that you know and all those you cannot know, you make something through your invention that is not a representation but a whole new thing truer than anything true and alive, and you make it alive, and if you make it well enough, you give it immortality."

For Hemingway, this making involved a carefully exercised restraint— the belief that saying less could express more. This is his principle of the iceberg. "If a writer of prose knows enough about what he is writing about," he observed, "he may omit things that he knows and the reader, if the writer is writing truly enough, will have a feeling of those things as strongly as though the writer had stated them. The dignity of movement of an iceberg is due to only one-eighth of it being above water."

When approaching Hemingway, the reader hence must focus on the surface in order to feel the emotional pressure, the weight of meaning, that exists below it. As "The Short Happy Life of Francis Macomber" at-tests, Hemingway's surfaces look simple but are highly complex. He is a bigger writer than he appears, which is why he is often misunderstood and taken for granted. Hemingway's style is subtle, sensitive, and, as in the story included here, evocative of searing pain and deep, if menaced, pleasure.

Biographies include Jeffrey Meyers, *Hemingway: A Biography* (1985); and James R. Mellow, *Hemingway: A Life Without Consequences* (1992). For biography and critical interpretation, see Kenneth S. Lynn, *Hemingway* (1987). Also helpful are *The Cambridge Companion to Hemingway*, ed. Scott Donaldson (1996); and *A Historical Guide to Ernest Hemingway*, ed. Linda Wagner-Martin (2000). Other resources are *New Critical Approaches to the Short Stories of Ernest Hemingway*, ed. Jackson J. Benson (1990); Charles M. Oliver, *Ernest Hemingway A to Z: The Essential Reference to the Life and Work* (1999); and Frederick Voss, *Picturing Hemingway: A Writer in His Time* (1999). Recent work includes Thomas F. Strychacz, *Hemingway's Theaters of Masculinity* (2003); *Hemingway: Eight Decades of Criticism*, ed. Linda Wagner-Martin (2009); and Robert Paul Lamb, *Art Matters: Hemingway, Craft, and the Creation of the Modern Short Story* (2010).

Ernest Hemingway, date unknown.

The Short Happy Life
of Francis Macomber

It was now lunch time and they were all sitting under the double green fly of the dining tent pretending that nothing had happened.

"Will you have lime juice or lemon squash?" Macomber asked.

"I'll have a gimlet,"[1] Robert Wilson told him.

"I'll have a gimlet too. I need something." Macomber's wife said.

"I suppose it's the thing to do," Macomber agreed. "Tell him to make three gimlets."

The mess boy had started them already, lifting the bottles out of the canvas cooling bags that sweated wet in the wind that blew through the trees that shaded the tents.

"What had I ought to give them?" Macomber asked.

"A quid[2] would be plenty," Wilson told him. "You don't want to spoil them."

"Will the headman distribute it?"

"Absolutely."

Francis Macomber had, half an hour before, been carried to his tent from the edge of the camp in triumph on the arms and shoulders of the cook, the personal boys, the skinner and the porters. The gun-bearers had

---

[1]A cocktail made with gin and lime juice.
[2]A sovereign; one pound sterling.

taken no part in the demonstration. When the native boys put him down at the door of his tent, he had shaken all their hands, received their congratulations, and then gone into the tent and sat on the bed until his wife came in. She did not speak to him when she came in and he left the tent at once to wash his face and hands in the portable wash basin outside and go over to the dining tent to sit in a comfortable canvas chair in the breeze and the shade.

"You've got your lion," Robert Wilson said to him," and a damned fine one too."

Mrs. Macomber looked at Wilson quickly. She was an extremely handsome and well-kept woman of the beauty and social position which had, five years before, commanded five thousand dollars as the price of endorsing, with photographs, a beauty product which she had never used. She had been married to Francis Macomber for eleven years.

"He is a good lion, isn't he?" Macomber said. His wife looked at him now. She looked at both these men as though she had never seen them before.

One, Wilson, the white hunter, she knew she had never truly seen before. He was about middle height with sandy hair, a stubby mustache, a very red face and extremely cold blue eyes with faint white wrinkles at the corners that grooved merrily when he smiled. He smiled at her now and she looked away from his face at the way his shoulders sloped in the loose tunic he wore with the four big cartridges held in loops where the left breast pocket should have been, at his big brown hands, his old slacks, his very dirty boots and back to his red face again. She noticed where the baked red of his face stopped in a white line that marked the circle left by his Stetson hat that hung now from one of the pegs of the tent pole.

"Well, here's to the lion," Robert Wilson said. He smiled at her again and, not smiling, she looked curiously at her husband.

Francis Macomber was very tall, very well built if you did not mind that length of bone, dark, his hair cropped like an oarsman, rather thin-lipped, and was considered handsome. He was dressed in the same sort of safari clothes that Wilson wore except that his were new, he was thirty-five years old, kept himself very fit, was good at court games, had a number of big-game fishing records, and had just shown himself, very publicly, to be a coward.

"Here's to the lion," he said. "I can't ever thank you for what you did." Margaret, his wife, looked away from him and back to Wilson.

"Let's not talk about the lion," she said.

Wilson looked over at her without smiling and now she smiled at him.

"It's been a very strange day," she said. "Hadn't you ought to put your hat on even under the canvas at noon? You told me that, you know."

"Might put it on," said Wilson.

"You know you have a very red face, Mr. Wilson," she told him and smiled again.

"Drink," said Wilson.

"I don't think so," she said. "Francis drinks a great deal, but his face is never red."

"It's red today," Macomber tried a joke.

"No," said Margaret. "It's mine that's red today. But Mr. Wilson's is always red."

"Must be racial," said Wilson. "I say, you wouldn't like to drop my beauty as a topic, would you?"

"I've just started on it."

"Let's chuck it," said Wilson.

"Conversation is going to be so difficult," Margaret said.

"Don't be silly, Margot," her husband said.

"No difficulty," Wilson said. "Got a damn fine lion."

Margot looked at them both and they both saw that she was going to cry. Wilson had seen it coming for a long time and he dreaded it. Macomber was past dreading it.

"I wish it hadn't happened. Oh, I wish it hadn't happened," she said and started for her tent. She made no noise of crying but they could see that her shoulders were shaking under the rose-colored, sun-proofed shirt she wore.

"Women upset," said Wilson to the tall man. "Amounts to nothing. Strain on the nerves and one thing'n another."

"No," said Macomber. "I suppose that I rate that for the rest of my life now."

"Nonsense. Let's have a spot of the giant killer," said Wilson. "Forget the whole thing. Nothing to it anyway."

"We might try," said Macomber. "I won't forget what you did for me though."

"Nothing," said Wilson. "All nonsense."

So they sat there in the shade where the camp was pitched under some wide-topped acacia trees with a boulder-strewn cliff behind them, and a stretch of grass that ran to the bank of a boulder-filled stream in front with forest beyond it, and drank their just-cool lime drinks and avoided one another's eyes while the boys set the table for lunch. Wilson could tell that the boys all knew about it now and when he saw Macomber's personal boy looking curiously at his master while he was putting dishes on the table he snapped at him in Swahili. The boy turned away with his face blank.

"What were you telling him?" Macomber asked.

"Nothing. Told him to look alive or I'd see he got about fifteen of the best."

"What's that? Lashes?"

"It's quite illegal," Wilson said. "You're supposed to fine them."

"Do you still have them whipped?"

"Oh, yes. They could raise a row if they chose to complain. But they don't. They prefer it to the fines."

"How strange!" said Macomber.

"Not strange, really," Wilson said. "Which would you rather do? Take a good birching or lose your pay?"

Then he felt embarrassed at asking it and before Macomber could answer he went on, "We all take a beating every day, you know, one way or another."

This was no better. "Good God," he thought. "I am a diplomat, aren't I?"

"Yes, we take a beating," said Macomber, still not looking at him. "I'm awfully sorry about that lion business. It doesn't have to go any further, does it? I mean no one will hear about it, will they?"

"You mean will I tell it at the Mathaiga Club?" Wilson looked at him now coldly. He had not expected this. So he's a bloody four-letter man[3] as well as a bloody coward, he thought. I rather liked him too until today. But how is one to know about an American?

"No," said Wilson. "I'm a professional hunter. We never talk about our clients. You can be quite easy on that. It's supposed to be bad form to ask us not to talk though."

He had decided now that to break would be much easier. He would eat, then, by himself and could read a book with his meals. They would eat by themselves. He would see them through the safari on a very formal basis—what was it the French called it? Distinguished consideration—and it would be a damn sight easier than having to go through this emotional trash. He'd insult him and make a good clean break. Then he could read a book with his meals and he'd still be drinking their whisky. That was the phrase for it when a safari went bad. You ran into another white hunter and you asked. "How is everything going?" and he answered, "Oh, I'm still drinking their whisky," and you knew everything had gone to pot.

"I'm sorry," Macomber said and looked at him with his American face that would stay adolescent until it became middle-aged, and Wilson noted his crew-cropped hair, fine eyes only faintly shifty, good nose, thin lips and handsome jaw. "I'm sorry I didn't realize that. There are lots of things I don't know."

So what could he do, Wilson thought. He was all ready to break it off quickly and neatly and here the beggar was apologizing after he had just insulted him. He made one more attempt. "Don't worry about me talking," he said. "I have a living to make. You know in Africa no woman ever misses her lion and no white man ever bolts."

"I bolted like a rabbit," Macomber said.

---

[3]An obnoxious person.

Now what in hell were you going to do about a man who talked like that, Wilson wondered.

Wilson looked at Macomber with his flat, blue, machine-gunner's eyes and the other smiled back at him. He had a pleasant smile if you did not notice how his eyes showed when he was hurt.

"Maybe I can fix it up on buffalo," he said. "We're after them next, aren't we?"

"In the morning if you like," Wilson told him. Perhaps he had been wrong. This was certainly the way to take it. You most certainly could not tell a damned thing about an American. He was all for Macomber again. If you could forget the morning. But, of course, you couldn't. The morning had been about as bad as they come.

"Here comes the Memsahib,"[4] he said. She was walking over from her tent looking refreshed and cheerful and quite lovely. She had a very perfect oval face, so perfect that you expected her to be stupid. But she wasn't stupid, Wilson thought, no, not stupid.

"How is the beautiful red-faced Mr. Wilson? Are you feeling better, Francis, my pearl?"

"Oh, much," said Macomber.

"I've dropped the whole thing," she said, sitting down at the table. "What importance is there to whether Francis is any good at killing lions? That's not his trade. That's Mr. Wilson's trade. Mr. Wilson is really very impressive killing anything. You do kill anything, don't you?"

"Oh, anything," said Wilson. "Simply anything." They are, he thought, the hardest in the world; the hardest, the cruelest, the most predatory and the most attractive and their men have softened or gone to pieces nervously as they have hardened. Or is it that they pick men they can handle? They can't know that much at the age they marry, he thought. He was grateful that he had gone through his education on American women before now because this was a very attractive one.

"We're going after buff in the morning," he told her.

"I'm coming," she said.

"No, you're not."

"Oh, yes, I am. Mayn't I, Francis?"

"Why not stay in camp?"

"Not for anything," she said. "I wouldn't miss something like today for anything."

When she left, Wilson was thinking, when she went off to cry, she seemed a hell of a fine woman. She seemed to understand, to realize, to be hurt for him and for herself and to know how things really stood. She is away for twenty minutes and now she is back, simply enamelled in

---

[4]An Indian term used to address a European lady or woman of rank.

that American female cruelty. They are the damnedest women. Really the damnedest.

"We'll put on another show for you tomorrow," Francis Macomber said.

"You're not coming," Wilson said.

"You're very mistaken," she told him. "And I want *so* to see you perform again. You were lovely this morning. That is if blowing things' heads off is lovely."

"Here's the lunch," said Wilson. "You're very merry, aren't you?"

"Why not? I didn't come out here to be dull."

"Well, it hasn't been dull," Wilson said. He could see the boulders in the river and the high bank beyond with the trees and he remembered the morning.

"Oh, no," she said. "It's been charming. And tomorrow. You don't know how I look forward to tomorrow."

"That's eland he's offering you," Wilson said.

"They're the big cowy things that jump like hares, aren't they?"

"I suppose that describes them," Wilson said.

"It's very good meat," Macomber said.

"Did you shoot it, Francis?" she asked.

"Yes."

"They're not dangerous, are they?"

"Only if they fall on you," Wilson told her.

"I'm so glad."

"Why not let up on the bitchery just a little, Margot," Macomber said, cutting the eland steak and putting some mashed potato, gravy and carrot on the down-turned fork that tined through the piece of meat.

"I suppose I could," she said, "since you put it so prettily."

"Tonight we'll have champagne for the lion," Wilson said. "It's a bit too hot at noon."

"Oh, the lion," Margot said. "I'd forgotten the lion!"

So, Robert Wilson thought to himself, she *is* giving him a ride, isn't she? Or do you suppose that's her idea of putting up a good show? How should a woman act when she discovers her husband is a bloody coward? She's damn cruel but they're all cruel. They govern, of course, and to govern one has to be cruel sometimes. Still, I've seen enough of their damn terrorism.

"Have some more eland," he said to her politely.

That afternoon, late, Wilson and Macomber went out in the motor car with the native driver and the two gun-bearers. Mrs. Macomber stayed in the camp. It was too hot to go out, she said, and she was going with them in the early morning. As they drove off Wilson saw her standing under the big tree, looking pretty rather than beautiful in her faintly rosy khaki, her dark hair drawn back off her forehead and gathered in a knot low on her neck, her face as fresh, he thought, as though she were in England. She waved to them as the car went off through the swale of high grass and curved around through the trees into the small hills of orchard bush.

In the orchard bush they found a herd of impala, and leaving the car they stalked one old ram with long, wide-spread horns and Macomber killed it with a very creditable shot that knocked the buck down at a good two hundred yards and sent the herd off bounding wildly and leaping over one another's backs in long, leg-drawn-up leaps as unbelievable and as floating as those one makes sometimes in dreams.

"That was a good shot," Wilson said. "They're a small target."

"Is it a worth-while head?" Macomber asked.

"It's excellent," Wilson told him. "You shoot like that and you'll have no trouble."

"Do you think we'll find buffalo tomorrow?"

"There's a good chance of it. They feed out early in the morning and with luck we may catch them in the open."

"I'd like to clear away that lion business," Macomber said. "It's not very pleasant to have your wife see you do something like that."

I should think it would be even more unpleasant to do it, Wilson thought, wife or no wife, or to talk about it having done it. But he said, "I wouldn't think about that any more. Any one could be upset by his first lion. That's all over."

But that night after dinner and a whisky and soda by the fire before going to bed, as Francis Macomber lay on his cot with the mosquito bar over him and listened to the night noises it was not all over. It was neither all over nor was it beginning. It was there exactly as it happened with some parts of it indelibly emphasized and he was miserably ashamed at it. But more than shame he felt cold, hollow fear in him. The fear was still there like a cold slimy hollow in all the emptiness where once his confidence had been and it made him feel sick. It was still there with him now.

It had started the night before when he had wakened and heard the lion roaring somewhere up along the river. It was a deep sound and at the end there were sort of coughing grunts that made him seem just outside the tent, and when Francis Macomber woke in the night to hear it he was afraid. He could hear his wife breathing quietly, asleep. There was no one to tell he was afraid, nor to be afraid with him, and, lying alone, he did not know the Somali proverb that says a brave man is always frightened three times by a lion; when he first sees his track, when he first hears him roar and when he first confronts him. Then while they were eating breakfast by lantern light out in the dining tent, before the sun was up, the lion roared again and Francis thought he was just at the edge of camp.

"Sounds like an old-timer," Robert Wilson said, looking up from his kippers and coffee. "Listen to him cough."

"Is he very close?"

"A mile or so up the stream."

"Will we see him?"

"We'll have a look."

"Does his roaring carry that far? It sounds as though he were right in camp."

"Carries a hell of a long way," said Robert Wilson. "It's strange the way it carries. Hope he's a shootable cat. The boys said there was a very big one about here."

"If I get a shot, where should I hit him," Macomber asked, "to stop him?"

"In the shoulders," Wilson said. "In the neck if you can make it. Shoot for bone. Break him down."

"I hope I can place it properly," Macomber said.

"You shoot very well," Wilson told him. "Take your time. Make sure of him. The first one in is the one that counts."

"What range will it be?"

"Can't tell. Lion has something to say about that. Don't shoot unless it's close enough so you can make sure."

"At under a hundred yards?" Macomber asked.

Wilson looked at him quickly.

"Hundred's about right. Might have to take him a bit under. Shouldn't chance a shot at much over that. A hundred's a decent range. You can hit him wherever you want at that. Here comes the Memsahib."

"Good morning," she said. "Are we going after that lion?"

"As soon as you deal with your breakfast," Wilson said. "How are you feeling?"

"Marvellous," she said. "I'm very excited."

"I'll just go and see that everything is ready." Wilson went off. As he left the lion roared again.

"Noisy beggar," Wilson said. "We'll put a stop to that."

"What's the matter, Francis?" his wife asked him.

"Nothing," Macomber said.

"Yes, there is," she said. "What are you upset about?"

"Nothing," he said.

"Tell me," she looked at him. "Don't you feel well?"

"It's that damned roaring," he said. "It's been going on all night, you know."

"Why didn't you wake me," she said. "I'd love to have heard it."

"I've got to kill the damned thing," Macomber said, miserably.

"Well, that's what you're out here for, isn't it?"

"Yes. But I'm nervous. Hearing the thing roar gets on my nerves."

"Well then, as Wilson said, kill him and stop his roaring."

"Yes, darling," said Francis Macomber. "It sounds easy, doesn't it?"

"You're not afraid, are you?"

"Of course not. But I'm nervous from hearing him roar all night."

"You'll kill him marvellously," she said. "I know you will. I'm awfully anxious to see it."

"Finish your breakfast and we'll be starting."

"It's not light yet," she said. "This is a ridiculous hour."

Just then the lion roared in a deep-chested moaning, suddenly guttural, ascending vibration that seemed to shake the air and ended in a sigh and a heavy, deep-chested grunt.

"He sounds almost here," Macomber's wife said.

"My God," said Macomber. "I hate that damned noise."

"It's very impressive."

"Impressive. It's frightful."

Robert Wilson came up then carrying his short, ugly, shockingly bigbored .505 Gibbs[5] and grinning.

"Come on," he said. "Your gun-bearer has your Springfield[6] and the big gun. Everything's in the car. Have you solids?"[7]

"Yes."

"I'm ready," Mrs. Macomber said.

"Must make him stop that racket," Wilson said. "You get in front. The Memsahib can sit back here with me."

They climbed into the motor car and, in the gray first daylight, moved off up the river through the trees. Macomber opened the breech of his rifle and saw he had metal-cased bullets, shut the bolt and put the rifle on safety. He saw his hand was trembling. He felt in his pocket for more cartridges and moved his fingers over the cartridges in the loops of his tunic front. He turned back to where Wilson sat in the rear seat of the doorless, box-bodied motor car beside his wife, them both grinning with excitement, and Wilson leaned forward and whispered.

"See the birds dropping. Means the old boy has left his kill."

On the far bank of the stream Macomber could see, above the trees, vultures circling and plummeting down.

"Chances are he'll come to drink along here," Wilson whispered. "Before he goes to lay up. Keep an eye out."

They were driving slowly along the high bank of the stream which here cut deeply to its boulder-filled bed, and they wound in and out through big trees as they drove. Macomber was watching the opposite bank when he felt Wilson take hold of his arm. The car stopped.

"There he is," he heard the whisper. "Ahead and to the right. Get out and take him. He's a marvellous lion."

Macomber saw the lion now. He was standing almost broadside, his great head up and turned toward them. The early morning breeze that blew toward them was just stirring his dark mane, and the lion looked huge,

---

[5]A .505 Gibbs Rimless Magnum action rifle, developed by George Gibbs around 1910.
[6]A hunting rifle.
[7]Bullets; specifically, steel-jacketed bullets that are copper-plated.

silhouetted on the rise of bank in the gray morning light, his shoulders heavy, his barrel of a body bulking smoothly.

"How far is he?" asked Macomber, raising his rifle.

"About seventy-five. Get out and take him."

"Why not shoot from where I am?"

"You don't shoot them from cars," he heard Wilson saying in his ear. "Get out. He's not going to stay there all day."

Macomber stepped out of the curved opening at the side of the front seat, onto the step and down onto the ground. The lion still stood looking majestically and coolly toward this object that his eyes only showed in silhouette, bulking like some super-rhino. There was no man smell carried toward him and he watched the object, moving his great head a little from side to side. Then watching the object, not afraid, but hesitating before going down the bank to drink with such a thing opposite him, he saw a man figure detach itself from it and he turned his heavy head and swung away toward the cover of the trees as he heard a cracking crash and felt the slam of a .30-06 220-grain solid bullet that bit his flank and ripped in sudden hot scalding nausea through his stomach. He trotted, heavy, big-footed, swinging wounded full-bellied, through the trees toward the tall grass and cover, and the crash came again to go past him ripping the air apart. Then it crashed again and he felt the blow as it hit his lower ribs and ripped on through, blood sudden hot and frothy in his mouth, and he galloped toward the high grass where he could crouch and not be seen and make them bring the crashing thing close enough so he could make a rush and get the man that held it.

Macomber had not thought how the lion felt as he got out of the car. He only knew his hands were shaking and as he walked away from the car it was almost impossible for him to make his legs move. They were stiff in the thighs, but he could feel the muscles fluttering. He raised the rifle, sighted on the junction of the lion's head and shoulders and pulled the trigger. Nothing happened though he pulled until he thought his finger would break. Then he knew he had the safety on and as he lowered the rifle to move the safety over he moved another frozen pace forward, and the lion seeing his silhouette flow clear of the silhouette of the car, turned and started off at a trot, and, as Macomber fired, he heard a whunk that meant that the bullet was home; but the lion kept on going. Macomber shot again and every one saw the bullet throw a spout of dirt beyond the trotting lion. He shot again, remembering to lower his aim, and they all heard the bullet hit, and the lion went into a gallop and was in the tall grass before he had the bolt pushed forward.

Macomber stood there feeling sick at his stomach, his hands that held the Springfield still cocked, shaking, and his wife and Robert Wilson were standing by him. Beside him too were the two gun-bearers chattering in Wakamba.[8]

"I hit him," Macomber said. "I hit him twice."

"You gut-shot him and you hit him somewhere forward." Wilson said without enthusiasm. The gun-bearers looked very grave. They were silent now.

"You may have killed him," Wilson went on. "We'll have to wait a while before we go in to find out."

"What do you mean?"

"Let him get sick before we follow him up."

"Oh," said Macomber.

"He's a hell of a fine lion," Wilson said cheerfully. "He's gotten into a bad place though."

"Why is it bad?"

"Can't see him until you're on him."

"Oh," said Macomber.

"Come on," said Wilson. "The Memsahib can stay here in the car. We'll go to have a look at the blood spoor."[9]

"Stay here, Margot," Macomber said to his wife. His mouth was very dry and it was hard for him to talk.

"Why?" she asked.

"Wilson says to."

"We're going to have a look," Wilson said. "You stay here. You can see even better from here."

"All right."

Wilson spoke in Swahili to the driver. He nodded and said, "Yes, Bwana."

Then they went down the steep bank and across the stream, climbing over and around the boulders and up the other bank, pulling up by some projecting roots, and along it until they found where the lion had been trotting when Macomber first shot. There was dark blood on the short grass that the gun-bearers pointed out with grass stems, and that ran away behind the river bank trees.

"What do we do?" asked Macomber.

"Not much choice," said Wilson. "We can't bring the car over. Bank's too steep. We'll let him stiffen up a bit and then you and I'll go in and have a look for him."

"Can't we set the grass on fire?" Macomber asked.

"Too green."

"Can't we send beaters?"

Wilson looked at him appraisingly. "Of course we can," he said. "But it's just a touch murderous. You see, we know the lion's wounded. You can

---

[8]The language of a tribe native to Kenya.
[9]The bloody track or trail of an injured wild animal pursued as game.

drive an unwounded lion—he'll move on ahead of a noise—but a wounded lion's going to charge. You can't see him until you're right on him. He'll make himself perfectly flat in cover you wouldn't think would hide a hare. You can't very well send boys in there to that sort of a show. Somebody bound to get mauled."

"What about the gun-bearers?"

"Oh, they'll go with us. It's their *shauri*.[10] You see, they signed on for it. They don't look too happy though, do they?"

"I don't want to go in there," said Macomber. It was out before he knew he'd said it.

"Neither do I," said Wilson very cheerily. "Really no choice though." Then, as an afterthought, he glanced at Macomber and saw suddenly how he was trembling and the pitiful look on his face.

"You don't have to go in, of course," he said. "That's what I'm hired for, you know. That's why I'm so expensive."

"You mean you'd go in by yourself? Why not leave him there?"

Robert Wilson, whose entire occupation had been with the lion and the problem he presented, and who had not been thinking about Macomber except to note that he was rather windy, suddenly felt as though he had opened the wrong door in a hotel and seen something shameful.

"What do you mean?"

"Why not just leave him?"

"You mean pretend to ourselves he hasn't been hit?"

"No. Just drop it."

"It isn't done."

"Why not?"

"For one thing, he's certain to be suffering. For another, some one else might run onto him."

"I see."

"But you don't have to have anything to do with it."

"I'd like to," Macomber said. "I'm just scared, you know."

"I'll go ahead when we go in," Wilson said, "with Kongoni tracking. You keep behind me and a little to one side. Chances are we'll hear him growl. If we see him we'll both shoot. Don't worry about anything. I'll keep you backed up. As a matter of fact, you know, perhaps you'd better not go. It might be much better. Why don't you go over and join the Memsahib while I just get it over with?"

"No, I want to go."

"All right," said Wilson. "But don't go in if you don't want to. This is my *shauri* now, you know."

"I want to go," said Macomber.

They sat under a tree and smoked.

---

[10]Problem.

"Want to go back and speak to the Memsahib while we're waiting?" Wilson asked.

"No."

"I'll just step back and tell her to be patient."

"Good," said Macomber. He sat there, sweating under his arms, his mouth dry, his stomach hollow feeling, wanting to find courage to tell Wilson to go on and finish off the lion without him. He could not know that Wilson was furious because he had not noticed the state he was in earlier and sent him back to his wife. While he sat there Wilson came up. "I have your big gun," he said. "Take it. We've given him time, I think. Come on."

Macomber took the big gun and Wilson said:

"Keep behind me and about five yards to the right and do exactly as I tell you." Then he spoke in Swahili to the two gun-bearers who looked the picture of gloom.

"Let's go," he said.

"Could I have a drink of water?" Macomber asked. Wilson spoke to the older gun-bearer, who wore a canteen on his belt, and the man unbuckled it, unscrewed the top and handed it to Macomber, who took it noticing how heavy it seemed and how hairy and shoddy the felt covering was in his hand. He raised it to drink and looked ahead at the high grass with the flat-topped trees behind it. A breeze was blowing toward them and the grass rippled gently in the wind. He looked at the gun-bearer and he could see the gun-bearer was suffering too with fear.

Thirty-five yards into the grass the big lion lay flattened out along the ground. His ears were back and his only movement was a slight twitching up and down of his long, black-tufted tail. He had turned at bay as soon as he had reached this cover and he was sick with the wound through his full belly, and weakening with the wound through his lungs that brought a thin foamy red to his mouth each time he breathed. His flanks were wet and hot and flies were on the little openings the solid bullets had made in his tawny hide, and his big yellow eyes, narrowed with hate, looked straight ahead, only blinking when the pain came as he breathed, and his claws dug in the soft baked earth. All of him, pain, sickness, hatred and all of his remaining strength, was tightening into an absolute concentration for a rush. He could hear the men talking and he waited, gathering all of himself into this preparation for a charge as soon as the men would come into the grass. As he heard their voices his tail stiffened to twitch up and down, and, as they came into the edge of the grass, he made a coughing grunt and charged.

Kongoni, the old gun-bearer, in the lead watching the blood spoor, Wilson watching the grass for any movement, his big gun ready, the second gun-bearer looking ahead and listening. Macomber close to Wilson, his rifle cocked, they had just moved into the grass when Macomber heard the blood-choked coughing grunt, and saw the swishing rush in the grass. The next thing he knew he was running; running wildly, in panic in the open, running toward the stream.

He heard the *ca-ra-wong!* of Wilson's big rifle, and again in a second crashing *carawong!* and turning saw the lion, horrible-looking now, with half his head seeming to be gone, crawling toward Wilson in the edge of the tall grass while the red-faced man worked the bolt on the short ugly rifle and aimed carefully as another blasting *carawong!* came from the muzzle, and the crawling, heavy, yellow bulk of the lion stiffened and the huge, mutilated head slid forward and Macomber, standing by himself in the clearing where he had run, holding a loaded rifle, while two black men and a white man looked back at him in contempt, knew the lion was dead. He came toward Wilson, his tallness all seeming a naked reproach, and Wilson looked at him and said:

"Want to take pictures?"

"No," he said.

That was all any one had said until they reached the motor car. Then Wilson had said:

"Hell of a fine lion. Boys will skin him out. We might as well stay here in the shade."

Macomber's wife had not looked at him nor he at her and he had sat by her in the back seat with Wilson sitting in the front seat. Once he had reached over and taken his wife's hand without looking at her and she had removed her hand from his. Looking across the stream to where the gun-bearers were skinning out the lion he could see that she had been able to see the whole thing. While they sat there his wife had reached forward and put her hand on Wilson's shoulder. He turned and she had leaned forward over the low seat and kissed him on the mouth.

"Oh, I say," said Wilson, going redder than his natural baked color.

"Mr. Robert Wilson," she said. "The beautiful red-faced Mr. Robert Wilson."

Then she sat down beside Macomber again and looked away across the stream to where the lion lay, with uplifted, white-muscled, tendon-marked naked forearms, and white bloating belly, as the black men fleshed away the skin. Finally the gun-bearers brought the skin over, wet and heavy, and climbed in behind with it, rolling it up before they got in, and the motor car started. No one had said anything more until they were back in camp.

That was the story of the lion. Macomber did not know how the lion had felt before he started his rush, nor during it when the unbelievable smash of the .505 with a muzzle velocity of two tons had hit him in the mouth, nor what kept him coming after that, when the second ripping crash had smashed his hind quarters and he had come crawling on toward the crashing, blasting thing that had destroyed him. Wilson knew something about it and only expressed it by saying, "Damned fine lion," but

Macomber did not know how Wilson felt about things either. He did not know how his wife felt except that she was through with him.

His wife had been through with him before but it never lasted. He was very wealthy, and would be much wealthier, and he knew she would not leave him ever now. That was one of the few things that he really knew. He knew about that, about motor cycles—that was earliest—about motor cars, about duck-shooting, about fishing, trout, salmon and big-sea, about sex in books, many books, too many books, about all court games, about dogs, not much about horses, about hanging on to his money, about most of the other things his world dealt in, and about his wife not leaving him. His wife had been a great beauty and she was still a great beauty in Africa, but she was not a great enough beauty any more at home to be able to leave him and better herself and she knew it and he knew it. She had missed the chance to leave him and he knew it. If he had been better with women she would probably have started to worry about him getting another new, beautiful wife; but she knew too much about him to worry about him either. Also, he had always had a great tolerance which seemed the nicest thing about him if it were not the most sinister.

All in all they were known as a comparatively happily married couple, one of those whose disruption is often rumored but never occurs, and as the society columnist put it, they were adding more than a spice of *adventure* to their much envied and ever-enduring *Romance* by a *Safari* in what was known as *Darkest Africa* until the Martin Johnson (1884–1937)[11] lighted it on so many silver screens where they were pursuing *Old Simba* the lion, the buffalo, *Tembo* the elephant and as well collecting specimens for the Museum of Natural History. This same columnist had reported them *on the verge* at least three times in the past and they had been. But they always made it up. They had a sound basis of union. Margot was too beautiful for Macomber to divorce her and Macomber had too much money for Margot ever to leave him.

It was now about three o'clock in the morning and Francis Macomber, who had been asleep a little while after he had stopped thinking about the lion, wakened and then slept again, woke suddenly, frightened in a dream of the bloody-headed lion standing over him, and listening while his heart pounded, he realized that his wife was not in the other cot in the tent. He lay awake with that knowledge for two hours.

At the end of that time his wife came into the tent, lifted her mosquito bar and crawled cozily into bed.

"Where have you been?" Macomber asked in the darkness.

"Hello," she said. "Are you awake?"

"Where have you been?"

"I just went out to get a breath of air."

[11]A reference to the adventurer/photographer Martin Johnson (1884–1937), best known for his silent film *Cannibals of the South Seas* (1918).

"You did, like hell."

"What do you want me to say, darling?"

"Where have you been?"

"Out to get a breath of air."

"That's a new name for it. You *are* a bitch."

"Well, you're a coward."

"All right," he said. "What of it?"

"Nothing as far as I'm concerned. But please let's not talk, darling, because I'm very sleepy."

"You think that I'll take anything."

"I know you will, sweet."

"Well, I won't."

"Please, darling, let's not talk. I'm so very sleepy."

"There wasn't going to be any of that. You promised there wouldn't be."

"Well, there is now," she said sweetly.

"You said if we made this trip that there would be none of that. You promised."

"Yes, darling. That's the way I meant it to be. But the trip was spoiled yesterday. We don't have to talk about it, do we?"

"You don't wait long when you have an advantage, do you?"

"Please let's not talk. I'm so sleepy, darling."

"I'm going to talk."

"Don't mind me then, because I'm going to sleep." And she did.

At breakfast they were all three at the table before daylight and Francis Macomber found that, of all the many men that he had hated, he hated Robert Wilson the most.

"Sleep well?" Wilson asked in his throaty voice, filling a pipe.

"Did you?"

"Topping," the white hunter told him.

You bastard, thought Macomber, you insolent bastard.

So she woke him when she came in, Wilson thought, looking at them both with his flat, cold eyes. Well, why doesn't he keep his wife where she belongs? What does he think I am, a bloody plaster saint? Let him keep her where she belongs. It's his own fault.

"Do you think we'll find buffalo?" Margot asked, pushing away a dish of apricots.

"Chance of it," Wilson said and smiled at her. "Why don't you stay in camp?"

"Not for anything," she told him.

"Why not order her to stay in camp?" Wilson said to Macomber.

"You order her," said Macomber coldly.

"Let's not have any ordering, nor," turning to Macomber, "any silliness, Francis," Margot said quite pleasantly.

"Are you ready to start?" Macomber asked.

"Any time," Wilson told him. "Do you want the Memsahib to go?"

"Does it make any difference whether I do or not?"

The hell with it, thought Robert Wilson. The utter complete hell with it. So this is what it's going to be like. Well, this is what it's going to be like, then.

"Makes no difference," he said.

"You're sure you wouldn't like to stay in camp with her yourself and let me go out and hunt the buffalo?" Macomber asked.

"Can't do that," said Wilson. "Wouldn't talk rot if I were you."

"I'm not talking rot. I'm disgusted."

"Bad word, disgusted."

"Francis, will you please try to speak sensibly," his wife said.

"I speak too damned sensibly," Macomber said. "Did you ever eat such filthy food?"

"Something wrong with the food?" asked Wilson quietly.

"No more than with everything else."

"I'd pull yourself together, laddybuck," Wilson said very quietly. "There's a boy waits at table that understands a little English."

"The hell with him."

Wilson stood up and puffing on his pipe strolled away, speaking a few words in Swahili to one of the gun-bearers who was standing waiting for him. Macomber and his wife sat on at the table. He was staring at his coffee cup.

"If you make a scene I'll leave you, darling," Margot said quietly.

"No, you won't."

"You can try it and see."

"You won't leave me."

"No," she said. "I won't leave you and you'll behave yourself."

"Behave myself? That's a way to talk. Behave myself."

"Yes. Behave yourself."

"Why don't *you* try behaving?"

"I've tried it so long. So very long."

"I hate that red-faced swine," Macomber said. "I loathe the sight of him."

"He's really *very* nice."

"Oh, *shut up*," Macomber almost shouted. Just then the car came up and stopped in front of the dining tent and the driver and the two gun-bearers got out. Wilson walked over and looked at the husband and wife sitting there at the table.

"Going shooting?" he asked.

"Yes," said Macomber, standing up. "Yes."

"Better bring a woolly. It will be cool in the car," Wilson said.

"I'll get my leather jacket," Margot said.

"The boy has it," Wilson told her. He climbed into the front with the driver and Francis Macomber and his wife sat, not speaking, in the back seat.

Hope the silly beggar doesn't take a notion to blow the back of my head off, Wilson thought to himself. Women *are* a nuisance on safari.

The car was grinding down to cross the river at a pebbly ford in the gray daylight and then climbed, angling up the steep bank, where Wilson had ordered a way shovelled out the day before so they could reach the parklike wooded rolling country on the far side.

It was a good morning, Wilson thought. There was a heavy dew and as the wheels went through the grass and low bushes he could smell the odor of the crushed fronds. It was an odor like verbena and he liked this early morning smell of the dew, the crushed bracken and the look of the tree trunks showing black through the early morning mist, as the car made its way through the untracked, parklike country. He had put the two in the back seat out of his mind now and was thinking about buffalo. The buffalo that he was after stayed in the daytime in a thick swamp where it was impossible to get a shot, but in the night they fed out into an open stretch of country and if he could come between them and their swamp with the car, Macomber would have a good chance at them in the open. He did not want to hunt buff with Macomber in thick cover. He did not want to hunt buff or anything else with Macomber at all, but he was a professional hunter and he had hunted with some rare ones in his time. If they got buff today there would only be rhino to come and the poor man would have gone through his dangerous game and things might pick up. He'd have nothing more to do with the woman and Macomber would get over that too. He must have gone through plenty of that before by the look of things. Poor beggar. He must have a way of getting over it. Well, it was the poor sod's own bloody fault.

He, Robert Wilson, carried a double size cot on safari to accommodate any windfalls he might receive. He had hunted for a certain clientele, the international, fast, sporting set, where the women did not feel they were getting their money's worth unless they had shared that cot with the white hunter. He despised them when he was away from them although he liked some of them well enough at the time, but he made his living by them; and their standards were his standards as long as they were hiring him.

They were his standards in all except the shooting. He had his own standards about the killing and they could live up to them or get some one else to hunt them. He knew, too, that they all respected him for this. This Macomber was an odd one though. Damned if he wasn't. Now the wife. Well, the wife. Yes, the wife. Hm, the wife. Well he'd dropped all that. He looked around at them. Macomber sat grim and furious. Margot smiled at him. She looked younger today, more innocent and fresher and not so professionally beautiful. What's in her heart God knows, Wilson thought. She hadn't talked much last night. At that it was a pleasure to see her.

The motor car climbed up a slight rise and went on through the trees and then out into a grassy prairie-like opening and kept in the shelter of the trees along the edge, the driver going slowly and Wilson looking

carefully out across the prairie and all along its far side. He stopped the
car and studied the opening with his field glasses. Then he motioned to
the driver to go on and the car moved slowly along, the driver avoiding
warthog holes and driving around the mud castles ants had built. Then,
looking across the opening, Wilson suddenly turned and said,

"By God, there they are!"

And looking where he pointed, while the car jumped forward and Wilson
spoke in rapid Swahili to the driver, Macomber saw three huge, black animals
looking almost cylindrical in their long heaviness, like big black tank cars,
moving at a gallop across the far edge of the open prairie. They moved at
a stiff-necked, stiff bodied gallop and he could see the upswept wide black
horns on their heads as they galloped heads out; the heads not moving.

"They're three old bulls," Wilson said. "We'll cut them off before they
get to the swamp."

The car was going a wild forty-five miles an hour across the open and
as Macomber watched, the buffalo got bigger and bigger until he could see
the gray, hairless, scabby look of one huge bull and how his neck was a
part of his shoulders and the shiny black of his horns as he galloped a little
behind the others that were strung out in that steady plunging gait; and
then, the car swaying as though it had just jumped a road, they drew up
close and he could see the plunging hugeness of the bull, and the dust in
his sparsely haired hide, the wide boss of horn and his outstretched, wide-
nostrilled muzzle, and he was raising his rifle when Wilson shouted, "Not
from the car, you fool!" and he had no fear, only hatred of Wilson, while
the brakes clamped on and the car skidded, plowing sideways to an almost
stop and Wilson was out on one side and he on the other, stumbling as his
feet hit the still speeding-by of the earth, and then he was shooting at
the bull as he moved away, hearing the bullets whunk into him, emptying
his rifle at him as he moved steadily away, finally remembering to get his
shots forward into the shoulder, and as he fumbled to re-load, he saw the
bull was down. Down on his knees, his big head tossing, and seeing the
other two still galloping he shot at the leader and hit him. He shot again
and missed and he heard the *carawonging* roar as Wilson shot and saw the
leading bull slide forward onto his nose.

"Get that other," Wilson said. "Now you're shooting!"

But the other bull was moving steadily at the same gallop and he
missed, throwing a spout of dirt, and Wilson missed and the dust rose
in a cloud and Wilson shouted, "Come on. He's too far!" and grabbed his
arm and they were in the car again, Macomber and Wilson hanging on the
sides and rocketing swayingly over the uneven ground, drawing up on the
steady, plunging, heavy-necked, straight-moving gallop of the bull.

They were behind him and Macomber was filling his rifle, dropping shells
onto the ground, jamming it, clearing the jam, then they were almost up
with the bull when Wilson yelled "Stop," and the car skidded so that it

almost swung over and Macomber fell forward onto his feet, slammed his bolt forward and fired as far forward as he could aim into the galloping, rounded black back, aimed and shot again, then again, then again, and the bullets, all of them hitting, had no effect on the buffalo that he could see. Then Wilson shot, the roar deafening him, and he could see the bull stagger. Macomber shot again, aiming carefully, and down he came, onto his knees.

"All right," Wilson said. "Nice work. That's the three."

Macomber felt a drunken elation.

"How many times did you shoot?" he asked.

"Just three," Wilson said. "You killed the first bull. The biggest one. I helped you finish the other two. Afraid they might have got into cover. You had them killed. I was just mopping up a little. You shot damn well."

"Let's go to the car," said Macomber. "I want a drink."

"Got to finish off that buff first," Wilson told him. The buffalo was on his knees and he jerked his head furiously and bellowed in pig-eyed, roaring rage as they came toward him.

"Watch he doesn't get up," Wilson said. Then, "Get a little broadside and take him in the neck just behind the ear."

Macomber aimed carefully at the center of the huge, jerking, rage-driven neck and shot. At the shot the head dropped forward.

"That does it," said Wilson. "Got the spine. They're a hell of a looking thing, aren't they?"

"Let's get the drink," said Macomber. In his life he had never felt so good.

In the car Macomber's wife sat very white-faced. "You were marvellous, darling," she said to Macomber. "What a ride."

"Was it rough?" Wilson asked.

"It was frightful. I've never been more frightened in my life."

"Let's all have a drink," Macomber said.

"By all means," said Wilson. "Give it to the Memsahib." She drank the neat whisky from the flask and shuddered a little when she swallowed. She handed the flask to Macomber who handed it to Wilson.

"It was frightfully exciting," she said. "It's given me a dreadful headache. I didn't know you were allowed to shoot them from cars though."

"No one shot from cars," said Wilson coldly.

"I mean chase them from cars."

"Wouldn't ordinarily," Wilson said. "Seemed sporting enough to me though while we were doing it. Taking more chance driving that way across the plain full of holes and one thing and another than hunting on foot. Buffalo could have charged us each time we shot if he liked. Gave him every chance. Wouldn't mention it to any one though. It's illegal if that's what you mean."

"It seemed very unfair to me," Margot said, "chasing those big helpless things in a motor car."

"Did it?" said Wilson.

"What would happen if they heard about it in Nairobi?"

"I'd lose my license for one thing. Other unpleasantnesses," Wilson said, taking a drink from the flask. "I'd be out of business."

"Really?"

"Yes, really."

"Well," said Macomber, and he smiled for the first time all day. "Now she has something on you."

"You have such a pretty way of putting things, Francis," Margot Macomber said. Wilson looked at them both. If a four-letter man marries a five-letter woman, he was thinking, what number of letters would their children be? What he said was, "We lost a gun-bearer. Did you notice it?"

"My God, no," Macomber said.

"Here he comes," Wilson said. "He's all right. He must have fallen off when we left the first bull."

Approaching them was the middle-aged gun-bearer, limping along in his knitted cap, khaki tunic, shorts and rubber sandals, gloomy-faced and disgusted looking. As he came up he called out to Wilson in Swahili and they all saw the change in the white hunter's face.

"What does he say?" asked Margot.

"He says the first bull got up and went into the bush," Wilson said with no expression in his voice.

"Oh," said Macomber blankly.

"Then it's going to be just like the lion," said Margot, full of anticipation.

"It's not going to be a damned bit like the lion," Wilson told her. "Did you want another drink, Macomber?"

"Thanks, yes," Macomber said. He expected the feeling he had had about the lion to come back but it did not. For the first time in his life he really felt wholly without fear. Instead of fear he had a feeling of definite elation.

"We'll go and have a look at the second bull," Wilson said. "I'll tell the driver to put the car in the shade."

"What are you going to do?" asked Margaret Macomber.

"Take a look at the buff," Wilson said.

"I'll come."

"Come along."

The three of them walked over to where the second buffalo bulked blackly in the open, head forward on the grass, the massive horns swung wide.

"He's a very good head," Wilson said. "That's close to a fifty-inch spread."

Macomber was looking at him with delight.

"He's hateful looking," said Margot. "Can't we go into the shade?"

"Of course," Wilson said. "Look," he said to Macomber, and pointed. "See that patch of bush?"

"Yes."

"That's where the first bull went in. The gun-bearer said when he fell off the bull was down. He was watching us helling along and the other two buff galloping. When he looked up there was the bull up and looking at him. Gun-bearer ran like hell and the bull went off slowly into that bush."

"Can we go in after him now?" asked Macomber eagerly.

Wilson looked at him appraisingly. Damned if this isn't a strange one, he thought. Yesterday he's scared sick and today he's a ruddy fire eater.

"No, we'll give him a while."

"Let's please go into the shade," Margot said. Her face was white and she looked ill.

They made their way to the car where it stood under a single, wide-spreading tree and all climbed in.

"Chances are he's dead in there," Wilson remarked. "After a little we'll have a look."

Macomber felt a wild unreasonable happiness that he had never known before.

"By God, that was a chase," he said. "I've never felt any such feeling. Wasn't it marvellous, Margot?"

"I hated it."

"Why?"

"I hated it," she said bitterly. "I loathed it."

"You know I don't think I'd ever be afraid of anything again," Macomber said to Wilson. "Something happened in me after we first saw the buff and started after him. Like a dam bursting. It was pure excitement."

"Cleans out your liver," said Wilson. "Damn funny things happen to people."

Macomber's face was shining. "You know something did happen to me," he said. "I feel absolutely different."

His wife said nothing and eyed him strangely. She was sitting far back in the seat and Macomber was sitting forward talking to Wilson who turned sideways talking over the back of the front seat.

"You know, I'd like to try another lion," Macomber said. "I'm really not afraid of them now. After all, what can they do to you?"

"That's it," said Wilson. "Worst one can do is kill you. How does it go? Shakespeare. Damned good. See if I can remember. Oh, damned good. Used to quote it to myself at one time. Let's see. 'By my troth, I care not; a man can die but once; we owe God a death and let it go which way it will, he that dies this year is quit for the next.' Damned fine, eh?"

He was very embarrassed, having brought out this thing he had lived by, but he had seen men come of age before and it always moved him. It was not a matter of their twenty-first birthday.

It had taken a strange chance of hunting, a sudden precipitation into action without opportunity for worrying beforehand, to bring this about with Macomber, but regardless of how it had happened it had most certainly happened. Look at the beggar now, Wilson thought. It's that some of them stay little boys so long. Wilson thought. Sometimes all their lives.

Their figures stay boyish when they're fifty. The great American boy-men. Damned strange people. But he liked this Macomber now. Damned strange fellow. Probably meant the end of cuckoldry too.[12] Well, that would be a damned good thing. Damned good thing. Beggar had probably been afraid all his life. Don't know what started it. But over now. Hadn't had time to be afraid with the buff. That and being angry too. Motor car too. Motor cars made it familiar. Be a damn fire eater now. He'd seen it in the war work the same way. More of a change than any loss of virginity. Fear gone like an operation. Something else grew in its place. Main thing a man had. Made him into a man. Women knew it too. No bloody fear.

From the far corner of the seat Margaret Macomber looked at the two of them. There was no change in Wilson. She saw Wilson as she had seen him the day before when she had first realized what his great talent was. But she saw the change in Francis Macomber now.

"Do you have that feeling of happiness about what's going to happen?" Macomber asked, still exploring his new wealth.

"You're not supposed to mention it," Wilson said, looking in the other's face. "Much more fashionable to say you're scared. Mind you, you'll be scared too, plenty of times."

"But you *have* a feeling of happiness about action to come?"

"Yes," said Wilson. "There's that. Doesn't do to talk too much about all this. Talk the whole thing away. No pleasure in anything if you mouth it up too much."

"You're both talking rot," said Margot. "Just because you've chased some helpless animals in a motor car you talk like heroes."

"Sorry," said Wilson. "I have been gassing too much." She's worried about it already, he thought.

"If you don't know what we're talking about why not keep out of it?" Macomber asked his wife.

"You've gotten awfully brave, awfully suddenly," his wife said contemptuously, but her contempt was not secure. She was very afraid of something.

Macomber laughed, a very natural hearty laugh. "You know I *have*," he said. "I really have."

"Isn't it sort of late?" Margot said bitterly. Because she had done the best she could for many years back and the way they were together now was no one person's fault.

"Not for me," said Macomber.

Margot said nothing but sat back in the corner of the seat.

"Do you think we've given him time enough?" Macomber asked Wilson cheerfully.

"We might have a look," Wilson said. "Have you any solids left?"

"The gun-bearer has some."

---

[12]Dishonoring a husband by engaging in adultery.

Wilson called in Swahili and the older gun-bearer, who was skinning out one of the heads, straightened up, pulled a box of solids out of his pocket and brought them over to Macomber, who filled his magazine and put the remaining shells in his pocket.

"You might as well shoot the Springfield," Wilson said. "You're used to it. We'll leave the Mannlicher in the car with the Memsahib. Your gun-bearer can carry your heavy gun. I've this damned cannon. Now let me tell you about them." He had saved this until the last because he did not want to worry Macomber. "When a buff comes he comes with his head high and thrust straight out. The boss of the horns covers any sort of a brain shot. The only shot is straight into the nose. The only other shot is into his chest or, if you're to one side, into the neck or the shoulders. After they've been hit once they take a hell of a lot of killing. Don't try anything fancy. Take the easiest shot there is. They've finished skinning out that head now. Should we get started?"

He called to the gun-bearers, who came up wiping their hands, and the older one got into the back.

"I'll only take Kongoni," Wilson said. "The other can watch to keep the birds away."

As the car moved slowly across the open space toward the island of brushy trees that ran in a tongue of foliage along a dry water course that cut the open swale, Macomber felt his heart pounding and his mouth was dry again, but it was excitement, not fear.

"Here's where he went in," Wilson said. Then to the gun-bearer in Swahili, "Take the blood spoor."

The car was parallel to the patch of bush. Macomber, Wilson and the gun-bearer got down. Macomber, looking back, saw his wife, with the rifle by her side, looking at him. He waved to her and she did not wave back.

The brush was very thick ahead and the ground was dry. The middle-aged gun-bearer was sweating heavily and Wilson had his hat down over his eyes and his red neck showed just ahead of Macomber. Suddenly the gun-bearer said something in Swahili to Wilson and ran forward.

"He's dead in there," Wilson said. "Good work," and he turned to grip Macomber's hand and as they shook hands, grinning at each other, the gun-bearer shouted wildly and they saw him coming out of the bush sideways, fast as a crab, and the bull coming, nose out, mouth tight closed, blood dripping, massive head straight out, coming in a charge, his little pig eyes bloodshot as he looked at them. Wilson, who was ahead, was kneeling shooting, and Macomber, as he fired, unhearing his shot in the roaring of Wilson's gun, saw fragments like slate burst from the huge boss of the horns, and the head jerked, he shot again at the wide nostrils and saw the horns jolt again and fragments fly, and he did not see Wilson now and, aiming carefully, shot again with the buffalo's huge bulk almost on him and his rifle almost level with the on-coming head, nose out, and he could see the little wicked eyes and the head started to lower and he felt a sudden white-hot, blinding flash explode inside his head and that was all he ever felt.

Wilson had ducked to one side to get in a shoulder shot. Macomber had stood solid and shot for the nose, shooting a touch high each time and hitting the heavy horns, splintering and chipping them like hitting a slate roof, and Mrs. Macomber, in the car, had shot at the buffalo with the 6.5 Maunlicher as it seemed about to gore Macomber and had hit her husband about two inches up and a little to one side of the base of his skull.

Francis Macomber lay now, face down, not two yards from where the buffalo lay on his side and his wife knelt over him with Wilson beside her.

"I wouldn't turn him over," Wilson said.

The woman was crying hysterically.

"I'd get back in the car," Wilson said. "Where's the rifle?"

She shook her head, her face contorted. The gun-bearer picked up the rifle.

"Leave it as it is," said Wilson. Then, "Go get Abdulla so that he may witness the manner of the accident."

He knelt down, took a handkerchief from his pocket, and spread it over Francis Macomber's crew-cropped head where it lay. The blood sank into the dry, loose earth.

Wilson stood up and saw the buffalo on his side, his legs out, his thinly-haired belly crawling with ticks. "Hell of a good bull," his brain registered automatically. "A good fifty inches, or better. Better." He called to the driver and told him to spread a blanket over the body and stay by it. Then he walked over to the motor car where the woman sat crying in the corner.

"That was a pretty thing to do," he said in a toneless voice. "He *would* have left you too."

"Stop it," she said.

"Of course it's an accident," he said. "I know that."

"Stop it," she said.

"Don't worry," he said. "There will be a certain amount of unpleasantness but I will have some photographs taken that will be very useful at the inquest. There's the testimony of the gun-bearers and the driver too. You're perfectly all right."

"Stop it," she said.

"There's a hell of a lot to be done," he said. "And I'll have to send a truck off to the lake to wireless for a plane to take the three of us into Nairobi. Why didn't you poison him? That's what they do in England."

"Stop it. Stop it. Stop it," the woman cried.

Wilson looked at her with his flat blue eyes.

"I'm through now," he said. "I was a little angry. I'd begun to like your husband."

"Oh, please stop it," she said. "Please stop it."

"That's better," Wilson said. "Please is much better. Now I'll stop."

[1936]

▪▪ CONTEXT AND RESPONSE ▪▪

Pío Baroja, From *The Chasm*

When a young Ernest Hemingway worked as a reporter, he had to write quickly, concisely, and vividly. Many critics credit the crisp, intense writing style of his fiction to his apprenticeship at the *Kansas City Star*. But another influence is evident: the plainspoken yet powerful style of Spanish novelist Pío Baroja. Baroja was a member of Spain's famous Generation of 1898, a group of artists and thinkers who aspired to awaken their country from its spiritual state of shock after a humbling defeat in the Spanish-American War of 1898. The Generation of 1898's creativity and national pride elevated Spanish contemporary literature to a renewed position of international prestige.

Baroja was a master of understatement: the excerpt from his short story "The Chasm" ("*La sima*") conveys a wrenching emotional realization through simple dialogue, uncomplicated sentences, and unsophisticated characters. Baroja's stark tale of a shepherd and the ugly fate of his beloved son is anything but sentimental. Hemingway, who lived in Spain for several years as an adult, was an avid reader of Baroja from his youth. Baroja's technique of communicating emotional motivation through action rather than explanation is echoed in Hemingway's own "iceberg" narrative style, in which he reveals only a fraction of his characters' complex emotional realities, buried beneath the surface of the narrative like the hidden bulk of a glacier. Furthermore, Hemingway is said to have written an admiring letter to Baroja in which he states that the older man should have won a Nobel Prize of his own.

PÍO BAROJA ▪ (1872–1956)

"Let's go back, boy," the shepherd said. "The sun is hiding."

The lad ran hastily back and forth, waving his arms, brandishing his staff, hitting the ground, shouting, and throwing stones until he had assembled the goats in a corner on the mountainside. The old man ordered their ranks; a he-goat, with a big bell on his neck, preceded them as a guide, and the flock began to descend to the plain. When the flock of goats stood out against the grass, it resembled a dark surge of waves furrowing a greenish sea. The cheerful ringing of their bells was uniform and rhythmic.

"Lad, have you seen whether old lady Remedios's he-goat is in the flock?" the sheperd asked.

"I saw him, grandfather," the boy replied.

"You have got to keep an eye on that animal, because may the devil take me if I don't have a dislike for the beast."

"Why do you feel that way, grandfather?"

"Don't you know that old lady Remedios has the reputation all over the village of being a witch?"

"And is it true, grandfather?"

"That's what the sacristan said the last time I was in the village. They also say she gives the evil eye to people and animals, and that she sells positions. The talk is that she was seen flying in the air amid groups of snakes."

The shepherd continued to relate what was said about the old lady in the village, and, while he conversed with his grandson in this manner, they both descended the mountain, from the trail to the path, from the path to the road, until they halted alongside the gate to an enclosure. Below that point the great hollow of the valley could be seen; in the distance shone the silver ribbon of the river, and next to that could be divined the mistshrouded village; and not far off, on the side of a mountain, there stood out prominently the ruins of the former castle of the local lords.

"Open the wattle, boy," the shepherd called to the lad.

The boy pulled out the poles that barred the fence gate, and the goats began to pass through it to the enclosure, crowding one another. In the course of this, one of the animals got frightened and, departing from the road, began to downhill speedily.

"Run, run after him, boy," the old man shouted, and then he incited the dog to pursue the runaway animal.

"Go on, Wolf! Go fetch him!"

The dog uttered a muffle bark, and set out like an arrow.

"Go! Catch up with him!" the shepherd went on shouting. "There he goes."

The he-goat leapt from rock to rock like a rubber ball; at times he turned around to look back, tall, erect, with his black fleece and his big devilish goatee. He hid among the blackberry and broom scrub, cutting capers and leaping in the air.

The dog followed him, gaining ground only with difficulty; the lad was following both of them, realizing that the pursuit would soon be over, because not far away the craggy mountainside ended in a sloping open area. On arriving there, the lad saw the he-goat running desperately, pursued by the dog; then he saw him approach a heap of rocks and vanish among them. Near those rocks was a vertical cave, which, according to some, was very deep; and, suspecting that the animal had fallen into it, the boy peered over the rim to look at the mouth of the cavern. On a scrub-covered shelf of rock jutting from the cavern wall was the he-goat.

The lad tried to grab him by a horn, lying on his stomach on the rim of the cave; but, seeing how impossible his attempt was, he returned to the spot where the shepherd was waiting and told him what had happened.

"Damned animal!" the old man muttered. "Now we'll go back, lad. First we've got to put the flock in the fold."

Between them they locked up the goats and, after doing that, the shepherd and his grandson descended to the open area and approached the rim of the chasm. The goat was still standing in the scrub. The dog was barking at him quietly from the perimeter.

"Give me your hand, grandfather. I'll let myself down," the lad said.

"Careful boy. I'm very frightened of your falling."

"Don't worry, grandfather."

The boy pushed aside the weeds at the mouth of the cave, sat down beside it, and turned his body around without supporting himself, until he was clinging with his hands from the very edge of the cavern; then he let his feet slide down its wall, until they were securely placed on one of the outcroppings near its entrance. He grasped the animal's horn with one hand, and pulled it. The goat, finding himself seized, gave such a tremendous backwards jerk that he lost his footing; he fell, and as he fell, he dragged the boy to the bottom of the abyss. Not a cry was heard, not a moan, not the slightest sound.

The shepherd peered into the mouth of the cavern.

"Lad, lad!" he called in despair.

Nothing; nothing was heard.

"Lad, lad!"

A sorrowful bleat, mingled with the rustling of the wind, seemed to be audible from the bottom of the cave.

Tormented by his parents (his father was a wealthy candy manufacturer perpetually at odds with his wife), ravaged by alcoholism, and conflicted by his homosexuality, Hart Crane nevertheless managed to produce an astonishing body of inventive and original poetry. Born in Garrettsville, Ohio, and brought up in Cleveland, Crane tried for four years while living in Cleveland to make his mark in business—which, he hoped, would give him financial support for a literary career. Between 1920 and 1922 he wrote a number of striking poems and initiated work on the erotic, mystical poetic sequence *Voyages*, several poems from which are included here. In 1923 he settled in New York City, where he had lived for a period among the avant-garde cultural community in 1916–17.

During the mid-1920s Crane completed *Voyages*, published his first book of poems, *White Buildings* (1926), and made considerable progress on a long work he envisioned that eventually became *The Bridge*, published in 1930. A banker and patron of the arts named Otto Kahn helped him financially, as did family members and friends and others in the literary world.

Crane viewed T. S. Eliot's *The Waste Land* (1922) as both a great achievement, revolutionary in form, and a danger, because of its bleakness and pessimism. "Good, of course," Crane concluded, "but so damned dead." He saw himself as a twentieth-century Walt Whitman who would soaringly affirm America, its people, and its technological prowess, geography, and history. But he would be modern in his techniques, structures, and organizations of language, learning from the innovations of Eliot, Ezra Pound, and the Irish poet William Butler Yeats. "The continuous and living evidence of the past in the inmost vital substance of the present"—this is the demanding subject that Crane, with huge ambition, sought to portray and evoke.

Christopher Marlowe, William Blake, Edgar Allan Poe, Herman Melville, and Fyodor Dostoyevsky, as well as Whitman and Eliot, were among Crane's chief influences and models. Classical music, grand symphonies above all, and the rhythms of jazz were also in the background of this poet's enterprise. As "To Brooklyn Bridge," included here, the opening of *The Bridge*, shows, Crane's poem has stunning passages and sequences. But the work as a whole, while admired by some, did not receive the high acclaim that Crane had hoped for. He had placed burdens on poetry and thus on himself he felt he had not overcome: "A poem is at least a stab at the truth....A single, new *word*." In despair, he committed suicide in April 1932 by jumping off a boat bound from Mexico (he had been struggling there with a new long poem) to New York City.

Crane often gives the impression of proclaiming his verse, and not being in control of it, rather than making it emerge securely and coherently from an authentically realized voice. "What I'm really handling, you see, is the

Myth of America": this was his grand subject, his great ambition. The curious result is that Crane can sound very public in his tone yet seem frustratingly private in his meanings. His metaphors are brilliant but sometimes elusive and enigmatic, hard to understand. There is a logic to them, Crane always insisted, but he is not always successful in conveying it to readers.

Ultimately, however, this does not limit Crane's power as a poet. When he operates at his best, as in "To Brooklyn Bridge" and the other poems presented here, his lyrics are as beautifully intense as any in the twentieth century.

Crane's *Collected Poems* were published in 1933, but this edition was superseded by *The Poems of Hart Crane*, ed. Marc Simon (1986).

An illuminating resource is *O My Land, My Friends: The Selected Letters of Hart Crane*, ed. Langdon Hammer and Brom Weber, introduction and commentary by Langdon Hammer (1997). Biographies include John Unterecker, *Voyager: A Life of Hart Crane* (1969); Paul Mariani, *The Broken Tower: A Life of Hart Crane* (1999); and Clive Fisher, *Hart Crane* (2002). For critical analysis, see R. W. B. Lewis, *The Poetry of Hart Crane: A Critical Study* (1967); Warner Berthoff, *Hart Crane, A Re-Introduction* (1989); and Thomas E. Yingling, *Hart Crane and the Homosexual Text: New Thresholds, New Anatomies* (1990).

Recent studies include Robert Rehder, *Stevens, Williams, Crane, and the Motive for Metaphor* (2005); Stephen Guy Bray, *Loving in Verse: Poetic Influence as Erotic* (2006); Brian M. Reed, *Hart Crane: After His Lights* (2006); Gordon A. Tapper, *The Machine That Sings: Modernism, Hart Crane, and the Culture of the Body* (2006); Peter Nickowitz, *Rhetoric and Sexuality: The Poetry of Hart Crane, Elizabeth Bishop, and James Merrill* (2006); Daniel Gabriel, *Hart Crane and the Modernist Epic: Canon and Genre Formation in Crane, Pound, Eliot, and Williams* (2007).

Brooklyn Bridge and New York skyline, 1925. Photograph by Irving Underhill (1872–1960).

At Melville's[1] Tomb

Often beneath the wave, wide from this ledge
The dice of drowned men's bones he saw bequeath
An embassy.[2] Their numbers as he watched,
Beat on the dusty shore and were obscured.

And wrecks passed without sound of bells,   5
The calyx[3] of death's bounty giving back
A scattered chapter, livid hieroglyph,
The portent wound in corridors of shells.

Then in the circuit calm of one vast coil,
Its lashings charmed and malice reconciled,   10
Frosted eyes there were that lifted altars;
And silent answers crept across the stars.

Compass, quadrant and sextant contrive
No farther tides...High in the azure steeps
Monody[4] shall not wake the mariner.   15
This fabulous shadow only the sea keeps.

                                                        [1926]

Voyages

I

Above the fresh ruffles of the surf
Bright striped urchins flay each other with sand.
They have contrived a conquest for shell shucks,
And their fingers crumble fragments of baked weed
Gaily digging and scattering.   5

And in answer to their treble interjections
The sun beats lightning on the waves,
The waves fold thunder on the sand;
And could they hear me I would tell them:

---

[1]Herman Melville (1819–91), American novelist best known for his stories about the sea, including his masterpiece *Moby-Dick* (1851). Melville is buried in Woodlawn Cemetery in New York City.
[2]A mission or message brought by an ambassador. Of this line, Crane notes, "Dice bequeath an embassy, in the first place, by being ground...in little cubes from the bones of drowned men by the action of the sea, and are finally thrown up on the sand, having 'numbers' but no identification. These being the bones of dead men who never completed their voyage, it seems legitimate to refer to them as the only surviving evidence of certain messages undelivered."
[3]The whorl of leaves forming the outer envelope in which a flower is enclosed while still in the bud stage. Of this line, Crane wrote, "The calyx refers in a double ironic sense both to the cornucopia and the vortex made by a sinking vessel. As soon as the water has closed over a ship this whirlpool sends up broken spars, wreckage, etc., which can be referred to as livid hieroglyphs, making a scattered chapter...."
[4]A lyric ode sung by a single voice, original to Greek tragedy; a mournful song or dirge.

O brilliant kids, frisk with your dog,   10
Fondle your shells and sticks, bleached
By time and the elements; but there is a line
You must not cross nor ever trust beyond it
Spry cordage of your bodies to caresses
Too lichen-faithful from too wide a breast.   15
The bottom of the sea is cruel.

II

—And yet this great wink of eternity,
Of rimless floods, unfettered leewardings,
Samite sheeted and processioned where
Her undinal vast belly moonward bends,
Laughing the wrapt inflections of our love;   20

Take this Sea, whose diapason knells
On scrolls of silver snowy sentences,
The sceptred terror of whose sessions rends
As her demeanors motion well or ill,
All but the pieties of lovers' hands.   25

And onward, as bells off San Salvador
Salute the crocus lustres of the stars,
In these poinsettia meadows of her tides,—
Adagios of islands, O my Prodigal,
Complete the dark confessions her veins spell.   30

Mark how her turning shoulders wind the hours,
And hasten while her penniless rich palms
Pass superscription of bent foam and wave,—
Hasten, while they are true,—sleep, death, desire,
Close round one instant in one floating flower.   35

Bind us in time, O Seasons clear, and awe.
O minstrel galleons of Carib fire,
Bequeath us to no earthly shore until
Is answered in the vortex of our grave
The seal's wide spindrift gaze toward paradise.   40

III

Infinite consanguinity it bears—
This tendered theme of you that light
Retrieves from sea plains where the sky
Resigns a breast that every wave enthrones;
While ribboned water lanes I wind
Are laved and scattered with no stroke   45

Wide from your side, whereto this hour
The sea lifts, also, reliquary[1] hands.

And so, admitted through black swollen gates
That must arrest all distance otherwise,—   50
Past whirling pillars and lithe pediments,
Light wrestling there incessantly with light,
Star kissing star through wave on wave unto
Your body rocking!
                                    and where death, if shed,   55
Presumes no carnage, but this single change,—
Upon the steep floor flung from dawn to dawn
The silken skilled transmemberment of song;

Permit me voyage, love, into your hands...

IV

Whose counted smile of hours and days, suppose
I know as spectrum of the sea and pledge   60
Vastly now parting gulf on gulf of wings
Whose circles bridge, I know, (from palms to the severe
Chilled albatross's white immutability)
No stream of greater love advancing now
Than, singing, this mortality alone   65
Through clay aflow immortally to you.

All fragrance irrefragably, and claim
Madly meeting logically in this hour
And region that is ours to wreathe again,
Portending eyes and lips and making told   70
The chancel port and portion of our June—

Shall they not stem and close in our own steps
Bright staves of flowers and quills today as I
Must first be lost in fatal tides to tell?

In signature of the incarnate word   75
The harbor shoulders to resign in mingling
Mutual blood, transpiring as foreknown
And widening noon within your breast for gathering
All bright insinuations that my years have caught
For islands where must lead inviolably   80
Blue latitudes and levels of your eyes,—

In this expectant, still exclaim receive
The secret oar and petals of all love.

[1]A small casket or shrine in which a relic or or other sacred object is kept.

V

Meticulous, past midnight in clear rime,[2]
Infrangible[3] and lonely, smooth as though cast   85
Together in one merciless white blade—
The bay estuaries fleck the hard sky limits.

—As if too brittle or too clear to touch!
The cables of our sleep so swiftly filed,
Already hang, shred ends from remembered stars.   90
One frozen trackless smile...What words
Can strangle this deaf moonlight? For we

Are overtaken, Now no cry, no sword
Can fasten or deflect this tidal wedge,
Slow tyranny of moonlight, moonlight loved   95
And changed..."There's

Nothing like this in the world," you say,
Knowing I cannot touch your hand and look
Too, into that godless cleft of sky
Where nothing turns but dead sands flashing.   100

"—And never to quite understand!" No,
In all the argosy of your bright hair I dreamed
Nothing so flagless as this piracy.

But now
Draw in your head, alone and too tall here.   105
Your eyes already in the slant of drifting foam;
Your breath sealed by the ghosts I do not know:
Draw in your head and sleep the long way home.

[1926]

VI

Where icy and bright dungeons lift
Of swimmers their lost morning eyes,   110
And ocean rivers, churning, shift
Green borders under stranger skies,

Steadily as a shell secretes
Its beating leagues of monotone,
Or as many waters trough the sun's   115
Red kelson past the cape's wet stone;

---

[2]Frost.
[3]Unbreakable.

O rivers mingling toward the sky
And harbor of the phoenix' breast—
My eyes pressed black against the prow,
—Thy derelict and blinded guest   120

Waiting, afire, what name, unspoke,
I cannot claim: let thy waves rear
More savage than the death of kings,
Some splintered garland for the seer.

Beyond siroccos harvesting   125
The solstice thunders, crept away,
Like a cliff swinging or a sail
Flung into April's inmost day—

Creation's blithe and petalled word
To the lounged goddess when she rose   130
Conceding dialogue with eyes
That smile unsearchable repose—

Still fervid covenant, Belle Isle,
—Unfolded floating dais before
Which rainbows twine continual hair—   135
Belle Isle, white echo of the oar!

The imaged Word, it is, that holds
Hushed willows anchored in its glow.
It is the unbetrayable reply
Whose accent no farewell can know.   140

[1926]

To Brooklyn Bridge

How many dawns, chill from his rippling rest
The seagull's wings shall dip and pivot him,
Shedding white rings of tumult, building high
Over the chained bay waters Liberty—

Then, with inviolate curve, forsake our eyes   5
As apparitional as sails that cross
Some page of figures to be filed away;
—Till elevators drop us from our day...

I think of cinemas, panoramic sleights
With multitudes bent toward some flashing scene   10
Never disclosed, but hastened to again,
Foretold to other eyes on the same screen;

And Thee, across the harbor, silver-paced
As though the sun took step of thee, yet left
Some motion ever unspent in thy stride,— 15
Implicitly thy freedom staying thee!

Out of some subway scuttle, cell or loft
A bedlamite[1] speeds to thy parapets,
Tilting there momently, shrill shirt ballooning,
A jest falls from the speechless caravan. 20

Down Wall, from girder into street noon leaks,
A rip-tooth of the sky's acetylene[2];
All afternoon the cloud-flown derricks[3] turn...
Thy cables breathe the North Atlantic still.

And obscure as that heaven of the Jews, 25
Thy guerdon[4]...Accolade thou dost bestow
Of anonymity time cannot raise:
Vibrant reprieve and pardon thou dost show.

O harp and altar, of the fury fused,
(How could mere toil align thy choiring strings!) 30
Terrific threshold of the prophet's pledge,
Prayer of pariah, and the lover's cry,—

Again the traffic lights that skim thy swift
Unfractioned idiom, immaculate sigh of stars,
Beading thy path—condense eternity: 35
And we have seen night lifted in thine arms.

Under thy shadow by the piers I waited;
Only in darkness is thy shadow clear.
The City's fiery parcels all undone,
Already snow submerges an iron year... 40

O Sleepless as the river under thee,
Vaulting the sea, the prairies' dreaming sod,
Unto us lowliest sometime sweep, descend
And of the curveship lend a myth to God.

[1927, 1930]

---

[1]A madman or lunatic. The original reference is to the Hospital of St. Mary of Bethlehem (pronounced "Bedlam"), a London insane asylum.
[2]A colorless gas used in welding.
[3]Cranes; machines used for hoisting or moving heavy weights; a hangman's gallows.
[4]Reward or recompense.

ALLEN TATE ■ (1899–1979)

The American poet, critic, and novelist Allen Tate was born in Winchester, Kentucky, and graduated from Vanderbilt University in 1922. With John Crowe Ransom (one of his teachers), Robert Penn Warren (one of his class-mates), and others, Tate founded *The Fugitive* (1922–25), a journal that reflected the literary, social, and political values of the conservative South. Two of his poems were published in the first issue, and four in the second. While still in his twenties, Tate also wrote biographies of the Confederate general Stonewall Jackson (1928) and the president of the Confederacy, Jefferson Davis (1929). He was a contributor, too, to an important southern manifesto, *I'll Take My Stand: The South and the Agrarian Tradition* (1930); his essay, an attack on abstraction and rationalism, is titled, "Remarks on the Southern Religion."

During the 1930s, Tate also worked on and published a novel, *The Fathers* (1938). This was a first-person narrative, set in Virginia, in which the 65-year-old Lacy Buchan recalls his past, surveying the decline and fall of the Old South and the order it embodied and the coming to prominence and power of a soulless modernity.

Tate was the resident fellow of poetry at Princeton (1939–42); he was the chair of poetry at the Library of Congress (1943–44); and he edited a literary journal, *The Sewanee Review* (1944–46). In 1950, he wrote of his poetry that "its main theme is man suffering from unbelief," and in this same year he became a convert to Roman Catholicism. From 1951 to 1968, he taught at the University of Minnesota. His critical writings—he was a leading figure in the New Criticism, which emphasized "close reading" of the texture and form of literature—include *Reactionary Essays on Poetry and Ideas* (1936), *On the Limits of Poetry* (1948), and *The Man of Letters in the Modern World* (1955).

Tate's distinguished literary career is summed up in his *Collected Poems, 1919–1976* (1977) and *Essays of Four Decades* (1969). His first marriage, to the fiction writer Caroline Gordon, was a troubled, complicated one; they married in 1924 and finally divorced in 1959. Tate married two more times, in 1959 and 1966. He died in 1979 and was buried in Sewanee, Tennessee.

Among Tate's best poems are "Ode to the Confederate Dead" (included here), "The Mediterranean," and "The Buried Lake." Significant influences on his poetry include Dante, Elizabethan and Jacobean tragedy, the French Symbolists (in particular, Charles Baudelaire and Stéphane Mallarmé), and T. S. Eliot—and the traditions and legacies (and perhaps the myths and idealizations) of the agrarian and anti-industrial South. Tate was, in liter-ary terms, conservative, traditionalist, and modernist, and both regional and cosmopolitan. He said that his technique as a poet consisted of "grad-ually circling round the subject, threatening it and filling it with suspense, and finally accomplishing its demise without ever quite using the ultimate violence upon it." Dense, allusive, symbolic, intense, with careful metrical patterns and rhythms; classical, Southern Gothic, baroque: Tate made highly wrought verse, and he had a major impact on Hart Crane, Robert Lowell, Randall Jarrell, and Theodore Roethke.

Tate wrote the "Ode to the Confederate Dead" in 1926 and published it in 1927; he published a revised version in 1930 and reprinted it in his *Selected Poems* (1937). As scholars have noted, the poem is not quite what the reader expects. To an extent, it is formal and public, an "ode" that honors the memory of those who died in battle. Yet, even more, it is private, meditative, a reflection, and an exploration of the meanings of change, time, and mortality. In reference to the "Ode to the Confederate Dead," the critic Lillian Feder has observed that Tate's poetry "speaks of the present only in relation to the past, and his view of the past is the epic view, heroic, exalted, the poet's past rather than the historian's." In this poem, another critic, Richard Gray, has said, there is "a constant tension between texture and structure: the language, packed and disruptive, the multiple levels of allusion and bitter ironies of feeling, are barely kept in control by the formal patterns of the verse." Ironic, pessimistic, complex, allusive, difficult: this poem is both conservative and modernist, remaking, with violence, the tradition it draws upon and honors.

For biography, see Radcliffe Squires, *Allen Tate: A Literary Biography* (1971); and Thomas A. Underwood, *Allen Tate: Orphan of the South* (2000). Scholarly studies include: *Allen Tate and His Work: Critical Evaluations*, ed. Radcliffe Squires (1972); R. K. Meiners, *The Last Alternatives: A Study of the Works of Allen Tate* (1973); and Robert S. Dupree, *Allen Tate and the Augustinian Imagination: A Study of the Poetry* (1983). See also: Walter Sullivan, *Allen Tate: A Recollection* (1988); and Langdon Hammer, *Hart Crane and Allen Tate: Janus-Faced Modernism* (1993). For cultural and historical contexts, see John L. Stewart, *The Burden of Time: The Fugitives and Agrarians: The Nashville Groups of the 1920s and 1930s, and the Writing of John Crowe Ransom, Allen Tate, and Robert Penn Warren* (1965); Daniel Joseph Singal, *The War Within: From Victorian to Modernist Thought in the South, 1919–1945* (1982); Robert H. Brinkmeyer Jr., *Three Catholic Writers of the Modern South* (1985); *The Southern Agrarians and the New Deal: Essays after I'll Take My Stand*, eds. Emily S. Bingham and Thomas A. Underwood (2001); and Paul V. Murphy, *The Rebuke of History: The Southern Agrarians and American Conservative Thought* (2001).

Ode to the Confederate Dead

Row after row with strict impunity
The headstones yield their names to the element,
The wind whirrs without recollection:
In the riven troughs the splayed leaves
Pile up, of nature the casual sacrament;   5

To the seasonal eternity of death;
Then driven by the fierce scrutiny
Of heaven to their election in the vast breath,
They sough the rumour of mortality.

Autumn is desolation in the plot   10
Of a thousand acres where these memories grow
From the inexhaustible bodies that are not
Dead, but feed the grass row after rich row.
Think of the autumns that have come and gone!—
Ambitious November with the humors of the year,   15
With a particular zeal for every slab,
Staining the uncomfortable angels that rot
On the slabs, a wing chipped here, an arm there:
The brute curiosity of an angel's stare
Turns you, like them, to stone,   20
Transforms the heaving air
Till plunged to a heavier world below
You shift your sea-space blindly
Heaving, turning like the blind crab.

    Dazed by the wind, only the wind   25
    The leaves flying, plunge

You know who have waited by the wall
The twilight certainty of an animal,
Those midnight restitutions of the blood
You know—the immitigable pines, the smoky frieze   30
Of the sky, the sudden call: you know the rage,
The cold pool left by the mounting flood,
Of muted Zeno and Parmenides.[1]
You who have waited for the angry resolution
Of those desires that should be yours tomorrow,   35
You know the unimportant shrift of death
And praise the vision
And praise the arrogant circumstance
Of those who fall
Rank upon rank, hurried beyond decision—   40
Here by the sagging gate, stopped by the wall.

---

[1]Zeno of Elea (c. 490 BCE–c. 430 BCE) was a pre-Socratic Greek philosopher and a follower of Parmenides; Parmenides of Elea (early 5th century BCE) was an ancient Greek philosopher who taught that the universe was single and unchanging.

Seeing, seeing only the leaves
Flying, plunge and expire

Turn your eyes to the immoderate past,
Turn to the inscrutable infantry rising   45
Demons out of the earth—they will not last.
Stonewall, Stonewall, and the sunken fields of hemp,[2]
Shiloh, Antietam, Malvern Hill, Bull Run.[3]
Lost in that orient of the thick-and-fast
You will curse the setting sun.   50

Cursing only the leaves crying
Like an old man in a storm

You hear the shout, the crazy hemlocks point
With troubled fingers to the silence which
Smothers you, a mummy, in time.   55
                        The hound bitch
Toothless and dying, in a musty cellar
Hears the wind only.

                    Now that the salt of their blood
Stiffens the saltier oblivion of the sea,   60
Seals the malignant purity of the flood,
What shall we who count our days and bow
Our heads with a commemorial woe
In the ribboned coats of grim felicity,
What shall we say of the bones, unclean,   65
Whose verdurous anonymity will grow?
The ragged arms, the ragged heads and eyes
Lost in these acres of the insane green?
The gray lean spiders come, they come and go;
In a tangle of willows without light   70
The singular screech-owl's tight
Invisible lyric seeds the mind
With the furious murmur of their chivalry.

We shall say only the leaves
Flying, plunge and expire   75

We shall say only the leaves whispering
In the improbable mist of nightfall
That flies on multiple wing;

---

[2]Thomas Jonathan "Stonewall" Jackson (1824–63), Confederate general during the American Civil War; accidentally shot by his own troops at the Battle of Chancellorsville, he died on May 2, 1863.
[3]Battles in the Civil War.

Night is the beginning and the end
And in between the ends of distraction   80
Waits mute speculation, the patient curse
That stones the eyes, or like the jaguar leaps
For his own image in a jungle pool, his victim.
What shall we say who have knowledge
Carried to the heart? Shall we take the act   85
To the grave? Shall we, more hopeful, set up the grave
In the house? The ravenous grave?

              Leave now
The shut gate and the decomposing wall:
The gentle serpent, green in the mulberry bush,   90
Riots with his tongue through the hush—
Sentinel of the grave who counts us all!

                         [1927; 1937]

STERLING A. BROWN ■ (1901–1989)

Sterling A. Brown was born in Washington, D.C. The son of an admired pastor and professor of divinity, Brown attended Dunbar High School, graduating with honors in 1918, and then Williams College in western Massachusetts, where he was elected to Phi Beta Kappa as a junior and compiled an outstanding record. He next attended Harvard for graduate work, studying with the eminent Shakespeare scholar G. L. Kittredge. Brown made the important discovery there of Louis Untermeyer's anthology *Modern American Poetry* (1919; rev. ed., 1921), which brought to his attention the poetry of Robert Frost, Carl Sandburg, Edwin Arlington Robinson, and others.

Brown then launched his career as a teacher at black colleges in the South, starting at Virginia Seminary and College from 1923 to 1926, and he delved deeply into African American folklore, tales, legends, and forms of music and oral tradition. In 1929 Brown accepted a position at Howard University in Washington, D.C., where he taught for four decades.

One of Brown's noteworthy achievements as a poet is his shrewd, insightful, and sometimes satirically or humorously edged exploration and development of folk materials alongside, and often in the midst, of conventional structures and genres—sonnet, villanelle, and ballad, for example. His main goal was fashioning an African American vernacular poetry that did not lapse into the stereotypical patterns and mannerisms of much so-called dialect verse. This interest in and respect for the vernacular gives a special power to Brown's poems of social protest, like those presented here.

Southern Road (1932) was Brown's first book of poetry, and it remains a seminal text in the African American literature of this period, along with Jean Toomer's *Cane* (1923) and Langston Hughes's *The Weary Blues* (1926). (Toomer was a high school classmate of Brown's.) As he noted in a lecture in the early 1940s, "I was first attracted by certain qualities that I thought the speech of the people had, and I wanted to get for my own writing a flavor, a color, a pungency of speech. Then later, I came to something more important—I wanted to get an understanding of people, to acquire an accuracy in the portrayal of their lives."

Brown was an active reviewer and essayist; the author of pioneering literary criticism in such books as *The Negro in American Fiction* (1937) and *Negro Poetry and Drama* (1937); and the coeditor or editor of groundbreaking literary anthologies, including *The Negro Caravan* (1941), an 1100-page collection of writings by African Americans. From the 1940s through the 1960s, Brown's work was mostly in literary criticism and editorial projects. He has long been influential, but only with the expansion of scholarly study of African American writers has the impact of his career as a poet, essayist, anthologist, and teacher gained the recognition it deserves.

Brown's *Collected Poems*, ed. Michael S. Harper, was published in 1980. See also *A Son's Return: Selected Essays of Sterling A. Brown*, ed. Mark A. Sanders (1996). For a brief biography, see Robert Stepto, "Sterling A. Brown," in *American National Biography* 3:734–736. For critical context and analysis: Joanne V. Gabbin, *Sterling A. Brown: Building the Black Aesthetic Tradition* (1985) and Mark A. Sanders, *Afro-Modernist Aesthetics and the Poetry of Sterling A. Brown* (1999). For a wide-ranging collection of critical and theoretical writings, see: *After Winter: The Art and Life of Sterling Brown*, eds. John Edgar Tidwell and Steven C. Tracy (2009).

He Was a Man

It wasn't about no woman,
   It wasn't about no rape,
He wasn't crazy, and he wasn't drunk,
   An' it wasn't no shooting scrape,
     He was a man, and they laid him down.   5

He wasn't no quarrelsome feller,
   And he let other folks alone,
But he took a life, as a man will do,
   In a fight for to save his own,
     He was a man, and they laid him down.   10

He worked on his little homeplace
   Down on the Eastern Shore;
He had his family, and he had his friends,
   And he didn't expect much more,
     He was a man, and they laid him down.   15

He wasn't nobody's great man,
   He wasn't nobody's good,
Was a po'boy tried to get from life
   What happiness he could,
     He was a man, and they laid him down.   20

He didn't abuse Tom Wickley,
   Said nothing when the white man curst,
But when Tom grabbed his gun, he pulled his own,
   And his bullet got there first,
     He was a man, and they laid him down.   25

Didn't catch him in no manhunt,
   But they took him from a hospital bed,
Stretched on his back in the nigger ward,
   With a bullet wound in his head,
     He was a man, and they laid him down.   30

It didn't come off at midnight
    Nor yet at the break of day,
It was in the broad noon daylight,
    When they put po' Will away,
        He was a man, and they laid him down. 35

Didn't take him to no swampland,
    Didn't take him to no woods,
Didn't hide themselves, didn't have no masks,
    Didn't wear no Ku Klux hoods,
        He was a man, and they laid him down.   40

They strung him up on Main Street,
    On a tree in the Court House Square,
And people came from miles around
    To enjoy a holiday there,
        He was a man, and they laid him down. 45

They hung him and they shot him,
    They piled packing cases around,
They burnt up Will's black body,
    'Cause he shot a white man down;
        "He was a man, and we'll lay him down." 50

It wasn't no solemn business,
    Was more like a barbecue,
The crackers yelled when the fire blazed,
    And the women and the children too—
        "He was a man, and we laid him down." 55

The Coroner and the Sheriff
    Said "Death by Hands Unknown."
The mob broke up by midnight,
    "Another uppity Nigger gone—
        He was a man, an' we laid him down." 60

                                                            [1932]

Break of Day

Big Jess fired on the Alabama Central,
Man in full, babe, man in full.
Been throwing on coal for Mister Murphy
From times way back, baby, times way back.

Big Jess had a pleasing woman, name of Mamie,   5
Sweet-hipted Mama, sweet-hipted Mame;
Had a boy growing up for to be a fireman,
Just like his pa, baby, like his pa.

Out by the roundhouse Jess had his cabin,
Longside the tracks, babe, long the tracks,   10
Jess pulled the whistle when they high-balled past it
"I'm on my way, baby, on my way."

Crackers craved the job what Jess was holding,
Times right tough, babe, times right tough,
Warned Jess to quit his job for a white man,   15
Jess he laughed, baby, he jes' laughed.

He picked up his lunch-box, kissed his sweet woman,
Sweet-hipted Mama, sweet-hipted Mame,
His son walked with him to the white-washed palings,
"Be seeing you soon, son, see you soon."   20

Mister Murphy let Big Jess talk on the whistle
"So long sugar baby, so long babe";
Train due back in the early morning
Breakfast time, baby, breakfast time.

Mob stopped the train crossing Black Bear Mountain   25
Shot rang out, babe, shot rang out.
They left Big Jess on the Black Bear Mountain,
Break of day, baby, break of day.

Sweet Mame sits rocking, waiting for the whistle
Long past due, babe, long past due.   30
The grits are cold, and the coffee's boiled over,
But Jess done gone, baby he done gone.

[1938]

Bitter Fruit of the Tree

They said to my grandmother: "Please do not be bitter,"
When they sold her first-born and let the second die,
When they drove her husband till he took to the swamplands,
And brought him home bloody and beaten at last.
They told her, "It is better you should not be bitter,   5
Some must work and suffer so that we, who must, can live,
Forgiving is noble, you must not be heathen bitter;
These are your orders: you *are* not to be bitter."
And they left her shack for their porticoed house.

They said to my father: "Please do not be bitter,"   10
When he ploughed and planted a crop not his,
When he weatherstripped a house that he could not enter,
And stored away a harvest he could not enjoy.
They answered his questions: "It does not concern you,
It is not for you to know, it is past your understanding,   15
All you need know is: you must not be bitter."

[1939]

LANGSTON HUGHES ■ (1902–1967)

Langston Hughes was an accomplished writer of short stories, a playwright, essayist, autobiographer, editor, and author of children's books. But he is known above all for his poetry, beginning in 1921 with "The Negro Speaks of Rivers" (included here), published in the magazine of the National Association of Colored People (NAACP), *The Crisis*. Hughes is the premier African American poet of the twentieth century and, in his adroit use of the rhythms and structures of music in his verse, one of the pioneering figures of modern American poetry in general.

Hughes was born in Joplin, Missouri, but he was raised in Lawrence, Kansas, with periods in Illinois, Ohio, and Mexico. He started as a student at Columbia University in 1921 but left in 1922 and worked at a number of low-paying jobs. He traveled to Africa and also, in 1924, to Paris.

Some scholars have noted Hughes's connections to Paul Laurence Dunbar and other dialect poets in the African American tradition, and also to such notable writers and intellectuals as W. E. B. Du Bois and James Weldon Johnson. But Hughes's central influences were Walt Whitman, and, even more, the popular poet Carl Sandburg, whom Hughes called "my guiding star" and who was himself interested in many forms of American music and song.

The pace, variations, and tone of the blues, mournful yet resilient, shape the poems that Hughes included in his first two books, *The Weary Blues* (1926) and *Fine Clothes to the Jew* (1927). He was a major figure in the Harlem or "New Negro" Renaissance of the 1920s and early 1930s, which led to a spirited array of race-conscious new production in literature and the arts. In an essay that became a manifesto for the movement, "The Negro and the Racial Mountain" (1926), Hughes maintained, "We younger Negro artists who create now intend to express our individual dark-skinned selves without fear or shame."

Hughes returned to his undergraduate studies, enrolling in Lincoln University in Pennsylvania, and he graduated in 1929. The late 1920s were also significant for the relationship he developed with a wealthy white woman, Mrs. Charlotte Mason, whom he termed his "Godmother." Serving as his devoted patroness, she gave Hughes much-needed support, but to an extent she also sought to dictate and control his literary work. In 1930 Hughes broke with her, and in the aftermath he suffered a serious depression. The poem "Poet to Patron," included here, reflects Hughes's realization that having a patron is a mixed blessing.

Hughes rallied, however, inspired by left-wing political groups with which he forged close connections. His poetry from the 1930s, including "Let America Be America Again," is radical, even revolutionary, in its point of view and themes. Hughes traveled and lived in the Soviet Union in 1932–33, and his support for it continued into the 1940s, solidified by the U.S.-Soviet alliance against Nazi Germany.

Of Hughes's many plays, the best is *Mulatto* (1935), which deals with miscegenation. His autobiographies, *The Big Sea* (1940) and *I Wonder Where I Wander* (1956), while secretive about his personal life, are absorbing. Many readers have taken pleasure in his short stories in *The Ways of White Folks*, but even better are the stories about an entertaining Harlem character named Jesse B. Semple ("Simple") and his associates and activities. Hughes published five collections of "Simple" stories, perhaps the best of which is the first, *Simple Speaks His Mind* (1950). But the great achievement amid Hughes's prolific output in the latter half of his career is *Montage of a Dream Deferred* (1951), a book of poems vivid with the rhythms of jazz and New York City, Harlem in particular, Hughes's home.

Hughes was, and remains, a popular, accessible writer, enjoyed by young and old alike. Some have observed that this popularity came at a cost—that Hughes produced most of his best poetry in the 1920s and thereafter, with the exception of *Montage of Dream Deferred*, he fell into decline, writing too much that was easy and not enough that challenged him or his readership. But in his best work, Hughes was highly original, both joyous and sorrowful, pointedly provocative in his insights into American and African American societies, and within both traditional and unconventional styles and genres. Beloved by many, he was referred to as "the Poet Laureate of the Negro Race."

Langston Hughes, photographed in 1964 by Jack Delano.

For biography, see Arnold Rampersad, *The Life of Langston Hughes*, 2 vols. (1986, 1988; 2nd ed., 2002). Critical studies include Onwuchekwa Jemie, *Langston Hughes: An Introduction to the Poetry* (1976); R. Baxter Miller, *The Art and Imagination of Langston Hughes* (1989); and *Langston Hughes: Critical Perspectives Past and Present*, ed. Henry Louis Gates Jr. and K. A. Appiah. See also: Hans Ostrom, *A Langston Hughes Encyclopedia* (2002). See also: *A Historical Guide to Langston Hughes*, ed. Steven C. Tracy (2004); R. Baxter Miller, *The Art and Imagination of Langston Hughes* (2006); Jonathan Scott, *Socialist Joy in the Writing of Langston Hughes* (2006); *Montage of a Dream: The Art and Life of Langston Hughes*, eds. John Edgar Tidwell and Cheryl R. Ragar; and W. Jason Miller, *Langston Hughes and American Lynching Culture* (2011).

The Negro Speaks of Rivers

I've known rivers:
I've known rivers ancient as the world and older than the
    flow of human blood in human veins.

My soul has grown deep like the rivers.

I bathed in the Euphrates when dawns were young.   5
I built my hut near the Congo and it lulled me to sleep.
I looked upon the Nile and raised the pyramids above it.

I heard the singing of the Mississippi when Abe Lincoln
    went down to New Orleans, and I've seen its muddy
    bosom turn all golden in the sunset.   10

I've known rivers:
Ancient, dusky rivers.

My soul has grown deep like the rivers.

[1921]

Mother to Son

Well, son, I'll tell you:
Life for me ain't been no crystal stair.
It's had tacks in it,
And splinters,
And boards torn up,   5
And places with no carpet on the floor—
Bare.
But all the time
I'se been a-climbin' on,
And reachin' landin's,   10

And turnin' corners,
And sometimes goin' in the dark
Where there ain't been no light.
So boy, don't you turn back.
Don't you set down on the steps   15
'Cause you finds it's kinder hard.
Don't you fall now—
For I'se still goin', honey,
I'se still climbin'
And life for me ain't been no crystal stair.   20

[1922]

The Weary Blues

Droning a drowsy syncopated tune,
Rocking back and forth to a mellow croon,
    I heard a Negro play.
Down on Lenox Avenue the other night
By the pale dull pallor of an old gas light   5
    He did a lazy sway....
    He did a lazy sway....
To the tune o' those Weary Blues.
With his ebony hands on each ivory key
He made that poor piano moan with melody.   10
    O Blues!
Swaying to and fro on his rickety stool
He played that sad raggy tune like a musical fool.
    Sweet Blues!
Coming from a black man's soul.   15
    O Blues!
In a deep song voice with a melancholy tone
I heard that Negro sing, that old piano moan—
    "Ain't got nobody in all this world,
        Ain't got nobody but ma self.   20
        I's gwine to quit ma frownin'
        And put ma troubles on the shelf."

Thump, thump, thump, went his foot on the floor.
He played a few chords then he sang some more—
    "I got the Weary Blues   25
        And I can't be satisfied.
        Got the Weary Blues
        And can't be satisfied—
        I ain't happy no mo'
        And I wish that I had died."   30

And far into the night he crooned that tune.
The stars went out and so did the moon.
The singer stopped playing and went to bed
While the Weary Blues echoed through his head.
He slept like a rock or a man that's dead.   35

[1925]

The South

The lazy, laughing South
With blood on its mouth.
The sunny-faced South,
    Beast-strong,
    Idiot-brained.   5
The child-minded South
Scratching in the dead fire's ashes
For a Negro's bones.
    Cotton and the moon,
    Warmth, earth, warmth,   10
    The sky the sun the stars
    The magnolia-scented South.
Beautiful, like a woman,
Seductive as a dark-eyed whore,
    Passionate, cruel,   15
    Honey-lipped, syphilitic—
    That is the South.
And I, who am black, would love her
But she spits in my face.
And I, who am black,   20
Would give her many rare gifts
But she turns her back upon me.
    So now I seek the North—
    The cold-faced North,
    For she, they say,   25
    Is a kinder mistress,
And in her house my children
May escape the spell of the South.

[1922]

Ruby Brown

She was young and beautiful
And golden like the sunshine
That warmed her body.
And because she was colored

Mayville had no place to offer her,   5
Nor fuel for the clean flame of joy
That tried to burn within her soul.

One day,
Sitting on old Mrs. Latham's back porch
Polishing the silver,   10
She asked herself two questions
And they ran something like this:
What can a colored girl do
On the money from a white woman's kitchen?
And ain't there any joy in this town?   15

Now the streets down by the river
Know more about this pretty Ruby Brown,
And the sinister shuttered houses of the bottoms
Hold a yellow girl
Seeking an answer to her questions.   20
The good church folk do not mention
Her name any more.

But the white men,
Habitués of the high shuttered houses,
Pay more money to her now   25
Than they ever did before,
When she worked in their kitchens.

                                              [1926]

Let America Be America Again

Let America be America again.
Let it be the dream it used to be.
Let it be the pioneer on the plain
Seeking a home where he himself is free.

(America never was America to me.)   5

Let America be the dream the dreamers dreamed—
Let it be that great strong land of love
Where never kings connive nor tyrants scheme
That any man be crushed by one above.

(It never was America to me.)   10

O, let my land be a land where Liberty
Is crowned with no false patriotic wreath,
But opportunity is real, and life is free,
Equality is in the air we breathe.

(There's never been equality for me,
Nor freedom in this "homeland of the free.")
Say, who are you that mumbles in the dark?
And who are you that draws your veil across the stars?

I am the poor white, fooled and pushed apart,
I am the Negro bearing slavery's scars.
I am the red man driven from the land,
I am the immigrant clutching the hope I seek—
And finding only the same old stupid plan
Of dog eat dog, of mighty crush the weak.

I am the young man, full of strength and hope,
Tangled in that ancient endless chain
Of profit, power, gain, of grab the land!
Of grab the gold! Of grab the ways of satisfying need!
Of work the men! Of take the pay!
Of owning everything for one's own greed!

I am the farmer, bondsman to the soil.
I am the worker sold to the machine.
I am the Negro, servant to you all.
I am the people, humble, hungry, mean—
Hungry yet today despite the dream.
Beaten yet today—O, Pioneers!
I am the man who never got ahead,
The poorest worker bartered through the years.

Yet I'm the one who dreamt our basic dream
In that Old World while still a serf of kings,
Who dreamt a dream so strong, so brave, so true,
That even yet its mighty daring sings
In every brick and stone, in every furrow turned
That's made America the land it has become.
O, I'm the man who sailed those early seas
In search of what I meant to be my home—
For I'm the one who left dark Ireland's shore,
And Poland's plain, and England's grassy lea,
And torn from Black Africa's strand I came
To build a "homeland of the free."

The free?

Who said the free? Not me?
Surely not me? The millions on relief today?
The millions shot down when we strike?
The millions who have nothing for our pay?
For all the dreams we've dreamed

15

20

25

30

35

40

45

50

55

And all the songs we've sung
And all the hopes we've held
And all the flags we've hung,
The millions who have nothing for our pay—   60
Except the dream that's almost dead today.

0, let America be America again—
The land that never has been yet—
And yet must be—the land where *every* man is free.
The land that's mine—the poor man's, Indian's, Negro's, ME—   65
Who made America,
Whose sweat and blood, whose faith and pain,
Whose hand at the foundry, whose plow in the rain,
Must bring back our mighty dream again.

Sure, call me any ugly name you choose—   70
The steel of freedom does not stain.
From those who live like leeches on the people's lives,
We must take back our land again,
America!

0, yes,   75
I say it plain,
America never was America to me,
And yet I swear this oath—
America will be!

Out of the rack and ruin of our gangster death,   80
The rape and rot of graft, and stealth, and lies,
We, the people, must redeem
The land, the mines, the plants, the rivers.
The mountains and the endless plain—
All, all the stretch of these great green states—   85
And make America again!

[1936]

Poet to Patron

What right has anyone to say
That I
Must throw out pieces of my heart
For pay?

For bread that helps to make   5
My heart beat true,
I must sell myself
To you?

A factory shift's better,
A week's meagre pay,   10
Than a perfumed note asking:
What poems today?

[1939]

Ballad of the Landlord

Landlord, landlord,
My roof has sprung a leak.
Don't you 'member I told you about it
Way last week?

Landlord, landlord,   5
These steps is broken down.
When you come up yourself
It's a wonder you don't fall down.

Ten Bucks you say I owe you?
Ten Bucks you say is due?   10
Well, that's Ten Bucks more'n I'll pay you
Till you fix this house up new.

What? You gonna get eviction orders?
You gonna cut off my heat?
You gonna take my furniture and   15
Throw it in the street?

Um-huh! You talking high and mighty.
Talk on—till you get through.
You ain't gonna be able to say a word
If I land my fist on you.   20

Police! Police!
Come and get this man!
He's trying to ruin the government
And overturn the land!

Copper's whistle!   25
Patrol bell!
Arrest.

Precinct Station.
Iron cell.
Headlines in press: 30

MAN THREATENS LANDLORD

•

• •

TENANT HELD NO BAIL

• •

JUDGE GIVES NEGRO 90 DAYS IN COUNTY JAIL

[1940]

Too Blue

I got those sad old weary blues.
I don't know where to turn.
I don't know where to go.
Nobody cares about you
When you sink so low.   5

What shall I do?
What shall I say?
Shall I take a gun
And put myself away?

I wonder if   10
One bullet would do?
As hard as my head is,
It would probably take two.

But I ain't got
Neither bullet nor gun—   15
And I'm too blue
To look for one.

[1943]

Theme for English B

The instructor said,

> Go home and write
> a page tonight.
> And let that page come out of you—
> Then, it will be true.   5

I wonder if it's that simple?
I am twenty-two, colored, born in Winston-Salem.
I went to school there, then Durham, then here
to this college on the hill above Harlem.

I am the only colored student in my class.   10
The steps from the hill lead down into Harlem,
through a park, then I cross St. Nicholas,
Eighth Avenue, Seventh, and I come to the Y,
the Harlem Branch Y, where I take the elevator
up to my room, sit down, and write this page: 15

It's not easy to know what is true for you or me
at twenty-two, my age. But I guess I'm what
I feel and see and hear. Harlem, I hear you:
hear you, hear me—we two—you, me, talk on this page.
(I hear New York, too.) Me—who?   20
Well, I like to eat, sleep, drink, and be in love.
I like to work, read, learn, and understand life.
I like a pipe for a Christmas present,
or records—Bessie,[1] bop, or Bach.[2]
I guess being colored doesn't make me *not* like   25
the same things other folks like who are other races.
So will my page be colored that I write?

Being me, it will not be white.
But it will be
a part of you, instructor.   30
You are white—
yet a part of me, as I am a part of you.
That's American.
Sometimes perhaps you don't want to be a part of me.
Nor do I often want to be a part of you.   35
But we are, that's true!
As I learn from you,
I guess you learn from me—
although you're older—and white—
and somewhat more free.   40

This is my page for English B.

[1949]

---

[1]Bessie Smith (1894–1937), a great classic blues singer of the 1920s.
[2]Johann Sebastian Bach (1685–1750), the great German baroque composer and organist. His most famous work is the *St. Matthew Passion*.

Poet to Bigot

I have done so little
For you,
And you have done so little
For me,
That we have good reason   5
Never to agree.

I, however,
Have such meagre
Power,
Clutching at a   10
Moment,
While you control
An hour.

But your hour is
A stone.   15

My moment is
A flower.

[1953]

I, Too

I, too, sing America.

I am the darker brother.
They send me to eat in the kitchen
When company comes,
But I laugh,   5
And eat well,
And grow strong.

Tomorrow,
I'll be at the table
When company comes.   10
Nobody'll dare
Say to me,
"Eat in the kitchen,"
Then.

Besides,   15
They'll see how beautiful I am
And be ashamed—

I, too, am America.

[1925]

COUNTEE CULLEN ■ (1903–1946)

At the height of his literary fame, Countee Cullen claimed that New York City was his birthplace, but earlier he had said it was Louisville, Kentucky, and some have even maintained that Cullen's real place of birth was Baltimore, Maryland. Not much is known about Cullen's youth; he was an adopted child (his name at birth was Countee Leroy Porter), but the reasons for the adoption are murky, and, a very private person, Cullen offered no explanations later. His adoptive father was a minister in Harlem, and father and son were close, even traveling together to Europe when Cullen was a boy.

Cullen performed well in his courses at DeWitt Clinton High School in New York City; he wrote some poetry and was involved with both the school newspaper and the literary magazine. From 1921 to 1925 Cullen attended New York University, and many of the poems in his volumes *Color* (1925), *Copper Sun* (1927), and *The Ballad of the Brown Girl* (1927) were composed at this time. He was something of a phenomenon, a talented young African American poet familiar with the traditions of English poetry and skillful at working with the sonnet, ballad, and other conventional forms.

Already an important, popular figure in the Harlem Renaissance, the flowering of African American literature, art, and music that occurred in the 1920s and early 1930s, Cullen from 1925 to 1927 was a student in the graduate program at Harvard University, receiving a master's degree in English and French. For his poetry he was awarded a number of prizes and fellowships. Though racial themes arise in his work, as in the poems included here, Cullen professed that he sought recognition "as a poet, not a Negro poet."

In April 1928 Cullen married Yolande Du Bois, the daughter of the African American intellectual, educator, and protest leader W. E. B. Du Bois. The wedding was a major event in Harlem, but the marriage turned out badly, ending in divorce two years later. Cullen remarried in 1940. Throughout these years he was part of the gay community of Harlem, and he had a number of male lovers in the United States and France.

Cullen's writings include *The Black Christ and Other Poems* (1929), the title poem of which focuses on the crime of lynching; *One Way to Heaven* (1934), a satiric novel; and two books of children's verse. During the 1930s he taught at Frederick Douglass Junior High School; one of his students was James Baldwin. Cullen's own selection of his best poems, *On These I Stand*, was published in 1947, a year after his death.

The best place to start is *My Soul's High Song: The Collected Writings of Countee Cullen, Voice of the Harlem Renaissance*, ed. Gerald L. Early (1991). For biography, critical study, and context, see Blanche E. Fergusson, *Countee Cullen and the Negro Renaissance* (1966); Houston A. Baker Jr., *A Many-Colored Coat of Dreams: The Poetry of Countee Cullen* (1974); and Alan R. Shucard, *Countee Cullen* (1984). See also: Caroline Goeser, *Picturing the New Negro: Harlem Renaissance Print Culture and Modern Black Identity* (2006); *The Harlem Renaissance Revisited: Politics, Arts, and Letters*, ed.

Jeffrey O. G. Ogbar (2010); and William W. Cook and James Tatum, *African American Writers and Classical Tradition* (2010). Also important is Charles Molesworth, *And Bid Him Sing: A Biography of Countee Cullen* (2012).

Yet Do I Marvel

I doubt not God is good, well-meaning, kind,
And did He stoop to quibble could tell why
The little buried mole continues blind,
Why flesh that mirrors Him must some day die,
Make plain the reason tortured Tantalus[1]   5
Is baited by the fickle fruit, declare
If merely brute caprice dooms Sisyphus
To struggle up a never-ending stair.
Inscrutable His ways are, and immune
To catechism by a mind too strewn   10
With petty cares to slightly understand
What awful brain compels His awful hand.
Yet do I marvel at his curious thing:
To make a poet black, and bid him sing!

[1925]

Incident

(For Eric Walrond)[1]

Once riding in old Baltimore,
    Heart-filled, head-filled with glee,
I saw a Baltimorean
    Keep looking straight at me.

Now I was eight and very small,   5
    And he was no whit bigger,
And so I smiled, but he poked out
    His tongue, and called me, "Nigger."

I saw the whole of Baltimore
    From May until December;   10
Of all the things that happened there
    That's all that I remember.

[1925]

---

[1]Tantalus and Sisyphus (line 10) are figures from Greek mythology doomed to suffer in Hades. Tantalus was condemned to forever rest his chin by a pool of water that retreated from his lips whenever he tried to slake his unbearable thirst. Sisyphus had to roll a heavy stone up a hill, only to have it roll back down again, forcing him to repeat the task for eternity.
[1]A journalist (1898–1966) who wrote many articles against racism, including the acclaimed essay "On Being Black," published in *The New Republic* (November 1922).

RICHARD WRIGHT ■ (1908–1960)

Richard Wright was born in Roxie, Mississippi, about twenty miles east of Natchez. His father, an illiterate sharecropper, deserted the family when Wright was seven. Moving from place to place and state to state, he was raised in poverty by his mother, his grandmother, and other devoutly religious relatives. "As the days slid past," Wright recalled, "the image of my father became associated with my pangs of hunger, and whenever I felt hunger I thought of him with a deep biological bitterness."

Wright's schooling ended when he was fifteen, and he then earned some money in a series of menial jobs. His intellectual and emotional breakthrough came when he discovered the writings of the literary and cultural critic H. L. Mencken, the novelist Theodore Dreiser, and other English and American authors. They opened up for him new worlds of imaginative experience and possibility, and they instilled in him the conviction that he could overcome the boundaries of race and class that confined him in the South.

In 1927 Wright, not yet twenty, decided to leave the South for Chicago, Illinois. Through the 1930s and into the early 1940s he was closely connected to the Communist Party. He published articles in *The Daily Worker* and *The New Masses*, prominent periodicals associated with the Communists, and, relocating to New York City in 1937, he became *The Daily Worker*'s Harlem editor and, briefly, the coeditor of a literary magazine, *New Challenge*. He had already begun to publish short stories; his first book was a collection of stories, *Uncle Tom's Children* (1938; rev. ed., 1940). The story "Long Black Song," from *Uncle Tom's Children*, is a brutal, bitter account of racial and sexual violence, unforgettable in its agonized rendering of a wife's pain, its depiction of her husband's rage at the injustices he suffers, and its terrible concluding spectacle of racist attack.

Native Son, published in 1940, was Wright's first published novel (he had been unable to find a publisher for an earlier novel in manuscript), and it had a shattering impact on American readers. Wright focuses with extraordinary intensity on a young black man, Bigger Thomas, who lives with his mother and sister in a broken-down tenement in Chicago; the protagonist's name and his behavior constitute an ironic rejoinder to Harriet Beecher Stowe's meek and submissive Uncle Tom in her 1852 novel *Uncle Tom's Cabin*. *Native Son* is passionate, angry, shocking, a narrative of murder and racial animosity and vengeance. "The day *Native Son* appeared," the critic Irving Howe stated, "American culture was changed forever." It was featured by the Book of the Month Club and was a best seller.

Black Boy (1945) followed; in it Wright describes his experiences as a boy and teenager in the segregated South. This volume was originally part of a longer autobiographical work in which Wright also recounted the story of his life and work in the North, especially among the members of the Communist Party. This section, however, was not published until 1977, with the title *American Hunger*.

Married to a white woman and wounded and weary from the racism he experienced in New York City, Wright, his wife, and their daughter moved in 1946 to Paris. There he met and became friends with Jean-Paul Sartre and Albert Camus. They viewed him as an African American proponent of existentialism, an influential philosophical movement among European intellectuals that centered on the plight of the individual who must assume responsibility for acts of free will without any certain knowledge of what is right or wrong. Wright's significant novels of the 1950s include *The Outsider* (1953) and *The Long Dream* (1958). During the 1950s he traveled widely, reporting on colonialism and postcolonialism and attending conferences and meetings on Pan-Africanism and other subjects. In *White Man Listen!* (1957), a collection of essays on racial oppression, literary tradition, and African nationalism, Wright linked the victimization of colonized peoples to the history of African Americans: "The great majority of the human race has undergone experiences comparable to those which Negroes in America have undergone for three centuries!"

In 1991 the Library of America published a two-volume edition of Wright's work, including *Native Son* and *Black Boy (American Hunger)* in their original versions. This edition restores passages cut by Wright's editors and publishers.

Biographies include Michel Fabre, *The Unfinished Quest of Richard Wright* (1973); and Hazel Rowley, *Richard Wright: The Life and Times* (2001). For critical analysis, see Joyce A. Joyce, *Richard Wright's Art of*

Negro tenant farmer, Jefferson County, Kansas, October 1938. Photograph by John Vachon, American photographer (1914–75).

Tragedy (1986); *Richard Wright: Critical Perspectives Past and Present*, eds.
Henry Louis Gates Jr. and K. A. Appiah (1993); and *The Critical Response
to Richard Wright*, ed. Robert J. Butler (1995). For contexts, see: James
Campbell, *Exiled in Paris: Richard Wright, James Baldwin, Samuel Beckett,
and Others on the Left Bank* (2003); Mary Hricko, *Genesis of the Chicago
Renaissance: Theodore Dreiser, Langston Hughes, Richard Wright, and James
T. Farrell* (2009); and Jeff Allred, *American Modernism and Depression
Documentary* (2010).

Long Black Song

I

> *Go t sleep, baby*
> *Papas gone t town*
> *Go t sleep, baby*
> *The suns goin down*
> *Go t sleep, baby*
> *To candys in the sack*
> *Go t sleep, baby*
> *Papas comin back...*

Over and over she crooned, and at each lull of her voice she rocked the
wooden cradle with a bare black foot. But the baby squalled louder, its wail
drowning out the song. She stopped and stood over the cradle, wondering what was bothering it, if its stomach hurt. She felt the diaper; it was
dry. She lifted it up and parted its back. Still it cried, longer and louder.
She put it back into the cradle and dangled a string of red beads before its
eyes. The little black fingers clawed them away. She bent over, frowning,
murmuring: "Whut's the mattah, chile? Yuh wan some watah?" She held a
dripping gourd to the black lips, but the baby turned its head and kicked
its legs. She stood a moment, perplexed. Whuts wrong wid tha chile? She
ain never carried on like this this tima day. She picked it up and went to
the open door. "See the sun, baby?" she asked, pointing to a big ball of red
dying between the branches of trees. The baby pulled back and strained its
round black arms and legs against her stomach and shoulders. She knew it
was tired; she could tell by the halting way it opened its mouth to draw in
air. She sat on a wooden stool, unbuttoned the front of her dress, brought
the baby closer and offered it a black teat. "Don baby wan suppah?" It
pulled away and went limp, crying softly, piteously, as though it would
never stop. Then it pushed its fingers against her breasts and wailed.
Lawd, chile, whut yuh wan? Yo ma cant hep yuh less she knows whut yuh
wan. Tears gushed; four white teeth flashed in red gums; the little chest
heaved up and down and round black fingers stretched floorward. Lawd,

chile, whuts wrong wid yuh? She stooped slowly, allowing her body to be guided by the downward tug. As soon as the little fingers touched the floor the wail quieted into a broken sniffle. She turned the baby loose and watched it crawl toward a corner. She followed and saw the little fingers reach for the tail-end of an old eight-day clock. "Yuh wan tha ol clock?" She dragged the clock into the center of the floor. The baby crawled after it, calling, "Ahh!" Then it raised its hands and beat on top of the clock Bink! Bink! Bink! "Naw, yuhll hurt yo hans!" She held the baby and looked around. It cried and struggled. "Wait, baby!" She fetched a small stick from the top of a rickety dresser. "Here," she said, closing the little fingers about it. "Beat wid this, see?" She heard each blow landing squarely on top of the clock Bang! Bang! Bang! And with each bang the baby smiled and said, "Ahh!" Mabbe thall keep yuh quiet erwhile. Mabbe Ah kin git some res now. She stood in the doorway. Lawd, tha chiles a pain! She mus be teethin. Er something...

She wiped sweat from her forehead with the bottom of her dress and looked out over the green fields rolling up the hillsides. She sighed, fighting a feeling of loneliness. Lawd, its sho hard t pass the days wid Silas gone. Been mos a week now since he took the wagon cutta here. Hope ain nothin wrong. He mus be buyin a heapa stuff there in Colwatah t be stayin all this time. Yes; maybe Silas would remember and bring that five-yard piece of red calico she wanted. Oh, Lawd! Ah *hope* he don fergit it!

She saw green fields wrapped in the thickening gloam.[1] It was as if they had left the earth, those fields, and were floating slowly skyward. The afterglow lingered, red, dying, somehow tenderly sad. And far away, in front of her, earth and sky met in a soft swoon of shadow. A cricket chirped, sharp and lonely; and it seemed she could hear it chirping long after it had stopped. Silas oughta c mon soon. Ahm tireda staying here by mahsef.

Loneliness ached in her. She swallowed, hearing Bang! Bang! Bang! Tom been gone t war mos a year now. N tha ol wars over n we ain heard nothin yit. Lawd, don let Tom be dead! She frowned into the gloam and wondered about that awful war so far away. They said it was over now. Yeah, Gawd had t stop em fo they killed everybody. She felt that merely to go so far away from home was a kind of death in itself. Just to go that far away was to be killed. Nothing good could come from men going miles across the seas to fight. N how come they wanna kill each other? How come they wanna make blood? Killing was not what men ought to do. Shucks! she thought.

She sighed, thinking of Tom, hearing Bang! Bang! Bang! She saw Tom, saw his big black smiling face; her eyes went dreamily blank, drinking in the red afterglow. Yes, God; it could have been Tom instead of Silas who

[1]Dusk.

was having her now. Yes; it could have been Tom she was loving. She smiled and asked herself, Lawd, Ah wondah how would it been wid Tom? Against the plush sky she saw a white bright day and a green cornfield and she saw Tom walking in his overalls and she was with Tom and he had his arm about her waist. She remembered how weak she had felt feeling his fingers sinking into the flesh of her hips. Her knees had trembled and she had had a hard time trying to stand up and not just sink right there to the ground. Yes; that was what Tom had wanted her to do. But she had held Tom up and he had held her up; they had held each other up to keep from slipping to the ground there in the green cornfield. Lawd! Her breath went and she passed her tongue over her lips. But that was not as exciting as that winter evening when the grey skies were sleeping and she and Tom were coming home from church down dark Lover's Lane. She felt the tips of her teats tingling and touching the front of her dress as she remembered how he had crushed her against him and hurt her. She had closed her eyes and was smelling the acrid scent of dry October leaves and had gone weak in his arms and had felt she could not breathe any more and had torn away and run, run home. And that sweet ache which had frightened her then was stealing back to her loins now with the silence and the cricket calls and the red afterglow and Bang! Bang! Bang! Lawd, Ah wondah how would it been wid Tom?

She stepped out on the porch and leaned against the wall of the house. Sky sang a red song. Fields whispered a green prayer. And song and prayer were dying in silence and shadow. Never in all her life had she been so much alone as she was now. Days were never so long as these days; and nights were never so empty as these nights. She jerked her head impatiently, hearing Bang! Bang! Bang! Shucks! she thought. When Silas had gone something had ebbed so slowly that at first she had not noticed it. Now she felt all of it as though the feeling had no bottom. She tried to think just how it had happened. Yes; there had been all her life the long hope of white bright days and the deep desire of dark black nights and then Silas had gone. Bang! Bang! Bang! There had been laughter and eating and singing and the long gladness of green cornfields in summer. There had been cooking and sewing and sweeping and the deep dream of sleeping grey skies in winter. Always it had been like that and she had been happy. But no more. The happiness of those days and nights, of those green cornfields and grey skies had started to go from her when Tom had gone to war. His leaving had left an empty black hole in her heart, a black hole that Silas had come in and filled. But not quite. Silas had not quite filled that hole. No; days and nights were not as they were before.

She lifted her chin, listening. She had heard something, a dull throb like she had heard that day Silas had called her outdoors to look at the airplane. Her eyes swept the sky. But there was no plane. Mabbe its behin the house? She stepped into the yard and looked upward through paling light. There were only a few big wet stars trembling in the east. Then she heard the throb again. She turned, looking up and down the road. The throb grew louder, droning; and she heard Bang! Bang! Bang! There! A car! Wondah whuts a car doin comin out here? A black car was winding over a dusty road, coming toward her. Mabbe some white mans bringing Silas home wida loada goods? But, Lawd, Ah *hope* its no trouble! The car stopped in front of the house and a white man got out. Wondah whut he wans? She looked at the car, but could not see Silas. The white man was young; he wore a straw hat and had no coat. He walked toward her with a huge black package under his arm.

"Well, howre yuh today, Aunty?"

"Ahm well. How yuh?"

"Oh, so-so. Its sure hot today, hunh?"

She brushed her hand across her forehead and sighed.

"Yeah; it is kinda warm."

"You busy?"

"Naw, Ah ain doin nothin."

"Ive got something to show you. Can I sit here, on your porch?"

"Ah reckon so. But, Mistah, Ah ain got no money."

"Havent you sold your cotton yet?"

"Silas gone t town wid it now."

"Whens he coming back?"

"Ah don know. Ahm waitin fer im."

She saw the white man take out a handkerchief and mop his face. Bang! Bang! Bang! He turned his head and looked through the open doorway, into the front room.

"Whats all that going on in there?"

She laughed.

"Aw, thas jus Ruth."

"Whats she doing?"

"She beatin tha ol clock."

"Beating a *clock*?"

She laughed again.

"She wouldnt go t sleep so Ah give her tha ol clock t play wid."

The white man got up and went to the front door; he stood a moment looking at the black baby hammering on the clock. Bang! Bang! Bang!

"But why let her tear your clock up?"

"It ain no good."

"You could have it fixed."

"We ain got no money t be fixin no clocks."

"Havent you got a clock?"

"Naw."

"But how do you keep time?"

"We git erlong widout time."

"But how do you know when to get up in the morning?"

"We jus git up, thas all."

"But how do you know what time it is when you get up?"

"We git up wid the sun."

"And at night, how do you tell when its night?"

"It gits dark when the sun goes down."

"Havent you ever had a clock?"

She laughed and turned her face toward the silent fields.

"Mistah, we don need no clock."

"Well, this beats everything! I dont see how in the world anybody can live without time."

"We jus don need no time, Mistah."

The white man laughed and shook his head; she laughed and looked at him. The white man was funny. Jus lika lil boy. Astin how do Ah know when t git up in the mawnin! She laughed again and mused on the baby, hearing Bang! Bang! Bang! She could hear the white man breathing at her side; she felt his eyes on her face. She looked at him; she saw he was looking at her breasts. Hes jus lika lil boy. Acks like he cant understan *nothin*!

"But you need a clock," the white man insisted. "Thats what Im out here for. Im selling clocks and graphophones. The clocks are made right into the graphophones, a nice sort of combination, hunh? You can have music and time all at once. Ill show you…"

"Mistah, we don need no clock!"

"You dont have to buy it. It wont cost you anything just to look."

He unpacked the big black box. She saw the strands of his auburn hair glinting in the afterglow. His back bulged against his white shirt as he stooped. He pulled out a square brown graphophone. She bent forward, looking. Lawd, but its pretty! She saw the face of a clock under the horn of the graphophone. The gilt on the corners sparkled. The color in the wood glowed softly. It reminded her of the light she saw sometimes in the baby's eyes. Slowly she slid a finger over a beveled edge; she wanted to take the box into her arms and kiss it.

"Its eight o'clock," he said.

"Yeah?"

"It only costs fifty dollars. And you dont have to pay for it all at once. Just five dollars down and five dollars a month."

She smiled. The white man was just like a little boy. Jus lika chile. She saw him grinding the handle of the box.

"Just listen to this," he said.

There was a sharp, scratching noise; then she moved nervously, her body caught in the ringing coils of music.

When the trumpet of the Lord shall sound…

She rose on circling waves of white bright days and dark black nights…. *and time shall be no more…*

Higher and higher she mounted.
And the morning breaks...
Earth fell far behind, forgotten.
...eternal, bright and fair...
Echo after echo sounded.
When the saved of the earth shall gather...
Her blood surged like the long gladness of summer.
...over on the other shore...
Her blood ebbed like the deep dream of sleep in winter.
And when the roll is called up yonder...
She gave up, holding her breath.
I'll be there...

A lump filled her throat. She leaned her back against a post, trembling, feeling the rise and fall of days and nights, of summer and winter; surging, ebbing, leaping about her, beyond her, far out over the fields to where earth and sky lay folded in darkness. She wanted to lie down and sleep, or else leap up and shout. When the music stopped she felt herself coming back, being let down slowly. She sighed. It was dark now. She looked into the doorway. The baby was sleeping on the floor. Ah gotta git up n put tha chile t bed, she thought.

"Wasnt that pretty?"

"It wuz pretty, awright."

"When do you think your husbands coming back?"

"Ah don know, Mistah."

She went into the room and put the baby into the cradle.

She stood again in the doorway and looked at the shadowy box that had lifted her up and carried her away. Crickets called. The dark sky had swallowed up the earth, and more stars were hanging, clustered, burning. She heard the white man sigh. His face was lost in shadow. She saw him rub his palms over his forehead. Hes jus lika lil boy.

"Id like to see your husband tonight," he said. "Ive got to be in Lilydale at six o'clock in the morning and I wont be back through here soon. I got to pick up my buddy over there and we're heading North."

She smiled into the darkness. He was just like a little boy. A little boy selling clocks.

"Yuh sell them things alla time?" she asked.

"Just for the summer," he said. "I go to school in winter. If I can make enough money out of this Ill go to Chicago to school this fall..."

"Whut yuh gonna be?"

"*Be?* What do you mean?"

"Whut yuh goin t school fer?"

"Im studying science."

"Whuts that?"

"Oh, er..." He looked at her. "Its about why things are as they are."

"Why things is as they *is*?"

"Well, its something like that."

"How come yuh wanna study tha?"

"Oh, you wouldnt understand."

She sighed.

"Naw, Ah guess Ah wouldnt."

"Well, I reckon Ill be getting along," said the white man. "Can I have a drink of water?"

"Sho. But we ain got nothin but well-watah, n yuhll have t come n git."

"Thats all right."

She slid off the porch and walked over the ground with bare feet. She heard the shoes of the white man behind her, falling to the earth in soft whispers. It was black dark now. She led him to the well, groped her way, caught the bucket and let it down with a rope; she heard a splash and the bucket grew heavy. She drew it up, pulling against its weight, throwing one hand over the other, feeling the cool wet of the rope on her palms.

"Ah don git watah outta here much," she said, a little out of breath. "Silas gits the watah mos of the time. This buckets too heavy fer me."

"Oh, wait! Ill help!"

His shoulder touched hers. In the darkness she felt his warm hands fumbling for the rope.

"Where is it?"

"Here."

She extended the rope through the darkness. His fingers touched her breasts.

"Oh!"

She said it in spite of herself. He would think she was thinking about that. And he was a white man. She was sorry she had said that.

"Wheres the gourd?" he asked. "Gee, its dark!"

She stepped back and tried to see him.

"Here."

"I cant see!" he said, laughing.

Again she felt his fingers on the tips of her breasts. She backed away, saying nothing this time. She thrust the gourd out from her. Warm fingers met her cold hands. He had the gourd. She heard him drink; it was the faint, soft music of water going down a dry throat, the music of water in a silent night. He sighed and drank again.

"I was thirsty," he said. "I hadnt had any water since noon."

She knew he was standing in front of her; she could not see him, but she felt him. She heard the gourd rest against the wall of the well. She turned, then felt his hands full on her breasts. She struggled back.

"Naw, Mistah!"

"Im not going to hurt you!"

White arms were about her, tightly. She was still. But hes a *white* man. A *white* man. She felt his breath coming hot on her neck and where his hands held her breasts the flesh seemed to knot. She was rigid, poised; she swayed backward, then forward. She caught his shoulders and pushed.

"Naw, naw...Mistah, Ah cant do that!"

She jerked away. He caught her hand.

"Please..."

"Lemme go!"

She tried to pull her hand out of his and felt his fingers tighten. She pulled harder, and for a moment they were balanced, one against the other. Then he was at her side again, his arms about her.

"I wont hurt you! I wont hurt you..."

She leaned backward and tried to dodge his face. Her breasts were full against him; she gasped, feeling the full length of his body. She held her head far to one side; she knew he was seeking her mouth. His hands were on her breasts again. A wave of warm blood swept into her stomach and loins. She felt his lips touching her throat and where he kissed it burned.

"Naw, naw..."

Her eyes were full of the wet stars and they blurred, silver and blue. Her knees were loose and she heard her own breathing; she was trying to keep from falling. But hes a *white* man! A *white* man! Naw! Naw! And still she would not let him have her lips; she kept her face away. Her breasts hurt where they were crushed against him and each time she caught her breath she held it and while she held it it seemed that if she would let it go it would kill her. Her knees were pressed hard against his and she clutched the upper parts of his arms, trying to hold on. Her loins ached. She felt her body sliding.

"Gawd..."

He helped her up. She could not see the stars now; her eyes were full of the feeling that surged over her body each time she caught her breath. He held her close, breathing into her ear; she straightened, rigidly, feeling that she had to straighten or die. And then her lips felt his and she held her breath and dreaded ever to breathe again for fear of the feeling that would sweep down over her limbs. She held tightly, hearing a mounting tide of blood beating against her throat and temples. Then she gripped him, tore her face away, emptied her lungs in one long despairing gasp and went limp. She felt his hand; she was still, taut, feeling his hand, then his fingers. The muscles in her legs flexed and she bit her lips and pushed her toes deep into the wet dust by the side of the well and tried to wait and tried to wait until she could wait no longer. She whirled away from him and a streak of silver and blue swept across her blood. The wet ground cooled her palms and knee-caps. She stumbled up and ran, blindly, her toes flicking warm, dry dust. Her numbed fingers grabbed at a rusty nail in the post at the porch and she pushed ahead of hands that held her breasts.

Her fingers found the door-facing; she moved into the darkened room, her hands before her. She touched the cradle and turned till her knees hit the bed. She went over, face down, her fingers trembling in the crumpled folds of his shirt. She moved and moved again and again, trying to keep ahead of the warm flood of blood that sought to catch her. A liquid metal covered her and she rode on the curve of white bright days and dark black nights and the surge of the long gladness of summer and the ebb of the deep dream of sleep in winter till a high red wave of hotness drowned her in a deluge of silver and blue that boiled her blood and blistered her flesh *bangbangbang*...

II

"Yuh bettah go," she said.

She felt him standing by the side of the bed, in the dark. She heard him clear his throat. His belt-buckle tinkled.

"Im leaving that clock and graphophone," he said.

She said nothing. In her mind she saw the box glowing softly, like the light in the baby's eyes. She stretched out her legs and relaxed.

"You can have it for forty instead of fifty. Ill be by early in the morning to see if your husbands in."

She said nothing. She felt the hot skin of her body growing steadily cooler.

"Do you think hell pay ten on it? Hell only owe thirty then."

She pushed her toes deep into the quilt, feeling a night wind blowing through the door. Her palms rested lightly on top of her breasts.

"Do you think hell pay ten on it?"

"Hunh?"

"Hell pay ten, wont he?"

"Ah don know," she whispered.

She heard his shoe hit against a wall; footsteps echoed on the wooden porch. She started nervously when she heard the roar of his car; she followed the throb of the motor till she heard it when she could hear it no more, followed it till she heard it roaring faintly in her ears in the dark and silent room. Her hands moved on her breasts and she was conscious of herself, all over; she felt the weight of her body resting heavily on shucks. She felt the presence of fields lying out there covered with night. She turned over slowly and lay on her stomach, her hands tucked under her. From somewhere came a creaking noise. She sat upright, feeling fear. The wind sighed. Crickets called. She lay down again, hearing shucks rustle. Her eyes looked straight up in the darkness and her blood sogged. She had lain a long time, full of a vast peace, when a far away tinkle made her feel the bed again. The tinkle came through the night; she listened, knowing that soon she would hear the rattle of Silas' wagon. Even then she tried to fight off the sound of Silas' coming, even then she wanted to feel the peace of night filling her again; but the tinkle grew louder and she heard the jangle of a wagon and the quick trot of horses. Thas Silas! She gave up and waited. She heard horses neighing. Out of the window bare feet whispered in the dust, then crossed the porch, echoing in soft booms. She closed her eyes and saw Silas come into the room in his dirty overalls as she had seen him come in a thousand times before.

"Yuh sleep, Sarah?"

She did not answer. Feet walked across the floor and a match scratched. She opened her eyes and saw Silas standing over her with a lighted lamp. His hat was pushed far back on his head and he was laughing.

"Ah reckon yuh thought Ah wuznt never comin back, hunh? Cant yuh wake up? See, Ah got that red cloth yuh wanted..." He laughed again and threw the red cloth on the mantel.

"Yuh hongry?" she asked.

"Naw, Ah kin make out till mawnin." Shucks rustled as he sat on the edge of the bed. "Ah got two hundred n fifty fer mah cotton."

"Two hundred n fifty?"

"Nothin different! N guess whut Ah done?"

"Whut?"

"Ah bought ten mo acres o lan. Got em from ol man Burgess. Paid im a hundred n fifty dollahs down. Ahll pay the res next year ef things go erlong awright. Ahma have t git a man to hep me nex spring..."

"Yuh mean hire somebody?"

"Sho, hire somebody! Whut yuh think? Ain tha the way the white folks do? Ef yuhs gonna git anywheres yuhs gotta do just like they do." He paused. "Whut yuh been doin since Ah been gone?"

"Nothin. Cookin, cleanin, n..."

"How Ruth?"

"She awright." She lifted her head. "Silas, yuh git any lettahs?"

"Naw. But Ah heard Tom wuz in town."

"In *town*?"

She sat straight up.

"Yeah thas whut the folks wuz sayin at the sto."

"Back from the war?"

"Ah ast erroun t see ef Ah could fin im. But Ah couldnt."

"Lawd Ah wish hed c mon home."

"Them white folks sho's glad the wars over. But things wuz kinda bad there in town. Everwhere Ah looked wuznt nothin but black n white soljers. N them white folks beat up a black soljer yistiddy. He wuz jus in from France. Wuz still wearin his soljers suit. They claimed he sassed a white woman..."

"Who wuz he?"

"Ah don know. Never saw im befo."

"Yuh see An Peel?"

"Naw."

"Silas!" she said reprovingly.

"Aw, Sarah, Ah jus couldnt git out there."

"What else yuh bring sides the cloth?"

"Ah got yuh some high-top shoes." He turned and looked at her in the dim light of the lamp. "Woman, ain yuh glad Ah bought yuh some shoes n cloth?" He laughed and lifted his feet to the bed. "Lawd, Sarah, yuhs sho sleepy, ain yuh?"

"Bettah put tha lamp out, Silas..."

"Aw..." He swung out of the bed and stood still for a moment. She watched him, then turned her face to the wall.

"Whuts that by the windah?" he asked.

She saw him bending over and touching the graphophone with his fingers.

"Thasa graphophone."

"Where yuh git it from?"

"A man lef it here."

"When he bring it?"

"Today."

"But how come he t leave it?"

"He says hell be out here in the mawnin t see ef yuh wans t buy it."

He was on his knees, feeling the wood and looking at the gilt on the edges of the box. He stood up and looked at her.

"Yuh ain never said yuh wanted one of these things."

She said nothing.

"Where wuz the man from?"

"Ah don know."

"He white?"

"Yeah."

He put the lamp back on the mantel. As he lifted the globe to blow out the flame, his hand paused.

"Whos hats this?"

She raised herself and looked. A straw hat lay bottom upwards on the edge of the mantel. Silas picked it up and looked back to the bed, to Sarah.

"Ah guess its the white mans. He must a lef it..."

"Whut he doin *in our room*?"

"He wuz talkin t me bout tha graphophone."

She watched him go to the window and stoop again to the box. He picked it up, fumbled with the price-tag and took the box to the light.

"Whut this thing cos?"

"Forty dollahs."

"But its marked fifty here."

"Oh, Ah means he said fifty..."

He took a step toward the bed.

"Yuh lyin t me!"

"Silas!"

He heaved the box out of the front door; there was a smashing, tinkling noise as it bounded off the front porch and hit the ground.

"Whut in hell yuh lie t me fer?"

"Yuh broke the box!"

"Ahma break yo Gawddam neck ef yuh don stop lyin t me!"

"Silas, Ah ain lied t yuh!"

"Shut up, Gawddammit! Yuh did!"

He was standing by the bed with the lamp trembling in his hand. She stood on the other side, between the bed and the wall.

"How come yuh tell me tha thing cos *forty* dollahs when it cos *fifty*?"

"Thas whut he tol me."

"How come he take *ten* dollahs off fer yuh?"

"He ain took nothin off fer me, Silas!"

"Yuh lyin t me! N yuh lied t me bout Tom, too!"

She stood with her back to the wall, her lips parted, looking at him silently, steadily. Their eyes held for a moment. Silas looked down, as though he were about to believe her. Then he stiffened.

"Whos this?" he asked, picking up a short yellow pencil from the crumpled quilt.

She said nothing. He started toward her.

"Yuh wan me t take mah raw-hide whip n make yuh talk?"

"Naw, naw, Silas! Yuh wrong! He wuz figgerin wid tha pencil!"

He was silent a moment, his eyes searching her face.

"Gawddam yo black soul t hell, don yuh try lyin t me! Ef yuh start layin wid white men Ahll hoss-whip yuh t a inch yo life. Shos theres a Gawd in Heaven Ah will! From sunup t sundown Ah works mah guts out t pay them white trash bastards whut Ah owe em, n then Ah comes n fins they been in mah house! Ah cant go into their houses, n yuh know Gawddam well Ah cant! They don have no mercy on no black folks; wes just like dirt under their feet! Fer ten years Ah slaves lika dog t git mah farm free, givin ever penny Ah kin t em, n then Ah comes n fins they been in mah house..." He was speechless with outrage. "Ef yuh wans t eat at mah table yuhs gonna keep them white trash bastards out, yuh hear? Tha white ape kin come n git tha damn box n Ah ain gonna pay im a cent! He had no bisness leavin it here, n yuh had no bisness lettin im! Ahma tell tha sonofabitch something when he comes out here in the mawnin, so hep me Gawd! Now git back in tha bed!"

She slipped beneath the quilt and lay still, her face turned to the wall. Her heart thumped slowly and heavily. She heard him walk across the floor in his bare feet. She heard the bottom of the lamp as it rested on the mantel. She stiffened when the room darkened. Feet whispered across the floor again. The shucks rustled from Silas' weight as he sat on the edge of the bed. She was still, breathing softly. Silas was mumbling. She felt sorry for him. In the darkness it seemed that she could see the hurt look on his black face. The crow of a rooster came from far away, came so faintly that it seemed she had not heard it. The bed sank and the shucks cried out in dry whispers; she knew Silas had stretched out. She heard him sigh. Then she jumped because he jumped. She could feel the tenseness of his body; she knew he was sitting bolt upright. She felt his hands fumbling jerkily under the quilt. Then the bed heaved amid a wild shout of shucks and Silas' feet hit the floor with a loud boom. She snatched herself to her elbows, straining her eyes in the dark, wondering what was wrong now. Silas was moving about, cursing under his breath.

"Don wake Ruth up!" she whispered.

"Ef yuh say one mo word t me Ahma slap yuh inter a black spasm!"

She grabbed her dress, got up and stood by the bed, the tips of her fingers touching the wall behind her. A match flared in yellow flame; Silas' face was caught in a circle of light. He was looking downward, staring intently at a white wad of cloth balled in his hand. His black cheeks were hard, set; his lips were tightly pursed. She looked closer; she saw that the white cloth was a man's handkerchief. Silas' fingers loosened; she heard the handkerchief hit the floor softly, damply. The match went out.

"Yuh little bitch!"

Her knees gave. Fear oozed from her throat to her stomach.

She moved in the dark toward the door, struggling with the dress, jamming it over her head. She heard the thick skin of Silas' feet swish across the wooden planks.

"Ah got mah raw-hide whip n Ahm takin yuh t the barn!"

She ran on tiptoe to the porch and paused, thinking of the baby. She shrank as something whined through air. A red streak of pain cut across the small of her back and burned its way into her body, deeply.

"Silas!" she screamed.

She grabbed for the post and fell in dust. She screamed again and crawled out of reach.

"Git t the barn, Gawddammit!"

She scrambled up and ran through the dark, hearing the baby cry. Behind her leather thongs hummed and feet whispered swiftly over the dusty ground.

"Cmere, yuh bitch! Cmere, Ah say!"

She ran to the road and stopped. She wanted to go back and get the baby, but she dared not. Not as long as Silas had that whip. She stiffened, feeling that he was near.

"Yuh jus as well c mon back n git yo beatin!"

She ran again, slowing now and then to listen. If she only knew where he was she would slip back into the house and get the baby and walk all the way to Aunt Peel's.

"Yuh ain comin back in mah house till Ah beat yuh!"

She was sorry for the anger she knew he had out there in the field. She had a bewildering impulse to go to him and ask him not to be angry; she wanted to tell him that there was nothing to be angry about; that what she had done did not matter; that she was sorry; that after all she was his wife and still loved him. But there was no way she could do that now; if she went to him be would whip her as she had seen him whip a horse.

"Sarah! Sarah!"

His voice came from far away. Ahm goin git Ruth. Back through dust she sped, going on her toes, holding her breath.

"Saaaarah!"

From far off his voice floated over the fields. She ran into the house and caught the baby in her arms. Again she sped through dust on her toes. She did not stop till she was so far away that his voice sounded like a faint echo falling from the sky. She looked up; the stars were paling a little. Mus be gittin near mawnin. She walked now, letting her feet sink softly into the cool dust. The baby was sleeping; she could feel the little chest swelling against her arm. She looked up again; the sky was solid black. Its gittin near mawnin. Ahma take Ruth t An Peels. N mabbe Ahll fin Tom... But she could not walk all that distance in the dark. Not now. Her legs were tired. For a moment a memory of surge and ebb rose in her blood; she felt her legs straining, upward. She sighed. Yes, she would go to the sloping hillside back of the garden and wait until morning. Then she would slip away. She stopped, listening. She heard a faint, rattling noise. She imagined Silas' kicking or throwing the smashed graphophone. Hes mad! Hes sho mad! Aw, Lawd!...She stopped stock still, squeezing the baby till it whimpered. What would happen when that white man came out in the morning? She had forgotten him. She would have to head him off and tell him. Yeah, cause Silas jus mad ernuff t kill! Lawd, hes mad ernuff t kill!

III

She circled the house widely, climbing a slope, groping her way, holding the baby high in her arms. After awhile she stopped and wondered where on the slope she was. She remembered there was an elm tree near the edge; if she could find it she would know. She groped farther, feeling with her feet. Ahm gittin los! And she did not want to fall with the baby. Ahma stop here, she thought. When morning came she would see the car of the white man from this hill and she would run down the road and tell him to go back; and then there would be no killing. Dimly she saw in her mind a picture of men killing and being killed. White men killed the black and black men killed the white. White men killed the black men because they could, and the black men killed the white men to keep from being killed. And killing was blood. Lawd, Ah wish Tom wuz here. She shuddered, sat on the ground and watched the sky for signs of morning. Mabbe Ah oughta walk on down the road? Naw...Her legs were tired. Again she felt her body straining. Then she saw Silas holding the white man's handkerchief. She heard it hit the floor, softly, damply. She was sorry for what she had done. Silas was as good to her as any black man could be to a black woman. Most of the black women worked in the fields as croppers. But Silas had given her her own home, and that was more than many others had done for their women. Yes, she knew how Silas felt. Always he had said he was as good as any white man. He had worked hard and saved his money and bought a farm so he could grow his own crops like white men. Silas hates white folks! Lawd, he sho hates em!

The baby whimpered. She unbuttoned her dress and nursed her in the dark. She looked toward the east. There! A tinge of grey hovered. It wont be long now. She could see ghostly outlines of trees. Soon she would see the elm, and by the elm she would sit till it was light enough to see the road.

The baby slept. Far off a rooster crowed. Sky deepened. She rose and walked slowly down a narrow, curving path and came to the elm tree. Standing on the edge of a slope, she saw a dark smudge in a sea of shifting shadows. That was her home. Wondah how come Silas didnt light the lamp? She shifted the baby from her right hip to her left, sighed, struggled against sleep. She sat on the ground again, caught the baby close and leaned against the trunk of a tree. Her eye-lids drooped and it seemed that a hard cold hand caught hold of her right leg—or was it her left leg? she did not know which—and began to drag her over a rough litter of shucks and when she strained to see who it was that was pulling her no one was in sight but far ahead was darkness and it seemed that out of the darkness some force came and pulled her like a magnet and she went sliding along over a rough bed of screeching shucks and it seemed that a wild fear made her want to scream but when she opened her mouth to scream she could not scream and she felt she was coming to a wide black hole and again she made ready to scream and then it was too late for she was already over the wide black hole falling falling falling...

She awakened with a start and blinked her eyes in the sunshine. She found she was clutching the baby so hard that it had begun to cry. She got to her feet, trembling from fright of the dream, remembering Silas and the white man and Silas' running her out of the house and the white man's coming. Silas was standing in the front yard; she caught her breath. Yes, she had to go and head that white man off! Naw! She could not do that, not with Silas standing there with that whip in his hand. If she tried to climb any of those slopes he would see her surely. And Silas would never forgive her for something like that. If it were anybody but a white man it would be different.

Then, while standing there on the edge of the slope looking wonderingly at Silas striking the whip against his overall-leg—and then, while standing there looking—she froze. There came from the hills a distant throb. Lawd! The baby whimpered. She loosened her arms. The throb grew louder, droning. Hes comin fas! She wanted to run to Silas and beg him not to bother the white man. But he had that whip in his hand. She should not have done what she had done last night. This was all her fault. Lawd, ef anything happens t im its mah blame...Her eyes watched a black car speed over the crest of a hill. She should have been out there on the road instead of sleeping here by the tree. But it was too late now. Silas was standing in the yard; she saw him turn with a nervous jerk and sit on the edge of the porch. He was holding the whip stiffly. The car came to a stop. A door swung open. A white man got out. Thas im! She saw another white man in the front seat of the car. N thats his buddy...The white man who had gotten out walked over the ground, going to Silas. They faced each other, the white man standing up and Silas sitting down; like two toy men they faced each other. She saw Silas point the whip to the smashed graphophone. The white man looked down and took a quick step backward. The white man's shoulders were bent and he shook his head from left to right. Then Silas got up and they faced each other again; like two dolls, a white doll and a black doll, they faced each other in the valley below. The white man pointed his finger into Silas' face. Then Silas' right arm went up; the whip flashed. The white man turned, bending, flinging his hands to shield his head. Silas' arm rose and fell, rose and fell. She saw the white man crawling in dust, trying to get out of reach. She screamed when she saw the other white man get out of the car and run to Silas. Then all three were on the ground, rolling in dust, grappling for the whip. She clutched the baby and ran. Lawd! Then she stopped, her mouth hanging open. Silas had broken loose and was running toward the house. She knew he was going for his gun.

"Silas!"

Running, she stumbled and fell. The baby rolled in the dust and bawled. She grabbed it up and ran again. The white men were scrambling for their car. She reached level ground, running. Hell be killed! Then again she stopped. Silas was on the front porch, aiming a rifle. One of the white men was climbing into the car. The other was standing, waving his arms, shouting at Silas. She tried to scream, but choked; and she could not scream till she heard a shot ring out.

"Silas!"

One of the white men was on the ground. The other was in the car. Silas was aiming again. The car started, running in a cloud of dust. She fell to her knees and hugged the baby close. She heard another shot, but the car was roaring over the top of the southern hill. Fear was gone now. Down the slope she ran. Silas was standing on the porch, holding his gun and looking at the fleeing car. Then she saw him go to the white man lying in dust and stoop over him. He caught one of the man's legs and dragged the body into the middle of the road. Then he turned and came slowly back to the house. She ran, holding the baby, and fell at his feet.

"Siiilas!"

IV

"Git up, Sarah!"

His voice was hard and cold. She lifted her eyes and saw blurred black feet. She wiped tears away with dusty fingers and pulled up. Something took speech from her and she stood with bowed shoulders. Silas was standing still, mute; the look on his face condemned her. It was as though he had gone far off and had stayed a long time and had come back changed even while she was standing there in the sunshine before him. She wanted to say something, to give herself. She cried.

"Git the chile up, Sarah!"

She lifted the baby and stood waiting for him to speak, to tell her something to change all this. But he said nothing. He walked toward the house. She followed. As she attempted to go in, he blocked the way. She jumped to one side as he threw the red cloth outdoors to the ground. The new shoes came next. Then Silas heaved the baby's cradle. It hit the porch and a rocker splintered; the cradle swayed for a second, then fell to the ground, lifting a cloud of brown dust against the sun. All of her clothes and the baby's clothes were thrown out.

"Silas!"

She cried, seeing blurred objects sailing through the air and hearing them hit softly in the dust.

"Git yo things n go!"

"Silas."

"Ain no use yuh sayin *nothin* now!"

"But theyll kill yuh!"

"There ain nothin Ah kin do. N there ain nothin yuh kin do. Yuh done done too Gawddam much awready. Git yo things n go!"

"Theyll kill yuh, Silas!"

He pushed her off the porch.

"GIT YO THINGS N GO T AN PEELS!"

"Les *both* go, Silas!"

"Ahm stayin here till they come back!"

She grabbed his arm and he slapped her hand away. She dropped to the edge of the porch and sat looking at the ground.

"Go way," she said quietly. "Go way fo they comes. Ah didnt mean no harm..."

"Go way fer whut?"

"Theyll *kill* yuh..."

"It don make no difference." He looked out over the sun-filled fields. "Fer ten years Ah slaved mah life out t git mah farm free..." His voice broke off. His lips moved as though a thousand words were spilling silently out of his mouth, as though he did not have breath enough to give them sound. He looked to the sky, and then back to the dust. "Now, its all gone. *Gone*...Ef Ah run erway, Ah ain got nothin. Ef Ah stay n fight, Ah ain got nothin. It don make no difference which way Ah go. Gawd! Gawd, Ah wish alla them white folks wuz dead! *Dead*, Ah tell yuh! Ah wish Gawd would kill em *all!*"

She watched him run a few steps and stop. His throat swelled. He lifted his hands to his face; his fingers trembled. Then he bent to the ground and cried. She touched his shoulders.

"Silas!"

He stood up. She saw he was staring at the white man's body lying in the dust in the middle of the road. She watched him walk over to it. He began to talk to no one in particular; he simply stood over the dead white man and talked out of his life, out of a deep and final sense that now it was all over and nothing could make any difference.

"The white folks ain never gimme a chance! They ain never give no black man a chance! There ain nothin in yo whole life yuh kin keep from em! They take yo lan! They take yo freedom! They take yo women! N then they take yo life!" He turned to her, screaming. "N then Ah gits stabbed in the back by mah own blood! When mah eyes is on the white folks to keep em from killin me, mah own blood trips me up!" He knelt in the dust again and sobbed; after a bit he looked to the sky, his face wet with tears. "Ahm gonna be hard like they is! So hep me, Gawd, Ah'm gonna be *hard!* When they come fer me Ah'm gonna *be* here! N when they git me outta here theys gonna *know* Ahm gone! Ef Gawd lets me live Ahm gonna make em *feel* it!" He stopped and tried to get his breath. "But, Lawd, Ah don wanna be this way! It don mean nothin! Yuh die ef yuh fight! Yuh die ef yuh don fight! Either way yuh die n it don mean nothin..."

He was lying flat on the ground, the side of his face deep in dust. Sarah stood nursing the baby with eyes black and stony. Silas pulled up slowly and stood again on the porch.

"Git on t An Peels, Sarah!"

A dull roar came from the south. They both turned. A long streak of brown dust was weaving down the hillside.

"Silas!"

"Go on cross the fiels, Sarah!"

"We kin *both* go! Git the hosses!"

He pushed her off the porch, grabbed her hand, and led her to the rear of the house, past the well, to where a path led up a slope to the elm tree.

"Silas!"

"Yuh git on fo they ketch yuh too!"

Blind from tears, she went across the swaying fields, stumbling over blurred grass. It ain no use! She knew it was now too late to make him change his mind. The calves of her legs knotted. Suddenly her throat tightened, aching. She stopped, closed her eyes and tried to stem a flood of sorrow that drenched her. Yes, killing of white men by black men and killing of black men by white men went on in spite of the hope of white bright days and the desire of dark black nights and the long gladness of green cornfields in summer and the deep dream of sleeping grey skies in winter. And when killing started it went on, like a red river flowing. Oh, she felt sorry for Silas! Silas...He was following that long river of blood. Lawd, how come he wans t stay there like tha? And he did not want to die; she knew he hated dying by the way he talked of it. Yet he followed the old river of blood, knowing that it meant nothing. He followed it, cursing and whimpering. But he followed it. She stared before her at the dry, dusty grass. Somehow, men, black men and white men, land and houses, green cornfields and grey skies, gladness and dreams, were all a part of that which made life good. Yes, somehow, they were linked, like the spokes in a spinning wagon wheel. She felt they were. She knew they were. She felt it when she breathed and knew it when she looked. But she could not say how; she could not put her finger on it and when she thought hard about it it became all mixed up, like milk spilling suddenly. Or else it knotted in her throat and chest in a hard aching lump, like the one she felt now. She touched her face to the baby's face and cried again.

There was a loud blare of auto horns. The growing roar made her turn round. Silas was standing, seemingly unafraid, leaning against a post of the porch. The long line of cars came speeding in clouds of dust. Silas moved toward the door and went in. Sarah ran down the slope a piece, coming again to the elm tree. Her breath was slow and hard. The cars stopped in front of the house. There was a steady drone of motors and drifting clouds of dust. For a moment she could not see what was happening. Then on all sides white men with pistols and rifles swarmed over the fields. She dropped to her knees, unable to take her eyes away, unable it seemed to breathe. A shot rang out. A white man fell, rolling over, face downward.

"Hes gotta gun!"

"Git back!"

"Lay down!"

The white men ran back and crouched behind cars. Three more shots came from the house. She looked, her head and eyes aching. She rested the baby in her lap and shut her eyes. Her knees sank into the dust. More shots came, but it was no use looking now. She knew it all by heart. She could feel it happening even before it happened. There were men killing and being killed. Then she jerked up, being compelled to look.

"Burn the bastard out!"

"Set the sonofabitch on fire!"

"Cook the coon!"

"Smoke im out!"

She saw two white men on all fours creeping past the well. One carried a gun and the other a red tin can. When they reached the back steps the one with the tin can crept under the house and crept out again. Then both rose and ran. Shots. One fell. A yell went up. A yellow tongue of fire licked out from under the back steps.

"Burn the nigger!"

"C mon out, nigger, n git yos!"

She watched from the hill-slope; the back steps blazed. The white men fired a steady stream of bullets. Black smoke spiraled upward in the sunshine. Shots came from the house. The white men crouched out of sight, behind their cars.

"Make up yo mind, nigger!"

"C mon out er burn, yuh black bastard!"

"Yuh think yuhre white now, nigger?"

The shack blazed, flanked on all sides by whirling smoke filled with flying sparks. She heard the distant hiss of flames. White men were crawling on their stomachs. Now and then they stopped, aimed, and fired into the bulging smoke. She looked with a tense numbness; she looked, waiting for Silas to scream, or run out. But the house crackled and blazed, spouting yellow plumes to the blue sky. The white men shot again, sending a hail of bullets into the furious pillars of smoke. And still she could not see Silas running out, or hear his voice calling. Then she jumped, standing. There was a loud crash; the roof caved in. A black chimney loomed amid crumbling wood. Flames roared and black smoke billowed, hiding the house. The white men stood up, no longer afraid. Again she waited for Silas, waited to see him fight his way out, waited to hear his call. Then she breathed a long, slow breath, emptying her lungs. She knew now. Silas had killed as many as he could and had stayed on to burn, had stayed without a murmur. She filled her lungs with a quick gasp as the walls fell in; the house was hidden by eager plumes of red. She turned and ran with the baby in her arms, ran blindly across the fields, crying, "Naw, Gawd!"

[1938]

MURIEL RUKEYSER ■ (1913–1980)

Muriel Rukeyser worked in a number of genres, including biography, novel, essay, drama, and even television script, but she is best known for her many volumes of poetry. Born in New York City, she studied at Vassar College and Columbia University. By her early teens she had already decided to become a writer, a vocation she combined with a lifelong dedication to social reform and radical politics that included a peace mission to Vietnam in 1972.

Rukeyser published her first book of poems, *Theory of Flight*, in 1935, and it was awarded the Yale Younger Poets prize. Later books of poetry include *U.S. 1* (1938), the centerpiece of which is the sequence "The Book of the Dead," based on research that Rukeyser had undertaken on the serious illnesses suffered by West Virginia coal miners; *A Turning Wind: Poems* (1939); *Beast in View* (1944); and *The Green Wave* (1948).

From the late 1940s onward, Rukeyser continued with verse—her poetic output is gathered in *The Collected Poems of Muriel Rukeyser* (1979)—but she also produced translations and other writings, including a meditative prose piece, *The Life of Poetry* (1949). After a period in California, where, unmarried, she gave birth to a son, she returned in the mid-1950s to the East, taking a position on the faculty of Sarah Lawrence College.

"Effort at Speech Between Two People," included here, is a probing poem about loss and love, notable in its structure for Rukeyser's handling of line and spacing. The speaker's "dreams of suicide" here look forward to the more powerful treatment of the theme in "Suicide Blues," a desperate, disturbing performance. Personal connection-making also figures in "Poem," from *The Speed of Darkness* (1968), but in this case Rukeyser states more explicitly the historical background within which desire and hope are expressed.

Rukeyser, like Walt Whitman, possesses a visionary power, tough-minded, pained, yet resilient and affirmative. "However confused the scene of our life appears," she observed, "however torn we may be who now do face that scene, it can be faced, and we can go on to be whole." Committed to peace, justice, and tolerance, Rukeyser insisted that poets and their readers always remember that "the universe is made of stories, not of atoms."

For critical interpretation and context, see Louise Kertesz, *The Poetic Vision of Muriel Rukeyser* (1980); and *How Shall We Tell Each Other of the Poet? The Life and Writing of Muriel Rukeyser*, eds. Anne F. Herzog and Janet E. Kaufman (1999). Tim Dayton, *Muriel Rukeyser's The Book of the Dead* (2003). An essential resource is *The Collected Poems of Muriel Rukeyser*, ed. Janet E. Kaufman and Anne F. Herzog (2005).

Effort at Speech Between Two People

Speak to me.   Take my hand.   What are you now?
I will tell you all.   I will conceal nothing.
When I was three, a little child read a story about a rabbit
who died, in the story, and I crawled under a chair:
a pink rabbit: it was my birthday, and a candle   5
burnt a sore spot on my finger, and I was told to be happy.

Oh, grow to know me.   I am not happy.   I will be open:
Now I am thinking of white sails against a sky like music,
like glad horns blowing, and birds tilting, and an arm about me.
There was one I loved, who wanted to live, sailing.   10

Speak to me.   Take my hand.   What are you now?
When I was nine, I was fruitily sentimental,
fluid: and my widowed aunt played Chopin,[1]
and I bent my head on the painted woodwork, and wept.
I want now to be close to you.   I would   15
link the minutes of my days close, somehow, to your days.

I am not happy.   I will be open.
I have liked lamps in evening corners, and quiet poems.
There has been fear in my life.   Sometimes I speculate
On what a tragedy his life was, really.   20

Take my hand.   Fist my mind in your hand.   What are you now?
When I was fourteen, I had dreams of suicide,
and I stood at a steep window, at sunset, hoping toward death:
if the light had not melted clouds and plains to beauty,
if light had not transformed that day, I would have leapt.   25
I am unhappy.   I am lonely.   Speak to me.

I will be open.   I think he never loved me:
he loved the bright beaches, the little lips of foam
that ride small waves, he loved the veer of gulls:
he said with a gay mouth: I love you.   Grow to know me.   30

What are you now?   If we could touch one another,
if these our separate entities could come to grips,
clenched like a Chinese puzzle...yesterday
I stood in a crowded street that was live with people,
and no one spoke a word, and the morning shone.   35
Everyone silent, moving....Take my hand.   Speak to me.

[1935]

---

[1]Frédéric François Chopin (1810–49) was a Polish composer known for his works for the piano.

Poem

I lived in the first century of world wars.
Most mornings I would be more or less insane,
The newspapers would arrive with their careless stories,
The news would pour out of various devices
Interrupted by attempts to sell products to the unseen.   5
I would call my friends on other devices;
They would be more or less mad for similar reasons.
Slowly I would get to pen and paper,
Make my poems for others unseen and unborn.
In the day I would be reminded of those men and women   10
Brave, setting up signals across vast distances,
Considering a nameless way of living, of almost unimagined values.
As the lights darkened, as the lights of night brightened,
We would try to imagine them, try to find each other.
To construct peace, to make love, to reconcile   15
Waking with sleeping, ourselves with each other,
Ourselves with ourselves. We would try by any means
To reach the limits of ourselves, to reach beyond ourselves,
To let go the means, to wake.

I lived in the first century of these wars.   20

[1968]

▪▪ GALLERY ▪▪

American Writers and the Great Depression

In courses on modern American literature, twentieth-century American literature, and modern American poetry, teachers and students focus on T. S. Eliot, Robert Frost, Ezra Pound, Edna St. Vincent Millay, Langston Hughes, Wallace Stevens, and others as though all of these writers shared a set of common themes and stylistic techniques. Yet once we enter deeply into the work of each of them, we realize how hard it is to describe each one in terms that apply to the others. The same holds true for fiction: Theodore Dreiser, Willa Cather, Ernest Hemingway, William Faulkner, Edith Wharton, and other major figures of the first three decades of the twentieth century fall within the same period, yet each developed a distinctive style that differentiates him or her from the rest. Perhaps for this reason, scholars sometimes propose that we should study each writer in his or her own right, not generalizing, not trying to impose patterns and similarities that the works of the writers cannot really support.

However, we might be able to say at least this much, taking as our cue Pound's injunction that modern writers "make it new." For many writers of this period this meant being innovative, risk-taking, experimental, unorthodox, unconventional. We see bold ventures of literary newness in the poetry of Eliot and Hughes, and in the prose of Hemingway and Faulkner. In a sense, taken as a whole these modern writers were creating a richer and more capacious democratic literature—not only in the voices in which they wrote and engaged readers but also in the range of views, voices, dialects, cultural and literary resources, forms of arts and media, regions, traditions, and histories that they relied on and explored in their work—and extended, tested, subverted, and reanimated.

American literature in the first decades of the twentieth century was becoming more expansive, and ever-expanding. It indeed was a more democratic, more inclusive national literature. It even could be considered a more democratic international or cosmopolitan literature, produced both by writers who remained in the United States and by writers who centered their literary lives in London or Paris or elsewhere abroad.

The great and familiar literary names of the modern period draw our attention and interest first, but through the efforts of literary scholars and historians we have come to understand how complicated each of them is in his or her Americanness—and the perspective that each of them offers on the American scene. We are aware as well of how much time has passed between their era and our own. The early poems of Eliot and Pound, the first stories and writing of Gertrude Stein and Sherwood Anderson, and the writings of others whom they influenced—like Hemingway and Fitzgerald for instance—are almost 100 years in the past. We have been reinterpreting, and are continuing to reinterpret, the classic modern authors and texts—their location in their time, and their changing significance in light of the decades of history and literature and criticism that have come after them. We realize the diversity of their remaking of American literature, their extension of the craft and idiom of writing done by Americans inside and beyond the borders of the United States from 1900 to 1930.

Slowly, but steadily too, we have come to understand that American literature continued to be rich and complex and diverse in the 1930s—often an overlooked decade in literary histories and course syllabi. On one level we have always known that there was much significant writing, important literature, in this decade. To take a single instance, the decade saw, at its beginning, Dashiell Hammett's detective novels, including *Red Harvest* (1929) and *The Maltese Falcon* (1930), and it concluded with those by Raymond Chandler, including *The Big Sleep* (1939) and *Farewell, My Lovely* (1940)—books that shaped the writing of crime fiction. But this decade of the Great Depression, which began with the Stock Market crash of late 1929, which the New Deal of President Franklin Delano Roosevelt defined, and which culminated in World War II, is one that we usually characterize above all not in literary, but in political, terms—the nation and the world in the midst of terrible and terrifying social and economic crisis.

A good case, though, could be made that in literature, art, music, and photography, in books and magazines and films and radio programs and in much more, the 1930s is among the great decades of American cultural achievement. Perhaps it rivaled, and even may have exceeded, the 1920s. The nation and the world were in the midst of an unprecedented crisis, of deprivation and suffering on a vast scale. Yet the 1930s was also in important respects a period of immense and varied creativity, of ongoing experiment and innovation as before, and of a thrilling, determined fighting spirit: writers and artists were caught up in a broken society, and were describing and documenting its inequalities and outrages, and were envisioning a better future—frequently with the financial support (modest, but crucial) given to them by federal art, culture, and literature projects that the Roosevelt administration had established. It seemed possible, even probable, that capitalism had expired, or would very soon. What would come next?

Not all writers became more liberal or radical, or turned to Marxism, socialism, or communism. Some, including Eliot and, at the extreme, Pound, moved aggressively to the political right and showed sympathy for a hard conservatism, even, as was true of Pound, fascism. Others wrote little about politics—though it was a difficult matter to ignore. But there were many major figures who became more directly political in their work; Hemingway, for instance, covered the Spanish Civil War as a journalist and at the end of the decade wrote *For Whom the Bell Tolls* (1940), which tells the story of a dedicated young American fighting with Spanish peasants against General Franco and his Fascist allies.

In their different ways, countless writers during the 1930s were inspired by the kind of social and political commitment that the literary scholar F. O. Matthiessen emphasized in his landmark volume *American Renaissance: Art and Expression in the Age of Emerson and Whitman*, published in 1941. He celebrated the writers of the nineteenth century who believed "there should be no split between art and the other functions of the community, that there should be an organic union between labor and culture." Matthiessen cited as a goal and a standard the words of the architect Louis Sullivan: "In a democracy there can be but one fundamental test of citizenship, namely: Are you using such gifts as you possess for or against the people?"

Before October 1929, nearly everyone had assumed that the American economy would continue to boom and prosper; the stock market was moving upward and the unemployment rate was 3.2 percent. But then, preceded by some weeks of fluctuation, the stock market crashed on October 29. In just several weeks' time, 30 billion dollars was lost in the value of stocks; translated into 2011–12 terms, this would be roughly 380 billion dollars. By the end of the year, and into the following year, the stock market had plummeted and the banking system had failed. The economy of the United States, and of the world, now was subjected to the consequences of extreme speculation, overproduction, too-easy credit and installment buying, and unregulated banking and stock-market practices— and from an excess of optimism and exuberance in the 1920s.

When President Roosevelt began his first term in March 1933, most of the banks in the United States were closed; the unemployment rate overall was 25 percent (perhaps as high as 33 percent), and among African Americans it was 50 percent. The gross national product (GDP) was cut in half. Agriculture was badly hit. Incomes in all nations of the world were slashed and international trade fell dramatically as the crisis continued. In the United States, the national income in 1930 was 87 billion dollars; in 1933, it was 40 billion dollars. For many Americans, the basics of food, clothing, and shelter were beyond reach; many families lost their jobs, their homes, and all of their savings. There was no unemployment insurance—no government agencies or institutions were in place that could aid and protect workers and families from disaster and misery.

Through his policy initiatives, including reforms in banking, job programs, public works (e.g., the Tennessee Value Authority, with its dams and electrification projects), President Roosevelt and his administration managed to restore industrial production and lower the high unemployment rate. But in 1937 the economy suffered the blow of "the recession within the depression" (as economic historians have termed it); production declined and severe unemployment took hold again. The Great Depression ended only because of the surge of manufacturing and industry that started with America's entry into World War II in December 1941.

This is the situation that American writers and artists faced in the 1930s, and, as the selections here suggest, they had to make fateful choices about the approach, voice, strategy, and point of view through which to take account of it in their work. These selections barely scratch the surface. Here, for example, we have included Thomas Wolfe and John Steinbeck, but we might also have given excerpts from John Dos Passos's experimental, panoramic survey of American society in the twentieth century, the U.S.A. trilogy: *The 42nd Parallel* (1930); *1919* (1932); and *The Big Money* (1936); James T. Farrell's *Studs Lonigan* trilogy about the Irish on the South Side of Chicago: *Young Lonigan* (1932), *The Young Manhood of Studs Lonigan* (1934), and *Judgment Day* (1935); Erskine Caldwell's novels *Tobacco Road* (1932), about Georgia sharecroppers, and *God's Little Acre* (1933), dealing with mill workers in the industrialized South; and Nathanael West's *Miss Lonelyhearts* (1933) and *The Day of the Locust* (1939), with their disturbing casts of misfits and grotesques. The selections here serve as a point of departure further exploration of fiction and verse, prose and drama, and other literary genres and types of art, music, and more.

FRANKLIN DELANO ROOSEVELT ■ (1882–1945)

Franklin Delano Roosevelt (1882–1945), known as FDR, was the Democratic Party's nominee for president in 1932, winning a landslide victory over the Republican incumbent, Herbert Hoover. A strong, active, confident leader and speaker—though his legs were paralyzed from polio he had contracted in 1921—Roosevelt quickly began to create a New Deal for Americans, a network of governmental policies, executive orders, and agencies designed to lift the nation from its severe economic hardships. The first American president elected to a third term, he was elected for a fourth term in 1944 but died in office and was succeeded by his vice president, Harry S. Truman. Here are key passages from his First Inaugural Address.

From First Inaugural Address

Washington, D.C., March 4, 1933

I am certain that my fellow Americans expect that on my induction into the Presidency I will address them with a candor and a decision which the present situation of our Nation impels. This is preeminently the time to speak the truth, the whole truth, frankly and boldly. Nor need we shrink from honestly facing conditions in our country today. This great Nation will endure as it has endured, will revive and will prosper. So, first of all, let me assert my firm belief that the only thing we have to fear is fear itself—nameless, unreasoning, unjustified terror which paralyzes needed efforts to convert retreat into advance. In every dark hour of our national life a leadership of frankness and vigor has met with that understanding and support of the people themselves which is essential to victory. I am convinced that you will again give that support to leadership in these critical days.

In such a spirit on my part and on yours we face our common difficulties. They concern, thank God, only material things. Values have shrunken to fantastic levels; taxes have risen; our ability to pay has fallen; government of all kinds is faced by serious curtailment of income; the means of exchange are frozen in the currents of trade; the withered leaves of industrial enterprise lie on every side; farmers find no markets for their produce; the savings of many years in thousands of families are gone.

More important, a host of unemployed citizens face the grim problem of existence, and an equally great number toil with little return. Only a foolish optimist can deny the dark realities of the moment.

Yet our distress comes from no failure of substance. We are stricken by no plague of locusts. Compared with the perils which our forefathers conquered because they believed and were not afraid, we have still much to be thankful for. Nature still offers her bounty and human efforts have multiplied it. Plenty is at our doorstep, but a generous use of it languishes in the very sight of the supply. Primarily this is because the rulers of the exchange of mankind's goods have failed, through their own stubbornness and their own incompetence, have admitted their failure, and abdicated. Practices of the unscrupulous money changers stand indicted in the court of public opinion, rejected by the hearts and minds of men.

True they have tried, but their efforts have been cast in the pattern of an outworn tradition. Faced by failure of credit they have proposed only the lending of more money. Stripped of the lure of profit by which to induce our people to follow their false leadership, they have resorted to exhortations, pleading tearfully for restored confidence. They know only the rules of a generation of self-seekers. They have no vision, and when there is no vision the people perish....

If I read the temper of our people correctly, we now realize as we have never realized before our interdependence on each other; that we can not merely take but we must give as well; that if we are to go forward, we must move as a trained and loyal army willing to sacrifice for the good of a common discipline, because without such discipline no progress is made, no leadership becomes effective. We are, I know, ready and willing to submit our lives and property to such discipline, because it makes possible a leadership which aims at a larger good. This I propose to offer, pledging that the larger purposes will bind upon us all as a sacred obligation with a unity of duty hitherto evoked only in time of armed strife.

With this pledge taken, I assume unhesitatingly the leadership of this great army of our people dedicated to a disciplined attack upon our common problems....

MARY HEATON VORSE ■ (1874–1966)

Born in New York City and raised in Amherst, Massachusetts, Mary Heaton Vorse (1874–1966) was a prolific journalist, an advocate for women's right to vote, a labor activist, and a novelist; her best-known novel is *Strike!* (1930), keyed to a strike at a textile mill that occurred in the late 1920s in Gastonia, North Carolina. The essay from which we have taken the following excerpt describes social and economic conditions in New York City, as the impact of the Great Depression spread.

From School for Bums

If you want to know how to make a bum out of a workingman who has had trade, home, security and ambition taken from him, talk to any of the young fellows on the breadline who have been in town long enough to have become experienced in misery. Say a man in this town goes to the Municipal Lodging House for his first night. Until lately, he would have been routed out at five in the morning. Now he can stay until six. He is given breakfast, then he must leave, blizzard or rain. He can go next to a Salvation Army shelter for a handout, and get down to the City Free Employment Bureau before it opens. Or he can find shelter in subways and mark the Want Ads in a morning paper.

If he decides on the Employment Bureau, he is wise to arrive there before the doors open. He will find himself in the midst of a huge company which augments all the time until the opening of the doors. He may have spent two hours there—from nine to eleven. After that, he will not have eaten since his handout at seven at the Salvation Army, and he will have walked quite a lot. The next thing to do will be to put himself on some other breadline. It will take him one and a half or two hours to get his noonday meal.

In the afternoon there isn't very much use hunting jobs; yet there may be a chance at something; at some of the agencies, or perhaps by looking through the scanty Want Ads in the afternoon papers. There is a question then as to how and where to spend the rest of the time. If he has good enough clothes he can kill some time in the library. With discretion, hours can be spent in the terminals of stations. He can go to a museum. If he has a nickel, he can "ride the subways." But if he can panhandle[1] some money, he can at least stay indoors in a speakeasy[2] or Bowery hotel.

---

[1] Beg in the street.
[2] An illicit liquor store or nightclub.

It will take him an hour and a half or two hours for his evening meal, and if he is going to the Municipal Lodging House again, he had best be early on the line.

Until recently the Municipal Lodging House was open only one night a month to non-residents and five nights to residents of New York. The restriction has now been removed. There are 3,300 people sleeping at the Municipal Lodging House, of which one hundred are women. The beds are full, and they are sleeping on benches, on the floor.

In the life of this drifting worker there is never any security. He is never sure where he is going to sleep. It is easy to learn to panhandle twenty-five or fifty cents for a night's flop. Between the agencies who help homeless men—the Salvation Army, Municipal lodging houses, the Y. M. C. A. and missions—there are not enough beds. Make a count of all the agencies, even including the new pier, which furnishes shelter for seven hundred more, and the Salvation Army boat that gives lodging to six hundred seamen, besides its other shelters. There is still a slack of thousands for whom there is no free accommodation at present in the city.

The present situation is indeed a school for bums. A thing to sap moral and physical strength. A situation which in a few weeks would make most employable men unemployable, and which puts a premium upon panhandling. It is the deadly frustration of each unsuccessful day of job hunting when, tired and footsore, a man again stands in the long gray queue of the breadline only to seek an uncertain shelter. It is astonishing how soon a newcomer learns the ropes, how quickly it spreads from mouth to mouth where food is better, where flops are to be had.

[1931]

ANONYMOUS

The Roosevelts received hundreds of thousands of cards and letters from American men, women, and children, wishing them well, praying for them, but, even more, detailing the hard times that so many in the country were experiencing and appealing for help.

Letter to Mr. and Mrs. Roosevelt

February 1936, Chicago, Illinois
Mr. and Mrs. Roosevelt,
Wash. D. C.
Dear Mr. President:

I'm a boy of 12 years. I want to tell you about my family. My father hasn't worked for 5 months. He went plenty times to relief, he filled out application. They won't give us anything. I don't know why. Please you do something. We haven't paid 4 months rent, Everyday the landlord rings the door bell, we don't open the door for him. We are afraid that will be put out, been put out before, and don't want to happen again. We haven't paid the gas bill, and the electric bill, haven't paid grocery bill for 3 months. My brother goes to Lane Tech. High School. he's eighteen years old, hasn't gone to school for 2 weeks because he got no carfare. I have a sister she's twenty years, she can't find work. My father he staying home. All the time he's crying because he can't find work. I told him why are you crying daddy, and daddy said why shouldn't I cry when there is nothing in the house. I feel sorry for him. That night I couldn't sleep. The next morning I wrote this letter to you. in my room. Were American citizens and were born in Chicago, IL. and I don't know why they don't help us Please answer right away because we need it. will starve Thank you.

God bless you.

[Anonymous]
Chicago, Ill.
[1936]

ROBERT JOHNSON ■ (1911–1938)

Robert Johnson is considered one of the greatest Blues singers, composers, and guitarists of all time. The twenty-nine songs that he recorded in 1936–37 give a vivid picture of African American life in the South during the Depression years.

Cross Road Blues

I went down to the crossroad
fell down on my knees
I went down to the crossroad
fell down on my knees
Asked the Lord above "Have mercy now   5
save poor Bob if you please"
Yeeooo, standin at the crossroad
tried to flag a ride
ooo ooo eee
I tried to flag a ride   10
Didn't nobody seem to know me babe
everybody pass me by
Standin at the crossroad babe
risin sun goin down
Standin at the crossroad babe   15
eee eee eee, risin sun goin down
I believe to my soul now,

Poor Bob is sinkin down
You can run, you can run
tell my friend Willie Brown[1]   20
You can run, you can run
tell my friend Willie Brown
(th)'at I got the crossroad blues this mornin Lord
babe, I'm sinkin down
And I went to the crossroad momma   25
I looked east and west
I went to the crossroad baby
I looked east and west
Lord, I didn't have no sweet woman
ooh-well babe, in my distress   30

[1936]

THOMAS WOLFE ■ (1900–1938)

Thomas Wolfe was born and raised in Asheville, North Carolina, and educated at the University of North Carolina and Harvard. His first and best
novel is *Look Homeward, Angel* (1929). Wolfe traveled to Germany in mid-
1936 and attended the Olympic games in Berlin. He drew upon this experience for *You Can't Go Home Again* (published posthumously in 1940),
which focuses on the writer George Webber and, in the Germany section,
his love affair with Else von Kohler.

Adolf Hitler (1889–1945), who had come to power in 1933, was determined to use the Olympics to promote the power and grandeur of the Nazi
regime. The African-American track and field star Jesse Owens (1913–80),
to whom Wolfe alludes in this excerpt, won four gold medals, which enraged Hitler, who said afterward that "colored" athletes should be excluded
from the Olympics in the future. Here, Wolfe conveys the frightening cha-
risma that Hitler possessed and the control over the German people he held.

From You Can't Go Home Again, (Book 6, Chapter 38, "The Dark Messiah")

It was the season of the great Olympic games, and almost every day George
and Else went to the stadium in Berlin. George observed that the organizing genius of the German people, which has been used so often to such
noble purpose, was now more thrillingly displayed than he had ever seen it
before. The sheer pageantry of the occasion was overwhelming, so much so
that he began to feel oppressed by it. There seemed to be something ominous in it. One sensed a stupendous concentration of effort, a tremendous

[1]An American delta blues guitarist and singer (1900–52).

drawing together and ordering in the vast collective power of the whole land. And the thing that made it seem ominous was that it so evidently went beyond what the games themselves demanded. The games were overshadowed, and were no longer merely sporting competitions to which other nations had sent their chosen teams. They became, day after day, an orderly and overwhelming demonstration in which the whole of Germany had been schooled and disciplined. It was as if the games had been chosen as a symbol of the new collective might, a means of showing to the world in concrete terms what this new power had come to be.

With no past experience in such affairs, the Germans had constructed a mighty stadium which was the most beautiful and most perfect in its design that had ever been built. And all the accessories of this monstrous plant—the swimming pools, the enormous halls, the lesser stadia—had been laid out and designed with this same cohesion of beauty and of use. The organization was superb. Not only were the events themselves, down to the minutest detail of each competition, staged and run off like clockwork, but the crowds—such crowds as no other great city has ever had to cope with, and the like of which would certainly have snarled and maddened the traffic of New York beyond hope of untangling—were handled with a quietness, order, and speed that was astounding.

The daily spectacle was breath-taking in its beauty and magnificence. The stadium was a tournament of color that caught the throat; the massed splendor of the banners made the gaudy decorations of America's great parades, presidential inaugurations, and World's Fairs seem like shoddy carnivals in comparison. And for the duration of the Olympics, Berlin itself was transformed into a kind of annex to the stadium. From one end of the city to the other, from the Lustgarten to the Brandenburger Tor, along the whole broad sweep of Unter den Linden, through the vast avenues of the faëry Tiergarten, and out through the western part of Berlin to the very portals of the stadium, the whole town was a thrilling pageantry of royal banners—not merely endless miles of looped-up bunting, but banners fifty feet in height, such as might have graced the battle tent of some great emperor.

And all through the day, from morning on, Berlin became a mighty Ear, attuned, attentive, focused on the stadium. Everywhere the air was filled with a single voice. The green trees along the Kurfürsten-damm began to talk: from loud-speakers concealed in their branches an announcer in the stadium spoke to the whole city—and for George Webber it was a strange experience to hear the familiar terms of track and field translated into the tongue that Goethe used. He would be informed now that the *Vorlauf* was about to be run—and then the *Zwischenlauf*—and at length the *Endlauf*—and the winner:

"Owens—Oo Ess Ah!"

Meanwhile, through those tremendous banner-laden ways, the crowds thronged ceaselessly all day long. The wide promenade of Unter den Linden was solid with patient, tramping German feet. Fathers, mothers, children, young folks, old—the whole material of the nation was there, from every corner of the land. From morn to night they trudged, wide-eyed, full of wonder, past the marvel of those banner-laden ways. And among them one saw the bright stabs of color of Olympic jackets and the glint of foreign faces: the dark features of Frenchmen and Italians, the ivory grimace of the Japanese, the straw hair and blue eyes of the Swedes, and the big Americans, natty in straw hats, white flannels, and blue coats crested with the Olympic seal.

And there were great displays of marching men, sometimes ungunned but rhythmic as regiments of brown shirts went swinging through the streets. By noon each day all the main approaches to the games, the embannered streets and avenues of the route which the Leader would take to the stadium, miles away, were walled in by the troops. They stood at ease, young men, laughing and talking with each other—the Leader's bodyguards, the Schutz Staffel units, the Storm Troopers, all the ranks and divisions in their different uniforms—and they stretched in two unbroken lines from the Wilhelm-strasse up to the arches of the Brandenburger Tor. Then, suddenly, the sharp command, and instantly there would be the solid smack of ten thousand leather boots as they came together with the sound of war.

It seemed if everything had been planned for this moment, shaped to this triumphant purpose. But the people—they had not been planned. Day after day, behind the unbroken wall of soldiers, they stood and waited in a dense and patient throng. These were the masses of the nation, the poor ones of the earth, the humble ones of life, the workers and the wives, the mothers and the children—and day after day they came and stood and waited. They were there because they did not have money enough to buy the little cardboard squares that would have given them places within the magic ring. From noon till night they waited for just two brief and golden moments of the day: the moment when the Leader went out to the stadium, and the moment when he returned.

At last he came—and something like a wind across a field of grass was shaken through that crowd, and from afar the tide rolled up with him, and in it was the voice, the hope, the prayer of the land. The Leader came by slowly in a shining car, a little dark man with a comic-opera mustache, erect and standing, moveless and unsmiling, with his hand upraised, palm outward, not in Nazi-wise salute, but straight up, in a gesture of blessing such as the Buddha or Messiahs use.

ALFRED KAZIN ■ (1915–1998)

One of the twentieth century's leading literary critics, Alfred Kazin was born in Brooklyn, the son of East European Jews who had immigrated to the United States. He was an essayist, reviewer, editor, and professor, who held academic appointments at Amherst College and other colleges and universities in the United States and abroad. His important literary studies include *On Native Grounds: An Interpretation of Modern American Prose Literature* (1942) and *An American Procession* (1984), which focuses on the period from 1830 to 1930. Kazin also wrote a number of evocative, arresting memoirs, including *A Walker in the City* (1951), which describes his childhood and education in Brooklyn, and *Starting Out in the Thirties* (1965), excerpted here, which recounts his emergence as a writer and literary critic and historian during the Great Depression decade.

From Starting Out in the Thirties

On Inaugural Day 1937, I went down to Washington to do an article on the great day, and though that morning of rain the flags flapped wetly against the posts and the streets seemed strangely empty, there, in the back of the car as it came out of the White House drive, was the fixedly smiling face that presided over our generation, and standing in the rain we cheered our President and all our own hopes.

Like all my friends, I distrusted Roosevelt as a wily politician and a professional charmer. Who was he behind that ever-smiling public face, and what reason did *he* have to care? But I could almost believe in him now, there was so much need of him to do the right thing. FDR's historical function was destined; everybody's was.

Not even the hack jobs I did for a living now seemed unworthy, for the issue raised in a book review, a street scene studied for an article, always fitted into my sense of the destiny and inclusiveness of history. So my parents' poverty had a mystique for me, and our loneliness a definite heroism—we were usually unhappy and always on each other's necks, but I saw us all moving forward on the sweep of great events. I believed that everyone was engulfed in politics, absorbed in issues that were the noble part of themselves. Despite the daily anxiety of trying to get a push up the inhumanly smooth wall of other people's jobs, I felt, with the outbreak of the Spanish Civil War, that the outrage of Franco, Mussolini and Hitler working together was a challenge, not a defeat; I trusted to the righteousness of history. Just as I was trying to break through, so history was seeking its appointed consummation. My interest and the genius of history simply had to coincide.

It did not matter how deceitful and murderous Stalin was showing himself to be in the purges; the Soviet Union, a "workers' state" stained only with the unaccountable sins of its leadership, still represented the irreversible movement of human progress. Even Hitler, by his total infamy, obviously represented a *deliberate* attempt to put the clock back; believing that the Jews, and especially Jewish intellectuals, had a mission to humanity, I never wondered why Jewish intellectuals particularly were hated by the Nazis. We were a moral ferment; easy to kill off, but an unsettling influence. Hitler destroyed German democracy, Dollfuss[1] the Austrian Socialists, Franco was destroying the Spanish Republic and Mussolini thousands of Ethiopians: the daily onrush of events fitted so easily into a general pattern of meaning, seemingly supplied by the age itself, that every day was like a smoothly rushing movie of the time—and I loved newsreels, documentary novels of Dos Passos with their own newsreels, documentary movies, especially now that in tribute to the emergency of the times there were movie houses in Times Square that showed nothing but newsreels. I was as excited by history as if it were a newsreel, and I saw history in every newsreel, my love and hatred of the historical actors rising to the music on the sound track like a swimmer to the surf.

AGNES SMEDLEY ■ (1892–1950)

Though Agnes Smedley is widely known for her autobiographically based novel *Daughter of Earth* (1929), she is perhaps even more significant for her articles and books of journalism and reportage about the Chinese Revolution, which she observed and experienced firsthand, beginning in 1929 and continuing throughout the 1930s and 1940s. So devoted was she to this cause that at one point she even sought—unsuccessfully—to become a member of the Chinese Communist Party. The following excerpt, the foreword from *China Fights Back* (1938), indicates the intensity of Smedley's commitment to the revolution and alerts us to the international scale and scope of the upheavals of the 1930s.

From China Fights Back: An American Woman with the Eighth Route Army

I'll keep sending you my articles. But I want you, when you read them, to realize that I am faced with great problems in my writing. My back is still so badly injured that I work in perpetual pain. And we never remain in one place more than two days at a time. We are always on the march. So I am always walking or in the saddle, and at the end of the day I must start work. Often I must work all night long if we remain but one day, or one night, in that place. I can do no polishing at all. I am so weary and often in such pain that I cannot retype and at times cannot even correct. So please correct my English and have my dispatches retyped. Cut out the repetitions and edit where necessary. Sell them wherever possible and use a part of the proceeds to pay for the typing. If I ever get well, and if we are ever long enough in one place, I can do my own editing.

We are moving through a region where not even ordinary rough paper can be bought. There are no nails, no oil or fat, no salt, no fuel for

---

[1]Engelbert Dollfuss (1892–1934), an Austrian minister, statesman, and chancellor, an anti-Nazi dictator, suppressed the Socialist movement in February 1934, assassinated by the Austrian Nazis.

fire. I shall be writing in the dead of winter without a blaze to warm me. And (need I tell you?) without sufficient food. Our food even now in the autumn is rice, or millet[1], as a base, with one vegetable. Today it was turnips, and yesterday it was turnips. Sometimes we have no vegetables at all. There are big armies here and there will be little even of the essentials. Sugar is simply unheard of.

You there can never conceive of the difficulties under which our army and other Chinese armies operate. The Japanese have trucks, airplanes and other efficient means of transport. We have donkeys, horses, a few mules, and men. Almost all of our army walks. No motorized units here!

I have one horse and one mule to carry the possessions of my party. Besides myself there are two newspapermen and three guards. We must carry many of our own things. Henceforth I shall carry not only my attaché case and my films from my saddle, but I shall have my typewriter strapped to my back. If my horse or mule should die, I am lost. I have less than one hundred Chinese dollars with me, which I borrowed from a friend, but almost all of it I use to buy corn for my horse and mule each day. Twice a week my party tries to buy a chicken to enrich our diet.

My companions have not a cent of money. I am the richest person in the army, with money I have borrowed. And this money I must use to feed my two precious animals so they can carry our baggage, typewriting paper, films, typewriter ribbons. I have one uniform and one winter coat and set of winter underwear. I have two pairs of shoes. The others in my party have only the shoes on their feet and they are wearing out. I don't know where we can get new shoes for them. Most of our army have no stockings at all.

I am not complaining when I write all this. These are the happiest, most purposeful days of my life. I prefer one bowl of rice a day and this life to all that "civilization" has to offer me. I prefer to work and ride with an injured back that would take six months to heal even if I should stay in bed. All this I prefer. I fear only that my injury will affect my work, has done so already. So I beg of you to help me by editing my manuscript—yet do not make it "literary".

[1937/38]

KENNETH FEARING ■ (1902–1961)

The son of a lawyer, Kenneth Fearing was born in Oak Park, Illinois. After graduating from the University of Wisconsin, he held a number of jobs, and then worked for *Time* magazine as a journalist.

Fearing viewed himself as a radical poet, a democratic writer "in the Whitman tradition." He used words and phrases on posters, billboards and signs; slang, the language of the city and streets; catchphrases and

---

[1]A fast-growing cereal plant.

slogans in advertising and popular media. We also see that poets E. A. Robinson and Carl Sandburg and the novelist John Dos Passos influenced Fearing. The poet and essayist Kenneth Rexroth said that Fearing wrote and thought "like a taxi driver reading a billboard while fighting traffic." He also was a writer of fiction, whose best novel is *The Big Clock* (1946). His *Complete Poems* was published in 1994.

Devil's Dream

But it could never be true; How could it ever happen, if it never did before, and it's not so now?

But suppose that the face behind those steel prison bars—
Why do you dream about a face lying cold in the trenches streaked with rain and dirt and blood?
Is it the very same face seen so often in the mirror? Just as though it could be true—

But what if it is, what if it is, what if it is, what if the thing that cannot happen really happens just the same,
Suppose the fever goes a hundred, then a hundred and one, What if Holy Savings Trust goes from 98 to 88 to 78 to 68, then drops down to 28 and 8 and out of sight,   5
And the fever shoots a hundred two, a hundred three, a hundred four, then a hundred five and out?

But now there's only the wind and the sky and sunlight and the clouds,
With everyday people walking and talking as they always have before along the everyday street,
Doing ordinary things with ordinary faces and ordinary voices in the ordinary way,
Just as they always will—   10

Then why does it feel like a bomb, why does it feel like a target, like standing on the gallows with the trap about to drop, why does it feel like a thunderbolt the second before it strikes, why does it feel like a tight-rope walk high over hell?

Because it is not, will not, never could be true That the whole wide, bright, green, warm, calm world goes: CRASH.

[1938]

JOHN STEINBECK ■ (1902–1968)

Recipient in 1962 of the Nobel Prize for Literature, the California-born John Steinbeck is the author of many novels and stories, including *Tortilla Flat* (1935), *Of Mice and Men* (1937), *In Dubious Battle* (1936), *Cannery Row* (1945), and *East of Eden* (1952). His most important work is *The Grapes of Wrath* (1940), a saga of an impoverished family's migration from drought-stricken Oklahoma to California. The renowned American director John Ford (1895–1973) adapted the novel for the screen in 1940; the film is more affirmative in its second half and more hopeful in its ending, but it is, nonetheless, stark and powerful, and Ford received the Academy Award for Best Director.

From The Grapes of Wrath, Chapter 5

The man sitting in the iron seat did not look like a man; gloved, goggled, rubber dust mask over nose and mouth, he was a part of the monster, a robot in the seat. The thunder of the cylinders sounded through the country, became one with the air and the earth, so that earth and air muttered in sympathetic vibration. The driver could not control it—straight across country it went, cutting through a dozen farms and straight back. A twitch at the controls could swerve the cat', but the driver's hands could not twitch because the monster that built the tractors, the monster that sent the tractor out, had somehow got into the driver's hands, into his brain and muscle, had goggled him and muzzled him—goggled his mind, muzzled his speech, goggled his perception, muzzled his protest. He could not see the land as it was, he could not smell the land as it smelled; his feet did not stamp the clods or feel the warmth and the power of the earth. He sat in an iron seat and stepped on iron pedals. He could not cheer or beat or curse or encourage the extension of his power, and because of this he could not cheer or whip or curse or encourage himself. He did not know or own or trust or beseech the land. If a seed dropped did not germinate, it was nothing. If the young thrusting plant withered in drought or drowned in a flood of rain, it was no more to the driver than to the tractor.

He loved the land no more than the bank loved the land. He could admire the tractor—its machined surfaces, its surge of power, the roar of its detonating cylinders; but it was not his tractor. Behind the tractor rolled the shining disks, cutting the earth with blades—not plowing but surgery, pushing the cut earth to the right where the second row of disks cut it and pushed it to the left; slicing blades shining, polished by the cut earth. And pulled behind the disks, the harrows combing with iron teeth so that the little clods broke up and the earth lay smooth. Behind the harrows, the long seeders—twelve curved iron penes [penises] erected in the foundry, orgasms set by gears, raping methodically, raping without passion. The driver sat in his iron seat and he was proud of the straight lines he did not will, proud of the tractor he did not own or love, proud of the power he could not control. And when that crop grew, and was harvested, no man had crumbled a hot clod in his fingers and let the earth sift past his fingertips. No man had touched the seed, or lusted for the growth. Men ate what they had not raised, had no connection with the bread. The land bore under iron, and under iron gradually died; for it was not loved or hated, it had no prayers to curses.

At noon the tractor driver stopped sometimes near a tenant house and opened his lunch: sandwiches wrapped in waxed paper, white bread, pickle, cheese, Spam, a piece of pie branded like an engine part. He ate without relish. And tenants not yet moved away came out to see him, looked curiously while the goggles were taken off, and the rubber dust mask, leaving white circles around the eyes and large white circle around nose and mouth. The exhaust of the tractor puttered on, for fuel is so cheap it is more efficient to leave the engine running than to heat the Diesel nose for a new start. Curious children crowded close, ragged children who ate their fried dough as they watched. They watched hungrily the unwrapping of the sandwiches, and their hunger-sharpened noses smelled the pickle, cheese, and Spam. They didn't speak to the driver. They watched his hand as it carried food to his mouth. They did not watch him chewing; their eyes followed the hand that held the sandwich. After awhile the tenant who could not leave the place came out and squatted in the shade beside the tractor.

"Why, you're Joe Davis's boy!"

"Sure," the driver said.

"Well, what you doing this kind of work for—against your own people?"

"Three dollars a day. I got damn sick of creeping for my dinner—and not getting it. I got a wife and kids. We got to eat. Three dollars a day, and it comes every day."

"That's right," the tenant said. "But for your three dollars a day fifteen or twenty families can't eat at all. Nearly a hundred people have to go out and wander on the roads for your three dollars a day. Is that right?"

And the driver said, "Can't think of that. Got to think of my own kids. Three dollars a day, and it comes every day. Times are changing, mister, don't you know? Can't make a living on the land unless you've got two, five, ten thousand acres and a tractor. Crop land isn't for little guys like us any more. You don't kick up a howl because you can't make Fords, or because you're not the telephone company. Well, crops are like that now. Nothing to do about it. You try to get three dollars a day someplace. That's the only way."

The tenant pondered. "Funny thing how it is. If a man owns a little property, that property is him, it's part of him, and it's like him. If he owns property only so he can walk on it and handle it and be sad when it isn't doing well, and feel fine when the rain falls on it, that property is him, and some way he's bigger because he owns it. Even if he isn't successful he's big with his property. That is so."

And the tenant pondered more. "But let a man get property he doesn't see, or can't take time to get his fingers in, or can't be there to walk on it—why, then the property is the man. He can't do what he wants, he can't think what he wants. The property is the man, stronger than he is. And he is small, not big. Only his possessions are big—and he's the servant of his property. That is so, too."

The driver munched the branded pie and threw the crust away. "Times are changed, don't you know? Thinking about stuff like that don't feed the kids. Get your three dollars a day, feed your kids. You got no call to worry about anybody's kids but your own. You get a reputation for talking like that, and you'll never get three dollars a day. Big shots won't give you three dollars a day if you worry about anything but your three dollars a day."

"Nearly a hundred people on the road for your three dollars. Where will we go?"

"And that reminds me," the driver said, "you better get out soon. I'm going through the dooryard after dinner."

"You filled in the well this morning."

"I know. Had to keep the line straight. But I'm going through the dooryard after dinner. Got to keep the lines straight. And—well, you know Joe Davis, my old man, so I'll tell you this. I got orders wherever there's a family not moved out—out if I have an accident—you know, get too close and cave the house in a little—well, I might get a couple of dollars. And my youngest kid never had no shoes yet."

"I built it with my hands. Straightened old nails to put the sheating on. Rafters are wired to the stringers with baling wire. It's mine. I built it. You bump it down—I'll be in the window with a rifle. You even come too close and I'll pot you like a rabbit."

"It's not me. There's nothing I can do. I'll lose my job if I don't do it. And look—suppose you kill me? They'll just hang you, but long before you're hung there'll be another guy on the tractor, and he'll bump the house down. You're not killing the right guy."

"That's so," the tenant said. "Who gave you orders? I'll go after him. He's the one to kill."

"You're wrong. He got his orders from the bank. The bank told him, 'Clear those people out or it's your job.'"

"Well, there's a president of the bank. There's a board of directors. I'll fill up the magazine of the rifle and go into the bank."

The driver said, "Fellow was telling me the bank gets orders from the East. The orders were, 'Make the land show profit or we'll close you up.'"

"But where does it stop? Who can we shoot? I don't aim to starve to death before I kill the man that's starving me."

"I don't know. Maybe there's nobody to shoot. Maybe the thing isn't men at all. Maybe like you said, the property's doing it. Anyway I told you my orders."

"I got to figure," the tenant said. "We all got to figure. There's some way to stop this. It's not like lightning or earthquakes. We've got a bad thing made by men, and by God that's something we can change." The tenant sat in his doorway, and the driver thundered his engine and started off, tracks falling and curving, harrows combing, and the phalli of the seeder slipping into the ground. Across the dooryard the tractor cut, and the hard, foot-beaten ground was seeded field, and the tractor cut through again; the uncut space was ten feet wide. And back he came. The iron guard bit into the house-corner, crumbled the wall, and wrenched the little house from its foundation so that it fell sideways, crushed like a bug. And the driver was goggled and a rubber mask covered his nose and mouth. The tractor cut a straight line on, and the air and the ground vibrated with its thunder. The tenant man stared after it, his rifle in his hand. His wife was beside him, and the quiet children behind. And all of them stared after the tractor.

[1939]

DOROTHEA LANGE ■ (1895–1965)

Dorothea Lange, one of America's outstanding photographers, was born in Hoboken, New Jersey, and as a young woman she worked and studied with the photographers Arnold Genthe and Clarence White. When the Great Depression struck, she dedicated her craft to depicting the conditions faced by the homeless and destitute.

Mexican Field Worker's Home, California

Migratory Mexican field worker's home on the edge of a frozen pea field. Imperial Valley, California (1937). Photograph by Dorothea Lange.

Members of the Mochida family awaiting evacuation bus. Identification tags were used to aid in keeping a family unit intact during all phases of evacuation. Mochida operated a nursery and five greenhouses on a two-acre site in Eden Township (May 8, 1942). Photograph by Dorothea Lange.

Along with other gifted photographers, such as Walker Evans and Arthur Rothstein, Lange was a member of the photographic section of the Resettlement Administration in Washington, D.C., organized and supervised by Roy Stryker. She not only documented the effects of the Great Depression in the Great Plains and in California, but later she took many photographs of the internment of Japanese Americans in the months following the entry in December 1941 of the United States into World War II.

WOODY GUTHRIE ■ (1912–1967)

Woodrow Wilson (Woody) Guthrie, born in Okemah, a small town in Oklahoma, is one of America's most influential folk singers and songwriters. He devoted his musical talents to chronicling the lives of the lowly and the dispossessed. During the Depression years, Guthrie traveled widely in the United States, frequently with migrant workers and families; his *Dust Bowl Ballads* (1940) testifies to the social and political themes of his songs and his populist activism.

Guthrie's semi-autobiography, *Bound for Glory*, was published in 1943 and is an account of his Dust Bowl years. Through his songs, poems, and prose, his impact was immense on Bob Dylan and others who were part

of the great "folk revival" of the late 1950s and 1960s. It continues to
this day with contemporary musicians such as Billy Bragg, Jonatha Brooke,
The Klezmatics, Dropkick Murphys, and Jay Farrar recording their music to
Woody Guthrie's lyrics.

This Land Is Your Land

This land is your land, this land is my land,
From California to the New York island;
From the red wood forest to the Gulf Stream waters
This land was made for you and me.

As I was walking that ribbon of highway,   5
I saw above me that endless skyway:
I saw below me that golden valley:
This land was made for you and me.

I've roamed and rambled and I followed my footsteps
To the sparkling sands of her diamond deserts;   10
And all around me a voice was sounding:
This land was made for you and me.

When the sun came shining, and I was strolling,
And the wheat fields waving and the dust clouds rolling,
As the fog was lifting a voice was chanting: 15
This land was made for you and me.

As I went walking I saw a sign there
And on the sign it said "No Trespassing."
But on the other side it didn't say nothing,
That side was made for you and me.   20

In the shadow of the steeple I saw my people,
By the relief office I seen my people;
As they stood there hungry, I stood there asking
Is this land made for you and me?

Nobody living can ever stop me,   25
As I go walking that freedom highway;
Nobody living can ever make me turn back
This land was made for you and me.

[1940, 1944]

American Prose
Since 1945

American Literature Since 1945, Cold War to Contemporary

Students come to courses on contemporary literature equipped with a story about "what happened" in American history and culture in the decades after World War II. It is a story that on the international scene highlights Cold War rivalry between the United States and the Soviet Union, and, furthermore, that emphasizes, on the domestic front, conservatism in the 1950s and protest and rebellion in the 1960s and early 1970s. This, the story continues, sparked a conservative reaction that led to the election of Richard Nixon to the White House in 1968 and again in 1972, and, eventually, to the landslide victories of Ronald Reagan in the presidential campaigns of 1980 and 1984.

There is truth to this story, and polling data suggest that students became more conservative themselves in the 1980s and into the 1990s, even during the presidency of the Democrat Bill Clinton (1992–2000). During Barack Obama's campaign for the presidency and at the time of his election in November 2008—the first African American president in the nation's history—young people did move in a more liberal direction. Voters under thirty backed Obama by a 2–1 ratio and many volunteered for door-to-door canvassing for voters, phone banks, and other activity. But the severe economic downturn that occurred in the first years of President Obama's first term and that extended into his second term caused a significant decline in his support among young people. While he won two elections, neither he and his administration nor the nation's other political and economic leaders were able to bring about a lower unemployment rate and prosperity. Perhaps not among the young themselves, but among many of their elders, the period immediately following the end of World War II in 1945 seemed, in retrospect, all the more a time of peace and plenty, when good jobs abounded, hope and optimism were in the air, and the American Dream of success was flourishing.

From a distance, it does appear that the 1950s was the decade of contentment with the status quo, followed in the 1960s by challenges to it, followed in turn in the next decades by a sharp shift to the right in political positions and attitudes, among Republicans and many Democrats as well, who were no longer the staunch liberals they once were. But there are complications to this story, as the literary and cultural works of these years testify.

The period from late 1945 through the 1950s especially merits more detailed, and complicating, attention. On one level, the nation was prosperous, and most people shared a common vision of success; the American Dream of career (for the husband, if not for the wife), family, and suburban home was alive and well and respected. But on another level, scholars and writers even then were criticizing the society the United States had become. The other, disquieting name for the American Dream, they argued, was conformity.

In *The Lonely Crowd*, published in 1950, the sociologist David Riesman studied "the changing American character" and reached unsettling conclusions about the spread of "conformity" and the loss of individualism. American society, he claimed, was evolving from "inner-directed" to "other-directed." Persons were influenced less by parents and "authority figures" than by their peers, whose approval they deemed essential. "The idea that men are created equal and free is both true and misleading," Riesman maintained. "Men are created different; they lose their social freedom and individual autonomy in seeking to become like another." Riesman struck a chord; his book sold hundreds of thousands of copies, and its title phrase even appeared in the third stanza of one of Bob Dylan's songs, "I Shall Be Released," in 1967.

The Lonely Crowd was the first of a number of sociological studies, novels, and films that, in the words of the critic Jonathan Yardley, "set middle-class America on a binge of self-scrutiny." These include Sloan Wilson's *The Man in the Gray Flannel Suit* (1955, and made into a movie the following year), which tells of a man discontented by corporate culture and material success and painfully seeking fulfillment at home, and William H. Whyte's *The Organization Man* (1956), which describes the networks of business bureaucracy that were producing conformity in the workplace and on the domestic scene, where safety, security, and comfort had become the rule. Also influential were Vance Packard's *The Hidden Persuaders* (1957), about the impact of advertising, and *The Status Seekers* (1961), about the increasing differences in social status that "affluence" created. "Under its gloss of prosperity," Packard stated in the latter book, the nation was growing divided as Americans everywhere sought "to find new ways to draw lines that will separate the elect from the non-elect."

Writing in 1960, the poet, novelist, and critic Paul Goodman defined the "organized society" America had turned into as "an apparently closed room in which there is a large rat race as the dominant center of attention." A few years later, the Beat author Jack Kerouac said, "You kill yourself to get to the grave. Especially you kill yourself to get to the grave before you even die, and the name of that grave is 'success.'" "Freedom," Goodman explained, was now "the most characteristic of all our dilemmas"; with "the maturation of automatic and computer technology, either people won't *have* to work and will degenerate; or there won't be anything for them to work *at*, and they will be unhappy spending their time in trivial leisure activities." "America is not so much a nightmare," reflected William Burroughs (1969),

> as a *non-dream*. The American non-dream is precisely a move to wipe the dream out
> of existence. The dream is a spontaneous happening and therefore dangerous to a
> control system set up by the non-dreamers.

Burroughs and the others were calling attention to tendencies they found troubling and angering in American society. Other voices—some scholarly and dispassionate, some fiercely critical—also made their views heard. The Swedish economist Gunnar Myrdal published a comprehensive study of American race relations, *An American Dilemma: The Negro Problem and Modern Democracy* (1944); the American professor and scholar Alfred Kinsey issued two reports, *Sexual Behavior in the Human Male* (1948) and *Sexual Behavior in the Human Female* (1953), which challenged prevailing norms of and attitudes toward sexual conduct; the classicist and philosopher Norman O. Brown wrote *Life Against Death* (1959) and *Love's Body* (1966), concluding in the latter, "Freedom is poetry, taking liberties with words, breaking the rules of normal speech, violating common sense. Freedom is violence"; and the novels of Henry Miller, full of exuberantly explicit sex scenes, became available in the United States in the 1960s (*The Tropic of Cancer* was first printed here in 1961, nearly three decades after its publication in Paris).

Sexuality, male authority and privilege, and gender roles came in for forceful analysis. An influential early book was the French writer (and long-time associate and lover of Jean-Paul Sartre) Simone de Beauvoir's *The Second Sex* (1953). Another, less keyed to women's issues but important for its critique of Freudian theory, was Herbert Marcuse's *Eros and Civilization* (1955). Among works of American writers, key texts include Betty Friedan's *The Feminine Mystique* (1963), exploring "the problem that has no name," the restless disenchantment experienced by women who, it seemed, had every reason—a husband, children, a nice home—to feel fulfilled and happy; and Kate Millett's *Sexual Politics* (1970), a stringent indictment of patriarchal values in classic and canonical literature.

Throughout the 1950s and into the 1960s, this critical, oppositional tone resonated in American writing. It is tempting, in fact, to propose that the 1960s simply made more starkly visible, more prominent in social and political life, the themes, arguments, and piercing critiques of writers and artists active in the late 1940s and 1950s.

A number of new writers made a sudden, electrifying impact: the poet Robert Lowell, for instance, whose first volume, *Lord Weary's Castle* (1946), won him rave reviews and the Pulitzer Prize; Norman Mailer, the author, at age 25, of *The Naked and the Dead* (1948), a novel about an army platoon in the Philippines toward the end of World War II; and the African American poet Gwendolyn Brooks, author of *A Street in Bronzeville* (1945) and *Annie Allen* (1949), the second of which received the Pulitzer Prize, making Brooks the first African American to gain this honor.

Still, there were literary continuities that should not be overlooked. Both William Faulkner and Ernest Hemingway were alive and stood as formidable authorities and influences. Faulkner published *Intruder in the Dust* (1948), *Collected Stories* (1950), and other books—he received the Nobel Prize in Literature in 1949—and Hemingway was awarded the Nobel Prize in Literature in 1954, not long after the publication of *The Old Man and the Sea* (1952). Robert Frost, T. S. Eliot, Wallace Stevens, Ezra Pound, William Carlos Williams, H. D., Marianne Moore, and E. E. Cummings, imposing figures from the first decades of the century and central to the emergence of modernism in the arts, remained active as writers, essayists, and speakers. The playwright Eugene O'Neill was active as well; perhaps his greatest works were produced or (having been written earlier) finally performed in the postwar years: *The Iceman Cometh* (1946); *Long Day's Journey into Night* (1956); *Hughie*, and *The Touch of the Poet* (both in 1958).

Critics had for some time been referring to and writing about these literary eminences in exalted terms. "It was given to Hawthorne to dramatize the human soul," stated John Peale Bishop in 1937. "In our time, Hemingway wrote the drama of its disappearance." "If there are any American novels of the present century which may be called great," observed Irving Howe of Faulkner in 1952, "and which bear comparison with the achievements of twentieth-century European literature, then surely *The Sound and the Fury* is among them." Another novelist, Henry James, on the cutting edge of modernism in *The Golden Bowl* (1904) and other late novels and stories, also was lionized and became a monumental literary presence. "Henry James stands astride two centuries and reaches backward to a third," said his biographer, Leon Edel, in 1953. "With him the American novel, in a single leap, attained a precocious maturity it has never surpassed. And it is now recognized that with Henry James the novel in English achieved its greatest perfection."

One might have predicted that the reputations won by James, Faulkner, Hemingway, and the others would loom over younger writers. How could they ever compete with *that*? But the effect was just the opposite. Hemingway, Eliot, and their fellow modernists had done the pioneering and pathbreaking; they articulated new conceptions of the writer's identity and mission and devised new styles and techniques. They showed that American writers could compete with English and European authors and establish themselves as forces to be reckoned with at home and abroad.

Cultural critics, writers, and scholars had been concerned since the early 1800s that there were not yet any truly major "American" writers, and, furthermore, that the democratic leveling encouraged by the nation's political principles and ideals of equality might prevent an authentic, independent literature from emerging. The modern American poets and novelists, whether based in the United States, Paris, London, or Rome, proved those fears wrong. Hemingway, Eliot, and Faulkner were American writers with international literary reputations.

This helps to explain why the poet-critic Louise Bogan could state in 1951, "The poet of the future need waste little time and energy in establishing the fact that his art has importance. Neither will he be forced to uncover for himself the scope and difficulty of that art." It is also why the poet Richard Wilbur could say in 1966:

> Most American poets of my generation were taught to admire the English Metaphysical poets of the seventeenth century and such contemporary masters of irony as [the poet, editor, and critic] John Crowe Ransom. We were led by our teachers and by the critics whom we read to feel that the most adequate and convincing poetry is that which accommodates mixed feelings, clashing ideas, and incongruous images. Poetry could not be honest, we thought, unless it began by acknowledging the full discordancy of modern life and consciousness. I still believe that to be a true view of poetry.

The authority of the earlier generation of writers was not burdensome but, instead, liberating. They had brilliantly made and secured the case for the significance of American literature. The new writers, after the war, could build on and take creative issue with their achievements.

Historical Background of the Period

The United States and its allies had triumphed over Germany, Italy, and Japan in World War II, defeating the forces of Nazism and Fascism. But the conclusion of the war in 1945 was both exhilarating and frightening, as atomic bombs were dropped on the Japanese cities of Hiroshima on August 6 ("a tremendous flash of light cut across the sky," John Hersey, *Hiroshima*, 1946) and Nagasaki on August 9, and as the horrors of the Nazi death camps were revealed. No sooner was the war against the Axis powers over than the United States was in the grip of a new "cold war" against the Soviet Union, its ally against the Nazis. Communism was portrayed as a dire and dreadful threat to the way of life held dear in the United States, and Americans feared the menacing power of the military might the Soviet Union had developed—and the hostility of Communism as an ideology to capitalism, democracy, and religion.

In 1949 Mao's Communist forces achieved victory in China, and in the same year the Soviet Union gained the power of atomic weaponry, accelerating an arms race that enabled it and the United States in some future conflict to annihilate the world. The United States fought an arduous war against Communist expansionism in Korea from 1950 to 1953, costing the lives of 50,000 U.S. soldiers and wounding 100,000 more, and in 1953 the Soviet Union announced it had possession of the hydrogen bomb, 100 to 1,000 times more powerful than an atomic bomb. During the Cuban missile crisis of October 1962, the two superpowers came perilously close to a nuclear holocaust. And as the 1960s unfolded, the United States, again in an effort to halt Communist advances, became increasingly mired in a terrible, tragic war in Vietnam. This peaked in the mid-1960s, and by the time it ended in the early 1970s, 58,000 U.S. soldiers had died and 313,000 more were wounded.

The decades from the 1970s to the present have seen many shocking events, including the Watergate scandal and the resignation of Richard Nixon as president in August 1974 under the threat of impeachment; the seizure of U.S. embassy personnel in Iran that occurred in November 1979 and concluded with their release in January 1981; the AIDS epidemic that caused the death of 460,000 Americans between 1981 and 2001 and that continues on its devastating course with the loss of millions of lives in countries around the world; the collapse of the former Soviet Union and the Communist nations of Eastern Europe in 1990–91; the first Persian Gulf War, January–February 1991; the terrorist attack in September 2001 on the Pentagon and the twin towers of the World Trade Center, which resulted in thousands of casualties; the U.S. assault, beginning in late 2001, on the repressive, terrorist-sponsoring Taliban government of Afghanistan; the second Persian Gulf War, in early 2003, which terminated the brutal regime of Saddam Hussein; the U.S. media release in 2004 of graphic photos of American soldiers abusing and sexually humiliating Iraqi prisoners at Abu Ghraib prison, in Baghdad, Iraq; and, in 2007, the shooting that took place on the campus of Virginia Polytechnic Institute and State University in Blacksburg, Virginia, in which the perpetrator killed 32 people and wounded 25 others before committing suicide—the deadliest shooting incident by a single gunman in American history.

Sometimes the pattern of U.S. and world history from the 1940s to the 1990s and beyond seems an unending series of crises (often accompanied by mass murder and atrocity)—preparing for crisis, experiencing it, confronting it and its consequences, and attempting somehow to be ready for the next crisis, not knowing what it will be. One of the essential tasks of literary studies is, through reading, discussion, and debate, to keep alive the memory, and to seek out the meanings, of what happened.

In the middle of a busy school year, filled with papers and exams and activities, keeping alive and vivid the memory and knowledge of the past can be a daunting assignment for teachers and students alike. To students, the Cold War in particular feels far away, yet, for many of their high school teachers and college professors the Cold War was the prevailing fact of life in their youth, an ongoing concern in otherwise stable-seeming lives.

As the cultural historian Alan Trachtenberg noted (1979):

> From the late 1940s to the middle 1960s, there was no doubt that a Cold War view of the world profoundly influenced the thinking of most Americans. The picture of a world divided between "us," "free" and democratic, and "them," totalitarian and "godless," seemed unshakable, as was the corollary of a need for military strength, preparedness, vigilance. The feeling of a superior virtue threatened by an insidious enemy reached a pitch of hysteria in the 1950s, a time of witch hunts, blacklists, loyalty oaths, charges of "subversion," trials for espionage and treason, and the jailing of Communists and other dissidents on charges of "conspiracy."

The central figure in the anti-Communist crusade was Republican Senator Joseph McCarthy, who declared that traitors in political, social, and cultural institutions were selling out the United States to the Soviet Union. McCarthy and his aides and supporters located few Communist subversives, but they did ruin many careers and provoked a determined hunt for Communists in schools, churches, and elsewhere. The atmosphere of repression, censorship, innuendo, ostracism, scapegoating, isolation, and intimidation prompted the playwright Arthur Miller to compose *The Crucible* (1953), his harrowing play about the witch-hunting hysteria of the 1690s in Salem, Massachusetts. It also led to the production of a classic western, *High Noon* (1952), starring Gary Cooper as a town marshal left alone by cowardly townspeople to face four killers.

The rhetoric deployed by both the United States and the Soviet Union was alarming. Soviet premier Nikita Khrushchev, in November 1956, told Western diplomats in the Kremlin, "Whether you like it or not, history is on our side. We will bury you." Republican Party leader Richard M. Nixon, in November 1964, emphasized, "The Cold War isn't thawing; it is burning with a deadly heat. Communism isn't sleeping; it is, as always, plotting, scheming, working, fighting."

Now, in the first decades of the twenty-first century, the Communist experiment in the Soviet Union and Eastern Europe has been thoroughly discredited, its panoramic trail of corruption, murder, and imprisonment having been made glaringly obvious for all to see. "We must conclude," the writer Salman Rushdie (born in India) said "that it is not only a particular political ideology that has failed, but the idea that men and women could ever define themselves in terms that exclude their spiritual needs."

Unrest and Its Impact on Literature and the Arts

The Soviet Union and the Iron Curtain are gone. But if we hope to understand the literature of the late 1940s and subsequent decades, we need to return imaginatively to the period of intense Cold War opposition and fear. The twin forces of conformity and anti-Communism (with its restrictions on free and open speech) proved stifling to authors, artists, and intellectuals, who then boldly challenged the status quo. One thinks, for example, of the poet Allen Ginsberg's lament and cry of pleasure, "Howl," published in 1956 when he was 30. An older poet, William Carlos Williams, concluded his introduction to *"Howl" and Other Poems* (1956): "Hold back the edges of your gowns, Ladies, we are going through hell." Ginsberg had first presented the poem in public in October 1955, in San Francisco, an event that for those in attendance was a transcendent experience that signified the rebellious, resistant, passionate energies swirling beneath the surface of the tranquil-appearing fifties. Ginsberg's biographer Michael Schumacher (1994) describes the scene:

> No one was prepared for the impact of Allen's dramatic reading of the poem. Allen had been drinking wine throughout the evening and, by his own later admission, he was intoxicated by the time the lights dimmed and he began his reading. Somewhat nervous, he started in a calm, quiet tone, letting the poem's words achieve their own impact, but before long he gained confidence and began to sway rhythmically with the music of his poetry, responding to the enthusiasm of the audience, which was transfixed by "Howl"'s powerful imagery. Jack Kerouac, sitting at the edge of the platform, pounded in accompaniment on a wine jug, shouting "GO!" at the end of each long line. The crowd quickly joined him in punctuating Allen's lines with shouts of encouragement, and Allen, inspired by the intensity of the room, responded with an even greater flourish to his reading. By the time he had concluded, he was in tears.... The audience erupted in appreciation of the work, as if each person in attendance recognized that literary history had been made.

"Howl" was a defiant blast against complacency. "I thought I wouldn't write a *poem*," Ginsberg said in 1958:

> but just write what I wanted to without fear, let my imagination go, open secrecy, and scribble magic lines from my real mind—sum up my life—something I wouldn't be able to show anybody, write for my own soul's ear and a few other golden ears.

Ginsberg seemed to be directing his work against the mentality that the widely distributed, glossy magazine *Life* had celebrated the previous month when it took a stand against America's literary malcontents:

> Ours is the most powerful nation in the world. It has had a decade of unparalleled prosperity. It has gone further than any other society in the history of man toward creating a truly classless society. Yet it is still producing a literature which sounds sometimes as if it were written by an unemployed homosexual living in a packing-box shanty on the city dump while awaiting admission to the county poorhouse.

Speaking in later years about "Howl," Ginsberg traced the social and political protests of the 1960s to the writers and artists, many of whom knew one another, who undertook daring, innovative work in the preceding decades:

> There are a lot of different themes that were either catalyzed, adapted, inaugurated, transformed or initiated by the literary movement of the fifties and a community of friends from the forties. The central theme was a transformation of consciousness, and as time unrolled, experiences... related to this notion—at least to widening the arena of consciousness.

In visual art, there were the action painters Jackson Pollock and Willem de Kooning, and in jazz, there were Thelonius Monk, Dizzy Gillespie, Charlie Parker, and Miles Davis. In rock and roll, Elvis Presley reigned supreme. Even as Irving Howe was maintaining (1954) that the postwar period was "the Age of Conformity," conformity itself was being assaulted on a wide front in advanced (and in some cases, like Presley's, very popular) forms of art, music, and literature.

Literature and art are oppositional to begin with; writers and artists have something critical to express and share with audiences. They destabilize conventional views and disorient habits of perception and thought. From the postwar period to the present, one can assemble list after list of novels, volumes of poetry, and plays that, tracing one topic or theme or another, demonstrate an inquiring, probing, unsettling attitude and spirit. One might consider the following novels—especially those by Heller and Pynchon—that explore the settings and events of World War II and its aftermath:

John Horne Burns, *The Gallery* (1947)

Norman Mailer, *The Naked and the Dead* (1948)

Irwin Shaw, *The Young Lions* (1948)

James Jones, *From Here to Eternity* (1951) and *The Thin Red Line* (1962)

Herman Wouk, *The Caine Mutiny* (1951)

Thomas Berger, *Crazy in Berlin* (1958)

Joseph Heller, *Catch-22* (1961)

Kurt Vonnegut, *Slaughterhouse-Five, or, The Children's Crusade: A Duty-Dance with Death* (1969)

Thomas Pynchon, *Gravity's Rainbow* (1973)

Leslie Marmon Silko, *Ceremony* (1977)

Even more, one could fasten on this next group of fictional and nonfictional works about the Vietnam War, which, as a group, depict the searing, surreal battles, the widespread antiwar demonstrations, and the struggles of soldiers and their families to readjust to life at home:

Norman Mailer, *The Armies of the Night* (1968)

Robert Stone, *Dog Soldiers* (1974)

Michael Herr, *Dispatches* (1977)

Philip Caputo, *A Rumor of War* (1977)

Jayne Anne Phillips, *Machine Dreams* (1984)

Bobbie Ann Mason, *In Country* (1985)

Larry Heinemann, *Paco's Story* (1986)

Tim O'Brien, *The Things They Carried* (1990)

Robert Olen Butler, *A Good Scent from a Strange Mountain* (1992)

As the Vietnam War raged, many authors condemned U.S. policies, among them the poets Robert Lowell, Allen Ginsberg, W. S. Merwin, Adrienne Rich, Denise Levertov, Robert Bly, and Galway Kinnell. They focused on the killing, the devastation, and they expressed their profound distrust of the government. American poets, critics, and novelists were public figures, making use of their talent and craft to assail U.S. military policy and to energize and compel their diverse audiences to mobilize on behalf of peace. They were literary figures and also campaigners for social justice, provoking readers to reexamine views taken for granted and to awaken their conscience.

From the atomic bombing of Hiroshima and Nagasaki in August 1945 to the attack on the World Trade Center in September 2001 and beyond, so much of the history of the past half-century is marked by terrible, tremendous acts of violence—by war and acts of terrorism, mass death, and political assassination. Much of American literature during this period depicts wrenching, even unbearable scenes of violence, or the preparation for or recovery from acts of violence.

In the short span from late 1963 to mid-1968, President Kennedy was killed, Malcolm X was assassinated, and both Martin Luther King Jr., and Robert Kennedy were gunned down. There were bloody, fiery urban riots, and every evening the Vietnam War was beamed into homes through TV newscasts. The lyrics of a popular hit song from 1965, Barry McGuire's "Eve of Destruction," catch something of the mood of the era:

> The Eastern World
> It is explodin'
> Violence flarin'
> Bullets loadin'
> You're old enough to kill
> But not for votin'
> You don't believe in war
> But what's that gun you're totin'
> And even the Jordan River has bodies floatin'
>
> But you tell me over, and over, and over again my friend
> Ah, you don't believe we're on the eve of destruction.

In 1969, shortly after race riots triggered by King's death and bruising battles between police and demonstrators in Chicago at the Democratic Party convention, the rock group Jefferson Airplane, in "Volunteers," went so far as to celebrate violent disturbances as thrilling signs of a transformation of American society, a revolution:

> Look what's happening out in the streets
>   Got a revolution, Got to revolution
> Hey I'm dancing down the streets
>   Got a revolution, Got to revolution.

American literature is violent, sometimes outrageously so, from the depictions by Europeans settlers of the torments and attacks they unleashed against America's indigenous peoples through Melville and Twain to Faulkner and O'Connor and to such writers of the present day as Russell Banks, Joyce Carol Oates, and Cormac McCarthy. In a notorious remark, the black militant H. Rap Brown declared, "Violence is as American as apple pie," and his claim may be as pertinent to our literature as to our society (where guns abound and murders number in the tens of thousands annually). One recalls in this context the statement of British writer and critic D. H. Lawrence in *Studies in Classic American*

Literature (1924): "[There] you have the myth of the essential white America. All the other stuff, the love, the democracy, the floundering into lust, is a sort of by-play. The essential American soul is hard, isolate, stoic, and a killer. It has never yet melted."

The critic F. O. Matthiessen drew attention early in the postwar period (1950) to the violent properties of much American literature, adding that this was an element—the "terrible underlying violence that has possessed the imaginations" of American writers—that European intellectuals, critics, and students seemed fascinated by: "It may seem a strange paradox that America, spared so far the worst violence of fascism and war, has imagined violence in a way that impresses men who have experienced the savage brutality of both."

This violence has been in American history from the first settlements in the Caribbean and in the Americas, in the seizure of territory from those who were already dwelling upon the land. The huge, horrid fact of slavery in the North American colonies and in the United States is the country's original sin, from which it is still straining to recover. Capture, enslavement, transport, separation of families, brutalization, torture, murder: this was the reality of slavery, and it did not end until Northern and Southern armies had let loose havoc upon one another in the 1860s during the Civil War. Nor did violence against African American minds and bodies end there, as the long, shameful record of terror, segregation, and lynching (thousands of blacks were lynched between 1889 and 1918, of which 350 were in Mississippi alone) amply attests.

African American Writers in the Postwar Period

All of the important African American writers of the postwar period witnessed and experienced acts of racist violence. Malcolm X's father was found dead in 1931, almost surely the victim of white supremacists; his son was six. When Lorraine Hansberry, author of *A Raisin in the Sun* (1959), was eight years old in 1938, she and her family were pelted with stones when they attempted to move into a white neighborhood in Chicago. Made bitter by racism, Hansberry's father decided in 1946 to relocate his family to Mexico but died before he could complete this plan. "American racism helped kill him," his daughter concluded.

Then again, the postwar record of African American progress is astonishing, if so slow in coming, as well. Jackie Robinson, in April 1947, began playing second base for the Brooklyn Dodgers, the first African American in the major leagues. In 1948 President Harry Truman ordered an end to segregation in the U.S. armed forces. The U.S. Supreme Court, in 1954, ruled segregated schools unconstitutional in *Brown v. Board of Education of Topeka, Kansas*. Boycotts, demonstrations, sit-ins, and many acts of civil disobedience under the leadership of Martin Luther King Jr. and other activists further weakened the South's segregationist codes, laws, and practices.

The climax was a series of legislative acts in the mid-1960s. The Civil Rights Act of 1964, supported and signed by President Lyndon Johnson, authorized the federal government to deny funding to segregated schools, prohibited discrimination by employers and labor unions, and brought an end to discrimination on the basis of race in public accommodations. The Voting Rights Act of 1965 expanded the power of the federal government to ensure African Americans free, unimpeded access to the vote. Finally, the Civil Rights Act of 1968 banned racial discrimination in housing and established stronger legal grounds for the enforcement and protection of civil rights.

Much of this remarkable advance, however, took place amid racial upheaval and rioting and angry, hostile words. During the turbulent 1960s, black writers often described America in stinging terms and argued for a style and strategy of militant confrontation. James Baldwin declared (1962), "At bottom, to be colored means that one has been caught in some utterly unbelievable cosmic joke, a joke so hideous and in such bad taste that it defeats all categories and definitions." The novelist, essayist, and professor John Killens said (1964), "We have to undo the millions of little white lies that America told itself and the world about the American Black man." Baldwin again (1965): "The country does not know what to do with its black population, now that they are no longer a source of wealth, are no longer to be bought and sold and bred like cattle."

Surveying the American scene and attuned to its bitter black voices, the white intellectual and social critic Susan Sontag (1966) concluded, "I do not think white America is committed to granting equality to the American Negro....This is a passionately racist country; it will continue to be so in the foreseeable future."

The work produced by African American writers since World War II in part sustains Sontag's judgment, but ultimately African American literature is a grandly hopeful, nurturing, invigorating tradition, with an extraordinary array of achievements, as this short list of postwar novels indicates:

Ann Petry, *The Street* (1946)
Dorothy West, *The Living Is Easy* (1948)
Ralph Ellison, *Invisible Man* (1952)
Paule Marshall, *Brown Girl, Brownstones* (1959)
Margaret Walker, *Jubilee* (1966)
Ernest Gaines, *The Autobiography of Miss Jane Pittman* (1971)
Gayl Jones, *Corregidora* (1975)
Alice Walker, *Meridian* (1976) and *The Color Purple* (1982)
Gloria Naylor, *The Women of Brewster Place* (1982)
Toni Morrison, *Beloved* (1987)
Terry McMillan, *Disappearing Acts* (1989)
Charles Johnson, *Middle Passage* (1990)
Jamaica Kincaid, *The Autobiography of My Mother* (1996)
Colson Whitehead, *John Henry Days* (2001)
Edward P. Jones, *The Known World* (2003)

Such a list, limited to novels, leaves out high points in poetry (e.g., Langston Hughes's *Montage of a Dream Deferred*, 1951); nonfictional prose (e.g., Baldwin's *Notes of a Native Son*, 1955); autobiography (e.g., *The Autobiography of Malcolm X*, 1965); and drama (e.g., August Wilson's *Fences*, 1987, and *Joe Turner's Come and Gone*, 1988). Across the genres, it is a rich, powerful body of work.

African American literature is the deepest and most developed of the racial and ethnic traditions of American literature. It has a special history of its own, with its own formative contexts, sources, and roots—and relationship to the white majority of the United States. But African American literature is also prophetic of the process that is underway in and that will expand and strengthen the literatures of America's other minority groups.

Not always are new or different groups treated well; sometimes they are treated very badly. But they strive, struggle, endure, build, create; they move forward and become part of the multicolored, diversely patterned, always expanding national quilt.

English as an Evolving Language

I keep referring to American literature, but I must acknowledge that some scholars have proposed that neither "American" nor "English" literature is any longer a meaningful classification. They would have us say instead "world literature written in English," which would equip teachers and students to recognize that writers around in the world, in Trinidad, India, South Africa, and many other countries, now use English as a literary language.

While it is true that English is now a global literary language, we cannot yet merge American literature into a non-national category. What Alfred Kazin proposed in the middle of the twentieth century is still convincing: "The single greatest fact about our modern American writing is our writers' absorption in every last detail of their American world together with their deep and subtle alienation from it." Inside and outside the American landscape, American writers engage classic American themes, visions, values, dreams, and nightmares; they make use of the resources of English to write about the United States and not some other place. There are writers worldwide who use English as their literary language, and there are American writers—our focus in this anthology—using English (itself influenced and informed by many languages and dialects) to articulate their complex, ambivalent, loving, and loathing connection to the United States.

As a language, American English has never stood still. It evolves, takes in, and transmutes terms, phrases, and expressions from other languages. It is a living language, and it is in diversities of speech where America's writers find their resources. Walt Whitman, in the essay "Slang in America" (1885), made the point cogently: "Viewed freely, the English language is the accretion and growth of every dialect, race, and range of time, and is both the free and compacted composition of all." As the poet William Carlos Williams explained (1948): "It is there, in the mouths of the living, that the language is changing and giving new means for expanded possibilities in literary expression and, I add, basic structure— the most important of all." Every true writer has an attraction to language, and the challenges to, and possibilities for, expression it offers. A writer diligently, devotedly labors with language because he or she has something compelling to say, or *attempts* to say. As one of T. S. Eliot's speakers declares (1936), "I've gotta use words when I talk to you."

Another poet, James Dickey, states concisely (1966) the painful quest for expression and understanding that a writer undertakes: "All poetry...is nothing more or less than an attempt to discover or invent conditions under which one can live with oneself." This relationship between language and life is one that all writers must deal with, even as they capitalize on the specific features of their own experience, background, history—and their identity as Americans. Derek Walcott (1988), a West Indian playwright, poet, and professor, insists that the English language, and the potential for creative work through it, belongs to everybody: "The English language is nobody's special property. It is the property of the imagination: it is the property of the language itself."

In a sense, all of American literature is a literature by and about immigrants, by persons who came here from elsewhere, and this is true even of the Indians of the Americas, who originated in northeastern Asia. More than a century ago, the historian Frederick Jackson Turner, in "The Significance of the Frontier in American History" (1893), described the colonial settlers in this way: "In the crucible of the frontier the immigrants were Americanized, liberated, and fused into a mixed race, English in neither nationality nor characteristics. The process has gone on from the early days to our own." American writers, notably in recent decades, have articulated both their desire for and resistance to such a fusion. This has long been an appealing, provocative subject for writers—the tension between seeking and gaining membership and regretting its psychological and emotional cost.

In the early 1960s, a distinguished literary scholar stated that immigrant writers could come into their own only by "dehyphenating" themselves; they must step out from "behind the minority barricade" and occupy a place in the "universal republic" of letters. But few writers, and few Americans, would ever accept a process that distorts who they are. Americans possess, embrace, and struggle with multiple identities *as* Americans; as a consequence, as the critic William Boelhower (1984) has said, "American literature is irremediably ethnic." Being American means learning to live with hyphens and treating other hyphenated Americans with the respect they deserve.

It is not easy to dispense with hyphens, though some of America's writers have tried. Bharati Mukherjee, for example, born in Calcutta, a PhD from the University of Iowa, a teacher at several U.S. colleges and universities, and the author of nonfiction and fiction about American and Indian societies and cultures, has rejected the category "Asian-American." She requests that she be known simply as an American writer: "The moment we say 'Asian-American,' we are implying that there is something that is the norm and that those we are hyphenating are different....Why should some of us, simply because of our race, color, etc., be specified as Asian-American?"

We might respectfully reply that the hyphen is hard, if not impossible, to lose, and that it is one of Mukherjee's distinctions as an American writer that she moves sensitively between cultures and perspectives. She negotiates this movement evocatively in her novels and stories (e.g., *The Middleman and Other Stories*, 1988). Eloquently describing her aims, she says:

> I'm giving you a version of America, your America, that you may not have chosen to see or may have missed. I used to travel on the train going out to my job in Queens from the Upper West Side. After a certain subway stop, the entire train is filled with non-whites. And those people are the people I am writing about, saying they have huge interesting lives. Let me tell you their stories. And how your lives have changed because of their being here.

Mukherjee is not simply presenting new and different versions of America to readers but also showing the authority that a new writer, of a kind who did not figure in the literary canon of the past, can claim, possess, demonstrate.

The literary scholar Louis Harap (1987) offers an instructive account of the development of multicultural and multiethnic American literature. He cites the novelist and critic William Dean Howells, who, in a 1915 essay, took issue with the bigoted contention, prevalent among the cultural elite, that Jews could never contribute to, or appreciate, the traditions of English and American literatures. As Howells put it, "Very possibly there may be at this moment a Russian or Polish Jew, born or bred on our East Side, who shall burst from his parental Yiddish, and from the local hydrants, as well as from the wells of English undefiled, slake our thirst of imaginative literature." Howells was a good prophet of the future of Jewish-American authorship. The short-story writer and novelist Bernard Malamud was born in 1914; the novelist and Nobel Prize winner Saul Bellow, born in Montreal in 1915, moved to Chicago when he was nine and was raised and educated there; and the essayist, literary historian, and autobiographer Alfred Kazin was born in 1915, as was the playwright Arthur Miller.

The process of multiculturalizing American literature, unfolding with such fervor and energy now, was given a significant boost in 1965 with the passage of the Immigration Act. As the literary scholars Katherine B. Payant and Toby Rose (1999) have shown, by abolishing the system of quotas this act made possible the entry into the country of many more immigrants and soon began to open up American literature, expanding its scale and scope.

As some students say on occasion, if anything there now seems *too much* American literature, too much to read, too many cultural traditions and religious, racial, and ethnic complications to get hold of—though this largeness of challenge is, I think, in keeping with the diversity, the boundary-breaking, of American culture and society in general. Where does one begin? Mexican-American/Latin-American/Hispanic writers include Tomas Rivera, Rolando Hinojosa-Smith, Rudolfo Anaya, Oscar Hijuelos, Richard Rodriguez, Sandra Cisneros, Lorna Dee Cervantes, Alberto Ríos, Jimmy Santiago Baca, Judith Ortiz Cofer, Gloria Anzaldúa, Aurora Levins Morales, and Cherrie Moraga. Asian-American writers include Hisaye Yamamoto, Maxine Hong Kingston, Amy Tan, Frank Chin, David Mura, Gish Jen, Garrett Hongo, Laureen Mar, Li-Young Lee, Cathy Song, Janice Mirikitani, and David Henry Hwang. As Elaine Kim (1982) has pointed out, the term *Asian-American* is itself fluid and multifarious, bringing together Chinese, Japanese, Korean, Filipino, Pakistani, and other writers.

Native American writers have also begun to appear on reading lists and syllabi and in campus bookstores. N. Scott Momaday, Paula Gunn Allen, Louise Erdrich, James Welch, Leslie Marmon Silko, Gerald Vizenor, Linda Hogan, Sherman Alexie, Joy Harjo, and Wendy Rose are just a few of them. It is becoming vividly clear to many teachers and students that Native American literature is the oldest American literature of all. "Native American literature has not 'just sprung up,'" Geary Hobson (1979) pointed out. "Native American literature, like the life and culture of which it is a part, is immeasurable centuries old— perhaps 30,000 years or more."

There are college and university courses, too, on postwar and contemporary gay and lesbian American writers such as Robert Duncan, Allen Ginsberg, Frank O'Hara, David Leavitt, Paul Monette, Adrienne Rich, Audre Lorde, Edmund White, Mark Doty, and Tony Kushner. Gay and lesbian writers have always been part of the literary canon. Walt Whitman is an obvious example. The difference is that today it is possible to speak openly about sexual choices and differences among writers, whereas in the past these were concealed or unknown and left unexplored. The nineteenth-century American literature course I took as a student in the early seventies made no reference to Whitman's sexuality or to homosexual and homoerotic themes in his poetry and prose. Such an approach was narrow and misleading; when we candidly deal with these dimensions of Whitman's life and work, we are making Whitman more interesting and complex, not less.

Sexual difference, gender, race, and ethnicity are topics present everywhere in American literature, and it is mistaken to identify an emphasis on them—as some critics of multiculturalism do—as reductive. The truth is exactly the opposite. It is the older literary canon, for all the riches it contained, that was reductive. It is the older approaches, however valuable they were up to a point, that limited our perception and understanding. Here, an observation by Ralph Ellison (1964) is pertinent: "A people must define itself, and minorities have the responsibility of having their ideals and images recognized as part of the composite image which is that of the still forming American people." "The extension of our sense of living by compelling us to contemplate a broader world," the critic F. O. Matthiessen wrote more than half a century ago, "is the chief gift that literature holds out to us."

On occasion all of us may feel that American literature, all literature, is endangered. There are so many forms of diversion and entertainment: television, radio, cell phone, movies, music, email, the Internet. "Popular art," popular culture, "is the dream of society," the Canadian writer Margaret Atwood remarked. "It does not examine itself." The statistics are dismaying. According to a recent study, Americans spend on the average only 24 minutes per day reading, and that means reading anything from a newspaper to *TV Guide* to a book about dieting. In contrast, they spend four hours each day watching television and three hours listening to music. Another even more recent study, in 2011, presents a somewhat different but related and maybe even more alarming picture: Americans spend, on average, three hours per day socializing on their mobile phones; more than sixty percent of Americans using their mobile phones play games on them every day; and hundreds of millions of YouTube views occur each day on American cell phones. Still, TV, with its endless array of channels, remains the archvillain. "Television is to blame," moaned John Updike (1996), "especially because it's come into the home. It has brought the fascination of the flickering image right into the house; like turning on a faucet, you can have it whenever you want." The computer and cell phone may displace it, though it is more likely to occupy additional hours at the expense of reading literature.

On the other hand, the Internet is already proving an impressively (if also bewilderingly) capacious home for literature. Many books, anthologies, sections from work in progress, poems, essays, stories, interviews with authors, and more—all of this can be found online, made available by publishers, institutions of all kinds, and private individuals who set up their own websites. The Internet makes available excerpts and reviews, and many texts in their entirety, and frequently it leads people to purchase "print" editions. In addition to the literary works in bookstores, there are now literary works in thousands of virtual bookstores and literary e-communities.

More than ever, then, American authors have countless opportunities to tell their stories, not only in print but also through other media. In both fictional and nonfictional forms, men and women of many backgrounds and nationalities have recounted their experiences—the scenes and settings of their youth, their families and relationships, their efforts to mediate between minority and majority cultures, the challenges they may have faced as a member of a particular racial, religious, or ethnic group. "Categories like black writer, woman writer, and Latin American writer aren't marginal anymore," Toni Morrison (1981) said. "We have to acknowledge that the thing we call 'literature' is more pluralistic now, just as society ought to be."

"Multiculturalism," the social critic and essayist Garry Wills rightly stressed,

> is the most obvious of global facts, in a world where the "natives" are telling Columbus how to behave, rather than the reverse. That, oddly, is a cause for celebration. The next century will not be North America's to call its own—or any other single nation's. We are all in a boat together, and Columbus must travel with us now as a fellow passenger, no longer the skipper.

On a related note, the poet Michael S. Harper (1983) commented, "A lyrical poet becomes absorbed in the difficulties of what it means to be historically responsible, and to become historically responsible means to open yourself up to options not immediately available." Harper is referring here to his own practices as a writer, and students who are creative writers may find his statement illuminating. But his words apply too to our experiences as readers, to the opening of ourselves to new perspectives we achieve through a multicultural approach to American and world literatures.

The novelist Saul Bellow (1982) no doubt has a point: "Readers don't like to be disturbed. They don't like either their habits or their expectations to be frustrated." But Bellow is not implying that a novelist should *avoid* disturbing his or her readers—that is a crucial aspect of the writer's task. It is not enough for us to find our conception of things confirmed by our reading. It has to be explored, tested, and delved into so it becomes more complex, so it grows.

"Poetry is not an expression of the party line," Allen Ginsberg said. "It's that time of night, lying in bed, thinking what you really think, making the private world public, that's what the poet does." And that is what the reader experiences. Poetry, Marianne Moore affirmed, is "a primal necessity." A person who is not in the midst of poetry, of literature, of American literature, is missing a basic dimension of life.

Thus it is not true to say that American literature, past or present, suffers from being too personal, private, or individual. As the novelist Robert Stone (2003) maintains, "Everybody has their own mythic story, whatever it is, their own personal mythology that is exclusive to themselves and how they relate to the world." These myths are sharable, communicable; this is how we learn from one another and how we perceive similarities and differences among the myths through which each of us gives expression to the self we have become and the world we inhabit. The critic Henry Louis Gates Jr. (1989), has suggested this: "The stories that we tell ourselves and our children function to order our world, serving to create both a foundation upon which each of us constructs our sense of reality and a filter through which we process each event that confronts us every day." These stories may be our own, but we tell them to others.

"Democracy is a collectivity of individuals," Ralph Ellison professed—individuals with their differences, yet differences kept in tense unity within the American social and political compact. American literature is a body of work by a rainbow coalition of individuals who participate in a collective, the collective enterprise that is the United States. In the nation, and in its literature, there is much argument, debate, dispute, disagreement, as voices demand to be heard. It is quite a "melee," Toni Morrison (1988) acknowledged, "but it's a provocative, healthy, explosive melee—extraordinarily profound work is being done."

Being done: Morrison reminds us that American literature has not ceased. Each syllabus for a course, each anthology, perhaps should end with three dots...in order to indicate that more could and should be added, and will be added, by the authors of the present and the future, and by authors of the past whose writings are being recovered, reprinted, and studied.

More than three decades ago, the African American novelist Ishmael Reed claimed, "Afro-American literature is food for a deep lifetime study, not something to be squeezed into a quarter or a semester." One could go further: American literature in general is food for a lifetime of deep study, and the courses we teach or take in school are only the beginning—a wonderful and rich point of departure for an intellectual, emotional, and spiritual journey. As has been said, we read in order to live, and if we do not read we will not know who we are and who we might become.

For further study, see *Harvard Guide to Contemporary American Writing*, ed. Daniel Hoffman (1979); Warner Berthoff, *A Literature Without Qualities: American Writing Since 1945* (1979); and Morris Dickstein, *Gates of Eden: American Culture in the Sixties* (1977; rpt. 1989) and *Leopards in the Temple: The Transformation of American Fiction, 1945–1970* (2002). See also Ethan Goffman, *Imagining Each Other: Blacks and Jews in Contemporary American Literature* (2000); Judith Oster, *Crossing Cultures: Creating Identity in Chinese and Jewish American Literature* (2003); Joanna Brooks, *American Lazarus: Religion and the Rise of African-American and Native American Literatures* (2003); Bill V. Mullen, *Afro-Orientalism* (2004); Dean J. Franco, *Ethnic American Literature: Comparing Chicano, Jewish, and African American Writing* (2006); Alicia A. Kent, *African, Native, and Jewish American Literature and the Reshaping of Modernism* (2007); and Claudia Sadowski-Smith, *Border Fictions: Globalization, Empire, and Writing at the Boundaries of the United States* (2008).

Allen Guttmann, *The Jewish Writer in America: Assimilation and the Crisis of Identity* (1971); Louis Harap, *The Mainstream: The Jewish Presence in Twentieth-Century American Literature, 1950s–1980s* (1987); Mark Shechner, *After the Revolution: Studies in the Contemporary Jewish American Imagination* (1987); and *Handbook of American-Jewish literature: An Analytical Guide to Topics, Themes, and Sources*, ed. Lewis Fried (1988). Also stimulating are Janet Burstein, *Telling the Little Secrets: American Jewish Writing since the 1980s* (2006); Hana Wirth-Nesher, *Call It English: The Languages of Jewish American Literature* (2006); *Modern Jewish Women Writers in America*, ed. Evelyn Avery (2007); Ezra Cappell, *American Talmud: The Cultural Work of Jewish American Fiction* (2007); and Julian Levinson, *Exiles on Main Street: Jewish American Writers and American Literary Culture* (2008).

Chant of Saints: A Gathering of Afro-American Literature, Art, and Scholarship, eds. Michael S. Harper and Robert B. Stepto (1979); *The Third Woman: Minority Women Writers of the United States*, ed. Dexter Fisher (1980); Bernard W. Bell, *The Afro-American Novel and Its Tradition* (1987); Houston A. Baker Jr., *Afro-American Poetics: Revisions of Harlem and the Black Aesthetic* (1988); Henry Louis Gates Jr., *The Signifying Monkey: A Theory of Afro-American Literary Criticism* (1988); and Ashraf H. A. Rushdy, *Remembering Generations: Race and Family in Contemporary African American Fiction* (2001). See also Madhu Dubey, *Signs and Cities: Black Literary Postmodernism* (2003); James Edward Smethurst, *The Black Arts Movement: Literary Nationalism in the 1960s and 1970s* (2005);

Cheryl A. Wall, *Worrying the Line: Black Women Writers, Lineage, and Literary Tradition* (2005); Thadious M. Davis, *Southcapes: Geographies of Race, Region, and Literature* (2011); Gene Andrew Jarrett, *Representing the Race: A New Political History of African American Literature* (2011); Julia H. Lee, *Interracial Encounters: Reciprocal Representations in African American and Asian American Literatures, 1896–1937* (2011); and Kenneth W. Warren, *What Was African American Literature?* (2011).

Studies in American Indian Literature: Critical Essays and Course Designs, ed. Paula Gunn Allen (1983); Paula Gunn Allen, *The Sacred Hoop: Recovering the Feminine in American Indian Traditions* (1986); David Murray, *Forked Tongues: Speech, Writing, and Representation in North American Indian Texts* (1991); and *Early Native American Writing: New Critical Essays*, ed. Helen Jaskoski (1996). Recent studies include Suzanne Evertsen Lundquist, *Native American Literatures: An Introduction* (2004); Matthew Herman, *Politics and Aesthetics in Contemporary Native American Literature: Across Every Border* (2010); and Christopher B. Teuton, *Deep Waters: The Textual Continuum in American Indian Literature* (2010).

Chicano Literature, ed. Charles M. Tatum (1982); *Chicano Literature: A Reference Guide*, eds. Julio A. Martínez and Francisco A. Lomelí (1985); *Criticism in the Borderlands: Studies in Chicano Literature, Culture, and Ideology*, eds. Héctor Calderón and José David Saldívar (1991); and Debra A. Castillo and María Socorro Tabuenca Córdoba, *Border Women: Writing from la Frontera* (2002). See also Sheila Marie Contreras, *Blood Lines: Myth, Indigenism, and Chicana/o Literature* (2008); Patrick L. Hamilton, *Of Space and Mind: Cognitive Mappings of Contemporary Chicano/a Fiction* (2011); and Marissa K. López, *Chicano Nations: The Hemispheric Origins of Mexican American Literature* (2011).

An Interethnic Companion to Asian American Literature, ed. King-Kok Cheung (1997); *Asian American Literature: Reviews and Criticism of Works by American Writers of Asian Descent*, ed. Lawrence J. Trudeau (1999); and *The Asian Pacific American Heritage: A Companion to Literature and Arts*, ed. George J. Leonard (1999).

Writers at Work: The Paris Review *Interviews* (1958); *Listen to the Voices: Conversations with Contemporary Writers*, ed. Jo Brans (1988); and *Alive and Writing: Interviews with American Authors of the 1980s*, ed. Larry McCaffery (1988).

For studies of poetry written since World War II, see Robert Pinsky, *The Situation of Poetry: Contemporary Poetry and Its Traditions* (1976); David Kalstone, *Five Temperaments: Elizabeth Bishop, Robert Lowell, James Merrill, Adrienne Rich, John Ashbery* (1977); Charles Molesworth, *The Fierce Embrace: A Study of Contemporary American Poetry* (1980); Randall Jarrell, *Kipling, Auden & Co.: Essays and Reviews, 1935–1964* (1980); Richard Howard, *Alone with America: Essays on the Art of Poetry in the United States Since 1950* (rev. ed., 1980); Cary Nelson, *Our Past First Poets: Vision and History in Contemporary American Poetry* (1981); James E. B. Breslin, *From Modern to Contemporary: American Poetry, 1945–1965* (1984); Alan Williamson, *Introspection and Contemporary Poetry* (1984); Robert von Hallberg, *American Poetry and Culture, 1945–1980* (1985); *Coming to Light: American Women Poets in the Twentieth Century*, eds. Diane Wood Middlebrook and Marilyn Yalom (1985); Lynn Keller, *Re-Making It New: Contemporary American Poetry and the Modernist Tradition* (1987); Helen Vendler, *The Music of What Happens: Poems, Poets, Critics* (1988); and Kevin Stein, *Private Poets, Worldly Acts: Public and Private History in Contemporary*

American Poetry (1996). See also David Lehman, *The Last Avant-Garde: The Making of the New York School of Poets* (1998); Thomas Travisano, *Midcentury Quartet: Bishop, Lowell, Jarrell, Berryman, and the Making of a Postmodern Aesthetic* (1999); Edward Brunner, *Cold War Poetry* (2001); Subarno Chattarji, *Memories of a Lost War: American Poetic Responses to the Vietnam War* (2001); and Norma C. Wilson, *The Nature of Native American Poetry* (2001).

Also rewarding are Stephen Yenser, *A Boundless Field: American Poetry at Large* (2002); Nick Halpern, *Everyday and Prophetic: The Poetry of Lowell, Ammons, Merrill, and Rich* (2003); Willard Spiegelman, *How Poets See the World: The Art of Description in Contemporary Poetry* (2005); Andrew Epstein, *Beautiful Enemies: Friendship and Postwar American Poetry* (2006); Jennifer Ashton, *From Modernism to Postmodernism: American Poetry and Theory in the Twentieth Century* (2005); Dan Chiasson, *One Kind of Everything: Poem and Person in Contemporary America* (2007); and G. Matthew Jenkins, *Poetic Obligation: Ethics in Experimental American Poetry After 1945* (2008).

Recent work also includes Josephine Nock-Hee Park, *Apparitions of Asia: Modernist Form and Asian American Poetics* (2008); Lesley Wheeler, *Voicing American Poetry: Sound and Performance from the 1920s to the Present* (2008); Jim Keller, *Writing Plural Worlds in Contemporary U.S. Poetry: Innovative Identities* (2009); Catherine Cucinella, *Poetics of the Body: Edna St. Vincent Millay, Elizabeth Bishop, Marilyn Chin, and Marilyn Hacker* (2010); Kevin Stein, *Poetry's Afterlife: Verse in the Digital Age* (2010); and Aidan Wasley, *The Age of Auden: Postwar Poetry and the American Scene* (2011).

Studies of fiction include Tony Tanner, *City of Words: American Fiction, 1950–1970* (1971); Alfred Kazin, *Bright Book of Life: American Novelists and Storytellers from Hemingway to Mailer* (1973); Marcus Klein, *After Alienation: American Novels in Mid-Century* (1978); Frederick R. Karl, *American Fictions, 1940–1980: A Comprehensive History and Critical Evaluation* (1983); and Thomas Schaub, *American Fiction in the Cold War* (1991). See also John Limon, *Writing After War: American War Fiction from Realism to Postmodernism* (1994); Elaine Tuttle Hansen, *Mother without Child: Contemporary Fiction and the Crisis of Motherhood* (1997); Reed Woodhouse, *Unlimited Embrace: A Canon of Gay Fiction, 1945–1995* (1998); Kathryn Hume, *American Dream, American Nightmare: Fiction since 1960* (2000); Kenneth Millard, *Contemporary American Fiction* (2000); Patricia Yaeger, *Dirt and Desire: Reconstructing Southern Women's Writing, 1930–1990* (2000); David Brauner, *Post-War Jewish Fiction: Ambivalence, Self-Explanation and Transatlantic Connections* (2001); Cyrus R. K. Patell, *Negative Liberties: Morrison, Pynchon, and the Problem of Liberal Ideology* (2001); Alan Bilton, *An Introduction to Contemporary American Fiction* (2003); Bernard W. Bell, *The Contemporary African American Novel: Its Folk Roots and Modern Literary Branches* (2004); Suzanne W. Jones, *Race Mixing: Southern Fiction since the Sixties* (2004); and Martyn Bone, *The Postsouthern Sense of Place in Contemporary Fiction* (2005).

Among other recent studies, see Jeremy Green, *Postmodernism: American Fiction at the Millennium* (2005); John A. McClure, *Partial Faiths: Postsecular Fiction in the Age of Pynchon and Morrison* (2007); David Simmons, *The Anti-Hero in the American Novel: From Joseph Heller to Kurt Vonnegut* (2008); Tim A. Ryan, *Calls and Responses: The American Novel of Slavery since Gone with the Wind* (2008); Dalia Kandiyoti, *Migrant Sites: America, Place, and Diaspora Literatures* (2009); Mark McGurl, *The Program Era: Postwar Fiction and the Rise of Creative Writing* (2009); Patrick O'Donnell, *The American Novel Now: Reading Contemporary American Fiction since 1980* (2010); Sally Bachner, *The Prestige of Violence: American Fiction, 1962–2007* (2011); and Steven Salaita, *Modern Arab American Fiction: A Reader's Guide* (2011).

On drama, see Gerald Clifford Weales, *American Drama since World War II* (1962); Elizabeth Brown-Guillory, *Their Place on the Stage: Black Women Playwrights in America* (1988); *Feminine Focus: The New Women Playwrights*, ed. Enoch Brater (1989); *Modern American Drama: The Female Canon*, ed. June Schlueter (1990); Thomas P. Adler, *American Drama, 1940–1960: A Critical History* (1994); Matthew C. Roudané, *American Drama since 1960: A Critical History* (1997); Robert J. Andreach, *Creating the Self in the Contemporary American Theatre* (1998); and Christopher Bigsby, *Contemporary American Playwrights* (1999) and *Modern American Drama, 1945–2000* (2000). See also Jorge A. Huerta, *Chicano Drama: Performance, Society, and Myth* (2000); Bruce A. McConachie, *American Theater in the Culture of the Cold War: Producing and Contesting Containment* (2003); David Krasner, *American Drama, 1945–2000: An Introduction* (2006); Zander Brietzke, *American Drama in the Age of Film* (2007); Lisa M. Anderson, *Black Feminism in Contemporary Drama* (2008); and Julius Novick, *Beyond the Golden Door: Jewish American Drama and Jewish American Experience* (2008).

EUDORA WELTY ▪ (1909–2001)

Eudora Welty was born in Jackson, Mississippi, and educated at Mississippi State College for Women and the University of Wisconsin. After a brief period (1930–31) in New York City, where she attended the Columbia University School of Business, she returned to Jackson. She worked as a journalist and, later in the 1930s, as part of a project for the federal government, took striking photographs of life in the South during the Great Depression. Soon, however, she devoted herself to the writing of fiction, publishing her first story, "Death of a Traveling Salesman," in 1936. Through two collections of stories, *A Curtain of Green* (1941) and *The Wide Net* (1943), Welty established her reputation as one of the premier practitioners of the genre. Her stature was secured by the publication of *The Golden Apples* (1949), a sequence of related stories Welty regarded as the best of her books.

Welty also wrote a number of novels and novellas, including *Delta Wedding* (1946), *The Ponder Heart* (1954), *Losing Battles* (1970), and the Pulitzer Prize winning *The Optimist's Daughter* (1972), in which a young woman recalls and strives to understand her parents' marriage. She assembled, too, a book of critical essays and reflections on the writer's craft, *The Eye of the Story: Selected Essays and Reviews* (1978), and composed a best-selling autobiography of her youth, *One Writer's Beginnings* (1984).

Highly skilled in portraying families, friends, neighbors, and their complex relationships, Welty has a wonderful way of depicting (sometimes to comic effect, as in *The Ponder Heart*) their gestures, manners, and forms of speech. Yet she is also adept at exploring the lives of lonely people, isolates, misfits, and outsiders. In her books, a community comes alive or is evoked as absent from the life of a character searching or wishing for it. Here she resembles, in her feeling for place, James Joyce in *Dubliners* and Sherwood Anderson in *Winesburg, Ohio*; both of these writers, along with Anton Chekhov, influenced Welty. "Place in fiction," she observed, "is the named, identified, concrete, exact and exacting, and therefore credible, gathering spot of all that has been felt, is about to be experienced.... Location pertains to feeling; feeling profoundly pertains to place; place in history partakes of feeling, as feeling about history partakes of place."

Other influences on Welty include Mark Twain, William Faulkner, Virginia Woolf, and the Anglo-Irish novelist and short-story writer Elizabeth Bowen. Welty, in turn, was a significant influence on the careers of such American southern writers as Carson McCullers, Flannery O'Connor, and Anne Tyler.

"A Worn Path," from *A Curtain of Green*, is unusual in the Welty canon because in it she focuses on an African American character, the elderly Phoenix Jackson, who is on a pilgrimage to get medicine for her grandson. Somewhat unfairly, Welty has been criticized on occasion for failing to confront racism and to depict race relations in the South. But this was not, for the most part, the area where she felt she possessed her greatest insight and expertise, as she sought to explain in an essay, "Must the Novelist Crusade?" Yet as "A Worn Path" shows, in its keen-eyed sympathy for its protagonist as she interacts with whites, Welty's range of characters is wider than is sometimes assumed. Determined, dignified, and perceptive, Phoenix Jackson lives on a higher moral level than do the white people she encounters.

Welty's *Collected Stories*, stunning in the depth and degree of originality it demonstrates from start to finish, was published in 1980. For biography, see Suzanne Marrs, *Eudora Welty: A Biography* (2006) as well as her *What There Is to Say We Have Said: The Correspondence of Eudora Welty and William Maxwell* (2011). For critical interpretation, see Peter Schmidt, *The Heart of the Story: Eudora Welty's Short Fiction* (1991); Jan Nordby Gretlund, *Eudora Welty's Aesthetics of Place* (1997); Carol Ann Johnston, *Eudora Welty: A Study of the Short Fiction* (1997); and Michael Kreyling, *Understanding Eudora Welty* (1999).

A Worn Path

It was December—a bright frozen day in the early morning. Far out in the country there was an old Negro woman with her head tied in a red rag, coming along a path through the pinewoods. Her name was Phoenix Jackson. She was very old and small and she walked slowly in the dark pine shadows, moving a little from side to side in her steps, with the balanced heaviness and lightness of a pendulum in a grandfather clock. She carried a thin, small cane made from an umbrella, and with this she kept tapping the frozen earth in front of her. This made a grave and persistent noise in the still air, that seemed meditative like the chirping of a solitary little bird.

She wore a dark striped dress reaching down to her shoe tops, and an equally long apron of bleached sugar sacks, with a full pocket: all neat and tidy, but every time she took a step she might have fallen over her shoelaces, which dragged from her unlaced shoes. She looked straight ahead. Her eyes were blue with age. Her skin had a pattern all its own of numberless branching wrinkles and as though a whole little tree stood in the middle of her forehead, but a golden color ran underneath, and the two knobs of her cheeks were illumined by a yellow burning under the dark. Under the red rag her hair came down on her neck in the frailest of ringlets, still black, and with an odor like copper.

Now and then there was a quivering in the thicket. Old Phoenix said, "Out of my way, all you foxes, owls, beetles, jack rabbits, coons and wild animals!...Keep out from under these feet, little bob-whites....Keep the big wild hogs out of my path. Don't let none of those come running my direction. I got a long way." Under her small black-freckled hand her cane, limber as a buggy whip, would switch at the brush as if to rouse up any hiding things.

On she went. The woods were deep and still. The sun made the pine needles almost too bright to look at, up where the wind rocked. The cones dropped as light as feathers. Down in the hollow was the mourning dove—it was not too late for him.

The path ran up a hill. "Seem like there is chains about my feet, time I get this far," she said, in the voice of argument old people keep to use with themselves. "Something always take a hold of me on this hill—pleads I should stay."

After she got to the top she turned and gave a full, severe look behind her where she had come. "Up through pines," she said at length. "Now down through oaks."

Her eyes opened their widest, and she started down gently. But before she got to the bottom of the hill a bush caught her dress.

Her fingers were busy and intent, but her skirts were full and long, so that before she could pull them free in one place they were caught in another. It was not possible to allow the dress to tear. "I in the thorny bush," she said. "Thorns, you doing your appointed work. Never want to let folks pass, no sir. Old eyes thought you was a pretty little *green* bush."

Finally, trembling all over, she stood free, and after a moment dared to stoop for her cane.

"Sun so high!" she cried, leaning back and looking, while the thick tears went over her eyes. "The time getting all gone here."

At the foot of this hill was a place where a log was laid across the creek.

"Now comes the trial," said Phoenix.

Putting her right foot out, she mounted the log and shut her eyes. Lifting her skirt, leveling her cane fiercely before her, like a festival figure in some parade, she began to march across. Then she opened her eyes and she was safe on the other side.

"I wasn't as old as I thought," she said.

But she sat down to rest. She spread her skirts on the bank around her and folded her hands over her knees. Up above her was a tree in a pearly cloud of mistletoe. She did not dare to close her eyes, and when a little boy brought her a plate with a slice of marble-cake on it she spoke to him. "That would be acceptable," she said. But when she went to take it there was just her own hand in the air.

So she left that tree, and had to go through a barbed-wire fence. There she had to creep and crawl, spreading her knees and stretching her fingers like a baby trying to climb the steps. But she talked loudly to herself: she could not let her dress be torn now, so late in the day, and she could not pay for having her arm or her leg sawed off if she got caught fast where she was.

At last she was safe through the fence and risen up out in the clearing. Big dead trees, like black men with one arm, were standing in the purple stalks of the withered cotton field. There sat a buzzard.

"Who you watching?"

In the furrow she made her way along.

"Glad this not the season for bulls," she said, looking sideways, "and the good Lord made his snakes to curl up and sleep in the winter. A pleasure I don't see no two-headed snake coming around that tree, where it come once. It took a while to get by him, back in the summer."

She passed through the old cotton and went into a field of dead corn. It whispered and shook and was taller than her head. "Through the maze now," she said, for there was no path.

Then there was something tall, black, and skinny there, moving before her.

At first she took it for a man. It could have been a man dancing in the field. But she stood still and listened, and it did not make a sound. It was as silent as a ghost.

"Ghost," she said sharply, "who be you the ghost of? For I have heard of nary death close by."

But there was no answer—only the ragged dancing in the wind.

She shut her eyes, reached out her hand, and touched a sleeve. She found a coat and inside that an emptiness, cold as ice.

"You scarecrow," she said. Her face lighted. "I ought to be shut up for good," she said with laughter. "My senses is gone. I too old. I the oldest people I ever know. Dance, old scarecrow," she said, "while I dancing with you."

She kicked her foot over the furrow, and with mouth drawn down, shook her head once or twice in a little strutting way. Some husks blew down and whirled in streamers about her skirts.

Then she went on, parting her way from side to side with the cane, through the whispering field. At last she came to the end, to a wagon track where the silver grass blew between the red ruts. The quail were walking around like pullets, seeming all dainty and unseen.

"Walk pretty," she said. "This the easy place. This the easy going."

She followed the track, swaying through the quiet bare fields, through the little strings of trees silver in their dead leaves, past cabins silver from weather, with the doors and windows boarded shut, all like old women under a spell sitting there. "I walking in their sleep," she said, nodding her head vigorously.

In a ravine she went where a spring was silently flowing through a hollow log. Old Phoenix bent and drank. "Sweet-gum makes the water sweet," she said, and drank more. "Nobody know who made this well, for it was here when I was born."

The track crossed a swampy part where the moss hung as white as lace from every limb. "Sleep on, alligators, and blow your bubbles." Then the track went into the road.

Deep, deep the road went down between the high green-colored banks. Overhead the live-oaks met, and it was as dark as a cave.

A black dog with a lolling tongue came up out of the weeds by the ditch. She was meditating, and not ready, and when he came at her she only hit him a little with her cane. Over she went in the ditch, like a little puff of milkweed.

Down there, her senses drifted away. A dream visited her, and she reached her hand up, but nothing reached down and gave her a pull. So she lay there and presently went to talking. "Old woman," she said to herself, "that black dog come up out of the weeds to stall you off, and now there he sitting on his fine tail, smiling at you."

A white man finally came along and found her—a hunter, a young man, with his dog on a chain.

"Well, Granny!" he laughed. "What are you doing there?"

"Lying on my back like a June-bug waiting to be turned over, mister," she said, reaching up her hand.

He lifted her up, gave her a swing in the air, and set her down. "Anything broken, Granny?"

"No sir, them old dead weeds is springy enough," said Phoenix, when she had got her breath. "I thank you for your trouble."

"Where do you live, Granny?" he asked, while the two dogs were growling at each other.

"Away back yonder, sir, behind the ridge. You can't even see it from here."

"On your way home?"

"No sir, I going to town."

"Why, that's too far! That's as far as I walk when I come out myself, and I get something for my trouble." He patted the stuffed bag he carried, and there hung down a little closed claw. It was one of the bob-whites, with its beak hooked bitterly to show it was dead. "Now you go on home, Granny!"

"I bound to go to town, mister," said Phoenix. "The time come around."

He gave another laugh, filling the whole landscape. "I know you old colored people! Wouldn't miss going to town to see Santa Claus!"

But something held old Phoenix very still. The deep lines in her face went into a fierce and different radiation. Without warning, she had seen with her own eyes a flashing nickel fall out of the man's pocket onto the ground.

"How old are you, Granny?" he was saying.

"There is no telling, mister," she said, "no telling."

Then she gave a little cry and clapped her hands and said, "Git on away from here, dog! Look! Look at that dog!" She laughed as if in admiration. "He ain't scared of nobody. He a big black dog." She whispered, "Sic him!"

"Watch me get rid of that cur," said the man. "Sic him, Pete! Sic him!"

Phoenix heard the dogs fighting, and heard the man running and throwing sticks. She even heard a gunshot. But she was slowly bending forward by that time, further and further forward, the lids stretched down over her eyes, as if she were doing this in her sleep. Her chin was lowered almost to her knees. The yellow palm of her hand came out from the fold of her apron. Her fingers slid down and along the ground under the piece of money with the grace and care they would have in lifting an egg from under a setting hen. Then she slowly straightened up, she stood erect, and the nickel was in her apron pocket. A bird flew by. Her lips moved. "God watching me the whole time. I come to stealing."

The man came back, and his own dog panted about them. "Well, I scared him off that time," he said, and then he laughed and lifted his gun and pointed it at Phoenix.

She stood straight and faced him.

"Doesn't the gun scare you?" he said, still pointing it.

"No, sir, I seen plenty go off closer by, in my day, and for less than what I done," she said, holding utterly still.

He smiled, and shouldered the gun. "Well, Granny," he said, "you must be a hundred years old, and scared of nothing. I'd give you a dime if I had any money with me. But you take my advice and stay home, and nothing will happen to you."

"I bound to go on my way, mister," said Phoenix. She inclined her head in the red rag. Then they went in different directions, but she could hear the gun shooting again and again over the hill.

She walked on. The shadows hung from the oak trees to the road like curtains. Then she smelled wood-smoke, and smelled the river, and she saw a steeple and the cabins on their steep steps. Dozens of little black children whirled around her. There ahead was Natchez shining. Bells were ringing. She walked on.

In the paved city it was Christmas time. There were red and green electric lights strung and criss-crossed everywhere, and all turned on in the daytime. Old Phoenix would have been lost if she had not distrusted her eyesight and depended on her feet to know where to take her.

She paused quietly on the sidewalk where people were passing by. A lady came along in the crowd, carrying an armful of red-, green- and silver-wrapped presents; she gave off perfume like the red roses in hot summer, and Phoenix stopped her.

"Please, missy, will you lace up my shoe?" She held up her foot.

"What do you want, Grandma?"

"See my shoe," said Phoenix. "Do all right for out in the country, but wouldn't look right to go in a big building."

"Stand still then, Grandma," said the lady. She put her packages down on the sidewalk beside her and laced and tied both shoes tightly.

"Can't lace 'em with a cane," said Phoenix. "Thank you, missy. I doesn't mind asking a nice lady to tie up my shoe, when I gets out on the street."

Moving slowly and from side to side, she went into the big building, and into a tower of steps, where she walked up and around and around until her feet knew to stop.

She entered a door, and there she saw nailed up on the wall the document that had been stamped with the gold seal and framed in the gold frame, which matched the dream that was hung up in her head.

"Here I be," she said. There was a fixed and ceremonial stiffness over her body.

"A charity case, I suppose," said an attendant who sat at the desk before her.

But Phoenix only looked above her head. There was sweat on her face, the wrinkles in her skin shone like a bright net.

"Speak up, Grandma," the woman said. "What's your name? We must have your history, you know. Have you been here before? What seems to be the trouble with you?"

Old Phoenix only gave a twitch to her face as if a fly were bothering her.

"Are you deaf?" cried the attendant.

But then the nurse came in.

"Oh, that's just old Aunt Phoenix," she said. "She doesn't come for herself—she has a little grandson. She makes these trips just as regular as clockwork. She lives away back off the Old Natchez Trace." She bent down. "Well, Aunt Phoenix, why don't you just take a seat? We won't keep you standing after your long trip." She pointed.

The old woman sat down, bolt upright in the chair.

"Now, how is the boy?" asked the nurse.

Old Phoenix did not speak.

"I said, how is the boy?"

But Phoenix only waited and stared straight ahead, her face very solemn and withdrawn into rigidity.

"Is his throat any better?" asked the nurse. "Aunt Phoenix, don't you hear me? Is your grandson's throat any better since the last time you came for the medicine?"

With her hands on her knees, the old woman waited, silent, erect and motionless, just as if she were in armor.

"You mustn't take up our time this way, Aunt Phoenix," the nurse said. "Tell us quickly about your grandson, and get it over. He isn't dead, is he?"

At last there came a flicker and then a flame of comprehension across her face, and she spoke.

"My grandson. It was my memory had left me. There I sat and forgot why I made my long trip."

"Forgot?" The nurse frowned. "After you came so far?"

Then Phoenix was like an old woman begging a dignified forgiveness for waking up frightened in the night. "I never did go to school, I was too old at the Surrender,"[1] she said in a soft voice. "I'm an old woman without an education. It was my memory fail me. My little grandson, he is just the same, and I forgot it in the coming."

"Throat never heals, does it?" said the nurse, speaking in a loud, sure voice to old Phoenix. By now she had a card with something written on it, a little list. "Yes. Swallowed lye. When was it?—January—two-three years ago—"

Phoenix spoke unasked now. "No, missy, he not dead, he just the same. Every little while his throat begin to close up again, and he not able to swallow. He not get his breath. He not able to help himself. So the time come around, and I go on another trip for the soothing medicine."

"All right. The doctor said as long as you came to get it, you could have it," said the nurse. "But it's an obstinate case."

"My little grandson, he sit up there in the house all wrapped up, waiting by himself," Phoenix went on. "We is the only two left in the world. He suffer and it don't seem to put him back at all. He got a sweet look. He going to last. He wear a little patch quilt and peep out holding his mouth open like a little bird. I remembers so plain now. I not going to forget him again, no, the whole enduring time. I could tell him from all the others in creation."

"All right." The nurse was trying to hush her now. She brought her a bottle of medicine. "Charity," she said, making a check mark in a book.

Old Phoenix held the bottle close to her eyes, and then carefully put it into her pocket.

"I thank you," she said.

"It's Christmas time, Grandma," said the attendant. "Could I give you a few pennies out of my purse?"

"Five pennies is a nickel," said Phoenix stiffly.

"Here's a nickel," said the attendant.

Phoenix rose carefully and held out her hand. She received the nickel and then fished the other nickel out of her pocket and laid it beside the new one. She stared at her palm closely, with her head on one side.

Then she gave a tap with her cane on the floor.

"This is what come to me to do," she said. "I going to the store and buy my child a little windmill they sells, made out of paper. He going to find it hard to believe there such a thing in the world. I'll march myself back where he waiting, holding it straight up in this hand."

She lifted her free hand, gave a little nod, turned around, and walked out of the doctor's office. Then her slow step began on the stairs, going down.

[1939]

---

[1] The end of the Civil War in 1865.

TENNESSEE WILLIAMS ■ (1911–1983)

Thomas Lanier Williams was born in Columbus, Mississippi, the son of a traveling salesman, a gambler who was frequently drunk and violent; his mother, pious and genteel, was an Episcopalian minister's daughter, and her relationship with her husband was tense and argumentative. Williams was sickly as a child, spending his days reading and playing games with his sister, Rose, who was two years older and who, suffering from emotional and mental problems, was institutionalized in 1937.

Williams began writing when he was eleven, soon after his mother gave him a typewriter. He developed his interests in literary work during three years at the University of Missouri, winning awards for fiction and poetry, but his father strongly disapproved and cut off support of his son.

Living in St. Louis, Williams worked for three years in a shoe warehouse and tried to keep up his writing in the evenings, but he suffered a breakdown in 1935. After some months of incapacitation, he began to recover while living at the home of his grandparents. He attended Washington University in St. Louis as well as the University of Iowa, where in 1938 he received his undergraduate degree. It was during the 1930s that Williams recognized he was homosexual, and biographers have said that his work gained much from his reading of the intense verse of the poet (and homosexual) Hart Crane, who in 1932 committed suicide. Williams observed of him, evocatively and enigmatically, "Perhaps it is only through self-immolation of such a nature that we living beings can offer to you the entire truth of ourselves." Other key influences are the French poet Arthur Rimbaud, the British poet and novelist D. H. Lawrence, and the Spanish poet Federico Garcia Lorca.

From 1939 into the early 1940s, Williams wrote one-act plays and other works, signing them (for reasons he never quite made clear) "Tennessee" Williams. His first big success came in 1945 with the Broadway production of *The Glass Menagerie*, a "memory play" about a brother and sister, their dreamy mother, and a "gentleman caller" friend of the brother's, whose visit shatters the family. In a comment pertinent to this play and others, Williams said, "Desire is rooted in a longing for companionship, a release from the loneliness that haunts every individual."

Williams's next triumph was *A Streetcar Named Desire* (1947), a desperate, brooding work about reality and illusion, sexual passion and sexual violence. Set in "Elysian Fields" in New Orleans, directed by Elia Kazan, and starring Jessica Tandy as the cultured, promiscuous, fading southern belle Blanche DuBois and the charismatic Marlon Brando in the role of the crude, sexually powerful Stanley Kowalski, the play ran on Broadway for two years. It has been termed a "revolutionary" work; as the director Richard Seyd noted, "It was one of the first times I think in the American theater, that working class figures were put on the stage within a very strong psychological context." The biographer Lyle Leverich adds that *Streetcar* fiercely dramatizes Williams's "main point—the breakdown of communication."

Williams was a major, perhaps the dominant, playwright (even more so than Arthur Miller) on the American scene from the late 1940s to about 1960. His work then began to fall out of favor, its lush and melancholy lyricism, and its brutality and violence, no longer exercising a strong hold on audiences. Williams himself became heavily dependent on drugs and liquor, obsessed by illness and death. Yet he remained productive and, often, highly accomplished in his work as a poet, essayist, fiction writer, and playwright.

Among Williams's other important plays are *The Rose Tattoo* (1951), *Cat on a Hot Tin Roof* (1955)—which Williams said came "closest to being both a work of art and a work of craft," *Suddenly Last Summer* (1958), and *The Night of the Iguana* (1961). A volume of essays, *Where I Live*, was published in 1978, and the *Collected Stories* in 1985.

Cat on a Hot Tin Roof, given here, a charged exploration of southern decadence, family dissolution, mendacity, greed, and sexual identity, was first performed in March 1955 and later in the year was awarded the Pulitzer Prize in drama.

Williams developed *Cat on a Hot Tin Roof* from a short story he had written in 1952, "Three Players of a Summer Game," reworking its storyline and characters. The focus of the play is on three members of a wealthy white family of humble origins gathered on their Mississippi Delta estate: Big Daddy, the father, who is unaware he is dying of cancer; Brick, one of his sons, an alcoholic ex-athlete who has been shattered by the discovery that his friend Skipper was homosexual—Skipper later killed himself; and Maggie (the "cat" of the title), Brick's wife, angry and sexually frustrated because her husband refuses to sleep with her. "Each of these characters," the Williams scholar Nancy M. Tischler said, "is at once individual, regional, and mythic."

Skipper is dead before the play begins, yet, as Mark Royden Winchell noted, his relationship with Brick is central to the action. This relationship "is never dramatized"; instead, "Williams gives us at least five different interpretations of that relationship" serving "a theatrical function somewhat similar to multiple points of view in a novel."

The play inspired a number of film adaptations. The best known, made in 1958 and downplaying the homosexual plot elements, starred Paul Newman as Brick, Elizabeth Taylor as Maggie, and Burl Ives as Big Daddy. Over the years Williams made revisions, changes, deletions, and substitutions in various editions of the play. The edition here is from 1974.

For biography, see Donald Spoto, *The Kindness of Strangers: The Life of Tennessee Williams* (1985), and Lyle Leverich, *Tom: The Unknown Tennessee Williams* (1995). See also, for additional biography and

Paul Newman and Elizabeth Taylor in a scene from the
film version of the Tennessee Williams play *Cat on a Hot
Tin Roof*, produced by MGM in 1958. Elizabeth Taylor
was nominated for an Academy Award for this role.

critical interpretation, Roger Boxill, *Tennessee Williams* (1987); *Tennessee
Williams: A Guide to Research and Performance*, ed. Philip C. Kolin (1998);
The Cambridge Companion to Tennessee Williams, ed. Matthew C. Roudané
(1997); and *Tennessee Williams: A Casebook*, ed. Robert F. Gross (2002).
Other important resources include Williams's *Memoirs* (1975, rpt. 2006)
and *Notebooks* (2006), from 1936 to 1981; and *The Tennessee Williams
Encyclopedia*, ed. Philip C. Kolin (2004).

Cat on a Hot Tin Roof

CHARACTERS

Margaret
Brick
Mae, *sometimes called Sister Woman*
Big Mama
Dixie, *a little girl*
Big Daddy

Reverend Tooker
Gooper, *sometimes called Brother Man*
Doctor Baugh, *pronounced "Baw"*
Lacey, *a Negro servant*
Sookey, *another*
Children

Notes for the Designer

The set is the bed-sitting-room of a plantation home in the Mississippi
Delta. It is along an upstairs gallery which probably runs around the entire
house; it has two pairs of very wide doors opening onto the gallery, showing white balustrades against a fair summer sky that fades into dusk and
night during the course of the play, which occupies precisely the time of
its performance, excepting, of course, the fifteen minutes of intermission.

Perhaps the style of the room is not what you would expect in the home
of the Delta's biggest cotton planter. It is Victorian with a touch of the Far
East. It hasn't changed much since it was occupied by the original owners of
the place, Jack Straw and Peter Ochello, a pair of old bachelors who shared
this room all their lives together. In other words, the room must evoke
some ghosts; it is gently and poetically haunted by a relationship that must
have involved a tenderness which was uncommon. This may be irrelevant
or unnecessary, but I once saw a reproduction of a faded photograph of the
verandah of Robert Louis Stevenson's home on that Samoan Island[1] where
he spent his last years, and there was a quality of tender light on weathered
wood, such as porch furniture made of bamboo and wicker, exposed to tropical suns and tropical rains, which came to mind when I thought about the
set for this play, bringing also to mind the grace and comfort of light, the
reassurance it gives, on a late and fair afternoon in summer, the way that no
matter what, even dread of death, is gently touched and soothed by it. For
the set is the background for a play that deals with human extremities of
emotion, and it needs that softness behind it.

The bathroom door, showing only pale-blue tile and silver towel racks,
is in one side wall; the hall door in the opposite wall. Two articles of furniture need mention: a big double bed which staging should make a functional part of the set as often as suitable, the surface of which should
be slightly raked to make figures on it seen more easily; and against the
wall space between the two huge double doors upstage: a monumental
monstrosity peculiar to our times, a *huge* console combination of radio-
phonograph (hi-fi with three speakers), TV set, *and* liquor cabinet, bearing and containing many glasses and bottles, all in one piece, which is a
composition of muted silver tones, and the opalescent tones of reflecting

---

[1]The Scottish writer Robert Louis Stevenson (1850–94), author of *Treasure Island* (1883) and other novels,
spent his final years living in Hawaii, Samoa, and elsewhere in the eastern and southern Pacific Ocean.

glass, a chromatic link, this thing, between the sepia (tawny gold) tones of the interior and the cool (white and blue) tones of the gallery and sky. This piece of furniture (?!), this monument, is a very complete and compact little shrine to virtually all the comforts and illusions behind which we hide from such things as the characters in the play are faced with....

The set should be far less realistic than I have so far implied in this description of it. I think the walls below the ceiling should dissolve mysteriously into air; the set should be roofed by the sky; stars and moon suggested by traces of milky pallor, as if they were observed through a telescope lens out of focus.

Anything else I can think of? Oh, yes, fan-lights (transoms shaped like an open glass fan) above all the doors in the set, with panes of blue and amber, and above all, the designer should take as many pains to give the actors room to move about freely (to show their restlessness, their passion for breaking out) as if it were a set for a ballet.

An evening in summer. The action is continuous with two intermissions.

ACT 1

(At the rise of the curtain someone is taking a shower in the bathroom, the door of which is half open. A pretty young woman, with anxious lines in her face, enters the bedroom and crosses to the bathroom door.)

Margaret (*shouting above roar of water*):   One of those no-neck monsters hit me with a hot buttered biscuit so I have t' change!

(Margaret's voice is both rapid and drawling. In her long speeches she has the vocal tricks of a priest delivering a liturgical chant, the lines are almost sung, always continuing a little beyond her breath so she has to gasp for another. Sometimes she intersperses the lines with a little wordless singing, such as "Da-da-daaaa!")

(Water turns off and Brick calls out to her, but is still unseen. A tone of politely feigned interest, masking indifference, or worse, is characteristic of his speech with Margaret.)

Brick: Wha'd you say, Maggie? Water was on s' loud I couldn't hearya....
Margaret: Well, I!—just remarked that!—one of th' no-neck monsters messed up m' lovely lace dress so I got t'—cha-a-ange....

(She opens and kicks shut drawers of the dresser.)

Brick: Why d'ya call Gooper's kiddies no-neck monsters?
Margaret: Because they've got no necks! Isn't that a good enough reason?
Brick: Don't they have any necks?
Margaret: None visible. Their fat little heads are set on their fat little bodies without a bit of connection.
Brick: That's too bad.

Margaret: Yes, it's too bad because you can't wring their necks if they've got no necks to wring! Isn't that right, honey?

(She steps out of her dress, stands in a slip of ivory satin and lace.)

Yep, they're no-neck monsters, all no-neck people are monsters...

(Children shriek downstairs.)

Hear them? Hear them screaming? I don't know where their voice boxes are located since they don't have necks. I tell you I got so nervous at that table tonight I thought I would throw back my head and utter a scream you could hear across the Arkansas border an' parts of Louisiana an' Tennessee. I said to your charming sister-in-law, Mae, honey, couldn't you feed those precious little things at a separate table with an oilcloth cover? They make such a mess an' the lace cloth looks *so* pretty! She made enormous eyes at me and said, "Ohhh, noooooo! On Big Daddy's birthday? Why, he would never forgive me!" Well, I want you to know, Big Daddy hadn't been at the table two minutes with those five no-neck monsters slobbering and drooling over their food before he threw down his fork an' shouted, "Fo' God's sake, Gooper, why don't you put them pigs at a trough in th' kitchen?"— Well, I swear, I simply could have di-ieed!

Think of it, Brick, they've got five of them and number six is coming. They've brought the whole bunch down here like animals to display at a county fair. Why, they have those children doin' tricks all the time! "Junior, show Big Daddy how you do this, show Big Daddy how you do that, say your little piece fo' Big Daddy, Sister. Show your dimples, Sugar. Brother, show Big Daddy how you stand on your head!"—It goes on all the time, along with constant little remarks and innuendos about the fact that you and I have not produced any children, are totally childless and therefore totally useless!—Of course it's comical but it's also disgusting since it's so obvious what they're up to!

Brick (*without interest*): What are they up to, Maggie?

Margaret: Why you know what they're up to!

Brick (*appearing*): No, I don't know what they're up to.

(He stands there in the bathroom doorway drying his hair with a towel and hanging onto the towel rack because one ankle is broken, plastered and bound. He is still slim and firm as a boy. His liquor hasn't started tearing him down outside. He has the additional charm of that cool air of detachment that people have who have given up the struggle. But now and then, when disturbed, something flashes behind it, like lightning in a fair sky, which shows that at some deeper level he is far from peaceful. Perhaps in a stronger light he would show some signs of deliquescence,[2] but the fading, still warm light from the gallery treats him gently.)

---

[2]To melt away, become fluid or soft.

Margaret: I'll tell you what they're up to, boy of mine!—They're up to cutting you out of your father's estate, and—

(She freezes momentarily before her next remark. Her voice drops as if it were somehow a personally embarrassing admission.)

—Now we know that Big Daddy's dyin' of—cancer....

(There are voices on the lawn below: long-drawn calls across distance. Margaret raises her lovely bare arms and powders her armpits with a light sigh.)

(She adjusts the angle of a magnifying mirror to straighten an eyelash, then rises fretfully saying:)

There's so much light in the room it—
Brick *(softly but sharply)*:   Do we?
Margaret: Do we what?
Brick: Know Big Daddy's dyin' of cancer?
Margaret: Got the report today.
Brick: Oh...
Margaret *(letting down bamboo blinds which cast long, gold-fretted shadows over the room)*:   Yep, got th' report just now... it didn't surprise me, Baby....

(Her voice has range, and music; sometimes it drops low as a boy's and you have a sudden image of her playing boy's games as a child.)

I recognized the symptoms soon's we got here last spring and I'm willin' to bet you that Brother Man and his wife were pretty sure of it, too. That more than likely explains why their usual summer migration to the coolness of the Great Smokies[3] was passed up this summer in favor of—hustlin' down here ev'ry whipstitch with their whole screamin' tribe! And why so many allusions have been made to Rainbow Hill lately. You know what Rainbow Hill is? Place that's famous for treatin' alcoholics an' dope fiends in the movies!
Brick: I'm not in the movies.
Margaret: No, and you don't take dope. Otherwise you're a perfect candidate for Rainbow Hill, Baby, and that's where they aim to ship you—over my dead body! Yep, over my dead body they'll ship you there, but nothing would please them better. Then Brother Man could get a-hold of the purse strings and dole out remittances to us, maybe get power of attorney and sign checks for us and cut off our credit wherever, whenever he wanted! Son-of-a-bitch!—How'd you like that, Baby?—Well, you've been doin' just about ev'rything in your power to bring it about, you've just been doin' ev'rything you can think of to aid and abet them in this scheme of theirs! Quittin' work, devoting yourself to the occupation of drinkin'!—Breakin' your ankle last night on the high school athletic field: doin' what? Jumpin' hurdles? At two

---

[3]The Great Smoky Mountains are a mountain range rising along the Tennessee/North Carolina border in the southeastern United States.

or three in the morning? Just fantastic! Got in the paper. *Clarksdale Register* carried a nice little item about it, human interest story about a well-known former athlete stagin' a one-man track meet on the Glorious Hill High School athletic field last night, but was slightly out of condition and didn't clear the first hurdle! Brother Man Gooper claims he exercised his influence t' keep it from goin' out over AP or UP or every goddamn "P."

But, Brick? You still have one big advantage!

(During the above swift flood of words, Brick has reclined with contrapuntual leisure on the snowy surface of the bed and has rolled over carefully on his side or belly.)

Brick (*wryly*):   Did you *say* something, Maggie?

Margaret: Big Daddy dotes on you, honey. And he can't stand Brother Man and Brother Man's wife, that monster of fertility, Mae. Know how I know? By little expressions that flicker over his face when that woman is holding fo'th on one of her choice topics such as—how she refused twilight sleep![4]—when the twins were delivered! Because she feels motherhood's an experience that a woman ought to experience fully!—in order to fully appreciate the wonder and beauty of it! HAH!—and how she made Brother Man come in an' stand beside her in the delivery room so he would not miss out on the "wonder and beauty" of it either!—producin' those no-neck monsters....

(A speech of this kind would be antipathetic from almost anybody but Margaret; she makes it oddly funny, because her eyes constantly twinkle and her voice shakes with laughter which is basically indulgent.)

—Big Daddy shares my attitude toward those two! As for me, well—I give him a laugh now and then and he tolerates me. In fact!—I sometimes suspect that Big Daddy harbors a little unconscious "lech" fo' me....

Brick: What makes you think that Big Daddy has a lech for you, Maggie?

Margaret: Way he always drops his eyes down my body when I'm talkin' to him, drops his eyes to my boobs an' licks his old chops! Ha ha!

Brick: That kind of talk is disgusting.

Margaret: Did anyone ever tell you that you're an ass-aching Puritan, Brick?

I think it's mighty fine that that ole fellow, on the doorstep of death, still takes in my shape with what I think is deserved appreciation!

---

[4]A state in which awareness of pain is dulled through medication.

And you wanta know something else? Big Daddy didn't know how many little Maes and Goopers had been produced! "How many kids have you got?" he asked at the table, just like Brother Man and his wife were new acquaintances to him! Big Mama said he was jokin', but that ole boy wasn't jokin', Lord, no!

And when they infawmed him that they had five already and were turning out number six!—the news seemed to come as a sort of unpleasant surprise...

(Children yell below.)

Scream, monsters!

(Turns to Brick with a sudden, gay, charming smile which fades as she notices that he is not looking at her but into fading gold space with a troubled expression.)

(It is constant rejection that makes her humor "bitchy.")

Yes, you should of been at that supper-table, Baby.

(Whenever she calls him "baby" the word is a soft caress.)

Y'know, Big Daddy, bless his ole sweet soul, he's the dearest ole thing in the world, but he does hunch over his food as if he preferred not to notice anything else. Well, Mae an' Gooper were side by side at the table, direckly across from Big Daddy, watchin' his face like hawks while they jawed an' jabbered about the cuteness an' brillance of th' no-neck monsters!

(She giggles with a hand fluttering at her throat and her breast and her long throat arched.)

(She comes downstage and recreates the scene with voice and gesture.)

And the no-neck monsters were ranged around the table, some in high chairs and some on th' *Books of Knowledge*, all in fancy little paper caps in honor of Big Daddy's birthday, and all through dinner, well, I want you to know that Brother Man an' his partner never once, for one moment, stopped exchanging pokes an' pinches an' kicks an' signs an' signals!—Why, they were like a couple of cardsharps fleecing a sucker.—Even Big Mama, bless her ole sweet soul, she isn't th' quickest an' brightest thing in the world, she finally noticed, at last, an' said to Gooper, "Gooper, what are you an' Mae makin' all these signs at each other about?"—I swear t' goodness, I nearly choked on my chicken!

(Margaret, back at the dressing table, still doesn't see Brick. He is watching her with a look that is not quite definable—Amused? shocked? contemptuous?—part of those and part of something else.)

Y'know—your brother Gooper still cherishes the illusion he took a giant step up on the social ladder when he married Miss Mae Flynn of the Memphis Flynns.

But I have a piece of Spanish news for Gooper. The Flynns never had a thing in this world but money and they lost that, they were nothing at all but fairly successful climbers. Of course, Mae Flynn came out in Memphis eight years before I made my debut in Nashville, but I had friends at Ward-Belmont who came from Memphis and they used to come to see me and I used to go to see them for Christmas and spring vacations, and so I know who rates an' who doesn't rate in Memphis society. Why, y'know ole Papa Flynn, he barely escaped doing time in the Federal pen for shady manipulations on th' stock market when his chain stores crashed, and as for Mae having been a cotton carnival queen, as they remind us so often, lest we forget, well, that's one honor that I don't envy her for!—Sit on a brass throne on a tacky float an' ride down Main Street, smilin', bowin', and blowin' kisses to all the trash on the street—

(She picks out a pair of jeweled sandals and rushes to the dressing table.)

Why, year before last, when Susan McPheeters was singled out fo' that honor, y' know what happened to her? Y'know what happened to poor little Susie McPheeters?

Brick *(absently)*:   No. What happened to little Susie McPheeters?

Margaret: Somebody spit tobacco juice in her face.

Brick *(dreamily)*:   Somebody spit tobacco juice in her face?

Margaret: That's right, some old drunk leaned out of a window in the Hotel Gayoso and yelled, "Hey, Queen, hey, hey, there, Queenie!" Poor Susie looked up and flashed him a radiant smile and he shot out a squirt of tobacco juice right in poor Susie's face.

Brick: Well, what d'you know about that.

Margaret *(gaily)*:   What do I know about it? I was there, I saw it!

Brick *(absently)*:   Must have been kind of funny.

Margaret: Susie didn't think so. Had hysterics. Screamed like a banshee.[5] They had to stop th' parade an' remove her from her throne an' go on with—

(She catches sight of him in the mirror, gasps slightly, wheels about to face him. Count ten.)

—Why are you looking at me like that?

Brick *(whistling softly, now)*:   Like what, Maggie?

Margaret *(intensely, fearfully)*:   The way y' were lookin' at me just now, befo' I caught your eye in the mirror and you started t' whistle! I don't know how t' describe it but it froze my blood!—I've caught you lookin' at me like that so often lately. What are you thinkin' of when you look at me like that?

[5]In Irish legend, a female spirit whose wailing warns of an impending death in a house.

Brick: I wasn't conscious of lookin' at you, Maggie.

Margaret: Well, I was conscious of it! What were you thinkin'?

Brick: I don't remember thinking of anything, Maggie.

Margaret: Don't you think I know that—? Don't you—?—Think I know that—?

Brick (*coolly*):   Know *what*, Maggie?

Margaret (*struggling for expression*):   That I've gone through this— *hideous!—transformation, become—hard! Frantic!*

(*Then she adds, almost tenderly:*)

—*cruel!!*

That's what you've been observing in me lately. How could y' help but observe it? That's all right. I'm not—thin-skinned any more, can't afford t' be thin-skinned any more.

(*She is now recovering her power.*)

—But Brick? Brick?

Brick: Did you say something?

Margaret: I was *goin' t'* say something: that I get—lonely. Very!

Brick: Ev'rybody gets that...

Margaret: Living with someone you love can be lonelier—than living entirely *alone!*—if the one that y' love doesn't love you....

(*There is a pause. Brick hobbles downstage and asks, without looking at her:*)

Brick: Would you like to live alone, Maggie?

(*Another pause: then—after she has caught a quick, hurt breath:*)

Margaret: *No!—God!—I wouldn't!*

(*Another gasping breath. She forcibly controls what must have been an impulse to cry out. We see her deliberately, very forcibly, going all the way back to the world in which you can talk about ordinary matters.*)

Did you have a nice shower?

Brick: Uh-huh.

Margaret: Was the water cool?

Brick: No.

Margaret: But it made y' feel fresh, huh?

Brick: Fresher....

Margaret: I know something would make y' feel *much* fresher!

Brick: What?

Margaret: An alcohol rub. Or cologne, a rub with cologne!

Brick: That's good after a workout but I haven't been workin' out, Maggie.

Margaret: You've kept in good shape, though.

Brick (*indifferently*):   You think so, Maggie?

Margaret: I always thought drinkin' men lost their looks, but I was plainly mistaken.

Brick (*wryly*):   Why, thanks, Maggie.

Margaret: You're the only drinkin' man I know that it never seems t' put fat on.

Brick: I'm gettin' softer, Maggie.

Margaret: Well, sooner or later it's bound to soften you up. It was just beginning to soften up Skipper when—

(*She stops short.*)

I'm sorry. I never could keep my fingers off a sore—I wish you *would* lose your looks. If you did it would make the martyrdom of Saint Maggie a little more bearable. But no such goddamn luck. I actually believe you've gotten better looking since you've gone on the bottle. Yeah, a person who didn't know you would think you'd never had a tense nerve in your body or a strained muscle.

(*There are sounds of croquet on the lawn below: the click of mallets, light voices, near and distant.*)

Of course, you always had that detached quality as if you were playing a game without much concern over whether you won or lost, and now that you've lost the game, not lost but just quit playing, you have that rare sort of charm that usually only happens in very old or hopelessly sick people, the charm of the defeated.—You look so cool, so cool, so enviably cool.

Reverend Tooker (*offstage right*):   Now looka here, boy, lemme show you how to get outa that!

Margaret: They're playing croquet. The moon has appeared and it's white, just beginning to turn a little bit yellow....

You were a wonderful lover....

Such a wonderful person to go to bed with, and I think mostly because you were really indifferent to it. Isn't that right? Never had any anxiety about it, did it naturally, easily, slowly, with absolute confidence and perfect calm, more like opening a door for a lady or seating her at a table than giving expression to any longing for her. Your indifference made you wonderful at lovemaking—*strange?*—but true....

Reverend Tooker: Oh! That's a beauty.

Doctor Baugh: Yeah. I got you boxed.

Margaret: You know, if I thought you would never, never, *never* make love to me again—I would go downstairs to the kitchen and pick out the longest and sharpest knife I could find and stick it straight into my heart, I swear that I would!

Reverend Tooker: Watch out, you're gonna miss it.

Doctor Baugh: You just don't know me, boy!

Margaret: But one thing I don't have is the charm of the defeated, my hat is still in the ring, and I am determined to win!

(There is the sound of croquet mallets hitting croquet balls.)

Reverend Tooker: Mmm—You're too slippery for me.

Margaret: —What is the victory of a cat on a hot tin roof?—I wish I knew....
        Just staying on it, I guess, as long as she can....

Doctor Baugh: Jus' like an eel, boy, jus' like an eel!

(More croquet sounds.)

Margaret: Later tonight I'm going to tell you I love you an' maybe by that time you'll be drunk enough to believe me. Yes, they're playing croquet....
        Big Daddy is dying of cancer....
        What were you thinking of when I caught you looking at me like that? Were you thinking of Skipper?

(Brick takes up his crutch, rises.)

Oh, excuse me, forgive me, but laws of silence don't work! No, laws of silence don't work....

(Brick crosses to the bar, takes a quick drink, and rubs his head with a towel.)

Laws of silence don't work....
        When something is festering in your memory or your imagination, laws of silence don't work, it's just like shutting a door and locking it on a house on fire in hope of forgetting that the house is burning. But not facing a fire doesn't put it out. Silence about a thing just magnifies it. It grows and festers in silence, becomes malignant....

(He drops his crutch.)

Brick: Give me my crutch.

(He has stopped rubbing his hair dry but still stands hanging onto the towel rack in a white towel-cloth robe.)

Margaret: Lean on me.

Brick: No, just give me my crutch.

Margaret: Lean on my shoulder.

Brick: *I don't want to lean on your shoulder, I want my crutch!*

(This is spoken like sudden lightning.)

Are you going to give me my crutch or do I have to get down on my knees on the floor and—

Margaret: *Here, here, take it, take it!*

(She has thrust the crutch at him.)

Brick *(hobbling out)*: Thanks...

Margaret: We mustn't scream at each other, the walls in this house have ears....

(He hobbles directly to liquor cabinet to get a new drink.)

    —but that's the first time I've heard you raise your voice in a long time, Brick. A crack in the wall?—Of composure?

    —I think that's a good sign....

    A sign of nerves in a player on the defensive!

(Brick turns and smiles at her coolly over his fresh drink.)

Brick: It just hasn't happened yet, Maggie.

Margaret: What?

Brick: The click I get in my head when I've had enough of this stuff to make me peaceful....

    Will you do me a favor?

Margaret: Maybe I will. What favor?

Brick: Just, just keep your voice down!

Margaret *(in a hoarse whisper)*: I'll do you that favor, I'll speak in a whisper, if not shut up completely, if *you* will do *me* a favor and make that drink your last one till after the party.

Brick: What party?

Margaret: Big Daddy's birthday party.

Brick: Is this Big Daddy's birthday?

Margaret: You know this is Big Daddy's birthday!

Brick: No, I don't, I forgot it.

Margaret: Well, I remembered it for you...

(They are both speaking as breathlessly as a pair of kids after a fight, drawing deep exhausted breaths and looking at each other with faraway eyes, shaking and panting together as if they had broken apart from a violent struggle.)

Brick: Good for you, Maggie.

Margaret: You just have to scribble a few lines on this card.

Brick: You scribble something, Maggie.

Margaret: It's got to be your handwriting; it's your present, I've given him my present; it's got to be your handwriting!

(The tension between them is building again, the voices becoming shrill once more.)

Brick: I didn't get him a present.

Margaret: I got one for you.

Brick: All right. You write the card, then.

Margaret: And have him know you didn't remember his birthday?

Brick: I didn't remember his birthday.

Margaret: You don't have to prove you didn't!

Brick: I don't want to fool him about it.

Margaret: Just write "Love, Brick!" for God's—

Brick: No.

Margaret: You've *got* to!

Brick: I don't have to do anything I don't want to do. You keep forgetting the conditions on which I agreed to stay on living with you.

Margaret (*out before she knows it*): I'm not living with you. We occupy
the same cage.

Brick: You've got to remember the conditions agreed on.

Sonny (*offstage*): Mommy, give it to me. I had it first.

Mae: Hush.

Margaret: They're impossible conditions!

Brick: Then why don't you—?

Sonny: I want it, I want it!

Mae: Get away!

Margaret: HUSH! Who is out there? Is somebody at the door?

(*There are footsteps in hall.*)

Mae (*outside*): May I enter a moment?

Margaret: Oh, *you!* Sure. Come in, Mae.

(*Mae enters bearing aloft the bow of a young lady's archery set.*)

Mae: Brick, is this thing yours?

Margaret: Why, Sister Woman—that's my Diana Trophy. Won it at the
intercollegiate archery contest on the Ole Miss campus.

Mae: It's a mighty dangerous thing to leave exposed round a house full
of nawmal rid-blooded children attracted t'weapons.

Margaret: "Nawmal rid-blooded children attracted t'weapons" ought t'be
taught to keep their hands off things that don't belong to them.

Mae: Maggie, honey, if you had children of your own you'd know how
funny that is. Will you please lock this up and put the key out of
reach?

Margaret: Sister Woman, nobody is plotting the destruction of your kiddies.—Brick and I still have our special archers' license. We're goin'
deerhuntin' on Moon Lake as soon as the season starts. I love to run
with dogs through chilly woods, run, run leap over obstructions—

(*She goes into the closet carrying the bow.*)

Mae: How's the injured ankle, Brick?

Brick: Doesn't hurt. Just itches.

Mae: Oh, my! Brick—Brick, you should've been downstairs after supper! Kiddies put on a show. Polly played the piano, Buster an' Sonny

drums, an then they turned out the lights an' Dixie an' Trixie puh-fawmed a toe dance in fairy costume with *spahkluhs*! Big Daddy just beamed! He just beamed!

Margaret (*from the closet with a sharp laugh*):   Oh, I bet. It breaks my heart that we missed it!

(*She reenters.*)

But Mae? Why did y'give dawgs' names to all your kiddies?

Mae: *Dogs'* names?

Margaret (*sweetly*):   Dixie, Trixie, Buster, Sonny, Polly!—Sounds like four dogs and a parrot...

Mae: Maggie?

(*Margaret turns with a smile.*)

Why are you so catty?

Margaret: Cause I'm a cat! But why can't *you* take a joke, Sister Woman?

Mae: Nothin' pleases me more than a joke that's funny. You know the real names of our kiddies. Buster's real name is Robert. Sonny's real name is Saunders. Trixie's real name is Marlene and Dixie's—

(*Gooper downstairs calls for her. "Hey, Mae! Sister Woman, intermission is over!"—She rushes to door, saying:*)

Intermission is over! See ya later!

Margaret: I wonder what Dixie's real name is?

Brick: Maggie, being catty doesn't help things any...

Margaret: I know! *WHY!*—Am I so catty?—Cause I'm consumed with envy an' eaten up with longing?—Brick, I'm going to lay out your beautiful Shantung silk suit from Rome and one of your monogrammed silk shirts. I'll put your cuff links in it, those lovely star sapphires I get you to wear so rarely....

Brick: I can't get trousers on over this plaster cast.

Margaret: Yes, you can, I'll help you.

Brick: I'm not going to get dressed, Maggie.

Margaret: Will you just put on a pair of white silk pajamas?

Brick: Yes, I'll do that, Maggie.

Margaret: *Thank* you, thank you so *much!*

Brick: Don't mention it.

Margaret: *Oh, Brick!* How long does it have t' go on? This punishment? Haven't I done time enough, haven't I served my term, can't I apply for a—pardon?

Brick: Maggie, you're spoiling my liquor. Lately your voice always sounds like you'd been running upstairs to warm somebody that the house was on fire!

Margaret: Well, no wonder, no wonder. Y'know what I feel like, Brick?

I feel all the time like a cat on a hot tin roof!

Brick: Then jump off the roof, jump off it, cats can jump off roofs and land on their four feet uninjured!

Margaret: Oh, yes!

Brick: Do it!—fo' God's sake, do it...

Margaret: Do what?

Brick: Take a lover!

Margaret: I can't see a man but you! Even with my eyes closed, I just see you! Why don't you get ugly, Brick, why don't you please get fat or ugly or something so I could stand it?

(She rushes to hall door, opens it, listens.)

The concert is still going on! Bravo, no-necks, bravo!

(She slams and locks door fiercely.)

Brick: What did you lock the door for?

Margaret: To give us a little privacy for a while.

Brick: You know better, Maggie.

Margaret: No, I don't know better....

(She rushes to gallery doors, draws the rose-silk drapes across them.)

Brick: Don't make a fool of yourself.

Margaret: I don't mind makin' a fool of myself over you!

Brick: I mind, Maggie. I feel embarrassed for you.

Margaret: Feel embarrassed! But don't continue my torture. I can't live on and on under these circumstances.

Brick: You agreed to—

Margaret: I know but—

Brick: —Accept that condition!

Margaret: *I CAN'T! CAN'T! CAN'T!*

(She seizes his shoulder.)

Brick: Let go!

(He breaks away from her and seizes the small boudoir chair and raises it like a lion-tamer facing a big circus cat.)

(Count five. She stares at him with her fist pressed to her mouth, then bursts into shrill, almost hysterical laughter. He remains grave for a moment, then grins and puts the chair down.)

(Big Mama calls through closed door.)

Big Mama: Son? Son? Son?

Brick: What is it, Big Mama?

Big Mama (*outside*):   Oh, son! We got the most wonderful news about Big
 Daddy. I just had t' run up an' tell you right this—

(She rattles the knob.)

—What's this door doin', locked faw? You all think there's robbers in
 the house?

Margaret: Big Mama, Brick is dressin, he's not dressed yet.

Big Mama: That's all right, it won't be the first time I've seen Brick not
 dressed. Come on, open this door!

*(Margaret, with a grimace, goes to unlock and open the hall door, as Brick
hobbles rapidly to the bathroom and kicks the door shut. Big Mama has
disappeared from the hall.)*

Margaret: Big Mama?

*(Big Mama appears through the opposite gallery doors behind Margaret,
huffing and puffing like an old bulldog. She is a short, stout woman; her
sixty years and 170 pounds have left her somewhat breathless most of the
time; she's always tensed like a boxer, or rather, a Japanese wrestler. Her
"family" was maybe a little superior to Big Daddy's, but not much. She
wears a black or silver lace dress and at least half a million in flashy gems.
She is very sincere.)*

Big Mama (*loudly, startling Margaret*):   Here—I come through Gooper's
 and Mae's gall'ry door. Where's Brick? *Brick*—Hurry on out of there
 son, I just have a second and want to give you the news about Big
 Daddy.—I hate locked doors in a house....

Margaret (*with affected lightness*):   I've noticed you do, Big Mama, but
 people have got to have *some* moments of privacy, don't they?

Big Mama: No, ma'am, not in *my* house. (*Without pause.*) Whacha took
 off you' dress faw? I thought that little lace dress was so sweet on
 yuh, honey.

Margaret: I thought it looked sweet on me, too, but one of m' cute little
 table-partners used it for a napkin so—!

Big Mama (*picking up stockings on floor*):   What?

Margaret: You know, Big Mama, Mae and Gooper's so touchy about those
 children—thanks, Big Mama...

*(Big Mama has thrust the picked-up stockings in Margaret's hand with a
grunt.)*

—that you just don't dare to suggest there's any room for improvement in their—

Big Mama: Brick, hurry out!—Shoot, Maggie, you just don't like
 children.

Margaret: I do SO like children! Adore them!—well brought up!

Big Mama (*gentle—loving*): Well, why don't you have some and bring them up well, then, instead of all the time pickin' on Gooper's an' Mae's?

Gooper (*shouting up the stairs*): Hey, hey, Big Mama, Betsy an' Hugh got to go, waitin' t' tell yuh g'by!

Big Mama: Tell 'em to hold their hawses, I'll be right down in a jiffy!

Gooper: Yes ma'am!

(*She turns to the bathroom door and calls out.*)

Big Mama: Son? Can you hear me in there?

(*There is a muffled answer.*)

We just got the full report from the laboratory at the Ochsner Clinic, completely negative, son, ev'rything negative, right on down the line! Nothin' a-tall's wrong with him but some little functional thing called a spastic colon. Can you hear me, son?

Margaret: He can hear you, Big Mama.

Big Mama: Then why don't he say something? God Almighty, a piece of news like that should make him shout. It made *me* shout, I can tell you. I shouted and sobbed and fell right down on my knees!—Look!

(*She pulls up her skirt.*)

See the bruises where I hit my kneecaps? Took both doctors to haul me back on my feet!

(*She laughs—she always laughs like hell at herself.*)

Big Daddy was furious with me! But ain't that wonderful news?

(*Facing bathroom again, she continues:*)

After all the anxiety we been through to git a report like that on Big Daddy's birthday? Big Daddy tried to hide how much of a load that news took off his mind, but didn't fool *me*. He was mighty close to crying about it *himself*!

(*Good-byes are shouted downstairs, and she rushes to door.*)

Gooper: Big Mama!

Big Mama: *Hold those people down there, don't let them go!*—Now, git dressed we're all comin' up to this room fo' Big Daddy's birthday party because of your ankle.—How's his ankle, Maggie?

Margaret: Well, he broke it, Big Mama.

Big Mama: I know he broke it.

(*A phone is ringing in hall. A Negro voice answers: "Mistuh Polly's res'dence."*)

I mean does it hurt him much still.

Margaret: I'm afraid I can't give you that information, Big Mama. You'll have to ask Brick if it hurts much still or not.

Sookey (*in the hall*):   It's Memphis, Mizz Polly, it's Miss Sally in Memphis.

Big Mama: Awright, Sookey.

(*Big Mama rushes into the hall and is heard shouting on the phone:*)

Hello, Miss Sally. How are you, Miss Sally?—Yes, well, I was just gonna call you about it. *Shoot!*—

Margaret: Brick, don't!

(*Big Mama raises her voice to a bellow.*)

Big Mama: *Miss Sally? Don't ever call me from the Gayoso Lobby, too much talk goes on in that hotel lobby, no wonder you can't hear me!* Now listen, Miss Sally. They's nothin' serious wrong with Big Daddy. We got the report just now, they's nothin' wrong but a thing called a—spastic! *SPASTIC!*—colon...

(*She appears at the hall door and calls to Margaret.*)

—Maggie, come out here and talk to that fool on the phone. I'm shouted breathless!

Margaret (*goes out and is heard sweetly at phone*):   Miss Sally? This is Brick's wife, Maggie. So nice to hear your voice. Can you hear *mine?* Well, *good!*—Big Mama just wanted you to know that they've got the report from the Ochsner Clinic and what Big Daddy has is a spastic colon. Yes. Spastic colon, Miss Sally. That's right, spastic colon. *G'bye, Miss Sally, hope I'll see you real soon!*

(*Hangs up a little before Miss Sally was probably ready to terminate the talk. She returns through the hall door.*)

She heard me perfectly. I've discovered with deaf people the thing to do is not shout at them but just enunciate clearly. My rich old Aunt Cornelia was deaf as the dead but I could make her hear me just by sayin' each word slowly, distinctly, close to her ear. I read her the *Commercial Appeal* ev'ry night, read her the classified ads in it, even, she never missed a word of it. But was she a mean ole thing! Know what I got when she died? Her unexpired subscriptions to five magazines and the Book-of-the-Month Club and a LIBRARY full of ev'ry dull book ever written! All else went to her hellcat of a sister... meaner than she was, even!

(*Big Mama has been straightening things up in the room during this speech.*)

Big Mama (*closing closet door on discarded clothes*):   *Miss Sally sure is a case!* Big Daddy says she's always got her hand out fo' something. He's not mistaken. That poor ole thing always has her hand out fo' somethin'. I don't think Big Daddy gives her as much as he should.

Gooper: Big Mama! Come on now! Betsy and Hugh can't wait no longer!
Big Mama (*shouting*): I'm comin'!

(*She starts out. At the hall door, turns and jerks a forefinger, first toward the bathroom door, then toward the liquor cabinet, meaning: "Has Brick been drinking?" Margaret pretends not to understand, cocks her head and raises her brows as if the pantomimic performance was completely mystifying to her.*)

(*Big Mama rushes back to Margaret:*)

Shoot! Stop playin' so dumb!—I mean has he been drinkin' that stuff much yet?

Margaret (*with a little laugh*): Oh! I think he had a highball after supper.
Big Mama: Don't laugh about it!—Some single men stop drinkin' when they git married and others start! Brick never touched liquor before he—!

Margaret (*crying out*): *THAT'S NOT FAIR!*

Big Mama: Fair or not fair I want to ask you a question, one question: D'you make Brick happy in bed?

Margaret: Why don't you ask if he makes *me* happy in bed?
Big Mama: Because I know that—
Margaret: *It works both ways!*
Big Mama: Something's not right! You're childless and my son drinks!
Gooper: Come on, Big Mama!

(*Gooper has called her downstairs and she has rushed to the door on the line above. She turns at the door and points at the bed.*)

—When a marriage goes on the rocks, the rocks are *there*, right *there*!

Margaret: *That's*—

(*Big Mama has swept out of the room and slammed the door.*)

—not—*fair...*

(*Margaret is alone, completely alone, and she feels it. She draws in, hunches her shoulders, raises her arms with fists clenched, shuts her eyes tight as a child about to be stabbed with a vaccination needle. When she opens her eyes again, what she sees is the long oval mirror and she rushes straight to it, stares into it with a grimace and says: "Who are you?"—Then she crouches a little and answers herself in a different voice which is high, thin, mocking: "I am Maggie the Cat!"—Straightens quickly as bathroom door opens a little and Brick calls out to her.*)

Brick: Has Big Mama gone?
Margaret: She's gone.

(He opens the bathroom door and hobbles out, with his liquor glass now empty, straight to the liquor cabinet. He is whistling softly. Margaret's head pivots on her long, slender throat to watch him.)

(She raises a hand uncertainly to the base of her throat, as if it was difficult for her to swallow, before she speaks:)

You know, our sex life didn't just peter out in the usual way, it was cut off short, long before the natural time for it to, and it's going to revive again, just as sudden as that. I'm confident of it. That's what I'm keeping myself attractive for. For the time when you'll see me again like other men see me. Yes, like other men see me. They still see me, Brick, and they like what they see. Uh-huh. Some of them would give their—

Look, Brick!

(She stands before the long oval mirror, touches her breast and then her hips with her two hands.)

How high my body stays on me!—Nothing has fallen on me—not a fraction....

(Her voice is soft and trembling: a pleading child's. At this moment as he turns to glance at her—a look which is like a player passing a ball to another player, third down and goal to go—she has to capture the audience in a grip so tight that she can hold it till the first intermission without any lapse of attention.)

Other men still want me. My face looks strained, sometimes, but I've kept my figure as well as you've kept yours, and men admire it. I still turn heads on the street. Why, last week in Memphis everywhere that I went men's eyes burned holes in my clothes, at the country club and in restaurants and department stores, there wasn't a man I met or walked by that didn't just eat me up with his eyes and turn around when I passed him and look back at me. Why, at Alice's party for her New York cousins, the best-lookin' man in the crowd—followed me upstairs and tried to force his way in the powder room with me, followed me to the door and tried to force his way in!

Brick: Why didn't you let him, Maggie?

Margaret: Because I'm not that common, for one thing. Not that I wasn't almost tempted to. You like to know who it was? It was Sonny Boy Maxwell, that's who!

Brick: Oh, yeah, Sonny Boy Maxwell, he was a good end-runner but had a little injury to his back and had to quit.

Margaret: He has no injury now and has no wife and still has a lech for me!

Brick: I see no reason to lock him out of a powder room in that case.

Margaret: And have someone catch me at it? I'm not that stupid. Oh, I might sometime cheat on you with someone, since you're so insultingly eager to have me do it!—But if I do, you can be damned sure it will be in a place and a time where no one but me and the man could possibly know. Because I'm not going to give you any excuse to divorce me for being unfaithful or anything else....

Brick: Maggie, I wouldn't divorce you for being unfaithful or anything else. Don't you know that? Hell. I'd be relieved to know that you'd found yourself a lover.

Margaret: Well, I'm taking no chances. No, I'd rather stay on this hot tin roof.

Brick: A hot tin roof's 'n uncomfo'table place t' stay on....

(He starts to whistle softly.)

Margaret *(through his whistle)*:   Yeah, but I can stay on it just as long as I have to.

Brick: You could leave me, Maggie.

(He resumes whistle. She wheels about to glare at him.)

Margaret: *Don't want to and will not!* Besides if I did, you don't have a cent to pay for it but what you get from Big Daddy and he's dying of cancer!

(For the first time a realization of Big Daddy's doom seems to penetrate to Brick's consciousness, visibly, and he looks at Margaret.)

Brick: Big Mama just said he *wasn't*, that the report was okay.

Margaret: That's what she thinks because she got the same story that they gave Big Daddy. And was just as taken in by it as he was, poor ole things....

But tonight they're going to tell her the truth about it. When Big Daddy goes to bed, they're going to tell her that he is dying of cancer.

(She slams the dresser drawer.)

—It's malignant and it's terminal.

Brick: Does Big Daddy know it?

Margaret: Hell, do they *ever* know it? Nobody says, "You're dying." You have to fool them. They have to fool *themselves*.

Brick: Why?

Margaret: *Why?* Because human beings dream of life everlasting, that's the reason! But most of them want it on earth and not in heaven.

(He gives a short, hard laugh at her touch of humor.)

Well....*(She touches up her mascara.)* That's how it is, anyhow....*(She looks about.)* Where did I put down my cigarette? Don't want to burn up the home-place, at least not with Mae and Gooper and their five monsters in it!

(She has found it and sucks at it greedily. Blows out smoke and continues:)

So this is Big Daddy's last birthday. And Mae and Gooper, they know it, oh, *they* know it, all right. They got the first information from the Ochsner Clinic. That's why they rushed down here with their no-neck monsters. Because. Do you know something? Big Daddy's made no will? Big Daddy's never made out any will in his life, and so this campaign's afoot to impress him, forcibly as possible, with the fact that you drink and I've borne no children!

(He continues to stare at her a moment, then mutters something sharp but not audible and hobbles rather rapidly out onto the long gallery in the fading, much faded, gold light.)

Margaret *(continuing her liturgical chant)*: Y'know, I'm *fond* of Big Daddy, I am genuinely fond of that old man, I really *am*, you know....

Brick *(faintly, vaguely)*: Yes, I know you are....

Margaret: I've always sort of admired him in spite of his coarseness, his four-letter words and so forth. Because Big Daddy *is* what he *is*, and he makes no bones about it. He hasn't turned gentleman farmer, he's still a Mississippi redneck, as much of a redneck as he must have been when he was just overseer here on the old Jack Straw and Peter Ochello place. But he got hold of it an' built it into th' biggest an' finest plantation in the Delta.—I've always *liked* Big Daddy....

(She crosses to the proscenium.)

Well, this is Big Daddy's last birthday. I'm sorry about it. But I'm facing the facts. It takes money to take care of a drinker and that's the office that I've been elected to lately.

Brick: You don't have to take care of me.

Margaret: Yes, I do. Two people in the same boat have got to take care of each other. At least you want money to buy more Echo Spring when this supply is exhausted, or will you be satisfied with a ten-cent beer?

Mae an' Gooper are plannin' to freeze us out of Big Daddy's estate because you drink and I'm childless. But we can defeat that plan. We're *going* to defeat that plan!

Brick, y'know, I've been so God damn disgustingly poor all my life!—That's the *truth*, Brick!

Brick: I'm not sayin' it isn't.

Margaret: Always had to suck up to people I couldn't stand because they had money and I was poor as Job's turkey.[6] You don't know what that's like. Well, I'll tell you, it's like you would feel a thousand miles away

---

[6]The Biblical character Job suffers and loses all of his possessions; the point of this 19C/20C American saying is that since Job is poor, any turkey he owns is poorer still.

from Echo Spring!—And had to get back to it on that broken ankle...
without a crutch!

That's how it feels to be as poor as Job's turkey and have to suck
up to relatives that you hated because they had money and all you
had was a bunch of hand-me-down clothes and a few old moldly three-
percent government bonds. My daddy loved his liquor, he fell in love
with his liquor the way you've fallen in love with Echo Spring!—And
my poor Mama, having to maintain some semblance of social position,
to keep appearances up, on an income of one hundred and fifty dollars
a month on those old government bonds!

When I came out, the year that I made my debut, I had just two
evening dresses! One Mother made me from a pattern in *Vogue*, the
other a hand-me-down from a snotty rich cousin I hated!

—The dress that I married you in was my grandmother's weddin'
gown....

So that's why I'm like a cat on a hot tin roof!

*(Brick is still on the gallery. Someone below calls up to him in a warm Negro
voice, "Hiya, Mistuh Brick, how yuh feelin'?" Brick raises his liquor glass as
if that answered the question.)*

Margaret: You can be young without money, but you can't be old without it. You've got to be old *with* money because to be old without it is
just too awful, you've got to be one or the other, either *young* or *with
money*, you can't be old and *without* it.—That's the *truth*, Brick....

(Brick whistles softly, vaguely.)

Well, now I'm dressed, I'm all dressed, there's nothing else for me
to do.

(Forlornly, almost fearfully.)

I'm dressed, all dressed, nothing else for me to do...

(She moves about restlessly, aimlessly, and speaks, as if to herself.)

What am I—? Oh!—my bracelets....

*(She starts working a collection of bracelets over her hands onto her wrists,
about six on each, as she talks.)*

I've thought a whole lot about it and now I know when I made my
mistake. Yes, I made my mistake when I told you the truth about
that thing with Skipper. Never should have confessed it, a fatal error,
tellin' you about that thing with Skipper.

Brick: Maggie, shut up about Skipper. I mean it, Maggie; you got to shut
up about Skipper.

Margaret: You ought to understand that Skipper and I—

Brick: You don't think I'm serious, Maggie? You're fooled by the fact that I am saying this quiet? Look, Maggie. What you're doing is a dangerous thing to do. You're—you're—you're—foolin' with something that—nobody ought to fool with.

Margaret: This time I'm going to finish what I have to say to you. Skipper and I made love, if love you could call it, because it made both of us feel a little bit closer to you. You see, you son of a bitch, you asked too much of people, of me, of him, of all the unlucky poor damned sons of bitches that happen to love you, and there was a whole pack of them, yes, there was a pack of them besides me and Skipper, you asked too goddamn much of people that loved you, you—superior creature!—you godlike being!—And so we made love to each other to dream it was you, both of us! Yes, yes, yes! Truth, truth! What's so awful about it? I like it, I think the truth is—yeah! I shouldn't have told you....

Brick (*holding his head unnaturally still and uptilted a bit*):   It was Skipper that told me about it. Not you, Maggie.

Margaret: I told you!

Brick: After he told me!

Margaret: What does it matter who—?

Dixie: I got your mallet, I got your mallet.

Trixie: Give it to me, give it to me. It's mine.

(*Brick turns suddenly out upon the gallery and calls:*)

Brick: Little girl! Hey, little girl!

Little Girl (*at a distance*):   What, Uncle Brick?

Brick: Tell the folks to come up!—Bring everybody upstairs!

Trixie: It's mine, it's mine.

Margaret: I can't stop myself! I'd go on telling you this in front of them all, if I had to!

Brick: Little girl! Go on, go on, will you? Do what I told you, call them!

Dixie: Okay.

Margaret: Because it's got to be told and you, you!—you never let me!

(*She sobs, then controls herself, and continues almost calmly.*)

It was one of those beautiful, ideal things they tell about in the Greek legends, it couldn't be anything else, you being you, and that's what made it so sad, that's what made it so awful, because it was love that never could be carried through to anything satisfying or even talked about plainly.

Brick: Maggie, you gotta stop this.

Margaret: Brick, I tell you, you got to believe me, Brick, I *do* understand all about it! I—I think it was—*noble!* Can't you tell I'm sincere when I say I respect it? My only point, the only point that I'm making, is

life has got to be allowed to continue even after the *dream* of life
is—all—over....

*(Brick is without his crutch. Leaning on furniture, he crosses to pick it up as
she continues as if possessed by a will outside herself:)*

Why I remember when we double dated at college, Gladys Fitzgerald
and I and you and Skipper, it was more like a date between you and
Skipper. Gladys and I were just sort of tagging along as if it was necessary to chaperone you!—to make a good public impression—

Brick *(turns to face her, half lifting his crutch)*: Maggie, you want me to
hit you with this crutch? Don't you know I could kill you with this
crutch?

Margaret: Good Lord, man, d' you think I'd care if you did?

Brick: One man has one great good true thing in his life. One great good
thing which is true!—I had friendship with Skipper.—You are naming
it dirty!

Margaret: I'm not naming it dirty! I am naming it clean.

Brick: Not love with you, Maggie, but friendship with Skipper was that
one great true thing, and you are naming it dirty!

Margaret: Then you haven't been listenin', not understood what I'm saying! I'm naming it so damn clean that it killed poor Skipper!—You two
had something that had to be kept on ice, yes, incorruptible, yes!—
and death was the only icebox where you could keep it....

Brick: I married you, Maggie. Why would I marry you, Maggie, if I was—?

Margaret: Brick, let me finish!—I know, believe me I know, that it was
only Skipper that harbored even any *unconscious* desire for anything
not perfectly pure between you two!—Now let me skip a little. You
married me early that summer we graduated out of Ole Miss, and we
were happy, weren't we, we were blissful, yes, hit heaven together
ev'ry time that we loved! But that fall you an' Skipper turned down
wonderful offers of jobs in order to keep on bein' football heroes—
pro-football heroes. You organized the Dixie Stars that fall, so you
could keep on bein' teammates forever! But somethin' was not right
with it!—*Me included!*—between you. Skipper began hittin' the bottle... you got a spinal injury—couldn't play the Thanksgivin' game
in Chicago, watched it on TV from a traction bed in Toledo. I joined
Skipper. The Dixie Stars lost because poor Skipper was drunk. We
drank together that night all night in the bar of the Blackstone and
when cold day was comin' up over the Lake an' we were comin' out
drunk to take a dizzy look at it, I said, "SKIPPER! STOP LOVIN' MY
HUSBAND OR TELL HIM HE'S GOT TO LET YOU ADMIT IT TO HIM!"—one
way or another!

HE SLAPPED ME HARD ON THE MOUTH!—then turned and ran without stopping once, I am sure, all the way back into his room at the Blackstone....

—When I came to his room that night, with a little scratch like a shy little mouse at his door, he made that pitiful, ineffectual little attempt to prove that what I had said wasn't true....

(Brick strikes at her with crutch, a blow that shatters the gemlike lamp on the table.)

—In this way, I destroyed him, by telling him truth that he and his world which he was born and raised in, yours and his world, had told him could not be told?

—From then on Skipper was nothing at all but a receptacle for liquor and drugs....

—*Who shot cock robin? I with my*—

(She throws back her head with tight shut eyes.)

—*merciful arrow!*

(Brick strikes at her; misses.)

Missed me!—Sorry,—I'm not tryin' to whitewash my behavior, Christ, no! Brick, I'm not good. I don't know why people have to pretend to be good, nobody's good. The rich or the well-to-do can afford to respect moral patterns, conventional moral patterns, but I could never afford to, yeah, but—I'm honest! Give me credit for just that, will you *please?*—Born poor, raised poor, expect to die poor unless I manage to get us something out of what Big Daddy leaves when he dies of cancer! But Brick?!—*Skipper is dead! I'm alive!* Maggie the cat is—

(Brick hops awkwardly forward and strikes at her again with his crutch.)

—*alive! I am alive, alive! I am...*

(He hurls the crutch at her, across the bed she took refuge behind, and pitches forward on the floor as she completes her speech.)

—*alive!*

(A little girl, Dixie, bursts into the room, wearing an Indian war bonnet and firing a cap pistol at Margaret and shouting: "Bang, bang, bang!")

(Laughter downstairs floats through the open hall door. Margaret had crouched gasping to bed at child's entrance. She now rises and says with cool fury:)

Little girl, your mother or someone should teach you—(*gasping*)—to knock at a door before you come into a room. Otherwise people might think that you—lack—good breeding....

Dixie: Yanh, yanh, yanh, what is Uncle Brick doin' on th' floor?

Brick: I tried to kill your Aunt Maggie, but I failed—and I fell. Little girl, give me my crutch so I can get up off th' floor.

Margaret: Yes, give your uncle his crutch, he's a cripple, honey, he broke his ankle last night jumping hurdles on the high school athletic field!

Dixie: What were you jumping hurdles for, Uncle Brick?

Brick: Because I used to jump them, and people like to do what they used to do, even after they've stopped being able to do it....

Margaret: That's right, that's your answer, now go away, little girl.

(Dixie fires cap pistol at Margaret three times.)

Stop, you stop that, monster! You little no-neck monster!

(She seizes the cap pistol and hurls it through gallery doors.)

Dixie   (*with a precocious instinct for the cruelest thing*): You're *jealous!*— You're just jealous because you can't have babies!

(She sticks out her tongue at Margaret as she sashays past her with her stomach stuck out, to the gallery. Margaret slams the gallery doors and leans panting against them. There is a pause. Brick has replaced his spilt drink and sits, faraway, on the great four-poster bed.)

Margaret: You see?—they gloat over us being childless, even in front of their five little no-neck monsters!

(Pauses. Voices approach on the stairs.)

Brick?—I've been to a doctor in Memphis, a—a gynecologist....
I've been completely examined, and there is no reason why we can't have a child whenever we want one. And this is my time by the calendar to conceive. Are you listening to me? Are you? Are you LISTENING TO ME!

Brick: Yes. I hear you, Maggie.

(His attention returns to her inflamed face.)

—But how in hell on earth do you imagine—that you're going to have a child by a man that can't stand you?

Margaret: That's a problem that I will have to work out.

(She wheels about to face the hall door.)

Mae (*offstage left*):   Come on, Big Daddy. We're all goin' up to Brick's room.

(From offstage left, voices: Reverend Tooker, Doctor Baugh, Mae.)

Margaret: *Here they come!*

(The lights dim.)

ACT 2

(There is no lapse of time. Margaret and Brick are in the same positions they held at the end of act 1.)

Margaret (*at door*): Here they come!

(Big Daddy appears first, a tall man with a fierce, anxious look, moving carefully not to betray his weakness even, or especially, to himself.)

Gooper: I read in the *Register* that you're getting a new memorial window.

(Some of the people are approaching through the hall, others along the gallery: voices from both directions. Gooper and Reverend Tooker become visible outside gallery doors, and their voices come in clearly.)

(They pause outside as Gooper lights a cigar.)

Reverend Tooker (*vivaciously*): Oh, but St. Paul's in Grenada has three memorial windows, and the latest one is a Tiffany stained-glass window that cost twenty-five hundred dollars, a picture of Christ the Good Shepherd with a Lamb in His arms.

Margaret: Big Daddy.

Big Daddy: Well, Brick.

Brick: Hello Big Daddy.—Congratulations!

Big Daddy: —Crap....

Gooper: Who give that window, Preach?

Reverend Tooker: Clyde Fletcher's widow. Also presented St. Paul's with a baptismal font.

Gooper: Y'know what somebody ought t' give your church is a *coolin'* system, Preach.

Mae (*almost religiously*): —Let's see now, they've had their *tyyy*-phoid shots, and their tetanus shots, their diphtheria shots and their hepatitis shots and their polio shots, they got *those* shots every month from May through September, and—Gooper? Hey! Gooper!—What all have the kiddies been shot faw?

Reverend Tooker: Yes, siree, Bob! And y'know what Gus Hamma's family gave in his memory to the church at Two Rivers? A complete new stone parish-house with a basketball court in the basement and a—

Big Daddy (*uttering a loud barking laugh which is far from truly mirthful*): Hey, Preach! What's all this talk about memorials, Preach? Y' think somebody's about t' kick off around here? 'S that it?

(Startled by this interjection, Reverend Tooker decides to laugh at the question almost as loud as he can.)

(How he would answer the question we'll never know, as he's spared that embarrassment by the voice of Gooper's wife, Mae, rising high and clear as she appears with "Doc" Baugh, the family doctor, through the ball door.)

Margaret (*overlapping a bit*): Turn on the hi-fi, Brick! Let's have some music t' start off th' party with!

Brick: You turn it on, Maggie.

(*The talk becomes so general that the room sounds like a great aviary of chattering birds. Only Brick remains unengaged, leaning upon the liquor cabinet with his faraway smile, an ice cube in a paper napkin with which he now and then rubs his forehead. He doesn't respond to Margaret's command. She bounds forward and stoops over the instrument panel of the console.*)

Gooper: We gave 'em that thing for a third anniversary present, got three speakers in it.

(*The room is suddenly blasted by the climax of a Wagnerian opera or a Beethoven symphony.*)

Big Daddy: *Turn that damn thing off!*

(*Almost instant silence, almost instantly broken by the shouting charge of Big Mama, entering through hall door like a charging rhino.*)

Big Mama: Wha's my Brick, wha's mah precious baby!!

Big Daddy: *Sorry! Turn it back on!*

(*Everyone laughs very loud. Big Daddy is famous for his jokes at Big Mama's expense, and nobody laughs louder at these jokes than Big Mama herself, though sometimes they're pretty cruel and Big Mama has to pick up or fuss with something to cover the hurt that the loud laugh doesn't quite cover.*)

(*On this occasion, a happy occasion because the dread in her heart has also been lifted by the false report on Big Daddy's condition, she giggles, grotesquely, coyly, in Big Daddy's direction and bears down upon Brick, all very quick and alive.*)

Big Mama: Here he is, here's my precious baby! What's that you've got in your hand? You put that liquor down, son, your hand was made fo' holdin' somethin' better than that!

Gooper: Look at Brick put it down!

(*Brick has obeyed Big Mama by draining the glass and handing it to her. Again everyone laughs, some high, some low.*)

Big Mama: Oh, you bad boy, you, you're my bad little boy. Give Big Mama a kiss, you bad boy, you!—Look at him shy away, will you? Brick never liked bein' kissed or made a fuss over, I guess because he's always had too much of it!

Son, you turn that thing off!

(*Brick has switched on the TV set.*)

I can't stand TV, radio was bad enough but TV has gone it one better, I mean—(*plops wheezing in chair*)—one worse, ha ha! Now what'm I sittin' down here faw? I want t' sit next to my sweetheart on the sofa, hold hands with him and love him up a little!

(*Big Mama has on a black and white figured chiffon. The large irregular patterns, like the markings of some massive animal, the luster of her great diamonds and many pearls, the brilliants set in the silver frames of her glasses, her riotous voice, booming laugh, have dominated the room since she entered. Big Daddy has been regarding her with a steady grimace of chronic annoyance.*)

Big Mama (*still louder*): Preacher, Preacher, hey, Preach! Give me you' hand an' help me up from this chair!
Reverend Tooker: None of your tricks, Big Mama!
Big Mama: What tricks? You give me you' hand so I can get up an'—

(*Reverend Tooker extends her his hand. She grabs it and pulls him into her lap with a shrill laugh that spans an octave in two notes.*)

Ever seen a preacher in a fat lady's lap? Hey, hey, folks! Ever seen a preacher in a fat lady's lap?

(*Big Mama is notorious throughout the Delta for this sort of inelegant horseplay. Margaret looks on with indulgent humor, sipping Dubonnet "on the rocks" and watching Brick, but Mae and Gooper exchange signs of humorless anxiety over these antics, the sort of behavior which Mae thinks may account for their failure to quite get in with the smartest young married set in Memphis, despite all. One of the Negroes, Lacey or Sookey, peeks in, cackling. They are waiting for a sign to bring in the cake and champagne. But Big Daddy's not amused. He doesn't understand why, in spite of the infinite mental relief he's received from the doctor's report, he still has these same old fox teeth in his guts. "This spastic condition is something else," he says to himself, but aloud he roars at Big Mama:*)

Big Daddy: *BIG MAMA, WILL YOU QUIT HORSIN'?*—You're too old an' too fat fo' that sort of crazy kid stuff an' besides a woman with your blood pressure—she had two hundred last spring!—is riskin' a stroke when you mess around like that....

(*Mae blows on a pitch pipe.*)

Big Mama: Here comes Big Daddy's birthday!

(*Negroes in white jackets enter with an enormous birthday cake ablaze with candles and carrying buckets of champagne with satin ribbons about the bottle necks.*)

(*Mae and Gooper strike up song, and everybody, including the Negroes and Children, joins in. Only Brick remains aloof.*)

Everyone: Happy birthday to you.
>   Happy birthday to you.
>   Happy birthday, Big Daddy—

(Some sing: "Dear, Big Daddy!")

>   Happy birthday to you.

(Some sing: "How old are you?")

(Mae has come down center and is organizing her children like a chorus. She gives them a barely audible: "One, two, three!" and they are off in the new tune.)

Children: Skinamarinka—dinka—dink
>   Skinamarinka—do
>   We love you.
>   Skinamarinka—dinka—dink
>   Skinamarinka—do.

(All together, they turn to Big Daddy.)

>   Big Daddy, you!

(They turn back front, like a musical comedy chorus.)

>   We love you in the morning;
>   We love you in the night.
>   We love you when we're with you,
>   And we love you out of sight.
>   Skinamarinka—dinka—dink
>   Skinamarinka—do.

(Mae turns to Big Mama.)

>   Big Mama, too!

(Big Mama bursts into tears. The Negroes leave.)

Big Daddy: Now Ida, what the hell is the matter with you?
Mae: She's just so happy.
Big Mama: I'm just so happy, Big Daddy, I have to cry or something.

(Sudden and loud in the hush:)

>   Brick, do you know the wonderful news that Doc Baugh got from the clinic about Big Daddy? Big Daddy's one hundred percent!
Margaret: Isn't that wonderful?
Big Mama: He's just one hundred percent. Passed the examination with flying colors. Now that we know there's nothing wrong with Big Daddy but a spastic colon, I can tell you something. I was worried sick half out of my mind, for fear that Big Daddy might have a thing like—

(Margaret cuts through this speech, jumping up and exclaiming shrilly:)

Margaret: Brick, honey, aren't you going to give Big Daddy his birthday present?

(Passing by him, she snatches his liquor glass from him.)

(She picks up a fancily wrapped package.)

Here it is, Big Daddy, this is from Brick!

Big Mama: This is the biggest birthday Big Daddy's ever had, a hundred presents and bushels of telegrams from—

Mae *(at same time)*:   What is it, Brick?

Gooper: I bet 500 to 50 that Brick don't *know* what it is.

Big Mama: The fun of presents is not knowing what they are till you open the package. Open your present, Big Daddy.

Big Daddy: Open it you'self. I want to ask Brick somethin! Come here, Brick.

Margaret: Big Daddy's callin' you, Brick.

(She is opening the package.)

Brick: Tell Big Daddy I'm crippled.

Big Daddy: I see you're crippled. I want to know how you got crippled.

Margaret *(making diversionary tactics)*:   *Oh, look, oh, look, why, it's a cashmere robe!*

(She holds the robe up for all to see.)

Mae: You sound surprised, Maggie.

Margaret: I never saw one before.

Mae: That's funny.—*Hah!*

Margaret *(turning on her fiercely, with a brilliant smile)*:   Why is it funny? All my family ever had was family—and luxuries such as cashmere robes still surprise me!

Big Daddy *(ominously)*:   Quiet!

Mae *(heedless in her fury)*:   I don't see how you could be so surprised when you bought it yourself at Loewenstein's in Memphis last Saturday. You know how I know?

Big Daddy: I said, Quiet!

Mae: —I know because the salesgirl that sold it to you waited on me and said, Oh, Mrs. Pollitt, your sister-in-law just bought a cashmere robe for your husband's father!

Margaret: Sister Woman! Your talents are wasted as a housewife and mother, you really ought to be with the FBI or—

Big Daddy: QUIET!

(Reverend Tooker's reflexes are slower than the others'. He finishes a sentence after the bellow.)

Reverend Tooker (*to Doc Baugh*):   —the Stork and the Reaper are running neck and neck!

(*He starts to laugh gaily when he notices the silence and Big Daddy's glare. His laugh dies falsely.*)

Big Daddy: Preacher, I hope I'm not butting in on more talk about memorial stained-glass windows, am I, Preacher?

(*Reverend Tooker laughs feebly, then coughs dryly in the embarrassed silence.*)

Preacher?

Big Mama: Now, Big Daddy, don't you pick on Preacher!

Big Daddy (*raising his voice*):   You ever hear that expression all hawk and no spit? You bring that expression to mind with that little dry cough of yours, all hawk an' no spit....

(*The pause is broken only by a short startled laugh from Margaret, the only one there who is conscious of and amused by the grotesque.*)

Mae (*raising her arms and jangling her bracelets*):   I wonder if the mosquitoes are active tonight?

Big Daddy: What's that, Little Mama? Did you make some remark?

Mae: Yes, I said I wondered if the mosquitoes would eat us alive if we went out on the gallery for a while.

Big Daddy: Well, if they do, I'll have your bones pulverized for fertilizer!

Big Mama (*quickly*):   Last week we had an airplane spraying the place and I think it done some good, at least I haven't had a—

Big Daddy (*cutting her speech*):   Brick, they tell me, if what they tell me is true, that you done some jumping last night on the high school athletic field?

Big Mama: Brick, Big Daddy is talking to you, son.

Brick (*smiling vaguely over his drink*):   What was that, Big Daddy?

Big Daddy: They said you done some jumping on the high school track field last night.

Brick: That's what they told me, too.

Big Daddy: Was it jumping or humping that you were doing out there? What were you doing out there at three a.m., layin' a woman on that cinder track?

Big Mama: Big Daddy, you are off the sick-list, now, and I'm not going to excuse you for talkin' so—

Big Daddy: Quiet!

Big Mama: —*nasty* in front of Preacher and—

Big Daddy: QUIET!—I ast you, Brick, if you was cuttin' yourself a piece o' poon-tang[7] last night on that cinder track? I thought maybe you were chasin' poon-tang on that track an' tripped over something in the heat of the chase—'sthat it?

[7]Sexual activity, perhaps from the French word "putain" (prostitute).

(Gooper laughs, loud and false, others nervously following suit. Big Mama stamps her foot, and purses her lips, crossing to Mae and whispering something to her as Brick meets his father's hard, intent, grinning stare with a slow, vague smile that he offers all situations from behind the screen of his liquor.)

Brick: No, sir, I don't think so....

Mae (*at the same time, sweetly*):   Reverend Tooker, let's you and I take a stroll on the widow's walk.

(She and the preacher go out on the gallery as Big Daddy says:)

Big Daddy: Then what the hell were you doing out there at three o'clock in the morning?

Brick: Jumping the hurdles, Big Daddy, runnin' and jumpin' the hurdles, but those high hurdles have gotten too high for me, now.

Big Daddy: Cause you was drunk?

Brick (*his vague smile fading a little*):   Sober I wouldn't have tried to jump the *low* ones....

Big Mama (*quickly*):   Big Daddy, blow out the candles on your birthday cake!

Margaret (*at the same time*):   I want to propose a toast to Big Daddy Pollitt on his sixty-fifth birthday, the biggest cotton planter in—

Big Daddy (*bellowing with fury and disgust*):   *I told you to stop it, now stop it, quit this—!*

Big Mama (*coming in front of Big Daddy with the cake*):   Big Daddy, I will not allow you to talk that way, not even on your birthday, I—

Big Daddy: I'll talk like I want to on my birthday, Ida, or any other god-damn day of the year and anybody here that don't like it knows what they can do!

Big Mama: You don't mean that!

Big Daddy: What makes you think I don't mean it?

(Meanwhile various discreet signals have been exchanged and Gooper has also gone out on the gallery.)

Big Mama: I just know you don't mean it.

Big Daddy: You don't know a goddamn thing and you never did!

Big Mama: Big Daddy, you don't mean that.

Big Daddy: Oh, yes, I do, oh, yes, I do, I mean it! I put up with a whole lot of crap around here because I thought I was dying. And you thought I was dying and you started taking over, well, you can stop taking over now, Ida, because I'm not gonna die, you can just stop now this business of taking over because you're not taking over be-cause I'm not dying, I went through the laboratory and the goddamn exploratory operation and there's nothing wrong with me but a spastic colon. And I'm not dying of cancer which you thought I was dying of. Ain't that so? Didn't you think that I was dying of cancer, Ida?

(Almost everybody is out on the gallery but the two old people glaring at each other across the blazing cake.)

(Big Mama's chest heaves and she presses a fat fist to her mouth.)

(Big Daddy continues, hoarsely:)

Ain't that so, Ida? Didn't you have an idea I was dying of cancer and now you could take control of this place and everything on it? I got that impression, I seemed to get that impression. Your loud voice everywhere, your fat old body butting in here and there!

Big Mama: Hush! The Preacher!

Big Daddy: Fuck the goddamn preacher!

(Big Mama gasps loudly and sits down on the sofa which is almost too small for her.)

Did you hear what I said? I said fuck the goddamn preacher!

(Somebody closes the gallery doors from outside just as there is a burst of fireworks and excited cries from the children.)

Big Mama: I never seen you act like this before and I can't think what's got in you!

Big Daddy: I went through all that laboratory and operation and all just so I would know if you or me was boss here! Well, now it turns out that I am and you ain't—and that's my birthday present—and my cake and champagne!—because for three years now you been gradually taking over. Bossing. Talking. Sashaying your fat old body around the place I made! I made this place! I was overseer on it! I was the overseer on the old Straw and Ochello plantation. I quit school at ten! I quit school at ten years old and went to work like a nigger in the fields. And I rose to be overseer of the Straw and Ochello plantation. And old Straw died and I was Ochello's partner and the place got bigger and bigger and bigger and bigger and bigger! I did all that myself with no goddamn help from you, and now you think you're just about to take over. Well, I am just about to tell you that you are not just about to take over, you are not just about to take over a God damn thing. Is that clear to you, Ida? Is that very plain to you, now? Is that understood completely? I been through the laboratory from A to Z. I've had the goddamn exploratory operation, and nothing is wrong with me but a spastic colon—made spastic, I guess, by *disgust!* By all the goddamn lies and liars that I have had to put up with and all the goddamn hypocrisy that I lived with all these forty years that we been livin' together!

Hey! Ida!! Blow out the candles on the birthday cake! Purse up your lips and draw a deep breath and blow out the goddamn candles on the cake!

Big Mama: Oh, Big Daddy, oh, oh, oh, Big Daddy!

Big Daddy: What's the matter with you?

Big Mama: *In all these years you never believed that I loved you??*

Big Daddy: Huh?

Big Mama: *And I did, I did so much, I did love you!*—I even loved your hate and your hardness, Big Daddy!

(She sobs and rushes awkwardly out onto the gallery.)

Big Daddy (*to himself*):   *Wouldn't it be funny if that was true....*

(A pause is followed by a burst of light in the sky from the fireworks.)
    BRICK! HEY, BRICK!

(He stands over his blazing birthday cake.)

(After some moments, Brick hobbles in on his crutch, holding his glass.)

(Margaret follows him with a bright, anxious smile.)

        I didn't call you, Maggie. I called Brick.

Margaret: I'm just delivering him to you.

(She kisses Brick on the mouth which he immediately wipes with the back of his hand. She flies girlishly back out. Brick and his father are alone.)

Big Daddy: Why did you do that?

Brick: Do what, Big Daddy?

Big Daddy: Wipe her kiss off your mouth like she'd spit on you.

Brick: I don't know. I wasn't conscious of it.

Big Daddy: That woman of yours has a better shape on her than Gooper's but somehow or other they got the same look about them.

Brick: What sort of look is that, Big Daddy?

Big Daddy: I don't know how to describe it but it's the same look.

Brick: They don't look peaceful, do they?

Big Daddy: No, they sure in hell don't.

Brick: They look nervous as cats?

Big Daddy: That's right, they look nervous as cats.

Brick: Nervous as a couple of cats on a hot tin roof?

Big Daddy: That's right, boy, they look like a couple of cats on a hot tin roof. It's funny that you and Gooper being so different would pick out the same type of woman.

Brick: Both of us married into society, Big Daddy.

Big Daddy: Crap...I wonder what gives them both that look?

Brick: Well. They're sittin' in the middle of a big piece of land, Big Daddy, twenty-eight thousand acres is a pretty big piece of land and so they're squaring off on it, each determined to knock off a bigger piece of it than the other whenever you let it go.

Big Daddy: I got a surprise for those women. I'm not gonna let it go for a long time yet if that's what they're waiting for.

Brick: That's right, Big Daddy. You just sit tight and let them scratch each other's eyes out....

Big Daddy: You bet your life I'm going to sit tight on it and let those sons of bitches scratch their eyes out, ha ha ha....

But Gooper's wife's a good breeder, you got to admit she's fertile. Hell, at supper tonight she had them all at the table and they had to put a couple of extra leafs in the table to make room for them, she's got five head of them, now, and another one's comin'.

Brick: Yep, number six is comin'...

Big Daddy: Six hell, she'll probably drop a litter next time. Brick, you know, I swear to God, I don't know the way it happens.

Brick: The way what happens, Big Daddy?

Big Daddy: You git you a piece of land, by hook or crook, an' things start growin' on it, things accumulate on it, and the first thing you know it's completely out of hand, completely out of hand!

Brick: Well, they say nature hates a vacuum, Big Daddy.

Big Daddy: That's what they say, but sometimes I think that a vacuum is a hell of a lot better than some of the stuff that nature replaces it with. Is someone out there by that door?

Gooper: Hey Mae.

Brick: Yep.

Big Daddy: Who?

(He has lowered his voice.)

Brick: Someone int'rested in what we say to each other.

Big Daddy: Gooper?—*GOOPER!*

(After a discreet pause, Mae appears in the gallery door.)

Mae: Did you call Gooper, Big Daddy?

Big Daddy: Aw, it was you.

Mae: Do you want Gooper, Big Daddy?

Big Daddy: No, and I don't want you. I want some privacy here, while I'm having a confidential talk with my son Brick. Now it's too hot in here to close them doors, but if I have to close those fuckin' doors in order to have a private talk with my son Brick, just let me know and I'll close 'em. Because I hate eavesdroppers, I don't like any kind of sneakin' an' spyin'.

Mae: Why, Big Daddy—

Big Daddy: You stood on the wrong side of the moon, it threw your shadow!

Mae: I was just—

Big Daddy: You was just nothing but *spyin'* an you *know* it!

Mae *(begins to sniff and sob)*:   Oh, Big Daddy, you're so unkind for some reason to those that really love you!

Big Daddy: Shut up, shut up, shut up! I'm going to move you and Gooper out of that room next to this! It's none of your goddamn business what goes on in here at night between Brick an' Maggie. You listen at night like a couple of rutten peekhole spies and go and give a report on what you hear to Big Mama an' she comes to me and says they say such and such and so and so about what they heard goin' on between Brick an' Maggie, and Jesus, it makes me sick. I'm goin' to move you an' Gooper out of that room, I can't stand sneakin' an' spyin', it makes me puke....

(Mae throws back her head and rolls her eyes heavenward and extends her arms as if invoking God's pity for this unjust martyrdom; then she presses a handkerchief to her nose and flies from the room with a loud swish of skirts.)

Brick (*now at the liquor cabinet*):   They listen, do they?

Big Daddy: Yeah. They listen and give reports to Big Mama on what goes on in here between you and Maggie. They say that—

(He stops as if embarrassed.)

   —You won't sleep with her, that you sleep on the sofa. Is that true or not true? If you don't like Maggie, get rid of Maggie!—What are you doin' there now?

Brick: Fresh'nin' up my drink.

Big Daddy: Son, you know you got a real liquor problem?

Brick: Yes, sir, yes, I know.

Big Daddy: Is that why you quit sports-announcing, because of this liquor problem?

Brick: Yes, sir, yes, sir, I guess so.

(He smiles vaguely and amiably at his father across his replenished drink.)

Big Daddy: Son, don't guess about it, it's too important.

Brick (*vaguely*):   Yes, sir.

Big Daddy: And listen to me, don't look at the damn chandelier....

(Pause. Big Daddy's voice is husky.)

   —Somethin' else we picked up at th' big fire-sale in Europe.

(Another pause.)

   Life is important. There's nothing else to hold onto. A man that drinks is throwing his life away. Don't do it, hold onto your life. There's nothing else to hold onto....

   Sit down over here so we don't have to raise our voices, the walls have ears in this place.

Brick (*hobbling over to sit on the sofa beside him*):   All right, Big Daddy.

Big Daddy: Quit!—how'd that come about? Some disappointment?

Brick: I don't know. Do you?

Big Daddy: I'm askin' you, God damn it! How in hell would I know if you don't?

Brick: I just got out there and found that I had a mouth full of cotton.
I was always two or three beats behind what was goin' on on the field
and so I—

Big Daddy: Quit!

Brick (*amiably*):   Yes, quit.

Big Daddy: Son?

Brick: Huh?

Big Daddy (*inhales loudly and deeply from his cigar; then bends suddenly
a little forward, exhaling loudly and raising a hand to his forehead*):
—Whew!—ha ha!—I took in too much smoke, it made me a little
lightheaded....

(*The mantel clock chimes.*)

Why is it so damn hard for people to talk?

Brick: Yeah....

(*The clock goes on sweetly chiming till it has completed the stroke of ten.*)

—Nice peaceful-soundin' clock, I like to hear it all night....

(*He slides low and comfortable on the sofa; Big Daddy sits up straight and
rigid with some unspoken anxiety. All his gestures are tense and jerky as he
talks. He wheezes and pants and sniffs through his nervous speech, glancing
quickly, shyly, from time to time, at his son.*)

Big Daddy: We got that clock the summer we wint to Europe, me an' Big
Mama on that damn Cook's Tour, never had such an awful time in my
life, I'm tellin' you, son, those gooks over there, they gouge your eyeballs out in their grand hotels. And Big Mama bought more stuff than
you could haul in a couple of boxcars, that's no crap. Everywhere she
wint on this whirlwind tour, she bought, bought, bought. Why, half that
stuff she bought is still crated up in the cellar, under water last spring!

(*He laughs.*)

That Europe is nothin' on earth but a great big auction, that's all
it is, that bunch of old worn-out places, it's just a big fire-sale, the
whole fuckin' thing, an' Big Mama wint wild in it, why, you couldn't
hold that woman with a mule's harness! Bought, bought, bought!—
lucky I'm a rich man, yes siree, Bob, an' half that stuff is mildewin' in
th' basement. It's lucky I'm a rich man, it sure is lucky, well, I'm a rich
man, Brick, yep, I'm a mighty rich man.

(*His eyes light up for a moment.*)

Y'know how much I'm worth? Guess, Brick! Guess how much I'm
worth!

(*Brick smiles vaguely over his drink.*)

Close on ten million in cash an' blue-chip stocks, outside, mind you, of twenty-eight thousand acres of the richest land this side of the valley Nile!

But a man can't buy his life with it, he can't buy back his life with it when his life has been spent, that's one thing not offered in the Europe fire-sale or in the American markets or any markets on earth, a man can't buy his life with it, he can't buy back his life when his life is finished....

That's a sobering thought, a very sobering thought, and that's a thought that I was turning over in my head, over and over—until today....

I'm wiser and sadder, Brick, for this experience which I just gone through. They's one thing else that I remember in Europe.

Brick: What is that, Big Daddy?

Big Daddy: The hills around Barcelona in the country of Spain and the children running over those bare hills in their bare skins beggin' like starvin' dogs with howls and screeches, and how fat the priests are on the streets of Barcelona, so many of them and so fat and so pleasant, ha ha!—Y'know I could feed that country? I got money enough to feed that goddamn country, but the human animal is a selfish beast and I don't reckon the money I passed out there to those howling children in the hills around Barcelona would more than upholster the chairs in this room, I mean pay to put a new cover on this chair!

Hell, I threw them money like you'd scatter feed corn for chickens, I threw money at them just to get rid of them long enough to climb back into th' car and—drive away....

And then in Morocco, them Arabs, why, I remember one day in Marrakech, that old walled Arab city, I set on a broken-down wall to have a cigar, it was fearful hot there and this Arab woman stood in the road and looked at me till I was embarrassed, she stood stock still in the dusty hot road and looked at me till I was embarrassed. But listen to this. She had a naked child with her, a little naked girl with her, barely able to toddle, and after a while she set this child on the ground and give her a push and whispered something to her.

This child come toward me, barely able t' walk, come toddling up to me and—

Jesus, it makes you sick t' remember a thing like this! It stuck out its hand and tried to unbutton my trousers!

That child was not yet five! Can you believe me? Or do you think that I am making this up? I wint back to the hotel and said to Big Mama, Git packed! We're clearing out of this country....

Brick: Big Daddy, you're on a talkin' jag tonight.

Big Daddy (*ignoring this remark*):   Yes, sir, that's how it is, the human animal is a beast that dies but the fact that he's dying don't give him pity for others, no, sir, it—

—Did you say something?

Brick: Yes.

Big Daddy: What?

Brick: Hand me over that crutch so I can get up.

Big Daddy: Where you goin?

Brick: I'm takin' a little short trip to Echo Spring.

Big Daddy: To where?

Brick: Liquor cabinet....

Big Daddy: Yes, sir, boy—

(*He hands Brick the crutch.*)

—the human animal is a beast that dies and if he's got money he buys and buys and buys and I think the reason he buys everything he can buy is that in the back of his mind he has the crazy hope that one of his purchases will be life everlasting!—Which it never can be.... The human animal is a beast that—

Brick (*at the liquor cabinet*):   Big Daddy, you sure are shootin' th' breeze here tonight.

(*There is a pause and voices are heard outside.*)

Big Daddy: I been quiet here lately, spoke not a word, just sat and stared into space. I had something heavy weighing on my mind but tonight that load was took off me. That's why I'm talking.—The sky looks diff'rent to me....

Brick: You know what I like to hear most?

Big Daddy: What?

Brick: Solid quiet. Perfect unbroken quiet.

Big Daddy: Why?

Brick: Because it's more peaceful.

Big Daddy: Man, you'll hear a lot of that in the grave.

(*He chuckles agreeably.*)

Brick: Are you through talkin' to me?

Big Daddy: Why are you so anxious to shut me up?

Brick: Well, sir, ever so often you say to me, Brick, I want to have a talk with you, but when we talk, it never materializes. Nothing is said. You sit in a chair and gas about this and that and I look like I listen. I try to look like I listen, but I don't listen, not much. Communication is—awful hard between people an'—somehow between you and me, it just don't—happen.

Big Daddy: Have you ever been scared? I mean have you ever felt down-
right terror of something?

(He gets up.)

Just one moment.

(He looks off as if he were going to tell an important secret.)

Brick?

Brick: What?

Big Daddy: Son, I thought I had it!

Brick: Had what? Had what, Big Daddy?

Big Daddy: Cancer!

Brick: Oh...

Big Daddy: I thought the old man made out of bones had laid his cold
and heavy hand on my shoulder!

Brick: Well, Big Daddy, you kept a tight mouth about it.

Big Daddy: A pig squeals. A man keeps a tight mouth about it, in spite
of a man not having a pig's advantage.

Brick: What advantage is that?

Big Daddy: Ignorance—of mortality—is a comfort. A man don't have
that comfort, he's the only living thing that conceives of death, that
knows what it is. The others go without knowing which is the way
that anything living should go, go without knowing, without any
knowledge of it, and yet a pig squeals, but a man sometimes, he can
keep a right mouth about it. Sometimes he—

(There is a deep, smoldering ferocity in the old man.)

—can keep a tight mouth about it. I wonder if—

Brick: What, Big Daddy?

Big Daddy: A whiskey highball would injure this spastic condition?

Brick: No, sir, it might do it good.

Big Daddy *(grins suddenly, wolfishly)*:   *Jesus, I can't tell you! The sky is
open! Christ, it's open again! It's open, boy, it's open!*

(Brick looks down at his drink.)

Brick: You feel better, Big Daddy?

Big Daddy: Better? Hell! I can breathe!—All of my life I been like a
doubled up fist....

(He pours a drink.)

—Poundin', smashin', drivin'!—now I'm going to loosen these
doubled-up hands and touch things *easy* with them....

(He spreads his hands as if caressing the air.)

You know what I'm contemplating?

Brick (*vaguely*):   No, sir. What are you contemplating?

Big Daddy: Ha ha!—*Pleasure!*—pleasure with *women!*

(*Brick's smile fades a little but lingers.*)

   —Yes, boy. I'll tell you something that you might not guess. I still have desire for women and this is my sixty-fifth birthday.

Brick: I think that's mighty remarkable, Big Daddy.

Big Daddy: Remarkable?

Brick: *Admirable*, Big Daddy.

Big Daddy: You're damn right it is, remarkable and admirable both. I realize now that I never had me enough. I let many chances slip by because of scruples about it, scruples, convention—crap....All that stuff is bull, bull, bull!—It took the shadow of death to make me see it. Now that shadow's lifted, I'm going to cut loose and have, what is it they call it, have me a—ball!

Brick: A ball, huh?

Big Daddy: That's right, a ball, a ball! Hell!—I slept with Big Mama till, let's see, five years ago, till I was sixty and she was fifty-eight, and never even liked her, never did!

(*The phone has been ringing down the hall. Big Mama enters, exclaiming:*)

Big Mama: Don't you men hear that phone ring? I heard it way out on the gall'ry.

Big Daddy: There's five rooms off this front gall'ry that you could go through. Why do you go through this one?

(*Big Mama makes a playful face as she bustles out the hall door.*)

   Hunh!—Why, when Big Mama goes out of a room, I can't remember what that woman looks like—

Big Mama: Hello.

Big Daddy: —But when Big Mama comes back into the room, boy, then I see what she looks like, and I wish I didn't!

(*Bends over laughing at this joke till it hurts his guts and he straightens with a grimace. The laugh subsides to a chuckle as he puts the liquor glass a little distrustfully down on the table.*)

Big Mama: Hello, Miss Sally.

(*Brick has risen and hobbled to the gallery doors.*)

Big Daddy: Hey! Where you goin'?

Brick: Out for a breather.

Big Daddy: Not yet you ain't. Stay here till this talk is finished, young fellow.

Brick: I thought it was finished, Big Daddy.

Big Daddy: It ain't even begun.

Brick: My mistake. Excuse me. I just wanted to feel that river breeze.
Big Daddy: Set back down in that chair.

(Big Mama's voice rises, carrying down the hall.)

Big Mama: Miss Sally, you're a case! You're a caution, Miss Sally.
Big Daddy: Jesus, she's talking to my old maid sister again.
Big Mama: Why didn't you give me a chance to explain it to you?
Big Daddy: Brick, this stuff burns me.
Big Mama: Well, good-bye, now, Miss Sally. You come down real soon. Big Daddy's dying to see you.
Big Daddy: Crap!
Big Mama: Yaiss, good-bye, Miss Sally....

(She hangs up and bellows with mirth. Big Daddy groans and covers his ears as she approaches.)

(Bursting in:)

   Big Daddy, that was Miss Sally callin' from Memphis again! You know what she done, Big Daddy? She called her doctor in Memphis to git him to tell her what that spastic thing is! Ha-*HAAAA!*—And called back to tell me how relieved she was that—Hey! Let me in!

(Big Daddy has been holding the door half closed against her.)

Big Daddy: Naw I ain't. I told you not to come and go through this room. You just back out and go through those five other rooms.
Big Mama: Big Daddy? Big Daddy? Oh, Big Daddy!—You didn't mean those things you said to me, did you?

(He shuts door firmly against her but she still calls.)

   Sweetheart? Sweetheart? Big Daddy? You didn't mean those awful things you said to me?—I know you didn't. I know you didn't mean those things in your heart....

(The childlike voice fades with a sob and her heavy footsteps retreat down the hall. Brick has risen once more on his crutches and starts for the gallery again.)

Big Daddy: All I ask of that woman is that she leave me alone. But she can't admit to herself that she makes me sick. That comes of having slept with her too many years. Should of quit much sooner but that old woman she never got enough of it—and I was good in bed...I never should of wasted so much of it on her....They say you got just so many and each one is numbered. Well, I got a few left in me, a few, and I'm going to pick me a good one to spend 'em on! I'm going to pick me a choice one, I don't care how much she costs, I'll smother her in—minks! Ha ha! I'll strip her naked and smother her in minks and choke her with diamonds! Ha ha! I'll strip her naked and choke her with diamonds and smother her with minks and hump her from hell to breakfast. *Ha aha ha ha ha!*

Mae (*gaily at door*):   Who's that laughin' in there?

Gooper: Is Big Daddy laughin' in there?

Big Daddy: Crap!—them two—*drips*....

(He goes over and touches Brick's shoulder.)

Yes, son. Brick, boy.—I'm—*happy!* I'm happy, son, I'm happy!

(He chokes a little and bites his under lip, pressing his head quickly, shyly against his son's head and then, coughing with embarrassment, goes uncertainly back to the table where he set down the glass. He drinks and makes a grimace as it burns his guts. Brick sighs and rises with effort.)

What makes you so restless? Have you got ants in your britches?

Brick: Yes, sir...

Big Daddy: Why?

Brick: —Something—hasn't—happened....

Big Daddy: Yeah? What is that!

Brick (*sadly*):   —the click....

Big Daddy: Did you say click?

Brick: Yes, click.

Big Daddy: What click?

Brick: A click that I get in my head that makes me peaceful.

Big Daddy: I sure in hell don't know what you're talking about, but it disturbs me.

Brick: It's just a mechanical thing.

Big Daddy: What is a mechanical thing?

Brick: This click that I get in my head that makes me peaceful. I got to drink till I get it. It's just a mechanical thing, something like a—like a—like a—

Big Daddy: Like a—

Brick: Switch clicking off in my head, turning the hot light off and the cool night on and—

(He looks up, smiling sadly.)

—all of a sudden there's—peace!

Big Daddy (*whistles long and soft with astonishment; he goes back to Brick and clasps his son's two shoulders*):   Jesus! I didn't know it had gotten that bad with you. Why, boy, you're—*alcoholic!*

Brick: That's the truth, Big Daddy. I'm alcoholic.

Big Daddy: This shows how I—let things go!

Brick: I have to hear that little click in my head that makes me peaceful. Usually I hear it sooner than this, sometimes as early as—noon, but—
—Today it's—dilatory[8]....
I just haven't got the right level of alcohol in my bloodstream yet!

(This last statement is made with energy as he freshens his drink.)

Big Daddy: Uh—huh. Expecting death made me blind. I didn't have no idea that a son of mine was turning into a drunkard under my nose.
Brick *(gently)*: Well, now you do, Big Daddy, the news has penetrated.
Big Daddy: Uh-huh, yes, now I do, the news has—penetrated....
Brick: And so if you'll excuse me—
Big Daddy: No, I won't excuse you.
Brick: —I'd better sit by myself till I hear that click in my head, it's just a mechanical thing but it don't happen except when I'm alone or talking to no one....
Big Daddy: You got a long, long time to sit still, boy, and talk to no one, but now you're talkin' to me. At least I'm talking to you. And you set there and listen until I tell you the conversation is over!
Brick: But this talk is like all the others we've ever had together in our lives! It's nowhere, nowhere!—it's—it's *painful*, Big Daddy....
Big Daddy: All right, then let it be painful, but don't you move from that chair!—I'm going to remove that crutch....

(He seizes the crutch and tosses it across room.)

Brick: I can hop on one foot, and if I fall, I can crawl!
Big Daddy: If you ain't careful you're gonna crawl off this plantation and then, by Jesus, you'll have to hustle your drinks along Skid Row!
Brick: That'll come, Big Daddy.
Big Daddy: Naw, it won't. You're my son and I'm going to straighten you out; now that *I'm* straightened out, I'm going to straighten out you!
Brick: Yeah?
Big Daddy: Today the report come in from Ochsner Clinic. Y'know what they told me?

(His face glows with triumph.)

The only thing that they could detect with all the instruments of science in that great hospital is a little spastic condition of the colon! And nerves torn to pieces by all that worry about it.

(A little girl bursts into room with a sparkler clutched in each fist, hops and shrieks like a monkey gone mad and rushes back out again as Big Daddy strikes at her.)

(Silence. The two men stare at each other. A woman laughs gaily outside.)

[8]Slow to act, intended to cause delay.

I want you to know I breathed a sigh of relief almost as powerful as the Vicksburg tornado![9]

(There is laughter outside, running footsteps, the soft, plushy sound and light of exploding rockets.)

(Brick stares at him soberly for a long moment; then makes a sort of startled sound in his nostrils and springs up on one foot and hops across the room to grab his crutch, swinging on the furniture for support. He gets the crutch and flees as if in horror for the gallery. His father seizes him by the sleeve of his white silk pajamas.)

Stay here, you son of a bitch!—till I say go!

Brick: I can't.

Big Daddy: You sure in hell will, God damn it.

Brick: No, I can't. We talk, you talk, in—circles! We get no where, no where! It's always the same, you say you want to talk to me and don't have a fuckin' thing to say to me!

Big Daddy: Nothin' to say when I'm tellin' you I'm going to live when I thought I was dying?!

Brick: Oh—*that!*—Is that what you have to say to me?

Big Daddy: Why, you son of a bitch! Ain't that, ain't that—*important?!*

Brick: Well, you said that, that's said, and now I—

Big Daddy: Now you set back down.

Brick: You're all balled up, you—

Big Daddy: I ain't balled up!

Brick: You are, you're all balled up!

Big Daddy: Don't tell me what I am, you drunken whelp! I'm going to tear this coat sleeve off if you don't set down!

Brick: Big Daddy—

Big Daddy: Do what I tell you! I'm the boss here, now! I want you to know I'm back in the driver's seat now!

(Big Mama rushes in, clutching her great heaving bosom.)

Big Mama: Big Daddy!

Big Daddy: What in hell do you want in here, Big Mama?

Big Mama: Oh, Big Daddy! Why are you shouting like that? I just cain't stainnnnnnnd—it....

Big Daddy *(raising the back of his hand above his head)*:   GIT—outa here.

(She rushes back out, sobbing.)

Brick *(softly, sadly)*:
   Christ....

---

[9]Tornado that struck Vicksburg, Mississippi, December 5, 1953, killing 38 and injuring 270.

Big Daddy (*fiercely*):
    Yeah! Christ!—is right....

(*Brick breaks loose and hobbles toward the gallery.*)

(*Big Daddy jerks his crutch from under Brick so he steps with the injured ankle. He utters a hissing cry of anguish, clutches a chair and pulls it over on top of him on the floor.*)

    Son of a—tub of—hog fat....
Brick: Big Daddy! Give me my crutch.

(*Big Daddy throws the crutch out of reach.*)

    Give me that crutch, Big Daddy.
Big Daddy: Why do you drink?
Brick: Don't know, give me my crutch!
Big Daddy: You better think why you drink or give up drinking!
Brick: Will you please give me my crutch so I can get up off this floor?
Big Daddy: First you answer my question. Why do you drink? Why are you throwing your life away, boy, like somethin' disgusting you picked up on the street?
Brick (*getting onto his knees*):   Big Daddy, I'm in pain, I stepped on that foot.
Big Daddy: Good! I'm glad you're not too numb with the liquor in you to feel some pain!
Brick: You—spilled my—drink...
Big Daddy: I'll make a bargain with you. You tell me why you drink and I'll hand you one. I'll pour you the liquor myself and hand it to you.
Brick: Why do I drink?
Big Daddy: Yea! Why?
Brick: Give me a drink and I'll tell you.
Big Daddy: Tell me first!
Brick: I'll tell you in one word.
Big Daddy: What word?
Brick: DISGUST!

(*The clock chimes softly, sweetly. Big Daddy gives it a short, outraged glance.*)

    Now how about that drink?
Big Daddy: What are you disgusted with? You got to tell me that, first. Otherwise being disgusted don't make no sense!
Brick: Give me my crutch.
Big Daddy: You heard me, you got to tell me what I asked you first.
Brick: I told you, I said to kill my disgust!
Big Daddy: DISGUST WITH WHAT!

Brick: You strike a hard bargain.

Big Daddy: What are you disgusted with?—an' I'll pass you the liquor.

Brick: I can hop on one foot, and if I fall, I can crawl.

Big Daddy: You want liquor that bad?

Brick (*dragging himself up, clinging to bedstead*):   Yeah, I want it that bad.

Big Daddy: If I give you a drink, will you tell me what it is you're disgusted with, Brick?

Brick: Yes, sir, I will try to.

(*The old man pours him a drink and solemnly passes it to him.*)

(*There is silence as Brick drinks.*)

Have you ever heard the word "mendacity"?

Big Daddy: Sure. Mendacity is one of them five-dollar words that cheap politicians throw back and forth at each other.

Brick: You know what it means?

Big Daddy: Don't it mean lying and liars?

Brick: Yes, sir, lying and liars.

Big Daddy: Has someone been lying to you?

Children (*chanting in chorus offstage*):   We want Big Dad-dee!

We want Big Dad-dee!

(*Gooper appears in the gallery door.*)

Gooper: Big Daddy, the kiddies are shouting for you out there.

Big Daddy (*fiercely*): Keep out, Gooper!

Gooper: 'Scuse me!

(*Big Daddy slams the doors after Gooper.*)

Big Daddy: Who's been lying to you, has Margaret been lying to you, has your wife been lying to you about something, Brick?

Brick: Not her. That wouldn't matter.

Big Daddy: Then who's been lying to you, and what about?

Brick: No one single person and no one lie....

Big Daddy: Then what, what then, for Christ's sake?

Brick: —The whole, the whole—thing....

Big Daddy: Why are you rubbing your head? You got a headache?

Brick: No, I'm tryin' to—

Big Daddy: —Concentrate, but you can't because your brain's all soaked with liquor, is that the trouble? Wet brain!

(*He snatches the glass from Brick's hand.*)

What do you know about this mendacity thing? Hell! I could write a book on it! Don't you know that? I could write a book on it and still not cover the subject? Well, I could, I could write a goddamn book on it and still not cover the subject anywhere near enough!!—Think of all the lies I got to put up with!—Pretenses! Ain't that mendacity? Having to pretend stuff you don't think or feel or have any idea of? Having for instance to act like I care for Big Mama!—I haven't been able to stand the sight, sound, or smell of that woman for forty years now!—even when I *laid* her!—regular as a piston....

Pretend to love that son of a bitch of a Gooper and his wife Mae and those five same screechers out there like parrots in a jungle? Jesus! Can't stand to look at 'em!

Church!—it bores the bejesus out of me but I go!—I go an' sit there and listen to the fool preacher!

Clubs!—Elks! Masons! Rotary!—*crap!*

(A spasm of pain makes him clutch his belly. He sinks to a chair and his voice is softer and hoarser.)

You I *do* like for some reason, did always have some kind of real feeling for—affection—respect—yes, always....

You and being a success as a planter is all I ever had any devotion to in my whole life!—and that's the truth....

I don't know why, but it is!

I've lived with mendacity!—Why can't *you* live with it? Hell, you *got* to live with it, there's nothing *else* to *live* with except mendacity, is there?

Brick: Yes, sir. Yes, sir there is something else that you can live with!

Big Daddy: What?

Brick *(lifting his glass)*:   This!—Liquor....

Big Daddy: That's not living, that's dodging away from life.

Brick: I want to dodge away from it.

Big Daddy: Then why don't you kill yourself, man?

Brick: I like to drink....

Big Daddy: Oh, God, I can't talk to you....

Brick: I'm sorry, Big Daddy.

Big Daddy: Not as sorry as I am. I'll tell you something. A little while back when I thought my number was up—

(This speech should have torrential pace and fury.)

—before I found out it was just this—spastic—colon. I thought about you. Should I or should I not, if the jig was up, give you this place when I go—since I hate Gooper an' Mae an' know that they hate me, and since all five same monkeys are little Maes an' Goopers.— And I thought, No!—Then I thought, Yes!—I couldn't make up my mind. I hate Gooper and his five same monkeys and that bitch Mae! Why should I turn over twenty-eight thousand acres of the richest land this side of the valley Nile to not my kind?—But why in hell, on the other hand, Brick—should I subsidize a goddamn fool on the bottle?—Liked or not liked, well, maybe even—*loved!*—Why should I do that?—Subsidize worthless behavior? Rot? Corruption?

Brick (*smiling*):   I understand.

Big Daddy: Well, if you do, you're smarter than I am, God damn it, because I don't understand. And this I will tell you frankly. I didn't make up my mind at all on that question and still to this day I ain't made out no will!—Well, now I don't *have* to. The pressure is gone. I can just wait and see if you pull yourself together or if you don't.

Brick: That's right, Big Daddy.

Big Daddy: You sound like you thought I was kidding.

Brick (*rising*):   No, sir, I know you're not kidding.

Big Daddy: But you don't care—?

Brick (*hobbling toward the gallery door*):   No, sir, I don't care....

(*He stands in the gallery doorway as the night sky turns pink and green and gold with successive flashes of light.*)

Big Daddy: *WAIT!*—Brick....

(*His voice drops. Suddenly there is something shy, almost tender, in his restraining gesture.*)

  Don't let's—leave it like this, like them other talks we've had, we've always—talked around things, we've—just talked around things for some fuckin' reason, I don't know what, it's always like something was left not spoken, something avoided because neither of us was honest enough with the—other....

Brick: I never lied to you, Big Daddy.

Big Daddy: Did I ever to *you?*

Brick: No, sir....

Big Daddy: Then there is at least two people that never lied to each other.

Brick: But we've never *talked* to each other.

Big Daddy: We can *now*.

Brick: Big Daddy, there don't seem to be anything much to say.

Big Daddy: You say that you drink to kill your disgust with lying.

Brick: You said to give you a reason.

Big Daddy: Is liquor the only thing that'll kill this disgust?

Brick: Now. Yes.

Big Daddy: But not once, huh?

Brick: Not when I was still young an' believing. A drinking man's someone who wants to forget he isn't still young an' believing.

Big Daddy: Believing what?

Brick: Believing....

Big Daddy: Believing *what?*

Brick (*stubbornly evasive*): Believing....

Big Daddy: I don't know what the hell you mean by believing and I don't think you know what you mean by believing, but if you still got sports in your blood, go back to sports announcing and—

Brick: Sit in a glass box watching games I can't play? Describing what I can't do while players do it? Sweating out their disgust and confusion in contests I'm not fit for? Drinkin' a coke, half bourbon, so I can stand it? That's no goddamn good any more, no help—time just outran me, Big Daddy—got there first...

Big Daddy: I think you're passing the buck.

Brick: You know many drinkin' men?

Big Daddy (*with a slight, charming smile*): I have known a fair number of that species.

Brick: Could any of them tell you why he drank?

Big Daddy: Yep, you're passin' the buck to things like time and disgust with "mendacity" and—crap!—if you got to use that kind of language about a thing, it's ninety-proof bull, and I'm not buying any.

Brick: I had to give you a reason to get a drink!

Big Daddy: You started drinkin' when your friend Skipper died.

(*Silence for five beats. Then Brick makes a startled movement, reaching for his crutch.*)

Brick: What are you suggesting?

Big Daddy: I'm suggesting nothing.

(*The shuffle and clop of Brick's rapid hobble away from his father's steady, grave attention.*)

—But Gooper an' Mae suggested that there was something not right exactly in your—

Brick (*stopping short downstage as if backed to a wall*): "Not right"?

Big Daddy: Not, well, exactly *normal* in your friendship with—

Brick: They suggested that, too? I thought that was Maggie's suggestion.

(*Brick's detachment is at last broken through. His heart is accelerated; his forehead sweat-beaded; his breath becomes more rapid and his voice hoarse. The thing they're discussing, timidly and painfully on the side of Big Daddy, fiercely, violently on Brick's side, is the inadmissible thing that Skipper died to disavow between them. The fact that if it existed it had to be disavowed to "keep face" in the world they lived in, may be at the heart of the "mendacity" that Brick drinks to kill his disgust with. It may be the root of his collapse. Or maybe it is only a single manifestation of it, not even the most important. The bird that I hope to catch in the net of this play is not the solution of one man's psychological problem. I'm trying to catch the true quality of experience in a group of people, that cloudy, flickering, evanescent—fiercely charged!—interplay of live human beings in the thundercloud of a common crisis. Some mystery should be left in the revelation of character in a play, just as a great deal of mystery is always left in the revelation of character in life, even in one's own character to himself. This does not absolve the playwright of his duty to observe and probe as clearly and deeply as he legitimately can: But it should steer him away from "pat" conclusions, facile definitions which make a play just a play, not a snare for the truth of human experience.)*

(The following scene should be played with great concentration, with most of the power leashed but palpable in what is left unspoken.)

> Who else's suggestion is it, is it *yours*? How many others thought that Skipper and I were—

Big Daddy (*gently*): Now, hold on, hold on a minute, son.—I knocked around in my time.

Brick: What's that got to do with—

Big Daddy: I said "Hold on!"—I bummed, I bummed this country till I was—

Brick: Whose suggestion, who else's suggestion is it?

Big Daddy: Slept in hobo jungles and railroad Y's and flophouses in all cities before I—

Brick: Oh, *you* think so, too, you call me your son and a queer. Oh! Maybe that's why you put Maggie and me in this room that was Jack Straw's and Peter Ochello's, in which that pair of old sisters slept in a double bed where both of 'em died!

Big Daddy: *Now just don't go throwing rocks at—*

(Suddenly Reverend Tooker appears in the gallery doors, his head slightly, playfully, fatuously cocked, with a practiced clergyman's smile, sincere as a bird-call blown on a hunter's whistle, the living embodiment of the pious, conventional lie.)

(Big Daddy gasps a little at this perfectly timed, but incongruous, apparition.)

> —What're you lookin' for, preacher?

Reverend Tooker: The gentleman's lavatory, ha ha!—heh, heh...

Big Daddy (*with strained courtesy*): —Go back out and walk down to the other end of the gallery, Reverend Tooker, and use the bathroom connected with my bedroom, and if you can't find it, ask them where it is!

Reverend Tooker: Ah, thanks.

(He goes out with a deprecatory chuckle.)

Big Daddy: It's hard to talk in this place...

Brick: Son of a—!

Big Daddy (*leaving a lot unspoken*):   —I seen all things and understood a lot of them, till 1910. Christ, the year that—I had worn my shoes through, hocked my—I hopped off a yellow dog freight car half a mile down the road, slept in a wagon of cotton outside the gin—Jack Straw an' Peter Ochello took me in. Hired me to manage this place which grew into this one.—When Jack Straw died—why, old Peter Ochello quit eatin' like a dog does when its master's dead, and died, too!

Brick: Christ!

Big Daddy: I'm just saying I understand such—

Brick (*violently*):   Skipper is dead. I have not quit eating!

Big Daddy: No, but you started drinking.

(*Brick wheels on his crutch and hurls his glass across the room shouting.*)

Brick: YOU THINK SO, TOO?

(*Footsteps run on the gallery. There are women's calls.*)

(*Big Daddy goes toward the door.*)

(*Brick is transformed, as if a quiet mountain blew suddenly up in volcanic flame.*)

Brick: You think so, too? You think so, too? You think me an' Skipper did, did, did!—*sodomy!*—together?

Big Daddy: Hold—!

Brick: That what you—

Big Daddy: —*ON*—a minute!

Brick: You think we did dirty things between us, Skipper an'—

Big Daddy: Why are you shouting like that? Why are you—

Brick: —Me, is that what you think of Skipper, is that—

Big Daddy: —so excited? I don't think nothing. I don't know nothing I'm simply telling you what—

Brick: You think that Skipper and me were a pair of dirty old men?

Big Daddy: Now that's—

Brick: Straw? Ochello? A couple of—

Big Daddy: Now just—

Brick: —fucking sissies? Queers? Is that what you—

Big Daddy: Shhh.

Brick: —think?

(*He loses his balance and pitches to his knees without noticing the pain. He grabs the bed and drags himself up.*)

Big Daddy: Jesus!—Whew....Grab my hand!

Brick: Naw, I don't want your hand...

Big Daddy: Well, I want yours. Git up!

(*He draws him up, keeps an arm about him with concern and affection.*)

    You broken out in a sweat! You're panting like you'd run a race with—

Brick (*freeing himself from his father's hold*): Big Daddy, you shock me, Big Daddy, you, you—*shock* me! Talkin' so—

(*He turns away from his father.*)

    —casually!—about a—thing like that...

    —Don't you know how people *feel* about things like that? How, how *disgusted* they are by things like that? Why, at Ole Miss when it was discovered a pledge to our fraternity, Skipper's and mine, did a, *attempted* to do a, unnatural thing with—

    We not only dropped him like a hot rock!—We told him to git off the campus, and he did, he got!—All the way to—

(*He halts, breathless.*)

Big Daddy: —Where?

Brick: —North Africa, last I heard!

Big Daddy: Well, I have come back from further away than that, I have just now returned from the other side of the moon, death's country, son, and I'm not easy to shock by anything here.

(*He comes downstage and faces out.*)

    Always, anyhow, lived with too much space around me to be infected by ideas of other people. One thing you can grow on a big place more important than cotton!—is *tolerance!*—I grown it.

(*He returns toward Brick.*)

Brick: Why can't exceptional friendship, *real, real, deep, deep friendship!* between two men be respected as something clean and decent without being thought of as—

Big Daddy: It can, it is, for God's sake.

Brick: —Fairies....

(*In his utterance of this word, we gauge the wide and profound reach of the conventional mores he got from the world that crowned him with early laurel.*)

Big Daddy: I told Mae an' Gooper—

Brick: Frig Mae and Gooper, frig all dirty lies and liars!—Skipper and me had a clean, true thing between us!—had a clean friendship, practically all our lives, till Maggie got the idea you're talking about. Normal? No!—It was too rare to be normal, any true thing between two people is too rare to be normal. Oh, once in a while he put his hand on my shoulder or I'd put mine on his, oh, maybe even, when we were touring the country in pro-football an' shared hotel rooms we'd reach

across the space between the two beds and shake hands to say good-
night, yeah, one or two times we—

Big Daddy: Brick, nobody thinks that that's not normal!

Brick: Well, they're mistaken, it was! It was a pure an' true thing an'
that's not normal.

Mae (*offstage*): Big Daddy, they're startin' the fireworks.

(*They both stare straight at each other for a long moment. The tension
breaks and both turn away as if tired.*)

Big Daddy: Yeah, it's—hard t'—talk....

Brick: All right, then, let's—let it go....

Big Daddy: Why did Skipper crack up? Why have you?

(*Brick looks back at his father again. He has already decided, without
knowing that he has made this decision, that he is going to tell his father
that he is dying of cancer. Only this could even the score between them: one
inadmissible thing in return for another.*)

Brick (*ominously*): All right. You're asking for it, Big Daddy. We're finally
going to have that real true talk you wanted. It's too late to stop it,
now, we got to carry it through and cover every subject.

(*He hobbles back to the liquor cabinet.*)

Uh-huh.

(*He opens the ice bucket and picks up the silver tongs with slow admiration
of their frosty brightness.*)

Maggie declares that Skipper and I went into pro-football after we
left Ole Miss because we were scared to grow up...

(*He moves downstage with the shuffle and clop of a cripple on a crutch. As
Margaret did when her speech became "recitative," he looks out into the
house, commanding its attention by his direct, concentrated gaze—a broken, "tragically elegant" figure telling simply as much as he knows of "the
Truth":*)

—Wanted to—keep on tossing—those long, long!—high, high!—
passes that—couldn't be intercepted except by time, the aerial attack
that made us famous! And so we did, we did, we kept it up for one
season, that aerial attack, we held it high!—Yeah, but—

—that summer, Maggie, she laid the law down to me, said, Now or
never, and so I married Maggie....

Big Daddy: How was Maggie in bed?

Brick (*wryly*): Great! the greatest!

(*Big Daddy nods as if he thought so.*)

She went on the road that fall with the Dixie Stars. Oh, she made a great show of being the world's best sport. She wore a—wore a—tall bearskin cap! A shako, they call it, a dyed moleskin coat, a moleskin coat dyed red!—Cut up crazy! Rented hotel ballrooms for victory celebrations, wouldn't cancel them when it—turned out—defeat....

MAGGIE THE CAT! Ha ha!

(Big Daddy nods.)

—But Skipper, he had some fever which came back on him which doctors couldn't explain and I got that injury—turned out to be just a shadow on the X-ray plate—and a touch of bursitis....

I lay in a hospital bed, watched our games on TV, saw Maggie on the bench next to Skipper when he was hauled out of a game for stumbles, fumbles!—Burned me up the way she hung on his arm!—Y'know, I think that Maggie had always felt sort of left out because she and me never got any closer together than two people just get in bed, which is not much closer than two cats on a—fence humping....

So! She took this time to work on poor dumb Skipper. He was a less than average student at Ole Miss, you know that, don't you?!—Poured in his mind the dirty, false idea that what we were, him and me, was a frustrated case of that ole pair of sisters that lived in this room, Jack Straw and Peter Ochello!—He, poor Skipper, went to bed with Maggie to prove it wasn't true, and when it didn't work out, he thought it *was* true!—Skipper broke in two like a rotten stick—nobody ever turned so fast to a lush—or died of it so quick....

—Now are you satisfied?

(Big Daddy has listened to this story, dividing the grain from the chaff. Now he looks at his son.)

Big Daddy: Are *you* satisfied?
Brick: With what?
Big Daddy: That half-ass story!
Brick: What's half-ass about it?
Big Daddy: Something's left out of that story. What did you leave out?

(The phone has started ringing in the hall.)

Gooper *(offstage)*:   Hello.

(As if it reminded him of something, Brick glances suddenly toward the sound and says:)

Brick: Yes!—I left out a long-distance call which I had from Skipper—
Gooper: Speaking, go ahead.
Brick: —In which he made a drunken confession to me and on which I hung up!

Gooper: No.

Brick: —Last time we spoke to each other in our lives...

Gooper: No, sir.

Big Daddy: You musta said something to him before you hung up.

Brick: What could I say to him?

Big Daddy: Anything. Something.

Brick: Nothing.

Big Daddy: Just hung up?

Brick: Just hung up.

Big Daddy: Uh-huh. Anyhow now!—we have tracked down the lie with which you're disgusted and which you are drinking to kill your disgust with, Brick. You been passing the buck. This disgust with mendacity is disgust with yourself.

You!—dug the grave of your friend and kicked him in it!—before you'd face truth with him!

Brick: *His* truth, not *mine!*

Big Daddy: His truth, okay! But you wouldn't face it with him!

Brick: Who *can* face truth? Can *you?*

Big Daddy: Now don't start passin' the rotten buck again, boy!

Brick: How about these birthday congratulations, these many, many happy returns of the day, when ev'rybody knows there won't be any except you!

(*Gooper, who has answered the hall phone, lets out a high, shrill laugh; the voice becomes audible saying: "No, no, you got it all wrong! Upside down! Are you crazy?"*)

(*Brick suddenly catches his breath as he realizes that he has made a shocking disclosure. He hobbles a few paces, then freezes, and without looking at his father's shocked face says:*)

Let's, let's—go out, now, and—watch the fireworks. Come on, Big Daddy.

(*Big Daddy moves suddenly forward and grabs hold of the boy's crutch like it was a weapon for which they were fighting for possession.*)

Big Daddy: Oh, no, no! No one's going out! What did you start to say?

Brick: I don't remember.

Big Daddy: "Many happy returns when they know there won't be any"?

Brick: Aw, hell, Big Daddy, forget it. Come on out on the gallery and look at the fireworks they're shooting off for your birthday....

Big Daddy: First you finish that remark you were makin' before you cut off. "Many happy returns when they know there won't be any"?— Ain't that what you just said?

Brick: Look, now. I can get around without that crutch if I have to but it would be a lot easier on the furniture an' glassware if I didn't have to go swinging along like Tarzan of th'—

Big Daddy: FINISH! WHAT YOU WAS SAYIN'!

(*An eerie green glow shows in sky behind him.*)

Brick: (*sucking the ice in his glass, speech becoming thick*):   Leave th' place to Gooper and Mae an' their five little same little monkeys. All I want is—

Big Daddy: "LEAVE TH' PLACE," did you say?

Brick (*vaguely*):   All twenty-eight thousand acres of the richest land this side of the valley Nile.

Big Daddy: Who said I was "leaving the place" to Gooper or anybody? This is my sixty-fifth birthday! I got fifteen years or twenty years left in me! I'll outlive *you!* I'll bury you an' have to pay for your coffin!

Brick: Sure. Many happy returns. Now let's go watch the fireworks, come on, let's—

Big Daddy: Lying, have they been lying? About the report from th'— clinic? Did they, did they—find something?—*Cancer.* Maybe?

Brick: Mendacity is a system that we live in. Liquor is one way out an' death's the other....

(*He takes the crutch from Big Daddy's loose grip and swings out on the gallery leaving the doors open.*)

(*A song, "Pick a Bale of Cotton," is heard.*)

Mae (*appearing in door*):   Oh, Big Daddy, the field hands are singin' fo' you!

Brick: I'm sorry, Big Daddy. My head don't work any more and it's hard for me to understand how anybody could care if he lived or died or was dying or cared about anything but whether or not there was liquor left in the bottle and so I said what I said without thinking. In some ways I'm no better than the others, in some ways worse because I'm less alive. Maybe it's being alive that makes them lie, and being almost *not* alive makes me sort of accidentally truthful—I don't know but—anyway—we've been friends...

—And being friends is telling each other the truth....

(*There is a pause.*)

You told *me!* I told *you!*

Big Daddy (*slowly and passionately*):   CHRIST—DAMN—

Gooper (*offstage*):   Let her go!

(*Fireworks offstage right.*)

Big Daddy: —ALL—LYING SONS OF—LYING BITCHES!

(He straightens at last and crosses to the inside door. At the door he turns and looks back as if he had some desperate question he couldn't put into words. Then he nods reflectively and says in a hoarse voice:)

Yes, all liars, all liars, all lying dying liars!

(This is said slowly, slowly, with a fierce revulsion. He goes on out.)

—Lying! Dying! Liars!

(Brick remains motionless as the lights dim out and the curtain falls.)

ACT 3

(There is no lapse of time. Big Daddy is seen leaving as at the end of act 2.)

Big Daddy: ALL LYIN'—DYIN'!—LIARS! LIARS!—LIARS!

(Margaret enters.)

Margaret: Brick, what in the name of God was goin' on in this room?

(Dixie and Trixie enter through the doors and circle around Margaret shouting. Mae enters from the lower gallery window.)

Mae: Dixie, Trixie, you quit that!

(Gooper enters through the doors.)

Gooper, will y' please get these kiddies to bed right now!

Gooper: Mae, you seen Big Mama?

Mae: Not yet.

(Gooper and kids exit through the doors. Reverend Tooker enters through the windows.)

Reverend Tooker: Those kiddies are so full of vitality. I think I'll have to be starting back to town.

Mae: Not yet, Preacher. You know we regard you as a member of this family, one of our closest an' dearest, so you just got t' be with us when Doc Baugh gives Big Mama th' actual truth about th' report from the clinic.

Margaret: Where do you think you're going?

Brick: Out for some air.

Margaret: Why'd Big Daddy shout "Liars"?

Mae: Has Big Daddy gone to bed, Brick?

Gooper *(entering)*:   Now where is that old lady?

Reverend Tooker: I'll look for her.

(He exits to the gallery.)

Mae: Cain'tcha find her, Gooper?

Gooper: She's avoidin' this talk.

Mae: I think she senses somethin'.

Margaret *(going out on the gallery to Brick)*:   Brick, they're goin' to tell Big Mama the truth about Big Daddy and she's goin' to need you.

Doctor Baugh: This is going to be painful.

Mae: Painful things caint always be avoided.

Reverend Tooker: I see Big Mama.

Gooper: Hey, Big Mama, come here.

Mae: Hush, Gooper, don't holler.

Big Mama *(entering)*:   Too much smell of burnt fireworks makes me feel a little bit sick at my stomach.—Where is Big Daddy?

Mae: That's what I want to know, where has Big Daddy gone?

Big Mama: He must have turned in, I reckon he went to baid...

Gooper: Well, then, now we can talk.

Big Mama: What *is* this talk, *what* talk?

(Margaret appears on the gallery, talking to Doctor Baugh.)

Margaret *(musically)*:   My family freed their slaves ten years before abolition. My great-great-grandfather gave his slaves their freedom five years before the War between the States started!

Mae: Oh, for God's sake! Maggie's climbed back up in her family tree!

Margaret *(sweetly)*:   What, Mae?

(The pace must be very quick: great Southern animation.)

Big Mama *(addressing them all)*:   I think Big Daddy was just worn out. He loves his family, he loves to have them around him, but it's a strain on his nerves. He wasn't himself tonight, Big Daddy wasn't himself, I could tell he was all worked up.

Reverend Tooker: I think he's remarkable.

Big Mama: Yaisss! Just remarkable. Did you all notice the food he ate at that table? Did you all notice the supper he put away? Why he ate like a hawss!

Gooper: I hope he doesn't regret it.

Big Mama: What? Why that man—ate a huge piece of cawn bread with molasses on it! Helped himself twice to hoppin' John.[10]

Margaret: Big Daddy loves hoppin' John.—We had a real country dinner.

Big Mama *(overlapping Margaret)*:   Yaiss, he simply adores it! an' candied yams? Son? That man put away enough food at that table to stuff a *field* hand!

Gooper *(with grim relish)*:   I hope he don't have to pay for it later on...

Big Mama *(fiercely)*:   What's *that*, Gooper?

Mae: Gooper says he hopes Big Daddy doesn't suffer tonight.

---

[10]A dish of black-eyed peas, spices, and bacon or salt pork, served with rice and cooked greens.

Big Mama: Oh, shoot, Gooper says, Gooper says! Why should Big Daddy
  suffer for satisfying a normal appetite? There's nothin' wrong with
  that man but nerves, he's sound as a dollar! And now he knows he is
  an' that's why he ate such a supper. He had a big load off his mind,
  knowin' he wasn't doomed t'—what he thought he was doomed to...
Margaret *(sadly and sweetly)*:   Bless his old sweet soul...
Big Mama *(vaguely)*:   Yais, bless his heart, where's Brick?
Mae: Outside.
Gooper: —Drinkin'...
Big Mama: I know he's drinkin'. Cain't I see he's drinkin' without you
  continually tellin' me that boy's drinkin'?
Margaret: Good for you, Big Mama!

(She applauds.)

Big Mama: Other people *drink* and *have* drunk an' will *drink*, as long as
  they make that stuff an' put it in bottles.
Margaret: That's the truth. I never trusted a man that didn't drink.
Big Mama: *Brick? Brick!*
Margaret: He's still on the gall'ry. I'll go bring him in so we can talk.
Big Mama *(worriedly)*:   I don't know what this mysterious family confer-
  ence is about.

*(Awkward silence. Big Mama looks from face to face, then belches slightly
and mutters, "Excuse me..." She opens an ornamental fan suspended about
her throat. A black lace fan to go with her black lace gown, and fans her
wilting corsage, sniffing nervously and looking from face to face in the uncomfortable silence as Margaret calls "Brick?" and Brick sings to the moon
on the gallery.)*

Margaret: Brick, they're gonna tell Big Mama the truth an' she's gonna
  need you.
Big Mama: I don't know what's wrong here, you all have such long faces!
  Open that door on the hall and let some air circulate through here,
  will you please, Gooper?
Mae: I think we'd better leave that door closed, Big Mama, till after the
  talk.
Margaret: Brick!
Big Mama: Reveren' Tooker, will *you* please open that door?
Reverend Tooker: I sure will, Big Mama.
Mae: I just didn't think we ought t' take any chance of Big Daddy hearin'
  a word of this discussion.
Big Mama: *I swan!* Nothing's going to be said in Big Daddy's house that
  he caint hear if he want to!
Gooper: Well, Big Mama, it's—

(Mae gives him a quick, hard poke to shut him up. He glares at her fiercely as she circles before him like a burlesque ballerina, raising her skinny bare arms over her head, jangling her bracelets, exclaiming:)

Mae: *A breeze! A breeze!*

Reverend Tooker: I think this house is the coolest house in the Delta.— Did you all know that Halsey Banks's widow put air-conditioning units in the church and rectory at Friar's Point in memory of Halsey?

(General conversation has resumed; everybody is chatting so that the stage sounds like a bird cage.)

Gooper: Too bad nobody cools your church off for you. I bet you sweat in that pulpit these hot Sundays, Reverend Tooker.

Reverend Tooker: Yes, my vestments are drenched. Last Sunday the gold in my chasuble faded into the purple.

Gooper: Reveren', you musta been preachin' hell's fire last Sunday.

Mae *(at the same time to Doctor Baugh)*:   You reckon those vitamin B12 injections are what they're cracked up t' be, Doc Baugh?

Doctor Baugh: Well, if you want to be stuck with something I guess they're as good to be stuck with as anything else.

Big Mama *(at the gallery door)*:   *Maggie, Maggie, aren't you comin' with Brick?*

Mae *(suddenly and loudly, creating a silence)*:   *I have a strange feeling, I have a peculiar feeling!*

Big Mama *(turning from the gallery)*:   What feeling?

Mae: That Brick said somethin' he shouldn't of said t' Big Daddy.

Big Mama: Now what on earth could Brick of said t' Big Daddy that he shouldn't say?

Gooper: Big Mama, there's somethin'—

Mae: NOW, WAIT!

(She rushes up to Big Mama and gives her a quick hug and kiss. Big Mama pushes her impatiently off.)

Doctor Baugh: In my day they had what they call the Keeley cure for heavy drinkers.

Big Mama: Shoot!

Doctor Baugh: But now I understand they just take some kind of tablets.

Gooper: They call them "Annie Bust" tablets.

Big Mama: *Brick don't need to take nothin'.*

(Brick and Margaret appear in gallery doors, Big Mama unaware of his presence behind her.)

That boy is just broken up over Skipper's death. You know how poor Skipper died. They gave him a big, big dose of that sodium amytal stuff at his home and then they called the ambulance and give him another big, big dose of it at the hospital and that and all of the alcohol in his system fo' months an' months just proved too much for his heart...I'm scared of needles! I'm more scared of a needle than the knife...I think more people have been needled out of this world than—

(She stops short and wheels about.)

Oh—here's. Brick! My precious baby—

(She turns upon Brick with short, fat arms extended, at the same time uttering a loud, short sob, which is both comic and touching. Brick smiles and bows slightly, making a burlesque gesture of gallantry for Margaret to pass before him into the room. Then he hobbles on his crutch directly to the liquor cabinet and there is absolute silence, with everybody looking at Brick as everybody has always looked at Brick when he spoke or moved or appeared. One by one he drops ice cubes in his glass, then suddenly, but not quickly, looks back over his shoulder with a wry, charming smile, and says:)

Brick: I'm sorry! Anyone else?

Big Mama *(sadly)*:   No, son. I *wish* you wouldn't!

Brick: I wish I didn't have to, Big Mama, but I'm still waiting for that click in my head which makes it all smooth out!

Big Mama: Ow, Brick, you—BREAK MY HEART!

Margaret *(at same time)*:   *Brick, go sit with Big Mama!*

Big Mama: I just cain't staiiiiii-nnnnnnnd-it...

(She sobs.)

Mae: Now that we're all assembled—

Gooper: We kin talk...

Big Mama: Breaks my heart...

Margaret: Sit with Big Mama, Brick, and hold her hand.

(Big Mama sniffs very loudly three times, almost like three drumbeats in the pocket of silence.)

Brick: You do that, Maggie. I'm a restless cripple. I got to stay on my crutch.

(Brick hobbles to the gallery door; leans there as if waiting.)

(Mae sits beside Big Mama, while Gooper moves in front and sits on the end of the couch, facing her. Reverend Tooker moves nervously into the space between them; on the other side, Doctor Baugh stands looking at nothing in particular and lights a cigar. Margaret turns away.)

Big Mama: Why're you all *surroundin'* me—like this? Why're you all starin' at me like this an' makin' signs at each other?

(Reverend Tooker steps back startled.)

Mae: Calm yourself, Big Mama.

Big Mama: Calm you'self, *you'self*, Sister Woman. How could I calm myself with everyone starin' at me as if big drops of blood had broken out
on m'face? What's this all about, annh! What?

(Gooper coughs and takes a center position.)

Gooper: Now, Doc Baugh.

Mae: Doc Baugh?

Gooper: Big Mama wants to know the complete truth about the report
we got from the Ochsner Clinic.

Mae (*eagerly*):   —on Big Daddy's condition!

Gooper: Yais, on Big Daddy's condition, we got to face it.

Doctor Baugh: Well...

Big Mama (*terrified, rising*):   Is there? Something? Something that I?
Don't—know?

*(In these few words, this startled, very soft, question, Big Mama reviews the
history of her forty-five years with Big Daddy, her great, almost embarrassingly true-hearted and simple-minded devotion to Big Daddy, who must have
had something Brick has, who made himself loved so much by the "simple
expedient" of not loving enough to disturb his charming detachment, also
once coupled, like Brick, with virile beauty).*

(Big Mama has a dignity at this moment; she almost stops being fat.)

Doctor Baugh (*after a pause, uncomfortably*):   Yes?—Well—

Big Mama: I!!!—want to—*knowwwwww...*

*(Immediately she thrusts her fist to her mouth as if to deny that statement.
Then for some curious reason, she snatches the withered corsage from her
breast and hurls it on the floor and steps on it with her short, fat feet.)*

       Somebody must be lyin!—I want to know!

Mae: Sit down, Big Mama, sit down on this sofa.

Margaret: Brick, go sit with Big Mama.

Big Mama: *What is it, what is it?*

Doctor Baugh: I never have seen a more thorough examination than Big
Daddy Pollitt was given in all my experience with the Ochsner Clinic.

Gooper: It's one of the best in the country.

Mae: It's THE best in the country—bar *none!*

*(For some reason she gives Gooper a violent poke as she goes past him. He
slaps at her hand without removing his eyes from his mother's face.)*

Doctor Baugh: Of course they were ninety-nine and nine-tenths percent
sure before they even started.

Big Mama: Sure of what, sure of what, sure of—*what?—what?*

(She catches her breath in a startled sob. Mae kisses her quickly. She thrusts Mae fiercely away from her, staring at the Doctor.)

Mae: Mommy, be a brave girl!

Brick (*in the doorway, softly*):   "By the light, by the light, Of the sil-ve-ry mo-oo-n...[11]"

Gooper: Shut up!—Brick.

Brick: Sorry...

(He wanders out on the gallery.)

Doctor Baugh: But now, you see, Big Mama, they cut a piece of this growth, a specimen of the tissue and—

Big Mama: Growth? You told Big Daddy—

Doctor Baugh: Now wait.

Big Mama (*fiercely*):   You told me and Big Daddy there wasn't a thing wrong with him but—

Mae: Big Mama, they always—

Gooper: Let Doc Baugh talk, will yuh?

Big Mama: —little spastic condition of—

(Her breath gives out in a sob.)

Doctor Baugh: Yes, that's what we told Big Daddy. But we had this bit of tissue run through the laboratory and I'm sorry to say the test was positive on it. It's—well—malignant...

(Pause.)

Big Mama: —Cancer?! Cancer?!

(Doctor Baugh nods gravely. Big Mama gives a long gasping cry.)

Mae and Gooper: Now, now, now, Big Mama, you had to know...

Big Mama: WHY DIDN'T THEY CUT IT OUT OF HIM? HANH? HANH?

Doctor Baugh: Involved too much, Big Mama, too many organs affected.

Mae: Big Mama, the liver's affected and so's the kidneys, both! It's gone way past what they call a—

Gooper: A surgical risk.

Mae: —Uh-huh...

(Big Mama draws a breath like a dying gasp.)

Reverend Tooker: Tch, tch, tch, tch, tch!

Doctor Baugh: Yes it's gone past the knife.

Mae: *That's why he's turned yellow, Mommy!*

Big Mama: *Git away from me, git away from me, Mae!*

(She rises abruptly.)

---

[11]"By The Light of the Silvery Moon" is a popular song, written and published by Gus Edwards and Edward Madden in 1909.

I want Brick! Where's Brick? Where is my only son?

Mae: Mama! Did she say "*only* son"?

Gooper: What does that make *me*?

Mae: A sober responsible man with five precious children!—*Six*!

Big Mama: I want Brick to tell me! Brick! Brick!

Margaret (*rising from her reflections in a corner*):   Brick was so upset he went back out.

Big Mama: *Brick*!

Margaret: Mama, let *me* tell you!

Big Mama: No, no, leave me alone, you're not my blood!

Gooper: *Mama, I'm your son*! Listen to *me*!

Mae: Gooper's your son, he's your first-born!

Big Mama: Gooper never liked Daddy.

Mae (*as if terribly shocked*):   That's not TRUE!

(*There is a pause. The minister coughs and rises.*)

Reverend Tooker (*to Mae*):   I think I'd better slip away at this point.

(*Discreetly.*)

Good night, good night, everybody, and God bless you all... on this place...

(*He slips out.*)

(*Mae coughs and points at Big Mama.*)

Gooper: Well, Big Mama...

(*He sighs.*)

Big Mama: It's all a mistake, I know it's just a bad dream.

Doctor Baugh: We're gonna keep Big Daddy as comfortable as we can.

Big Mama: Yes, it's just a bad dream, that's all it is, it's just an awful dream.

Gooper: In my opinion Big Daddy is having some pain but won't admit that he has it.

Big Mama: Just a dream, a bad dream.

Doctor Baugh: That's what lots of them do, they think if they don't admit they're having the pain they can sort of escape the fact of it.

Gooper (*with relish*):   Yes, they get sly about it, they get real sly about it.

Mae: Gooper and I think—

Gooper: Shut up, Mae! Big Mama, I think—Big Daddy ought to be started on morphine.

Big Mama: Nobody's going to give Big Daddy morphine.

Doctor Baugh: Now, Big Mama, when that pain strikes it's going to strike mighty hard and Big Daddy's going to need the needle to bear it.

Big Mama:　I tell you, nobody's going to give him morphine.

Mae:　Big Mama, you don't want to see Big Daddy suffer, you know you—

(Gooper, standing beside her, gives her a savage poke.)

Doctor Baugh *(placing a package on the table)*:　I'm leaving this stuff here, so if there's a sudden attack you all won't have to send out for it.

Mae:　I know how to give a hypo.

Big Mama:　Nobody's gonna give Big Daddy morphine.

Gooper:　Mae took a course in nursing during the war.

Margaret:　Somehow I don't think Big Daddy would want Mae to give him a hypo.

Mae:　You think he'd want *you* to do it?

Doctor Baugh:　Well...

(Doctor Baugh rises.)

Gooper:　Doctor Baugh is goin'.

Doctor Baugh:　Yes, I got to be goin'. Well, keep your chin up, Big Mama.

Gooper *(with jocularity)*:　She's gonna keep *both* chins up, aren't you, Big Mama?

(Big Mama sobs.)

　　Now stop that, Big Mama.

Gooper *(at the door with Doctor Baugh)*:　Well, Doc, we sure do appreciate all you done. I'm telling you, we're surely obligated to you for—

(Doctor Baugh has gone out without a glance at him.)

　　—I guess that doctor has got a lot on his mind but it wouldn't hurt him to act a little more human...

(Big Mama sobs.)

　　Now be a brave girl, Mommy.

Big Mama:　It's not true, I know that it's just not true!

Gooper:　Mama, those tests are infallible!

Big Mama:　Why are you so determined to see your father daid?

Mae:　Big Mama!

Margaret *(gently)*:　I know what Big Mama means.

Mae *(fiercely)*:　Oh, do you?

Margaret *(quietly and very sadly)*:　Yes, I think I do.

Mae:　For a newcomer in the family you sure do show a lot of understanding.

Margaret:　Understanding is needed on this place.

Mae:　I guess you must have needed a lot of it in your family, Maggie, with your father's liquor problem and now you've got Brick with his!

Margaret: Brick does not have a liquor problem at all. Brick is devoted to Big Daddy. This thing is a terrible strain on him.

Big Mama: Brick is Big Daddy's boy, but he drinks too much and it worries me and Big Daddy, and, Margaret, you've got to cooperate with us, you've got to cooperate with Big Daddy and me in getting Brick straightened out. Because it will break Big Daddy's heart if Brick don't pull himself together and take hold of things.

Mae: Take hold of *what* things, Big Mama?

Big Mama: The place.

(There is a quick violent look between Mae and Gooper.)

Gooper: Big Mama, you've had a shock.

Mae: Yais, we've all had a shock, but...

Gooper: Let's be realistic—

Mae: —Big Daddy would never, would *never*, be foolish enough to—

Gooper: —put this place in irresponsible hands!

Big Mama: Big Daddy ain't going to leave the place in anybody's hands; Big Daddy is *not* going to die. I want you to get that in your heads, all of you!

Mae: Mommy, Mommy, Big Mama, we're just as hopeful an' optimistic as you are about Big Daddy's prospects, we have faith in *prayer*—but nevertheless there are certain matters that have to be discussed an' dealt with, because otherwise—

Gooper: Eventualities have to be considered and now's the time...Mae, will you please get my brief case out of our room?

Mae: Yes, honey.

(She rises and goes out through the hall door.)

Gooper *(standing over Big Mama)*:   Now, Big Mom. What you said just now was not at all true and you know it. I've always loved Big Daddy in my own quiet way. I never made a show of it, and I know that Big Daddy has always been fond of me in a quiet way, too, and he never made a show of it neither.

(Mae returns with Gooper's brief case.)

Mae: Here's your brief case, Gooper, honey.

Gooper *(handing the brief case back to her)*:   Thank you...Of cou'se, my relationship with Big Daddy is different from Brick's.

Mae: You're eight years older'n Brick an' always had t' carry a bigger load of th' responsibilities than Brick ever had t' carry. He never carried a thing in his life but a football or a highball.

Gooper: Mae, will y' let me talk, please?

Mae: Yes, honey.

Gooper: Now, a twenty-eight-thousand-acre plantation's a mighty big thing t' run.

Mae: Almost singlehanded.

(Margaret has gone out onto the gallery and can be heard calling softly to Brick.)

Big Mama: You never had to run this place! What are you talking about? As if Big Daddy was dead and in his grave, you had to run it? Why, you just helped him out with a few business details and had your law practice at the same time in Memphis!

Mae: Oh, Mommy, Mommy, Big Mommy! Let's be fair!

Margaret: Brick!

Mae: Why, Gooper has given himself body and soul to keeping this place up for the past five years since Big Daddy's health started failing.

Margaret: Brick!

Mae: Gooper won't say it, Gooper never thought of it as a duty, he just did it. And what did Brick do? Brick kept living in his past glory at college! Still a football player at twenty-seven!

Margaret *(returning alone)*:   Who are you talking about now? Brick? A football player? He isn't a football player and you know it. Brick is a sports announcer on TV and one of the best-known ones in the country!

Mae: I'm talking about what he was.

Margaret: Well, I wish you would just stop talking about my husband.

Gooper: I've got a right to discuss my brother with other members of MY OWN family, which don't include *you*. Why don't you go out there and drink with Brick?

Margaret: I've never seen such malice toward a brother.

Gooper: How about his for me? Why, he can't stand to be in the same room with me!

Margaret: This is a deliberate campaign of vilification for the most disgusting and sordid reason on earth, and I know what it is! It's *avarice, avarice, greed, greed!*

Big Mama: *Oh, I'll scream! I will scream in a moment unless this stops!*

(Gooper has stalked up to Margaret with clenched fists at his sides as if he would strike her. Mae distorts her face again into a hideous grimace behind Margaret's back.)

Big Mama *(sobs)*:   Margaret. Child. Come here. Sit next to Big Mama.

Margaret: Precious Mommy. I'm sorry, I'm sorry, I—!

(She bends her long graceful neck to press her forehead to Big Mama's bulging shoulder under its black chiffon.)

Mae: How beautiful, how touching, this display of devotion! Do you know why she's childless? She's childless because that big beautiful athlete husband of hers won't go to bed with her!

Gooper: You jest won't let me do this in a nice way, will yah? Aw right— I don't give a goddamn if Big Daddy likes me or don't like me or did or never did or will or will never! I'm just appealing to a sense of common decency and fair play. I'll tell you the truth. I've resented Big Daddy's partiality to Brick ever since Brick was born, and the way I've been treated like I was just barely good enough to spit on and sometimes not even good enough for that. Big Daddy is dying of cancer, and it's spread all through him and it's attacked all his vital organs including the kidneys and right now he is sinking into uremia, and you all know what uremia is, it's poisoning of the whole system due to the failure of the body to eliminate its poisons.

Margaret (*to herself, downstage, hissingly*):   *Poisons, poisons! Venomous thoughts and words! In hearts and minds!—That's poisons!*

Gooper (*overlapping her*):   I am asking for a square deal, and, by God, I expect to get one. But if I don't get one, if there's any peculiar she-nanigans going on around here behind my back, well, I'm not a cor-poration lawyer for nothing, I know how to protect my own interests.

(*Brick enters from the gallery with a tranquil, blurred smile, carrying an empty glass with him.*)

Brick: Storm coming up.

Gooper: Oh! A late arrival!

Mae: Behold the conquering hero comes!

Gooper: The fabulous Brick Pollitt! Remember him?—Who could forget him!

Mae: He looks like he's been injured in a game!

Gooper: Yep, I'm afraid you'll have to warm the bench at the Sugar Bowl this year, Brick!

(*Mae laughs shrilly.*)

Or was it the Rose Bowl that he made that famous run in?—

(*Thunder.*)

Mae: The punch bowl, honey. It was in the punch bowl, the cut-glass punch bowl!

Gooper: Oh, that's right, I'm getting the bowls mixed up!

Margaret: Why don't you stop venting your malice and envy on a sick boy?

Big Mama: *Now you two hush, I mean it, hush, all of you, hush!*

Daisy, Sookey: Storm! Storm comin'! Storm! Storm!

Lacey: Brightie, close them shutters.

Gooper: Lacey, put the top up on my Cadillac, will yuh?

Lacey: Yes, suh, Mistah Pollitt!

Gooper (*at the same time*):   Big Mama, you know it's necessary for me t' go back to Memphis in th' mornin' t' represent the Parker estate in a lawsuit.

(*Mae sits on the bed and arranges papers she has taken from the brief case.*)

Big Mama: Is it, Gooper?

Mae: Yaiss.

Gooper: That's why I'm forced to—to bring up a problem that—

Mae: Somethin' that's too important t' be put off!

Gooper: If Brick was sober, he ought to be in on this.

Margaret: Brick is present; we're present.

Gooper: Well, good. I will now give you this outline my partner, Tom Bullitt, an' me have drawn up—a sort of dummy—trusteeship.

Margaret: Oh, that's it! You'll be in charge an' dole out remittances, will you?

Gooper: This we did as soon as we got the report on Big Daddy from th' Ochsner Laboratories. We did this thing, I mean we drew up this dummy outline with the advice and assistance of the Chairman of the Boa'd of Directors of th' Southern Plantahs Bank and Trust Company in Memphis, C. C. Bellowes, a man who handles estates for all th' prominent fam'lies in West Tennessee and th' Delta.

Big Mama: Gooper?

Gooper (*crouching in front of Big Mama*):   Now this is not—not final, or anything like it. This is just a preliminary outline. But it does provide a basis—a design—a—possible, feasible—*plan!*

Margaret: Yes, I'll bet it's a plan.

(*Thunder.*)

Mae: It's a plan to protect the biggest estate in the Delta from irresponsibility an'—

Big Mama: Now you listen to me, all of you, you listen here! They's not goin' to be any more catty talk in my house! And Gooper, you put that away before I grab it out of your hand and tear it right up! I don't know what the hell's in it, and I don't want to know what the hell's in it. I'm talkin' in Big Daddy's language now; I'm his *wife*, not his *widow*, I'm still his *wife!* And I'm talkin' to you in his language an'—

Gooper: Big Mama, what I have here is—

Mae (*at the same time*):   Gooper explained that it's just a plan...

Big Mama: I don't care what you got there. Just put it back where it came from, an' don't let me see it again, not even the outside of the envelope of it! Is that understood? Basis! Plan! Preliminary! Design! I say—what is it Big Daddy always says when he's disgusted?

Brick (*from the bar*):   Big Daddy says "crap" when he's disgusted.
Big Mama (*rising*):   That's right—CRAP! I say CRAP too, like Big Daddy!

(*Thunder.*)

Mae: Coarse language doesn't seem called for in this—
Gooper: Somethin' in me is *deeply outraged* by hearin' you talk like this.
Big Mama: *Nobody's goin' to take nothin'!*—till Big Daddy lets go of it—
maybe, just possibly, not—not even then! No, not even then!

(*Thunder.*)

Mae: Sookey, hurry up an' git that po'ch furniture covahed; want th'
paint to come off?
Gooper: Lacey, put mah car away!
Lacey: Caint, Mistah Pollitt, you got the keys!
Gooper: Naw, you got 'em, man. Where th' keys to th' car, honey?
Mae: You got 'em in your pocket!
Brick: "You can always hear me singin' this song, Show me the way to
go home."

(*Thunder distantly.*)

Big Mama: Brick! Come here, Brick, I need you. Tonight Brick looks like
he used to look when he was a little boy, just like he did when he
played wild games and used to come home when I hollered myself
hoarse for him, all sweaty and pink cheeked and sleepy, with his—red
curls shining...

(*Brick draws aside as he does from all physical contact and continues the
song in a whisper, opening the ice bucket and dropping in the ice cubes one
by one as if he were mixing some important chemical formula.*)

(*Distant thunder.*)

Time goes by so fast. Nothin' can outrun it. Death commences
too early—almost before you're half acquainted with life—you
meet the other... Oh, you know we just got to love each other an'
stay together, all of us, just as close as we can, especially now that
such a *black* thing has come and moved into this place without
invitation.

(*Awkwardly embracing Brick, she presses her head to his shoulder.*)

(*A dog howls offstage.*)

Oh, Brick, son of Big Daddy, Big Daddy does so love you. Y'know
what would be his fondest dream come true? If before he passed on, if
Big Daddy has to pass on...

(*A dog howls.*)

> ...you give him a child of yours, a grandson as much like his son
> as his son is like Big Daddy...

Margaret: I know that's Big Daddy's dream.

Big Mama: That's his dream.

Mae: Such a pity that Maggie and Brick can't oblige.

Big Daddy (*off downstage right on the gallery*):   Looks like the wind was
takin' liberties with this place.

Servant (*offstage*):   Yes, sir, Mr. Pollitt.

Margaret (*crossing to the right door*):   Big Daddy's on the gall'ry.

(*Big Mama has turned toward the hall door at the sound of Big Daddy's
voice on the gallery.*)

Big Mama: I can't stay here. He'll see somethin' in my eyes.

(*Big Daddy enters the room from upstage right.*)

Big Daddy: Can I come in?

(*He puts his cigar in an ash tray.*)

Margaret: Did the storm wake you up, Big Daddy?

Big Daddy: Which stawm are you talkin' about—th' one outside or th'
hullballoo in here?

(*Gooper squeezes past Big Daddy.*)

Gooper: 'Scuse me.

(*Mae tries to squeeze past Big Daddy to join Gooper, but Big Daddy puts his
arm firmly around her.*)

Big Daddy: I heard some mighty loud talk. Sounded like somethin' important was bein' discussed. What was the powwow about?

Mae (*flustered*):   Why—nothin', Big Daddy...

Big Daddy (*crossing to extreme left center, taking Mae with him*):   What is
that pregnant-lookin' envelope you're puttin' back in your brief case,
Gooper?

Gooper (*at the foot of the bed, caught, as he stuffs papers into envelope*):
That? Nothin', suh—nothin' much of anythin' at all...

Big Daddy: Nothin'? It looks like a whole lot of nothin'!

(*He turns upstage to the group.*)

You all know th' story about th' young married couple—

Gooper: Yes, sir!

Big Daddy: Hello, Brick—

Brick: Hello, Big Daddy.

(*The group is arranged in a semicircle above Big Daddy, Margaret at the
extreme right, then Mae and Gooper, then Big Mama, with Brick at the left.*)

Big Daddy: Young married couple took Junior out to th' zoo one Sunday, inspected all of God's creatures in their cages, with satisfaction.

Gooper: Satisfaction.

Big Daddy (*crossing to upstage center, facing front*):   This afternoon was a warm afternoon in spring an' that ole elephant had somethin' else on his mind which was bigger'n peanuts. You know this story, Brick?

(*Gooper nods.*)

Brick: No, sir, I don't know it.

Big Daddy: Y'see, in th' cage adjoinin' they was a young female elephant in heat!

Big Mama (*at Big Daddy's shoulder*):   Oh, Big Daddy!

Big Daddy: What's the matter, preacher's gone, ain't he? All right. That female elephant in the next cage was permeatin' the atmosphere about her with a powerful and excitin' odor of female fertility! Huh! Ain't that a nice way to put it, Brick?

Brick: Yes, sir, nothin' wrong with it.

Big Daddy: Brick says th's nothin' wrong with it!

Big Mama: Oh, Big Daddy!

Big Daddy (*crossing to downstage center*):   So this ole bull elephant still had a couple of fornications left in him. He reared back his trunk an' got a whiff of that elephant lady next door!—began to paw at the dirt in his cage an' butt his head against the separatin' partition and, first thing y'know, there was a conspicuous change in his *profile*—very *conspicuous!* Ain't I tellin' this story in decent language, Brick?

Brick: Yes, sir, too fuckin' decent!

Big Daddy: So, the little boy pointed at it and said, "What's that?" His mama said, "Oh, that's—nothin'!"—His papa said, "She's spoiled!"

(*Big Daddy crosses to Brick at left.*)

      You didn't laugh at that story, Brick.

(*Big Mama crosses to downstage right crying. Margaret goes to her. Mae and Gooper bold upstage right center.*)

Brick: No, sir, I didn't laugh at that story.

Big Daddy: What is the smell in this room? Don't you notice it, Brick? Don't you notice a powerful and obnoxious odor of mendacity in this room?

Brick: Yes, sir, I think I do, sir.

Gooper: Mae, Mae...

Big Daddy: There is nothing more powerful. Is there, Brick?

Brick: No, sir. No, sir, there isn't, an' nothin' more obnoxious.

Big Daddy: Brick agrees with me. The odor of mendacity is a powerful and obnoxious odor an' the stawm hasn't blown it away from this room yet. You notice it, Gooper?

Gooper: What, sir?

Big Daddy: How about you, Sister Woman? You notice the unpleasant odor of mendacity in this room?

Mae: Why, Big Daddy, I don't even know what that is.

Big Daddy: You can smell it. Hell it smells like death!

(Big Mama sobs. Big Daddy looks toward her.)

What's wrong with that fat woman over there, loaded with diamonds? Hey, what's-you-name, what's the matter with you?

Margaret (*crossing toward Big Daddy*):   She had a slight dizzy spell, Big Daddy.

Big Daddy: You better watch that, Big Mama. A stroke is a bad way to go.

Margaret (*crossing to Big Daddy at center*):   Oh, Brick, Big Daddy has on your birthday present to him, Brick, he has on your cashmere robe, the softest material I have ever felt.

Big Daddy: Yeah, this is my soft birthday, Maggie...Not my gold or my silver birthday, but my soft birthday, everything's got to be soft for Big Daddy on this soft birthday.

(Maggie kneels before Big Daddy at center.)

Margaret: Big Daddy's got on his Chinese slippers that I gave him, Brick. Big Daddy, I haven't given you my big present yet, but now I will, now's the time for me to present it to you! I have an announcement to make!

Mae: What? What kind of announcement?

Gooper: A sports announcement, Maggie?

Margaret: Announcement of life beginning! A child is coming, sired by Brick, and out of Maggie the Cat! I have Brick's child in my body, an' that's my birthday present to Big Daddy on this birthday!

(Big Daddy looks at Brick who crosses behind Big Daddy to downstage portal, left.)

Big Daddy: Get up, girl, get up off your knees, girl.

(Big Daddy helps Margaret to rise. He crosses above her, to her right, bites off the end of a fresh cigar, taken from his bathrobe pocket, as he studies Margaret.)

Uh huh, this girl has life in her body, that's no lie!

Big Mama: BIG DADDY'S DREAM COME TRUE!

Brick: JESUS!

Big Daddy (*crossing right below wicker stand*):   Gooper, I want my lawyer in the mornin'.

Brick: Where are you goin', Big Daddy?

Big Daddy: Son, I'm goin' up on the roof, to the belvedere on th' roof to look over my kingdom before I give up my kingdom—twenty-eight thousand acres of th' richest land this side of the valley Nile!

(He exits through right doors, and down right on the gallery.)

Big Mama (following): Sweetheart, sweetheart, sweetheart—can I come with you?

(She exits downstage right.)

(Margaret is downstage center in the mirror area. Mae has joined Gooper and she gives him a fierce poke, making a low hissing sound and a grimace of fury.)

Gooper (pushing her aside): Brick, could you possibly spare me one small shot of that liquor?

Brick: Why, help yourself, Gooper boy.

Gooper: I will.

Mae (shrilly): Of course we know that this is—a lie.

Gooper: Be still, Mae.

Mae: I won't be still! I know she's made this up!

Gooper: Goddamn it, I said shut up!

Margaret: Gracious! I didn't know that my little announcement was going to provoke such a storm!

Mae: That woman isn't pregnant!

Gooper: Who said she was?

Mae: She did.

Gooper: The doctor didn't. Doc Baugh didn't.

Margaret: I haven't gone to Doc Baugh.

Gooper: Then who'd you go to, Maggie?

Margaret: One of the best gynecologists in the South.

Gooper: Uh huh, uh huh!—I see...

(He takes out a pencil and notebook.)

—May we have his name, please?

Margaret: No, you may not, Mister Prosecuting Attorney!

Mae: He doesn't have any name, he doesn't exist!

Margaret: Oh, he exists all right, and so does my child, Brick's baby!

Mae: You can't conceive a child by a man that won't sleep with you unless you think you're—

(Brick has turned on the phonograph. A scat song cuts Mae's speech.)

Gooper: Turn that off!

Mae: We know it's a lie because we hear you in here; he won't sleep with you, we hear you! So don't imagine you're going to put a trick over on us, to fool a dying man with a—

(A long drawn cry of agony and rage fills the house. Margaret turns the phonograph down to a whisper. The cry is repeated.)

Mae: Did you hear that, Gooper, did you hear that?
Gooper: Sounds like the pain has struck.
Mae: Go see, Gooper!
Gooper: Come along and leave these lovebirds together in their nest!

(He goes out first. Mae follows but turns at the door, contorting her face and hissing at Margaret.)

Mae: *Liar!*

(She slams the door.)

(Margaret exhales with relief and moves a little unsteadily to catch hold of Brick's arm.)

Margaret: Thank you for—keeping still...
Brick: O.K., Maggie.
Margaret: It was gallant of you to save my face!

(He now pours down three shots in quick succession and stands waiting, silent. All at once he turns with a smile and says:)

Brick: *There!*
Margaret: What?
Brick: The *click*...

(His gratitude seems almost infinite as he hobbles out on the gallery with a drink. We hear his crutch as he swings out of sight. Then, at some distance, he begins singing to himself a peaceful song. Margaret holds the big pillow forlornly as if it were her only companion, for a few moments, then throws it on the bed. She rushes to the liquor cabinet, gathers all the bottles in her arms, turns about undecidedly, then runs out of the room with them, leaving the door ajar on the dim yellow hall. Brick is heard hobbling back along the gallery, singing his peaceful song. He comes back in, sees the pillow on the bed, laughs lightly, sadly, picks it up. He has it under his arm as Margaret returns to the room. Margaret softly shuts the door and leans against it, smiling softly at Brick.)

Margaret: Brick, I used to think that you were stronger than me and I didn't want to be overpowered by you. But now, since you've taken to liquor—you know what?—I guess it's bad, but now I'm stronger than you and I can love you more truly! Don't move that pillow. I'll move it right back if you do!—Brick?

(She turns out all the lamps but a single rose-silk-shaded one by the bed.)

I really have been to a doctor and I know what to do and—
Brick?—this is my time by the calendar to conceive?

Brick: Yes, I understand, Maggie. But how are you going to conceive a child by a man in love with his liquor?

Margaret: By locking his liquor up and making him satisfy my desire before I unlock it!

Brick: Is that what you've done, Maggie?

Margaret: Look and see. That cabinet's mighty empty compared to before!

Brick: Well, I'll be a son of a—

(He reaches for his crutch but she beats him to it and rushes out on the gallery, hurls the crutch over the rail, and comes back in, panting.)

Margaret: And so tonight we're going to make the lie true, and when that's done, I'll bring the liquor back here and we'll get drunk together, here, tonight, in this place that death has come into...—What do you say?

Brick: I don't say anything. I guess there's nothing to say.

Margaret: Oh, you weak people, you weak, beautiful people!—who give up with such grace. What you want is someone to—

(She turns out the rose-silk lamp.)

—take hold of you.—Gently, gently with love hand your life back to you, like somethin' gold you let go of. I *do* love you, Brick, *I do!*

Brick *(smiling with charming sadness)*: Wouldn't it be funny if that was true?

The Curtain Comes Down

[1955]

▪▪▪ CONTEXT AND RESPONSE ▪▪▪

Carson McCullers, from *The Member of the Wedding*

The Southern Gothic literary genre groups together writers of the Southern United States whose works, set in the South, include eccentric characters enmeshed in bizarre or dreamlike situations. Well-known Southern Gothic writers include Flannery O'Connor, Truman Capote, William Faulkner, and Tennessee Williams. In the 1940s, the newly successful Williams became friends with and encouraged the career of a contemporary, Georgia-born Carson McCullers, who had already become a successful writer while still in her early twenties. McCullers's novels and short stories map the interior lives of lonely characters trying to connect with others. Her first novel, *The Heart Is a Lonely Hunter* (1940), was swiftly followed by *Reflections in a Golden Eye* (1941) and *The Member of the Wedding* (1946). Williams urged McCullers to adapt *The Member of the Wedding* into a play and she took his advice. The successful Broadway production was adapted into a movie in 1952.

The Member of the Wedding centers on around an imaginative and awkward girl, Frankie, on the brink between childhood and adolescence, who becomes obsessed with the specialness of her brother's upcoming marriage. She idealizes the rather ordinary event into something transcendent that, in her yearning to transform herself, she longs to take part in. That Tennessee Williams felt a connection to the work of McCullers is not surprising: both writers sympathetically examine the plight of the sensitive social outcast. These fragile characters often collide with harsh realities, as does Frankie as soon as she begins to see her brother's wedding as her escape from loneliness and the beginning of belonging. In the following excerpt from the novel's first chapter, Frankie gives voice to her fascination with the union of Jarvis and his bride.

CARSON MCCULLERS ▪ (1917–1967)

It happened that green and crazy summer when Frankie was twelve years old. This was the summer when for a long time she had not been a member. She belonged to no club and was a member of nothing in the world. Frankie had become an unjoined person who hung around in doorways, and she was afraid. In June the trees were bright dizzy green, but later the leaves darkened, and the town turned black and shrunken under the glare of the sun. At first Frankie walked around doing one thing and another. The sidewalks of the town were gray in the early morning and at night, but the noon sun put a glaze on them, so that the cement burned and glittered like glass. The sidewalks finally became too hot for Frankie's feet, and also she got herself in trouble. She was in so much secret trouble that she thought it was better to stay at home—and at home there was only Berenice Sadie Brown and John Henry West. The three of them sat at the kitchen table, saying the same things over and over, so that by August the words began to rhyme with each other and sound strange. The world seemed to die each afternoon and nothing moved any longer. At last the summer was like a green sick dream, or like a silent crazy jungle under glass. And then, on the last Friday of August, all this was changed: it was so sudden that Frankie puzzled the whole blank afternoon, and still she did not understand.

"It is so very queer," she said. "The way it all just happened."

"Happened? Happened?" said Berenice.

John Henry listened and watched them quietly.

"I have never been so puzzled."

"But puzzled about what?"

"The whole thing," Frankie said.

And Berenice remarked: "I believe the sun has fired your brains."

"Me too." John Henry whispered.

Frankie herself almost admitted maybe so. It was four o'clock in the afternoon and the kitchen was square and gray and quiet. Frankie sat at the table with her eyes half closed, and she thought about a wedding. She saw a silent church, a strange snow slanting down against the colored windows. The groom in the wedding was her brother, and there was a brightness where his face should be. The bride was there in a long white train, and the bride also was faceless. There was something about this wedding that gave Frankie a feeling she could not name.

"Look here at me," said Berenice. "You jealous?"

"Jealous?"

"Jealous because your brother is going to be married?"

"No," said Frankie. "I just never saw any two people like them. When they walked in the house today it was so queer."

"You jealous," said Berenice. "Go and behold yourself in the mirror. I can see from the color in your eye."

There was a watery kitchen mirror hanging above the sink. Frankie looked, but her eyes were gray as they always were. This summer she was grown so tall that she was almost a big freak, and her shoulders were narrow, her legs too long. She wore a pair of blue black shorts, a

B.V.D. undervest, and she was barefooted. Her hair had been cut like a boy's, but it had not been cut for a long time and was now not even parted. The reflection in the glass was warped and crooked, but Frankie knew well what she looked like; she drew up her left shoulder and turned her head aside.

"Oh," she said. "They were the two prettiest people I ever saw. I just can't understand how it happened."

"But what, Foolish?" said Berenice. "Your brother come home with the girl he means to marry and took dinner today with you and your Daddy. They intend to marry at her home in Winter Hill this coming Sunday. You and your Daddy are going to the wedding. And that is the A and the Z of the matter. So whatever ails you?"

"I don't know," said Frankie. "I bet they have a good time every minute of the day."

"Less us have a good time," John Henry said.

"Us have a good time?" Frankie asked. "Us?"

JOHN CHEEVER ■ (1912–1982)

John Cheever was born in Quincy, Massachusetts, the son of a shoe salesman who lost his job and fortune in the 1920s. His mother took on the responsibility of providing for the family, operating a gift shop. Cheever attended Thayer Academy in Braintree, Massachusetts, but was expelled for smoking and bad grades, and he then started working as a writer (and living more or less in poverty) in New York City. Cheever was close to his brother, Fred, with whom he later shared an apartment in Boston, and in the 1930s Fred helped to support Cheever as he worked on his fiction. A number of Cheever's novels and stories (e.g., "The Brothers") delve into the complexities of fraternal relationships and, more broadly, examine the tensions, connections, and exclusions within families and in the community.

Cheever's first story, "Expelled," based on his own experience, was published in *The New Republic* in 1930; a few years later he began a literary relationship with *The New Yorker* magazine, where many of his stories appeared. In *The Way Some People Live* (1943), *The Enormous Radio and Other Stories* (1953), and *The Housebreaker of Shady Hill and Other Stories* (1958), Cheever presented men and women in urban and, especially, suburban settings, highlighting the disjunction between their material comforts and their disordered and strife-laden emotional, sexual, and spiritual lives. Cheever's own life was a painful, difficult one; he suffered from alcoholism, severe bouts of depression, and other serious ailments, including cancer, from which he died. In a journal entry, he observed, "There is no home, there is no surety or permanence in this world."

Cheever's first novel, *The Wapshot Chronicle* (1957), describing a wealthy Massachusetts family, was honored with the National Book Award. *Falconer* (1977), his fourth novel, about a character in prison who falls in love with another man and undergoes a religious awakening, was a best seller. His collected *Stories* (1978) received the Pulitzer Prize and the National Book Critics Circle Award.

The Sorrows of Gin" is an adroit, powerful piece of short-story writing about affluent suburbia told from the point of view of eight-year old Amy as she surveys, experiences, and responds to the emptiness, disconnection, and hypocrisy (and alcoholism and partying) of her parents. Amy is both observant and naïve, dreamy, alienated, a child interacting with parents who are self-absorbed and imperceptive about their daughter's thoughts, feelings, and uncertainties, and with maids, cooks, and babysitters who inadequately perform a role for Amy that her parents do not. Mr. Lawton, the father, relies on liquor to block his engagement with others, above all with his own child. His and his wife's lives, neglectful and corrupt, are perhaps most accurately defined and represented by the amount of gin they consume.

Biographical works include Blake Bailey, *Cheever: A Life* (2009); and Susan Cheever, *Home Before Dark: A Biographical Memoir of John Cheever*

Lower Manhattan skyline, 1948. Photograph by Jack Delano.

by His Daughter (1984). See also the novel by Cheever's son Benjamin, *The Plagiarist* (1992). For literary interpretation, see Lynne Waldeland, *John Cheever* (1979); *Critical Essays on John Cheever*, ed. R. G. Collins (1982); George W. Hunt, *John Cheever: The Hobgoblin Company of Love* (1983); and James E. O'Hara, *John Cheever: A Study of the Short Fiction* (1989).

The Sorrows of Gin

It was Sunday afternoon, and from her bedroom Amy could hear the Beardens coming in, followed a little while later by the Farquarsons and the Parminters. She went on reading *Black Beauty* until she felt in her bones that they might be eating something good. Then she closed her book and went down the stairs. The living-room door was shut, but through it she could hear the noise of loud talk and laughter. They must have been gossiping or worse, because they all stopped talking when she entered the room.

"Hi, Amy," Mr. Farquarson said.

"Mr. Farquarson spoke to you, Amy," her father said.

"Hello, Mr. Farquarson," she said. By standing outside the group for a minute, until they had resumed their conversation, and then by slipping past Mrs. Farquarson, she was able to swoop down on the nut dish and take a handful.

"Amy!" Mr. Lawton said.

"I'm sorry, Daddy," she said, retreating out of the circle, toward the piano.

"Put those nuts back," he said.

"I've handled them, Daddy," she said.

"Well, pass the nuts, dear," her mother said sweetly. "Perhaps someone else would like nuts."

Amy filled her mouth with the nuts she had taken, returned to the coffee table, and passed the nut dish.

"Thank you, Amy," they said, taking a peanut or two.

"How do you like your new school, Amy?" Mrs. Bearden asked.

"I like it," Amy said. "I like private schools better than public schools. It isn't so much like a factory."

"What grade are you in?" Mr. Bearden asked.

"Fourth," she said.

Her father took Mr. Parminter's glass and his own, and got up to go into the dining room and refill them. She fell into the chair he had left vacant.

"Don't sit in your father's chair, Amy," her mother said, not realizing that Amy's legs were worn out from riding a bicycle, while her father had done nothing but sit down all day.

As she walked toward the French doors, she heard her mother beginning to talk about the new cook. It was a good example of the interesting things they found to talk about.

"You'd better put your bicycle in the garage," her father said, returning with the fresh drinks. "It looks like rain."

Amy went out onto the terrace and looked at the sky, but it was not very cloudy, it wouldn't rain, and his advice, like all the advice he gave her, was superfluous. They were always at her. "Put your bicycle away." "Open the door for Grandmother, Amy." "Feed the cat." "Do your homework." "Pass the nuts." "Help Mrs. Bearden with her parcels." "Amy, please try and take more pains with your appearance."

They all stood, and her father came to the door and called her. "We're going over to the Parminters' for supper," he said. "Cook's here, so you won't be alone. Be sure and go to bed at eight like a good girl. And come and kiss me good night."

After their cars had driven off, Amy wandered through the kitchen to the cook's bedroom beyond it and knocked on the door. "Come in," a voice said, and when Amy entered, she found the cook, whose name was Rosemary, in her bathrobe, reading the Bible. Rosemary smiled at Amy. Her smile was sweet and her old eyes were blue. "Your parents have gone out again?" she asked. Amy said that they had, and the old woman invited her to sit down. "They do seem to enjoy themselves, don't they? During the four days I've been here, they've been out every night, or had people in." She put the Bible face down on her lap and smiled, but not at Amy. "Of course, the drinking that goes on here is all sociable, and what your parents do is none of my business, is it? I worry about drink more than most people, because of my poor sister. My poor sister drank too much.

For ten years, I went to visit her on Sunday afternoons, and most of the time she was *non compos mentis.*[1] Sometimes I'd find her huddled up on the floor with one or two sherry bottles empty beside her. Sometimes she'd seem sober enough to a stranger, but I could tell in a second by the way she spoke her words that she'd drunk enough not to be herself any more. Now my poor sister is gone, I don't have anyone to visit at all."

"What happened to your sister?" Amy asked.

"She was a lovely person, with a peaches-and-cream complexion and fair hair," Rosemary said. "Gin makes some people gay—it makes them laugh and cry—but with my sister it only made her sullen and withdrawn. When she was drinking, she would retreat into herself. Drink made her contrary. If I'd say the weather was fine, she'd tell me I was wrong. If I'd say it was raining, she'd say it was clearing. She'd correct me about everything I said, however small it was. She died in Bellevue Hospital one summer while I was working in Maine. She was the only family I had."

The directness with which Rosemary spoke had the effect on Amy of making her feel grown, and for once politeness came to her easily. "You must miss your sister a great deal," she said.

"I was just sitting here now thinking about her. She was in service, like me, and it's lonely work. You're always surrounded by a family, and yet you're never a part of it. Your pride is often hurt. The Madams seem condescending and inconsiderate. I'm not blaming the ladies I've worked for. It's just the nature of the relationship. They order chicken salad, and you get up before dawn to get ahead of yourself, and just as you've finished the chicken salad, they change their minds and want crab-meat soup."

"My mother changes her mind all the time," Amy said.

"Sometimes you're in a country place with nobody else in help. You're tired, but not too tired to feel lonely. You go out onto the servants' porch when the pots and pans are done, planning to enjoy God's creation, and although the front of the house may have a fine view of the lake or the mountains, the view from the back is never much. But there is the sky and the trees and the stars and the birds singing and the pleasure of resting your feet. But then you hear them in the front of the house, laughing and talking with their guests and their sons and daughters. If you're new and they whisper, you can be sure they're talking about you. That takes all the pleasure out of the evening."

"Oh," Amy said.

"I've worked all kinds of places—places where there were eight or nine in help and places where I was expected to burn the rubbish myself, on winter nights, and shovel the snow. In a house where there's a lot of help, there's usually some devil among them—some old butler or parlormaid—who tries to make your like miserable from the beginning. 'The Madam

[1]Latin, literally "not having control of one's mind."

doesn't like it this way,' and 'The Madam doesn't like it that way,' and 'I've been with the Madam for twenty years,' they tell you. It takes a diplomat to get along. Then there is the rooms they give you, and every one of them I've ever seen is cheerless. If you have a bottle in your suitcase, it's a terrible temptation in the beginning not to take a drink to raise your spirits. But I have a strong character. It was different with my poor sister. She used to complain about nervousness, but, sitting here thinking about her tonight, I wonder if she suffered from nervousness at all. I wonder if she didn't make it all up. I wonder if she just wasn't meant to be in service. Toward the end, the only work she could get was out in the country, where nobody else would go, and she never lasted much more than a week or two. She'd take a little gin for her nervousness, then a little for her tiredness, and when she'd drunk her own bottle and everything she could steal, they'd hear about it in the front part of the house. There was usually a scene, and my poor sister always liked to have the last word. Oh, if I had had my way, they'd be a law against it! It's not my business to advise you to take anything from your father, but I'd be proud of you if you'd empty his gin bottle into the sink now and then—the filthy stuff! But it's made me feel better to talk with you, sweetheart. It's made me not miss my poor sister so much. Now I'll read a little more in my Bible, and then I'll get you some supper."

THE LAWTONS had had a bad year with cooks—there had been five of them. The arrival of Rosemary had made Marcia Lawton think back to a vague theory of dispensations; she had suffered, and now she was being rewarded. Rosemary was clean, industrious, and cheerful, and her table—as the Lawtons said—was just like the Chambord. On Wednesday night after dinner, she took the train to New York, promising to return on the evening train Thursday. Thursday morning, Marcia went into the cook's room. It was a distasteful but a habitual precaution. The absence of anything personal in the room—a package of cigarettes, a fountain pen, an alarm clock, a radio, or anything else that could tie the old woman to the place—gave her the uneasy feeling that she was being deceived, as she had so often been deceived by cooks in the past. She opened the closet door and saw a single uniform hanging there and, on the closet floor, Rosemary's old suitcase and the white shoes she wore in the kitchen. The suitcase was locked, but when Marcia lifted it, it seemed to be nearly empty.

Mr. Lawton and Amy drove to the station after dinner on Thursday to meet the eight-sixteen train. The top of the car was down, and the brisk air, the starlight, and the company of her father made the little girl feel kindly toward the world. The railroad station in Shady Hill resembled the railroad stations in old movies she had seen on television, where detectives and spies, bluebeards and their trusting victims, were met to be driven off to remote country estates. Amy liked the station, particularly toward dark. She imagined that the people who traveled on the locals were engaged on errands that were more urgent and sinister than commuting. Except when there was a heavy fog or a snowstorm, the club car that her father traveled on seemed to have the gloss and the monotony of the rest of his life. The locals that ran at odd hours belonged to a world of deeper contrasts, where she would like to live.

They were a few minutes early, and Amy got out of the car and stood on the platform. She wondered what the fringe of string that hung above the tracks at either end of the station was for, but she knew enough not to ask her father, because he wouldn't be able to tell her. She could hear the train before it came into view, and the noise excited her and made her happy. When the train drew in to the station and stopped, she looked in the lighted windows for Rosemary and didn't see her. Mr. Lawton got out of the car and joined Amy on the platform. They could see the conductor bending over someone in a seat, and finally the cook arose. She clung to the conductor as he led her out to the platform of the car, and she was crying. "Like peaches and cream," Amy heard her sob. "A lovely, lovely person." The conductor spoke to her kindly, put his arm around her shoulders, and eased her down the steps. Then the train pulled out, and she stood there drying her tears. "Don't say a word, Mr. Lawton," she said, "and I won't say anything." She held out a small paper bag. "Here's a present for you, little girl."

"Thank you, Rosemary," Amy said. She looked into the paper bag and saw that it contained several packets of Japanese water flowers.

Rosemary walked toward the car with the caution of someone who can hardly find her way in the dim light. A sour smell came from her. Her best coat was spotted with mud and ripped in the back. Mr. Lawton told Amy to get in the back seat of the car, and made the cook sit in front, beside him. He slammed the car door shut after her angrily, and then went around to the driver's seat and drove home. Rosemary reached into her handbag and took out a Coca-Cola bottle with a cork stopper and took a drink. Amy could tell by the smell that the Coca-Cola bottle was filled with gin.

"Rosemary!" Mr. Lawton said.

"I'm lonely," the cook said. "I'm lonely, and I'm afraid, and it's all I've got."

He said nothing more until he had turned into their drive and brought the car around to the back door. "Go and get your suitcase, Rosemary," he said. "I'll wait here in the car."

As soon as the cook had staggered into the house, he told Amy to go in by the front door. "Go upstairs to your room and get ready for bed."

Her mother called down the stairs when Amy came in, to ask if Rosemary had returned. Amy didn't answer. She went to the bar, took an open gin bottle, and emptied it into the pantry sink. She was nearly crying when she encountered her mother in the living room, and told her that her father was taking the cook back to the station.

When Amy came home from school the next day, she found a heavy, black-haired woman cleaning the living room. The car Mr. Lawton usually drove to the station was at the garage for a checkup, and Amy drove to the station with her mother to meet him. As he came across the station platform, she could tell by the lack of color in his face that he had had a hard day. He kissed her mother, touched Amy on the head, and got behind the wheel.

"You know," her mother said, "there's something terribly wrong with the guest-room shower."

"Damn it, Marcia," he said, "I wish you wouldn't always greet me with bad news!"

His grating voice oppressed Amy, and she began to fiddle with the button that raised and lowered the window.

"Stop that, Amy!" he said.

"Oh, well, the shower isn't important," her mother said. She laughed weakly.

"When I got back from San Francisco last week," he said, "you couldn't wait to tell me that we need a new oil burner."

"Well, I've got a part-time cook. That's good news."

"Is she a lush?" her father asked.

"Don't be disagreeable, dear. She'll get us some dinner and wash the dishes and take the bus home. We're going to the Farquarsons'."

"I'm really too tired to go anywhere," he said.

"Who's going to take care of me?" Amy asked.

"You always have a good time at the Farquarsons'," her mother said.

"Well, let's leave early," he said

"Who's going to take care of me?" Amy asked.

"Mrs. Henlein," her mother said.

When they got home, Amy went over to the piano.

Her father washed his hands in the bathroom off the hall and then went to the bar. He came into the living room holding the empty gin bottle. "What's her name?" he asked.

"Ruby," her mother said.

"She's exceptional. She's drunk a quart of gin on her first day."

"Oh dear!" her mother said. "Well, let's not make any trouble now."

"Everybody is drinking my liquor," her father shouted, "and I am God-damned sick and tired of it!"

"There's plenty of gin in the closet," her mother said. "Open another bottle."

"We paid that gardener three dollars an hour and all he did was sneak in here and drink up my Scotch. The sitter we had before we got Mrs. Henlein used to water my bourbon, and I don't have to remind you about Rosemary. The cook before Rosemary not only drank everything in my liquor cabinet but she drank all the rum, kirsch, sherry, and wine that we had in the kitchen for cooking. Then, there's that Polish woman we had last summer. Even that old laundress. *And* the painters. I think they must have put some kind of a mark on my door. I think the agency must have checked me off as an easy touch."

"Well, let's get through dinner, and then you can speak to her."

"The hell with that!" he said. "I'm not going to encourage people to rob me. *Ruby!*" He shouted her name several times, but she didn't answer. Then she appeared in the dining-room doorway anyway, wearing her hat and coat.

"I'm sick," she said. Amy could see that she was frightened.

"I should think that you would be," her father said.

"I'm sick," the cook mumbled, "and I can't find anything around here, and I'm going home."

"Good," he said. "Good! I'm through with paying people to come in here and drink my liquor."

The cook started out the front way, and Marcia Lawton followed her into the front hall to pay her something. Amy had watched this scene from the piano bench, a position that was withdrawn but that still gave her a good view. She saw her father get a fresh bottle of gin and make a shaker of Martinis. He looked very unhappy.

"Well," her mother said when she came back into the room. "You know, she didn't look drunk."

"Please don't argue with me, Marcia," her father said. He poured two cocktails, said "Cheers," and drank a little. "We can get some dinner at Orpheo's," he said.

"I suppose so," her mother said. "I'll rustle up something for Amy." She went into the kitchen, and Amy opened her music to "Reflets d'Automne." "COUNT," her music teacher had written. "COUNT and lightly, lightly . . ." Amy began to play. Whenever she made a mistake, she said "Darn it!" and started at the beginning again. In the middle of "Reflets d'Automne" it struck her that *she* was the one who had emptied the gin bottle. Her perplexity was so intense that she stopped playing, but her feelings did not go beyond perplexity, although she did not have the strength to continue playing the piano. Her mother relieved her. "Your supper's in the kitchen dear," she said. "And you can take a popsicle out of the deep freeze for dessert. Just one."

Marcia Lawton held her empty glass toward her husband, who filled it from the shaker. Then she went upstairs. Mr. Lawton remained in the room, and, studying her father closely, Amy saw that his tense look had begun to soften. He did not seem so unhappy any more, and as she passed him on her way to the kitchen, he smiled at her tenderly and patted her on the top of the head.

When Amy had finished her supper, eaten her popsicle, and exploded the bag it came in, she returned to the piano and played "Chopsticks" for a while. Her father came downstairs in his evening clothes, put his drink on the mantelpiece, and went to the French doors to look at his terrace and his garden. Amy noticed that the transformation that had begun with a softening of his features was even more advanced. At last, he seemed happy. Amy wondered if he was drunk, although his walk was not unsteady. If anything, it was more steady.

Her parents never achieved the kind of rolling, swinging gait that she saw impersonated by a tightrope walker in the circus each year while the band struck up "Show Me the Way to Go Home" and that she liked to imitate herself sometimes. She liked to turn round and round and round on the lawn, until, staggering and a little sick, she would whoop, "I'm drunk! I'm a drunken man!" and reel over the grass, righting herself as she was about to fall and finding herself not unhappy at having lost for second her ability to see the world. But she had never seen her parents like that. She had never seen them hanging on to a lamppost and singing and reeling, but she had seen them fall down. They were never indecorous—they seemed to get more decorous and formal the more they drank—but sometimes her father would get up to fill everybody's glass and he would walk straight enough but his shoes would seem to stick to the carpet. And sometimes, when he got to the dining-room door, he would miss it by a foot or more. Once, she had seen him walk into the wall with such force that he collapsed onto the floor and broke most of the glasses he was carrying. One or two people laughed, but the laughter was not general or hearty, and most of them pretended that he had not fallen down at all. When her father got to his feet, he went right on to the bar as if nothing had happened. Amy had once seen Mrs. Farquarson miss the chair she was about to sit in, by a foot, and thump down onto the floor, but nobody laughed then, and they pretended that Mrs. Farquarson hadn't fallen down at all. They seemed like actors in a play. In the school play, when you knocked over a paper tree you were supposed to pick it up without showing what you were doing, so that you would not spoil the illusion of being in a deep forest, and that was the way *they* were when somebody fell down.

Now her father had that stiff, funny walk that was so different from the way he tramped up and down the station platform in the morning, and she could see that he was looking for something. He was looking for his drink. It was right on the mantelpiece, but he didn't look there. He looked on all the tables in the living room. Then he went out onto the terrace and looked there, and then he came back into the living room and looked on all the tables again. Then he went back onto the terrace, and then back over the living-room tables, looking three times in the same place, although he was always telling her to look intelligently when she lost her sneakers or her raincoat. "Look for it, Amy," he was always saying. "Try and remember where you left it. I can't buy you a new raincoat every time it rains." Finally he gave up and poured himself a cocktail in another glass.

"I'm going to get Mrs. Henlein," he told Amy, as if this were an important piece of information.

Amy's only feeling for Mrs. Henlein was indifference, and when her father returned with the sitter, Amy thought of the nights, stretching into weeks—the years, almost—when she had been cooped up with Mrs. Henlein. Mrs. Henlein was very polite and was always telling Amy what was ladylike and what was not. Mrs. Henlein also wanted to know where Amy's parents were going and what kind of a party it was, although it was none of her business. She always sat down on the sofa as if she owned the place, and talked about people she had never even been introduced to, and asked Amy to bring her the newspaper, although she had no authority at all.

When Marcia Lawton came down, Mrs. Henlein wished her good evening. "Have a lovely party," she called after the Lawtons as they went out the door. Then she turned to Amy. "Where are your parents going, sweetheart?

"But you must know, sweetheart. Put on your thinking cap and try and remember. Are they going to the club?"

"No," Amy said.

"I wonder if they could be going to the Trenchers'," Mrs. Henlein said. "The Trenchers' house was lighted up when we came by."

"They're not going to the Trenchers'," Amy said. "They hate the Trenchers."

"Well, where are they going, sweetheart?" Mrs. Henlein asked.

"They're going to the Farquarsons'," Amy said.

"Well, that's all I wanted to know, sweetheart," Mrs. Henlein said, "Now get me the newspaper and hand it to me politely. *Politely,*" she said, as Amy approached her with the paper. "It doesn't mean anything when you do things for your elders unless you do them politely." She put on her glasses and began to read the paper.

Amy went upstairs to her room. In a glass on her table were the Japanese flowers that Rosemary had brought her, blooming stately in water that was colored pink for the dyes. Amy went down the back stairs and through the kitchen into the dining room. Her father's cocktail things were spread over the bar. She emptied the gin bottle into the pantry sink and then put it back where she had found it. It was too late to ride her bicycle and too early to go to bed, and she knew that if she got anything interesting on the television, like a murder, Mrs. Henlein would make her turn it off. Then she remembered that her father had brought her home from his trip West a book about horses, and she ran cheerfully up the back stairs to read her new book.

It was after two when the Lawtons returned. Mrs. Henlein, asleep on the living-room sofa dreaming about a dusty attic, was awakened by their voices in the hall. Marcia Lawton paid her, and thanked her, and asked if anyone had called, and then went upstairs. Mr. Lawton was in the dining room, rattling the bottles around. Mrs. Henlein, anxious to get into her own bed and back to sleep, prayed that he wasn't going to pour himself another drink, as they so often did. She was driven home night after night by drunken gentlemen. He stood in the door of the dining room, holding an empty bottle in his hand. "You must be stinking, Mrs. Henlein," he said.

"Hmm," she said. She didn't understand.

"You drank a full quart of gin," he said.

The lackluster old woman—half between wakefulness and sleep—gathered together her bones and groped for her gray hair. It was in her nature to collect stray cats, pile the bathroom up to the ceiling with interesting and valuable newspapers, rouge, talk to herself, sleep in her underwear in case of fire, quarrel over the price of soup bones, and have it circulated around the neighborhood that when she finally died in her dusty junk heap, the mattress would be full of bankbooks and the pillow stuffed with hundred-dollar bills. She had resisted all these rich temptations in order to appear a lady, and she was repaid by being called a common thief. She began to scream at him.

"You take that back, Mr. Lawton! You take back every one of those words you just said! I never stole anything in my whole life, and nobody in my family ever stole anything, and I don't have to stand here and be insulted by a drunk man. Why, as for drinking, I haven't drunk enough to fill an eyeglass for twenty-five years. Mr. Henlein took me to a place of refreshment twenty-five years ago, and I drank two Manhattan cocktails that made me so sick and dizzy that I've never liked the stuff ever since. How dare you speak to me like this! Calling me a thief and a drunken woman! Oh, you disgust me—you disgust me in your ignorance of all the trouble I've had. Do you know what I had for Christmas dinner last year? I had a bacon sandwich. Son of a bitch!" She began to weep. "I'm glad I said it!" she screamed. "It's the first time I've used a dirty word in my whole life and I'm glad I said it. Son of a bitch!" A sense of liberation, as if she stood at the bow of a great ship, came over her. "I lived in this neighborhood my whole life. I can remember when it was full of good farming people and there was fish in the rivers. My father had four acres of sweet meadowland and a name that was known far and wide, and on my mother's side I'm descended from patroons, Dutch nobility. My mother was the spit and image of Queen Wilhelmina[2]. You think you can get away with insulting me, but you're very, very, very much mistaken." She went to the telephone and, picking up the receiver, screamed, "Police! Police! Police! This is Mrs. Henlein, and I'm over at the Lawtons'. He's drunk, and he's calling me insulting names, and I want you to come over here and arrest him!"

[2]Wilhelmina Helena Pauline Maria (1880–1962) was Queen regnant of the Kingdom of the Netherlands from 1890 to 1948.

The voices woke Amy, and, lying in her bed, she perceived vaguely the pitiful corruption of the adult world; how crude and frail it was, like a piece of worn burlap, patched with stupidities and mistakes, useless and ugly, and yet they never saw its worthlessness, and when you pointed it out to them, they were indignant. But as the voices went on and she heard the cry "Police! Police!" she was frightened. She did not see how they could arrest her, although they could find her fingerprints on the empty bottle, but it was not her own danger that frightened her but the collapse, in the middle of the night, of her father's house. It was all her fault, and when she heard her father speaking into the extension telephone in the library, she felt sunk in guilt. Her father tried to be good and kind— and, remembering the expensive illustrated book about horses that he had brought her from the West, she had to set her teeth to keep from crying. She covered her head with a pillow and realized miserably that she would have to go away. She had plenty of friends from the time when they used to live in New York, or she could spend the night in the Park or hide in a museum. She would have to go away.

"GOOD MORNING," her father said at breakfast. "Ready for a good day!" Cheered by the swelling light in the sky, by the recollection of the manner in which he had handled Mrs. Henlein and kept the police from coming, refreshed by his sleep, and pleased at the thought of playing golf. Mr. Lawton spoke with feeling, but the words seemed to Amy offensive and fatuous; they took away her appetite, and she slumped over her cereal bowl, stirring it with a spoon. "Don't slump, Amy," he said. Then she remembered the night, the screaming, the resolve to go. His cheerfulness refreshed her memory. Her decision was settled. She had a ballet lesson at ten, and she was going to have lunch with Lillian Towele. Then she would leave.

Children prepare for a sea voyage with a toothbrush and a Teddy bear; they equip themselves for a trip around the world with a pair of odd socks, a conch shell, and a thermometer; books and stones and peacock feathers, candy bars, tennis balls, soiled handkerchiefs, and skeins of old string appear to them to be the necessities of travel, and Amy packed, that afternoon, with the impulsiveness of her kind. She was late coming home from lunch, and her getaway was delayed, but she didn't mind. She could catch one of the late-afternoon locals; one of the cooks' trains. Her father was playing golf and her mother was off somewhere. A part-time worker was cleaning the living room. When Amy had finished packing, she went into her parents' bedroom and flushed the toilet. While the water murmured, she took a twenty-dollar bill from her mother's desk. Then she went downstairs and left the house and walked around Blenhollow Circle and down Alewives Lane to the station. No regrets or goodbyes formed in her mind. She went over the names of the friends she had in the city, in case she decided not to spend the night in a museum. When she opened the door of the waiting room, Mr. Flanagan, the stationmaster, was poking his coal fire.

"I want to buy a ticket to New York," Amy said.

"One-way or round-trip?"

"One-way, please."

Mr. Flanagan went through the door into the ticket office and raised the glass window. "I'm afraid I haven't got a half-fare ticket for you, Amy," he said. "I'll have to write one."

"That's all right," she said. She put twenty-dollar bill on the counter.

"And in order to change that," he said, "I'll have to go over to the other side. Here's the four-thirty-two coming in now, but you'll be able to get the five-ten." She didn't protest, and went and sat beside her cardboard suitcase, which was printed with European hotel and place names. When the local had come and gone, Mr. Flanagan shut his glass window and walked over the footbridge to the northbound platform and called the Lawtons'. Mr. Lawton had just come in from his game and was mixing himself a cocktail. "I think your daughter's planning to take some kind of a trip," Mr. Flanagan said.

It was dark by the time Mr. Lawton got down to the station. He saw his daughter through the station window. The girl sitting on the bench, the rich names on her paper suitcase, touched him as it was in her power to touch him only when she seemed helpless or when she was very sick. Someone had walked over his grave! He shivered with longing, he felt his skin coarsen as when, driving home late and alone, a shower of leaves on the wind crossed the beam of his headlights, liberating him for a second at the most from the literal symbols of his life—the buttonless shirts, the vouchers and bank statements, the order blanks, and the empty glasses. He seemed to listen—God knows for what. Commands, drums, the crackle of signal fires, the music of the glockenspiel[3]—how sweet it sounds on the Alpine air—singing from a tavern in the pass, the honking of wild swans; he seemed to smell the salt air in the churches of Venice. Then, as it was with the leaves, the power of her figure to trouble him was ended; his gooseflesh vanished. He was himself. Oh, why should she want to run away? Travel—and who know better than a man who spent three days of every fortnight on the road—was a world of overheated plane cabins and repetitious magazines, where even the coffee, even the champagne, tasted of plastics. How could he teach her that home sweet home was the best place of all?

[1953]

---

[3] A musical percussion instrument having a set of tuned metal pieces mounted in a frame and struck with small hammers.

RALPH ELLISON ■ (1914–1994)

It is a loss to American literature that Ralph Ellison was unable to complete his second novel, which he labored over and struggled with from the early 1950s until his death. But the novel he did complete, *Invisible Man*, published in 1952, is one of the major literary works of the twentieth century—a profound, daring, original achievement that few of his contemporaries came close to rivaling. Ellison also published a number of vivid short stories, sections from his novel-in-progress, and brilliant essays in literary and cultural criticism, many of which he included in *Shadow and Act* (1964) and *Going to the Territory* (1986). He was a brilliant interview, as *Conversations with Ralph Ellison* (1995) testifies, and he was the author as well of witty, incisive letters, a number of which, exchanged with his lifelong friend and fellow writer Albert Murray, are gathered in *Trading Twelves: The Selected Letters of Ralph Ellison and Albert Murray* (2000).

Ellison was born in Oklahoma City, Oklahoma, and named by his father after Ralph Waldo Emerson, the Transcendentalist poet-essayist and celebrator of self-reliance. Ellison aspired first to be a musician, and he studied classical music in high school and, beginning in 1933, at Tuskegee Institute in Alabama. At Tuskegee, however, Ellison discovered the poetry of T. S. Eliot, which dazzled and inspired him and kindled a new ambition: to become a writer. Modern literature, jazz, African American folklore—all of these were part of Ellison's literary and cultural background, and all of them he later drew upon for *Invisible Man*.

In the summer of 1936, Ellison traveled to New York City, where he met Richard Wright, who as the editor of a literary journal gave Ellison his first writing assignments. Ellison learned much from Wright's passionate example as a fiction writer in *Uncle Tom's Children* and *Native Son*, and he defended Wright against critics who found these books shocking in their depiction of the African American experience. But Ellison wanted to do more than that in his own work. As James Alan McPherson noted, "Ellison was trying to solve the central problem of American literature. He was trying to find forms invested with enough familiarity to reinvent a much broader and much more diverse world for those who take their provisional identities from groups." This is what Ellison accomplished in *Invisible Man*, with its complex integration of sources from Wright and Eliot to Dostoyevsky, James Joyce, jazz great Louis Armstrong, and countless others. A masterpiece of African American, American, and world literatures, its first chapter, describing a racist-arranged "battle royal," was originally published in the British magazine *Horizon* in October 1947.

Robert O'Meally, in *The Craft of Ralph Ellison* (1980), cogently surveys the life and writings. For a range of critical perspectives, see *Speaking for You: The Vision of Ralph Ellison* (1980), ed. Kimberly W. Benston. Lawrence Jackson's richly detailed *Ralph Ellison: Emergence of Genius* (2002) is illuminating but covers Ellison's life only up to 1952. Parts of Ellison's unfinished second novel have been published with the title *Juneteenth*, ed. John F. Callahan (1999). An essential resource is Arnold Rampersad, *Ralph Ellison: A Biography* (2007). *Three Days Before the Shooting...: The Unfinished Second Novel*, ed. John F. Callahan and Adam Bradley (2010), is a massive volume that gathers the multiple versions, parts, and fragments of his next great work that Ellison left behind at the time of his death.

Battle Royal

Chapter I

It goes a long way back, some twenty years. All my life I had been looking for something, and everywhere I turned someone tried to tell me what it was. I accepted their answers too, though they were often in contradiction and even self-contradictory. I was naïve. I was looking for myself and asking everyone except myself questions which I, and only I, could answer. It took me a long time and much painful boomeranging of my expectations to achieve a realization everyone else appears to have been born with: That I am nobody but myself. But first I had to discover that I am an invisible man!

And yet I am no freak of nature, nor of history. I was in the cards, other things having been equal (or unequal) eighty-five years ago. I am not ashamed of my grandparents for having been slaves. I am only ashamed of myself for having at one time been ashamed. About eighty-five years ago they were told that they were free, united with others of our country in everything pertaining to the common good, and, in everything social, separate like the fingers of the hand.[1] And they believed it. They exulted in it. They stayed in their place, worked hard, and brought up my father to do the same. But my grandfather is the one. He was an odd old guy, my grandfather, and I am told I take after him. It was he who caused the trouble. On his death-bed he called my father to him and said, "Son, after I'm gone I want you to keep up the good fight. I never told you, but our life is a war and I have been a traitor all my born days, a spy in the enemy's country ever since I give up my gun back in the Reconstruction. Live with your head in the lion's mouth. I want you to overcome 'em with yeses, undermine 'em with grins, agree 'em to death and destruction, let 'em swoller you till they vomit or bust wide open." They thought the old man had gone out of his mind. He had been the meekest of men. The younger children were rushed from the room, the shades drawn and the flame of the lamp turned so low that it sputtered on the wick like the old man's breathing. "Learn it to the younguns," he whispered fiercely; then he died.

---

[1]Here and later, the narrator quotes from the "Atlanta Exposition Address" (1895) by the African-American educator, leader, and author Booker T. Washington (1856–1915). Seeking to enlist the support of the white South, Washington stated in his speech that African Americans would commit themselves to making progress in education and in work (especially in agriculture and in carpentry, brick-making, and other trades) and would not agitate for social and political equality.

But my folks were more alarmed over his last words than over his dying. It was as though he had not died at all, his words caused so much anxiety. I was warned emphatically to forget what he had said and, indeed, this is the first time it has been mentioned outside the family circle. It had a tremendous effect upon me, however. I could never be sure of what he meant. Grandfather had been a quiet old man who never made any trouble, yet on his deathbed he had called himself a traitor and a spy, and he had spoken of his meekness as a dangerous activity. It became a constant puzzle which lay unanswered in the back of my mind. And whenever things went well for me I remembered my grandfather and felt guilty and uncomfortable. It was as though I was carrying out his advice in spite of myself. And to make it worse, everyone loved me for it. I was praised by the most lily-white men of the town. I was considered an example of desirable conduct—just as my grandfather had been. And what puzzled me was that the old man had defined it as *treachery*. When I was praised for my conduct I felt a guilt that in some way I was doing something that was really against the wishes of the white folks, that if they had understood they would have desired me to act just the opposite, that I should have been sulky and mean, and that that really would have been what they wanted, even though they were fooled and thought they wanted me to act as I did. It made me afraid that some day they would look upon me as a traitor and I would be lost. Still I was more afraid to act any other way because they didn't like that at all. The old man's words were like a curse. On my graduation day I delivered an oration in which I showed that humility was the secret, indeed, the very essence of progress. (Not that I believed this—how could I, remembering my grandfather?—I only believed that it worked.) It was a great success. Everyone praised me and I was invited to give the speech at a gathering of the town's leading white citizens. It was a triumph for our whole community.

It was in the main ballroom of the leading hotel. When I got there I discovered that it was on the occasion of a smoker, and I was told that since I was to be there anyway I might as well take part in the battle royal to be fought by some of my schoolmates as part of the entertainment. The battle royal came first.

All of the town's big shots were there in their tuxedoes, wolfing down the buffet foods, drinking beer and whiskey and smoking black cigars. It was a large room with a high ceiling. Chairs were arranged in neat rows around three sides of a portable boxing ring. The fourth side was clear, revealing a gleaming space of polished floor. I had some misgivings over the battle royal, by the way. Not from a distaste for fighting, but because I didn't care too much for the other fellows who were to take part. They were tough guys who seemed to have no grandfather's curse worrying their minds. No one could mistake their toughness. And besides, I suspected that fighting a battle royal might detract from the dignity of my speech. In those pre-invisible days I visualized myself as a potential

Booker T. Washington. But the other fellows didn't care too much for me either, and there were nine of them. I felt superior to them in my way, and I didn't like the manner in which we were all crowded together into the servants' elevator. Nor did they like my being there. In fact, as the warmly lighted floors flashed past the elevator we had words over the fact that I, by taking part in the fight, had knocked one of their friends out of a night's work.

We were led out of the elevator through a rococo hall into an anteroom and told to get into our fighting togs. Each of us was issued a pair of boxing gloves and ushered out into the big mirrored hall, which we entered looking cautiously about us and whispering, lest we might accidentally be heard above the noise of the room. It was foggy with cigar smoke. And already the whiskey was taking effect. I was shocked to see some of the most important men of the town quite tipsy. They were all there—bankers, lawyers, judges, doctors, fire chiefs, teachers, merchants. Even one of the more fashionable pastors. Something we could not see was going on up front. A clarinet was vibrating sensuously and the men were standing up and moving eagerly forward. We were a small tight group, clustered together, our bare upper bodies touching and shining with anticipatory sweat; while up front the big shots were becoming increasingly excited over something we still could not see. Suddenly I heard the school superintendent, who had told me to come, yell, "Bring up the shines, gentlemen! Bring up the little shines!"

We were rushed up to the front of the ballroom, where it smelled even more strongly of tobacco and whiskey. Then we were pushed into place. I almost wet my pants. A sea of faces, some hostile, some amused, ringed around us, and in the center, facing us, stood a magnificent blonde—stark naked. There was dead silence. I felt a blast of cold air chill me. I tried to back away, but they were behind me and around me. Some of the boys stood with lowered heads, trembling. I felt a wave of irrational guilt and fear. My teeth chattered, my skin turned to goose flesh, my knees knocked. Yet I was strongly attracted and looked in spite of myself. Had the price of looking been blindness, I would have looked. The hair was yellow like that of a circus kewpie doll, the face heavily powdered and rouged, as though to form an abstract mask, the eyes hollow and smeared a cool blue, the color of a baboon's butt. I felt a desire to spit upon her as my eyes brushed slowly over her body. Her breasts were firm and round as the domes of East Indian temples, and I stood so close as to see the fine skin texture and beads of pearly perspiration glistening like dew around the pink and erected buds of her nipples. I wanted at one and the same time to run from the room, to sink through the floor, or go to her and cover her from my eyes and the eyes of the others with my body; to feel the soft thighs, to caress her and destroy her, to love her and murder her, to hide from her, and yet to stroke where below the small American flag tattooed upon her belly her thighs formed a capital V. I had a notion that of all in the room she saw only me with her impersonal eyes.

And then she began to dance, a slow sensuous movement; the smoke of a hundred cigars clinging to her like the thinnest of veils. She seemed like a fair bird-girl girdled in veils calling to me from the angry surface of some gray and threatening sea. I was transported. Then I became aware of the clarinet playing and the big shots yelling at us. Some threatened us if we looked and others if we did not. On my right I saw one boy faint. And now a man grabbed a silver pitcher from a table and stepped close as he dashed ice water upon him and stood him up and forced two of us to support him as his head hung and moans issued from his thick bluish lips. Another boy began to plead to go home. He was the largest of the group, wearing dark red fighting trunks much too small to conceal the erection which projected from him as though in answer to the insinuating low-registered moaning of the clarinet. He tried to hide himself with his boxing gloves.

And all the while the blonde continued dancing, smiling faintly at the big shots who watched her with fascination, and faintly smiling at our fear. I noticed a certain merchant who followed her hungrily, his lips loose and drooling. He was a large man who wore diamond studs in a shirt-front which swelled with the ample paunch underneath, and each time the blonde swayed her undulating hips he ran his hand through the thin hair of his bald head and, with his arms upheld, his posture clumsy like that of an intoxicated panda, wound his belly in a slow and obscene grind. This creature was completely hypnotized. The music had quickened. As the dancer flung herself about with a detached expression on her face, the men began reaching out to touch her. I could see their beefy fingers sink into the soft flesh. Some of the others tried to stop them and she began to move around the floor in graceful circles, as they gave chase, slipping and sliding over the polished floor. It was mad. Chairs went crashing, drinks were spilt, as they ran laughing and howling after her. They caught her just as she reached a door, raised her from the floor, and tossed her as college boys are tossed at a hazing, and above her red, fixed-smiling lips I saw the terror and disgust in her eyes, almost like my own terror and that which I saw in some of the other boys. As I watched, they tossed her twice and her soft breasts seem to flatten against the air and her legs flung wildly as she spun. Some of the more sober ones helped her to escape. And I started off the floor, heading for the anteroom with the rest of the boys.

Some were still crying and in hysteria. But as we tried to leave we were stopped and ordered to get into the ring. There was nothing to do but what we were told. All ten of us climbed under the ropes and allowed ourselves to be blindfolded with broad bands of white cloth. One of the men seemed to feel a bit sympathetic and tried to cheer us up as we stood with our backs against the ropes. Some of us tried to grin. "See that boy over there?" one of the men said. "I want you to run across at the bell and give it to him right in the belly. If you don't get him, I'm going to get you. I don't like his looks." Each of us was told the same. The blindfolds were put on. Yet even then I had been going over my speech. In my mind each word was as bright as flame. I felt the cloth pressed into place, and frowned so that it would be loosened when I relaxed.

But now I felt a sudden fit of blind terror. I was unused to darkness. It was as though I had suddenly found myself in a dark room filled with poisonous cottonmouths. I could hear the bleary voices yelling insistently for the battle royal to begin.

"Get going in there!"

"Let me at that big nigger!"

I strained to pick up the school superintendent's voice, as though to squeeze some security out of that slightly more familiar sound.

"Let me at those black sonsabitches!" someone yelled.

"No, Jackson, no!" another voice yelled. "Here, somebody, help me hold Jack."

"I want to get at that ginger-colored nigger. Tear him limb from limb," the first voice yelled.

I stood against the ropes trembling. For in those days I was what they called ginger-colored, and he sounded as though he might crunch me between his teeth like a crisp ginger cookie.

Quite a struggle was going on. Chairs were being kicked about and I could hear voices grunting as with a terrific effort. I wanted to see, to see more desperately than ever before. But the blindfold was tight as a thick skin-puckering scab and when I raised my gloved hands to push the layers of white aside a voice yelled, "Oh, no you don't, black bastard! Leave that alone!"

"Ring the bell before Jackson kills him a coon!" someone boomed in the sudden silence. And I heard the bell clang and the sound of the feet scuffling forward.

A glove smacked against my head. I pivoted, striking out stiffly as someone went past, and felt the jar ripple along the length of my arm to my shoulder. Then it seemed as though all nine of the boys had turned upon me at once. Blows pounded me from all sides while I struck out as best I could. So many blows landed upon me that I wondered if I were not the only blindfolded fighter in the ring, or if the man called Jackson hadn't succeeded in getting me after all.

Blindfolded, I could not longer control my motions. I had no dignity. I stumbled about like a baby or a drunken man. The smoke had become thicker and with each new blow it seemed to sear and further restrict my lungs. My saliva became like hot bitter glue. A glove connected with my head, filling my mouth with warm blood. It was everywhere. I could not tell if the moisture I felt upon my body was sweat or blood. A blow landed hard against the nape of my neck. I felt myself going over, my head hitting the floor. Streaks of blue light filled the black world behind the blindfold. I lay prone, pretending that I was knocked out, but felt myself seized by hands and yanked to my feet. "Get going, black boy! Mix it up!" My arms were like lead, my head smarting from blows. I managed to feel my way to the ropes and held on, trying to catch my breath. A glove landed in my mid-section and I went over again, feeling as though the smoke had become a knife jabbed into my guts. Pushed this way and that by the legs milling around me, I finally pulled erect and discovered that I could see the black, sweat-washed forms weaving in the smoky-blue atmosphere like drunken dancers weaving to the rapid drum-like thuds of blows.

Everyone fought hysterically. It was complete anarchy. Everybody fought everybody else. No group fought together for long. Two, three, four, fought one, then turned to fight each other, were themselves attacked. Blows landed below the belt and in the kidney, with the gloves open as well as closed, and with my eye partly opened now there was not so much terror. I moved carefully, avoiding blows, although not too many to attract attention, fighting from group to group. The boys groped about like blind, cautious crabs crouching to protect their mid-sections, their heads pulled in short against their shoulders, their arms stretched nervously before them, with their fists testing the smoke-filled air like the knobbed feelers of hypersensitive snails. In one corner I glimpsed a boy violently punching the air and heard him scream in pain as he smashed his hand against a ring post. For a second I saw him bent over holding his hand, then going down as a blow caught his unprotected head. I played one group against the other, slipping in and throwing a punch then stepping out of range while pushing the others into the melee to take the blows blindly aimed at me. The smoke was agonizing and there were no rounds, no bells at three minute intervals to relieve our exhaustion. The room spun around me, a swirl of lights, smoke, sweating bodies surrounded by tense white faces. I bled from both nose and mouth, the blood spattering upon my chest.

The men kept yelling, "Slug him, black boy! Knock his guts out!"

"Uppercut him! Kill him! Kill that big boy!"

Taking a fake fall, I saw a boy going down heavily beside me as though we were felled by a single blow, saw a sneaker-clad foot shoot into his groin as the two who had knocked him down stumbled upon him. I rolled out of range, feeling a twinge of nausea.

The harder we fought the more threatening the men became. And yet, I had begun to worry about my speech again. How would it go? Would they recognize my ability? What would they give me?

I was fighting automatically when suddenly I noticed that one after another of the boys was leaving the ring. I was surprised, filled with panic, as though I had been left alone with an unknown danger. Then I understood. The boys had arranged it among themselves. It was the custom for the two men left in the ring to slug it out for the winner's prize. I discovered this too late. When the bell sounded two men in tuxedoes leaped into the ring and removed the blindfold. I found myself facing Tatlock, the biggest of the gang. I felt sick at my stomach. Hardly had the bell stopped ringing in my ears than it clanged again and I saw him moving swiftly toward me. Thinking of nothing else to do I hit him smash on the nose. He kept coming, bringing the rank sharp violence of stale sweat. His face was a black blank of a face, only his eyes alive—with hate of me and aglow with a feverish terror from what had happened to us all. I became anxious. I wanted to deliver my speech and he came at me as though he meant to beat it out of me. I smashed him again and again, taking his blows as they came. Then on a sudden impulse I struck him lightly and as we clinched, I whispered, "Fake like I knocked you out, you can have the prize."

"I'll break your behind," he whispered hoarsely.

"For *them*?"

"For *me*, sonofabitch!"

They were yelling for us to break it up and Tatlock spun me half around with a blow, and as a joggled camera sweeps in a reeling scene, I saw the howling red faces crouching tense beneath the cloud of blue-gray smoke. For a moment the world wavered, unraveled, flowed, then my head cleared and Tatlock bounced before me. That fluttering shadow before my eyes was his jabbing left hand. Then falling forward, my head against his damp shoulder, I whispered.

"I'll make it five dollars more."

"Go to hell!"

But his muscles relaxed a trifle beneath my pressure and I breathed, "Seven?"

"Give it to your ma," he said, ripping me beneath the heart.

And while I still held him I butted him and moved away. I felt myself bombarded with punches. I fought back with hopeless desperation. I wanted to deliver my speech more than anything else in the world, because I felt that only these men could judge truly my ability, and now this stupid clown was ruining my chances. I began fighting carefully now, moving in to punch him and out again with my greater speed. A lucky blow to his chin and I had him going too—until I heard a loud voice yell, "I got my money on the big boy."

Hearing this, I almost dropped my guard. I was confused: Should I try to win against the voice out there? Would not this go against my speech, and was not this a moment for humility, for nonresistance? A blow to my head as I danced about sent my right eye popping like a jack-in-the-box and settled my dilemma. The room went red as I fell. It was a dream fall, my body languid and fastidious as to where to land, until the floor became impatient and smashed up to meet me. A moment later I came to. An hypnotic voice said FIVE emphatically. And I lay there, hazily watching a dark red spot of my own blood shaping itself into a butterfly, glistening and soaking into the soiled gray world of the canvas.

When the voice drawled TEN I was lifted up and dragged to a chair. I sat dazed. My eye pained and swelled with each throb of my pounding heart and I wondered if now I would be allowed to speak. I was wringing wet, my mouth still bleeding. We were grouped along the wall now. The other boys ignored me as they congratulated Tatlock and speculated as to how much they would be paid. One boy whimpered over his smashed hand. Looking up front, I saw attendants in white jackets rolling the portable ring away and placing a small square rug in the vacant space surrounded by chairs. Perhaps, I thought, I will stand on the rug to deliver my speech.

Then the M.C.[2] called to us, "Come on up here boys and get your money."

We ran forward to where the men laughed and talked in their chairs, waiting. Everyone seemed friendly now.

"There it is on the rug," the man said. I saw the rug covered with coins of all dimensions and a few crumpled bills. But what excited me, scattered here and there, were the gold pieces.

"Boys, it's all yours," the man said. "You get all you grab."

"That's right, Sambo,"[3] a blond man said, winking at me confidentially.

I trembled with excitement, forgetting my pain. I would get the gold and the bills, I thought. I would use both hands. I would throw my body against the boys nearest me to block them from the gold.

"Get down around the rug now," the man commanded, "and don't anyone touch it until I give the signal."

"This ought to be good," I heard.

As told, we got around the square rug on our knees. Slowly the man raised his freckled hand as we followed it upward with our eyes.

I heard, "These niggers look like they're about to pray!"

Then, "Ready," the man said. "Go!"

I lunged for a yellow coin lying on the blue design of the carpet, touching it and sending a surprised shriek to join those rising around me. I tried frantically to remove my hand but could not let go. A hot, violent force tore through my body, shaking me like a wet rat. The rug was electrified. The hair bristled up on my head as I shook myself free. My muscles jumped, my nerves jangled, writhed. But I saw that this was not stopping the other boys. Laughing in fear and embarrassment, some were holding back and scooping up the coins knocked off by the painful contortions of the others. The men roared above us as we struggled.

"Pick it up, goddamnit, pick it up!" someone called like a bass-voiced parrot. "Go on, get it!"

I crawled rapidly around the floor, picking up the coins, trying to avoid the coppers and to get greenbacks and the gold. Ignoring the shock by

---

[2]Master of Ceremonies.
[3]An offensive, insulting term for a Black person.

laughing, as I brushed the coins off quickly, I discovered that I could contain the electricity—a contradiction, but it works. Then the men began to push us onto the rug. Laughing embarrassedly, we struggled out of their hands and kept after the coins. We were all wet and slippery and hard to hold. Suddenly I saw a boy lifted into the air, glistening with sweat like a circus seal, and dropped, his wet back landing flush upon the charged rug, heard him yell and saw him literally dance upon his back, his elbows beating a frenzied tattoo upon the floor, his muscles twitching like the flesh of a horse stung by many flies. When he finally rolled off, his face was gray and no one stopped him when he ran from the floor amid booming laughter.

"Get the money," the M.C. called. "That's good hard American cash!"

And we snatched and grabbed, snatched and grabbed. I was careful not to come too close to the rug now, and when I felt the hot whiskey breath descend upon me like a cloud of foul air I reached out and grabbed the leg of a chair. It was occupied and I held on desperately.

"Leggo, nigger! Leggo!"

The huge face wavered down to mine as he tried to push me free. But my body was slippery and he was too drunk. It was Mr. Colcord, who owned a chain of movie houses and "entertainment palaces." Each time he grabbed me I slipped out of his hands. It became a real struggle. I feared the rug more than I did the drunk, so I held on, surprising myself for a moment by trying to topple *him* upon the rug. It was such an enormous idea that I found myself actually carrying it out. I tried not to be obvious, yet when I grabbed his leg, trying to tumble him out of the chair, he raised up roaring with laughter, and, looking at me with soberness dead in the eye, kicked me viciously in the chest. The chair leg flew out of my hand and I felt myself going and rolled. It was as though I had rolled through a bed of hot coals. It seemed a whole century would pass before I would roll free, a century in which I was seared through the deepest levels of my body to the fearful breath within me and the breath seared and heated to the point of explosion. It'll all be over in a flash, I thought as I rolled clear. It'll all be over in a flash.

But not yet, the men on the other side were waiting, red faces swollen as though from apoplexy as they bent forward in their chairs. Seeing their fingers coming toward me I rolled away as a fumbled football rolls off the receiver's fingertips, back into the coals. That time I luckily sent the rug sliding out of place and heard the coins ringing against the floor and the boys scuffling to pick them up and the M.C. calling, "All right, boys, that's all. Go get dressed and get your money."

I was limp as a dish rag. My back felt as though it had been beaten with wires.

When we had dressed the M.C. came in and gave us each five dollars, except Tatlock, who got ten for being last in the ring. Then he told us to leave. I was not to get a chance to deliver my speech, I thought. I was going out into the dim alley in despair when I was stopped and told to go back. I returned to the ballroom, where the men were pushing back their chairs and gathering in groups to talk.

The M.C. knocked on a table for quiet. "Gentlemen," he said, "we almost forgot an important part of the program. A most serious part, gentlemen. This boy was brought here to deliver a speech which he made at his graduation yesterday..."

"Bravo!"

"I'm told that he is the smartest boy we've got out there in Greenwood. I'm told that he knows more big words than a pocket-sized dictionary."

Much applause and laughter.

"So now, gentlemen, I want you to give him your attention."

There was still laughter as I faced them, my mouth dry, my eye throbbing. I began slowly, but evidently my throat was tense, because they began shouting, "Louder! Louder!"

"We of the younger generation extol the wisdom of that great leader and educator," I shouted, "who first spoke these flaming words of wisdom: 'A ship lost at sea for many days suddenly sighted a friendly vessel. From the mast of the unfortunate vessel was seen a signal: "Water, water; we die of thirst!" The answer from the friendly vessel came back: "Cast down your bucket where you are." The captain of the distressed vessel, at last heeding the injunction, cast down his bucket, and it came up full of fresh sparkling water from the mouth of the Amazon River.' And like him I say, and in his words, 'To those of my race who depend upon bettering their condition in a foreign land, or who underestimate the importance of cultivating friendly relations with the Southern white man, who is his next-door neighbor, I would say: "Cast down your bucket where you are"— cast it down in making friends in every manly way of the people of all races by whom we are surrounded...'"

I spoke automatically and with such fervor that I did not realize that the men were still talking and laughing until my dry mouth, filling up with blood from the cut, almost strangled me. I coughed, wanting to stop and go to one of the tall brass, sand-filled spittoons to relieve myself, but a few of the men, especially the superintendent, were listening and I was afraid. So I gulped it down, blood, saliva and all, and continued. (What powers of endurance I had during those days! What enthusiasm! What a belief in the rightness of things!) I spoke even louder in spite of the pain. But still they talked and still they laughed, as though deaf with cotton in dirty ears. So I spoke with greater emotional emphasis. I closed my ears and swallowed blood until I was nauseated. The speech seemed a hundred times as long as before, but I could not leave out a single word. All had to be said, each memorized nuance considered, rendered. Nor was that all. Whenever I uttered a word of three or more syllables a group of voices would yell for me to repeat it. I used the phrase "social responsibility," and they yelled:

"What's that word you say, boy?"

"Social responsibility," I said.

"What?"

"Social..."

"Louder."

"...responsibility."

"More!"

"Respon—"

"Repeat!"

"...sibility."

The room filled with the uproar of laughter until, no doubt, distracted by having to gulp down my blood, I made a mistake and yelled a phrase I had often seen denounced in newspaper editorials, heard debated in private.

"Social..."

"What?" they yelled.

"...equality—"

The laughter hung smokelike in the sudden stillness. I opened my eyes, puzzled. Sounds of displeasure filled the room. The M.C. rushed forward. They shouted hostile phrases at me. But I did not understand.

A small dry mustached man in the front row blared out, "Say that slowly, son!"

"What, sir?"

"What you just said!"

"Social responsibility, sir," I said.

"You weren't being smart, were you, boy?" he said, not unkindly.

"No, sir!"

"You sure that about 'equality' was a mistake?"

"Oh, yes, sir," I said. "I was swallowing blood."

"Well, you had better speak more slowly so we can understand. We mean to do right by you, but you've got to know your place at all times. All right, now, go on with your speech."

I was afraid. I wanted to leave but I wanted also to speak and I was afraid they'd snatch me down.

"Thank you, sir," I said, beginning where I had left off, and having them ignore me as before.

Yet when I finished there was a thunderous applause. I was surprised to see the superintendent come forth with a package wrapped in white tissue paper, and, gesturing for quiet, address the men.

"Gentlemen, you see that I did not overpraise the boy. He makes a good speech and some day he'll lead his people in the proper paths. And I don't have to tell you that that is important in these days and times. This is a good, smart boy, and so to encourage him in the right direction, in the name of the Board of Education I wish to present him a prize in the form of this..."

He paused, removing the tissue paper and revealing a gleaming calfskin brief case.

"...in the form of this first-class article from Shad Whitmore's shop."

"Boy," he said, addressing me, "take this prize and keep it well. Consider it a badge of office. Prize it. Keep developing as you are and some day it will be filled with important papers that will help shape the destiny of your people."

I was so moved that I could hardly express my thanks. A rope of bloody saliva forming a shape like an undiscovered continent drooled upon the leather and I wiped it quickly away. I felt an importance that I had never dreamed.

"Open it and see what's inside," I was told.

My fingers a-tremble, I complied, smelling the fresh leather and finding an official-looking document inside. It was a scholarship to the state college for Negroes. My eyes filled with tears and I ran awkwardly off the floor.

I was overjoyed; I did not even mind when I discovered that the gold pieces I had scrambled for were brass pocket tokens advertising a certain make of automobile.

When I reached home everyone was excited. Next day the neighbors came to congratulate me. I even felt safe from grandfather, whose death-bed curse usually spoiled my triumphs. I stood beneath his photograph with my brief case in hand and smiled triumphantly into his stolid black peasant's face. It was a face that fascinated me. The eyes seemed to follow everywhere I went.

That night I dreamed I was at a circus with him and that he refused to laugh at the clowns no matter what they did. Then later he told me to open my brief case and read what was inside and I did, finding an official envelope stamped with the state seal; and inside the envelope I found another and another, endlessly, and I thought I would fall of weariness. "Them's years," he said. "Now open that one." And I did and in it I found an engraved document containing a short message in letters of gold. "Read it," my grandfather said. "Out loud!"

"To Whom It May Concern," I intoned. "Keep This Nigger-Boy Running."

I awoke with the old man's laughter ringing in my ears.

(It was a dream I was to remember and dream again for many years after. But at that time I had no insight into its meaning. First I had to attend college.)

[1952]

GRACE PALEY ■ (1922–2007)

The poet, essayist, political activist, and short-story writer Grace Paley was born in New York City, the daughter of Russian Jewish immigrants from Ukraine, and was raised in the midst of three languages—Yiddish, Russian, and English. In an interview she noted that "one of the major influences on my writing is the street in which I grew up":

> I was out in it all the time. And the language of my family which was English and Russian and some Yiddish running back and forth a lot at great speed, and the life they talked about, the life they led. That language that I heard, and the language of the street, of the kids and also of the grown ups, who hung out in the street a lot in those days, that was as great an influence on my writing as anything I've read.

Paley attended Hunter College and New York University, and, in 1959, published her first collection of stories, *The Little Disturbances of Man*. Among the authors she admires are Anton Chekhov, James Joyce, Gertrude Stein, and Virginia Woolf. Paley's later collections include *Enormous Changes at the Last Minute* (1974). Her *Collected Stories* was published in 1994. Other works include a collection of essays. *Just As I Thought* (1998) and several volumes of poetry. A film adaptation of three stories from *Enormous Changes at the Last Minute* was released in 1983. A documentary about her life and work, "grace," was released in 2008.

Paley is skilled at capturing the nuances and tones of voice of her characters; and she again calls attention to the sounds, rhythms, and stories of her youth: "That's what you listen for and what you expect when you are a kid; the next conversation will tell you what it's all about, if you only listen to it."

Subtle, probing, with an understanding of and feeling for complexity, Paley is one of the most honest and adept American practitioners of the short-story form. In "The Loudest Voice," below, the first-person narrator Shirley Abramowitz tells of her experience as a Jewish girl in the 1930s when, because of her firm, clear, expressive voice, she was chosen to narrate her school's Christmas play. With insight and sensitivity, Paley describes the performance and then the later conversation between Shirley's immigrant parents, which the girl overhears. Paley explores the meanings and implications of American, Jewish, and Jewish-American identities in a Christian-majority society and culture.

Secondary sources include Sara Poli, *Grace Paley* (1983); and Jacqueline Taylor, *Grace Paley: Illuminating the Dark Lives* (1990).

The Loudest Voice

There is a certain place where dumbwaiters[1] boom, doors slam, dishes crash; every window is a mother's mouth bidding the street shut up, go skate somewhere else, come home. My voice is the loudest.

There, my own mother is still as full of breathing as me and the grocer stands up to speak to her. "Mrs. Abramowitz," he says, "people should not be afraid of their children."

"Ah, Mr. Bialik," my mother replies, "if you say to her or her father 'Ssh,' they say, 'In the grave it will be quiet.' "

"From Coney Island to the cemetery," says my papa. "It's the same subway, it's the same fare."

I am right next to the pickle barrel. My pinky is making tiny whirlpools in the brine. I stop a moment to announce: "Campbell's Tomato Soup Campbell's Vegetable Beef Soup. Campbell's S-c-otch Broth..."

"Be quiet," the grocer says, "the labels are coming off."

"Please, Shirley, be a little quiet," my mother begs me.

In that place the whole street groans: Be quiet! Be quiet! But steals from the happy chorus of my inside self not a tittle or a jot.

There, too, but just around the corner, is a red brick building that has been old for many years. Every morning the children stand before it in double lines which must be straight. They are not insulted. They are waiting anyway.

I am usually among them. I am, in fact, the first, since I begin with "A".

One cold morning the monitor tapped me on the shoulder. "Go to Room 409, Shirley Abramowitz" he said. I did as I was told. I went in a hurry up a down staircase to Room 409, which contained sixth-graders. I had to wait at the desk without wiggling until Mr. Hilton, their teacher, had time to speak.

After five minutes he said, "Shirley?"

"What?" I whispered.

He said, "My! My! Shirley Abramowitz! They told me you had a particularly loud, clear voice and read with lots of expression. Could that be true?"

"Oh yes," I whispered.

"In that case, don't be silly; I might very well be your teacher someday. Speak up, speak up."

"Yes," I shouted"

"More like it," he said. "Now, Shirley, can you put a ribbon in your hair or a bobby pin? It's too messy."

"Yes!" I bawled.

"Now, now, calm down." He turned to the class. "Children, not a sound. Open at page 39. Read till 52. When you finish, start again." He looked me

---

[1] A small elevator for carrying things, esp. food and dishes, between the floors of a building.

over once more. "Now, Shirley, you know, I suppose, that Christmas is coming. We are preparing a beautiful play. Most of the parts have been given out. But I still need a child with a strong voice, lots of stamina. Do you know what stamina is? You do? Smart kid. You know, I heard you read "The Lord is my shepherd"[2] in Assembly yesterday. I was very impressed. Wonderful delivery. Mrs. Jordan, your teacher, speaks highly of you. Now listen to me, Shirley Abramowitz, if you want to take the part and be in the play, repeat after me, 'I swear to work harder than I ever did before.' "

I looked to heaven and said at once, "Oh, I swear." I kissed my pinky and looked at God.

"That is an actor's life, my dear," he explained. "Like a soldier's, never tardy or disobedient to his general, the director. Everything," he said, "absolutely everything will depend on you."

That afternoon, all over the building, children scraped and scrubbed the turkeys and the sheaves of corn off the schoolroom windows. Goodbye Thanksgiving. The next morning a monitor brought red paper and green paper from the office. We made new shapes and hung them on the walls and glued them to the doors.

The teachers became happier and happier. Their heads were ringing like the bells of childhood. My best friend, Evie, was prone to evil, but she did not get a single demerit for whispering. We learned, "Holy Night" without an error. "How wonderful!" said Miss Glace, the student teacher. "To think that some of you don't even speak the language!" We learned "Deck the Halls" and "Hark! The Herald Angels" ... they weren't ashamed and we weren't embarrassed.

Oh, but when my mother heard about it all, she said to my father, "Misha, you don't know what's going on there. Cramer is the heard of the Tickets Committee."

"Who?" asked my father. "Cramer? Oh yes, an active woman."

"Active? Active has to have a reason. Listen," she said sadly, "I'm surprised to see my neighbors making tra-la-la for Christmas."

My father couldn't think of what to say to that. Then he decided: "You're in America Clara, you wanted to come here. In Palestine the Arabs would be eating you alive. Europe you had pogroms.[3] Argentina is full of Indians. Here you got Christmas ... Some joke, Ha?"

"Very funny, Misha. What is becoming of you? If we came to a new country a long time ago to run away from tyrants, and instead we fall into a creeping pogrom, that our children learn a lot of lies, so what's the joke? Ach, Misha, your idealism is going away."

"So is your sense of humor."

"That I never had, but idealism you had a lot of."

---

[2]The first words of Psalm 23 in the Hebrew Bible/Old Testament.
[3]An organized massacre of a particular ethnic group, in particular that of Jews in Russia or eastern Europe.

"I'm the same Misha Abramovitch, I didn't change an iota. Ask anyone."

"Only ask me," says my mama, may she rest in peace. "I got the answer."

Meanwhile the neighbors had to think of what to say too.

Marty's father said: "You know, he has a very important part, my boy."

"Mine also," said Mr. Sauerfeld.

"Not my boy!" said Mrs. Kleig. "I said to him no. The answer is no. When I say no! I mean no!"

The rabbi's wife said, "It's disgusting!" But no one listened to her. Under the narrow sky of God's great wisdom she wore a strawberry-blond wig.

Every day was busy and full of experience. I was Right-hand Man. Mr. Hilton said: "How could I get along without you, Shirley!"

He said: "Your mother and father ought to get down on their knees every night and thank God for giving them a child like you."

He also said: "You're absolutely a pleasure to work with, my dear, dear child."

Sometimes he said: "For godsakes, what did I do with the script? Shirley! Shirley! Find it."

Then I answered quietly: "Here it is, Mr. Hilton."

Once in a while, when he was very tired, he would cry out: "Shirley, I'm just tired of screaming at those kids. Will you tell Ira Pushkov not to come in till Lester points to that star the second time?"

Then I roared: "Ira Pushkov, what's the matter with you? Dope! Mr. Hilton told you five times already, don't come in till Lester points to that star the second time."

"Ach, Clara," my father asked, "what does she do there till six o'clock she can't even put the plates on the table?"

"Christmas," said my mother coldly.

"Ho! Ho!" my father said. "Christmas. What's the harm? After all, history teaches everyone. We learn from reading this is a holiday from pagan times also, candles, lights, even Hanukkah. So if they think it's a private holiday, they're only ignorant, not patriotic. What belongs to history belongs to all men. You want to go back to the Middle Ages? Is it better to shave your head with a second-hand razor? Does it hurt Shirley to learn to speak up? It does not. So maybe someday she won't live between the kitchen and the shop. She's not a fool."

I thank you, Papa, for your kindness. It is true about me to this day. I am foolish but I am not a fool.

That night my father kissed me and said with great interest in my career, "Shirley, tomorrow's your big day. Congrats."

"Save it," my mother said. Then she shut all the windows in order to prevent tonsillitis.

In the morning it snowed. On the street corner a tree had been decorated for us by a kind city administration. In order to miss its chilly shadow our neighbors walked three blocks east to buy a loaf of bread. The butcher pulled down black window shades to keep the colored lights from shining on his chickens. Oh, not me. On the way to school, with both my hands I tossed it a kiss of tolerance. Poor thing, it was a stranger in Egypt.

I walked straight into the auditorium past the staring children. "Go ahead, Shirley!" said the monitors. Four boys, big for their age, had already started work as propmen and stagehands.

Mr. Hilton was very nervous. He was not even happy. Whatever he started to say ended in a sideward look of sadness. He sat slumped in the middle of the first row and asked me to help Miss Glace. I did this, although she thought my voice too resonant and said, "Show-off!"

Parents began to arrive long before we were ready. They wanted to make a good impression. From among the yards of drapes I peeked out at the audience. I saw my embarrassed mother.

Ira, Lester, and Meyer were pasted to their beards by Miss Glace. She almost forgot to thread the star on its wire, but I reminded her. I coughed a few times to clear my throat. Miss Glace looked around and saw that everyone was in costume and on line waiting to play his part. She whispered, "All right..."

Then:

Jackie Sauerfield, the prettiest boy in the first grade, parted the curtains with his skinny elbows and in a high voice sang out:

Parents dear
We are here
To make a Christmas play in time.
It we give
In narrative
And illustrate with pantomime.

He disappeared.

My voice burst immediately from the wings to the great shock of Ira, Lester, and Meyer, who were waiting for it but were surprised all the same.

"I remember, I remember, the house where I was born..."

Miss Glace yanked the curtain open and there it was, the house—an old hayloft, where Celia Kornbluh lay in the straw with Cindy Lou, her favorite doll. Ira, Lester and Meyer moved slowly from the wings toward her, sometimes pointing to a moving star and sometimes ahead to Cindy Lou.

It was a long story and it was a sad story. I carefully pronounced all the words about my lonesome childhood, while little Eddie Braunstein wandered upstage and down with his shepherd's stick, looking for sheep. I brought up lonesomeness again, and not being understood at all except by some women everybody hated. Eddie was too small for that and Marty Groff took his place, wearing his father's prayer shawl. I announced twelve friends, and half the boys in the fourth grade gathered round Marty, who stood on an orange crate while my voice harangued. Sorrowful and loud, I declaimed about love and God and Man, but because of the terrible deceit of Abie Stock we came suddenly to a famous moment. Marty, whose remembering tongue I was, waited at the foot of the cross. He stared desperately at the audience. I groaned, "My God, my God, why has thou forsaken me?" the soldiers who were sheiks grabbed poor Marty to pin him up to die, but he wrenched free, turned again to the audience, and spread his arms aloft to show despair and the end. I murmured at the top of my voice, "The rest is silence, but as everyone in this room, in this city—in this world—now knows, I shall have life eternal."

That night Mrs. Kornbluh visited our kitchen for a glass of tea.

"How's the virgin?" asked my father with a look of concern.

"For a man with a daughter, you got a fresh mouth, Abramovitch."

"Here," said my father kindly, "have some lemon, it'll sweeten your disposition."

They debated a little in Yiddish, then fell in a puddle of Russian and Polish. What I understood next was my father, who said, "Still and all, it was certainly a beautiful affair, you have to admit, introducing us to the beliefs of a different culture."

"Well, yes," said Mrs. Kornbluh. "The only thing ... you know Charlie Turner—that cute boy in Celia's class—a couple others? They got very small parts or no part at all. In very bad taste, it seemed to me. After all, it's their religion."

"Ach," explained my mother, "what could Mr. Hilton do? They got very small voice; after all, why should they holler? The English language they know from the beginning by heart. They're blond like angels. You think it's so important they should get in the play? Christmas ... the whole piece of goods ... they own it."

I listened and listened until I couldn't listen anymore. Too sleepy, I climbed out of bed and kneeled. I made a little church of my hands and said, "Hear, O Israel..." Then I called out in Yiddish, "Please, good night, good night. Ssh." My father said, "Ssh yourself," and slammed the kitchen door.

I was happy. I fell asleep at once. I had prayed for everybody: my talking family, cousins far away, passersby, and all the lonesome Christians. I expected to be heard. My voice was certainly the loudest.

[1959]

JAMES BALDWIN ▪ (1924–1987)

Harlem-born James Baldwin was the author of a number of compelling short stories, gathered in the collection *Going to Meet the Man* (1965), and powerful, if uneven, novels, including *Go Tell It on the Mountain* (1953), *Giovanni's Room* (1956), and *Another Country* (1962). But his best work is his nonfiction, and it includes some of the most vivid, provocative essays of the post–World War II period. *Notes of a Native Son* (1955), *Nobody Knows My Name* (1961), and *The Fire Next Time* (1963) are classics of modern American prose and essential reading for the study of race, racism, and race relations in the United States.

Sharply objective, bitterly ironic, eloquent in imagery and tone, Baldwin's style derives from a diverse range of sources, among them the black church, the prophets of the Old Testament, the novels of Charles Dickens and Henry James, and the traditions of African American oratory from Frederick Douglass in the nineteenth century to W. E. B. Du Bois in the twentieth. As his career as a writer developed, Baldwin's style and point of view also came to reflect his status as an expatriate in Paris. He spent much of his life from the 1950s onward in France and Turkey, although he was a force on the American scene during periodic visits to the United States, speaking and writing on behalf of civil rights. An expatriate, a black man, a gay man, and an American who both loved and loathed his native land, Baldwin is a fascinating figure who expressed and explored (sometimes explicitly, sometimes implicitly) his multiple identities in his extraordinary body of essays.

Baldwin's nonfiction is collected in *The Price of the Ticket* (1985). For biography and critical interpretation, see Horace Porter, *Stealing the Fire: The Art and Protest of James Baldwin* (1989); William J. Weatherby, *James Baldwin: Artist on Fire* (1989); and James Campbell, *Talking at the Gates: A Life of James Baldwin* (1991).

Notes of a Native Son

I

On the 29th of July, in 1943, my father died. On the same day, a few hours later, his last child was born. Over a month before this, while all our energies were concentrated in waiting for these events, there had been, in Detroit, one of the bloodiest race riots[1] of the century. A few hours after

[1] The demand for factory workers during World War II nearly doubled the African American population in Detroit in only ten years. Racial tensions in the city grew dramatically in 1943, with some blacks engaging in a bumping campaign (walking into whites on the streets and bumping them off the sidewalks, or nudging them in elevators). On June 20, 1943, blacks and whites clashed in a relatively minor skirmish on Belle Isle. But a false rumor spread at the black-run Forest Social Club that whites had thrown a black woman and her baby off the Belle Isle Bridge. Another rumor spread in white neighborhoods that black men had raped and murdered a white woman, also on the Belle Isle Bridge. Angry crowds clashed in Woodward, the unofficial racial dividing line between Detroit neighborhoods, around 4:00 a.m. The police could not control the riot. Street warfare ensued, with both blacks and whites being dragged from cars or from sidewalks and beaten to death or injured by angry rioters. Detroit mayor Edward Jeffries Jr., and Michigan governor Harry Kelly asked President Franklin D. Roosevelt to send federal troops to restore order. In thirty-six hours of rioting, thirty-four people were killed and more than 1,800 were arrested for looting and other incidents.

my father's funeral, while he lay in state in the undertaker's chapel, a race riot broke out in Harlem. On the morning of the 3rd of August, we drove my father to the graveyard through a wilderness of smashed plate glass.

The day of my father's funeral had also been my nineteenth birthday. As we drove him to the graveyard, the spoils of injustice, anarchy, discontent, and hatred were all around us. It seemed to me that God himself had devised, to mark my father's end, the most sustained and brutally dissonant of codas. And it seemed to me, too, that the violence which rose all about us as my father left the world had been devised as a corrective for the pride of his eldest son. I had declined to believe in that apocalypse which had been central to my father's vision; very well, life seemed to be saying, here is something that will certainly pass for an apocalypse until the real thing comes along. I had inclined to be contemptuous of my father for the conditions of his life, for the conditions of our lives. When his life had ended I began to wonder about that life and also, in a new way, to be apprehensive about my own.

I had not known my father very well. We had got on badly, partly because we shared, in our different fashions, the vice of stubborn pride. When he was dead I realized that I had hardly ever spoken to him. When he had been dead a long time I began to wish I had. It seems to be typical of life in America, where opportunities, real and fancied, are thicker than anywhere else on the globe, that the second generation has no time to talk to the first. No one, including my father, seems to have known exactly how old he was, but his mother had been born during slavery. He was of the first generation of free men. He, along with thousands of other Negroes, came North after 1919 and I was part of that generation which had never seen the landscape of what Negroes sometimes call the Old Country.

He had been born in New Orleans and had been a quite young man there during the time that Louis Armstrong,[2] a boy, was running errands for the dives and honky-tonks of what was always presented to me as one of the most wicked of cities—to this day, whenever I think of New Orleans, I also helplessly think of Sodom and Gomorrah.[3] My father never mentioned Louis Armstrong, except to forbid us to play his records; but there was a picture of him on our wall for a long time. One of my father's strong-willed female relatives had placed it there and forbade my father to take it down. He never did, but he eventually maneuvered her out of the house and when, some years later, she was in trouble and near death, he refused to do anything to help her.

---

[2]Born in New Orleans, Louis Armstrong (1901–71) is considered the greatest jazz musician of the twentieth century.

[3]As described in the biblical book of Genesis, God decides to destroy the cities of Sodom and Gomorrah for their citizens' sinful ways and wickedness. "Then the Lord rained brimstone and fire on Sodom and Gomorrah, from the Lord out of the heavens." (Genesis 19:24) "Turning the cities of Sodom and Gomorrah into ashes, condemned them to destruction, making them an example to those who afterward would live ungodly." (II Peter 2:6)

He was, I think, very handsome. I gather this from photographs and from my own memories of him, dressed in his Sunday best and on his way to preach a sermon somewhere, when I was little. Handsome, proud, and ingrown, "like a toe-nail," somebody said. But he looked to me, as I grew older, like pictures I had seen of African tribal chieftains: he really should have been naked, with war-paint on and barbaric mementos, standing among spears. He could be chilling in the pulpit and indescribably cruel in his personal life and he was certainly the most bitter man I have ever met; yet it must be said that there was something else in him, buried in him, which lent him his tremendous power and, even, a rather crushing charm. It had something to do with his blackness, I think—he was very black—with his blackness and his beauty, and with the fact that he knew that he was black but did not know that he was beautiful. He claimed to be proud of his blackness but it had also been the cause of much humiliation and it had fixed bleak boundaries to his life. He was not a young man when we were growing up and he had already suffered many kinds of ruin; in his outrageously demanding and protective way he loved his children, who were black like him and menaced, like him; and all these things sometimes showed in his face when he tried, never to my knowledge with any success, to establish contact with any of us. When he took one of his children on his knee to play, the child always became fretful and began to cry; when he tried to help one of us with our homework the absolutely unabating tension which emanated from him caused our minds and our tongues to become paralyzed, so that he, scarcely knowing why, flew into a rage and the child, not knowing why, was punished. If it ever entered his head to bring a surprise home for his children, it was, almost unfailingly, the wrong surprise and even the big watermelons he often brought home on his back in the summertime led to the most appalling scenes. I do not remember, in all those years, that one of his children was ever glad to see him come home. From what I was able to gather of his early life, it seemed that this inability to establish contact with other people had always marked him and had been one of the things which had driven him out of New Orleans. There was something in him, therefore, groping and tentative, which was never expressed and which was buried with him. One saw it most clearly when he was facing new people and hoping to impress them. But he never did, not for long. We went from church to smaller and more improbable church, he found himself in less and less demand as a minister, and by the time he died none of his friends had come to see him for a long time. He had lived and died in an intolerable bitterness of spirit and it frightened me, as we drove him to the graveyard through those unquiet, ruined streets, to see how powerful and overflowing this bitterness could be and to realize that this bitterness now was mine.

When he died I had been away from home for a little over a year. In that year I had had time to become aware of the meaning of all my father's bitter warnings, had discovered the secret of his proudly pursed lips and rigid carriage: I had discovered the weight of white people in the world. I saw that this had been for my ancestors and now would be for me an awful thing to live with and that the bitterness which had helped to kill my father could also kill me.

He had been ill a long time—in the mind, as we now realized, reliving instances of his fantastic intransigence in the new light of his affliction and endeavoring to feel a sorrow for him which never, quite, came true. We had not known that he was being eaten up by paranoia, and the discovery that his cruelty, to our bodies and our minds, had been one of the symptoms of his illness was not, then, enough to enable us to forgive him. The younger children felt, quite simply, relief that he would not be coming home any more. My mother's observation that it was he, after all, who had kept them alive all these years meant nothing because the problems of keeping children alive are not real for children. The older children felt, with my father gone, that they could invite their friends to the house without fear that their friends would be insulted or, as had sometimes happened with me, being told that their friends were in league with the devil and intended to rob our family of everything we owned. (I didn't fail to wonder, and it made me hate him, what on earth we owned that anybody else would want.)

His illness was beyond all hope of healing before anyone realized that he was ill. He had always been so strange and had lived, like a prophet, in such unimaginably close communion with the Lord that his long silences which were punctuated by moans and hallelujahs and snatches of old songs while he sat at the living-room window never seemed odd to us. It was not until he refused to eat because, he said, his family was trying to poison him that my mother was forced to accept as a fact what had, until then, been only an unwilling suspicion. When he was committed, it was discovered that he had tuberculosis and, as it turned out, the disease of his mind allowed the disease of his body to destroy him. For the doctors could not force him to eat, either, and, though he was fed intravenously, it was clear from the beginning that there was no hope for him.

In my mind's eye I could see him, sitting at the window, locked up in his terrors; hating and fearing every living soul including his children who had betrayed him, too, by reaching toward the world which had despised him. There were nine of us. I began to wonder what it could have felt like for such a man to have had nine children whom he could barely feed. He used to make little jokes about our poverty, which never, of course, seemed very funny to us; they could not have seemed very funny to him, either, or else our all too feeble response to them would never have caused such rages. He spent great energy and achieved, to our chagrin, no small amount of success in keeping us away from the people who surrounded us, people who had all-night rent parties to which we listened when we should have been sleeping, people who cursed and drank and flashed razor blades on Lenox Avenue. He could not understand why, if they had so much energy to spare, they could not use it to make their lives better. He treated almost everybody on our block with a most uncharitable asperity and neither they, nor, of course, their children were slow to reciprocate.

The only white people who came to our house were welfare workers and bill collectors. It was almost always my mother who dealt with them, for my father's temper, which was at the mercy of his pride, was never to be trusted. It was clear that he felt their very presence in his home to be a violation: this was conveyed by his carriage, almost ludicrously stiff, and by his voice, harsh and vindictively polite. When I was around nine or ten I wrote a play which was directed by a young, white schoolteacher, a woman, who then took an interest in me, and gave me books to read and, in order to corroborate my theatrical bent, decided to take me to see what she somewhat tactlessly referred to as "real" plays. Theater-going was forbidden in our house, but, with the really cruel intuitiveness of a child, I suspected that the color of this woman's skin would carry the day for me. When, at school, she suggested taking me to the theater, I did not, as I might have done if she had been a Negro, find a way of discouraging her, but agreed that she should pick me up at my house one evening. I then, very cleverly, left all the rest to my mother, who suggested to my father, as I knew she would, that it would not be very nice to let such a kind woman make the trip for nothing. Also, since it was a schoolteacher, I imagine that my mother countered the idea of sin with the idea of "education," which word, even with my father, carried a kind of bitter weight.

Before the teacher came my father took me aside to ask *why* she was coming, what *interest* she could possibly have in our house, in a boy like me. I said I didn't know but I, too, suggested that it had something to do with education. And I understood that my father was waiting for me to say something—I didn't quite know what; perhaps that I wanted his protection against this teacher and her "education." I said none of these things and the teacher came and we went out. It was clear, during the brief interview in our living room, that my father was agreeing very much against his will and that he would have refused permission if he had dared. The fact that he did not dare caused me to despise him: I had no way of knowing that he was facing in that living room a wholly unprecedented and frightening situation.

Later, when my father had been laid off from his job, this woman became very important to us. She was really a very sweet and generous woman and went to a great deal of trouble to be of help to us, particularly during one awful winter. My mother called her by the highest name she knew: she said she was a "christian." My father could scarcely disagree but during the four or five years of our relatively close association he never trusted her and was always trying to surprise in her open, Midwestern face the genuine, cunningly hidden, and hideous motivation. In later years, particularly when it began to be clear that this "education" of mine was going to lead me to perdition, he became more explicit and warned me that my white friends in high school were not really my friends and that I would see, when I was older, how white people would do anything to keep a Negro down. Some of them could be nice, he admitted, but none of them were to be trusted and most of them were not even nice. The best thing was to have as little to do with them as possible. I did not feel this way and I was certain, in my innocence, that I never would.

But the year which preceded my father's death had made a great change in my life. I had been living in New Jersey, working in defense plants,[4] working and living among southerners, white and black. I knew about the south, of course, and about how southerners treated Negroes and how they expected them to behave, but it had never entered my mind that anyone would look at me and expect *me* to behave that way. I learned in New Jersey that to be a Negro meant, precisely, that one was never looked at but was simply at the mercy of the reflexes the color of one's skin caused in other people. I acted in New Jersey as I had always acted, that is as though I thought a great deal of myself—I had to *act* that way— with results that were, simply, unbelievable. I had scarcely arrived before I had earned the enmity, which was extraordinarily ingenious, of all my superiors and nearly all my co-workers. In the beginning, to make matters worse, I simply did not know what was happening. I did not know what I had done, and I shortly began to wonder what *anyone* could possibly do, to bring about such unanimous, active, and unbearably vocal hostility. I knew about jim-crow[5] but I had never experienced it. I went to the same self-service restaurant three times and stood with all the Princeton boys before the counter, waiting for a hamburger and coffee; it was always an extraordinarily long time before anything was set before me; but it was not until the fourth visit that I learned that, in fact, nothing had ever been set before me: I had simply picked something up. Negroes were not served there, I was told, and they had been waiting for me to realize that I was always the only Negro present. Once I was told this, I determined to go there all the time. But now they were ready for me and, though some dreadful scenes were subsequently enacted in that restaurant, I never ate there again.

It was the same story all over New Jersey, in bars, bowling alleys, diners, places to live. I was always being forced to leave, silently, or with

---

[4]Factories supporting the war effort during World War II.

[5]The practice of legal racial discrimination against African Americans, a feature of the post–Civil War South. In addition to political and economic disenfranchisement, African Americans were barred from eating at whites-only restaurants, required to attend segregated schools, forced to use separate washrooms and water fountains, and relegated to the back of buses and trains. The name "Jim Crow" is from an African American character featured in nineteenth-century musical productions in which white performers wore blackface.

mutual imprecations. I very shortly became notorious and children giggled behind me when I passed and their elders whispered or shouted—they really believed that I was mad. And it did begin to work on my mind, of course; I began to be afraid to go anywhere and to compensate for this I went places to which I really should not have gone and where, God knows, I had no desire to be. My reputation in town naturally enhanced my reputation at work and my working day became one long series of acrobatics designed to keep me out of trouble. I cannot say that these acrobatics succeeded. It began to seem that the machinery of the organization I worked for was turning over, day and night, with but one aim: to eject me. I was fired once, and contrived, with the aid of a friend from New York, to get back on the payroll; was fired again, and bounced back again. It took a while to fire me for the third time, but the third time took. There were no loopholes anywhere. There was not even any way of getting back inside the gates.

That year in New Jersey lives in my mind as though it were the year during which, having an unsuspected predilection for it, I first contracted some dread, chronic disease, the unfailing symptom of which is a kind of blind fever, a pounding in the skull and fire in the bowels. Once this disease is contracted, one can never be really carefree again, for the fever, without an instant's warning, can recur at any moment. It can wreck more important things than race relations. There is not a Negro alive who does not have this rage in his blood—one has the choice, merely, of living with it consciously or surrendering to it. As for me, this fever has recurred in me, and does, and will until the day I die.

My last night in New Jersey, a white friend from New York took me to the nearest big town, Trenton, to go to the movies and have a few drinks. As it turned out, he also saved me from, at the very least, a violent whipping. Almost every detail of that night stands out very clearly in my memory. I even remember the name of the movie we saw because its title impressed me as being so patly ironical. It was a movie about the German occupation of France, starring Maureen O'Hara and Charles Laughton and called *This Land Is Mine*. I remember the name of the diner we walked into when the movie ended: it was the "American Diner." When we walked in the counterman asked what we wanted and I remember answering with the casual sharpness which had become my habit: "We want a hamburger and a cup of coffee, what do you think we want?" I do not know why, after a year of such rebuffs, I so completely failed to anticipate his answer, which was, of course, "We don't serve Negroes here." This reply failed to discompose me, at least for the moment. I made some sardonic comment about the name of the diner and we walked out into the streets.

This was the time of what was called the "brown-out," when the lights in all American cities were very dim. When we re-entered the streets something happened to me which had the force of an optical illusion, or a nightmare. The streets were very crowded and I was facing north. People were moving in every direction but it seemed to me, in that instant, that all of the people I could see, and many more than that, were moving toward me, against me, and that everyone was white. I remember how their faces gleamed. And I felt, like a physical sensation, a *click* at the nape of my neck as though some interior string connecting my head to my body had been cut. I began to walk. I heard my friend call after me, but I ignored him. Heaven only knows what was going on in his mind, but he had the good sense not to touch me—I don't know what would have happened if he had—and to keep me in sight. I don't know what was going on in my mind, either; I certainly had no conscious plan. I wanted to do something to crush these white faces, which were crushing me. I walked for perhaps a block or two until I came to an enormous, glittering, and fashionable restaurant in which I knew not even the intercession of the Virgin[6] would cause me to be served. I pushed through the doors and took the first vacant seat I saw, at a table for two, and waited.

I do not know how long I waited and I rather wonder, until today, what I could possibly have looked like. Whatever I looked like, I frightened the waitress who shortly appeared, and the moment she appeared all of my fury flowed toward her. I hated her for her white face, and for her great, astounded, frightened eyes. I felt that if she found a black man so frightening I would make her fright worth-while.

She did not ask me what I wanted, but repeated, as though she had learned it somewhere, "We don't serve Negroes here." She did not say it with the blunt, derisive hostility to which I had grown so accustomed, but, rather, with a note of apology in her voice, and fear. This made me colder and more murderous than ever. I felt I had to do something with my hands. I wanted her to come close enough for me to get her neck between my hands.

So I pretended not to have understood her, hoping to draw her closer. And she did step a very short step closer, with her pencil poised incongruously over her pad, and repeated the formula: "...don't serve Negroes here."

Somehow, with the repetition of that phrase, which was already ringing in my head like a thousand bells of a nightmare, I realized that she would never come any closer and that I would have to strike from a distance. There was nothing on the table but an ordinary water-mug half full of water, and I picked this up and hurled it with all my strength at her. She ducked and it missed her and shattered against the mirror behind the bar. And, with that sound, my frozen blood abruptly thawed, I returned from wherever I had been, I *saw*, for the first time, the restaurant, the people with their mouths open, already, as it seemed to me, rising as one

[6]The Virgin Mary.

man, and I realized what I had done, and where I was, and I was frightened. I rose and began running for the door. A round, potbellied man grabbed me by the nape of the neck just as I reached the doors and began to beat me about the face. I kicked him and got loose and ran into the streets. My friend whispered, "*Run!*" and I ran.

My friend stayed outside the restaurant long enough to misdirect my pursuers and the police, who arrived, he told me, at once. I do not know what I said to him when he came to my room that night. I could not have said much. I felt, in the oddest, most awful way, that I had somehow betrayed him. I lived it over and over and over again, the way one relives an automobile accident after it has happened and one finds oneself alone and safe. I could not get over two facts, both equally difficult for the imagination to grasp, and one was that I could have been murdered. But the other was that I had been ready to commit murder. I saw nothing very clearly but I did see this: that my life, my *real* life, was in danger, and not from anything other people might do but from the hatred I carried in my own heart.

II

I had returned home around the second week in June—in great haste because it seemed that my father's death and my mother's confinement were both but a matter of hours. In the case of my mother, it soon became clear that she had simply made a miscalculation. This had always been her tendency and I don't believe that a single one of us arrived in the world, or has since arrived anywhere else, on time. But none of us dawdled so intolerably about the business of being born as did my baby sister. We sometimes amused ourselves, during those endless, stifling weeks, by picturing the baby sitting within in the safe, warm dark, bitterly regretting the necessity of becoming a part of our chaos and stubbornly putting it off as long as possible. I understood her perfectly and congratulated her on showing such good sense so soon. Death, however, sat as purposefully at my father's bedside as life stirred within my mother's womb and it was harder to understand why he so lingered in that long shadow. It seemed that he had bent, and for a long time, too, all of his energies toward dying. Now death was ready for him but my father held back.

All of Harlem, indeed, seemed to be infected by waiting. I had never before known it to be so violently still. Racial tensions throughout this country were exacerbated during the early years of the war, partly because the labor market brought together hundreds of thousands of ill-prepared people and partly because Negro soldiers, regardless of where they were born, received their military training in the south. What happened in defense plants and army camps had repercussions, naturally, in every Negro ghetto. The situation in Harlem had grown bad enough for clergymen, policemen, educators, politicians, and social workers to assert in one breath that there was no "crime wave" and to offer, in the very next breath, suggestions as to how to combat it. These suggestions always seemed to involve playgrounds, despite the fact that racial skirmishes were occurring in the playgrounds, too. Playground or not, crime wave or not, the Harlem police force had been augmented in March, and the unrest grew—perhaps, in fact, partly as a result of the ghetto's instinctive hatred of policemen. Perhaps the most revealing news item, out of the steady parade of reports of muggings, stabbings, shootings, assaults, gang wars, and accusations of police brutality, is the item concerning six Negro girls who set upon a white girl in the subway because, as they all too accurately put it, she was stepping on their toes. Indeed she was, all over the nation.

I had never before been so aware of policemen, on foot, on horseback, on corners, everywhere, always two by two. Nor had I ever been so aware of small knots of people. They were on stoops and on corners and in doorways, and what was striking about them, I think, was that they did not seem to be talking. Never, when I passed these groups, did the usual sound of a curse or a laugh ring out and neither did there seem to be any hum of gossip. There was certainly, on the other hand, occurring between them communication extraordinarily intense. Another thing that was striking was the unexpected diversity of the people who made up these groups. Usually, for example, one would see a group of sharpies standing on the street corner, jiving the passing chicks; or a group of older men, usually, for some reason, in the vicinity of a barber shop, discussing baseball scores, or the numbers, or making rather chilling observations about women they had known. Women, in a general way, tended to be seen less often together—unless they were church women, or very young girls, or prostitutes met together for an unprofessional instant. But that summer I saw the strangest combinations: large, respectable, churchly matrons standing on the stoops or the corners with their hair tied up, together with a girl in sleazy satin whose face bore the marks of gin and the razor, or heavy-set, abrupt, no-nonsense older men, in company with the most disreputable and fanatical "race" men, or these same "race" men with the sharpies, or these sharpies with the churchly women. Seventh Day Adventists and Methodists and Spiritualists seemed to be hobnobbing with Holyrollers and they were all, alike, entangled with the most flagrant disbelievers; something heavy in their stance seemed to indicate that they had all, incredibly, seen a common vision, and on each face there seemed to be the same strange, bitter shadow.

The churchly women and the matter-of-fact, no-nonsense men had children in the Army. The sleazy girls they talked to had lovers there, the sharpies and the "race" men had friends and brothers there. It would have demanded an unquestioning patriotism, happily as uncommon in this country as it is undesirable, for these people not to have been disturbed by the bitter letters they received, by the newspaper stories they read, not to have been enraged by the posters, then to be found all over New York, which described the Japanese as "yellow-bellied Japs." It was only the "race" men, to be sure, who spoke ceaselessly of being revenged—how this vengeance was to be exacted was not clear—for the indignities and dangers suffered by Negro boys in uniform; but everybody felt a directionless, hopeless bitterness, as well as that panic which can scarcely be suppressed when one knows that a human being one loves is beyond one's reach, and in danger. This helplessness and this gnawing uneasiness does something, at length, to even the toughest mind. Perhaps the best way to sum all this up is to say that the people I knew felt, mainly, a peculiar kind of relief when they knew that their boys were being shipped out of the south, to do battle overseas. It was, perhaps, like feeling that the most dangerous part of a dangerous journey had been passed and that now, even if death should come, it would come with honor and without the complicity of their countrymen. Such a death would be, in short, a fact with which one could hope to live.

It was on the 28th of July, which I believe was a Wednesday, that I visited my father for the first time during his illness and for the last time in his life. The moment I saw him I knew why I had put off this visit so long. I had told my mother that I did not want to see him because I hated him. But this was not true. It was only that I *had* hated him and I wanted to hold on to this hatred. I did not want to look on him as a ruin: it was not a ruin I had hated. I imagine that one of the reasons people cling to their hates so stubbornly is because they sense, once hate is gone, that they will be forced to deal with pain.

We traveled out to him, his older sister and myself, to what seemed to be the very end of a very Long Island. It was hot and dusty and we wrangled, my aunt and I, all the way out, over the fact that I had recently begun to smoke and, as she said, to give myself airs. But I knew that she wrangled with me because she could not bear to face the fact of her brother's dying. Neither could I endure the reality of her despair, her unstated bafflement as to what had happened to her brother's life, and her own. So we wrangled and I smoked and from time to time she fell into a heavy reverie. Covertly, I watched her face, which was the face of an old woman; it had fallen in, the eyes were sunken and lightless; soon she would be dying, too.

In my childhood—it had not been so long ago—I had thought her beautiful. She had been quick-witted and quick-moving and very generous with all the children and each of her visits had been an event. At one time one of my brothers and myself had thought of running away to live with her. Now she could no longer produce out of her handbag some unexpected and yet familiar delight. She made me feel pity and revulsion and fear. It was awful to realize that she no longer caused me to feel affection. The closer we came to the hospital the more querulous she became and at the same time, naturally, grew more dependent on me. Between pity and guilt and fear I began to feel that there was another me trapped in my skull like a jack-in-the-box who might escape my control at any moment and fill the air with screaming.

She began to cry the moment we entered the room and she saw him lying there, all shriveled and still, like a little black monkey. The great, gleaming apparatus which fed him and would have compelled him to be still even if he had been able to move brought to mind, not beneficence, but torture; the tubes entering his arm made me think of pictures I had seen when a child, of Gulliver,[7] tied down by the pygmies on that island. My aunt wept and wept, there was a whistling sound in my father's throat; nothing was said; he could not speak. I wanted to take his hand, to say something. But I do not know what I could have said, even if he could have heard me. He was not really in that room with us, he had at last really embarked on his journey; and though my aunt told me that he said he was going to meet Jesus, I did not hear anything except that whistling in his throat. The doctor came back and we left, into that unbearable train again, and home. In the morning came the telegram saying that he was dead. Then the house was suddenly full of relatives, friends, hysteria, and confusion and I quickly left my mother and the children to the care of those impressive women, who, in Negro communities at least, automatically appear at times of bereavement armed with lotions, proverbs, and patience, and an ability to cook. I went downtown. By the time I returned, later the same day, my mother had been carried to the hospital and the baby had been born.

III

For my father's funeral I had nothing black to wear and this posed a nagging problem all day long. It was one of those problems, simple, or impossible of solution, to which the mind insanely clings in order to avoid the mind's real trouble. I spent most of that day at the downtown apartment of a girl I knew, celebrating my birthday with whiskey and wondering what to wear that night. When planning a birthday celebration one naturally does not expect that it will be up against competition from a funeral and this girl had anticipated taking me out that night, for a big dinner and a night club afterwards. Sometime during the course of that long day we decided that we would go out anyway, when my father's funeral service was over. I imagine *I* decided it, since, as the funeral hour approached, it became clearer and clearer to me that I would not know what to do with myself when it was over. The girl, stifling her very lively concern as to the possible effects of the whiskey on one of my father's chief mourners, concentrated on being conciliatory and practically helpful.

[7]The title character of Jonathan Swift's (1667–1745) satiric novel *Gulliver's Travels* (1726), in which the shipwrecked Lemuel Gulliver wakes to find himself on Lilliput, an island inhabited by tiny people.

She found a black shirt for me somewhere and ironed it and, dressed in the darkest pants and jacket I owned, and slightly drunk, I made my way to my father's funeral.

The chapel was full, but not packed, and very quiet. There were, mainly, my father's relatives, and his children, and here and there I saw faces I had not seen since childhood, the faces of my father's one-time friends. They were very dark and solemn now, seeming somehow to suggest that they had known all along that something like this would happen. Chief among the mourners was my aunt, who had quarreled with my father all his life; by which I do not mean to suggest that her mourning was insincere or that she had not loved him. I suppose that she was one of the few people in the world who had, and their incessant quarreling proved precisely the strength of the tie that bound them. The only other person in the world, as far as I knew, whose relationship to my father rivaled my aunt's in depth was my mother, who was not there.

It seemed to me, of course, that it was a very long funeral. But it was, if anything, a rather shorter funeral than most, nor, since there were no overwhelming, uncontrollable expressions of grief, could it be called—if I dare to use the word—successful. The minister who preached my father's funeral sermon was one of the few my father had still been seeing as he neared his end. He presented to us in his sermon a man whom none of us had ever seen—a man thoughtful, patient, and forbearing, a Christian inspiration to all who knew him, and a model for his children. And no doubt the children, in their disturbed and guilty state, were almost ready to believe this; he had been remote enough to be anything and, anyway, the shock of the incontrovertible, that it was really our father lying up there in that casket, prepared the mind for anything. His sister moaned and this grief-stricken moaning was taken as corroboration. The other faces held a dark, noncommittal thoughtfulness. This was not the man they had known, but they had scarcely expected to be confronted with *him*; this was, in a sense deeper than questions of fact, the man they had not known, and the man they had not known may have been the real one. The real man, whoever he had been, had suffered and now he was dead: this was all that was sure and all that mattered now. Every man in the chapel hoped that when his hour came he, too, would be eulogized, which is to say forgiven, and that all of his lapses, greeds, errors, and strayings from the truth would be invested with coherence and looked upon with charity. This was perhaps the last thing human beings could give each other and it was what they demanded, after all, of the Lord. Only the Lord saw the midnight tears, only He was present when one of His children, moaning and wringing hands, paced up and down the room. When one slapped one's child in anger the recoil in the heart reverberated through heaven and became part of the pain of the universe. And when the children were hungry and sullen and distrustful and one watched them, daily, growing wilder, and further away, and running headlong into danger, it was the Lord who knew what the charged heart endured as the strap was laid to the backside; the Lord alone who knew what one *would* have said if one had had, like the Lord, the gift of the living word. It was the Lord who knew of the impossibility every parent in that room faced: how to prepare the child for the day when the child would be despised and how to *create* in the child—by what means?—a stronger antidote to this poison than one had found for oneself. The avenues, side streets, bars, billiard halls, hospitals, police stations, and even the playgrounds of Harlem—not to mention the houses of correction, the jails, and the morgue—testified to the potency of the poison while remaining silent as to the efficacy of whatever antidote, irresistibly raising the question of whether or not such an antidote existed; raising, which was worse, the question of whether or not an antidote was desirable; perhaps poison should be fought with poison. With these several schisms in the mind and with more terrors in the heart than could be named, it was better not to judge the man who had gone down under an impossible burden. It was better to remember: *Thou knowest this man's fall; but thou knowest not his wrassling.*

While the preacher talked and I watched the children—years of changing their diapers, scrubbing them, slapping them, taking them to school, and scolding them had had the perhaps inevitable result of making me love them, though I am not sure I knew this then—my mind was busily breaking out with a rash of disconnected impressions. Snatches of popular songs, indecent jokes, bits of books I had read, movie sequences, faces, voices, political issues—I thought I was going mad; all these impressions suspended, as it were, in the solution of the faint nausea produced in me by the heat and liquor. For a moment I had the impression that my alcoholic breath, inefficiently disguised with chewing gum, filled the entire chapel. Then someone began singing one of my father's favorite songs and, abruptly, I was with him, sitting on his knee, in the hot, enormous, crowded church which was the first church we attended. It was the Abyssinian Baptist Church on 138th Street. We had not gone there long. With this image, a host of others came. I had forgotten, in the rage of my growing up, how proud my father had been of me when I was little. Apparently, I had had a voice and my father had liked to show me off before the members of the church. I had forgotten what he had looked like when he was pleased but now I remembered that he had always been grinning with pleasure when my solos ended. I even remembered certain expressions on his face when he teased my mother—had he loved her? I would never know. And when had it all begun to change? For now it seemed that he had not always been cruel. I remembered being taken for a haircut and scraping my knee on the footrest of the barber's chair and I remembered my father's face as he soothed my crying and applied the stinging iodine. Then I remembered our fights, fights which had been of the worst possible kind because my technique had been silence.

I remembered the one time in all our life together when we had really spoken to each other.

It was on a Sunday and it must have been shortly before I left home. We were walking, just the two of us, in our usual silence, to or from church. I was in high school and had been doing a lot of writing and I was, at about this time, the editor of the high school magazine. But I had also been a Young Minister and had been preaching from the pulpit. Lately, I had been taking fewer engagements and preached as rarely as possible. It was said in the church, quite truthfully, that I was "cooling off."

My father asked me abruptly, "You'd rather write than preach, wouldn't you?"

I was astonished at his question—because it was a real question. I answered, "Yes."

That was all we said. It was awful to remember that that was all we had *ever* said.

The casket now was opened and the mourners were being led up the aisle to look for the last time on the deceased. The assumption was that the family was too overcome with grief to be allowed to make this journey alone and I watched while my aunt was led to the casket and, muffled in black, and shaking, led back to her seat. I disapproved of forcing the children to look on their dead father, considering that the shock of his death, or, more truthfully, the shock of death as a reality, was already a little more than a child could bear, but my judgment in this matter had been overruled and there they were, bewildered and frightened and very small, being led, one by one, to the casket. But there is also something very gallant about children at such moments. It has something to do with their silence and gravity and with the fact that one cannot help them. Their legs, somehow, seem *exposed*, so that it is at once incredible and terribly clear that their legs are all they have to hold them up.

I had not wanted to go to the casket myself and I certainly had not wished to be led there, but there was no way of avoiding either of these forms. One of the deacons led me up and I looked on my father's face. I cannot say that it looked like him at all. His blackness had been equivocated by powder and there was no suggestion in that casket of what his power had or could have been. He was simply an old man dead, and it was hard to believe that he had ever given anyone either joy or pain. Yet, his life filled that room. Further up the avenue his wife was holding his newborn child. Life and death so close together, and love and hatred, and right and wrong, said something to me which I did not want to hear concerning man, concerning the life of man.

After the funeral, while I was downtown desperately celebrating my birthday, a Negro soldier, in the lobby of the Hotel Braddock, got into a fight with a white policeman over a Negro girl. Negro girls, white policemen, in or out of uniform, and Negro males—in or out of uniform—were part of the furniture of the lobby of the Hotel Braddock and this was certainly not the first time such an incident had occurred. It was destined, however, to receive an unprecedented publicity, for the fight between the policeman and the soldier ended with the shooting of the soldier. Rumor, flowing immediately to the streets outside, stated that the soldier had been shot in the back, an instantaneous and revealing invention, and that the soldier had died protecting a Negro woman. The facts were somewhat different—for example, the soldier had not been shot in the back, and was not dead, and the girl seems to have been as dubious a symbol of womanhood as her white counterpart in Georgia usually is, but no one was interested in the facts. They preferred the invention because this invention expressed and corroborated their hates and fears so perfectly. It is just as well to remember that people are always doing this. Perhaps many of those legends, including Christianity, to which the world clings began their conquest of the world with just some such concerted surrender to distortion. The effect, in Harlem, of this particular legend was like the effect of a lit match in a tin of gasoline. The mob gathered before the doors of the Hotel Braddock simply began to swell and to spread in every direction, and Harlem exploded.

The mob did not cross the ghetto lines. It would have been easy, for example, to have gone over Morningside Park on the west side or to have crossed the Grand Central railroad tracks at 125th Street on the east side, to wreak havoc in white neighborhoods. The mob seems to have been mainly interested in something more potent and real than the white face, that is, in white power, and the principal damage done during the riot of the summer of 1943 was to white business establishments in Harlem. It might have been a far bloodier story, of course, if, at the hour the riot began, these establishments had still been open. From the Hotel Braddock the mob fanned out, east and west along 125th Street, and for the entire length of Lenox, Seventh, and Eighth avenues. Along each of these avenues, and along each major side street—116th, 125th, 135th, and so on—bars, stores, pawnshops, restaurants, even little luncheonettes had been smashed open and entered and looted—looted, it might be added, with more haste than efficiency. The shelves really looked as though a bomb had struck them. Cans of beans and soup and dog food, along with toilet paper, corn flakes, sardines, and milk tumbled every which way, and abandoned cash registers and cases of beer leaned crazily out of the splintered windows and were strewn along the avenues. Sheets, blankets, and clothing of every description formed a kind of path, as though people had dropped them while running. I truly had not realized that Harlem *had* so many stores until I saw them all smashed open; the first time the word *wealth* ever entered my mind in relation to Harlem was when I saw it scattered in the streets. But one's first, incongruous impression of plenty was countered immediately by an impression of waste. None of this was doing anybody any good. It would have been better to have left the plate glass as it had been and the goods lying in the stores.

It would have been better, but it would also have been intolerable, for Harlem had needed something to smash. To smash something is the ghetto's chronic need. Most of the time it is the members of the ghetto who smash each other, and themselves. But as long as the ghetto walls are standing there will always come a moment when these outlets do not work. That summer, for example, it was not enough to get into a fight on Lenox Avenue, or curse out one's cronies in the barber shops. If ever, indeed, the violence which fills Harlem's churches, pool halls, and bars erupts outward in a more direct fashion, Harlem and its citizens are likely to vanish in an apocalyptic flood. That this is not likely to happen is due to a great many reasons, most hidden and powerful among them the Negro's real relation to the white American. This relation prohibits, simply, anything as uncomplicated and satisfactory as pure hatred. In order really to hate white people, one has to blot so much out of the mind—and the heart—that this hatred itself becomes an exhausting and self-destructive pose. But this does not mean, on the other hand, that love comes easily: the white world is too powerful, too complacent, too ready with gratuitous humiliation, and, above all, too ignorant and too innocent for that. One is absolutely forced to make perpetual qualifications and one's own reactions are always canceling each other out. It is this, really, which has driven so many people mad, both white and black. One is always in the position of having to decide between amputation and gangrene. Amputation is swift but time may prove that the amputation was not necessary—or one may delay the amputation too long. Gangrene is slow, but it is impossible to be sure that one is reading one's symptoms right. The idea of going through life as a cripple is more than one can bear, and equally unbearable is the risk of swelling up slowly, in agony, with poison. And the trouble, finally, is that the risks are real even if the choices do not exist.

"But as for me and my house,"[8] my father had said, "we will serve the Lord." I wondered, as we drove him to his resting place, what this line had meant for him. I had heard him preach it many times. I had preached it once myself, proudly giving it an interpretation different from my father's. Now the whole thing came back to me, as though my father and I were on our way to Sunday school and I were memorizing the golden text: *And if it seem evil unto you to serve the Lord, choose you this day whom you will serve; whether the gods which your fathers served that were on the other side of the flood, or the gods of the Amorites, in whose land ye dwell: but as for me and my house, we will serve the Lord.* I suspected in these familiar lines a meaning which had never been there for me before. All of my father's texts and songs, which I had decided were meaningless, were

[8]Joshua 24:14–15.

arranged before me at his death like empty bottles, waiting to hold the meaning which life would give them for me. This was his legacy: nothing is ever escaped. That bleakly memorable morning I hated the unbelievable streets and the Negroes and whites who had, equally, made them that way. But I knew that it was folly, as my father would have said, this bitterness was folly. It was necessary to hold on to the things that mattered. The dead man mattered, the new life mattered; blackness and whiteness did not matter; to believe that they did was to acquiesce in one's own destruction. Hatred, which could destroy so much, never failed to destroy the man who hated and this was an immutable law.

It began to seem that one would have to hold in the mind forever two ideas which seemed to be in opposition. The first idea was acceptance, the acceptance, totally without rancor, of life as it is, and men as they are: in the light of this idea, it goes without saying that injustice is a commonplace. But this did not mean that one could be complacent, for the second idea was of equal power: that one must never, in one's own life, accept these injustices as commonplace but must fight them with all one's strength. This fight begins, however, in the heart and it now had been laid to my charge to keep my own heart free of hatred and despair. This intimation made my heart heavy and, now that my father was irrecoverable, I wished that he had been beside me so that I could have searched his face for the answers which only the future would give me now.

[1955]

FLANNERY O'CONNOR ■ (1925–1964)

Flannery O'Connor is the author of two strange, macabre short novels, *Wise Blood* (1952) and *The Violent Bear It Away* (1960), and many gripping stories, often violent and grotesque in their action and characterizations. Her *Complete Stories* was published in 1971.

O'Connor was born in Savannah, Georgia, where she attended Catholic elementary schools, and later she studied at the Georgia State College for Women and at the University of Iowa. For most of her life, she lived on her mother's farm in Milledgeville, Georgia. She sometimes gave readings of her work at universities and colleges, but her travel was limited because of the serious disease, lupus, she contracted in 1950.

O'Connor was a devout believer in the Catholic faith, with a gothic sense of menacing humor, and much of her work reflects her own and her characters' painful, sometimes bewildered, even fanatical quest for redemption, as the story "Revelation" vividly shows. She was also a deeply Southern writer, once remarking, "Anything that comes out of the South is going to be called grotesque by the Northern reader, unless it is grotesque, in which case it is going to be called realistic." She also said, "If you start with a real personality, a real character, then something is bound to happen." And also, "The action of grace changes a character...All of my stories are about the action of grace on a character who is not very willing to support it."

O'Connor's nonfiction is collected in *Mystery and Manners: Occasional Prose*, eds. Sally and Robert Fitzgerald (1969), and her letters in *The Habit of Being*, ed. Sally Fitzgerald (1979). For critical discussion, see *Critical Essays on Flannery O'Connor*, eds. Melvin J. Friedman and Beverly Lyon Clark (1985); Richard Giannone, *Flannery O'Connor and the Mystery of Love* (1989) and *Flannery O'Connor, Hermit Novelist* (2000); Katherine Hemple Prown, *Revising Flannery O'Connor: Southern Literary Culture and the Problem of Female Authorship* (2001); and Brad Gooch, *Flannery: A Life of Flannery O'Connor* (2010).

Revelation

The doctor's waiting room, which was very small, was almost full when the Turpins entered and Mrs. Turpin, who was very large, made it look even smaller by her presence. She stood looming at the head of the magazine table set in the center of it, a living demonstration that the room was inadequate and ridiculous. Her little bright black eyes took in all the patients as she sized up the seating situation. There was one vacant chair and a place on the sofa occupied by a blond child in a dirty blue romper who should have been told to move over and make room for the lady. He was five or six, but Mrs. Turpin saw at once that no one was going to tell him to move over. He was slumped down in the seat, his arms idle at his sides and his eyes idle in his head; his nose ran unchecked.

Mrs. Turpin put a firm hand on Claud's shoulder and said in a voice that included anyone who wanted to listen, "Claud, you sit in that chair there," and gave him a push down into the vacant one. Claud was florid and bald and sturdy, somewhat shorter than Mrs. Turpin, but he sat down as if he were accustomed to doing what she told him to.

Mrs. Turpin remained standing. The only man in the room besides Claud was a lean stringy old fellow with a rusty hand spread out on each knee, whose eyes were closed as if he were asleep or dead or pretending to be so as not to get up and offer her his seat. Her gaze settled agreeably on a well-dressed gray-haired lady whose eyes met hers and whose expression said: if that child belonged to me, he would have some manners and move over—there's plenty of room there for you and him too.

Claud looked up with a sigh and made as if to rise.

"Sit down," Mrs. Turpin said. "You know you're not supposed to stand on that leg. He has an ulcer on his leg," she explained.

Claud lifted his foot onto the magazine table and rolled his trouser leg up to reveal a purple swelling on a plump marble-white calf.

"My!" the pleasant lady said. "How did you do that?"

"A cow kicked him," Mrs. Turpin said.

"Goodness!" said the lady.

Claud rolled his trouser leg down.

"Maybe the little boy would move over," the lady suggested, but the child did not stir.

"Somebody will be leaving in a minute," Mrs. Turpin said. She could not understand why a doctor—with as much money as they made charging five dollars a day to just stick their head in the hospital door and look at you—couldn't afford a decent-sized waiting room. This one was hardly bigger than a garage. The table was cluttered with limp-looking magazines and at one end of it there was a big green glass ash tray full of cigarette butts and cotton wads with little blood spots on them. If she had had anything to do with the running of the place, that would have been emptied every so often. There were no chairs against the wall at the head of the room. It had a rectangular-shaped panel in it that permitted a view of the office where the nurse came and went and the secretary listened to the radio. A plastic fern in a gold pot sat in the opening and trailed its fronds down almost to the floor. The radio was softly playing gospel music.

Just then the inner door opened and a nurse with the highest stack of yellow hair Mrs. Turpin had ever seen put her face in the crack and called for the next patient. The woman sitting beside Claud grasped the two arms of her chair and hoisted herself up; she pulled her dress free from her legs and lumbered through the door where the nurse had disappeared.

Mrs. Turpin eased into the vacant chair, which held her tight as a corset. "I wish I could reduce," she said, and rolled her eyes and gave a comic sigh.

"Oh, *you* aren't fat," the stylish lady said.

"Ooooo I am too," Mrs. Turpin said. "Claud he eats all he wants to and never weighs over one hundred and seventy-five pounds, but me I just look at something good to eat and I gain some weight," and her stomach and shoulders shook with laughter. "You can eat all you want to, can't you, Claud?" she asked, turning to him.

Claud only grinned.

"Well, as long as you have such a good disposition," the stylish lady said, "I don't think it makes a bit of difference what size you are. You just can't beat a good disposition."

Next to her was a fat girl of eighteen or nineteen, scowling into a thick blue book which Mrs. Turpin saw was entitled *Human Development*. The girl raised her head and directed her scowl at Mrs. Turpin as if she did not like her looks. She appeared annoyed that anyone should speak while she tried to read. The poor girl's face was blue with acne and Mrs. Turpin thought how pitiful it was to have a face like that at that age. She gave the girl a friendly smile but the girl only scowled the harder. Mrs. Turpin herself was fat but she had always had good skin, and, though she was forty-seven years old, there was not a wrinkle in her face except around her eyes from laughing too much.

Next to the ugly girl was the child, still in exactly the same position, and next to him was a thin leathery old woman in a cotton print dress. She and Claud had three sacks of chicken feed in their pump house that was in the same print. She had seen from the first that the child belonged with the old woman. She could tell by the way they sat—kind of vacant and white-trashy, as if they would sit there until Doomsday if nobody called and told them to get up. And at right angles but next to the well-dressed pleasant lady was a lank-faced woman who was certainly the child's mother. She had on a yellow sweat shirt and wine-colored slacks, both gritty-looking, and the rims of her lips were stained with snuff. Her dirty yellow hair was tied behind with a little piece red paper ribbon. Worse than niggers any day, Mrs. Turpin thought.

The gospel hymn playing was, "When I looked up and He looked down," and Mrs. Turpin, who knew it, supplied the last line mentally, "And wona these days I know I'll we-eara crown."

Without appearing to, Mrs. Turpin always noticed people's feet. The well-dressed lady had on red and gray suede shoes to match her dress. Mrs. Turpin had on her good black patent leather pumps. The ugly girl had on Girl Scout shoes and heavy socks. The old woman had on tennis shoes and the white-trashy mother had on what appeared to be bedroom slippers, black straw with gold braid threaded through them—exactly what you would have expected her to have on.

Sometimes at night when she couldn't go to sleep, Mrs. Turpin would occupy herself with the question of who she would have chosen to be if she couldn't have been herself. If Jesus had said to her before he made her,

"There's only two places available for you. You can either be a nigger or white-trash," what would she have said? "Please, Jesus, please," she would have said, "just let me wait until there's another place available," and he would have said, "No, you have to go right now and I have only those two places so make up your mind." She would have wiggled and squirmed and begged and pleaded but it would have been no use and finally she would have said, "All right, make me a nigger then—but that don't mean a trashy one." And he would have made her a neat lean respectable Negro woman, herself but black.

Next to the child's mother was a red-headed youngish woman, reading one of the magazines and working a piece of chewing gum, hell for leather, as Claud would say. Mrs. Turpin could not see the woman's feet. She was not white-trash, just common. Sometimes Mrs. Turpin occupied herself at night naming the classes of people. On the bottom of the heap were most colored people, not the kind she would have been if she had been one, but most of them; then next to them—not above, just away from—were the white-trash; then above them were the home-owners, and above them the home-and-land owners, to which she and Claud belonged. Above she and Claud were people with a lot of money and much bigger houses and much more land. But here the complexity of it would begin to bear in on her, for some of the people with a lot of money were common and ought to be below she and Claud and some of the people who had good blood had lost their money and had to rent and then there were colored people who owned their homes and land as well. There was a colored dentist in town who had two red Lincolns and a swimming pool and a farm with registered white-face cattle on it. Usually by the time she had fallen asleep all the classes of people were moiling and roiling around in her head, and she would dream they were all crammed in together in a box car, being ridden off to be put in a gas oven.

"That's a beautiful clock," she said and nodded to her right. It was a big wall clock, the face encased in a brass sunburst.

"Yes, it's very pretty," the stylish lady said agreeably. "And right on the dot too," she added, glancing at her watch.

The ugly girl beside her cast an eye upward at the clock, smirked, then looked directly at Mrs. Turpin and smirked again. Then she returned her eyes to her book. She was obviously the lady's daughter because, although they didn't look anything alike as to disposition, they both had the same shape of face and the same blue eyes. On the lady they sparkled pleasantly but in the girl's seared face they appeared alternately to smolder and to blaze.

What if Jesus had said, "All right, you can be white-trash or a nigger or ugly"!

Mrs. Turpin felt an awful pity for the girl, though she thought it was one thing to be ugly and another to act ugly.

The woman with the snuff-stained lips turned around in her chair and looked up at the clock. Then she turned back and appeared to look a little to the side of Mrs. Turpin. There was a cast in one of her eyes. "You want to know wher you can get you one of themther clocks?" she asked in a loud voice.

"No, I already have a nice clock," Mrs. Turpin said. Once somebody like her got a leg in the conversation, she would be all over it.

"You can get you one with green stamps," the woman said. "That's most likely wher he got hisn. Save you up enough, you can get you most anythang. I got me some joo'ry."

Ought to have got you a wash rag and some soap, Mrs. Turpin thought.

"I get contour sheets with mine," the pleasant lady said.

The daughter slammed her book shut. She looked straight in front of her, directly through Mrs. Turpin and on through the yellow curtain and the plate glass window which made the wall behind her. The girl's eyes seemed lit all of a sudden with a peculiar light, an unnatural light like night road signs give. Mrs. Turpin turned her head to see if there was anything going on outside that she should see, but she could not see anything. Figures passing cast only a pale shadow through the curtain. There was no reason the girl should single her out for her ugly looks.

"Miss Finley," the nurse said, cracking the door. The gum-chewing woman got up and passed in front of her and Claud and went into the office. She had on red high-heeled shoes.

Directly across the table, the ugly girl's eyes were fixed on Mrs. Turpin as if she had some very special reason for disliking her.

"This is wonderful weather, isn't it?" the girl's mother said.

"It's good weather for cotton if you can get the niggers to pick it," Mrs. Turpin said, "but niggers don't want to pick cotton any more. You can't get the white folks to pick it and now you can't get the niggers—because they got to be right up there with the white folks."

"They gonna *try* any ways," the white-trash woman said, leaning forward.

"Do you have one of the cotton-picking machines?" the pleasant lady asked.

"No," Mrs. Turpin said, "they leave half the cotton in the field. We don't have much cotton anyway. If you want to make it farming now, you have to have a little of everything. We got a couple of acres of cotton and a few hogs and chickens and just enough white-face that Claud can look after them himself."

"One thang I don't want," the white-trash woman said, wiping her mouth with the back of her hand. "Hogs. Nasty stinking things, a-gruntin and a-rootin all over the place."

Mrs. Turpin gave her the merest edge of her attention. "Our hogs are not dirty and they don't stink," she said. "They're cleaner than some children I've seen. Their feet never touch the ground. We have a pig-parlor—that's where you raise them on concrete," she explained to the

pleasant lady, "and Claud scoots them down with the hose every afternoon and washes off the floor." Cleaner by far than that child right there,
she thought. Poor nasty little thing. He had not moved except to put the
thumb of his dirty hand into his mouth.

The woman turned her face away from Mrs. Turpin. "I know I wouldn't
scoot down no hog with no hose," she said to the wall.

You wouldn't have no hog to scoot down, Mrs. Turpin said to herself.

"A-gruntin and a-rootin and a-groanin," the woman muttered.

"We got a little of everything," Mrs. Turpin said to the pleasant lady. "It's
no use in having more than you can handle yourself with help like it is. We
found enough niggers to pick our cotton this year but Claud he has to go after them and take them home again in the evening. They can't walk that half
a mile. No they can't, I tell you," she said and laughed merrily, "I sure am
tired of buttering up niggers, but you got to love em if you want em to work
for you. When they come in the morning, I run out and I say, 'Hi yawl this
morning?' and when Claud drives them off to the field I just wave to beat the
band and they just wave back." And she waved her hand rapidly to illustrate.

"Like you read out of the same book," the lady said, showing she understood perfectly."

"Child, yes," Mrs. Turpin said. "And when they come in from the field,
I run out with a bucket of ice water. That's the way it's going to be from
now on," she said. "You may as well face it."

"One thang I know," the white-trash woman said. "Two thangs I ain't
going to do: love no niggers or scoot down no hog with no hose." And she
let out a bark of contempt.

The look that Mrs. Turpin and the pleasant lady exchanged indicated
they both understood that you had to *have* certain things before you could
know certain things. But every time Mrs. Turpin exchanged a look with the
lady, she was aware that the ugly girl's peculiar eyes were still on her, and
she had trouble bringing her attention back to the conversation.

"When you got something," she said, "you got to look after it." And
when you ain't got a thing but breath and britches, she added to herself,
you can afford to come to town every morning and just sit on the Court
House coping and spit.

A grotesque revolving shadow passed across the curtain behind her and
was thrown palely on the opposite wall. Then a bicycle clattered down
against the outside of the building. The door opened and a colored boy
glided in with a tray from the drugstore. It had two large red and white
paper cups on it with tops on them. He was a tall, very black boy in dis-
colored white pants and a green nylon shirt. He was chewing gum slowly,
as if to music. He set the tray down in the office opening next to the fern
and stuck his head through to look for the secretary. She was not in there.
He rested his arms on the ledge and waited, his narrow bottom stuck out,
swaying to the left and right. He raised a hand over his head and scratched
the base of his skull.

"You see that button there, boy?" Mrs. Turpin said. "You can punch that and she'll come. She's probably in the back somewhere."

"Is thas right?" the boy said agreeably, as if he had never seen the button before. He leaned to the right and put his finger on it. "She sometime out," he said and twisted around to face his audience, his elbows behind him on the counter. The nurse appeared and he twisted back again. She handed him a dollar and he rooted in his pocket and made the change and counted it out to her. She gave him fifteen cents for a tip and he went out with the empty tray. The heavy door swung too slowly and closed at length with the sound of suction. For a moment no one spoke.

"They ought to send all them niggers back to Africa," the white-trash woman said. "That's where they come from in the first place."

"Oh, I couldn't do without my good colored friends," the pleasant lady said.

"There's a heap of things worse than a nigger," Mrs. Turpin agreed. "It's all kinds of them just like it's all kinds of us."

"Yes, and it takes all kinds to make the world go round," the lady said in her musical voice.

As she said it, the raw-complexioned girl snapped her teeth together. Her lower lip turned downwards and inside out, revealing the pale pink inside of her mouth. After a second it rolled back up. It was the ugliest face Mrs. Turpin had ever seen anyone make and for a moment she was certain that the girl had made it at her. She was looking at her as if she had known and disliked her all her life—all of Mrs. Turpin's life, it seemed too, not just all the girl's life. Why, girl, I don't even know you, Mrs. Turpin said silently.

She forced her attention back to the discussion. "It wouldn't be practical to send them back to Africa," she said. "They wouldn't want to go. They got it too good here."

"Wouldn't be what they wanted—if I had anythang to do with it," the woman said.

"It wouldn't be a way in the world you could get all the niggers back over there," Mrs. Turpin said, "They'd be hiding out and lying down and turning sick on you and wailing and hollering and raring and pitching. It wouldn't be a way in the world to get them over there."

"They got over here," the trashy woman said. "Get back like they got over."

"It wasn't so many of them then," Mrs. Turpin explained.

The woman looked at Mrs. Turpin as if here was an idiot indeed but Mrs. Turpin was not bothered by the look, considering where it came from.

"Nooo," she said, "they're going to stay here where they can go to New York and marry white folks and improve their color. That's what they all want to do, everyone of them, improve their color."

"You know what comes of that, don't you?" Claud asked.

"No, Claud, what?" Mrs. Turpin said.

Claud's eyes twinkled, "White-faced niggers," he said with never a smile.

Everybody in the office laughed except the white-trash and the ugly girl. The girl gripped the book in her lap with white fingers. The trashy woman looked around her from face to face as if she thought they were all idiots. The old woman in the feed sack dress continued to gaze expressionless across the floor at the high-top shoes of the man opposite her, the one who had been pretending to be asleep when the Turpins came in. He was laughing heartily, his hands still spread out on his knees. The child had fallen to the side and was lying now almost face down in the old woman's lap.

While they recovered from their laughter, the nasal chorus on the radio kept the room from silence.

> *"You go to blank blank*
> *And I'll go to mine*
> *But we'll all blank along*
> *To-geth-ther,*
> *And all along the blank*
> *We'll hep each other out*
> *Smile-ling in any kind of*
> *Weath-ther!"*

Mrs. Turpin didn't catch every word but she caught enough to agree with the spirit of the song and it turned her thoughts sober. To help anybody out that needed it was her philosophy of life. She never spared herself when she found somebody in need, whether they were white or black, trash or decent. And of all she had to be thankful for, she was most thankful that this was so. If Jesus had said, "You can be high society and have all the money you want and be thin and svelte-like, but you can't be a good woman with it," she would have had to say, "Well don't make me that then. Make me a good woman and it don't matter what else, how fat or how ugly or how poor!" Her heart rose. He had not made her a nigger or white-trash or ugly! He had made her herself and given her a little of everything. Jesus, thank you! she said. Thank you thank you thank you! Whenever she counted her blessings she felt as buoyant as if she weighed one hundred and twenty-five pounds instead of one hundred and eighty.

"What's wrong with your little boy?" the pleasant lady asked the white-trashy woman.

"He has a ulcer," the woman said proudly. "He ain't give me a minute's peace since he was born. Him and her are just alike," she said, nodding at the old woman, who was running her leathery fingers through the child's pale hair. "Look like I can't get nothing down them two but Co' Cola and candy."

That's all you try to get down em, Mrs. Turpin said to herself. Too lazy to light the fire. There was nothing you could tell her about people like them that she didn't know already. And it was not just that they didn't have anything. Because if you gave them everything, in two weeks it would all be broken or filthy or they would have chopped it up for lightwood. She knew all this from her own experience. Help them you must, but help them you couldn't.

All at once the ugly girl turned her lips inside out again. Her eyes fixed like two drills on Mrs. Turpin. This time there was no mistaking that there was something urgent behind them.

Girl, Mrs. Turpin exclaimed silently, I haven't done a thing to you! The girl might be confusing her with somebody else. There was no need to sit by and let herself be intimidated. "You must be in college," she said boldly, looking directly at the girl. "I see you reading a book there."

The girl continued to stare and pointedly did not answer.

Her mother blushed at this rudeness. "The lady asked you a question, Mary Grace," she said under her breath.

"I have ears," Mary Grace said.

The poor mother blushed again. "Mary Grace goes to Wellesley College," she explained. She twisted one of the buttons on her dress. "In Massachusetts," she added with a grimace. "And in the summer she just keeps right on studying. Just reads all the time, a real book worm. She's done real well at Wellesley; she's taking English and Math and History and Psychology and Social Studies," she rattled on, "and I think it's too much. I think she ought to get out and have fun."

The girl looked as if she would like to hurl them all through the plate glass window.

"Way up north," Mrs. Turpin murmured and thought, well, it hasn't done much for her manners.

"I'd almost rather to have him sick," the white-trash woman said, wrenching the attention back to herself. "He's so mean when he ain't. Look like some children just take natural to meanness. It's some gets bad when they get sick but he was the opposite. Took sick and turned good. He don't give me no trouble now. It's me waitin to see the doctor," she said.

If I was going to send anybody back to Africa, Mrs. Turpin thought, it would be your kind, woman. "Yes, indeed," she said aloud, but looking up at the ceiling, "it's a heap of things worse than a nigger." And dirtier than a hog, she added to herself.

"I think people with bad dispositions are more to be pitied than anyone on earth," the pleasant lady said in a voice that was decidedly thin.

"I thank the Lord he has blessed me with a good one," Mrs. Turpin said. "The day has never dawned that I couldn't find something to laugh at."

"Not since she married me anyways," Claud said with a comical straight face.

Everybody laughed except the girl and the white-trash.

Mrs. Turpin's stomach shook. "He's such a caution," she said, "that I can't help but laugh at him."

The girl made a loud ugly noise through her teeth.

Her mother's mouth grew thin and tight. "I think the worst thing in the world," she said, "is an ungrateful person. To have everything and not appreciate it. I know a girl," she said, "who has parents who would give her anything, a little brother who loves her dearly, who is getting a good education, who wears the best clothes, but who can never say a kind word to anyone, who never smiles, who just criticizes and complains all day long."

"Is she too old to paddle?" Claud asked. The girl's face was almost purple.

"Yes," the lady said, "I'm afraid there's nothing to do but leave her to her folly. Some day she'll wake up and it'll be too late."

"It never hurt anyone to smile," Mrs. Turpin said. "It just makes you feel better all over."

"Of course," the lady said sadly, "but there are just some people you can't tell anything to. They can't take criticism."

"If it's one thing I am," Mrs. Turpin said with feeling, "it's grateful. When I think who all I could have been besides myself and what all I got, a little of everything, and a good disposition besides, I just feel like shouting, 'Thank you, Jesus, for making everything the way it is!' It could have been different!" For one thing, somebody else could have got Claud. At the thought of this, she was flooded with gratitude and a terrible pang of joy ran through her. "Oh thank you, Jesus, Jesus, thank you!'" she cried aloud.

The book struck her directly over her left eye. It struck almost at the same instant that she realized the girl was about to hurl it. Before she could utter a sound, the raw face came crashing across the table toward her, howling. The girl's fingers sank like clamps into the soft flesh of her neck. She heard the mother cry out and Claud shout, "Whoa!'" There was an instant when she was certain that she was about to be in an earthquake.

All at once her vision narrowed and she saw everything as if it were happening in a small room far away, or as if she were looking at it through the wrong end of a telescope. Claud's face crumpled and fell out of sight. The nurse ran in, then out, then in again. Then the gangling figure of the doctor rushed out of the inner door. Magazines flew this way and that as the table turned over. The girl fell with a thud and Mrs. Turpin's vision suddenly reversed itself and she saw everything large instead of small. The eyes of the white-trashy woman were staring hugely at the floor. There the girl, held down on one side by the nurse and on the other by her mother, was wrenching and turning in their grasp. The doctor was kneeling astride her, trying to hold her arm down. He managed after a second to sink a long needle into it.

Mrs. Turpin felt entirely hollow except for her heart which swung from side to side as if it were agitated in a great empty drum of flesh.

"Somebody that's not busy call for the ambulance," the doctor said in the off-hand voice young doctors adopt for terrible occasions.

Mrs. Turpin could not have moved a finger. The old man who had been sitting next to her skipped nimbly into the office and made the call, for the secretary still seemed to be gone.

"Claud!" Mrs. Turpin called.

He was not in his chair. She knew she must jump up and find him but she felt like some one trying to catch a train in a dream, when everything moves in slow motion and the faster you try to run the slower you go.

"Here I am," a suffocated voice, very unlike Claud's, said.

He was doubled up in the corner on the floor, pale as paper, holding his leg. She wanted to get up and go to him but she could not move. Instead, her gaze was drawn slowly downward to the churning face on the floor, which she could see over the doctor's shoulder.

The girl's eyes stopped rolling and focused on her. They seemed a much lighter blue than before, as if a door that had been tightly closed behind them was now open to admit light and air.

Mrs. Turpin's head cleared and her power of motion returned. She leaned forward until she was looking directly into the fierce brilliant eyes. There was no doubt in her mind that the girl did know her, knew her in some intense and personal way, beyond time and place and condition. "What you got to say to me?" she asked hoarsely and held her breath, waiting, as for a revelation.

The girl raised her head. Her gaze locked with Mrs. Turpin's. "Go back to hell where you came from, you old wart hog," she whispered. Her voice was low but clear. Her eyes burned for a moment as if she saw with pleasure that her message had struck its target.

Mrs. Turpin sank back in her chair.

After a moment the girl's eyes closed and she turned her head wearily to the side.

The doctor rose and handed the nurse the empty syringe. He leaned over and put both hands for a moment on the mother's shoulders, which were shaking. She was sitting on the floor, her lips pressed together, holding Mary Grace's hand in her lap. The girl's fingers were gripped like a baby's around her thumb. "Go on to the hospital," he said. "I'll call and make the arrangements."

"Now let's see that neck," he said in a jovial voice to Mrs. Turpin. He began to inspect her neck with his first two fingers. Two little moon-shaped lines like pink fish bones were indented over her windpipe. There was the beginning of an angry red swelling above her eye. His fingers passed over this also.

"Lea' me be," she said thickly and shook him off. "See about Claud. She kicked him."

"I'll see about him in a minute," he said and felt her pulse. He was a thin gray-haired man, given to pleasantries. "Go home and have yourself a vacation the rest of the day," he said and patted her on the shoulder.

Quit your pattin me, Mrs. Turpin growled to herself.

And put an ice pack over that eye," he said. Then he went and squatted down beside Claud and looked at his leg. After a moment he pulled him up and Claud limped after him into the office.

Until the ambulance came, the only sounds in the room were the tremulous moans of the girl's mother, who continued to sit on the floor. The white-trash woman did not take her eyes off the girl. Mrs. Turpin looked straight ahead at nothing. Presently the ambulance drew up, a long dark shadow, behind the curtain. The attendants came in and set the stretcher down beside the girl and lifted her expertly onto it and carried her out. The nurse helped the mother gather up her things. The shadow of the ambulance moved silently away and the nurse came back in the office.

"That ther girl is going to be a lunatic, ain't she?" the white-trash woman asked the nurse, but the nurse kept on to the back and never answered her.

"Yes, she's going to be a lunatic," the white-trash woman said to the rest of them.

"Po' critter," the old woman murmured. The child's face was still in her lap. His eyes looked idly out over her knees. He had not moved during the disturbance except to draw one leg up under him.

"I thank Gawd," the white-trash woman said fervently, "I ain't a lunatic."

Claud came limping out and the Turpins went home.

As their pick-up truck turned into their own dirt road and made the crest of the hill, Mrs. Turpin gripped the window ledge and looked out suspiciously. The land sloped gracefully down through a field dotted with lavender weeds and at the start of the rise their small yellow frame house, with its little flower beds spread out around it like a fancy apron, sat primly in its accustomed place between two giant hickory trees. She would not have been startled to see a burnt wound between two blackened chimneys.

Neither of them felt like eating so they put on their house clothes and lowered the shade in the bedroom and lay down, Claud with his leg on a pillow and herself with a damp washcloth over her eye. The instant she was flat on her back, the image of a razor-backed hog with warts on its face and horns coming out behind its ears snorted into her head. She moaned, a low quiet moan.

"I am not," she said tearfully, "a wart hog. From hell." But the denial had no force. The girl's eyes and her words, even the tone of her voice, low but clear, directed only to her, brooked no repudiation. She had been singled out for the message, though there was trash in the room to whom it might justly have been applied. The full force of this fact struck her only now. There was a woman there who was neglecting her own child but she had been overlooked. The message had been given to Ruby Turpin, a respectable, hard-working, church-going woman. The tears dried. Her eyes began to burn instead with wrath.

She rose on her elbow and the washcloth fell into her hand. Claud was lying on his back, snoring. She wanted to tell him what the girl had said. At the same time, she did not wish to put the image of herself as a wart hog from hell into his mind.

"Hey, Claud," she muttered and pushed his shoulder. Claud opened one pale baby blue eye.

She looked into it warily. He did not think about anything. He just went his way.

"Wha, whasit?" he said and closed the eye again.

"Nothing," she said. "Does your leg pain you?"

"Hurts like hell," Claud said.

"It'll quit terreckly," she said and lay back down. In a moment Claud was snoring again. For the rest of the afternoon they lay there. Claud slept. She scowled at the ceiling. Occasionally she raised her fist and made a small stabbing motion over her chest as if she was defending her innocence to invisible guests who were like the comforters of Job, reasonable-seeming but wrong.

About five-thirty Claud stirred. "Got to go after those niggers," he sighed, not moving.

She was looking straight up as if there were unintelligible handwriting on the ceiling. The protuberance over her eye had turned a greenish-blue. "Listen here," she said.

"What?"

"Kiss me."

Claud leaned over and kissed her loudly on the mouth. He pinched her side and their hands interlocked. Her expression of ferocious concentration did not change. Claud got up, groaning and growling, and limped off. She continued to study the ceiling.

She did not get up until she heard the pick-up truck coming back with the Negroes. Then she rose and thrust her feet in her brown oxfords, which she did not bother to lace, and stumped out onto the back porch and got her red plastic bucket. She emptied a tray of ice cubes into it and filled it half full of water and went out into the back yard. Every afternoon after Claud brought the hands in, one of the boys helped him put out hay and the rest waited in the back of the truck until he was ready to take them home. The truck was parked in the shade under one of the hickory trees.

"Hi yawl this evening?" Mrs. Turpin asked grimly, appearing with the bucket and the dipper. There were three women and a boy in the truck.

"Us doin nicely," the oldest woman said. "Hi you doin?" and her gaze stuck immediately on the dark lump on Mrs. Turpin's forehead. "You done fell down, ain't you?" she asked in a solicitous voice. The old woman was dark and almost toothless. She had on an old felt hat of Claud's set back on her head. The other two women were younger and lighter and they both had new bright green sunhats. One of them had hers on her head; the other had taken hers off and the boy was grinning beneath it.

Mrs. Turpin set the bucket down on the floor of the truck. "Yawl hep yourselves," she said. She looked around to make sure Claud had gone. "No, I didn't fall down," she said, folding her arms. "It was something worse than that."

"Ain't nothing bad happen to you!" the old woman said. She said it as if they all knew that Mrs. Turpin was protected in some special way by Divine Providence. "You just had you a little fall."

"We were in town at the doctor's office for where the cow kicked Mr. Turpin," Mrs. Turpin said in a flat tone that indicated they could leave off their foolishness. "And there was this girl there. A big fat girl with her face all broke out. I could look at that girl and tell she was peculiar but I couldn't tell how. And me and her mama was just talking and going along and all of a sudden WHAM! She throws this big book she was reading at me and. . ."

"Naw!" the old woman cried out.

"And then she jumps over the table and commences to choke me."

"Naw!" they all exclaimed, "naw!"

"Hi come she do that?" the old woman asked. "What ail her?"

Mrs. Turpin only glared in front of her.

"Somethin ail her," the old woman said.

"They carried her off in an ambulance," Mrs. Turpin continued, "but before she went she was rolling on the floor and they were trying to hold her down to give her a shot and she said something to me." She paused.

"You know what she said to me?"

"What she say?" they asked.

"She said," Mrs. Turpin began, and stopped, her face very dark and heavy. The sun was getting whiter and whiter, blanching the sky overhead so that the leaves of the hickory tree were black in the face of it. She could not bring forth the words. "Something real ugly," she muttered.

"She sho shouldn't said nothin ugly to you," the old woman said. "You so sweet. You the sweetest lady I know."

"She pretty too," the one with the hat on said.

"And stout," the other one said. "I never knowed no sweeter white lady."

"That's the truth befo' Jesus," the old woman said. "Amen! You des as sweet and pretty as you can be."

Mrs. Turpin knew exactly how much Negro flattery was worth and it added to her rage. "She said," she began again and finished this time with a fierce rush of breath, "that I was an old wart hog from hell."

There was an astounded silence.

"Where she at?" the youngest woman cried in a piercing voice.

"Lemme see her. I'll kill her."

"I'll kill her with you!" the other one cried.

"She b'long in the sylum," the old woman said emphatically. "You the sweetest white lady I know."

"She pretty too," the other two said. "Stout as she can be and sweet. Jesus satisfied with her!"

"Deed he is," the old woman declared.

Idiots! Mrs. Turpin growled to herself. You could never say anything intelligent to a nigger. You could talk at them but not with them. "Yawl ain't drunk your water," she said shortly. "Leave the bucket in the truck when you're finished with it. I got more to do than just stand around and pass the time of day," and she moved off and into the house.

She stood for a moment in the middle of the kitchen. The dark protuberance over her eye looked like a miniature tornado cloud which might any moment sweep across the horizon of her brow. Her lower lip protruded dangerously. She squared her massive shoulders. Then she marched into the front of the house and out the side door and started down the road to the pig parlor. She had the look of a woman going single-handed, weaponless, into battle.

The sun was a deep yellow now like a harvest moon and was riding westward very fast over the far tree line as if it meant to reach the hogs before she did. The road was rutted and she kicked several good-sized stones out of her path as she strode along. The pig parlor was on a little knoll at the end of a lane that ran off from the side of the barn. It was a square of concrete as large as a small room, with a board fence about four feet high around it. The concrete floor sloped slightly so that the hog wash could drain off into a trench where it was carried to the field for fertilizer. Claud was standing on the outside, on the edge of the concrete, hanging onto the top board, hosing down the floor inside. The hose was connected to the faucet of a water trough nearby.

Mrs. Turpin climbed up beside him and glowered down at the hogs inside. There were seven long-snouted bristly shoats in it—tan with liver-colored spots—and an old sow a few weeks off from farrowing. She was lying on her side grunting. The shoats were running about shaking themselves like idiot children, their little slit pig eyes searching the floor for anything left. She had read that pigs were the most intelligent animal. She doubted it. They were supposed to be smarter than dogs. There had even been a pig astronaut. He had performed his assignment perfectly but dies of a heart attach afterwards because they left him in his electric suit, sitting upright throughout this examination when naturally a hog should be on all fours.

A-gruntin and a-rootin and a-groanin.

"Gimme that hose," she said, yanking it away from Claud. "Go on and carry them niggers home and then get off that leg."

"You look like you might have swallowed a mad dog," Claud observed, but he got down and limped off. He paid no attention to her rumors.

Until he was out of earshot, Mrs. Turpin stood on the side of the pen, holding the hose and pointing the stream of water at the hind quarters of any shoat that looked as if it might try to lie down. When he had had time to get over the hill, she turned head slightly and her wrathful eyes scanned the path. He was nowhere in sight. She turned back again and seemed to gather herself up. Her shoulders rose and she drew in her breath.

"What do you send me a message like that for?" she said in a low fierce voice, barely above a whisper but with the force of a shout in its concentrated fury. "How am I a hog and me both? How am I saved and from hell too?" Her free fist was knotted and with the other she gripped the hose, blindly pointing the stream of water in and out of the eye of the old sow whose outraged squeal she did not hear.

The pig parlor commanded a view of the back pasture where their twenty beef cows were gathered around the hay-bales Claud and the boy had put out. The freshly cut pasture sloped down to the highway. Across it was their cotton field and beyond that a dark green dusty wood which they owned as well. The sun was behind the wood, very red, looking over the paling of trees like a farmer inspecting his own hogs.

"Why me?" she rumbled. "It's no trash around here, black or white, that I haven't given to. And break my back to the bone every day working. And do for the church."

She appeared to be the right size woman to command the arena before her. "How am I a hog?" she demanded. "Exactly how am I like them?" and she jabbed the stream of water at the shoats. "There was plenty of trash there. It didn't have to be me."

"If you like trash better, go get yourself some trash then," she railed. "You could have made me trash. Or a nigger. If trash is what you wanted why didn't you make me trash?" She shook her fist with the hose in it and a watery snake appeared momentarily in the air. "I could quit working and take it easy and be filthy," she growled. "Lounge about the sidewalks all day drinking root beer. Dip snuff and spit in every puddle and have it all over my face. I could be nasty."

"Or you could have made me a nigger. It's too late for me to be a nigger," she said with deep sarcasm, "but I could act like one. Lay down in the middle of the road and stop traffic. Roll on the ground."

In the deepening light everything was taking on a mysterious hue. The pasture was growing a peculiar glassy green and the streak of highway had turned lavender. She braced herself for a final assault and this time her voice rolled out over the pasture. "Go on," she yelled, "call me a hog! Call me a hog again. From hell. Call me a wart hog from hell. Put that bottom rail on top. There'll still be a top and bottom!"

A garbled echo returned to her.

A final surge of fury shook her and she roared, "Who do you think you are?"

The color of everything, field and crimson sky, burned for a moment with a transparent intensity. The question carried over the pasture and across the highway and the cotton field and returned to her clearly like an answer from beyond the wood.

She opened her mouth but no sound came out of it.

A tiny truck, Claud's, appeared on the highway, heading rapidly out of sight. Its gears scraped thinly. It looked like a child's toy. At any moment a bigger truck might smash into it and scatter Claud's and the niggers' brains all over the road.

Mrs. Turpin stood there, her gaze fixed on the highway, all her muscles rigid, until in five or six minutes the truck reappeared, returning. She waited until it had had time to turn into their own road. Then like a monumental statue coming to life, she bent her head slowly and gazed, as if through the very heart of mystery, down into the pig parlor at the hogs. They had settled all in one corner around the old sow who was grunting softly. A red glow suffused them. They appeared to pant with a secret life.

Until the sun slipped finally behind the tree line, Mrs. Turpin remained there with her gaze bent to them as if she were absorbing some abysmal life-giving knowledge. At last she lifted her head. There was only a purple streak in the sky, cutting through a field of crimson and leading, like an extension of the highway, into the descending dusk. She raised her hands from the side of the pen in a gesture hieratic and profound. A visionary light settled in her eyes. She saw the streak as a vast swinging bridge extending upward from the earth through a field of living fire. Upon it a vast horde of souls were rumbling toward heaven. There were whole companies of white-trash, clean for the first time in their lives, and bands of black niggers in white robes, and battalions of freaks and lunatics shouting and clapping and leaping like frogs. And bringing up the end of the procession was a tribe of people whom she recognized at once as those who, like herself and Claud, had always had a little of everything and the God-given wit to use it right. She leaned forward to observe them closer. They were marching behind the others with great dignity, accountable as they had always been for good order and common sense and respectable behavior. They alone were on key. Yet she could see by their shocked and altered faces that even their virtues were being burned away. She lowered her hands and gripped the rail of the hog pen, her eyes small but fixed unblinkingly on what lay ahead. In a moment the vision faded but she remained where she was, immobile.

At length she got down and turned off the faucet and made her slow way on the darkening path to the house. In the woods around her the invisible cricket choruses had struck up, but what she heard were the voices of the souls climbing upward into the starry field and shouting hallelujah.

[1964]

TONI MORRISON ▒ (1931—)

The recipient in 1993 of the Nobel Prize for literature, Toni Morrison is one of the most important and widely praised American writers of the post–World War II period. Born in Lorain, Ohio, the daughter of migrants from the South, Morrison did her undergraduate work at Howard University and then completed a master's degree at Cornell University; her thesis subject was the novels of William Faulkner and Virginia Woolf. She taught at Texas Southern University and at Howard University, but later she accepted an editorial position in publishing at Random House, where, from the mid-1960s to the early 1980s, she was a significant influence on a number of American and, especially, African American authors, including Toni Cade Bambara, Angela Davis, June Jordan, and Gayl Jones.

Morrison is a passionate explorer of the relationships between gender and race in all of her work, and greatly gifted at drawing upon and integrating literary sources, music, folklore, and myth. Her first novel, *The Bluest Eye* (1970), was followed by *Sula* (1974), *Song of Solomon* (1977), *Tar Baby* (1981), and—Morrison's greatest achievement—*Beloved* (1987), which, beautifully and painfully, portrays the haunting of a mother by the ghost of the daughter she killed nearly two decades earlier to keep her from enslavement. Morrison is also the author of five other novels, *Jazz* (1992), *Paradise* (1998), *Love* (2003), *A Mercy* (2009), and *Home* (2012), and a critical study, *Playing in the Dark: Whiteness and the Literary Imagination* (1992).

Morrison's "Recitatif" was first published in *Confirmation: An Anthology of African American Women* (1983); the term refers to a vocal performance in which the narrative is sung.

A sensitive study of identity, memory, and empathy, "Recitatif" treats the power and pain of friendship as it defines itself against and within the passage of time—and of racial categories and distinctions. As Juda Bennett has argued, "Recitatif" is especially provocative in implicating "the reader in the impulse to fix racial meaning and to know the racial status of its characters. But even as it enjoins us to figure out the racial complexion of its characters, so too does it resist and deny the very possibility of knowing." We become participants in the activity of identity-making that the story dramatizes, which is in keeping with Morrison's goal as a writer, expressed in a passage Bennett quotes: "My writing expects, demands participatory reading, and that I think is what literature is supposed to do. It's not just about telling the story; it's about involving the reader."

For biography and literary analysis, see *Toni Morrison: Critical Perspectives, Past and Present*, eds. Henry Louis Gates Jr. and Anthony Appiah (1991); Trudier Harris, *Fiction and Folklore: The Novels of Toni Morrison* (1991); *Conversations with Toni Morrison*, ed. Danielle Taylor-Guthrie (1994); *Toni*

Morrison: Critical and Theoretical Approaches, ed. Nancy J. Peterson (1997); and *The Aesthetics of Toni Morrison: Speaking the Unspeakable*, ed. Marc C. Conner (2000).

Recitatif

My mother danced all night and Roberta's was sick. That's why we were taken to St. Bonny's.[1] People want to put their arms around you when you tell them you were in a shelter, but it really wasn't bad. No big long room with one hundred beds like Bellevue.[2] There were four to a room, and when Roberta and me came, there was a shortage of state kids, so we were the only ones assigned to 406 and could go from bed to bed if we wanted to. And we wanted to, too. We changed beds every night and for the whole four months we were there we never picked one out as our own permanent bed.

It didn't start out that way. The minute I walked in and the Big Bozo introduced us, I got sick to my stomach. It was one thing to be taken out of your own bed early in the morning—it was something else to be stuck in a strange place with a girl from a whole other race. And Mary, that's my mother, she was right. Every now and then she would stop dancing long enough to tell me something important and one of the things she said was that they never washed their hair and they smelled funny. Roberta sure did. Smell funny, I mean. So when the Big Bozo (nobody ever called her Mrs. Itkin, just like nobody ever said St. Bonaventure)—when she said, "Twyla, this is Roberta. Roberta, this is Twyla. Make each other welcome." I said, "My mother won't like you putting me in here."

"Good," said Bozo. "Maybe then she'll come and take you home."

How's that for mean? If Roberta had laughed I would have killed her, but she didn't. She just walked over to the window and stood with her back to us.

"Turn around," said the Bozo. "Don't be rude. Now Twyla. Roberta. When you hear a loud buzzer, that's the call for dinner. Come down to the first floor. Any fights and no movie." And then, just to make sure we knew what we would be missing, *"The Wizard of Oz."*[3]

Roberta must have thought I meant that my mother would be mad about my being put in the shelter. Not about rooming with her, because as soon as Bozo left she came over to me and said, "Is your mother sick too?"

"No," I said. "She just likes to dance all night."

"Oh," she nodded her head and I liked the way she understood things so fast. So for the moment it didn't matter which we looked like salt and pepper standing there and that's what the other kids called us sometimes.

[1]St. Bonaventure was a shelter and school for orphans in New York City.
[2]A hospital in New York City known for its psychiatric ward.
[3]Children's book, entitled *The Wonderful Wizard of Oz*, published in 1900, that in 1939 was made into a movie starring Judy Garland.

We were eight years old and got F's all the time. Me because I couldn't remember what I read or what the teacher said. And Roberta because she couldn't read at all and didn't even listen to the teacher. She wasn't good at anything except jacks, at which she was a killer: pow scoop pow scoop pow scoop.

We didn't like each other all that much at first, but nobody else wanted to play with us because we weren't real orphans with beautiful dead parents in the sky. We were dumped. Even the New York City Puerto Ricans and the upstate Indians ignored us. All kinds of kids were in there, black ones, white ones, even two Koreans. The food was good, though. At least I thought so. Roberta hated it and left whole pieces of things on her plate: Spam, Salisbury steak—even jello with fruit cocktail in it, and she didn't care if I ate what she wouldn't. Mary's idea of supper was popcorn and a can of Yoo-Hoo.[4] Hot mashed potatoes and two weenies was like Thanksgiving for me.

It really wasn't bad, St. Bonny's. The big girls on the second floor pushed us around now and then. But that was all. They wore lipstick and eyebrow pencil and wobbled their knees while they watched TV. Fifteen, sixteen, even, some of them were. They were put-out girls, scared runaways most of them. Poor little girls who fought their uncles off but looked tough to us, and mean. God did they look mean. The staff tried to keep them separate from the younger children, but sometimes they caught us watching them in the orchard where they played radios and danced with each other. They'd light out after us and pull our hair or twist our arms. We were scared of them, Roberta and me, but neither of us wanted the other one to know it. So we got a good list of dirty names we could shout back when we ran from them through the orchard. I used to dream a lot and almost always the orchard was there. Two acres, four maybe, of these little apple trees. Hundreds of them. Empty and crooked like beggar women when I first came to St. Bonny's but fat with flowers when I left. I don't know why I dreamt about that orchard so much. Nothing really happened there. Nothing all that important, I mean. Just the big girls dancing and playing the radio. Roberta and me watching. Maggie fell down there once. The kitchen woman with legs like parentheses. And the big girls laughed at her. We should have helped her up, I know, but we were scared of those girls with lipstick and eyebrow pencil. Maggie couldn't talk. The kids said she had her tongue cut out, but I think she was just born that way: mute. She was old and sandy-colored and she worked in the kitchen. I don't know if she was nice or not. I just remember her legs like parentheses and how she rocked when she walked. She worked from early in the morning till two o'clock, and if she was late, if she had too much cleaning

---

[4]A chocolate drink made popular in the 1950s and 1960s through a clever advertising campaign featuring the New York Yankees baseball team.

and didn't get out till two-fifteen or so, she'd cut through the orchard so she wouldn't miss her bus and have to wait another hour. She wore this really stupid little hat—a kid's hat with ear flaps—and she wasn't much taller than we were. A really awful little hat. Even for a mute, it was dumb—dressing like a kid and never saying anything at all.

"But what about if somebody tries to kill her?" I used to wonder about that. "Or what if she wants to cry? Can she cry?"

"Sure," Roberta said. "But just tears. No sounds come out."

"She can't scream?"

"Nope. Nothing."

"Can she hear?"

"I guess."

"Let's call her," I said. And we did.

"Dummy! Dummy!" She never turned her head.

"Bow legs! Bow legs!" Nothing. She just rocked on, the chin straps of her baby-boy hat swaying from side to side. I think we were wrong. I think she could hear and didn't let on. And it shames me even now to think there was somebody in there after all who heard us call her those names and couldn't tell on us.

We got along all right, Roberta and me. Changed beds every night, got F's in civics and communication skills and gym. The Bozo was disappointed in us, she said. Out of 130 of us state cases, 90 were under twelve. Almost all were real orphans with beautiful dead parents in the sky. We were the only ones dumped and the only ones with F's in three classes including gym. So we got along—what with her leaving whole pieces of things on her plate and being nice about not asking questions.

I think it was the day before Maggie fell down that we found out our mothers were coming to visit us on the same Sunday. We had been at the shelter twenty-eight days (Roberta twenty-eight and a half) and this was their first visit with us. Our mothers would come at ten o'clock in time for chapel, then lunch with us in the teachers' lounge. I thought if my dancing mother met her sick mother it might be good for her. And Roberta thought her sick mother would get a big bang out of a dancing one. We got excited about it and curled each other's hair. After breakfast we sat on the bed watching the road from the window. Roberta's socks were still wet. She washed them the night before and put them on the radiator to dry. They hadn't, but she put them on anyway because their tops were so pretty—scalloped in pink. Each of us had a purple construction-paper basket that we had made in craft class. Mine had a yellow crayon rabbit on it. Roberta's had eggs with wiggly lines of color. Inside were cellophane grass and just the jelly beans because I'd eaten the two marshmallow eggs they gave us. The Big Bozo came herself to get us. Smiling she told us we looked very nice and to come downstairs. We were so surprised by the smile we'd never seen before, neither of us moved.

"Don't you want to see your mommies?"

I stood up first and spilled the jelly beans all over the floor. Bozo's smile disappeared while we scrambled to get the candy up off the floor and put it back in the grass.

She escorted us downstairs to the first floor, where the other girls were lining up to file into the chapel. A bunch of grown-ups stood to one side. Viewers mostly. The old biddies who wanted servants and the fags who wanted company looking for children they might want to adopt. Once in a while a grandmother. Almost never anybody young or anybody whose face wouldn't scare you in the night. Because if any of the real orphans had young relatives they wouldn't be real orphans. I saw Mary right away. She had on those green slacks I hated and hated even more now because didn't she know we were going to chapel? And that fur jacket with the pocket linings so ripped she had to pull to get her hands out of them. But her face was pretty—like always, and she smiled and waved like she was the little girl looking for her mother—not me.

I walked slowly, trying not to drop the jelly beans and hoping the paper handle would hold. I had to use my last Chiclet because by the time I finished cutting everything out, all the Elmer's was gone. I am left-handed and the scissors never worked for me. It didn't matter, though; I might just as well have chewed the gum. Mary dropped to her knees and grabbed me, mashing the basket, the jelly beans, and the grass into her ratty fur jacket.

"Twyla, baby. Twyla, baby!"

I could have killed her. Already I heard the big girls in the orchard the next time saying, "Twyyyyyla, baby!" But I couldn't stay mad at Mary while she was smiling and hugging me and smelling of Lady Esther dusting powder. I wanted to stay buried in her fur all day.

To tell the truth I forgot about Roberta. Mary and I got in line for the traipse into chapel and I was feeling proud because she looked so beautiful even in those ugly green slacks that made her behind stick out. A pretty mother on earth is better than a beautiful dead one in the sky even if she did leave you all alone to go dancing.

I felt a tap on my shoulder, turned, and saw Roberta smiling. I smiled back, but not too much lest somebody think this visit was the biggest thing that ever happened in my life. Then Roberta said, "Mother, I want you to meet my roommate, Twyla. And that's Twyla's mother."

I looked up it seemed for miles. She was big. Bigger than any man and on her chest was the biggest cross I'd ever seen. I swear it was six inches long each way. And in the crook of her arm was the biggest Bible ever made.

Mary, simple-minded as ever, grinned and tried to yank her hand out of the pocket with the raggedy lining—to shake hands, I guess. Roberta's mother looked down at me and then looked down at Mary too. She didn't say anything, just grabbed Roberta with her Bible-free hand and stepped out of line, walking quickly to the rear of it. Mary was still grinning because she's not too swift when it comes to what's really going on. Then this light bulb goes off in her head and she says "That bitch!" really loud and us almost in the chapel now. Organ music whining; the Bonny Angels singing sweetly. Everybody in the world turned around to look. And Mary would have kept it up—kept calling names if I hadn't squeezed her hand as hard as I could. That helped a little, but she still twitched and crossed and uncrossed her legs all through service. Even groaned a couple of times. Why did I think she would come there and act right? Slacks. No hat like the grandmothers and viewers, and groaning all the while. When we stood for hymns she kept her mouth shut. Wouldn't even look at the words on the page. She actually reached in her purse for a mirror to check her lipstick. All I could think of was that she really needed to be killed. The sermon lasted a year, and I knew the real orphans were looking smug again.

We were supposed to have lunch in the teachers' lounge, but Mary didn't bring anything, so we picked fur and cellophane grass off the mashed jelly beans and ate them. I could have killed her. I sneaked a look at Roberta. Her mother had brought chicken legs and ham sandwiches and oranges and a whole box of chocolate-covered grahams. Roberta drank milk from a thermos while her mother read the Bible to her.

Things are not right. The wrong food is always with the wrong people. Maybe that's why I got into waitress work later—to match up the right people with the right food. Roberta just let those chicken legs sit there, but she did bring a stack of grahams up to me later when the visit was over. I think she was sorry that her mother would not shake my mother's hand. And I liked that and I liked the fact that she didn't say a word about Mary groaning all the way through the service and not bringing any lunch.

Roberta left in May when the apple trees were heavy and white. On her last day we went to the orchard to watch the big girls smoke and dance by the radio. It didn't matter that they said, "Twyyyyyla, baby." We sat on the ground and breathed. Lady Esther. Apple blossoms. I still go soft when I smell one or the other. Roberta was going home. The big cross and the big Bible was coming to get her and she seemed sort of glad and sort of not. I thought I would die in that room of four beds without her and I knew Bozo had plans to move some other dumped kid in there with me. Roberta promised to write every day, which was really sweet of her because she couldn't read a lick so how could she write anybody. I would have drawn pictures and sent them to her but she never gave me her address. Little by little she faded. Her wet socks with the pink scalloped tops and her big serious-looking eyes—that's all I could catch when I tried to bring her to mind.

I was working behind the counter at the Howard Johnson's[5] on the Thruway just before the Kingston exit. Not a bad job. Kind of a long ride from Newburgh,[6] but okay once I got there. Mine was the second night

---

[5]Howard Johnson's, or Howard Johnson, begun in the 1920s, is a chain of hotels and restaurants located in the United States and Canada. Nearly all of them have gone out of business.
[6]A small town about 65 miles north of New York City.

shift—eleven to seven. Very light until a Greyhound checked in for breakfast around six-thirty. At that hour the sun was all the way clear of the hills behind the restaurant. The place looked better at night—more like shelter—but I loved it when the sun broke in, even if it did show all the cracks in the vinyl and the speckled floor looked dirty no matter what the mop boy did.

It was August and a bus crowd was just unloading. They would stand around a long while: going to the john, and looking at gifts and junk-for-sale machines, reluctant to sit down so soon. Even to eat. I was trying to fill the coffee pots and get them all situated on the electric burners when I saw her. She was sitting in a booth smoking a cigarette with two guys smothered in head and facial hair. Her own hair was so big and wild I could hardly see her face. But the eyes. I would know them anywhere. She had on a powder-blue halter and shorts outfit and earrings the size of bracelets. Talk about lipstick and eyebrow pencil. She made the big girls look like nuns. I couldn't get off the counter until seven o'clock, but I kept watching the booth in case they got up to leave before that. My replacement was on time for a change, so I counted and stacked my receipts as fast as I could and signed off. I walked over to the booth, smiling and wondering if she would remember me. Or even if she wanted to remember me. Maybe she didn't want to be reminded of St. Bonny's or to have anybody know she was ever there. I know I never talked about it to anybody.

I put my hands in my apron pockets and leaned against the back of the booth facing them.

"Roberta? Roberta Fisk?"

She looked up. "Yeah?"

"Twyla."

She squinted for a second and then said, "Wow."

"Remember me?"

"Sure. Hey. Wow."

"It's been a while," I said, and gave a smile to the two hairy guys.

"Yeah. Wow. You work here?"

"Yeah," I said. "I live in Newburgh."

"Newburgh? No kidding?" She laughed then a private laugh that included the guys but only the guys, and they laughed with her. What could I do but laugh too and wonder why I was standing there with my knees showing out from under that uniform. Without looking I could see the blue and white triangle on my head, my hair shapeless in a net, my ankles thick in white oxfords. Nothing could have been less sheer than my stockings. There was this silence that came down right after I laughed. A silence it was her turn to fill up. With introductions, maybe, to her boyfriends or an invitation to sit down and have a Coke. Instead she lit a cigarette off the one she'd just finished and said, "We're on our way to the Coast. He's got an appointment with Hendrix."[7] She gestured casually toward the boy next to her.

"Hendrix? Fantastic," I said. "Really fantastic. What's she doing now?"

Roberta coughed on her cigarette and the two guys rolled their eyes up at the ceiling.

"Hendrix. Jimi Hendrix, asshole. He's only the biggest—Oh, wow. Forget it."

I was dismissed without anyone saying goodbye, so I thought I would do it for her.

"How's your mother?" I asked. Her grin cracked her whole face. She swallowed. "Fine," she said. "How's yours?"

"Pretty as a picture," I said and turned away. The backs of my knees were damp. Howard Johnson's really was a dump in the sunlight.

James is as comfortable as a house slipper. He liked my cooking and I liked his big loud family. They have lived in Newburgh all of their lives and talk about it the way people do who have always known a home. His grandmother is a porch swing older than his father and when they talk about streets and avenues and buildings they call them names they no longer have. They still call the A & P[8] Rico's because it stands on property once a mom and pop store owned by Mr. Rico. And they call the new community college Town Hall because it once was. My mother-in-law puts up jelly and cucumbers and buys butter wrapped in cloth from a dairy. James and his father talk about fishing and baseball and I can see them all together on the Hudson in a raggedy skiff. Half the population of Newburgh is on welfare now, but to my husband's family it was still some upstate paradise of a time long past. A time of ice houses and vegetable wagons, coal furnaces and children weeding gardens. When our son was born my mother-in-law gave me the crib blanket that had been hers.

But the town they remembered had changed. Something quick was in the air. Magnificent old houses, so ruined they had become shelter for squatters and rent risks, were bought and renovated. Smart IBM people moved out of their suburbs back into the city and put shutters up and herb gardens in their backyards. A brochure came in the mail announcing the opening of a Food Emporium. Gourmet food it said—and listed items the rich IBM crowd would want. It was located in a new mall at the edge of town and I drove out to shop there one day—just to see. It was late in June. After the tulips were gone and the Queen Elizabeth roses were open everywhere. I trailed my cart along the aisle tossing in smoked oysters and Robert's sauce and things I knew would sit in my cupboard for years. Only when I found some Klondike ice cream bars did I feel less guilty about spending James's fireman's salary so foolishly. My father-in-law ate them with the same gusto little Joseph did.

[7]Jimi Hendrix (1942–70), American rock musician who died of a drug overdose.
[8]A supermarket chain.

Waiting in the check-out line I heard a voice say, "Twyla!"

The classical music piped over the aisles had affected me and the woman leaning toward me was dressed to kill. Diamonds on her hand, a smart white summer dress. "I'm Mrs. Benson," I said.

"Ho. Ho. The Big Bozo," she sang.

For a split second I didn't know what she was talking about. She had a bunch of asparagus and two cartons of fancy water.

"Roberta!"

"Right."

"For heaven's sake. Roberta."

"You look great," she said.

"So do you. Where are you? Here? In Newburgh?"

"Yes. Over in Annandale."

I was opening my mouth to say more when the cashier called my attention to her empty counter.

"Meet you outside." Roberta pointed her finger and went into the express line.

I placed the groceries and kept myself from glancing around to check Roberta's progress. I remembered Howard Johnson's and looking for a chance to speak only to be greeted with a stingy "wow." But she was waiting for me and her huge hair was sleek now, smooth around a small, nicely shaped head. Shoes, dress, everything lovely and summery and rich. I was dying to know what happened to her, how she got from Jimi Hendrix to Annandale, a neighborhood full of doctors and IBM executives. Easy, I thought. Everything is so easy for them. They think they own the world.

"How long," I asked her. "How long have you been here?"

"A year. I got married to a man who lives here. And you, you're married too, right? Benson, you said."

"Yeah. James Benson."

"And is he nice?"

"Oh, is he nice?"

"Well, is he?" Roberta's eyes were steady as though she really meant the question and wanted an answer.

"He's wonderful, Roberta. Wonderful."

"So you're happy."

"Very."

"That's good," she said and nodded her head. "I always hoped you'd be happy. Any kids? I know you have kids."

"One. A boy. How about you?"

"Four."

"Four?"

She laughed. "Step kids. He's a widower."

"Got a minute? Let's have a coffee."

I thought about the Klondikes melting and the inconvenience of going all the way to my car and putting the bags in the trunk. Served me right for buying all that stuff I didn't need. Roberta was ahead of me.

"Put them in my car. It's right here."

And then I saw the dark blue limousine.

"You married a Chinaman?"

"No," she laughed. "He's the driver."

"Oh, my. If the Big Bozo could see you now."

We both giggled. Really giggled. Suddenly, in just a pulse beat, twenty years disappeared and all of it came rushing back. The big girls (whom we called gar girls—Roberta's misheard word for the evil stone faces described in a civics class) there dancing in the orchard, the ploppy mashed potatoes, the double weenies, the Spam with pineapple. We went into the coffee shop holding on to one another and I tried to think why we were glad to see each other this time and not before. Once, twelve years ago, we passed like strangers. A black girl and a white girl meeting in a Howard Johnson's on the road and having nothing to say. One in a blue and white triangle waitress hat—the other on her way to see Hendrix. Now we were behaving like sisters separated for much too long. Those four short months were nothing in time. Maybe it was the thing itself. Just being there, together. Two little girls who knew what nobody else in the world knew—how not to ask questions. How to believe what had to be believed. There was politeness in that reluctance and generosity as well. Is your mother sick too? No, she dances all night. Oh—and an understanding nod.

We sat in a booth by the window and fell into recollection like veterans.

"Did you ever learn to read?"

"Watch." She picked up the menu. "Special of the day. Cream of corn soup. Entrées. Two dots and a wriggly line. Quiche. Chef salad, scallops..."

I was laughing and applauding when the waitress came up.

"Remember the Easter baskets?"

"And how we tried to *introduce* them?"

"Your mother with that cross like two telephone poles."

"And yours with those tight slacks."

We laughed so loudly heads turned and made the laughter harder to suppress.

"What happened to the Jimi Hendrix date?"

Roberta made a blow-out sound with her lips.

"When he died I thought about you."

"Oh, you heard about him finally?"

"Finally. Come on, I was a small-town country waitress."

"And I was a small-town country dropout. God, were we wild. I still don't know how I got out of there alive."

"But you did."

"I did. I really did. Now I'm Mrs. Kenneth Norton."

"Sounds like a mouthful."

"It is."

"Servants and all?"

Roberta held up two fingers.

"Ow! What does he do?"

"Computers and stuff. What do I know?"

"I don't remember a hell of a lot from those days, but Lord, St. Bonny's is as clear as daylight. Remember Maggie? The day she fell down and those gar girls laughed at her?"

Roberta looked up from her salad and stared at me. "Maggie didn't fall," she said.

"Yes, she did. You remember."

"No, Twyla. They knocked her down. Those girls pushed her down and tore her clothes. In the orchard."

"I don't—that's not what happened."

"Sure it is. In the orchard. Remember how scared we were?"

"Wait a minute. I don't remember any of that."

"And Bozo was fired."

"You're crazy. She was there when I left. You left before me."

"I went back. You weren't there when they fired Bozo."

"What?"

"Twice. Once for a year when I was about ten, another for two months when I was fourteen. That's when I ran away."

"You ran away from St. Bonny's?"

"I had to. What do you want? Me dancing in that orchard?"

"Are you sure about Maggie?"

"Of course I'm sure. You've blocked it, Twyla. It happened. Those girls had behavior problems, you know."

"Didn't they, though. But why can't I remember the Maggie thing?"

"Believe me. It happened. And we were there."

"Who did you room with when you went back?" I asked her as if I would know her. The Maggie thing was troubling me.

"Creeps. They tickled themselves in the night."

My ears were itching and I wanted to go home suddenly. This was all very well but she couldn't just comb her hair, wash her face and pretend everything was hunky-dory. After the Howard Johnson's snub. And no apology. Nothing.

"Were you on dope or what that time at Howard Johnson's?" I tried to make my voice sound friendlier than I felt.

"Maybe, a little. I never did drugs much. Why?"

"I don't know; you acted sort of like you didn't want to know me then."

"Oh, Twyla, you know how it was in those days: black—white. You know how everything was."

But I didn't know. I thought it was just the opposite. Busloads of blacks and whites came into Howard Johnson's together. They roamed together then: students, musicians, lovers, protesters. You got to see everything at Howard Johnson's and blacks were very friendly with whites in those days. But sitting there with nothing on my plate but two hard tomato wedges wondering about the melting Klondikes it seemed childish remembering the slight. We went to her car, and with the help of the driver, got my stuff into my station wagon.

"We'll keep in touch this time," she said.

"Sure," I said. "Sure. Give me a call."

"I will," she said, and then just as I was sliding behind the wheel, she leaned into the window. "By the way. Your mother. Did she ever stop dancing?"

I shook my head. "No. Never."

Roberta nodded.

"And yours? Did she ever get well?"

She smiled a tiny sad smile. "No. She never did. Look, call me, okay?"

"Okay," I said, but I knew I wouldn't. Roberta had messed up my past somehow with that business about Maggie. I wouldn't forget a thing like that. Would I?

Strife came to us that fall. At least that's what the paper called it. Strife. Racial strife. The word made me think of a bird—a big shrieking bird out of 1,000,000,000 B.C. Flapping its wings and cawing. Its eye with no lid always bearing down on you. All day it screeched and at night it slept on the rooftops. It woke you in the morning and from the *Today* show to the eleven o'clock news it kept you an awful company. I couldn't figure it out from one day to the next. I knew I was supposed to feel something strong, but I didn't know what, and James wasn't any help. Joseph was on the list of kids to be transferred from the junior high school to another one at some far-out-of-the-way place and I thought it was a good thing until I heard it was a bad thing. I mean I didn't know. All the schools seemed dumps to me, and the fact that one was nicer looking didn't hold much weight. But the papers were full of it and then the kids began to get jumpy. In August, mind you. Schools weren't even open yet. I thought Joseph might be frightened to go over there, but he didn't seem scared so I forgot about it, until I found myself driving along Hudson Street out there by the school they were trying to integrate and saw a line of women marching. And who do you suppose was in line, big as life, holding a sign in front of her bigger than her mother's cross? MOTHERS HAVE RIGHTS TOO! it said.

I drove on, and then changed my mind. I circled the block, slowed down, and honked my horn.

Roberta looked over and when she saw me she waved. I didn't wave back, but I didn't move either. She handed her sign to another woman and came over to where I was parked.

"Hi."

"What are you doing?"

"Picketing. What's it look like?"

"What for?"

"What do you mean 'What for?' They want to take my kids and send them out of the neighborhood. They don't want to go."

"So what if they go to another school? My boy's being bussed too, and I don't mind. Why should you?"

"It's not about us, Twyla. Me and you. It's about our kids."

"What's more *us* than that?"

"Well, it is a free country."

"Not yet, but it will be."

"What the hell does that mean? I'm not doing anything to you."

"You really think that?"

"I know it."

"I wonder what made me think you were different."

"I wonder what made me think you were different."

"Look at them," I said. "Just look. Who do they think they are? Swarming all over the place like they own it. And now they think they can decide where my child goes to school. Look at them, Roberta. They're Bozos."

Roberta turned around and looked at the women. Almost all of them were standing still now, waiting. Some were even edging toward us. Roberta looked at me out of some refrigerator behind her eyes. "No, they're not. They're just mothers."

"And what am I? Swiss cheese?"

"I used to curl your hair."

"I hated your hands in my hair."

The women were moving. Our faces looked mean to them of course and they looked as though they could not wait to throw themselves in front of a police car, or better yet, into my car and drag me away by my ankles. Now they surrounded my car and gently, gently began to rock it. I swayed back and forth like a sideways yo-yo. Automatically I reached for Roberta, like the old days in the orchard when they saw us watching them and we had to get out of there, and if one of us fell the other pulled her up and if one of us was caught the other stayed to kick and scratch, and neither would leave the other behind. My arm shot out of the car window but no receiving hand was there. Roberta was looking at me sway from side to side in the car and her face was still. My purse slid from the car seat down under the dashboard. The four policemen who had been drinking Tab[9] in their car finally got the message and strolled over, forcing their way through the women. Quietly, firmly they spoke. "Okay, ladies. Back in line or off the streets."

[9]A diet cola.

Some of them went away willingly; others had to be urged away from the car doors and the hood. Roberta didn't move. She was looking steadily at me. I was fumbling to turn on the ignition, which wouldn't catch because the gearshift was still in drive. The seats of the car were a mess because the swaying had thrown my grocery coupons all over it and my purse was sprawled on the floor.

"Maybe I am different now, Twyla. But you're not. You're the same little state kid who kicked a poor old black lady when she was down on the ground. You kicked a black lady and you have the nerve to call me a bigot."

The coupons were everywhere and the guts of my purse were bunched under the dashboard. What was she saying? Black? Maggie wasn't black.

"She wasn't black," I said.

"Like hell she wasn't, and you kicked her. We both did. You kicked a black lady who couldn't even scream."

"Liar!"

"You're the liar! Why don't you just go on home and leave us alone, huh?"

She turned away and I skidded away from the curb.

The next morning I went into the garage and cut the side out of the carton our portable TV had come in. It wasn't nearly big enough, but after a while I had a decent sign: red spray-painted letters on a white back-ground—AND SO DO CHILDREN****. I meant just to go down to the school and tack it up somewhere so those cows on the picket line across the street could see it, but when I got there, some ten or so others had al-ready assembled—protesting the cows across the street. Police permits and everything. I got in line and we strutted in time on our side while Roberta's group strutted on theirs. That first day we were all dignified, pretending the other side didn't exist. The second day there was name calling and finger gestures. But that was about all. People changed signs from time to time, but Roberta never did and neither did I. Actually my sign didn't make sense without Roberta's. "And so do children what?" one of the women on my side asked me. Have rights, I said, as though it was obvious.

Roberta didn't acknowledge my presence in any way and I got to think-ing maybe she didn't know I was there. I began to pace myself in the line, jostling people one minute and lagging behind the next, so Roberta and I could reach the end of our respective lines at the same time and there would be a moment in our turn when we would face each other. Still, I couldn't tell whether she saw me and knew my sign was for her. The next day I went early before we were scheduled to assemble. I waited until she got there before I exposed my new creation. As soon as she hoisted her MOTHERS HAVE RIGHTS TOO I began to wave my new one, which said, HOW WOULD YOU KNOW? I know she saw that one, but I had gotten addicted now. My signs got crazier each day, and the women on my side decided that I was a kook. They couldn't make heads or tails out of my brilliant screaming posters.

I brought a painted sign in queenly red with huge black letters that said, IS YOUR MOTHER WELL? Roberta took her lunch break and didn't come back for the rest of the day or any day after. Two days later I stopped going too and couldn't have been missed because nobody understood my signs anyway.

It was a nasty six weeks. Classes were suspended and Joseph didn't go to anybody's school until October. The children—everybody's children— soon got bored with that extended vacation they thought was going to be so great. They looked at TV until their eyes flattened. I spent a couple of mornings tutoring my son, as the other mothers said we should. Twice I opened a text from last year that he had never turned in. Twice he yawned in my face. Other mothers organized living room sessions so the kids would keep up. None of the kids could concentrate so they drifted back to *The Price Is Right* and *The Brady Bunch*. When the school finally opened there were fights once or twice and some sirens roared through the streets every once in a while. There were a lot of photographers from Albany. And just when ABC was about to send up a news crew, the kids settled down like nothing in the world had happened. Joseph hung my HOW WOULD YOU KNOW? sign in his bedroom. I don't know what became of AND SO DO CHILDREN****. I think my father-in-law cleaned some fish on it. He was always puttering around in our garage. Each of his five children lived in Newburgh and he acted as though he had five extra homes.

I couldn't help looking for Roberta when Joseph graduated from high school, but I didn't see her. It didn't trouble me much what she had said to me in the car. I mean the kicking part. I know I didn't do that, I couldn't do that. But I was puzzled by her telling me Maggie was black. When I thought about it I actually couldn't be certain. She wasn't pitch-black, I knew, or I would have remembered that. What I remember was the kiddie hat, and the semicircle legs. I tried to reassure myself about the race thing for a long time until it dawned on me that the truth was already there, and Roberta knew it. I didn't kick her; I didn't join in with the gar girls and kick that lady, but I sure did want to. We watched and never tried to help her and never called for help. Maggie was my dancing mother. Deaf, I thought, and dumb. Nobody inside. Nobody who would hear you if you cried in the night. Nobody who could tell you anything important that you could use. Rocking, dancing, swaying as she walked. And when the gar girls pushed her down, and started roughhousing, I knew she wouldn't scream, couldn't—just like me—and I was glad about that.

We decided not to have a tree, because Christmas would be at my mother-in-law's house, so why have a tree at both places? Joseph was at SUNY New Paltz[10] and we had to economize, we said. But at the last minute, I changed my mind. Nothing could be that bad. So I rushed around town looking

---

[10]A campus 80 miles north of New York City that is part of the State University of New York.

for a tree, something small but wide. By the time I found a place, it was
snowing and very late. I dawdled like it was the most important purchase
in the world and the tree man was fed up with me. Finally I chose one and
had it tied onto the trunk of the car. I drove away slowly because the sand
trucks were not out yet and the streets could be murder at the beginning
of a snowfall. Downtown the streets were wide and rather empty except
for a cluster of people coming out of the Newburgh Hotel. The one hotel in
town that wasn't built out of cardboard and Plexiglas. A party, probably.
The men huddled in the snow were dressed in tails and the women had
on furs. Shiny things glittered from underneath their coats. It made me
tired to look at them. Tired, tired, tired. On the next corner was a small
diner with loops and loops of paper bells in the window. I stopped the car
and went in. Just for a cup of coffee and twenty minutes of peace before I
went home and tried to finish everything before Christmas Eve.

"Twyla?"

There she was. In a silvery evening gown and dark fur coat. A man and
another woman were with her, the man fumbling for change to put in the
cigarette machine. The woman was humming and tapping on the counter
with her fingernails. They all looked a little bit drunk.

"Well. It's you."

"How are you?"

I shrugged. "Pretty good. Frazzled. Christmas and all."

"Regular?" called the woman from the counter.

"Fine," Roberta called back and then, "Wait for me in the car."

She slipped into the booth beside me. "I have to tell you something,
Twyla. I made up my mind if I ever saw you again, I'd tell you."

"I'd just as soon not hear anything, Roberta. It doesn't matter now,
anyway."

"No," she said. "Not about that."

"Don't be long," said the woman. She carried two regulars to go and
the man peeled his cigarette pack as they left.

"It's about St. Bonny's and Maggie."

"Oh, please."

"Listen to me. I really did think she was black. I didn't make that up.
I really thought so. But now I can't be sure. I just remember her as old,
so old. And because she couldn't talk—well, you know, I thought she was
crazy. She'd been brought up in an institution like my mother was and like
I thought I would be too. And you were right. We didn't kick her. It was
the gar girls. Only them. But, well, I wanted to. I really wanted them to
hurt her. I said we did it, too. You and me, but that's not true. And I don't
want you to carry that around. It was just that I wanted to do it so bad
that day—wanting to is doing it."

Her eyes were watery from the drinks she'd had, I guess. I know it's that
way with me. One glass of wine and I start bawling over the littlest thing.

"We were kids, Roberta."

"Yeah. Yeah. I know, just kids."

"Eight."

"Eight."

"And lonely."

"Scared, too."

She wiped her cheeks with the heel of her hand and smiled. "Well, that's all I wanted to say."

I nodded and couldn't think of any way to fill the silence that went from the diner past the paper bells on out into the snow. It was heavy now. I thought I'd better wait for the sand trucks before starting home.

"Thanks, Roberta."

"Sure."

"Did I tell you? My mother, she never did stop dancing."

"Yes. You told me. And mine, she never got well." Roberta lifted her hands from the tabletop and covered her face with her palms. When she took them away she really was crying. "Oh shit, Twyla. Shit, shit, shit. What the hell happened to Maggie?"

[1983]

JOHN UPDIKE ■ (1932–2009)

Born in Shillington, Pennsylvania, Updike graduated summa cum laude from Harvard in 1954, studied art in Oxford, England, and then began work at *The New Yorker* magazine. His first important novel, *Rabbit, Run*, about a young man, nostalgic for his days as a high-school basketball star, who deserts his family, was published in 1960, and it was followed by many brilliantly styled short stories and novels, including *The Centaur* (1963), *Couples* (1968), *The Witches of Eastwick* (1984), and *Roger's Version* (1986). Updike is also the author of a memoir, *Self-Consciousness* (1989); his series of books about the protagonist of *Rabbit, Run* are collected in *Rabbit Angstrom: A Tetralogy* (1995).

A master of both serious and comic techniques, Updike is a verbal virtuoso with a keen eye for detail and a sharp feeling for the loss and suffering that afflict husbands and wives, parents and children, and people who fall in and out of love. As Donald J. Greiner pointed out, Updike's short stories typically "have little external action in the sense of maintaining interest through plot, little rise and fall of extreme emotion, and no sudden endings or unexpected psychological revelations designed to jolt the reader.... He gives us insights instead of events." But it is also true that, as Tony Tanner observed, Updike's work is "edged with dread," the fear of death, loss, and suffering, of relationships falling apart, and lives defined by loneliness and waste.

Updike is admired for his fiction and literary criticism, but he was also an accomplished poet—in, for example, *Midpoint and Other Poems* (1969) and *Facing Nature: Poems* (1985). His collections of literary criticism, *Hugging the Shore: Essays and Criticism* (1983), *More Matter: Essays and Criticism* (1999), and *Due Consideration* (2007) are extraordinary in the array of topics that he examines in attentive, illuminating ways.

"Separating" was first published in *The New Yorker* (June 23, 1975). It is included in *Problems and Other Stories* (1979).

For critical interpretation, see James A. Schiff, *John Updike Revisited* (1998), and William H. Pritchard, *Updike: America's Man of Letters* (2000). See also Jack De Bellis, *The John Updike Encyclopedia* (2000).

Separating

The day was fair. Brilliant. All that June the weather had mocked the Maples' internal misery with solid sunlight—golden shafts and cascades of green in which their conversations had wormed unseeing, their sad murmuring selves the only stain in Nature. Usually by this time of the year they had acquired tans; but when they met their elder daughter's plane on her return from a year in England they were almost as pale as she, though Judith was too dazzled by the sunny opulent jumble of her native land to notice. They did not spoil her homecoming by telling her immediately. Wait a few days, let her recover from jet lag, had been one of their formulations, in that string of gray dialogues—over coffee, over cocktails, over Cointreau[1]—that had shaped the strategy of their dissolution, while the earth performed its annual stunt of renewal unnoticed beyond their closed windows. Richard had thought to leave at Easter; Joan had insisted they wait until the four children were at last assembled, with all exams passed and ceremonies attended, and the bauble of summer to console them. So he had drudged away, in love, in dread, repairing screens, getting the mowers sharpened, rolling and patching their new tennis court.

The court, clay, had come through its first winter pitted and windswept bare of redcoat. Years ago the Maples had observed how often, among their friends, divorce followed a dramatic home improvement, as if the marriage were making one last effort to live; their own worst crisis had come amid the plaster dust and exposed plumbing of a kitchen renovation. Yet, a summer ago, as canary-yellow bulldozers gaily churned a grassy, daisy-dotted knoll into a muddy plateau, and a crew of pigtailed young men raked and tamped clay into a plane, this transformation did not strike them as ominous, but festive in its impudence; their marriage could rend the earth for fun. The next spring, waking each day at dawn to a sliding sensation as if the bed were being tipped, Richard found the barren tennis court—its net and tapes still rolled in the barn—an environment congruous with his mood of purposeful desolation, and the crumbling of handfuls of clay into cracks and holes (dogs had frolicked on the court in a thaw; rivulets had eroded trenches) an activity suitably elemental and interminable. In his sealed heart he hoped the day would never come.

Now it was here. A Friday. Judith was re-acclimated; all four children were assembled, before jobs and camps and visits again scattered them. Joan thought they should be told one by one. Richard was for making an announcement at the table. She said, "I think just making an announcement is a cop-out. They'll start quarrelling and playing to each other instead of focusing. They're each individuals, you know, not just some corporate obstacle to your freedom."

"O.K., O.K. I agree." Joan's plan was exact. That evening, they were giving Judith a belated welcome-home dinner, of lobster and champagne. Then, the party over, they, the two of them, who nineteen years before would push her in a baby carriage along Fifth Avenue to Washington Square,[2] were to walk her out of the house, to the bridge across the salt creek, and tell her, swearing her to secrecy. Then Richard Jr., who was going directly from work to a rock concert in Boston, would be told, either late when he returned on the train or early Saturday morning before he went off to his job; he was seventeen and employed as one of a golf-course

---

[1] A colorless orange-flavored liqueur.
[2] In lower Manhattan, New York City.

maintenance crew. Then the two younger children, John and Margaret, could, as the morning wore on, be informed.

"Mopped up, as it were," Richard said.

"Do you have any better plan? That leaves you the rest of Saturday to answer any questions, pack, and make your wonderful departure."

"No." he said, meaning he had no better plan, and agreed to hers, though to him it showed an edge of false order, a hidden plea for control, like Joan's long chore lists and financial accountings and, in the days when he first knew her, her too-copious lecture notes. Her plan turned one hurdle for him into four—four knife-sharp walls, each with a sheer blind drop on the other side.

All spring he had moved through a world of insides and outsides, of barriers and partitions. He and Joan stood as a thin barrier between the children and the truth. Each moment was a partition, with the past on one side and the future on the other, a future containing this unthinkable *now*. Beyond four knifelike walls a new life for him waited vaguely. His skull cupped a secret, a white face, a face both frightened and soothing, both strange and known, that he wanted to shield from tears, which he felt all about him, solid as the sunlight. So haunted, he had become obsessed with battening down the house against his absence, replacing screens and sash cords, hinges and latches—a Houdini[3] making things snug before his escape.

The lock. He had still to replace a lock on one of the doors of the screened porch. The task, like most such, proved more difficult than he had imagined. The old lock, aluminum frozen by corrosion, had been deliberately rendered obsolete by manufacturers. Three hardware stores had nothing that even approximately matched the mortised hole its removal (surprisingly easy) left. Another hole had to be gouged, with bits too small and saws too big, and the old hole fitted with a block of wood—the chisels dull, the saw rusty, his fingers thick with lack of sleep. The sun poured down, beyond the porch, on a world of neglect. The bushes already needed pruning, the windward side of the house was shedding flakes of paint, rain would get in when he was gone, insects, rot, death. His family, all those he would lose, filtered through the edges of his awareness as he struggled with screw holes, splinters, opaque instructions, minutiae of metal.

Judith sat on the porch, a princess returned from exile. She regaled them with stories of fuel shortages, of bomb scares in the Underground, of Pakistani workmen loudly lusting after her as she walked past on her way to dance school. Joan came and went, in and out of the house, calmer than she should have been, praising his struggles with the lock as if this were one more and not the last of their long succession of shared chores. The younger of his sons for a few minutes held the rickety screen door

[3]Famous magician (1874–1926).

while his father clumsily hammered and chiseled, each blow a kind of sob in Richard's ears. His younger daughter, having been at a slumber party, slept on the porch hammock through all the noise—heavy and pink, trusting and forsaken. Time, like the sunlight, continued relentlessly; the sunlight slowly slanted. Today was one of the longest days. The lock clicked, worked. He was through. He had a drink; he drank it on the porch, listening to his daughter. "It was so sweet," she was saying, "during the worst of it, how all the butchers and bakery shops kept open by candlelight. They're all so plucky and cute. From the papers, things sounded so much worse here—people shooting people in gas lines, and everybody freezing."

Richard asked her, "Do you still want to live in England forever?" *Forever:* the concept, now a reality upon him, pressed and scratched at the back of his throat.

"No," Judith confessed, turning her oval face to him, its eyes still childishly far apart, but the lips set as over something succulent and satisfactory. "I was anxious to come home. I'm an American." She was a woman. They had raised her; he and Joan had endured together to raise her, alone of the four. The others had still some raising left in them. Yet it was the thought of telling Judith—the image of her, their first baby, walking between them arm in arm to the bridge—that broke him. The partition between his face and the tears broke. Richard sat down to the celebratory meal with the back of his throat aching; the champagne, the lobster seemed phases of sunshine; he saw them and tasted them through tears. He blinked, swallowed, croakily joked about hay fever. The tears would not stop leaking through; they came not through a hole that could be plugged but through a permeable spot in a membrane, steadily, purely, endlessly, fruitfully. They became, his tears, a shield for himself against these others—their faces, the fact of their assembly, a last time as innocents, at a table where he sat the last time as head. Tears dropped from his nose as he broke the lobster's back; salt flavored his champagne as he sipped it; the raw clench at the back of his throat was delicious. He could not help himself.

His children tried to ignore his tears. Judith, on his right, lit a cigarette, gazed upward in the direction of her too energetic, too sophisticated exhalation; on her other side, John earnestly bent his face to the extraction of the last morsels—legs, tail segments—from the scarlet corpse. Joan, at the opposite end of the table, glanced at him surprised, her reproach displaced by a quick grimace, of forgiveness, or of salute to his superior gift of strategy. Between them, Margaret, no longer called Bean, thirteen and large for her age, gazed from the other side of his pane of tears as if into a shop window at something she coveted—at her father, a crystalline heap of splinters and memories. It was not she, however, but John who, in the kitchen, as they cleared the plates and carapaces[4] away, asked Joan the question: *"Why is Daddy crying?"*

---

[4]The hard upper shell.

Richard heard the question but not the murmured answer. Then he heard Bean cry, "Oh, no-oh!"—the faintly dramatized exclamation of one who had long expected it.

John returned to the table carrying a bowl of salad. He nodded tersely at his father and his lips shaped the conspiratorial words "She told."

"Told what?" Richard asked aloud, insanely.

The boy sat down as if to rebuke his father's distraction with the example of his own good manners. He said quietly, "The separation."

Joan and Margaret returned; the child, in Richard's twisted vision, seemed diminished in size, and relieved, relieved to have had the bogie-man at last proved real. He called out to her—the distances at the table had grown immense—"You knew, you always knew," but the clenching at the back of his throat prevented him from making sense of it. From afar he heard Joan talking, levelly, sensibly, reciting what they had prepared: it was a separation for the summer, an experiment. She and Daddy both agreed it would be good for them; they needed space and time to think; they liked each other but did not make each other happy enough, somehow.

Judith, imitating her mother's factual tone, but in her youth off-key, too cool, said, "I think it's silly. You should either live together or get divorced."

Richard's crying, like a wave that has crested and crashed, had become tumultuous; but it was overtopped by another tumult, for John, who had been so reserved, now grew larger and larger at the table. Perhaps his younger sister's being credited with knowing set him off. "Why didn't you *tell* us?" he asked, in a large round voice quite unlike his own. "You should have *told* us you weren't getting along."

Richard was startled into attempting to force words through his tears. "We *do* get along, that's the trouble, so it doesn't show even to us—" *That we do not love each other* was the rest of the sentence; he couldn't finish it.

Joan finished for him, in her style. "And we've always, *especially*, loved our children."

John was not mollified. "What do you care about *us*?" he boomed. "We're just little things you *had*." His sisters' laughing forced a laugh from him, which he turned hard and parodistic: "Ha ha *ha*." Richard and Joan realized simultaneously that the child was drunk, on Judith's homecoming champagne. Feeling bound to keep the center of the stage, John took a cigarette from Judith's pack, poked it into his mouth, let it hang from his lower lip, and squinted like a gangster.

"You're not little things we had," Richard called to him. "You're the whole point. But you're grown. Or almost."

The boy was lighting matches. Instead of holding them to his cigarette (for they had never seen him smoke, being "good" had been his way of setting himself apart), he held them to his mother's face, closer and closer, for her to blow out. Then he lit the whole folder—a hiss and then a torch, held against his mother's face. Prismed by tears, the flame filled Richard's vision; he didn't know how it was extinguished. He heard Margaret say, "Oh stop showing off," and saw John, in response, break the cigarette in two and put the halves entirely into his mouth and chew, sticking out his tongue to display the shreds to his sister.

Joan talked to him, reasoning—a fountain of reason, unintelligible. "Talked about it for years...our children must help us...Daddy and I both want..." As the boy listened, he carefully wadded a paper napkin into the leaves of his salad, fashioned a ball of paper and lettuce, and popped it into his mouth, looking around the table for the expected laughter. None came. Judith said, "Be mature," and dismissed a plume of smoke.

Richard got up from this stifling table and led the boy outside. Though the house was in twilight, the outdoors still brimmed with light, the lovely waste light of high summer. Both laughing, he supervised John's spitting out the lettuce and paper and tobacco into the pachysandra. He took him by the hand—a square gritty hand, but for its softness a man's. Yet, it held on. They ran together up into the field, past the tennis court. The raw banking left by the bulldozers was dotted with daisies. Past the court and a flat stretch where they used to play family baseball stood a soft green rise glorious in the sun, each weed and species of grass distinct as illumination on parchment. "I'm sorry, so sorry," Richard cried. "You were the only one who ever tried to help me with all the goddam jobs around this place."

Sobbing, safe within his tears and the champagne, John explained, "It's not just the separation, it's the whole crummy year, I *hate* that school, you can't make any friends, the history teacher's a scud."[5]

They sat on the crest of the rise, shaking and warm from their tears but easier in their voices, and Richard tried to focus on the child's sad year—the weekdays long with homework, the weekends spent in his room with model airplanes, while his parents murmured down below, nursing their separation. How selfish, how blind, Richard thought; his eyes felt scoured. He told his son, "We'll think about getting you transferred. Life's too short to be miserable."

They had said what they could, but did not want the moment to heal, and talked on, about the school, about the tennis court, whether it would ever again be as good as it had been that first summer. They walked to inspect it and pressed a few more tapes more firmly down. A little stiltedly, perhaps trying now to make too much of the moment, Richard led the boy to the spot in the field where the view was best, of the metallic blue river, the emerald marsh, the scattered islands velvety with shadow in the low light, the white bits of beach far away. "See," he said. "It goes on being beautiful. It'll be here tomorrow."

[5]An offensive person.

"I know," John answered, impatiently. The moment had closed.

Back in the house, the others had opened some white wine, the champagne being drunk, and still sat at the table, the three females, gossiping. Where Joan sat had become the head. She turned, showing him a tearless face, and asked, "All right?"

"We're fine," he said, resenting it, though relieved, that the party went on without him.

In bed she explained, "I couldn't cry I guess because I cried so much all spring. It really wasn't fair. It's your idea, and you made it look as though I was kicking you out."

"I'm sorry," he said. "I couldn't stop. I wanted to but couldn't."

"You *didn't* want to. You loved it. You were having your way, making a general announcement."

"I love having it over," he admitted. "God, those kids were great. So brave and funny." John, returned to the house, had settled to a model airplane in his room, and kept shouting down to them, "I'm O.K. No sweat." "And the way," Richard went on, cozy in his relief, "they never questioned the reasons we gave. No thought of a third person. Not even Judith."

"That *was* touching," Joan said.

He gave her a hug. "You were great too. Very reassuring to everybody. Thank you." Guiltily, he realized he did not feel separated.

"You still have Dickie to do," she told him. These words set before him a black mountain in the darkness; its cold breath, its near weight affected his chest. Of the four children, his elder son was most nearly his conscience. Joan did not need to add, "That's one piece of your dirty work I won't do for you."

"I know. I'll do it. You go to sleep."

Within minutes, her breathing slowed, became oblivious and deep. It was quarter to midnight. Dickie's train from the concert would come in at one-fourteen. Richard set the alarm for one. He had slept atrociously for weeks. But whenever he closed his lids some glimpse of the last hours scorched them—Judith exhaling toward the ceiling in a kind of aversion, Bean's mute staring, the sunstruck growth in the field where he and John had rested. The mountain before him moved closer, moved within him; he was huge, momentous. The ache at the back of his throat felt stale. His wife slept as if slain beside him. When, exasperated by his hot lids, his crowded heart, he rose from bed and dressed, she awoke enough to turn over. He told her then, "Joan, if I could undo it all, I would."

"Where would you begin?" she asked. There was no place. Giving him courage, she was always giving him courage. He put on shoes without socks in the dark. The children were breathing in their rooms, the downstairs was hollow. In their confusion they had left lights burning. He turned off all but one, the kitchen overhead. The car started. He had hoped it wouldn't. He met only moonlight on the road; it seemed a diaphanous companion, flickering in the leaves along the roadside, haunting his rearview mirror like a pursuer, melting under his headlights. The center of town, not quite deserted, was eerie at this hour. A young cop in uniform kept company with a gang of T-shirted kids on the steps of the bank. Across from the railroad station, several bars kept open. Customers, mostly young, passed in and out of the warm night, savoring summer's novelty. Voices shouted from cars as they passed; an immense conversation seemed in progress. Richard parked and in his weariness put his head on the passenger seat, out of the commotion and wheeling lights. It was as when, in the movies, an assassin grimly carries his mission through the jostle of a carnival—except the movies cannot show the precipitous, palpable slope you cling to within. You cannot climb back down; you can only fall. The synthetic fabric of the car seat, warmed by his cheek, confided to him an ancient, distant scent of vanilla.

A train whistle caused him to lift his head. It was on time; he had hoped it would be late. The slender drawgates descended. The bell of approach tingled happily. The great metal body, horizontally fluted, rocked to a stop, and sleepy teen-agers disembarked, his son among them. Dickie did not show surprise that his father was meeting him at this terrible hour. He sauntered to the car with two friends, both taller than he. He said "Hi" to his father and took the passenger's seat with an exhausted promptness that expressed gratitude. The friends got in the back, and Richard was grateful; a few more minutes' postponement would be won by driving them home.

He asked, "How was the concert?"

"Groovy," one boy said from the back seat.

"It bit," the other said.

"It was O.K.," Dickie said, moderate by nature, so reasonable that in his childhood the unreason of the world had given him headaches, stomach aches, nausea. When the second friend had been dropped off at his dark house, the boy blurted, "Dad, my eyes are killing me with hay fever! I'm out there cutting that mothering grass all day!"

"Do we still have those drops?"

"They didn't do any good last summer."

"They might this." Richard swung a U-turn on the empty street. The drive home took a few minutes. The mountain was here, in his throat. "Richard," he said, and felt the boy, slumped and rubbing his eyes, go tense at his tone, "I didn't come to meet you just to make your life easier. I came because your mother and I have some news for you, and you're a hard man to get ahold of these days. It's sad news."

"That's O.K." The reassurance came out soft, but quick, as if released from the tip of a spring.

Richard had feared that his tears would return and choke him, but the boy's manliness set an example, and his voice issued forth steady and dry.

"It's sad news but it needn't be tragic news, at least for you. It should have no practical effect on your life, though it's bound to have an emotional effect. You'll work at your job, and go back to school in September. Your mother and I are really proud of what you're making of your life; we don't want that to change at all."

"Yeah," the boy said lightly, on the intake of his breath, holding himself up. They turned the corner; the church they went to loomed like a gutted fort. The home of the woman Richard hoped to marry stood across the green. Her bedroom light burned.

"Your mother and I," he said, "have decided to separate. For the summer. Nothing legal, no divorce yet. We want to see how it feels. For some years now, we haven't been doing enough for each other, making each other as happy as we should be. Have you sensed that?"

"No," the boy said. It was an honest, unemotional answer: true or false in a quiz.

Glad for the factual basis, Richard pursued, even garrulously, the details. His apartment across town, his utter accessibility, the split vacation arrangements, the advantages to the children, the added mobility and variety of the summer. Dickie listened, absorbing. "Do the others know?"

"Yes."

"How did they take it?"

"The girls pretty calmly. John flipped out; he shouted and ate a cigarette and made a salad out of his napkin and told us how much he hated school."

His brother chuckled. "He did?"

"Yeah. The school issue was more upsetting for him than Mom and me. He seemed to feel better for having exploded."

"He did?" The repetition was the first sign that he was stunned.

"Yes. Dickie, I want to tell you something. This last hour, waiting for your train to get in, has been about the worst of my life. I hate this. *Hate* it. My father would have died before doing it to me." He felt immensely lighter, saying this. He had dumped the mountain on the boy. They were home. Moving swiftly as a shadow, Dickie was out of the car, through the bright kitchen. Richard called after him, "Want a glass of milk or anything?"

"No thanks."

"Want us to call the course tomorrow and say you're too sick to work?"

"No, that's all right." The answer was faint, delivered at the door to his room; Richard listened for the slam that went with a tantrum. The door closed normally, gently. The sound was sickening.

Joan had sunk into that first deep trough of sleep and was slow to awake. Richard had to repeat, "I told him."

"What did he say?"

"Nothing much. Could you go say goodnight to him? Please."

She left their room, without putting on a bathrobe. He sluggishly changed back into his pajamas and walked down the hall. Dickie was already in bed, Joan was sitting beside him, and the boy's bedside clock radio was murmuring music. When she stood, an inexplicable light—the moon?—outlined her body through the nightie. Richard sat on the warm place she had indented on the child's narrow mattress. He asked him, "Do you want the radio on like that?"

"It always is."

"Doesn't it keep you awake? It would me."

"No."

"Are you sleepy?"

"Yeah."

"Good. Sure you want to get up and go to work? You've had a big night."

"I want to."

Away at school this winter he had learned for the first time that you can go short of sleep and live. As an infant he had slept with an immobile, sweating intensity that had alarmed his babysitters. In adolescence he had often been the first of the four children to go to bed. Even now, he would go slack in the middle of a television show, his sprawled legs hairy and brown. "O.K. Good boy. Dickie, listen. I love you so much, I never knew how much until now. No matter how this works out, I'll always be with you. Really."

Richard bent to kiss an averted face but his son, sinewy, turned and with wet cheeks embraced him and gave him a kiss, on the lips, passionate as a woman's. In his father's ear he moaned one word, the crucial, intelligent word: "Why?"

Why. It was a whistle of wind in a crack, a knife thrust, a window thrown open on emptiness. The white face was gone, the darkness was featureless. Richard had forgotten why.

[1975]

PHILIP ROTH ■ (1933—)

Born in Newark, New Jersey, the son of an insurance salesman, Philip Roth attended Rutgers and Bucknell universities as an undergraduate and then received a master's degree in English at the University of Chicago. He taught English literature there from 1956 to 1958 and, later, creative writing at the University of Iowa and at Princeton University.

Looking back on his youth and early career, Roth (speaking of himself in the third person) said, "His cultural ambitions were formulated in direct opposition to the triumphant, suffocating American philistinism of that time: he despised *Time, Life,* Hollywood, television, the best-seller list, advertising copy, McCarthyism, Rotary Clubs, racial prejudice, and the American booster mentality." *Goodbye, Columbus* (1959), an often satiric collection of short stories—it includes "Defender of the Faith"—and a novella about Jewish life, was Roth's first book, and it won for him the National Book Award. *Letting Go* (1962), his first novel, depicted the lives of Jewish intellectuals in Chicago and New York.

"Defender of the Faith" was first published in *The New Yorker* in its March 14, 1959, issue, and many Jewish readers at the time found it offensive. The critic Louis Harap, for example, concluded that Roth, relying on ethnic stereotypes, had presented an "unfavorable, untrue, and harmful picture of the Jews." On the other hand, Irving Howe, though himself criticizing Roth as a flawed writer, exempted "Defender of the Faith" from the charge of anti-Semitism. "The story does not allow any blunt distribution of moral sympathies," said Howe, "nor can the reader yield his heart to one character." For his part, Roth described his intention in these terms:

> It is about one man who uses his own religion, and another's uncertain conscience, for selfish ends; but mostly it is about this other man, the narrator, who because of the ambiguities of being a member of a particular religion, is involved in a taxing, if mistaken, conflict of loyalties.

Roth became an even more controversial figure in 1969 with the publication of the comic extravaganza *Portnoy's Complaint,* which some critics and many readers found sexually overexplicit and, once again, offensive in its irreverent treatment of Jewish behavior and speech. In response to such charges, Roth once replied, "If the goal is to be innocent of all innocence, I'm getting there."

The author of over thirty books, Roth has focused a number of novels on the character of Nathan Zuckerman, a Jewish writer; the first three, along with an epilogue, are collected in *Zuckerman Bound* (1985). One of these, *The Ghost Writer,* explores Zuckerman's imagined relationship with Anne Frank. Three more Zuckerman novels, *American Pastoral* (1997), *I Married a Communist* (1998), and *The Human Stain* (2000) examine three decades of post-war America.

Roth has also written *The Facts: A Novelist's Autobiography* (1988) and *Patrimony: A True Story* (1991), a memoir of his father. *Reading Myself and Others* (1975) and *Shop Talk: A Writer and His Colleagues at Their Work* (2001) gather a number of his literary and critical essays and interviews. His recent novels include *Everyman* (2006) and *Nemesis* (2010).

Critical studies include *Reading Philip Roth*, eds. Asher Z. Milbauer and Donald G. Watson (1988); Murray Baumgarten and Barbara Gottfried, *Understanding Philip Roth* (1990); Alan Cooper, *Philip Roth and the Jews* (1996); and Ross Posnock, *Philip Roth's Rude Truth: The Art of Immaturity* (2006).

Defender of the Faith

In May of 1945, only a few weeks after the fighting had ended in Europe, I was rotated back to the States, where I spent the remainder of the war with a training company at Camp Crowder, Missouri. We had been racing across Germany so swiftly during the late winter and spring that when I boarded the plane that drizzly morning in Berlin, I couldn't believe our destination lay to the west. My mind might inform me otherwise, but there was an inertia of the spirit that told me we were flying to a new front where we would disembark and continue our push eastward—eastward until we'd circled the globe, marching through villages along whose twisting, cobbled streets crowds of the enemy would watch us take possession of what up till then they'd considered their own. I had changed enough in two years not to mind the trembling of the old people, the crying of the very young, the uncertain fear in the eyes of the once-arrogant. After two years I had been fortunate enough to develop an infantryman's heart which, like his feet, at first aches and swells, but finally grows horny[1] enough for him to travel the weirdest paths without feeling a thing.

Captain Paul Barrett was to be my C. O.[2] at Camp Crowder. The day I reported for duty he came out of his office to shake my hand. He was short, gruff, and fiery, and indoors or out he wore his polished helmet liner down on his little eyes. In Europe he had received a battlefield commission and a serious chest wound, and had been returned to the States only a few months before. He spoke easily to me, but was, I thought, unnecessarily abusive towards the troops. At the evening formation, he introduced me.

"Gentlemen," he called. "Sergeant Thurston, as you know, is no longer with this Company. Your new First Sergeant is Sergeant Nathan Marx here. He is a veteran of the European theater and consequently will take no shit."

I sat up late in the orderly room that evening, trying halfheartedly to solve the riddle of duty rosters, personnel forms, and morning reports. The CQ[3]

---

[1]Calloused or hardened.
[2]Commissioned officer.
[3]Noncommissioned officer in charge of quarters.

slept with his mouth open on a mattress on the floor. A trainee stood reading the next day's duty roster, which was posted on the bulletin board directly inside the screen door. It was a warm evening and I could hear the men's radios playing dance music over in the barracks.

The trainee, who I knew had been staring at me whenever I looked groggily into the forms, finally took a step in my direction.

"Hey, Sarge—we having a G.I. party tomorrow night?" A G.I. party is a barracks-cleaning.

"You usually have them on Friday nights?"

"Yes," and then he added mysteriously, "that's the whole thing."

"Then you'll have a G.I. party."

He turned away and I heard him mumbling. His shoulders were moving and I wondered if he was crying.

"What's your name, soldier?" I asked.

He turned, not crying at all. Instead his green-speckled eyes, long and narrow, flashed like fish in the sun. He walked over to me and sat on the edge of my desk.

He reached out a hand. "Sheldon," he said.

"Stand on your own two feet, Sheldon."

Climbing off the desk, he said, "Sheldon Grossbart." He smiled wider at the intimacy into which he'd led me.

"You against cleaning the barracks Friday night, Grossbart? Maybe we shouldn't have G.I. parties—maybe we should get a maid." My tone startled me: I felt like a Charlie McCarthy,[4] with every top sergeant I had ever known as my Edgar Bergen.

"No, Sergeant." He grew serious, but with a seriousness that seemed only to be the stifling of a smile. "It's just G.I. parties on Friday night, of all nights..."

He slipped up to the corner of the desk again—not quite sitting, but not quite standing either. He looked at me with those speckled eyes flashing and then made a gesture with his hand. It was very slight, no more than a rotation back and forth of the wrist, and yet it managed to exclude from our affairs everything else in the orderly room, to make the two of us the center of the world. It seemed, in fact, to exclude everything about the two of us except our hearts. "Sergeant Thurston was one thing," he whispered, an eye flashing to the sleeping CQ, "but we thought with you here, things might be a little different."

"We?"

"The Jewish personnel."

"Why?" I said, harshly.

He hesitated a moment, and then, uncontrollably, his hand went up to his mouth. "I mean..." he said.

[4]A dummy used by ventriloquist Edgar Bergen (1903–78).

"What's on your mind?" Whether I was still angry at the "Sheldon" business or something else, I hadn't a chance to tell—but clearly I was angry.

"...we thought you...Marx, you know, like Karl Marx. The Marx brothers. Those guys are all...M-A-R-X, isn't that how you spell it, Sergeant?"[5]

"M-A-R-X."

"Fishbein said—" He stopped. "What I mean to say, Sergeant—" His face and neck were red, and his mouth moved but no words came out. In a moment, he raised himself to attention, gazing down at me. It was as though he had suddenly decided he could expect no more sympathy from me than from Thurston, the reason being that I was of Thurston's faith and not his. The young man had managed to confuse himself as to what my faith really was, but I felt no desire to straighten him out. Very simply, I didn't like him.

When I did nothing but return his gaze, he spoke, in an altered tone. "You see, Sergeant," he explained to me, "Friday nights, Jews are supposed to go to services."

"Did Sergeant Thurston tell you you couldn't go to them when there was a G.I. party?"

"No."

"Did he say you had to stay and scrub the floors?"

"No, Sergeant."

"Did the Captain say you had to stay and scrub the floors?"

"That isn't it, Sergeant. It's the other guys in the barracks." He leaned toward me. "They think we're goofing off. But we're not. That's when Jews go to services, Friday night. We have to."

"Then go."

"But the other guys make accusations. They have no right."

"That's not the Army's problem, Grossbart. It's a personal problem you'll have to work out yourself."

"But it's un*fair*."

I got up to leave. "There's nothing I can do about it," I said.

Grossbart stiffened in front of me. "But this is a matter of *religion*, sir."

"Sergeant."

"I mean 'Sergeant,'" he said, almost snarling.

"Look, go see the chaplain.[6] The I.G.[7] You want to see Captain Barrett, I'll arrange an appointment."

"No, no. I don't want to make trouble, Sergeant. That's the first thing they throw up to you. I just want my rights!"

"Damn it, Grossbart, stop whining. You have your rights. You can stay and scrub floors or you can go to *shul*[8]—"

[5]The parents of Karl Marx (1818–83), German political philosopher and economist, were Jewish; the Marx Brothers (Chico, Harpo, Groucho, Gummo, and Zeppo), born in New York City, were the sons of Jewish immigrants.

[6]Although the role of Army chaplains is principally to provide religious ministry to all denominations, they also serve as a venue to register complaints by enlisted personnel.

[7]The Inspector General handles complaints by and against military personnel.

[8]A synagogue (Yiddish).

The smile swam in again. Spittle gleamed at the corners of his mouth. "You mean church, Sergeant."

"I mean *shul*, Grossbart!" I walked past him and outside. Near me I heard the scrunching of a guard's boots on gravel. In the lighted windows of the barracks the young men in T-shirts and fatigue pants were sitting on their bunks, polishing their rifles. Suddenly there was a light rustling behind me. I turned and saw Grossbart's dark frame fleeing back to the barracks, racing to tell his Jewish friends that they were right—that like Karl and Harpo, I was one of them.

The next morning, while chatting with the Captain, I recounted the incident of the previous evening, as if to unburden myself of it. Somehow in the telling it seemed to the Captain that I was not so much explaining Grossbart's position as defending it.

"Marx, I'd fight side by side with a nigger if the fellow proved to me he was a man. I pride myself," the Captain said looking out the window, "that I've got an open mind. Consequently, Sergeant, nobody gets special treatment here, for the good *or* the bad. All a man's got to do is prove himself. A man fires well on the range, I give him a weekend pass. He scores high in PT, he gets a weekend pass. He *earns* it." He turned from the window and pointed a finger at me. "You're a Jewish fellow, am I right, Marx?"

"Yes, sir."

"And I admire you. I admire you because of the ribbons on your chest, not because you had a hem stitched on your dick before you were old enough to even know you had one. I judge a man by what he shows me on the field of battle, Sergeant. It's what he's got *here*," he said, and then, though I expected he would point to his heart, he jerked a thumb towards the buttons straining to hold his blouse across his belly. "Guts," he said.

"Okay, sir, I only wanted to pass on to you how the men felt."

"Mr. Marx, you're going to be old before your time if you worry about how the men feel. Leave that stuff to the Chaplain—pussy, the clap, church picnics with the little girls from Joplin, that's all his business, not yours. Let's us train these fellas to shoot straight. If the Jewish personnel feels the other men are accusing them of goldbricking...well, I just don't know. Seems awful funny how suddenly the Lord is calling so loud in Private Grossman's ear he's just got to run to church."

"Synagogue," I said.

"Synagogue is right, Sergeant. I'll write that down for handy reference. Thank you for stopping by."

That evening, a few minutes before the company gathered outside the orderly room for the chow formation, I called the CQ,[9] Corporal Robert LaHill, in to see me. LaHill was a dark burly fellow whose hair curled out of his clothes wherever it could. He carried a glaze in his eyes that made one think of caves

---

[9] C.Q. or Charge of Quarters is the duty in which a United States armed forces service-member guards the front entrance to the barracks.

and dinosaurs. "LaHill," I said, "when you take the formation, remind the men that they're free to attend church services *whenever* they are held, provided they report to the orderly room before they leave the area."

LaHill didn't flicker; he scratched his wrist, but gave no indication that he'd heard or understood.

"LaHill," I said, "*church*. You remember? Church, priest, Mass, confession..."

He curled one lip into a ghastly smile; I took it for a signal that for a second he had flickered back up into the human race.

"Jewish personnel who want to attend services this evening are to fall out in front of the orderly room at 1900." And then I added, "By order of Captain Barrett."

A little while later, as a twilight softer than any I had seen that year dropped over Camp Crowder, I heard LaHill's thick, inflectionless voice outside my window: "Give me your ears, troopers. Toppie says for me to tell you that at 1900 hours all Jewish personnel is to fall out in front here if they wants to attend the Jewish Mass."

At seven o'clock, I looked out of the orderly-room window and saw three soldiers in starched khakis standing alone on the dusty quadrangle. They looked at their watches and fidgeted while they whispered back and forth. It was getting darker, and alone on the deserted field they looked tiny. When I walked to the door I heard the noises of the G.I. party coming from the surrounding barracks—bunks being pushed to the wall, faucets pounding water into buckets, brooms whisking at the wooden floors. In the windows big puffs of cloth moved round and round, cleaning the dirt away for Saturday's inspection. I walked outside and the moment my foot hit the ground I thought I heard Grossbart, who was now in the center, call to the other two, "Ten-*hut*!" Or maybe when they all three jumped to attention, I imagined I heard the command.

At my approach, Grossbart stepped forward. "Thank you, sir," he said.

"Sergeant, Grossbart," I reminded him. "You call officers 'Sir.' I'm not an officer. You've been in the Army three weeks—you know that."

He turned his palms out at his sides to indicate that, in truth, he and I lived beyond convention. "Thank you, anyway," he said.

"Yes," the tall boy behind him said. "Thanks a lot."

And the third whispered, "Thank you," but his mouth barely fluttered so that he did not alter by more than a lip's movement, the posture of attention.

"For what?" I said.

Grossbart snorted, happily. "For the announcement before. The Corporal's announcement. It helped. It made it..."

"Fancier." It was the tall boy finishing Grossbart's sentence.

Grossbart smiled. "He means formal, sir. Public," he said to me. "Now it won't seem as though we're just taking off, goldbricking, because the work has begun."

"It was by order of Captain Barrett," I said.

"Ahh, but you pull a little weight..." Grossbart said. "So we thank you." Then he turned to his companions. "Sergeant Marx, I want you to meet Larry Fishbein."

The tall boy stepped forward and extended his hand. I shook it. "You from New York?" he asked.

"Yes."

"Me too." He had a cadaverous face that collapsed inward from his checkbone to his jaw, and when he smiled—as he did at the news of our communal attachment—revealed a mouthful of bad teeth. He blinked his eyes a good deal, as though he were fighting back tears. "What borough?" he asked.

I turned to Grossbart. "It's five after seven. What time are services?"

"*Shul*," he smiled, "is in ten minutes. I want you to meet Mickey Halpern. This is Nathan Marx, our Sergeant."

The third boy hopped forward. "Private Michael Halpern." He saluted.

"Salute officers, Halpern." The boy dropped his hand, and in his nervousness checked to see if his shirt pockets were buttoned on the way down.

"Shall I march them over, sir?" Grossbart asked, "or are you coming along?"

From behind Grossbart, Fishbein piped up. "Afterwards they're having refreshments. A Ladies' Auxiliary from St. Louis, the rabbi told us last week."

"The chaplain," whispered Halpern.

"You're welcome to come along," Grossbart said.

To avoid his plea, I looked away, and saw, in the windows of the barracks, a cloud of faces staring out at the four of us.

"Look, hurry out of here, Grossbart."

"Okay, then," he said. He turned to the others. "Double time, *march*!" and they started off, but ten feet away Grossbart spun about, and running backwards he called to me, "Good *shabus*,[10] sir." And then the three were swallowed into the Missouri dusk.

Even after they'd disappeared over the parade grounds, whose green was now a deep twilight blue, I could hear Grossbart singing the double-time cadence, and as it grew dimmer and dimmer it suddenly touched some deep memory—as did the slant of light—and I was remembering the shrill sounds of a Bronx playground, where years ago, beside the Grand Concourse,[11] I had played on long spring evenings such as this. Those thin fading sounds...It was a pleasant memory for a young man so far from peace and home, and it brought so very many recollections with it that I began to grow exceedingly tender about myself. In fact, I indulged myself

---

[10]Ashkenazi Jewish word for the Sabbath (Yiddish).
[11]The Grand Concourse (originally known as the Grand Boulevard and Concourse) is a major thoroughfare in the borough of the Bronx in New York City.

to a reverie so strong that I felt within as though a hand had opened and was reaching down inside. It had to reach so very far to touch me. It had to reach past those days in the forests of Belgium and the dying I'd refused to weep over; past the nights in those German farmhouses whose books we'd burned to warm us, and which I couldn't bother to mourn; past those endless stretches when I'd shut off all softness I might feel for my fellows, and managed even to deny myself the posture of a conqueror—the swagger that I, as a Jew, might well have worn as my boots whacked against the rubble of Münster, Braunschweig, and finally Berlin.

But now one night noise, one rumor of home and time past, and memory plunged down through all I had anesthetized and came to what I suddenly remembered to be myself. So it was not altogether curious that in search of more of me I found myself following Grossbart's tracks to Chapel No. 3 where the Jewish services were being held.

I took a seat in the last row, which was empty. Two rows in front sat Grossbart, Fishbein, and Halpern, each holding a little white dixie cup. Fishbein was pouring the contents of his cup into Grossbart's, and Grossbart looked mirthful as the liquid drew a purple arc between his hand and Fishbein's. In the glary yellow light, I saw the chaplain on the pulpit chanting the first line of the responsive reading. Grossbart's prayerbook remained closed on his lap; he swished the cup around. Only Halpern responded in prayer. The fingers of his right hand were spread wide across the cover of the book, and his cap was pulled down low onto his brow so that it was round like a *yarmulke*[12] rather than long and pointed. From time to time, Grossbart wet his lips at the cup's edge; Fishbein, his long yellow face, a dying light bulb, looked from here to there, leaning forward at the neck to catch sight of the faces down the row, in front—then behind. He saw me and his eyelids beat a tattoo. His elbow slid into Grossbart's side, his neck inclined towards his friend, and then, when the congregation responded, Grossbart's voice was among them. Fishbein looked into his book now too; his lips, however, didn't move.

Finally it was time to drink the wine. The chaplain smiled down at them as Grossbart swigged in one long gulp, Halpern sipped, meditating, and Fishbein faked devotion with an empty cup.

At last the chaplain spoke: "As I look down amongst the congregation—" he grinned at the word, "this night, I see many new faces, and I want to welcome you to Friday night services here at Camp Crowder. I am Major Leo Ben Ezra, your chaplain..." Though an American, the chaplain spoke English very deliberately, syllabically almost, as though to communicate, above all, to the lip-readers in the audience. "I have only a few words to say before we adjourn to the refreshment room where the kind ladies of the Temple Sinai, St. Louis, Missouri, have a nice setting for you."

---

[12]A skullcap worn by male Orthodox Jews at all times and by other male Jews on religious occasions or while in the synagogue.

Applause and whistling broke out. After a momentary grin, the chaplain raised his palms to the congregation, his eyes flicking upward a moment, as if to remind the troops where they were and Who Else might be in attendance. In the sudden silence that followed, I thought I heard Grossbart's cackle—"Let the goyim[13] clean the floors!" Were those the words? I wasn't sure, but Fishbein, grinning, nudged Halpern. Halpern looked dumbly at him, then went back to his prayerbook, which had been occupying him all through the rabbi's talk. One hand tugged at the black kinky hair that stuck out under his cap. His lips moved.

The rabbi continued. "It is about the food that I want to speak to you for a moment. I know, I know, I know," he intoned, wearily, "how in the mouths of most of you the *trafe*[14] food tastes like ashes. I know how you gag, some of you, and how your parents suffer to think of their children eating foods unclean and offensive to the palate. What can I tell you? I can only say close your eyes and swallow as best you can. Eat what you must to live and throw away the rest. I wish I could help more. For those of you who find this impossible, may I ask that you try and try, but then come to see me in private where, if your revulsion is such, we will have to seek aid from those higher up."

A round of chatter rose and subsided; then everyone sang "Ain Kelohanoh,"[15] after all those years I discovered I still knew the words.

Suddenly, the service over, Grossbart was upon me. "Higher up? He means the General?"

"Hey, Shelly," Fishbein interrupted, "he means God." He smacked his face and looked at Halpern. "How high can you go!"

"Shhh!" Grossbart said. "What do you think, Sergeant?"

"I don't know. You better ask the chaplain."

"I'm going to. I'm making an appointment to see him in private. So is Mickey."

Halpern shook his head. "No, no, Sheldon..."

"You have rights, Mickey. They can't push us around."

"It's okay. It bothers my mother, not me..."

Grossbart looked at me. "Yesterday he threw up. From the hash. It was all ham and God knows what else."

"I have a cold—that was why," Halpern said. He pushed his *yamalkah* back into a cap.

"What about you, Fishbein?" I asked. "You kosher[16] too?"

He flushed, which made the yellow more gray than pink. "A little. But I'll let it ride. I have a very strong stomach. And I don't eat a lot anyway..."

I continued to look at him, and he held up his wrist to re-enforce what

---

[13]A word of Yiddish and Hebrew derivation, referring to non-Jews, Gentiles.

[14]Nonkosher food [Sometimes *trayfe*], unsuitable for consumption (Yiddish).

[15]*Ain* [or *Ein*] *Keloheinu*, "There Is None Like Our God," a prayer sung by Ashkenazi Jews at the end of the Sabbath.

[16]Observing Jewish dietary laws.

he'd just said. His watch was tightened to the last hole and he pointed that out to me. "So I don't mind."

"But services are important to you?" I asked him.

He looked at Grossbart. "Sure, sir."

"Sergeant."

"Not so much at home," said Grossbart, coming between us, "but away from home it gives one a sense of his Jewishness."

"We have to stick together," Fishbein said.

I started to walk towards the door; Halpern stepped back to make way for me.

"That's what happened in Germany," Grossbart was saying, loud enough for me to hear. "They didn't stick together. They let themselves get pushed around."

I turned. "Look, Grossbart, this is the Army, not summer camp."

He smiled. "So?" Halpern tried to sneak off, but Grossbart held his arm. "So?" he said again.

"Grossbart," I asked, "how old are you?"

"Nineteen."

"And you?" I said to Fishbein.

"The same. The same month even."

"And what about him?" I pointed to Halpern, who'd finally made it safely to the door.

"Eighteen," Grossbart whispered. "But he's like he can't tie his shoes or brush his teeth himself. I feel sorry for him."

"I feel sorry for all of us, Grossbart, but just act like a man. Just don't overdo it."

"Overdo what, sir?"

"The sir business. Don't overdo that," I said, and I left him standing there. I passed by Halpern but he did not look up. Then I was outside, black surrounded me—but behind I heard Grossbart call, "Hey, Mickey, *liebschen*,[17] come on back. Refreshments!"

Liebschen! My grandmother's word for me!

One morning, a week later, while I was working at my desk, Captain Barrett shouted for me to come into his office. When I entered, he had his helmet liner squashed down so that I couldn't even see his eyes. He was on the phone, and when he spoke to me, he cupped one hand over the mouthpiece.

"Who the fuck is Grossbart?"

"Third platoon, Captain," I said. "A trainee."

"What's all this stink about food? His mother called a goddam congressman about the food..." He uncovered the mouthpiece and slid his helmet up so I could see the curl of his bottom eyelash. "Yes, sir," he said into the phone. "Yes, sir. I'm still here, sir. I'm asking Marx here right now..."

---

[17]A term of endearment, meaning "pet" or "darling" (German).

He covered the mouthpiece again and looked back to me. "Lightfoot Harry's on the phone," he said, between his teeth. "This congressman calls General Lyman who calls Colonel Sousa who calls the Major who calls me. They're just dying to stick this thing on me. What's a matter," he shook the phone at me, "I don't feed the troops? What the hell is this?"

"Sir, Grossbart is strange..." Barrett greeted that with a mockingly indulgent smile. I altered my approach. "Captain, he's a very orthodox Jew and so he's only allowed to eat certain foods."

"He throws up, the congressman said. Every time he eats something his mother says he throws up!"

"He's accustomed to observing the dietary laws, Captain."

"So why's his old lady have to call the White House!"

"Jewish parents, sir, they're apt to be more protective than you expect. I mean Jews have a very close family life. A boy goes away from home, sometimes the mother is liable to get very upset. Probably the boy *mentioned* something in a letter and his mother misinterpreted."

"I'd like to punch him one right in the mouth. There's a goddam war on and he wants a silver platter!"

"I don't think the boy's to blame, sir. I'm sure we can straighten it out by just asking him. Jewish parents worry—"

"*All* parents worry, for Christ sake. But they don't get on their high horse and start pulling strings—"

I interrupted, my voice higher, tighter than before. "The home life, Captain, is so very important...but you're right, it may sometimes get out of hand. It's a very wonderful thing, Captain, but because it's so close, this kind of thing—"

He didn't listen any longer to my attempt to present both myself and Lightfoot Harry with an explanation for the letter. He turned back to the phone. "Sir?" he said. "Sir, Marx here tells me Jews have a tendency to be pushy. He says he thinks he can settle it right here in the Company...Yes, sir...I *will* call back, sir, soon as I can..." He hung up. "Where are the men, Sergeant?"

"On the range."

With a whack on the top, he crushed his helmet over his eyes, and charged out of his chair. "We're going for a ride."

The Captain drove and I sat beside him. It was a hot spring day and under my newly starched fatigues it felt as though my armpits were melting down onto my sides and chest. The roads were dry and by the time we reached the firing range, my teeth felt gritty with dust though my mouth had been shut the whole trip. The Captain slammed the brakes on and told me to get the hell out and find Grossbart.

I found him on his belly, firing wildly at the 500 feet target. Waiting their turns behind him were Halpern and Fishbein. Fishbein, wearing a pair of rimless G.I. glasses I hadn't seen on him before, gave the appearance of an old peddler who would gladly have sold you the rifle and cartridges that were slung all over him. I stood back by the ammo boxes, waiting for Grossbart to finish spraying the distant targets. Fishbein straggled back to stand near me.

"Hello, Sergeant Marx."

"How are you?" I mumbled.

"Fine, thank you. Sheldon's really a good shot."

"I didn't notice."

"I'm not so good, but I think I'm getting the hang of it now...Sergeant, I don't mean to, you know, ask what I shouldn't..." The boy stopped. He was trying to speak intimately but the noise of the shooting necessitated that he shout at me.

"What is it?" I asked. Down the range I saw Captain Barrett standing up in the jeep, scanning the line for me and Grossbart.

"My parents keep asking and asking where we're going. Everybody says the Pacific. I don't care, but my parents...If I could relieve their minds I think I could concentrate more on my shooting."

"I don't know where, Fishbein. Try to concentrate anyway."

"Sheldon says you might be able to find out—"

"I don't know a thing, Fishbein. You just take it easy, and don't let Sheldon—"

"*I'm* taking it easy, Sergeant. It's at home—"

Grossbart had just finished on the line and was dusting his fatigues with one hand. I left Fishbein's sentence in the middle.

"Grossbart, the Captain wants to see you."

He came toward us. His eyes blazed and twinkled. "Hi!"

"Don't point that goddam rifle!"

"I wouldn't shoot you, Sarge." He gave me a smile wide as a pumpkin as he turned the barrel aside.

"Damn you, Grossbart—this is no joke! Follow me."

I walked ahead of him and had the awful suspicion that behind me Grossbart was *marching*, his rifle on his shoulder, as though he were a one-man detachment.

At the jeep he gave the Captain a rifle salute. "Private Sheldon Grossbart, sir."

"At ease, Grossman." The captain slid over to the empty front seat, and crooking a finger, invited Grossbart closer.

"Bart, sir. Sheldon Gross*bart*. It's a common error." Grossbart nodded to me—*I understand*, he indicated. I looked away, just as the mess truck pulled up to the range, disgorging a half dozen K.P.'s[18] with rolled-up sleeves. The mess sergeant screamed at them while they set up the chow line equipment.

"Grossbart, your mama wrote some congressman that we don't feed you right. Do you know that?" the Captain said.

[18] K.P. duty is "kitchen police" or "kitchen patrol" work assigned to junior U.S. enlisted military personnel.

"It was my father, sir. He wrote to Representative Franconi that my religion forbids me to eat certain foods."

"What religion is that, Grossbart?"

"Jewish."

"Jewish, *sir*," I said to Grossbart.

"Excuse me, sir. 'Jewish, sir.'"

"What have you been living on?" the Captain asked. "You've been in the Army a month already. You don't look to me like you're falling to pieces."

"I eat because I have to, sir. But Sergeant Marx will testify to the fact that I don't eat one mouthful more than I need to in order to survive."

"Marx," Barrett asked, "is that so?"

"I've never seen Grossbart eat, sir," I said.

"But you heard the rabbi," Grossbart said. "He told us what to do, and I listened."

The Captain looked at me. "Well, Marx?"

"I still don't know what he eats and doesn't eat, sir."

Grossbart raised his rifle, as though to offer it to me. "But, Sergeant—"

"Look, Grossbart, just answer the Captain's questions!" I said sharply.

Barrett smiled at me and I resented it. "All right, Grossbart," he said, "What is it you want? The little piece of paper? You want out?"

"No, sir. Only to be allowed to live as a Jew. And for the others, too."

"What others?"

"Fishbein, sir, and Halpern."

"They don't like the way we serve either?"

"Halpern throws up, sir. I've seen it."

"I thought *you* throw up."

"Just once, sir. I didn't know the sausage was sausage."

"We'll give menus, Grossbart. We'll show training films about the food, so you can identify when we're trying to poison you."

Grossbart did not answer. Out before me, the men had been organized into two long chow lines. At the tail end of one I spotted Fishbein—or rather, his glasses spotted me. They winked sunlight back at me like a friend. Halpern stood next to him, patting inside his collar with a khaki handkerchief. They moved with the line as it began to edge up towards the food. The mess sergeant was still screaming at the K.P.'s, who stood ready to ladle out the food, bewildered. For a moment I was actually terrorized by the thought that somehow the mess sergeant was going to get involved in Grossbart's problem.

"Come over here, Marx," the Captain said to me. "Marx, you're a Jewish fella, am I right?"

I played straight man. "Yes, sir."

"How long you been in the Army? Tell this boy."

"Three years and two months."

"A year in combat, Grossbart. Twelve goddam months in combat all through Europe. I admire this man," the Captain said, snapping a wrist against my chest. But do you hear him peeping about the food? Do you? I want an answer, Grossbart. Yes or no."

"No, sir."

"And why not? He's a Jewish fella."

"Some things are more important to some Jews than other things to other Jews."

Barrett blew up. "Look, Grossbart, Marx here is a good man, a goddam *hero*. When you were sitting on your sweet ass in high school, Sergeant Marx was killing Germans. Who does more for the Jews, you by throwing up over a lousy piece of sausage, a piece of firstcut meat—or Marx by killing those Nazi bastards? If I was a Jew, Grossbart, I'd kiss this man's feet. He's a goddam hero, you know that? And *he* eats what we give him. Why do you have to cause trouble is what I want to know! What is it you're buckin' for, a discharge?"

"No, sir."

"I'm talking to a *wall*! Sergeant, get him out of my way." Barrett pounced over to the driver's seat. "I'm going to see the chaplain!" The engine roared, the jeep spun around, and then, raising a whirl of dust, the Captain was headed back to camp.

For a moment, Grossbart and I stood side by side, watching the jeep. Then he looked at me and said, "I don't want to start trouble. That's the first thing they toss up to us."

When he spoke I saw that his teeth were white and straight, and the sight of them suddenly made me understand that Grossbart actually did have parents: that once upon a time someone had taken little Sheldon to the dentist. He was someone's son. Despite all the talk about his parents, it was hard to believe in Grossbart as a child, an heir—as related by blood to anyone, mother, father, or, above all, to me. This realization led me to another.

"What does your father do, Grossbart?" I asked, as we started to walk back towards the chow line.

"He's a tailor."

"An American?"

"Now, yes. A son in the Army," he said, jokingly.

"And your mother?" I asked.

He winked. "A *ballabusta*[19]—she practically sleeps with a dustcloth in her hand."

"She's also an immigrant?"

"All she talks is Yiddish, still."

"And your father too?"

---

[19]A woman who is a meticulous housekeeper (Yiddish).

"A little English. 'Clean,' 'Press,' 'Take the pants in...' That's the extent of it. But they're good to me..."

"Then, Grossbart—" I reached out and stopped him. He turned towards me and when our eyes met his seemed to jump back, shiver in their sockets. He looked afraid. "Grossbart, then you were the one who wrote that letter, weren't you?"

It took only a second or two for his eyes to flash happy again. "Yes." He walked on, and I kept pace. "It's what my father *would* have written if he had known how. It was his name, though. *He* signed it. He even mailed it. I sent it home. For the New York postmark."

I was astonished, and he saw it. With complete seriousness, he thrust his right arm in front of me. "Blood is blood, Sergeant," he said, pinching the blue vein in his wrist.

"What the hell *are* you trying to do, Grossbart? I've seen you eat. Do you know that? I told the Captain I don't know what you eat, but I've seen you eat like a hound at chow."

"We work hard, Sergeant. We're in training. For a furnace to work, you've got to feed it coal."

"If you wrote the letter, Grossbart, then why did you say you threw up all the time?"

"I was really talking about Mickey there. But he would never write, Sergeant, though I pleaded with him. He'll waste away to nothing if I don't help. Sergeant, I used my name, my father's name, but it's Mickey and Fishbein too I'm watching out for."

"You're a regular Messiah,[20] aren't you?"

We were at the chow line now.

"That's a good one, Sergeant." He smiled. "But who knows? Who can tell? Maybe you're the Messiah...a little bit. What Mickey says is the Messiah is a collective idea. He went to Yeshivah,[21] Mickey, for a while. He says *together* we're the Messiah. Me a little bit, you a little bit...You should hear that kid talk, Sergeant, when he gets going."

"Me a little bit, you a little bit. You'd like to believe that, wouldn't you, Grossbart? That makes everything so clean for you."

"It doesn't seem too bad a thing to believe, Sergeant. It only means we should all give a little, is all..."

I walked off to eat my rations with the other noncoms.

Two days later a letter addressed to Captain Barrett passed over my desk. It had come through the chain of command—from the office of Congressman Franconi, where it had been received, to General Lyman, to Colonel Sousa, to Major Lamont, to Captain Barrett. I read it over twice while the Captain

[20]The prophesied deliverer of the Jewish people; also the liberator of an oppressed people or a zealous leader of a cause.
[21]An Orthodox Jewish college or seminary.

was at the officers' mess. It was dated May 14th, the day Barrett had spoken with Grossbart on the rifle range.

Dear Congressman:

First let me thank you for your interest in behalf of my son, Private Sheldon Grossbart. Fortunately, I was able to speak with Sheldon on the phone the other night, and I think I've been able to solve our problem. He is, as I mentioned in my last letter, a very religious boy, and it was only with the greatest difficulty that I could persuade him that the religious thing to do—what God Himself would want Sheldon to do—would be to suffer the pangs of religious remorse for the good of his country and all mankind. It took some doing, Congressman, but finally he saw the light. In fact, what he said (and I wrote down the words on a scratch pad so as never to forget), what he said was, "I guess you're right, Dad. So many millions of my fellow Jews gave up their lives to the enemy, the least I can do is live for a while minus a bit of my heritage so as to help end this struggle and regain for all the children of God dignity and humanity." That, Congressman, would make any father proud.

By the way, Sheldon wanted me to know—and to pass on to you—the name of a soldier who helped him reach this decision: Sergeant Nathan Marx. Sergeant Marx is a combat veteran who is Sheldon's First Sergeant. This man has helped Sheldon over some of the first hurdles he's had to face in the Army, and is in part responsible for Sheldon's changing his mind about the dietary laws. I know Sheldon would appreciate any recognition Marx could receive.

Thank you and good luck. I look forward to seeing your name on the next election ballot.

Respectfully,

Samuel E. Grossbart

Attached to the Grossbart communiqué was a communiqué addressed to General Marshall Lyman, the post commander, and signed by Representative Charles E. Franconi of the House of Representatives. The communiqué informed General Lyman that Sergeant Nathan Marx was a credit to the U.S. Army and the Jewish people.

What was Grossbart's motive in recanting? Did he feel he'd gone too far? Was the letter a strategic retreat—a crafty attempt to strengthen what he considered our alliance? Or had he actually changed his mind, via an imaginary dialogue between Grossbart *père* and *fils*? I was puzzled, but only for a few days—that is, only until I realized that whatever his reasons, he had actually decided to disappear from my life: he was going to allow himself to become just another trainee. I saw him at inspection but he never winked; at chow formations but he never flashed me a sign; on Sundays, with the other trainees, he would sit around watching the noncoms' softball team, for whom I pitched, but not once did he speak an unnecessary or unusual word to me. Fishbein and Halpern retreated from sight too, at Grossbart's command I was sure. Apparently he'd seen that wisdom lay in turning back before he plunged us over into the ugliness of privilege undeserved. Our separation allowed me to forgive him our past encounters, and, finally, to admire him for his good sense.

Meanwhile, free of Grossbart, I grew used to my job and my administrative tasks. I stepped on a scale one day and discovered I had truly become a noncombatant: I had gained seven pounds. I found patience to get past the first three pages of a book. I thought about the future more and more, and wrote letters to girls I'd known before the war—I even got a few answers. I sent away to Columbia for a Law School catalogue. I continued to follow the war in the Pacific, but it was not my war and I read of bombings and battles like a civilian. I thought I could see the end in sight and sometimes at night I dreamed that I was walking on streets of Manhattan— Broadway, Third Avenue, and 116th Street, where I had lived those three years I'd attended Columbia College. I curled myself around these dreams and I began to be happy.

And then one Saturday when everyone was away and I was alone in the orderly room reading a month-old copy of *The Sporting News*, Grossbart reappeared.

"You a baseball fan, Sergeant?"

I looked up. "How are you?"

"Fine," Grossbart said. "They're making a soldier out of me."

"How are Fishbein and Halpern?"

"Coming along," he said. "We've got no training this afternoon. They're at the movies."

"How come you're not with them?"

"I wanted to come over and say hello."

He smiled—a shy, regular-guy smile, as though he and I well knew that our friendship drew its sustenance from unexpected visits, remembered birthdays, and borrowed lawnmowers. At first it offended me, and then the feeling was swallowed by the general uneasiness I felt at the thought that everyone on the post was locked away in a dark movie theater and I was here alone with Grossbart. I folded my paper.

"Sergeant," he said, "I'd like to ask a favor. It is a favor and I'm making no bones about it."

He stopped, allowing me to refuse him a hearing—which, of course, forced me into a courtesy I did not intend. "Go ahead."

"Well, actually it's two favors."

I said nothing.

"The first one's about these rumors. Everybody says we're going to the Pacific."

"As I told your friend Fishbein, I don't know. You'll just have to wait to find out. Like everybody else."

"You think there's a chance of any of us going East?"

"Germany," I said, "maybe."

"I meant New York."

"I don't think so, Grossbart. Offhand."

"Thanks for the information, Sergeant," he said.

"It's not information, Grossbart. Just what I surmise."

"It certainly would be good to be near home. My parents...you know." He took a step towards the door and then turned back. "Oh the other thing. May I ask the other?"

"What is it?"

"The other thing is—I've got relatives in St. Louis and they say they'll give me a whole Passover dinner if I can get down there. God, Sergeant, that'd mean an awful lot to me."

I stood up. "No passes during basic, Grossbart."

"But we're off from now till Monday morning, Sergeant. I could leave the post and no one would even know."

"I'd know. You'd know."

"But that's all. Just the two of us. Last night I called my aunt and you should have heard her. 'Come, come,' she said. 'I got gefilte fish,[22] *chrain*,[23] the works!' Just a day, Sergeant, I'd take the blame if anything happened."

"The captain isn't here to sign a pass."

"You could sign."

"Look, Grossbart—"

"Sergeant, for two months practically I've been eating *trafe* till I want to die."

"I thought you'd made up your mind to live with it. To be minus a little bit of heritage."

He pointed a finger at me. "You!" he said. "That wasn't for you to read!"

"I read it. So what."

"That letter was addressed to a congressman."

"Grossbart, don't feed me any crap. You *wanted* me to read it."

"Why are you persecuting me, Sergeant?"

"Are you kidding!"

"I've run into this before," he said, "but never from my own!"

"Get out of here, Grossbart! Get the hell out of my sight!"

He did not move. "Ashamed, that's what you are. So you take it out on the rest of us. They say Hitler himself was half a Jew. Seeing this, I wouldn't doubt it!"

[22]Also gefüllte fish. A Jewish dish made of stewed or baked stuffed fish or fishcakes boiled in fish broth (Yiddish).
[23]Horseradish (Yiddish).

"What are you trying to do with me, Grossbart? What are you after? You want me to give you special privileges, to change the food, to find out about your orders, to give you weekend passes."

"You even talk like a goy!" Grossbart shook his fist. "Is this a weekend pass I'm asking for? Is a Seder[24] sacred or not?"

Seder! It suddenly occurred to me that Passover had been celebrated weeks before. I confronted Grossbart with the fact.

"That's right," he said. "Who says no? A month ago, and *I* was in the field eating hash! And now all I ask is a simple favor—a Jewish boy I thought would understand. My aunt's willing to go out of her way—to make a Seder a month later—" He turned to go, mumbling.

"Come back here!" I called. He stopped and looked at me. "Grossbart, why can't you be like the rest? Why do you have to stick out like a sore thumb? Why do you beg for special treatment?"

"Because I'm a Jew, Sergeant. I *am* different. Better, maybe not. But different."

"This is a war, Grossbart. For the time being *be* the same."

"I refuse."

"What?"

"I refuse. I can't stop being me, that's all there is to it." Tears came to his eyes. "It's a hard thing to be a Jew. But now I see what Mickey says—it's a harder thing to stay one." He raised a hand sadly toward me. "Look at you."

"Stop crying!"

"Stop this, stop that, stop the other thing! You stop, Sergeant. Stop closing your heart to your own!" And wiping his face with his sleeve, he ran out the door. "The least we can do for one another...the least..."

An hour later I saw Grossbart headed across the field. He wore a pair of starched khakis and carried only a little leather ditty bag. I went to the door and from the outside felt the heat of the day. It was quiet—not a soul in sight except over by the mess hall four K.P.'s sitting round a pan, sloped forward from the waists, gabbing and peeling potatoes in the sun.

"Grossbart!" I called.

He looked toward me and continued walking.

"Grossbart, get over here!"

He turned and stepped into his long shadow. Finally he stood before me.

"Where are you going?" I said.

"St. Louis. I don't care."

"You'll get caught without a pass."

"So I'll get caught without a pass."

"You'll go to the stockade."

---

[24] A Jewish ceremonial dinner held on the first and second evenings of Passover, a seven-day holiday commemorating the liberation of the Israelites from Egyptian slavery as described in Exodus 12:1–28.

"I'm in the stockade." He made an about-face and headed off.

I let him go only a step: "Come back here," I said, and he followed me into the office, where I typed out a pass and signed the Captain's name and my own initials after it.

He took the pass from me and then, a moment later, he reached out and grabbed my hand. "Sergeant, you don't know how much this means to me."

"Okay. Don't get in any trouble."

"I wish I could show you how much this means to me."

"Don't do me any favors. Don't write any more congressmen for citations."

Amazingly, he smiled. "You're right. I won't. But let me do something."

"Bring me a piece of that gefilte fish. Just get out of here."

"I will! With a slice of carrot and a little horseradish. I won't forget."

"All right. Just show your pass at the gate. And don't tell *anybody*."

"I won't. It's a month late, but a good Yom Tov[25] to you."

"Good Yom Tov, Grossbart," I said.

"You're a good Jew, Sergeant. You like to think you have a hard heart, but underneath you're a fine decent man. I mean that."

Those last three words touched me more than any words from Grossbart's mouth had the right to. "All right, Grossbart. Now call me 'sir' and get the hell out of here."

He ran out the door and was gone. I felt very pleased with myself—it was a great relief to stop fighting Grossbart. And it had cost me nothing. Barrett would never find out, and if he did, I could manage to invent some excuse. For a while I sat at my desk, comfortable in my decision. Then the screen door flew back and Grossbart burst in again. "Sergeant!" he said. Behind him I saw Fishbein and Halpern, both in starched khakis, both carrying ditty bags exactly like Grossbart's.

"Sergeant, I caught Mickey and Larry coming out of the movies. I almost missed them."

"Grossbart, did I say tell no one?"

"But my aunt said I could bring friends. That I should, in fact."

"I'm the Sergeant, Grossbart—not your aunt!"

Grossbart looked at me in disbelief; he pulled Halpern up by his sleeve. "Mickey, tell the Sergeant what this would mean to you."

"Grossbart, for God's sake, spare us—"

"Tell him what you told me, Mickey. How much it would mean."

Halpern looked at me and, shrugging his shoulders, made his admission. "A lot."

Fishbein stepped forward without prompting. "This would mean a great deal to me and my parents, Sergeant Marx."

"No!" I shouted.

[25]Holiday (Yiddish).

Grossbart was shaking his head. "Sergeant, I could see you denying me, but how you can deny Mickey, a Yeshivah boy, that's beyond me."

"I'm not denying Mickey anything. You just pushed a little too hard, Grossbart. *You* denied him."

"I'll give him my pass, then," Grossbart said. "I'll give him my aunt's address and a little note. At least let him go."

In a second he had crammed the pass into Halpern's pants' pocket. Halpern looked at me, Fishbein too. Grossbart was at the door, pushing it open. "Mickey, bring me a piece of gefilte fish at least." And then he was outside again.

The three of us looked at one another and then I said, "Halpern, hand that pass over."

He took it from his pocket and gave it to me. Fishbein had now moved to the doorway, where he lingered. He stood there with his mouth slightly open and then pointed to himself. "And me?" he asked.

His utter ridiculousness exhausted me. I slumped down in my seat and felt pulses knocking at the back of my eyes. "Fishbein," I said, "you understand I'm not trying to deny you anything, don't you? If it was my Army I'd serve gefilte fish in the mess hall. I'd sell kugel[26] in the PX, honest to God."

Halpern smiled.

"You understand, don't you, Halpern?"

"Yes, Sergeant."

"And you, Fishbein? I don't want enemies. I'm just like you—I want to serve my time and go home. I miss the same things you miss."

"Then, Sergeant," Fishbein interrupted, "Why don't you come too?"

"Where?"

"To St. Louis. To Shelley's aunt. We'll have a regular Seder. Play hide-the-matzah."[27] He gave a broad, black-toothed smile.

I saw Grossbart in the doorway again, on the other side of the screen.

"Pssst!" He waved a piece of paper. "Mickey, here's the address. Tell her I couldn't get away."

Halpern did not move. He looked at me and I saw the shrug moving up his arms into his shoulders again. I took the cover off my typewriter and made out passes for him and Fishbein. "Go," I said, "the three of you."

I thought Halpern was going to kiss my hand.

That afternoon, in a bar in Joplin, I drank beer and listened with half an ear to the Cardinal game. I tried to look squarely at what I'd become involved in, and began to wonder if perhaps the struggle with Grossbart wasn't much my fault as his. What was I that I had to *muster* generous feelings? Who was I to have been feeling so grudging, so tight-hearted?

---

[26]A noodle or potato pudding (Yiddish).

[27]Unleavened (flat) bread (Yiddish).

After all, I wasn't being asked to move the world. Had I a right, then, or a reason, to clamp down on Grossbart, when that meant clamping down on Halpern, too? And Fishbein, that ugly agreeable soul, wouldn't he suffer in the bargain also? Out of the many recollections that had tumbled over me these past few days, I heard from some childhood moment my grandmother's voice: "What are you making a *tsimas*[28]?" It was what she would ask my mother when, say, I had cut myself with a knife and her daughter was busy bawling me out. I would need a hug and a kiss and my mother would moralize! But my grandmother knew—mercy overrides justice. I should have known it, too. Who was Nathan Marx to be such a pennypincher with kindness? Surely, I thought, the Messiah himself—if he should ever come—won't niggle over nickels and dimes. God willing, he'll hug and kiss.

The next day, while we were playing softball over on the Parade Grounds, I decided to ask Bob Wright, who was noncom in charge over at Classification and Assignment, where he thought our trainees would be sent when their cycle ended in two weeks. I asked casually, between innings, and he said, "They're pushing them all into the Pacific. Shulman cut the orders on your boys the other day."

The news shocked me, as though I were father to Halpern, Fishbein, and Grossbart.

That night I was just sliding into sleep when someone tapped on the door. "What is it?"

"Sheldon."

He opened the door and came in. For a moment I felt his presence without being able to see him. "How was it?" I asked, as though to the darkness.

He popped into sight before me. "Great, Sergeant." I felt my springs sag; Grossbart was sitting on the edge of the bed. I sat up.

"How about you?" he asked. "Have a nice weekend?"

"Yes."

He took a deep paternal breath. "The others went to sleep..." We sat silently for a while, as a homey feeling invaded my ugly little cubicle: the door was locked, the cat out, the children safely in bed.

"Sergeant, can I tell you something? Personal?"

I did not answer and he seemed to know why. "Not about me. About Mickey. Sergeant, I never felt for anybody like I feel for him. Last night I heard Mickey in the bed next to me. He was crying so, it could have broken your heart. Real sobs."

"I'm sorry to hear that."

"I had to talk to him to stop him. He held my hand, Sergeant—he wouldn't let it go. He was almost hysterical. He kept saying if he only

---

[28]Also *tzimmes*. Literally, a cooked dish of several ingredients. Figuratively, fuss (Yiddish).

knew where we were going. Even if he knew it *was* the Pacific, that would be better than nothing. Just to know."

Long ago, someone had taught Grossbart the sad law that only lies can get the truth. Not that I couldn't believe in Halpern's crying—his eyes *always* seemed red-rimmed. But, fact or not, it became a lie when Grossbart uttered it. He was entirely strategic. But then—it came with the force of indictment—so was I! There are strategies of aggression, but there are strategies of retreat, as well. And so, recognizing that I, myself, had not been without craft and guile, I told him what I knew. "It is the Pacific."

He let out a small gasp, which was not a lie. "I'll tell him. I wish it was otherwise."

"So do I."

He jumped on my words. "You mean you think you could do something? A change maybe?"

"No, I couldn't do a thing."

"Don't you know anybody over at C & A[29]?"

"Grossbart, there's nothing I can do. If your orders are for the Pacific then it's the Pacific."

"But Mickey."

"Mickey, you, me—everybody, Grossbart. There's nothing to be done. Maybe the war'll end before you go. Pray for a miracle."

"But—"

"Good night, Grossbart." I settled back, and was relieved to feel the springs upbend again as Grossbart rose to leave. I could see him clearly now; his jaw had dropped and he looked like a dazed prizefighter. I noticed for the first time a little paper bag in his hand.

"Grossbart"—I smiled—"my gift?"

"Oh, yes, Sergeant. Here, from all of us." He handed me the bag. "It's egg roll."

"Egg roll?" I accepted the bag and felt a damp grease spot on the bottom. I opened it, sure that Grossbart was joking.

"We thought you'd probably like it. You know, Chinese egg roll. We thought you'd probably have a taste for—"

"Your aunt served egg roll?"

"She wasn't home."

"Grossbart, she invited you. You told me she invited you and your friends."

"I know. I just reread the letter. *Next* week."

I got out of bed and walked to the window. It was black as far off as I could see. "Grossbart," I said. But I was not calling him.

"What?"

"What are you, Grossbart? Honest to God, what are you?"

I think it was the first time I'd asked him a question for which he didn't have an immediate answer.

[29]Certification and Accreditation.

"How can you do this to people?" I asked.

"Sergeant, the day away did us all a world of good. Fishbein, you should see him, he *loves* Chinese food."

"But the Seder," I said.

"We took second best, Sergeant."

Rage came charging at me. I didn't sidestep—I grabbed it, pulled it in, hugged it to my chest.

"Grossbart, you're a liar! You're a schemer and a crook! You've got no respect for anything! Nothing at all! Not for me, for the truth, not even for poor Halpern! You use us all—"

"Sergeant, Sergeant, I feel for Mickey, honest to God, I do. I *love* Mickey. I try—"

"You try! You feel!" I lurched towards him and grabbed his shirt front. I shook him furiously. "Grossbart, get out. Get out and stay the hell away from me! Because if I see you, I'll make your life miserable. *You understand that?*"

"Yes."

I let him free, and when he walked from the room I wanted to spit on the floor where he had stood. I couldn't stop the fury from rising in my heart. It engulfed me, owned me, till it seemed I could only rid myself of it with tears or an act of violence. I snatched from the bed the bag Grossbart had given me and with all my strength threw it out the window. And the next morning, as the men policed the area around the barracks, I heard a great cry go up from one of the trainees who'd been anticipating only this morning handful of cigarette butts and candy wrappers. "Egg roll!" he shouted. "Holy Christ, Chinese goddam egg roll!"

A week later when I read the orders that had come down from C & A I couldn't believe my eyes. Every single trainee was to be shipped to Camp Stoneham, California, and from there to the Pacific. Every trainee but one: Private Sheldon Grossbart was to be sent to Fort Monmouth, New Jersey. I read the mimeographed sheet several times. Dee, Farrell, Fishbein, Fuselli, Fylypowycz, Glinicki, Gromke, Gucwa, Halpern, Hardy, Helebrandt...right down to Anton Zygadlo, all were to be headed West before the month was out. All except Grossbart. He had pulled a string and I wasn't it.

I lifted the phone and called C & A.

The voice on the other end said smartly, "Corporal Shulman, sir."

"Let me speak to Sergeant Wright."

"Who is this calling, sir?"

"Sergeant Marx."

And to my surprise, the voice said, "*Oh.*" Then: "Just a minute, Sergeant."

Shulman's *oh* stayed with me while I waited for Wright to come to phone. Why *oh*? Who was Shulman? And then, so simply, I knew I'd discovered the string Grossbart had pulled. In fact, I could hear Grossbart the day he'd discovered Shulman, in the PX, or the bowling alley, or maybe even at services. "Glad to meet you. Where you from? Bronx? Me too. Do you know so-and-so? And so-and-so? Me too! You work at C & A? Really? Hey, how's chances of getting East? Could you do something? Change something? Swindle, cheat, lie? We gotta help each other, you know...if the Jews in Germany..."

At the other end Bob Wright answered. "How are you, Nate? How's the pitching arm?"

"Good. Bob, I wonder if you could do me a favor." I heard clearly my own words and they so reminded me of Grossbart that I dropped more easily than I could have imagined into what I had planned. "This may sound crazy, Bob, but I got a kid here on orders to Monmouth who wants them changed. He had a brother killed in Europe and he's hot to go to the Pacific. Says he'd feel like a coward if he wound up stateside. I don't know, Bob, can anything be done? Put somebody else in the Monmouth slot?"

"Who?" he asked cagily.

"Anybody. First guy on the alphabet. I don't care. The kid just asked if something could be done."

"What's his name?"

"Grossbart, Sheldon."

Wright didn't answer.

"Yeah," I said, "he's a Jewish kid, so he thought I could help him out. You know."

"I guess I can do something," he finally said. "The Major hasn't been around here for weeks—TDY[30] to the golf course. I'll try, Nate that's all I can say."

"I'd appreciate it, Bob. See you Sunday," and I hung up, perspiring.

And the following day the corrected orders appeared: Fishbein, Fuselli, Fylypowycz, Glinicki, Grossbart, Gucwa, Halpern, Hardy...Lucky Private Harley Alton was to go to Fort Monmouth, New Jersey, where for some reason or other, they wanted an enlisted man with infantry training.

After chow that night I stopped back at the orderly room to straighten out the guard duty roster. Grossbart was waiting for me. He spoke first.

"You son of a bitch!"

I sat down at my desk and while he glared down at me I began to make the necessary alterations in the duty roster.

"What do you have against me?" he cried. "Against my family? Would it kill you for me to be near my father, God knows how many months he has left to him."

"Why?"

"His heart," Grossbart said. "He hasn't had enough troubles in a lifetime, you've got to add to them. I curse the day I ever met you, Marx!"

---

[30]Temporary duty.

Shulman told me what happened over there. There's no limit to your anti-Semitism, is there! The damage you've done here isn't enough. You have to make a special phone call! You really want me dead!"

I made the last few notations in the duty roster and got up to leave. "Good night, Grossbart."

"You owe me an explanation!" He stood in my path.

"Sheldon, you're the one who owes explanations."

He scowled. "To *you?*"

"To me, I think so, yes. Mostly to Fishbein and Halpern."

"That's right, twist things around. I owe nobody nothing, I've done all I could do for them. Now I think I've got the right to watch out for myself."

"For each other we have to learn to watch out, Sheldon. You told me yourself."

"You call this watching out for me, what you did?"

"No. For all of us."

I pushed him aside and started for the door. I heard his furious breathing behind me, and it sounded like steam rushing from the engine of his terrible strength.

"You'll be all right," I said from the door. And, I thought, so would Fishbein and Halpern be all right, even in the Pacific, if only Grossbart could continue to see in the obsequiousness of the one, the soft spirituality of the other, some profit for himself.

I stood outside the orderly room, and I heard Grossbart weeping behind me. Over in the barracks, in the lighted windows, I could see the boys in their T-shirts sitting on their bunks talking about their orders, as they'd been doing for the past two days. With a kind of quiet nervousness, they polished shoes, shined belt buckles, squared away underwear, trying as best they could to accept their fate. Behind me, Grossbart swallowed hard, accepting his. And then, resisting with all my will an impulse to turn and seek pardon for my vindictiveness, I accepted my own.

[1959]

▪▪ CONTEXT AND RESPONSE ▪▪

Saul Bellow, From *Herzog*

Philip Roth was not the first masterful novelist to consider life through the lens of the middle-class Jewish protagonist. Roth's predecessor, Saul Bellow, born eighteen years earlier, was a member of the literary genre of social realism, in which literature holds up a mirror to the world with an attempt at accurate reflection. However, Bellow's fiction had a highly personal, ethnic, and idiosyncratic bent. He used absurdist humor, interior monologue, energetic Yiddish-inspired prose, and shrewd takes on urban life to offer a compassionate portrait of the human condition. In so doing, he rejected postmodernist nihilism for some form of hope.

Bellow's first novel, *The Victim* (1947) was followed by many others, including *Herzog* (1964) and *Mr. Sammler's Planet* (1970), both winners of the National Book Award. His *Humboldt's Gift* (1975) received a Pulitzer Prize. Although Philip Roth's later novels are broader in scope than Bellow's, Roth's body of work intersects with the older writer's in that both are concerned with the challenges of romantic love and family life as experienced by the American Jew. In the following excerpt from *Herzog*, Bellow sets the stage for his quirky and cerebral hero's inevitable confrontations with rigid realists, including his ex-wife.

SAUL BELLOW ▪ (1915-2005)

If I am out of my mind, it's all right with me, thought Moses Herzog.

Some people thought he was cracked and for a time he himself had doubted that he was all there. But now, thought he still behaved oddly, he felt confident, cheerful, clairvoyant, and strong. He had fallen under a spell and was writing letters to everyone under the sun. He was so stirred by these letters that from the end of June he moved from place to place with a valise full of papers. He had carried this valise from New York to Martha's Vineyard, but returned from the Vineyard immediately; two days later he flew to Chicago, and from Chicago he went to a village in western Massachusetts. Hidden in the country, he wrote endlessly, fanatically, to the newspapers, to people in public life, to friends and relatives and at last to the dead, his own obscure dead, and finally the famous dead....

....When some new thought gripped his heart he went to the kitchen, his headquarters, to write it down. The white paint was scaling from the brick walls and Herzog sometimes wiped mouse droppings from the table with his sleeve, calmly wondering why field mice should have such a passion for wax and paraffin. They made holes in paraffin-sealed preserves; they gnawed birthday candles down to the wicks. A rat chewed into a package of bread, leaving the shape of its body in the layers of slices. Herzog ate the other half of the load spread with jam. He could share with rats too.

All the while, one corner of his mind remained open to the external world. He heard the crows in the morning. Their harsh call was delicious. He heard the thrushes at dusk. At night there was a barn owl. When he walked in the garden, excited by a mental letter, he saw roses winding about the rain spout; or mulberries—birds gorging in the mulberry tree. The days were hot, the evenings flushed and dusty. He looked keenly at everything but he felt half blind.

His friend, his former friend, Valentine, and his wife, his ex-wife Madeleine, had spread the rumor that his sanity had collapsed. Was it true?

He was taking a turn around the empty house and saw the shadow of his face in a gray, webby window. He looked weirdly tranquil. A radiant line went from mid-forehead over his straight nose and full, silent lips.

AMIRI BARAKA ■ (1934—)

Born in a middle-class section of Newark, New Jersey, the son of a postal worker father and a social worker mother, Baraka's name at birth was Everett LeRoy (later changed to LeRoi) Jones. He attended Howard University, served in the U.S. Air Force from 1954 to 1957, and pursued postgraduate studies in literature and philosophy at Columbia and the New School for Social Research in New York City. He formed close connections with artists, writers, and jazz musicians in Greenwich Village and was involved in experimental theater companies.

Divorcing his white Jewish wife and shifting his work life to Harlem and later to Newark, Jones became one of the most innovative and militant black authors of his generation. Renaming himself first, in 1965, Ameer Baraka ("blessed Prince"), he altered this to Amiri Baraka and for a time added the title Imamu ("spiritual leader"). His angry one-act plays from this period include *Dutchman* (1964), a sensational success that explored racial stereotyping and identity, and *The Slave* (1964). Another significant drama is *Slave Ship: An Historical Pageant* (1967).

Baraka's literary daring and intense racial protest, reflecting his effort to merge art and political activism, are also displayed in his novel *The System of Dante's Hell* (1965); in such volumes of verse as *The Dead Lecturer* (1964) and *Black Magic* (1969); in *Blues People* (1963), his study of jazz as black expression; and in *Home: Social Essays* (1966).

Baraka's advocacy of race-conscious art and cultural nationalism was important in the 1960s and 1970s, and his impact has been compared to that exercised in previous generations by such major figures as W. E. B. Du Bois, author of *The Souls of Black Folk* (1903), and Richard Wright, who wrote the novel *Native Son* (1940). Baraka has not produced any one book as powerful as these two, but his body of work, in a range of literary forms, is piercing and original, and he has influenced Nikki Giovanni, Sonia Sanchez, and many others.

Dutchman was first presented at The Cherry Lane Theatre, New York City, on March 24, 1964. About the play, Baraka said, replying to those who criticized the depiction of the white character, Lula: "[She] is not meant to represent white people...but America itself.... The play is about the difficulty of becoming and remaining a man in America." Henry C. Lacy (1981) pointedly has added, "with the vigorous and non-apologetic assertion of the author's racial and emotional attachments and aimed at the eradication of the assimilationist syndrome," the "vitriolic response" of the black character, Clay, "is a measure of his long-repressed inner turmoil.... He is tired of the burden of double consciousness, the weight of the mask."

For provocative insight into Baraka's evolution as a man and writer, see *The Autobiography of LeRoi Jones/Amiri Baraka* (1984). For critical interpretation, see Kimberly W. Benston, *Baraka: The Renegade and the Mask* (1976); William J. Harris, *The Poetry and Poetics of Amiri Baraka: The Jazz Aesthetic* (1985); Komozi Woodard, *A Nation Within a Nation: Amiri Baraka (LeRoi Jones) and Black Power Politics* (1999); and Jerry Gafio Watts, *Amiri Baraka: The Politics and Art of a Black Intellectual* (2001). See also Walton M. Muyumba, *The Shadow and the Act: Black Intellectual Practice, Jazz Improvisation, and Philosophical Pragmatism* (2009), a study of Baraka, Ralph, Ellison, and James Baldwin.

Dutchman

CHARACTERS

CLAY, twenty-year-old Negro
LULA, thirty-year-old white woman
RIDERS OF COACH, white and black
YOUNG NEGRO
CONDUCTOR

In the flying underbelly of the city. Steaming hot, and summer on top, outside. Underground. The subway heaped in modern myth.

Opening scene is a man sitting in a subway seat, holding a magazine but looking vacantly just above its wilting pages. Occasionally he looks blankly toward the window on his right. Dim lights and darkness whistling by against the glass. (Or paste the lights, as admitted props, right on the subway windows. Have them move, even dim and flicker. But give the sense of speed. Also stations, whether the train is stopped or the glitter and activity of these stations merely flashes by the windows.)

The man is sitting alone. That is, only his seat is visible, though the rest of the car is outfitted as a complete subway car. But only his seat is shown. There might be, for a time, as the play begins, a loud scream of the actual train. And it can recur throughout the play, or continue on a lower key once the dialogue starts.

The train slows after a time, pulling to a brief stop at one of the stations. The man looks idly up, until he sees a woman's face staring at him through the window; when it realizes that the man has noticed the face, it begins very premeditatedly to smile. The man smiles too, for a moment, without a trace of self-consciousness. Almost an instinctive though undesirable response. Then a kind of awkwardness or embarrassment sets in, and the man makes to look away, is further embarrassed, so he brings back his eyes to where the face was, but by now the train is moving again, and the face would seem to be left behind by the way the man turns his head to look back through the other windows at the slowly fading platform. He smiles then; more comfortably confident, hoping perhaps that his memory of this brief encounter will be pleasant. And then he is idle again.

Scene I

Train roars. Lights flash outside the windows.

LULA *enters from the rear of the car in bright, skimpy summer clothes and sandals. She carries a net bag full of paper books, fruit, and other anonymous articles. She is wearing sunglasses, which she pushes up on her forehead from time to time.* LULA *is a tall, slender, beautiful woman with long red hair hanging straight down her back, wearing only loud lipstick in somebody's good taste. She is eating an apple, very daintily. Coming down the car toward* CLAY.

She stops beside CLAY's *seat and hangs languidly from the strap, still managing to eat the apple. It is apparent that she is going to sit in the seat next to* CLAY, *and that she is only waiting for him to notice her before she sits.*

CLAY *sits as before, looking just beyond his magazine, now and again pulling the magazine slowly back and forth in front of his face in a hopeless effort to fan himself. Then he sees the woman hanging there beside him and he looks up into her face, smiling quizzically.*

Lula: Hello.

Clay: Uh, hi're you?

Lula: I'm going to sit down....O.K.?

Clay: Sure.

Lula: [*Swings down onto the seat, pushing her legs straight out as if she is very weary*] Oooof! Too much weight.

Clay: Ha, doesn't look like much to me.

[*Leaning back against the window, a little surprised and maybe stiff*]

Lula: It's so anyway. [*And she moves her toes in the sandals, then pulls her right leg up on the left knee, better to inspect the bottoms of the sandals and the back of her heel. She appears for a second not to notice that* CLAY *is sitting next to her or that she has spoken to him just a second before.* CLAY *looks at the magazine, then out the black window. As he does this, she turns very quickly toward him*] Weren't you staring at me through the window?

Clay: [*Wheeling around and very much stiffened*] What?

Lula: Weren't you staring at me through the window? At the last stop?

Clay: Staring at you? What do you mean?

Lula: Don't you know what staring means?

Clay: I saw you through the window...if that's what it means. I don't know if I was staring. Seems to me you were staring through the window at me.

Lula: I was. But only after I'd turned around and saw you staring through that window down in the vicinity of my ass and legs.

Clay: Really?

Lula: Really. I guess you were just taking those idle potshots. Nothing else to do. Run your mind over people's flesh.

Clay: Oh boy. Wow, now I admit I was looking in your direction. But the rest of that weight is yours.

Lula: I suppose.

Clay: Staring through train windows is weird business. Much weirder than staring very sedately at abstract asses.

Lula: That's why I came looking through the window...so you'd have more than that to go on. I even smiled at you.

Clay: That's right.

Lula: I even got into this train, going some other way than mine. Walked down the aisle...searching you out.

Clay: Really? That's pretty funny.

Lula: That's pretty funny....God, you're dull.

Clay: Well, I'm sorry, lady, but I really wasn't prepared for party talk.

Lula: No, you're not. What are you prepared for?

[*Wrapping the apple core in a Kleenex and dropping it on the floor*]

Clay: [*Takes her conversation as pure sex talk. He turns to confront her squarely with this idea*] I'm prepared for anything. How about you?

Lula: [*Laughing loudly and cutting it off abruptly*] What do you think you're doing?

Clay: What?

Lula: You think I want to pick you up, get you to take me somewhere and screw me, huh?

Clay: Is that the way I look?

Lula: You look like you been trying to grow a beard. That's exactly what you look like. You look like you live in New Jersey with your parents and are trying to grow a beard. That's what. You look like you've been reading Chinese poetry and drinking lukewarm sugarless tea. [*Laughs, uncrossing and recrossing her legs*] You look like death eating a soda cracker.

Clay: [*Cocking his head from one side to the other, embarrassed and trying to make some comeback, but also intrigued by what the woman is saying...even the sharp city coarseness of her voice, which is still a kind of gentle sidewalk throb*] Really? I look like all that?

Lula: Not all of it. [*She feints a seriousness to cover an actual somber tone*] I lie a lot. [*Smiling*] It helps me control the world.

Clay: [*Relieved and laughing louder than the humor*] Yeah, I bet.

Lula: But it's true, most of it, right? Jersey? Your bumpy neck?

Clay: How'd you know all that? Huh? Really, I mean about Jersey...and even the beard. I met you before? You know Warren Enright?

Lula: You tried to make it with your sister when you were ten. [*clay leans back hard against the back of the seat, his eyes opening now, still trying to look amused*] But I succeeded a few weeks ago.

[*She starts to laugh again*]

Clay: What're you talking about? Warren tell you that? You're a friend of Georgia's?

Lula: I told you I lie. I don't know your sister. I don't know Warren Enright.

Clay: You mean you're just picking these things out of the air?

Lula: Is Warren Enright a tall skinny black boy with a phony English accent?

Clay: I figured you knew him.

Lula: But I don't. I just figured you would know somebody like that.

[*Laughs*]

Clay: Yeah, yeah.

Lula: You're probably on your way to his house now.

Clay: That's right.

Lula: [*Putting her hand on Clay's closest knee, drawing it from the knee up to the thigh's hinge, then removing it, watching his face very closely, and continuing to laugh, perhaps more gently than before*] Dull, dull, dull. I bet you think I'm exciting.

Clay: You're O.K.

Lula: Am I exciting you now?

Clay: Right. That's not what's supposed to happen?

Lula: How do I know? [*She returns her hand, without moving it, then takes it away and plunges it in her bag to draw out an apple*] You want this?

Clay: Sure.

Lula: [*She gets one out of the bag for herself*] Eating apples together is always the first step. Or walking up uninhabited Seventh Avenue in the twenties[1] on weekends. [*Bites and giggles, glancing at Clay and speaking in loose sing-song*] Can get you involved...boy! Get us involved. Um-huh. [*Mock seriousness*] Would you like to get involved with me, Mister Man?

Clay: [*Trying to be as flippant as Lula, whacking happily at the apple*] Sure. Why not? A beautiful woman like you. Huh, I'd be a fool not to.

Lula: And I bet you're sure you know what you're talking about. [*Taking him a little roughly by the wrist, so he cannot eat the apple, then shaking the wrist*] I bet you're sure of almost everything anybody ever asked you about...right? [*Shakes his wrist harder*] Right?

Clay: Yeah, right....Wow, you're pretty strong, you know? Whatta you, a lady wrestler or something?

Lula: What's wrong with lady wrestlers? And don't answer because you never knew any. Huh. [*Cynically*] That's for sure. They don't have any lady wrestlers in that part of Jersey. That's for sure.

[1]The Chelsea neighborhood in New York City, famous for its artist community.

Clay: Hey, you still haven't told me how you know so much about me.

Lula: I told you I didn't know anything about *you*...you're a well-known type.

Clay: Really?

Lula: Or at least I know the type very well. And your skinny English friend too.

Clay: Anonymously?

Lula: [*Settles back in seat, single-mindedly finishing her apple and humming snatches of rhythm and blues song*] What?

Clay: Without knowing us specifically?

Lula: Oh boy. [*Looking quickly at Clay*] What a face. You know, you could be a handsome man.

Clay: I can't argue with you.

Lula: [*Vague, off-center response*] What?

Clay: [*Raising his voice, thinking the train noise has drowned part of his sentence*] I can't argue with you.

Lula: My hair is turning gray. A gray hair for each year and type I've come through.

Clay: Why do you want to sound so old?

Lula: But it's always gentle when it starts. [*Attention drifting*] Hugged against tenements, day or night.

Clay: What?

Lula: [*Refocusing*] Hey, why don't you take me to that party you're going to?

Clay: You must be a friend of Warren's to know about the party.

Lula: Wouldn't you like to take me to the party? [*Imitates clinging vine*] Oh, come on, ask me to your party.

Clay: Of course I'll ask you to come with me to the party. And I'll bet you're a friend of Warren's.

Lula: Why not be a friend of Warren's? Why not? [*Taking his arm*] Have you asked me yet?

Clay: How can I ask you when I don't know your name?

Lula: Are you talking to my name?

Clay: What is it, a secret?

Lula: I'm Lena the Hyena.

Clay: The famous woman poet?

Lula: Poetess! The same!

Clay: Well, you know so much about me...what's my name?

Lula: Morris the Hyena.

Clay: The famous woman poet?

Lula: The same. [*Laughing and going into her bag*] You want another apple?

Clay: Can't make it, lady. I only have to keep one doctor away a day.

Lula: I bet your name is...something like...uh, Gerald or Walter. Huh?

Clay: God, no.

Lula: Lloyd, Norman? One of those hopeless colored names creeping out
of New Jersey. Leonard? Gag....

Clay: Like Warren?

Lula: Definitely. Just exactly like Warren. Or Everett.[2]

Clay: Gag....

Lula: Well, for sure, it's not Willie.

Clay: It's Clay.

Lula: Clay? Really? Clay what?

Clay: Take your pick. Jackson, Johnson, or Williams.

Lula: Oh, really? Good for you. But it's got to be Williams. You're too
pretentious to be a Jackson or Johnson.

Clay: Thass right.

Lula: But Clay's O.K.

Clay: So's Lena.

Lula: It's Lula.

Clay: Oh?

Lula: Lula the Hyena.

Clay: Very good.

Lula: [*Starts laughing again*] Now you say to me, "Lula, Lula, why don't
you go to this party with me tonight?" It's your turn, and let those be
your lines.

Clay: Lula, why don't you go to this party with me tonight, Huh?

Lula: Say my name twice before you ask, and no huh's.

Clay: Lula, Lula, why don't you go to this party with me tonight?

Lula: I'd like to go, Clay, but how can you ask me to go when you barely
know me?

Clay: That is strange, isn't it?

Lula: What kind of reaction is that? You're supposed to say, "Aw, come
on, we'll get to know each other better at the party."

Clay: That's pretty corny.

Lula: What are you into anyway? [*Looking at him half sullenly but still
amused*] What thing are you playing at, Mister? Mister Clay Williams?
[*Grabs his thigh, up near the crotch*] What are *you* thinking about?

Clay: Watch it now, you're gonna excite me for real.

Lula: [*Taking her hand away and throwing her apple core through the
window*] I bet.

[*She slumps in the seat and is heavily silent*]

Clay: I thought you knew everything about me? What happened? [LULA
*looks at him, then looks slowly away, then over where the other aisle
would be. Noise of the train. She reaches in her bag and pulls out one of
the paper books. She puts it on her leg and thumbs the pages listlessly.*
CLAY *cocks his head to see the title of the book. Noise of the train.* LULA

---

[2]A reference to Baraka's birth name, Everett Leroy Jones.

flips pages and her eyes drift. Both remain silent] Are you going to the party with me, Lula?

Lula: [*Bored and not even looking*] I don't even know you.

Clay: You said you know my type.

Lula: [*Strangely irritated*] Don't get smart with me, Buster. I know you like the palm of my hand.

Clay: The one you eat the apples with?

Lula: Yeh. And the one I open doors late Saturday evening with. That's my door. Up at the top of the stairs. Five flights. Above a lot of Italians and lying Americans. And scrape carrots with. Also...[*Looks at him*] the same hand I unbutton my dress with, or let my skirt fall down. Same hand. Lover.

Clay: Are you angry about anything? Did I say something wrong?

Lula: Everything you say is wrong. [*Mock smile*] That's what makes you so attractive. Ha. In that funnybook jacket with all the buttons. [*More animate, taking hold of his jacket*] What've you got that jacket and tie on in all this heat for? And why're you wearing a jacket and tie like that? Did your people ever burn witches or start revolutions over the price of tea? Boy, those narrow-shoulder clothes come from a tradition you ought to feel oppressed by. A three-button suit. What right do you have to be wearing a three-button suit and striped tie? Your grandfather was a slave, he didn't go to Harvard.

Clay: My grandfather was a night watchman.

Lula: And you went to a colored college where everybody thought they were Averell Harriman.[3]

Clay: All except me.

Lula: And who did you think you were? Who do you think you are now?

Clay: [*Laughs as if to make light of the whole trend of the conversation*] Well, in college I thought I was Baudelaire.[4] But I've slowed down since.

Lula: I bet you never once thought you were a black nigger. [*Mock serious, then she howls with laughter.* CLAY *is stunned but after initial reaction, he quickly tries to appreciate the humor.* LULA *almost shrieks*] A black Baudelaire.

Clay: That's right.

Lula: Boy, are you corny. I take back what I said before. Everything you say is not wrong. It's perfect. You should be on television.

Clay: You act like you're on television already.

Lula: That's because I'm an actress.

[3]William Averell Harriman (1891–1986) was a politician from a wealthy family known for his political diplomacy. He held government appointments made by presidents Roosevelt, Truman, Kennedy, and Johnson and served as governor of New York from 1954 to 1959.

[4]Charles Baudelaire (1821–67) was a French poet, translator, and literary and art critic best known for his sensual *Les Fleurs du Mal* ("The Flowers of Evil"), published in 1857, an influential and introspective poetry collection popular in Europe. He was deeply interested in the power of symbolism.

Clay: I thought so.

Lula: Well, you're wrong. I'm no actress. I told you I always lie. I'm nothing, honey, and don't you ever forget it. [*Lighter*] Although my mother was a Communist. The only person in my family ever to amount to anything.

Clay: My mother was a Republican.

Lula: And your father voted for the man rather than the party.

Clay: Right!

Lula: Yea for him. Yea, yea for him.

Clay: Yea!

Lula: And yea for America where he is free to vote for the mediocrity of his choice! Yea!

Clay: Yea!

Lula: And yea for both your parents who even though they differ about so crucial a matter as the body politic still forged a union of love and sacrifice that was destined to flower at the birth of the noble Clay... what's your middle name?

Clay: Clay.

Lula: A union of love and sacrifice that was destined to flower at the birth of the noble Clay Clay Williams. Yea! And most of all yea yea for you, Clay Clay. The Black Baudelaire! Yes! [*And with knifelike cynicism*] My Christ. My Christ.

Clay: Thank you, ma'am.

Lula: May the people accept you as a ghost of the future. And love you, that you might not kill them when you can.

Clay: What?

Lula: You're a murderer, Clay, and you know it. [*Her voice darkening with significance*] You know goddamn well what I mean.

Clay: I do?

Lula: So we'll pretend the air is light and full of perfume.

Clay: [*Sniffing at her blouse*] It is.

Lula: And we'll pretend the people cannot see you. That is, the citizens. And that you are free of your own history. And I am free of my history. We'll pretend that we are both anonymous beauties smashing along through the city's entrails. [*She yells as loud as she can*] GROOVE!

[*Black*]

SCENE II

Scene is the same as before, though now there are other seats visible in the car. And throughout the scene other people get on the subway. There are maybe one or two seated in the car as the scene opens, though neither CLAY nor LULA notices them. CLAY's tie is open. LULA is hugging his arm.

Clay: The party!

Lula: I know it'll be something good. You can come in with me, looking casual and significant. I'll be strange, haughty, and silent, and walk with long slow strides.

Clay: Right.

Lula: When you get drunk, pat me once, very lovingly on the flanks, and I'll look at you cryptically, licking my lips.

Clay: It sounds like something we can do.

Lula: You'll go around talking to young men about your mind, and to old men about your plans. If you meet a very close friend who is also with someone like me, we can stand together, sipping our drinks and exchanging codes of lust. The atmosphere will be slithering in love and half-love and very open moral decision.

Clay: Great. Great.

Lula: And everyone will pretend they don't know your name, and then... [*She pauses heavily*] later, when they have to, they'll claim a friendship that denies your sterling character.

Clay: [*Kissing her neck and fingers*] And then what?

Lula: Then? Well, then we'll go down the street, late night, eating apples and winding very deliberately toward my house.

Clay: Deliberately?

Lula: I mean, we'll look in all the shopwindows, and make fun of the queers. Maybe we'll meet a Jewish Buddhist and flatten his conceits[5] over some very pretentious coffee.

Clay: In honor of whose God?

Lula: Mine.

Clay: Who is...?

Lula: Me...and you?

Clay: A corporate Godhead.

Lula: Exactly. Exactly.

[*Notices one of the other people entering*]

Clay: Go on with the chronicle. Then what happens to us?

Lula: [*A mild depression, but she still makes her description triumphant and increasingly direct*] To my house, of course.

Clay: Of course.

Lula: And up the narrow steps of the tenement.

Clay: You live in a tenement?

Lula: Wouldn't live anywhere else. Reminds me specifically of my novel form of insanity.

Clay: Up the tenement stairs.

Lula: And with my apple-eating hand I push open the door and lead you, my tender big-eyed prey, into my...God, what can I call it...into my hovel.

Clay: Then what happens?

---

[5]An unduly high opinion of one's own abilities or worth; an ingenious or witty turn of phrase or thought.

Lula: After the dancing and games, after the long drinks and long walks, the real fun begins.

Clay: Ah, the real fun. [*Embarrassed, in spite of himself*] Which is...?

Lula: [*Laughs at him*] Real fun in the dark house. Hah! Real fun in the dark house, high up above the street and the ignorant cowboys. I lead you in, holding your wet hand gently in my hand...

Clay: Which is not wet?

Lula: Which is dry as ashes.

Clay: And cold?

Lula: Don't think you'll get out of your responsibility that way. It's not cold at all. You Fascist! Into my dark living room. Where we'll sit and talk endlessly, endlessly.

Clay: About what?

Lula: About what? About your manhood, what do you think? What do you think we've been talking about all this time?

Clay: Well, I didn't know it was that. That's for sure. Every other thing in the world but that. [*Notices another person entering, looks quickly, almost involuntarily up and down the car, seeing the other people in the car*] Hey, I didn't even notice when those people got on.

Lula: Yeah, I know.

Clay: Man, this subway is slow.

Lula: Yeah, I know.

Clay: Well, go on. We were talking about my manhood.

Lula: We still are. All the time.

Clay: We were in your living room.

Lula: My dark living room. Talking endlessly.

Clay: About my manhood.

Lula: I'll make you a map of it. Just as soon as we get to my house.

Clay: Well, that's great.

Lula: One of the things we do while we talk. And screw.

Clay: [*Trying to make his smile broader and less shaky*] We finally got there.

Lula: And you'll call my rooms black as a grave. You'll say, "This place is like Juliet's tomb."[6]

Clay: [*Laughs*] I might.

Lula: I know. You've probably said it before.

Clay: And is that all? The whole grand tour?

Lula: Not all. You'll say to me very close to my face, many, many times, you'll say, even whisper, that you love me.

Clay: Maybe I will.

---

[6]A reference to Shakespeare's *Romeo and Juliet* (1595) and to a poem by T. S. Eliot (1888–1965), "Portrait of a Lady" (1917). "Among the smoke and fog of a December afternoon / You have the scene arrange itself—as it will seem to do— / With 'I have saved this afternoon for you'; / And four wax candles in the darkened room, / Four rings of light upon the ceiling overhead, / An atmosphere of Juliet's tomb / Prepared for all the things to be said, or left unsaid."

Lula: And you'll be lying.

Clay: I wouldn't lie about something like that.

Lula: Hah. It's the only kind of thing you will lie about. Especially if you think it'll keep me alive.

Clay: Keep you alive? I don't understand.

Lula: [*Bursting out laughing, but too shrilly*] Don't understand? Well, don't look at me. It's the path I take, that's all. Where both feet take me when I set them down. One in front of the other.

Clay: Morbid. Morbid. You sure you're not an actress? All that self-aggrandizement.

Lula: Well, I told you I wasn't an actress...but I also told you I lie all the time. Draw your own conclusions.

Clay: Morbid. Morbid. You sure you're not an actress? All scribed? There's no more?

Lula: I've told you all I know. Or almost all.

Clay: There's no funny parts?

Lula: I thought it was all funny.

Clay: But you mean peculiar, not ha-ha.

Lula: You don't know what I mean.

Clay: Well, tell me the almost part then. You said almost all. What else? I want the whole story.

Lula: [*Searching aimlessly through her bag. She begins to talk breathlessly, with a light and silly tone*] All stories are whole stories. All of 'em. Our whole story ... nothing but change. How could things go on like that forever? Huh? [*Slaps him on the shoulder, begins finding things in her bag, taking them out and throwing them over her shoulder into the aisle*] Except I do go on as I do. Apples and long walks with deathless intelligent lovers. But you mix it up. Look out the window, all the time. Turning pages. Change change change. Till, shit, I don't know you. Wouldn't, for that matter. You're too serious. I bet you're even too serious to be psychoanalyzed. Like all those Jewish poets from Yonkers, who leave their mothers looking for other mothers, or others' mothers, on whose baggy tits they lay their fumbling heads. Their poems are always funny, and all about sex.

Clay: They sound great. Like movies.

Lula: But you change. [*Blankly*] And things work on you till you hate them.

[*More people come into the train. They come closer to the couple, some of them not sitting, but swinging drearily on the straps, staring at the two with uncertain interest*]

Clay: Wow. All these people, so suddenly. They must all come from the same place.

Lula: Right. That they do.

Clay: Oh? You know about them too?

Lula: Oh yeah. About them more than I know about you. Do they frighten you?

Clay: Frighten me? Why should they frighten me?

Lula: 'Cause you're an escaped nigger.

Clay: Yeah?

Lula: 'Cause you crawled through the wire and made tracks to my side.

Clay: Wire?

Lula: Don't they have wire around plantations?

Clay: You must be Jewish. All you can think about is wire. Plantations didn't have any wire. Plantations were big open whitewashed places like heaven, and everybody on 'em was grooved to be there. Just strummin' and hummin' all day.

Lula: Yes, yes.

Clay: And that's how the blues was born.

Lula: Yes, yes. And that's how the blues was born. [*Begins to make up a song that becomes quickly hysterical. As she sings she rises from her seat, still throwing things out of her bag into the aisle, beginning a rhythmical shudder and twistlike wiggle, which she continues up and down the aisle, bumping into many of the standing people and tripping over the feet of those sitting. Each time she runs into a person she lets out a very vicious piece of profanity, wiggling and stepping all the time*] And that's how the blues was born. Yes. Yes. Son of a bitch, get out of the way. Yes. Quack. Yes. Yes. And that's how the blues was born. Ten little niggers sitting on a limb, but none of them ever looked like him. [*Points to* CLAY, *returns toward the seat, with her hands extended for him to rise and dance with her*] And that's how blues was born. Yes. Come on, Clay. Let's do the nasty. Rub bellies. Rub bellies.

Clay: [*Waves his hands to refuse. He is embarrassed, but determined to get a kick out of the proceedings*] Hey, what was in those apples? Mirror, mirror on the wall, who's the fairest one of all? Snow White, baby, and don't you forget it.

Lula: [*Grabbing for his hands, which he draws away*] Come on, Clay. Let's rub bellies on the train. The nasty. The nasty. Do the gritty grind, like your ol' rag-head mammy. Grind till you lose your mind. Shake it, shake it, shake it, shake it! OOOOweeee! Come on, Clay. Let's do the choo-choo train shuffle, the navel scratcher.

Clay: Hey, you coming on like the lady who smoked up her grass skirt.

Lula: [*Becoming annoyed that he will not dance, and becoming more animated as if to embarrass him still further*] Come on, Clay...let's do the thing. Uhh! Uhh! Clay! Clay! You middle-class black bastard. Forget your social-working mother for a few seconds and let's knock stomachs. Clay, you liver-lipped white man. You would-be Christian. You ain't no nigger, you're just a dirty white man. Get up, Clay. Dance with me, Clay.

Clay: Lula! Sit down, now. Be cool.

Lula: [*Mocking him, in wild dance*] Be cool. Be cool. That's all you know...
shaking that wildroot cream-oil on your knotty head, jackets button-
ing up to your chin, so full of white man's words. Christ. God. Get up
and scream at these people. Like scream meaningless shit in these
hopeless faces. [*She screams at people in train, still dancing*] Red trains
cough Jewish underwear for keeps! Expanding smells of silence. Gravy
snot whistling like sea birds. Clay. Clay, you got to break out. Don't sit
there dying the way they want you to die. Get up.

Clay: Oh, sit the fuck down. [*He moves to restrain her*] Sit down, goddamn it.

Lula: [*Twisting out of his reach*] Screw yourself, Uncle Tom.[7] Thomas
Woolly-head. [*Begins to dance a kind of jig, mocking Clay with loud
forced humor*] There is Uncle Tom...I mean, Uncle Thomas Woolly-
Head. With old white matted mane. He hobbles on his wooden cane.
Old Tom. Old Tom. Let the white man hump his ol' mama, and he jes'
shuffle off in the woods and hide his gentle gray head. Ol' Thomas
Woolly-Head.

[*Some of the other riders are laughing now. A drunk gets up and joins* LULA
in her dance, singing, as best he can, her "song." CLAY *gets up out of his seat
and visibly scans the faces of the other riders*]

Clay: Lula! Lula! [*She is dancing and turning, still shouting as loud as she
can. The drunk too is shouting, and waving his hands wildly*] Lula...you
dumb bitch. Why don't you stop it? [*He rushes half stumbling from his
seat, and grabs one of her flailing arms*]

Lula: Let me go! You black son of a bitch. [*She struggles against him*] Let
me go! Help!

[CLAY *is dragging her towards her seat, and the drunk seeks to interfere. He
grabs* CLAY *around the shoulders and begins wrestling with him.* CLAY *clubs the
drunk to the floor without releasing* LULA, *who is still screaming.* CLAY *finally
gets her to the seat and throws her into it*]

Clay: Now you shut the hell up. [*Grabbing her shoulders*] Just shut up.
You don't know what you're talking about. You don't know anything.
So just keep your stupid mouth closed.

Lula: You're afraid of white people. And your father was. Uncle Tom Big
Lip!

Clay: [*Slaps her as hard as he can, across the mouth.* LULA's *head bangs
against the back of the seat. When she raises it again,* CLAY *slaps her
again*] Now shut up and let me talk. [*He turns toward the other riders,*

---

[7]The title character in the anti-slavery novel *Uncle Tom's Cabin* (1852) by Harriet Beecher Stowe
(1811–96), a character often criticized for being too deferential and submissive.

some of whom are sitting on the edge of their seats. The drunk is on one knee, rubbing his head, and singing softly the same song. He shuts up too when he sees CLAY *watching him. The others go back to newspapers or stare out the windows*] Shit, you don't have any sense, Lula, nor feelings either. I could murder you now. Such a tiny ugly throat. I could squeeze it flat, and watch you turn blue, on a humble. For dull kicks. And all these weak-faced ofays squatting around here, staring over their papers at me. Murder them too. Even if they expected it. That man there...[*Points to well-dressed man*] I could rip that *Times* right out of his hand, as skinny and middle-classed as I am, I could rip that paper out of his hand and just as easily rip out his throat. It takes no great effort. For what? To kill you soft idiots? You don't understand anything but luxury.

Lula: You fool!

Clay: [*Pushing her against the seat*] I'm not telling you again, Tallulah Bankhead![8] Luxury. In your face and your fingers. You telling me what I ought to do. [*Sudden scream frightening the whole coach*] Well, don't! Don't you tell me anything! If I'm a middle-class fake white man...let me be. And let me be in the way I want. [*Through his teeth*] I'll rip your lousy breasts off! Let me be who I feel like being. Uncle Tom. Thomas. Whoever. It's none of your business. You don't know anything except what's there for you to see. An act. Lies. Device. Not the pure heart, the pumping black heart. You don't ever know that. And I sit here, in this buttoned-up suit, to keep myself from cutting all your throats. I mean wantonly. You great liberated whore! You fuck some black man, and right away you're an expert on black people. What a lotta shit that is. The only thing you know is that you come if he bangs you hard enough. And that's all. The belly rub? You wanted to do the belly rub? Shit, you don't even know how. You don't know how. That ol' dipty-dip shit you do, rolling your ass like an elephant. That's not my kind of belly rub. Belly rub is not Queens. Belly rub is dark places, with big hats and overcoats held up with one arm. Belly rub hates you. Old bald-headed four-eyed ofays popping their fingers...and don't know yet what they're doing. They say, "I love Bessie Smith."[9] And don't even understand that Bessie Smith is saying, "Kiss my ass, kiss my black unruly ass." Before love, suffering, desire, anything you can explain, she's saying, and very plainly, "Kiss my black ass." And if you don't know that, it's you that's doing the kissing.

[8]Flamboyant actress (1902–68) who performed in silent and talking films and on the stage. In addition to her acting career, she was known for her many affairs, her long parties, and for calling everyone "daahling."

[9]African American classic blues singer (1895–1937) of the 1920s, considered by many critics the finest female blues singer of her day. Smith was known to be wild, promiscuous, and violent. Many of her songs lament social and political inequalities between the white and African American communities.

Charlie Parker?[10] Charlie Parker. All the hip white boys scream for Bird. And Bird saying, "Up your ass, feebleminded ofay! Up your ass." And they sit there talking about the tortured genius of Charlie Parker. Bird would've played not a note of music if he just walked up to East Sixty-seventh Street and killed the first ten white people he saw. Not a note! And I'm the great would-be poet. Yes. That's right! Poet. Some kind of bastard literature...all it needs is a simple knife thrust. Just let me bleed you, you loud whore, and one poem vanished. A whole people of neurotics, struggling to keep from being sane. And the only thing that would cure the neurosis would be your murder. Simple as that. I mean if I murdered you, then other white people would begin to understand me. You understand? No. I guess not. If Bessie Smith had killed some white people she wouldn't have needed that music. She could have talked very straight and plain about the world. No metaphors. No grunts. No wiggles in the dark of her soul. Just straight two and two are four. Money. Power. Luxury. Like that. All of them. Crazy niggers turning their backs on sanity. When all it needs is that simple act. Murder. Just murder! Would make us all sane. [*Suddenly weary*] Ahhh. Shit. But who needs it? I'd rather be a fool. Insane. Safe with my words, and no deaths, and clean, hard thoughts, urging me to new conquests. My people's madness. Hah! That's a laugh. My people. They don't need me to claim them. They got legs and arms of their own. Personal insanities. Mirrors. They don't need all those words. They don't need any defense. But listen, though, one more thing. And you tell this to your father, who's probably the kind of man who needs to know at once. So he can plan ahead. Tell him not to preach so much rationalism and cold logic to these niggers. Let them alone. Let them sing curses at you in code and see your filth as simple lack of style. Don't make the mistake, through some irresponsible surge of Christian charity, of talking too much about the advantages of Western rationalism, or the great intellectual legacy of the white man, or maybe they'll begin to listen. And then, maybe one day, you'll find they actually do understand exactly what you are talking about, all these fantasy people. All these blues people. And on that day, as sure as shit, when you really believe you can "accept" them into your fold, as half-white trusties late of the subject peoples. With no more blues, except the very old ones, and not a watermelon in sight, the great missionary heart will have triumphed, and all of those ex-coons will be stand-up Western men, with eyes for clean hard useful lives, sober, pious and

---

[10]Charlie "Bird" or "Yardbird" Parker (1920–55) is considered one of the most influential African American jazz soloists of the twentieth century. He was a central figure in the development of bop in the 1940s.

sane, and they'll murder you. They'll murder you, and have very
rational explanations. Very much like your own. They'll cut your
throats, and drag you out to the edge of your cities so the flesh can
fall away from your bones, in sanitary isolation.

Lula: [*Her voice takes on a different, more businesslike quality*] I've heard
enough.

Clay: [*Reaching for his books*] I bet you have. I guess I better collect my
stuff and get off this train. Looks like we won't be acting out that
little pageant you outlined before.

lula: No. We won't. You're right about that, at least. [*She turns to look
quickly around the rest of the car*] All right!

[*The others respond*]

Clay: [*Bending across the girl to retrieve his belongings*] Sorry, baby, I
don't think we could make it. [*As he is bending over her, the girl brings
up a small knife and plunges it into* CLAY's *chest. Twice. He slumps across
her knees, his mouth working stupidly*]

Lula: Sorry is right. [*Turning to the others in the car who have already
gotten up from their seats*] Sorry is the rightest thing you've said. Get
this man off me! Hurry, now! [*The others come and drag* CLAY's *body
down the aisle*] Open the door and throw his body out. [*They throw
him off*] And all of you get off at the next stop.

[LULA *busies herself straightening her things. Getting everything in order. She
takes out a notebook and makes a quick scribbling note. Drops it in her bag.
The train apparently stops and all the others get off, leaving her alone in the
coach.*

[*Very soon a young Negro of about twenty comes into the coach, with a
couple of books under his arm. He sits a few seats in back of* LULA. *When
he is seated she turns and gives him a long slow look. He looks up from his
book and drops the book on his lap. Then an old Negro conductor comes into
the car, doing a sort of restrained soft shoe, and half mumbling the words of
some song. He looks at the young man, briefly, with a quick greeting*]

conductor: Hey, brother!
young man: Hey.

[*The conductor continues down the aisle with his little dance and the mumbled song.* LULA *turns to stare at him and follows his movements down the
aisle. The conductor tips his hat when he reaches her seat, and continues out
the car.*]

CURTAIN

[1964]

JOYCE CAROL OATES ■ (1938—)

Joyce Carol Oates has been criticized for writing too much, but the main point to be made about her is that much of her writing, and in many genres, is very good. Sometimes compared to William Faulkner, whose fictional landscape of Yoknapatawpha County in Mississippi has its parallel in her fictional Eden County in New York State, Oates writes material that is often violent and grotesque, disturbing, and provocative, as she explores what she has described as "the phantasmagoria of personality."

A professor for many years at Princeton University—she satirized the academic life in *Unholy Loves* (1979)—Oates was born and raised in Erie County, New York, outside Buffalo. She earned her undergraduate degree from Syracuse University and then took a master's degree in English at the University of Wisconsin. She published her first collection of short stories, *By the North Gate*, in 1963, and since then has produced somewhere in the neighborhood of one hundred books—novels, short stories, essays, plays, poems, literary criticism, and journalism. She has also published a number of novels under pseudonyms. One of her most intriguing performances is a collection of stories, *Marriages and Infidelities* (1972), in which she revises, with an American setting, such classic tales as Chekhov's "The Lady with the Pet Dog" and Kafka's "The Metamorphosis."

A collection of Oates's astute literary criticism is *Contraries: Essays* (1981). Her recent books include *The Collector of Hearts: New Tales of the Grotesque* (1998); *Blonde: A Novel* (2000), a dark, desperate, penetrating masterpiece modeled on the life of Marilyn Monroe; *The Tattooed Girl: A Novel* (2003); *The Faith of a Writer: Life, Craft, Art* (2003); *High Lonesome New and Selected Stories* (2004); *Little Bird of Heaven* (2009); and *A Widow's Story: A Memoir* (2011).

The best places to begin for critical interpretation and biographical context are three books by Greg Johnson: *Understanding Joyce Carol Oates* (1987), *Joyce Carol Oates: A Study of the Short Fiction* (1994), and *Invisible Writer: A Biography of Joyce Carol Oates* (1998).

For insight into and context for the following story, see *"Where Are You Going, Where Have You Been?"* ed. Elaine Showalter (1994) in the *Women Writers: Texts and Contexts* series. Inspired by a magazine story about a serial killer and focused on the themes of sexual victimization, adolescent sexuality, and male violence, this compelling story was originally published in *Epoch* in fall 1966.

Where Are You Going, Where Have You Been?

FOR BOB DYLAN[1]

Her name was Connie. She was fifteen and she had a quick, nervous giggling habit of craning her neck to glance into mirrors or checking other people's faces to make sure her own was all right. Her mother, who noticed everything and knew everything and who hadn't much reason any longer to look at her own face, always scolded Connie about it. "Stop gawking at yourself. Who are you? You think you're so pretty?" she would say. Connie would raise her eyebrows at these familiar old complaints and look right through her mother, into a shadowy vision of herself as she was right at that moment: she knew she was pretty and that was everything. Her mother had been pretty once too, if you could believe those old snapshots in the album, but now her looks were gone and that was why she was always after Connie.

"Why don't you keep your room clean like your sister? How've you got your hair fixed—what the hell stinks? Hair spray? You don't see your sister using that junk."

Her sister June was twenty-four and still lived at home. She was a secretary in the high school Connie attended, and if that wasn't bad enough—with her in the same building—she was so plain and chunky and steady that Connie had to hear her praised all the time by her mother and her mother's sisters. June did this, June did that, she saved money and helped clean the house and cooked and Connie couldn't do a thing, her mind was all filled with trashy daydreams. Their father was away at work most of the time and when he came home he wanted supper and he read the newspaper at supper and after supper he went to bed. He didn't bother talking much to them, but around his bent head Connie's mother kept picking at her until Connie wished her mother was dead and she herself was dead and it was all over. "She makes me want to throw up sometimes," she complained to her friends. She had a high, breathless, amused voice that made everything she said sound a little forced, whether it was sincere or not.

There was one good thing: June went places with girl friends of hers, girls who were just as plain and steady as she, and so when Connie wanted to do that her mother had no objections. The father of Connie's best girl friend drove the girls the three miles to town and left them at a shopping plaza so they could walk through the stores or go to a movie, and when he came to pick them up again at eleven he never bothered to ask what they had done.

[1]Oates has said that Bob Dylan's song "It's All Over Now, Baby Blue" was an inspiration for her story.

They must have been familiar sights, walking around the shopping plaza in their shorts and flat ballerina slippers that always scuffed the sidewalk, with charm bracelets jingling on their thin wrists; they would lean together to whisper and laugh secretly if someone passed who amused or interested them. Connie had long dark blond hair that drew anyone's eye to it, and she wore part of it pulled up on her head and puffed out and the rest of it she let fall down her back. She wore a pullover jersey blouse that looked one way when she was at home and another way when she was away from home. Everything about her had two sides to it, one for home and one for anywhere that was not home: her walk, which could be child-like and bobbing, or languid enough to make anyone think she was hearing music in her head; her mouth, which was pale and smirking most of the time, but bright and pink on these evenings out; her laugh, which was cynical and drawling at home—"Ha, ha, very funny"—but high-pitched and nervous anywhere else, like the jingling of the charms on her bracelet.

Sometimes they did go shopping or to a movie, but sometimes they went across the highway, ducking fast across the busy road, to a drive-in restaurant where older kids hung out. The restaurant was shaped like a big bottle, though squatter than a real bottle, and on its cap was a revolving figure of a grinning boy holding a hamburger aloft. One night in mid-summer they ran across, breathless with daring, and right away someone leaned out a car window and invited them over, but it was just a boy from high school they didn't like. It made them feel good to be able to ignore him. They went up through the maze of parked and cruising cars to the bright-lit, fly-infested restaurant, their faces pleased and expectant as if they were entering a sacred building that loomed up out of night to give them what haven and blessings they yearned for. They sat at the counter and crossed their legs at the ankles, their thin shoulders rigid with excite-ment, and listened to the music that made everything so good: the music was always in the background, like music at a church service; it was some-thing to depend upon.

A boy named Eddie came in to talk with them. He sat backwards on his stool, turning himself jerkily around in semicircles and then stopping and turning back again, and after a while he asked Connie if she would like something to eat. She said she would and so she tapped her friend's arm on her way out—her friend pulled her face up into a brave, droll look—and Connie said she would meet her at eleven, across the way. "I just hate to leave her like that," Connie said earnestly, but the boy said that she wouldn't be alone for long. So they went out to his car, and on the way Connie couldn't help but let her eyes wander over the windshields and faces all around her, her face gleaming with a joy that had nothing to do with Eddie or even this place; it might have been the music. She drew her shoulders up and sucked in her breath with the pure pleasure of being alive, and just at that moment she happened to glance at a face just a few feet from hers. It was a boy with shaggy black hair, in a convertible jalopy painted gold. He stared at her and then his lips widened into a grin. Connie slit her eyes at him and turned away, but she couldn't help glancing back and there he was, still watching her. He wagged a finger and laughed and said, "Gonna get you, baby," and Connie turned away again without Eddie noticing anything.

She spent three hours with him, at the restaurant where they ate hamburgers and drank Cokes in wax cups that were always sweating, and then down an alley a mile or so away, and when he left her off at five to eleven only the movie house was still open at the plaza. Her girl friend was there, talking with a boy. When Connie came up, the two girls smiled at each other and Connie said, "How was the movie?" and the girl said, "*You* should know." They rode off with the girl's father, sleepy and pleased, and Connie couldn't help but look back at the darkened shopping plaza with its big empty parking lot and its signs that were faded and ghostly now, and over at the drive-in restaurant where cars were still circling tirelessly. She couldn't hear the music at this distance.

Next morning June asked her how the movie was and Connie said, "So-so."

She and that girl and occasionally another girl went out several times a week, and the rest of the time Connie spent around the house—it was summer vacation—getting in her mother's way and thinking, dreaming about the boys she met. But all the boys fell back and dissolved into a single face that was not even a face but an idea, a feeling, mixed up with the urgent insistent pounding of the music and the humid night of July. Connie's mother kept dragging her back to the daylight by finding things for her to do or saying suddenly, "What's this about the Pettinger girl?"

And Connie would say nervously, "Oh, her. That dope." She always drew thick clear lines between herself and such girls, and her mother was simple and kind enough to believe it. Her mother was so simple, Connie thought, that it was maybe cruel to fool her so much. Her mother went scuffling around the house in old bedroom slippers and complained over the telephone to one sister about the other, then the other called up and the two of them complained about the third one. If June's name was mentioned her mother's tone was approving, and if Connie's name was mentioned it was disapproving. This did not really mean she disliked Connie, and actually Connie thought that her mother preferred her to June just because she was prettier, but the two of them kept up a pretense of exasperation, a sense that they were tugging and struggling over something of little value to either of them. Sometimes, over coffee, they were almost friends, but something would come up—some vexation that was like a fly buzzing suddenly around their heads—and their faces went hard with contempt.

One Sunday Connie got up at eleven—none of them bothered with church—and washed her hair so that it could dry all day long in the sun.

Her parents and sister were going to a barbecue at an aunt's house and Connie said no, she wasn't interested, rolling her eyes to let her mother know just what she thought of it. "Stay home alone then," her mother said sharply. Connie sat out back in a lawn chair and watched them drive away, her father quiet and bald, hunched around so that he could back the car out, her mother with a look that was still angry and not at all softened through the windshield, and in the back seat poor old June, all dressed up as if she didn't know what a barbecue was, with all the running yelling kids and the flies. Connie sat with her eyes closed in the sun, dreaming and dazed with the warmth about her as if this were a kind of love, the caresses of love, and her mind slipped over onto thoughts of the boy she had been with the night before and how nice he had been, how sweet it always was, not the way someone like June would suppose but sweet, gentle, the way it was in movies and promised in songs; and when she opened her eyes she hardly knew where she was, the back yard ran off into weeds and a fence-like line of trees and behind it the sky was perfectly blue and still. The asbestos "ranch house" that was now three years old startled her—it looked small. She shook her head as if to get awake.

It was too hot. She went inside the house and turned on the radio to drown out the quiet. She sat on the edge of her bed, barefoot, and listened for an hour and a half to a program called XYZ Sunday Jamboree, record after record of hard, fast, shrieking songs she sang along with, interspersed by exclamations from "Bobby King[2]": "An' look here, you girls at Napoleon's—Son and Charley want you to pay real close attention to this song coming up!"

And Connie paid close attention herself, bathed in a glow of slow-pulsed joy that seemed to rise mysteriously out of the music itself and lay languidly about the airless little room, breathed in and breathed out with each gentle rise and fall of her chest.

After while she heard a car coming up the drive. She sat up at once, startled, because it couldn't be her father so soon. The gravel kept crunching all the way in from the road—the driveway was long—and Connie ran to the window. It was a car she didn't know. It was an open jalopy, painted a bright gold that caught the sunlight opaquely. Her heart began to pound and her fingers snatched at her hair, checking it, and she whispered, "Christ, Christ," wondering how bad she looked. The car came to a stop at the side door and the horn sounded four short taps, as if this were a signal Connie knew.

She went into the kitchen and approached the door slowly, then hung out the screen door, her bare toes curling down off the step. There were two boys in the car and now she recognized the driver: he had shaggy, shabby black hair that looked crazy as a wig and he was grinning at her.

"I ain't late, am I?" he said.

"Who the hell do you think you are?" Connie said.

[2]Bobby King (b. 1944), an American gospel-style, rhythm and blues, and soul singer.

"Toldja I'd be out, didn't I?"

"I don't even know who you are."

She spoke sullenly, careful to show no interest or pleasure, and he spoke in a fast, bright monotone. Connie looked past him to the other boy, taking her time. He had fair brown hair, with a lock that fell onto his forehead. His sideburns gave him a fierce, embarrassed look, but so far he hadn't even bothered to glance at her. Both boys wore sunglasses. The driver's glasses were metallic and mirrored everything in miniature.

"You wanta come for a ride?" he said.

Connie smirked and let her hair fall loose over one shoulder.

"Don'tcha like my car? New paint job," he said. "Hey."

"What?"

"You're cute."

She pretended to fidget, chasing flies away from the door.

"Don'tcha believe me, or what?" he said.

"Look, I don't even know who you are," Connie said in disgust.

"Hey, Ellie's got a radio, see. Mine broke down." He lifted his friend's arm and showed her the little transistor radio the boy was holding, and now Connie began to hear the music. It was the same program that was playing inside the house.

"Bobby King?" she said.

"I listen to him all the time. I think he's great."

"He's kind of great," Connie said reluctantly.

"Listen, that guy's *great*. He knows where the action is."

Connie blushed a little, because the glasses made it impossible for her to see just what this boy was looking at. She couldn't decide if she liked him or if he was just a jerk, and so she dawdled in the doorway and wouldn't come down or go back inside. She said, "What's all that stuff painted on your car?"

"Can'tcha read it?" He opened the door very carefully, as if he were afraid it might fall off. He slid out just as carefully, planting his feet firmly on the ground, the tiny metallic world in his glasses slowing down like gelatin hardening, and in the midst of it Connie's bright green blouse. "This here is my name, to begin with," he said. ARNOLD FRIEND was written in tarlike black letters on the side, with a drawing of a round, grinning face that reminded Connie of a pumpkin, except it wore sunglasses. "I wanta introduce myself, I'm Arnold Friend and that's my real name and I'm gonna be your friend, honey, and inside the car's Ellie Oscar, he's kinda shy." Ellie brought his transistor radio up to his shoulder and balanced it there. "Now, these numbers are a secret code, honey," Arnold Friend explained. He read off the numbers 33, 19, 17 and raised his eyebrows at her to see what she thought of that, but she didn't think much of it. The left rear fender had been smashed and around it was written, on the gleaming gold background: DONE BY CRAZY WOMAN DRIVER. Connie had to laugh at that.

Arnold Friend was pleased at her laughter and looked up at her. "Around the other side's a lot more—you wanta come and see them?"

"No."

"Why not?"

"Why should I?"

"Don'tcha wanta see what's on the car? Don'tcha wanta go for a ride?"

"I don't know."

"Why not?"

"I got things to do."

"Like what?"

"Things."

He laughed as if she had said something funny. He slapped his thighs. He was standing in a strange way, leaning back against the car as if he were balancing himself. He wasn't tall, only an inch or so taller than she would be if she came down to him. Connie liked the way he was dressed, which was the way all of them dressed: tight faded jeans stuffed into black, scuffed boots, a belt that pulled his waist in and showed how lean he was, and a white pullover shirt that was a little soiled and showed the hard small muscles of his arms and shoulders. He looked as if he probably did hard work, lifting and carrying things. Even his neck looked muscular. And his face was a familiar face, somehow: the jaw and chin and cheeks slightly darkened because he hadn't shaved for a day or two, and the nose long and hawklike, sniffing as if she were a treat he was going to gobble up and it was all a joke.

"Connie, you ain't telling the truth. This is your day set aside for a ride with me and you know it," he said, still laughing. The way he straightened and recovered from his fit of laughing showed that it had been all fake.

"How do you know what my name is?" she said suspiciously.

"It's Connie."

"Maybe and maybe not."

"I know my Connie," he said, wagging his finger. Now she remembered him even better, back at the restaurant, and her cheeks warmed at the thought of how she had sucked in her breath just at the moment she passed him—how she must have looked to him. And he had remembered her. "Ellie and I come out here especially for you," he said. "Ellie can sit in back. How about it?"

"Where?"

"Where what?"

"Where're we going?"

He looked at her. He took off the sunglasses and she saw how pale the skin around his eyes was, like holes that were not in shadow but instead in light. His eyes were like chips of broken glass that catch the light in an amiable way. He smiled. It was as if the idea of going for a ride somewhere, to someplace, was a new idea to him.

"Just for a ride, Connie sweetheart."

"I never said my name was Connie," she said.

"But I know what it is. I know your name and all about you, lots of things," Arnold Friend said. He had not moved yet but stood still leaning back against the side of his jalopy. "I took a special interest in you, such a pretty girl, and found out all about you—like I know your parents and sister are gone somewheres and I know where and how long they're going to be gone, and I know who you were with last night, and your best girl friend's name is Betty. Right?"

He spoke in a simple lilting voice, exactly as if he were reciting the words to a song. His smile assured her that everything was fine. In the car Ellie turned up the volume on his radio and did not bother to look around at them.

"Ellie can sit in the back seat," Arnold Friend said. He indicated his friend with a casual jerk of his chin, as if Ellie did not count and she should not bother with him.

"How'd you find out all that stuff?" Connie said.

"Listen: Betty Schultz and Tony Fitch and Jimmy Pettinger and Nancy Pettinger," he said in a chant. "Raymond Stanley and Bob Hutter—"

"Do you know all those kids?"

"I know everybody."

"Look, you're kidding. You're not from around here."

"Sure."

"But—how come we never saw you before?"

"Sure you saw me before," he said. He looked down at his boots, as if he were a little offended. "You just don't remember."

"I guess I'd remember you," Connie said.

"Yeah?" He looked up at this, beaming. He was pleased. He began to mark time with the music from Ellie's radio, tapping his fists lightly together. Connie looked away from his smile to the car, which was painted so bright it almost hurt her eyes to look at it. She looked at that name, ARNOLD FRIEND. And up at the front fender was an expression that was familiar—MAN THE FLYING SAUCERS. It was an expression kids had used the year before but didn't use this year. She looked at it for a while as if the words meant something to her that she did not yet know.

"What're you thinking about? Huh?" Arnold Friend demanded. "Not worried about your hair blowing around in the car, are you?"

"No."

"Think I maybe can't drive good?"

"How do I know?"

"You're a hard girl to handle. How come?" he said. "Don't you know I'm your friend? Didn't you see me put my sign in the air when you walked by?"

"What sign?"

"My sign." And he drew an X in the air, leaning out toward her. They were maybe ten feet apart. After his hand fell back to his side the X was still in the air, almost visible. Connie let the screen door close and stood perfectly still inside it, listening to the music from her radio and the boy's blend together. She stared at Arnold Friend. He stood there so stiffly relaxed, pretending to be relaxed, with one hand idly on the door handle as if he were keeping himself up that way and had no intention of ever moving again. She recognized most things about him, the tight jeans that showed his thighs and buttocks and the greasy leather boots and the tight shirt, and even that slippery friendly smile of his, that sleepy dreamy smile that all the boys used to get across ideas they didn't want to put into words. She recognized all this and also the singsong way he talked, slightly mocking, kidding, but serious and a little melancholy, and she recognized the way he tapped one fist against the other in homage to the perpetual music behind him. But all these things did not come together.

She said suddenly, "Hey, how old are you?"

His smile faded. She could see then that he wasn't a kid, he was much older—thirty, maybe more. At this knowledge her heart began to pound faster.

"That's a crazy thing to ask. Can'tcha see I'm your own age?"

"Like hell you are."

"Or maybe a coupla years older. I'm eighteen."

"Eighteen?" she said doubtfully.

He grinned to reassure her and lines appeared at the corners of his mouth. His teeth were big and white. He grinned so broadly his eyes became slits and she saw how thick the lashes were, thick and black as if painted with a black tarlike material. Then, abruptly, he seemed to become embarrassed and looked over his shoulder at Ellie. "*Him,* he's crazy," he said. "Ain't he a riot? He's a nut, a real character." Ellie was still listening to the music. His sunglasses told nothing about what he was thinking. He wore a bright orange shirt unbuttoned halfway to show his chest, which was a pale, bluish chest and not muscular like Arnold Friend's. His shirt collar was turned up all around and the very tips of the collar pointed out past his chin as if they were protecting him. He was pressing the transistor radio up against his ear and sat there in a kind of daze, right in the sun.

"He's kinda strange," Connie said.

"Hey, she says you're kinda strange! Kinda strange!" Arnold Friend cried. He pounded on the car to get Ellie's attention. Ellie turned for the first time and Connie saw with shock that he wasn't a kid either—he had a fair, hairless face, cheeks reddened slightly as if the veins grew too close to the surface of his skin, the face of a forty-year-old baby. Connie felt a wave of dizziness rise in her at this sight and she stared at him as if waiting for something to change the shock of the moment, make it all right again. Ellie's lips kept shaping words, mumbling along with the words blasting in his ear.

"Maybe you two better go away," Connie said faintly.

"What? How come?" Arnold Friend cried. "We come out here to take you for a ride. It's Sunday." He had the voice of the man on the radio now. It was the same voice, Connie thought: "Don'tcha know it's Sunday all day? And honey, no matter who you were with last night, today you're with Arnold Friend and don't you forget it! Maybe you better step out here," he said, and this last was in a different voice. It was a little flatter, as if the heat was finally getting to him.

"No. I got things to do."

"Hey."

"You two better leave."

"We ain't leaving until you come with us."

"Like hell I am—"

"Connie, don't fool around with me. I mean—I mean, don't fool *around,*" he said, shaking his head. He laughed incredulously. He placed his sunglasses on top of his head, carefully, as if he were indeed wearing a wig, and brought the stems down behind his ears. Connie stared at him, another wave of dizziness and fear rising in her so that for a moment he wasn't even in focus but was just a blur standing there against his gold car, and she had the idea that he had driven up the driveway all right but had come from nowhere before that and belonged nowhere and that everything about him and even about the music that was so familiar to her was only half real.

"If my father comes and sees you—"

"He ain't coming. He's at a barbecue."

"How do you know that?"

"Aunt Tillie's. Right now they're—uh—they're drinking. Sitting around," he said vaguely, squinting as if he were staring all the way to town and over to Aunt Tillie's back yard. Then the vision seemed to get clear and he nodded energetically. "Yeah. Sitting around. There's your sister in a blue dress, huh? And high heels, the poor sad bitch—nothing like you, sweetheart! And your mother's helping some fat woman with the corn, they're cleaning the corn—husking the corn—"

"What fat woman?" Connie cried.

"How do I know what fat woman, I don't know every goddamn fat woman in the world!" Arnold Friend laughed.

"Oh, that's Mrs. Hornsby....Who invited her?" Connie said. She felt a little lightheaded. Her breath was coming quickly.

"She's too fat. I don't like them fat. I like them the way you are, honey," he said, smiling sleepily at her. They stared at each other for a while through the screen door. He said softly, "Now, what you're going to do is this: you're going to come out that door. You're going to sit up front with me and Ellie's going to sit in the back, the hell with Ellie, right? This isn't Ellie's date. You're my date. I'm your lover, honey."

"What? You're crazy—"

"Yes, I'm your lover. You don't know what that is but you will," he said. "I know that too. I know all about you. But look: it's real nice and you couldn't ask for nobody better than me, or more polite. I always keep my word. I'll tell you how it is, I'm always nice at first, the first time. I'll hold you so tight you won't think you have to try to get away or pretend anything because you'll know you can't. And I'll come inside you where it's all secret and you'll give in to me and you'll love me—"

"Shut up! You're crazy!" Connie said. She backed away from the door. She put her hands up against her ears as if she'd heard something terrible, something not meant for her. "People don't talk like that, you're crazy," she muttered. Her heart was almost too big now for her chest and its pumping made sweat break out all over her. She looked out to see Arnold Friend pause and then take a step toward the porch, lurching. He almost fell. But, like clever drunken man, he managed to catch his balance. He wobbled in his high boots and grabbed hold of one of the porch posts.

"Honey?" he said. "You still listening?"

"Get the hell out of here!"

"Be nice, honey. Listen."

"I'm going to call the police—"

He wobbled again and out of the side of his mouth came a fast spat curse, an aside not meant for her to hear. But even this "Christ!" sounded forced. Then he began to smile again. She watched this smile come, awkward as if he were smiling from inside a mask. His whole face was a mask, she thought wildly, tanned down to his throat but then running out as if he had plastered makeup on his face but had forgotten about his throat.

"Honey—? Listen, here's how it is. I always tell the truth and I promise you this: I ain't coming in that house after you."

"You better not! I'm going to call the police if you—if you don't—"

"Honey," he said, talking right through her voice, "honey, I'm not coming in there but you are coming out here. You know why?"

She was panting. The kitchen looked like a place she had never seen before, some room she had run inside but that wasn't good enough, wasn't going to help her. The kitchen window had never had a curtain, after three years, and there were dishes in the sink for her to do—probably—and if you ran your hand across the table you'd probably feel something sticky there.

"You listening, honey? Hey?"

"—going to call the police—"

"Soon as you touch the phone I don't need to keep my promise and can come inside. You won't want that."

She rushed forward and tried to lock the door. Her fingers were shaking. "But why lock it," Arnold Friend said gently, talking right into her face. It's just a screen door. It's just nothing." One of his boots was at a strange angle, as if his foot wasn't in it. It pointed out to the left, bent at the ankle. "I mean, anybody can break through a screen door and glass and wood and iron or anything else if he needs to, anybody at all, and specially Arnold Friend. If the place got lit up with a fire, honey, you'd come runnin' out into my arms, right into my arms an' safe at home—like you knew I was your lover and'd stopped fooling around." Part of those words were spoken with a slight rhythmic lilt, and Connie somehow recognized them—the echo of a song from last year, about a girl rushing into her boy friend's arms and coming home again—

Connie stood barefoot on the linoleum floor, staring at him. "What do you want?" she whispered.

"I want you," he said.

"What?"

"Seen you that night and thought, that's the one, yes sir. I never needed to look anymore."

"But my father's coming back. He's coming to get me. I had to wash my hair first—" She spoke in a dry, rapid voice, hardly raising it for him to hear.

"No, your daddy is not coming and yes, you had to wash your hair and you washed it for me. It's nice and shining and all for me. I thank you sweetheart," he said with a mock bow, but again he almost lost his balance. He had to bend and adjust his boots. Evidently his feet did not go all the way down; the boots must have been stuffed with something so that he would seem taller. Connie stared out at him and behind him at Ellie in the car, who seemed to be looking off toward Connie's right, into nothing. This Ellie said, pulling the words out of the air one after another as if he were just discovering them, "You want me to pull out the phone?"

"Shut your mouth and keep it shut," Arnold Friend said, his face red from bending over or maybe from embarrassment because Connie had seen his boots. "This ain't none of your business."

"What—what are you doing? What do you want?" Connie said. "If I call the police they'll get you, they'll arrest you—"

"Promise was not to come in unless you touch that phone, and I'll keep that promise," he said. He resumed his erect position and tried to force his shoulders back. He sounded like a hero in a movie, declaring something important. But he spoke too loudly and it was as if he were speaking to someone behind Connie. "I ain't made plans for coming in that house where I don't belong but just for you to come out to me, the way you should. Don't you know who I am?"

"You're crazy," she whispered. She backed away from the door but did not want to go into another part of the house, as if this would give him permission to come through the door. "What do you...you're crazy, you..."

"Huh? What're you saying, honey?"

Her eyes darted everywhere in the kitchen. She could not remember what it was, this room.

"This is how it is, honey: you come out and we'll drive away, have a nice ride. But if you don't come out we're gonna wait till your people come home and then they're all going to get it."

"You want that telephone pulled out?" Ellie said.

He held the radio away from his ear and grimaced, as if without the radio the air was too much for him.

"I toldja shut up, Ellie," Arnold Friend said, "you're deaf, get a hearing aid, right? Fix yourself up. This little girl's no trouble and's gonna be nice to me, so Ellie keep to yourself, this ain't your date—right? Don't hem in on me, don't hog, don't crush, don't bird dog, don't trail me," he said in a rapid, meaningless voice, as if he were running through all the expressions he'd learned but was no longer sure which of them was in style, then rushing on to new ones, making them up with his eyes closed. "Don't crawl under my fence, don't squeeze in my chipmunk hole, don't sniff my glue, suck my popsicle, keep your own greasy fingers on yourself!" He shaded his eyes and peered in at Connie, who was backed against the kitchen table. "Don't mind him, honey, he's just a creep. He's a dope. Right? I'm the boy for you and like I said, you come out here nice like a lady and give me your hand, and nobody else gets hurt, I mean, your nice old bald-headed daddy and your mummy and your sister in her high heels. Because listen: why bring them in this?"

"Leave me alone," Connie whispered.

"Hey, you know that old woman down the road, the one with the chickens and stuff—you know her?"

"She's dead!"

"Dead? What? You know her?" Arnold Friend said.

"She's dead—"

"Don't you like her?"

"She's dead—she's—she isn't here any more—"

"But don't you like her, I mean, you got something against her? Some grudge or something?" Then his voice dipped as if he were conscious of a rudeness. He touched the sunglasses perched up on top of his head as if to make sure they were still there. "Now, you be a good girl."

"What are you going to do?"

"Just two things, or maybe three," Arnold Friend said. "But I promise it won't last long and you'll like me the way you get to like people you're close to. You will. It's all over for you here, so come on out. You don't want your people in any trouble, do you?"

She turned and bumped against a chair or something, hurting her leg, but she ran into the back room and picked up the telephone. Something roared in her ear, a tiny roaring, and she was so sick with fear that she could do nothing but listen to it—the telephone was clammy and very heavy and her fingers groped down to the dial but were too weak to touch it. She began to scream into the phone, into the roaring. She cried out, she cried for her mother, she felt her breath start jerking back and forth in her lungs as if it were something Arnold Friend was stabbing her with again and again with no tenderness. A noisy sorrowful wailing rose all about her and she was locked inside it the way she was locked inside this house.

After a while she could hear again. She was sitting on the floor with her wet back against the wall.

Arnold Friend was saying from the door, "That's a good girl. Put the phone back."

She kicked the phone away from her.

"No, honey. Pick it up. Put it back right."

She picked it up and put it back. The dial tone stopped.

"That's a good girl. Now, you come outside."

She was hollow with what had been fear but what was now just an emptiness. All that screaming had blasted it out of her. She sat, one leg cramped under her, and deep inside her brain was something like a pinpoint of light that kept going and would not let her relax. She thought, I'm not going to see my mother again. She thought, I'm not going to sleep in my bed again. Her bright green blouse was all wet.

Arnold Friend said, in a gentle-loud voice that was like a stage voice, "The place where you came from ain't there any more, and where you had in mind to go is cancelled out. This place you are now—inside your daddy's house—is nothing but a cardboard box I can knock down any time. You know that and always did know it. You hear me?"

She thought, I have got to think. I have got to know what to do.

"We'll go out to a nice field, out in the country here where it smells so nice and it's sunny," Arnold Friend said, "I'll have my arms tight around you so you won't need to try to get away and I'll show you what love is like, what it does. The hell with this house! It looks solid all right," he said. He ran a fingernail down the screen and the noise did not make Connie shiver, as it would have the day before. "Now, put your hand on your heart, honey. Feel that? That feels solid too but we know better. Be nice to me, be sweet like you can because what else is there for a girl like you but to be sweet and pretty and give in?—and get away before her people come back?"

She felt her pounding heart. Her hand seemed to enclose it. She thought for the first time in her life that it was nothing that was hers, that belonged to her, but just a pounding, living thing inside this body that wasn't really hers either.

"You don't want them to get hurt," Arnold Friend went on. "Now, get up, honey. Get up all by yourself."

She stood.

"Now, turn this way. That's right. Come over here to me.—Ellie, put that away, didn't I tell you? You dope. You miserable creepy dope," Arnold Friend said. His words were not angry but only part of an incantation. The incantation was kindly. "Now, come out through the kitchen to me, honey, and let's see a smile, try it, you're a brave, sweet little girl and now they're eating corn and hot dogs cooked to bursting over an outdoor fire, and they don't know one thing about you and never did and honey, you're better than them because not a one of them would have done this for you."

Connie felt the linoleum under her feet; it was cool. She brushed her hair back out of her eyes. Arnold Friend let go of the post tentatively and opened his arms for her, his elbows pointing in toward each other and his wrists limp, to show that this was an embarrassed embrace and a little mocking, he didn't want to make her self-conscious.

She put out her hand against the screen. She watched herself push the door slowly open as if she were back safe somewhere in the other doorway, watching this body and this head of long hair moving out into the sunlight where Arnold Friend waited.

"My sweet little blue-eyed girl," he said in a half-sung sigh that had nothing to do with her brown eyes but was taken up just the same by the vast sunlit reaches of the land behind him and on all sides of him—so much land that Connie had never seen before and did not recognize except to know that she was going to it.

[1966]

RAYMOND CARVER ■ (1938–1988)

The poet, short-story writer, and essayist Raymond Carver was born in Oregon and raised in Yakima, Washington. Married and the father of two children by age twenty, he relocated with his family to California, and at Chico State College he studied with the novelist John Gardner. One of Carver's former students recalled that Carver always "felt Gardner looking over his shoulder when he wrote, approving or disapproving of certain words, phrases, and strategies." Later he developed his craft at the University of Iowa's Writers' Workshop. He worked at an assortment of jobs, suffered from alcoholism, and smoked heavily, which led to the cancer that caused his death at age fifty. "I began as a poet," Carver observed. "My first publication was a poem. So I suppose on my tombstone I'd be very pleased if they put 'Poet and short-story writer—and occasional essayist' in that order."

Often referred to as a minimalist because of his lean, focused prose, Carver is one of the most noteworthy short-story writers of the post–World War II period, and perhaps the most influential. He usually takes as his subject the lives—frustrated, adrift, struggling to make ends meet—of working-class and blue-collar Americans. His first important book, *Will You Please Be Quiet, Please?*, was published in 1976. It was followed by *What We Talk About When We Talk About Love* (1981), *Cathedral* (1983), and *Where I'm Calling From* (1988). *All of Us: The Collected Poems* was published in 1998. Carver's writing style is deceptively simple: "It is possible to write a line of seemingly innocuous dialogue and have it send a chill along the reader's spine—the source of artistic delight, as [Vladimir] Nabokov would have it. That's the kind of writing that most interests me" (Carver, in the *New York Times*, February 15, 1981). "Cathedral," the story that follows, considers the significance of the act of seeing in a way that is more than merely physical.

For biography and literary context, see *Conversations with Raymond Carver*, eds. Marshall Bruce Gentry and William L. Stull (1990). Critical studies include Randolph Paul Runyon, *Reading Raymond Carver* (1992); and Arthur F. Bethea, *Technique and Sensibility in the Fiction and Poetry of Raymond Carver* (2001). See also *Remembering Ray: A Composite Biography of Raymond Carver*, eds. William L. Stull and Maureen P. Carroll (1993); Sam Halpert, *Raymond Carver: An Oral Biography* (1995); and *Raymond Carver: A Writer's Life* (2009) by Carol Sklenicka.

Cathedral

This blind man, an old friend of my wife's, he was on his way to spend the night. His wife had died. So he was visiting the dead wife's relatives in Connecticut. He called my wife from his in-laws'. Arrangements were made.

He would come by train, a five-hour trip, and my wife would meet him at the station. She hadn't seen him since she worked for him one summer in Seattle ten years ago. But she and the blind man had kept in touch. They made tapes and mailed them back and forth. I wasn't enthusiastic about his visit. He was no one I knew. And his being blind bothered me. My idea of blindness came from the movies. In the movies, the blind moved slowly and never laughed. Sometimes they were led by seeing-eye dogs. A blind man in my house was not something I looked forward to.

That summer in Seattle she had needed a job. She didn't have any money. The man she was going to marry at the end of the summer was in officers' training school. He didn't have any money, either. But she was in love with the guy, and he was in love with her, etc. She'd seen something in the paper: HELP WANTED—*Reading to Blind Man*, and a telephone number. She phoned and went over, was hired on the spot. She'd worked with this blind man all summer. She read stuff to him, case studies, reports, that sort of thing. She helped him organize his little office in the county social-service department. They'd become good friends, my wife and the blind man. How do I know these things? She told me. And she told me something else. On her last day in the office, the blind man asked if he could touch her face. She agreed to this. She told me he touched his fingers to every part of her face, her nose—even her neck! She never forgot it. She even tried to write a poem about it. She was always trying to write a poem. She wrote a poem or two every year, usually after something really important had happened to her.

When we first started going out together, she showed me the poem. In the poem, she recalled his fingers and the way they had moved around over her face. In the poem, she talked about what she had felt at the time, about what went through her mind when the blind man touched her nose and lips. I can remember I didn't think much of the poem. Of course, I didn't tell her that. Maybe I just don't understand poetry. I admit it's not the first thing I reach for when I pick up something to read.

Anyway, this man who'd first enjoyed her favors, the officer-to-be, he'd been her childhood sweetheart. So okay. I'm saying that at the end of the summer she let the blind man run his hands over her face, said good-bye to him, married her childhood etc., who was now a commissioned officer, and she moved away from Seattle. But they'd kept in touch, she and the blind man. She made the first contact after a year or so. She called him up one night from an Air Force base in Alabama. She wanted to talk. They talked. He asked her to send a tape and tell him about her life. She did this. She sent the tape. On the tape, she told the blind man about her husband and about their life together in the military. She told the blind man she loved her husband but she didn't like it where they lived and she didn't like it that he was part of the military-industrial thing. She told the blind man she'd written a poem and he was in it. She told him that she was writing a poem about what it was like to be an Air Force officer's wife. The poem wasn't finished yet. She was still writing it. The blind man made a tape. He sent her the tape. She made a tape. This went on for years. My wife's officer was posted to one base and then another. She sent tapes from Moody AFB, McGuire, McConnell, and finally Travis, near Sacramento, where one night she got to feeling lonely and cut off from people she kept losing in that moving-around life. She got to feeling she couldn't go it another step. She went in and swallowed all the pills and capsules in the medicine chest and washed them down with a bottle of gin. Then she got into a hot bath and passed out.

But instead of dying, she got sick. She threw up. Her officer—why should he have a name? he was the childhood sweetheart, and what more does he want?—came home from somewhere, found her, and called the ambulance. In time, she put it all on a tape and sent the tape to the blind man. Over the years, she put all kinds of stuff on tapes and sent the tapes off lickety-split. Next to writing a poem every year, I think it was her chief means of recreation. On one tape, she told the blind man she'd decided to live away from her officer for a time. On another tape, she told him about her divorce. She and I began going out, and of course she told her blind man about it. She told him everything, or so it seemed to me. Once she asked me if I'd like to hear the latest tape from the blind man. This was a year ago. I was on the tape, she said. So I said okay, I'd listen to it. I got us drinks and we settled down in the living room. We made ready to listen. First she inserted the tape into the player and adjusted a couple of dials. The she pushed a lever. The tape squeaked and someone began to talk in this loud voice. She lowered the volume. After a few minutes of harmless chitchat, I heard my own name in the mouth of this stranger, this blind man I didn't even know! And then this: "From all you've said about him, I can only conclude—" But we were interrupted, a knock at the door, something, and we didn't ever get back to the tape. Maybe it was just as well. I'd heard all I wanted to.

Now this same blind man was coming to sleep in my house.

"Maybe I could take him bowling," I said to my wife. She was at the draining board doing scalloped potatoes. She put down the knife she was using and turned around.

"If you love me," she said, "you can do this for me. If you don't love me, okay. But if you had a friend, any friend, and the friend came to visit, I'd make him feel comfortable." She wiped her hands with the dish towel.

"I don't have any blind friends," I said.

"You don't have *any* friends," she said. "Period. Besides," she said, "goddamn it, his wife's just died! Don't you understand that? The man's lost his wife!"

I didn't answer. She'd told me a little about the blind man's wife. Her name was Beulah. Beulah! That's a name for a colored woman.

"Was his wife a Negro?" I asked.

"Are you crazy?" my wife said. "Have you just flipped or something?" She picked up a potato. I saw it hit the floor, then roll under the stove. "What's wrong with you?" she said. "Are you drunk?"

"I'm just asking," I said.

Right then my wife filled me in with more detail than I cared to know. I made a drink and sat at the kitchen table to listen. Pieces of the story began to fall into place.

Beulah had gone to work for the blind man the summer after my wife had stopped working for him. Pretty soon Beulah and the blind man had themselves a church wedding. It was a little wedding—who'd want to got to such a wedding in the first place?—just the two of them, plus the minister and the minister's wife. But it was a church wedding just the same. It was what Beulah had wanted, he'd said. But even then Beulah must have been carrying the cancer in her glands. After they had been inseparable for eight years—my wife's word, *inseparable*—Beulah's health went into a rapid decline. She died in a Seattle hospital room, the blind man sitting beside the bed and holding on to her hand. They'd married, lived and worked together, slept together—had sex, sure—and then the blind man had to bury her. All this without his having ever seen what the goddamned woman looked like. It was beyond my understanding. Hearing this, I felt sorry for the blind man for a little bit. And then I found myself thinking what a pitiful life this woman must have led. Imagine a woman who could never see herself as she was seen in the eyes of her loved one. A woman who could go on day after day and never receive the smallest compliment from her beloved. A woman whose husband could never read the expression on her face, be it misery or something better. Someone who could wear makeup or not—what difference to him? She could, if she wanted, wear green eye-shadow around one eye, a straight pin in her nostril, yellow slacks, and purple shoes, no matter. And then to slip off into death, the blind man's hand on her hand, his blind eyes streaming tears—I'm imagining now—her last thought maybe this: that he never even knew what she looked like, and she on an express to the grave. Robert was left with a small insurance policy and a half of a twenty-peso Mexican coin. The other half of the coin went into the box with her. Pathetic.

So when the time rolled around, my wife went to the depot to pick him up. With nothing to do but wait—sure, I blamed him for that—I was having a drink and watching the TV when I heard the car pull into the drive. I got up from the sofa with my drink and went to the window to have a look.

I saw my wife laughing as she parked the car. I saw her get out of the car and shut the door. She was still wearing a smile. Just amazing. She went around to the other side of the car to where the blind man was already starting to get out. This blind man, feature this, he was wearing a full beard! A beard on a blind man! Too much, I say. The blind man reached into the backseat and dragged out a suitcase. My wife took his arm, shut the car door, and, talking all the way, moved him down the drive and then up the steps to the front porch. I turned off the TV. I finished my drink, rinsed the glass, dried my hands. Then I went to the door.

My wife said, "I want you to meet Robert. Robert, this is my husband. I've told you all about him." She was beaming. She had this blind man by his coat sleeve.

The blind man let go of his suitcase and up came his hand.

I took it. He squeezed hard, held my hand, and then he let it go.

"I feel like we've already met," he boomed.

"Likewise," I said. I didn't know what else to say. Then I said, "Welcome. I've heard a lot about you." We began to move then, a little group, from the porch into the living room, my wife guiding him by the arm. The blind man was carrying his suitcase in his other hand. My wife said things like, "To your left here, Robert. That's right. Now watch it, there's a chair. That's it. Sit down right here. This is the sofa. We just bought this sofa two weeks ago."

I started to say something about the old sofa. I'd liked that old sofa. But I didn't say anything. Then I wanted to say something else, small-talk, about the scenic ride along the Hudson. How going *to* New York, you should sit on the right-hand side of the train, and coming *from* New York, the left-hand side.

"Did you have a good train ride?" I said. "Which side of the train did you sit on, by the way?"

"What a question, which side!" my wife said. "What's it matter which side?" she said.

"I just asked," I said.

"Right side," the blind man said. "I hadn't been on a train in nearly forty years. Not since I was a kid. With my folks. That's been a long time. I'd nearly forgotten the sensation. I have winter in my beard now," he said. "So I've been told, anyway. Do I look distinguished, my dear?" the blind man said to my wife.

"You look distinguished, Robert," she said. "Robert," she said. "Robert, it's just so good to see you."

My wife finally took her eyes off the blind man and looked at me. I had the feeling she didn't like what she saw. I shrugged.

I've never met, or personally known, anyone who was blind. This blind man was late forties, a heavy-set, balding man with stooped shoulders, as if he carried a great weight there. He wore brown slacks, brown shoes, a light-brown shirt, a tie, a sports coat. Spiffy. He also had this full beard. But he didn't use a cane and he didn't wear dark glasses. I'd always thought dark glasses were a must for the blind. Fact was, I wished he had a pair. At first glance, his eyes looked like anyone else's eyes. But if you looked close, there was something different about them. Too much white in the iris, for one thing, and the pupils seemed to move around in the sockets without his knowing it or being able to stop it. Creepy. As I stared at his face, I saw the left pupil turn in toward his nose while the other made an effort to keep in one place. But it was only an effort, for that eye was on the roam without his knowing it or wanting it to be.

I said, "Let me get you a drink. What's your pleasure? We have a little of everything. It's one of our pastimes."

"Bub, I'm a Scotch man myself," he said fast enough in this big voice.

"Right," I said. Bub! "Sure you are. I knew it."

He let his fingers touch his suitcase, which was sitting alongside the sofa. He was taking his bearings. I didn't blame him for that.

"I'll move that up to your room," my wife said.

"No, that's fine," the blind man said loudly. "It can go up when I go up."

"A little water with the Scotch?" I said.

"Very little," he said.

"I knew it," I said.

He said, "Just a tad. The Irish actor, Barry Fitzgerald?[1] I'm like that fellow. When I drink water, Fitzgerald said, I drink water. When I drink whiskey, I drink whiskey." My wife laughed. The blind man brought his hand up under his beard. He lifted his beard slowly and let it drop.

I did the drinks, three big glasses of Scotch with a splash of water in each. Then we made ourselves comfortable and talked about Robert's travels. First the long flight from the West Coast to Connecticut, we covered that. Then from Connecticut up here by train. We had another drink concerning that leg of the trip.

I remembered having read somewhere that the blind didn't smoke because, as speculation had it, they couldn't see the smoke they exhaled. I thought I knew that much and that much only about blind people. But this blind man smoked his cigarette down to the nubbin and then lit another one. This blind man filled his ashtray and my wife emptied it.

When we sat down at the table for dinner, we had another drink. My wife heaped Robert's plate with cube steak, scalloped potatoes, green beans. I buttered him up two slices of bread. I said, "Here's bread and butter for you." I swallowed some of my drink. "Now let us pray," I said, and the blind man lowered his head. My wife looked at me, her mouth agape. "Pray the phone won't ring and the food doesn't get cold," I said.

We dug in. We ate everything there was to eat on the table. We ate like there was no tomorrow. We didn't talk. We ate. We scarfed. We grazed that table. We were into serious eating. The blind man had right away located his foods, he knew just where everything was on his plate. I watched with admiration as he used his knife and fork on the meat. He'd cut two pieces of meat, fork the meat into his mouth, and then go all

[1] Barry Fitzgerald (1888–1961), born in Dublin, was a stage, film, and television actor.

out for the scalloped potatoes, the beans next, and then he'd tear off a hunk of buttered bread and eat that. He'd follow this up with a big drink of milk. It didn't seem to brother him to use his fingers once in a while, either.

We finished everything, including half a strawberry pie. For a few moments, we sat as if stunned. Sweat beaded on our faces. Finally, we got up from the table and left the dirty plates. We didn't look back. We took ourselves into the living room and sank into our places again. Robert and my wife sat on the sofa. I took the big chair. We had us two or three more drinks while they talked about the major things that had come to pass for them in the past ten years. For the most part, I just listened. Now and then I joined in. I didn't want him to think I'd left the room, and I didn't want her to think I was feeling left out. They talked of things that had happened to them—to them!—these past ten years. I waited in vain to hear my name on my wife's sweet lips: "And then my dear husband came into my life"—something like that. But I heard nothing of the sort. More talk of Robert. Robert had done a little of everything, it seemed, a regular blind jack-of-all-trades. But most recently he and his wife had had an Amway distributorship, from which, I gathered, they'd earned their living, such as it was. The blind man was also a ham radio operator. He talked in his loud voice about conversations he'd had with fellow operators in Guam, in the Philippines, in Alaska, and even in Tahiti. He said he'd have a lot of friends there if he ever wanted to go visit those places. From time to time, he'd turn his blind face toward me, put his hand under his beard, ask me something. How long had I been in my present position? (Three years.) Did I like my work? (I didn't.) Was I going to stay with it? (What were the options?) Finally, when I thought he was beginning to run down, I got up and turned on the TV.

My wife looked at me with irritation. She was heading toward a boil. Then she looked at the blind man and said, "Robert, do you have a TV?"

The blind man said, "My dear, I have two TVs. I have a color set and black-and-white thing, an old relic. It's funny, but if I turn the TV on, said I'm always turning it on, I turn on the color set. It's funny, don't you think?"

I didn't know what to say to that. I had absolutely nothing to say to that. No opinion. So I watched the news program and tried to listen to what the announcer was saying.

"This is a color TV," the blind man said. "Don' ask me how, but I can tell."

"We traded up a while ago," I said.

The blind man had another taste of his drink. He lifted his beard, sniffed it, and let it fall. He leaned forward on the sofa. He positioned his ashtray on the coffee table, then put the lighter to his cigarette. He leaned back on the sofa and crossed his legs at the ankles.

My wife covered her mouth, and then she yawned. She stretched. She said, "I think I'll go upstairs and put on my robe. I think I'll change into something else. Robert, you make yourself comfortable," she said.

"I'm comfortable," the blind man said.

"I want you to feel comfortable in this house," she said.

"I am comfortable," the blind man said.

After she'd left the room, he and I listened to the weather report and then to the sports roundup. By that time, she'd been gone so long I didn't know if she was going to come back. I thought she might have gone to bed. I wished she'd come back downstairs. I didn't want to be left alone with a blind man. I asked him if he wanted another drink, and he said sure. Then I asked if he wanted to smoke some dope with me. I said I'd just rolled a number. I hadn't, but I planned to do so in about two shakes.

"I'll try some with you," he said.

"Damn right," I said. "That's the stuff."

I got our drinks and sat down on the sofa with him. Then I rolled us two fat numbers. I lit one and passed it. I brought it to his fingers. He took it and inhaled.

"Hold it as long as you can," I said. I could tell he didn't know the first thing.

My wife came back downstairs wearing her pink robe and her pink slippers.

"What do I smell?" she said.

"We thought we'd have us some cannabis," I said.

My wife gave me a savage look. Then she looked at the blind man and said, "Robert, I didn't know you smoked."

He said, "I do now, my dear. There's a first time for everything. But I don't feel anything yet."

"This stuff is pretty mellow," I said. "This stuff is mild. It's dope you can reason with," I said. "It doesn't mess you up."

"Not much it doesn't, bub," he said, and laughed.

My wife sat on the sofa between the blind man and me. I passed her the number. She took it and toked and then passed it back to me. "Which way is this going?" she said. Then she said, "I shouldn't be smoking this. I can hardly keep my eyes open as it is. That dinner did me in. I shouldn't have eaten so much."

"It was the strawberry pie," the blind man said. "That's what did it," he said, and he laughed his big laugh. Then he shook his head.

"There's more strawberry pie," I said.

"Do you want some more, Robert?" my wife said.

"Maybe in a little while," he said.

We gave our attention to the TV. My wife yawned again. She said. "Your bed is made up when you feel like going to bed, Robert. I know you must have had a long day. When you're ready to go to bed, say so." She pulled his arm. "Robert?"

He came to and said, "I've had a real nice time. This beats tapes, doesn't it?"

I said, "Coming at you," and I put the number between his fingers. He inhaled, held the smoke, and then let it go. It was like he'd been doing it since he was nine years old.

"Thanks, bub," he said. "But I think this is all for me. I think I'm beginning to feel it," he said. He held the burning roach out for my wife.

"Same here," she said. "Ditto. Me, too." She took the roach and passed it to me. "I may just sit here for a while between you two guys with my eyes closed. But don't let me bother you, okay? Either one of you. If it bothers you, say so. Otherwise, I may just sit here with my eyes closed until you're ready to go to bed," she said. "Your bed's made up, Robert, when you're ready. It's right next to our room at the top of the stairs. We'll show you up when you're ready. You wake me up now, you guys, if I fall asleep." She said that and then she closed her eyes and went to sleep.

The news program ended. I got up and changed the channel. I sat back down on the sofa. I wished my wife hadn't pooped out. Her heady lay across the back of the sofa, her mouth open. She'd turned so that her robe slipped away from her legs, exposing a juicy thigh. I reached to draw her robe back over her, and it was then that I glanced at the blind man. What the hell! I flipped the robe open again.

"You say when you want some strawberry pie," I said.

"I will," he said.

I said, "Are you tired? Do you want me to take you up to your bed? Are you ready to hit the hay?"

"Not yet," he said. "No, I'll stay up with you, bub. If that's all right. I'll stay up until you're ready to turn in. We haven't had a chance to talk. Know what I mean? I feel like me and her monopolized the evening." He lifted his beard and he let it fall. He picked up his cigarettes and his lighter.

"That's all right," I said. Then I said, "I'm glad for the company."

And I guess I was. Every night I smoked dope and stayed up as long as I could before I fell asleep. My wife and I hardly ever went to bed at the same time. When I did go to sleep, I had these dreams. Sometimes I'd wake up from one of them, my heart going crazy.

Something about the church and the Middle Ages was on the TV. Not your run-of-the mill TV fare. I wanted to watch something else. I turned to the other channels. But there was nothing on them, either. So I turned back to the first channel and apologized.

"Bub, it's all right," the blind man said. "It's fine with me. Whatever you want to watch is okay. I'm always learning something. Learning never ends. It won't hurt me to learn something tonight. I got ears," he said.

We didn't say anything for a time. He was leaning forward with his head turned at me, his right ear aimed in the direction of the set. Very disconcerting. Now and then his eyelids drooped and then they snapped open again. Now and then he put his fingers into his beard and tugged, like he was thinking about something he was hearing on the television.

On the screen, a group of men wearing cowls was being set upon and tormented by men dressed in skeleton costumes and men dressed as devils. The men dressed as devils wore devil masks, horns, and long tails. This pageant was part of a procession. The Englishman who was narrating the thing said it took place in Spain once a year. I tried to explain to the blind man what was happening.

"Skeletons," he said. "I know about skeletons," he said, and he nodded.

The TV showed this one cathedral. Then there was a long, slow look at another one. Finally, the picture switched to the famous one in Paris, with its flying buttresses and its spires reaching up to the clouds. The camera pulled away to show the whole of the cathedral rising above the skyline.

There were times when the Englishman who was telling the thing would shut up, would simply let the camera move around the cathedrals. Or else the camera would tour the countryside, men in fields walking behind oxen. I waited as long as I could. Then I felt I had to say something. I said, "They're showing the outside of this cathedral now. Gargoyles. Little statues carved to look like monsters. Now I guess they're in Italy. Yeah, they're in Italy. There's paintings on the walls of this one church."

"Are those fresco paintings, bub?" he asked, and he sipped from his drink.

I reached for my glass. But it was empty. I tried to remember what I could remember. "You're asking me are those frescoes?" I said. "That's a good question. I don't know."

The camera moved to a cathedral outside Lisbon. The differences in the Portuguese cathedral compared with the French and Italian were not that great. But they were there. Mostly the interior stuff. Then something occurred to me, and I said, "Something has occurred to me. Do you have any idea what a cathedral is? What they look like, that is? Do you follow me? If somebody says cathedral to you, do you have any notion what they're talking about? Do you know the difference between that and a Baptist church, say?"

He let the smoke dribble from his mouth. "I know they took hundreds of workers fifty or a hundred years to build," he said. "I just heard the man say that, of course. I know generations of the same families worked on a cathedral. I heard him say that, too. The men who began their life's work on them, they never lived to see the completion of their work. In that wise, bub, they're no different from the rest of us, right?" He laughed. Then his eyelids drooped again. His head nodded. He seemed to be snoozing. Maybe he was imaging himself in Portugal. The TV was showing another cathedral now. This one was in Germany. The Englishman's voice droned on. "Cathedrals," the blind man said. He sat up and rolled his head back and forth. "If you want the truth, bub, that's about all I know. What I just said. What I heard him say. But maybe you could describe one to me? I wish you'd do it. I'd like that. If you want to know, I really don't have a good idea."

I stared hard at the shot of the cathedral on the TV. How could I even begin to describe it? But say my life depended on it. Say my life was being threatened by an insane guy who said I had to do it or else.

I stared some more at the cathedral before the picture flipped off into the countryside. There was no use. I turned to the blind man and said, "To begin with, they're very tall." I was looking around the room for clues. "They reach way up. Up and up. Toward the sky. They're so big, some of them, they have to have these supports. To help hold them up, so to speak. These supports are called buttresses. They remind me of viaducts, for some reason. But maybe you don't know viaducts, either? Sometimes the cathedrals have devils and such carved into the front. Sometimes lords and ladies. Don't ask me why this is," I said.

He was nodding. The whole upper part of his body seemed to be moving back and forth.

"I'm not doing so good, am I?" I said.

He stopped nodding and leaned forward on the edge of the sofa. As he listened to me, he was running his fingers through his beard. I wasn't getting through to him, I could see that. But he waited for me to go on just the same. He nodded, like he was trying to encourage me. I tried to think what else to say. "They're really big," I said. "They're massive. They're built of stone. Marble, too, sometimes. In those olden days, when they build cathedrals, men wanted to be close to God. In those olden days, God was an important part of everyone's life. You could tell this from their cathedral-building. I'm sorry," I said, "but it looks like that's the best I can do for you. I'm just no good at it."

"That's all right, bub," the blind man said. "Hey, listen. I hope you don't mind my asking you. Can I ask you something? Let me ask you a simple question, yes or no. I'm just curious and there's no offense. You're my host. But let me ask if you are in any way religious? You don't mind my asking?"

I shook my head. He couldn't see that, though. A wink is the same as a nod to a blind man. "I guess I don't believe in it. In anything. Sometimes it's hard. You know what I'm saying?"

"Sure, I do," he said.

"Right," I said.

The Englishman was still holding forth. My wife sighed in her sleep. She drew a long breath and went on with her sleeping.

"You'll have to forgive me," I said. "But I can't tell you what a cathedral looks like. It just isn't in me to do it. I can't do any more than I've done."

The blind man sat very still, his head down, as he listened to me.

I said, "The truth is, cathedrals don't mean anything special to me. Nothing, Cathedrals. They're something to look at on late-night TV. That's all they are."

It was then that the blind man cleared his throat. He brought something up. He took a handkerchief from his back pocket. Then he said, "I get it, bub. It's okay. It happens. Don't worry about it," he said. "Hey, listen to me. Will you do me a favor? I got an idea. Why don't you find us some heavy paper? And a pen. We'll do something. We'll draw one together. Get us a pen and some heavy paper. Go on, bub, get the stuff," he said.

So I went upstairs. My legs felt like they didn't have any strength in them. They felt like they did after I'd done some running. In my wife's room I looked around. I found some ballpoints in a little basket on her table. And then I tried to think where to look for the kind of paper he was talking about.

Downstairs, in the kitchen, I found a shopping bag with onion skins in the bottom of the bag. I emptied the bag and shook it. I brought it into the living room and sat down with it near his legs. I moved some things, smoothed the wrinkles from the bag, spread it out on the coffee table.

The blind man got down from the sofa and sat next to me on the carpet.

He ran his fingers over the paper. He went up and down the sides of the paper. The edges, even the edges. He fingered the corners.

"All right," he said. "All right, let's do her."

He found my hand, the hand with the pen. He closed his hand over my hand. "Go ahead, bub, draw," he said. "Draw. You'll see. I'll follow along with you. It'll be okay. Just begin now like I'm telling you. You'll see. Draw," the blind man said.

So I began. First I drew a box that looked like a house. It could have been the house I lived in. Then I put a roof on it. At either end of the roof, I drew spires. Crazy.

"Swell," he said. "Terrific. You're doing fine," he said. "Never thought anything like this could happen in your lifetime, did you, bub? Well, it's strange life, we all know that. Go on now. Keep it up."

I put in windows with arches. I drew flying buttresses. I hung great doors. I couldn't stop. The TV station went off the air. I put down the pen and closed and opened my fingers. The blind man felt around over the paper. He moved the tips of his fingers over the paper, all over what I had drawn, and he nodded.

"Doing fine," the blind man said.

I took up the pen again, and he found my hand. I kept at it. I'm no artist. But I kept drawing just the same.

My wife opened up her eyes and gazed at us. She sat up on the sofa, her robe hanging open. She said, "What are you doing? Tell me, I want to know."

I didn't answer her.

The blind man said, "We're drawing a cathedral. Me and him are working on it. Press hard," he said to me. "That's right. That's good," he said. "Sure. You got it, bub, I can tell. You didn't think you could. But you can, can't you? You're cooking with gas now. You know what I'm saying? We're going to really have us something here in a minute. How's the old arm? "he said. "Put some people in there now. What's a cathedral without people?"

My wife said, "What's going on? Robert, what are you doing? What's going on?"

"It's all right," he said to her. "Close your eyes now," the blind man said to me.

I did it. I closed them just like he said.

"Are they closed?" he said. "Don't fudge."

"They're closed," I said.

"Keep them that way," he said. He said, "Don't stop now. Draw."

So we kept on with it. His fingers rode my fingers as my hand went over the paper. It was like nothing else in my life up to now.

Then he said, "I think that's it. I think you got it," he said. "Take a look. What do you think?"

But I had my eyes closed. I thought I'd keep them that way for a little longer. I thought it was something I ought to do.

"Well?" he said. "Are you looking?"

My eyes were still closed. I was in my house. I knew that. But I didn't feel like I was inside anything.

"It's really something," I said.

[1981]

TONI CADE BAMBARA ■ (1939–1995)

The author of a much admired and influential multilayered, experimental novel, *The Salt Eaters* (1980), which explores religious and spiritual traditions in the town of Claybourne, Georgia, in the 1970s, and two collections of short stories, Toni Cade Bambara was born in New York City. She absorbed the sights and sounds of African American politics and music (she said that jazz and other kinds of musicians educated her about "voice and pace and pitch") and, later, found support and inspiration in Toni Morrison, who became her friend as well as her editor.

Bambara graduated from Queens College in 1959, honored already for her fiction-writing and journalism. She then attended graduate school at Columbia University while employed in New York City as a social worker. During the 1960s and 1970s she was active in social protest movements and theater groups, published many essays and stories, and taught at a number of colleges and universities. Bambara edited two noteworthy anthologies, *The Black Woman* (1970) and *Tales and Stories for Black Folks* (1971), and published her first book of stories, *Gorilla, My Love* (1972), from which the following story, a vibrant, incisive rendering of a narrator's voice is taken. This story shows Bambara's creative, affectionate response to and understanding of the rhythms of urban speech—its energy, speed, and complexity. As her career progressed, Bambara became a writer of and narrator for a number of documentary films, including one on Malcolm X and another on the jazz saxophonist John Coltrane. *The Sea Birds Are Still Alive: Collected Stories* was published in 1977. A posthumously published novel, *Those Bones Are Not My Child*, based in the Atlanta Child Murders of the early eighties, appeared in 2000.

For further reading, see *Toni Cade Bambara, Deep Sightings and Rescue Missions: Fiction, Essays, and Conversations* (1996). For critical discussion, see Susan Willis, *Specifying: Black Women Writing the American Experience* (1987); and Elliott Butler-Evans, *Race, Gender, and Desire: Narrative Strategies in the Fiction of Toni Cade Bambara, Toni Morrison, and Alice Walker* (1989).

The Lesson

Back in the days when everyone was old and stupid or young and foolish and me and Sugar were the only ones just right, this lady moved on our block with nappy hair and proper speech and no makeup. And quite naturally we laughed at her, laughed the way we did at the junk man who went about his business like he was some big-time president and his sorry-ass horse his secretary. And we kinda hated her too, hated the way we did the winos who cluttered up our parks and pissed on our handball walls and stank up our hallways and stairs so you couldn't halfway play hide-and-seek without a goddamn gas mask. Miss Moore was her name. The only woman on the block with no first name. And she was black as hell, cept for her feet, which were fish-white and spooky. And she was always planning these boring-ass things for us to do, us being my cousin, mostly, who lived on the block cause we all moved North the same time and to the same apartment then spread out gradual to breathe. And our parents would yank our heads into some kinda shape and crisp up our clothes so we'd be presentable for travel with Miss Moore, who always looked like she was going to church, though she never did. Which is just one of things the grownups talked about when they talked behind her back like a dog. But when she came calling with some sachet she'd sewed up or some gingerbread she'd made or some book, why then they'd all be too embarrassed to turn her down and we'd get handed over all spruced up. She'd been to college and said it was only right that she should take responsibility for the young ones' education, and she not even related by marriage or blood. So they'd go for it. Specially Aunt Gretchen. She was the main gofer in the family. You got some ole dumb shit foolishness you want somebody to go for, you send for Aunt Gretchen. She been screwed into the go-along for so long, it's a blood-deep natural thing with her. Which is how she got saddled with me and Sugar and junior in the first place while our mothers were in a la-de-da apartment up the block having a good ole time.

So this one day Miss Moore rounds us all up at the mailbox and it's puredee hot and she's knockin herself out about arithmetic. And school suppose to let up in summer I heard, but she don't never let up. And the starch in my pinafore scratching the shit outta me and I'm really hating this nappy-head bitch and her goddamn college degree. I'd much rather go to the pool or to the show where it's cool. So me and Sugar leaning on the mailbox being surly, which is a Miss Moore word. And Flyboy checking out what everybody brought for lunch. And Fat Butt already wasting his peanut-butter-and-jelly sandwich like the pig he is. And Junebug punchin on Q.T.'s arm for potato chips. And Rosie Giraffe shifting from one hip to the other waiting for somebody to step on her foot or ask her if she from Georgia so she can kick ass, preferably Mercedes'. And Miss Moore asking us do we know what money is, like we a bunch of retards. I mean real money, she say, like it's only poker chips or monopoly papers we lay on the grocer. So right away I'm tired of this and say so. And would much rather snatch Sugar and go to the Sunset and terrorize the West Indian kids and take their hair ribbons and their money too. And Miss Moore files that remark away for next week's lesson on brotherhood, I can tell. And finally I say we oughta get to the subway cause it's cooler and besides we might meet some cute boys. Sugar done swiped her mama's lipstick, so we ready.

So we heading down the street and she's boring us silly about what things cost and what our parents make and how much goes for rent and how money ain't divided up right in this country. And then she gets to the part about we all poor and live in the slums, which I don't feature. And I'm ready to speak on that, but she steps out in the street and hails two cabs just like that. Then she hustles half the crew in with her and hands me a five-dollar bill and tells me to calculate 10 percent tip for the driver. And we're off. Me and Sugar and Junebug and Flyboy hangin out the window and hollering to everybody, putting lipstick on each other cause Flyboy a faggot anyway, and making farts with our sweaty armpits. But I'm mostly trying to figure how to spend this money. But they all fascinated with the meter ticking and Junebug starts laying bets as to how much it'll read when Flyboy can't hold his breath no more. Then Sugar lays bets as to how much it'll be when we get there. So I'm stuck. Don't nobody want to go for my plan, which is to jump out at the next light and run off to the first bar-b-que we can find. Then the driver tells us to get the hell out cause we there already. And the meter reads eighty-five cents. And I'm stalling to figure out the tip and Sugar say give him a dime. And I decide he don't need it bad as I do, so later for him. But then he tries to take off with Junebug foot still in the door so we talk about his mama something ferocious. Then we check out that we on Fifth Avenue[1] and everybody dressed up in stockings. One lady in a fur coat, hot as it is. White folks crazy.

"This is the place," Miss Moore say, presenting it to us in the voice she uses at the museum. "Let's look in the windows before we go in."

"Can we steal?" Sugar asks very serious like she's getting the ground rules squared away before she plays, "I beg your pardon," say Miss Moore, and we fall out. So she leads us around the windows of the toy store and me and Sugar screamin, "This is mine, that's mine, I gotta have that, that was made for me, I was born for that," till Big Butt drowns us out.

"Hey, I'm goin to buy that there."

"That there? You don't even know what it is, stupid."

"I do so," he say punchin on Rosie Giraffe. "It's a microscope."

"Whatcha gonna do with a microscope, fool?"

"Look at things."

"Like what, Ronald?" ask Miss Moore. And Big Butt ain't got the first notion. So here go Miss Moore gabbing about the thousands of bacteria in a drop of water and the somethinorother in a speck of blood and the million and one living things in the air around us is invisible to the naked eye. And what she say that for? Junebug go to town on that "naked" and we rolling. Then Miss Moore ask what it cost. So we all jam into the window smudgin it up and the price tag say $300. So then she ask how long'd take for Big Butt and Junebug to save up their allowances, "Too long," I say. "Yeh," adds Sugar, "outgrown it by that time." And Miss Moore say no, you never outgrow learning instruments. "Why, even medical students and interns and," blah, blah, blah. And we ready to choke Big Butt for bringing it up in the first damn place.

[1]A fashionable street in Manhattan.

"This here costs four hundred eighty dollars," say Rosie Giraffe. So we pile up all over her to see what she pointin out. My eyes tell me it's a chunk of glass cracked with something heavy, and different-color inks dripped into the splits, then the whole thing put into a oven or something. But for $480 it don't make sense.

"That's a paperweight made of semi-precious stones fused together under tremendous pressure," she explains slowly, with her hands doing the mining and all the factory work.

"So what's a paperweight?" asks Rosie Giraffe.

"To weigh paper with, dumbbell," say Flyboy, the wise man from the East.

"Not exactly," say Miss Moore, which is what she say when you warm or way off too. "It's to weigh paper down so it won't scatter and make your desk untidy." So right away me and Sugar curtsy to each other and then to Mercedes who is more the tidy type.

"We don't keep paper on top of the desk in my class," say Junebug, figuring Miss Moore crazy or lyin one.

"At home, then," she say. "Don't you have a calendar and a pencil case and a blotter and a letter-opener on your desk at home where you do your homework?" And she know damn well what our homes look like cause she nosys around in them every chance she gets.

"I don't even have a desk," say Junebug. "Do we?"

"No. And I don't get no homework neither," say Big Butt.

"And I don't even have a home," say Flyboy like he do at school to keep the white folks off his back and sorry for him. Send this poor kid to camp posters, is his specialty.

"I do," says Mercedes. "I have a box of stationery on my desk and a picture of my cat. My godmother bought the stationery and the desk. There's a big rose on each sheet and the envelopes smell like roses."

"Who wants to know about your smelly-ass stationery," say Rosie Giraffe fore I can get my two cents in.

"It's important to have a work area all your own so that..."

"Will you look at this sailboat, please," say Flyboy, cuttin her off and pointin to the thing like it was his. So once again we tumble all over each other to gaze at this magnificent thing in the toy store which is just big enough to maybe sail two kittens across the pond if you strap them to the posts tight. We all start reciting the price tag like we in assembly. "Handcrafted sailboat of fiberglass at one thousand one hundred ninety-five dollars."

"Unbelievable," I hear myself say and am really stunned. I read it again for myself just in case the group recitation put me in a trance. Same thing. For some reason this pisses me off. We look at Miss Moore and she lookin at us, waiting for I dunno what.

"Who'd pay all that when you can buy a sailboat set for a quarter at Pop's, a tube of glue for a dime, and a ball of string for eight cents?"

"It must have a motor and a whole lot else besides," I say. "My sailboat cost me about fifty cents."

"But will it take water?" say Mercedes with her smart ass.

"Took mine to Alley Pond Park once," say Flyboy. "String broke. Lost it. Pity."

"Sailed mine in Central Park and it keeled over and sank. Had to ask my father for another dollar."

"And you got the strap," laugh Big Butt. "The jerk didn't even have a string on it. My old man wailed on his behind."

Little Q.T. was staring hard at the sailboat and you could see he wanted it bad. But he too little and somebody'd just take it from him. So what the hell. "This boat for kids, Miss Moore?"

"Parents silly to buy something like that just to get all broke up," say Rosie Giraffe.

"That much money it should last forever," I figure.

"My father'd buy it for me if I wanted it."

"Your father, my ass," say Rosie Giraffe getting a chance to finally push Mercedes.

"Must be rich people shop here," say Q.T.

"You are a very bright boy," say Flyboy. "What was your first clue?" And he rap him on the head with the back of his knuckles, since Q.T. the only one he could get away with. Though Q.T. liable to come up behind you years later and get his licks in when you half expect it.

"What I want to know is," I says to Miss Moore though I never talk to her. I wouldn't give the bitch that satisfaction, "is how much a real boat costs? I figure a thousand'd get you a yacht any day."

"Why don't you check that out," she says, "and report back to the group?" Which really pains my ass. If you gonna mess up a perfectly good swim day least you could do is have some answers. "Let's go in," she say like she got something up her sleeve. Only she don't lead the way. So me and Sugar turn the corner to where the entrance is, but when we get there I kinda hang back. Not that I'm scared, what's there to be afraid of, just a toy store. But I feel funny, shame. But what I got to be shamed about? Got as much right to go in as anybody. But somehow I can't seem to get hold of the door, so I step away for Sugar to lead. But she hangs back too. And I look at her and she looks at me and this is ridiculous. I mean, damn, I have never ever been shy about doing nothing or going nowhere. But then Mercedes steps up and then Rosie Giraffe and Big Butt crowd in behind and shove, and next thing we all stuffed into the doorway with only Mercedes squeezing past us, smoothing out her jumper and walking right down the aisle. Then the rest of us tumble in like a glued-together jigsaw done all wrong. And people lookin at us. And it's like the time me and Sugar crashed into the Catholic church on a dare. But once we got in there and everything so hushed and holy and the candles and the bowin and the handkerchiefs on all the drooping heads. I just couldn't go through with the plan. Which was for me to run up to the altar and do a tap dance while Sugar played the nose flute and messed around in the holy water. And Sugar kept givin me the elbow. Then later teased me so bad I tied her up in the shower and turned it on and locked her in. And she'd be there till this day if Aunt Gretchen hadn't finally figured I was lyin about the boarder takin a shower.

Same thing in the store. We all walkin on tiptoe and hardly touchin the games and puzzles and things. And I watched Miss Moore who is steady watchin us like she waitin for a sign. Like Mama Drewery watches the sky and sniffs the air and takes note of just how much slant is in the bird formation. Then me and Sugar bump smack into each other, so busy gazing at the toys, 'specially the sailboat. But we don't laugh and go into our fat-lady bump-stomach routine. We just stare at that price tag. Then Sugar run a finger over the whole boat. And I'm jealous and want to hit her. Maybe not her, but I sure want to punch somebody in the mouth.

"Watcha bring us here for, Miss Moore?"

"You sound angry, Sylvia. Are you mad about something?" Givin me one of them grins like she tellin a grown-up joke that never turns out to be funny. And she's lookin very closely at me like maybe she plannin to do my portrait from memory. I'm mad, but I won't give her that satisfaction. So I slouch around the store bein very bored and say, "Let's go."

Me and Sugar at the back of the train watchin the tracks whizzin by large then small then gettin gobbled up in the dark. I'm thinkin about this tricky toy I saw in the store. A clown that somersaults on a bar then does chin-ups just cause you yank lightly at his leg. Cost $35. I could see me askin my mother for a $35 birthday clown. "You wanna who that costs what?" she'd say, cocking her head to the side to get a better view of the hole in my head. Thirty-five dollars could buy new bunk beds for Junior and Gretchen's boy. Thirty-five dollars and the whole household could go visit Granddaddy Nelson in the country. Thirty-five dollars would pay for the rent and the piano bill too. Who are these people that spend that much for performing clowns and $1,000 for toy sailboats? What kinda work they do and how they live and how come we ain't in on it? Where we are is who we are, Miss Moore always pointin out. But it don't necessarily have to be that way, she always adds then waits for somebody to say that poor people have to wake up and demand their share of the pie and don't none of us know what kind of pie she talkin about in the first damn place. But she ain't so smart cause I still got her four dollars from the taxi and she sure ain't gettin it. Messin up my day with this shit. Sugar nudges me in my pocket and winks.

Miss Moore lines us up in front of the mailbox where we started from, seem like years ago, and I got a headache for thinkin so hard. And we lean all over each other so we can hold up under the draggy-ass lecture she always finishes us off with at the end before we thank her for borin us to tears. But she just looks at us like she readin tea leaves. Finally she say, "Well, what did you think of F.A.O. Schwarz?"[2]

Rosie Giraffe mumbles, "White folks crazy."

"I'd like to go there again when I get my birthday money," says Mercedes, and we shove her out the pack so she has to lean on the mailbox by herself.

"I'd like a shower. Tiring day," say Flyboy.

Then Sugar surprises me by sayin, "You know, Miss Moore, I don't think all of us here put together eat in a year what that sailboat costs." And Miss Moore lights up like somebody goosed her. "And?" she say, urging Sugar on. Only I'm standin on her foot so she don't continue.

"Imagine for a minute what kind of society it is in which some people can spend on a toy what it would cost to feed a family of six or seven. What do you think?"

"I think," say Sugar pushing me off her feet like she never done before, cause I whip her ass in a minute, "that this is not much of a democracy if you ask me. Equal chance to pursue happiness means an equal crack at the dough, don't it?" Miss Moore is besides herself and I am disgusted with Sugar's treachery. So I stand on her foot one more time to see if she'll shove me. She shuts up, and Miss Moore looks at me, sorrowfully I'm thinkin. And somethin weird is goin on, I can feel it in my chest.

"Anybody else learn anything today?" lookin dead at me.

I walk away and Sugar has to run to catch up and don't even seem to notice when I shrug her arm off my shoulder.

"Well, we got four dollars anyway," she says.

"Uh hunh."

"We could go to Hascombs and get half a chocolate layer and then go to the Sunset and still have plenty money for potato chips and ice-cream sodas."

"Uh hunh."

"Race you to Hascombs," she say.

We start down the block and she gets ahead which is O.K. by me cause I'm goin to the West End and then over to the Drive to think this day through. She can run if she want to and even run faster. But ain't nobody gonna beat me at nuthin.

[1972]

---

[2]An upscale toy store located on Fifth Avenue, New York City.

TERRENCE MCNALLY ■ (1939–)

"I'm a gay man who writes plays," Terrence McNally has said. One of America's leading dramatists, the winner of numerous fellowships and honors (including four Tony Awards), he was born in St. Petersburg, Florida, grew up in Corpus Christi, Texas, and received his undergraduate degree at Columbia University. By his mid-twenties he was already an esteemed playwright, especially for his comedies, but his first major success came with *Frankie and Johnny at the Claire de Lune* (1987), which he later adapted for a film starring Al Pacino and Michelle Pfeiffer.

Recent work includes *Lips Together, Teeth Apart* (1991), which deals with prejudice against homosexuals and AIDS victims; the musical adaptation (1992) of Manuel Puig's *Kiss of the Spider Woman* (1992), about two men imprisoned in South America; *Love! Valour! Compassion!* (1994), dealing with the relationships of eight gay men who spend summer weekends together in a house in upstate New York; *Master Class* (1995), on the opera star Maria Callas; the musical adaptation (1997) of E. L. Doctorow's novel *Ragtime; Corpus Christi* (1997), a highly controversial drama that depicts Jesus and his apostles as homosexuals; and the musical *The Full Monty* (2000), about a group of men in need of money who launch a striptease act.

Andre's Mother is the original version (1988) of a play exploring the relationship between the mother of a young man who has died from AIDS and his lover, which McNally later expanded and revised for a television production (1990) for which he was awarded an Emmy for Best Writing in a Miniseries or Special.

For biography and context, see interviews in *A Search for a Postmodern Theater: Interviews with Contemporary Playwrights*, ed. John L. DiGaetani (1991), 219–228; *The Playwright's Art: Conversations with Contemporary American Dramatists*, ed. Jackson R. Bryer (1995), 182–204; and *Speaking on Stage: Interviews with Contemporary American Playwrights*, ed. Philip C. Kolin and Colby H. Kullman (1996), 332–345.

Andre's Mother

CHARACTERS

Cal, *a young man*
Arthur, *his father*
Penny, *his sister*
Andre's Mother

Time. *Now*
Place. *New York City, Central Park*

Four people—Cal, Arthur, Penny, and Andre's Mother—enter. They are nicely dressed and each carries a white helium-filled balloon on a string.

Cal: You know what's really terrible? I can't think of anything terrific to say. Goodbye. I love you. I'll miss you. And I'm supposed to be so great with words!

Penny: What's that over there?

Arthur: Ask your brother.

Cal: It's a theatre. An outdoor theatre. They do plays there in the summer. Shakespeare's plays. (*To Andre's Mother.*) God, how much he wanted to play Hamlet again. He would have gone to Timbuktu to have another go at that part. The summer he did it in Boston, he was so happy!

Penny: Cal, I don't think she...! It's not the time. Later.

Arthur: Your son was a...the Jews have a word for it...

Penny (*quietly appalled*): Oh my God!

Arthur: Mensch,[1] I believe it is, and I think I'm using it right. It means warm, solid, the real thing. Correct me if I'm wrong.

Penny: Fine, Dad, fine. Just quit while you're ahead.

Arthur: I won't say he was like a son to me. Even my son isn't always like a son to me. I mean...! In my clumsy way, I'm trying to say how much I liked Andre. And how much he helped me to know my own boy. Cal was always two handsful but Andre and I could talk about anything under the sun. My wife was very fond of him, too.

Penny: Cal, I don't understand about the balloons.

Cal: They represent the soul. When you let go, it means you're letting his soul ascend to Heaven. That you're willing to let go. Breaking the last earthly ties.

Penny: Does the Pope know about this?

Arthur: Penny!

Penny: Andre loved my sense of humor. Listen, you can hear him laughing. (*She lets go of her white balloon.*) So long, you glorious, wonderful, I-know-what-Cal-means-about-words...*man*! God forgive me for wishing you were straight every time I laid eyes on you. But if any man was going to have you, I'm glad it was my brother! Look how fast it went up. I bet that means something. Something terrific.

Arthur (*lets his balloon go*): Goodbye. God speed.

Penny: Cal?

Cal: I'm not ready yet.

Penny: Okay. We'll be over there. Come on, Pop, you can buy your little girl a Good Humor.[2]

---

[1]A person of high integrity, morals, and honor (Yiddish).
[2]An ice cream bar on a stick, originally sold from trucks.

Arthur: They still make Good Humor?

Penny: Only now they're called Dove Bars[3] and they cost twelve dollars.

(Penny takes Arthur off. Cal and Andre's Mother stand with their balloons.)

Cal: I wish I knew what you were thinking. I think it would help me. You know almost nothing about me and I only know what Andre told me about you. I'd always had it in my mind that one day we would be friends, you and me. But if you didn't know about Andre and me... If this hadn't happened, I wonder if he would have ever told you. When he was sick, if I asked him once I asked him a thousand times, tell her. She's your mother. She won't mind. But he was so afraid of hurting you and of your disapproval. I don't know which was worse. *(No response. He sighs.)* God, how many of us live in this city because we don't want to hurt our mothers and live in mortal terror of their disapproval. We lose ourselves here. Our lives aren't furtive, just our feelings toward people like you are! A city of fugitives from our parents' scorn or heartbreak. Sometimes he'd seem a little down and I'd say, "What's the matter, babe?" and this funny sweet, sad smile would cross his face and he'd say, "Just a little homesick, Cal, just a little bit." I always accused him of being a country boy just playing at being a hotshot, sophisticated New Yorker. *(He sighs.)*

It's bullshit. It's all bullshit. *(Still no response.)*

Do you remember the comic strip *Little Lulu*?[4] Her mother had no name, she was so remote, so formidable to all the children. She was just Lulu's mother. "Hello, Lulu's Mother," Lulu's friends would say. She was almost anonymous in her remoteness. You remind me of her. Andre's mother. Let me answer the questions you can't ask and then I'll leave you alone and you won't ever have to see me again. Andre died of AIDS.[5] I don't know how he got it. I tested negative. He died bravely. You would have been proud of him. The only thing that frightened him was you. I'll have everything that was his sent to you. I'll pay for it. There isn't much. You should have come up the summer he played Hamlet. He was magnificent. Yes, I'm bitter. I'm bitter I've lost him. I'm bitter what's happening. I'm bitter even now, after all this, I can't reach you. I'm beginning to feel your disapproval and it's making me ill. *(He looks at his balloon.)* Sorry, old friend. I blew it. *(He lets go of the balloon.)*

[3] An ice cream bar.

[4] The *Little Lulu* comic strip was created by Marjorie (Marge) Henderson Buell in 1935.

[5] HIV (human immunodeficiency virus) weakens the body's immune defenses by destroying T-cell lymphocytes, rendering the body vulnerable to many types of opportunistic infections, cancers, and neurological illnesses. The entire spectrum of symptoms and illnesses that can occur when HIV infection depletes the immune system's defenses is called AIDS (acquired immunodeficiency syndrome).

Good night, sweet prince,[6] and flights of angels sing thee to thy
rest!

(*Beat.*)

Goodbye, Andre's mother.

(*He goes. Andre's Mother stands alone holding her white balloon. Her lips
tremble. She looks on the verge of breaking down. She is about to let go of
the balloon when she pulls it down to her. She looks at it awhile before she
gently kisses it. She lets go of the balloon. She follows it with her eyes as it
rises and rises. The lights are beginning to fade. Andre's Mother's eyes are
still on the balloon. The lights fade.*)

(1988)

---

[6]A quote from Shakespeare's tragedy *Hamlet*, spoken by Horatio on Hamlet's death (Act V. ii. 359–360).

ALICE WALKER ■ (1944—)

A skillful writer in a range of genres, including the novel, poem, short story, and essay, Alice Walker arrived on the American literary scene in a major way with the publication of *The Color Purple* in 1982, winner of both the Pulitzer Prize and the National Book Award. In 1985 the novel served as the basis for a film directed by Steven Spielberg, and in 2005 it was adopted as a Broadway musical. But Walker had already written a number of significant books, including two novels, *The Third Life of Grange Copeland* (1970) and *Meridian* (1976); two collections of short stories, *In Love and Trouble* (1973, which includes the story "Everyday Use") and *You Can't Keep a Good Woman Down* (1981); and several volumes of verse. Innovative and experimental in her approach to literary forms, Walker has explored—often controversially—the topics of race, religion, class, sexuality, and gender from multiple points of view.

Walker was born in Eatonton, Georgia, the eighth child of a sharecropper and a part-time maid. She was an outstanding student in high school and attended Spelman College and Sarah Lawrence College. She next lived in New York City, working for the Welfare Department, but following her marriage to Mel Leventhal, a Jewish lawyer and civil rights activist, she returned to the South, settling with her husband in Jackson, Mississippi. There she was involved in the campaign against racism and segregation even as she produced a number of her best literary works. "Writing," she observed, "saved me from the sin and inconvenience of violence."

Walker has taught at many colleges and universities, and through her teaching and critical writing she has helped to launch important changes in the literary canon and curriculum. In her collection *In Search of Our Mothers' Gardens* (1983) and other books, Walker effectively called, for example, for a renewed attention to Zora Neale Hurston, whose book *Their Eyes Were Watching God* (1937) is now widely regarded as a classic of modern American and African American fiction. And Walker's treatment of the bonds between and among African American women writers has not only enriched the understanding of this body of work but also stimulated a lively discussion and debate about its relationship to the traditions of white southern writing in William Faulkner, Flannery O'Connor (about whom Walker said, she is "the first great modern writer from the South"), Eudora Welty, and others.

Walker's other books include the novels *The Temple of My Familiar* (1989) and *Possessing the Secret of Joy* (1992). Her poetry collections include *Now Is the Time to Open Your Heart* (2005), *Her Blue Body Everything We Know: Earthling Poems, 1965–1990* (1991), and *Hard Times Require Furious Dancing: A Year of Poems* (2010).

"Everyday Use," her best-known story, shows Walker's interest in the sometimes divisive, sometimes nurturing, tensions between mothers and daughters, the pains and rewards of family life, and the complex impact—both a burden and a blessing—of racial heritage upon identity.

For critical response and context, see Donna Haisty Winchell, *Alice Walker* (1992); *Alice Walker: Critical Perspectives Past and Present*, eds. Henry Louis Gates Jr. and K. A. Appiah (1993); and Ikenna Dieke, *Critical Essays on Alice Walker* (1999). A biography, *Alice Walker: A Life*, by Evelyn C. White, was published in 2005.

Everyday Use

For Your Grandmama

I will wait for her in the yard that Maggie and I made so clean and wavy yesterday afternoon. A yard like this is more comfortable than most people know. It is not just a yard. It is like an extended living room. When the hard clay is swept clean as a floor and the fine sand around the edges lined with tiny, irregular grooves, anyone can come and sit and look up into the elm tree and wait for the breezes that never come inside the house.

Maggie will be nervous until after her sister goes: she will stand hopelessly in corners, homely and ashamed of the burn scars down her arms and legs, eyeing her sister with a mixture of envy and awe. She thinks her sister has held life always in the palm of one hand, that "no" is a word the world never learned to say to her.

You've no doubt seen those TV shows where the child who has "made it" is confronted, as a surprise, by her own mother and father, tottering in weakly from backstage. (A pleasant surprise, of course: What would they do if parent and child came on the show only to curse out and insult each other?) On TV mother and child embrace and smile into each other's faces. Sometimes the mother and father weep, the child wraps them in her arms and leans across the table to tell how she would not have made it without their help. I have seen these programs.

Sometimes I dream a dream in which Dee and I are suddenly brought together on a TV program of this sort. Out of a dark and soft-seated limousine I am ushered into a bright room filled with many people. There I meet a smiling, gray, sporty man like Johnny Carson[1] who shakes my hand and tells me what a fine girl I have. Then we are on the stage and Dee is embracing me with tears in her eyes. She pins on my dress a large orchid, even though she has told me once that she thinks orchids are tacky flowers.

In real life I am a large, big-boned woman with rough, man-working hands. In the winter I wear flannel nightgowns to bed and overalls during the day. I can kill and clean a hog as mercilessly as a man. My fat keeps me hot in zero weather. I can work outside all day, breaking ice to get water for washing; I can eat pork liver cooked over the open fire minutes after it

---

[1]John William "Johnny" Carson (1925-2005) was an American television host and comedian, known for thirty years as host of *The Tonight Show Starring Johnny Carson* (1962–92).

comes steaming from the hog. One winter I knocked a bull calf straight in the brain between the eyes with a sledge hammer and had the meat hung up to chill before nightfall. But of course all this does not show on television. I am the way my daughter would want me to be: a hundred pounds lighter, my skin like an uncooked barley pancake. My hair glistens in the hot bright lights. Johnny Carson has much to do to keep up with my quick and witty tongue.

But that is a mistake. I know even before I wake up. Who ever knew a Johnson with a quick tongue? Who can even imagine me looking a strange white man in the eye? It seems to me I have talked to them always with one foot raised in flight, with my head turned in whichever way is farthest from them. Dee, though. She would always look anyone in the eye. Hesitation was no part of her nature.

"How do I look, Mama?" Maggie says, showing just enough of her thin body enveloped in pink skirt and red blouse for me to know she's there, almost hidden by the door.

"Come out into the yard," I say.

Have you ever seen a lame animal, perhaps a dog run over by some careless person rich enough to own a car, sidle up to someone who is ignorant enough to be kind to them? That is the way my Maggie walks. She has been like this, chin on chest, eyes on ground, feet in shuffle, ever since the fire that burned the other house to the ground.

Dee is lighter than Maggie, with nicer hair and a fuller figure. She's a woman now, though sometimes I forget. How long ago was it that the other house burned? Ten, twelve years? Sometimes I can still hear the flames and feel Maggie's arms sticking to me, her hair smoking and her dress falling off her in little black papery flakes. Her eyes seemed stretched open, blazed open by the flames reflected in them. And Dee. I see her standing off under the sweet gum tree she used to dig gum out of; a look of concentration on her face as she watched the last dingy gray board of the house fall in toward the red-hot brick chimney. Why don't you do a dance around the ashes? I'd wanted to ask her. She had hated the house that much.

I used to think she hated Maggie, too. But that was before we raised the money, the church and me, to send her to Augusta to school. She used to read to us without pity; forcing words, lies, other folks' habits, whole lives upon us two, sitting trapped and ignorant underneath her voice. She washed us in a river of make-believe, burned us with a lot of knowledge we didn't necessarily need to know. Pressed us to her with the serious way she read, to shove us away at just the moment, like dimwits, we seemed about to understand.

Dee wanted nice things. A yellow organdy dress to wear to her graduation from high school; black pumps to match a green suit she'd made from an old suit somebody gave me. She was determined to stare down any disaster in her efforts. Her eyelids would not flicker for minutes at a time. Often I fought off the temptation to shake her. At sixteen she had a style of her own: and knew what style was.

I never had an education myself. After second grade the school was closed down. Don't ask me why: in 1927 colored asked fewer questions than they do now. Sometimes Maggie reads to me. She stumbles along good-naturedly but can't see well. She knows she is not bright. Like good looks and money, quickness passed her by. She will marry John Thomas (who has mossy teeth in an earnest face) and then I'll be free to sit here and I guess just sing church songs to myself. Although I never was a good singer. Never could carry a tune. I was always better at a man's job. I used to love to milk till I was hooked in the side in '49. Cows are soothing and slow and don't bother you, unless you try to milk them the wrong way.

I have deliberately turned my back on the house. It is three rooms, just like the one that burned, except the roof is tin; they don't make shingle roofs any more. There are no real windows, just some holes cut in the sides, like the portholes in a ship, but not round and not square, with rawhide holding the shutters up on the outside. This house is in a pasture, too, like the other one. No doubt when Dee sees it she will want to tear it down. She wrote me once that no matter where we "choose" to live, she will manage to come see us. But she will never bring her friends. Maggie and I thought about this and Maggie asked me, "Mama, when did Dee ever *have* any friends?"

She had a few. Furtive boys in pink shirts hanging about on washday after school. Nervous girls who never laughed. Impressed with her they worshiped the well-turned phrase, the cute shape, the scalding humor that erupted like bubbles in lye. She read to them.

When she was courting Jimmy T she didn't have much time to pay to us, but turned all her faultfinding power on him. He *flew* to marry a cheap city girl from a family of ignorant flashy people. She hardly had time to recompose herself.

When she comes I will meet—but there they are!

Maggie attempts to make a dash for the house, in her shuffling way, but I stay her with my hand. "Come back here," I say. And she stops and tries to dig a well in the sand with her toe.

It is hard to see them clearly through the strong sun. But even the first glimpse of leg out of the car tells me it is Dee. Her feet were always neat-looking, as if God himself had shaped them with a certain style. From the other side of the car comes a short, stocky man. Hair is all over his head a foot long and hanging from his chin like a kinky mule tail. I hear Maggie suck in her breath. "Uhnnnh," is what it sounds like. Like when you see the wriggling end of a snake just in front of your foot on the road. "Uhnnnh."

Dee next. A dress down to the ground, in this hot weather. A dress so loud it hurts my eyes. There are yellows and oranges enough to throw back the light of the sun. I feel my whole face warming from the heat waves it throws out. Earrings gold, too, and hanging down to her shoulders. Bracelets dangling and making noises when she moves her arm up to shake the folds of the dress out of her armpits. The dress is loose and flows, and as she walks closer, I like it. I hear Maggie go "Uhnnnh" again. It is her sister's hair. It stands straight up like the wool on a sheep. It is black as night and around the edges are two long pigtails that rope about like small lizards disappearing behind her ears.

"Wa-su-zo-Tean-o!" she says, coming on in that gliding way the dress makes her move. The short stocky fellow with the hair to his navel is all grinning and he follows up with "Asalamalakim, my mother and sister!" He moves to hug Maggie but she falls back, right up against the back of my chair. I feel her trembling there and when I look up I see the perspiration falling off her chin.

"Don't get up," says Dee. Since I am stout it takes something of a push. You can see me trying to move a second or two before I make it. She turns, showing white heels through her sandals, and goes back to the car. Out she peeks next with a Polaroid. She stoops down quickly and lines up picture after picture of me sitting there in front of the house with Maggie cowering behind me. She never takes a shot without making sure the house is included. When a cow comes nibbling around the edge of the yard she snaps it and me and Maggie *and* the house. Then she puts the Polaroid in the back seat of the car, and comes up and kisses me on the forehead.

Meanwhile Asalamalakim is going through motions with Maggie's hand. Maggie's hand is as limp as a fish, and probably as cold, despite the sweat, and she keeps trying to pull it back. It looks like Asalamalakim wants to shake hands but wants to do it fancy. Or maybe he don't know how people shake hands. Anyhow, he soon gives up on Maggie.

"Well," I say. "Dee."

"No, Mama," she says. "Not 'Dee,' Wangero Leewanika Kemanjo!"

"What happened to 'Dee'?" I wanted to know.

"She's dead," Wangero said. "I couldn't bear it any longer, being named after the people who oppress me."

"You know as well as me you was named after your aunt Dicie," I said. Dicie is my sister. She named Dee. We called her "Big Dee" after Dee was born.

"But who was *she* named after?" asked Wangero.

"I guess after Grandma Dee," I said.

"And who was she named after?" asked Wangero.

"Her mother," I said, and saw Wangero was getting tired. "That's about as far back as I can trace it," I said. Though, in fact, I probably could have carried it back beyond the Civil War through the branches.

"Well," said Asalamalakim, "there you are."

"Uhnnnh," I heard Maggie say.

"There I was not," I said, "before 'Dicie' cropped up in our family, so why should I try to trace it that far back?"

He just stood there grinning, looking down on me like somebody inspecting a Model A car. Every once in a while he and Wangero sent eye signals over my head.

"How do you pronounce this name?" I asked.

"You don't have to call me by it if you don't want to," said Wangero.

"Why shouldn't I?" I asked. "If that's what you want us to call you, we'll call you."

"I know it might sound awkward at first," said Wangero.

"I'll get used to it," I said. "Ream it out again."

Well, soon we got the name out of the way. Asalamalakim had a name twice as long and three times as hard. After I tripped over it two or three times he told me to just call him Hakim-a-barber. I wanted to ask him was he a barber, but I didn't really think he was, so I didn't ask.

"You must belong to those beef-cattle peoples down the road," I said. They said "Asalamalakim" when they met you, too, but they didn't shake hands. Always too busy: feeding the cattle, fixing the fences, putting up salt-lick shelters, throwing down hay. When the white folks poisoned some of the herd the men stayed up all night with rifles in their hands. I walked a mile and a half just to see the sight.

Hakim-a-barber said, "I accept some of their doctrines, but farming and raising cattle is not my style." (They didn't tell me, and I didn't ask, whether Wangero [Dee] had really gone and married him.)

We sat down to eat and right away he said he didn't eat collards and pork was unclean. Wangero, though, went on through the chitlins and corn bread, the greens and everything else. She talked a blue streak over the sweet potatoes. Everything delighted her. Even the fact that we still used the benches her daddy made for the table when we wouldn't afford to buy chairs.

"Oh, Mama!" she cried. Then turned to Hakim-a-barber. "I never knew how lovely these benches are. You can feel the rump prints," she said, running her hands underneath her and along the bench. Then she gave a sigh and her hand closed over Grandma Dee's butter dish. "That's it!" she said. "I knew there was something I wanted to ask you if I could have." She jumped up from the table and went over to the corner where the churn stood, the milk in it clabber by now. She looked at the churn and looked at it.

"This churn top is what I need," she said. "Didn't Uncle Buddy whittle it out of a tree you all used to have?"

"Yes," I said.

"Uh huh," she said happily. "And I want the dasher, too."

"Uncle Buddy whittle that, too?" asked the barber.

Dee (Wangero) looked up at me.

"Aunt Dee's first husband whittled the dash," said Maggie so low you almost couldn't hear her. "His name was Henry, but they called him Stash."

"Maggie's brain is like an elephant's," Wangero said, laughing. "I can use the churn top as a centerpiece for the alcove table," she said, sliding a plate over the churn, "and I'll think of something artistic to do with the dasher."

When she finished wrapping the dasher the handle stuck out. I took it for a moment in my hands. You didn't even have to look close to see where hands pushing the dasher up and down to make butter had left a kind of sink in the wood. In fact, there were a lot of small sinks; you could see where thumbs and fingers had sunk into the wood. It was beautiful light yellow wood, from a tree that grew in the yard where Big Dee and Stash had lived.

After dinner Dee (Wangero) went to the trunk at the foot of my bed and started rifling through it. Maggie hung back in the kitchen over the dishpan. Out came Wangero with two quilts. They had been pieced by Grandma Dee and then Big Dee and me had hung them on the quilt frames on the front porch and quilted them. One was in the Lone Star pattern. The other was Walk Around the Mountain. In both of them were scraps of dresses Grandma Dee had worn fifty and more years ago. Bits and pieces of Grandpa Jarrell's Paisley shirts. And one teeny faded blue piece, about the size of a penny matchbox, that was from Great Grandpa Ezra's uniform that he wore in the Civil War.

"Mama," Wangero said sweet as a bird. "Can I have these old quilts?"

I heard something fall in the kitchen, and a minute later the kitchen door slammed.

"Why don't you take one or two of the others?" I asked. "These old things were just done by me and Big Dee from some tops your grandma pieced before she died."

"No," said Wangero. "I don't want those. They are stitched around the borders by machine."

"That'll make them last better," I said.

"That's not the point," said Wangero. "These are all pieces of dresses Grandma used to wear. She did all this stitching by hand. Imagine!" She held the quilts securely in her arms, stroking them.

"Some of the pieces, like those lavender ones, come from old clothes her mother handed down to her," I said, moving up to touch the quilts. Dee (Wangero) moved back just enough so that I couldn't reach the quilts. They already belong to her.

"Imagine!" she breathed again, clutching them closely to her bosom.

"The truth is," I said, "I promised to give them quilts to Maggie, for when she marries John Thomas."

She gasped like a bee had stung her.

"Maggie can't appreciate these quilts!" she said. "She'd probably be backward enough to put them to everyday use."

"I reckon she would," I said. "God knows I been saving 'em for long enough with nobody using 'em. I hope she will!" I didn't want to bring up how I had offered Dee (Wangero) a quilt when she went away to college. Then she told me they were old-fashioned, out of style.

"But they're *priceless*!" she was saying now, furiously; for she has a temper. "Maggie would put them on the bed and in five years they'd be rags. Less than that!"

"She can always make some more," I said. "Maggie knows how to quilt."

Dee (Wangero) looked at me with hatred. "You just will not understand. The point is these quilts, *these* quilts!"

"Well," I said, stumped. "What would *you* do with them?"

"Hang them," she said. As if that was the only thing you *could* do with quilts.

Maggie by now was standing on the door. I could almost hear the sound her feet made as they scraped over each other.

"She can have them, Mama," she said, like somebody used to never winning anything, or having anything reserved for her. "I can 'member Grandma Dee without the quilts."

I looked at her hard. She had filled her bottom lip with checkerberry snuff and it gave her a face a kind of dopey, hangdog look. It was Grandma Dee and Big Dee who taught her how to quilt herself. She stood there with her scarred hands hidden in the folds of her skirt. She looked at her sister with something like fear but she wasn't mad at her. This was Maggie's portion. This was the way she knew God to work.

When I looked at her like that something hit me in the top of my head and ran down to the soles of my feet. Just like when I'm in church and the spirit of God touches me and I get happy and shout. I did something I never had done before: hugged Maggie to me, then dragged her on into the room, snatched the quilts out of Miss Wangero's hands and dumped them into Maggie's lap. Maggie just sat there on my bed with her mouth open.

"Take one or two of the others," I said to Dee.

But she turned without a word and went out to Hakim-a-barber.

"You just don't understand," she said, as Maggie and I came out to the car.

"What don't I understand?" I wanted to know.

"Your heritage," she said. And then she turned to Maggie, kissed her, and said, "You ought to try to make something of yourself, too, Maggie. It's really a new day for us. But from the way you and Mama still live you'd never know it."

She put on some sunglasses that hid everything above the tip of her nose and her chin.

Maggie smiled; maybe at the sunglasses. But a real smile, not scared. After we watched the car dust settle I asked Maggie to bring me a dip of snuff. And then the two of us sat there just enjoying, until it was time to go in the house and go to bed.

[1973]

TIM O'BRIEN ■ (1946—)

Born in Austin, Minnesota, the novelist and short-story writer Tim O'Brien was educated at Macalester College, where he was the president of the student body and a *summa cum laude* major in political science. He was drafted into the U.S. army during the Vietnam War and wounded at My Lai. His wartime experiences have been at the center of much of his writing. His first book, *If I Die in a Combat Zone, Box Me Up and Ship Me Home* (1973), is a series of sketches about his life as a soldier; his second book, a novel called *Northern Lights* (1974), set in Minnesota, examines the relationship between a returning veteran and his brother; his third, parts of which were first published as stories, is another novel, *Going After Cacciato* (1978), and it too deals with the war. Recent work includes *July, July* (2002), a novel keyed to the thirtieth reunion of a college class that graduated in 1969.

The brilliantly designed and paced "The Things They Carried," included in a book of the same title (1990), is one of O'Brien's best stories. O'Brien has described himself as a "strict realist," but the term underplays the innovative styles and complex points of view that impel his work, which often surveys the boundaries between fact and fiction. "As a storyteller and as a person who trusts story," O'Brien stated, "I think a well-told story, a good story, addresses not just the head. It addresses the whole human body: the tear ducts, the scalp, the back of your neck and spine, even the stomach."

See Steven Kaplan, *Understanding Tim O'Brien* (1995); Tobey C. Herzog, *Tim O'Brien* (1997); and Mark A. Heberle, *A Trauma Artist: Tim O'Brien and the Fiction of Vietnam* (2001).

U.S. Marine gunner and rifleman in the Demilitarized Zone (DMZ), which
separated North and South Vietnam, 1966.

The Things They Carried

First Lieutenant Jimmy Cross carried letters from a girl named Martha, a junior at Mount Sebastian College in New Jersey. They were not love letters, but Lieutenant Cross was hoping, so he kept them folded in plastic at the bottom of his rucksack. In the late afternoon, after a day's march, he would dig his foxhole, wash his hands under a canteen, unwrap the letters, hold them with the tips of his fingers, and spend the last hour of light pretending. He would imagine romantic camping trips into the White Mountains in New Hampshire. He would sometimes taste the envelope flaps, knowing her tongue had been there. More than anything, he wanted Martha to love him as he loved her, but the letters were mostly chatty, elusive on the matter of love. She was a virgin, he was almost sure. She was an English major at Mount Sebastian, and she wrote beautifully about her professors and roommates and midterm exams, about her respect for Chaucer and her great affection for Virginia Woolf. She often quoted lines of poetry; she never mentioned the war, except to say, Jimmy, take care of yourself. The letters weighed 10 ounces. They were signed Love, Martha, but Lieutenant Cross understood that Love was only a way of signing and did not mean what he sometimes pretended it meant. At dusk, he would carefully return the letters to his rucksack. Slowly, a bit distracted, he would get up and move among his men, checking the perimeter, then at full dark he would return to his hole and watch the night and wonder if Martha was a virgin.

The things they carried were largely determined by necessity. Among the necessities or near-necessities were P-38 can openers, pocket knives, heat tabs, wristwatches, dog tags, mosquito repellent, chewing gum, candy, cigarettes, salt tablets, packets of Kool-Aid, lighters, matches, sewing kits, Military Payment Certificates, C rations, and two or three canteens of water. Together, these items weighed between 15 and 20 pounds, depending upon a man's habits or rate of metabolism. Henry Dobbins, who was a big man, carried extra rations; he was especially fond of canned peaches in heavy syrup over pound cake. Dave Jensen, who practiced field hygiene, carried a toothbrush, dental floss, and several hotel-sized bars of soap he'd stolen on R&R[1] in Sydney, Australia. Ted Lavender, who was scared, carried tranquilizers until he was shot in the head outside the village of Than Khe in mid-April. By necessity, and because it was SOP,[2] they all carried steel helmets that weighed 5 pounds including the liner and camouflage cover. They carried the standard fatigue jackets and trousers. Very few carried underwear. On their feet they carried jungle boots—2.1 pounds—and Dave Jensen carried three pairs of socks and a can of Dr. Scholl's foot powder as a precaution against trench foot. Until he was shot, Ted Lavender carried six or seven ounces of premium dope, which for him was

---

[1]Rest and rehabilitation leave.
[2]Standard operating procedure.

a necessity. Mitchell Sanders, the RTO,[3] carried condoms. Norman Bowker carried a diary. Rat Kiley carried comic books. Kiowa, a devout Baptist, carried an illustrated New Testament that had been presented to him by his father, who taught Sunday school in Oklahoma City, Oklahoma. As a hedge against bad times, however, Kiowa also carried his grandmother's distrust of the white man, his grandfather's old hunting hatchet. Necessity dictated. Because the land was mined and booby-trapped, it was SOP for each man to carry a steel-centered, nylon-covered flak jacket, which weighed 6.7 pounds, but which on hot days seemed much heavier. Because you could die so quickly, each man carried at least one large compress bandage, usually in the helmet band for easy access. Because the nights were cold, and because the monsoons were wet, each carried a green plastic poncho that could be used as a raincoat or groundsheet or makeshift tent. With its quilted liner, the poncho weighed almost two pounds, but it was worth every ounce. In April, for instance, when Ted Lavender was shot, they used his poncho to wrap him up, then to carry him across the paddy, then to lift him into the chopper that took him away.

They were called legs or grunts.

To carry something was to hump it, as when Lieutenant Jimmy Cross humped his love for Martha up the hills and through the swamps. In its intransitive form, to hump meant to walk, or to march, but it implied burdens far beyond the intransitive.

Almost everyone humped photographs. In his wallet, Lieutenant Cross carried two photographs of Martha. The first was a Kodacolor snapshot signed Love, though he knew better. She stood against a brick wall. Her eyes were gray and neutral, her lips slightly open as she stared straight-on at the camera. At night, sometimes, Lieutenant Cross wondered who had taken the picture, because he knew she had boyfriends, because he loved her so much, and because he could see the shadow of the picture-taker spreading out against the brick wall. The second photograph had been clipped from the 1968 Mount Sebastian yearbook. It was an action shot—women's volleyball—and Martha was bent horizontal to the floor, reaching, the palms of her hands in sharp focus, the tongue taut, the expression frank and competitive. There was no visible sweat. She wore white gym shorts. Her legs, he thought, were almost certainly the legs of a virgin, dry and without hair, the left knee cocked and carrying her entire weight, which was just over one hundred pounds. Lieutenant Cross remembered touching that left knee. A dark theater, he remembered, and the movie was *Bonnie and Clyde*,[4] and Martha wore a tweed skirt, and during the final scene, when he touched her knee, she turned and looked at him in a sad, sober way that made him pull his hand back, but he would always remember the feel of the tweed skirt and the knee beneath it and the sound of

---

[3]Radio and telephone operator.
[4]*Bonnie and Clyde* is a violent 1967 American crime film directed by Arthur Penn and starring Warren Beatty and Faye Dunaway.

the gun-fire that killed Bonnie and Clyde, how embarrassing it was, how slow and oppressive. He remembered kissing her good night at the dorm door. Right then, he thought, he should have done something brave. He should've carried her up the stairs to her room and tied her to the bed and touched that left knee all night long. He should've risked it. Whenever he looked at the photographs, he thought of new things he should've done.

What they carried was partly a function of rank, partly of field specialty.

As a first lieutenant and platoon leader, Jimmy Cross carried a compass, maps, code books, binoculars, and a .45-caliber pistol that weighed 2.9 pounds fully loaded. He carried a strobe light and the responsibility for the lives of his men.

As an RTO, Mitchell Sanders carried the PRC-25 radio, a killer, 26 pounds with its battery.

As a medic, Rat Kiley carried a canvas satchel filled with morphine and plasma and malaria tablets and surgical tape and comic books and all the things a medic must carry, including M&M's[5] for especially bad wounds, for a total weight of nearly 20 pounds.

As a big man, therefore a machine gunner, Henry Dobbins carried the M-60, which weighed 23 pounds unloaded, but which was almost always loaded. In addition, Dobbins carried between 10 and 15 pounds of ammunition draped in belts across his chest and shoulders.

As PFCs or Spec 4s, most of them were common grunts and carried the standard M-16 gas-operated assault rifle. The weapon weighed 7.5 pounds unloaded, 8.2 pounds with its full 20-round magazine. Depending on numerous factors, such as topography and psychology, the riflemen carried anywhere from 12 to 20 magazines, usually in cloth bandoliers, adding on another 8.4 pounds at minimum, 14 pounds at maximum. When it was available, they also carried M-16 maintenance gear—rods and steel brushes and swabs and tubes of LSA oil—all of which weighed about a pound. Among the grunts, some carried the M-79 grenade launcher, 5.9 pounds unloaded, a reasonably light weapon except for the ammunition, which was heavy. A single round weighed 10 ounces. The typical load was 25 rounds. But Ted Lavender, who was scared, carried 34 rounds when he was shot and killed outside Than Khe, and he went down under an exceptional burden, more than 20 pounds of ammunition, plus the flak jacket and helmet and rations and water and toilet paper and tranquilizers and all the rest, plus the unweighed fear. He was dead weight. There was no twitching or flopping. Kiowa, who saw it happen, said it was like watching a rock fall, or a big sandbag or something—just boom, then down—not like the movies where the dead guy rolls around and does fancy spins and goes ass over teakettle—not like that, Kiowa said, the poor bastard just flat-fuck fell. Boom. Down. Nothing else. It was a bright morning in mid-April. Lieutenant Cross

---

[5]Joking term for medical supplies.

felt the pain. He blamed himself. They stripped off Lavender's canteens and ammo, all the heavy things, and Rat Kiley said the obvious, the guy's dead, and Mitchell Sanders used his radio to report one U.S. KIA[6] and to request a chopper. Then they wrapped Lavender in his poncho. They carried him out to a dry paddy, established security, and sat smoking the dead man's dope until the chopper came. Lieutenant Cross kept to himself. He pictured Martha's smooth young face, thinking he loved her more than anything, more than his men, and now Ted Lavender was dead because he loved her so much and could not stop thinking about her. When the dustoff arrived, they carried Lavender aboard. Afterward they burned Than Khe. They marched until dusk, then dug their holes, and that night Kiowa kept explaining how you had to be there, how fast it was, how the poor guy just dropped like so much concrete. Boom-down, he said. Like cement.

In addition to the three standard weapons—the M-60, M-16, and M-79—they carried whatever presented itself, or whatever seemed appropriate as a means of killing or staying alive. They carried catch-as-catch-can. At various times, in various situations, they carried M-14s and CAR-15s and Swedish Ks and grease guns and captured AK-47s and Chi-Coms and RPGs and Simonov carbines and black market Uzis and .38-caliber Smith & Wesson handguns and 66 mm LAWs and shotguns and silencers and blackjacks and bayonets and C-4 plastic explosives. Lee Strunk carried a slingshot; a weapon of last resort, he called it. Mitchell Sanders carried brass knuckles. Kiowa carried his grandfather's feathered hatchet. Every third or fourth man carried a Claymore antipersonnel mine—3.5 pounds with its firing device. They all carried fragmentation grenades—14 ounces each. They all carried at least one M-18 colored smoke grenades—24 ounces. Some carried CS or tear gas grenades. Some carried white phosphorus grenades. They carried all they could bear, and then some, including a silent awe for the terrible power of the things they carried.

In the first week of April, before Lavender died, Lieutenant Jimmy Cross received a good-luck charm from Martha. It was a simple pebble, an ounce at most. Smooth to the touch, it was a milky white color with flecks of orange and violet, oval-shaped, like a miniature egg. In the accompanying letter, Martha wrote that she had found the pebble on the Jersey shoreline, precisely where the land touched water at high tide, where things came together but also separated. It was this separate-but-together quality, she wrote, that had inspired her to pick up the pebble and to carry it in her breast pocket for several days, where it seemed weightless, and then to send it through the mail, by air, as a token of her truest feelings for him. Lieutenant Cross found this romantic. But he wondered what her truest feelings were, exactly, and what she meant by separate-but-together. He wondered how the tides and waves had come into play on that afternoon

[6]Killed in action.

along the Jersey shoreline when Martha saw the pebble and bent down to rescue it from geology. He imagined bare feet. Martha was a poet, with the poet's sensibilities, and her feet would be brown and bare, the toenails unpainted, the eyes chilly and somber like the ocean in March, and though it was painful, he wondered who had been with her that afternoon. He imagined a pair of shadows moving along the strip of sand where things came together but also separated. It was phantom jealousy, he knew, but he couldn't help himself. He loved her so much. On the march, through the hot days of early April, he carried the pebble in his mouth, turning it with his tongue, tasting sea salt and moisture. His mind wandered. He had difficulty keeping his attention on the war. On occasion he would yell at his men to spread out the column, to keep their eyes open, but then he would slip away into daydreams, just pretending, walking barefoot along the Jersey shore, with Martha, carrying nothing. He would feel himself rising. Sun and waves and gentle winds, all love and lightness.

What they carried varied by mission.

When a mission took them to the mountains, they carried mosquito netting, machetes, canvas tarps, and extra bug juice.

If a mission seemed especially hazardous, or if it involved a place they knew to be bad, they carried everything they could. In certain heavily mined AOs,[7] where the land was dense with Toe Poppers and Bouncing Betties,[8] they took turns humping a 28-pound mine detector. With its headphones and big sensing plate, the equipment was a stress on the lower back and shoulders, awkward to handle, often useless because of the shrapnel in the earth, but they carried it anyway, partly for safety, partly for the illusion of safety.

On ambush, or other night missions, they carried peculiar little odds and ends. Kiowa always took along his New Testament and a pair of moccasins for silence. Dave Jensen carried night-sight vitamins high in carotene. Lee Strunk carried his slingshot; ammo, he claimed, would never be a problem. Rat Kiley carried brandy and M&M's candy. Until he was shot, Ted Lavender carried the starlight scope, which weighed 6.3 pounds with its aluminum carrying case. Henry Dobbins carried his girlfriend's pantyhose wrapped around his neck as a comforter. They all carried ghosts. When dark came, they would move out single file across the meadows and paddies to their ambush coordinates, where they would quietly set up the Claymores and lie down and spend the night waiting.

Other missions were more complicated and required special equipment. In mid-April, it was their mission to search out and destroy the elaborate tunnel complexes in the Than Khe area south of Chu Lai. To blow the tunnels, they carried one-pound blocks of pentrite high explosives, four blocks to man, 68 pounds in all. They carried wiring, detonators, and

---

[7]Areas of operation.
[8]Dangerous, lethal land mines.

battery-powered clackers. Dave Jensen carried earplugs. Most often, before blowing the tunnels, they were ordered by higher command to search them, which was considered bad news, but by and large they just shrugged and carried out orders. Because he was a big man, Henry Dobbins was excused from tunnel duty. The others would draw numbers. Before Lavender died there were 17 men in the platoon, and whoever drew the number 17 would strip off his gear and crawl in headfirst with a flashlight and Lieutenant Cross's .45-caliber pistol. The rest of them would fan out as security. They would sit down or kneel, not facing the hole, listening to the ground beneath them, imagining cobwebs and ghosts, whatever was down there—the tunnel walls squeezing in—how the flashlight seemed impossibly heavy in the hand and how it was tunnel vision in the very strictest sense, compression in all ways, even time, and how you had to wiggle in—ass and elbows—a swallowed-up feeling—and how you found yourself worrying about odd things: Will your flashlight go dead? Do rats carry rabies? If you screamed, how far would the sound carry? Would your buddies hear it? Would they have the courage to drag you out? In some respects, though not many, the waiting was worse than the tunnel itself. Imagination was a killer.

On April 16, when Lee Strunk drew the number 17, he laughed and muttered something and went down quickly. The morning was hot and very still. Not good, Kiowa said. He looked at the tunnel opening, then out across a dry paddy toward the village of Than Khe. Nothing moved. No clouds or birds or people. As they waited, the men smoked and drank Kool-Aid, not talking much, feeling sympathy for Lee Strunk but also feeling the luck of the draw. You win some, you lose some, said Mitchell Sanders, and sometimes you settle for a rain check. It was a tired line and no one laughed.

Henry Dobbins ate a tropical chocolate bar. Ted Lavender popped a tranquilizer and went off to pee.

After five minutes, Lieutenant Jimmy Cross moved to the tunnel, leaned down, and examined the darkness. Trouble, he thought—a cave-in maybe. And then suddenly, without willing it, he was thinking about Martha. The stresses and fractures, the quick collapse, the two of them buried alive under all that weight. Dense, crushing love. Kneeling, watching the hole, he tried to concentrate on Lee Strunk and the war, all the dangers, but his love was too much for him, he felt paralyzed, he wanted to sleep inside her lungs and breathe her blood and be smothered. He wanted her to be a virgin and not a virgin, all at once. He wanted to know her. Intimate secrets: Why poetry? Why so sad? Why that grayness in her eyes? Why so alone? Not lonely, just alone—riding her bike across campus or sitting off by herself in the cafeteria—even dancing, she danced alone—and it was the aloneness that filled him with love. He remembered telling her that one evening. How she nodded and looked away. And how, later, when he kissed her, she received the kiss without returning it, her eyes wide open, not afraid, not a virgin's eyes, just flat and uninvolved.

Lieutenant Cross gazed at the tunnel. But he was not there. He was buried with Martha under the white sand at the Jersey shore. They were pressed together, and the pebble in his mouth was her tongue. He was smiling. Vaguely, he was aware of how quiet the day was, the sullen paddies, yet he could not bring himself to worry about matters of security. He was beyond that. He was just a kid at war, in love. He was twenty-four years old. He couldn't help it.

A few moments later Lee Strunk crawled out of the tunnel. He came up grinning, filthy but alive. Lieutenant Cross nodded and closed his eyes while the others clapped Strunk on the back and made jokes about rising from the dead.

Worms, Rat Kiley said. Right out of the grave. Fuckin' zombie.

The men laughed. They all felt great relief.

Spook city, said Mitchell Sanders.

Lee Strunk made a funny ghost sound, a kind of moaning, yet very happy, and right then, when Strunk made that high happy moaning sound, when he went *Ahhooooo*, right then Ted Lavender was shot in the head on his way back from peeing. He lay with his mouth open. The teeth were broken. There was a swollen black bruise under his left eye. The cheekbone was gone. Oh shit, Rat Kiley said, the guy's dead. The guy's dead, he kept saying, which seemed profound—the guy's dead. I mean really.

The things they carried were determined to some extent by superstition. Lieutenant Cross carried his good-luck pebble. Dave Jensen carried a rabbit's foot. Norman Bowker, otherwise a very gentle person, carried a thumb that had been presented to him as a gift by Mitchell Sanders. The thumb was dark brown, rubbery to the touch, and weighed four ounces at most. It had been cut from a VC corpse, a boy of fifteen or sixteen. They'd found him at the bottom of an irrigation ditch, badly burned, flies in his mouth and eyes. The boy wore black shorts and sandals. At the time of his death he had been carrying a pouch of rice, a rifle, and three magazines of ammunition.

You want my opinion, Mitchell Sanders said, there's a definite moral here.

He put his hand on the dead boy's wrist. He was quiet for a time, as if counting a pulse, then he patted the stomach, almost affectionately, and used Kiowa's hunting hatchet to remove the thumb.

Henry Dobbins asked what the moral was.

Moral?

You know. *Moral*.

Sanders wrapped the thumb in toilet paper and handed it across to Norman Bowker. There was no blood. Smiling, he kicked the boy's head, watched the flies scatter, and said, It's like with that old TV show—Paladin.[9] Have gun, will travel.

Henry Dobbins thought about it.

[9]TV western (1957–63).

Yeah, well, he finally said. I don't see no moral.

There it *is*, man.

Fuck off.

They carried USO[10] stationery and pencils and pens. They carried Sterno, safety pins, trip flares, signal flares, spools of wire, razor blades, chewing tobacco, liberated joss sticks and statuettes of the smiling Buddha, candles, grease pencils, The Stars and Stripes, fingernail clippers, Psy Ops leaflets, bush hats, bolos, and much more. Twice a week, when the resupply choppers came in, they carried hot chow in green Mermite cans and large canvas bags filled with iced beer and soda pop. They carried plastic water containers, each with a two-gallon capacity. Mitchell Sanders carried a set of starched tiger fatigues for special occasions. Henry Dobbins carried Black Flag insecticide. Dave Jensen carried empty sandbags that could be filled at night for added protection. Lee Strunk carried tanning lotion. Some things they carried in common. Taking turns, they carried the big PRC-77 scrambler radio, which weighed 30 pounds with its battery. They shared the weight of memory. They took up what others could no longer bear. Often, they carried each other, the wounded or weak. They carried infections. They carried chess sets, basketballs, Vietnamese-English dictionaries, insignia of rank, Bronze Stars and Purple Hearts, plastic cards imprinted with the Code of Conduct. They carried diseases, among them malaria and dysentery. They carried lice and ringworm and leeches and paddy algae and various rots and molds. They carried the land itself—Vietnam, the place, the soil—a powdery orange-red dust that covered their boots and fatigues and faces. They carried the sky. The whole atmosphere, they carried it, the humidity, the monsoons, the stink of fungus and decay, all of it, they carried gravity. They moved like mules. By daylight they took sniper fire, at night they were mortared, but it was not battle, it was just the endless march, village to village, without purpose, nothing won or lost. They marched for the sake of the march. They plodded along slowly, dumbly, leaning forward against the heat, unthinking, all blood and bone, simple grunts, soldiering with their legs, toiling up the hills and down into the paddies and across the rivers and up again and down, just humping, one step and then the next and then another, but no volition, no will, because it was automatic, it was anatomy, and the war was entirely a matter of posture and carriage, the hump was everything, a kind of inertia, a kind of emptiness, a dullness of desire and intellect and conscience and hope and human sensibility. Their principles were in their feet. Their calculations were biological. They had no sense of strategy or mission. They searched the villages without knowing what to look for, not caring, kicking over jars of rice, frisking children and old men, blowing tunnels, sometimes setting fires and sometimes not, then forming up and moving on to the next village, then other villages, where it would always be the same.

[10]United Service Organizations.

They carried their own lives. The pressures were enormous. In the heat of early afternoon, they would remove their helmets and flak jackets, walking bare, which was dangerous but which helped ease the strain. They would often discard things along the route of march. Purely for comfort, they would throw away rations, blow their Claymores and grenades, no matter, because by nightfall the resupply choppers would arrive with more of the same, then a day or two later still more, fresh watermelons and crates of ammunition and sunglasses and woolen sweaters—the resources were stunning—sparklers for the Fourth of July, colored eggs for Easter—it was the great American war chest—the fruits of science, the smokestacks, the canneries, the arsenals at Hartford, the Minnesota forests, the machine shops, the vast fields of corn, and wheat—they carried like freight trains; they carried it on their backs and shoulders—and for all the ambiguities of Vietnam, all the mysteries and unknowns, there was at least the single abiding certainty that they would never be at a loss for things to carry.

After the chopper took Lavender away, Lieutenant Jimmy Cross led his men into the village of Than Khe. They burned everything. They shot chickens and dogs, they trashed the village well, they called in artillery and watched the wreckage, then they marched for several hours through the hot afternoon, and then at dusk, while Kiowa explained how Lavender died, Lieutenant Cross found himself trembling.

He tried not to cry. With his entrenching tool, which weighed five pounds, he began digging a hole in the earth.

He felt shame. He hated himself. He had loved Martha more than his men, and as a consequence Lavender was now dead, and this was something he would have to carry like a stone in his stomach for the rest of the war.

All he could do was dig. He used his entrenching tool like an ax, slashing, feeling both love and hate, and then later, when it was full dark, he sat at the bottom of his foxhole and wept. It went on for a long while. In part, he was grieving for Ted Lavender, but mostly it was for Martha, and for himself, because she belonged to another world, which was not quite real, and because she was a junior at Mount Sebastian College in New Jersey, a poet and a virgin and uninvolved, and because he realized she did not love him and never would.

Like cement, Kiowa whispered in the dark. I swear to God—boom, down. Not a word.

I've heard this, said Norman Bowker.

A pisser, you know? Still zipping himself up. Zapped while zipping.

All right, fine. That's enough.

Yeah, but you had to see it, the guy just—

I *heard*, man. Cement. So why not shut the fuck *up*?

Kiowa shook his head sadly and glanced over at the hole where Lieutenant Jimmy Cross sat watching the night. The air was thick and wet.

A warm dense fog had settled over the paddies and there was the stillness that precedes rain.

After a time Kiowa sighed.

One thing for sure, he said. The lieutenant's in some deep hurt. I mean that crying jag—the way he was carrying on—it wasn't fake or anything, it was real heavy-duty hurt. The man cares.

Sure, Norman Bowker said.

Say what you want, the man does care.

We all got problems.

Not Lavender.

No, I guess not, Bowker said.

Do me a favor, though.

Shut up?

That's a smart Indian. Shut up.

Shrugging, Kiowa pulled off his boots. He wanted to say more, just to lighten up his sleep, but instead he opened his New Testament and arranged it beneath his head as a pillow. The fog made things seem hollow and unattached. He tried not to think about Ted Lavender, but then he was thinking how fast it was, no drama, down and dead, and how it was hard to feel anything except surprise. It seemed unchristian. He wished he could find some great sadness, or even anger, but the emotion wasn't there and he couldn't make it happen. Mostly he felt pleased to be alive. He liked the smell of the New Testament under his cheek, the leather and ink and paper and glue, whatever the chemicals were. He liked hearing the sounds of night. Even his fatigue, it felt fine, the stiff muscles and the prickly awareness of his own body, a floating feeling. He enjoyed not being dead. Lying there, Kiowa admired Lieutenant Jimmy Cross's capacity for grief. He wanted to share the man's pain, he wanted to care as Jimmy Cross cared. And yet when he closed his eyes, all he could think was Boom-down, and all he could feel was the pleasure of having his boots off and the fog curling in around him and the damp soil and the Bible smells and the plush comfort of night.

After a moment Norman Bowker sat up in the dark.

What the hell, he said. You want to talk, *talk*. Tell it to me.

Forget it.

No, man, go on. One thing I hate, it's a silent Indian.

For the most part they carried themselves with poise, a kind of dignity. Now and then, however, there were times of panic, when they squealed or wanted to squeal but couldn't, when they twitched and made moaning sounds and covered their heads and said Dear Jesus and flopped around on the earth and fired their weapons blindly and cringed and sobbed and begged for the noise to stop and went wild and made stupid promises to themselves and to God and to their mothers and fathers, hoping not to die. In different ways, it happened to all of them. Afterward, when the firing ended, they would blink and peek up. They would touch their bodies, feeling shame, then quickly hiding it. They would force themselves to stand. As if in slow motion, frame by frame, the world would take on the old logic—absolute silence, then the wind, then sunlight, then voices. It was the burden of being alive. Awkwardly, the men would reassemble themselves, first in private, then in groups, becoming soldiers again. They would repair the leaks in their eyes. They would check for casualties, call in dustoffs, light cigarettes, try to smile, clear their throats and spit and begin cleaning their weapons. After a time someone would shake his head and say, No lie, I almost shit my pants, and someone else would laugh, which meant it was bad, yes, but the guy had obviously not shit his pants, it wasn't that bad, and in any case nobody would ever do such a thing and then go ahead and talk about it. They would squint into the dense, oppressive sunlight. For a few moments, perhaps, they would fall silent, lighting a joint and tracking its passage from man to man, inhaling, holding in the humiliation. Scary stuff, one of them might say. But then someone else would grin or flick his eyebrows and say, Roger-dodger, almost cut me a new asshole, *almost*.

There were numerous such poses. Some carried themselves with a sort of wistful resignation, others with pride or stiff soldierly discipline or good humor or macho zeal. They were afraid of dying but they were even more afraid to show it.

They found jokes to tell.

They used a hard vocabulary to contain the terrible softness. *Greased* they'd say. *Offed, lit up, zapped while zipping*. It wasn't cruelty, just stage presence. They were actors. When someone died, it wasn't quite dying, because in a curious way it seemed scripted, and because they had their lines mostly memorized, irony mixed with tragedy, and because they called it by other names, as if to encyst and destroy the reality of death itself. They kicked corpses. They cut off thumbs. They talked grunt lingo. They told stories about Ted Lavender's supply of tranquilizers, how the poor guy didn't feel a thing, how incredibly tranquil he was.

There's a moral here, said Mitchell Sanders.

They were waiting for Lavender's chopper, smoking the dead man's dope.

The moral's pretty obvious, Sanders said, and winked. Stay away from drugs. No joke, they'll ruin your day every time.

Cute, said Henry Dobbins.

Mind blower, get it? Talk about wiggy. Nothing left, just blood and brains.

They made themselves laugh.

There it is, they'd say. Over and over—there it is, my friend, there it is—as if the repetition itself were an act of poise, a balance between crazy and almost crazy, knowing without going, there it is, which meant be cool, let it ride, because Oh yeah, man, you can't change what can't be changed, there it is, there it absolutely and positively and fucking well *is*.

They were tough.

They carried all the emotional baggage of men who might die. Grief, terror, love, longing—these were intangibles, but the intangibles had their own mass and specific gravity, they had tangible weight. They carried shameful memories. They carried the common secret of cowardice barely restrained, the instinct to run or freeze or hide, and in many respects this was the heaviest burden of all, for it could never be put down, it required perfect balance and perfect posture. They carried their reputations. They carried the soldier's greatest fear, which was the fear of blushing. Men killed, and died, because they were embarrassed not to. It was what had brought them to the war in the first place, nothing positive, no dreams of glory or honor, just to avoid the blush of dishonor. They died so as not to die of embarrassment. They crawled into tunnels and walked point and advanced under fire. Each morning, despite the unknowns, they made their legs move. They endured. They kept humping. They did not submit to the obvious alternative, which was simply to close the eyes and fall. So easy, really. Go limp and tumble to the ground and let the muscles unwind and not speak and not budge until your buddies picked you up and lifted you into the chopper that would roar and dip its nose and carry you off into the world. A mere matter of falling, yet no one ever fell. It was not courage, exactly; the object was not valor. Rather, they were too frightened to be cowards.

By and large they carried these things inside, maintaining the masks of composure. They sneered at sick call. They spoke bitterly about guys who had found release by shooting off their own toes or fingers. Pussies, they'd say. Candy-asses. It was fierce, mocking talk, with only a trace of envy or awe, but even so the image played itself out behind their eyes.

They imagined the muzzle against flesh. So easy: squeeze the trigger and blow away a toe. They imagined it. They imagined the quick, sweet pain, then the evacuation to Japan, then a hospital with warm beds and cute geisha nurses.

And they dreamed of freedom birds.

At night, on guard, staring into the dark, they were carried away by jumbo jets. They felt the rush of takeoff. *Gone!* they yelled. And then velocity—wings and engines—a smiling stewardess—but it was more than a plane, it was a real bird, a big sleek silver bird with feathers and talons and high screeching. They were flying. The weights fell off; there was nothing to bear. They laughed and held on tight, feeling the cold slap of wind and altitude, soaring, thinking *It's over, I'm gone!*—they were naked, they were light and free—it was all lightness, bright and fast and buoyant, light as light, a helium buzz in the brain, a giddy bubbling in the lungs as they were taken up over the clouds and the war, beyond duty, beyond gravity and mortification and global entanglements—*Sin loi!*[11] they yelled. *I'm sorry, motherfuckers, but I'm out of it, I'm goofed, I'm on a space cruise, I'm gone!*—and it was a restful, unencumbered sensation, just riding the light waves, sailing that big silver freedom bird over the mountains and oceans, over America, over the farms and great sleeping cities and cemeteries and highways and the golden arches of McDonald's. It was flight, a kind of fleeing, a kind of falling, falling higher and higher, spinning off the edge of the earth and beyond the sun and through the vast, silent vacuum where there were no burdens and where everything weighed exactly nothing—*Gone!* they screamed. *I'm sorry but I'm gone!*—and so at night, not quite dreaming, they gave themselves over to lightness, they were carried, they were purely borne.

On the morning after Ted Lavender died, First Lieutenant Jimmy Cross crouched at the bottom of his foxhole and burned Martha's letters. Then he burned the two photographs. There was a steady rain falling, which made it difficult, but he used heat tabs and Sterno to build a small fire, screening it with his body, holding the photographs over the tight blue flame with the tips of his fingers.

He realized it was only a gesture. Stupid, he thought. Sentimental, too, but mostly just stupid.

Lavender was dead. You couldn't burn the blame.

Besides, the letters were in his head. And even now, without photographs, Lieutenant Cross could see Martha playing volleyball in her white gym shorts and yellow T-shirt. He could see her moving in the rain.

When the fire died out, Lieutenant Cross pulled his poncho over his shoulders and ate breakfast from a can.

There was no great mystery, he decided.

In those burned letters Martha had never mentioned the war, except to say, Jimmy, take care of yourself. She wasn't involved. She signed the letters Love, but it wasn't love, and all the fine lines and technicalities did not matter. Virginity was no longer an issue. He hated her. Yes, he did. He hated her. Love, too, but it was a hard, hating kind of love.

The morning came up wet and blurry. Everything seemed part of everything else, the fog and Martha and the deepening rain.

He was a soldier, after all.

Half smiling, Lieutenant Jimmy Cross took out his maps. He shook his head hard, as if to clear it, then bent forward and began planning the day's march. In ten minutes, or maybe twenty, he would rouse the men and they would pack up and head west, where the maps showed the country to be green and inviting. They would do what they had always done. The rain might add some weight, but otherwise it would be one more day layered upon all the other days.

[11]Sorry.

He was realistic about it. There was that new hardness in his stomach. He loved her but he hated her.

No more fantasies, he told himself.

Henceforth, when he thought about Martha, it would be only to think that she belonged elsewhere. He would shut down the daydreams. This was not Mount Sebastian, it was another world, where there were no pretty poems or midterm exams, a place where men died because of carelessness and gross stupidity. Kiowa was right. Boom-down, and you were dead, never partly dead.

Briefly, in the rain, Lieutenant Cross saw Martha's gray eyes gazing back at him.

He understood.

It was very sad, he thought. The things men carried inside. The things men did or felt they had to do.

He almost nodded at her, but didn't.

Instead he went back to his maps. He was now determined to perform his duties firmly and without negligence. It wouldn't help Lavender, he knew that, but from this point on he would comport himself as an officer. He would dispose of his good-luck pebble. Swallow it, maybe, or use Lee Strunk's slingshot, or just drop it along the trail. On the march he would impose strict field discipline. He would be careful to send out flank security, to prevent straggling or bunching up, to keep his troops moving at the proper pace and at the proper interval. He would insist on clean weapons. He would confiscate the remainder of Lavender's dope. Later in the day, perhaps, he would call the men together and speak to them plainly. He would accept the blame for what had happened to Ted Lavender. He would be a man about it. He would look them in the eyes, keeping his chin level, and he would issue the new SOPs in a calm, impersonal tone of voice, a lieutenant's voice, leaving no room for argument or discussion. Commencing immediately, he'd tell them, they would no longer abandon equipment along the route of march. They would police up their acts. They would get their shit together, and keep it together, and maintain it neatly and in good working order.

He would not tolerate laxity. He would show strength, distancing himself.

Among the men there would be grumbling, of course, and maybe worse, because their days would seem longer and their loads heavier, but Lieutenant Jimmy Cross reminded himself that his obligation was not to be loved but to lead. He would dispense with love; it was not now a factor. And if anyone quarreled or complained, he would simply tighten his lips and arrange his shoulders in the correct command posture. He might give a curt little nod. Or he might not. He might just shrug and say, Carry on, then they would saddle up and form into a column and move out toward the villages west of Than Khe.

[1986, 1990]

LESLIE MARMON SILKO ■ (1948–)

Of mixed Laguna, Mexican, and white ancestry, Leslie Marmon Silko was born in Albuquerque, New Mexico. She grew up 50 miles away in Old Laguna, hearing and learning stories from her female relatives. She has said of herself, "I am of mixed-breed ancestry, but what I know is Laguna. This place I am from is everything I am as a writer and human being." She also said, "I suppose at the core of my writing is the attempt to identify what it is to be a half-breed or mixed blooded person; what it is to grow up neither white nor fully traditional Indian."

Silko received her undergraduate degree, majoring in English, from the University of New Mexico in 1969 and then studied law there in a special program for Native Americans. Her first book, *Laguna Woman* (1974), was a collection of poems. It was followed by the highly successful, critically esteemed *Ceremony* (1977), the story of a mixed-ancestry veteran of World War II who saves himself by regaining connection to his native origins.

Possibly her best book is *Storyteller* (1981), from which "Lullaby", is taken, a multigenre work that blends poetry, photography, autobiography, excerpts from letters, short stories, and family histories, and that makes uses of Inuit myths that Silko discovered during a period in the 1970s when she lived in a remote village in Alaska.

Silko's literary work also includes *The Delicacy and Strength of Lace* (1986), an exchange of letters with the poet James Wright; *Almanac of the Dead* (1991), an ambitiously conceived "moral history of the Americas"; *Yellow Woman and a Beauty of the Spirit* (1996), a gathering of essays; and *Gardens in the Dunes* (1999), a novel, set on the California-Arizona border at the turn of the twentieth century, that deals with the relationship between an orphaned Native American girl and a white woman. *The Turquoise Ledge: A Memoir* was published in 2010.

In all of her writings, Silko has explored the themes of memory, storytelling, and tradition, and the relationships among identity, place, and culture. "Lullaby," a story of loss, pain, and grief, is a wounding, beautifully told account of a mother's bond with her children. Estranged from her husband, Ayah reflects on her children who have died and on others of her children from whom she is now separated. As Helen Jaskoski (1999), has noted, these losses are connected to Ayah's "no less felt loss of heritage, culture, and way of life. There will be no children and grandchildren to teach and nurture in the way her mother and grandmother had educated and cared for Ayah, no infants to be lulled by the lyrics she sings to herself at the end of the story. Art, religion, language, natural history—all are being lost."

For critical discussion, see Gregory Sayler, *Leslie Marmon Silko* (1997); Helen Jaskowski, *Leslie Marmon Silko: A Study of the Short Fiction* (1998); and *Leslie Marmon Silko: A Collection of Critical Essays*, eds. Louis K. Barnett and James L. Thorson (1999).

Lullaby

The sun had gone down but the snow in the wind gave off its own light. It came in thick tufts like new wool—washed before the weaver spins it. Ayah reached out for it like her own babies had, and she smiled when she remembered how she had laughed at them. She was an old woman now, and her life had become memories. She sat down with her back against the wide cottonwood tree, feeling the rough bark on her back bones; she faced east and listened to the wind and snow sing a high-pitched Yeibechei[1] song. Out of the wind she felt warmer, and she could watch the wide fluffy snow fill in her tracks, steadily, until the direction she had come from was gone. By the light of the snow she could see the dark outline of the big arroyo[2] a few feet away. She was sitting on the edge of Cebolleta Creek, where in the springtime the thin cows would graze on grass already chewed flat to the ground. In the wide deep creek bed where only a trickle of water flowed in the summer, the skinny cows would wander, looking for new grass along winding paths splashed with manure.

Ayah pulled the old Army blanket over her head like a shawl. Jimmie's blanket—the one he had sent to her. That was a long time ago and the green wool was faded, and it was unraveling on the edges. She did not want to think about Jimmie. So she thought about the weaving and the way her mother had done it. On the tall wooden loom set into the sand under a tamarack tree for shade. She could see it clearly. She had been only a little girl when her grandma gave her the wooden combs to pull the twigs and burrs from the raw, freshly washed wool. And while she combed the wool, her grandma sat beside her, spinning a silvery strand of yarn around the smooth cedar spindle. Her mother worked at the loom with yarns dyed bright yellow and red and gold. She watched them dye the yarn in boiling black pots full of beeweed petals, juniper berries, and sage. The blankets her mother made were soft and woven so tight that rain rolled off them like birds' feathers. Ayah remembered sleeping warm on cold windy nights, wrapped in her mother's blankets on the hogan's[3] sandy floor.

The snow drifted now, with the northwest wind hurling it in gusts. It drifted up around her black overshoes—old ones with little metal buckles. She smiled at the snow which was trying to cover her little by little. She could remember when they had no black rubber overshoes; only the high buckskin leggings that they wrapped over their elkhide moccasins. If the snow was dry or frozen, a person could walk all day and not get wet; and in the evenings the beams of the ceiling would hang with lengths of pale buckskin leggings, drying out slowly.

---

[1] A sacred song of the Navajo. The Navajo Yeibechei is a nine-day sacred healing ceremony performed only in the winter months.
[2] The bed of a stream or a gully (Spanish).
[3] A Navajo hut made of mud and logs or a similar dwelling of other American Indian peoples of the southwestern United States.

She felt peaceful remembering. She didn't feel cold any more. Jimmie's blanket seemed warmer than it had ever been. And she could remember the morning he was born. She could remember whispering to her mother, who was sleeping on the other side of the hogan, to tell her it was time now. She did not want to wake the others. The second time she called to her, her mother stood up and pulled on her shoes; she knew. They walked to the old stone hogan together, Ayah walking a step behind her mother. She waited alone, learning the rhythms of the pains while her mother went to call the old woman to help them. The morning was already warm even before dawn and Ayah smelled the bee flower blooming and the young willow growing at the springs. She could remember that so clearly, but his birth merged into the births of the other children and to her it became all the same birth. They named him for the summer morning and in English they called him Jimmie.

It wasn't like Jimmie died. He just never came back, and one day a dark blue sedan with white writing on its doors pulled up in front of the boxcar shack where the rancher let the Indians live. A man in a khaki uniform trimmed in gold gave them a yellow piece of paper and told them that Jimmie was dead. He said the Army would try to get the body back and then it would be shipped to them; but it wasn't likely because the helicopter had burned after it crashed. All of this was told to Chato because he could understand English. She stood inside the doorway holding the baby while Chato listened. Chato spoke English like a white man and he spoke Spanish too. He was taller than the white man and he stood straighter too. Chato didn't explain why; he just told the military man they could keep the body if they found it. The white man looked bewildered; he nodded his head and he left. Then Chato looked at her and shook his head, and then he told her, "Jimmie isn't coming home anymore," and when he spoke, he used the words to speak of the dead. She didn't cry then, but she hurt inside with anger. And she mourned him as the years passed, when a horse fell with Chato and broke his leg, and the white rancher told them he wouldn't pay Chato until he could work again. She mourned Jimmie because he would have worked for his father then; he would have saddled the big bay horse and ridden the fence lines each day, with wire cutters and heavy gloves, fixing the breaks in the barbed wire and putting the stray cattle back inside again.

She mourned him after the white doctors came to take Danny and Ella away. She was at the shack alone that day they came. It was back in the days before they hired Navajo women to go with them as interpreters. She recognized one of the doctors. She had seen him at the children's clinic at Cañoncito about a month ago. They were wearing khaki uniforms and they waved papers at her and a black ball-point pen, trying to make her understand their English words. She was frightened by the way they looked at the children, like the lizard watches the fly. Danny was swinging on the tire swing on the elm tree behind the rancher's house, and Ella was toddling around the front door, dragging the broomstock horse Chato made for her. Ayah could see they wanted her to sign the papers, and Chato had taught her to sign her name. It was something she was proud of. She only wanted them to go, and to take their eyes away from her children.

She took the pen from the man without looking at his face and she signed the papers in three different places he pointed to. She stared at the ground by their feet and waited for them to leave. But they stood there and began to point and gesture at the children. Danny stopped swinging. Ayah could see his fear. She moved suddenly and grabbed Ella into her arms; the child squirmed, trying to get back to her toys. Ayah ran with the baby toward Danny; she screamed for him to run and then she grabbed him around his chest and carried him too. She ran south into the foothills of juniper trees and black lava rock. Behind her she heard the doctors running, but they had been taken by surprise, and as the hills became steeper and the cholla cactus were thicker, they stopped. When she reached the top of the hill, she stopped to listen in case they were circling around her. But in a few minutes she heard a car engine start and they drove away. The children had been too surprised to cry while she ran with them. Danny was shaking and Ella's little fingers were gripping Ayah's blouse.

She stayed up in the hills for the rest of the day, sitting on a black lava boulder in the sunshine where she could see for miles all around her. The sky was light blue and cloudless, and it was warm for late April. The sun warmth relaxed her and took the fear and anger away. She lay back on the rock and watched the sky. It seemed to her that she could walk into the sky, stepping through clouds endlessly. Danny played with little pebbles and stones, pretending they were birds eggs and then little rabbits. Ella sat at her feet and dropped fistfuls of dirt into the breeze, watching the dust and particles of sand intently. Ayah watched a hawk soar high above them, dark wings gliding; hunting or only watching, she did not know. The hawk was patient and he circled all afternoon before he disappeared around the high volcanic peak the Mexicans called Guadalupe.

Late in the afternoon, Ayah looked down at the gray boxcar shack with the paint all peeled from the wood; the stove pipe on the roof was rusted and crooked. The fire she had built that morning in the oil drum stove had burned out. Ella was asleep in her lap now and Danny sat close to her, complaining that he was hungry; he asked when they would go to the house. "We will stay up here until your father comes," she told him, "because those white men were chasing us." The boy remembered then and he nodded at her silently.

If Jimmie had been there he could have read those papers and explained to her what they said. Ayah would have known then, never to sign them. The doctors came back the next day and they brought a BIA[4]

---

[4]Bureau of Indian Affairs.

policeman with them. They told Chato they had her signature and that was all they needed. Except for the kids. She listened to Chato sullenly; she hated him when he told her it was the old woman who died in the winter, spitting blood; it was her old grandma who had given the children this disease. "They don't spit blood," she said coldly. "The whites lie." She held Ella and Danny close to her, ready to run to the hills again. "I want a medicine man first," she said to Chato, not looking at him. He shook his head. "It's too late now. The policeman is with them. You signed the paper." His voice was gentle.

It was worse than if they had died: to lose the children and to know that somewhere, in a place called Colorado, in a place full of sick and dying strangers, her children were without her. There had been babies that died soon after they were born, and one that died before he could walk. She had carried them herself, up to the boulders and great pieces of the cliff that long ago crashed down from Long Mesa; she laid them in the crevices of sandstone and buried them in fine brown sand with round quartz pebbles that washed down the hills in the rain. She had endured it because they had been with her. But she could not bear this pain. She did not sleep for a long time after they took her children. She stayed on the hill where they had fled the first time, and she slept rolled up in the blanket Jimmie had sent her. She carried the pain in her belly and it was fed by everything she saw: the blue sky of their last day together and the dust and pebbles they played with; the swing in the elm tree and broomstick horse choked life from her. The pain filled her stomach and there was no room for food or for her lungs to fill with air. The air and the food would have been theirs.

She hated Chato, not because he let the policeman and doctors put the screaming children in the government car, but because he had taught her to sign her name. Because it was like the old ones always told her about learning their language or any of their ways: it endangered you. She slept alone on the hill until the middle of November when the first snows came. Then she made a bed for herself where the children had slept. She did not lie down beside Chato again until many years later, when he was sick and shivering and only her body could keep him warm. The illness came after the white rancher told Chato he was too old to work for him anymore, and Chato and his old woman should be out of the shack by the next afternoon because the rancher had hired new people to work there. That had satisfied her. To see how the white man repaid Chato's years of loyalty and work. All of Chato's fine-sounding English talk didn't change things.

It snowed steadily and the luminous light from the snow gradually diminished into the darkness. Somewhere in Cebolleta a dog barked and other village dogs joined with it. Ayah looked in the direction she had come, from the bar where Chato was buying the wine. Sometimes he told her to go on ahead and wait; and then he never came. And when she finally went back looking for him, she would find him passed out at the bottom of the wooden steps to Azzie's Bar. All the wine would be gone and most of the money too, from the pale blue check that came to them once a month in a government envelope. It was then that she would look at his face and his hands, scarred by ropes and the barbed wire of all those years, and she would think, this man is a stranger; for forty years she had smiled at him and cooked his food, but he remained a stranger. She stood up again, with the snow almost to her knees, and she walked back to find Chato.

It was hard to walk in the deep snow and she felt the air burn in her lungs. She stopped a short distance from the bar to rest and readjust the blanket. But this time he wasn't waiting for her on the bottom step with his old Stetson hat pulled down and his shoulders hunched up in his long wool overcoat.

She was careful not to slip on the wooden steps. When she pushed the door open, warm air and cigarette smoke hit her face. She looked around slowly and deliberately, in every corner, in every dark place that the old man might find to sleep. The bar owner didn't like Indians in there, especially Navajos, but he let Chato come in because he could talk Spanish like he was one of them. The men at the bar stared at her, and the bartender saw that she left the door open wide. Snowflakes were flying inside like moths and melting into a puddle on the oiled wood floor. He motioned to her to close the door, but she did not see him. She held herself straight and walked across the room slowly, searching the room with every step. The snow in her hair melted and she could feel it on her forehead. At the far corner of the room, she saw red flames at the mica[5] window of the old stove door; she looked behind the stove just to make sure. The bar got quiet except for the Spanish polka music playing on the jukebox. She stood by the stove and shook the snow from her blanket and held it near the stove to dry. The wet wool smell reminded her of new-born goats in early March, brought inside to warm near the fire. She felt calm.

In past years they would have told her to get out. But her hair was white now and her face was wrinkled. They looked at her like she was a spider crawling slowly across the room. They were afraid; she could feel the fear. She looked at their faces steadily. They reminded her of the first time the white people brought her children back to her that winter. Danny had been shy and hid behind the thin white woman who brought them. And the baby had not known her until Ayah took her into her arms, and then Ella had nuzzled close to her as she had when she was nursing. The blonde woman was nervous and kept looking at a dainty gold watch on her wrist. She sat on the bench near the small window and watched the dark snow clouds gather around the mountains; she was worrying about the

[5] A crystalline mineral. The crystalline structure of mica forms layers that can be split into thin light-weight sheets that are transparent to opaque.

unpaved road. She was frightened by what she saw inside too: the strips of venison drying on a rope across the ceiling and the children jabbering excitedly in a language she did not know. So they stayed for only a few hours. Ayah watched the government car disappear down the road and she knew they were already being weaned from these lava hills and from this sky. The last time they came was in early June, and Ella stared at her the way the men in the bar were now staring. Ayah did not try to pick her up; she smiled at her instead and spoke cheerfully to Danny. When he tried to answer her, he could not seem to remember and he spoke English words with the Navajo. But he gave her a scrap of paper that he had found somewhere and carried in his pocket; it was folded in half, and he shyly looked up at her and said it was a bird. She asked Chato if they were home for good this time. He spoke to the white woman and she shook her head. "How much longer?" he asked, and she said she didn't know; but Chato saw how she stared at the boxcar shack. Ayah turned away then. She did not say good-bye.

She felt satisfied that the men in the bar feared her. Maybe it was her face and the way she held her mouth with teeth clenched tight, like there was nothing anyone could do to her now. She walked north down the road, searching for the old man. She did this because she had the blanket, and there would be no place for him except with her and the blanket in the old adobe[6] barn near the arroyo. They always slept there when they came to Cebolleta. If the money and the wine were gone, she would be relieved because then they could go home again; back to the old hogan with a dirt roof and rock walls where she herself had been born. And the next day the old man could go back to the few sheep they still had, to follow along behind them, guiding them, into dry sandy arroyos where sparse grass grew. She knew he did not like walking behind old ewes when for so many years he rode big quarter horses and worked with cattle. But she wasn't sorry for him; he should have known all along what would happen.

There had not been enough rain for their garden in five years; and that was when Chato finally hitched a ride into the town and brought back brown boxes of rice and sugar and big tin cans of welfare peaches. After that, at the first of the month they went to Cebolleta to ask the postmaster for the check; and then Chato would go to the bar and cash it. They did this as they planted the garden every May, not because anything would survive the summer dust, but because it was time to do this. The journey passed the days that smelled silent and dry like the caves above the canyon with yellow painted buffaloes on their walls.

He was walking along the pavement when she found him. He did not stop or turn around when he heard her behind him. She walked beside him and

---

[6]Sun-dried bricks.

she noticed how slowly he moved now. He smelled strongly of woodsmoke and urine. Lately he had been forgetting. Sometimes he called her by his sister's name and she had been gone for a long time. Once she had found him wandering on the road to the white man's ranch, and she asked him why he was going that way; he laughed at her and said, "You know they can't run that ranch without me," and he walked on determined, limping on the leg that had been crushed many years before. Now he looked at her curiously, as if for the first time, but he kept shuffling along, moving slowly along the side of the highway. His gray hair had grown long and spread out on the shoulders of the long overcoat. He wore the old felt hat pulled down over his ears. His boots were worn out at the toes and he had stuffed pieces of an old red shirt in the holes. The rags made his feet look like little animals up to their ears in snow. She laughed at his feet; the snow muffled the sound of her laugh. He stopped and looked at her again. The wind had quit blowing and the snow was falling straight down; the southeast sky was beginning to clear and Ayah could see a star.

"Let's rest awhile," she said to him. They walked away from the road and up the slopes to the giant boulders that had tumbled down from the red sandrock mesa throughout the centuries of rainstorms and earth tremors. In a place where the boulders shut out the wind, they sat down with their backs against the rock. She offered half of the blanket to him and they sat wrapped together.

The storm passed swiftly. The clouds moved east. They were massive and full, crowding together across the sky. She watched them with the feeling of horses—steely blue-gray horses startled across the sky. The powerful haunches pushed into the distances and the tail hairs streamed white mist behind them. The sky cleared. Ayah saw that there was nothing between her and the stars. The light was crystalline. There was no shimmer, no distortion through earth haze. She breathed the clarity of the night sky; she smelled the purity of the half moon and the stars. He was lying on his side with his knees pulled up near his belly for warmth. His eyes were closed now, and in the light from the stars and the moon, he looked young again.

She could see it descend out of the night sky: an icy stillness from the edge of the thin moon. She recognized the freezing. It came gradually, sinking snowflake by snowflake until the crust was heavy and deep. It had the strength of the stars in Orion,[7] and its journey was endless. Ayah knew that with the wine he would sleep. He would not feel it. She tucked the blanket around him, remembering how it was when Ella had been with her; and she felt the rush so big inside her heart for the babies. And she sang the only song she knew to sing for babies. She could not remember if she

---

[7] A large, bright constellation described as a hunter with a belt and sword.

had ever sung it to her children, but she knew that her grandmother had
sung it and her mother had sung it:

> The earth is your mother,
> > she holds you.
>
> The sky is your father,
> > he protects you.
>
> Sleep,
> sleep.
>
> Rainbow is your sister,
> > she loves you.
>
> The winds are your brothers,
> > they sing to you.
>
> Sleep,
> sleep.
>
> We are together always
> We are together always
> There never was a time
> when this
> was not so.

[1981]

African American novelist and short-story writer Edward Paul Jones was born in 1950 in Washington, D.C., the only son of a hotel maid estranged from her husband. He was an early and avid reader, discovering African American novelists such as Ethel Waters and Richard Wright at the age of thirteen. "I felt as if they were talking to me.... I was shocked to learn black people could write such things," he recalled in an interview with *Publisher's Weekly*.

Jones attended the College of the Holy Cross in Worcester, Massachusetts, where he wrote his first attempts at fiction during his sophomore year. He earned his BA from Holy Cross in 1972. Jones, who showed writing talent early but did not at first consider writing a viable career, sold his first story to *Essence* magazine in 1975 at a low point in his life, when, after the death of his mother and between jobs, he was reduced to staying in a city mission. In 1979, Jones began studying creative writing at the University of Virginia, where he earned an MFA in 1981. For more than a decade, starting in 1990, he earned a steady living not by writing fiction, but as a proofreader and later a columnist at a newsletter for tax professionals.

Known in his work for evoking the far-reaching ravages of slavery and the lives of working-class African Americans, Jones debuted his breakthrough collection of short stories, *Lost in the City*, in 1993. Consciously inspired by his admiration for James Joyce's *Dubliners*, Jones opened his readers' eyes to the inhabitants of Washington, D.C., in the 1950s and 1960s through a frank examination of individual souls. *Lost in the City* was widely praised, winning the PEN/Hemingway Award and a nomination for a National Book Award. What followed, however, was ten years of silence.

In spite of the glittering critical acclaim under his belt, Jones hesitated to commit to writing full-time, even as ideas for a new work percolated in his mind. Only after he was laid off from his day job in 2002 did he begin his next novel in earnest. *The Known World* (2003) is the morally complex tale of Henry Townsend, a slave who eventually becomes a slave owner himself. This long-awaited second work was greeted by even more accolades than Jones's first book. In addition to winning the 2004 Pulitzer Prize for Fiction, Jones was one of twenty-three recipients of the MacArthur Foundation "genius grant" that same year. Jones's third book, another collection of short stories titled *All Aunt Hagar's Children* (2006), returned to the working-class world of Washington, D.C., that he examined in his first book.

"Blindsided," appears in *All Aunt Hagar's Children*. The story is told from the point of view of a woman who is past her "partying years." Roxanne dismays everyone around her by mysteriously going blind. She ultimately learns that even those blind from birth can read signs.

For commentary and discussion: Wyatt Mason, "Ballad for Americans: The Stories of Edward P. Jones," *Harper's Magazine*, September 2006. See also Lawrence P. Jackson, "An Interview with Edward P. Jones," *African American Review* 34:1 (2000): 95-103.; and Maryemma Graham, "An Interview with Edward P. Jones," *African American Review* 42:3/4 (Fall/Winter 2008): 421–438.

Blindsided

After the white woman Roxanne Stapleton worked for in Silver Spring gave her a ride across the northern border into Washington, Roxanne, without much waiting, was able to catch the D.C. Transit bus heading down 14th Street, N.W. The bus going down 11th Street would have put her closer to her room on 10th, but it was still early Friday evening and the show at the Howard Theater wasn't until eight-thirty, and the white woman would be far away in another world until Monday. And, too, going down 14th had always been good luck: long ago she had met Cedric on a 14th Street bus. Dark Cedric with green eyes. Cedric of the two and a half years. She had once found a twenty-dollar bill on a 14th Street bus. So because there was time to spare, she took the 14th Street bus.

The bus was half full and Roxanne managed to get the first seat after the side door, her favorite spot. "Now you be sure to have a good weekend, Roxanne," the white woman she worked for had said, the same thing she had been saying for four years. Her white woman was to tut-tut over the telephone on Monday morning and ask, "Did you injure yourself inadvertently over the weekend, Roxanne? Maybe at one of your Negro functions?" The white woman had her ideas about what black people did with their lives, especially on weekends, and just about everything they did in her mind could lead to blindness.

By the time the bus reached Rittenhouse Street, a woman had sat down beside Roxanne and the haze was already over her eyes. Roxanne blinked once, and her eyes started to clear, and then she blinked twice more and all was as before. Between Randolph Street and Park Road the haze returned and refused to go away with more blinking. It was October, the days growing shorter as they rushed toward the end, and she, ever a poor daughter of the universe, attributed the haze to the world's gradual loss of daylight. And she was exhausted. Oh, but the things the body did when it was tired. Gonna make you a little blind, Roxanne, so you can't see that stage at the Howard Theater tonight. What will Sam Cooke[1] sound like when you blind, child? The universe told her to smile. But after they crossed Harvard Street and before they could reach Girard Street, with the bus now offering standing room only, she became worried because the haze remained steadfast. She considered herself a woman of some refinement and would not

---

[1] Samuel Cook (1931–64), known by his stage name Sam Cooke, was an American recording artist and singer-songwriter.

talk to just anyone on a bus, but she was so worried that she turned to the woman beside her and asked, "Miss, you see somethin on my eyes?" Leaning toward the woman, Roxanne opened her eyes as wide as she could.

"Lemme see," the woman said and took Roxanne's chin in her hand and pulled it to her. Some people thought nothing of taking large liberties when a small one was all that was needed. "No, they just look like regular eyes to me. You got somethin in your eyes?"

"There's something growin over my eyes, thas all. It's like cheese-cloth."

"Cheesecloth?" the woman said. She had a southern accent so thick it insulted Roxanne's ears. She was much older than Roxanne was when she came to Washington with her own accent, so the woman would probably never speak any other way, as Roxanne had succeeded in doing. "Whas cheesecloth?" And she was louder than she needed to be in public.

"I just can't see the way I usually see, thas what I'm sayin." Roxanne closed her eyes and used her index fingers to massage her temples. Just relax, she told herself. Her Catholic friend, Agnes Simmons, had prayers to some saint for every ailment. Who was the saint for blind people and had he himself been struck blind?

At Clifton Street, the bus stopped for some time after a man got on and dropped the twenty-five pennies he had for his fare. Not one fell into the fare box. People laughed as the bus driver said to no one in particular that they should outlaw paying with pennies. "I pay your salary with these pennies," the man said at one point, down on his hands and knees. Each time he found a penny he would stand up and drop it in the box. "You don't pay my salary with nothin," said the driver, who refused to move until the man had paid his full fare. "Oh, yes, I do, too. Here. Here's little bit of it now," and he stood and put in a penny. "All right, yall," a man seated behind the driver said. He had roses in one arm, cradled there like a small child. "I'll pay his G-D fare and you just get this bus goin." People applauded. He leaned over the penny man on the floor and put a quarter in the box, the roses still nestled in his arm, and the driver pulled back into traffic. The man with the pennies stayed on the floor and the bus driver said he would have to move behind the white line, as required by the laws and regulations of Washington, D.C. "On that floor is my tip for you," the man said and stood up.

Roxanne, trying to remember if she had seen any white people on the bus, did not laugh with everyone else. She had kept her eyes closed once the woman next to her had looked into them, but before the intersection at Florida Avenue, she opened them and there was nothing but darkness. Her heart sank and she gave up a tiny yelp. "Lady," she said to the woman beside her, "I think I'm blind. I don't know what I'm gonna do."

"You a blind lady?" Yes, Roxanne decided, the accent was eternal. "How long you been blind, honey?"

"Just now. It just happened. You have to tell the bus driver because I don't know what I'm goin to do."

"You blind? You do good to be blind. I wouldn't go about if I was blind, I can tell you that."

"Please, just tell the driver. I got here seein and now I can't see. Tell him that. Please."

"Oh, you just *got* blind? Thas what you sayin?"

"Yes, just now. I could see all day, but now I can't."

"Dear Jesus sittin on the throne!" The woman stood up. "Driver, we have a poor blind woman here. You hear me!"

The word was taken forward. "We got a blind woman that want off this bus, driver," people from Roxanne up to the front began saying. "Driver, ain't you listenin?" the penny man said. "Thas just like D.C. Transist to hold a blind woman up."

The driver stopped between Swann and S Streets. "What is this commotion?" he said after he stood up and looked back. His view was not good because of the standing people. "Somebody hurt?"

"There a blind woman that wants off," said the penny man, who was standing midway between the driver and Roxanne. What he said was repeated until it reached Roxanne, who said as loud as her dignity would permit, "No, please. I was just now struck blind. I could see when I got on, and now I can't. I was just struck blind."

"She was struck blind on your rickety-ass bus," a woman across from Roxanne said. "I hope she sue D.C. Transit for everything yall got."

"You workin for that blind lady now, bigshot," the penny man said to the driver, who was making his slow way back to Roxanne. "Try bein nasty to your new boss lady and see how long you keep your job. Fire him right now, lady. He made you blind."

The driver reached Roxanne. "Lady, why ain't you tell me you was blind when you got on? I coulda put you by me and it woulda made things easier."

Roxanne thought she remembered his face, the bill of the hat cocked a bit more up than it should be, and a face too womanish to suit her. "Is your fellow a handsome colored man, Roxanne?" her white woman had once asked. "Thas just it," Roxanne said to the driver. "I wasn't blind when I got on." And the driver was also short. Cedric and Ray and Casey and all the rest had been tall men of long shadows. Her new man, Melvin, was a good foot taller than she was. "Can't you understand? I was just now struck blind." But was this driver really short, or had that been the one yesterday? Last week? How can a blind woman trust her memory?

"Right now? Right here? On my bus?"

"Yes. I could see when I paid my fare." She sighed because at last her words and his words made it all real, for herself, for the entire bus: Roxanne Stapleton was blind. "I could see," she said, and the words were only a few degrees above a whisper, which was how she liked to speak in public. People said she got loud when she drank, but she didn't believe them. I ain't just like every colored person from every corner of the world.

"I just can't see now." Would the show at Howard Theater ever come back? Was Sam Cooke the kind of man to wait for a blind woman?

"You wanna go to the hospital?" the driver said.

"I don't know. There's no pain. I do know I wanna get home now."

"Where you live?"

"Seventeen-oh-eight 10th Street."

"I know where that is," the penny man said. He had followed the driver through the standing crowd. "Round the corner from the fire station on R Street. Right?"

"Yes," Roxanne said. Please, Lord, give me help from anybody but this jackass.

"You mind takin her home?" the driver said.

The man leaned over and looked out a window, up and down 14th Street. When he rose up again, pennies in his pockets jangled. "This way before my stop," the man said, "but I could see her home."

"You want this man to see you home, lady?"

She would have preferred anyone but the absurd man with his pennies, but in the end Roxanne nodded her head. "I'd appreciate it."

The driver led her to the front and wrote down her name and address and her friend Agnes's telephone number because Roxanne used her money for clothes rather than a telephone. "I'm sorry bout all this," the driver said and placed in her hand a slip of paper with the names of the D.C. Transit people she should contact. Then he opened the door and people started saying, "Good luck to you, lady. Good luck to you, blind lady." The man went down the steps first, his pennies jangling with each movement, and then he reached up and took her hand and guided her down. The door of the bus closed and it went on, and the sound of it leaving was the saddest sound she had heard in a long time.

At the corner of S and 14th Streets she asked the man where they were. She was surprised when he told her because she had thought they were still on the other side of Florida Avenue. She knew the area well, the liquor store at the corner, the office of her notorious landlord, Roscoe L. Jones, behind her at the corner of Swann, and across 14th on S was a little restaurant Melvin had taken her to on their first date. But maybe this wasn't the place. Maybe this was Southeast and everyone was out to get her.

"If you get a good night's sleep, your sight might come back," the man said, placing her right hand around his left upper arm. "Whas your name again, lady?"

She told him.

"I'm Lowell and I'll see you home safe." He did not sound like a man so down in the world that he had only pennies for money.

"I really appreciate this, Lowell." Two weeks ago a woman on New Jersey Avenue returning home from work had been robbed and hit twice in the head with a gun, the worst crime many had heard about in some time.

Roxanne was realizing that Washington was getting less and less safe for people like her. The good and the decent. Men with little in their pockets had done the city in. "I've told Mr. Shepherd we just cannot chance coming into the city after dark, Roxanne," her white woman in Silver Spring had said once. "It is not a city for the good and the decent anymore the way it was when Mr. Truman and General Eisenhower were here. There are new elements there."

Lowell said, "No big deal. I knowed a blind woman when I was a boy in Anacostia.[2] She raised five children by herself after her husband died walkin to work. That lady could fill your cup up to the top and not spill a drop while she was doin it."

They turned and went up 10th and within a few steps they could smell what was left of the storefront church that had burned down just the Sunday before. "I hope nobody was hurt," Lowell said, looking through the skeletal thing all the way into the back. It was a frightening mess, and the man was tempted to tell her that she was lucky she could not see it. The church's reverend was to knock at Roxanne's door within the week, having heard about what had happened to her. She would talk to him only at the door, would not allow him in, thinking that he was looking for a donation to help rebuild the church. He would see that in her face. "I only came," Reverend Saunders said, putting a basket of fruit in her hands, "because God would not allow me to do otherwise."

At her building, a lime-green two-story brick structure, she wanted to know if there was a light on in the basement, and when he said there was, she asked that he go down and knock at the door. Mary Benoit and her two children lived there. Mary wasn't a drinker, a partyer, but she and Roxanne, ever a woman in search of a good time, were friendly enough. She wanted now to be with people she knew, hear voices she recognized. Mary's nine-year-old daughter, Adele, came out. "Hi you, Miss Roxanne?"

"I'm blind, honey. It just happened."

"Blind? Oh, no, Miss Roxanne. You want me to help you?"

"Your mother home yet?" Lowell had placed Roxanne's hand on the railing before knocking, and now he took that hand and put in the girl's hand.

"My mama not home yet," Adele said, "but Taylor, he home." The girl began rubbing the hand Lowell had given her, rubbing it in both of hers, the way she had seen people in the movies do with someone's cold hands.

"I best get on," Lowell said. "Less you need me for somethin else."

"Oh, no," Roxanne said. "You been so good to me. Lemme give you a little somethin for all your trouble. I know you went out your way." She began to open her pocketbook, but he put his hand over hers. "I don't need your money, lady. Just try to get better, thas all." He stepped away.

"Adele, baby, would you see me to my place?" Her room was on the first floor, a few feet beyond the front door, a large room with a sink and

[2] A historic neighborhood in Washington, D.C.

an icebox and a stove, along with a bed and dresser and everything else she needed to make a good life. She had been there six years. Adele unlocked the door and Roxanne switched on the light just inside the door and stepped inside. The room smelled the same—Spice and Span mingling with the perfume she had put on the morning before going out to clean her white woman's house and cook her food. Suddenly, taking small steps into the room, both hands out before her, she could see herself the day she picked up the box of Spic and Span at the Safeway on 7th Street, had taken it from a shelf two up from the bottom and looked at the price to compare it with the larger size one shelf up. No, she had told herself, the small size will do for now; the price had been in blue numbers on a tiny white sticker. She could also see herself the Sunday she got the perfume at Peoples Drug at 7th and M. She had gone in with Melvin; he bought prophylactics in a red box, and she wandered over to the perfume kiosk. "Pick one, and I'll buy it for you," he had said and kissed her shoulder from behind. But, no, had that been Melvin, or Cedric of a long time ago, Cedric of two and a half years?

Roxanne sat on the bed. Adele helped her take off her sweater.

"Miss Roxanne, you really blind?"

"Why would I lie bout something like that, girl?" There was an edge in her voice, and Adele, not used to it, closed down. "Why would a body lie bout bein less than what they was?" Roxanne had a daughter, way back in Louisiana, nine ugly miles outside of Baton Rouge. But she had not raised the daughter, and she had not seen her in two years, the last time Roxanne had visited Antibes Nouveau. Had left that place, without planning to, for good at twenty-six years of age in the middle of the night with two men friends as the daughter, then three years, slept at the home of Roxanne's parents. Sipping rum and Coke, Roxanne and the two men had only planned to visit four juke joints before morning. I be back fore breakfast, she had said to her parents when she left the girl at nine o'clock that night. But she did not see Louisiana or the daughter again for a year. Long before they hit the second juke joint, one of the men, the driver, had suggested that they drive all the way to Washington, where folks partied seven days a week. Of the three, only Roxanne knew geography and distance, but the rum said she did not know what she thought she did. On the third day, more than halfway to Washington, somewhat sober and committed now to nothing else but salvaging a bad idea, the man spoke not about parties but about his third cousin who knew how to get well-paying jobs in the federal government. After finding a pathetic government job in Washington, Roxanne telegraphed her parents eight days later, after they had already begun rehearsing how to tell their granddaughter her mother was dead. *Will send for Carolyn soon. Give me a few months to save for her ticket.* She was hungover when she telegraphed, and she would be hungover the times over the years when she started her visits home from Union Station. But every year as she set out for Antibes Nouveau, Washington was ever in her heart and mind a new city, still a place with men who did not yet know about "the Jewel of Louisiana," still a place where she needed to be.

There was a picture of her daughter in a gold-looking metal frame on the tiny table beside the bed in her room; the girl was five years old in the picture, but that had been six years ago. Roxanne turned now to Adele and said, trying to put a little warmth in her voice, "Baby girl, would you mind hangin up my sweater?" The room had no closet, just a long wooden rack that Roxanne hung all her clothes on. Her daughter had never seen Washington. "I don't think I can reach up there, Miss Roxanne, less I get on the chair." "Well, just hang it on the back of the chair." During the visit to Antibes Nouveau two years before, her daughter had first avoided her, and then, on the eve of her return to Washington, the child had begged her not to go.

With Roxanne still on the bed, Adele remained near the chair, which was unlike her when around Roxanne. When grown-ups talked mean, the child liked to stay to herself.

"Adele?"

"Ma'am?" Next to the chair was a tiny table, a twin to the one at the bed, and on it was a record player. The records were on the one shelf below that.

"You lookin at me?"

"Yes, ma'am, but I whatn't starin hard or nothin." She was not a child of lies.

"Come over here. I'm still the same Miss Roxanne." She opened her arms, and the girl put her head into the woman's lap. Roxanne felt herself wanting to cry; maybe this wasn't just something to mess up her weekend. Maybe this was always and always. "You go on back downstairs and tell you mama to come up when she get here."

"I can stay if you want me to. I'll stay with you."

"No." Roxanne told her to take the lock off the door and pull it shut. Behind her room were stairs that went down to the basement and she could hear Adele going down. Long ago she had heard of a man in a foreign country, a man the doctors had made into a woman. If they could do that, then they could restore her sight. Those doctors had had a long way to go, for the man had never been a woman. They might not have to go as far with her, for she had known sight all her life.

She stood and put her arms out. This how blind people act, she thought. This how all them poor blind people act. At the mirror over the sink, she blinked and blinked, hoping. She put her face close to the mirror, so close that the breath came out of her and bounced against the glass and returned to warm her nose. "You look like a million dollars to a man that been poor all his life," a boyfriend had said not long after she arrived in Washington. Pulling her head back, she reached up and touched the mirror. She was beautiful, and the whole world had always told her so. That boyfriend was dead now. And being that he was dead, and being that she was blind, how true were the words? Fine, fine Roxanne, the best thing ever to come out of Louisiana. "You could be one of those colored models they say your people have," her white woman had said. What would happen to her beautiful face now? She tapped the mirror and then touched all the features of her face. What would happen? She had not learned very many big things about herself while living in Washington, but one big thing she had learned was that if she was not first beautiful in her own eyes, then she was beautiful in no one's eyes.

Agnes Simmons got off the D.C. Transit but at R and 11th Streets, N.W., and stopped at Cohen's grocery store on the corner. She knew she needed something, but she couldn't remember what. Bread, yes. Eggs? Was it eggs? She bought bread and told herself she would just have to come back if she had no eggs. Her friend Roxanne was not a lender. *I work hard for what I got, Agnes...* She walked to 10th on the southern side of R to see if Tenth Street Baptist Church had changed the signboard in their yard. For nearly three years of living above Roxanne, she had enjoyed the little sayings they put there, though lately they had been rather tame. A year ago they had had the best yet: I COMPLAINED BECAUSE I HAD NO SHOES UNTIL I MET A MAN WHO HAD NO FEET. That had touched the Catholic soul in her, something she still thought about as she closed her eyes and opened her mouth and accepted the host. *This is my flesh...* She was twenty-eight and had never been married and had not had a steady boyfriend in four years, but she was not in pain. *This is my flesh...* No one had told her she was beautiful in a very long time, since before the last boyfriend who had wanted only one thing. Beware of boys who want only one thing, her Catholic mother had warned as they shopped for Agnes's first brassiere.

The church's signboard that night had nothing but the names of the church and the pastor and the times of services. *Eat...*

She knocked at Roxanne's door and Roxanne said to come in.

"Where the hell you been, Agnes? I been waitin and waitin for you. Where the hell you been?"

"Why? What's wrong?"

"I been struck blind, thas what's wrong." Roxanne was in the easy chair in front of the large front window.

Agnes laughed. "Oh, just give me another one, because that one won't do it." She had been educated in Washington's Catholic schools and worked now across from the gas company in a shop on 11th Street that sold buttons and sewing supplies and cloth and all else that a woman needed to help make a good home. Becoming the manager after five years of service. Once, looking out the store's window, Agnes had seen passing two former teachers, nuns, from Holy Redeemer and had gone out to them. But as she watched their sturdy backs, the ironed perfection of their long, black habits that seemed not to swish one bit from side to side like women's dresses, she had said nothing. Agnes's mother had always prayed that she would become a nun, but her mother was dead now, and so there was no one to want such a life for her anymore. Her father had converted to marry her mother. His good Catholic wife had suffered up to her last moment of life, and the kneeling convert had raised his bowed head at her funeral mass and never lowered it again. "Agnes," he told her whenever she asked if he had been to mass, "you can be Catholic for both of us now."

"I should slap your damn face!" Roxanne shouted.

"Why? What did I do, Roxanne?" Agnes came in and set down her grocery bag and purse next to the door, something she always did so as not to forget things on her way out.

"'What did I do, Roxanne? What did I do?'" Roxanne stood up and nearly fell, and when she took a step, she bumped into the small table beside the chair. "'What did I do, Roxanne?' You make me so sick! I tell you I went blind and all you can do is laugh."

Agnes went to her "But I thought you were kidding, Roxanne. You know how you kid sometimes." Agnes touched her arm.

"Well, I'm not kiddin now, you dumb bitch." Roxanne pulled away. "I don't know why I bother with you. Why do I waste my damn time with someone like you?"

"I'm sorry, Roxanne. I really am. Here, why don't you sit down. Please tell me what happened? Dear Jesus." Agnes made the sign of the cross.

"'Dear Jesus. Dear Jesus.' For Chrissakes!" Roxanne sat again and misjudged where she was and so sat on the arm and tumbled onto the seat. "Get me a little vodka from the icebox, and mix some orange juice in it." Why had she lost her sight and Agnes hadn't? What did Agnes do with her sight all day anyway? Sell a few buttons here, a few needles there. Not even anough makeup on her face to cover a roach's back.

Agnes brought the glass with three-quarters vodka and one-fourth orange juice, the way Roxanne liked it. "Here it is." She waited until Roxanne had a firm grip on the glass and then released it. Roxanne drank nearly half of it in one gulp. They were both facing the large window onto 10th Street, and Agnes looked down to see two boys on the sidewalk counting money and Roxanne heard first a car honking its horn all the way up to R Street, followed by a pickup chugging along. Two cars with well-tuned engines came after the pickup. Roxanne was listening for Melvin's car. Three more cars went almost silently past her window. It was like Melvin to be late when he knew she needed him. Agnes remembered that soon everyone would have to turn their clocks back one hour. Fall back, spring forward, that was the rule from the nuns arrayed in their black. *Black is not my color, Mama." "Black's everyone's color, Agnes."*

There were playful taps at the door and Roxanne called out, "Melvin? Melvin? That you?" Melvin foster came in and started singing a medley of Sam Cooke songs. "If he can't make it," Melvin said, "I'm gonna go up on that state and replace him." He was in a dark blue suit and a bright gray tie, Agnes saw, and he was wearing black Swiss Ballys, the kind with the graceful stitching at the toes. She had seen such in the window of Rich's on F Street, as she strolled about on her lunch hour.

"Oh, Melvin," Roxanne said, "where you been, honey?"

"I'm real early," he said, "so don't give me none a your stuff."

"She's blind, Melvin."

"She's blind, she's blind as a bat," Melvin sang. When neither woman responded, he stopped, took off his hat, and put it on a peg on the wooden rack. He was nothing if not a man who took the awful silence of women seriously. "Temporary, temporary," he said after Roxanne had explained as he sat on the arm of the easy chair, his arm around Roxanne as she drank a second vodka. "Fuckin temporary, baby." Agnes was now only a few feet beyond the door. He remembered how religious Agnes was and he looked at her and said, "Just temporary."

In the end, Melvin said they had best get to Freedmen's Hospital, and Agnes asked if she should accompany them.

"Of course, you should," Roxanne said. "What kinda stupid-ass question is that?"

"Let her alone, Roxanne. She ain't responsible for this," Melvin said.

It snowed that night in October, two inches, and people said that was one for the record books.

Through the months of the fall and the winter, Roxanne saw a series of ophthalmologists, neurosurgeons, and psychiatrists from Freedmen's to D.C. General, and none could tell her where her sight had gone. "It may well be, Miss Stapleton," a psychiatrist in a darkened, borrowed office at D.C. General said to Roxanne late one morning as Agnes sat in a chair beside the door, "that you could awaken tomorrow and your eyesight will be back." This woman, who had been imported from Georgetown University, was herself losing her sight, though none of her patients—many of whom were prisoners from the D.C. Jail next to the hospital—had been informed. She saw Roxanne alone that morning for some forty-five minutes and then brought in Agnes, who had been accompanying her friend to many of the doctors' visits. And when Agnes was not able to come, Melvin had been there. So many of the friends Roxanne lived to party with had drifted away. They might catch her blindness, and blind people couldn't dance very well, and they certainly weren't known as partyers. "Or it could be," the psychiatrist continued, "that when you are sixty or seventy or eighty, you will awaken and be able to see again." A social worker at Howard University had thought a psychiatrist going blind would know the proper things to say to a woman who was already there. "But then, too, you might die without ever seeing again." Some of the jail's prisoners, who knew what no one had told them, called her the Bat, and others called her the Mole behind her back. It was like God to do that shit to a colored woman, the prisoners said—make her a doctor with one hand and make her blind with the other.

That lousy bitch doctor!" Roxanne complained as Agnes led her out to the D.C. General entrance where Melvin, who had driven them there and was outside smoking, was to pick them up. "That lousy, no-good bitch!"

"There is hope there somewhere," Agnes said quietly.

"Let me fuckin go!" Roxanne pulled her arm away. "You worse than she is, you silly-ass thing. Take that hope shit and stick it up some priest's ass!" People stopped and stared at her, but Roxanne did not know.

Agnes stood with her arms at her sides, and when Roxanne heard nothing from her, she swung at the place where she had last heard Agnes speak. "You worse than nothin!" It had been more or less this way between them for some time, though the effort to strike Agnes was at the end of a very long road. Neither woman would know it for some time. Agnes leaned to the left and Roxanne hit nothing, then stumbled and caught herself before she fell.

"Hey! Hey!" Roxanne could hear Melvin coming closer. "What the hell you doin out here, Roxanne? Why you actin up?"

"Oh, Melvin baby, I'm tired of this stuff from her and everybody else." He took her gently by the arm and led her to the nearest wall.

"I know," he said. "I can only think I know." He held her shoulder for several moments, and then he turned and faced Agnes, who had a look he could not fathom. He reached across to Agnes and touched her cheek with his open hand. People watched the two. As far as either Melvin or Agnes could remember, this was the first time they had ever touched in such a way. Agnes closed her eyes and moved into his hand.

This was late April, and up until then spring had not been unkind to Washington. It stayed that way until mid-June when the humidity hit, thick and mean and unforgiving, and ordinary people with ordinary lives had to slog and claw their way into a more horrendous beast of an August where they lived each day thinking September would bring them relief. That was not to be so.

"I sometime think I'm gonna lose my mind," Roxanne said now, and Melvin returned to her.

"You made of better stuff than that," Melvin said. Agnes went toward the door; he could not make out anything bad in her walking, not hatred or bitterness or even resentment. There was merely—or so it seemed as he saw her step onto the rubber pad before the electric doors and watch them, first one and then the other, open to her—there was just a passable day out beyond the door that she wanted to enjoy before returning to many hours at the shop.

"I useta think I was, honey," Roxanne said. "I really useta think so."

Weeks before this, in March, after the city government people had officially declared her "a blind entity with no feeble mindedness," the social worker at Howard and some D.C. government people got Roxanne into a program aimed at teaching the handicapped, especially the blind, how to live like everyone else. Someone, for three days, came to the homes of the five blind students then in the program to show them how to maneuver around their "habitable space." Then Roxanne and the four other blind people began to learn the basics of accounting and how to operate tiny stores that were in various federal government office buildings around the city. The stores sold snacks and cigarettes and newspapers and small packets of Kleenex that could be tucked into a woman's pocketbook. The instructor, an accountant with a blind husband who ran his own little store at the Justice Department, told her students at the end of the first day that the federal government employed people who would be mostly honest customers but that there were some who did not have the fear of God. "They will give you a dollar and swear to their thieving and useless god it was five dollars," she said. "But our all-seeing god is a money God and knows money backwards and forwards. He will guide you."

The store they ultimately gave Roxanne was on the sixth floor of a ten-story building at Thomas Circle, with a large window that faced Vermont Avenue. On the building's seventh floor was an outpost of the Atomic Energy Commission with people who did nothing but read reports only from scientists based in Nevada and Utah and the southeastern portion of North Dakota. In time, as these people came to know her, they would come into the store and joke with Roxanne that if her doughnuts weren't fresh enough, they would "atomize" her and her stale doughnuts. On the fifth floor and on her own sixth floor there were outposts of the Internal Revenue Service and the Department of Commerce. These were primarily silent people, except for the Negroes who laughed with Roxanne as they complained that the federal government had outlawed soul food. A good part of the rest of the building were D.C. government employees, and though they came and went all day and were as friendly as any of the federal people, few of the federal people knew exactly what their jobs were.

It became not such a bad life, the life of a small store operator, and by the beginning of August Roxanne had assured herself that she could conquer "this blindness thing," or at least learn to live side by side with it. She had worried that she would become a next to nothing, floating out in the universe alone and penniless. She could see herself becoming like the blind man with his milky gray eyes she used to see sitting on a wooden folding chair on the corner of 9th and F Streets, N.W., his quart-sized mason jar of donated bills and coins on a green handkerchief on the ground in front of him. Blowing on a silver harmonica when he wasn't mumbling to himself. "Blind man here, blind man here, blind man here just tryin to get by," he sang to passersby.

On the Monday evening of that second week in August, the accountant instructor took Roxanne to dinner at Scholl's Cafeteria just down the street from her job on Vermont Avenue and then saw her home. "I'm so proud of you, Roxanne," the woman said. "You and me both," Roxanne said before she got out of the car and unfolded her white cane. Once in her room, after she had turned on the fan, she banged on the ceiling with a pole—a device to open high windows—for Agnes to come down to her. The pole had been given to her by Melvin, back when the blindness was such a new thing to them all. Roxanne hit the ceiling five times and waited, but Agnes did not come down. She waited several minutes more and hit the ceiling again. She thought she had heard footsteps above her, but she knew by now that blindness played tricks with the rest of her senses. She got a beer from the icebox and sat in her easy chair in shorts and an old Dr. Ben Casey[3] shirt from Melvin. The oscillating fan blew on her and then blew to the nothing on either side of her.

Upstairs, Agnes sat on her bed. She also had one room but, unlike Roxanne, there was a small kitchen attached to hers. After Agnes had heard the first banging, she had immediately stopped walking across the floor, and then, as quiet as an old thief, she had gone lightly to the bed and sat as the listened to the second round of banging. "I want you to write a letter to my parents when I get home tonight," Roxanne had told her that morning. Now, Agnes looked down at the red fingernail polish she had applied two evenings before. It had taken her more than an hour. She had long ago seen Roxanne paint her own nails in less than ten minutes. Agnes touched the nails, the redness, the smoothness. They were cut short to suit a functional life. "Is this not pride before a fall?" she said of the polish and waited for the pole to hit her floor again. She had tried putting on lipstick that morning, but the face she saw in the mirror with the lipstick was such an alien one that she was forced to wipe it off. The three of them, Agnes, Roxanne, and Melvin, had been sitting on the porch two evenings before, enjoying the sight and sound of children playing along 10th Street. Roxanne had gotten up and made her way upstairs to the building's only bathroom. Agnes and Melvin could, despite the sounds of the street, hear Roxanne's hands along the wall behind them as she made her way. No sooner was she on the stairs going to the second floor than Melvin looked at Agnes for a long time without words. She blushed and took her eyes to her lap. "I think I'll go for a walk. Please tell Roxanne," Melvin said as he stood. He went down two steps to the sidewalk and turned and looked up at her. Less than fifteen minutes before, Roxanne had said to Agnes, "Go get me another beer." "I'll get it," Melvin had said. "No, I told Agnes, honey." On the sidewalk, Melvin looked up the two steps at Agnes and said, "Why you scared to even put lipstick on?" He seemed more hurt than anything else. He left without an answer. And as she heard Roxanne making her way back down, Agnes picked up the beer that was still cold even with the crushing heat about them and asked herself who would know if she spit in the can. She had had confession that Saturday and had escaped

[3]*Ben Casey* was a TV medical drama, 1961–66.

from the confessional with a penance of only two Our Fathers and two Hail Marys. "Go in peace," the priest had told her. She put the can back down in the same place.

Agnes now got up from the bed and went into the kitchen, not caring what sounds she made along the floor. A third round of banging began, but she ignored it and prepared her dinner. Across the city, on North Capitol Street, Melvin sat in a booth in Mojo's and thought how nice it would be to have another beer. He had told Roxanne that he needed to visit a sick relative in Arlington for a few days, but she did not know that all his kin there had died out a long time ago. He took his time with two more beers, and then, a little before midnight, he got in his car and traveled to S Street, N.W., between 10th and 11th. He parked and the time went on and on until it was nearly one thirty in the morning. He had a job to go to in a few hours, but he was lovesick and no job in the universe could matter now. The beer had taken him there, but as he sat in the car and smoked cigarettes, the beer lost its hold and he gradually became just a man thinking about a skinny woman, not altogether attractive with her eyeglasses and her unpainted lips and the habit of crossing herself whenever a dead person's name was mentioned.

Melvin got out of the car and went around the corner and up 10th Street to where Roxanne and Agnes lived. He took the outside stairs slowly, one at a time, and walked by Roxanne's door. Agnes opened her door after the third knock and stood with her robe tightly around her nightgown, one hand holding the bunched cloth at the neck. It would be like you, Melvin thought, to have on a nightgown in this weather. She squinted without her eyeglasses. She had a life that burrowed through the world with few surprises, and there was no surprise on her face now. It was as if, every day over years and years, he had said to her, "On such and such a night, I will knock at your door and I want you to answer without giving it any thought."

"It's late," he said as she stood in the space the partly opened door made.

"I know," she said. They were not whispering and it was nearly two in the morning. Roxanne had stopped banging on the ceiling after about half an hour, and she had not sent anyone to get Agnes.

"You can shut that door in my face and I'll turn around and leave," he said.

"Leave? And go back downstairs?" she said. They had never spoken man-and-woman talk like that, but no one listening would have known this.

"I didn't come from downstairs."

Once he was inside, she put on her eyeglasses and fixed him a cup of coffee while he sat at the small table at the window, and again she moved about her place without thinking once of the woman below her. The world outside her window looked different to Melvin from one floor up.

"I've been thinking of moving from here," she said after placing the cup and saucer before him and taking the seat across from him.

He said, "I would miss you. It would be like all the pain in the world if I couldn't see you again."

The priest who would instruct him in the Catholic faith told him he would have to choose a middle name for himself. "Why?" Melvin would ask. "Because there was no Saint Melvin, and God wants you to have a saint's name." Agnes's father, a Catholic no more, unearthed a small book giving all the saints' names and why they had been canonized. "Pick one," his father-in-law-to-be said. "George. Sebastian. John. Pick one ... But try to stay away from Xavier. I don't remember what he did, but that name ain't done all that right by me."

For weeks, Agnes and Melvin did no more than talk in the night when the human beings in that building were all away in sleep. And when the talking was done sometime near dawn, he would stand, stretch, drink the last of his coffee, and go off to work. Then, late one night in October, a year after she went blind, Roxanne got up from her bed to go upstairs to the bathroom. Melvin had told her he would be away again that day. Before she had even reached the top of the stairs, she heard a most unfamiliar sound from Agnes's place—the sound of a woman moaning in pleasure. She knew the sounds Melvin made when he made love, but she did not have to hear him to know he was with Agnes. All that her life was at that moment told her he was in there. And that life, such as it was, flowed out of her and she fell back and had to catch herself before falling down the stairs. She went down four steps and was in such pain that she had to sit. She wanted to cry out, but she prevented that by putting the sleeve of her nightgown in her mouth. I must get back to my place, she thought, even though she knew she lacked the strength. Melvin had always been such a good man, even as she had strayed a few times. What could have happened to him? And to be with such a wretch of a woman. Perhaps, just perhaps, she thought after some time, it was not herself who had been beautiful all those years, but maybe it had always been Agnes.

He came to her three days later, planning to tell her he was taking his life in a different direction and not knowing she had heard Agnes with him. He picked up the chair under the wooden rack and sat across from Roxanne as she sat in the easy chair. He said a great deal but none of it contained the right words, and in the end they heard Agnes moving about upstairs and Roxanne turned to accuse him and he looked away because her eyes were the same as always—not at all milky and full of nothing like those of other blind women. They were as full of life as ever and they told him she saw all as before. They were silent for a time. "You'd best go now," Roxanne said, "your whore be callin you." "You got no call." "I got every call in the world," and that was the last time for the couple.

The next month Agnes moved away. And a week later a woman, Mercy, came into Roxanne's store, a woman she had known from all her partying years, a woman she had not seen in a long time. "You still look as good as ever," the woman said. "Oh, go on away from here," Roxanne said. They were the best words she had heard since going up that night to the bathroom. "I mean it, girl. I still run across men who go on and on about you. 'Roxanne this, Roxanne that.'" She invited Roxanne to a party that Saturday night, and Roxanne said as she gave the woman change, "Why not? Why the hell not?" It was so good to talk to the woman Mercy that Roxanne told her to take whatever she wanted, and Mercy took three packs of cigarettes, a package of doughnuts, and two sodas, though she told Roxanne she was taking only one soda and no cigarettes.

She had a sweet old time at the party—her first since Melvin went out of her life. The music, the cigarette smoke, the voices, a woman shrieking with laughter across the room—it was all familiar, and it was all her. Being blind might not be so bad. That Monday a fellow she had met at the party called her job and asked her out to lunch, but she said no. His voice had not grabbed her, and he had held her as they slow-dragged in that way of desperate men—as if he wanted to melt his body into hers. Two days after his call she received a letter from her parents, who asked for the tenth time that year if she wanted them to come up to her. "Don't fight alone," they said. "That would be just like you." Her parents also wrote that Roxanne's daughter—who had only been told in October, the month before, what had happened to her mother—had been trying to think of what to write. "She needs the time to take it in," her parents said in a letter of one page. Roxanne had Adele's brother, Taylor, write a letter to them and get a money order for their train tickets to Washington for an extended Christmas visit. Had it not been for the party, for Mercy telling everyone at the party that the Jewel of Louisiana was back and better than ever, she might have had him write, "My boyfriend abandoned me and I am utterly alone." "Utterly" was one of the favorite words of an early boyfriend after she first arrived in Washington. *"I'm utterly ashamed, baby." "I'm utterly hungry." "He was utterly dead."*

When Taylor had finished the letter, he sat in the chair under the wooden rack and studied the stamp on the envelope to make certain all the edges adhered. And after he knew the stamp would stay in place all the way to Antibes Nouveau, he said, "It hurt to be blind, Miss Roxanne?" She had become close to him and his sister and their mother, but the boy was nothing if not a barrel of questions. Maybe that came from having a mother who was a nondrinker. No parties. A life that seemed devoted only to her children. A boy with a mother like that could stop being afraid of asking grown people questions.

"Whatcha think, Taylor?" She was at the sink, putting a wet washcloth to her face.

"I say yes, but Mama said no. It hurt in other ways."

She touched the washcloth to her throat. The cloth was cool, but she knew that in moments her body would warm it. "Your mama right, Taylor." She faced the mirror and saw darkness and then turned and could make out the faintest of light in the rest of the room. Would her own daughter be like this boy? Questions, questions, always questions. Blind people, she remembered from the days when she could see, had that jumping thing with their eyes, and she wondered if she would get that, too. One more blow to a beautiful face. Adele had told her only two days ago that her eyes looked like regular eyes. But whatever could that mean? "I suppose blind people hurt in ways you don't understand now, Taylor." Maybe it was only people who had been blind for a very long time who got that jumping disease, people who had never learned to teach their eyes to pretend that they could see. She was coming to understand that it was not the questions, but the fear that she would not have the proper answers, answers that would not stand the test of time. If Taylor was this way, how much worse would it be with her own daughter? Who knew what kind of girl she had grown into? "Well, is it like pins in the arm or somethin?" the boy said. "O gettin shot by a BB gun?"

In the end, she put him off by telling him to put on a record Taylor's mother had given her on Thanksgiving. It was a 45, and on it a Puerto Rican was singing about the Earth as an apple moving silently through space. "I love his voice," Mary had said, "and I thought you might, too." Roxanne had not learned until much later, from someone at work, that the singer was blind.

Mercy took her to three office parties that second week in December. The morning after the third, Roxanne, hungover, could barely pull herself out of bed to get ready for work. Mercy came by her job near the end of the day and laughed that Roxanne would be drummed out of the blind people's union because she was having more fun than blind people were allowed.

A Saturday party at a house before the Tuesday her people were to arrive was the best in years. She had been introduced early to a man Mercy said was her third cousin "once removed," but Roxanne tried to discourage him from monopolizing her time. Still, he had a wonderful way about him. The Kearney Street, N.E., event was cut short at about midnight because it began to snow, and while the house where the party was held was nice enough, it would not comfortably keep the fifty or so people throughout a snowbound weekend.

Roxanne and Mercy and her boyfriend and her third cousin returned to 10th Street just before twelve thirty. The cousin had a wreck of a stomach and was living on practically nothing but baby food, so he was the only one who had not been drinking. He had put his hand on Roxanne's knee during the ride from Kearney Street, but she had not minded that. Indeed, she found it rather pleasant.

The boyfriend parked only two doors from Roxanne's place, and they got out of the car, giggling and dancing through the snow, which was already coming to an end. Just inside the front door, in the hallway, the cousin began kissing Roxanne and then the boyfriend began kissing Mercy. "Oh, whas this," Roxanne laughed, "an early Christmas present?" "Thas what it feels like to me," Mercy said. "Well," Roxanne said, "the least you could do is find us some mistletoe."

"Just shut up and enjoy it," the cousin said and placed his open mouth violently over hers so that his expelling breath went rushing into her body. His tongue pushed in and down her throat. His mouth was at an angle to hers, as boys have been taught to do, but in its violence, the mouth covered one of her nostrils, and the free nostril was the only way she could breathe, but that one had a very hard time of it. She felt as if she were drowning. She struggled, for breath and for freedom from the prison of his body. Then he put his hand between her legs, and that seemed to pull her back from drowning. Finally she pulled her face away and managed an insignificant scream. "Stop! Stop!" She thought, *I done seen this before. I done been in this play before.*

"Oh, Roxanne," Mercy said, "just lay back and enjoy it. It's Christmas, for God's sake. It's Christmastime."

Roxanne began punching the cousin's back. The accumulation of hits must have said something to him, because he pulled back and said to her, "You blind bitch! You should be happy a man like me would even give something like you the time a day." He tapped her jaw with his open hand, the one that had been between her legs. She hit the back of his head, and again he placed his mouth over hers. *I have no memory of singin this song. Dancin this dance ...* His hand returned to that place between her legs.

Roxanne heard two yips, and then a little voice called her name. "Agnes," Roxanne said, "is that you out there? Please, Agnes, is that you? Agnes?" Adele asked, "Miss Roxanne, you all right?" Roxanne could see herself through the child's eyes—a blind woman being assaulted in a hall. By a man she had been weak in the knees for only an hour earlier. Was the desperation plain as well? In a hall with two drunks doing what no child should see. *I done danced his dance and sung this song before ... This is what happens to blind people in the end.* "You betta leave Miss Roxanne alone," Adele said. There was no other sound in the hall but the tiny voice of the child. The third cousin pulled back. In the dim light of the hall, Adele was standing in her nightgown holding the puppy her mother had given her children early for Christmas. "Call Mr. Young for me, baby," Roxanne said. "Call him. Call your mama."

The cousin stepped back. He turned to Mercy and her boyfriend, who had not stopped kissing, and said, "Les blow this scene, yall." Once they were gone, Roxanne turned to the wall and began crying. She could still see what Adele was seeing. She had never felt more vulnerable, and never so small. The child put down the puppy and stayed where she was and the dog went to the woman. "If," Adele's mother had explained to Roxanne a week before, "it was a doll or a bicycle, I could hold it back from em till Christmas. But it's a puppy. It's life, and I can't keep that from em." The puppy sniffed at Roxanne's heels, and then Adele came to her. "I was goin to the bathroom," the girl said. "Number two. I tried to make him stay downstairs, but he jus a baby and won't listen." Adele picked up the puppy. Roxanne turned around and reached for the child and the puppy licked her hand. "You want me to stay with you, Miss Roxanne? We all be missin Miss Agnes."

At about six that morning, she got out of bed and stood there and felt the precious life that was the sleeping Adele. The puppy scrambled from its bed of blankets and came to her heels and sniffed. "We will have to do something for you, or you'll piss and shit up my house," she said to him. She went to the window. *I shoulda wrote you and told you what to expect when you get here. A daughter deserves that...* During the night the snow had returned briefly. It amounted to next to nothing, but after Roxanne raised the window a bit, she could smell that far, far more was on the way. She wondered what someone looking in the window would see—would they see a blind woman who was trying to get on with the rest of her life? She began humming the song by the blind Puerto Rican, about the Earth as an apple moving quietly through the universe. In her mind the world was moving through heavy snow. She boiled water and waited for the snow to come into their lives. When the coffee was ready, she took the cup with both hands and blew into it and sipped. Too much sugar, but the cream was just right. She sat in the easy chair. *I am you mother. That is first,* she should have had Taylor write. *Before there was anything else in the world for you, I was your mother...*

The snow came, and she felt it begin to cover and silence the world. She took another sip of the coffee, and as she did the snow grew heavier. Did her daughter like pancakes? She closed her eyes. Adele turned in her sleep. *In the beginning, before there was any breath in your body, you had your mother...* The puppy came up to her feet and turned around and around until it found a comfortable place beside her. She reached down and patted its back. *I am blind and that is all there is to it.* Eyes closed, she listened to the snow falling, each flake supplying a note in a long and wondrous song, and in moments, as the song played on, she was sitting on the giant apple that was the Earth and that was taking her through the snowy universe. They were moving away from the sun because she had all the heat she needed, so there was no reason to go that way. She leaned against the stem of the apple that was the Earth. As she and the apple neared Mars, she turned to the right and saw the puppy, but it was all grown up and was a dog that she had known back home when she was a girl no bigger than Adele, no bigger than her daughter in the picture on the table beside the bed. She pointed to Mars because she knew the dog, being as smart as he was, would appreciate the sight, and as she took her hand down, she saw Adele beside her on the left on the apple that was the Earth moving through the universe.

"You cold?" Roxanne asked the girl.

"No, ma'am," the child said. "The snow is warm, Miss Roxanne."

The woman and the girl and the dog looked at Mars, and after a long time, they were past it, and the girl sighed that Mars was now gone and Roxanne told her that they would see it again. The three were some ways from Jupiter when Roxanne began to worry that she would not remember the proper order of the planets. Could she be true to memory? She knew for sure that Jupiter was next, but was Uranus or Saturn after that? She knew all that once upon a time, could stand in front of the class-room nine ugly miles from the capital of Louisiana and recite their order and how far they were from the sun. What did she know now? On the apple, still traveling silently through the universe, she crossed her legs at the ankles and wiggled the toes of the foot on top. Then, as Jupiter showed itself hundreds and hundreds of thousands of miles away, she pulled the girl and the dog closer to her and the stem of the apple grew a covering as soft as that on her easy chair. It would be Uranus next if that was what she wanted it to be. She would put rings around it and give it a million moons, each a different color. Could she be true to memory? Maybe memory was what you made of it. She looked and the dog nodded Yes, ma'am, memory was what you made of it. Yes, then, rings around Uranus and Neptune. And she would put all the best singers and all the best dancing bands on Pluto, which was still a hundred million miles away, and on the outside of that planet, in blue and orange neon letters that even those blind from birth could read, she would put a sign that said Pluto was open all the time to all of God's children. Yes, open even to the least of them.

[2006]

AMY TAN ■ (1952–)

Amy Tan was born in Oakland, California, of Chinese immigrant parents. After the deaths of her father and brother, she and her mother moved to Montreux, Switzerland, where she attended high school. Returning to the United States, she enrolled at Linfield College in Oregon, and then transferred to San Jose State University where, while working two part-time jobs, she became an honors student and a President's Scholar.

In 1973 Tan earned a master's degree in linguistics, also at San Jose State, and enrolled in the doctoral program at the University of California, Berkeley; she left before completing the requirements for the degree. For the next five years Tan worked as a language development consultant and a project director, and then she became a freelance business writer. In 1986 she published her first short story; it was reprinted in *Seventeen* magazine, where it was noticed by an agent, who encouraged Tan to continue writing fiction.

Tan's collection of linked short stories, *The Joy Luck Club* (1989), which includes "Two Kinds," focuses on Chinese-American women and their immigrant mothers. Tan explained to an interviewer that while writing the book, she felt "as if she were merely taking dictation from an invisible storyteller" (*New York Times*, July 4, 1989):

> When I wrote these stories, it was as much a discovery to me as to any reader reading them for the first time. Things would surprise me. I would sit there laughing and I would say, "Oh, you're kidding!" It was like people telling me the stories, and I would write them down as fast as I could.

In the same interview, Tan noted that *The Joy Luck Club* arose from her desire to examine her relationship with her own mother and understand the reasons for their disagreements.

> When I was writing, it was so much for my mother and myself. I wanted her to know what I thought about China and what I thought about growing up in this country. And I wanted those words to almost fall off the page so that she could just see the story, that the language would be simple enough, almost like a little curtain that would fall away.

"Two Kinds" is at once a comic and a serious story. The comedy is evident in, for example, the mother's singlemindedness and in the daughter's absurd hope that the piano recital may be going all right, even though she is hitting all the wrong notes. The seriousness is suggested by the conflict between the mother and the daughter, the mother's passionate love, the daughter's rebelliousness, and her later recognition that her mother loved her deeply. There is a special power, too, in Tan's depiction of the daughter's deepening perception of her Chinese heritage.

Tan's other books include *The Kitchen God's Wife* (1991), *The Hundred Secret Senses* (1995), *The Bonesetter's Daughter* (2001), *Saving Fish from Drowning* (2005), and *Rules for Virgins* (2011), a 43-page story about 1912 Shanghai. Tan has also written two books for children, *The Moon Lady* (1992) and *SAGWA, the Chinese Siamese Cat* (1994).

See E. D. Huntley, *Amy Tan: A Critical Companion* (1998).

Two Kinds

My mother believed you could be anything you wanted to be in America. You could open a restaurant. You could work for the government and get good retirement. You could buy a house with almost no money down. You could become rich. You could become instantly famous.

"Of course you can be prodigy, too," my mother told me when I was nine. "You can be best anything. What does Auntie Lindo know? Her daughter, she is only best tricky."

America was where all my mother's hopes lay. She had come here in 1949 after losing everything in China: her mother and father, her family home, her first husband, and two daughters, twin baby girls. But she never looked back with regret. There were so many ways for things to get better.

We didn't immediately pick the right kind of prodigy. At first my mother thought I could be a Chinese Shirley Temple.[1] We'd watch Shirley's old movies on TV as though they were training films. My mother would poke my arm and say, "*Ni kan*"—You watch. And I would see Shirley tapping her feet, or singing a sailor song, or pursing her lips into a very round O while saying, "Oh my goodness."

"*Ni kan*," said my mother as Shirley's eyes flooded with tears. "You already know how. Don't need talent for crying!"

Soon after my mother got this idea about Shirley Temple, she took me to a beauty training school in the Mission district and put me in the hands of a student who could barely hold the scissors without shaking. Instead of getting big fat curls, I emerged with an uneven mass of crinkly black fuzz. My mother dragged me off to the bathroom and tried to wet down my hair.

"You look like Negro Chinese," she lamented, as if I had done this on purpose.

The instructor of the beauty training school had to lop off these soggy clumps to make my hair even again. "Peter Pan is very popular these days," the instructor assured my mother. I now had hair the length of a boy's, with

---

[1]United States film actress (b.1928) famous for child roles in the 1930s.

straight-across bangs that hung at a slant two inches above my eyebrows. I liked the haircut and it made me actually look forward to my future fame.

In fact, in the beginning, I was just as excited as my mother, maybe even more so. I pictured this prodigy part of me as many different images, trying each one on for size. I was a dainty ballerina girl standing by the curtains, waiting to hear the right music that would send me floating on my tiptoes. I was like the Christ child lifted out of the straw manger, crying with holy indignity. I was Cinderella stepping from her pumpkin carriage with sparkly cartoon music filling the air.

In all of my imaginings, I was filled with a sense that I would soon become *perfect*. My mother and father would adore me. I would be beyond reproach. I would never feel the need to sulk for anything.

But sometimes the prodigy in me became impatient. "If you don't hurry up and get me out of here, I'm disappearing for good," it warned. "And then you'll always be nothing."

Every night after dinner, my mother and I would sit at the Formica kitchen table. She would present new tests, taking her examples from stories of amazing children she had read in *Ripley's Believe It or Not,* or *Good Housekeeping, Reader's Digest,* and a dozen other magazines she kept in a pile in our bathroom. My mother got these magazines from people whose houses she cleaned. And since she cleaned many houses each week, we had a great assortment. She would look through them all, searching for stories about remarkable children.

The first night she brought out a story about a three-year-old boy who knew the capitals of all the states and even most of the European countries. A teacher was quoted as saying the little boy could also pronounce the names of the foreign cities correctly.

"What's the capital of Finland?" my mother asked me, looking at the magazine story.

All I knew was the capital of California, because Sacramento was the name of the street we lived on in Chinatown. "Nairobi!" I guessed, saying the most foreign word I could think of. She checked to see if that was possibly one way to pronounce "Helsinki" before showing me the answer.

The tests got harder—multiplying numbers in my head, finding the queen of hearts in a deck of cards, trying to stand on my head without using my hands, predicting the daily temperatures in Los Angeles, New York, and London.

One night I had to look at a page from the Bible for three minutes and then report everything I could remember. "Now Jehoshaphat had riches and honor in abundance and...that's all I remember, Ma," I said.

And after seeing my mother's disappointed face once again, something inside of me began to die. I hated the tests, the raised hopes and failed expectations. Before going to bed that night, I looked in the mirror above the bathroom sink and when I saw only my face staring back—and that it would always be this ordinary face—I began to cry. Such a sad, ugly girl! I made high-pitched noises like a crazed animal, trying to scratch out the face in the mirror.

And then I saw what seemed to be the prodigy side of me—because I had never seen that face before. I looked at my reflection, blinking so I could see more clearly. The girl staring back at me was angry, powerful. This girl and I were the same. I had new thoughts, willful thoughts, or rather thoughts filled with lots of won'ts. I won't let her change me, I promised myself. I won't be what I'm not.

So now on nights when my mother presented her tests, I performed listlessly, my head propped on one arm. I pretended to be bored. And I was. I got so bored I started counting the bellows of the foghorns out on the bay while my mother drilled me in other areas. The sound was comforting and reminded me of the cow jumping over the moon. And the next day, I played a game with myself, seeing if my mother would give up on me before eight bellows. After a while I usually counted only one, maybe two bellows at most. At last she was beginning to give up hope.

Two or three months had gone by without any mention of my being a prodigy again. And then one day my mother was watching *The Ed Sullivan Show*[2] on TV. The TV was old and the sound kept shorting out. Every time my mother got halfway up from the sofa to adjust the set, the sound would go back on and Ed would be talking. As soon as she sat down, Ed would go silent again. She got up, the TV broke into loud piano music. She sat down. Silence. Up and down, back and forth, quiet and loud. It was like a stiff embraceless dance between her and the TV set. Finally she stood by the set with her hand on the sound dial.

She seemed entranced by the music, a little frenzied piano piece with this mesmerizing quality, sort of quick passages and then teasing lilting ones before it returned to the quick playful parts.

"*Ni kan*," my mother said, calling me over with hurried hand gestures, "Look here."

I could see why my mother was fascinated by the music. It was being pounded out by a little Chinese girl, about nine years old, with a Peter Pan haircut. The girl had the sauciness of a Shirley Temple. She was proudly modest like a proper Chinese child. And she also did this fancy sweep of a curtsy, so that the fluffy skirt of her white dress cascaded slowly to the floor like the petals of a large carnation.

In spite of these warning signs, I wasn't worried. Our family had no piano and we couldn't afford to buy one, let alone reams of sheet music and piano lessons. So I could be generous in my comments when my mother bad-mouthed the little girl on TV.

[2]Popular variety show on TV (1948–71).

"Play note right, but doesn't sound good! No singing sound," complained my mother.

"What are you picking on her for?" I said carelessly. "She's pretty good. Maybe she's not the best, but she's trying hard." I knew almost immediately I would be sorry I said that.

"Just like you," she said. "Not the best. Because you not trying." She gave a little huff as she let go of the sound dial and sat down on the sofa.

The little Chinese girl sat down also to play an encore of "Anitra's Dance" by Grieg.[3] I remember the song, because later on I had to learn how to play it.

Three days after watching *The Ed Sullivan Show,* my mother told me what my schedule would be for piano lessons and piano practice. She had talked to Mr. Chong, who lived on the first floor of our apartment building. Mr. Chong was a retired piano teacher and my mother had traded housecleaning services for weekly lessons and a piano for me to practice on every day, two hours a day, from four until six.

When my mother told me this, I felt as though I had been sent to hell. I whined and then kicked my foot a little when I couldn't stand it anymore.

"Why don't you like me the way I am? I'm *not* a genius! I can't play the piano. And even if I could, I wouldn't go on TV if you paid me a million dollars!" I cried.

My mother slapped me. "Who ask you be genius?" she shouted. "Only ask you be your best. For you sake. You think I want you be genius? Hnnh! What for! Who ask you!"

"So ungrateful," I heard her mutter in Chinese. "If she had as much talent as she had temper, she would be famous now."

Mr. Chong, whom I secretly nicknamed Old Chong, was very strange, always tapping his fingers to the silent music of an invisible orchestra. He looked ancient in my eyes. He had lost most of the hair on top of his head and he wore thick glasses and had eyes that always looked tired and sleepy. But he must have been younger than I thought, since he lived with his mother and was not yet married.

I met Old Lady Chong once and that was enough. She had this peculiar smell like a baby that had done something in his pants. And her fingers felt like a dead person's, like an old peach I once found in the back of the refrigerator; the skin just slid off the meat when I picked it up.

I soon found out why Old Chong had retired from teaching piano. He was deaf. "Like Beethoven!" he shouted to me. "We're both listening only in our head!" And he would start to conduct his frantic silent sonatas.

---

[3]Edward Grieg (1843–1907), Norwegian composer.

Our lessons went like this. He would open the book and point to different things, explaining their purpose: "Key! Treble! Bass! No sharps or flats! So this is C major! Listen now and play after me!"

And then he would play the C scale a few times, a simple chord, and then, as if inspired by an old, unreachable itch, he gradually added more notes and running trills and a pounding bass until the music was really something quite grand.

I would play after him, the simple scale, the simple chord, and then I just played some nonsense that sounded like a cat running up and down on top of garbage cans. Old Chong smiled and applauded and then said, "Very good! But now you must learn to keep time!"

So that's how I discovered that Old Chong's eyes were too slow to keep up with the wrong notes I was playing. He went through the motions in half-time. To help me keep rhythm, he stood behind me, pushing down on my right shoulder for every beat. He balanced pennies on top of my wrists so I would keep them still as I slowly played scales and arpeggios. He had me curve my hand around an apple and keep that shape when playing chords. He marched stiffly to show me how to make each finger dance up and down, staccato like an obedient little soldier.

He taught me all these things, and that was how I also learned I could be lazy and get away with mistakes, lots of mistakes. If I hit the wrong notes because I hadn't practiced enough, I never corrected myself. I just kept playing in rhythm. And Old Chong kept conducting his own private reverie.

So maybe I never really gave myself a fair chance. I did pick up the basics pretty quickly, and I might have become a good pianist at that young age. But I was so determined not to try, not to be anybody different that I learned to play only the most ear-splitting preludes, the most discordant hymns.

Over the next year, I practiced like this, dutifully in my own way. And then one day I heard my mother and her friend Lindo Jong both talking in a loud bragging tone of voice so others could hear. It was after church, and I was leaning against the brick wall wearing a dress with stiff white petticoats. Auntie Lindo's daughter, Waverly, who was about my age, was standing farther down the wall about five feet away. We had grown up together and shared all the closeness of two sisters squabbling over crayons and dolls. In other words, for the most part, we hated each other. I thought she was snotty. Waverly Jong had gained a certain amount of fame as "Chinatown's Littlest Chinese Chess Champion."

"She bring home too many trophy," lamented Auntie Lindo that Sunday. "All day she play chess. All day I have no time do nothing but dust off her winnings." She threw a scolding look at Waverly, who pretended not to see her.

"You lucky you don't have this problem," said Auntie Lindo with a sigh to my mother.

And my mother squared her shoulders and bragged: "Our problem worser than yours. If we ask Jing-mei wash dish, she hear nothing but music. It's like you can't stop this natural talent."

And right then, I was determined to put a stop to her foolish pride.

A few weeks later, Old Chong and my mother conspired to have me play in a talent show which would be held in the church hall. By then, my parents had saved up enough to buy me a secondhand piano, a black Wurlitzer spinet with a scarred bench. It was the showpiece of our living room.

For the talent show, I was to play a piece called "Pleading Child" from Schumann's[4] *Scenes from Childhood.* It was a simple, moody piece that sounded more difficult than it was. I was supposed to memorize the whole thing, playing the repeat parts twice to make the piece sound longer. But I dawdled over it, playing a few bars and then cheating, looking up to see what notes followed. I never really listened to what I was playing. I daydreamed about being somewhere else, about being someone else.

The part I liked to practice best was the fancy curtsy: right foot out, touch the rose on the carpet with a pointed foot, sweep to the side, left leg bends, look up and smile.

My parents invited all the couples from the Joy Luck Club to witness my debut. Auntie Lindo and Uncle Tin were there. Waverly and her two older brothers had also come. The first two rows were filled with children both younger and older than I was. The littlest ones got to go first. They recited simple nursery rhymes, squawked out tunes on miniature violins, twirled Hula Hoops, pranced in pink ballet tutus, and when they bowed or curtsied, the audience would sigh in unison, "Awww," and then clap enthusiastically.

When my turn came, I was very confident. I remember my childish excitement. It was as if I knew, without a doubt, that the prodigy side of me really did exist. I had no fear whatsoever, no nervousness. I remember thinking to myself, This is it! This is it! I looked out over the audience, at my mother's blank face, my father's yawn, Auntie Lindo's stiff-lipped smile, Waverly's sulky expression. I had on a white dress layered with sheets of lace, and a pink bow in my Peter Pan haircut. As I sat down I envisioned people jumping to their feet and Ed Sullivan rushing up to introduce me to everyone on TV.

And I started to play. It was so beautiful. I was so caught up in how lovely I looked at first I didn't worry how I would sound. So it was a surprise to me when I hit the first wrong note and I realized something didn't sound quite right. And then I hit another and another followed that. A chill started at the top of my head and began to trickle down. Yet I couldn't stop playing, as though my hands were bewitched. I kept thinking

---

[4]A set of thirteen pieces of music for piano written in 1838 by Robert Schumann (1810–56).

my fingers would adjust themselves back, like a train switching to the right track. I played this strange jumble through two repeats, the sour notes staying with me all the way to the end.

When I stood up, I discovered my legs were shaking. Maybe I had just been nervous and the audience, like Old Chong, had seen me go through the right motions and had not heard anything wrong at all. I swept my right foot out, went down on my knee, looked up and smiled. The room was quiet, except for Old Chong, who was beaming and shouting, "Bravo! Bravo! Well done!" But then I saw my mother's face, her stricken face. The audience clapped weakly, and as I walked back to my chair, with my whole face quivering as I tried not to cry, I heard a little boy whisper loudly to his mother, "That was awful," and the mother whispered back, "Well, she certainly tried."

And now I realized how many people were in the audience, the whole world it seemed. I was aware of eyes burning into my back. I felt the shame of my mother and father as they sat stiffly throughout the rest of the show.

We could have escaped during intermission. Pride and some strange sense of honor must have anchored my parents to their chairs. And so we watched it all: the eighteen-year-old boy with a fake mustache who did a magic show and juggled flaming hoops while riding a unicycle. The breasted girl with white makeup who sang from *Madama Butterfly*[5] and got honorable mention. And the eleven-year-old boy who won first prize play-ing a tricky violin song that sounded like a busy bee.

After the show, the Hsus, the Jongs, and the St. Clairs from the Joy Luck Club came up to my mother and father.

"Lots of talented kids," Auntie Lindo said vaguely, smiling broadly.

"That was somethin' else," said my father, and I wondered if he was referring to me in a humorous way, or whether he even remembered what I had done.

Waverly looked at me and shrugged her shoulders. "You aren't a genius like me," she said matter-of-factly. And if I hadn't felt so bad, I would have pulled her braids and punched her stomach.

But my mother's expression was what devastated me: a quiet, blank look that said she had lost everything. I felt the same way, and it seemed as if everybody were now coming up, like gawkers at the scene of an accident, to see what parts were actually missing. When we got on the bus to go home, my father was humming the busy-bee tune and my mother was silent. I kept thinking she wanted to wait until we got home before shouting at me. But when my father unlocked the door to our apartment, my mother walked in and then went to the back, into the bedroom. No accusations. No blame. And in a way, I felt disappointed. I had been waiting for her to start shout-ing, so I could shout back and cry and blame her for all my misery.

---

[5]*Madama Butterfly* (*Madame Butterfly*) is an opera in three acts (originally two acts) by Giacomo Puccini (1858–1924).

I assumed my talent-show fiasco meant I never had to play the piano again. But two days later, after school, my mother came out of the kitchen and saw me watching TV.

"Four clock," she reminded me as if it were any other day. I was stunned, as though she were asking me to go through the talent-show torture again. I wedged myself more tightly in front of the TV.

"Turn off TV," she called from the kitchen five minutes later.

I didn't budge. And then I decided. I didn't have to do what my mother said anymore. I wasn't her slave. This wasn't China. I had listened to her before and look what happened. She was the stupid one.

She came out of the kitchen and stood in the arched entryway of the living room. "Four clock," she said once again, louder.

"I'm not going to play anymore," I said nonchalantly. "Why should I? I'm not a genius."

She walked over and stood in front of the TV. I saw her chest was heaving up and down in an angry way.

"No!" I said, and I now felt stronger, as if my true self had finally emerged. So this was what had been inside me all along.

"No! I won't!" I screamed.

She yanked me by the arm, pulled me off the floor, snapped off the TV. She was frighteningly strong, half pulling, half carrying me toward the piano as I kicked the throw rugs under my feet. She lifted me up and onto the hard bench. I was sobbing by now, looking at her bitterly. Her chest was heaving even more and her mouth was open, smiling crazily as if she were pleased I was crying.

"You want me to be someone that I'm not!" I sobbed. "I'll never be the kind of daughter you want me to be!"

"Only two kinds of daughters," she shouted in Chinese. "Those who are obedient and those who follow their own mind! Only one kind of daughter can live in this house. Obedient daughter!"

"Then I wish I wasn't your daughter. I wish you weren't my mother," I shouted. As I said these things I got scared. It felt like worms and toads and slimy things crawling out of my chest, but it also felt good, as if this awful side of me had surfaced, at last.

"Too late change this," said my mother shrilly.

And I could sense her anger rising to its breaking point. I wanted to see it spill over. And that's when I remembered the babies she had lost in China, the ones we never talked about. "Then I wish I'd never been born!" I shouted. "I wish I were dead! Like them."

It was as if I had said the magic words. Alakazam!—and her face went blank, her mouth closed, her arms went slack, and she backed out of the room, stunned, as if she were blowing away like a small brown leaf, thin, brittle, lifeless.

It was not the only disappointment my mother felt in me. In the years that followed, I failed her so many times, each time asserting my own will, my right to fall short of expectations. I didn't get straight As. I didn't become class president. I didn't get into Stanford. I dropped out of college.

For unlike my mother, I did not believe I could be anything I wanted to be. I could only be me.

And for all those years, we never talked about the disaster at the recital or my terrible accusations afterward at the piano bench. All that remained unchecked, like a betrayal that was now unspeakable. So I never found a way to ask her why she had hoped for something so large that failure was inevitable.

And even worse, I never asked her what frightened me the most: Why had she given up hope?

For after our struggle at the piano, she never mentioned my playing again. The lessons stopped. The lid to the piano was closed, shutting out the dust, my misery, and her dreams.

So she surprised me. A few years ago, she offered to give me the piano, for my thirtieth birthday. I had not played in all those years. I saw the offer as a sign of forgiveness, a tremendous burden removed.

"Are you sure?" I asked shyly. "I mean, won't you and Dad miss it?"

"No, this your piano," she said firmly. "Always your piano. You only one can play."

"Well, I probably can't play anymore," I said. "It's been years."

"You pick up fast," said my mother, as if she knew this was certain. "You have natural talent. You could been genius if you want to."

"No I couldn't."

"You just not trying," said my mother. And she was neither angry nor sad. She said it as if to announce a fact that could never be disproved. "Take it," she said.

But I didn't at first. It was enough that she had offered to me. And after that, every time I saw it in my parent's living room, standing in front of the bay windows, it made me feel proud, as if it were a shiny trophy I had won back.

Last week I sent a tuner over to my parents' apartment and had the piano reconditioned, for purely sentimental reasons. My mother had died a few months before and I had been getting things in order for my father, a little bit at a time. I put the jewelry in special silk pouches. The sweaters she had knitted in yellow, pink, bright orange—all the colors I hated—I put those in moth-proof boxes. I found some old Chinese silk dresses, the kind with little slits up the sides. I rubbed the old silk against my skin, then wrapped them in tissue and decided to take them home with me.

After I had the piano tuned, I opened the lid and touched the keys. It sounded even richer than I remembered. Really, it was a very good piano.

Inside the bench were the same exercise notes with handwritten scales, the same secondhand music books with their covers held together with yellow tape.

I opened up the Schumann book to the dark little piece I had played at the recital. It was on the left-hand side of the page, "Pleading Child." It looked more difficult than I remembered. I played a few bars, surprised at how easily the notes came back to me.

And for the first time, or so it seemed, I noticed the piece on the right-hand side. It was called "Perfectly Contented." I tried to play this one as well. It had a lighter melody but the same flowing rhythm and turned out to be quite easy. "Pleading Child" was shorter but slower; "Perfectly Contented" was longer, but faster. And after I played them both a few times, I realized they were two halves of the same song.

[1989]

LOUISE ERDRICH ■ (1954–)

The eldest of seven children, Louise Erdrich was born in Little Falls, Minnesota, and raised in Wahpeton, North Dakota, on the Minnesota border. Her father (German-American) and mother (French-Chippewa) worked for the Bureau of Indian Affairs, and they introduced Erdrich at an early age to a love for literature. In later interviews she acknowledged their impact on her own work:

> The people in our families made everything into a story. They love to tell a good story. People just sit and the stories start coming, one after another. You just sort of grab the tail of the last person's story: it reminds you of something and you keep going on. I suppose that when you grow up constantly hearing the stories rise, break and fall, it gets into you somehow.

Erdrich enrolled at Dartmouth College in Hanover, New Hampshire, in 1972, studying there with the author and anthropologist Michael Dorris, the director of its Native American Studies program. She received awards for her poetry and fiction and, after graduation, entered the creative writing department at Johns Hopkins University, where she received a master's degree. She became a writer-in-residence at Dartmouth and for many years worked closely with Dorris, whom she married in 1981. They separated in the mid-1990s, and he committed suicide in 1997. The mother of five children, Erdrich now lives in Minneapolis.

A key figure in the resurgence of Native American literature, Erdrich made her mark on the literary scene with the novel *Love Medicine* (1984), which, ranging widely over time, explores the lives and experiences of Chippewa families. "The Red Convertible," is part of *Love Medicine* but stands as a self-contained narrative about brotherly love and loss.

In three later novels, Erdrich continued her explorations of the families portrayed in *Love Medicine*: *The Beet Queen* (1986), *Tracks* (1988), and *The Bingo Palace* (1994). She also published a new and expanded edition of *Love Medicine* (1993), adding chapters that integrate it more fully with the scenes and situations of *The Bingo Palace*. Other novels include *The Master Butchers Singing Club* (2003), *The Plague of Doves* (2008), and *Shadow Tag* (2010). *The Red Convertible: Collected and New Stories* appeared in 2009.

For critical context and commentary, see Peter G. Beidler and Gay Barton, *A Reader's Guide to the Novels of Louise Erdrich* (1999); Lorena L. Stookey, *Louise Erdrich: A Critical Companion* (1999); and *The Chippewa Landscape of Louise Erdrich*, ed. Allan Chavkin (1999). See also *Conversations with Louise Erdrich and Michael Dorris*, eds. Allan Chavkin and Nancy Feyl Chavkin (1994); and *Louise Erdrich's* Love Medicine: *A Casebook*, ed. Hertha Dawn Wong (2000).

The Red Convertible

I was the first one to drive a convertible on my reservation. And of course it was red, a red Olds. I owned that car along with my brother Henry Junior. We owned it together until his boots filled with water on a windy night and he bought out my share. Now Henry owns the whole car, and his younger brother Lyman (that's myself), Lyman walks everywhere he goes.

How did I earn enough money to buy my share in the first place? My one talent was I could always make money. I had a touch for it, unusual in a Chippewa. From the first I was different that way, and everyone recognized it. I was the only kid they let in the American Legion Hall to shine shoes, for example, and one Christmas I sold spiritual bouquets for the mission door to door. The nuns let me keep a percentage. Once I started, it seemed the more money I made the easier the money came. Everyone encouraged it. When I was fifteen I got a job washing dishes at the Joliet Café, and that was where my first big break happened.

It wasn't long before I was promoted to bussing tables, and then the short-order cook quit and I was hired to take her place. No sooner than you know it I was managing the Joliet. The rest is history. I went on managing. I soon become part owner, and of course there was no stopping me then. It wasn't long before the whole thing was mine.

After I'd owned the Joliet for one year, it blew over in the worst tornado ever seen around here. The whole operation was smashed to bits. A total loss. The fryalator was up in a tree, the grill torn in half like it was paper. I was only sixteen. I had it all in my mother's name, and I lost it quick, but before I lost it I had every one of my relatives, and their relatives, to dinner, and I also bought that red Olds I mentioned, along with Henry.

The first time we saw it! I'll tell you when we first saw it. We had gotten a ride up to Winnipeg, and both of us had money. Don't ask me why, because we never mentioned a car or anything, we just had all our money. Mine was cash, a big bankroll from the Joliet's insurance. Henry had two checks—a week's extra pay for being laid off, and his regular check from the Jewel Bearing Plant.

We were walking down Portage anyway, seeing the sights, when we saw it. There it was, parked, large as life. Really as *if* it was alive. I thought of the word *repose,* because the car wasn't simply stopped, parked, or whatever. That car reposed calm and gleaming, a FOR SALE sign in its left front window. Then, before we had thought it over at all, the car belonged to us and our pockets were empty. We had just enough money for gas back home.

We went places in that car, me and Henry. We took off driving all one whole summer. We started off toward the Little Knife River and Mandaree in Fort Berthold and then we found ourselves down in Wakpala somehow, and then suddenly we were over in Montana on the Rocky Boy, and yet the summer was not even half over. Some people hang on to details when they travel, but we didn't let them bother us and just lived our everyday lives here to there.

I do remember this one place with willows. I remember I laid under those trees and it was comfortable. So comfortable. The branches bent down all around me like a tent or a stable. And quiet, it was quiet, even though there was a powwow close enough so I could see it going on. The air was not too still, not too windy either. When the dust rises up and hangs in the air around the dancers like that, I feel good. Henry was asleep with his arms thrown wide. Later on, he woke up and we started driving again. We were somewhere in Montana, or maybe on the Blood Reserve—it could have been anywhere. Anyway it was where we met the girl.

All her hair was in buns around her ears, that's the first thing I noticed about her. She was posed alongside the road with her arm out, so we stopped. That girl was short, so short her lumber shirt looked comical on her, like a nightgown. She had jeans on and fancy moccasins and she carried a little suitcase.

"Hop on in," says Henry. So she climbs in between us.

"We'll take you home," I says. "Where do you live?"

"Chicken," she says.

"Where the hell's that?" I ask her.

"Alaska."

"Okay," says Henry, and we drive.

We got up there and never wanted to leave. The sun doesn't truly set there in summer, and the night is more a soft dusk. You might doze off, sometimes, but before you know it you're up again, like an animal in nature. You never feel like you have to sleep hard or put away the world. And things would grow up there. One day just dirt or moss, the next day flowers and long grass. The girl's name was Susy. Her family really took to us. They fed us and put us up. We had our own tent to live in by their house, and the kids would be in and out of there all day and night. They couldn't get over me and Henry being brothers, we looked so different. We told them we knew we had the same mother, anyway.

One night Susy came in to visit us. We sat around in the tent talking of this thing and that. The season was changing. It was getting darker by that time and the cold was even getting just a little mean. I told her it was time for us to go. She stood up on a chair.

"You never seen my hair," Susy said.

That was true. She was standing on a chair, but still, when she unclipped her buns the hair reached all the way to the ground. Our eyes opened. You couldn't tell how much hair she had when it was rolled up so neatly. Then my brother Henry did something funny. He went up to the chair and said, "Jump on my shoulders." So she did that, and her hair reached down past his waist, and he started twirling, this way and that, so her hair was flung out from side to side.

"I always wondered what it was like to have long pretty hair," Henry says. Well we laughed. It was a funny sight, the way he did it. The next morning we got up and took leave of those people.

On to greener pastures, as they say. It was down through Spokane and across Idaho then Montana and very soon we were racing the weather right along under the Canadian border through Columbus, Des Lacs, and then we were in Bottineau County and soon home. We'd made most of the trip, that summer, without putting up the car hood at all. We got home just in time it turned out, for the army to remember Henry had signed up to join it.

I don't wonder that the army was so glad to get my brother that they turned him into a Marine. He was built like a brick outhouse anyway. We liked to tease him that they really wanted him for his Indian nose. He had a nose big and sharp as a hatchet, like the nose on Red Tomahawk, the Indian who killed Sitting Bull, whose profile is on signs all along the North Dakota highways. Henry went off to training camp, came home once during Christmas, then the next thing you know we got an overseas letter from him. It was 1970, and he said he was stationed up in the northern hill country. Whereabouts I did not know. He wasn't such a hot letter writer, and only got off two before the enemy caught him. I could never keep it straight, which direction those good Vietnam soldiers were from.

I wrote him back several times, even though I didn't know if those letters would get through. I kept him informed all about the car. Most of the time I had it up on blocks in the yard or half taken apart, because that long trip did a hard job on it under the hood.

I always had good luck with numbers,[1] and never worried about the draft myself. I never even had to think about what my numbers was. But Henry was never lucky in the same way as me. It was at least three years before Henry came home. By then I guess the whole war was solved in the government's mind, but for him it would keep on going. In those years I'd put his car into almost perfect shape. I always thought of it as his car while he was gone, even though when he left he said, "Now it's yours," and threw me his key.

"Thanks for the extra key," I'd said. "I'll put it up in your drawer just in case I need it." He laughed.

When he came home, though, Henry was very different, and I'll say this: the change was no good. You could hardly expect him to change for the better, I know. But he was quiet, so quiet, and never comfortable sitting still anywhere but always up and moving around. I thought back to times

---

[1]Beginning in 1969, the United States held a draft lottery for military service.

we'd sat still for whole afternoons, never moving a muscle, just shifting our weight along the ground, talking to whoever sat with us, watching things. He'd always had a joke, then, too, and now you couldn't get him to laugh, or when he did it was more the sound of a man choking, a sound that stopped up the throats of other people around him. They got to leaving him alone most of the time, and I didn't blame them. It was a fact: Henry was jumpy and mean.

I'd bought a color TV set for my mom and the rest of us while Henry was away. Money still came very easy. I was sorry I'd ever bought it though, because of Henry. I was also sorry I'd bought color, because with black-and-white the pictures seem older and farther away. But what are you going to do? He sat in front of it, watching it, and that was the only time he was completely still. But it was the kind of stillness that you see in a rabbit when it freezes and before it will bolt. He was not easy. He sat in his chair gripping the armrests with all his might, as if the chair itself was moving at a high speed and if he let go at all he would rocket forward and maybe crash right through the set.

Once I was in the room watching TV with Henry and I heard his teeth click at something. I looked over, and he'd bitten' through his lip. Blood was going down his chin. I tell you right then I wanted to smash that tube to pieces. I went over to it but Henry must have known what I was up to. He rushed from his chair and shoved me out of the way, against the wall. I told myself he didn't know what he was doing.

My mom came in, turned the set off real quiet, and told us she had made something for supper. So we went and sat down. There was still blood going down Henry's chin, but he didn't notice it and no one said anything, even though every time he took a bite of his bread his blood fell onto it until he was eating his own blood mixed in with the food.

While Henry was not around we talked about what was going to happen to him. There were no Indian doctors on the reservation, and my mom was afraid of trusting Old Man Pillager because he courted her long ago and was jealous of her husbands. He might take revenge through her son. We were afraid that if we brought Henry to a regular hospital they would keep him.

"They don't fix them in those places," Mom said; "they just give them drugs."

"We wouldn't get him there in the first place," I agreed, "so let's just forget about it."

Then I thought about the car.

Henry had not even looked at the car since he'd gotten home, though like I said, it was in tip-top condition and ready to drive. I thought the car might bring the old Henry back somehow. So I bided my time and waited for my chance to interest him in the vehicle.

One night Henry was off somewhere. I took myself a hammer. I went out to that car and I did a number on its underside. Whacked it up. Bent the tail pipe double. Ripped the muffler loose. By the time I was done with the car it looked worse than any typical Indian car that has been driven all its life on reservation roads, which they always say are like government promises—full of holes. It just about hurt me, I'll tell you that! I threw dirt in the carburetor and I ripped all the electric tape off the seats. I made it look just as beat up as I could. Then I sat back and waited for Henry to find it.

Still, it took him over a month. That was all right, because it was just getting warm enough, not melting, but warm enough to work outside.

"Lyman," he says, walking in one day, "that red car looks like shit."

"Well it's old," I says. "You got to expect that."

"No way," says Henry. "That car's a classic! But you went and ran the piss right out of it, Lyman, and you know it don't deserve that. I kept that car in A-one shape. You don't remember. You're too young. But when I left, that car was running like a watch. Now I don't even know if I can get it to start again, let alone get it anywhere near its old condition."

"Well you try," I said, like I was getting mad, "but I say it's a piece of junk."

Then I walked out before he could realize I knew he'd strung together more than six words at once.

After that I thought he'd freeze himself to death working on that car. He was out there all day, and at night he rigged up a little lamp, ran a cord out the window, and had himself some light to see by while he worked. He was better than he had been before, but that's still not saying much. It was easier for him to do the things the rest of us did. He ate more slowly and didn't jump up and down during the meal to get this or that or look out the window. I put my hand in the back of the TV set, I admit, and fiddled around with it good, so that it was almost impossible now to get a clear picture. He didn't look at it very often anyway. He was always out with that car or going off to get parts for it. By the time it was really melting outside, he had it fixed.

I had been feeling down in the dumps about Henry around this time. We had always been together before. Henry and Lyman. But he was such a loner now that I didn't know how to take it. So I jumped at the chance one day when Henry seemed friendly. It's not that he smiled or anything. He just said, "Let's take that old shitbox for a spin." Just the way he said it made me think he could be coming around.

We went out to the car. It was spring. The sun was shining very bright. My only sister, Bonita, who was just eleven years old, came out and made us stand together for a picture. Henry leaned his elbow on the red car's windshield, and he took his other arm and put it over my shoulder, very carefully, as though it was heavy for him to lift and he didn't want to bring the weight down all at once.

"Smile," Bonita said, and he did.

That picture. I never look at it anymore. A few months ago, I don't know why, I got his picture out and tacked it on the wall. I felt good about Henry at the time, close to him. I felt good having his picture on the wall, until one night when I was looking at television. I was a little drunk and stoned. I looked up at the wall and Henry was staring at me. I don't know what it was, but his smile had changed, or maybe it was gone. All I know is I couldn't stay in the same room with that picture. I was shaking. I got up, closed the door, and went into the kitchen. A little later my friend Ray came over and we both went back into that room. We put the picture in a brown bag, folded the bag over and over tightly, then put it way back in a closet.

I still see that picture now, as if it tugs at me, whenever I pass that closet door. The picture is very clear in my mind. It was so sunny that day Henry had to squint against the glare. Or maybe the camera Bonita held flashed like a mirror, blinding him, before she snapped the picture. My face is right out in the sun, big and round. But he might have drawn back, because the shadows on his face are deep as holes. There are two shadows curved like little hooks around the ends of his smile, as if to frame it and try to keep it there—that one, first smile that looked like it might have hurt his face. He has his field jacket on and the worn-in clothes he'd come back in and kept wearing ever since. After Bonita took the picture, she went into the house and we got into the car. There was a full cooler in the trunk. We started off, east, toward Pembina and the Red River because Henry said he wanted to see the high water.

The trip over there was beautiful. When everything starts changing, drying up, clearing off, you feel like your whole life is starting. Henry felt it, too. The top was down and the car hummed like a top. He'd really put it back in shape, even the tape on the seats was very carefully put down and glued back in layers. It's not that he smiled again or even joked, but his face looked to me as if it was clear, more peaceful. It looked as though he wasn't thinking of anything in particular except the bare fields and windbreaks and houses we were passing.

The river was high and full of winter trash when we got there. The sun was still out, but it was colder by the river. There were still little clumps of dirty snow here and there on the banks. The water hadn't gone over the banks yet, but it would, you could tell. It was just at its limit, hard swollen, glossy like an old gray scar. We made ourselves a fire, and we sat down and watched the current go. As I watched it I felt something squeezing inside me and tightening and trying to let go all at the same time. I knew I was not just feeling it myself; I knew I was feeling what Henry was going through at that moment. Except that I couldn't stand it, the closing and opening. I jumped to my feet. I took Henry by the shoulders and I started shaking him. "Wake up," I says, "wake up, wake up, wake up!" I didn't know what had come over me. I sat down beside him again.

His face was totally white and hard. Then it broke, like stones break all of a sudden when water boils up inside them.

"I know it," he says. "I know it. I can't help it. It's no use."

We start talking. He said he knew what I'd done with the car. It was obvious it had been whacked out of shape and not just neglected. He said he wanted to give the car to me for good now, it was no use. He said he'd fixed it just to give it back and I should take it.

"No way," I says, "I don't want it."

"That's okay," he says, "you take it."

"I don't want it, though," I says back to him, and then to emphasize, just to emphasize, you understand, I touch his shoulder. He slaps my hand off.

"Take that car," he says.

"No," I say, "make me," I say and then he grabs my jacket and rips the arm loose. That jacket is a class act, suede with tags and zippers. I push Henry backwards, off the log. He jumps up and bowls me over. We go down in a clinch and come up swinging hard, for all we're worth, with our fists. He socks my jaw so hard I feel like it swings loose. Then I'm at his ribcage and land a good one under his chin so his head snaps back. He's dazzled. He looks at me and I look at him and then his eyes are full of tears and blood and at first I think he's crying. But no, he's laughing. "Ha! Ha!" he says. "Ha! Ha! Take good care of it."

"Okay," I says, "okay, no problem. Ha! Ha!"

I can't help it, and I start laughing, too. My face feels fat and strange, and after a while I get a beer from the cooler in the trunk, and when I hand it to Henry he takes his shirt and wipes my germs off. "Hoof-and-mouth disease," he says. For some reason this cracks me up, and so we're really laughing for a while, and then we drink all the rest of the beers one by one and throw them in the river and see how far, how fast, the current takes them before they fill up and sink.

"You want to go on back?" I ask after a while. "Maybe we could snag a couple nice Kashpaw girls."

He says nothing. But I can tell his mood is turning again. "They're all crazy, the girls up here, every damn one of them."

"You're crazy too," I say, to jolly him up. "Crazy Lamartine boys!"

He looks as though he will take this wrong at first. His face twists, then clears, and he jumps up on his feet. "That's right!" he says. "Crazier'n hell. Crazy Indians!"

I think it's the old Henry again. He throws off his jacket and starts swinging his legs out from the knees like a fancy dancer. He's down doing something between a grouse dance and a bunny hop, no kind of dance I ever saw before, but neither has anyone else on all this green growing earth. He's wild. He wants to pitch whoopee! He's up and at me and all over. All this time I'm laughing so hard, so hard my belly is getting tied up in a knot.

"Got to cool me off!" he shouts all of a sudden. Then he runs over to the river and jumps in.

There's boards and other things in the current. It's so high. No sound comes from the river after the splash he makes, so I run right over. I look around. It's getting dark. I see he's halfway across the water already, and I know he didn't swim there but the current took him. It's far. I hear his voice, though, very clearly across it.

"My boots are filling," he says.

He says this in a normal voice, like he just noticed and he doesn't know what to think of it. Then he's gone. A branch comes by, Another branch. And I go in.

By the time I get out of the river, off the snag I pulled myself onto, the sun is down. I walk back to the car, turn on the high beams, and drive it up the bank. I put it in first gear and then I take my foot off the clutch. I get out, close the door, and watch it plow softly into the water. The headlights reach in as they go down, searching, still lighted even after the water swirls over the back end. I wait. The wires short out. It is all finally dark. And then there is only the water, the sound of it going and running and going and running and running.

[1984]

DAVID HENRY HWANG ▪ (1957–)

Born and raised in the Los Angeles area, David Henry Hwang is the son of Asian parents who came to the United States in the early 1950s. His father, born in China, worked as an accountant and later was the president of a bank, and his mother, born in the Philippines, was a gifted pianist and teacher. She was also a devout Christian, and Hwang's father converted to Christianity at the time of his marriage. Hwang's own work reflects his interest in religious and cultural elements and themes from both Eastern and Western traditions.

Hwang graduated from Stanford University in 1979. A play he wrote and directed during his senior year, titled *FOB* (i.e., "fresh off the boat," a phrase used of recent immigrants), was produced in New York City, where it received an Obie award for best play. It focuses on several young men, one of whom has just arrived in the United States from China, and their difficulties in accommodating themselves to American life.

Hwang's best-known work is *M. Butterfly* (the play has connections to Puccini's opera *Madame Butterfly*, 1906), which opened on Broadway in 1988. It recounts a French diplomat's 20-year affair with a member of the Peking Opera Company, whom he eventually learns is not a woman, as he had assumed, but a man and, furthermore, a spy for Communist China.

Hwang's plays include *Family Devotions* (1981), *Rich Relations* (1986), and *Golden Child* (1996). He has also undertaken collaborations with the composer Philip Glass (*1000 Airplanes on the Roof*, 1989, and *The Voyage*, 1992), and with the popular musician Elton John (*Aida*, 2000). Hwang is an accomplished violinist, and he has often investigated and developed relationships between written text and music, opera, and dance.

Hwang described *The Sound of a Voice* (1983), given here, as a change of direction in his work as an author—a "Japanese" play, one of the first he wrote that "didn't deal with being Chinese-American, with race and assimilation." He termed it "a tragic love story."

For further study, see Bonnie Lyons, "'Making His Muscles Work for Himself': An Interview with David Henry Hwang," *Literary Review: An International Journal of Contemporary Writing* 42:2 (Winter 1999), 230–244; and Misha Berson, "The Demon in David Henry Hwang," *American Theatre* 15:4 (April 1998), 14–18, 50–52. See also *Staging Difference: Cultural Pluralism in American Theatre and Drama*, ed. Marc Maufort (1995); and Josephine Lee, *Performing Asian America: Race and Ethnicity on the Contemporary Stage* (1997). Hwang's *Chinatown: Selected Plays* (1999) includes *The Sound of a Voice* and seven other works.

The Sound of a Voice

Characters

Man, *fifties, Japanese*
Woman, *fifties, Japanese*
   Setting. Woman's house, in a remote corner of the forest.

Scene I

Woman pours tea for Man. Man rubs himself, trying to get warm.

Man: You're very kind to take me in.
Woman: This is a remote corner of the world. Guests are rare.
Man: The tea—you pour it well.
Woman: No.
Man: The sound it makes—in the cup—very soothing.
Woman: That is the tea's skill, not mine. (*She hands the cup to him.*) May
   I get you something else? Rice, perhaps?
Man: No.
Woman: And some vegetables?
Man: No, thank you.
Woman: Fish? (*Pause.*) It is at least two days' walk to the nearest village.
   I saw no horse. You must be very hungry. You would do a great honor
   to dine with me. Guests are rare.
Man: Thank you.
Woman   (*Woman gets up, leaves. Man holds the cup in his hands, using
   it to warm himself. He gets up, walks around the room. It is sparsely
   furnished, drab, except for one shelf on which stands a vase of brightly
   colored flowers. The flowers stand out in sharp contrast to the stark-
   ness of the room. Slowly, he reaches out towards them. He touches
   them. Quickly, he takes one of the flowers from the vase, hides it in his
   clothes. He returns to where he had sat previously. He waits. Woman re-
   enters. She carries a tray with food.*): Please. Eat. It will give me great
   pleasure.
Man: This—this is magnificent.
Woman: Eat.
Man: Thank you. (*He motions for Woman to join him.*)
Woman: No, thank you.
Man: This is wonderful. The best I've tasted.
Woman: You are reckless in your flattery. But anything you say, I will
   enjoy hearing. It's not even the words. It's the sound of a voice, the
   way it moves through the air.
Man: How long has it been since you last had a visitor? (*Pause.*)
Woman: I don't know.
Man: Oh?

Woman: I lose track. Perhaps five months ago, perhaps ten years, perhaps yesterday. I don't consider time when there is no voice in the air. It's pointless. Time begins with the entrance of a visitor, and ends with his exit.

Man: And in between? You don't keep track of the days? You can't help but notice—

Woman: Of course I notice.

Man: Oh.

Woman: I notice, but I don't keep track. (*Pause.*) May I bring out more?

Man: More? No. No. This was wonderful.

Woman: I have more.

Man: Really—the best I've had.

Woman: You must be tired. Did you sleep in the forest last night?

Man: Yes.

Woman: Or did you not sleep at all?

Man: I slept.

Woman: Where?

Man: By a waterfall. The sound of the water put me to sleep. It rumbled like the sounds of a city. You see, I can't sleep in too much silence. It scares me. It makes me feel that I have no control over what is about to happen.

Woman: I feel the same way.

Man: But you live here—alone?

Woman: Yes.

Man: It's so quiet here. How can you sleep?

Woman: Tonight, I'll sleep. I'll lie down in the next room, and hear your breathing through the wall, and fall asleep shamelessly. There will be no silence.

Man: You're very kind to let me stay here.

Woman: This is yours. (*She unrolls a mat; there is a beautiful design of a flower on the mat. The flower looks exactly like the flowers in the vase.*)

Man: Did you make it yourself?

Woman: Yes. There is a place to wash outside.

Man: Thank you.

Woman: Goodnight.

Man: Goodnight. (*Man starts to leave.*)

Woman: May I know your name?

Man: No. I mean, I would rather not say. If I gave you a name, it would only be made-up. Why should I deceive you? You are too kind for that.

Woman: Then what should I call you? Perhaps—"Man Who Fears Silence"?

Man: How about, "Man Who Fears Women"?

Woman: That name is much too common.

Man: And you?

Woman: Yokiko.

Man: That's your name?

Woman: It's what you may call me.

Man: Goodnight, Yokiko. You are very kind.

Woman: You are very smart. Goodnight. (*Man exits. Hanako goes to the mat. She tidies it, brushes it off. She goes to the vase. She picks up the flowers, studies them. She carries them out of the room with her. Man re-enters. He takes off his outer clothing. He glimpses the spot where the vase used to sit. He reaches into his clothing, pulls out the stolen flower. He studies it. He puts it underneath his head as he lies down to sleep, like a pillow. He starts to fall asleep. Suddenly, a start. He picks up his head. He listens.*)

Scene II

Dawn. Man is getting dressed. Woman enters with food.

Woman: Good morning.

Man: Good morning, Yokiko.

Woman: You weren't planning to leave?

Man: I have quite a distance to travel today.

Woman: Please. (*She offers him food.*)

Man: Thank you.

Woman: May I ask where you're travelling to?

Man: It's far.

Woman: I know this region well.

Man: Oh? Do you leave the house often?

Woman: I used to. I used to travel a great deal. I know the region from those days.

Man: You probably wouldn't know the place I'm headed.

Woman: Why not?

Man: It's new. A new village. It didn't exist in "those days." (*Pause.*)

Woman: I thought you said you wouldn't deceive me.

Man: I didn't. You don't believe me, do you?

Woman: No.

Man: Then I didn't deceive you. I'm travelling. That much is true.

Woman: Are you in such a hurry?

Man: Travelling is a matter of timing. Catching the light. (*Woman exits; Man finishes eating, puts down his bowl. Woman re-enters with the vase of flowers.*) Where did you find those? They don't grow native around these parts, do they?

Woman: No; they've all been brought in. They were brought in by visitors. Such as yourself. They were left here. In my custody.

Man: But—they look so fresh, so alive.

Woman: I take care of them. They remind me of the people and places outside this house.

Man: May I touch them?

Woman: Certainly.

Man: These have just blossomed.

Woman: No; they were in bloom yesterday. If you'd noticed them before, you would know that.

Man: You must have received these very recently. I would guess—within five days.

Woman: I don't know. But I wouldn't trust your estimate. It's all in the amount of care you show to them. I create a world which is outside the realm of what you know.

Man: What do you do?

Woman: I can't explain. Words are too inefficient. It takes hundreds of words to describe a single act of caring. With hundreds of acts, words become irrelevant. (*Pause.*) But perhaps you can stay.

Man: How long?

Woman: As long as you'd like.

Man: Why?

Woman: To see how I care for them.

Man: I am tired.

Woman: Rest.

Man: The light?

Woman: It will return.

Scene III

Man is carrying chopped wood. He is stripped to the waist. Woman enters.

Woman: You're very kind to do that for me.

Man: I enjoy it, you know. Chopping wood. It's clean. No questions. You take your axe, you stand up the log, you aim—pow!—you either hit it or you don't. Success or failure.

Woman: You seem to have been very successful today.

Man: Why shouldn't I be? It's a beautiful day. I can see to those hills. The trees are cool. The sun is gentle. Ideal. If a man can't be successful on a day like this, he might as well kick the dust up into his own face. (*Man notices Woman staring at him. Man pats his belly, looks at her.*) Protection from falls.

Woman: What? (*Man pinches his belly, showing some fat.*) Oh. Don't be silly. (*Man begins slapping the fat on his belly to a rhythm.*)

Man: Listen—I can make music—see?—that wasn't always possible. But now—that I've developed this—whenever I need entertainment.

Woman: You shouldn't make fun of your body.

Man: Why not? I saw you. You were staring.

Woman: I wasn't making fun. (*Man inflates his cheeks.*) I was just—stop that!

Man: Then why were you staring?

Woman: I was—

Man: Laughing?

Woman: No.

Man: Well?

Woman: I was—Your body. It's...strong. (*Pause.*)

Man: People say that. But they don't know. I've heard that age brings wisdom. That's a laugh. The years don't accumulate here. They accumulate here. (*Pause; he pinches his belly.*) But today is a day to be happy, right? The woods. The sun. Blue. It's a happy day. I'm going to chop wood.

Woman: There's nothing left to chop. Look.

Man: Oh, I guess...that's it.

Woman: Sit. Here.

Man: But—

Woman: There's nothing left. (*Man sits; Woman stares at his belly.*) Learn to love it.

Man: Don't be ridiculous.

Woman: Touch it.

Man: It's flabby.

Woman: It's strong.

Man: It's weak.

Woman: And smooth.

Man: Do you mind if I put on my shirt?

Woman: Of course not. Shall I get it for you?

Man: No. No. Just sit there. (*Man starts to put on his shirt. He pauses, studies his body.*) You think it's cute, huh?

Woman: I think you should learn to love it. (*Man pats his belly, talks to it.*)

Man (*To belly*): You're okay, sir. You hang onto my body like a great horseman.

Woman: Not like that.

Man (*Ibid.*): You're also faithful. You'll never leave me for another man.

Woman: No.

Man: What do you want me to say? (*Woman walks over to Man. She touches his belly with her hand. They look at each other.*)

Scene IV

Night. Man is alone. Flowers are gone from stand. Mat is unrolled. Man lies on it, sleeping. Suddenly, he starts. He lifts up his head. He listens. Silence. He goes back to sleep. Another start. He lifts up his head, strains to hear. Slowly, we begin to make out the strains of a single shakuhachi[1] *playing a haunting line. It is very soft. He strains to hear it. The instrument slowly*

---

[1]Japanese bamboo flute.

fades out. He waits for it to return, but it does not. He takes out the stolen flower. He stares into it.

Scene V

Day. Woman is cleaning, while Man relaxes. She is on her hands and knees, scrubbing. She is dressed in a simple outfit, for working. Her hair is tied back. Man is sweating. He has not, however, removed his shirt.

Man: I heard your playing last night.

Woman: My playing?

Man: *Shakuhachi.*

Woman: Oh.

Man: You played very softly. I had to strain to hear it. Next time, don't be afraid. Play out. Fully. Clear. It must've been very beautiful, if only I could've heard it clearly. Why don't you play for me sometime?

Woman: I'm very shy about it.

Man: Why?

Woman: I play for my own satisfaction. That's all. It's something I developed on my own. I don't know if it's at all acceptable by outside standards.

Man: Play for me. I'll tell you.

Woman: No; I'm sure you're too knowledgeable in the arts.

Man: Who? Me?

Woman: You being from the city and all.

Man: I'm ignorant, believe me.

Woman: I'd play, and you'd probably bite your cheek.

Man: Ask me a question about music. Any question. I'll answer incorrectly. I guarantee it.

Woman: Look at this.

Man: What?

Woman: A stain.

Man: Where?

Woman: Here? See? I can't get it out.

Man: Oh. I hadn't noticed it before.

Woman: I notice it every time I clean.

Man: Here. Let me try.

Woman: Thank you.

Man: Ugh. It's tough.

Woman: I know.

Man: How did it get here?

Woman: It's been there as long as I've lived here.

Man: I hardly stand a chance. (*Pause.*) But I'll try. Uh—one—two—three—four! One—two—three—four! See, you set up...gotta set up...a rhythm—two—three—four. Like fighting! Like battle!

One—two—three—four! Used to practice with a rhythm...beat...battle! Yes! (*The stain starts to fade away.*) Look—it's—yes!—whoo!—there it goes—got the sides—the edges—yes!—fading quick—fading away—ooo—here we come—towards the center—to the heart—two—three—four—slow—slow death—tough—dead! (*Man rolls over in triumphant laughter.*)

Woman: Dead.

Man: I got it! I got it! Whoo! A little rhythm! All it took! Four! Four!

Woman: Thank you.

Man: I didn't think I could do it—but there—it's gone—I did it!

Woman: Yes. You did.

Man: And you—you were great.

Woman: No—I was carried away.

Man: We were a team! You and me!

Woman: I only provided encouragement.

Man: You were great! You were! (*Man grabs Woman. Pause.*)

Woman: It's gone. Thank you. Would you like to hear me play *shakuhachi*?

Man: Yes I would.

Woman: I don't usually play for visitors. It's so...I'm not sure. I developed it—all by myself—in times when I was alone. I heard nothing—no human voice. So I learned to play *shakuhachi*. I tried to make these sounds resemble the human voice. The *shakuhachi* became my weapon. To ward off the air. It kept me from choking on many a silent evening.

Man: I'm here. You can hear my voice.

Woman: Speak again.

Man: I will.

Scene VI

Night. Man is sleeping. Suddenly, a start. He lifts his head up. He listens. Silence. He strains to hear. The shakuhachi *melody rises up once more. This time, however, it becomes louder and more clear than before. He gets up. He cannot tell from what direction the music is coming. He walks around the room, putting his ear to different places in the wall, but he cannot locate the sound. It seems to come from all directions at once, as omnipresent as the air. Slowly, he moves towards the wall with the sliding panel through which the Woman enters and exits. He puts his ear against it, thinking the music may be coming from there. Slowly, he slides the door open just a crack, ever so carefully. He peeks through the crack. As he peeks through, the Upstage wall of the set becomes transparent, and through the scrim, we are able to see what he sees. Woman is Upstage of the scrim. She is tending a room filled with potted and vased flowers of all variety. The lushness and beauty of the room Upstage of the scrim stands out in stark contrast to the barrenness of the main set. She is also transformed. She is a young woman. She is beautiful. She wears a brightly colored kimono. Man*

*observes this scene for a long time. He then slides the door shut. The scrim
returns to opaque. The music continues. He returns to his mat. He picks up
the stolen flower. It is brown and wilted, dead. He looks at it. The music
slowly fades out.*

Scene VII

*Morning. Man is half-dressed. He is practicing sword maneuvers. He practices
with the feel of a man whose spirit is willing, but the flesh is inept. He tries
to execute deft movements, but is dissatisfied with his efforts. He curses
himself, and returns to basic exercises. Suddenly, he feels something buzzing
around his neck—a mosquito. He slaps his neck, but misses it. He sees it flying near him. He swipes at it with his sword. He keeps missing. Finally, he
thinks he's hit it. He runs over, kneels down to recover the fallen insect. He
picks up two halves of a mosquito on two different fingers. Woman enters the
room. She looks as she normally does. She is carrying a vase of flowers, which
she places on its shelf.*

Man: Look.

Woman: I'm sorry?

Man: Look.

Woman: What? (*He brings over the two halves of mosquito to show her.*)

Man: See?

Woman: Oh.

Man: I hit it—chop!

Woman: These are new forms of target practice?

Man: Huh? Well—yes—in a way.

Woman: You seem to do well at it.

Man: Thank you. For last night. I heard your *shakuhachi.* It was very
    loud, strong—good tone.

Woman: Did you enjoy it? I wanted you to enjoy it. If you wish, I'll play
    it for you every night.

Man: Every night!

Woman: If you wish.

Man: No—I don't—I don't want you to treat me like a baby.

Woman: What? I'm not.

Man: Oh, yes. Like a baby. Who you must feed in the middle of the night
    or he cries. Waaah! Waaah!

Woman: Stop that!

Man: You need your sleep.

Woman: I don't mind getting up for you. (*Pause.*) I would enjoy playing
    for you. Every night. While you sleep. It will make me feel—like I'm
    shaping your dreams. I go through long stretches when there is no
    one in my dreams. It's terrible. During those times, I avoid my bed as
    much as possible. I paint. I weave. I play *shakuhachi.* I sit on mats and

rub powder into my face. Anything to keep from facing a bed with no
dreams. It is like sleeping on ice.

Man: What do you dream of now?

Woman: Last night—I dreamt of you. I don't remember what happened.
But you were very funny. Not in a mocking way. I wasn't laughing at
you. But you made me laugh. And you were very warm. I remember
that. (*Pause.*) What do you remember about last night?

Man: Just your playing. That's all. I got up, listened to it, and went back
to sleep. (*Man gets up, resumes practicing with his sword.*)

Woman: Another mosquito bothering you?

Man: Just practicing. Ah! Weak! Too weak! I tell you, it wasn't always
like this. I'm telling you, there were days when I could chop the fruit
from a tree without ever taking my eyes off the ground. (*He continues
practicing.*) You ever use one of these?

Woman: I've had to pick one up, yes.

Man: Oh?

Woman: You forget—I live alone—out here—there is...not much to sustain me but what I manage to learn myself. It wasn't really a matter
of choice.

Man: I used to be very good, you know. Perhaps I can give you some
pointers.

Woman: I'd really rather not.

Man: C'mon—a woman like you—you're absolutely right. You need to
know how to defend yourself.

Woman: As you wish.

Man: Do you have something to practice with?

Woman: Yes. Excuse me. (*She exits. He practices more. She re-enters with
two wooden sticks. He takes one of them.*) Will these do?

Man: Nice. Now, show me what you can do.

Woman: I'm sorry?

Man: Run up and hit me.

Woman: Please.

Man: Go on—I'll block it.

Woman: I feel so...undignified.

Man: Go on. (*She hits him playfully with stick.*) Not like that!

Woman: I'll try to be gentle.

Man: What?

Woman: I don't want to hurt you.

Man: You won't—Hit me! (*Woman charges at Man, quickly, deftly. She
scores a hit.*) Oh!

Woman: Did I hurt you?

Man: No—you were—let's try that again. (*They square off again. Woman
rushes forward. She appears to attempt a strike. He blocks that apparent
strike, which turns out to be a feint. She scores.*) Huh?

Woman: Did I hurt you? I'm sorry.

Man: No.

Woman: I hurt you.

Man: No.

Woman: Do you wish to hit me?

Man: No.

Woman: Do you want me to try again?

Man: No.

Woman: Thank you.

Man: Just practice there—by yourself—let me see you run through some maneuvers.

Woman: Must I?

Man: Yes! Go! (*She goes to an open area.*) My greatest strength was always as a teacher. (*Woman executes a series of deft movements. Her whole manner is transformed. Man watches with increasing amazement. Her movements end. She regains her submissive manner.*)

Woman: I'm so embarrassed. My skills—they're so—inappropriate. I look like a man.

Man: Where did you learn that?

Woman: There is much time to practice here.

Man: But you—the techniques.

Woman: I don't know what's fashionable in the outside world. (*Pause.*) Are you unhappy?

Man: No.

Woman: Really?

Man: I'm just...surprised.

Woman: You think it's unbecoming for a woman.

Man: No, no. Not at all.

Woman: You want to leave.

Man: No!

Woman: All visitors do. I know. I've met many. They say they'll stay. And they do. For a while. Until they see too much. Or they learn something new. There are boundaries outside of which visitors do not want to see me step. Only who knows what those boundaries are? Not I. They change with every visitor. You have to be careful not to cross them, but you never know where they are. And one day, inevitably, you step outside the lines. The visitor knows. You don't. You didn't know that you'd done anything different. You thought it was just another part of you. The visitor sneaks away. The next day, you learn that you had stepped outside his heart. I'm afraid you've seen too much.

Man: There are stories.

Woman: What?

Man: People talk.

Woman: Where? We're two days from the nearest village.

Man: Word travels.

Woman: What are you talking about?

Man: There are stories about you. I heard them. They say that your visitors never leave this house.

Woman: That's what you heard?

Man: They say you imprison them.

Woman: Then you were a fool to come here.

Man: Listen.

Woman: Me? Listen? You. Look! Where are these prisoners? Have you seen any?

Man: They told me you were very beautiful.

Woman: Then they are blind as well as ignorant.

Man: You are.

Woman: What?

Man: Beautiful.

Woman: Stop that! My skin feels like seaweed.

Man: I didn't realize it at first. I must confess—I didn't. But over these few days—your face has changed for me. The shape of it. The feel of it. The color. All changed. I look at you now, and I'm no longer sure you are the same woman who had poured tea for me just a week ago. And because of that I remembered—how little I know about a face that changes in the night. (*Pause.*) Have you heard those stories?

Woman: I don't listen to old wives' tales.

Man: But have you heard them?

Woman: Yes. I've heard them. From other visitors—young—hotblooded—or old—who came here because they were told great glory was to be had by killing the witch in the woods.

Man: I was told that no man could spend time in this house without falling in love.

Woman: Oh? So why did you come? Did you wager gold that you could come out untouched? The outside world is so flattering to me. And you—are you like the rest? Passion passing through your heart so powerfully that you can't hold onto it?

Man: No! I'm afraid!

Woman: Of what?

Man: Sometimes—when I look into the flowers, I think I hear a voice—from inside—a voice beneath the petals. A human voice.

Woman: What does it say? "Let me out"?

Man: No. Listen. It hums. It hums with the peacefulness of one who is completely imprisoned.

Woman: I understand that if you listen closely enough, you can hear the ocean.

Man: No. Wait. Look at it. See the layers? Each petal—hiding the next. Try and see where they end. You can't. Follow them down, further down, around—and as you come down—faster and faster—the breeze picks up. The breeze becomes a wail. And in that rush of air—in the silent midst of it—you can hear a voice.

Woman (WOMAN *grabs flower from* MAN.):   So, you believe I water and prune my lovers? How can you be so foolish? (*She snaps the flower in half, at the stem. She throws it to the ground.*) Do you come only to leave again? To take a chunk of my heart, then leave with your booty on your belt, like a prize? You say that I imprison hearts in these flowers? Well, bits of my heart are trapped with travellers across this land. I can't even keep track. So kill me. If you came here to destroy a witch, kill me now. I can't stand to have it happen again.

Man: I won't leave you.

Woman: I believe you. (*She looks at the flower that she has broken, bends to pick it up. He touches her. They embrace.*)

Scene VIII

Day. Woman wears a simple undergarment, over which she is donning a brightly colored kimono, the same one we saw her wearing Upstage of the scrim. Man stands apart.

Woman: I can't cry. I don't have the capacity. Right from birth, I didn't cry. My mother and father were shocked. They thought they'd given birth to a ghost, a demon. Sometimes I've thought myself that. When great sadness has welled up inside me, I've prayed for a means to release the pain from my body. But my prayers went unanswered. The grief remained inside me. It would sit like water, still. (*Pause; she models her kimono.*) Do you like it?

Man: Yes, it's beautiful.

Woman: I wanted to wear something special today.

Man: It's beautiful. Excuse me. I must practice.

Woman: Shall I get you something?

Man: No.

Woman: Some tea, maybe?

Man: No. (*Man resumes swordplay.*)

Woman: Perhaps later today—perhaps we can go out—just around here. We can look for flowers.

Man: All right.

Woman: We don't have to.

Man: No. Let's.

Woman: I just thought if—

Man: Fine. Where do you want to go?

Woman: There are very few recreational activities around here, I know.

Man: All right. We'll go this afternoon. (*Pause.*)

Woman: Can I get you something?

Man   (*Turning around.*): What?

Woman: You might be—

Man: I'm not hungry or thirsty or cold or hot.

Woman: Then what are you?

Man: Practicing. (*Man resumes practicing; Woman exits. As soon as she exits, he rests. He sits down. He examines his sword. He runs his finger along the edge of it. He takes the tip, runs it against the soft skin under his chin. He places the sword on the ground with the tip pointed directly upwards. He keeps it from falling by placing the tip under his chin. He experiments with different degrees of pressure. Woman re-enters. She sees him in this precarious position. She jerks his head upward; the sword falls.*)

Woman: Don't do that!

Man: What?

Woman: You can hurt yourself!

Man: I was practicing!

Woman: You were playing!

Man: I was practicing!

Woman: It's dangerous.

Man: What do you take me for—a child?

Woman: Sometimes wise men do childish things.

Man: I knew what I was doing!

Woman: It scares me.

Man: Don't be ridiculous. (*He reaches for the sword again.*)

Woman: Don't! Don't do that!

Man: Get back! (*He places the sword back in its previous position, suspended between the floor and his chin, upright.*)

Woman: But—

Man: Sssssh!

Woman: I wish—

Man: Listen to me! The slightest shock, you know—the slightest shock—surprise—it might make me jerk or—something—and then...so you must be perfectly still and quiet.

Woman: But I—

Man: Sssssh! (*Silence.*) I learned this exercise from a friend—I can't even remember his name—good swordsman—many years ago. He called it his meditation position. He said, like this, he could feel the line between this world and the others because he rested on it. If he saw something in another world that he liked better, all he would have to do is let his head drop, and he'd be there. Simple. No fuss. One day, they found him with the tip of his sword run clean out the back of his neck. He was smiling. I guess he saw something he liked. Or else he'd fallen asleep.

Woman: Stop that.

Man: Stop what?

Woman: Tormenting me.

Man: I'm not.

Woman: Take it away!

Man: You don't have to watch, you know.

Woman: Do you want to die that way—an accident?

Man: I was doing this before you came in.

Woman: If you do, all you need to do is tell me.

Man: What?

Woman: I can walk right over. Lean on the back of your head.

Man: Don't try to threaten—

Woman: Or jerk your sword up.

Man: Or scare me. You can't threaten—

Woman: I'm not. But if that's what you want.

Man: You can't threaten me. You wouldn't do it.

Woman: Oh?

Man: Then I'd be gone. You wouldn't let me leave that easily.

Woman: Yes, I would.

Man: You'd be alone.

Woman: No. I'd follow you. Forever. (*Pause.*) Now, let's stop this nonsense.

Man: No! I can do what I want! Don't come any closer!

Woman: Then release your sword.

Man: Come any closer and I'll drop my head.

Woman   (*Woman slowly approaches Man. She grabs the hilt of the sword. She looks into his eyes. She pulls it out from under his chin.*): There will be no more of this. (*She exits with the sword. He starts to follow her, then stops. He touches under his chin. On his finger, he finds a drop of blood.*)

Scene IX

Night. Man is leaving the house. He is just about out, when he hears a shakuhachi *playing. He looks around, trying to locate the sound. Woman appears in the doorway to the outside.* shakuhachi *slowly fades out.*

Woman: It's time for you to go?

Man: Yes. I'm sorry.

Woman: You're just going to sneak out? A thief in the night? A frightened child?

Man: I care about you.

Woman: You express it strangely.

Man: I leave in shame because it is proper. (*Pause.*) I came seeking glory.

Woman: To kill me? You can say it. You'll be surprised at how little I blanche. As if you'd said, "I came for a bowl of rice," or "I came seeking love" or "I came to kill you."

Man: Weakness. All weakness. Too weak to kill you. Too weak to kill myself. Too weak to do anything but sneak away in shame. (*Woman brings out Man's sword.*)

Woman: Were you even planning to leave without this? (*He takes sword.*) Why not stay here?

Man: I can't live with someone who's defeated me.

Woman: I never thought of defeating you. I only wanted to take care of you. To make you happy. Because that made me happy and I was no longer alone.

Man: You defeated me.

Woman: Why do you think that way?

Man: I came here with a purpose. The world was clear. You changed the shape of your face, the shape of my heart—rearranged everything—created a world where I could do nothing.

Woman: I only tried to care for you.

Man: I guess that was all it took. (*Pause.*)

Woman: You still think I'm a witch. Just because old women gossip. You are so cruel. Once you arrived, there were only two possibilities; I would die or you would leave. (*Pause.*) If you believe I'm a witch, then kill me. Rid the province of one more evil.

Man: I can't—

Woman: Why not? If you believe that about me, then it's the right thing to do.

Man: You know I can't.

Woman: Then stay.

Man: Don't try and force me.

Woman: I won't force you to do anything. (*Pause.*) All I wanted was an escape—for both of us. The sound of a human voice—the simplest thing to find, and the hardest to hold onto. This house—my loneliness is etched into the walls. Kill me, but don't leave. Even in death, my spirit would rest here and be comforted by your presence.

Man: Force me to stay.

Woman: I won't. (*Man starts to leave.*) Beware.

Man: What?

Woman: The ground on which you walk is weak. It could give way at any moment. The crevice beneath is dark.

Man: Are you talking about death? I'm ready to die.

Woman: Fear for what is worse than death.

Man: What?

Woman: Falling. Falling through the darkness. Waiting to hit the ground. Picking up speed. Waiting for the ground. Falling faster. Falling alone. Waiting. Falling. Waiting. Falling.

(*Woman wails and runs out through the door to her room. Man stands, confused, not knowing what to do. He starts to follow her, then hesitates, and rushes out the door to the outside. Silence. Slowly, he re-enters from the outside. He looks for her in the main room. He goes slowly towards the panel to her room. He throws down his sword. He opens the panel. He goes inside. He comes out. He unrolls his mat. He sits on it, cross-legged. He looks out into space. He notices near him a* shakuhachi. *He picks it up. He begins to blow into it. He tries to make sounds. He continues trying through the end of the play. The Upstage scrim lights up. Upstage, we see the Woman. She is young. She is hanging from a rope suspended from the roof. She has hung herself. Around her are scores of vases with flowers in them whose blossoms have been blown off. Only the stems remain in the vases. Around her swirl the thousands of petals from the flowers. They fill the Upstage scrim area like a blizzard of color. Man continues to attempt to play. Lights fade to black.)*

[1983]

JHUMPA LAHIRI ■ (1967–)

Jhumpa Lahiri's debut story collection, *Interpreter of Maladies*, won the Pulitzer Prize for fiction in 2000. Born in London to Bengali parents, she grew up in Rhode Island where her father worked as a university librarian. After graduating from Barnard College, she received three master's degrees and a PhD from Boston University. Her first collection of stories was followed by a novel, *The Namesake* (2003). Her second collection, *Unaccustomed Earth* (2008), debuted at Number 1 on *The New York Times* best-seller list.

Acclaimed for the quiet eloquence of her prose, Jhumpa Lahiri has been compared to the Canadian writer Alice Munro, not only for her grave and stately style but also for the way her work has helped to renew popular interest in the short story form. She is also considered a leading light among a number of talented transnational writers (Junot Diaz from the Dominican Republic, Aleksander Hemon from Bosnia, Edwidge Danticat from Haiti) whose fiction is redefining the immigrant experience, and thus the American experience, for the twenty-first century.

In an essay entitled, *My Two Lives* (2006), Lahiri describes her efforts as an Indian-American to "be the two things, loyal to the old world and fluent in the new, approved of on either side of the hyphen.":

> When I first started writing, I was not conscious that my subject was the Indian-American experience. What drew me to my craft was the desire to force the two worlds I occupied to mingle on the page as I was not brave enough, or mature enough, to allow in life.... The immigrant's journey, no matter how ultimately rewarding, is founded on departure and deprivation, but it secures for the subsequent generation a sense of arrival and advantage. I can see a day coming when my American side, lacking the counterpoint India has until now maintained, begins to gain ascendancy and weight. It is in fiction that I will continue to interpret the term 'Indian-American,' calculating that shifting equation, whatever answers it might yield.

In the sharply focused, wide-ranging "Hell—Heaven," a sensitive character study of marriage and inter-racial relationships, Lahiri examines love, loss, identity, and family. These are themes that she has engaged subtly and profoundly throughout her work.

For critical discussion: *Naming Jhumpa Lahiri: Canons and Controversies*, eds. Lavina Dhingra and Floyd Cheung (2011). See also the chapter on Lahiri in Paul Brians, *Modern South Asian Literature in English* (2003).

Hell–Heaven

Pranab Chakraborty wasn't technically my father's younger brother. He was a fellow Bengali from Calcutta who had washed up on the barren shores of my parents' social life in the early seventies, when they lived in a rented apartment in Central Square[1] and could number their acquaintances on one hand. But I had no real uncles in America, and so I was taught to call him Pranab Kaku. Accordingly, he called my father Shyamal Da, always addressing him in the polite form, and he called my mother Boudi, which is how Bengalis are supposed to address an older brother's wife, instead of using her first name, Aparna. After Pranab Kaku was befriended by my parents, he confessed that on the day we met him he had followed my mother and me for the better part of an afternoon around the streets of Cambridge, where she and I tended to roam after I got out of school. He had trailed behind us along Massachusetts Avenue and in and out of the Harvard Coop,[2] where my mother liked to look at discounted housewares. He wandered with us into Harvard Yard, where my mother often sat on the grass on pleasant days and watched the stream of students and professors filing busily along the paths, until, finally, as we were climbing the steps to Widener Library so that I could use the bathroom he tapped my mother on the shoulder and inquired, in English, if she might be a Bengali. The answer to his question was clear, given that my mother was wearing the red and white bangles unique to Bengali married women, and a common Tangail sari, and had a thick stem of vermillion powder in the center parting of her hair, and the full round face and large dark eyes that are so typical of Bengali women. He noticed the two or three safety pins she wore fastened to the thin gold bangles that were behind the red and white ones, which she would use to replace a missing hook on a blouse or to draw a string through a petticoat at a moment's notice, a practice he associated strictly with his mother and sisters and aunts in Calcutta. Moreover, Pranab Kaku had overheard my mother speaking to me in Bengali, telling me that I couldn't buy an issue of *Archie*[3] at the Coop. But back then, he also confessed, he was so new to America that he took nothing for granted and doubted even the obvious.

My parents and I had lived in Central Square for three years prior to that day; before that, we lived in Berlin, where I was born and where my father had finished his training in microbiology before accepting a position as a researcher at Mass General, and before Berlin my mother and father had lived in India, where they were strangers to each other, and where their marriage had been arranged. Central Square is the first place I can recall living, and in my memories of our apartment, in a dark brown shingled house on Ashburton Place, Pranab Kaku is always there. According to the story he liked to recall often, my mother invited him to accompany us back to our apartment that very afternoon and prepared tea for the two of them; then, after learning that he had not had a proper Bengali meal

---

[1]An area in Cambridge, Massachusetts.
[2]The Harvard/MIT Cooperative Society (or The Coop), a large store in Harvard Square, is a Cambridge, Massachusetts-based cooperative serving the Harvard University and MIT campuses.
[3]Archie Andrews, created in 1941 by Vic Bloom and Bob Montana, is a fictional character in an American comic book series.

in more than three months, she served him the leftover curried mackerel and rice that we had eaten for dinner the night before. He remained into the evening for a second dinner after my father got home, and after that he showed up for dinner almost every night, occupying the fourth chair at our square Formica kitchen table and becoming a part of our family in practice as well as in name.

He was from a wealthy family in Calcutta and had never has to do so much as pour himself a glass of water before moving to America, to study engineering at MIT. Life as a graduate student in Boston was a cruel shock, and in his first month he lost nearly twenty pounds. He had arrived in January, in the middle of a snowstorm, and at the end of a week he had packed his bags and gone to Logan, prepared to abandon the opportunity he'd worked toward all his life, only to change his mind at the last minute. He was living on Trowbridge Street in the home of a divorced woman with two young children who were always screaming and crying. He rented a room in the attic and was permitted to use the kitchen only at specified times of the day and instructed always to wipe down the stove with Windex and a sponge. My parents agreed that it was a terrible situation, and if they'd had a bedroom to spare they would have offered it to him. Instead, they welcomed him to our meals and opened up our apartment to him at any time, and soon it was there he went between classes and on his days off, always leaving behind some vestige of himself: a nearly finished pack of cigarettes, a newspaper, a piece of mail he had not bothered to open, a sweater he had taken off and forgotten in the course of his stay.

I remember vividly the sound of his exuberant laughter and the sight of his lanky body slouched or sprawled on the dull, mismatched furniture that had come with our apartment. He had a striking face, with a high forehead and a thick mustache, and overgrown, untamed hair that my mother said made him look like the American hippies who were everywhere in those days. His long legs jiggled rapidly up and down wherever he sat, and his elegant hands trembled when he held a cigarette between his fingers, tapping the ashes into a teacup that my mother began to set aside for this exclusive purpose. Though he was a scientist by training, there was nothing rigid or predictable or orderly about him. He always seemed to be starving, walking through the door and announcing that he hadn't had lunch, and then he would eat ravenously, reaching behind my mother to steal cutlets as she was frying them, before she had a chance to set them properly on a plate with red onion salad. In private, my parents remarked that he was a brilliant student, a star at Jadavpur who had come to MIT with an impressive assistantship, but Pranab Kaku was cavalier about his classes, skipping them with frequency. "These Americans are learning equations I knew at Usha's age," he would complain. He was stunned that my second-grade teacher didn't assign any homework and that at the age of seven I hadn't yet been taught square roots or the concept of pi.

He appeared without warning, never phoning beforehand but simply knocking on the door the way people did in Calcutta and calling out "Boudi!" as he waited for my mother to let him in. Before we met him, I would return from school and find my mother with her purse in her lap and her trench coat on, desperate to escape the apartment where she had spent the day alone. But now I would find her in the kitchen, rolling out dough for luchis, which she normally made only on Sundays for my father and me, or putting up new curtains she'd bought at Woolworth's.[4] I did not know, back then, that Pranab Kaku's-visits were what my mother looked forward to all day, that she changed into a new sari and combed her hair in anticipation of his arrival, and that she planned, days in advance, the snacks she would serve him with such nonchalance. That she lived for the moment she heard him call out "Boudi!" from the porch and that she was in a foul humor on the days he didn't materialize.

It must have pleased her that I looked forward to his visits as well. He showed me card tricks and an optical illusion in which he appeared to be severing his own thumb with enormous struggle and strength and taught me to memorize multiplication tables well before I had to learn them in school. His hobby was photography. He owned an expensive camera that required thought before you pressed the shutter, and I quickly became his favorite subject, round-faced, missing teeth, thick bangs in need of a trim. They are still the pictures myself I like best, for they convey that confidence of youth I no longer possess, especially in front of a camera. I remember having to run back and forth in Harvard Yard as he stood with camera, trying to capture me in motion, or posing on the steps of university buildings and on the street and against the trunks of trees. There is only one photograph in which my mother appears; she is holding me as I sit straddling her lap, her head tilted toward me, her hands pressed to my ears as if to prevent me from hearing something. In that picture, Pranab Kaku's shadow, his two arms raised at angles to hold the camera to face, hovers in the corner of the frame, his darkened, featureless shape superimposed on one side of my mother's body. It was always the three of us. I was always there when he visited. It would have been inappropriate for my mother to receive him in the apartment alone; this was something that went without saying.

They had in common all the things she and my father did not: a love of music, film, leftist politics, poetry. They were from the same neighborhood in North Calcutta, their family homes within walking distance, the facades familiar to them once the exact locations were described. They knew the same shops, the same bus and tram routes, the same holes-in-the-wall for the best jelabis and moghlai parathas. My father, on the other hand, came from a suburb twenty miles outside Calcutta, an area that my mother considered the wilderness, and even her bleakest hours of homesickness she

---

[4]Chain of retail stores in the U.S. and elsewhere (1879–1970).

was grateful that my father had at least spared her a life in the stern house of her in-laws, where she would have had to keep her head covered with the end of her sari at all times and use an outhouse that was nothing but a raised platform with a hole, and where, in the rooms, there was not a single painting hanging on the walls. Within a few weeks, Pranab Kaku had brought his reel-to-reel over to our apartment, and he played for my mother medley after medley of songs from the Hindi films of their youth. They were cheerful songs of courtship, which transformed the quiet life in our apartment and transported my mother back to the world she'd left behind in order to marry my father. She and Pranab Kaku would try to recall which scene in which movie the songs were from, who the actors were and what they were wearing. My mother would describe Raj Kapoor and Nargis singing under umbrellas in the rain, or Dev Anand strumming a guitar on the beach in Goa. She and Pranab Kaku would argue passionately about these matters, raising their voices in playful combat, confronting each other in a way she and my father never did.

Because he played the part of a younger brother, she felt free to call him Pranab, whereas she never called my father by his first name. My father was thirty-seven then, nine years older than my mother. Pranab Kaku was twenty-five. My father was a lover of silence and solitude. He had married my mother to placate his parents; they were willing to accept his desertion as long as he had a wife. He was wedded to his work, his research, and he existed in a shell that neither my mother nor I could penetrate. Conversation was a chore for him; it required an effort he preferred to expend at the lab. He disliked excess in anything, voiced no cravings or needs apart from the frugal elements of his daily routine: cereal and tea in the mornings, a cup of tea after he got home, and two different vegetable dishes every night with dinner. He did not eat with the reckless appetite of Pranab Kaku. My father had a survivor's mentality. From time to time, he liked to remark, in mixed company and often with no relevant provocation, that starving Russians under Stalin had resorted to eating the glue off the back of their wallpaper. One might think that he would have slightly jealous, or at the very least suspicious, about the regularity of Pranab Kaku's visits and the effect they had on mother's behavior and mood. But my guess is that my father was grateful to Pranab Kaku for the companionship he provided, freed from the sense of responsibility he must have for forcing her to leave India, and relieved, perhaps, to see her happy for a change.

In the summer, Pranab Kaku bought a navy-blue Volkswagen Beetle and began to take my mother and me for drives through Boston and Cambridge, and soon outside the city, flying down the highway. He would take us to India Tea Spices in Watertown, and one time he drove us all the way to New Hampshire to look at the mountains. As the weather grew hotter, we started going, once or twice a week, to Walden Pond. My mother always prepared a picnic of hard-boiled eggs and cucumber sandwiches and talked fondly about the winter picnics of her youth, grand expeditions with fifty of her relatives, all taking the train into the West Bengal countryside. Pranab Kaku listened to these stories with interest, absorb the vanishing details of her past. He did not turn a deaf ear to her nostalgia, like my father, or listen uncomprehending, me. At Walden Pond, Pranab Kaku would coax my mother through the woods, and lead her down the steep slope to water's edge. She would unpack the picnic things and sit and watch us as we swam. His chest was matted with thick dark hair, all the way to his waist. He was an odd sight, with his pole-thin legs and a small, flaccid belly, like an otherwise svelte woman who has had a baby and not bothered to tone abdomen. "You're making me fat, Boudi," he would complain after gorging himself on my mother's cooking. He swam noisily, clumsily, his head always above the water; he didn't know how to blow bubbles or hold his breath, as I had learned swimming class. Wherever we went, any stranger would have naturally assumed that Pranab Kaku was my father, that my mother was his wife.

It is clear to me now that my mother was in love with him. He wooed her as no other man had, with the innocent affection of a brother-in-law. In my mind, he was just a family member, a cross between an uncle and a much older brother, for in certain respects my parents sheltered and cared for him in much the same way they cared for me. He was respectful of my father, always seeking his advice about making a life in the West, about setting up a bank account and getting a job, and deferring to his opinions about Kissinger and Watergate.[5] Occasionally, my mother would tease him about women, asking about female Indian students at MIT or showing him pictures of her younger cousins in India. "What do you think of her?" she would ask. "Isn't she pretty?" She knew that she could never have Pranab Kaku for herself, and I suppose it was her attempt to keep him in the family. But, most important, in the beginning he was totally dependent on her, needing her for those months in a way my father never did in the whole history of their marriage. He brought to my mother the first and, I suspect, the only pure happiness she ever felt. I don't think even my birth made her as happy. I was evidence of her marriage to my father, an assumed consequence of the life she had been raised to lead. But Pranab Kaku was different. He was the one totally unanticipated pleasure in her life.

In the fall of 1974, Pranab Kaku met a student at Radcliffe named Deborah, an American, and she began to accompany him to our house. I called Deborah by her first name, as my parents did, but Pranab Kaku taught her to call my father Shyamal Da and my mother Boudi, something with which Deborah gladly complied. Before they came to dinner for the first time, I asked my mother, as she was straightening up the living room, if I ought

[5]Henry Kissinger: born in Germany (1923), U.S. statesman and diplomat and secretary of state, 1973–77; Watergate: a political scandal in which an attempt to spy on the national headquarters of the Democratic Party (in the Watergate building in Washington, DC) led to the resignation of President Nixon (1974).

to address her as Deborah Kakima, turning her into an aunt as I had turned Pranab into an uncle. "What's the point?" my mother said, looking back at me sharply. "In a few weeks, the fun will be over and she'll leave him." And yet Deborah remained by his side, attending the weekend parties that Pranab Kaku and my parents were becoming more involved with, gatherings that were exclusively Bengali with the exception of her. Deborah was very tall, taller than both my parents and nearly as tall as Pranab Kaku. She wore her long brass-colored hair center-parted, as my mother did, but it was gathered into a low ponytail instead of a braid, or it spilled messily over her shoulders and down her back in a way that my mother considered indecent. She wore small silver spectacles and not a trace of makeup, and she studied philosophy. I found her utterly beautiful, but according to my mother she had spots on her face, and her hips were too small.

For a while, Pranab Kaku still showed up once a week for dinner on his own, mostly asking my mother what she thought of Deborah. He sought her approval, telling her that Deborah was the daughter of professors at Boston College, that her father published poetry, and that both her parents had PhDs. When he wasn't around, my mother complained about Deborah's visits, about having to make the food less spicy, even though Deborah said she liked spicy food, and feeling embarrassed to put a fried fish head in the dal. Pranab Kaku taught Deborah to say *khub bhalo* and *aacha* and to pick up certain foods with her fingers instead of with a fork. Sometimes they ended up feeding each other, allowing their fingers to linger in each other's mouth, causing my parents to look down at their plates and wait for the moment to pass. At larger gatherings, they kissed and held hands in front of everyone, and when they were out of earshot my mother would talk to the other Bengali women. "He used to be so different. I don't understand how a person can change so suddenly. It's just hell–heaven, the difference," she would say, always using the English words for her self-concocted, backward metaphor.

The more my mother began to resent Deborah's visits, the more I began to anticipate them. I fell in love with Deborah, the way young girls often fall in love with women who are not their mothers. I loved her serene gray eyes, the ponchos and denim wrap skirts and sandals she wore, her straight hair that she let me manipulated into all sorts of silly styles. I longed for her casual appearance; my mother insisted whenever there was a gathering that I wear one of my ankle-length, faintly Victorian dresses, which she referred to as maxis, and have party hair, which meant taking a strand from either side of my head and joining them with a barrette at the back. At parties, Deborah would, eventually, politely slip away, much to the relief of the Bengali women with whom she was expected to carry on a conversation, and she would play with me. I was older than all my parents' friends' children, but with Deborah I had a companion. She knew all about the books I read, about Pippi Long-stocking and Anne of Green Gables. She gave me the sorts of gifts my parents had neither the money nor the

inspiration to buy: a large book of Grimm's *Fairy Tales* with watercolor illustrations on thick, silken pages, wooden puppets with hair fashioned
from yarn. She told me about her family, three older sisters and two brothers, the youngest of whom was closer to my age than to hers. Once, after
visiting her parents, she brought back three Nancy Drews,[6] her name written in a girlish hand at the top of the first page, and an old toy she'd had,
a small paper theater set with interchangeable backdrops, the exterior of
a castle and a ballroom and an open field. Deborah and I spoke freely in
English, a language in which, by that age, I expressed myself more easily
than Bengali, which I was required to speak at home. Sometimes she asked
me how to say this or that in Bengali; once, she asked me what *asobbho*
meant. I hesitated, then told her it was what my mother called me if I had
done something extremely naughty, and Deborah's face clouded. I felt protective of her, aware that she was unwanted, that she was resented, aware
of the nasty things people said.

Outings in the Volkswagen now involved the four of us, Deborah in the
front, her hand over Pranab Kaku's while it rested on the gearshift, my
mother and I in the back. Soon, my mother began coming up with reasons
to excuse herself, headaches and incipient colds, and so I became part of
a new triangle. To my surprise, my mother allowed me to go with them, to
the Museum of Fine Arts and the Public Garden and the Aquarium. She was
waiting for the affair to end, for Deborah to break Pranab Kaku's heart and
for him to return to us, scarred and penitent. I saw no sign of their relationship foundering. Their open affection for each other, their easily expressed happiness, was a new and romantic thing to me. Having me in the
backseat allowed Pranab Kaku and Deborah to practice for the future, to
try on the idea of a family of their own. Countless photographs were taken
of me and Deborah, of me sitting on Deborah's lap, holding her hand, kissing her on the cheek. We exchanged what I believed were secret smiles,
and in those moments I felt that she understood me better than anyone
else in the world. Anyone would have said that Deborah would make an
excellent mother one day. But my mother refused to acknowledge such
a thing. I did not know at the time that my mother allowed me to go off
with Pranab Kaku and Deborah because she was pregnant for the fifth time
since my birth and was so sick and exhausted and fearful of losing another
baby that she slept most of the day. After ten weeks, she miscarried once
again and was advised by her doctor to stop trying.

By summer, there was a diamond on Deborah's left hand, something my
mother had never been given. Because his own family lived so far away,
Pranab Kaku came to the house alone one day, to ask for my parents'
blessing before giving her the ring. He showed us the box, opening it and
taking out the diamond nestled inside. "I want to see how it looks on

[6]A fictional character in a mystery fiction series launched in 1930; published under the collective
pseudonym Carolyn Keene, the books have been written by a number of authors.

someone," he said, urging my mother to try it on, but she refused. I was the one who stuck out my hand, feeling the weight of the ring suspended at the base of my finger. Then he asked for a second thing: he wanted my parents to write to his parents, saying that they had met Deborah and that they thought highly of her. He was nervous, naturally, about telling his family that he intended to marry an American girl. He had told his parents all about us, and at one point my parents had received a letter from them, expressing appreciation for taking such good care of their son and for giving him a proper home in America. "It needn't be long," Pranab Kaku said. "Just a few lines. They'll accept it more easily if it comes from you." My father thought neither ill nor well of Deborah, never commenting or criticizing as my mother did, but he assured Pranab Kaku that a letter of endorsement would be on its way to Calcutta by the end of the week. My mother nodded her assent, but the following day I saw the teacup Pranab Kaku had used all this time as an ashtray in the kitchen garbage can, in pieces, and three Band-Aids taped to my mother's hand.

Pranab Kaku's parents were horrified by the thought of their only son marrying an American woman, and a few weeks later our telephone rang in the middle of the night: it was Mr. Chakraborty telling my father that they could not possibly bless such a marriage, that it was out of the question, that if Pranab Kaku dared to marry Deborah he would no longer acknowledge him as a son. Then his wife got on the phone, asking to speak to my mother and attacked her as if they were intimate, blaming my mother for allowing the affair to develop. She said that they had already chosen a wife for him in Calcutta, that he'd left for America with the understanding that he'd go back after he had finished his studies and marry this girl. They had bought the neighboring flat in their building for Pranab and his betrothed, and it was sitting empty, waiting for his return. "We thought we could trust you, and yet you have betrayed us deeply," his mother said, taking out her anger on a stranger in a way she could not with her son. "Is this what happens to people in America?" For Pranab Kaku's sake, my mother defended the engagement, telling his mother that Deborah was a polite girl from a decent family. Pranab Kaku's parents pleaded with mine to talk him out of the engagement, but my father refused, deciding that it was not their place to get embroiled. "We are not his parents" he told my mother. "We can tell him they don't approve but nothing more." And so my parents told Pranab Kaku nothing about how his parents had berated them, and blamed them, and threatened to disown Pranab Kaku, only that they have refused to give him their blessing. In the face of this refusal Pranab Kaku shrugged. "I don't care. Not everyone can be open-minded as you," he told my parents. "Your blessing is blessing enough."

After the engagement, Pranab Kaku and Deborah began drifting out of our lives. They moved in together, to an apartment in Boston, in the South

End, a part of the city my parents considered unsafe. We moved as well, to a house in Natick.[7] Though my parents had bought the house, they occupied it as if they were still tenants, touching up scuff marks with leftover paint and reluctant to put holes in the walls, and every afternoon when the sun shone through the living-room window mother closed the blinds so that our new furniture would not fade. A few weeks before the wedding, my parents invited Pranab Kaku to the house alone, and my mother prepared special meal to mark the end of his bachelorhood. It would be the only Bengali aspect of the wedding; the rest of it would be strictly American, with a cake and a minister and Deborah in a long white dress and veil. There is a photograph of the dinner taken by my father, the only picture, to my knowledge, in which my mother and Pranab Kaku appear together. The picture is slightly blurry; I remember Pranab Kaku explaining to my father how to work the camera, and so he is captured looking up from the kitchen table and the elaborate array of food my mother had prepared in his honor, his mouth open, his long arm outstretched and his finger pointing, instructing my father how to read the light meter or some such thing. My mother stands beside him, one hand placed on top of his head in a gesture of blessing, the first and last time she was to touch him in her life. "She will leave him," my mother told her friends afterward. "He is throwing his life away."

The wedding was at a church in Ipswich,[8] with a reception at a country club. It was going to be a small ceremony, which my parents took to mean one or two hundred people as opposed to three or four hundred. My mother was shocked that fewer than thirty people had been invited, and she was more perplexed than honored that, of all the Bengalis Pranab Kaku knew by then, we were the only ones on the list. At the wedding we sat, like the other guests, first on the hard wooden pews of the church and then at a long table that had been set up for lunch. Though we were the closest thing Pranab Kaku had to a family that day, we were not included in the group photographs that were taken on the grounds of the country club, with Deborah's parents and grandparents and her many siblings, and neither my mother nor my father got up to make a toast. My mother did not appreciate the fact that Deborah had made sure that my parents, who did not eat beef, were given fish instead of filet mignon like everyone else. She kept speaking in Bengali, complaining about the formality of the proceedings, and the fact that Pranab Kaku, wearing a tuxedo, barely said a word to us because he was too busy leaning over the shoulders of his new American in-laws as he circled the table. As usual, my father said nothing in response to my mother's commentary, quietly and methodically working through his meal, his fork an occasionally squeaking against the surface of the china, because he was accustomed to eating with his hands. He cleared his plate and then my mother's, for she had pronounced the food inedible, and then he announced that he had overeaten had a stomachache. The

---

[7] A town approximately twenty miles west of Boston.
[8] Ipswich is a coastal town, thirty miles north of Boston, in Essex County, Massachusetts.

only time my mother forced a smile was when Deborah appeared behind her chair, kissing her on the cheek and asking if we were enjoying ourselves. When the dancing started, my parents remained at the drinking tea, and after two or three songs they decided that it was time for us to go home, my mother shooting me looks that effect across the room, where I was dancing in a circle Pranab Kaku and Deborah and the other children at the wedding. I wanted to stay, and when, reluctantly, I walked over to where my parents sat, Deborah followed me. "Boudi, let Usha stay. She's having such a good time," she said to my mother. "Lots of people will be heading back your way, someone will drop her off in a little while." But my mother said no, I had plenty of fun already and forced me to put on my coat over long puff-sleeved dress. As we drove home from the wedding I told my mother, for the first but not the last time in my life, that I hated her.

The following year, we received a birth announcement from the Chakrabortys, a picture of twin girls, which my mother did not paste into an album or display on the refrigerator door. The girls were named Srabani and Sabitri but were called Bonny and Sara. Apart from a thank-you card for our wedding gift, it was their only communication; we were not invited to the new house in Marblehead, bought after Pranab Kaku got a high-paying job at Stone & Webster.[9] For a while, my parents and their friends continued to invite the Chakrabortys to gatherings, but because they never came, or left after staying only an hour, the invitations stopped. Their absences were attributed, by my parents and their circle, to Deborah, and it was universally agreed that she had stripped Pranab Kaku not only of his origins but of his independence. She was the enemy, he was her prey, and their example was invoked as a warning, and as vindication, that mixed marriages were a doomed enterprise. Occasionally, they surprised everyone, appearing at a pujo for a few hours with their two identical little girls who barely looked Bengali and spoke only English and were being raised so differently from me and most of the other children. They were not taken to Calcutta every summer, they did not have parents who were clinging to another way of life and exhorting their children to do the same. Because of Deborah, they were exempt from all that, and for this reason I envied them. "Usha, look at you, all grown up and so pretty," Deborah would say whenever she saw me, rekindling, if only for a minute, our bond of years before. She had cut off her beautiful long hair by then, and had a bob. "I bet you'll be old enough to babysit soon," she would say. "I'll call you—the girls would love that." But she never did.

I began to grow out of my girlhood, entering middle school and developing crushes on the American boys in my class. The crushes amounted to nothing; in spite of Deborah's compliments, I was always overlooked at that age. But my mother must have picked up on something, for she forbade

---

[9]An American engineering company based in Stoughton, Massachusetts, founded by electrical engineers Charles Stone and Edwin Webster in 1889.

me to attend the dances that were held the last Friday of every month in the school cafeteria, and it was an unspoken law that I was not allowed to date. "Don't think you'll get away with marrying an American, the way Pranab Kaku did," she would say from time to time. I was thirteen, the thought of marriage irrelevant to my life. Still, her words upset me, and I felt her grip on me tighten. She would fly into a rage when I told her I wanted to start wearing a bra, or if I wanted to go to Harvard Square with a friend. In the middle of our arguments, she often conjured Deborah as her antithesis, the sort of woman she refused to be. "If she were your mother, she would let you do whatever you wanted, because she wouldn't care. Is that what you want, Usha, a mother who doesn't care?" When I began menstruating, the summer before I started ninth grade, my mother gave me a speech, telling me that I was to let no boy touch me, and then she asked if I knew how a woman became pregnant. I told her what I had been taught in science, about the sperm fertilizing the egg, and then she asked if I knew how, exactly, that happened. I saw the terror in her eyes and so, though I knew that aspect of procreation as well, I lied, and told her it hadn't been explained to us.

I began keeping other secrets from her, evading her with the aid of my friends. I told her I was sleeping over at a friend's when really I went to parties, drinking beer and allowing boys to kiss me and fondle my breasts and press their erections against my hip as we lay groping on a sofa or the backseat of a car. I began to pity my mother; the older I got, the more I saw what a desolate life she led. She had never worked, and during the day she watched soap operas to pass the time. Her only job, every day, was to clean and cook for my father and me. We rarely went to restaurants, my father always pointing out, even in cheap ones, how expensive they were compared with eating at home. When my mother complained to him about how much she hated life in the suburbs and how lonely she felt, he said nothing to placate her. "If you are so unhappy, go back to Calcutta," he would offer, making it clear that their separation would not affect him one way or the other. I began to take my cues from my father in dealing with her, isolating her doubly. When she screamed at me for talking too long on the telephone, or for staying too long in my room, I learned to scream back, telling her that she was pathetic, that she knew nothing about me, and it was clear to us both that I had stopped needing her, definitively and abruptly, just as Pranab Kaku had.

Then, the year before I went off to college, my parents and I were invited to the Chakrabortys' home for Thanksgiving. We were not the only guests from my parents' old Cambridge crowd; it turned out that Pranab kaku and Deborah wanted to have a sort of reunion of all the people they had been friendly with back then. Normally, my parents did not celebrate Thanksgiving; the ritual of a large sit-down dinner and the foods that one was supposed to eat was lost on them. They treated it as if it were Memorial Day or Veterans Day—just another holiday in the American year.

But we drove out to Marblehead,[10] to an impressive stone-faced house with a semicircular gravel driveway clogged with cars. The house was a short walk from the ocean; on our way, we had driven by the harbor overlooking the cold, glittering Atlantic, and when we stepped out of the car we were greeted by the sound of gulls and waves. Most of the living-room furniture had been moved to the basement and extra tables joined to the main one to form a giant U. They were covered with tablecloths, set with white plates and silverware, and had centerpieces of gourds. I was struck by the toys and dolls that were everywhere, dogs that shed long yellow hairs on everything, all the photographs of Bonny and Sara and Deborah decorating the walls, still more plastering the refrigerator door. Food was being prepared when we arrived, something my mother always frowned upon, the kitchen a chaos of people and smells and enormous dirtied bowls.

Deborah's family, whom we remembered dimly from the wedding, was there, her parents and her brothers and sisters and their husbands and wives and boyfriends and babies. Her sisters were in their thirties, but like Deborah, they could have been mistaken for college students, wearing jeans and clogs and fisherman sweaters, and her brother Matty, with whom I had danced in a circle at the wedding, was now a freshman at Amherst, with wide set green eyes and wispy brown hair and a complexion that reddened easily. As soon as I saw Deborah's siblings, joking with one another as they chopped and stirred things in the kitchen, I was furious with my mother for making a scene before we left the house and forcing me to wear a shalwar kameez. I knew they assumed, from my clothing, that I had more in common with the other Bengalis than with them. But Deborah insisted on including me, setting me to work peeling apples with Matty, and out of my parents' sight I was given beer to drink. When the meal was ready, we were told where to sit, in an alternating boy-girl formation that made the Bengalis uncomfortable. Bottles of wine were lined up on the table. Two turkeys were brought out, one stuffed with sausage and one without. My mouth watered at the food, but I knew that afterward, on our way home, my mother would complain that it was all tasteless and bland. "Impossible," my mother said, shaking her hand over the top of her glass when someone tried to pour her a little wine.

Deborah's father, Gene, got up to say grace, and asked everyone at the table to join hands. He bowed his head and closed his eyes. "Dear Lord, we thank you today for the food we are about to receive," he began. My parents were seated next to each other, and I was stunned to see that they complied, that my father's brown fingers lightly clasped my mother's pale ones. I noticed Matty seated on the other side of the room and saw him glancing at me as his father spoke. After the chorus of Amens, Gene raised his glass and said, "Forgive me, but I never thought I'd have the opportunity to say this: Here's to Thanksgiving with the Indians." Only a few people laughed at the joke.

[10]Prosperous coastal town sixteen miles north of Boston.

Then Pranab Kaku stood up and thanked everyone for coming. He was relaxed from alcohol, his once wiry body beginning to thicken. He started to talk sentimentally about his early days in Cambridge, and then suddenly he recounted the story of meeting me and my mother for the first time, telling the guests about how he had followed us that afternoon. The people who did not know us laughed, amused by the description of the encounter, and by Pranab Kaku's desperation. He walked around the room to where my mother was sitting and draped a lanky arm around her shoulder, forcing her, for a brief moment, to stand up. "This woman," he declared, pulling her close to his side, "this woman hosted my first real Thanksgiving in America. It might have been an afternoon in May, but that first meal at Boudi's table was Thanksgiving to me. If it weren't for that meal, I would have gone back to Calcutta." My mother looked away, embarrassed. She was thirty-eight, already going gray, and she looked closer to my father's age than to Pranab Kaku's; regardless of his waistline, he retained his handsome, carefree looks. Pranab Kaku went back to his place at the head of the table, next to Deborah, and concluded, "And if that had been the case I'd have never met you, my darling," and he kissed her on the mouth in front of everyone, to much applause, as if it were their wedding day all over again.

After the turkey, smaller forks were distributed and orders were taken for three different kinds of pie, written on small pads by Deborah's sisters, as if they were waitresses. After dessert, the dogs needed to go out, and Pranab Kaku volunteered to take them. "How about a walk on the beach?" he suggested, and Deborah's side of the family agreed that that was an excellent idea. None of the Bengalis wanted to go, preferring to sit with their tea and cluster together, at last, at one end of the room, speaking freely after the forced chitchat with the Americans during the meal. Matty came over and sat in the chair beside me that was now empty, encouraging me to join the walk. When I hesitated, pointing to my inappropriate clothes and shoes but also aware of my mother's silent fury at the sight of us together, he said, "I'm sure Deb can lend you something." So I went upstairs, where Deborah gave me a pair of her jeans and a thick sweater and some sneakers, so that I looked like her and her sisters.

She sat on the edge of her bed, watching me change, as if we were girlfriends, and she asked if I had a boyfriend. When I told her no, she said, "Matty thinks you're cute."

"He told you?"

"No, but I can tell."

As I walked back downstairs, emboldened by this information, in the jeans I'd had to roll up and in which I felt finally like myself, I noticed my mother lift her eyes from her teacup and stare at me, but she said nothing, and off I went, with Pranab Kaku and his dogs and his in-laws, along a road and then down some steep wooden steps to the water. Deborah and one of her sisters stayed behind, to begin the cleanup and see to the needs of those who remained. Initially, we all walked together, in a single row across the sand, but then I noticed Matty hanging back, and so the two of us trailed behind, the distance between us and the others increasing. We began flirting, talking of things I no longer remember, and eventually we wandered into a rocky inlet and Matty fished a joint out of his pocket. We turned our backs to the wind and smoked it, our cold fingers touching in the process, our lips pressed to the same damp section of the rolling paper. At first I didn't feel any effect, but then, listening to him talk about the band he was in, I was aware that his voice sounded miles away, and that I had the urge to laugh, even though what he was saying was not terribly funny. It felt as if we were apart from the group for hours, but when we wandered back to the sand we could still see them, walking out onto a promontory to watch the sun set.

It was dark by the time we all headed back to the house, and I dreaded seeing my parents while I was still high. But when we got there Deborah told me that my parents, feeling tired, had left, agreeing to let someone drive me home later. A fire had been lit and I was told to relax and have more pie as the leftovers were put away and the living room slowly put back in order. Of course, it was Matty who drove me home, and sitting in my parents' driveway I kissed him, at once thrilled and terrified that my mother might walk onto the lawn in her nightgown and discover us. I gave Matty my phone number, and for a few weeks I thought of him constantly, and hoped foolishly that he would call.

In the end, my mother was right, and fourteen years after that Thanksgiving, after twenty-three years of marriage, Pranab Kaku and Deborah got divorced. It was he who had strayed, falling in love with a married Bengali woman, destroying two families in the process. The other woman was someone my parents knew, though not very well. Deborah was in her forties by then, Bonny and Sara away at college. In her shock and grief, it was my mother whom Deborah turned to, calling and weeping into the phone. Somehow, through all the years, she had continued to regard us as quasi in-laws, sending flowers when my grandparents died and giving me a compact edition of the *O.E.D.*[11] as a college-graduation present. "You knew him so well. How could he do something like this?" Deborah asked my mother. And then, "Did you know anything about it?" My mother answered truthfully that she did not. Their hearts had been broken by the same man, only my mother's had long ago mended, and in an odd way, as my parents approached their old age, she and my father had grown fond of each other, out of habit if nothing else. I believe my absence from the house, once I left for college, had something to do with this, because over the years, when I visited, I noticed a warmth between my parents that had not been there before, a quiet teasing, a solidarity, a concern when one of them fell ill. My mother and I had also made peace; she had accepted the fact that I was not only her daughter but a child of America as well. Slowly, she accepted that I dated one American man, and then another, and then yet another, that I slept with them, and

---

[11]The Oxford English Dictionary.

even that I lived with one though we were not married. She welcomed my boyfriends into our home and when things didn't work out she told me I would find someone better. After years of being idle, she decided, when she turned fifty, to get a degree in library science at a nearby university.

On the phone, Deborah admitted something that surprised my mother: that all these years she had felt hopelessly shut out of a part of Pranab Kaku's life. "I was so horribly jealous of you back then, for knowing him, understanding him in a way I never could. He turned his back on his family, on all of you, really but I still felt threatened. I could never get over that." She told my mother that she had tried, for years, to get Pranab Kaku to reconcile with his parents, and that she had also encouraged him to maintain ties with other Bengalis, but he had resisted. It had been Deborah's idea to invite us to their Thanksgiving; ironically, the other woman had been there, too. "I hope you don't blame me for taking him away from your lives, Boudi. I always worried that you did."

My mother assured Deborah that she blamed her for nothing. She confessed nothing to Deborah about her own jealousy of decades before, only that she was sorry for what had happened, that it was a sad and terrible thing for their family. She did not tell Deborah that a few weeks after Pranab Kaku's wedding, while I was at a Girl Scout meeting and my father was at work, she had gone through the house, gathering up all the safety pins that lurked in drawers and tins, and adding them to the few fastened to her bracelets. When she'd found enough, she pinned them to her sari one by one, attaching the front piece to the layer of material underneath, so that no one would be able to pull the garment off her body. Then she took a can of lighter fluid and a box kitchen matches and stepped outside, into our chilly backyard, which was full of leaves needing to be raked. Over her sari she was wearing a knee-length lilac trench coat, and to any neighbor she must have looked as though she'd simply stepped out for some fresh air. She opened up the coat and removed the tip from the can of lighter fluid and doused herself, then buttoned and belted the coat. She walked over to the garbage barrel behind our house and disposed of the fluid, then returned to the middle of the yard with the box of matches in her coat pocket. For nearly an hour she stood there, looking at our house, trying to work up the courage to strike a match. It was not I who saved her, or my father, but our next-door neighbor, Mrs. Holcomb, with whom my mother had never been particularly friendly. She came out to rake the leaves in her yard, calling out to my mother and remarking how beautiful the sunset was. "I see you've been admiring it for a while now," she said. My mother agreed, and then she went back into the house. By the time my father and I came home in the early evening, she was in the kitchen boiling rice for our dinner, as if it were any other day.

My mother told Deborah none of this. It was to me that she confessed, after my own heart was broken by a man I'd hoped to marry.

[2004]

▪▪ **GALLERY** ▪▪

Postmodernism

Perhaps the best approach to postmodernism is through specific examples, because the term itself is extremely—some would say, notoriously—difficult to define. While many scholars, critics, and theorists have studied postmodernism, there is little to no consensus about what it means.

The scholar Ihab Hassan, writing in 2000, states the point this way: "What was postmodernism, and what is it still? I believe it is a revenant, the return of the irrepressible; every time we are rid of it, its ghost rises back. And like a ghost, it eludes definition." More recently, a curator presenting a major exhibition on postmodernism at London's Victoria and Albert Museum said: "We talked about it endlessly for three years. There were many, many definitions that we put forward."

The only thing that commentators agree about is that the postmodernism is highly complex and multifaceted—so much so that, according to some, the term escapes clear definition altogether. No one is certain whether postmodernism is the same as, similar to, or different from modern, late modern, and contemporary.

Sometimes postmodernism in art and architecture, and in music and literature, is defined as a break or departure, post-1945, from modernism—as a momentous trend or tendency on the other side of World War II, the Holocaust, and the U.S. military's nuclear bombing of Japan. Postmodernists, it is said, inhabit a post-Holocaust, post-nuclear world, one that is increasingly saturated in media, and, as we move further into the twenty-first century, in near-instantaneous forms of video and audio communication and display. The novelist John Barth touched on this point when he observed that "what makes a text postmodern" is not "literary strategies in isolation, but rather their connection through complex feedback loops with postmodernism as a cultural dominant."

Postmodernist theorists reject capacious explanations and elaborate analytical constructs, large overviews, and totalizing narratives. "I define postmodern," says Jean-François Lyotard, "as incredulity toward metanarratives"—that is, capacious explanatory arguments, and grand narratives of decline and progress. According to one recent scholar, Postmodernism, says Anna Copeland, is "a reaction to intellectual traditions that attempt to explain the world using universal concepts such as Freudian models of the personality, Marxist theories of economics, or the cause-and-effect explanations used by historians. Postmodernism views life in the late twentieth century as a series of disconnected events, a smorgasbord of narratives or discourses that compete for attention."

A manifestation of this attitude is the denial by some theorists of distinct categories of knowledge and cultural production. This is why one

of them has said, "Postmodernism is the new philosophy of the skeptical." Nothing is intrinsically literature or art, or, rather, anything and everything is literature or art, at least potentially. Postmodernism breaks,
disrupts, challenges boundaries, including our understanding of what it
means to be a human being, a person.

For this reason it is often claimed that postmodernism is antihuman,
antihumanist. Technology rules. Yet on occasion it may seem to us that
postmodernism really means everything that a person now can do and
control and organize with a cell phone. Each person is the center of his
or her world, is the maker or convener or facilitator of a world. What
is real and what is not: who could presume to say what the distinction
is? Is there any distinction? What is a postmodern person? Possibly such
large and daunting questions, for a postmodernist, no longer matter and
are unanswerable. Too much is happening, nothing stands still for inspection. Life is incessant movement, flux, variation. As the novelist Jonathan
Franzen has noted, all around us we see "fresh outrageousness being
manufactured daily."

It may be, then, that no one can identify what postmodernism is
because postmodernism is networked with all that makes and remakes us
in a super-technological environment. Everyone is a postmodernist or soon
will be, as technology captivates and captures more and more of the globe.
Persons who are not on the Internet are not persons in the way that others
are who are electronically connected. Postmodernism hence is a dimension
or an aspect of (or a code name for) unstoppable technological innovation
and corporate power.

Many who seek to define postmodernism, whatever their suspicion of
grand narratives, nevertheless are inclined to connect it to developments
on the national and international scenes—and to the assault by the present on the past. To these scholars, critics, and intellectuals, postmodernism is critical, oppositional, aggressive; the scholar and museum curator
Glenn Adamson insists: "Postmodernism was an attack on what had come
before; it was an attack on modernism." This may be the case, but then
again postmodernism also could be understood as an antimodernism that is
bound up with everything that modernism led to and prepared the ground
for: post-structuralism, post-industrialism, post-nationalism, late capitalism, and globalization.

At this juncture, some who have written about postmodernism would
urge us to slow down, to tone it down. They have stressed that we should
be more restrained, more modest, in our characterizations of the way we
live now and they temper the claims that postmodernists have made and
that others have made about them. Postmodernism, they propose, does
not really exist: there was modernism, and there remains modernism.
Postmodernism, such advocates of modernism say, is not new or different
from what preceded it. Instead it is a continuation, an extension, of the

avant-garde achievements of Joyce, Pound, Eliot, Kafka, Gertrude Stein, Faulkner, Stevens, William Carlos Williams, among others in literature. Picasso and Matisse in art; Schoenberg, Stravinsky, and Charles Ives in music. Has anyone since surpassed the original, experimental, innovative work that these modern or modernist writers, artists, and composers produced? It could be claimed that no one is more postmodern than these modernists.

This explains why some scholars and writers are impatient when they hear high praise for the newness of postmodernism. No break from the modernist past has occurred, they say, but, rather, the past—the achievement of modernism and its impact—has continued into the twenty-first century and defines (and always will define) the present. To many, modernist art has become a familiar topic in scholarly books and college classrooms, yet it remains disorienting, hard to understand, strange, difficult. A character on *The Simpsons* TV show says: postmodern means "weird for the sake of weird." One could imagine the same being said of the modernists Picasso, Joyce, and Stravinsky.

The art critic Clement Greenberg pointed out that the great nineteenth- and twentieth-century painters have at least one thing in common: each was attacked for the "ugliness" of his work. As Greenberg says, in each instance the ugliness to which the critics called attention reflected the newness, the originality, of the work: the painter was doing something radically unconventional—something modern. Manet in the 1860s and 1870s; Picasso in the 1900s and 1910s; Pollock in the 1940s: each was disdained at first for being ugly, but now we esteem them for being modern and for striking us today as more modern than ever.

In other words: the only term we may need is "modern" or "modernist," a term that makes forceful sense whenever radically new works of art, literature, and music arrive on the contemporary scene. Postmodern means modern that remains modern, that never becomes conventional, clear or simple or distinct. Is one of Picasso's analytic Cubist paintings from 1909 to 1912 modern or postmodern? This is art that has retained its beguiling, disconcerting, not-really-understandable modernism. On one level it is familiar: we can buy a Cubist poster to hang on a wall. Yet on another level we wonder what this work means, how we should respond to it, and what Picasso is doing in it and why.

Are we, then, still in the middle of modernism, or have we moved beyond it into something different and unprecedented? The debate continues, unresolved, even as critics and scholars come forward with arguments for what, in their view, postmodernism is, or was.

In, for example, a survey (published in 1991) of American literature, Richard Ruland and Malcolm Bradbury maintain, as have others, that in the United States we experienced a postmodernist phase of literary production that has ended—it was over and done with several decades ago, "a stylistic phase that ran from the 1960s to the 1980s." The problem with this claim and others like it is, again, that the most powerful figures in late nineteenth- and early twentieth-century thought and culture, such as Nietzsche, Freud, and Heidegger, and Eliot and Faulkner, and Kafka and Gide, are as provocative as ever, dizzying, and exhilarating in their styles and strategies as anyone in literature or philosophy whom we might nominate as a postmodernist. The Marxist political theorist Alex Callinicos has said: "postmodernism is now history." Possibly. But if it is, when exactly was it that it ended, detaching itself from the present and becoming the past that we can bracket in a set of decades?

Modernism meant manifestoes, critiques of mass society, cutting-edge uses of technology, fascinated forays into anthropology, psychology, and other fields and disciplines, a rigorous and determined effort to jettison the past and contest boundaries and (as Pound said) "make it new." When literary historians describe modernism, they highlight its mixing of high and low culture, its fondness for parody and pastiche, its pervasive irony, and its stylistic difficulty—to the point of a willingness to be misunderstood or not to be understood at all. This sounds similar to many accounts given of postmodernism.

Modernism or postmodernism itself, as a twentieth- and twenty-first century phenomenon, might be too limited as a pairing, conceptually and chronologically. It could be that our chronology is mistaken, too recent. There are scholars who have suggested that we see vivid signs and forms of postmodernism as early as the eighteenth century in the English novelist Laurence Sterne's *Tristram Shandy* (1759–67) and, further back, in Cervantes's satiric romance *Don Quixote* (1605–15), and still further back, in the French writer François Rabelais's *Gargantua* (1534) and *Pantagruel* (1532). Should we say that these writers anticipated and prophesied postmodernism or, instead, that they are postmodernist?

Where does all of this leave us? We could try to sum up by saying that postmodernism began—with antecedents in prior centuries!—in the modernist decades of the early twentieth-century, moved into and through the middle of the century, altered and transformed during the 1960s and later, and now lives an animated, always-being-renewed life among us. This might sound too loose and generalized, not helpful in historical terms, not precise enough. But some postmodernists have said that historical thinking is what postmodernism makes difficult, even impossible. The literary theorist and cultural critic Fredric Jameson contends that defining postmodernism—thinking about what it was and what it is—is "an attempt to think the present historically in an age that has forgotten how to think historically in the first place."

Postmodernism either is new or not new, depending on the perspective of the teacher, scholar, or student seeking to define and describe it. If there is a difference, in broad terms, between modernism and postmodernism it may be that modern writers and artists faced an incoherent, disordered world and sought through their work to make a new, intricate, complex, and subversive sense of it. Postmodernists, on the other hand, delight in disorder and disarray—they take inspiration from it; they take for granted the incoherence they see and hear, and they engage in serious and radical play and performance with it.

The critic and novelist Raymond Federman, writing in 1981, argued that the "most striking aspects" of postmodern fiction are "its semblance of disorder and its deliberate incoherency." With so much text around, everywhere, who would presume to say what is literature and what is not? Everything is wide open, anything goes. As one commentator has observed, postmodernism is "shopping": "the world and all of history is a vast supermarket, and you can just pick out the ingredients you like, and assemble them into your own version of something." The pop artist Andy Warhol said in a similar vein: "I never think that people die. They just go to department stores."

Postmodernists whose names we encounter in histories and textbooks include the architects Robert Venturi and Philip Johnson, the musician John Cage, the artists Jasper Johns, Robert Rauschenberg, and Andy Warhol. The cultural world of postmodernism includes the films *Blade Runner* (1982); *Blue Velvet* (1986), *Pulp Fiction* (1994), *Memento* (2000), and *Minority Report* (2002); the TV shows *The Simpsons* (1989–), *Seinfeld* (1990–98), and *Game of Thrones* (2011), as well as countless "reality TV" shows, including *Survivor*, *American Idol*, *America's Next Top Model*, and *Dancing with the Stars*, and many "celebrity TV" shows that depict this or that celebrity going about the tasks, trials, and tribulations of daily life. But consider also two of the best shows in TV history: *The Sopranos* (1999–2007) and *The Wire* (2002–08). Are these modern or postmodern, or should we say rather that they are or were contemporary? Sometimes these shows are compared favorably to the best Victorian novels by Dickens, Trollope, and others. Is there something, then, Victorian in *The Sopranos* and something modern, postmodern, or contemporary in Dickens?

A list of postmodernist writers—subject to dispute—might include the Irish novelist and playwright Samuel Beckett; the Argentine short-story author, poet, and essayist Jorge Luis Borges; and, from the United States, Vladimir Nabokov (who settled in the U.S. in 1940), William Burroughs, John Barth, Kurt Vonnegut, William Gaddis, and Thomas Pynchon. One could add many other names, including Robert Coover, Philip Roth, Ishmael Reed, Don DeLillo, Kathy Acker, William Gibson, Paul Auster, Richard Powers, William T. Vollmann, J. G. Ballard, Bret Easton Ellis, Dave Eggers, Nicole Krauss, Jonathan Safran Foer, Kathryn Davis, David Markson, Evan Dara, and David Foster Wallace.

Names, lists, and groupings of writers and artists; and elusive questions about meaning and significance: it is not evident that finally these lead us to know what postmodernism takes in and gives back, what it embraces. Our broad definitions of terms do and do not help us. Perhaps, then, we do understand best what postmodernism is, or might be, when we select and ponder specific examples—instances and forms of postmodernism—to which we now will turn.

CARL ANDRE ■ (1935–)

Born in Quincy, Massachusetts, Carl Andre studied art at Phillips Academy (1951–53) in Andover, Massachusetts, served a year in the U.S. army, and then in 1956 moved to New York City, sharing studio space with his friend and Phillips Academy classmate Frank Stella, a painter and printmaker. The first exhibition of Andre's work was in New York City in 1965, and it was followed by a number of other shows and exhibitions. His arrangement of fireplace bricks, *Equivalent VIII*, was constructed in 1966 and acquired by the Tate Gallery in London in 1972. For several years it was exhibited without controversy or incident. But when it was included in an exhibition in 1976, it was attacked in a newspaper editorial as a waste of taxpayers' money. After all, it was just a collection of bricks, arranged in two layers, in a ten-by-six rectangle—an extreme simplicity of form that art historians and critics have referred to as "minimalism," and that unsympathetic critics and members of the media derided as "not real art" at all.

Surely, Andre's critics charged, *Equivalent VIII* was not and is not art. But it was Andre's claim that it was, and that it endures as art. Critics and scholars who admire Andre have said that *Equivalent VIII* is "a typically postmodernist object," noting that it is not engaging to look at and even could be considered boring. There it is, however, in a major art museum, which in turn raises the question—one that Andre intends to provoke—why this simple-seeming, repeatable arrangement of bricks is there. A further, and postmodern, irony is that Andre's sculpture is immediately accessible—the viewer knows what it is—but at the same time it is perplexing, even mysterious, in its meaning and significance.

In its guidebook the Tate Gallery says this: "'The sensation of these pieces was that they come above your ankles, as if you were wading in bricks', Andre has commented. 'It was like stepping from water of one depth to water of another depth.' This was the last in his series of *Equivalent* sculptures, each consisting of a rectangular con-figuration of 120 firebricks. Although the shape of each arrangement is different, they all have the same height, mass and volume, and are therefore 'equivalent' to each other."

Andre's *Equivalent VIII* makes the viewer think yet it gives no guidance about the direction that this thinking should take. Andre describes his intention thus: "My art springs from my desire to have things in the world which would otherwise never be there."

Please do not cross this line

Carl Andre, Equivalent VIII (1966). Photograph by Brian Harris.

Christopher Butler

On Equivalent VIII, From Postmodernism: A Very Short Introduction

Carl Andre's rectangular pile of bricks, *Equivalent VIII* (1966), annoyed lots of people when shown at the Tate Gallery, London, in 1976. It is a typically postmodernist object. Now re-enshrined in the Tate Modern, it doesn't resemble much in the canon of modernist sculpture. It is not formally complex or expressive or particularly engaging to look at, indeed it can soon be boring. It is easy to repeat.

Lacking any features to sustain interest in itself (except perhaps to Pythagorean number mystics[1]) it inspires us to ask questions about its context rather than its content: "What is the point of this?" or "Why is this displayed in a museum?" Some theory about the work has to be brought in to fill the vacuum of interest, and this is also fairly typical. It might inspire the question "Is it really art, or just a heap of bricks pretending to be art?" But this is not a question that makes much sense in the postmodernist era, in which it seems to be generally accepted that it is the institution or gallery, rather than anything else, which has made it, de facto, a "work of art." The visual arts just are what museum curators show us, from Picasso to sliced-up cows, and it is up to us to keep up with the ideas surrounding these works.

[2002]

FRANK GEHRY ■ (1929–)

Born in Toronto, Canada, but a resident of Los Angeles, California, for most of his life and professional career, Frank Gehry is one of the most important architects of the twentieth and twenty-first centuries.

---

[1]It is said of the ancient philosopher Pythagoras (570–595 BCE) that he saw numbers in everything.

His important works include the Guggenheim Museum in Bilbao, Spain; MIT Stata Center in Cambridge, Massachusetts; Walt Disney Concert Hall in downtown Los Angeles; Experience Music Project in Seattle, Washington; and Weisman Art Museum in Minneapolis, Minnesota.

Scholars and architectural historians have associated Gehry with the style of Deconstructivism, a form of postmodernist architecture that came to prominence in the 1980s. It is surprising, unpredictable, flamboyant, beautiful, complex, disconcerting, provocative. "Controlled chaos" is a phrase that is sometimes used about it, and about the amazing, wonderful shapes, structures, and spaces that Gehry has designed. He sees each new architectural project as, in his words, "a sculptural object, a spatial container, a space with light and air." "The idea of doing something special architecturally," said Gehry in 2007, "means it will look weird when you first see it."

The photograph here is of the Walt Disney Concert Hall (WDCH), Los Angeles, California, May 2003. Opened on October 24, 2003, WDCH received enthusiastic responses from scholars, critics, and the general public, and it is now the city's landmark building. It was an extraordinary act of construction, and it is perhaps worth noting that, in a postmodernist paradox, Gehry said in reference to it: "buildings under construction look nicer than buildings finished."

Walt Disney Concert Hall (2003). Photograph by Carol M. Highsmith.

The contemporary sculptor and earth/land artist Michael Heizer was born in Berkeley, California, the son of Robert Heizer, an eminent archaeologist. He began as an artist in painting and sculpture in New York City in the mid-1960s, but at the end of the decade he relocated to the West, working on a large-scale in the California and Nevada deserts—making, for example, large holes or gaps in the land, using dyes to "paint" the landscape, moving vast amounts of earth, and arranging huge granite slabs or boulders in his various artistic projects.

Heizer's recent work includes the captivating and thrilling *Levitated Mass*, for the Los Angeles County Museum of Art (LACMA). It took many years and 10 million dollars (paid for by private donors) for Heizer to bring *Levitated Mass* to completion. It is a 340-ton rock, 21.5 feet wide and 21.5 feet high, which the artist located in a quarry in Riverside, California—he paid $70,000 for it.

On the grounds of the Museum, a 700-ton crane installed the rock atop a concrete trench, *The Slot*, which is 456 feet in length and 15 feet wide. The trench enables the viewer to walk underneath the massive rock as if it were buoyant, floating (i.e., levitating) overhead. The rock seems to be passing over the viewer: this is a piece of sculpture placed so that we can see the bottom, the underside, of the work.

Heizer has said little about the meaning of *Levitated Mass*, but he has stated that it is intended to endure for 3500 years. In a brief interview he added: "The size thing is not some gimmick or attention-getting trick but a genuine undercurrent of the work. Frank Gehry for instance likes to imagine his buildings as sculptures. I like to imagine my sculptures as architectural."

Michael Govan, director of LACMA, has described *Levitated Mass* as a "masterpiece": "Obviously it's made now by a living artist, but it has echoes of the most ancient aspects of art and art history. And transporting the 900-million-year-old rock has two meanings. One, it refers very specifically to the origins of civilization and the early impulse to move megaliths [that is, a large stone that forms a prehistoric monument]. Plus, it's interesting to replay that in a contemporary context with modern engineering." *Levitated Mass*, as Govan and others have noted, is one of the largest "environmental art creations" situated in the context of a major city—a megalith marking a cultural center.

Though the quarry is not far from the museum—roughly an hour by car on the freeway—the trip made by *Levitated Mass* from there to the installation site took eleven days, from late February to mid-March 2012. The custom-built transport-truck—200 feet long, three highway lanes wide, and with 196 wheels—that carried the massive rock could travel only at night and at no more than 5–7 miles per hour, and it had to make a long, winding journey through twenty-two cities in four counties. Street and block parties and even a wedding proposal occurred when the truck from time to time made its rest stops. More than 20,000 people gathered in Long Beach for a street festival. Among the songs played along the route were "Rocky Mountain High," "We Will Rock You," and "I Love Rock and Roll."

Levitated Mass is a complex, sophisticated work of design and engineering, and partly for this reason it has been cited as an example of avant-garde art. From another point of view, however, Heizer is practicing his craft with the most ancient material in the world—a rock many millions of years old. A postmodern dimension to *Levitated Mass* thus is its ironic relationship between the very distant past and the immediate present, and also, the future into which it is projected. One of the implications of this sublime work is that it will be where it now is for thousands of years, outlasting the museum itself and probably most or all the city of Los Angeles.

Levitated Mass (2012)

FREDRIC JAMESON ■ (1934–)

Fredric Jameson is an important, influential American literary critic and Marxist political theorist. His major books include: *Marxism and Form: Twentieth Century Dialectical Theories of Literature* (1971); *The Political Unconscious: Narrative as a Socially Symbolic Act* (1981); and *Postmodernism: The Cultural Logic of Late Capitalism* (1991).

From Postmodernism and the Consumer Society

The essay excerpted here was originally a lecture presented at the Whitney Museum of American Art (New York City) in fall 1982.

One of the most significant features or practices in postmodernism today is pastiche. I must first explain this term, which people generally tend to confuse with or assimilate to that related verbal phenomenon called parody. Both pastiche and parody involve the imitation or, better still, the mimicry of other styles and particularly of the mannerisms and stylistic twitches of other styles. It is obvious that modern literature in general offers a very rich field for parody, since the great modern writers have all been defined by the invention or production of rather unique styles: think of the Faulknerian long sentence or of D. H. Lawrence's characteristic nature imagery; think of Wallace Stevens's peculiar way of using abstractions; think also of the mannerisms of the philosophers, of Heidegger for example, or Sartre[1]; think of the musical styles of Mahler or Prokofiev.[2] All of these styles, however different from each other, are comparable in this: each is quite unmistakable; once one is learned, it is not likely to be confused with something else.

Now parody capitalizes on the uniqueness of these styles and seizes on their idiosyncrasies and eccentricities to produce an imitation which mocks the original. I won't say that the satiric impulse is conscious in all forms of parody. In any case, a good or great parodist has to have some secret sympathy for the original, just as a great mimic has to have the capacity to put himself or herself in the place of the person imitated, still, the general effect of parody is—whether in sympathy or with malice—to cast ridicule on the private nature of these stylistic mannerisms and their excessiveness and eccentricity with respect to the way people normally speak or write. So there remains somewhere behind all parody the feeling that there is a linguistic norm in contrast to which the styles of the great modernists can be mocked.

[1]Heidegger, Sartre: Martin Heidegger (1889–1976), German philosopher; Jean-Paul Sartre (1905–80), French philosopher, novelist, playwright, and critic.
[2]Mahler, Prokofiev: Gustav Mahler (1860–1911), Austrian composer, conductor, and pianist; Sergei Prokofiev (1891–1953), Russian composer.

But what would happen if one no longer believed in the existence of normal language, of ordinary speech, of the linguistic norm (the kind of clarity and communicative power celebrated by Orwell in his famous essay, for example)?[3] One could think of it in this way: perhaps the immense fragmentation and privatization of modern literature—its explosion into a host of distinct private styles and mannerisms—foreshadows deeper and more general tendencies in social life as a whole.

Supposing that modern art and modernism—far from being a kind of specialized aesthetic curiosity—actually anticipated social developments along these lines; supposing that in the decades since the emergence of the great modern styles society has itself begun to fragment in this way, each group coming to speak a curious private language of its own, each profession developing its private code or idiolect, and finally each individual coming to be a kind of linguistic island, separated from everyone else? But then in that case, the very possibility of any linguistic norm in terms of which one could ridicule private languages and idiosyncratic styles would vanish, and we would have nothing but stylistic diversity and heterogeneity.

That is the moment at which pastiche appears and parody has become impossible. Pastiche is, like parody, the imitation of a peculiar or unique style, the wearing of a stylistic mask, speech in a dead language: but it is a neutral practice of such mimicry, without parody's ulterior motive, without the satirical impulse, without laughter, without that still latent feeling that there exists something normal compared to which what is being imitated is rather comic. Pastiche is blank parody, parody that has lost its sense of humor.

[1988]

SHERRIE LEVINE ▦ (1947–)

Sometimes described as a photographer, sometimes as a rephotographer, and sometimes as an appropriation artist, Sherrie Levine was born in Hazleton, Pennsylvania, and received her BA (1969) and MA (1973) degrees from the University of Wisconsin. Her most important and influential work is her series *After Walker Evans* (1903–75), in which she photographed Depression-era photographs by Walker Evans (1903–75) from an Evans exhibition catalog. Levine did not change or alter the photographs that Evans had taken. She took photographs of his photographs and presented them under her own name.

When museum-goers first see this photograph on the wall, or when readers glance at it in a book, they identify it as a famous

---

[3]Orwell in his famous essay: "Politics and the English Language," published in 1946, by the English novelist and essayist George Orwell (1903–1950).

photograph from the 1930s by Walker Evans, one of America's greatest modern photographers. It is not, however, a photograph by Evans. Rather, it is a photograph by Sherrie Levine—a photograph of a photograph (i.e., the reproduction of a photograph) by Evans. This prompts a number of postmodernist questions: what is an original and what is a copy? To whom does this photograph belong, to Evans or Levine? Is the later artist paying tribute to the first, or mocking and parodying him? Does Jameson's term "pastiche" apply to this photograph? What is the artistic worth, the monetary value, the long-term significance, of a photograph like this?

Such is the strength and the limitation of much postmodernist photography: often it is keyed to—it dramatizes—theoretical issues and hence privileges idea as much (or even more) than image. To its critics, it seems less about art than about philosophy, while to its admirers, it is all the more rewarding because of the philosophical arguments and debates that it fosters.

Allie Mae Burroughs, wife of Floyd Burroughs, sharecropper.
Hale County, Alabama. July, 1936. Photograph by Sherrie Levine.

BATMAN AND THE JOKER ■ (2008)

Batman and The Joker appear in *The Dark Knight* (2008), a film featuring the hero Batman, which was cowritten, directed, and produced
by Christopher Nolan. Christian Bale performed the leading role, and
Heath Ledger was The Joker. Ledger died of an overdose of prescription drugs in January 2008, a few months after he had completed
filming and six months before the film's release. One of the highest-
grossing films of all-time, *The Dark Knight* was nominated for eight
Academy Awards; the Best Supporting Actor award was given posthumously to Ledger.

The character of the masked-hero Batman was introduced in a
comic book in 1939 and became very popular. As the critic Monica
Hafer has noted: "Tales of the hero Batman can be found in old radio
show scripts, novels, numerous comic books, graphic novels, television series (both animated and live action), and movies. Batman
represents the expression of the general culture of American society
(as that society has changed over time) and has given his readers a
way to deal with the unique psychological challenges faced by the
postmodern mind." Batman has no special superpowers; he is smart,
shrewd, strong, courageous, and skilled in technology. His real-life
disguise is Bruce Wayne, a wealthy businessman and philanthropist
whose parents were murdered and who has dedicated his Batman-life
to fighting crime.

Nolan's film quickly took on canonical status for its depiction of
postmodern reality. In the words of the film critic Tina Beattie: "It
is a shifting, sliding, disintegrating world that Nolan evokes in *The
Dark Knight*. Gotham is the postmodern state and we are its citizens.
The choices we face are not those which are ranged around good and
evil, right and wrong. They are the vicious and dreadful dilemmas we
face when our own survival is a gamble which pits us against shadowy
and unpredictable enemies who infiltrate and infect all our social and
political institutions with fear and mistrust." Batman is a figure of
exhausting, brooding, violent goodness, matched against the sheer,
chaos-engendering evil of The Joker, a character who, according to
Nolan, has "no arc, no development"—he is an "absolute." One
reviewer termed The Joker "the poster boy for postmodernism,"
someone who believes that "everything is relative, that the world
would be better off if it let go of its delusions of order and a civilized
society governed by laws."

At one point in *The Dark Knight* The Joker is asked what his
"plan" is, to which he replies: "Do I really look like a guy with a
plan? You know what I am? I'm a dog chasing cars. I wouldn't know
what to do with one if I caught it. You know? I just do things. The

Heath Ledger as The Joker and Christian Bale as Batman in Warner Bros.
Pictures' and Legendary Pictures' action drama *The Dark Knight*.
TM & © DC Comics. Photo by Stephen Vaughan.

Mob has plans. The cops have plans. [Police Commissioner] Gordon's
got plans. You know, they're schemers. Schemers trying to control
their little worlds. I'm not a schemer. I try to show the schemers how
pathetic their attempts to control things really are."

MADONNA ■ (1958–)

Madonna, the American pop singer and film actress, was born
Madonna Louise Ciccone, in Bay City, Michigan. An excellent student
in high school, she dropped out of the University of Michigan and
moved to New York City, where she worked as a dancer and singer. Albums such as *Like a Virgin* (1984), *True Blue* (1986), and *Like a Prayer*

(1989), and her status as a sex symbol, a paragon of daring fashion and costume, and a brilliant self-creator and self-reinventor brought her national and international stardom in the mid-1980s.

Madonna has sold hundreds of millions of recordings; she is the top-selling female recording artist of all time. In an interview in 2011 she said: "I may be dressing the typical bimbo, whatever, but I'm in charge. You know. I'm in charge of my fantasies. I put myself in these situations with men, you know, and people don't think of me as a person who's not in charge of my career or my life, okay. And isn't that what feminism is all about, you know, equality for men and women? And aren't I in charge of my life, doing the things I want to do? Making my own decisions?" Subversive, controversial, an extraordinary performer and a master-mistress of disguise and illusion, rebel and individualist, Madonna is one of the icons of postmodernism, a performer for whom life is virtual and image is everything.

Madonna performs during the Super Bowl XLVI half-time show on February 5, 2012, at Lucas Oil Stadium in Indianapolis, Indiana.

The American novelist and essayist Jonathan Franzen was born in Western Springs, Illinois. He graduated from Swarthmore College, majoring in German, in 1981. His novels include *The Corrections* (2001) and *Freedom* (2010). Often termed a postmodern writer, Franzen has said that he began writing novels to create a "conversation with the great sixties and seventies Postmoderns."

From On Rainer Maria Rilke

In the following excerpt, which is taken from an interview, Franzen refers to *The Notebooks of Malte Laurids Brigge*, the only novel by Rainer Maria Rilke (1875–1926), the Austrian writer best-known for his poetry in *The Duino Elegies* and *Sonnets to Orpheus*, both published in 1923. The novel was written while Rilke lived in Paris, and it was published in 1910. Malte Laurids Brigge is a young Danish nobleman and poet who lives in Paris.

The most terrifying scene in Rilke's *Malte Laurids Brigge* is the one in which Malte, as a boy, starts putting on party masks from a trunk in his family's attic, one after another, until finally one of them takes control of him. He sees his masked self in the mirror and goes momentarily insane with terror that there is no him, there's only the mask. Years later, as an adult, walking around in Paris, he sees a woman on a park bench who puts her face in her hands and then looks up with a naked face, a horrifying Nothing, having left the mask in her hands. Malte is essentially the story of a young writer working through a fear of masks to a recognition of their necessity.

Rilke anticipated the postmodern insight that there is no personality, there are just these various intersecting fields: that personality is socially, genetically, linguistically constructed by upbringing. Where the postmoderns go wrong is in positing a nullity behind all that. It's not a nullity, it's something raw and frightening and bottomless.

[2010]

Cynthia "Cindy" Morris Sherman was born in Glen Ridge, New Jersey, and grew up in Huntington, Long Island. While an undergraduate at State University of New York, Buffalo, Sherman first focused on painting but soon gave it up: "There was nothing more to say. I was meticulously copying other art and then I realized I could just use a camera and put my time into an idea instead." In her first year of college, she enrolled in a photography course—which she failed. She took the course a second time, crediting her teacher with stimulating her interesting in conceptual art.

Upon completion of her BA in 1976, Sherman moved to New York City and began taking photographs of herself, and this has been her practice ever since, working alone in her studio. The photographs from the late 1970s, the Untitled Film Stills, show Sherman in a fascinating and compelling range of roles. These are not portraits of herself, not portraits of Cindy Sherman. Sherman instead makes creative use of wigs, clothes, hats, and other materials and settings (including yards, swimming pools, interiors) to represent someone other than herself, a person (or is it a type of person?) whom she has imagined, enacted, and then photographed.

Commenting on her art in an interview in 2001, Sherman said: "I'm good at using my face as a canvas... I'll see a photograph of a character and try to copy them on to my face. I think I'm really observant, and thinking how a person is put together, seeing them on the street and noticing subtle things about them that make them who they are." In a later series in the late 1980s, The History Portraits, Sherman casts herself in roles that she derives and develops from well-known paintings.

Sherman examines the nature of photography: what does it mean to be a photographer, what does it mean to be the subject of one? She also explores gender roles, sexual identities, women in society, and the media. As she noted in a 1997 interview, "the world is so drawn toward beauty that I became interested in things that are normally considered grotesque or ugly, seeing them as more fascinating and beautiful. Also, I like making images that from a distance seem kind of seductive, colorful, luscious and engaging, and then you realize what you're looking at is something totally opposite. It seems boring to me to pursue the typical idea of beauty, because that is the easiest or the most obvious way to see the world. It's more challenging to look at the other side."

Sherman once was asked whether she understood herself to be an "actress" in her photographs, to which she replied: "I never thought I was acting." In an interview in 1990, she said: "I feel I'm anonymous in my work. When I look at the pictures, I never see myself; they aren't self-portraits. Sometimes I disappear." In 2012, the Museum of Modern Art presented "Cindy Sherman," a major exhibition that surveyed and chronicled Sherman's work from the mid-1970s and that included more than 170 photographs. She has become highly successful; in May 2011, one of her photographs sold for 3.9 million dollars.

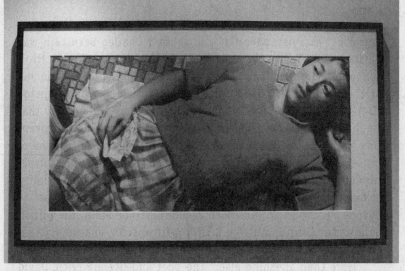

MOSCOW, RUSSIA. APRIL 1, 2011. Cindy Sherman's Untitled #96 on display at Christie's preview in Moscow. Photograph by Krasilnikov Stanislav.

DIANE WILLIAMS ▪ (1946–)

The American short-story writer and editor Diane Williams attended the University of Pennsylvania, studying English, sculpture, drawing, and creative writing (one of her teachers there was the novelist Philip Roth). Later, in New York City, she was a member of writing workshops taught by the literary editor and author Gordon Lish.

Williams has written a number of books, including *Some Sexual Success Stories Plus Other Stories in Which God Might Choose to Appear* (1992), *The Stupefaction* (1996), and *Excitability: Selected Stories* (1998). The novelist Jonathan Franzen has said that Williams is "one of the true living heroes of the American avant-garde. Her fiction makes very familiar things very, very weird"; the novelist and essayist Ben Marcus, describing Williams's stories, observes: "this is writing of the future, a prose of sophisticated disturbance and sorrow."

In a postmodernist affirmation, Williams has stated: "Experience on the page is equivalent to life and taking it up godlike with high hopes for vibrancy and drama is outrageous, but necessary." She also has said: "I'm not interested at all in any experience that I have previously organized, synthesized and formed an opinion about. All I want is to take experience and rearrange it and come up with something completely new."

Human Being

Now I have a baby boy and a five-year-old girl.

Being married, I thought I'd always be married to Wayne because he tried to be perfect. What more could he ask for?

The poet, essayist, theorist, and scholar Charles Bernstein was born in New York City and was educated at the Bronx High School of Science and at Harvard University (BA, 1972). He is one of the founders and most important practitioners of Language (L=A=N=G=U=A=G=E) poetry, a postmodern theory and practice that emphasizes the written dimension of poetry rather than the spoken; that favors disjunction in the use of language and the disruption of conventional syntax and narrative; and, influenced by post-struc-turalism and deconstruction, that explores the self-referentiality of language. Influences on Bernstein's poetic theory and practice include the expatriate American author Gertrude Stein, the British philosopher (born in Austria) Ludwig Wittgenstein, and the Harvard philosopher Stanley Cavell.

"More than anything else," the poet and literary critic David Lehman has remarked, "postmodernism is an attitude, and that attitude is definitively ironic. It revels in comedy and exalts the spirit of parody and play. It treats the monuments of tradition in particular with irreverence. The distinction between artifacts of high and low culture gets leveled. Characters and lives are confused. Poems based on intricate rules are written in a kind of partnership with the language, an attempt to bring out the poetry latent in the language rather than to impose meaning on language." The poet-critic Ron Silliman, associated with Language poetry, has observed, "Form is of interest only to the extent that it empowers liberation." Lyn Hejinian, another Language poet, critic, and translator, has made a related point: this poetry "invites participation, rejects the authority of the writer over the reader and thus, by analogy, the authority implicit in other (social, economic, cultural) hierarchies." "I want to engage the materials of the culture," Bernstein has said, "derange them as they have deranged me, sound them out, as they sound me out."

thinking i think i think

What are aesthetic values and why do
there appear to be lesser & fewer of
them? Quick: define the difference
between arpeggio & Armani. The baby
cries because the baby likes crying.
The baby cries because a pin is
sticking into the baby. The baby
is not crying but it is called
crying. Who's on first, what's

5

shortstop. The man the man declined
to be, appraised at auction at
eighty percent of surface volume.
Cube steak on rye amusing twist
on lay demo cells, absolutely no
returns. *Damaged goods are the only
kind of goods I ever cared about.*
The lacuna misplaced the ladle,
the actor aborted the fable. Fold
your caps into Indians &
flaps. Dusting the rigor mortis
for compos mentis. Rune is busting
out all over—perfidious quarrel
sublates even the heckling at
the Ponderosa. A bevy of belts.
Burl Ives turned to burlap. Who
yelled that? Lily by the lacquer
(laparotomy). *I'm here strictly on
business, literary business.* May
I propose the codicil-ready cables?
Like slips gassing in the night.
Chorus of automatic exclusions.
Don't give me no label as long as I
am able. Search & displace, curse
& disgrace. Suppose you suppose,
circumstances remonstrating. Crest
envy. Don't give me the Bronx
when you mean the Bronx. *This
one thing I know for she loathes
me so:* Ketchup will pass for blood
only under highly limited conditions.
I had a red ball / I watched it
fall. *Help me so that I may exist
again.* It's the billyclub not the
Billy that needs watching. Keep
your eye on the balloon (cartoon)!
Budge, but then move back into
position. In other words, steal
my car but don't steal my sister's
hood. Ironclad comeuppance. Breakfast
at the Eiffel tower, lunch at the
Kremlin, dinner at the Taj Mahal.
In other words, *hurt me
but don't hurt me so bad.*
May files / So June can hold

10

15

20

25

30

35

40

45

50

July. That's no arrow that's a 55
diversionary tactic. That's no
spastic that's my elocutionary
lodge. When all the cares
have become little tiny porous
creatures, buckling under the weight 60
of the remorse. The barfly butters
his bread on all sides of the
collective agency, while even at home
the Colonel takes out the garbage.
You will find a moist towelette 65
with your porridge. Then just say so.
Cratylus, Cratylus, wilt thou be
mine? As I is the starch from
yesterday's yawning. *Cure me*
so that I will smoke yet not be 70
consumed (at least not at a
discount). *Pools rush in*
where barriers have not been
fortified. Rule rules
where furriers redesign. "Amish 75
modern." French poetry is looking
for a way out of "French poetry."
Ne touchez pas cette button. The
color of baloney. WWW.TheSirens.Org.
Ne touchez pas ma bologna. Her 80
hair was auburn her eyes like amber.
Honest to gosh gullies: arraignment
of a power untapped & untappable.
Quittez votre place (Kitaj dislikes
his place). Emboss my fiduciary 85
capitulations! The bellicose churning
of the unsettled stomach. *National*
Geographic's "Robot" issue:
The Wilderness of the Future, e.g.,
the Gates Robot Preserve, the 90
American Robotic Conservancy,
the Fund for Robotic Culture,
the National Endowment for Robots
(a.k.a. U.S. Congress). Millions
for automation but not one cent 95
for elegy. Eight elephants dancing
deliriously to the wail of the
bumble bees. *So long, sailor /*

goodbye failure. Or let the pail
wear the head of the lotion. Here 100
is smoldering continuation. The
smell of green tea on Greene Street.
Bottled reticence. *Gimme gimme
gone.* Guilt in the form of guilt.
  "& even then my heart was aching 105
  For I am yours, just for the taking..."

[2001]

MICK STEVENS

OMG! I just got born!

Published in *The New Yorker*, March 15, 2010

The New Yorker accepted a cartoon by Mick Stevens in 1979, and since then his work has been published in many journals and magazines.

A L A N   K I R B Y

Alan Kirby is an Oxford-based cultural critic and author of *Digimodernism: How New Technologies Dismantle the Postmodern and Reconfigure Our Culture* (2009).

From The Death of Postmodernism and Beyond

Somewhere in the late 1990s or early 2000s, the emergence of new technologies restructured, violently and forever, the nature of the author, the reader and the text, and the relationships between them.

Postmodernism, like modernism and romanticism before it, fetishized (i.e., placed supreme importance on) the author, even when the author chose to indict or pretended to abolish himself or herself. But the culture we have now fetishizes the recipient of the text to the degree that they become a partial or whole author of it. Optimists may see this as the democratization of culture; pessimists will point to the excruciating banality and vacuity of the cultural products thereby generated (at least so far)....

Postmodernism conceived of contemporary culture as a spectacle before which the individual sat powerless, and within which questions of the real were problematized. It therefore emphasized the television or the cinema screen. Its successor, which I will call digimodernism, makes the individual's action the necessary condition of the cultural product.

Digimodernism includes all television or radio programs or parts of programs, all "texts," whose content and dynamics are invented or directed by the participating viewer or listener (although these latter terms, with their passivity and emphasis on reception, are obsolete....

The digimodern cultural phenomenon par excellence is the Internet. Its central act is that of the individual clicking on his or her mouse to move through pages in a way which cannot be duplicated, inventing a pathway through cultural products which has never existed before and never will again. This is a far more intense engagement with the cultural process than anything literature can offer, and gives the undeniable sense (or illusion) of the individual controlling, managing, running, making up his or her involvement with the cultural product. Internet pages are not "authored" in the sense that anyone knows who wrote them, or cares. The majority either require the individual to make them work, like Streetmap or Route Planner, or permit him or her to add to them, like Wikipedia, or through feedback on, for instance, media Web sites. In all cases, it is intrinsic to the Internet that you can easily make up pages yourself (e.g., blogs).

If the Internet and its use define and dominate digimodernism, the new era has also seen the revamping of older forms along its lines. Cinema in the digimodern age looks more and more like a computer game. Its images, which once came from the "real" world—framed, lit, soundtracked, and edited together by ingenious directors to guide the viewer's thoughts or emotions—are now increasingly created through a computer. And they look it. Where once special effects were supposed to make the impossible appear credible, CGI (Computer-Generated Imagery) frequently works to make the possible look artificial, as in much of *Lord of the Rings* or *Gladiator*. Battles involving thousands of individuals have really happened; digimodern cinema makes them look as if they have only ever happened in cyberspace. And so cinema has given cultural ground not merely to the computer as a generator of its images, but to the computer game as the model of its relationship with the viewer....

A digimodern text lasts an exceptionally brief time.... Reality TV programs cannot be repeated in their original form, since the phone-ins cannot be reproduced, and without the possibility of phoning-in they become a different and far less attractive entity....

If scholars give the date they referenced an Internet page, it is because the pages disappear or get radically recast so quickly. Text messages and e-mails are extremely difficult to keep in their original form; printing out e-mails does convert them into something more stable, like a letter, but only by destroying their essential, electronic state. Radio phone-ins, computer games—their shelf-life is short, they are very soon obsolete. A culture based on these things can have no memory—certainly not the burdensome sense of a preceding cultural inheritance which informed modernism and postmodernism. Non-reproducible and evanescent, digimodernism is thus also amnesiac: these are cultural actions in the present moment with no sense of either past or future.

The cultural products of digimodernism are also exceptionally banal. The content of digimodern films tends to be solely the acts which beget and end life. This puerile primitivism of the script stands in stark contrast to the sophistication of contemporary cinema's technical effects. Much text messaging and e-mailing is vapid in comparison with what people of all educational levels used to put into letters. A triteness, a shallowness dominates all. The digimodern era, at least so far, is a cultural desert. Although we may grow so used to the new terms that we can adapt them for meaningful artistic expression (and then the pejorative label I have given digimodernism may no longer be appropriate), for now we are confronted by a storm of human activity producing almost nothing of any lasting or even reproducible cultural value—anything which human beings might look at again and appreciate in fifty or two hundred years time.

The roots of digimodernism can be traced back through the years dominated by postmodernism. Dance music and industrial pornography, for instance, products of the late 70s and 80s, tend to the ephemeral, to the vacuous on the level of signification, and to the unauthored (dance much more so than pop or rock). They also foreground the activity of their "reception": dance music is to be danced to, porn is not to be read or watched but used, in a way which generates the digimodern illusion of participation. In music, the digimodern superseding of the artist-dominated album as monolithic text by the downloading and mix-and-matching of individual tracks on to an iPod, selected by the listener, was certainly prefigured by the music fan's creation of compilation tapes a generation ago. But a shift has occurred: what was a marginal pastime of the fan has become the dominant and definitive way of consuming music, rendering the idea of the album as a coherent work of art, a body of integrated meaning, obsolete.

To a degree, digimodernism is no more than a technologically motivated shift to the cultural center of something which has always existed (similarly, metafiction has always existed, but was never so fetishized as it was by postmodernism). Television has always used audience participation, just as theater and other performing arts did before it; but as an option, not as a necessity: digimodern TV programs have participation built into them. There have long been very "active" cultural forms, too, from carnival to pantomime. But none of these implied a written or otherwise material text, and so they dwelt in the margins of a culture which fetishized such texts—whereas the digimodern text, with all its peculiarities, stands as the central, dominant, paradigmatic form of cultural product today, although culture, in its margins, still knows other kinds.

Nor should these other kinds be stigmatized as "passive" against digimodernity's "activity." Reading, listening, watching always had their kinds of activity; but there is a physicality to the actions of the digimodern text-maker, and a necessity to his or her actions as regards the composition of the text, as well as a domination which has changed the cultural balance of power (note how cinema and TV, yesterday's giants, have bowed before it). It forms the twenty-first century's social-historical-cultural hegemony. Moreover, the activity of digimodernism has its own specificity: it is electronic, and textual, but ephemeral.

In postmodernism, one read, watched, listened, as before. In digimodernism one phones, clicks, presses, surfs, chooses, moves, downloads. There is a generation gap here, roughly separating people born before and after 1980. Those born later might see their peers as free, autonomous, inventive, expressive, dynamic, empowered, independent, their voices unique, raised and heard: postmodernism and everything before it will by contrast seem elitist, dull, a distant and droning monologue which oppresses and occludes them.

Those born before 1980 may see, not the people, but contemporary texts which are alternately violent, pornographic, unreal, trite, vapid, conformist, consumerist, meaningless and brainless…. To them what came before digimodernism will increasingly seem a golden age of intelligence, creativity, rebellion and authenticity. Hence the name "digimodernism" also connotes the tension between the sophistication of the technological means, and the vapidity or ignorance of the content conveyed by it—a cultural moment summed by the fatuity of the mobile phone user's "I'm on the bus."

Whereas postmodernism called "reality" into question, digimodernism defines the real implicitly as myself, now, "interacting" with its texts.

[2012]

ANDY WARHOL ■ (1928–1987)

The painter, graphic artist, and filmmaker Andy Warhol was born Andrew Warhola in Pittsburgh, Pennsylvania. A major exponent of pop art, he achieved fame for a series of silkscreen prints and acrylic paintings of familiar objects (such as Campbell's soup cans) and famous people (such as Marilyn Monroe and Elvis Presley), which he treated with objectivity and precision—and without any indication of his own response to and interpretation of them. Many have criticized Warhol as commercial, shallow, and superficial. Many others have pointed to him as one of the great exemplars of postmodernism: he has been called "the most brilliant mirror of our times."

About his embrace of Hollywood, mass media, and celebrity culture, Warhol said in a comment that typifies his uncanny, deadpan postmodernist self-presentation: "I love Los Angeles. I love Hollywood. They're so beautiful. Everything's plastic, but I love plastic. I want to be plastic." Elsewhere he has said, in what might be his philosophy of life: "Sometimes people let the same problems make them miserable for years when they should just say, So what. That's one of my favorite things to say.

Museum-goer viewing Campbell's Soup Cans by Andy Warhol, 1962, MOMA.
Photograph by El Chapulin.

So what." To Warhol, "an artist is somebody who produces things that people don't need to have." People may not need them but they definitely want them. One of Warhol's works featuring a "Campbell's Soup Can" (1962) sold in 2010 for 24 million dollars. His "Eight Elvises" (1963) sold at auction in 2008 for even more—100 million dollars.

This is the Museum of Modern Art gallery text for "Campbell's Soup Cans" (1962): "When Warhol first exhibited these thirty-two canvases in 1962, each one simultaneously hung from the wall like a painting and rested on a shelf like groceries in a store. The number of canvases corresponds to the varieties of soup then sold by the Campbell Soup Company. Warhol assigned a different flavor to each painting, referring to a product list supplied by Campbell's. There is no evidence that Warhol envisioned the canvases in a particular sequence. Here, they are arranged in rows that reflect the chronological order in which they were introduced, beginning with 'Tomato' in the upper left, which debuted in 1897."

MARK TANSEY ■ (1949–)

Born in San Jose, California, Mark Tansey attended schools on the west coast and visited museums and art galleries there, and then in the mid-1970s moved to New York City. He completed his training in art at Hunter College, where he now has his studio.

On first encounter, Tansey's paintings seem realistic, human figures in a narrative situation or scene. But on closer inspection, the viewer notices oddities, anomalies, visual puns, and contradictions that blur and complicate the distinctions that we imagine we can make and sustain between reality and representation. Perhaps the central and abiding subject of Tansey's postmodern art is his exploration of the nature of meaning, perception, and interpretation.

"In my work," Tansey has said, "I'm searching for pictorial functions that are based on the idea that the painted picture knows itself to be metaphorical rhetorical, transformational, fictional. I'm not doing pictures of things that actually exist in the world. The narratives never actually occurred. In contrast to the assertion of one reality, my work investigates how different realities interact and abrade. And the understanding is that the abrasions start within the medium itself." Influenced by post-structuralist and postmodernist theory, Tansey has stressed that in his painting he is not seeking to "capture the real." His aim instead is to represent "how different realities interact with each other."

In "The Innocent Eye Test," a cow stands in front of the Dutch painter Paulus Potter's "The Young Bull" (1647), while the human observers and experts await its response to this painting and perhaps also to Claude Monet's "Grainstack" (1890–91), located on the wall to the right.

The Innocent Eye Test (1981). Photography by Peter Horree.

JEFF KOONS ■ (1955–)

The American artist Jeff Koons was born in York, Pennsylvania. He studied painting at the School of the Art Institute of Chicago and the Maryland Institute College of Art, gaining prominence and notoriety for his artistic work in the mid-1980s.

In his 16,000 square-foot Chelsea (New York City) studio, Koon employs 90–100 assistants who assist him in the production of his sculptures. Hugely popular and successful—his art works sell for millions of dollars—Koons has made sculptures of rabbits, dogs, the pop singer Michael Jackson, and much else. He maintains that his work contains no ironies, no hidden meanings, and no critiques. Some scholars and critics have praised Koons as brilliant and dazzlingly creative, whereas others contend that he is a banal and unimaginative. There is no doubt that he is significant, as someone who forthrightly rejects distinctions between high and low art and seeks (in his words) to exploit "mass culture iconography." The critic Norman Holland has made this observation: "Koons, it seems to me, is very postmodern in that he works more with my relation to the object he creates than with the object itself.... My thought is his medium."

This is Koon's interesting commentary on the art object illustrated here.

JEFF KOONS: My father was an interior decorator, so I grew up around objects being displayed. And I think that influenced me very much, and that's how I could envision and make a work like this.

I've always enjoyed display. And the *New Hoover Convertibles*, *Double-decker*, it's just displaying itself. It's like an individual displaying themselves. My work I believe is always directed toward what

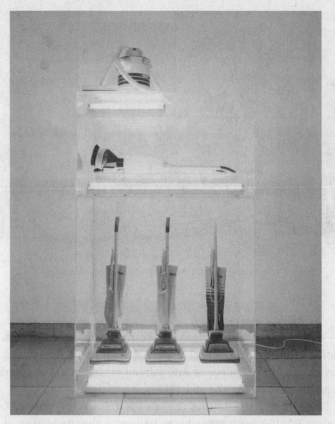

New Hoover Convertibles, Green, Blue; New Hoover
Convertibles, Green, Blue; Double-Decker, 1981–87.

it means to be alive, what it means to be a human being in the world
we live. And these are breathing machines. They are like individuals.
And the first thing that we do when we come into this world to be
alive is to breathe. I also enjoy the sexual quality of the work where
some vacuum cleaners may read more feminine, other more mascu-
line. I've created some double deckers, it's almost like a family unit,
like a momma bear, a poppa bear, and a baby bear.

I think the work has a form of visual beauty, but I think that
the work's really more about a philosophical and psychological ideal.
These vacuums—these vacuum cleaners are like eternal virgins.
They're brand new. The object has its greatest amount of integrity
before it ever participates in the world. Their cords are wrapped up
just as they came out of the box. They've never been turned on.
They're never participated.

I've always kind of enjoyed the idea of showing Hoover vacuum
cleaners. When I grew up there were still people coming door to door
selling vacuum cleaners. And I felt that I was kind of doing that with
my artwork. I was a young artist saying, look here, I have something, and I'd like to participate. I'd like to get my foot in the door.

TO THE READER

American Poetry Since 1945

ROBERT PENN WARREN ■ (1905–1989)

Responding to the question "How do poems grow?" Robert Penn Warren answered, "They grow out of your life." "For what is a poem," he added, "but a hazardous attempt at self-understanding: it is the deepest part of autobiography."

Born in Guthrie, Kentucky, Warren pursued his undergraduate studies at Vanderbilt University, becoming the youngest of the Fugitive poets, a group that included John Crowe Ransom, Allen Tate, and other southerners who published their work in *The Fugitive* magazine (1922–25). This experience deepened Warren's interest in southern history and tradition—one that had begun in his childhood (both of his grandfathers had fought for the Confederacy) and that he carried further in his contribution to *I'll Take My Stand* (1930), a polemical volume criticizing northern industrialism and defending the southern agrarian way of life.

During the late 1920s, Warren was a teaching fellow at the University of California at Berkeley and then a Rhodes Scholar at Oxford University in England. He held teaching positions at Vanderbilt, Louisiana State, the University of Minnesota, and Yale. His many publications include, with his friend and fellow southerner Cleanth Brooks, *Understanding Poetry* (1938, rev. 1950), an influential textbook that emphasized "close reading" and detailed interpretation of the language of poetry. Warren was also, again with Brooks, a founding editor of *The Southern Review*, a literary quarterly that numbered Eudora Welty, W. H. Auden, and many other important authors among its contributors.

Warren is best known for his novels, especially *All the King's Men* (1946), based on the life of the corrupt Louisiana politician Huey Long. He was a sensitive literary critic and a passionate, probing writer about American history and race relations as well. But Warren viewed himself above all as a poet, and he received many honors and awards for his verse; among them was his appointment in 1985 as the first Poet Laureate of the United States. The range and depth of his achievement can be studied in *New and Selected Poems 1923–1985* (1985) and *The Collected Poems* (1998).

In many of his best poems, including those given here, Warren shows a brooding, anguished, brave response to the erosions of meaning by time. The fact of death, and the threat of its finality, its negation of everything, looms in "Bearded Oaks" and "Mortal Limit", which uses the figure (a favorite of Warren's) of a hawk, in flight "over Wyoming," to ponder the theme of death and the possibility of transcendence.

These poems testify to the conception of the poet's vocation and craft that Warren articulated in interviews and literary essays. As he explained in an interview (1956), "If I had to say what I would try to hunt for in a poem—would hunt for in a poem, or would expect from a poem that I would call a poem—it would be some kind of vital image, a vital and evaluating image, of vitality." "Writing is the process," he noted in a later interview (1970), "in which the imagination takes the place of literal living; by moving toward values and modifying, testing, and exfoliating older values."

See Joseph Blotner, *Robert Penn Warren: A Biography* (1997); and *Selected Letters of Robert Penn Warren*, 5 vols, ed. William Bedford Clark (2000). Studies of the poetry include Victor H. Strandberg, *A Colder Fire: The Poetry of Robert Penn Warren* (1975); Floyd C. Watkins, *Then and Now: The Personal Past in the Poetry of Robert Penn Warren* (1982); Calvin Bedient, *In the Heart's Last Kingdom: Robert Penn Warren's Major Poetry* (1984); and Lesa Carnes Corrigan, *Poems of Pure Imagination: Robert Penn Warren and the Romantic Tradition* (1999).

The Legacy of Robert Penn Warren, ed. David Madden (2000), includes cogent essays on the poetry. Also illuminating are Charlotte H. Beck, *Robert Penn Warren: Critic* (2006); and Joseph R. Millichap, *Robert Penn Warren after Audubon: The Work of Aging and the Quest for Transcendence in His Later Poetry* (2009), which deals with poems written after Warren's *Audubon: A Vision* (1969).

From left to right: The southern writers Allen Tate, Merrill Moore, Robert Penn Warren, John Crowe Ransom, and Donald Davidson, photographed May 4, 1956. Vanderbilt University Special Collections and University Archives.

Bearded Oaks

The oaks, how subtle and marine,
Bearded, and all the layered light
Above them swims; and thus the scene,
Recessed, awaits the positive night.

So, waiting, we in the grass now lie   5
Beneath the languorous tread of light:
The grasses, kelp-like, satisfy
The nameless motions of the air.

Upon the floor of light, and time,
Unmurmuring, of polyp made,   10
We rest; we are, as light withdraws,
Twin atolls on a shelf of shade.

Ages to our construction went,
Dim architecture, hour by hour:
And violence, forgot now, lent   15
The present stillness all its power.

The storm of noon above us rolled,
Of light the fury, furious gold,
The long drag troubling us, the depth:
Dark is unrocking, unrippling, still.   20

Passion and slaughter, ruth, decay
Descend, minutely whispering down,
Silted down swaying streams, to lay
Foundation for our voicelessness.

All our debate is voiceless here,   25
As all our rage, the rage of stone
If hope is hopeless, then fearless is fear,
And history is thus undone.

Our feet once wrought the hollow street
With echo when the lamps were dead   30
At windows, once our headlight glare
Disturbed the doe that, leaping, fled.

I do not love you less that now
The caged heart makes iron stroke,
Or less that all that light once gave   35
The graduate dark should now revoke.

We live in time so little time
And we learn all so painfully,
That we may spare this hour's term
To practice for eternity.   40

[1942]

Mortal Limit

I saw the hawk ride updraft in the sunset over Wyoming.
It rose from coniferous darkness, past gray jags
Of mercilessness, past whiteness, into the gloaming
Of dream-spectral light above the last purity of snow-snags.
There—west—were the Tetons.[1] Snow-peaks would soon be   5
In dark profile to break constellations. Beyond what height
Hangs now the black speck? Beyond what range will gold eyes see
New ranges rise to mark a last scrawl of light?

Or, having tasted that atmosphere's thinness, does it
Hang motionless in dying vision before   10
It knows it will accept the mortal limit,
And swing into the great circular downwardness that will restore

The breath of earth? Of rock? Of rot? Of other such
Items, and the darkness of whatever dream we clutch?

[1985]

---

[1]A mountain range in northwest Wyoming.

THEODORE ROETHKE ■ (1908–1963)

It could be said that Theodore Roethke, born in Saginaw, Michigan, received his early training as a poet when he spent many days as an observer in the greenhouse (the largest in the United States) that his father and uncle owned, paying close and steady attention to flowers and other plants. He did his undergraduate work at the University of Michigan and later took courses in law at Michigan and in literature in the graduate program at Harvard. His first book, *Open House* (1941), ten years in the making, was reviewed favorably; his second, *The Lost Son and Other Poems* (1948), which includes a stunning sequence recalling and exploring the boy's experiences amid the flowers in the greenhouse, made even more of an impact, and his reputation and influence grew with each new book he published.

Lyrical, intense, highly structured at the outset but later, in *The Far Field* (1964), more free-form, with lines that extend across the page like Whitman's, Roethke's impressive body of verse is gathered in *Collected Poems* (1966). *On the Poet and His Craft: Selected Prose* (1966) is noteworthy as well.

Importance influences on Roethke include Ralph Waldo Emerson, Henry David Thoreau, Walt Whitman, Emily Dickinson, and T. S. Eliot among American writers, and William Blake, Gerard Manley Hopkins, William Butler Yeats, and Dylan Thomas from the English tradition. His poetry was enriched, too, by his friendships with W. H. Auden, William Carlos Williams, Louise Bogan, Stanley Kunitz, and other contemporaries. It was shaped also through his work with gifted students and aspiring poets, especially at the University of Washington, where Roethke was poet-in-residence, which led to his mentoring of David Wagoner, Richard Hugo, and Carolyn Kizer. Roethke's poetry was an inspiration and a resource for many of the best poets of the period, including Sylvia Plath, Anne Sexton, and James Dickey.

"Frau Bauman, Frau Schmidt, and Frau Schwartze," the first poem included here, is keyed to the greenhouse world, which, Roethke said, symbolized for him "both heaven and hell, a kind of tropics created in the savage climate of Michigan, where austere German-Americans turned their love of order and their terrifying efficiency into something truly beautiful." The critic Richard Allen Blessing observed of this poem, "Through the Fraus who were, through the Fraus mythologized, and through the Fraus who remain as a felt presence, [Roethke] has made a poetic representation of the living extension of the past into the ever-moving present." In contrast, the more personal "My Papa's Waltz" touches on Roethke's relationship with his father, who died of cancer when Roethke was fifteen and whom he both admired and feared.

"The Waking" also has a personal component, reflecting ("This shaking keeps me steady") the bouts of mental illness, depression, and alcoholism that afflicted Roethke. "Night Crow," less directly, may as well, and "In a

Dark Time" certainly does. These episodes were frightening, yet they also enabled Roethke, he claimed, to "reach a new level of reality."

Between these two poems, in a different tone and manner, is "I Knew a Woman," a witty, engaging, ironic love poem that recalls the lyrics and love poems of Shakespeare and other Elizabethan poets.

The poet and essayist Mark Doty cogently described Roethke's vision:

> For Roethke, boundaries between outer and inner dissolve; the natural world seems a vast landscape of the psyche, just as the voyage inward leads to natural things—roots, leaves, and flowers—as emblems of the recesses of the self. To travel either outward or inward is to encounter the self, and the voyage in either direction is fraught with the possibilities of transcendence, dissolution, or both.

For a helpful survey, see George Wolff, *Theodore Roethke* (1981). For biography, see Allan Seager, *The Glass House: The Life of Theodore Roethke* (1968). Critical studies include Jay Parini, *Theodore Roethke: An American Romantic* (1979); Don Bogen, *Theodore Roethke and the Writing Process* (1991); Peter Balakian, *Theodore Roethke's Far Fields: The Evolution of His Poetry* (1989); and Walter B. Kalaidjian, *Understanding Theodore Roethke* (1987). Another important resource is *Straw for the Fire: From the Notebooks of Theodore Roethke, 1943–63*, ed. David Wagoner (2nd ed., 2006).

Frau[1] Bauman, Frau Schmidt, and Frau Schwartze[2]

Gone the three ancient ladies
Who creaked on the greenhouse ladders,
Reaching up white strings
To wind, to wind
The sweet-pea tendrils, the smilax,[3]   5
Nasturtiums, the climbing
Roses, to straighten
Carnations, red
Chrysanthemums; the stiff
Stems, jointed like corn,   10
They tied and tucked,—
These nurses of nobody else
Quicker than birds, they dipped
Up and sifted the dirt;
They sprinkled and shook;   15
They stood astride pipes,

---

[1]The German title for a married woman, equivalent to Mrs. in English.
[2]Women who worked in a greenhouse owned by Roethke's father.
[3]A twining plant of the *Smilaceæ* genus; its rootstalks are used to make sarsaparilla.

Their skirts billowing out wide into tents,
Their hands twinkling with wet;
Like witches they flew along rows
Keeping creation at ease;   20
With a tendril for needle
They sewed up the air with a stem;
They teased out the seed that the cold kept asleep,—
All the coils, loops, and whorls,
They trellised the sun; they plotted for more than themselves.   25

I remember how they picked me up, a spindly kid,
Pinching and poking my thin ribs
Till I lay in their laps, laughing,
Weak as a whiffet;[4]   30
Now, when I'm alone and cold in my bed,
They still hover over me,
These ancient leathery crones,
With their bandannas stiffened with sweat,
And their thorn-bitten wrists,   35
And their snuff-laden breath blowing lightly over me in
      my first sleep.

                                                   [1948]

My Papa's Waltz

The whiskey on your breath
Could make a small boy dizzy;
But I hung on like death:
Such waltzing was not easy.

We romped until the pans   5
Slid from the kitchen shelf;
My mother's countenance
Could not unfrown itself.

The hand that held my wrist
Was battered on one knuckle;   10
At every step you missed
My right ear scraped a buckle.

You beat time on my head
With a palm caked hard by dirt,
Then waltzed me off to bed   15
Still clinging to your shirt.

                                                   [1948]

---

[4]An insignificant young person, from the word *whippet*, used to describe a small dog; a whippersnapper.

The Waking

I wake to sleep, and take my waking slow.
I feel my fate in what I cannot fear.
I learn by going where I have to go.

We think by feeling. What is there to know?
I hear my being dance from ear to ear.   5
I wake to sleep, and take my waking slow.

Of those so close beside me, which are you?
God bless the Ground! I shall walk softly there,
And learn by going where I have to go.

Light takes the Tree; but who can tell us how?   10
The lowly worm climbs up a winding stair;
I wake to sleep, and take my waking slow.

Great Nature has another thing to do
To you and me; so take the lively air,
And, lovely, learn by going where to go.   15

This shaking keeps me steady. I should know.
What falls away is always. And is near.
I wake to sleep, and take my waking slow.
I learn by going where I have to go.

[1953]

Night Crow

When I saw that clumsy crow
Flap from a wasted tree,
A shape in the mind rose up:
Over the gulfs of dream
Flew a tremendous bird   5
Further and further away
Into a moonless black,
Deep in the brain, far back.

[1948]

I Knew a Woman

I knew a woman, lovely in her bones,
When small birds sighed, she would sigh back at them;
Ah, when she moved, she moved more ways than one:
The shapes a bright container can contain!
Of her choice virtues only gods should speak,   5

Or English poets who grew up on Greek
(I'd have them sing in chorus,[1] cheek to cheek).

How well her wishes went! She stroked my chin,
She taught me Turn, and Counter-turn, and Stand;[2]
She taught me Touch, that undulant white skin;   10
I nobbled meekly from her proffered hand;
She was the sickle; I, poor I, the rake,
Coming behind her for her pretty sake
(But what prodigious mowing we did make).

Love likes a gander, and adores a goose: 15
Her full lips pursed, the errant note to seize;
She played it quick, she played it light and loose;
My eyes, they dazzled at her flowing knees;
Her several parts could keep a pure repose,
Or one hip quiver with a mobile nose   20
(She moved in circles, and those circles moved).

Let seed be grass, and grass turn into hay:
I'm martyr to a motion not my own;
What's freedom for? To know eternity.
I swear she cast a shadow white as stone.   25
But who would count eternity in days?
These old bones live to learn her wanton ways:
(I measure time by how a body sways).

                                                            [1958]

In a Dark Time

In a dark time, the eye begins to see,
I meet my shadow in the deepening shade;
I hear my echo in the echoing wood—
A lord of nature weeping to a tree.
I live between the heron and the wren,   5
Beasts of the hill and serpents of the den.

What's madness but nobility of soul
At odds with circumstance? The day's on fire!
I know the purity of pure despair,
My shadow pinned against a sweating wall.   10

---

[1] A reference to the classical chorus used in Greek drama, which provided important background and summary information on the play's events and articulated moral and religious sentiments on the action of the play.
[2] In classical Greek theater, these terms refer to *strophe, antistrophe,* and *epode*—respectively, the three-part stanza structure of a choral ode. The strophe presents an ideological position, the antistrophe presents the other side of this position, and the epode summarizes both.

That place among the rocks—is it a cave,
Or winding path? The edge is what I have.

A steady storm of correspondences!
A night flowing with birds, a ragged moon,
And in broad day the midnight come again!   15
A man goes far to find out what he is—
Death of the self in a long, tearless night,
All natural shapes blazing unnatural light.

Dark, dark my light, and darker my desire.
My soul, like some heat-maddened summer fly,   20
Keeps buzzing at the sill. Which I is *I*?
A fallen man, I climb out of my fear.
The mind enters itself, and God the mind,
And one is One, free in the tearing wind.

[1964]

CHARLES OLSON ■ (1910–1970)

Charles Olson was born in Worcester, Massachusetts, and received his undergraduate and master's degrees at Wesleyan University in Middletown, Connecticut. After two years of teaching at Clark University in Worcester, Olson entered the graduate program in American Civilization at Harvard, where he studied with the distinguished literary historian F. O. Matthiessen and did pioneering work on Herman Melville's novels, *Moby-Dick* in particular, which he developed and later published as *Call Me Ishmael* (1947). Olson chose, however, not to remain in the academy and instead accepted a position in the foreign language section of the Office of War Information, which he held until 1944.

Moving to Key West, Florida, to concentrate on his literary work, Olson in 1950 published an important essay, "Projective Verse," in which he maintained that poets should rely on breath and the natural rhythm of thought in organizing lines of verse. "A poem is energy transferred from where the poet got it (he will have some several causations), by way of the poem itself to, all the way over to, the reader.... The poem itself must, at all points, be a high energy-construct and, at all points, an energy-discharge." Perception leads to perception, sound takes priority over sense, and that is how the poem attains its structure, rather than through logical argument. "The Kingfishers," the longest and best poem in Olson's first book, *In Cold Hell, in Thicket* (1953), is his most noteworthy embodiment of the "projective" theory.

Also in the early 1950s, Olson traveled to the Yucatan Peninsula, in southeast Mexico and extending into Guatemala, for the purpose of examining Mayan temples and artifacts. He was especially intrigued by Mayan hieroglyphs, and his responses to and speculations about them were presented in *Mayan Letters* (1953), a series of letters to his friend and fellow poet Robert Creeley.

In 1948 Olson had begun teaching at the experimental liberal arts school Black Mountain College in North Carolina. Through his poetry, essays, and example as a teacher, he influenced Robert Duncan, Denise Levertov, and other significant writers of the 1950s and 1960s. With the closing of Black Mountain in 1956, Olson moved to the seacoast town of Gloucester, Massachusetts.

Olson's major achievement is *The Maximus Poems*, titled after a fourth-century mystic and alluding also, it is said, to Olson's 6-foot, 8-inch height. Modeled on Ezra Pound's *Cantos*, *The Maximus Poems* are "a poem of a person and a place," exploring the speaker's relationship to contemporary Gloucester and the American past. Ranging widely and drawing on anthropology, mythology, geography, and other disciplines and fields of knowledge, Olson started on these poems sometime in the mid-1940s. The first volume appeared in 1960, followed by volumes later in 1960 and 1975. The *Collected Poems*, which excludes *The Maximus Poems*, was published in 1987.

"Maximus, to Himself," the poem given here, is meditative and self-critical.

For biography, see Ralph Maud, *Charles Olson's Reading: A Biography* (1996); and Tom Clark, *Charles Olson: The Allegory of a Poet's Life* (2000). Also important are *Charles Olson and Robert Creeley: The Complete Correspondence*, eds. George F. Buttrick and Richard Blevins, 9 vols. (1980–90); *Charles Olson: Collected Prose*, eds. Donald Allen and Benjamin Friedlander (1997); and *Muthologos Charles Olson: Lectures and Interviews*, ed. Ralph Maud (2nd ed., 2010). On *The Maximus Poems*, see George F. Butterick, *A Guide to the Maximus Poems of Charles Olson* (1978); and Don Byrd, *Charles Olson's Maximus* (1980). Surveys of the career and major themes include Robert Von Hallberg, *Charles Olson: The Scholar's Art* (1978); Sherman Paul, *Olson's Push: Origin, Black Mountain, and Recent American Poetry* (1978); Thomas F. Merrill, *The Poetry of Charles Olson: A Primer* (1982); and Stephen Fredman, *The Grounding of American Poetry: Charles Olson and the Emersonian Tradition* (1993).

Maximus, to Himself

I have had to learn the simplest things
last. Which made for difficulties.
Even at sea I was slow, to get the hand out, or to cross
a wet deck.

       The sea was not, finally, my trade.   5
But even my trade, at it, I stood estranged
from that which was most familiar.[1] Was delayed,
and not content with the man's argument
that such postponement
is now the nature of   10
obedience,

       that we are all late
       in a slow time,
       that we grow up many
       And the single   15
       is not easily
       known

It could be, though the sharpness (the *achiote*[2])
I note in others,
makes more sense   20
than my own distances. The agilities

       they show daily

---

[1] An allusion to the pre-Socratic Greek philosopher Heraclitus (535–475 BCE), who said, "Man is estranged from that with which he is most familiar."
[2] The seeds of the anatto tree (Bixa orellana), which are used to make a bright red dye (Spanish).

                    who do the world's
                    businesses
                    And who do nature's   25
                    as I have no sense
                    I have done either

I have made dialogues,
have discussed ancient texts,
have thrown what light I could, offered   30
what pleasures
doceat[3] allows

            But the known?
This, I have had to be given,
a life, love, and from one man   35
the world.

            Tokens.
            But sitting here
            I look out as a wind
            and water man, testing   40
            And missing
            some proof

I know the quarters
of the weather, where it comes from,
where it goes. But the stem of me,   45
this I took from their welcome,
or their rejection, of me

            And my arrogance
            was neither diminished
            nor increased,   50
            by the communication

2

It is undone business
I speak of, this morning,
with the sea
stretching out   55
from my feet

                                              [1953]

[3]"That he teach" (Latin).

ELIZABETH BISHOP ■ (1911–1979)

Born in 1911 in Worcester, Massachusetts, Elizabeth Bishop suffered the loss of both parents when she was still a child; her father died of Bright's disease in 1911, and her mother was committed to an institution for the mentally ill in 1916—Bishop never saw her again (the mother died in 1934). Bishop then lived with her mother's parents in Great Village, Nova Scotia, on the east coast of Canada.

This period came to a harsh end when she was moved back to Worcester to live with her father's parents. "I felt myself aging," she recalled, "even dying. I was bored and lonely with Grandma, my silent grandpa, the dinners alone.... At night I lay blinking my flashlight off and on, and crying."

After boarding school in Massachusetts, Bishop went on to Vassar College, where she majored in English, founded a literary magazine, and edited the college yearbook. During her senior year she met the poet Marianne Moore, who became a mentor, source of inspiration, and lifelong friend; Moore included a number of Bishop's poems in an anthology, *Trial Balances*, published in 1935. After graduation in 1934, Bishop spent much of the next years traveling in Europe and northern Africa before settling in Key West, Florida. Her travels to and experiences of places are featured in her first book, *North and South*, published in 1946.

In New York, in 1942, Bishop had met Lota de Macedo Soares, a young Brazilian woman, and the two became lovers. Bishop first visited Brazil in November 1951, and the country so enchanted her that she decided to move there with Lota. Bishop felt fulfilled emotionally, though disappointed by the slow pace of her work as a poet. She was burdened by depression, asthma, and alcoholism, as well as periods of difficulty and turbulence in her relationship with Lota, who committed suicide when she and Bishop were on a visit to New York City in September 1967.

Bishop was named poet-in-residence at Harvard in 1969, and students there valued the quiet effectiveness and clarity of her teaching. During this period she also formed a relationship with a woman named Alice Methfessel and completed work on her final volume, *Geography III*, published in 1976.

A brilliant maker of images, penetrating in her wit and piercingly intelligent, Bishop is one of the foremost poets of the latter half of the twentieth century, highly admired and influential even though she wrote only about a hundred poems. Bishop's major books are *The Complete Poems 1927–1979* (1983); *The Collected Prose* (1984); and *One Art: Selected Letters* (1993). For many years described as a "poet's poet" because of the sheer excellence of her craft—she spoke of her "passion for accuracy"—Bishop has grown increasingly popular, beloved by a wide readership.

As the poet Alfred Corn noted, Bishop's work is "a perfected transparence of expression, warmth of tone, and a singular blend of sadness and good humor, of pain and acceptance—a radiant patience few people ever achieve and few writers ever successfully render." As the following poems, spanning her career, testify, few poets more artfully investigate the mysteries of landscape, the relationship of human beings to creatures (and to themselves), and the challenge of giving form and coherence to a complex, multifarious world.

For biography, see Brett C. Millier, *Elizabeth Bishop: Life and the Memory of It* (1993); and Gary Fountain and Peter Brazeau, *Remembering Elizabeth Bishop: An Oral Biography* (1994). See also Carmen L. Oliveira, *Rare and Commonplace Flowers: The Story of Elizabeth Bishop and Lota de Macedo Soares* (trans. 2002). Among many critical studies, the following are especially helpful: Robert Dale Parker, *The Unbeliever: The Poetry of Elizabeth Bishop* (1988); Thomas Travisano, *Elizabeth Bishop: Her Artistic Development* (1988); Bonnie Costello, *Elizabeth Bishop: Questions of Mastery* (1991); and C. K. Doreski, *Elizabeth Bishop: The Restraints of Language* (1993). Also stimulating are *Elizabeth Bishop and Her Art*, eds. Lloyd Schwartz and Sybil P. Estess (1983); Peter Nickowitz, *Rhetoric and Sexuality: The Poetry of Hart Crane, Elizabeth Bishop, and James Merrill* (2006); and Peggy Samuels, *Deep Skin: Elizabeth Bishop and Visual Art* (2010). Highly recommended is the Library of America volume of Bishop's *Poems, Prose, and Letters*, eds. Robert Giroux and Lloyd Schwartz (2008).

The Fish

I caught a tremendous fish
and held him beside the boat
half out of water, with my hook
fast in a corner of his mouth.
He didn't fight.   5
He hadn't fought at all.
He hung a grunting weight,
battered and venerable
and homely. Here and there
his brown skin hung in strips   10
like ancient wallpaper,
and its pattern of darker brown
was like wallpaper:
shapes like full-blown roses
stained and lost through age.   15
He was speckled with barnacles,
fine rosettes of lime,
and infested
with tiny white sea-lice,
and underneath two or three   20

rags of green weed hung down.
While his gills were breathing in
the terrible oxygen
—the frightening gills,
fresh and crisp with blood,   25
that can cut so badly—
I thought of the coarse white flesh
packed in like feathers,
the big bones and the little bones,
the dramatic reds and blacks   30
of his shiny entrails,
and the pink swim-bladder
like a big peony.
I looked into his eyes
which were far larger than mine   35
but shallower, and yellowed,
the irises backed and packed
with tarnished tinfoil
seen through the lenses
of old scratched isinglass.[1]   40
They shifted a little, but not
to return my stare.
—It was more like the tipping
of an object toward the light.
I admired his sullen face,   45
the mechanism of his jaw,
and then I saw
that from his lower lip
—if you could call it a lip—
grim, wet, and weaponlike,   50
hung five old pieces of fish-line,
or four and a wire leader
with the swivel still attached,
with all their five big hooks
grown firmly in his mouth.   55
A green line, frayed at the end
where he broke it, two heavier lines,
and a fine black thread
still crimped from the strain and snap
when it broke and he got away.   60
Like medals with their ribbons
frayed and wavering,

[1] A semi transparent whitish substance.

a five-haired beard of wisdom
trailing from his aching jaw.
I stared and stared   65
and victory filled up
the little rented boat,
from the pool of bilge
where oil had spread a rainbow
around the rusted engine   70
to the bailer rusted orange,
the sun—cracked thwarts,
the oarlocks on their strings,
the gunnels—until everything
was rainbow, rainbow, rainbow!   75
And I let the fish go.

                                                          [1946]

Sestina[1]

September rain falls on the house.
In the failing light, the old grandmother
sits in the kitchen with the child
beside the Little Marvel Stove,[2]
reading the jokes from the almanac,   5
laughing and talking to hide her tears.

She thinks that her equinoctial tears
and the rain that beats on the roof of the house
were both foretold by the almanac,
but only known to a grandmother.   10
The iron kettle sings on the stove.
She cuts some bread and says to the child,

It's time for tea now; but the child
is watching the teakettle's small hard tears
dance like mad on the hot black stove,   15
the way the rain must dance on the house.
Tidying up, the old grandmother
hangs up the clever almanac

on its string. Birdlike, the almanac
hovers half open above the child,   20
hovers above the old grandmother

---

[1]A poem of six six-line stanzas in which the last word of each line of the first stanza is repeated, but in a different order, in the other five stanzas.
[2]Type of cast-iron stove used for cooking and heating, made by Marvel Company.

and her teacup full of dark brown tears.
She shivers and says she thinks the house
feels chilly, and puts more wood in the stove.

It was to be, says the Marvel Stove.   25
I know what I know, says the almanac.
With crayons the child draws a rigid house
and a winding pathway. Then the child
puts in a man with buttons like tears
and shows it proudly to the grandmother.   30

But secretly, while the grandmother
busies herself about the stove,
and the little moons fall down like tears
from between the pages of the almanac
into the flower bed the child   35
has carefully placed in the front of the house.

Time to plant tears, says the almanac.
The grandmother sings to the marvellous stove
and the child draws another inscrutable house.

[1956]

In the Waiting Room

In Worcester, Massachusetts,
I went with Aunt Consuelo
to keep her dentist's appointment
and sat and waited for her
in the dentist's waiting room.   5
It was winter. It got dark
early. The waiting room
was full of grown-up people,
arctics and overcoats,
lamps and magazines.   10
My aunt was inside
what seemed like a long time
and while I waited I read
the *National Geographic*
(I could read) and carefully   15
studied the photographs:
the inside of a volcano,
black, and full of ashes;
then it was spilling over
in rivulets of fire.   20

Osa and Martin Johnson[1]
dressed in riding breeches,
laced boots, and pith helmets.
A dead man slung on a pole
—"Long Pig,"[2] the caption said.   25
Babies with pointed heads
wound round and round with string;
black, naked women with necks
wound round and round with wire
like the necks of light bulbs.   30
Their breasts were horrifying.
I read it right straight through.
I was too shy to stop.
And then I looked at the cover:
the yellow margins, the date.   35

Suddenly, from inside,
came an *oh!* of pain
—Aunt Consuelo's voice—
not very loud or long.
I wasn't at all surprised;   40
even then I knew she was
a foolish, timid woman.
I might have been embarrassed,
but wasn't. What took me
completely by surprise   45
was that it was *me:*
my voice, in my mouth.
Without thinking at all
I was my foolish aunt,
I—we—were falling, falling,   50
our eyes glued to the cover
of the *National Geographic,*
February, 1918.

I said to myself: three days
and you'll be seven years old.   55
I was saying it to stop
the sensation of falling off
the round, turning world
into cold, blue-black space.

[1]Osa (Leighty) Johnson (1894–1953) and Martin Johnson (1884–1937) were explorers and documentary
filmmakers who traveled extensively in the South Pacific and Africa.
[2]The Polynesian cannibal term for a human carcass, as described in Osa Johnson's memoir, *I Married
Adventure* (1940).

But I felt: you are an *I*,
you are an *Elizabeth*,
you are one of *them*.
Why should you be one, too?
I scarcely dared to look
to see what it was I was.
I gave a sidelong glance
—I couldn't look any higher—
at shadowy gray knees,
trousers and skirts and boots
and different pairs of hands
lying under the lamps.
I knew that nothing stranger
had ever happened, that nothing
stranger could ever happen.
Why should I be my aunt,
or me, or anyone?
What similarities—
boots, hands, the family voice
I felt in my throat, or even
the *National Geographic*
and those awful hanging breasts—
held us all together
or made us all just one?
How—I didn't know any
word for it—how "unlikely"...
How had I come to be here,
like them, and overhear
a cry of pain that could have
got loud and worse but hadn't?

The waiting room was bright
and too hot. It was sliding
beneath a big black wave,
another, and another.

Then I was back in it.
The War was on. Outside,
in Worcester, Massachusetts,
were night and slush and cold,
and it was still the fifth
of February, 1918.

60
65
70
75
80
85
90
95

[1976]

The Moose

For Grace Bulmer Bowers[1]

From narrow provinces
of fish and bread and tea,
home of the long tides
where the bay leaves the sea
twice a day and takes   5
the herrings long rides,

where if the river
enters or retreats
in a wall of brown foam
depends on if it meets   10
the bay coming in,
the bay not at home;

where, silted red,
sometimes the sun sets
facing a red sea,   15
and others, veins the flats'
lavender, rich mud
in burning rivulets;

on red, gravelly roads,
down rows of sugar maples,   20
past clapboard farmhouses
and neat, clapboard churches,
bleached, ridged as clamshells,
past twin silver birches,

through late afternoon   25
a bus journeys west,
the windshield flashing pink,
pink glancing off of metal,
brushing the dented flank
of blue, beat-up enamel;   30

down hollows, up rises,
and waits, patient, while
a lone traveller gives
kisses and embraces

---

[1] Grace Bulmer Bowers (1889–1977) was Bishop's favorite maternal aunt.

to seven relatives
and a collie supervises.   35

Goodbye to the elms,
to the farm, to the dog.
The bus starts. The light
grows richer; the fog,   40
shifting, salty, thin,
comes closing in.

Its cold, round crystals
form and slide and settle
in the white hens' feathers,   45
in gray glazed cabbages,
on the cabbage roses
and lupins[1] like apostles;

the sweet peas cling
to their wet white string   50
on the whitewashed fences;
bumblebees creep
inside the foxgloves,
and evening commences.

One stop at Bass River.   55
Then the Economies—
Lower, Middle, Upper;
Five Islands, Five Houses,[2]
where a woman shakes a tablecloth
out after supper.   60

A pale flickering. Gone.
The Tantramar marshes[3]
and the smell of salt hay.
An iron bridge trembles
and a loose plank rattles   65
but doesn't give way.

On the left, a red light
swims through the dark:
a ship's port lantern.

---

[1]A plant of the genus *Lupinus* (family *Leguminosæ*), with blue, purple, white, or yellow flowers that
grow in clusters on long, tapering spikes.
[2]Small towns and villages near Halifax, Nova Scotia, Canada.
[3]The Tantramar marshes, known for its wide variety of waterfowl, stretch across the Isthmus of
Chignecto, which joins Nova Scotia to the Canadian mainland. The noise caused by the large number of
waterfowl inspired the local inhabitants to nickname the region Tintamarre, meaning "din" or "racket."

Two rubber boots show,   70
illuminated, solemn.
A dog gives one bark.

A woman climbs in
with two market bags,
brisk, freckled, elderly.   75
"A grand night. Yes, sir,
all the way to Boston."
She regards us amicably.

Moonlight as we enter
the New Brunswick[4] woods,   80
hairy, scratchy, splintery;
moonlight and mist
caught in them like lamb's wool
on bushes in a pasture.

The passengers lie back.   85
Snores. Some long sighs.
A dreamy divagation[5]
begins in the night,
a gentle, auditory,
slow hallucination....   90

In the creakings and noises,
an old conversation
—not concerning us,
but recognizable, somewhere,
back in the bus: 95
Grandparents' voices

uninterruptedly
talking, in Eternity:
names being mentioned,
things cleared up finally;   100
what he said, what she said,
who got pensioned;

deaths, deaths and sicknesses;
the year he remarried;
the year (something) happened.   105
She died in childbirth.
That was the son lost
when the schooner foundered.

[4]One of Canada's maritime provinces, bordering the U.S. state of Maine.
[5]Digression.

He took to drink. Yes.
She went to the bad.
When Amos began to pray   110
even in the store and
finally the family had
to put him away.

"Yes..." that peculiar
affirmative. "Yes..."   115
A sharp, indrawn breath,
half groan, half acceptance,
that means "Life's like that.
We know *it* (also death)."   120

Talking the way they talked
in the old featherbed,
peacefully, on and on,
dim lamplight in the hall,
down in the kitchen, the dog   125
tucked in her shawl.

Now, it's all right now
even to fall asleep
just as on all those nights.
—Suddenly the bus driver   130
stops with a jolt,
turns off his lights.

A moose has come out of
the impenetrable wood
and stands there, looms, rather,   135
in the middle of the road.
It approaches; it sniffs at
the bus's hot hood.

Towering, antlerless,
high as a church,   140
homely as a house
(or, safe as houses).
A man's voice assures us
"Perfectly harmless...."

Some of the passengers   145
exclaim in whispers,
childishly, softly,

"Sure are big creatures."
"It's awful plain."
"Look! It's a she!"   150

Taking her time,
she looks the bus over,
grand, otherworldly.
Why, why do we feel
(we all feel) this sweet   155
sensation of joy?

"Curious creatures,"
says our quiet driver,
rolling his *r*'s.
"Look at that, would you."   160
Then he shifts gears.
For a moment longer,

by craning backward,
the moose can be seen
on the moonlit macadam;[6]   165
then there's a dim
smell of moose, an acrid
smell of gasoline.

[1976]

One Art

The art of losing isn't hard to master;
so many things seem filled with the intent
to be lost that their loss is no disaster.

Lose something every day. Accept the fluster
of lost door keys, the hour badly spent.   5
The art of losing isn't hard to master.

Then practice losing farther, losing faster:
places, and names, and where it was you meant
to travel. None of these will bring disaster.

I lost my mother's watch. And look! my last, or   10
next-to-last, of three loved houses went.
The art of losing isn't hard to master.

I lost two cities, lovely ones. And, vaster,

---

[6]A road constructed using the paving method devised by Scotsman John Loudon McAdam (1756–1836) in the nineteenth century. This method is the foundation of modern road construction.

some realms I owned, two rivers, a continent.
I miss them, but it wasn't a disaster.   15

—Even losing you (the joking voice, a gesture
I love) I shan't have lied. It's evident
the art of losing's not too hard to master
though it may look like (*Write* it!) like disaster.

[1976]

ROBERT HAYDEN ■ (1913–1980)

Robert Hayden grew up poor in a racially mixed neighborhood called "Paradise Valley" in Detroit, Michigan, moving back and forth between his own family (his parents separated soon after he was born) and a foster family that lived nearby. His childhood was abusive and traumatic, and it led later in life to bouts of depression that Hayden described as "my dark nights of the soul."

After graduation from high school in 1932, Hayden spent several years at Detroit City College (now Wayne State University), majoring in Spanish but not completing his degree. From 1936 to 1938 he researched African American folklore, culture, and history for the Federal Writers Project, one of the relief programs launched by President Roosevelt in the midst of the Great Depression.

Hayden's first book of poems, *Heart-Shape in the Dust*, was published in 1940, the same year as his marriage to Erma Morris, a pianist, composer, and music teacher. He enrolled the following year in the graduate program in English at the University of Michigan. There, one of his teachers was the poet-critic W. H. Auden, who emphasized to Hayden the importance of formal control and disciplined craft. Auden demonstrated, Hayden said, "the modernist poetry of technical and meditative complexity, in which judicious erudition and imagination, rather than pseudo-folk simplicity or didacticism, were vital elements." In addition to Auden, Hayden was influenced by Edna St. Vincent Millay and Carl Sandburg as well as by Langston Hughes (whom Hayden met in college), Jean Toomer, and other writers in the African American tradition.

Hayden taught from 1944 to 1946 at the University of Michigan and then accepted an appointment at Fisk University in Nashville, Tennessee, where he remained for more than two decades. Hayden returned to the University of Michigan for the final phase of his teaching career.

Like Ralph Ellison, Hayden stressed that the "black experience" in America, while richly significant in its own terms, provided a means through which to express and explore universal themes of identity, memory, heroism, and history—elements of what Hayden identified as "the long human struggle toward freedom." Also like Ellison, Hayden came under fire from black nationalists and militants during the 1960s and early 1970s who maintained his work lacked radical content and revolutionary commitment. Hayden, hurt by these criticisms, nonetheless rejected the notion that he should be a "spokesman for his race," a category that, in his view, would place an African American author in a "kind of literary ghetto where the standards applied to other writers are not likely to be applied to him."

The winner of many awards and prizes, Hayden was the first African American to be named Consultant in Poetry to the Library of Congress (later, this distinction was termed the Poet Laureate). His work is best approached through the *Collected Poems* (1985, rpt. 1996) and *Collected Prose* (1984). As the critic Mark A. Sanders observed, "with emotional intensity achieved through technical mastery, Hayden's poetry renders a world fraught with anguish, yet one gesturing toward liberating possibility."

The poems here include "Homage to the Empress of the Blues," a tribute to the blues singer Bessie Smith; "Those Winter Sundays," a painful recollection of his father; and "Frederick Douglass," a passionate portrait of the great nineteenth-century African American writer and orator.

For an introduction, see Fred M. Fetrow, *Robert Hayden* (1984). See also John Hatcher, *From the Auroral Darkness: The Life and Poetry of Robert Hayden* (1984). For discussion of the poems, see Pontheolla T. Williams, *Robert Hayden: A Critical Analysis of His Poetry* (1987); and *Robert Hayden: Essays on the Poetry*, eds. Laurence Goldstein and Robert Chrisman (2001).

Portrait of Bessie Smith by Carl Van Vechten, 1936.

Homage to the Empress of the Blues[1]

Because there was a man somewhere in a candystripe silk shirt,
gracile and dangerous as a jaguar and because a woman moaned
for him in sixty-watt gloom and mourned him Faithless Love
Twotiming Love Oh Love Oh Careless Aggravating Love,

    She came out on the stage in yards of pearls, emerging like   5
    a favorite scenic view, flashed her golden smile and sang.

Because grey laths[2] began somewhere to show from underneath
torn hurdygurdy[3] lithographs of dollfaced heaven;
and because there were those who feared alarming fists of snow
on the door and those who feared the riot-squad of statistics,   10

    She came out on the stage in ostrich feathers, beaded satin,
    and shone that smile on us and sang.

[1962]

[1]Bessie Smith (1895–1937), an African American classic blues singer of the 1920s. She was considered
by many to be the finest female blues singer of her day.
[2]Thin, narrow strips of wood that form a backing for plaster walls.
[3]A barrel organ, played by turning a crank; here, perhaps a disreputable dance hall.

Those Winter Sundays

Sundays too my father got up early
and put his clothes on in the blueblack cold,
then with cracked hands that ached
from labor in the weekday weather made
banked fires blaze. No one ever thanked him.　　　　5

I'd wake and hear the cold splintering, breaking.
When the rooms were warm, he'd call,
and slowly I would rise and dress,
fearing the chronic angers of that house,

Speaking indifferently to him,　　　　10
who had driven out the cold
and polished my good shoes as well.
What did I know, what did I know
of love's austere and lonely offices?

[1962]

Frederick Douglass[1]

When it is finally ours, this freedom, this liberty, this beautiful
and terrible thing, needful to man as air,
usable as earth; when it belongs at last to all,
when it is truly instinct, brain matter, diastole, systole,[2]
reflex action; when it is finally won; when it is more　　　　5
than the gaudy mumbo jumbo of politicians:
this man, this Douglass, this former slave, this Negro
beaten to his knees, exiled, visioning a world
where none is lonely, none hunted, alien,
this man, superb in love and logic, this man　　　　10
shall be remembered. Oh, not with statues' rhetoric,
not with legends and poems and wreaths of bronze alone,
but with the lives grown out of his life, the lives
fleshing his dream of the beautiful, needful thing.

[1962]

---

[1]Frederick Douglass (1818–95) is considered the foremost African American abolitionist. Born Frederick Augustus Washington Bailey, he endured life as a slave in Maryland until 1838, when he escaped to New York and adopted the last name of Douglass. He married a free African American woman, settled in New Bedford, Massachusetts, and became involved in the antislavery movement. In 1841, at an abolitionist meeting in Nantucket, he delivered a rousing speech about his experiences as a slave and was hired as a lecturer by the Massachusetts Antislavery Society. Some of his friends convinced him to write his autobiography; he published *The Narrative of the Life of Frederick Douglass* in 1845. The book, however, marked him as a fugitive slave, and he fled to England for several years, earning money to buy his freedom. He returned to New York in 1847 and began publishing a newspaper, *The North Star*. Douglass advised President Abraham Lincoln during the Civil War and continued to serve in politics until his death.
[2]Referring to the pumping action of the heart. *Diastole* is the period of relaxation of the heart muscle; *systole* is the period of contraction by the heart muscle.

WILLIAM STAFFORD ■ (1914–1993)

William Stafford was born in Hutchinson, Kansas, the son of parents who, he recalled, loved literature and "luxuriated in stories." A conscientious objector during World War II, he spent four years in work camps in Arkansas and California, an experience he described in *Down in My Heart* (1947).

Stafford attended the University of Kansas for his bachelor's and master's degrees, and then went on to the graduate program at the University of Iowa, receiving his PhD in 1954. He began teaching in 1948 at Lewis and Clark College, in Portland, Oregon, and he remained there his entire career. His students and fellow poets greatly admired him as a teacher, generous and kind but dedicated every day to the practice of poetry.

As a teacher, Stafford accented the "process" of writing rather than the final result; "lower your standards" was a favorite principle, implying that a writer should be open to the flow and movement of his or her writing and not overplay the role of self-critic and self-censor. Two collections illustrate Stafford's approach to poetry and poetry-writing: *Writing the Australian Crawl: Views on the Writer's Vocation* (1978) and *Crossing Unmarked Snow: Further Views on the Writer's Vocation* (1998).

In an interview, Stafford offered these observations about what writing meant to him:

> It's a confirming, satisfying activity to do. And it's almost devotional. Maybe that's too strong, but it's as if a day of my life deserves a little attention from life. It's my kind of attention to stop long enough, to let the evaluative, the speculative, the exploratory impulses that are native to that portion of my time be manifest in a sustained way so that I can recognize them and get sustenance from them.

Many of Stafford's poems focus on Midwest scenes and settings, but he is known in particular for his poems about the Pacific Northwest, and its landscapes are often the basis for the speaker's personal reflection and quiet contemplation. Stafford's first book, which he published in his late forties, was *Traveling Through the Dark* (1962). The title poem, given here, a restrained but wounding meditation on technology, nature, and death, had its origin in Stafford's own experience:

> The poem concerns my finding a dead deer on the highway. This grew out of an actual experience of coming around a bend on the Wilson River Road near Jordan Creek in Oregon, and finding this deer, dead. As I was recounting the story to my kids the next day, I discovered by the expressions on their faces that I was arriving at some area of enhancement in the narrative.

The poet-essayist Charles Simic said about Stafford, "At the end of his great poems we are always alone, their fateful acts and consequences now our own to consider," and this insight is especially pertinent to the close of "Traveling Through the Dark."

For biographical background and context, see William Stafford, *Down in My Heart* (1998); and Kim Stafford, *Early Morning: Remembering My Father, William Stafford* (2002). For an introduction, see Jonathan Holden, *The Mark to Turn: A Reading of William Stafford's Poetry* (1976). See also *On William Stafford: The Worth of Local Things*, ed. Tom Andrews (1993); and Judith Kitchen, *Writing the World: Understanding William Stafford* (1999). See also *The Answers Are Inside the Mountains: Meditations on the Writing Life*, eds. Paul Merchant and Vincent Wixon (2003), a collection of material by Stafford that includes unpublished interviews, poems, articles, aphorisms, and writing exercises.

Traveling Through the Dark

Traveling through the dark I found a deer
dead on the edge of the Wilson River road.
It is usually best to roll them into the canyon:
that road is narrow; to swerve might make more dead.

By glow of the tail-light I stumbled back of the car   5
and stood by the heap, a doe, a recent killing;
she had stiffened already, almost cold.
I dragged her off; she was large in the belly.

My fingers touching her side brought me the reason—
her side was warm; her fawn lay there waiting,   10
alive, still, never to be born.
Beside that mountain road I hesitated.

The car aimed ahead its lowered parking lights;
under the hood purred the steady engine.
I stood in the glare of the warm exhaust turning red;   15
around our group I could hear the wilderness listen.

I thought hard for us all—my only swerving—,
then pushed her over the edge into the river.

[1962]

RANDALL JARRELL ▪ (1914–1965)

Randall Jarrell has been highly praised for both his poetry and his literary essays and reviews. The critic Delmore Schwartz said of his book of essays and reviews, *Poetry and the Age* (1953), that it was "perhaps the most comprehensive and certainly the most detailed of all studies of modern poetry"; and the poet John Berryman added that Jarrell was "the most powerful reviewer of poetry active in the country." The poet-critic Karl Shapiro observed about Jarrell's poetry: "He is the one poet of my generation who made an art of American speech as it is, who advanced beyond Robert Frost in using not only a contemporary idiom but the actual rhythms of our speech."

Born in Nashville, Tennessee, Jarrell received his bachelor's and master's degrees from Vanderbilt University. From 1937 to 1939 he taught at Kenyon College in Gambier, Ohio. During the years at Vanderbilt and Kenyon, Jarrell came to know and learned much from the poet-critics John Crowe Ransom, Allen Tate, and Robert Penn Warren, as well as Robert Lowell (with whom Jarrell shared a room for a time at Kenyon) and the fiction-writer Peter Taylor.

From 1939 to 1942, Jarrell was an instructor in the English department at the University of Texas, Austin. He published his first book of poems, *Blood for a Stranger*, in 1942, and in the same year he enlisted in the Army Air Corps. While he was in the service, his second book, an exploration of the lives and experiences of young men in the military entitled *Little Friend, Little Friend* (1945), appeared. After the war Jarrell taught at the Woman's College of the University of North Carolina, Greensboro, remaining there until his death.

Jarrell could be scathing in his literary criticism when reviewing poets whose work fell below his exacting standards (he said one poet's work seemed to have "been written on a typewriter by a typewriter"). But he was a passionate advocate of the poets, past and present, whom he valued, and—penetrating, lucid, and briskly engaging as a stylist—he played a crucial role in securing the canonical status of Walt Whitman, Robert Frost, William Carlos Williams, Robert Lowell, Elizabeth Bishop, and others.

The author of a satiric novel, *Pictures from an Institution* (1954), and children's books, Jarrell translated fairy tales and the work of the German authors Goethe and Rilke. His poetry (see *Complete Poems*, 1969; reissued 1996) displays technical skill, especially in the handling of meter and rhythm, combined with a keen feeling for colloquial speech. Noteworthy for their sympathetic insight, Jarrell's poems show a sharp, sometimes harrowing, feeling for life's losses and pains.

Two poems are presented here: "The Death of the Ball Turret Gunner," a grimly focused war poem; and "The Woman at the Washington Zoo," which depicts a woman reflecting on her age and isolation. As the critic Richard Fein remarked, and as these poems in their different ways suggest, "People in Jarrell's poetry awake to the dark knowledge of their death, their awareness of being caught in the grip of great forces."

The poet-critic Adrienne Rich has described Jarrell's significance in these terms: "He was a kind of conscience of poetry.... His influence on the poetry of his time has yet to be fathomed: it worked through his own poems, his published criticism, his teaching, his involvement with the work of his friends. For many of us, if asked that old question: 'To what or whom do you address your poems?' the truthful answer would be: 'To the mind of Randall Jarrell.'"

For biography, see William H. Pritchard, *Randall Jarrell: A Literary Life* (1990); Mary von Schrader Jarrell, *Remembering Randall: A Memoir of Poet, Critic, and Teacher Randall Jarrell* (1999); and Stephen Burt, *Randall Jarrell and His Age* (2002). For a range of critical interpretations, see *Randall Jarrell, 1914–1965*, eds. Robert Lowell, Peter Taylor, and Robert Penn Warren (1967); and *Critical Essays on Randall Jarrell*, ed. Suzanne Ferguson (1983). See also Suzanne Ferguson, *The Poetry of Randall Jarrell* (1971); and J. A. Bryant Jr., *Understanding Randall Jarrell* (1986).

The Death of the Ball Turret Gunner[1]

From my mother's sleep I fell into the State,
And I hunched in its belly till my wet fur froze.
Six miles from earth, loosed from its dream of life,
I woke to black flak[2] and the nightmare fighters.
When I died they washed me out of the turret with a hose.   5

[1945]

A B-17 bomber, nicknamed the "Flying Fortress," discharging a bomb
on an enemy target during World War II.

[1]A ball turret was a plexiglass dome in the belly of a B-17 or B-24 bomber. Two .50-caliber machine guns were operated by a small man who fit inside the sphere. The gunner, hunched up like a fetus, would revolve with the turret as he tracked enemy plans with his machine guns.
[2]The bursting shells of antiaircraft guns.

The Woman at the Washington Zoo

The saris go by me from the embassies.[1]

Cloth from the moon. Cloth from another planet.
They look back at the leopard like the leopard.

And I....
        this print of mine, that has kept its color   5
Alive through so many cleanings; this dull null
Navy I wear to work, and wear from work, and so
To my bed, so to my grave, with no
Complaints, no comment: neither from my chief,
The Deputy Chief Assistant, nor his chief—   10
Only I complain.... this serviceable
Body that no sunlight dyes, no hand suffuses
But, dome-shadowed, withering among columns,
Wavy beneath fountains—small, far-off, shining
In the eyes of animals, these beings trapped   15
As I am trapped but not, themselves, the trap,
Aging, but without knowledge of their age,
Kept safe here, knowing not of death, for death—
Oh, bars of my own body, open, open!

The world goes by my cage and never sees me.   20
And there comes not to me, as come to these,
The wild beasts, sparrows pecking the llamas' grain,
Pigeons settling on the bears' bread, buzzards
Tearing the meat the flies have clouded....
        Vulture,   25
When you come for the white rat that the foxes left,
Take off the red helmet of your head, the black
Wings that have shadowed me, and step to me as man:
The wild brother at whose feet the white wolves fawn,
To whose hand of power the great lioness
Stalks, purring....   30
        You know what I was,
You see what I am: change me, change me!

[1960]

---

[1]Jarrell composed this poem when he worked in Washington, D.C. as poetry consultant for the Library of Congress; the poem is set at the National Zoo in Rock Creek Park.

JOHN BERRYMAN ■ (1914–1972)

Born in the rural town of MacAlester, Oklahoma, John Berryman's given name was John Smith Jr. His parents' marriage was a bitterly unhappy one, and in 1926—this loss haunted Berryman his entire life—his father died in Tampa, Florida, of a self-inflicted gunshot wound. His mother remarried, to a stylish fellow from Georgia, John Berryman—which led John Smith Jr. to be given the name John Berryman Jr.

As an undergraduate at Columbia University (BA, 1936), Berryman benefited from the mentoring of the poet-critic Mark Van Doren. He was awarded a fellowship for two years' study at Cambridge University in England, where he met the poets William Butler Yeats, T. S. Eliot, Dylan Thomas, and W. H. Auden. This period abroad prompted Berryman to adopt a British accent and manner and tweedy clothing.

Berryman taught at Wayne State University, Princeton, Harvard, and, from 1955 to 1972, the University of Minnesota, but in both his academic work and disorderly personal life (he was married three times and had numerous affairs) he was plagued by alcoholism. In 1972 he jumped to his death from a bridge over the Mississippi River.

Despite his emotional trials and psychological problems, Berryman was a compelling and challenging lecturer and teacher. The poet Philip Levine recalled, "He put more energy and more time and more study into surveying our work and making suggestions, and encouraging us. Although he'd be very tough on us, I thought he was never cruel, because he was always looking for something to praise as well. But when he didn't like what he didn't like, he didn't make any bones about it."

Berryman was also a gifted, though erratic, literary critic and scholar, the author of a probing study of Stephen Crane (1950) and of a number of essays, included in *The Freedom of the Poet* (1976). For many years he labored on a big book about Shakespeare; it was never completed, but much of the project is now available in *Berryman's Shakespeare*, ed. John Haffenden (1999).

"Homage to Mistress Bradstreet" (1953, 1956) was Berryman's first important poem, a long work (fifty-seven stanzas) in which he assumes the voice of Anne Bradstreet, a New England Puritan poet of the seventeenth century. His best-known book is the brilliant if uneven *Dream Songs* (first published in 1964, later expanded as *The Dream Songs*, 1969), which draws on his own experiences, mood swings, bouts of anger, and laments. The form of these poems (ultimately there were 385 of them) is sonnetlike, and they are dazzling in their diction, comic and extravagant in their performance of voices, amazing and disorienting in their jumps from image to image, point to point, and in their sudden shifts from exuberance to utter despair.

Taken as a whole, *The Dream Songs*, according to Berryman, looks back to Walt Whitman's "Song of Myself," the centerpiece poem of *Leaves of Grass* (1855): "I think the model in *The Dream Songs* was the other greatest American poem—I am very ambitious—"Song of Myself"—a very long poem, about sixty pages." But in truth, Berryman's sequence, focused on the intense and often feverish and frantic exchanges between Henry, a white American of middle age, and an unnamed Friend, is far more manic and hyped up than Whitman's richly affirmative poem.

Berryman stressed that *Dream Songs* should not be interpreted autobiographically:

> The poem then, whatever its wide cast of characters, is essentially about an imaginary character (not the poet, not me) named Henry, a white American in early middle age sometimes in blackface, who has suffered an irreversible loss and talks about himself sometimes in the first person, sometimes in the third, sometimes even in the second; he has a friend, never named, who addresses him as Mr. Bones and variants thereof.

Yet many readers, including Berryman's friends and fellow-poets, have argued that *Dream Songs* gains whatever unity it possesses as an intense, multiple series of reflections of Berryman himself. The poet Robert Lowell in 1964 observed:

> The dreams are not real dreams but a waking hallucination in which anything that might have happened to the author can be used at random. Anything he has seen, overheard, or imagined can go in. The poems are about Berryman, or rather they are about a person he calls Henry. Henry is Berryman seen as himself, as poète maudit [accursed poet, a poet living outside or against society], child and puppet. He is tossed about with a mixture of tenderness and absurdity, pathos and hilarity that would have been impossible if the author had spoken in the first person.

For brief introductions, see J. M. Linebarger, *John Berryman* (1974); and Joel Conarroe, *John Berryman: An Introduction to the Poetry* (1977). For biography, see Eileen Simpson, *Poets in Their Youth* (1982), a memoir of her marriage to Berryman (they divorced in 1956), which includes revealing portraits of Randall Jarrell, Robert Lowell, and others; John Haffenden, *The Life of John Berryman* (1982); *We Dream of Honour: John Berryman's Letters to His Mother*, ed. Richard J. Kelly (1988); and Paul Mariani, *Dream Song: The Life of John Berryman* (1990). Discussions of the poetry include Stephen Matterson, *Berryman and Lowell: The Art of Losing* (1988); *Recovering Berryman: Essays on a Poet*, eds. Richard J. Kelly and Alan K. Lathrop (1993); and Thomas Travisano, *Midcentury Quartet: Bishop, Lowell, Jarrell, Berryman, and the Making of a Postmodern Aesthetic* (1999).

From The Dream Songs: 14

Life, friends, is boring. We must not say no.
After all, the sky flashes, the great sea yearns,
we ourselves flash and yearn,
and moreover my mother told me as a boy
(repeatingly) 'Ever to confess you're bored   5
means you have no

Inner Resources.' I conclude now I have no
inner resources, because I am heavy bored.
Peoples bore me,
literature bores me, especially great literature,   10
Henry bores me, with his plights & gripes
as bad as achilles,[1]

who loves people and valiant art, which bores me.
And the tranquil hills, & gin, look like a drag
and somehow a dog   15
has taken itself & its tail considerably away
into mountains or sea or sky, leaving
behind: me, wag.

[1964]

From The Dream Songs: 29

There sat down, once, a thing on Henry's heart
so heavy, if he had a hundred years
& more, & weeping, sleepless, in all them time
Henry could not make good.
Starts again always in Henry's ears   5
the little cough somewhere, an odour, a chime.

And there is another thing he has in mind
like a grave Sienese[1] face a thousand years
would fail to blur the still profiled reproach of. Ghastly,
with open eyes, he attends, blind.   10
All the bells say: too late. This is not for tears;
thinking.

But never did Henry, as he thought he did,
end anyone and hacks her body up

---

[1]The Greek hero of Homer's *Iliad* who, angry that his honor had been slighted, remained in his tent and refused to accompany the Greeks into battle against the Trojans.
[1]Allusion to an Italian school of painting, developed at Siena during the fourteenth and fifteenth centuries, that featured somber portraits of religious figures.

and hide the pieces, where they may be found. 15
He knows: he went over everyone, & nobody's missing.
Often he reckons, in the dawn, them up.
Nobody is ever missing.

[1964]

From The Dream Songs: 40

I'm scared a lonely. Never see my son,
easy be not to see anyone,
combers[1] out to sea
know they're goin somewhere but not me.
Got a little poison, got a little gun, 5
I'm scared a lonely.

I'm scared a only one thing, which is me,
from othering I don't take nothin, see,
for any hound dog's sake.
But this is where I livin, where I rake 10
my leaves and cop[2] my promise, this' where we
cry oursel's awake.

Wishin was dyin but I gotta make
it all this way to that bed on these feet
where peoples said to meet. 15
Maybe but even if I see my son
forever never, get back on the take,
free, black & forty-one.[3]

[1968]

From The Dream Songs: 45

He stared at ruin. Ruin stared straight back.
He thought they was old friends. He felt on the stair
where her papa found them bare
they became familiar. When the papers were lost
rich with pals' secrets, he thought he had the knack 5
of ruin. Their paths crossed

and once they crossed in jail; they crossed in bed;
and over an unsigned letter their eyes met,
and in an Asian city

[1]Long, curling waves.
[2]Slang for pile or heap, bank up; also, steal or swipe.
[3]A play on the phrase "free, white, and twenty-one," referring to legal independence.

directionless & lurchy at two & three,   10
or trembling to a telephone's fresh threat,
and when some wired his head

to reach a wrong opinion, 'Epileptic'.
But he noted now that: they were not old friends.
He did not know this one.   15
This one was a stranger, come to make amends
for all the imposters, and to make it stick.
Henry nodded, un-.

                                                                   [1968]

From The Dream Songs: 385

My daughter's heavier. Light leaves are flying.
Everywhere in enormous numbers turkeys will be dying
and other birds, all their wings.
They never greatly flew. Did they wish to?
I should know. Off away somewhere once I knew   5
such things.

Or good Ralph Hodgson[1] back then did, or does.
The man is dead whom Eliot[2] praised. My praise
follows and flows too late.
Fall is grievy, brisk. Tears behind the eyes   10
almost fall. Fall comes to us as a prize
to rouse us toward our fate.

My house is made of wood and it's made well,
unlike us. My house is older than Henry;
that's fairly old.   15
If there were a middle ground between things and the soul
or if the sky resembled more the sea,
I wouldn't have to scold
                                                   my heavy daughter.

                                                                   [1968]

---

[1]English poet (1871–1962) whose poem "Hymn to Moloch" protests the commercial slaughter of birds.
[2]T. S. Eliot, American poet and literary critic (1888–1965).

ROBERT LOWELL ▩ (1917–1977)

On his mother's side, Robert Lowell's lineage reached back to the Winslow family, which sailed to America on the *Mayflower*; on his father's side he was related to the nineteenth-century poet, essayist, and man-of-letters James Russell Lowell and the modern poet Amy Lowell. Born in 1917, Lowell attended the prestigious St. Mark's School, located in central Massachusetts, and from there went on to Harvard College. He performed poorly in his studies, and his emotional life was often in turmoil, as his parents fought with one another and he battled with them.

Through the intercession of Merrill Moore (a Tennessee-born writer but also a psychiatrist practicing in Boston), Lowell was befriended by the poet Allen Tate, and he left the Boston/Cambridge area to live with Tate and his wife in Clarksville, Tennessee. He then enrolled at Kenyon College in Gambier, Ohio, where he excelled, graduating *summa cum laude* with a major in classics. He was mentored by the poet-critic John Crowe Ransom and became friends with the fiction-writer Peter Taylor and the poet-essayist Randall Jarrell. In 1940 Lowell married Jean Stafford, a novelist, and converted to Catholicism.

Lowell spent a year in the graduate program at Louisiana State University in Baton Rouge, working with two important teachers and critics, Robert Penn Warren and Cleanth Brooks. In 1943 he declared himself a conscientious objector and was sentenced to jail for five months. His first book, *The Land of Unlikeness*, was published in 1944; it was followed, in 1946, by *Lord Weary's Castle*, metrically complex, packed with fierce and complicated imagery and metaphor, strained and daunting in syntax.

Lowell's most important book is *Life Studies* (1959), a vivid self-portrait charged with the pain of mental crisis and the wrenching effort to recover from its impact. Its intimate exposures of Lowell's experience led critics to stress a new term, "confessional poetry," with *Life Studies* as the pioneering example of the genre. *Life Studies* revolutionized the writing of poetry, crucially affecting the work of Allen Ginsberg (whose "Howl" had earlier influenced Lowell), Sylvia Plath, Anne Sexton, John Berryman, and many others.

Lowell's next volumes, *For the Union Dead* (1964) and *Near the Ocean* (1967), are related in tone, atmosphere, and style to *Life Studies*, but these took his explorations into new, more political terrain marked by the antiwar movement and the campaign for civil rights, causes in which he was active.

Lowell and Stafford had separated in 1946, and in 1949 he had married the essayist and novelist Elizabeth Hardwick. Living in New York City, spending summers in Maine, and teaching poetry each spring semester at Harvard, Lowell remained afflicted through the 1950s and into the early to mid-1960s by periods of grievous mental and emotional distress; on a number of occasions he was hospitalized for manic-depressive illness.

His next volume, *Notebook 1967–1968* (1969), a set of unrhymed sonnets, was later expanded and revised into *Notebook* (1970) and then into

History and *For Lizzie and Harriet* (1973). These were daring, shocking books that made use of private letters to Lowell from Elizabeth Hardwick, from whom Lowell had separated. He now was residing in England, married to the writer Lady Caroline Blackwood. He was writing with such revelatory drive, and with such painful consequences for those closest to him, that his friend and fellow-poet Elizabeth Bishop wondered, "Is art worth this?"

The Dolphin (1973), part of this same period of literary production, is a sequence of sonnets keyed to his marriage to Caroline Blackwood. Lowell's final book, *Day by Day* (1977), is more restrained, more reflective, than his work earlier in the decade.

Lowell also was the author of sharp essays and portraits of friends, poets, and teachers; he translated plays by Aeschylus and Racine; and he adapted stories by Nathaniel Hawthorne and Herman Melville for production on stage. He was a prominent literary figure, an acclaimed poet and spokesman for literature who enjoyed a celebrity status among writers and the reading public and who was in the middle of the social and political crises of his era.

Five poems are given here: "Mr. Edwards and the Spider," which revolves around the figure of Jonathan Edwards (1703–58), an eminent Puritan theologian and preacher, author of "Sinners in the Hands of an Angry God" and other gripping sermons and essays; "Memories of West Street and Lepke," which deals with Lowell's imprisonment in the 1940s and which refers to Lepke Buchalter, the head of an organized crime syndicate, Murder Incorporated; "Skunk Hour," a grim work that, as the critic Steven Gould Axelrod said, shows Lowell "confronting death...not a death leading to resurrection, but an existential death, yielding nothingness"; "Night Sweat," an intense, frightening work; and "For the Union Dead," which focuses on Robert Gould Shaw (1837–63), the commanding officer of a regiment of black troops, who was killed in the Union Army's assault on Fort Wagner, South Carolina, and the monument to Shaw and his men, by the sculptor Augustus Saint-Gaudens, located on the Boston Common, opposite the State House. About this last poem, generally considered Lowell's masterpiece, the essayist Ernest Hilbert observed, "It stands as a warning and admonition, holding a mirror to the country's deeply-rooted political hypocrisy, its civic indifference, self-absorption, and arrogance."

Lowell's work is perhaps best approached through the *Selected Poems* (1976, rev. ed. 1977). But for a full account, the place to turn is *Robert Lowell: Collected Poems*, eds. Frank Bidart and David Gewanter (2003).

Good points of departure include Richard J. Fein, *Robert Lowell* (2nd ed., 1979); Mark Rudman, *Robert Lowell: An Introduction to the Poetry* (1983); and Philip Hobsbaum, *A Reader's Guide to Robert Lowell* (1988). For biography, see Ian Hamilton, *Robert Lowell: A Biography* (1982); *Robert Lowell: Interviews and Memoirs*, ed. Jeffrey Meyers (1988); and Paul Mariani, *Lost Puritan: A Life of Robert Lowell* (1994). For critical interpretation, see Steven Gould Axelrod, *Robert Lowell: Life and Art* (1978); Vereen

Bell, *Robert Lowell: Nihilist as Hero* (1983); *Robert Lowell: Essays on the Poetry*, eds. Steven Gould Axelrod and Helen Deese (1986); and *The Critical Response to Robert Lowell*, ed. Steven Gould Axelrod (1999). See also *The Letters of Robert Lowell*, ed. Saskia Hamilton (2005); and *Words in Air: The Complete Correspondence Between Elizabeth Bishop and Robert Lowell*, ed. Thomas Travisano, with Saskia Hamilton (2008).

Mr. Edwards and the Spider[1]

I saw the spiders marching through the air,
Swimming from tree to tree that mildewed day
   In latter August when the hay
   Came creaking to the barn. But where
     The wind is westerly,   5
Where gnarled November makes the spiders fly
Into the apparitions of the sky,
They purpose nothing but their ease and die
Urgently beating east to sunrise and the sea;

What are we in the hands of the great God?   10
It was in vain you set up thorn and briar
   In battle array against the fire
   And treason crackling in your blood;
     For the wild thorns grow tame
And will do nothing to oppose the flame;   15
Your lacerations tell the losing game
You play against a sickness past your cure.
How will the hands be strong? How will the heart endure?[2]

A very little thing, a little worm,
Or hourglass-blazoned spider,[3] it is said,   20
   Can kill a tiger. Will the dead
   Hold up his mirror and affirm
     To the four winds the smell
And flash of his authority? It's well
If God who holds you to the pit of hell,   25
   Much as one holds a spider, will destroy,

---

[1] A reference to the sermon "Sinners in the Hands of an Angry God" (1741) by the strict American minister Jonathan Edwards (1703–1758), in which he states, "The God that holds you over the pit of hell, much as one holds a spider, or some loathsome insect over the fire, abhors you, and is dreadfully provoked."
[2] Edwards writes of the wrath of God, "Oh! then, what will be the consequence! What will become of the poor worms that shall suffer it! Whose hands can be strong? And whose heart can endure?"
[3] The deadly black widow spider, which has a marking resembling an hourglass on its abdomen.

Baffle and dissipate your soul. As a small boy

> On Windsor Marsh,[4] I saw the spider die
> When thrown into the bowels of fierce fire:
>> There's no long struggle, no desire   30
>> To get up on its feet and fly—
>>> It stretches out its feet
> And dies. This is the sinner's last retreat;
> Yes, and no strength exerted on the heat
> Then sinews the abolished will, when sick   35
And full of burning, it will whistle on a brick.

> But who can plumb the sinking of that soul?
> Josiah Hawley,[5] picture yourself cast
>> Into a brick-kiln where the blast
>> Fans your quick vitals to a coal—   40
>>> If measured by a glass,
> How long would it seem burning! Let there pass
> A minute, ten, ten trillion; but the blaze
> Is infinite, eternal: this is death,
To die and know it. This is the Black Widow, death.   45

[1946]

Memories of West Street and Lepke[1]

Only teaching on Tuesdays, book-worming
in pajamas fresh from the washer each morning,
I hog a whole house on Boston's
"hardly passionate Marlborough Street,"[2]
where even the man   5
scavenging filth in the back alley trash cans,
has two children, a beach wagon, a helpmate,
and is a "young Republican."
I have a nine months' daughter,
young enough to be my granddaughter.   10
Like the sun she rises in her flame-flamingo infants' wear.

---

[4]Jonathan Edwards's birthplace in East Windsor, Connecticut.

[5]Edward's uncle, who committed suicide.

[1]In 1943, Lowell served a year in prison for refusing to serve in the Armed Forces. While awaiting transfer to a prison in Danbury, Connecticut, Lowell was briefly held in the West Street Jail, where Louis "Lepke" Buchalter (1897–1944), the infamous Jewish mob boss, was also incarcerated. Lepke was the leader of Murder Incorporated, an organized crime syndicate. He was executed by electric chair in Sing Sing Prison.

[2]The phrase used by philosopher William James (1842–1910) to describe the affluent Back Bay area of Boston, Massachusetts, where Lowell lived in the 1950s.

These are the tranquillized *Fifties*,
and I am forty. Ought I to regret my seedtime?
I was a fire-breathing Catholic C.O.,[3]
and made my manic statement,   15
telling off the state and president, and then
sat waiting sentence in the bull pen
beside a Negro boy with curlicues
of marijuana in his hair.

Given a year,   20
I walked on the roof of the West Street Jail, a short
enclosure like my school soccer court,
and saw the Hudson River once a day
through sooty clothesline entanglements
and bleaching khaki tenements.   25
Strolling, I yammered metaphysics with Abramowitz,
a jaundice-yellow ("it's really tan")
and fly-weight pacifist,
so vegetarian,
he wore rope shoes and preferred fallen fruit.   30
He tried to convert Bioff and Brown,
the Hollywood pimps, to his diet.
Hairy, muscular, suburban,
wearing chocolate double-breasted suits,
they blew their tops and beat him black and blue.   35

I was so out of things, I'd never heard
of the Jehovah's Witnesses.[4]
"Are you a C.O.?" I asked a fellow jailbird.
"No," he answered, "I'm a J.W."
He taught me the "hospital tuck,"[5]   40
and pointed out the T shirted back
of *Murder Incorporated's* Czar Lepke,
there piling towels on a rack,
or dawdling off to this little segregated cell full
of things forbidden the common man: 45
a portable radio, a dresser, two toy American
flags tied together with a ribbon of Easter palm.
Flabby, bald, lobotomized,
he drifted in a sheepish calm,
where no agonizing reappraisal   50

[3]Conscientious objector.
[4]A religious sect whose members strongly oppose military service and the government's right to dictate matters of moral conscience.
[5]Referring to the secure and efficient bed-making style common in hospitals.

jarred his concentration on the electric chair—
hanging like an oasis in his air
of lost connections....

[1959]

Skunk Hour

(For Elizabeth Bishop)[1]

Nautilus Island's[2] hermit
heiress still lives through winter in her Spartan[3] cottage;
her sheep still graze above the sea.
Her son's a bishop. Her farmer
is first selectman in our village;   5
she's in her dotage.

Thirsting for
the hierarchic privacy
of Queen Victoria's century,[4]
she buys up all   10
the eyesores facing her shore,
and lets them fall.

The season's ill—
we've lost our summer millionaire,
who seemed to leap from an L.L. Bean   15
catalogue.[5] His nine-knot yawl[6]
was auctioned off to lobstermen.
A red fox stain covers Blue Hill.[7]

And now our fairy
decorator brightens his shop for fall;   20
his fishnet's filled with orange cork,
orange, his cobbler's bench and awl;
there is no money in his work,
he'd rather marry.

---

[1]Massachusetts poet and contemporary (1911–79) of Lowell. This poem is written in response to Bishop's poem, "The Armadillo."
[2]An island off of the coast of Castine, Maine, where Lowell had a summer home. Castine is west of the town of Blue Hill, about 45 minutes south of Bar Harbor.
[3]Distinguished by simplicity and frugality. The reference is to the Spartans of ancient Greece, who lived a militaristic lifestyle.
[4]The nineteenth century. The English Queen Victoria (1819–1901) reigned from 1837 to 1901.
[5]L.L. Bean is a company headquartered in Freeport, Maine, known for its sporting and outdoor gear and practical, rugged clothing.
[6]A small sailboat.
[7]See note 2.

One dark night,   25
my Tudor Ford climbed the hill's skull;
I watched for love-cars. Lights turned down,
they lay together, hull to hull,
where the graveyard shelves on the town....
My mind's not right.   30

A car radio bleats,
"Love, O careless Love..." I hear
my ill-spirit sob in each blood cell,
as if my hand were at its throat....
I myself am hell;[8]   35
nobody's here—

only skunks, that search
in the moonlight for a bite to eat.
They march on their soles up Main Street:
white stripes, moonstruck eyes' red fire   40
under the chalk-dry and spar spire
of the Trinitarian Church.[9]

I stand on top
of our back steps and breathe the rich air—
a mother skunk with her column of kittens swills the garbage
pail.   45
She jabs her wedge-head in a cup
of sour cream, drops her ostrich tail,
and will not scare.

                                                                     [1959]

Night Sweat

Work-table, litter, books and standing lamp,
plain things, my stalled equipment, the old broom—
but I am living in a tidied room,
for ten nights now I've felt the creeping damp
float over my pajamas' wilted white...   5
Sweet salt embalms me and my head is wet,
everything streams and tells me this is right;
my life's fever is soaking in night sweat—
one life, one writing! But the downward glide
and bias of existing wrings us dry—   10
always inside me is the child who died,

---

[8]Words spoken by Satan in *Paradise Lost* (1667, 1674), by the English poet John Milton (1608–74):
"Which way I fly is Hell, myself am Hell."
[9]Perhaps a playful allusion to Trinity Church, located in the Back Bay of Boston, Massachusetts,
designed by the architect H. H. Richardson (1838–86) and built 1872–77.

always inside me is his will to die—
one universe, one body... in this urn
the animal night sweats of the spirit burn.

Behind me! You! Again I feel the light   15
lighten my leaded eyelids, while the gray
skulled horses whinny for the soot of night.
I dabble in the dapple of the day,
a heap of wet clothes, seamy, shivering,
I see my flesh and bedding washed with light,   20
my child exploding into dynamite,
my wife...your lightness alters everything,
and tears the black web from the spider's sack,
as your heart hops and flutters like a hare.
Poor turtle, tortoise, if I cannot clear   25
the surface of these troubled waters here,
absolve me, help me, Dear Heart, as you bear
this world's dead weight and cycle on your back.

[1964]

For the Union Dead

"Relinquunt Omnia Servare Rem Publicam."[1]

The old South Boston Aquarium stands
in a Sahara of snow now. Its broken windows are boarded.
The bronze weathervane cod has lost half its scales.
The airy tanks are dry.

Once my nose crawled like a snail on the glass;   5
my hand tingled
to burst the bubbles
drifting from the noses of the cowed, compliant fish.

My hand draws back. I often sigh still
for the dark downward and vegetating kingdom   10
of the fish and reptile. One morning last March,
I pressed against the new barbed and galvanized

fence on the Boston Common. Behind their cage,
yellow dinosaur steamshovels were grunting
as they cropped up tons of mush and grass   15
to gouge their underworld garage.

[1]"They give up everything to serve the Republic" (Latin). The phrase is inscribed on the bronze memorial, designed by Augustus Saint-Gaudens (1848–1907), to Colonel Robert Gould Shaw (1837–63) and members of the Negro Fifty-fourth Massachusetts Volunteers. The statue stands opposite the Massachusetts State House at one corner of Boston Common. Lowell changed the word *reliquit* ("he gives up") in the original inscription to *relinquunt* ("they give up"). Shaw led the first African American regiment of the Union forces in the Civil War and was killed in battle at Fort Wagner, South Carolina.

Parking spaces luxuriate like civic
sandpiles in the heart of Boston.
A girdle of orange, Puritan-pumpkin colored girders
braces the tingling Statehouse,   20

shaking over the excavations, as it faces Colonel Shaw
and his bell-cheeked Negro infantry
on St. Gaudens' shaking Civil War relief,
propped by a plank splint against the garage's earthquake.

Two months after marching through Boston,   25
half the regiment was dead;
at the dedication,
William James[2] could almost hear the bronze Negroes breathe.

Their monument sticks like a fishbone
in the city's throat.   30
Its Colonel is as lean
as a compass-needle.

He has an angry wrenlike vigilance,
a greyhound's gentle tautness;
he seems to wince at pleasure,   35
and suffocate for privacy.

He is out of bounds now. He rejoices in man's lovely,
peculiar power to choose life and die—
when he leads his black soldiers to death,
he cannot bend his back.   40

On a thousand small town New England greens,
the old white churches hold their air
of sparse, sincere rebellion; frayed flags
quilt the graveyards of the Grand Army of the Republic.

The stone statues of the abstract Union Soldier   45
grow slimmer and younger each year—
wasp-waisted, they doze over muskets
and muse through their sideburns....

Shaw's father wanted no monument[3]
except the ditch,   50

[2]The philosopher William James (1842–1910) gave the unveiling address of Saint-Gaudens's statue in 1897. In a letter to his brother, novelist Henry James, he wrote, "There on foot go the dark outcasts, so true to nature that one can almost hear them breathing as they march."
[3]Shaw was killed while leading the charge. His body was stripped by the Confederate commander of the fort and thrown into a ditch with his soldiers, denying him the traditional officer's burial. When efforts were later made to rebury him, Shaw's parents rejected the offer, commenting that there was "no holier place" for Shaw than to be "surrounded by his brave and devoted soldiers."

where his son's body was thrown
and lost with his "niggers."

The ditch is nearer.
There are no statues for the last war here;[4]
on Boylston Street,[5] a commercial photograph   55
shows Hiroshima boiling

over a Mosler Safe, the "Rock of Ages"
that survived the blast. Space is nearer.
When I crouch to my television set,
the drained faces of Negro school-children[6] rise like balloons.   60

Colonel Shaw
is riding on his bubble,
he waits
for the blessèd break.

The Aquarium is gone. Everywhere,   65
giant finned cars nose forward like fish;
a savage servility
slides by on grease.

[1960, 1964]

The Shaw Memorial, by Augustus Saint-Gaudens, Boston Common, photograph taken sometime
between 1900 and 1915.

[4]World War II.
[5]A main street in Boston.
[6]News coverage connected to the controversial desegregation of schools. In 1964, President Lyndon
Baines Johnson enforced an act specifically prohibiting discrimination in voting, education, and the use
of public facilities. Title VI of the act barred the use of federal funds for segregated programs and schools.

GWENDOLYN BROOKS ■ (1917–2000)

The author of poems, novels, essays, reviews, and books for children, Gwendolyn Brooks was born in Topeka, Kansas, but soon after she was born, her family moved to Chicago, Illinois, the city with which throughout her productive career Brooks has been closely identified. She was educated at three different high schools, and then took a degree at Wilson Junior College. Her first poem appeared in 1930, and, with the support and encouragement of African American writers Langston Hughes and James Weldon Johnson, Brooks became a dedicated, prolific poet. Many of her poems during the 1930s appeared in *The Chicago Defender*, an important weekly with a wide readership in the African American community. Her first book of verse, *A Street in Bronzeville* (1945), was highly praised, and her second, *Annie Allen* (1949), was awarded the Pulitzer Prize, making Brooks the first African American poet to receive this honor.

Sometimes Brooks is too quickly characterized (and undervalued) as a "protest" poet, in part because of her involvement in the Black Arts movement of the 1960s and 1970s, which sought to merge aesthetics and radical politics and thereby ground African American literary production in the needs, desires, and demands of black people. Yet, if one takes her work as a whole, Brooks capitalizes on a rich, complicated blend of influences and shows more range than the term *protest* implies. Committed to black people and influenced by Hughes, Countee Cullen, and other African American poets, Brooks also drew from Emily Dickinson and Walt Whitman as well as seventeenth-century English poets (e.g., John Donne), and she was keenly aware of the modernist work of Ezra Pound, T. S. Eliot, and E. E. Cummings. She is a vivid observer and storyteller, sensitive to both the wonder and hardness of urban experience.

"We Real Cool" and "Martin Luther King, Jr." are lean, potent poems. The first catches the cocky tone of pool players who have dropped out of school—and whose lives are doomed, as they sense themselves. The second laments King's death—he was killed by a gunman in Memphis, Tennessee, on April 4, 1968—and affirms that those still living must heed his message and bring it to fulfillment.

For biography, see George E. Kent, *A Life of Gwendolyn Brooks* (1990). For a helpful critical study, see D. H. Melhem, *Gwendolyn Brooks: Poetry and the Heroic Voice* (1987). Also valuable are *A Life Distilled: Gwendolyn Brooks, Her Poetry and Fiction*, eds. Maria K. Mootry and Gary Smith (1987); and *On Gwendolyn Brooks: Reliant Contemplation*, ed. Stephen Caldwell Wright (1996). In *Of Women, Poetry, and Power: Strategies of Address in Dickinson, Miles, Brooks, Lorde, and Angelou* (2002), Zofia Burr examines Brooks and other contemporary women poets in relation to the legacy of Emily Dickinson's life and work.

We Real Cool

The Pool Players.
Seven at the Golden Shovel.

We real cool. We
Left school. We

Lurk late. We
Strike straight. We

Sing sin. We   5
Thin gin. We

Jazz June. We
Die soon.

[1960]

Martin Luther King, Jr.

A man went forth with gifts.
He was a prose poem.
He was a tragic grace.
He was a warm music.

He tried to heal the vivid volcanoes.   5
His ashes are
      reading the world

His Dream still wishes to anoint
      the barricades of faith and of control

His word still burns the center of the sun   10
      above the thousands and the
      hundred thousands

The word was Justice. It was spoken.

So it shall be spoken.
So it shall be done.   15

[1969]

LAWRENCE FERLINGHETTI ▪ (1919–)

The poet, essayist, translator, editor, and publisher Lawrence Ferlinghetti was one of the central figures in the Beat (both "beaten up" and "beatific") movement of the 1950s and a self-described "enemy of the state" who believed that poetry and politics are part of the same project of social engagement. As he said on more than one occasion, "Only the dead are disengaged."

Born in Yonkers, New York, Ferlinghetti was educated at the University of North Carolina, Columbia University, and the Sorbonne in Paris, where in 1951 he received a doctoral degree in poetry. Settling in San Francisco, he taught French in an adult education program, but then, in 1953, he became copublisher of *City Lights* magazine and co-owner of City Lights Books Shop (it was the first bookstore in the United States to specialize in paperback books). In 1955 he founded City Lights Books, which published and promoted the work of Beat writers—hip, alienated, dynamic, daring, satiric visionaries.

As an editor and publisher, Ferlinghetti was willing to make trouble on behalf of writers and causes he believed in. In 1956, for example, he was arrested on obscenity charges for publishing Allen Ginsberg's "Howl"; his trial (he was acquitted) made Ferlinghetti a figure of national renown (and also, to some, national infamy) and helped to give the prophetic and exuberant Beats—Ginsberg, Jack Kerouac, Kenneth Rexroth, and Gary Snyder—literary and cultural prominence.

Ferlinghetti's many volumes of verse include *A Coney Island of the Mind* (1958), which for many years was a poetry best seller, *The Secret Meaning of Things* (1969), and *These Are My Rivers: New & Selected Poems, 1955–1993* (1993). He is also the author of eight plays and the novels *Love in the Days of Rage* (1988) and *Her* (1966).

Like other Beat writers, Ferlinghetti enjoyed shocking the sensibilities of the middle class and challenging convention and entrenched forms of cultural and political authority and power. But as the following work, "Constantly risking absurdity," indicates, Ferlinghetti also wrote with insight, comic poise, and subtlety about the nature of the poet's craft.

For bibliography and critical discussion, see Neeli Cherkovski, *Ferlinghetti: A Biography* (1979); Larry Smith, *Lawrence Ferlinghetti, Poet-at-Large* (1983); and Barry Silesky, *Ferlinghetti, The Artist in His Time* (1990).

Constantly risking absurdity

Constantly risking absurdity
                              and death
          whenever he performs
                    above the heads
                                        of his audience   5
      the poet like an acrobat
                  climbs on rime
                        to a high wire of his own making
and balancing on eyebeams
                        above a sea of faces   10
          paces his way
                      to the other side of the day
          performing entrechats[1]
                        and sleight-of-foot tricks
      and other high theatrics   15
                        and all without mistaking
                  any thing
                        for what it may not be
        For he's the super realist
                        who must perforce perceive   20
                  taut truth
                        before the taking of each stance or step
    in his supposed advance
                        toward that still higher perch
where Beauty stands and waits   25
                  with gravity
                        to start her death-defying leap
          And he
              a little charleychaplin[2] man
                        who may or may not catch   30
              her fair eternal form
                          spreadeagled in the empty air
          of existence

                                                              [1958]

---

[1]A vertical jump during which the dancer repeatedly crosses the feet and beats them together.
[2]Charlie Chaplin (1889–1977) was an actor, producer, screenwriter, director, and composer. He is best known for his trademark character the Little Tramp, who sported a little moustache and was clad in a bowler hat, cane, baggy pants, and oversized shoes.

ROBERT DUNCAN ■ (1919–1988)

Robert Duncan was born in Oakland, California, attended high school in Bakersfield, and then, for two years, the University of California at Berkeley. He moved in 1938 to New York City and quickly became a member of the advanced art and literary groups there, numbering among his friends the painters Roberto Matta and Hans Hofmann. Duncan's own contributions to the cause of the cultural avant-garde included the *Experimental Review*, which published the work of Anaïs Nin, Henry Miller, Kenneth Patchen, and Lawrence Durrell.

Returning to Berkeley in 1946, Duncan was a key poet in the San Francisco Renaissance, along with Jack Spicer, Robin Blaser, and Kenneth Rexroth. He and they sought, in his words, "a reinterpretation of the work of Stein, Joyce, Pound, H. D., Williams, D. H. Lawrence, not as 'we moderns' but as links in a spiritual "tradition."

An even more important development for Duncan came the following year, when he met the poet Charles Olson, an influential writer and instructor at Black Mountain College, an experimental liberal arts institution located in North Carolina. In 1956, at Olson's invitation, Duncan began teaching at Black Mountain, and there he wrote many of the poems gathered in *The Opening of the Field* (1960), which he regarded as his first major book. Olson had called for "projective verse" and "open forms," the poem as "a field of action," thus urging that poetic composition be formed according to the poet's "breath" rather than based on the standard rhythmic and metrical rules and conventions. Duncan extended this theory into a view of verse as "grand collage," with the poem on the page as a "compositional field." "Few poets," the scholar George F. Butterick has noted about Duncan, "have written more articulately and self-consciously about their own intentions and understanding of poetry."

Duncan was a mythmaker, spiritualist, and mystic, long interested in world religions, philosophy, magic, and the occult. Duncan also was gay and the author, in 1944, of a brave, groundbreaking article, "The Homosexual in Society," in *Politics* magazine. His love lyrics are erotic and beautiful, and his longer poems, testifying to his passionate interest in Dante and Whitman, Blake and H. D., are intellectually ambitious and evocative.

Perhaps the most noteworthy volumes of Duncan's productive career are *Ground Work: Before the War* (1983) and *Ground Work II: In the Dark* (1987). The *Selected Poems* (2nd ed., 1997), edited by Robert J. Bertholf, suggest the richness and breadth of his work.

For biography and critical interpretation, see Ekbert Faas, *Young Robert Duncan: Portrait of the Poet as Homosexual in Society* (1983); Mark Andrew Johnson, *Robert Duncan* (1988); Edward Halsey Foster, *Understanding the Black Mountain Poets* (1995); and Peter O'Leary, *Gnostic Contagion: Robert*

Duncan and the Poetry of Illness (2002). A good collection of essays in
Robert Duncan: Scales of the Marvelous, eds. Robert J. Bertholf and Ian
W. Reid (1979). Also significant are *The Letters of Robert Duncan and Denise
Levertov*, eds. Robert J. Bertholf and Albert Gelpi (2003); and the essays
included in *Robert Duncan and Denise Levertov: The Poetry of Politics, the
Politics of Poetry*, eds. Albert Gelpi and Robert J. Bertholf (2006). The
University of California Press launched its Collected Writings of Robert Dun-
can in 2011 with *The H.D. Book*, a fascinating 700-page work that Duncan
wrote in 1960–61 on modern poetry (keyed to the poet H. D.) and poetics.

Often I Am Permitted to Return to a Meadow

as if it were a scene made-up by the mind,
that is not mine, but is a made place,

that is mine, it is so near to the heart,
an eternal pasture folded in all thought
so that there is a hall therein   5

that is a made place, created by light
wherefrom the shadows that are forms fall.

Wherefrom fall all architectures I am
I say are likenesses of the First Beloved
whose flowers are flames lit to the Lady.   10

She it is Queen Under The Hill
whose hosts are a disturbance of words within words
that is a field folded.

It is only a dream of the grass blowing
east against the source of the sun   15
in an hour before the sun's going down

whose secret we see in a children's game
of ring a round of roses told.

Often I am permitted to return to a meadow
as if it were a given property of the mind   20
that certain bounds hold against chaos,

that is a place of first permission,
everlasting omen of what is.

[1960]

Interrupted Forms

Long slumbering, often coming forward,
haunting the house I am the house I live in
resembles so, does he recall me or I
recall him? Seeing you the other day
long I lookt to see your face his, longing   5
without reason. I meant to tell
or spell your name, to dwell in the charm
I almost felt in the stone, the impassive
weight of old feeling, the cold awakening
I meant to tell you of, as if telling could reach you,   10
at last come into your embrace again, my arms
hold you, mounting, coming into your life
my life and interruption of all long lasting
    inertia in feeling,
arousal.   15

       In dreams
insubstantially you have come before my eyes'
expectations, and, even in waking,
taking over the field of sight fleetingly
stronger than what my eyes see,   20
the thought of you thought has eyes to see
has eyes to meet your answering eyes
thought raises. I am speaking of a ghost
the heart is glad to have return, of a room
I have often been lonely in, of a desertion   25
that remains even where I am most cherisht
and surrounded by Love's company, of a form,
wholly fulfilling the course of my life, interrupted,
of a cold in the full warmth of the sunlight
that seeks to come in close to your heart
          for warmth.   30

[1984]

RICHARD WILBUR ▧ (1921—)

Born in New York City, raised on a farm in rural New Jersey, Richard Wilbur is an accomplished poet, a perceptive essayist and editor, and a skillful translator of Molière, Racine, Apollinaire, and other authors. His early books include *The Beautiful Changes and Other Poems* (1947), *Ceremony and Other Poems* (1950), and *Things of This World* (1956), for which he was awarded the Pulitzer Prize and the National Book Award. His *New and Collected Poems* was published in 1988, and *Anterooms: New Poems and Translations* was published in 2010.

Wilbur attended Amherst College, graduating in 1942, and then served in the U.S. Army, first as a cryptographer (i.e., code breaker) and then as an infantryman who experienced combat against the Germans in Italy and elsewhere. After the war, Wilbur took a master's degree in English at Harvard and was a member for three years of the prestigious Harvard Society of Fellows. There his teachers included the American literary historian F. O. Matthiessen and the literary critic and theorist I. A. Richards. Wilbur also became friends with Robert Frost, whose poetry, along with Marianne Moore's and, to a lesser extent, Wallace Stevens's, was crucial in the development of Wilbur's own style and voice. He taught at Harvard, Wesleyan, Wellesley, and Smith, and in 1987 was named Poet Laureate of the United States.

Wilbur is a polished, elegant, witty, ironic, balanced craftsman, and his procedures have been both honored and treated with a measure of detachment. The poet-critic Randall Jarrell, reviewing *Ceremony*, observed, "Mr. Wilbur never goes too far, but he never goes far enough." Some have criticized him for failing to give sufficient notice to social, political, and historical issues. The better way to frame the point, however, is to say that Wilbur defined the imaginative territory that he feels best equipped to explore. As he stated in an interview (2009), in reference to his focus on metaphor, "Poetry is concerned with things, and with making them vivid, and what metaphor does is to render some part of the world more vivid by comparing it—sometimes violently—to something else." In its focus and precision of phrase and image, Wilbur's work is a criticism of theatricality, cant, pretense, and unearned piety, and it seeks distance from the kind of posturing that Jarrell's claim might tend to encourage.

In an essay on William Carlos Williams, Wilbur observes:

> Every poem begins, or ought to, by a disorderly retreat to defensible positions. Or, rather, by a perception of the hopelessness of direct combat, and a resort to the warfare of spells, effigies, and prophecies. The relation between the artist and reality is an oblique one, and indeed there is no good art which is not consciously oblique. If you respect the reality of the world, you know that you can approach that reality only by indirect means.

Listened to closely, these words intimate the doubt, peril, and fear that Wilbur's verse both fends off and discreetly, shrewdly, looks into. Perhaps the best approach to the following poems, "Years-End" and "Love Calls Us to the Things of This World," is to attend to the complexities and tensions that animate and threaten, if just barely, to break through the poised shape of the lines and control of the imagery.

For critical interpretation, see Donald L. Hill, *Richard Wilbur* (1967); *Richard Wilbur's Creation*, ed. Wendy Salinger (1983); Bruce Michelson, *Wilbur's Poetry: Music in a Scattering Time* (1991); and Rodney Stenning Edgecombe, *A Reader's Guide to the Poetry of Richard Wilbur* (1995).

Years-End

Now winter downs the dying of the year,
And night is all a settlement of snow;
From the soft street the rooms of houses show
A gathered light, a shapen atmosphere,
Like frozen-over lakes whose ice is thin   5
And still allows some stirring down within.

I've known the wind by water banks to shake
The late leaves down, which frozen where they fell
And held in ice as dancers in a spell
Fluttered all winter long into a lake;   10
Graved on the dark in gestures of descent,
They seemed their own most perfect monument.

There was perfection in the death of ferns
Which laid their fragile cheeks against the stone
A million years. Great mammoths overthrown   15
Composedly have made their long sojourns,
Like palaces of patience, in the gray
And changeless lands of ice. And at Pompeii[1]

The little dog lay curled and did not rise
But slept the deeper as the ashes rose   20
And found the people incomplete, and froze
The random hands, the loose unready eyes
Of men expecting yet another sun
To do the shapely thing they had not done.

---

[1]On August 24, AD 79, the Italian Mount Vesuvius erupted, burying the Roman resort town of Pompeii and nearby Herculaneum under volcanic ash. The towns were rediscovered in the eighteenth century, with many of the inhabitants preserved in their death poses.

These sudden ends of time must give us pause.   25
We fray into the future, rarely wrought
Save in the tapestries of afterthought.
More time, more time. Barrages of applause
Come muffled from a buried radio.
The New-year bells are wrangling with the snow.   30

[1950]

Love Calls Us to the Things of This World

    The eyes open to a cry of pulleys,
And spirited from sleep, the astounded soul
Hangs for a moment bodiless and simple
As false dawn.
                Outside the open window   5
The morning air is all awash with angels.

    Some are in bed-sheets, some are in blouses,
Some are in smocks: but truly there they are.
Now they are rising together in calm swells
Of halcyon[1] feeling, filling whatever they wear   10
With the deep joy of their impersonal breathing;

    Now they are flying in place, conveying
The terrible speed of their omnipresence, moving
And staying like white water; and now of a sudden
They swoon down into so rapt a quiet   15
That nobody seems to be there.
                    The soul shrinks

    From all that it is about to remember,
From the punctual rape of every blessèd day,
And cries,   20
           "Oh, let there be nothing on earth but laundry,
Nothing but rosy hands in the rising steam
And clear dances done in the sight of heaven."

    Yet, as the sun acknowledges
With a warm look the world's hunks and colors,   25
The soul descends once more in bitter love
To accept the waking body, saying now
In a changed voice as the man yawns and rises,

---

[1]Calm and peaceful. The word refers to a mythical bird that was fabled to breed during the time of the
winter solstice in a nest floating in the sea, thus charming the wind and waves.

"Bring them down from their ruddy gallows;
Let there be clean linen for the backs of thieves;   30
Let lovers go fresh and sweet to be undone,
And the heaviest nuns walk in a pure floating
Of dark habits,
                    keeping their difficult balance."

[1956]

JAMES DICKEY ■ (1923–1997)

James Dickey's fame as the author of the best-selling novel *Deliverance* (1970), which describes the nightmarish adventures of four Atlanta businessmen on a weekend canoe trip and which Dickey then adapted for a film (1972), has led readers to neglect or undervalue his superb poetry. As the following poems suggest, he explores the themes of mortality and transcendence, especially in his early work, with a rare power and insight.

Dickey's reputation has faltered for other reasons as well. Whenever he talked about his life, he freely mixed fact with fiction, and, when he became well known and traveled to college campuses to give readings or lectures, he often behaved in embarrassingly flamboyant, out-of-control ways. "James Dickey was hugely gifted and hugely flawed," the critic Peter Davison said, "a tremendous reader and a born writer, an athlete and an intellectual, a deep thinker and a drinker, a composer of burly and extremist poetry, an excessive performer, a hopeless liar, an inveterate womanizer, a father who gave himself airs."

Dickey was born in Atlanta, Georgia, attended Clemson A & M College (now Clemson University) in South Carolina for only a year, and then enlisted in the Army Air Corps, serving in the South Pacific during World War II. When the war ended, he enrolled at Vanderbilt University in Nashville, Tennessee, where he benefited from the advice and support of the poet Donald Davidson and the literary critic Monroe K. Spears. An avid reader of the Romantic poet and adventurer Lord Byron as well as the contemporary (and often strained and apocalyptic) poets Kenneth Patchen and Dylan Thomas, Dickey published his first poem in *The Sewanee Review*, an important literary journal, during his senior year. But he was slow to publish his first book, largely because, after a period as a teacher at Rice University in Texas and the University of Florida, he was busy working for advertising agencies in New York and Atlanta—he stated that he was "selling his soul to the devil in the daytime and buying it back at night." Dickey's first book, *Into the Stone*, was published in 1960, and it led him to give up advertising and return to the academy, where he held positions at a number of universities until settling in 1968 at the University of South Carolina as poet-in-residence and professor of English.

In his third volume, *Buckdancer's Choice* (1965), Dickey introduced a new technique, the "split line," that gave his poetry a new look and a changed rhythm. Each line is divided ("split") into phrases, separated from one another by spaces rather than by punctuation. Dickey sought to reveal and dramatize the sudden, sharp movements of thought and feeling, especially in moments of high intensity and crisis. For *Buckdancer's Choice*, Dickey was awarded the National Book Award in Poetry, and his stylistic innovation was and is admired by many readers, saying it liberated his voice. But over time, Dickey's verse grew self-indulgent and overly rhetorical, prompted in that direction by the too-easy freedoms the split line encouraged.

The authentic core of Dickey's achievement is in the work he did from the late 1950s to the late 1960s. It reached its height with the publication of *Poems 1957–1967* (1967); *Babel to Byzantium* (1968), a collection of reviews and essays; and *Self-Interviews* (1970), a vigorous, probing account of his literary career and commentary on his poems.

The pre-1965 poems presented here show Dickey's strong, indeed magnificent, kind of simplicity and focus. His speakers take forays into the self, penetrating deeper, feeling the disturbances, inquiring and wondering about the relationship between mind and heart. As the poet Stanley Plumly recalled, with Dickey "you had the sense about him that he was caged, and that he had something powerful in him he wanted to say." Yet the danger, the tension, while there, is restrained, and the language and the forms are beautifully handled. At his best, Dickey is an observant and profound Nature poet, a seeker for what it means to be a person and an explorer of the zones of life and death. As he explained in an interview (1976), a poet is "someone who notices and is enormously taken by things that somebody else would walk by." Even more: a poet "has got to find some way to love that white empty page, those words he hasn't said yet."

For biography, see Henry Hart, *James Dickey: The World as a Lie* (2000). See also Neal Bowers, *James Dickey: The Poet as Pitchman* (1985); and Christopher Dickey, *Summer of Deliverance: A Memoir of Father and Son* (1998). Helpful critical studies include *The Imagination as Glory: The Poetry of James Dickey*, eds. Bruce Weigl and T. R. Hummer (1984); Ronald Baughman, *Understanding James Dickey* (1985); Robert Kirschten, *James Dickey and the Gentle Ecstasy of Earth: A Reading of the Poems* (1988); and Gordon Van Ness, *Outbelieving Existence: The Measured Motion of James Dickey* (1992). On Dickey's fiction, see Casey Howard Clabough, *Elements: The Novels of James Dickey* (2002), which examines the three published novels as well as unpublished manuscripts and notes. For primary sources and commentary, see also *The Once Voice of James Dickey: His Letters and Life, 1942–1969*, ed. Gordon Van Ness (2003).

Drowning With Others

There are moments a man turns from us
Whom we have all known until now.
Upgathered, we watch him grow,
Unshipping his shoulder bones

Like human, everyday wings
That he has not ever used,
Releasing his hair from his brain,
A kingfisher's crest, confused

5

By the God-tilted light of Heaven.
His deep, window-watching smile   10
Comes closely upon us in waves,
And spreads, and now we are

At last within it, dancing.
Slowly we turn and shine
Upon what is holding us,   15
As under our feet he soars,

Struck dumb as the angel of Eden,[1]
In wide, eye-opening rings.
Yet the hand on my shoulder fears
To feel my own wingblades spring,   20

To feel me sink slowly away
In my hair turned loose like a thought
Of a fisherbird dying in flight.
If I opened my arms, I could hear

Every shell in the sea find the word   25
It has tried to put into my mouth.
Broad flight would become of my dancing,
And I would obsess the whole sea,

But I keep rising and singing
With my last breath. Upon my back,   30
With his hand on my unborn wing,
A man rests easy as sunlight

Who has kept himself free of the forms
Of the deaf, down-soaring dead,
And me laid out and alive   35
For nothing at all, in his arms.

[1962]

The Heaven of Animals

Here they are. The soft eyes open.
If they have lived in a wood
It is a wood.
If they have lived on plains
It is grass rolling   5
Under their feet forever.

---

[1]Referring to the cherubim who guard the entrance to Eden after God casts out Adam and Eve. "He drove Adam out and...placed the cherubim and a flaming sword turning every way to guard the path to the tree of life." (Genesis 3:24)

Having no souls, they have come,
Anyway, beyond their knowing.
Their instincts wholly bloom
And they rise.
The soft eyes open.   10

To match them, the landscape flowers,
Outdoing, desperately
Outdoing what is required:
The richest wood,   15
The deepest field.

For some of these,
It could not be the place
It is, without blood.
These hunt, as they have done,   20
But with claws and teeth grown perfect,

More deadly than they can believe.
They stalk more silently,
And crouch on the limbs of trees,
And their descent   25
Upon the bright backs of their prey

May take years
In a sovereign floating of joy.
And those that are hunted
Know this as their life,   30
Their reward: to walk

Under such trees in full knowledge
Of what is in glory above them,
And to feel no fear,
But acceptance, compliance.   35
Fulfilling themselves without pain

At the cycle's center,
They tremble, they walk
Under the tree,
They fall, they are torn,   40
They rise, they walk again.

                                                          [1962]

MITSUYE YAMADA ■ (1923—)

Mitsuye Yamada, the daughter of Japanese immigrants to the United States, was born in Japan during her mother's return visit to her native land. Yamada was raised in Seattle, Washington, but in 1942 she and her family were incarcerated and then relocated to a camp in Idaho. This was the result of Executive Order 9066, signed by President Roosevelt in February 1942. The order, in the aftermath of the Japanese attack on Pearl Harbor in December 1941, gave military authorities the right to remove any and all persons from "military areas." In the mid-1950s Yamada became an American citizen, and, in the 1960s, she joined the English department at Cypress College in Seattle, where she taught literature and creative writing until her retirement in 1989.

In addition to *Camp Notes and Other Poems* (1992), Yamada has written *Desert Run: Poems and Stories* (1988) and edited *Sowing TI Leaves: Writings by Multicultural Women* (1991).

For further study, see *And Justice for All: An Oral History of the Japanese American Detention Camps*, ed. John Tateishi (1984); *Only What We Could Carry: The Japanese American Internment Experience*, ed. Lawson Fusao Inada (2000); Greg Robinson, *By Order of the President: FDR and the Internment of Japanese Americans* (2001); and Caroline Chung Simpson, *An Absent Presence: Japanese Americans in Postwar American Culture, 1945–1960* (2001). See also Brian Masaru Hayashi, *Democratizing the Enemy: The Japanese American Internment* (2008); Alice Yang Murray, *Historical Memories of the Japanese American Internment and the Struggle for Redress* (2008); and Todd Stewart, *Placing Memory: A Photographic Exploration of Japanese American Internment* (2008), which provides a detailed visual and factual survey of the camps and color photographs of the sites as they appear today.

To the Lady

The one in San Francisco who asked:
Why did the Japanese Americans let
the government put them in
those camps without protest?

Come to think of it I   5
    should've run off to Canada
    should've hijacked a plane to Algeria
    should've pulled myself up from my
    bra straps
    and kicked'm in the groin   10
    should've bombed a bank

should've tried self-immolation
should've holed myself up in a
woodframe house
and let you watch me
burn up on the six o'clock news   15
should've run howling down the street
naked and assaulted you at breakfast
by AP[1] wirephoto
should've screamed bloody murder
like Kitty Genovese[2]   20

Then
YOU would've
come to my aid in shining armor
laid yourself across the railroad track
marched on Washington
tatooed a Star of David[3] on your arm
written six million enraged   25
letters to Congress

But we didn't draw the line
anywhere
law and order Executive Order 9066[4]
social order moral order internal order

You let'm   30
I let'm
All are punished.

[1976]

---

[1]The Associated Press, an international news agency.
[2]On March 13, 1964, Catherine "Kitty" Genovese, age 28, was murdered steps away from her apartment building in New York City. Police discovered that thirty-eight of her neighbors had witnessed at least one of her killer's three attacks over a thirty-minute span, but not a single person came to her aid or called the police. The one call made to the police came after Genovese was dead. Her name soon became symbolic in the public mind for American ambivalence—the dark side of a nation of people too indifferent, alienated, or self-absorbed to get involved to save a fellow human being in dire trouble. The term *Genovese syndrome* was coined to describe this attitude.
[3]The Mogen David (shield of David), shaped like a six-pointed star, a symbol most commonly associated with Judaism. In Nazi Germany, Jews were ordered to wear arm badges bearing the symbol.
[4]Under Executive Order 9066, signed by President Franklin D. Roosevelt on February 19, 1942, all Japanese and Americans of Japanese ancestry were forced to move from Western coastal regions to guarded camps in the interior of the United States.

DENISE LEVERTOV ■ (1923–1997)

Denise Levertov was born in England. Her father was a Hasidic Jew who had converted to Christianity and become an Anglican parson, preacher, and scholar; her mother, from Wales, was a lover of literature who read classic works to the family and educated her daughter at home. At the age of twelve, Levertov mailed some of her poetry to T. S. Eliot; he responded to her supportively, and by the time she reached her seventeenth birthday she was a published poet.

During and after her service as a nurse in England during World War II, Levertov continued to work on her verse; her first book, *The Double Image*, was published in 1946. A year later she married, and the following year she and her husband relocated to the United States. Levertov became a U.S. citizen in 1956.

Levertov immersed herself during the 1950s in the work of such American writers as Ralph Waldo Emerson and Henry David Thoreau, and she studied the literary innovations introduced by Ezra Pound and William Carlos Williams, among the modernists. Williams in particular, she recalled, "was a sort of gateway into my own development as a poet. He opened up a new way of handling language." If she had lacked his example and inspiration, she noted, "I could not have developed from a British Romantic with an almost Victorian background to an American poet of any vitality."

Among her more immediate contemporaries, Levertov was influenced by Robert Creeley, Charles Olson, Robert Duncan, and other writers connected with the experimental Black Mountain College, founded in the 1930s in North Carolina. Though she remained (in her phrase) "obstinately precise" and meticulous as a craftswoman, Levertov's poetry grew more flexible and open, and through her next two books, *Here and Now* (1956) and *With Eyes at the Back of Our Heads* (1959), she secured a place as a leading poet, one that she reinforced during her years (1961, 1963–65) as poetry editor of *The Nation* magazine. In the 1960s and 1970s, her work was informed by the feminist and antiwar movements, and she produced a number of powerful, and controversial, poems (e.g., "What Were They Like?" included here) on these and related subjects.

Levertov's later volumes of verse include *Collected Earlier Poems 1940–1960* (1979); *Poems 1960–1967* (1983); *The Life Around Us: Selected Poems on Nature* (1997); and *The Stream and the Sapphire: Selected Poems on Religious Themes* (1997). She also published translations and critical and literary essays, many of which are included in *New and Selected Essays* (1992).

Levertov's comments on her work form a rich context for the voices she speaks through in her poetry. Here are three examples, all taken from an interview she gave near the end of her life, when she was suffering from complications of lymphoma:

> I've been writing poetry for many, many decades. In talking about the process, I'm almost obliged to say, "First you do this. Then you

do that. Then you stand back. Then you do that." But these things overlap and flow into each other. One has to use that linear description of a process that is actually much less linear, much more intuitive, doubling back on itself. But it's only for convenience sake that one has to talk about them as a sequence of discreet events, because they really aren't.

Some poems come into being and don't need revising. They emerge out of nowhere. You have to recognize they are complete and not mess around with them. This certainly doesn't happen with every poem. But you would be mistaken to suppose that every poem has to go through many revisions. You're bound to develop some craft confidence in all this after you've been doing it for a while.

When you're really caught up in writing a poem, it can be a form of prayer. I'm not very good at praying, but what I experience when I'm writing a poem is close to prayer. I feel it in different degrees and not with every poem. But in certain ways writing is a form of prayer.

For interpretation and context, see Linda Wagner-Martin, *Denise Levertov* (1967); Audrey T. Rodgers, *Denise Levertov: The Poetry of Engagement* (1993); *Denise Levertov: Selected Criticism*, ed. Albert Gelpi (1993); *Denise Levertov: New Perspectives*, eds. Anne Colclough Little and Susie Paul (2000), and *The Letters of Robert Duncan and Denise Levertov*, eds. Robert J. Bertholf and Albert Gelpi (2003). See also the essays included in *Robert Duncan and Denise Levertov: The Poetry of Politics, the Politics of Poetry*, eds. Albert Gelpi and Robert J. Bertholf (2006).

In Mind

There's in my mind a woman
of innocence, unadorned but

fair-featured, and smelling of
apples or grass. She wears

a utopian smock or shift, her hair   5
is light brown and smooth, and she

is kind and very clean without
ostentation—

    but she has
no imagination.   10

    And there's a
turbulent moon-ridden girl

or old woman, or both,
dressed in opals and rags, feathers

and torn taffeta,
who knows strange songs—

but she is not kind.

[1964]

September 1961

This is the year the old ones,
the old great ones
leave us alone on the road.

The road leads to the sea.
We have the words in our pockets,   5
obscure directions. The old ones

have taken away the light of their presence,
we see it moving away over a hill
off to one side.

They are not dying,   10
they are withdrawn
into a painful privacy

learning to live without words.
E.P.[1] "It looks like dying"—Williams:[2] "I can't
describe to you what has been   15

happening to me"—
H.D.[3] "unable to speak."
The darkness
twists itself in the wind, the stars
are small, the horizon   20
ringed with confused urban light-haze.

They have told us
the road leads to the sea,
and given

[1]Ezra Pound (1885–1972), American poet and critic, who in his final years fell silent, not speaking at all for days at a time.
[2]William Carlos Williams (1883–1963), who suffered several paralyzing strokes before his death.
[3]The Imagist poet Hilda Doolittle (1886–1961), who died of a heart attack in Zurich, Switzerland, in September 1961 after suffering a stroke earlier that year. In 1913, Pound persuaded Doolittle to sign herself "H. D., Imagiste."

the language into our hands.   25
We hear
our footsteps each time a truck

has dazzled past us and gone
leaving us a new silence.
One can't reach   30

the sea on this endless
road to the sea unless
one turns aside at the end, it seems,

follows
the owl that silently glides above it
aslant, back and forth,   35

and away into deep woods.

But for us the road
unfurls itself, we count the
words in our pockets, we wonder

how it will be without them, we don't   40
stop walking, we know
there is far to go, sometimes

we think the night wind carries
a smell of the sea...

[1964]

What Were They Like?

1) Did the people of Viet Nam
   use lanterns of stone?
2) Did they hold ceremonies
   to reverence the opening of buds?
3) Were they inclined to quiet laughter?   5
4) Did they use bone and ivory,
   jade and silver, for ornament?
5) Had they an epic poem?
6) Did they distinguish between speech and singing?

1) Sir, their light hearts turned to stone.   10
   It is not remembered whether in gardens
   stone lanterns illumined pleasant ways.

2) Perhaps they gathered once to delight in blossom,
   but after their children were killed
   there were no more buds.   15
3) Sir, laughter is bitter to the burned mouth.
4) A dream ago, perhaps. Ornament is for joy.
   All the bones were charred.
5) It is not remembered. Remember,
   most were peasants; their life   20
   was in rice and bamboo.
   When peaceful clouds were reflected in the paddies
   and the water buffalo stepped surely along terraces,
   maybe fathers told their sons old tales.
   When bombs smashed those mirrors   25
   there was time only to scream.
6) There is an echo yet, it is said,
   of their speech which was like a song.
   It was reported their singing resembled
   the flight of moths in moonlight.   30
   Who can say? It is silent now.

                                              [1971]

An American military advisor, a South Vietnamese soldier, and children whose village, thought to
have been a Viet Cong stronghold, had been burned by government troops, 1963.

Zeroing In

'I am a landscape,' he said,
'a landscape and a person walking in that landscape.
There are daunting cliffs there,
and plains glad in their way
of brown monotony. But especially   5
there are sinkholes, places
of sudden terror, of small circumference
and malevolent depths.'
'I know,' she said. 'When I set forth
to walk in myself, as it might be   10
on a fine afternoon, forgetting,
sooner or later I come to where sedge
and clumps of white flowers, rue perhaps,
mark the bogland, and I know
there are quagmires there that can pull you   15
down, and sink you in bubbling mud.'
'We had an old dog,' he told her, 'when I was a boy,
a good dog, friendly. But there was an injured spot
on his head, if you happened
just to touch it he'd jump up yelping   20
and bite you. He bit a young child,
they had to take him down to the vet's and destroy him.'
'No one knows where it is,' she said,
'and even by accident no one touches it.
It's inside my landscape, and only I, making my way   25
preoccupied through my life, crossing my hills,
sleeping on green moss of my own woods,
I myself without warning touch it,
and leap up at myself—'
'—or flinch back   30
just in time.'

          'Yes, we learn that.
It's not terror, it's pain we're talking about:
those places in us, like your dog's bruised head,
that are bruised forever, that time   35
never assuages, never.'

[1987]

A. R. AMMONS ■ (1926–2001)

Born on a small tobacco farm near Whiteville, North Carolina, A. R. Ammons first composed poetry while serving in the U.S. Navy during World War II. He later attended Wake Forest University, and then held several jobs before beginning a teaching career at Cornell University in Ithaca, New York, in 1964. The author of many books of poetry, Ammons was widely admired and much honored, receiving many prestigious fellowships and prizes, including the National Book Award for *Collected Poems 1951–1971* (1972). His major publications include *The Selected Poems: Expanded Edition* (1986) and *Set in Motion: Essays, Interviews, and Dialogues* (1996).

"You can't write out of just what you know," Ammons observed in an interview:

> There's no motivation for that. And so I feel always in agreement with that thing that Emerson said in the essay *Nature*, where he says let me record from day to day my honest thought. Today, I say exactly the way things seem to me. Tomorrow, I also say, and it may differ somewhat from what I said the day before, but the difference, while it may be interesting, is not as important as the hope, which he expresses, that if you go on doing this somehow or other you will come to know a deeper thing that unifies all these days. Whereas if you had tried to plunge towards that deeper symmetry directly, there would be no way you could get there.

"Corsons Inlet," keyed to its speaker's walk along a narrow strait that leads from the Atlantic Ocean through barrier islands on the southeast coast of New Jersey, is Ammons's best-known poem, and it reflects the exploratory quality that he speaks of here.

As the critic John Elder noted, "the Jersey shore, where Ammons lived at one time, figures in many of his poems: its constant motion of wind and sand meets the movement of his accommodating mind.... [The poem] is not a self-contained poetic artifact but a terrain into which the reader may step." Indeed, the organization of the words on the page enacts both the walk and the movement of the speaker's mind, in its shifts, turns, changes of direction, and ongoing observation and inquiry.

As certain details and images imply, Walt Whitman is a poetic presence in "Corsons Inlet," especially "As I Ebb'd with the Ocean of Life," which Whitman included in the 1860 edition of *Leaves of Grass*. In this respect, "Corsons Inlet" is a poem about the art of poetry, the development and shape of Ammons's career, and his relation to his American literary precursors—not only Whitman but also William Carlos Williams and Gary Snyder, among others, who also experimented with line length and typography and who are also, in their different ways, astute observers of land, space, and geography. Ralph Waldo Emerson, Wallace Stevens, and Elizabeth Bishop are in the background of Ammons's great and ambitious poem as well.

For Ammons, as "Corsons Inlet" bears witness, freedom lies in flux, in process, and hence he resists fixity. He sights and wanders through and contests boundaries, even as he maintains creative control—an orderliness—throughout the action of his poem.

For an overview, see Alan Holder, *A. R. Ammons* (1979). For critical interpretation, see Steven Paul Schneider, *A. R. Ammons and the Poetics of Widening Scope* (1994); *Critical Essays on A. R. Ammons*, ed. Robert Kirschten (1997); and *Complexities of Motion: New Essays on A. R. Ammons' Long Poems*, ed. Steven Paul Schneider (1999). See also Nick Halpern, *Everyday and Prophetic: The Poetry of Lowell, Ammons, Merrill, and Rich* (2003); and *Considering the Radiance: Essays on the Poetry of A. R. Ammons*, eds. David Burak and Roger Gilbert (2005), a wide-ranging, stimulating collection.

Corsons Inlet[1]

I went for a walk over the dunes again this morning
to the sea,
then turned right along
    the surf
           rounded a naked headland   5
        and returned

    along the inlet shore:

it was muggy sunny, the wind from the sea steady and high,
crisp in the running sand,
        some breakthroughs of sun   10
    but after a bit

continuous overcast:

the walk liberating, I was released from forms,
from the perpendiculars,
        straight lines, blocks, boxes, binds   15
of thought
into the hues, shadings, rises, flowing bends and blends
        of sight:

           I allow myself eddies of meaning:
yield to a direction of significance   20
running
like a stream through the geography of my work:
        you can find

[1]Corsons Inlet is located in southeast New Jersey, near Ocean City.

in my sayings
     swerves of action   25
      like the inlet's cutting edge:
  there are dunes of motion,
organizations of grass, white sandy paths of remembrance
in the overall wandering of mirroring mind:

but Overall is beyond me: is the sum of these events 30
I cannot draw, the ledger I cannot keep, the accounting
beyond the account:

in nature there are few sharp lines: there are areas of
primrose
    more or less dispersed;   35
disorderly orders of bayberry; between the rows
of dunes,
irregular swamps of reeds,
though not reeds alone, but grass, bayberry, yarrow, all...
predominantly reeds: 40

I have reached no conclusions, have erected no boundaries,
shutting out and shutting in, separating inside
    from outside: I have
    drawn no lines:
    as   45

manifold events of sand
change the dune's shape that will not be the same shape
tomorrow,

so I am willing to go along, to accept
the becoming   50
thought, to stake off no beginnings or ends, establish
    no walls:

by transitions the land falls from grassy dunes to creek
to undercreek: but there are no lines, though
    change in that transition is clear   55
    as any sharpness: but "sharpness" spread out,
allowed to occur over a wider range
than mental lines can keep:

the moon was full last night: today, low tide was low:
black shoals of mussels exposed to the risk   60
of air
and, earlier, of sun,
waved in and out with the waterline, waterline inexact,

caught always in the event of change:
> a young mottled gull stood free on the shoals   65
> and ate
to vomiting: another gull, squawking possession, cracked a crab,
picked out the entrails, swallowed the soft-shelled legs, a ruddy
turnstone[2] running in to snatch leftover bits:

risk is full: every living thing in   70
siege: the demand is life, to keep life: the small
white blacklegged egret, how beautiful, quietly stalks and spears
> > the shallows, darts to shore
> > > to stab—what? I couldn't
> > see against the black mudflats—a frightened   75
> > fiddler crab?

> > > the news to my left over the dunes and
reeds and bayberry clumps was
> > fall: thousands of tree swallows
> > gathering for flight: 80
> > an order held
> > > in constant change: a congregation
rich with entropy: nevertheless, separable, noticeable
> > as one event,
> > > > not chaos: preparations for   85
flight from winter,
cheet, cheet, cheet, cheet, wings rifling the green clumps,
beaks
at the bayberries
> > a perception full of wind, flight, curve,   90
> > sound:
> > the possibility of rule as the sum of rulelessness:
the "field" of action
with moving, incalculable center:

in the smaller view, order tight with shape: 95
blue tiny flowers on a leafless weed: carapace[3] of crab:
snail shell:
> > pulsations of order
> > in the bellies of minnows: orders swallowed,
broken down, transferred through membranes   100
to strengthen larger orders: but in the large view, no

---

[2]*Arenaria interpres,* a small, short-legged shore bird.
[3]Shell.

lines or changeless shapes: the working in and out, together
       and against, of millions of events: this,
          so that I make
          no form of   105
          formlessness:

orders as summaries, as outcomes of actions override
or in some way result, not predictably (seeing me gain
the top of a dune,
the swallows   110
could take flight—some other fields of bayberry
       could enter fall
          berryless) and there is serenity:

       no arranged terror: no forcing of image, plan,
or thought: 115
no propaganda, no humbling of reality to precept:

terror pervades but is not arranged, all possibilities
of escape open: no route shut, except in
the sudden loss of all routes:

       I see narrow orders, limited tightness, but will   120
not run to that easy victory:
       still around the looser, wider forces work:
       I will try
    to fasten into order enlarging grasps of disorder, widening
scope, but enjoying the freedom that   125
Scope eludes my grasp, that there is no finality of vision,
that I have perceived nothing completely,
       that tomorrow a new walk is a new walk.

                                [1965]

JAMES MERRILL ■ (1926–1995)

James Merrill, born in New York City, was the son of Charles Merrill, co-founder of the brokerage firm Merrill, Lynch & Company. His background of wealth and privilege enabled him to attend exclusive schools and focus on literature, art, and music and to pursue a career as a poet. Later, in the mid-1950s, through an inheritance, Merrill established the Ingram Merrill Foundation, which has awarded hundreds of grants to writers and artists.

Merrill was an undergraduate at Amherst College, where he made the acquaintance of Robert Frost and the eminent literary critic Reuben Brower. Service in the U.S. Army disrupted his college years; he graduated in 1947, *summa cum laude* and Phi Beta Kappa, the author of a senior thesis on the modern French novelist Marcel Proust, and a poet whose work had been published in *Poetry* magazine and *The Kenyon Review*, a distinguished literary quarterly.

Merrill then taught at Barnard College, but he left after a year to spend two and a half years traveling in Europe. His *First Poems* was published in 1951, followed by *The Country of a Thousand Years of Peace* (1959) and *Water Street* (1962). Critics praised all three for their elegance and skill, but some called attention to an overrefinement in the tone and sensibility—too much art for art's sake alone. Merrill's next three books, *Nights and Days* (1966), which won the National Book Award for poetry, *The Fire Screen* (1969), and *Braving the Elements* (1972), received high praise for their lyric poise and insight, especially on the subject of love, and secured his position as a major voice, worthy to be mentioned in the same breath with such canonical figures as W. H. Auden and Wallace Stevens.

In 1955 Merrill and his companion David Jackson settled in Stonington, Connecticut, though from 1959 to 1979 they lived part of each year in Athens, Greece, and over the years spent a good deal of time in Key West, Florida, as well. Merrill died of AIDS in 1995.

The author of novels and autobiographical works, Merrill was above all a major, influential poet whose other enduring books include *Divine Comedies* (1976); *The Changing Light at Sandover* (1982), which reflects Merrill's and Jackson's interest in the occult and the world of spirits; *From the First Nine: Poems 1946–1976* (1982); *Selected Poems 1946–1985* (1992); and *Collected Poems* (2001). About *Collected Poems*, the critic Helen Vendler said, "If you have despaired of finding words subtle enough for all that goes on between lovers over time; if you are delighted by poetic invention, Merrill will please you. If you are eager for a window into the pangs and pleasures of gay existence, or if you want to know what a person of ever-attentive receptivity might have seen between 1926 and 1995, Merrill will please you."

In the memory poem, "The Broken Home," from *Nights and Days* (1966), Merrill recalls his parents' marriage, which ended in divorce. Speaking of this poem in an interview (1982), Merrill noted:

> History in our time has cut loose, has broken faith with Nature. But poems, even those of the most savage incandescence, can't deal frontally with such huge, urgent subjects without sounding grumpy or dated when they should still be in their prime. So my parents' divorce dramatized on a human scale a subject that couldn't have been handled otherwise. Which is what a "poetic" turn of mind allows for. You don't see eternity except in the grain of sand, or history except at the family dinner table.

Playful in places, bitter in others, risking but not lapsing into self-pity, sensitive to and ironic about everyday idioms and commonplace sayings, "The Broken Home" shows Merrill's power to seize on an incident or moment or relationship (often one from his own life) and reveal its deep mythic significance. "His common style is a net of loose talk tightening to verse," the literary critic Denis Donoghue observed, "a mode in which anything can be said with grace." "Chronicles of love and loss" was Merrill's own phrase for his practice as a poet, and "The Broken Home" is an example of how love's wounds and losses can be faced, given form, and worked through.

For biographical context, see Alison Lurie, *Familiar Spirits: A Memoir of James Merrill and David Jackson* (2001). See also Merrill's memoir, *A Different Person* (1994). For critical discussion, the following are recommended: *James Merrill, Essays in Criticism*, eds. David Lehman and Charles Berger (1983); Stephen Yenser, *The Consuming Myth: The Work of James Merrill* (1987); *Critical Essays on James Merrill*, ed. Guy L. Rotella (1996); and Timothy Materer, *James Merrill's Apocalypse* (2000). See also Nick Halpern, *Everyday and Prophetic: The Poetry of Lowell, Ammons, Merrill, and Rich* (2003). For further study of Merrill in relation to other modern and contemporary poets, see Ann Keniston, *Overheard Voices: Address and Subjectivity in Postmodern American Poetry* (2006); and Siobhan Phillips, *The Poetics of the Everyday: Creative Repetition in Modern American Verse* (2010). On sexual themes, see Peter Nickowitz, *Rhetoric and Sexuality: The Poetry of Hart Crane, Elizabeth Bishop, and James Merrill* (2006); and Piotr K. Gwiazda, *James Merrill and W. H. Auden: Homosexuality and Poetic Influence* (2007).

The Broken Home

Crossing the street,
I saw the parents and the child
At their window, gleaming like fruit
With evening's mild gold leaf.

In a room on the floor below,   5
Sunless, cooler—a brimming
Saucer of wax, marbly and dim—
I have lit what's left of my life.

I have thrown out yesterday's milk
And opened a book of maxims.   10
The flame quickens. The word stirs.

Tell me, tongue of fire,
That you and I are real
At least as the people upstairs.
My father, who had flown in World War I,   15
Might have continued to invest his life
In cloud banks well above Wall Street and wife.
But the race was run below, and the point was to win.

Too late now, I make out in his blue gaze
(Through the smoked glass of being thirty-six)   20
The soul eclipsed by twin black pupils, sex
And business; time was money in those days.

Each thirteenth year he married. When he died
There were already several chilled wives
In sable orbit—rings, cars, permanent waves.   25
We'd felt him warming up for a green bride.

He could afford it. He was "in his prime"
At three score ten. But money was not time.

When my parents were younger this was a popular act:
A veiled woman would leap from an electric, wine-dark car   30
To the steps of no matter what—the Senate or the Ritz Bar—
And bodily, at newsreel speed, attack.

No matter whom—Al Smith[1] or José Maria Sert[2]
Or Clemenceau[3]—veins standing out on her throat
As she yelled *War mongerer! Pig! Give us the vote!*,[4]   35
And would have to be hauled away in her hobble skirt.

---

[1]Alfred E. Smith (1873–1944), a New York politician who served as governor (elected in 1918, defeated in 1920, and reelected 1922–28) and ran for president (1928).
[2]Spanish painter (1876–1945) noted for his paintings in the lobby in the Waldorf-Astoria Hotel in New York City.
[3]Georges Clemenceau (1841–1929), French statesman and prime minister (1906–09, 1917–20), who was a vocal opponent of women's suffrage.
[4]Women could not vote in the United States until 1920, when the Nineteenth Amendment to the Constitution was ratified.

What had the man done? Oh, made history.
Her business (he had implied) was giving birth,
Tending the house, mending the socks.

Always that same old story—   40
Father Time and Mother Earth,[5]
A marriage on the rocks.

One afternoon, red, satyr-thighed
Michael, the Irish setter, head
Passionately lowered, led   45
The child I was to a shut door. Inside,

Blinds beat sun from the bed.
The green-gold room throbbed like a bruise.
Under a sheet, clad in taboos
Lay whom we sought, her hair undone, outspread,   50

And of a blackness found, if ever now, in old
Engravings where the acid bit.
I must have needed to touch it
Or the whiteness—was she dead?
Her eyes flew open, startled strange and cold.   55
The dog slumped to the floor. She reached for me. I fled.

Tonight they have stepped out onto the gravel.
The party is over. It's the fall
Of 1931. They love each other still.

She: Charlie, I can't stand the pace.   60
He: Come on, honey—why, you'll bury us all!

A lead soldier guards my windowsill:
Khaki rifle, uniform, and face.
Something in me grows heavy, silvery, pliable.

How intensely people used to feel!   65
Like metal poured at the close of a proletarian novel,[6]
Refined and glowing from the crucible,
I see those two hearts, I'm afraid,
Still. Cool here in the graveyard of good and evil,
They are even so to be honored and obeyed.   70

...Obeyed, at least, inversely. Thus
I rarely buy a newspaper, or vote.

---

[5]A possible reference to the tumultuous union of Cronus, the Greek god of time, and his wife, Rhea, mother
of the gods. Rhea plotted to overthrow Cronus because he ate his children as soon as they were born.
[6]A novel that extols the struggles of the working classes.

To do so, I have learned, is to invite
The tread of a stone guest[7] within my house.
Shooting this rusted bolt, though, against him,   75
I trust I am no less time's child than some
Who on the heath impersonate Poor Tom[8]
Or on the barricades risk life and limb.

Nor do I try to keep a garden, only
An avocado in the glass of water—   80
Roots pallid, gemmed with air. And later,

When the small gilt leaves have grown
Fleshy and green, I let them die, yes, yes,
And start another. I am earth's no less.

A child, a red dog roam the corridors,   85
Still, of the broken home. No sound. The brilliant
Rag runners halt before wide-open doors.
My old room! Its wallpaper—cream, medallioned
With pink and brown—brings back the first nightmares,
Long summer colds, and Emma, sepia-faced,   90
Perspiring over broth carried upstairs
Aswim with golden fats I could not taste.

The real house became a boarding-school.
Under the ballroom ceiling's allegory
Someone at last may actually be allowed   95
To learn something; or, from my window, cool
With the unstiflement of the entire story,
Watch a red setter stretch and sink in cloud.

                                                              [1966]

---

[7]A character in Mozart's opera *Don Giovanni* (1787).
[8]A reference to Shakespeare's *King Lear*, in which Edgar, disowned by his father, wanders the heath
disguised as an insane beggar called Poor Tom.

ROBERT CREELEY ■ (1926–2005)

The poet and essayist John Ashbery said of Robert Creeley, "His poetry is as basic and necessary as the air we breathe; as hospitable, plain and open as our continent itself. He is about the best we have."

Creeley was born in Arlington, Massachusetts, a few miles west of Boston. His father, a doctor, died when Creeley was four years old. Raised in a family of women, "I was shy of the word 'poet,'" he recalled, "and all its associations in a world I was then intimate with. It was not, in short, a fit attention for a young man raised in the New England manner, compact of Puritanically deprived senses of speech and sensuality." He attended Harvard University in the mid-1940s but did not graduate. For a time he worked as a farmer in New Hampshire and attempted to launch a literary magazine with Charles Olson, with whom he started a wide-ranging exchange of letters. Hundreds of these letters have now been published (nine volumes, 1980–90), and at one juncture Creeley was spending as many as eight hours per day on them.

Olson had perhaps the greatest impact on Creeley's formation as a poet, though he also drew upon Walt Whitman, Hart Crane, Ezra Pound, and William Carlos Williams as well as abstract art and jazz (he responded to the improvisational spirit of the music and its deployment of sound and silence). Creeley also benefited from the support of the Boston writer and poet Cid Corman, editor of the literary magazine *Origin*.

During the early 1950s, Creeley lived with his wife in France, and there they established a press that published work by Creeley himself, Olson, Robert Duncan, and others. Olson then invited him to teach at Black Mountain College, an experimental liberal arts school in North Carolina, which led to Creeley's founding of *The Black Mountain Review* (1954–57).

Creeley's first books of poetry appeared in a cluster: *Le Fou* (1952); *The Kind of Act Of* (1953); *The Immoral Proposition* (1953); *All That Is Lovely in Men* (1955); and *If You* (1956). Divorced and remarried, he lived and taught in New Mexico in the late 1950s before moving to the Buffalo campus of the State University of New York. Already an influential literary figure, he won national critical acclaim with the publication of *For Love: Poems 1950–1960* in 1962.

The critic Nicholas Everett described Creeley's style as a "unique brand of vigilant minimalism," calling attention to the typical shortness of the lines and stanzas, the terse statements, the deliberately limited vocabulary, and the use of free verse—qualities the following poems display. "Form is never more than an extension of content," Creeley professed. He noted too, "There's an appropriate way of saying something inherent in the thing to be said."

Much of Creeley's best work is highly concentrated in its organizations of language—"You can't derail a train by standing directly in front of it, or, not quite. But, a tiny piece of steel, properly placed...." Sometimes obscure and elliptical in its movements and transitions (which may not be there in the poem at all), Creeley's most memorable work dwells on the complex experience of love—difficult to come by and secure (Creeley divorced and remarried a third time in 1977), tempered by doubt, driven by desire, its bodily yearning and instinct held back by mind. Summing up his aims as a poet, Creeley said: "I write to realize the world as one has come to live in it, thus to give testament. I write to move in words, a human delight. I write when no other act is possible."

Creeley has been extraordinarily prolific; he is the author of more than sixty books of poetry. He has observed, "Why poetry? Its materials are so constant, simple, elusive, specific. It costs so little and so much. It preoccupies a life, yet can only find one living. It is a music, a playful construct of feeling, a last word and communion." The core of his achievement can be examined in *The Collected Poems, 1945–1975* (1982), which should be supplemented by the *Collected Prose* (1984) and *Collected Essays* (1989).

Introductory studies include Arthur L. Ford, *Robert Creeley* (1978); and Cynthia Dubin Edelberg, *Robert Creeley's Poetry: A Critical Introduction* (1978). For biography, see Ekbert Faas with Maria Trombacco, *Robert Creeley: A Biography* (2001). Recommended too is *Robert Creeley: The Poet's Workshop*, ed. Carroll F. Terrell (1984); and *Robert Creeley's Life and Work: A Sense of Increment*, ed. John Wilson (1987). See also *Form, Power, and Person in Robert Creeley's Life and Work*, eds. Stephen Fredman and Steve McCaffery (2010).

For Love

for Bobbie[1]

Yesterday I wanted to
speak of it, that sense above
the others to me
important because all

that I know derives   5
from what it teaches me.
today, what is it that
is finally so helpless,

different, despairs of its own
statement, wants to   10
turn away, endlessly
to turn away.

If the moon did not...
no, if you did not
I wouldn't either, but   15
what would I not

---

[1]Creeley's second wife.

do, what prevention, what
thing so quickly stopped.
That is love yesterday
or tomorrow, not   20

now. Can I eat
what you give me. I
have not earned it. Must
I think of everything

as earned. Now love also   25
becomes a reward so
remote from me I have
only made it with my mind.

Here is tedium,
despair, a painful   30
sense of isolation and
whimsical if pompous

self-regard. But that image
is only of the mind's
vague structure, vague to me   35
because it is my own.

Love, what do I think
to say. I cannot say it.
What have you become to ask,
what have I made you into,   40

companion, good company,
crossed legs with skirt, or
soft body under
the bones of the bed.

Nothing says anything   45
but that which it wishes
would come true, fears
what else might happen in

some other place, some
other time not this one.   50
A voice in my place, an
echo of that only in yours,

Let me stumble into
not the confession but
the obsession I begin with   55
now. For you

also (also)
some time beyond place, or
place beyond time, no
mind left to   60

say anything at all,
that face gone, now.
Into the company of love[1]
it all returns.

[1962]

The Messengers

for Allen Ginsberg[1]

The huge dog, Broderick, and
the smile of the quick eyes
of Allen light a kind world.

Their feelings, under some distance
of remote skin, must touch,   5
wondering at what impatience does

block them. So little love
to share among so many, so much
yellow-orange hair, on the one,

and on the other, such a darkness   10
of long hanging hair now, such
slightness of body, and a voice that

rises on the sounds of feeling.
Aie! It raises the world, lifts,
falls, like a sudden sunlight, like   15

that edge of the black night sweeps
the low lying fields, of soft grasses,
bodies, fills them with quiet longing.

[1967]

---

[1]From the poem "The Broken Tower," by Hart Crane (1899–1932). "And so it was I entered the broken world / To trace the visionary company of love, its voice / An instant in the wind (I know not whither hurled) / But not for long to hold each desperate choice."
[1]American poet (1926–97) known for pioneering the Beat Movement. He helped to lead the revolt against "academic poetry" and the cultural and political establishment of the 1950s and 1960s.

Allen Ginsberg was born in Newark, New Jersey, the son of Russian Jewish immigrants. His father was a teacher, a poet, and a socialist; and his mother, a Communist, suffered periods of extreme mental disorder and distress. Ginsberg attended Columbia University (his goal was a career as a radical labor lawyer), and during these years in New York City he became friends with Jack Kerouac and William S. Burroughs.

After graduation and a few odd jobs, Ginsberg traveled to San Francisco, drawn to its atmosphere of radical politics, anarchist thought, and rebellious bohemian lifestyles. There he became a leader of the Beat movement (beaten down and beatific), whose members were disaffected and alienated, the restless and hip nay-sayers and joy-seekers, hungry for liberation.

Ginsberg's arrival on the literary scene was the publication in 1956 of the fervent, fiery, bardic *Howl and Other Poems*—a book that led to the arrest of its publisher, Lawrence Ferlinghetti, because of the explicitly sexual and scandalous language it contained. Ginsberg first presented the poem in an oral performance in October 1955, an event that has assumed legendary proportions in the history of American literature and counterculture.

Ginsberg's next book was *Kaddish and Other Poems* (1961); the title poem (twice as long as "Howl") is a passionate lament for his deceased mother, a grim and moving work that the poet Robert Lowell called a "terrible masterpiece." Ginsberg himself judged "Kaddish" the best poem he ever wrote, though in literary historical terms its impact was less momentous than that of "Howl."

Ginsberg wrote many books in later years, gave countless readings and speeches, traveled widely, and served as a counterculture representative par excellence during the 1960s and beyond, the embodiment of "Beat." He was active in the civil rights and antiwar movements and, later, in the cause of gay liberation. Influences on his work range from William Blake and Walt Whitman to the French poet Arthur Rimbaud and the Czech-born German writer Franz Kafka to the American poet William Carlos Williams (to whom the young Ginsberg wrote letters and who in turn wrote the Introduction to *Howl and Other Poems*), Greenwich Village gay bars, mysticism, Zen Buddhism, and marijuana and LSD.

"Howl" celebrates the lives of those who live at high intensity, even as it attacks the forces of materialism and conformity that harass, oppress, and destroy them. Carl Solomon, to whom the poem is dedicated, was such a figure himself, a poet whom Ginsberg first met in a mental hospital in the late 1940s, where they were being treated. Ginsberg described his intention as follows:

> I wouldn't write a *poem*, but just write what I wanted to without fear, let my imagination go, open secrecy, and scribble magic lines from my real mind.... Something I wouldn't be able to show anybody, writ for my own soul's ear and a few other golden ears.

Big, bold, highly personal, provocative, brashly and outrageously direct about sex and politics, Ginsberg's poem injected a new energy and excitement and sense of possibility into American poetry. The singer-songwriter Bob Dylan observed, "Ginsberg is both tragic and dynamic, a lyrical genius, con-man extraordinaire and probably the single greatest influence on American poetical voice since Walt Whitman." The critic Helen Vendler added that his "powerful mixture of Blake, Whitman, Pound, and Williams, to which he added his own volatile, grotesque, and tender humor, has assured him a memorable place in modern poetry."

Two comments from mid-1990s interviews with Ginsberg offer insights into the conception of poetry he embraced and had put into action four decades earlier:

> Poetry's role is to provide spontaneous individual candor as distinct from manipulators and brainwash.

> Poetry is the one place where people can speak their original human mind. It is the outlet for people to say in public what is known in private.

Important primary sources are Ginsberg's *Collected Poems, 1947–1997* (2006); *The Book of Martyrdom and Artifice: First Journals and Poems, 1937–1952* (2008), eds. Juanita Lieberman-Plimpton and Bill Morgan; and *The Letters of Allen Ginsberg*, ed. Bill Morgan (2008). Biographies include Barry Miles, *Ginsberg: A Biography* (1989); and Graham Caveney, *Screaming with Joy: The Life of Allen Ginsberg* (1999). See also James Campbell, *This Is the Beat Generation: New York, San Francisco, Paris* (2001). Also illuminating is *Spontaneous Mind: Selected Interviews, 1958–1996, Allen Ginsberg*, ed. David Carter (2001). For critical interpretation, see *On the Poetry of Allen Ginsberg*, ed. Lewis Hyde (1984); and John Lardas, *The Bop Apocalypse: The Religious Visions of Kerouac, Ginsberg, and Burroughs* (2001). See also for biography and context Bill Morgan, *I Celebrate Myself: The Somewhat Private Life of Allen Ginsberg* (2006). On the poem "Howl": Jonah Raskin, *Allen Ginsberg's Howl and the Making of the Beat Generation* (2004); and Jason Shinder, *The Poem That Changed America: Howl Fifty Years Later*, ed. Jason Shinder (2006).

Howl

For Carl Solomon[1]

I

I saw the best minds of my generation destroyed by madness,
    starving hysterical naked,

---

[1]One of Ginsberg's friends had been using his apartment to store stolen goods used to support a drug habit. To avoid prosecution as an accomplice, Ginsberg pleaded insanity and in 1949 spent eight months at Columbia Psychiatric Institute, where he met Carl Solomon (1928–93), a patient who was receiving shock therapy at the hospital.

dragging themselves through the negro streets at dawn looking for
    an angry fix,

angelheaded hipsters burning for the ancient heavenly connection   5
    to the starry dynamo in the machinery of night,

who poverty and tatters and hollow-eyed and high sat up smoking
    in the supernatural darkness of cold-water flats floating across
    the tops of cities contemplating jazz,

who bared their brains to Heaven under the El[2] and saw   10
    Mohammedan angels[3] staggering on tenement roofs
    illuminated,

who passed through universities with radiant cool eyes
    hallucinating Arkansas and Blake-light[4] tragedy among the
    scholars of war,   15

who were expelled from the academies for crazy & publishing
    obscene odes on the windows of the skull,[5]

who cowered in unshaven rooms in underwear, burning their
    money in wastebaskets and listening to the Terror through the
    wall,   20

who got busted in their pubic beards returning through Laredo[6]
    with a belt of marijuana for New York,

who ate fire in paint hotels or drank turpentine in Paradise Alley,[7]
    death, or purgatoried their torsos night after night

with dreams, with drugs, with waking nightmares, alcohol and   25
    cock and endless balls,

incomparable blind streets of shuddering cloud and lightning in
    the mind leaping toward poles of Canada & Paterson,[8]
    illuminating all the motionless world of Time between,

Peyote solidities of halls, backyard green tree cemetery dawns,   30
    wine drunkenness over the rooftops, storefront boroughs of
    teahead joyride neon blinking traffic light, sun and moon and
    tree vibrations in the roaring winter dusks of Brooklyn, ashcan
    rantings and kind king light of mind,

who chained themselves to subways for the endless ride from   35
    Battery to holy Bronx[9] on benzedrine until the noise of wheels
    and children brought them down shuddering mouth-wracked

[2]The elevated train in New York City. Also, the Hebrew word for "God."

[3]Relating to Muhammad. When used in place of *Muslim* or *Islamic*, the term is now seen as deprecatory or offensive because it makes a human being central in their religion, a position that Muslims believe only Allah should occupy.

[4]Alluding to the English poet William Blake (1757–1827).

[5]In 1945, while a student at Columbia University, Ginsberg was suspended for writing (ironic) anti-Semitic remarks on his dormitory window.

[6]An industrial port city in southern Texas.

[7]A depressed area of New York's Lower East Side, not far from the Five Points slum and gang area, and the setting of the novel *The Subterraneans* (1958), by Jack Kerouac (1922–69).

[8]The city in New Jersey, near Newark, where Ginsberg was born. The town is celebrated in the poem "Paterson" by William Carlos Williams (1883–1963), a friend and mentor of Ginsberg's.

[9]The opposite ends of New York City. The Battery is at the southern tip of Manhattan; the Bronx is the northernmost borough.

and battered bleak of brain all drained of brilliance in the
  drear light of Zoo,
who sank all night in submarine light of Bickford's floated out   40
  and sat through the stale beer afternoon in desolate
  Fugazzi's[10] listening to the crack of doom on the hydrogen
  jukebox,
who talked continuously seventy hours from park to pad to bar to
  Bellevue[11] to museum to the Brooklyn Bridge,   45
a lost battalion of platonic conversationalists jumping down the
  stoops off fire escapes off windowsills off Empire State out of
  the moon,
yacketayakking screaming vomiting whispering facts and memories
  and anecdotes and eyeball kicks and shocks of hospitals[12] and   50
  jails and wars,
whole intellects disgorged in total recall for seven days and nights
  with brilliant eyes, meat for the Synagogue cast on the pavement,
who vanished into nowhere Zen New Jersey leaving a trail of   55
  ambiguous picture postcards of Atlantic City Hall,
suffering Eastern sweats and Tangerian bone-grindings and
  migraines of China[13] under junk-withdrawal in Newark's bleak
  furnished room,
who wandered around and around at midnight in the railroad yard   60
  wondering where to go, and went, leaving no broken hearts,
who lit cigarettes in boxcars boxcars boxcars racketing through
  snow toward lonesome farms in grandfather night,
who studied Plotinus[14] Poe[15] St. John of the Cross[16] telepathy and bop[17]
  kaballah[18] because the cosmos instinctively vibrated at their feet   65
  in Kansas,
who loned it through the streets of Idaho seeking visionary indian
  angels who were visionary indian angels,
who thought they were only mad when Baltimore gleamed in
  supernatural ecstasy,   70

[10]A bar in Greenwich Village that was a hangout for the Beats. Ginsberg was a leader of the Beat movement, which originally comprised young writers and artists who adopted unconventional dress, habits, and manners as a form of self-expression and social protest.
[11]A hospital in New York City known for its psychiatric ward.
[12]Shock therapy used on psychiatric patients, including Carl Solomon, to whom Ginsberg's poem is dedicated.
[13]Allusions to the negative effects of drugs, especially heroin. Ginsberg's friend, William S. Burroughs (1914–97), described heroin withdrawal in his *Letters to Allen Ginsberg* (1953–57).
[14]The Greek philosopher Plotinus (204–270) is considered the founder of Neo-Platonism. Building from the teachings of Plato, Plotinus postulated that all existence emanates from the union of three hypostases: the one, the intelligence, and the soul.
[15]American poet and writer (1809–49), known for his dark tales of the supernatural.
[16]John de Yepes (1542–91), a Spanish mystic poet who was canonized as a saint in 1726. He is best known for his work *The Dark Night of the Soul*.
[17]Be-bop music, developed in the early 1940s, was an extension of jazz, featuring harmonic complexity and rapid tempos.
[18]The teachings of Jewish mysticism.

who jumped in limousines with the Chinaman of Oklahoma on the
impulse of winter midnight streetlight smalltown rain,

who lounged hungry and lonesome through Houston seeking jazz
or sex or soup, and followed the brilliant Spaniard to
converse about America and Eternity, a hopeless task, and so 75
took ship to Africa,

who disappeared into the volcanoes of Mexico leaving behind
nothing but the shadow of dungarees and the lava and ash of
poetry scattered in fireplace Chicago,

who reappeared on the West Coast investigating the F.B.I. in 80
beards and shorts with big pacifist eyes sexy in their dark skin
passing out incomprehensible leaflets,

who burned cigarette holes in their arms protesting the narcotic
tobacco haze of Capitalism,

who distributed Supercommunist pamphlets in Union Square 85
weeping and undressing while the sirens of Los Alamos[19] wailed
them down, and wailed down Wall,[20] and the Staten Island
ferry also wailed,

who broke down crying in white gymnasiums naked and trembling
before the machinery of other skeletons, 90

who bit detectives in the neck and shrieked with delight in
policecars for committing no crime but their own wild
cooking pederasty and intoxication,

who howled on their knees in the subway and were dragged off
the roof waving genitals and manuscripts, 95

who let themselves be fucked in the ass by saintly motorcyclists,
and screamed with joy,

who blew and were blown by those human seraphim, the sailors,
caresses of Atlantic and Caribbean love,

who balled in the morning in the evenings in rosegardens and the 100
grass of public parks and cemeteries scattering their semen
freely to whomever come who may,

who hiccupped endlessly trying to giggle but wound up with a sob
behind a partition in a Turkish Bath when the blonde &
naked angel came to pierce them with a sword,[21] 105

who lost their loveboys to the three old shrews of fate[22] the one
eyed shrew of the heterosexual dollar the one eyed shrew that
winks out of the womb and the one eyed shrew that does

---

[19]The location in New Mexico of the headquarters of the center responsible for the development of the atomic bomb.

[20]A reference to both Wall Street and the Western (or "Wailing") Wall in Jerusalem, a public place for the expression of grief by Jews.

[21]A reference to the sculpture *The Ecstasy of St. Teresa* by Lorenzo Bernini (1598–1680). It is based on the vision of St. Teresa (1515–82), in which she was visited by an angel who pierced her with the love of God.

[22]In Greek and Roman mythology, the three Fates were goddesses who controlled everyone's destiny. Clotho spun the thread of a person's life. Lachesis decided how long the thread would be. Atropos cut the thread.

nothing but sit on her ass and snip the intellectual golden
    threads of the craftsman's loom,   110
who copulated ecstatic and insatiate with a bottle of beer a
    sweetheart a package of cigarettes a candle and fell off the
    bed, and continued along the floor and down the hall and
    ended fainting on the wall with a vision of ultimate cunt and
    come eluding the last gyzym of consciousness,   115
who sweetened the snatches of a million girls trembling in the
    sunset, and were red eyed in the morning but prepared to
    sweeten the snatch of the sunrise, flashing buttocks under
    barns and naked in the lake,
who went out whoring through Colorado in myriad stolen night   120
    cars, N.C.,[23] secret hero of these poems, cocksman and
    Adonis[24] of Denver—joy to the memory of his innumerable lays
    of girls in empty lots & diner backyards, moviehouses' rickety
    rows, on mountaintops in caves or with gaunt waitresses in
    familiar roadside lonely petticoat upliftings & especially secret   125
    gas-station solipsisms of johns, & hometown alleys too,
who faded out in vast sordid movies, were shifted in dreams, woke
    on a sudden Manhattan, and picked themselves up out of
    basements hungover with heartless Tokay[25] and horrors of
    Third Avenue iron dreams & stumbled to unemployment   130
    offices,
who walked all night with their shoes full of blood on the
    snowbank docks waiting for a door in the East River to open
    to a room full of steamheat and opium,
who created great suicidal dramas on the apartment cliff-banks of   135
    the Hudson under the wartime blue floodlight of the moon &
    their heads shall be crowned with laurel in oblivion,
who ate the lamb stew of the imagination or digested the crab at
    the muddy bottom of the rivers of Bowery[26]
who wept at the romance of the streets with their pushcarts full of   140
    onions and bad music,
who sat in boxes breathing in the darkness under the bridge, and
    rose up to build harpsichords in their lofts,
who coughed on the sixth floor of Harlem crowned with flame
    under the tubercular sky surrounded by orange crates of   145
    theology,
who scribbled all night rocking and rolling over lofty incantations
    which in the yellow morning were stanzas of gibberish,

[23]Neal Cassady, a Beat generation author (1926–68) with whom Ginsberg had a sexual relationship.
[24]In ancient Greek mythology, Adonis was a beautiful youth who was beloved by Aphrodite.
[25]A sweet wine.
[26]A main street on New York's Lower East Side known to be frequented by transients and alcoholics.

who cooked rotten animals lung heart feet tail borscht & tortillas
    dreaming of the pure vegetable kingdom, 150
who plunged themselves under meat trucks looking for an egg,
who threw their watches off the roof to cast their ballot for
    Eternity outside of Time, & alarm clocks fell on their heads
    every day for the next decade,
who cut their wrists three times successively unsuccessfully, gave 155
    up and were forced to open antique stores where they thought
    they were growing old and cried,
who were burned alive in their innocent flannel suits on Madison
    Avenue[27] amid blasts of leaden verse & the tanked-up clatter of
    the iron regiments of fashion & the nitroglycerine shrieks of 160
    the fairies of advertising & the mustard gas of sinister
    intelligent editors, or were run down by the drunken taxicabs
    of Absolute Reality,
who jumped off the Brooklyn Bridge this actually happened and
    walked away unknown and forgotten into the ghostly daze of 165
    Chinatown soup alleyways & firetrucks, not even one free
    beer,
who sang out of their windows in despair, fell out of the subway
    window, jumped in the filthy Passaic,[28] leaped on negroes, cried
    all over the street, danced on broken wineglasses barefoot 170
    smashed phonograph records of nostalgic European 1930's
    German jazz finished the whiskey and threw up groaning into
    the bloody toilet, moans in their ears and the blast of colossal
    steamwhistles,
who barreled down the highways of the past journeying to each 175
    other's hotrod-Golgotha[29] jail-solitude watch or Birmingham
    jazz incarnation,
who drove crosscountry seventytwo hours to find out if I had a
    vision or you had a vision or he had a vision to find out
    Eternity, 180
who journeyed to Denver,[30] who died in Denver, who came back to
    Denver & waited in vain, who watched over Denver &
    brooded & loned in Denver and finally went away to find out
    the Time, & now Denver is lonesome for her heroes,
who fell on their knees in hopeless cathedrals praying for each 185
    other's salvation and light and breasts, until the soul
    illuminated its hair for a second,

[27]Street recognized as the center of New York advertising and marketing agencies.
[28]The river that runs past Paterson, New Jersey.
[29]The hill on which Jesus was said to be crucified.
[30]A reference to lines by Kerouac—"Down in Denver, / Down in Denver, / All I did was die"—that
appear in drafts for his poem *Shroudy Stranger of the Night*.

who crashed through their minds in jail waiting for impossible
　criminals with golden heads and the charm of reality in their
　hearts who sang sweet blues to Alcatraz,[31]　　　　190
who retired to Mexico to cultivate a habit, or Rocky Mount to
　tender Buddha or Tangiers to boys or Southern Pacific to the
　black locomotive or Harvard to Narcissus to Woodlawn[32] to
　the daisychain or grave,
who demanded sanity trials accusing the radio of hypnotism &　　195
　were left with their insanity & their hands & a hung jury,
who threw potato salad at CCNY[33] lecturers on Dadaism[34] and
　subsequently presented themselves on the granite steps of the
　madhouse with shaven heads and harlequin speech of suicide,
　demanding instantaneous lobotomy,　　　　200
and who were given instead the concrete void of insulin metrasol
　electricity hydrotherapy psychotherapy occupational therapy
　pingpong & amnesia,
who in humorless protest overturned only one symbolic pingpong
　table, resting briefly in catatonia,　　　　205
returning years later truly bald except for a wig of blood, and tears
　and fingers, to the visible madman doom of the wards of the
　madtowns of the East,
Pilgrim State's Rockland's and Greystone's foetid halls,[35] bickering
　with the echoes of the soul, rocking and rolling in the　　　210
　midnight solitude-bench dolmen realms[36] of love, dream of life
　a nightmare, bodies turned to stone as heavy as the moon,
with mother finally ******, and the last fantastic book flung out of
　the tenement window, and the last door closed at 4 AM and
　the last telephone slammed at the wall in reply and the last　　215
　furnished room emptied down to the last piece of mental
　furniture, a yellow paper rose twisted on a wire hanger in the
　closet, and even that imaginary, nothing but a hopeful little
　bit of hallucination—
ah, Carl, while you are not safe I am not safe, and now you're　　220
　really in the total animal soup of time—
and who therefore ran through the icy streets obsessed with a

[31]An island in San Francisco Bay known for its inescapable prison.
[32]A cemetery in the Bronx.
[33]City College of New York.
[34]The theory applied to an early twentieth-century international movement in art and literature that
challenged and rejected traditional conventions and reason and was intended to shock.
[35]Psychiatric hospitals near New York. Solomon spent time at both Pilgrim State and Rockland.
Ginsberg's mother was institutionalized at Greystone, in New Jersey, and died there in 1956, the year
after "Howl" was published.
[36]A Paleolithic tomb or prehistoric structure consisting of a large, flat stone supported on two or more
smaller upright stones.

sudden flash of the alchemy of the use of the ellipse the
catalog the meter & the vibrating plane,

who dreamt and made incarnate gaps in Time & Space through   225
images juxtaposed, and trapped the archangel of the soul
between 2 visual images and joined the elemental verbs and
set the noun and dash of consciousness together, jumping with
sensation of Pater Omnipotens Aeterna Deus[37]

to recreate the syntax and measure of poor human prose and stand   230
before you speechless and intelligent and shaking with shame,
rejected yet confessing out the soul to conform to the rhythm
of thought in his naked and endless head,

the madman bum and angel beat in Time, unknown, yet putting
down here what might be left to say in time come after death,   235

and rose incarnate in the ghostly clothes of jazz in the goldhorn
shadow of the band and blew the suffering of America's
naked mind for love into an eli eli lamma lamma sabacthani[38]
saxophone cry that shivered the cities down to the last radio

with the absolute heart of the poem of life butchered out of their   240
own bodies good to eat a thousand years.

II

What sphinx of cement and aluminum bashed open their skulls
and ate up their brains and imagination?

Moloch![39] Solitude! Filth! Ugliness! Ashcans and unobtainable
dollars! Children screaming under the stairways! Boys   245
sobbing in armies! Old men weeping in the parks!

Moloch! Moloch! Nightmare of Moloch! Moloch the loveless!
Mental Moloch! Moloch the heavy judger of men!

Moloch the incomprehensible prison! Moloch the crossbone
soulless jailhouse and Congress of sorrows! Moloch whose   250
buildings are judgement! Moloch the vast stone of war!
Moloch the stunned governments!

Moloch whose mind is pure machinery! Moloch whose blood is
running money! Moloch whose fingers are ten armies!
Moloch whose breast is a cannibal dynamo! Moloch whose   255
ear is a smoking tomb!

[37]All-powerful Father, eternal God" (Latin).
[38]Christ's last words before dying upon the cross: "My God, My God, why have you forsaken me?"
(Aramaic), Matthew 27:46.
[39]Canaanite and Phoenician god of fire to whom children were sacrificed. "And thou shalt not let any
of thy seed pass through the fire to Moloch" (Leviticus 18:21) [Ginsberg's note].

Moloch whose eyes are a thousand blind windows! Moloch whose
    skyscrapers stand in the long streets like endless Jehovahs!
    Moloch whose factories dream and croak in the fog!
    Moloch whose smokestacks and antennae crown the cities!   260
Moloch whose love is endless oil and stone! Moloch whose soul is
    electricity and banks! Moloch whose poverty is the
    specter of genius! Moloch whose fate is a cloud of sexless
    hydrogen! Moloch whose name is the Mind!
Moloch in whom I sit lonely! Moloch in whom I dream Angels!   265
    Crazy in Moloch! Cocksucker in Moloch! Lacklove and
    manless in Moloch!
Moloch who entered my soul early! Moloch in whom I am a
    consciousness without a body! Moloch who frightened me
    out of my natural ecstasy! Moloch whom I abandon!   270
    Wake up in Moloch! Light streaming out of the sky!
Moloch! Moloch! Robot apartments! invisible suburbs!
    skeleton treasuries! blind capitals! demonic industries!
    spectral nations! invincible madhouses! granite cocks!
    monstrous bombs!   275
They broke their backs lifting Moloch to Heaven! Pavements,
    trees, radios, tons! lifting the city to Heaven which exists
    and is everywhere about us!
Visions! omens! hallucinations! miracles! ecstasies! gone down
    the American river!   280
Dreams! adorations! illuminations! religions! the whole
    boatload of sensitive bullshit!
Breakthroughs! over the river! flips and crucifixions! gone down
    the flood! Highs! Epiphanies! Despairs! Ten years'
    animal screams and suicides! Minds! New loves! Mad   285
    generation! down on the rocks of Time!
Real holy laughter in the river! They saw it all! the wild eyes!
    the holy yells! They bade farewell! They jumped off the
    roof! to solitude! waving! carrying flowers! Down to
    the river! into the street!   290

III

Carl Solomon! I'm with you in Rockland
    where you're madder than I am
I'm with you in Rockland
    where you must feel very strange
I'm with you in Rockland   295
    where you imitate the shade of my mother
I'm with you in Rockland
    where you've murdered your twelve secretaries

I'm with you in Rockland
    where you laugh at this invisible humor   300

I'm with you in Rockland
    where we are great writers on the same dreadful typewriter

I'm with you in Rockland
    where your condition has become serious and is reported
    on the radio   305

I'm with you in Rockland
    where the faculties of the skull no longer admit the worms
    of the senses

I'm with you in Rockland
    where you drink the tea of the breasts of the spinsters of   310
    Utica

I'm with you in Rockland
    where you pun on the bodies of your nurses the harpies[40] of
    the Bronx

I'm with you in Rockland   315
    where you scream in a straightjacket that you're losing the
    game of the actual pingpong of the abyss

I'm with you in Rockland
    where you bang on the catatonic piano the soul is innocent
    and immortal it should never die ungodly in an armed madhouse   320

I'm with you in Rockland
    where fifty more shocks will never return your soul to its
    body again from its pilgrimage to a cross in the void

I'm with you in Rockland   325
    where you accuse your doctors of insanity and plot the
    Hebrew socialist revolution against the fascist national
    Golgotha

I'm with you in Rockland
    where you split the heavens of Long Island and resurrect   330
    your living human Jesus from the superhuman tomb

I'm with you in Rockland
    where there are twentyfive-thousand mad comrades all
    together singing the final stanzas of the Internationale

I'm with you in Rockland   335
    where we hug and kiss the United States under our
    bedsheets the United States that coughs all night and won't
    let us sleep

I'm with you in Rockland
    where we wake up electrified out of the coma by our own   340
    souls' airplanes roaring over the roof they've come to drop

---

[40]In Greek mythology, winged monsters with the faces of ugly hags and crooked, sharp talons. They
carried off their victims to the underworld to punish and torture them.

angelic bombs the hospital illuminates itself imaginary
   walls collapse O skinny legions run outside O starry-
   spangled shock of mercy the eternal war is here O victory
   forget your underwear we're free   345
I'm with you in Rockland
   in my dreams you walk dripping from a sea-journey on the
   highway across America in tears to the door of my cottage
   in the Western night.

                                        San Francisco, 1955–1956

                                                          [1956]

FRANK O'HARA ■ (1926–1966)

Frank O'Hara was born in Baltimore, Maryland, but was raised in Grafton, central Massachusetts. After serving in the South Pacific in the U.S. Navy, 1944–46, he attended Harvard College, majoring in music (he had been a student of the piano for a number of years) and graduating in 1950. O'Hara pursued graduate work in comparative literature at the University of Michigan (MA, 1951), and then moved to New York City, where he held a position at the Museum of Modern Art and became closely involved with new movements in American art, abstract expressionism in particular. From 1953 to 1955, O'Hara was a member of the editorial staff of the magazine *Art News*, to which his friends and fellow poets John Ashbery and James Schuyler also contributed. He stayed on at the Museum of Modern Art and in 1960 was appointed an assistant curator. In July 1966, O'Hara was killed in an accident on Fire Island, off Long Island, New York.

During his years as a Harvard student, O'Hara had begun to develop an interest in literature, taking courses in creative writing taught by the poet John Ciardi. He met Ashbery there, published poems in the *Harvard Advocate*, and decided to major in English rather than music. His first book, *A City Winter and Other Poems* (1952), reflected O'Hara's engagement with the New York cultural scene and his connection to the painters he admired and about whom he was writing brilliantly in essays and reviews for art periodicals. "To us he seemed to dance from canvas to canvas," recalled the composer Morton Feldman, "from party to party, from poem to poem—a Fred Astaire with the whole art community as his Ginger Rogers."

O'Hara is often grouped with Ashbery, Schuyler, and Kenneth Koch as a member of the New York School of poets, which marks their relationship with the New York School of abstract expressionist painters, among them Jackson Pollock, Willem De Kooning, and Franz Kline. Both O'Hara's first book (which included two drawings by the artist Larry Rivers) and his second, *Oranges* (1953), were published by Tibor de Nagy art gallery. Except for a writing workshop he led in 1963, O'Hara never took a position as a teacher, which made him unusual among poets of his generation, so many of whom held professorships in colleges and universities.

The critic Mark Ford described O'Hara's poems as "a heady mixture of Whitmanian enthusiasm and explosive surrealism." They are playful, ironic, full of references to O'Hara's life in the city, his passion for music and art (his work includes collaborative projects with artists), and his gay love affairs and many friendships. O'Hara was a filmmaker and a playwright as well as a poet, and his sharply intelligent, cool, urbane poems, blending the languages of the street with the experimental discourses of modern art and avant-garde literature, integrating the spirit of improvisation with a deft sense of structure, show a wonderful feeling for the dramatization of voice, style, and manner.

O'Hara's *Art Chronicles, 1954–1966* (1974) and *Selected Plays* (1978) are well worth reading, but the *Collected Poems* (1971) is the best point of departure for appreciating this multitalented author. Yet this book is, in a sense, an inadequate guide to O'Hara's literary production and achievement, as the poet-critic Mark Doty noted: "O'Hara composed huge numbers of poems with apparent spontaneity and ease; a friend estimates that his vast *Collected Poems* contains perhaps only a third of his work, which was often scribbled or typed quickly, stuffed in drawers or left about in stacks." A poem, said O'Hara, should be "between two persons instead of two pages", he characterized himself as an "I do this I do that" poet because of the seemingly casual, conversational quality of his verse, as though it consisted of entries in a diary.

Two poems are given here: "To the Harbormaster," a love poem for the painter Larry Rivers, and "The Day Lady Died," an elegy for the great jazz singer Billie Holiday. These poems suggest the distinctive features of O'Hara's poetry, nicely summarized by the critic David Lehman:

> O'Hara made poetry seem continuous with the rest of his life.
> He took it with him into the streets, galleries, beaches and bars
> he frequented, shedding the uptight decorousness that verse in
> the 1950s and '60s was expected to have. Colloquial, quick-witted,
> autobiographical without being confessional and charged with
> wonderment, his poetry helped instigate a revolution in diction....
> He wrote verse in recognizably the same language we use in talking.

For an overview of the life and work, see Alan Feldman, *Frank O'Hara* (1979). For biography, see Brad Gooch, *City Poet: The Life and Times of Frank O'Hara* (1993). For a good critical study, see Marjorie Perloff, *Frank O'Hara: Poet Among Painters* (1977; new ed., 1998). See also *Frank O'Hara: To Be True to a City*, ed. Jim Elledge (1990). On O'Hara and art, see Russell Ferguson, *In Memory of My Feelings: Frank O'Hara and American Art* (1999); and Paul R. Cappucci, *William Carlos Williams, Frank O'Hara, and the New York Art Scene* (2010). See also Geoff Ward, *Statutes of Liberty: The New York School of Poets* (2001), on O'Hara, James Schuyler, and John Ashbery.

To the Harbormaster

I wanted to be sure to reach you;
though my ship was on the way it got caught
in some moorings. I am always tying up
and then deciding to depart. In storms and
at sunset, with the metallic coils of the tide   5
around my fathomless arms, I am unable
to understand the forms of my vanity
or I am hard alee with my Polish rudder

in my hand and the sun sinking. To
you I offer my hull and the tattered cordage   10
of my will. The terrible channels where
the wind drives me against the brown lips
of the reeds are not all behind me. Yet
I trust the sanity of my vessel; and
if it sinks, it may well be in answer   15
to the reasoning of the eternal voices,
the waves which have kept me from reaching you.

[1957]

The Day Lady Died[1]

It is 12:20 in New York a Friday
three days after Bastille day,[2] yes
it is 1959 and I go get a shoeshine
because I will get off the 4:19 in Easthampton[3]
at 7:15 and then go straight to dinner   5
and I don't know the people who will feed me

I walk up the muggy street beginning to sun
and have a hamburger and a malted and buy
an ugly new world writing to see what the poets
in Ghana are doing these days   10
                    I go on to the bank
and Miss Stillwagon (first name Linda I once heard)
doesn't even look up my balance for once in her life
and in the golden griffin[4] I get a little Verlaine[5]
for Patsy[6] with drawings by Bonnard[7] although I do   15
think of Hesiod,[8] trans. Richmond Lattimore[9] or
Brendan Behan's[10] new play, or *Le Balcon* or *Les Nègres*
of Genet,[11] but I don't, I stick with Verlaine
after practically going to sleep with quandariness

---

[1]A reference to Billie Holiday (1915–59), the blues singer nicknamed Lady Day.
[2]French Independence Day, celebrated on July 14.
[3]A town on the south shore of Long Island, New York.
[4]A bookstore near the Museum of Modern Art in New York City.
[5]Paul Verlaine (1844–96), a French Symbolist poet.
[6]Patsy Southgate, a poet and friend of O'Hara who was married to his friend Mike Goldberg.
[7]Pierre Bonnard (1867–1947), a French painter.
[8]A Greek poet who wrote during the eighth century BCE Hesiod's works were translated by Richmond Lattimore in 1959.
[9]Classicist and poet (1906–84), best known for his many translations from Greek into English, most notably Homer's *Iliad* (1951) and Aristophanes's *Frogs* (1961).
[10]Irish playwright (1923–64).
[11]Jean Genet (1910–86), a controversial French playwright whose works included *Le Balcon* ("The Balcony") and *Les Nègres* ("The Blacks").

and for Mike[12] I just stroll into the park lane   20
Liquor Store and ask for a bottle of Strega and
then I go back where I came from to 6th Avenue
and the tobacconist in the Ziegfeld Theatre[13] and
casually ask for a carton of Gauloises and a carton
of Picayunes,[14] and a new york post with her face on it   25

and I am sweating a lot by now and thinking of
leaning on the john door in the 5 spot
while she whispered a song along the keyboard
to Mal Waldron[15] and everyone and I stopped breathing

[1959]

---

[12]Mike Goldberg (1924–2007), a painter and friend of O'Hara. See note 6.
[13]Famous theater in New York.
[14]French cigarette brands.
[15]Malcolm Earl Waldron (1925–2002), American jazz pianist; he was Billie Holiday's regular accompanist from 1957 until her death in 1959.

GALWAY KINNELL ■ (1927–)

Galway Kinnell has been much admired for his poetry about nature, and the poem "The Porcupine," is a notable example. Yet he emphasized in an interview (*The Cortland Review*, August 2001) that he does not consider himself a "nature poet" as such:

> I don't think of myself as a "nature poet." I don't recognize the distinction between nature poetry and—what would be the other thing?—human civilization poetry. We are creatures of the earth. All the creatures have their intricate ways of living on earth. Humans are unique in one respect: we've taken over. We've taken over so successfully that we've become a threat to many of the other creatures and even a danger to the earth itself, so that's why I don't think of myself as a "nature poet." Poems about other creatures may have political and social implications for us.

Recipient of the Pulitzer Prize and the National Book Award for his *Selected Poems* (1980), Kinnell is the author of both poetry and translations. He was born in Providence, Rhode Island, and was an undergraduate at Princeton University (BA, *summa cum laude,* 1948) and a graduate student at the University of Rochester (MA, 1949). Kinnell has taught creative writing in the United States and abroad and, recently, has served as the Director of the Graduate Writing Division of New York University. A *New Selected Poems* was published in 2000.

In his poems on nature topics and themes, Kinnell examines settings, scenes, and creatures as part of a process of self-examination in an effort to discover the relationship of the self to forms of existence outside, and seemingly different from, the self. As the critic Richard Gray observed, Kinnell's speakers bring themselves ever closer to "the natural world, sharing in the primal experiences of birth and death." Striking for both its humor and, as it develops, its horror, "The Porcupine" dramatizes the speaker's kinship with the natural world with an almost unbearable intensity. "Few writers," states Karen Maceira, "have embraced the contemporary existential view of life with as much grace and affirmation as Kinnell. In his poetry, he has made the shift successfully from the theistic framework of our forebears to the secular one our culture has claimed as its own, a shift, for Kinnell, that does not leave behind the sacred but weaves it into the very air we breathe."

For a survey, see Richard J. Calhoun, *Galway Kinnell* (1992). Critical studies include Lee Zimmerman, *Intricate and Simple Things: The Poetry of Galway Kinnell* (1987); *On the Poetry of Galway Kinnell: The Wages of Dying*, ed. Howard Nelson (1987); and *Critical Essays on Galway Kinnell*, ed. Nancy Lewis Tuten (1996).

The Porcupine

1

Fatted
on herbs, swollen on crabapples,
puffed up on bast and phloem,[1] ballooned
on willow flowers, poplar catkins, first
leafs of aspen and larch,   5
the porcupine
drags and bounces his last meal through ice,
mud, roses and goldenrod, into the stubbly high fields.

2

In character
he resembles us in seven ways: 10
he puts his mark on outhouses,
he alchemizes[2] by moonlight,
he shits on the run,
he uses his tail for climbing,
he chuckles softly to himself when scared,   15
he's overcrowded if there's more than one of him per five acres,
his eyes have their own inner redness.

3

Digger of
goings across floors, of hesitations
at thresholds, of   20
handprints of dread
at doorpost or window jamb, he would
gouge the world
empty of us, hack and crater
it   25
until it is nothing, if that
could rinse it of all our sweat and pathos.

Adorer of ax
handles aflow with grain, of arms
of Morris chairs,[3] of hand   30
crafted objects
steeped in the juice of fingertips,

---

[1]The soft, inner portion of the fibrovascular tissue of trees, as distinct from the hard, outer bark.
[2]Referring to alchemy, the medieval form of chemistry that sought to transform base metal, such as
lead, into gold; a miraculous transformation.
[3]A chair of a type designed by the English artist and writer William Morris (1834–96) at the end of the
nineteenth century, usually an easy chair with open padded arms and an adjustable back.

of surfaces wetted down
with fist grease and elbow oil,
of clothespins that have   35
grabbed our body-rags by underarm and crotch...

Unimpressed—bored—
by the whirl of the stars, by *these*
he's astonished, ultra-
Rilkean angel![4]   40

for whom the true
portion of the sweetness of earth
is one of those bottom-heavy, glittering, saccadic
bits
of salt water that splash down   45
the haunted ravines of a human face.

4

A farmer shot a porcupine three times
as it dozed on a tree limb. On
the way down it tore open its belly
on a broken   50
branch, hooked its gut,
and went on falling. On the ground
it sprang to its feet, and
paying out gut heaved
and spartled through a hundred feet of goldenrod   55
before
the abrupt emptiness.

5

The Avesta[5]
puts porcupine killers
into hell for nine generations, sentencing them   60
to gnaw out
each other's hearts for the
salts of desire.

I roll
this way and that in the great bed, under   65
the quilt
that mimics this country of broken farms and woods,

[4]Rainer Maria Rilke (1875–1926), German poet who wrote of his *Duino Elegies* (1923) that "the 'angel'
of the Elegies has nothing to do with the angel of the Christian heaven....The angel of the Elegies is
that being which stands for the idea of recognizing a higher order of reality in invisibility."
[5]Book of sacred scripture from the Persian religion Zoroastrianism.

the fatty sheath of the man
melting off,
the self-stabbing coil 70
of bristles reversing, blossoming outward—
a red-eyed, hard-toothed, arrow-stuck urchin
tossing up mattress feathers,
pricking the
woman beside me until she cries. 75

6

In my time I have
crouched, quills erected,
Saint
Sebastian[6] of the
scared heart, and been
beat dead with a locust club 80
on the bare snout.
And fallen from high places
I have fled, have
jogged
over fields of goldenrod, 85
terrified, seeking home,
and among flowers
I have come to myself empty, the rope
strung out behind me
in the fall sun 90
suddenly glorified with all my blood.

7

And tonight I think I prowl broken
skulled or vacant as a
sucked egg in the wintry meadow, softly chuckling, blank 95
template of myself, dragging
a starved belly through the lichflowered acres,
where
burdock[7] looses the ark of its seed
and thistle holds up its lost blooms 100
and rosebushes in the wind scrape their dead limbs
for the forced-fire
of roses.

[1969]

---

[6]A Christian martyr and former Roman soldier who was shot full of arrows, miraculously survived, but later was clubbed to death.
[7]A coarse weed with prickly flowers called burrs.

JOHN ASHBERY ■ (1927—)

The author of more than twenty books of poetry and the winner of many awards and prizes both in the United States and abroad, John Ashbery was born in Rochester, New York, and raised on a farm nearby. He graduated from Harvard in 1949, majoring in English, and then attended Columbia University for graduate school in the same field (MA, 1951). During 1955–56 he was a Fulbright scholar in Paris, and there, from 1958 to 1966, he wrote art criticism for the *Herald Tribune*, *Art News*, and *Arts International*. He continued working as an art critic and editor on his return to New York City in 1966, and then in 1974 he took an academic appointment in the creative writing program at Brooklyn College.

The French poets whom Ashbery studied, as well as Wallace Stevens and W. H. Auden (the subject of Ashbery's senior thesis at Harvard), were important influences on *Some Trees*, his first book, published in 1956, from which "Illustration," following, is taken. His second book, *The Tennis Court Oath*, published in 1962, was a foray into a more experimental, fragmentary style, but it met with mixed responses from critics, who found it perplexing, elusive, and incoherent.

Ashbery's later books, such as *Rivers and Mountains* (1966), have received more favorable notices. His most popular, best-known publication is *Self-Portrait in a Convex Mirror* (1976); the title poem, keyed to a self-portrait by the sixteenth-century Italian painter Parmigianino, delves into the relationship of art and life and the fragility of constructions of the self, two of Ashbery's abiding themes. One critic identified it as "the touchstone for poets who have continued to write in its aftermath. It is generally considered the most compelling and influential poem written by an American since the Second World War."

Ashbery's verse is highly self-conscious, always reflecting on its own operations, techniques, and strategies. He is a difficult, disorienting poet, inviting and seductive, masterful in his array of tones and diction but challenging to the sense-making efforts of readers. As the literary historian David Perkins remarked:

> For both Stevens and Ashbery the imagination creates, destroys, and immediately creates another vision of reality, but in Ashbery the process is enormously speeded up. His envisionings of reality are not merely provisional; they transform themselves and disappear in the very process of being proposed.

The reason for this is Ashbery's fascination with language, its powers and limitations, and its rich, and yet so limited, relationship to reality—to a reality that exists only in the transient forms language gives it. Another poet might find in such a prospect a reason for despair, but Ashbery finds it opening up endless possibilities for poetic recreation and self-exploration. "I don't think there are any things that can't be written about in poetry—it all depends on how it's done," he has said. He is a poet absorbed in the pleasures and pains of organizing literary works that resist, even as they solicit and reward, the reader's efforts at interpretation. He is, too, a poet both seriously and playfully committed to ongoing artistic change and development. As Harold Bloom, writing in the 1990s, has observed, "Ashbery follows Stevens and Yeats in the amazing trait of achieving fresh greatness as a poet, instead of ebbing or merely repeating himself. More than ever, Ashbery seems to be the second half of our century what Stevens and Yeats were to the first."

A good beginning: David Shapiro, *John Ashbery: An Introduction to the Poetry* (1979). Interpretive studies include *Beyond Amazement: New Essays on John Ashbery*, ed. David Lehman (1980); John Shoptaw, *On the Outside Looking Out: John Ashbery's Poetry* (1994); and David Herd, *John Ashbery and American Poetry* (2000). Ashbery's *Other Traditions* (2000) explores the poet's craft through a series of studies of poets not in the mainstream of literary tradition; and his *Selected Prose*, ed. Eugene Richie (2004), includes pieces on Gertrude Stein, Frank O'Hara, Marianne Moore, and other writers and artists. See also John Ashbery, *Collected Poems, 1956–1987*, ed. Mark Ford (2008); and *Notes from the Air: Selected Later Poems* (2007). For further critical discussion, see Helen Vendler, *Invisible Listeners: Lyric Intimacy in Herbert, Whitman, and Ashbery* (2005); and Ellen Levy, *Criminal Ingenuity: Moore, Cornell, Ashbery, and the Struggle Between the Arts* (2011).

Illustration

I

A novice[1] was sitting on a cornice
High over the city. Angels

Combined their prayers with those
Of the police, begging her to come off it.

One lady promised to be her friend.   5
"I do not want a friend," she said.

A mother offered her some nylons
Stripped from her very legs. Others brought

Little offerings of fruit and candy,
The blind man all his flowers. If any   10

Could be called successful, these were,
For that the scene should be a ceremony

---

[1]A student in the first stage of becoming a nun.

Illustration **1287**

Was what she wanted. "I desire
Monuments," she said. "I want to move

Figuratively, as waves caress   15
The thoughtless shore. You people I know

Will offer me every good thing
I do not want. But please remember

I died accepting them." With that, the wind
Unpinned her bulky robes, and naked   20

As a roc's egg,[2] she drifted softly downward
Out of the angels' tenderness and the minds of men.

II

Much that is beautiful must be discarded
So that we may resemble a taller

Impression of ourselves. Moths climb in the flame,   25
Alas, that wish only to be the flame:

They do not lessen our stature.
We twinkle under the weight

Of indiscretions. But how could we tell
That of the truth we know, she was   30

The somber vestment? For that night, rockets sighed
Elegantly over the city, and there was feasting:

There is so much in that moment!
So many attitudes toward that flame,

We might have soared from earth, watching her glide   35
Aloft, in her peplum[3] of bright leaves.

But she, of course, was only an effigy
Of indifference, a miracle

Not meant for us, as the leaves are not
Winter's because it is the end.   40

[1956]

---

[2]In Arabian legends, the roc is an enormous bird of prey. Its eggs are described by Sinbad the Sailor, a character in *The Thousand and One Nights*, as measuring up to fifty paces in circumference.
[3]A veil or tunic.

The Lament upon the Waters

For the disciple nothing had changed. The mood was still
Gray tolerance, as the road marched along
Singing its little song of despair. Once, a cry
Started up out of the hills. That old, puzzling persuasion
Again. Sex was part of this,   5
And the shock of day turning into night.
Though we always found something delicate (too delicate
For some tastes, perhaps) to touch, to desire.

And we made much of this sort of materiality
That clogged the weight of starlight, made it seem   10
Fibrous, yet there was a chance in this
To see the present as it never had existed,

Clear and shapeless, in an atmosphere like cut glass.
At Latour-Maubourg you said this was a good thing, and on the steps
Of Métro Jasmin[1] the couriers nodded to us correctly, and the   15
Pact was sealed in the sky. But now moments surround us

Like a crowd, some inquisitive faces, some hostile ones,
Some engimatic or turned away to an anterior form of time
Given once and for all. The jetstream inscribes a final flourish
That melts as it stays. The problem isn't how to proceed   20

But is one of being: whether this ever was, and whose
It shall be. To be starting out, just one step
Off the sidewalk, and as such pulled back into the glittering
Snowstorm of stinging tentacles of how that would be worked out

If we ever work it out. And the voice came back at him   25
Across the water, rubbing it the wrong way: "Thou
Canst but undo the wrong thou hast done." The sackbuts[2]
Embellish it, and we are never any closer to the collision

Of the waters, the peace of light drowning light,
Grabbing it, holding it up streaming. It is all one. It lies   30
All around, its new message, guilt, the admission
Of guilt, your new act. Time buys

The receiver, the onlooker of the earlier system, but cannot
Buy back the rest. It is night that fell
At the edge of your footsteps as the music stopped.   35
And we heard the bells for the first time. It is your chapter, I said.

[1977]

[1]Latour-Maubourg and Métro Jasmin are both stops on the Paris subway system.
[2]A sackbut was a musical instrument of the Renaissance period. It resembled a bass trumpet with a
trombone-like slide used to alter pitch.

W. S. Merwin is, in the words of a recent critic, "our strongest poet of silence and doubt, vacancy and absence, deprival and dispossession." He was born in New York City and raised in Union City, New Jersey, and Scranton, Pennsylvania. The son of a Presbyterian minister, Merwin recalled that he "started writing hymns for my father as soon as I could write at all."

Merwin was an English major at Princeton, where his teachers included the poet-critics John Berryman and R. P. Blackmur. After a year of graduate study at Princeton, where he focused on Romance languages, Merwin traveled abroad, spending time in France, Spain, and England before settling in 1950 in Majorca in the western Mediterranean. There he worked as a tutor to the son of the poet, critic, and mythologist Robert Graves.

Relocating to London in the early 1950s, Merwin made his living as a translator, even as he composed and arranged poems for his first book, *A Mask for Janus* (1952), which was acclaimed for its display of technical skill and craftsmanship. It was followed by *The Dancing Bears* (1954), *Green with Beasts* (1956), *The Drunk in the Furnace* (1960), *The Moving Target* (1963), *The Lice* (1967), and *The Carrier of Ladders* (1970). Commenting in 1970 on this body of work, the poet-essayist Adrienne Rich said, "For years now, W. S. Merwin has been working more privately, profoundly, and daringly than any other American poet of my generation. He has been developing a language and a poetic landscape which are both severe and sensuous, in which the silences—as in human intercourse—are as essential as the speech."

Merwin's later volumes, which include *The Rain in the Trees* (1988), *Travels* (1993), and *The Vixen* (1996), while making use (as he did his previous books) of classical and mythological topics, themes, and references, became still more personal and reflective, more experimental and looser, more open, in structure, and more expressive of his commitments to pacifism and the preservation of the environment. The poet-critic Neal Bowers, writing in 1990, has remarked in this context: "Merwin's poetry—stylistically, aesthetically, philosophically—in every way is engaged in the struggle for form." "Our importance," Merwin noted in an interview, "is based on a feeling of responsibility and awareness of all life, the fact that we are a part of the entire universe and our importance is not different from the importance of the rest of the universe." His recent poetry reflects, too, the settings and landscapes of Hawaii, where he has lived since 1975.

Merwin is an accomplished translator of French, Spanish, and Italian writers, as two notable books attest: *Selected Translations, 1948–1968* (1968) and *Selected Translations, 1968–1978* (1979). But his central achievement as a writer is best appreciated through his *Selected Poems* (1988), which offers a selection of some one hundred pieces from the eleven volumes (totaling 630 poems) he published between 1952 and 1988. Other significant books include *Unframed Originals: Recollections* (1982), an autobiographical study that is especially revealing about Merwin's up-bringing among family members who were uninterested in art and litera-ture; and *Regions of Memory: Uncollected Prose, 1949–1982 (*1987), which gathers book reviews, essays on politics and society, memoirs, stories, and a wide-ranging interview. A wide-ranging writer and intellectual, Merwin has defined the social role of the poet in these both forthright and modest terms: "One is trying to say everything that can be said for the things that one loves while there's still time.... We keep expressing our anger and our love, and we hope, hopelessly perhaps, that it will have some effect."

For introductions, see Mark Christhilf, *W. S. Merwin, the Mythmaker* (1986); and H. L. Hix, *Understanding W. S. Merwin* (1997). For further critical analysis, see Cheri Davis, *W. S. Merwin* (1981); *W. S. Merwin: Essays on the Poetry*, eds. Cary Nelson and Ed Folsom (1987); and Edward J. Brunner, *Poetry as Labor and Privilege: The Writings of W. S. Merwin* (1991). See also Jane Frazier, *From Origin to Ecology: Nature and the Poetry of W. S. Merwin* (1999); and Leonard M. Scigaj, *Sustainable Poetry: Four American Ecopoets* (1999), which examines Merwin, Wendell Berry, A. R. Ammons, and Gary Snyder.

For the Anniversary of My Death

Every year without knowing it I have passed the day
When the last fires will wave to me
And the silence will set out
Tireless traveler
Like the beam of a lightless star   5

Then I will no longer
Find myself in life as in a strange garment
Surprised at the earth
And the love of one woman
And the shamelessness of men   10
As today writing after three days of rain
Hearing the wren sing and the falling cease
And bowing not knowing to what

[1967]

For a Coming Extinction

Gray whale
Now that we are sending you to The End
That great god
Tell him
That we who follow you invented forgiveness   5
And forgive nothing

I write as though you could understand
And I could say it
One must always pretend something
Among the dying   10
When you have left the seas nodding on their stalks
Empty of you
Tell him that we were made
On another day

The bewilderment will diminish like an echo   15
Winding along your inner mountains
Unheard by us
And find its way out
Leaving behind it the future
Dead   20
And ours

When you will not see again
The whale calves trying the light
Consider what you will find in the black garden
And its court   25
The sea cows the Great Auks the gorillas[1]
The irreplaceable hosts ranged countless
And fore-ordaining as stars
Our sacrifices
Join your word to theirs   30
Tell him
That it is we who are important

[1967]

---

[1]All animals that are either extinct or endangered. The Great Auk is a large, flightless bird that became
extinct in the mid-19th century.

JAMES WRIGHT ■ (1927–1980)

James Wright was born in Martins Ferry, Ohio, the son of hardworking parents, neither of whom had more than an eighth-grade education. Wright described his father, a worker for fifty years in a glass factory, as "a handsome man of great physical strength and the greatest human strength of all, an enduring gentleness in the presence of the hardship that the Great Depression brought to everyone." After entering the army in 1946 and serving for a period in Japan, Wright returned to the United States and attended Kenyon College, which he said was "the most literary enclave in the state of Ohio," studying with the poet-critic John Crowe Ransom.

Wright traveled to the University of Vienna in the early 1950s as a Fulbright fellow, and then took his master's and doctoral degrees (his PhD thesis was on Charles Dickens) at the University of Washington, where his teachers included Theodore Roethke and Stanley Kunitz. He held several teaching positions and published a number of noteworthy volumes of verse even as he struggled with the demons of depression and alcoholism.

Significant influences on Wright's work include Robert Frost, the British author Thomas Hardy, and the American poet, essayist, and teacher Robert Bly. He is best approached through *Above the River: The Complete Poems* (1992) and *Collected Prose* (1983). As a writer for the *New York Times* noted, "Lucidity, precision, rhythmical poise, sentiment, intelligence, and the rigors of a conscious craft that liberated the imagination—these were the poetic values Wright cherished."

Wright wrote a good deal of socially conscious poetry, and this concern is intimated in "Autumn Begins in Martins Ferry, Ohio," following, which dates from 1963. But Wright's most enduring works are his lyric explorations of the self and nature, the speaker and the landscape he surveys and to which he seeks to relate and connect himself. Often Wright's poems lead to a sudden or surprising discovery, a revelation. So much is this the case that the critic David Pink characterized Wright as "a poet of epiphany."

For critical studies, see Kevin Stein, *James Wright: The Poetry of a Grown Man* (1989); and Andrew Elkins, *The Poetry of James Wright* (1991). See also *The Pure Clear Word: Essays on the Poetry of James Wright*, ed. Dave Smith (1982); and *James Wright: The Heart of the Light*, eds. Peter Stitt and Frank Graziano (1990). *A Wild Perfection: The Selected Letters of James Wright*, eds. Anne Wright and Saundra Rose Maley, with Jonathan Blunk (2005), includes letters to Wright's fellow poets Theodore Roethke, Galway Kinnell, James Dickey, and others dealing with the creative process and his struggles with depression and illness.

Autumn Begins in Martins Ferry, Ohio

In the Shreve High football stadium,
I think of Polacks nursing long beers in Tiltonsville,
And gray faces of Negroes in the blast furnace at Benwood,[1]
And the ruptured night watchman of Wheeling Steel,[2]
Dreaming of heroes.   5

All the proud fathers are ashamed to go home.
Their women cluck like starved pullets,[3]
Dying for love.

Therefore,
Their sons grow suicidally beautiful   10
At the beginning of October,
And gallop terribly against each other's bodies.

[1963]

To the Evening Star: Central Minnesota

Under the water tower at the edge of town
A huge Airedale[1] ponders a long ripple
In the grass fields beyond.
Miles off, a whole grove silently
Flies up into the darkness.
One light comes on in the sky,   5
One lamp on the prairie.

Beautiful daylight of the body, your hands carry seashells.
West of this wide plain,
Animals wilder than ours
Come down from the green mountains in the darkness.   10
Now they can see you, they know
The open meadows are safe.

[1963]

A Blessing

Just off the highway to Rochester, Minnesota,
Twilight bounds softly forth on the grass.
And the eyes of those two Indian ponies
Darken with kindness.

[1]Tiltonsville and Benwood are towns near Martins Ferry.
[2]A steel mill located in Benwood, Ohio.
[3]Young hens.
[1]Airedale terriers are a breed of large dog.

They have come gladly out of the willows 5
To welcome my friend and me.
We step over the barbed wire into the pasture
Where they have been grazing all day, alone.
They ripple tensely, they can hardly contain their
    happiness 10
That we have come.
They bow shyly as wet swans. They love each other.
There is no loneliness like theirs.
At home once more,
They begin munching the young tufts of spring in the 15
    darkness.
I would like to hold the slenderer one in my arms,
For she has walked over to me
And nuzzled my left hand.
She is black and white, 20
Her mane falls wild on her forehead,
And the light breeze moves me to caress her long ear
That is delicate as the skin over a girl's wrist.
Suddenly I realize
That if I stepped out of my body I would break 25
Into blossom.

[1963]

PHILIP LEVINE ■ (1928—)

Born in Detroit, Michigan, Philip Levine saw the economic fortunes of his Russian-Jewish immigrant family decline during his childhood years. "Although I was born into the middle class," he said, "my father died before I was old enough to enjoy my station." His family moved from one apartment to the next, each smaller than the one before, and Levine was obliged to earn money for the family. He spent most of his twenties in Detroit factories, a worker performing hard, tiring jobs. Though he is now the author of many books of poetry and prose, his subject often is the immigrant neighborhood and the people and scenes he experienced in his boyhood and blue-collar period in Detroit.

Levine is a writer with a tough, gritty humor, and a keen sympathy for hardworking people, but also a poet of loss and lament. "The American experience," he observed, "is to return and discover one cannot even find the way, for the streets abruptly end, replaced by freeways, the houses have been removed for urban renewal that never takes place, and nothing remains."

The big break for Levine came when he left Detroit to attend the Iowa Writers' Workshop at the University of Iowa, studying with Robert Lowell and John Berryman and making a commitment to poetry writing. Levine's recent volumes include *What Work Is* (1991); *The Simple Truth* (1994), which presents elegies the critic Harold Bloom said possess a "controlled pathos" that rivals Walt Whitman's; and *The Mercy* (1998), which one reviewer praised as "a book for the twenty-first century, revealing the diversity out of which Americans emerged and toward which we continue." Levine has been widely honored for his work and is the recipient of prestigious fellowships.

The poem "Starlight" focuses on Levine's father. It is an absorbing study of character, a recollection of a person with whom Levine was intimate, and yet from whom, through his literary work, he has become separated. In a sense, these poems are as much about Levine as they are about his parents. He has noted that in the poems he values most, "I make a lot of discoveries about voice, about subject, about what my real feelings are."

For biographical and critical contexts, see Philip Levine, *The Bread of Time: Toward an Autobiography* (1994); *Don't Ask* (1981); and *So Ask: Essays, Conversations, and Interviews* (2002). For critical discussion, see *On the Poetry of Philip Levine: Stranger to Nothing*, ed. Christopher Buckley (1991).

Starlight

My father stands in the warm evening
on the porch of my first house.
I am four years old and growing tired.
I see his head among the stars,
the glow of his cigarette, redder   5

than the summer moon riding
low over the old neighborhood. We
are alone, and he asks me if I am happy.
"Are you happy?" I cannot answer.
I do not really understand the word, 10
and the voice, my father's voice, is not
his voice, but somehow thick and choked,
a voice I have not heard before, but
heard often since. He bends and passes
a thumb beneath each of my eyes. 15
The cigarette is gone, but I can smell
the tiredness that hangs on his breath.
He has found nothing, and he smiles
and holds my head with both his hands.
Then he lifts me to his shoulder, 20
and now I too am there among the stars,
as tall as he. Are you happy? I say.
He nods in answer, Yes! oh yes! oh yes!
And in that new voice he says nothing,
holding my head tight against his head, 25
his eyes closed up against the starlight,
as though those tiny blinking eyes
of light might find a tall, gaunt child
holding his child against the promises
of autumn, until the boy slept 30
never to waken in that world again.

[1979]

Ellis Island and harbor, New York City, with the Statue of Liberty to the left, in the early 1900s.

ANNE SEXTON ■ (1928–1974)

Anne Sexton suffered throughout her life from serious and sustained mental and emotional problems, and, unable to resolve them, she took her own life. Through her verse she managed to achieve for a time a measure of focus and control, and her body of work, which probes deeply, painfully, and provocatively into women's issues and concerns, stands as one of the important achievements in American poetry of the 1950s and 1960s.

Sexton was born in Newton, Massachusetts, the daughter of middle-class parents whose New England ancestors reached back to the seventeenth century. Her childhood was unpleasant and disturbing. She felt badly at odds with her parents, and her biographer Diane Middlebrook suggested that Sexton (for whom incest became an abiding literary theme) may have been the victim of sexual abuse—and that, later, she may have abused her own children.

Married at age nineteen, Sexton gave birth to two daughters in the early 1950s. She was beautiful and worked for a time as a fashion model. Lonely, anguished by extreme mood swings, sexually promiscuous, dependent on drugs and liquor, and suicidal, Sexton sought in her poetry to delve into the conflicts between a woman's desire for creativity and the restrictive conventions that in her era governed the shape of women's lives.

During one of her treatments for depression, Sexton's psychiatrist recommended she explore an interest in writing that had arisen during her years in high school. In fall 1957, Sexton enrolled in a workshop on poetry offered by John Holmes at the Boston Center for Adult Education; one of her classmates was Maxine Kumin, later a close friend and an accomplished poet in her own right. As Kumin noted, Sexton learned her craft quickly and soon was "writing openly about menstruation, abortion, masturbation, incest, adultery, and drug addiction at a time when the proprieties embraced none of these as proper topics for poetry." The poet and essayist Katha Pollitt made a similar point: "At a time when American poetry was nearly as male-dominated as football, Sexton wrote frankly, extravagantly, and without apology about the experience of women."

Sexton was praised for her technical skill and for the audaciously personal power of her poetry, which was linked by reviewers and critics to the intimate, intensely confessional poetry of W. D. Snodgrass (with whom Sexton studied in 1958) as well as of Robert Lowell and Sylvia Plath (both of whom Sexton came to know in writing workshops at Boston University). She received many prizes, honors, awards, and honorary degrees for her work. Her books include *To Bedlam and Part Way Back* (1960), poems about madness and the struggle to return from it; *All My Pretty Ones* (1962), which takes its title from a line in *Macbeth* and confronts the death of loved ones; *Live or Die* (1966), winner of the Pulitzer Prize; *Love Poems* (1969); and *Transformations* (1971), an edgy, daring, comic (often uproarious and outrageous) set of feminist poems keyed to *Grimm's Fairy Tales*. But Sexton is encountered most directly through *The Complete Poems* (1981) and *Anne Sexton: A Self-Portrait in Letters* (1977). Poetry, Sexton insisted, "should be a shock to the senses. It should also hurt."

The following poems are "The Truth the Dead Know," a "strange, bitter elegy," as one critic called it; and "Sylvia's Death," which takes as its point of departure Plath's self-destruction at age thirty-one. A fierce poet and the mother of two children, Plath committed suicide in February 1963 by gassing herself in the oven of her kitchen. Eleven years later, Sexton, taking a tragic cue from her friend's example, gassed herself in the garage of her home.

For an introduction, see Caroline King Barnard, *Anne Sexton* (1989). For biography, see Diane Wood Middlebrook, *Anne Sexton: A Biography* (1991). These books give a range of critical responses: *Anne Sexton: The Artist and Her Critics*, ed. J. D. McClatchy (1978); *Anne Sexton: Telling the Tale*, ed. Steven E. Colburn (1988); *Original Essays on the Poetry of Anne Sexton*, ed. Frances Bixler (1988); and *Critical Essays on Anne Sexton*, ed. Linda Wagner-Martin (1989). See also Linda Gray Sexton, *Searching for Mercy Street: My Journey Back to My Mother* (1994), an intimate account of a complex, painful mother-daughter relationship; and Jo Gill, *Anne Sexton's Confessional Poetics* (2007).

The Truth the Dead Know

For my mother, born March 1902, died March 1959
and my father, born February 1900, died June 1959

Gone, I say and walk from church,
refusing the stiff procession to the grave,
letting the dead ride alone in the hearse.   5
It is June. I am tired of being brave.

We drive to the Cape.[1] I cultivate
myself where the sun gutters from the sky,
where the sea swings in like an iron gate
and we touch. In another country people die.   10

My darling, the wind falls in like stones
from the whitehearted water and when we touch
we enter touch entirely. No one's alone.
Men kill for this, or for as much.

And what of the dead? They lie without shoes   15
in their stone boats. They are more like stone
than the sea would be if it stopped. They refuse
to be blessed, throat, eye and knucklebone.

[1962]

---

[1]Cape Cod, Massachusetts.

Sylvia's Death

for Sylvia Plath[1]

0 Sylvia, Sylvia,
with a dead box of stones and spoons,

with two children, two meteors
wandering loose in the tiny playroom,

with your mouth into the sheet,   5
into the roofbeam, into the dumb prayer,

(Sylvia, Sylvia,
where did you go
after you wrote me
from Devonshire   10
about raising potatoes
and keeping bees?)

what did you stand by,
just how did you lie down into?

Thief!—   15
how did you crawl into,

crawl down alone
into the death I wanted so badly and for so long,

the death we said we both outgrew,
the one we wore on our skinny breasts,   20

the one we talked of so often each time
we downed three extra dry martinis in Boston,

the death that talked of analysts and cures,
the death that talked like brides with plots,

the death we drank to,   25
the motives and then the quiet deed?

(In Boston
the dying
ride in cabs,
yes death again,   30
that ride home
with *our* boy.)

0 Sylvia, I remember the sleepy drummer
who beat on our eyes with an old story,

[1]American poet (1932–63) and friend of Sexton's who committed suicide by inhaling gas from a kitchen oven. Her children were in the next room.

how we wanted to let him come   35
like a sadist or a New York fairy

to do his job,
a necessity, a window in a wall or a crib,

and since that time he waited   40
under our heart, our cupboard,

and I see now that we store him up
year after year, old suicides

and I know at the news of your death,
a terrible taste for it, like salt.

(And me,   45
me too.
And now, Sylvia,
you again
with death again,
that ride home   50
with *our* boy.)

And I say only
with my arms stretched out into that stone place,

what is your death
but an old belonging,   55

a mole that fell out
of one of your poems?

(0 friend,
while the moon's bad,
and the king's gone,   60
and the queen's at her wit's end
the bar fly ought to sing!)

0 tiny mother,
you too!
0 funny duchess!   65
0 blonde thing!

February 17, 1963
[1966]

ADRIENNE RICH ■ (1929—2012)

Born in Baltimore, Maryland, Adrienne Rich attended Radcliffe College. She graduated in 1951, the same year she received the Yale Series of Younger Poets Award for *A Change of World*. Still in her twenties, while married and raising three children, Rich produced a second book, *The Diamond Cutters* (1955).

Rich came into her own as a writer in the early 1960s with the publication of *Snapshots of a Daughter-in-Law* (1963), which articulates and examines the tensions between a traditional female role and a commitment to a career as an author. This work arose from Rich's immediate observations and experiences, and from her family background; her father was a doctor and professor at Johns Hopkins University, and her mother was a composer and a skillful pianist who had turned away from these pursuits to become a wife and mother. *Snapshots of a Daughter-in-Law* was criticized by reviewers for its bitterness and anger and for the absence of the taut formal discipline Rich's first books demonstrated. But for her it was a breakthrough. Her poems reflected, and helped to create, a process of radical change in her understanding of herself and of female identity.

During the 1960s and 1970s, Rich took part in the political causes and reform movements of the era. Her books of this period include *Necessities of Life* (1966), *Leaflets* (1969), *The Will to Change* (1971), and *Diving Into the Wreck* (1973). After the death of her husband in 1970, Rich moved even more prominently into the campaigns for women's rights and sexual liberation, seeking "to write directly and overtly as a woman, out of a woman's body and experience." "Poetry," she affirmed, should "consciously situate itself amid political conditions."

From the 1970s to her death Rich continued her activity as a poet, but she also published a number of nonfiction works on feminist theory, women writers, lesbianism, and other topics. These include *Of Woman Born: Motherhood as Experience and Institution* (1976); *On Lies, Secrets, and Silence: Selected Prose, 1966–1978* (1979); and *Blood, Bread, and Poetry: Selected Prose, 1979–1985* (1986). As one scholar has said, "There is no writer of comparable influence and achievement in so many areas of the contemporary women's movement as the poet and theorist Adrienne Rich."

Rich offers these illuminating statements about her vocation and intention as a poet:

> A poem can't free us from the struggle for existence, but it can uncover desires and appetites buried under the accumulating emergencies of our lives, the fabricated wants and needs we have had urged on us, have accepted as our own. It's not a philosophical or psychological blueprint; it's an instrument for embodied experience. But we seek that experience, or recognize it when it is offered to us, because it reminds us in some way of our need. After that rearousal of desire, the task of acting on that truth, or making love, or meeting other needs, is ours. (1993)

[P]oetry is liberative language, connecting the fragments within us, connecting us to others like and unlike ourselves, replenishing our desire. It's potentially catalytic speech because it's more than speech: it is associative, metaphoric, dialectical, visual, musical; in poetry words can say more than they mean and mean more than they say. In a time of frontal assaults both on language and on human solidarity, poetry can remind us of all we are in danger of losing—disturb us, embolden us out of resignation. (1998)

Below, are two powerful poems, each differently composed and organized. The first is "Storm Warnings," compelling for its finely crafted restraint, which expresses the pressures of human adjustment to the changing seasons, the passing of time, and the effort to stabilize the self in the aftermath of heightened feeling. The second is "Diving Into the Wreck," one of the most important poems of the women's movement, an exploration and critique of the myths that have defined sexual roles. Yet the explorer is, it seems, both male and female, suggesting that women and men alike must undertake an heroic journey into the self and its conditioning circumstances. "Diving Into the Wreck" is a brave, inspiring, anguished poem that speaks, above all, to women afflicted by patriarchy even as it achieves a grandeur of application to all persons willing to face and learn from its insights and its appeal for new myths to replace the old.

Critical studies include Claire Keyes, *The Aesthetics of Power: The Poetry of Adrienne Rich* (1986); and Alice Templeton, *The Dream and the Dialogue: Adrienne Rich's Feminist Poetics* (1994). See also *Reading Adrienne Rich: Reviews and Re-Visions, 1951–1981*, ed. Jane Roberta Cooper (1984); and Craig Werner, *Adrienne Rich: The Poet and Her Critics* (1988). For further analysis and context, see Wendy Martin, *An American Triptych: Anne Bradstreet, Emily Dickinson, Adrienne Rich* (1984); and Paula Bennett, *My Life, a Loaded Gun: Female Creativity and Feminist Poetics* (1986). Also significant are Rich's *Arts of the Possible: Essays and Conversations* (2001); and *What Is Found There: Notebooks on Poetry and Politics* (2003).

Storm Warnings

The glass[1] has been falling all the afternoon,
And knowing better than the instrument
What winds are walking overhead, what zone
Of gray unrest is moving across the land,
I leave the book upon a pillowed chair   5
And walk from window to closed window, watching
Boughs strain against the sky

---

[1]Barometer.

And think again, as often when the air
Moves inward toward a silent core of waiting,
How with a single purpose time has traveled   10
By secret currents of the undiscerned
Into this polar realm. Weather abroad
And weather in the heart alike come on
Regardless of prediction.

Between foreseeing and averting change   15
Lies all the mastery of elements
Which clocks and weatherglasses cannot alter.
Time in the hand is not control of time,
Nor shattered fragments of an instrument
A proof against the wind; the wind will rise,   20
We can only close the shutters.

I draw the curtains as the sky goes black
And set a match to candles sheathed in glass
Against the keyhole draught, the insistent whine
Of weather through the unsealed aperture.[2]   25
This is our sole defense against the season;
These are the things that we have learned to do
Who live in troubled regions.

[1951]

Diving Into the Wreck

First having read the book of myths,
and loaded the camera,
and checked the edge of the knife-blade,
I put on
the body-armor of black rubber   5
the absurd flippers
the grave and awkward mask.
I am having to do this
not like Cousteau[1] with his
assiduous team   10
aboard the sun-flooded schooner
but here alone.

There is a ladder.
The ladder is always there
hanging innocently   15

[2]An opening, gap, or hole.
[1]Jacques Cousteau (1910–97), French underwater explorer and oceanographer.

close to the side of the schooner.
We know what it is for,
we who have used it.
Otherwise
it's a piece of maritime floss   20
some sundry equipment.

I go down.
Rung after rung and still
the oxygen immerses me
the blue light   25
the clear atoms
of our human air.
I go down.
My flippers cripple me,
I crawl like an insect down the ladder   30
and there is no one
to tell me when the ocean
will begin.

First the air is blue and then
it is bluer and then green and then   35
black I am blacking out and yet
my mask is powerful
it pumps my blood with power
the sea is another story
the sea is not a question of power   40
I have to learn alone
to turn my body without force
in the deep element.

And now: it is easy to forget
what I came for   45
among so many who have always
lived here
swaying their crenellated² fans
between the reefs
and besides   50
you breathe differently down here.

I came to explore the wreck.
The words are purposes.
The words are maps.
I came to see the damage that was done   55

²Scalloped or crimped.

and the treasures that prevail.
I stroke the beam of my lamp
slowly along the flank
of something more permanent
than fish or weed   60

the thing I came for:
the wreck and not the story of the wreck
the thing itself and not the myth
the drowned face³ always staring
toward the sun   65
the evidence of damage
worn by salt and sway into this threadbare beauty
the ribs of the disaster
curving their assertion
among the tentative haunters.   70

This is the place.
And I am here, the mermaid whose dark hair
streams black, the merman in his armored body
We circle silently
about the wreck   75
we dive into the hold.
I am she: I am he

whose drowned face sleeps with open eyes
whose breasts still bear the stress
whose silver, copper, vermeil cargo lies   80
obscurely inside barrels
half-wedged and left to rot
we are the half-destroyed instruments
that once held to a course
the water-eaten log   85
the fouled compass

We are, I am, you are
by cowardice or courage
the one who find our way
back to this scene   90
carrying a knife, a camera
a book of myths
in which
our names do not appear.

                                                        [1973]

---

³Referring to the ornamental figureheads of women that adorned the bows of sailing ships.

GARY SNYDER ▪ (1930—)

Gary Snyder was born in San Francisco, California, and attended Reed College in Portland, Oregon, where he majored in a combination of literature, anthropology, and environmental studies. His life and work experiences are extremely diverse; he was a logger on the West Coast, a seaman, an explorer of Native American cultures, a member of the graduate program in linguistics at Indiana University, a student (1953–56) of Oriental languages at the Berkeley campus of the University of California, a lookout for forest fires (which inspired the following poem, "August on Sourdough"), a friend to members of the Beat Generation (Jack Kerouac, Allen Ginsberg, and others), a resident (1956–64) of Japan and a devout scholar of Buddhism, a prize-winning author, a builder of his own house in the Sierra Nevadas, a teacher of literature and "wilderness thought" at the University of California's Davis campus, and much more.

As a poet, Snyder is distinctive for the clarity and precision of his lines and for the sensitivity of his inquiries into and statements about the meanings and purposes of nature and humankind's relationship to it. Influenced by the poets Ezra Pound and Charles Olson and by Henry David Thoreau, Snyder writes with directness and honesty; everything is authentically felt and described with wit, sometimes playfulness, and wisdom.

Snyder's first book was *Riprap* (the word means a foundation or wall of stones, or a layering of stone or rock deployed to prevent erosion), published in 1959 and later included in a single volume with one of his best books, *Cold Mountain Poems* (1965, 1991), a contemplative exploration of nature and the wilderness that reflects the disciplined attentiveness that Snyder achieved through his long study of Buddhist thought and practice. "I try to hold both history and the wilderness in mind," he observed, "that my poems may approach the true measure of things and stand against the unbalance and ignorance of our times." Elsewhere he emphasized his belief in "the fertility of the soil, the magic of animals, the power-vision in solitude, the terrifying initiation and rebirth, the love and ecstasy of the dance, the common work of the tribe." One of his books, *Earth House Hold* (1969), is an influential text for those dedicated to the care and preservation of the planet, its organic wholeness and interdependence ("interconnected, interpenetrating, mutually reflecting, and mutually embracing").

"Rhythm" is an important term and technique for Snyder—the rhythm of nature, the rhythm of persons rightly at home in nature, the rhythm of forms of work, the rhythm of the well-made poem. "My poems," he noted, "follow the rhythms of the physical work I'm doing and the life I'm leading at any given time." This commitment, in poetry, is evident in such later books as *Regarding Wave* (1970), *Turtle Island* (1974), and, especially, in the focused structures in *Axe Handles* (1983). "What we want poetry to do," Snyder maintained, "is guide lovers toward ecstasy, give witness to the dignity of old people, intensify human bonds, elevate the community, and improve the public spirit."

An excellent point of departure for surveying Snyder's career as a poet is *No Nature: New and Selected Poems* (1993). Also noteworthy are Snyder's collection of new and selected prose, *A Place in Space* (1995) and *Back on the Fire: Essays* (2007). *The Gary Snyder Reader: Prose, Poetry, and Translations, 1952–1998* (1999) and *Look Out: A Selection of Writings* (2002) are good resources for surveying the shape of Snyder's career.

Summing up his commitment to poetry, Snyder stated:

> The act of making something, bringing elements together and creating a new thing with craft and wit hidden in it, is a great pleasure. It's not the only sort of pleasure, but it is challenging and satisfying, and not unlike other sorts of creating and building. In Greek "poema" means "makings." It doesn't change with the years, or with the centuries.

For the best introduction, see Charles Molesworth, *Gary Snyder's Vision: Poetry and the Real Work* (1983). See also Tim Dean, *Gary Snyder and the American Unconscious: Inhabiting the Ground* (1991); and Patrick D. Murphy, *A Place for Wayfaring: The Poetry and Prose of Gary Snyder* (2000). For further commentary and discussion, see *Gary Snyder: Dimensions of a Life*, ed. Jon Halper (1991); *Critical Essays on Gary Snyder*, ed. Patrick D. Murphy (1991); and Timothy Gray, *Gary Snyder and the Pacific Rim: Creating Countercultural Community* (2006).

Riprap[1]

Lay down these words
Before your mind like rocks.
   placed solid, by hands
In choice of place, set
Before the body of the mind   5
   in space and time:
Solidity of bark, leaf, or wall
   riprap of things:
Cobble of milky way,
   straying planets,   10
These poems, people,
   lost ponies with
Dragging saddles—
   and rocky sure-foot trails.

---

[1]Loose stone used to cover slippery trails or embankments.

The worlds like an endless 15
    four-dimensional
Game of *Go*.[2]
    ants and pebbles
In the thin loam, each rock a word
    a creek-washed stone 20
Granite: ingrained
    with torment of fire and weight
Crystal and sediment linked hot
    all change, in thoughts,
As well as things. 25

[1959]

August on Sourdough,[1] a Visit from Dick Brewer[2]

You hitched a thousand miles
    north from San Francisco
Hiked up the mountainside   a mile in the air
The little cabin—one room—
    walled in glass 5
Meadows and snowfields,   hundreds of peaks.
We lay in our sleeping bags
    talking half the night;
Wind in the guy-cables   summer mountain rain.
Next morning I went with you 10
    as far as the cliffs.
Loaned you my poncho—   the rain across the shale—
You down the snowfield
    flapping in the wind
Waving a last goodbye   half hidden in the clouds 15
To go on hitching
    clear to New York;
Me back to my mountain   and far, far, west.

[1968]

Ripples on the Surface

"Ripples on the surface of the water—
were silver salmon passing under—different
from the ripples caused by breezes"

---

[2]A Japanese game played with black and white stones on a checkered board.
[1]A mountain in the Far West where Snyder once worked.
[2]Dick Brewer, one of Snyder's friends, a professional surfer and surfboard builder, also interested in Buddhism.

A scudding plume on the wave—
a humpback whale is   5
breaking out in air up
gulping herring
        —Nature, not a book, but a *performance,* a
high old culture

Ever-fresh events   10
scraped out, rubbed out, and used, used, again—
the braided channels of the rivers
hidden under fields of grass—

The vast wild
        the house, alone.   15
The little house in the wild,
        the wild in the house.
Both forgotten.

                    No nature
            Both together, one big empty house.   20
                                        [1993]

SYLVIA PLATH ■ (1932–1963)

During the 1960s and 1970s, many viewed Sylvia Plath as a martyr-poet, a woman writer driven to her death by a cruelly self-absorbed husband and, more generally, by the difficult, if not impossible, challenge of both caring for young children and pursuing a literary career. This remains an important, although controversial and much-debated, dimension of Plath's life and work, but biographers and critics have in recent years explored as well the complex and conflicted nature of Plath's own personality. There is more to the story than her victimization, and the result is that her poetry has gained in depth and power.

Plath was born in Boston, Massachusetts. Her father, a German immigrant, was a professor at Boston University, and her mother was one of his former students. Plath grew up in the nearby coastal town of Winthrop, but, with her mother and brother, she moved at age ten to Wellesley, 12 miles to the west. Her father had died two years earlier, and the loss of this figure she loved and loathed lacerated Plath her entire life.

Brilliant, high-achieving, yet troubled and insecure, Plath attended Smith College in western Massachusetts, where she excelled as a student and won awards and published poems and stories. During her junior year, however, Plath suffered a breakdown, attempted suicide, and was hospitalized for six months (her therapy included electric shock treatments) before she managed to return to school.

Graduating *summa cum laude* from Smith in 1955, Plath traveled on a Fulbright fellowship to Cambridge University in England, where she met the poet Ted Hughes, marrying him in 1956. During the first six years of their marriage, they supported each other's literary endeavors. "Our minds," Hughes recalled, "soon became two parts of one operation. We dreamed a lot of shared or complementary dreams." He made his mark first, with much advice and help from her, through the publication of *The Hawk in the Rain*, an acclaimed volume of poems, in 1957. She, meanwhile, was unable to find a publisher for a collection of poems she had written. Hughes and Plath spent extended time in both Massachusetts and England and had two children, a daughter born in 1960 and a son born in 1962.

Plath's first book, *The Colossus and Other Poems*, appeared in 1960, and she also completed a novel, *The Bell Jar*, which was published early in 1963. Her marriage suffered strains in mid-1962 and shattered when Plath learned that Hughes was involved in a relationship with another woman. By fall 1962 they had separated, and soon thereafter Plath produced, in a span of about two months, her most brilliant, unforgettable poetry—bitter and agonized in tone, packed with rage and despair and desperation, craving love and understanding, ferocious and blazing in style and imagery. "I am writing the best poems of my life," she said in a letter to her mother. "They will make my name."

Low on money, Plath settled with her children in London in December 1962 during one of the coldest winters on record. She soon fell into a terrible depression, and in February she committed suicide. For insight into the dazzling, tormented mind of this driven, desperate writer, perhaps one should turn directly to *Ariel* (1965), which gathers the fierce, stunning poems Plath wrote in her final months of life. Her *Collected Poems* (1981) provides the full range of her work and can be supplemented by *Letters Home: Correspondence 1950–1963* (1975, containing correspondence between herself and her mother) and the *Unabridged Journals of Sylvia Plath, 1950–1962* (2000).

Plath's focus on private and personal experiences and her intense, even violent imagery have led her to be termed a "confessional" poet, associated in style and theme with Robert Lowell, John Berryman, Anne Sexton, and others. She made a version of this point herself in an interview published in October 1962:

> I've been very excited by what I feel is the new breakthrough that came with, say, Robert Lowell's *Life Studies*, this intense breakthrough into very serious, very personal, emotional experience which I feel has been partly taboo. Robert Lowell's poems about his experience in a mental hospital, for example, interested me very much. These peculiar, private and taboo subjects, I feel, have been explored in recent American poetry. I think particularly the poetess Anne Sexton, who writes about her experiences as a mother, as a mother who has had a nervous breakdown, is an extremely emotional and feeling young woman and her poems are wonderfully craftsman-like poems and yet they have a kind of emotional and psychological depth which I think is something perhaps quite new, quite exciting.

Ted Hughes in an interview (*The Paris Review*, 1995) decades after Plath's death, offered a related comment:

> Sylvia went furthest in the sense that her secret was most dangerous to her. She desperately needed to reveal it. You can't overestimate her compulsion to write like that. She had to write those things—even against her most vital interests.... She had to get them out. She had to tell everybody.

All of the poems here—"Morning Song," "Lady Lazarus," "Ariel," and "Daddy"—are included in *Ariel*. The writing of poetry exhilarated Plath. When asked whether poetry had been a "great satisfaction," she replied:

> Oh, satisfaction! I don't think I could live without it. It's like water or bread, or something absolutely essential to me. I find myself absolutely fulfilled when I have written a poem, when I'm writing one. Having written one, then you fall away very rapidly from having been a poet to becoming a sort of poet in rest, which isn't the same thing at all. But I think the actual experience of writing a poem is a magnificent one.

It was just after she said this that she wrote the poems in *Ariel* and then, one day, after placing cups of milk by the bedsides of her children, she wedged towels in the cracks of the kitchen door and killed herself by inhaling gas from the oven.

For studies that combine biography and critical interpretation, see Linda Wagner-Martin, *Sylvia Plath: A Biography* (1987; 2nd ed., 2003); Anne Stevenson, *Bitter Fame: A Life of Sylvia Plath* (1989); Jacqueline Rose, *The Haunting of Sylvia Plath* (1992). See also Janet Malcolm, *The Silent Woman: Sylvia Plath and Ted Hughes* (1994); and Erica Wagner, *Ariel's Gift: Ted Hughes, Sylvia Plath, and the Story of* Birthday Letters (2001). For literary analysis, see *Sylvia Plath: New Views on the Poetry*, ed. Gary Lane (1979); *Critical Essays on Sylvia Plath* (1984) and *Sylvia Plath: The Critical Heritage* (1988), ed. Linda W. Wagner; and Christina Britzolakis, *Sylvia Plath and the Theatre of Mourning* (1999). An importance primary source is *Ariel: The Restored Edition* (2004), which presents facsimile pages of the manuscript and other notes. See also Tim Kendall, *Sylvia Plath: A Critical Study* (2001); Dianne Middlebrook, *Her Husband: Hughes and Plath—A Marriage* (2003); and Heather L. Clark, *The Grief of Influence: Sylvia Plath and Ted Hughes* (2011). Other significant biographies include: Carl Rollyson, *American Isis: The Life and Art of Sylvia Plath* (2013); Andrew Wilson, *Mad Girl's Love Song: Sylvia Plath and Life Before Ted* (2013); and Elizabeth Winder, *Pain, Parties, Work: Sylvia Plath in New York, Summer 1953* (2013).

Morning Song

Love set you going like a fat gold watch.
The midwife slapped your footsoles, and your bald cry
Took its place among the elements.

Our voices echo, magnifying your arrival. New statue.
In a drafty museum, your nakedness   5
Shadows our safety. We stand round blankly as walls.

I'm no more your mother
Than the cloud that distils a mirror to reflect its own slow
Effacement at the wind's hand.

All night your moth-breath   10
Flickers among the flat pink roses. I wake to listen:
A far sea moves in my ear.

One cry, and I stumble from bed, cow-heavy and floral
In my Victorian nightgown.
Your mouth opens clean as a cat's. The window square   15

Whitens and swallows its dull stars. And now you try
Your handful of notes;
The clear vowels rise like balloons.

[1961, 1966]

Lady Lazarus[1]

I have done it again.
One year in every ten
I manage it—

A sort of walking miracle, my skin
Bright as a Nazi lampshade,[2]   5
My right foot

A paperweight,
My face a featureless, fine
Jew linen.

Peel off the napkin   10
O my enemy.
Do I terrify?—

The nose, the eye pits, the full set of teeth?
The sour breath
Will vanish in a day.   15

Soon, soon the flesh
The grave cave ate will be
At home on me

And I a smiling woman.
I am only thirty.   20
And like the cat I have nine times to die.

This is Number Three.
What a trash
To annihilate each decade.

What a million filaments.   25
The peanut-crunching crowd
Shoves in to see

Them unwrap me hand and foot—
The big strip tease.
Gentlemen, ladies   30

---

[1] In the Bible, John 11:1–44 relates the story of how Jesus raises his beloved friend Lazarus from the dead at the request of Lazarus's sisters, Martha and Mary of Bethany.
[2] In Nazi death camps, the skins of some victims were used to make lampshades.

These are my hands
My knees.
I may be skin and bone,

Nevertheless, I am the same, identical woman.
The first time it happened I was ten.   35
It was an accident.

The second time I meant
To last it out and not come back at all.
I rocked shut

As a seashell.   40
They had to call and call
And pick the worms off me like sticky pearls.

Dying
Is an art, like everything else.
I do it exceptionally well.   45

I do it so it feels like hell.
I do it so it feels real.
I guess you could say I've a call.

It's easy enough to do it in a cell.
It's easy enough to do it and stay put.   50
It's the theatrical

Comeback in broad day
to the same place, the same face, the same brute
Amused shout:

"A miracle!"   55
That knocks me out.
There is a charge

For the eyeing of my scars, there is a charge
For the hearing of my heart—
It really goes.   60

And there is a charge, a very large charge
For a word or a touch
Or a bit of blood

Or a piece of my hair or my clothes.
So, so, Herr Doktor.[3]   65
So, Herr Enemy.[4]

---

[3]Mr. Doctor (German).
[4]Located on the coast of Cape Cod, Massachusetts.

I am your opus,
I am your valuable,
The pure gold baby

That melts to a shriek.   70
I turn and burn.
Do not think I underestimate your great concern.

Ash, ash—
You poke and stir.
Flesh, bone, there is nothing there—   75

A cake of soap,
A wedding ring,
A gold filling.[5]

Herr God, Herr Lucifer[6]
Beware   80
Beware.

Out of the ash[7]
I rise with my red hair
And I eat men like air.

[1962, 1966]

Ariel[1]

Stasis in darkness.
Then the substanceless blue
Pour of tor[2] and distances.

God's lioness,[3]
How one we grow,   5
Pivot of heels and knees!—The furrow

Splits and passes, sister to
The brown arc
Of the neck I cannot catch,

Nigger-eye   10
Berries cast dark
Hooks—

[5]The Nazis scavenged the bodies of the victims of the death camps for gold fillings and jewelry.
[6]Satan; the devil.
[7]A reference to the phoenix, a mythical bird that is consumed by fire and then reborn from its own ashes. Also an allusion to the crematoriums used at the Nazi death camps to burn the bodies of their victims.
[1]A character in Shakespeare's play *The Tempest* who is a spirit of the air. Ariel was also the name of a horse owned by Plath when she wrote this poem. In Hebrew, Ariel literally translates to "lion of God."
[2]A high, rocky peak.
[3]See note 1.

Black sweet blood mouthfuls,
Shadows.
Something else   15

Hauls me through air—
Thighs, hair;
Flakes from my heels.

White
Godiva,[4] I unpeel—   20
Dead hands, dead stringencies.

And now I
Foam to wheat, a glitter of seas.
The child's cry

Melts in the wall.   25
And I
Am the arrow,

The dew that flies
Suicidal, at one with the drive
Into the red   30

Eye, the cauldron of morning.

                                                         [1962, 1966]

Daddy

You do not do, you do not do
Any more, black shoe
In which I have lived like a foot
For thirty years, poor and white,
Barely daring to breathe or Achoo.   5

Daddy, I have had to kill you.
You died before I had time—
Marble-heavy, a bag full of God,
Ghastly statue with one gray toe
Big as a Frisco seal   10

And a head in the freakish Atlantic
Where it pours bean green over blue
In the waters off beautiful Nauset.[5]

---

[4]A reference to Lady Godiva, who rode naked on her horse through the streets of Coventry, England, in 1040 to gain a remission from taxes for the subjects in her shire.
[5]Located on the coast of Cape Cod, Massachusetts.

I used to pray to recover you.
Ach, du.[1]   15

In the German tongue, in the Polish town
Scraped flat by the roller
Of wars, wars, wars.
But the name of the town is common.
My Polack friend   20

Says there are a dozen or two.
So I never could tell where you
Put your foot, your root,
I never could talk to you.
The tongue stuck in my jaw.   25

I stuck in a barb wire snare.
Ich, ich, ich, ich,[2]
I could hardly speak.
I thought every German was you.
And the language obscene   30

An engine, an engine
Chuffing me off like a Jew.
A Jew to Dachau, Auschwitz, Belsen.[3]
I began to talk like a Jew.
I think I may well be a Jew.   35

The snows of the Tyrol, the clear beer of Vienna
Are not very pure or true.
With my gipsy ancestress and my weird luck
And my Taroc[4] pack and my Taroc pack
I may be a bit of a Jew.   40

I have always been scared of *you,*
With your Luftwaffe,[5] your gobbledygoo.
And your neat mustache
And your Aryan eye, bright blue.
Panzer-man,[6] panzer-man, O You—   45

Not God but a swastika[7]
So black no sky could squeak through.
Every woman adores a Fascist,

[1] O, you (German).
[2] The first-person pronoun, I (German).
[3] Nazi concentration camps.
[4] Taroc, or tarot, is an old European card-game.
[5] German air force.
[6] Member of a tank crew.
[7] An ancient symbol in the form of an equal-armed cross with each arm continued at a right angle, used as the emblem of the German Nazi Party.

The boot in the face, the brute
Brute heart of a brute like you.   50

You stand at the blackboard, daddy,
In the picture I have of you,
A cleft in your chin instead of your foot
But no less a devil for that, no not
Any less the black man who   55

Bit my pretty red heart in two.
I was ten when they buried you.
At twenty I tried to die
And get back, back, back to you.
I thought even the bones would do.   60

But they pulled me out of the sack,
And they stuck me together with glue.
And then I knew what to do.
I made a model of you,
A man in black with a Meinkampf[8] look   65

And a love of the rack and the screw.
And I said I do, I do.
So daddy, I'm finally through.
The black telephone's off at the root,
The voices just can't worm through.   70

If I've killed one man, I've killed two—
The vampire who said he was you
And drank my blood for a year,
Seven years, if you want to know.
Daddy, you can lie back now.   75

There's a stake in your fat black heart
And the villagers never liked you.
They are dancing and stamping on you.
They always *knew* it was you.
Daddy, daddy, you bastard, I'm through.   80

[1962, 1966]

---

[8]*Mein Kampf* ("My Struggle") is the title of Adolf Hitler's autobiography, written when he was sent to prison for treason in 1923.

LINDA PASTAN ■ (1932—)

Born and raised in New York City, Linda Pastan received her undergraduate degree from Radcliffe College and her master's degree from Brandeis University. A resident of Potomac, Maryland, outside Washington, D.C., she served as Maryland's poet laureate from 1991 to 1994.

Pastan focuses in her best work on love, death, the family, and other fundamental themes and settings of everyday experience, often with an ironic edge and an incisive humor. She gives close attention to persons and feelings close to home; as she says in one of her poems, "Let the eye enlarge with all it beholds."

One critic noted about Pastan that she "in large measure [has] fulfilled Emerson's dream—the revelation of the miraculous in the common." Another observed, "She is a poet of a hundred small delights, celebrations, responses, satisfactions, pleasures."

For surveying Pastan's achievement, explore *Carnival Evening: New and Selected Poems, 1968–1998* (1998), which shows her command of domestic scenes and relationships even as its extends her range into new areas and features her skill as a lyric storyteller. Since the publication of this volume, Pastan has written three more collections of poems: *The Last Uncle* (2002), *Queen of a Rainy Country* (2006), and *Traveling Light* (2011).

For secondary sources, see *Dictionary of Literary Biography, Volume 5: American Poets Since World War II*, first series, edited Donald J. Greiner (1980), 158–163.

Marks

My husband gives me an A
for last night's supper,
an incomplete for my ironing,
a B plus in bed.
My son says I am average,   5
an average mother, but if
I put my mind to it
I could improve.
My daughter believes
in Pass/Fail and tells me   10
I pass. Wait 'til they learn
I'm dropping out.

[1978]

AMIRI BARAKA■ (1934–)

A Poem for Black Hearts

For Malcolm's[1] eyes, when they broke
the face of some dumb white man, For
Malcolm's hands raised to bless us
all black and strong in his image
of ourselves. For Malcolm's words   5
fire darts, the victor's tireless
thrusts, words hung above the world
change as it may, he said it, and
for this he was killed, for saying,
and feeling, and being/change, all   10
collected hot in his heart. For Malcolm's
heart, raising us above our filthy cities,
for his stride, and his beat, and his address
to the gray monsters of the world. For Malcolm's
pleas for your dignity, black men, for your life,   15
black man, for the filling of your minds
with righteousness. For all of him dead and
gone and vanished from us, and all of him which
clings to our speech black god of our time.
For all of him, and all of yourself, look up,   20
black man, quit stuttering and shuffling, look up,
black man, quit whining and stooping, for all of him.
For Great Malcolm a prince of the earth, let nothing in us rest
until we avenge ourselves for his death, stupid animals
that killed him, let us never breathe a pure breath if   25
we fail and white men call us faggots[2] till the end of
the earth.

[1969]

---

[1]Malcolm X (1925–65), a militant black leader who rose to prominence as a Black Muslim. Suspended
from the Black Muslims, he formed his own organization, the Muslim Mosque. In 1964 he converted to
orthodox Islam and proclaimed the brotherhood of blacks and whites, although he continued to support black nationalism. He was shot to death in 1965, perhaps as an act of vengeance by Black Muslims.
[2]Faggot is an offensive term for a male homosexual.

MARY OLIVER ■ (1935–)

Mary Oliver was born in Maple Heights, a suburb of Cleveland, Ohio, and attended Ohio State University (1955–56) and Vassar College (1956–57). A major influence on her literary development was the work of the modern lyric poet Edna St. Vincent Millay, but, as critics have noted, Oliver's style, approach to the poetic line, and piercing clarity connect her as well to the Romantic poet William Blake and to Emily Dickinson. Other scholars call attention to Oliver's affinities with D. H. Lawrence, Marianne Moore, and Elizabeth Bishop, and, even more, to Theodore Roethke and James Wright.

Oliver is distinctive for her attentiveness to nature, to nature tinged by loss and regret and touched inevitably by the presence of death. The poet Maxine Kumin said about Oliver that she is "an indefatigable guide to the natural world," and this guidance is connected to her feeling for the movement of time, shadowing everything. Oliver's style is lucidly controlled, yet subtle, expressive, affectingly engaged with its subject, always "warmly human and open," as the poet-critic Sandra M. Gilbert remarked. In an interview (1992), Oliver said: "I decided very early that I wanted to write. But I didn't think of it as a career. I didn't even think of it as a profession.... It was the most exciting thing, the most powerful thing, the most wonderful thing to do with my life." In a later interview (2011), she described herself as a poet in this way: "I consider myself kind of a reporter—one who uses words that are more like music and that have a choreography."

Oliver's books include *No Voyage and Other Poems* (1963, expanded edition, 1965), *Twelve Moons* (1978), *American Primitive* (1983, winner of the Pulitzer Prize), and *Dream Work* (1986). Oliver's significant publications are *New and Selected Poems* (1992), for which she was honored with the National Book Award, and *A Poetry Handbook* (1994). She also is the author of *Long Life: Essays and Other Writings* (2004) and *New and Selected Poems*, volume 2 (2005).

For background and context, see *Dictionary of Literary Biography, Volume 5: American Poets Since World War II* (1980). See also Diane S. Bonds, "The Language of Nature in the Poetry of Mary Oliver," *Women's Studies* 21:1 (1992), 1–15; and David Barber, review of *New and Selected Poems* in *Poetry* 162:4 (July 1993), 233–242.

The Black Snake

When the black snake
flashed onto the morning road,
and the truck could not swerve—
death, that is how it happens.

Now he lies looped and useless   5
as an old bicycle tire.
I stop the car
and carry him into the bushes.

He is as cool and gleaming
as a braided whip, he is as beautiful and quiet   10
as a dead brother.
I leave him under the leaves

and drive on, thinking
about *death:* its suddenness,
its terrible weight,   15
its certain coming. Yet under

reason burns a brighter fire,
which the bones
have always preferred.
It is the story of endless good fortune.   20
It says to oblivion: not me!

It is the light at the center of every cell.
It is what sent the snake coiling and flowing forward
happily all spring through the green leaves before
he came to the road.   25

[1979]

Hawk

This morning
   the hawk
      rose up
         out of the meadow's browse

and swung over the lake—   5
   it settled
      on the small black dome
         of a dead pine,

alert as an admiral,
   its profile   10
      distinguished with sideburns
         the color of smoke,

and I said: remember
　　this is not something
　　　　of the red fire, this is
　　　　　　heaven's fistful

of death and destruction,
　　and the hawk hooked
　　　　one exquisite foot
　　　　　　onto a last twig

to look deeper
　　into the yellow reeds
　　　　along the edges of the water
　　　　　　and I said: remember

the tree, the cave,
　　the white lily of resurrection,
　　　　and that's when it simply lifted
　　　　　　its golden feet and floated

into the wind, belly-first,
　　and then it cruised along the lake—
　　　　all the time its eyes fastened
　　　　　　harder than love on some

unimportant rustling in the
　　yellow reeds—and then it
　　　　seemed to crouch high in the air, and then it
　　　　　　turned into a white blade, which fell.

[1992]

The poet Lucille Clifton was born in Depew, New York, and educated at Howard University in Washington, D.C., where her teachers included the poets Sterling Brown and Amiri Baraka, and at Fredonia State College in southwest New York. Clifton began her writing career in 1969 with the publication of a book of poems, *Good Times*; later the author of a number of books for young people, she was at this time the mother of six children, all under the age of ten.

A poet of the commonplace and everyday, of the family and community, Clifton is subtle and provocative, more so than the spare surface of her work might at first suggest. Her poetry, the critic Mari Evans has said, is "a conscious, quiet introduction to the real world of Black sensitivities." Another critic, Ronald Baughman, commented that Clifton's "pride in being black and in being a woman helps her transform difficult circumstances into a qualified affirmation about the black urban world she portrays."

Clifton herself emphasized the centrality to her art of her African American identity, observing in an interview (1998):

> A person can, I hope, enjoy the poetry without knowing that I am black or female. But it adds to their understanding if they do know it—that is, that I am black and female. To me, that I am what I am is all of it; all of what I am is relevant.

The best points of departure for the appreciation of Clifton's verse are *Good Woman: Poems and a Memoir, 1969–1980* (1987); *Next: New Poems* (1987); and *Blessing the Boats: New and Selected Poems, 1988–2000* (2000). She is the author of *Generations* (1976), which traces her family history amid the history of slavery, segregation, and racial oppression.

For commentary, see Alicia Ostriker, "Kith and Kin: The Poetry of Lucille Clifton," *American Poetry Review* 22 (1993), 41–48; and Robin Becker, "The Poetics of Engagement," *American Poetry Review* 30:6 (November–December 2001), 11–17. See also Wallace R. Peppers, "Lucille Clifton," *Dictionary of Literary Biography* 41 (1985), 55–60; Hilary Holladay, *Wild Blessings: The Poetry of Lucille Clifton* (2004); and Mary Jane Lupton, *Lucille Clifton: Her Life and Letters* (2006).

In the Inner City

in the inner city
or
like we call it
home
we think a lot about uptown   5

and the silent nights
and the houses straight as
dead men
and the pastel lights
and we hang on to our no place   10
happy to be alive
and in the inner city
or
like we call it
home   15

[1987]

MICHAEL S. HARPER ■ (1938—)

Born in Brooklyn, New York, Michael S. Harper moved with his family in 1951 to a predominantly white neighborhood in Los Angeles. Harper's father, a postal worker, and his mother, a medical stenographer, hoped their son would become a doctor, but he resisted this career path. He attended Los Angeles City College and then Los Angeles State College, taking courses while holding a job in the post office. In 1961, having written a few poems, Harper enrolled in the Iowa Writer's Workshop (he was assigned to segregated housing). He received an MFA in 1963 and soon thereafter began his career as a teacher.

Harper's first book of poems was *Dear John, Dear Coltrane* (1970); the title poem, following, refers to the African American saxophonist John Coltrane, whose albums include *A Love Supreme* (1964). It dramatizes Harper's interest in jazz—note too, the poem on another jazz saxophonist, Charlie Parker, nicknamed "The Bird"—as a form of expression at once personal, historical, and mythic in its power. As the critic Brian A. Spillane observed, Harper is attuned to the verbal and musical resources of Black people, yet ultimately he draws on "African-American, white, and even Native American history and traditions, and is truly an American poet, reflecting the complexity of the country as a whole."

Harper published *Images of Kin: New and Selected Poems* in 1977. It has since been superseded by *Songlines in Michaeltree: New and Collected Poems* (2000). Harper is also coeditor, with Robert B. Stepto, of an important anthology of texts and criticism, *Chant of Saints: A Gathering of Afro-American Literature, Art, and Scholarship* (1979). He served as poet laureate of Rhode Island and for many years has taught as a member of the English Department of Brown University. Harper's recent publications include *Use Trouble: Poems* (2009). About this book, the scholar Anthony Walton has made this forceful comment: "From tragic meditations on American public life and history to searingly perceptive ruminations on the griefs and epiphanies of a private soul, [Harper] uses *trouble* to illuminate and document his complicated life's journey as a son, father, poet, American, and black man. His perceptions of trouble wind, float, and burn through the mind in a way that is echoed in the lines and forms of the poems themselves, forcing and allowing us as readers ever closer to the actual processes of poetic vision and interpretation."

For further study, see Robert B. Stepto, "Michael S. Harper, Poet as Kinsman: The Family Sequences," *Massachusetts Review* 17 (Autumn 1976): 477–502, and "After Modernism, After Hibernation: Michael Harper, Robert Hayden and Jay Wright," in *Chant of Saints: A Gathering of Afro-American Literature, Art, and Scholarship*, eds. Michael S. Harper and Robert B. Septo, 470–486; Gunter H. Lenz, "Black Poetry and Black Music: History and Tradition: Michael Harper and John Coltrane," in *History and*

Tradition in Afro-American Culture* (1984), 277–319; Joseph Brown, "Their Long Scars Touch Ours: A Reflection on the Poetry of Michael Harper," *Callaloo* 9, no. 1 (1986): 209–220; and "Michael S. Harper: American Poet," special issue of *Callaloo* 13, no. 4 (Fall 1990): 749–829.

Dear John, Dear Coltrane[1]

> *a love supreme, a love supreme*
> *a love supreme, a love supreme*

Sex fingers toes
in the marketplace
near your father's church
in Hamlet, North Carolina—   5
witness to this love
in this calm fallow
of these minds,
there is no substitute for pain:
genitals gone or going,   10
seed burned out,
you tuck the roots in the earth,
turn back, and move
by river through the swamps,
singing: *a love supreme, a love supreme;*   15
what does it all mean?
Loss, so great each black
woman expects your failure
in mute change, the seed gone.
You plod up into the electric city—   20
your song now crystal and
the blues. You pick up the horn
with some will and blow
into the freezing night: 25
a love supreme, a love supreme—

Dawn comes and you cook
up the thick sin 'tween
impotence and death, fuel
the tenor sax cannibal   30
heart, genitals and sweat
that makes you clean—
a love supreme, a love supreme—

---

[1]John Coltrane (1926–67) was a saxophonist, composer, bandleader, and seminal figure of the free jazz movement of the 1960s. *A Love Supreme* is considered his most influential work.

Why you so black?
cause I am   35
why you so funky?
cause I am
why you so black?
cause I am
why you so sweet?   40
cause I am
why you so black?
cause I am
a love supreme, a love supreme:

So sick   45
you couldn't play *Naima,*[2]
so flat we ached
for song you'd concealed
with your own blood,
your diseased liver gave   50
out its purity,
the inflated heart
pumps out, the tenor kiss,
tenor love:
a love supreme, a love supreme—   55
a love supreme, a love supreme—

[1970]

John Coltrane, 1960.

[2]"Naima" is a ballad composed by John Coltrane in 1959, and named after his then-wife, Juanita Naima
Grubbs.

Martin's[1] Blues

He came apart in the open,
the slow motion cameras
falling quickly
neither alive nor kicking;
stone blind dead   5
on the balcony
that old melody
etched his black lips
in a pruned echo:
We shall overcome   10
some day—
Yes we did!
Yes we did!

[1971]

"Bird Lives": Charles Parker[1] in St. Louis

Last on legs, last on sax,
last in Indian wars, last on *smack*,
Bird is specious, *Bird* is alive,
horn, unplayable, before, after,
right now: it's heroin time: 5
smack, in the melody a trip;
smack, in the Mississippi;
smack, in the drug merchant trap;
smack, in St. Louis, Missouri.

We knew you were through—   10
trying to get out of town,
unpaid bills, connections
unmet, unwanted, unasked,
Bird's in the last arc
of his own light: *blow Bird!*   15
And you did—
screaming, screaming, baby,
for life, after it, around it,
screaming for life, *blow Bird!*

---

[1]Martin Luther King Jr. (1929–68), American civil rights leader who was assassinated on a motel
balcony in Memphis, Tennessee, April 4, 1968.
[1]Charlie "Yardbird" Parker (1920–55) is considered one of the major influential African American jazz
soloists of the twentieth century. In the 1940s he was a central figure in the development of bop.

What is the meaning of music?   20
What is the meaning of war?
What is the meaning of oppression?
Blow Bird! Ripped up and down
into the interior of life, the pain,
Bird, the embraceable you,[2]   25
how many brothers gone,
smacked out: blues and racism,
the hardest, longest penis
in the Mississippi urinal:
Blow Bird!   30

Taught more musicians, then forgot,
space loose, fouling the melodies,
the marching songs, the fine white
geese from the plantations,
syrup in this pork barrel,   35
Kansas City, the even teeth
of the mafia, the big band:
Blow Bird! Inside out Charlie's
guts, *Blow Bird!* get yourself killed.

In the first wave, the musicians,   40
out there, alone, in the first wave;
everywhere you went, Massey Hall,
Sweden, New Rochelle, *Birdland*,
nameless bird, Blue Note, Carnegie,[3]
tuxedo junction, out of nowhere,   45
confirmation, confirmation, confirmation:
Bird Lives! Bird Lives! and you do:
Dead—

                                                          [1971]

---

[2]The title of a song made famous by Charlie Parker in 1950.
[3]Places where Charlie Parker performed.

FRANK BIDART ■ (1939—)

Frank Bidart is one of America's most innovative and intense contemporary poets, the author of bold, provocative work in both style and theme. He was born in Bakersfield, California, and received his BA from the University of California, Riverside, and his MA from Harvard, where he studied and became friends with Robert Lowell and Elizabeth Bishop. Bidart lives in Cambridge, Massachusetts, and since 1972 he has taught literature and creative writing at Wellesley College. He has received many awards, including, in 2007, the Bollingen Prize in American Poetry, one of the most significant of literary honors.

The following poem, "Self-Portrait, 1969," is included in *Golden State*, Bidart's first book (1973), which was followed by *The Book of the Body* (1977). His major book of the 1980s was *The Sacrifice*, and he concluded the decade with *In the Western Night: Collected Poems* (1990). His other books include *Desire* (1997), *Music Like Dirt* (2002), *Star Dust* (2005), *Watching the Spring Festival* (2008), and *Metaphysical Dog* (2013). Of his poetry, the poet Louise Glück has said, "Since the publication, in 1973, of *Golden State*, Frank Bidart has patiently amassed as profound and original a body of work as any now being written in this country."

In interviews and prose pieces, Bidart has noted important influences on his development as a writer, including Ezra Pound, T. S. Eliot, Sylvia Plath, and Lowell—he is (with David Gewanter) the editor of *The Collected Poems of Robert Lowell* (2002). He has spoken in particular about the impact of reading Pound's *Cantos*: "They were tremendously liberating in the way that they say that anything can be gotten into a poem, that it doesn't have to change its essential identity to enter the poem—if you can create a structure that is large enough or strong enough, anything can retain its own identity and find its place there." For Bidart, a poet becomes original, making something new, through reading and absorbing the poets in the literary tradition. As he observed in an interview (2007): "On the one hand one feels a work is powerful and original when the writer's eye is on those animating insights that lead one to write the poem in the first place, and you're not saying *look how clever I am in relation to the tradition*. But, in fact, you are using something from the tradition; you are using a form or container, but you are making it seem so necessitous, it is so animated by a sense that *this is how I must speak*, that it feels fresh and original."

Throughout his career, Bidart has shown great daring in the structure of his verse, in its arrangement on the page, with vivid, startling choices in lineation, typography, and quotation—he makes frequent strategic use, for example, of italicized and capitalized words, and sometimes he shifts from verse into prose and back again. What Bidart writes about and the voices through which he writes are provocative, even shocking and near-scandalous: the subjects of his poems include a psychopathic child-murderer, an amputee, a suicidal anorexic, and a pair of incestuous lovers, and his autobiographical exploration and revelation in his writing are both disturbing and riveting, brilliant, full of anguish, guilt, and illumination, of extremity, paradox, and contradiction.

Bidart is best known for his long, detailed, meditative, and thrilling dramatic monologues. A case in point is his thirty-page "The War of Vaslav Nijinsky," included in *The Sacrifice*. But Bidart also has written many sharply concentrated shorter poems, such as "Self-Portrait, 1969," in which the poet's scrutiny of self occurs through a third-person gaze and reflection. "One thing art, again and again, has done," Bidart has said, "is to create a structure where the things that are beneath the surface in ordinary life are revealed. And, I think, one of the things we all crave is for what is real to be revealed." "But," he adds, "it's often frightening," as this poem attests.

For commentary and interpretation, the best place to begin is *On Frank Bidart: Fastening the Voice to the Page*, eds. Liam Rector and Tree Swenson (2007), which includes interviews and essays by a wide range of poets and critics. Also stimulating are Calvin Bedient, "Frank Bidart: Tragedian," *Salmagundi* 118–119 (Spring-Summer 1998), 328–336—this essay is reprinted in *On Frank Bidart*; and William Olsen, "Poetry and Emotion," *Chicago Review*, 44:3/4 (1998), 328–336. See also the interviews with Bidart in *Ploughshares* 9:1 (1983), 11–32; *Chicago Review* 47:3 (Fall 2001), 21–42; and *Literary Review* 53:1 (Fall 2009), 191–198.

Self-Portrait, 1969

He's still young—; thirty, but looks younger—
or does he?... In the eyes and cheeks, tonight,
turning in the mirror, he saw his mother,—
puffy; angry; bewildered... Many nights,
now, when he stares there, he gets angry:—   5
something *unfulfilled* there, something dead
to what he once thought he surely could be—
Now, just the glamour of habits...

                        Once, instead,
he thought insight would remake him, he'd reach   10
—what? The thrill, the exhilaration
unravelling disaster, that seemed to teach
necessary knowledge... became just jargon.

Sick of being decent, he craves another
crash. What *reaches* him except disaster?   15

                                     [1973]

The poet laureate of the United States from 2001 to 2003, and professor at Lehman College of the City University of New York, Billy Collins was born in New York City. He was educated in Catholic grammar and high schools, received his BA from the College of the Holy Cross (1963), and then his MA and PhD from the University of California, Riverside.

Collins is the most popular poet in the United States, admired by many for his insight, imagination, and wit, as can be seen in the poem "Sonnet," which is a clever, agile exploration of the "sonnet" genre itself. "The Names," although also adroit and even playful in its verbal maneuvers, is a more reflective and somber work, a poem that Collins composed to commemorate the victims of the terrorist attacks of September 11, 2001, aimed at New York City and Washington, D.C. He read "The Names" at a special joint session of Congress, September 6, 2002, and he has chosen not to include it in any of the books of poetry that he has published.

Some have criticized Collins for being too explicit in his aims and themes, even for being too clear, conversational, and accessible. But this is his intention; he seeks to be clear and accessible to readers—which is not the same as being easy or simple. As Collins explained in an interview (2004), he believes that he changed for the better as a poet when he "began to dare to be clear, because I think clarity is the real risk in poetry because you are exposed. You're out in the open field. You're actually saying things that are comprehensible, and it's easy to criticize something you can understand." The critic John Taylor has noted in this regard that there is more to a poem by Collins than a reader might initially assume: "Rarely has anyone written poems that appear so transparent on the surface yet become so ambiguous, thought-provoking, or simply wise once the reader has peered into the depths."

In an interview (2005), Collins offered this insight into how readers can best appreciate his own and others' poems: We should

> substitute for the question "What does this poem mean?" the question "How does this poem go?" In other words, how does this poem move? You could compare it to maneuvers on a basketball court. How does this poem find its way down the court? One way is to start to look at the very beginning of the poem to see where we are, then look at the end of the poem and see where we end up.

Describing his response to Collins, the poet Stephen Dunn has made a related observation: "We seem to always know where we are in a Billy Collins poem, but not necessarily where he is going. I love to arrive with him at his arrivals. He doesn't hide things from us, as I think lesser poets do. He allows us to overhear, clearly, what he himself has discovered."

Collins's books of poetry include *Sailing Alone Around the Room: New and Selected Poems* (2001); *The Trouble with Poetry and Other Poems* (2007); and *Horoscopes for the Dead* (2011). For a commentary on Collins's work, see Dennis O'Driscoll, review of *Sailing Alone Around the Room*, in *Poetry*, 180:1 (April 2002), 32–39. See also the wide-ranging interview with Collins published in *The Paris Review*, 43 (Fall 2001), 182–216.

Sonnet[1]

All we need is fourteen lines, well, thirteen now,
and after this next one just a dozen
to launch a little ship on love's storm-tossed seas,
then only ten more left like rows of beans.
How easily it goes unless you get Elizabethan   5
and insist the iambic bongos must be played
and rhymes positioned at the ends of lines,
one for every station of the cross.[2]
But hang on here while we make the turn
into the final six where all will be resolved,   10
where longing and heartache will find an end,
where Laura will tell Petrarch to put down his pen,[3]
take off those crazy medieval tights,
blow out the lights, and come at last to bed.

[2001]

The Names

Yesterday, I lay awake in the palm of the night.
A soft rain stole in, unhelped by any breeze,
And when I saw the silver glaze on the windows,
I started with A, with Ackerman, as it happened,
Then Baxter and Calabro,   5
Davis and Eberling, names falling into place
As droplets fell through the dark.
Names printed on the ceiling of the night.
Names slipping around a watery bend.
Twenty-six willows on the banks of a stream.   10
In the morning, I walked out barefoot

---

[1]A poem of fourteen lines, usually in iambic pentameter (ten syllables, in a unstressed/stressed pattern), with rhymes arranged according to one of certain definite schemes. The Italian (Petrarchan—see below) form is divided into a major group of eight lines (the octave) followed by a minor group of six lines (the sestet), and the common English (Shakespearean) form into three quatrains followed by a rhyming couplet.
[2]The Stations of the Cross are the depiction, in fourteen scenes, of the final hours (or Passion) of Jesus and the devotion commemorating the Passion.
[3]The Italian poet and scholar Petrarch (1304–74) composed a series of sonnets to his beloved, Laura.

Among thousands of flowers
Heavy with dew like the eyes of tears,
And each had a name—
Fiori inscribed on a yellow petal 　　　　　　　　　　15
Then Gonzalez and Han, Ishikawa and Jenkins.
Names written in the air
And stitched into the cloth of the day.
A name under a photograph taped to a mailbox.
Monogram on a torn shirt, 　　　　　　　　　　　　20
I see you spelled out on storefront windows
And on the bright unfurled awnings of this city.
I say the syllables as I turn a corner—
Kelly and Lee,
Medina, Nardella, and O'Connor. 　　　　　　　　　25
When I peer into the woods,
I see a thick tangle where letters are hidden
As in a puzzle concocted for children.
Parker and Quigley in the twigs of an ash,
Rizzo, Schubert, Torres, and Upton, 　　　　　　　　30
Secrets in the boughs of an ancient maple.
Names written in the pale sky.
Names rising in the updraft amid buildings.
Names silent in stone
Or cried out behind a door. 　　　　　　　　　　　35
Names blown over the earth and out to sea.
In the evening—weakening light, the last swallows.
A boy on a lake lifts his oars.
A woman by a window puts a match to a candle,
And the names are outlined on the rose clouds— 　　40
Vanacore and Wallace,
(let X stand, if it can, for the ones unfound)
Then Young and Ziminsky, the final jolt of Z.
Names etched on the head of a pin.
One name spanning a bridge, another undergoing a tunnel. 　45
A blue name needled into the skin.
Names of citizens, workers, mothers and fathers,
The bright-eyed daughter, the quick son.
Alphabet of names in a green field.
Names in the small tracks of birds. 　　　　　　　　50
Names lifted from a hat
Or balanced on the tip of the tongue.
Names wheeled into the dim warehouse of memory.
So many names, there is barely room on the walls of the heart.

　　　　　　　　　　　　　　　　　　　　　[2002]

GLORIA ANZALDÚA ■ (1942–2004)

The Chicana lesbian author Gloria Anzaldúa was born and raised in South Texas. When she was eleven her family moved to Hargill, Texas, and in the next few years the family traveled as migrant workers between Texas and Arkansas. She attended Pan American University, the University of Texas, and the University of California, Santa Cruz. She makes use of, explores, and blends genres (including poetry, essay, short story), as her most important book, *Borderlands/La Frontera: The New Mestiza* (1987), from which the following poem is reprinted, demonstrates. *Borderlands* was chosen one of the best books of 1987 by Library Journal. Her work also received the Lambda Lesbian Small Book Press Award and the Before Columbus Foundation American Book Award. Anzaldúa is the editor of two influential volumes: (with Cherrie Moraga) *The Bridge Called My Back: Writings by Radical Women of Color* (1981) and *Making Face, Making Soul/ Haciendo Caras: Creative and Critical Perspectives by Women of Color* (1990).

See "Gloria Anzaldúa," in *Dictionary of Literary Biography, Volume 122: Chicano Writers*, second series (1992), 8–17. See also *The Gloria Anzaldúa Reader*, ed. AnaLouise Keating (2009), a posthumous volume that includes poetry, prose, fiction, and experimental autobiographical writing.

To live in the Borderlands means you

To live in the Borderlands means you
    are neither *hispana india negra española*
    ni gabacha, eres mestiza, mulata,[1] half-breed
    caught in the crossfire between camps
    while carrying all five races on your back
    not knowing which side to turn to, run from;   5

To live in the Borderlands means knowing
    that the *india* in you, betrayed for 500 years,
    is no longer speaking to you,
    that *mexicanas* call you *rajetas,*[2]
    that denying the Anglo inside you   10
    is as bad as having denied the Indian or Black;

Cuando vives en la frontera[3]
    people walk through you, the wind steals your voice,
    you're a *burra, buey,*[4] scapegoat,

---

[1] Neither Spanish Indian black Spanish woman, nor white, you are mixed, a mixed breed.
[2] Split, having betrayed your word [Author's note].
[3] When you live in the borderlands.
[4] Donkey, ox [Author's note].

forerunner of a new race,   15
half and half—both woman and man, neither—
a new gender;

To live in the Borderlands means to
    put *chile* in the borscht,
    eat whole wheat *tortillas,*   20
    speak Tex-Mex with a Brooklyn accent;
    be stopped by *la migra*[5] at the border checkpoints;

Living in the Borderlands means you fight hard to
    resist the gold elixir beckoning from the bottle,
    the pull of the gun barrel,   25
    the rope crushing the hollow of your throat;

In the Borderlands
    you are the battleground
    where enemies are kin to each other;
    you are at home, a stranger,   30
    the border disputes have been settled
    the volley of shots have shattered the truce
    you are wounded, lost in action
    dead, fighting back;

To live in the Borderlands means   35
    the mill with the razor white teeth wants to shred off
    your olive-red skin, crush out the kernel, your heart
    pound you pinch you roll you out
    smelling like white bread but dead;

To survive the Borderlands   40
    you must live *sin fronteras*[6]
    be a crossroads.

                                                          [1987]

---

[5]Immigration officials.
[6]Without borders.

JOSEPH BRUCHAC III ■ (1942–)

The Native American (Abenaki) short-story writer, essayist, and poet Joseph Bruchac, author of more than thirty books, is dedicated to the understanding and propagation of the experiences and cultures of his people. This body of work, he has said, enabled his own sons to "grow up taking such things as sweat lodges and powwows and pride in Indian ancestry for granted. The small amount that I have learned I've tried, when right to do so, to share with others."

As the following poem, "Ellis Island," indicates, Bruchac is also Slovak (and English) in his ancestry. Growing up in the Adirondack Mountains of upstate New York, he did not make connections with Native Americans and their communities until his teenage years.

Bruchac's diverse publications include *Indian Mountain and Other Poems* (1971); *Turkey Brother and Other Tales* (1976); *The Dreams of Jesse Brown* (1977, novel); *Walking with My Sons and Other Poems* (1986); *Survival This Way: Interviews with Native American Poets* (1987); *Long Memory and Other Poems* (1989); *Turtle Meat and Other Stories* (1992); and *Bowman's Store: A Journey to Myself* (1997, autobiography). In an interview (1999), Bruchac expressed his vision as a human being and as a writer: "We need to listen to each other. We need to remember we were given two ears so we can always hear in more than one direction. I think we also need to remember that every human being shares the drumbeat of the heart. As much as we need to recognize those things that are different between us and celebrate our diversity, we also need to remember that we all share the heartbeat of the earth."

For further study, see *Ellis Island: An Illustrated History of the Immigrant Experience*, Ivan Chermayeff, designer, Fred Wasserman, editor, Mary J. Shapiro, writer (1991); Orm Øverland, *Immigrant Minds, American Identities: Making the United States Home, 1870–1930* (2000); and Nancy Foner, *From Ellis Island to JFK: New York's Two Great Waves of Immigration* (2000). See also Bruchac's *Ndakinna = Our Land: New and Selected Poems* (2003).

Ellis Island[1]

Beyond the red brick of Ellis Island
where the two Slovak children
who became my grandparents
waited the long days of quarantine,
after leaving the sickness,   5

---

[1]Ellis Island, located in the upper New York Bay, a short distance from the New Jersey shore, was the gateway for more than half of the immigrants entering the United States between 1892 and 1924. Ellis Island was closed to immigration in 1954.

the old Empires of Europe,
a Circle Line ship slips easily
on its way to the island
of the tall woman, green
as dreams of forests and meadows   10
waiting for those who'd worked

a thousand years
yet never owned their own.

Like millions of others,
I too come to this island,   15
nine decades the answerer
of dreams.

Yet only one part of my blood loves that memory.
Another voice speaks
of native lands   20
within this nation.
Lands invaded
when the earth became owned.
Lands of those who followed
the changing Moon,   25
knowledge of the seasons
in their veins.

[1978]

SHARON OLDS ■ (1942—)

"I write the way I perceive," Sharon Olds said in an interview (1999), acknowledging that her work is more accessible than that of many other poets:

> It's not really simple, I don't think, but it's about ordinary things—feeling about things, about people. I'm not an intellectual. I'm not an abstract thinker. And I'm interested in ordinary life. So I think that our writing reflects us.

In her poems Olds uses powerful and "accurate" (a word she values) imagery to examine sexuality, the family, intense and tormented relationships between parents and children, and forms of violence. Perhaps her best-known book is her second, *The Dead and the Living* (1984), from which both of the following poems are taken and for which Olds received the Lamont Poetry Prize and the National Book Critics Circle Award. As one critic, Carolyn Wright, wrote of *The Dead and the Living*, "What makes these poems gripping is not only their humanity, the recognizable and plausibly complex rendering of character and representative episode, but their language—direct, down to earth, immersed in the essential implements and processes of daily living."

Olds was born in San Francisco, California. She did her undergraduate work at Stanford University (BA, 1964), and then received her PhD from Columbia University (her dissertation was on Ralph Waldo Emerson) in 1972. She chose, however, not to pursue a career as a literary scholar, and instead she devoted a number of years to developing and honing her craft as a creative writer, benefiting in particular from the teaching and mentoring she received from the poet Muriel Rukeyser.

Olds's first book, *Satan Says*, was published in 1980, and it reflected her preoccupations:

> Questions that interest me include: Is there anything that shouldn't or can't be written about in a poem? Is what has never been written about a poem? What is the use, function, service of poetry in society? For whom are you writing (the dead, the unborn, the woman in front of you at the checkout line in Safeway)?

Olds is a member of the Creative Writing Program at New York University. She also is the founding chair of the Writing Program at Goldwater Hospital (New York City) for the severely physically disabled. The program began in 1984 when an arts organization invited Olds to give an eight-week workshop at the hospital, and she developed this relationship with Goldwater into a long-term expanded program.

Later books include *The Dead and the Living* (1983), *The Gold Cell* (1987), *The Father* (1992), and *The Unswept Room* (2002). Perhaps the most rewarding point of departure is *Strike Sparks: Selected Poems, 1980–2002* (2004). Olds's "best work," the writer David Leavitt has said, "exhibits a lyrical acuity which is both purifying and redemptive."

For further study, *see* Laurel Blossom, "Sharon Olds: An Interview," *Poets and Writers* (September/October 1993): 30–32; Alicia Ostriker, "American Poetry, Now Shaped by Women," *New York Times Book Review*, March 9, 1986, 27–28; and Peggy Phelan, "Intimation of Mortality," *The Women's Review of Books* (February 1984): 16–17.

Rite of Passage

As the guests arrive at my son's party
they gather in the living room—
short men, men in first grade
with smooth jaws and chins.
Hands in pockets, they stand around   5
jostling, jockeying for place, small fights
breaking out and calming. One says to another
How old are you? Six. I'm seven. So?
They eye each other, seeing themselves
tiny in the other's pupils. They clear their   10
throats a lot, a room of small bankers,
they fold their arms and frown. *I could beat you
up,* a seven says to a six,
the dark cake, round and heavy as a
turret, behind them on the table. My son,   15
freckles like specks of nutmeg on his cheeks,
chest narrow as the balsa[1] keel of a
model boat, long hands
cool and thin as the day they guided him
out of me, speaks up as a host   20
for the sake of the group.
We could easily kill a two-year-old,
he says in his clear voice. The other
men agree, they clear their throats
like Generals, they relax and get down to   25
playing war, celebrating my son's life.

[1983]

The Victims

When Mother divorced you, we were glad. She took it and
took it, in silence, all those years and then

[1]An extremely lightweight wood.

kicked you out, suddenly, and her
kids loved it. Then you were fired, and we
grinned inside, the way people grinned when   5
Nixon's[1] helicopter lifted off the South
Lawn[2] for the last time. We were tickled
to think of your office taken away,
your secretaries taken away,
your lunches with three double bourbons,   10
your pencils, your reams of paper. Would they take your
suits back, too, those dark
carcasses hung in your closet, and the black
noses of your shoes with their large pores?
She had taught us to take it, to hate you and take it   15
until we pricked with her for your
annihilation, Father. Now I
pass the bums in doorways, the white
slugs of their bodies gleaming through slits in their
suits of compressed silt, the stained   20
flippers of their hands, the underwater
fire of their eyes, ships gone down with the
lanterns lit, and I wonder who took it and
took it from them in silence until they had
given it all away and had nothing   25
left but this.

                                                           [1984]

[1]Richard M. Nixon (1913–94) was the thirty-seventh president of the United States. After his final election campaign in 1972, he soon became embroiled in the Watergate scandal, which began with a break-in, linked to Republicans, at the national headquarters of the Democratic Party. Subpoenaed tapes revealed that Nixon obstructed justice in stopping an FBI probe of the burglary. On August 9, 1974, he became the first U.S. president to resign from office.
[2]The south lawn of the White House.

DAVE SMITH ▪ (1942—)

One of the South's, and contemporary America's, most admired poets, Dave Smith was born in Portsmouth, Virginia, and received his BA from the University of Virginia (1965), his MA from Southern Illinois University (1969), and his PhD from Ohio University (1976). Smith is best known for his many volumes of poetry, in particular *The Wick of Memory: New and Selected Poems, 1970–2000* (2000) and *Little Boats, Unsalvaged: Poems, 1992–2004* (2005). He also has written a novel, *Onliness* (1981), short stories, and essays; he has edited books and anthologies, including *The William Morrow Anthology of Younger American Poets* (1985); and he has received a number of prestigious awards and fellowships for his work. An experienced, highly respected teacher, Smith has taught widely in the United States and currently is a professor in the Writing Seminars program at Johns Hopkins.

Influenced by Robert Penn Warren and James Dickey, among others, Smith has a vivid sense of place and region—wistful, affectionate, nostalgic, gritty, tough-minded—especially of coastal Virginia. "Regional identity," he has said, "is central to poetry's power. Great poetry cannot be divorced from an intimate, organic link to place." Smith indeed is a southern writer, yet, as much or more, he describes the South's landscape and geography, as in the following poem, "Tide Pools," as an occasion for broad and deep exploration of the self and its relationship to home, family, memory, and history.

Smith has made a version of this point: "In the course of my life, poetry has often been the way that I could both record experience and come to some understanding of it that otherwise was inaccessible to me." As he explained in an interview (2002): "The joy is in the writing, in the present moment, not in what is on the horizon. And it is, it must be, entirely personal, writing to the self's sense of what matters, albeit with a healthy respect for good readers, or else you cannot achieve what is yours to do and you will drift out on time's tide as valueless as any piece of old plastic or wood."

"Tide Pools" bears witness, furthermore, to Smith's love of language, his pleasure in the richness and energy of the words and phrases and images that are his literary resource. As he noted in another interview (2009), "A poet loves the color and texture and weight and airiness, the tensile strength and useless delicacy and wicked weaponry of words." Concentrated and forceful, lively, passionate, striking in its combination of the elegant and the prosaic, Smith's poetry repays rereading, reflection, and intensive study.

Smith's recent work includes *Hunting Men: Reflections on a Life in American Poetry* (2006), a collection of essays on southern poetry and poets, including Poe, Ransom, Warren, and Dickey, and interviews; and *Hawks on Wires: Poems, 2005–2010* (2011). For critical interpretation, see

Stephen Yenser, "Sea Changes: On Dave Smith," *American Poetry Review*, 11:1 (January/February 1982), 32–35; Phoebe Pettingell, "Dave Smith's Voice," *Poetry*, 147:6 (March 1986), 346–350; "'Unfold the Fullness': Dave Smith's Poetry and Fiction," *Sewanee Review*, 91:3 (Summer 1983), 483–490; and Mark Johnson, "The Dangerous Poems of Dave Smith," *Southern Literary Journal*, 38:1 (Fall 2005), 91–114.

Tide Pools[1]

At dusk and long-distance they are the mouths
to another world, caves of silence that speak
only in light and, tonight, family packed
for home travel, we take a last, slow route
over sand the sea has been all day cleaning.
At driftwood the children stop, first veering
off wordlessly, and kneel to know some texture
of wood, or stand merely to dream themselves
freely into the gathering shadows of the land.
As we go ahead of them, we imagine their hands
collecting what seems to have waited for each,

shells, starfish, agates like a lover's eyes.
Then we also drift apart, each following deep
runnels the tide has left, and after a while
I see you hunched on a rock, almost part of it.

The light is almost gone and the wind chills me
so I think of my father's whistle, how it called
the sundered shadows of a family into the house.
But do not whistle now, through the lips he made,
for somehow we have come where we may be apart
and whole. Instead, I walk farther to the north,
until you are all taken into shapes of this place.

Then I find it, the deepest pool, rock-vaulted,
light bending and alive in water faintly moving.
I see the lacey deceptions, creatures disguised
as rock whose breath flutes in quick freshets.
A killdeer[2] cries from the dark suck of the surf
and, though sweet, that darkness is not wanted.
This hole is filled with the last golden light
and by it I learn to see what I always suspected,

---

[1] Or, tidal pool, a pool left (as in a rock basin reef, or beach) after the tide has receded.
[2] A plover, a bird with a much-repeated cry that is plaintive and penetrating.

the small, quiet, incessant outcroppings of life.
For a while I state into the spooling depth, for
here are hard black eyes and iron-shells, glitter
of hulls laid forever side by side like the dead
caught at last unwarily, perfect and untouchable.

When finally I whistle there is almost no light,
but there's enough. You come, then, invisible,
a sound made by the sand, a mingling of laughter,
and I duck under just in time, holding my breath.
How I love your squeal of delight when I burst up
like a king from underground! Soon we are all in,
all naked, splashing and crying like white birds.
The road home will be long and dark, the stars cold,
but collected, like this, we will be buoyed beyond
the dark snags and splinters of what we once were.

NIKKI GIOVANNI ■ (1943—)

The African American poet and essayist Yolande Cornelia "Nikki" Giovanni was born in Knoxville, Tennessee, and raised in Cincinnati, Ohio, though she and her sister returned each summer to Knoxville to spend time with their grandparents, and in 1957 she moved in with them. "My grandfather," she recalled, "was a Latin scholar and he loved the myths, and my mother is big romanticist, so we heard a lot of stories growing up." Giovanni began her undergraduate studies at Fisk University in Nashville, Tennessee, in 1960, but, not ready for the demands of college life, she left after a short period and did not return until 1964. She graduated in 1967 with a major in history, having served as the editor of the campus literary magazine. She is professor of English and Gloria D. Smith Professor of Black Studies at Virginia Polytechnic Institute and State University, Blacksburg.

Giovanni's first books, published after she had settled in New York City, were revolutionary in their politics and committed to the power of black identity and experience: *Black Feeling, Black Talk* (1968), *Black Judgement* (1969/70), and *Re: Creation* (1970). In 1971 she made a recording of a number of her poems to the accompaniment of gospel music, and the album, *Truth Is on Its Way*, was highly successful.

Several of Giovanni's next publications, written while she was a single mother, were collections of verse for children: *Spin a Soft Black Song* (1971), *Ego-Tripping* (1973), and *Vacation Time* (1979). As one reviewer noted, Giovanni's "poems for children, like her adult works, exhibit a combination of casual energy and sudden wit. No cheek-pinching auntie, she explores the contours of childhood with honest affection, sidestepping both nostalgia and condescension."

Giovanni has continued to write poetry, has lectured widely, and throughout her career has received many honors and awards. Her books include *Gemini* (1971), an autobiographical work; *Sacred Cows...and Other Edibles* (1988), a book of essays; and *Racism 101* (1994), another group of essays. *A Dialogue: James Baldwin and Nikki Giovanni* (1973) and *A Poetic Equation: Conversations Between Nikki Giovanni and Margaret Walker* (1974) are also noteworthy.

For an appreciation of Giovanni's poetry, the best starting point is *The Selected Poems of Nikki Giovanni, 1968–1995* (1996) or, even more up to date, *The Collected Poetry of Nikki Giovanni, 1968–1998* (2003). It should be supplemented by *Love Poems* (1997); *Blues for All the Changes: New Poems* (1999); and *Quilting the Black-Eyed Pea: Poems and Not-Quite Poems* (2002).

Giovanni has long viewed herself as a poet of the people somewhat akin to Langston Hughes—a popular poet using language in vivid, direct, expressive ways. The poem "Nikki-Rosa" attests to this conception of her art. "I appreciated the quality and the rhythm of the telling of the stories," she said, "and I know when I started to write that I wanted to retain that—I didn't want to become the kind of writer that was stilted or that used language in ways that could not be spoken. I use a very natural rhythm; I want my writing to sound like I talk."

For an interpretive study, see Virginia C. Fowler, *Nikki Giovanni* (1992). Also valuable are an interview, "A MELUS Interview: Nikki Giovanni," with Arlene Elder, *MELUS* 9:3 (Winter 1982), 61–75; and the collection *Conversations with Nikki Giovanni*, ed. Virginia Fowler (1992).

Nikki-Rosa

childhood remembrances are always a drag
if you're Black
you always remember things like living in Woodlawn[1]
with no inside toilet
and if you become famous or something   5
they never talk about how happy you were to have your mother
all to yourself and
how good the water felt when you got your bath from one of those
big tubs[2] that folk in chicago barbecue in
and somehow when you talk about home   10
it never gets across how much you
understood their feelings
as the whole family attended meetings about Hollydale[3]
and even though you remember
your biographers never understand   15
your father's pain as he sells his stock
and another dream goes
And though you're poor it isn't poverty that
concerns you
and though they fought a lot   20
it isn't your father's drinking that makes any difference
but only that everybody is together and you
and your sister have happy birthdays and very good Christmasses
and I really hope no white person ever has cause to write about me
because they never understand Black love is Black wealth and they'll   25
probably talk about my hard childhood and never understand that
all the while I was quite happy

[1968]

---

[1] An economically depressed area of Chicago.
[2] Large metal tubs for bathing. The family has no running water.
[3] Possibly a housing community in Woodlawn. During the 1960s, community residents began to organize protests to demand better conditions in Woodlawn.

"From the time, at four or five or six," the poet and essayist Louise Glück said,

> I first started reading poems, first thought of the poets I read as
> my companions, my predecessors—from the beginning I preferred
> the simplest vocabulary. What fascinated me were the possibilities
> of context. What I responded to, on the page, was the way a poem
> could liberate, by means of a word's setting, through subtleties of
> timing, of pacing, that word's full and surprising range of meaning.
> It seemed to me that simple language best suited this enterprise;
> such language, in being generic, is likely to contain the greatest
> and most dramatic variety of meaning within individual words.

Glück was born in New York City, raised on Long Island, and attended
Sarah Lawrence College and Columbia University. She is now a senior
lecturer in English at Williams College in Williamstown, Massachusetts, and
lives in Cambridge, Massachusetts. As her verse and prose pieces testify,
Glück is, in the phrase of the critic Helen Vendler, a writer "of strong and
haunting presence." Her poems, the poet Stanley Kunitz has remarked,
"are delicately intense, spun out of fire and air, with a tensile strength
that belies their fragility."

A good start for the study and appreciation of Glück's work is *The First
Four Books of Poems* (2nd ed., 1996), which includes *Firstborn* (1968), *The
House on Marshland* (1975), *Descending Figure* (1980), and *The Triumph
of Achilles* (1985). Prolific, accomplished, and intense, a writer whose focused, challenging, often melancholy lines linger in the reader's mind,
Glück has also published *Ararat* (1990), *The Wild Iris* (1992), *Meadowlands*
(1996), *Vita Nova* (1999), and *The Seven Ages* (2001). Her recent books of
poems include *Averno* (2007) and *A Village Life* (2009). She is the author
as well of a book of essays, *Proofs and Theories* (1994), in which she examines poets, such as T. S. Eliot and George Oppen, and a number of topics, including courage, sincerity, and disinterestedness. In 2003, Glück was
named United States Poet Laureate. In an interview, (2006), Glück spoke
eloquently about the relationship between her life and her approach to the
writing of poetry:

> I draw on the materials my life has given me, but what interests me
> isn't that they happen to me, what interests me is that they seem,
> as I look around, paradigmatic. We're all born mortal. We have to
> contend with the idea of mortality. We all, at some point, love, with
> the risks involved, the vulnerabilities involved, the disappointments
> and great thrills of passion. This is common human experience,
> so what you use is the self as a laboratory, in which to practice,
> master, what seem to you central human dilemmas.

For interpretation, see Lynn Keller, "'Free/of Blossom and Subterfuge': Louise Glück and the Language of Renunciation," in *World, Self, Poem: Essays on Contemporary Poetry from the "Jubilation of Poets,"* ed. Leonard M. Trawick (1990); Elizabeth Dodd, *The Veiled Mirror and the Woman Poet: H. D., Louise Bogan, Elizabeth Bishop, and Louise Glück* (1992); James Longenbach, "Louise Glück's Nine Lives," *Southwest Review* 84:2 (Spring 1999), 184–198; Bonnie Costello, "*Meadowlands*: Trustworthy Speakers," *PN Review* 25:6 (July–August 1999), 14–19; Linda Gregerson, "The Sower Against Gardens," *Kenyon Review* 23:1 (Winter 2001), 115–133; and Brian Henry, "To Speak of Woe," *Kenyon Review* 23:1 (Winter 2001), 166–172. See also Ann Keniston, *Overheard Voices: Address and Subjectivity in Postmodern American Poetry* (2006). For the full span of Glück's achievement: *Poems, 1962–2012* (2012).

The Drowned Children

You see, they have no judgment.
So it is natural that they should drown,
first the ice taking them in
and then, all winter, their wool scarves
floating behind them as they sink   5
until at last they are quiet.
And the pond lifts them in its manifold dark arms.

But death must come to them differently,
so close to the beginning.
As though they had always been   10
blind and weightless. Therefore
the rest is dreamed, the lamp,
the good white cloth that covered the table,
their bodies.

And yet they hear the names they used   15
like lures slipping over the pond:
What are you waiting for
come home, come home, lost
in the waters, blue and permanent.

[1980]

Gretel in Darkness[1]

This is the world we wanted.
All who would have seen us dead
are dead. I hear the witch's cry
break in the moonlight through a sheet
of sugar: God rewards.   5
Her tongue shrivels into gas....

      Now, far from women's arms
and memory of women, in our father's hut
we sleep, are never hungry.
Why do I not forget?   10
My father bars the door, bars harm
from this house, and it is years.

No one remembers. Even you, my brother,
summer afternoons you look at me as though
you meant to leave,   15
as though it never happened.
But I killed for you. I see armed firs,
the spires of that gleaming kiln—

Nights I turn to you to hold me
but you are not there.   20
Am I alone? Spies
hiss in the stillness, Hansel,
we are there still and it is real, real,
that black forest and the fire in earnest.

                        [1975]

---

[1]Hansel and Gretel is a well-known German fairy-tale about a brother and sister menaced by a cannibal-istic witch.

KAY RYAN ■ (1945–)

Kay Ryan was born in San José, California, and grew up in Rosamond, a town in the Mojave Desert. She received her BA (1967) and MA (1968) degrees from UCLA, and, after much hard work and a long apprenticeship as a poet, she self-published her first collection of poems, *Dragon Acts to Dragon Ends*, in 1983. Ryan began to receive wide recognition in the 1990s, and she was appointed Poet Laureate of the United States in 2008, serving until 2010, and in 2011 she was awarded a prestigious MacArthur Fellowship for her creative achievement and promise. Since 1971 Ryan has lived in Marin County and taught part-time at the College of Marin in Kentifield, north of San Francisco.

The poet J. D. McClatchy has observed about Ryan that she is "as intense and elliptical as Dickinson, as buoyant and rueful as Frost." She suggests major themes through concise, focused, precisely shaped and organized lines and sentences. She also possesses a keen sense of humor and takes pleasure in subtle irony. In an interview (2008), Ryan said: "I can't bear work that takes itself too seriously, but that doesn't mean that my work isn't serious."

Ryan has noted, furthermore, that she enjoys exploring the meanings and implications of everyday remarks, truisms, and clichés: "I often find myself thinking in clichés. I'll urge myself on with various bromides and chasten myself with others. When I want to write they're one way to start thinking because they're so metaphorically rich." Both of the poems included here, "A Certain Kind of Eden" and "Home to Roost," especially the second, show this strategy, an attentiveness to what we often say and might find rewarding to think about in some detail and depth. Ryan writes poems that at first glance might appear simple on the page, but the truth is quite the opposite. She is a dark and deep poet, surprising, sometimes even shocking, a writer whose work has a special kind of exactness of statement and intellectual power.

Ryan's *The Best of It: New and Selected Poems* (2010), which won the Pulitzer Prize for poetry, is the best place to begin. See also two interviews, the first in *The Paris Review*, 187 (Winter 2008), 49–79, and the second in *American Poetry Review*, 38 (July/August 2009), 43–47.

A Certain Kind of Eden[1]

It seems like you could, but
you can't go back and pull
the roots and runners and replant.
It's all too deep for that.
You've overprized intention,   5

---

[1] The garden where Adam and Eve lived before the Fall (Genesis 2:8); more generally, any delightful region or abode; paradise, a state of perfect happiness or bliss.

have mistaken any bent you're given
for control. You thought you chose
the bean and chose the soil.
You even thought you abandoned
one or two gardens. But those things   10
keep growing where we put them—
if we put them at all.
A certain kind of Eden holds us thrall.
Even the one vine that tendrils out alone
in time turns on its own impulse,   15
twisting back down its upward course
a strong and then a stronger rope,
the greenest saddest strongest
kind of hope.

[1994]

Home to Roost[1]

The chickens
are circling and
blotting out the
day. The sun is
bright, but the   5
chickens are in
the way. Yes,
the sky is dark
with chickens,
dense with them.   10
They turn and
then they turn
again. These
are the chickens
you let loose   15
one at a time
and small—
various breeds.
Now they have
come home   20
to roost—all
the same kind
at the same speed.

[2005]

---

[1]When we use the expression "the chickens are coming home to roost," we mean that actions taken in
the past are beginning to cause problems, that we are facing the consequences of our mistakes.

YUSEF KOMUNYAKAA ■ (1947–)

Yusef Komunyakaa, an African American poet and Vietnam veteran, was born in Bogalusa, Louisiana, "a typical Southern town," he said—"one paper mill that dominated the place, and a public library that did not admit blacks." After he graduated from high school in 1965, he joined the U.S. Army and was sent to Vietnam, where he wrote for (and later edited) a military newspaper. When his period of army service ended, Komunyakaa entered the University of Colorado; he began to discover his talents as an author in a workshop on the short story and received his BA degree in 1975. He next attended Colorado State University, enrolling in the graduate program in writing and receiving his MA in 1978. His first two books, *Dedications and Other Darkhorses* (1977) and *Lost in the Bonewheel Factory* (1979), he published himself.

Komunyakaa received a second MA from the University of California, Irvine, in 1980, and then joined the Provincetown Fine Arts Work Center, where he developed his craft as a poet in workshops on writing. His third book, *Copacetic* (meaning "fine, smooth, mellow"), was published in 1981, and it shows his engagement with the realities of race and racism in America, especially in the South, and his interest in the expressive and healing power of jazz and the blues.

Komunyakaa next taught at the University of New Orleans, and then in 1985 moved to Indiana University in Bloomington, and then, in 1997, to Princeton University. His later books include two powerful collections delving into his Vietnam experiences, *Toys in a Field* (1987) and *Dien Cai Dau* (1988; the title means "crazy" in Vietnamese), in which "Facing It" appears; *February in Sydney* (1989), which blends Komunyakaa's enthusiasm for jazz and Australian society and culture; and *Magic City* (1992), about his Louisiana boyhood. Among his other publications are *Blue Notes: Essays, Interviews, and Commentaries* (2000); and *Pleasure Dome: New and Collected Poems* (2001). He has won many prizes, awards, and fellowships and currently is professor of creative writing at New York University. His recent books of poetry include *Taboo* (2004) and *Warhorses* (2008).

Komunyakaa noted that the poems about his Vietnam experiences "uncapped a hidden place" inside himself: "I tend to tell people that we are walking reservoirs of images. We take in everything, even what we're not overly conscious of, it's still there, pulsating in the psyche." He said of the poetic process, "A sort of unearthing has to take place.... Sometimes one has to remove layers of facades and superficialities. The writer has to get down to the guts of the thing and rediscover the basic timbre of his or her existence."

In "Facing It," Komunyakaa, facing the Vietnam Veterans Memorial in Washington, D.C., confronts his own painful memories. As he, a black man, looks at his reflection in the black wall, he finds the reflection disappearing, even as recollections of the war catch hold of him. The detail at the end, of the woman brushing the boy's hair, dramatizes the difference between those who took part in the war and those who did not—the difference between *them* and *us*. Yet it also implies a life of everyday gestures and the hope embodied in the next generation. Komunyakaa thus expresses terrible loss even as he evokes the present that he and other survivors occupy and where human ties remain.

For critical discussion, see Kevin Stein, "Vietnam and the 'Voice Within': Public and Private History in Yusef Komunyakaa's *Dien Cai Dau*," *Massachusetts Review*, 36:4 (Winter 1995/96), 541–561; and Angela M. Salas, "'Flashbacks Through the Heart': Yusef Komunyakaa and the Poetry of Self-Assertion," in *The Furious Flowering of African American Poetry*, ed. Joanne V. Gabbin (1999). See also interviews with Komunyakaa published in *New England Review: Middlebury Series,* 16:1 (Winter 1994), 141–147; *Kenyon Review,* 20:3–4 (Summer/Fall 1998), 5–29; and *Southbound: Interviews with Southern Poets*, compiled by Ernest Suarez with T. W. Stanford III and Amy Verner (1999). Also stimulating is *Conversations with Yusef Komunyakaa*, ed. Shirley A. James Hanshaw (2010).

Vietnam Veterans Memorial, West Potomac Park, Washington, D.C.

Facing It

My black face fades,
hiding inside the black granite.
I said I wouldn't,
dammit: No tears.
I'm stone. I'm flesh.   5
My clouded reflection eyes me
like a bird of prey, the profile of night
slanted against morning. I turn
this way—the stone lets me go.
I turn that way—I'm inside   10
the Vietnam Veterans Memorial
again, depending on the light
to make a difference.
I go down the 58,022 names,
half-expecting to find   15
my own in letters like smoke.
I touch the name Andrew Johnson;
I see the booby trap's white flash.
Names shimmer on a woman's blouse
but when she walks away   20
the names stay on the wall.
Brushstrokes flash, a red bird's
wings cutting across my stare.
The sky. A plane in the sky.
A white vet's image floats   25
closer to me, then his pale eyes
look through mine. I'm a window.
He's lost his right arm
inside the stone. In the black mirror
a woman's trying to erase names: 30
No, she's brushing a boy's hair.

[1988]

Carolyn D. "C. D." Wright, one of this country's most skillful poets of place, and of its regional voices, was born in Mountain Home, a town of 5,000 in the Ozark Mountains, Arkansas. In reference to Arkansas, she has said: "I am a stalwart believer in the bearing a particular geography can have on a writer. I am not just talking about individual experience, but about the effects of temperature, vegetation, animal life, waterways, human structures and institutions. And I have long been an advocate of the integrity of that place in the writing."

Wright received her BA in 1971 from Memphis State College, attended law school for a brief period, enrolled at the University of Arkansas, where in 1976 she received her MFA degree, and then lived and worked in San Francisco and became involved there in the poetry scene. Since 1983, Wright has been a professor of English at Brown University, in Providence, Rhode Island. In 1994 she was named Rhode Island's Poet Laureate.

Wright is the author of many volumes of poetry. The best starting points for entering into her work are *Steal Away: New and Selected Poems* (2002) and *Like Something Flying Backwards: New and Selected Poems* (2007). These books need to be supplemented by her more recent work, including *Cooling Time: An American Poetry Vigil* (2005); *Rising, Falling, Hovering* (2008); and *One with Others* (2010), a 150-page poem which mixes poetry and investigative journalism dealing with a Civil Rights march in Arkansas, and which won the National Book Critics Circle award for poetry in 2011. With the photographer Deborah Luster, Wright has written *One Big Self: Prisoners of Louisiana* (2003), which documents her visits to three Louisiana state prisons.

Wright is unique, distinctive—the critic Joel Brouwer has said that she "belongs to a school of exactly one." Another critic, Ben Marcus, with admiration says that she "defies full understanding." The terms used about Wright's art are both suggestive and contradictory, indicating the diverse elements and styles that she brings together in the practice of her craft: southern, nonconformist, socially conscious, idiosyncratic, political, regional, experimental, prosy, hermetic, restless, Biblical, down-home, radical, edgy, innovative. Some commentators, such as Stephen Burt, have described her as "elliptical"—difficult to understand; expressed with extreme or excessive economy; relieved of irrelevant matter; tending to be ambiguous, cryptic, or obscure.

Difficult and obscure: these are terms that readers and critics tend to apply to poets who challenge expectations, presenting us with poems that, in their organization of language and articulation of voice, strike us as different—too different. What this really means, in the case of such modernists as T. S. Eliot and Wallace Stevens, and such contemporaries (so unlike one another) as Jorie Graham and Wright, is that the poet is searching and striving for ways to be new—for finding forms ad exploring themes that must be different, that demand to be.

In an interview (2001), Wright has made the case well:

> My work is not obscure, it's maybe cranky,
> idiosyncratic, privately allusive, but I am not as
> conceptual as even I would want to be. Nor do I
> attempt to pander. It's project by project for me—by
> any means necessary; that's enough of a directive. I'm
> fairly aware of the contradictions in my work and
> personality. I'm country but sophisticated. I'm
> particular and concrete.

Then again, perhaps Wright, as the following poems attest, is not as difficult as she is sometimes made out to be. "Tours," for instance, focuses, with fearful clarity, on a domestic scene, moving back and forth from concise colloquial phrases (e.g., "doors bang") to stunning similes and images ("like a boy with an orchid"), and concluding with a haunting moment that somehow combines nightmare and repose. And "Personals": Wright here is working with a type of writing familiar to us in the worlds of both print and Internet, adapting and mimicking it in a manner that is both precise and loose, specific and murky—how many voices (one, many?) are speaking in this poem? Even more than the beautifully composed "Tours," "Personals" is a surprising poem that calls for and rewards rereading and study.

For biography and criticism, see Stephen Burt, "'I Came to Talk You into Physical Splendor'": On the Poetry of C. D. Wright," *Boston Review*, 22:6 (December 1997/January 1998), 31–33; Jenny Goodman, "Politics and the Personal Lyric in the Poetry of Joy Harjo and C. D. Wright," *MELUS*, 19:2 (Summer 1994), 35–56; Nadia Herman Colburn, "About C. D. Wright," *Ploughshares*, 28:4 (Winter 2002/2003), 204–209; and Lynn Keller, "'Ink and Eyes and Veins and Phonemes': C. D. Wright's Eclectic Poetics," *Arizona Quarterly*, 59:3 (Autumn 2003), 115–149.

Tours

A girl on the stairs listens to her father
Beat up her mother.
Doors bang.
She comes down in her nightgown.

The piano stands there in the dark   5
Like a boy with an orchid.

She plays what she can
Then she turns the lamp on.

Her mother's music is spread out
On the floor like brochures.   10

She hears her father
Running through the leaves.

The last black key
She presses stays down, makes no sound
Someone putting their tongue where their tooth had been.   15

[1982]

Personals

Some nights I sleep with my dress on. My teeth
are small and even. I don't get headaches.
Since 1971 or before, I have hunted a bench
where I could eat my pimento cheese in peace.
If this were Tennessee and across that river, Arkansas,   5
I'd meet you in West Memphis tonight. We could
have a big time. Danger, shoulder soft.
Do not lie or lean on me. I'm still trying to find a job
for which a simple machine isn't better suited.
I've seen people die of money. Look at Admiral Benbow.[1] I wish   10
like certain fishes, we came equipped with light organs.
Which reminds me of a little known fact:
if we were going the speed of light, this dome
would be shrinking while we were gaining weight.
Isn't the road crooked and steep.   15
In this humidity, I make repairs by night. I'm not one
among millions who saw Monroe's[2] face
in the moon. I go blank looking at that face.
If I could afford it I'd live in hotels. I won awards
in spelling and the Australian crawl.[3] Long long ago.   20
Grandmother married a man named Ivan. The men called him
Eve. Stranger, to tell the truth, in dog years I am up there.

[2002]

---

[1] John Benbow (1653–1702), English admiral; the name is best known from a location, "The Admiral Benbow Inn," in Robert Louis Stevenson's novel *Treasure Island* (1883).
[2] Marilyn Monroe (1926–62), American actress and Hollywood sex symbol.
[3] A type of swimming stroke.

JORIE GRAHAM ▓ (1950—)

Born in New York City in 1950, Jorie Graham—"one of the best, and most intelligent, poets in the language," says the poet-critic Stephen Burt—spent her early years in Rome, and was educated at schools in France. At the Sorbonne in Paris, she studied philosophy but was expelled for taking part in student protests. She then did her undergraduate degree at New York University, majoring in film. She received her MFA from the University of Iowa, and since 1999 she has taught in the English department at Harvard.

Graham's books include *The Dream of the Unified Field, Selected Poems, 1974–1994* (1996), winner of the Pulitzer Prize in Poetry; *The Errancy* (1997); *Swarm* (2000); *Never* (2002); *Overlord* (2005); and *Sea Change* (2008). She also is the editor of two anthologies: *The Best American Poetry, 1990*; and *Earth Took of Earth: 100 Great Poems of the English Language* (1996).

Graham is a major poet, a cosmopolitan, and an intellectual, widely read in literature, art, philosophy, fluent in three languages. She has deeply studied and absorbed and worked her way into and through the modernist tradition, especially the poetry of Yeats, Eliot, and Stevens. Often it is said that Graham is a difficult poet—extreme in her complexity, hermetic, obscure, hard to understand. But these criticisms point not to a limitation in her poetry but, rather, to its ambition and boldness. Graham frequently moves her phrases, lines, images, structures and organizations of lines and stanzas into unfamiliar territory. She confronts readers with styles and themes that at first might seem to them unrecognizable, indeed too difficult.

In her Introduction, *Best American Poetry, 1990*, Graham focuses on this feature of her own and others' work:

> [T]he difficulty of poetry, even for its most sympathetic readers, is a real one. Or rather it is both real and imagined. Much of it dissipates as one opens up to the experience of poetry. To comprehend poetry one must, after all, practice by reading it. As to "see" modern dance, one must at least know its vocabulary, its texture, what the choreographer chose not to do. As to understand good carpentry one must be able to grasp what the maker's options were, what the tradition is, what the nature of wood is, what the structural necessities were: what is underpinning, what flourish and passion, what décor.

"Poetry can also be difficult, though," Graham continues,

> because much of it attempts to render aspects of experience that occur outside the provinces of logic and reason, outside the realm of narrative realism. The ways in which dreams proceed, or magic, or mystical vision, or memory, are often models for poetry's methods: what we remember upon waking, what we remember at birth—all the brilliant Irrational in the human sensibility.

The following poem, "Sea-Blue Aubade," from the mid-1990s, is in fact less difficult than many of Graham's poems. Perhaps it is less difficult than elusive, suggestive, concrete in its choices of words and images yet, nonetheless, not easily or entirely graspable. For the reader the poem is enthralling because of the description, even more because of the exploration, that through her speaker Graham presents in it. Her mind is captivating, and the reader is drawn to what this mind depicts and reflects upon and seeks to know.

The critic David Baker has stated the point well:

> I can think of no other current American poet who has employed and exposed the actual mechanics of narrative, of form, of strategic inquiry more fully than she has—at least no other readable poet—and no other poet able to deploy so fruitfully and invitingly the diverse systems of philosophy, science, and history. If anyone can unify the disjoined fields of contemporary discourse, I think it might be Jorie Graham.

See the interview with Graham, *The Paris Review*, 165 (Spring 2003), 52–97. For interpretation, see Helen Vendler, *The Breaking of Style: Hopkins, Heaney, Graham* (1995); *Jorie Graham: Essays on the Poetry*, ed. Thomas Gardner (2005), an excellent, diverse collection; Catherine Sona Karagueuzian, *"No Image There and the Gaze Remains": The Visual in the Work of Jorie Graham* (2005), dealing with the connection between Graham's work and the legacy of American Modernism; Kirstin Hotelling Zona, "Jorie Graham and American Poetry," *Contemporary Literature*, 46:4 (Winter 2005), 667–687; and Willard Spiegelman, "Jorie Graham Talking," *Kenyon Review*, 28:4 (Fall 2006), 175–185.

Sea-Blue Aubade[1]

Dawn—or is it sea-blue—fills the square.
Two in a room asleep with that window
And dark thinning inside the view.
And human breathing.
And freedom in the room like a thin gray floating.   5
And doctrine.
And other kinds of shine rising off the edges of things
as if the daylight were a doctor arriving,
each thing needing to be seen ....
Soon the sunlight   10
will want to be changed.
Will want to be caught up in the weavings of freedom.
To be caught up in the wide net and made to have edges
light coming in, so acidly, with the strength of wind or an ox ....

[1]A poem or piece of music appropriate to the dawn or early morning, musical announcement of the dawn.

Outside, slowly, the grapes seem fatter.   15
The cat moves its tail once in sleep.
The silence is largest wherever an eye falls.
Somebody's glance smokes through the blues until they start to
feel... ?
But it is all chalky.   20
All asleep, all unalive.
An icy thing, even in its fluency
the tree, the stone heroically built-up into a wall,
each stone in the mind of its mason, elsewhere, asleep,
the eat in the sleep of its owner, the purple light, muscular,   25
more days, more nights, more roads, shouts, flowers,
all making towards what pebbled shore,
each changing place with that which went before
and forwards, forwards, how it all contends,
across the crookedness to 'be itself, to be at last, the crown,   30
the jeweled asterisk that stops that very moment still,
the place the parallels, the cruelties, do, for just a fraction
of a pebbled instant,
meet—(save that I die I leave my love alone
possibly rain oncoming—on the sidewalk down below   35
could it be steps, or is it just the clock
does it arrive and dissipate
no, it splatters like
thousands of thoughts,
replacing all the listening   40
sea of ideas—so blue
although you can hear something like cuts in the blue
and one can feel how the boat feels
all of the freedom swirling and slapping round the keel, the here,
foaming round, as feelings—and still the pitch of the dawn   45
grasping at transparence, as if something like an hour were
trying
to plash in, and make, and make...what would it make
and in the suddenly awakening one:
an upward glance, one take—a main-mast starting up   50
sails glimpsing about, quick rules and suppositions—coalescings
and then the single sturdier open gaze cast up a stare: a fear:
why is father lashed to it?
Why is mother singing?

[1995]

J O Y   H A R J O ▪ (1951—)

In an interview given in 1985, Joy Harjo explained that she began to take a serious interest in a literary career when she was in her early twenties. Her focus had been painting, and she majored in art for her first three years at the University of New Mexico. During her senior year Harjo switched to the English department so she could major in creative writing. She recalled, "I found that language, through poetry, was taking on more magical qualities than my painting. I could say more when I wrote. Soon it wasn't a choice. Poetry-speaking called me in a sense. And I couldn't say no." After graduation in 1976 Harjo went on to the University of Iowa, where in 1978 she received an MFA in creative writing.

Harjo's father was Creek, and her mother was part Cherokee, part French. Born in Tulsa, Oklahoma, Harjo has emphasized that as a Native American woman, writing functions as a "means of survival."

> On both a personal level and a larger, communal level, I don't believe I would be alive today if it hadn't been for writing. There were times when I was conscious of holding onto a pen and letting the words flow, painful and from the gut, to keep from letting go of it all. Now, this was when I was much younger, and full of self-hatred. Writing helped me give voice to turn around a terrible silence that was killing me. And on a larger level, if we, as Indian people, Indian women, keep silent, then we will disappear, at least in this level of reality.

Harjo has also been a teacher, an editor, and a musician (she plays the saxophone). For her poetry she draws upon her vigorous response to art and music, her love for the Southwest landscape, and her exploration of Native American myth and symbolism. Among her books are *A Map to the Next World: Poetry and Tales* (1998) and *How We Became Human: New and Selected Poems* (2002). Of the following poems, "Call It Fear" and "White Bear" first appeared in *She Had Some Horses* (1983), and "Eagle Poem" in *In Mad Love and War* (1990).

Reviewing this second volume, a critic in *The Kenyon Review* observed:

> Nearly all these poems seem written in a moment of urgency, fed by deeply rooted memory or longing, sometimes by defiance, and always by a warriorlike compassion that sees through the split between people and their histories, people and their hearts, people and the natural world.

For biography and context, see *The Spiral of Memory: Interviews—Joy Harjo*, ed. Laura Coltelli (1996). See also Joy Harjo and Tanaya Winder, *Soul Talk, Song Language: Conversations with Joy Harjo* (2011), which includes personal essays, interviews, and newspaper columns.

Call It Fear

There is this edge where shadows
and bones of some of us walk
                    backwards.
Talk backwards. There is this edge
call it an ocean of fear of the dark. Or   5
name it with other songs. Under our ribs
our hearts are bloody stars. Shine on
shine on, and horses in their galloping flight
strike the curve of ribs.
                    Heartbeat   10
and breathe back sharply. Breath
                    backwards
There is this edge within me
                    I saw it once
an August Sunday morning when the heat hadn't   15
left this earth. And Goodluck
sat sleeping next to me in the truck.
We had never broken through the edge of the
singing at four a.m.
                    We had only wanted to talk, to hear   20
any other voice to stay alive with.
                    And there was this edge—
not the drop of sandy rock cliff
bones of volcanic earth into
                    Albuquerque.¹   25
Not that,
        but a string of shadow horses kicking
and pulling me out of my belly,
        not into the Rio Grande² but into the music
barely coming through   30
                    Sunday church singing
from the radio. Battery worn-down but the voices
talking backwards.

                                        [1983]

White Bear

She begins to board the flight
    to Albuquerque. Late night.

---

¹Albuquerque, New Mexico.
²A river that extends from Colorado to the Gulf of Mexico. The middle Rio Grande runs through New Mexico.

But stops in the corrugated tunnel,
   a space between leaving and staying,
where the night sky catches   5

       her whole life

she has felt like a woman
   balancing on a wooden nickle heart
approaching herself from here to
   there, Tulsa or New York   10
with knives or corn meal.

The last flight someone talked
   about how coming from Seattle
the pilot flew a circle
   over Mt. St. Helens;[1] she sat   15
quiet. (But had seen the eruption
   as the earth beginning
to come apart, as in birth
   out of violence.)

She watches the yellow lights   20
   of towns below the airplane flicker,
fade and fall backwards. Somewhere,
   she dreamed, there is the white bear
moving down from the north, motioning her paws
   like a long arctic night, that kind   25
of circle and the whole world balanced in
   between carved of ebony and ice

       oh so hard

the clear black nights
   like her daughter's eyes, and the white   30
bear moon, cupped like an ivory rocking
cradle, tipping back it could go
either way
       all darkness
           is open to all light.

                        [1983]

---

[1]An active volcano in Washington state. On May 18, 1980, Mount St. Helens erupted for nine hours after being shaken by an earthquake. Nearly 230 square miles of forest were blown up and a mushroom-shaped column of ash rose thousands of feet skyward and drifted downwind, turning the sky as dark as night and covering eastern Washington with gray ash.

Eagle Poem

To pray you open your whole self
To sky, to earth, to sun, to moon
To one whole voice that is you.
And know there is more
That you can't see, can't hear,   5
Can't know except in moments
Steadily growing, and in languages
That aren't always sound but other
Circles of motion.
Like eagle that Sunday morning   10
Over Salt River.[1] Circled in blue sky
In wind, swept our hearts clean
With sacred wings.
We see you, see ourselves and know
That we must take the utmost care   15
And kindness in all things.
Breathe in, knowing we are made of
All this, and breathe, knowing
We are truly blessed because we
Were born, and die soon within a   20
True circle of motion,
Like eagle rounding out the morning
Inside us.
We pray that it will be done   25
In beauty.
In beauty.

[1990]

---

[1]A 200-mile stream in the state of Arizona.

ANDREW HUDGINS ■ (1951—)

Born in Killeen, Texas, educated at Huntingdon College in Montgomery, Alabama, the University of Alabama, and the University of Iowa (MFA, 1983), and now a professor in the English department at Ohio State University, Andrew Hudgins has won wide recognition for both his poems and essays. His *American Rendering: New and Selected Poems* (2010) is a captivating volume, consisting of twenty-four new poems and a selection from Hudgins's six previous books of poetry. This is a wonderful, comic, erotic, dark, grim array of work that shows the influence of William Faulkner, Flannery O'Connor, and James Dickey, but in a voice, or voices, uniquely Hudgins's own. As one critic has said, Hudgins is that rare writer "of the American South who can be both solemn and side-splitting in a single poem."

A nonfiction book *The Glass Anvil* (1997) assembles essays by Hudgins on his life and work, on poets past and present, such as Galway Kinnell, and on his responses to and explorations of race and racism, southern literature, and religion. Another collection of nonfiction, *Diary of a Poem* (2011), includes not only essays on Allen Tate, Donald Justice, and other poets, but also pieces on gardening, unread books, an interaction with Hudgins's father-in-law, and the rock 'n' roll singer guitarist Johnny Winter. He also has written *The Joker: A Memoir* (2013), an exploration of jokes, humor, and vulgar speech.

The poet Mark Strand has noted about Hudgins's poetry: "there is a beautiful oddness about it. Dark moments seem charged with an eerie luminosity and the most humdrum events assume a startling lyric intensity." This intensity often derives from Hudgins's management of humor, a crucial element of poetry as he practices it. "Humor," he observes, "is a complex and often dirty business. As the ancient playwrights knew, everything depends on where the Wheel of Fortune stops, or more accurately, pauses, hesitates, or trembles, before it starts spinning again." The following poem, "Death and Doom," is more restrained, quieter, than many others that Hudgins has composed. Yet it, too, has its sly and wry turns and twists of humor in the speaker's voice—in the rhetorical question in line 4, for instance. In this poem Hudgins also moves with precision and control among different levels of word-choice and phrase. There is the short and so-direct "I hate," but then, attached to it, are "paradigm," "thralldom," and "diadem." Even here, then, in "Death and Doom," Hudgins makes clear his pleasure in words and in the artful combinations he can make with them.

Hudgins also has written two compelling poetic sequences. The first is *After the Lost War: A Narrative* (1988), which explores the post-bellum South through the musician and poet Sidney Lanier's voice, following this Confederate soldier and writer from the first years of the war to his death. This book is a sequence of poems, and also a historical novel and a biography. The second narrative poem, *The Glass Hammer: A Southern Childhood*

(1994), which Hudgins vowed to write while he was "still angry" about the injustices he faced as a child at the hands of his parents, tells the story of a boy brought up in a military family in Texas and Alabama.

For further reading, see Daniel Cross Turner, "Restoration, Metanostalgia, and Critical Memory: Forms of Nostalgia in Contemporary Southern Poetry," *Southern Literary Journal*, 40:2 (Spring 2008), 182–206; and Nick Norwood, "The Plain Style in Southern Poetry," *Southern Literary Journal*, 43:1 (Fall 2010), 109–124.

Death and Doom

I longed for martyrdom
as a boy—saintdom or stardom.
some way to swindle doom.
by which I meant death. Dumb?
Perhaps. I'm quick to condemn　　　　　　　　　　5
the boy I was, his quondam[1]
terror now turned to dim
hopes of a durable kingdom—
heaven or the boredom
of someone reading in a dorm　　　　　　　　　　10
—at the lash of academe!—
these words I deem wisdom.
But what do they redeem?
(That and, at one time, a dime.)
Art's memorandum　　　　　　　　　　15
to the future is seldom,
if read, respected.
　　　　　　　Doom,
I'd love to call death doom,
and untrifle it, though, damn,　　　　　　　　　　20
I hate the paradigm:
departures thralldom
to drama's diadem.[2]
May death—mine, yours—seldom
be doom but gently random,　　　　　　　　　　25
merely an addendum
to life's agenda, and doom.
when doom must come in tandem.
bring respite before freedom.

[2007]

[1]That once was, former; from Latin, "formerly."
[2]A jeweled crown or headband worn as a symbol of sovereignty.

JIMMY SANTIAGO BACA ■ (1952–)

Born in Santa Fe, New Mexico, Jimmy Santiago Baca somehow survived brutalizing experiences as a child and young adult. Because his parents were unable to care for him—his mother was murdered by her second husband, and his father died of alcoholism—he was sent at age two to an orphanage. He ran away when he was twelve and fell into crime, street violence, and drugs. Arrested at age eighteen for drug possession, he spent five years in the early 1970s in the federal prison in Florence, Arizona, where, despite harsh treatment, he taught himself to read and write and began making himself into a powerful poet.

In an interview published in the early 1990s, Baca vividly described the grim conditions and circumstances of his upbringing that inform the situations and feelings he depicts in his poetry and prose:

> I grew up in a world that considered brown, dirt. I remember very distinctly being told by several people that God hated you, and other people saying, "your language is dirty, don't speak Spanish, your skin is dirty and you can't be white." So when you have that kind of baggage, it begins to rot inside of you and you become gangrenous, you know, and that gangrene spreads into the emotions, into your thinking, and I didn't go to school at all, I was not a school person. I was in the streets most of the time.

He continues:

> So consequently, what happened was my relationships with people were based on destruction. It was like a fuse, a time bomb. Every minute I had with people, with women especially, with friends of mine, it was a ticking, it was a burning of a fuse.... Everything was always pointed towards destruction. So, I didn't know what to do with myself because my relationship to the world was destructive, because my relationship to myself was very destructive. I was no good. I had no right to exist.... If my body felt danger, I lashed out violence. So, I was continually fighting the police. I think that by the time I was sixteen I had been in the county jail maybe about twenty times for assault and battery with the police. I mean it was a war in the streets.

In another interview, published in the journal *Callaloo* in 1994, Baca explained the extraordinary transformation that took place during his prison years:

> I was writing things that I remember doing as a kid and as an adult and so forth. And what happened was that, in a place like prison where all sensory enjoyment was deprived, language became more real, more tangible than bars or concrete, than the structure of buildings in the landscape. So I began to read, to read and write in the sense that,

metaphorically, I wrapped myself in this cocoon of language, and when I came back out, I was no longer the caterpillar: I was a butterfly.

Baca proceeded to earn a BA in English from the University of New Mexico in 1984 and to progress year by year toward his PhD in literature, awarded in 2003, also from the University of New Mexico. Among his books are the following collections of poems: *Immigrants in Our Own Land* (1979), *Martín and Meditations on the South Valley* (1987), and *Black Mesa Poems* (1989). He is the author of a book of essays, *Working in the Dark: Reflections on a Poet in the Barrio* (1992). Nationally and internationally, Baca is a dedicated, inspiring, and energizing writer and activist, lecturing, reading from his work, conducting workshops, advocating drug-free behavior, promoting literary activity and publishing among Hispanic and Native American young people and adults, and emphasizing the need for education and critical thinking. His recent publications include *Winter Poems Along the Rio Grande* (2004), *Spring Poems Along the Rio Grande* (2007), and *The Importance of a Piece of Paper* (2004), a collection of stories.

The following poem is taken from *Immigrants in Our Own Land*, a book that has as its center Baca's experiences in prison. "Poetry," he has said,

> gives us courage and faith to live with open wounds. Poetry gives us the means to understand pain in a meaningless age. Language gives us insight into the darkness that we all stumble into today. So, I don't know if it heals, but I do know that it provides us with what we lack. Language provides us with something that we desperately need. Not to close the wound, but not to forget it. Language makes us not forget what we went through.

For critical analysis, see George Moore, "Beyond Cultural Dialogues: Identities in the Interstices of Culture in Jimmy Santiago Baca's *Martín and Meditations on the South Valley*," *Western American Literature* 33:2 (Summer 1998), 153–177. See also Gabriel Meléndez, "Carrying the Magic of His People's Heart: An Interview with Jimmy Santiago Baca," *The Americas Review: A Review of Hispanic Literature and Art of the USA* 19:3–4 (Winter 1991), 64–86; and John Keene, "'Poetry Is What We Speak to Each Other': An Interview with Jimmy Santiago Baca,"*Callaloo* 17:1 (Winter 1994), 33–51.

So Mexicans are Taking Jobs from Americans

O Yes? Do they come on horses
with rifles, and say,
   Ese gringo,[1] gimmee your job?

---

[1]Hey, whitey.

And do you, gringo, take off your ring,
drop your wallet into a blanket   5
spread over the ground, and walk away?

I hear Mexicans are taking your jobs away.
Do they sneak into town at night,
and as you're walking home with a whore,
do they mug you, a knife at your throat,   10
saying, I want your job?

Even on TV, an asthmatic leader
crawls turtle heavy, leaning on an assistant,
and from a nest of wrinkles on his face,
a tongue paddles through flashing waves   15
of lightbulbs, of cameramen, rasping
"They're taking our jobs away."

Well, I've gone about trying to find them,
asking just where the hell are these fighters.

The rifles I hear sound in the night   20
are white farmers shooting blacks and browns
whose ribs I see jutting out
and starving children,
I see the poor marching for a little work,
I see small white farmers selling out   25
to clean-suited farmers living in New York,
who've never been on a farm,
don't know the look of a hoof or the smell
of a woman's body bending all day long in fields.

I see this, and I hear only a few people   30
got all the money in this world, the rest
count their pennies to buy bread and butter.

Below that cool green sea of money,
millions and millions of people fight to live,
search for pearls in the darkest depths   35
of their dreams, hold their breath for years
trying to cross poverty to just having something.

The children are dead already. We are killing them,
that is what America should be saying;
on TV, in the streets, in offices, should be saying,   40
"We aren't giving the children a chance to live."
Mexicans are taking our jobs, they say instead.
What they really say is, let them die,
and the children too.   [1979]

RITA DOVE ■ (1952–)

Rita Dove was born in Akron, Ohio, to parents who valued literature and classical music; she graduated *summa cum laude* in 1973 from Miami University (Ohio); she then resided in Germany as a Fulbright scholar. Upon her return to the United States, Dove enrolled in the Creative Writing Program at the University of Iowa, receiving her MFA in 1977. Her first book of poems, *The Yellow House on the Corner*, was published in 1980. Her next books were a second volume of poems, *Museum* (1983), and a collection of short stories, *Fifth Sunday* (1985).

For *Thomas and Beulah* (1986), based on the lives of her maternal grandparents, Dove was awarded the Pulitzer Prize for poetry. While continuing to write poetry, she has also published a novel, *Through the Ivory Tower* (1992); a play about slavery, miscegenation, and rebellion in the antebellum South, *The Darker Face of the Earth* (1994); and a set of lectures, *The Poet's World* (1995). The first African American to be named Poet Laureate of the United States (1993–95), the recipient of many honors for her sensitive and poised literary work, and currently the Commonwealth Professor of English at the University of Virginia, Dove is best approached through her *Selected Poems* (1993); *American Smooth: Poems* (2004); and *Conversations with Rita Dove*, ed. Earl G. Ingersoll (2003).

Economical, disciplined, richly attentive to the history of African American people even as she moves through it to touch on and explore universal themes and feelings, alert to the connections between personal and national histories, Dove is one of the foremost American poets. She is one of the foremost African American women poets as well, a designation she herself commented on in an interview published in 1995:

> I've never been sure what exactly it's supposed to mean, to be called an African-American poet or a woman poet. I'm a woman, I'm an African-American. My poems often reflect those two aspects of myself. With some of my poems, obviously, you cannot tell race or gender....My own reluctance with being labelled an African-American poet comes from battling the assumption that this means writing in a racially programmatic way. As far as I'm concerned no programmatic poetry, no matter how well meant the ideology, can be truly free. So long as we agree that that's not what you mean, I'll say yes, I'm an African-American poet; I'm a woman poet; I'm an American poet: all those things. But I'm a poet first.

For critical discussion, see Arnold Rampersad, "The Poems of Rita Dove," *Callaloo* 9:1 (Winter 1986), 52–60; Helen Vendler, "Rita Dove: Identity Markers," *Callaloo* 17:2 (Summer 1994), 381–398; and Therese Steffen, *Crossing Color: Transcultural Space and Place in Rita Dove's Poetry, Fiction, and Drama* (2001). See also Malin Pereira, "An Interview with Rita Dove," *Contemporary*

Literature 40:2 (Summer 1999), 182–213. See also Malin Pereira, *Rita Dove's Cosmopolitanism* (2003); and Pat Righelato, *Understanding Rita Dove* (2006). Also noteworthy is Dove's editing of *The Penguin Anthology of Twentieth-Century American Poetry* (2011).

Daystar

She wanted a little room for thinking:
but she saw diapers steaming on the line,
a doll slumped behind the door.

So she lugged a chair behind the garage
to sit out the children's naps.   5

Sometimes there were things to watch—
the pinched armor of a vanished cricket,
a floating maple leaf. Other days
she stared until she was assured
when she closed her eyes   10
she'd see only her own vivid blood.

She had an hour, at best, before Liza appeared
pouting from the top of the stairs.
And just *what* was mother doing
out back with the field mice? Why,   15

building a palace. Later
that night when Thomas rolled over and
lurched into her, she would open her eyes
and think of the place that was hers
for an hour—where   20
she was nothing,
pure nothing, in the middle of the day.

[1986]

Adolescence—I

In water-heavy nights behind grandmother's porch
We knelt in the tickling grasses and whispered:
Linda's face hung before us, pale as a pecan,
And it grew wise as she said:
       "A boy's lips are soft,   5
       As soft as baby's skin."
The air closed over her words.
A firefly whirred near my ear, and in the distance
I could hear streetlamps ping

Into miniature suns   10
Against a feathery sky.

[1980]

Adolescence—II

Although it is night, I sit in the bathroom, waiting.
Sweat prickles behind my knees, the baby-breasts are alert.
Venetian blinds slice up the moon; the tiles quiver in pale strips.

Then they come, the three seal men with eyes as round
As dinner plates and eyelashes like sharpened tines.[1]   5
They bring the scent of licorice. One sits in the washbowl,

One on the bathtub edge; one leans against the door.
"Can you feel it yet?" they whisper.
I don't know what to say, again. They chuckle,

Patting their sleek bodies with their hands.   10
"Well, maybe next time." And they rise,
Glittering like pools of ink under moonlight,

And vanish. I clutch at the ragged holes
They leave behind, here at the edge of darkness.
Night rests like a ball of fur on my tongue.   15

[1980]

Straw Hat

In the city, under the saw-toothed leaves of an oak
overlooking the tracks, he sits out
the last minutes before dawn, lucky
to sleep third shift. Years before
he was anything, he lay on   5
so many kinds of grass, under stars,
the moon's bald eye opposing.

He used to sleep like a glass of water
held up in the hand of a very young girl.
Then he learned he wasn't perfect, that   10
no one was perfect. So he made his way
North under the bland roof of a tent
too small for even his lean body.

---

[1]Prongs.

The mattress ticking he shares in the work barracks
is brown and smells   15
from the sweat of two other men.
One of them chews snuff:
he's never met either.
To him, work is a narrow grief
and the music afterwards   20
is like a woman
reaching into his chest
to spread it around. When he sings

he closes his eyes.
He never knows when she'll be coming   25
but when she leaves, he always
tips his hat.

                                                                                    [1986]

Missing

I am the daughter who went out with the girls,
never checked back in and nothing marked my "last
known whereabouts," not a single glistening petal.

Horror is partial; it keeps you going. A lost
child is a fact hardening around its absence,   5
a knot in the breast purring *Touch, and I will*

come true. I was "returned," I watched her
watch as I babbled *It could have been worse....*
Who can tell
what penetrates? Pity is the brutal   10
discipline. Now I understand she can never
die, just as nothing can bring me back—

I am the one who comes and goes;
I am the footfall that hovers.

                                                                                    [1995]

JUDITH ORTIZ COFER ■ (1952—)

Born in Puerto Rico, Judith Ortiz Cofer immigrated with her family to the United States in 1954. In an interview (1993), she noted she was raised "bilingual and bicultural" in Paterson, New Jersey, as a "navy child"—which informs the poem "My Father in the Navy." She added, "My father being in the navy put me at the center of my family's life since my mother did not know much English. Therefore I became the translator, the interpreter, the decision maker, very early in my life."

In a second interview (1997), Cofer stressed the significance of "storytelling" in her upbringing and its impact on the narrative element of her poems as well as of her stories:

> The women in my family were wonderful storytellers who infected me at a very early age with the desire to tell stories. I used to try to impress my father, who was hard to impress, by telling him stories.... It was at that early stage that I realized I could gain power and attention in this way, and I became hooked on it.

Cofer received her BA in English (1974) from Augusta College, and her MA in English from Florida Atlantic University (1977). Since the mid-1980s she has been a member of the English department at the University of Georgia, where she is now the Franklin Professor of English and Creative Writing. Among her books are *The Year of Our Revolution: Selected and New Prose and Poetry* (1998); *Sleeping with One Eye Open: Women Writers and the Art of Survival* (1999), coedited by Marilyn Kallet; and *Woman in Front of the Sun: On Becoming a Writer* (2000). "Art," Cofer said, "is taking the ordinary and trying to give it enough levels so that it becomes universal. I make people laugh when I say that my unschooled grandmother and Virginia Woolf were two of my literary ancestors. As different as they were they shared one thing: They knew that the word was empowering in a way that nothing else was." Cofer's recent work includes *The Latin Deli: Prose and Poetry* (2010), collection of poems, personal essays, and short stories in which the subject—the lives of Puerto Ricans in a New Jersey barrio—is drawn from the author's own childhood.

For biographical background and context, see the interviews with Cofer in the following publications: *Bilingual Review* 17 (May–August 1992); *MELUS* 18:3 (Fall 1993); *Callaloo* 17:3 (Summer 1994); and *Speaking of the Short Story: Interviews with Contemporary Writers*, eds. Farhat Iftekharuddin and Mary Rohrberger (1997).

My Father in the Navy

Stiff and immaculate
in the white cloth of his uniform
and a round cap on his head like a halo,
he was an apparition on leave from a shadow-world
and only flesh and blood when he rose from below   5
the waterline where he kept watch over the engines
and dials making sure the ship parted the waters
on a straight course.
Mother, Brother, and I kept vigil
on the nights and dawns of his arrivals,   10
watching the corner beyond the neon sign of a quasar[1]
for the flash of white, our father like an angel
heralding a new day.
His homecomings were the verses
we composed over the years making up   15
the siren's song that kept him coming back
from the bellies of iron whales
and into our nights
like the evening prayer.

[1987]

---

[1]When radio telescopes were first used to explore space, point sources of radio waves were detected along the Milky Way. Astronomers examined these areas and found phenomena such as remnants of a supernova, a large star-birth region. In some places, however, no visible source other than a starlike shape was found. These objects were called *quasars*. They are now believed to be the centers of distant galaxies where some sort of energetic action is occurring, probably due to the presence of a massive black hole.

ALBERTO RÍOS ■ (1952—)

"I was born in Nogales [Arizona], on the border of Mexico," Alberto Ríos said in a lecture given in the mid-1990s. He went on:

> My father was from Tapachula, Chiapas, Mexico, and my mother from Warrington, Lancashire, England. I grew up around my father's family, but I look like my mother--which means I got to see two worlds from the beginning. I could even physically experience the difference growing up where I did: I could put, every day of my life, one foot in Mexico and one foot in the United States, at the same time.

Ríos attended the University of Arizona, receiving his BA in psychology in 1974 and his MFA in creative writing in 1979. Among his books are *Whispering to Fool the Wind: Poems* (1982), *The Iguana Killer: Twelve Stories of the Heart* (1984), *Five Indiscretions: A Book of Poems* (1985), *The Lime Orchard Woman: Poems* (1988), *Teodora Luna's Two Kisses: Poems* (1990), *The Curtain of Trees: Stories* (1999), *Pig Cookies and Other Stories* (1995), and *Capirotada: A Nogales Memoir* (1999). Ríos is the recipient of many honors and awards, and his poems are widely anthologized. He is professor of English at Arizona State University.

Ríos has described the interrelations between the Chicano and American dimensions of his cultural background and heritage, especially the feeling for words and things he gained from his intimate knowledge of two languages. "I have been around other languages all my life, particularly Spanish," he explained, "and have too often thought of the act of translation as simply giving something two names. But it is not so, not at all. Rather than filling out, a second name for something pushes it forward, forward and backward, and gives it another life."

"Wet Camp", is included in *Whispering to Fool the Wind*, and "Advice to a First Cousin" appears in *Five Indiscretions*. Both poems evoke and dramatize the conception of language, and its relation to the world, that Ríos has expressed in essays and interviews, as in this revealing passage:

> I look for things that have a voice of their own. I try to listen before I speak. In this way, I try not to be simply a user, but a partner to those things in the world around and inside and beyond me; on their own terms and in their own languages. This is how writing comes to me, and how I give it back.

Ríos's recent work includes *The Smallest Muscle in the Human Body* (2002), poems that make use of parable, fable, and legend, in the mode of magical realism; *The Theater of Night* (2007), poems that present the story of Ventura and Clements Rios, a married couple living near the U.S.-Mexico border in the first half of the twentieth century; and *The Dangerous Shirt* (2009), a collection of poems.

For discussion and context, see "'Words Like the Wind': An Interview with Alberto Ríos," The *Americas Review: A Review of Hispanic Literature and Art of the USA* 24: 3–4 (Fall–Winter 1996), 116–129; Joseph Deters, "Fireworks on the Borderlands: A Blending of Cultures in the Poetry of Alberto Ríos," *Confluencia: Revista Hispánica de Cultura y Literatura* 15:2 (Spring 2000), 28–35; and Richard Vela, "The Idea of Boundaries in the Work of Alberto Ríos," *Pembroke Magazine* 34 (2002), 115–122.

Wet Camp

We have been here before, but we are lost.
The earth is black and the trees are bent
and broken and piled as if the game
of pick-up-sticks were ready and the children
hiding, waiting their useless turns.   5
The west bank of the river is burned
and the Santa Cruz has poured onto it.
The grit brown ponds
sit like dirty lilies in the black.
The afternoon is gone grazing   10
over the thin mountains.
The night is colder here without leaves.
Nothing holds up the sky.

[1982]

Advice to a First Cousin

The way the world works is like this:
for the bite of scorpions, she says,
my grandmother to my first cousin,
because I might die and someone must know,
go to the animal jar   5
the one with the soup of green herbs
mixed with the scorpions I have been putting in
still alive. Take one out
put it on the bite. It has had time to think
there with the others—put the lid back tight—   10
and knows that a biting is not the way to win
a finger or a young girl's foot.
It will take back into itself the hurting
the redness and the itching and its marks.
But the world works like this, too: 15
look out for the next scorpion you see,

she says, and makes a big face to scare me
thereby instructing my cousin, look out!
for one of the scorpion's many
illegitimate and unhappy sons.   20
It will be smarter, more of the devil.
It will have lived longer than these dead ones.
It will know from them something more
about the world, in the way mothers know
when something happens to a child, or how   25
I knew from your sadness you had been bitten.
It will learn something stronger than biting.
Look out most for that scorpion, she says,
making a big face to scare me again and it works
I go—crying—she lets me go—they laugh,   30
the way you must look out for men
who have not yet bruised you.

                                                        [1985]

MARK DOTY ■ (1953–)

The author of eight books of poetry and three memoirs, and a book of literary criticism, Mark Doty was born in Maryville, Tennessee. He received his BA from Drake University in Des Moines, Iowa, and his MFA from Goddard College in Plainfield, Vermont. He teaches at Rutgers University and lives in New York City and Fire Island, New York.

Doty is perhaps best known for three powerful, affecting books dealing with the AIDS crisis and the death of his partner, Wally Roberts, from the disease. In an interview (2011), Doty said: "Before the crisis years of the AIDS epidemic I had that sense that one does of a long, expansive living ahead of me. When my friends and my partner began to sicken and die around me, that shifted everything in a sense that you just don't know what prospect is ahead of you."

The first of these books is *My Alexandria* (1993), which the critic Mark Wunderlich has termed "the finest in-depth literary investigation of the AIDS crisis, and at its center is the anticipation of tremendous loss, an ache that pervades each of the poems." The second, *Atlantis* (1995), is a complex, sensuous series of poems about love, death, loss, and grief, with vivid descriptions of Provincetown, Massachusetts, on the tip of Cape Cod, where Doty and Roberts lived—Roberts died in February 1994; the title-poem is especially strong and forthright, beautifully written, as is the charged, bold, angry poem, "Homo Will Not Inherit." The third, *Heaven's Coast: A Memoir* (1997), is a prose work that focuses on the period in Doty's and Roberts's lives that began in May 1989 when Roberts was told that he was HIV-positive (Doty tested negative). In memoir form, Doty tells the story of Roberts's decline and death, and other losses that he suffered (including the death of another close friend from AIDS), and the network of gay and lesbian friends and supporters (Doty includes parts of letters from these friends) who consoled and sustained him.

Doty's literary precursors and influences, as gay poets, include Walt Whitman and the Greek writer C. P. Cavafy (1863–1933). But it is important to recognize the significance and impact of the original work, as a gay writer of prose and poetry, that Doty has done. As Mark Wunderlich has observed: "Simply by being open about his sexuality, by using it as a subject for his poems without having it to be *the* subject, Doty created a new model for gay and lesbian poets and poetry."

Another of Doty's noteworthy books is *Firebird* (1999), a memoir of growing up gay, from age six to sixteen. He also is the author of *Dog Years* (2007), a *New York Times* best seller, about Doty's relationship with his two dogs, Beau and Arden. A book of literary criticism, *The Art of Description*

(2010), offers a stimulating account of what "description" is, how it works, and how it is performed by a range of poets, such as Hart Crane, Elizabeth Bishop, and Allen Ginsberg.

To appreciate the range and depth of Doty's achievement as a poet, the best beginning is *Fire to Fire: New and Selected Poems* (2008), winner of the National Book Award for poetry. The poet Philip Levine has paid tribute to this body of work: "If it were mine to invent the poet to complete the century of William Carlos Williams and Wallace Stevens, I would create Mark Doty just as he is, a maker of big, risky fearless poems in which ordinary human experience becomes music."

See the biographical profile by Mark Wunderlich, *Ploughshares*, 25:1 (Spring 1999), 183–189. Also an interview with Mark Doty, *Five Points: A Journal of Literature and Art*, 12:2 (2008) 111–128. For a good example of Doty's skill as a literary critic, see "Form, Eros, and the Unspeakable: Whitman's Stanzas," *Virginia Quarterly Review*, 81:2 (Spring 2005), 66–78.

Photograph of the NAMES Project AIDS Memorial quilt, Washington, D.C., by Carol M. Highsmith. Often abbreviated to the AIDS Memorial quilt, this enormous quilt weighs 54 tons and was made as a memorial to and a celebration of the lives of those who died of AIDS-related illness. The first showing of the quilt was in 1987 on the National Mall in Washington, D.C., and was last displayed in full on the Mall in 1996.

Golden Retrievals[1]

Fetch? Balls and sticks capture my attention
seconds at a time. Catch? I don't think so.
Bunny, tumbling leaf, a squirrel who's—oh
joy—actually scared. Sniff the wind, then

I'm off again: muck, pond, ditch, residue   5
of any thrillingly dead thing. And you?
Either you're sunk in the past, half our walk,
thinking of what you never can bring back,

or else you're off in some fog concerning
—tomorrow, is that what you call it? My work: 10
to unsnare time's warp (and woof!), retrieving,
my haze-headed friend, you. This shining bark,

a Zen[2] master's bronzy[3] gong, calls you here,
entirely, now: bow-wow, bow-wow, bow-wow.

                                                          [1998]

At the Gym

This salt-stain spot
marks the place where men
lay down their heads,
back to the bench,

and hoist nothing   5
that need be lifted
but some burden they've chosen
this time: more reps,

more weight, the upward shove
of it leaving, collectively,   10
this sign of where we've been:
shroud-stain, negative

flashed onto the vinyl
where we push something
unyielding skyward,   15
gaining some power

---

[1]In an author's note, Mark Doty says that this poem, "for Robert Jones, is spoken by Beau." Jones is
one of his friends and his editor, and Beau is the name of one of Doty's dogs.
[2]Zen, a Japanese school of Mahayana Buddhism emphasizing the value of meditation and intuition.
[3] Bronze.

at least over flesh,
which goads with desire,
and terrifies with frailty.
Who could say who's   20

added his heat to the nimbus
of our intent, here where
we make ourselves:
something difficult

lifted, pressed or curled,   25
Power over beauty,
power over power!
Though there's something more

tender, beneath our vanity,
our will to become objects   30
of desire: we sweat the mark
of our presence onto the cloth.

Here is some halo
the living made together.

[2002]

AURORA LEVINS MORALES ■ (1954–)

Born in Puerto Rico, Aurora Levins Morales came to the United States with her family in 1967. She has lived in Illinois and New Hampshire and now resides in the San Francisco Bay area. The author of stories, essays, prose poems, and poems, she has held teaching positions at the University of California at Berkeley, the University of Minnesota, and Pacifica Graduate Institute.

"Child of the Americas" is from a book written by Levins Morales and her mother, Rosario Morales, *Getting Home Alive* (1986), which includes essays, stories, and poems about their lives, languages, cultures, and religions. Rosario Morales was born in Puerto Rico, the daughter of Russian-Jewish immigrants who moved to New York when she was a child. In *Medicine Stories: History, Culture, and the Politics of Integrity* (1998), Levins Morales presents essays on social identity, ecology, children's liberation, and other topics. Her *Remedios: Stories of Earth and Iron from the History of Puertorriqueflas* (1998) is a prose poetry retelling of Latina history.

For further study, see *Biographical Dictionary of Hispanic Literature in the United States: The Literature of Puerto Ricans, Cuban Americans, and Other Hispanic Writers*, ed. Nicolás Kanellos (1989); *Puerto Rican Writers at Home in the USA: An Anthology*, ed. Faythe Turner (1991); and Lisa Sánchez-González, *Boricua Literuature: A Literary History of the Puerto Rican Diaspora* (2001).

Child of the Americas

I am a child of the Americas.
a light-skinned mestiza[1] of the Caribbean,
a child of many diaspora,[2] born into this continent at a crossroads.

I am a U.S. Puerto Rican Jew,
a product of the ghettos of New York I have never known.   5
An immigrant and the daughter and granddaughter of immigrants.
I speak English with passion: it's the tongue of my consciousness,
a flashing knife blade of crystal, my tool, my craft.

I am Caribeña, island grown. Spanish is in my flesh,
ripples from my tongue, lodges in my hips: 10
the language of garlic and mangoes,
the singing in my poetry, the flying gestures of my hands.

---

[1] A woman of mixed racial ancestry (Spanish).
[2] Originally referring to the dispersion of Jews from Israel around the sixth century BCE. It now may mean the dispersion of any group of people from their original homeland.

I am of Latinoamerica, rooted in the history of my continent:
I speak from that body.

I am not african. Africa is in me, but I cannot return.   15
I am not taína.[3] Taíno is in me, but there is no way back.
I am not european. Europe lives in me, but I have no home there.

I am new. History made me. My first language was spanglish.[4]
I was born at the crossroads
and I am whole.   20

[1986]

---

[3]A native people of the Caribbean. Taíno culture was highly developed when Columbus reached
Hispaniola in 1492. Most information regarding Taíno society comes from sixteenth-century Spanish
chronicles and archaeological excavation. The Taíno legacy survives in the ethnic heritage of many
Caribbean peoples and in words borrowed from their language, including *barbecue, canoe, hammock,*
and *hurricane.*
[4]A mixture of Spanish and English, Spanglish often involves the conversion of an English word to a
Spanish one.

Born in San Francisco, California, Lorna Dee Cervantes founded a press and a poetry magazine, *Mango*, focusing on Chicano literature. In 1978 she received a fellowship from the National Endowment for the Arts, and in 1981 she published her first book of poems, *Emplumada*. It includes "Refugee Ship," about a speaker isolated from her origins and uncertain about her future. Her other books include *Drive: The First Quartet: New Poems, 1980–2005* (2006).

For background, see Alfred Arteaga, *Chicano Poetics: Heterotexts and Hybridities* (1997); Louis Gerard Mendoza, *Historia: The Literary Making of Chicana and Chicano Cultural Studies in the 21st Century*, eds. Arturo J. Aldama and Naomi H. Quìnonez (2002).

Refugee Ship

Like wet cornstarch, I slide
past my grandmother's eyes. Bible
at her side, she removes her glasses.
The pudding thickens.

Mama raised me without language.   5
I'm orphaned from my Spanish name.
The words are foreign, stumbling
on my tongue. I see in the mirror
my reflection: bronzed skin, black hair.

I feel I am a captive   10
aboard the refugee ship.
The ship that will never dock.
El barco que nunca atraca.[1]

[1981]

---

[1]The boat that never docks (Spanish).

CATHY SONG ▓ (1955—)

Born in Hawaii of Chinese and Korean heritage, Cathy Song attended the University of Hawaii, where she studied with the poet-critic John Unterecker, and then Wellesley College (BA, 1977) and Boston University (MA, 1981). Her books include *Picture Bride* (1983, winner of the Yale Younger Poets Award), *Squares of Light* (1988), *School Figures* (1994), *The Land of Bliss* (2001), and *Cloud Moving Hands* (2007). Song has received many honors and prizes for her work. She lives in Honolulu with her husband and three children.

Song is one of the major voices in Asian American poetry, yet at the same time, as one critic noted, she "has consistently maintained that the rich world she creates within her narrative poetry transcends her own ethnic and regional background, and resists classification as an 'Asian American' or 'Hawaiian' writer.... The moral ties that bind women to children and parents, to their community, to tradition, and to the land are continuously interwoven throughout her verse." Song thus places special emphasis on the role of the imagination as the element that connects poet and reader. In response to an interviewer who asked if the imagination "liberates" the reader, she replied:

> Exactly. To appreciate a good book, to be able to respond to a piece of music, a work of art, a human situation, then be able to make sense of it all through language. We're all going to toil. We desperately need our imagination.

For critical discussion, *see* Gayle K. Fujita-Sato, "'Third World' as Place and Paradigm in Cathy Song's *Picture Bride*," *MELUS* 15 (Spring 1988), 49–72; and "Cathy Song," in *Dictionary of Literary Biography, Volume 169: American Poets Since World War II*, ed. Joseph Conte (1996), 267–274.

The White Porch

I wrap the blue towel
after washing,
around the damp
weight of hair, bulky
as a sleeping cat,   5
and sit out on the porch.
Still dripping water,
it'll be dry by supper,
by the time the dust
settles off your shoes,   10
though it's only five

past noon. Think
of the luxury: how to use
the afternoon like the stretch
of lawn spread before me. 15
There's the laundry,
sun-warm clothes at twilight,
and the mountain of beans
in my lap. Each one,
I'll break and snap 20
thoughtfully in half.

But there is this slow arousal.
The small buttons
of my cotton blouse
are pulling away from my body. 25
I feel the strain of threads,
the swollen magnolias
heavy as a flock of birds
in the tree. Already,
the orange sponge cake 30
is rising in the oven.
I know you'll say it makes
your mouth dry
and I'll watch you
drench your slice of it 35
in canned peaches
and lick the plate clean.

So much hair, my mother
used to say, grabbing
the thick braided rope 40
in her hands while we washed
the breakfast dishes, discussing
dresses and pastries.
My mind often elsewhere
as we did the morning chores together. 45
Sometimes, a few strands
would catch in her gold ring.
I worked hard then,
anticipating the hour
when I would let the rope down 50
at night, strips of sheets,
knotted and tied,
while she slept in tight blankets.
My hair, freshly washed

like a measure of wealth,
like a bridal veil.
Crouching in the grass,
you would wait for the signal,
for the movement of curtains
before releasing yourself   60
from the shadow of moths.
Cloth, hair and hands,
smuggling you in.

[1983]

Chinatown

1

Chinatowns: they all look alike.
In the heart
of cities. Dead
center: fish eyes
blinking between   5
red-light & ghetto,
sleazy movie houses
& oily joints.

A network of yellow tumors,
throbbing insect wings.
Lanterns of moths   10
and other shady characters:
cricket bulbs & roach eggs
hatching in the night.

2

Grandmother is gambling.
Her teeth rattle: Mah-Jongg tiles.[1]   15

She is the blood bank
we seek
for wobbly supports.

Building
on top of one another,   20
bamboo chopstick tenements

[1]A Chinese game for four people. Introduced into Europe and North America in the early 1920s, mah-jongg is played with 136 small tiles divided into several suits representing natural and mythological entities, such as dragons and winds.

pile up like noodles.
Fungus mushrooming,
hoarding sunlight
from the neighbors   25
as if it were rice.

Lemon peels
off the walls so thin,
abalone[2] skins.
Everyone can hear.   30

3

First question,
Can it be eaten?
If not, what good
is it, is anything?

Father's hair is gleaming   35
like black shoe polish.
Chopping pork & prawns,
his fingers emerge
unsliced, all ten intact.

Compact muscles taut,   40
the burning cigarette
dangling from his mouth,
is the fuse to the dynamite.

Combustible material.
Inflammable.   45
Igniting each other
when the old men talk
stories on street corners.
Words spark & flare out,
firecrackers popping on sidewalks.   50
Spitting insults, hurled garbage
exploding into rancid odors:
urine & water chestnuts.

4

Mother is swollen again.
Puffy & waterlogged.   55
Sour plums
fermenting in dank cellars.

[2]A mollusk; also called an ear-shell or sea-ear.

She sends the children
up for air.
Sip it like tea.   60

5

The children are the dumplings
set afloat.
Little boats
bobbing up to surface
in the steamy cauldron.   65

The rice & the sunlight
have been saved for this:

Wrap the children
in wonton skins,
bright quilted bundles   70
sewn warm with five spices.

Jade, ginger root,
sesame seed, mother-of-pearl
& ivory.

Light incense to a strong wind.   75
Blow the children away,
one at a time.

                                        [1983]

Heaven

He thinks when we die we'll go to China.
Think of it—a Chinese heaven
where, except for his blond hair,
the part that belongs to his father,
everyone will look like him.   5
China, that blue flower on the map,
bluer than the sea
his hand must span like a bridge
to reach it.
An octave away.   10

I've never seen it.
It's as if I can't sing that far.
But look—
on the map, this black dot.
Here is where we live,   15

on the pancake plains
just east of the Rockies,
on the other side of the clouds.
A mile above the sea,
the air is so thin, you can starve on it.   20
No bamboo trees
but the alpine equivalent,
reedy aspen with light, fluttering leaves.
Did a boy in Guangzhou[1] dream of this
as his last stop?   25

I've heard the trains at night
whistling past our yards,
what we've come to own,
the broken fences, the whiny dog, the rattletrap cars.
It's still the wild west,   30
mean and grubby,
the shootouts and fistfights in the back alley.
With my son the dreamer
and my daughter, who is too young to walk,
I've sat in this spot   35
and wondered why here?
Why in this short life,
this town, this creek they call a river?

He had never planned to stay,
the boy who helped to build   40
the railroads for a dollar a day.[2]
He had always meant to go back.
When did he finally know
that each mile of track led him further away,
that he would die in his sleep,   45
dispossessed,
having seen Gold Mountain,[3]
the icy wind tunneling through it,
these landlocked, makeshift ghost towns?

It must be in the blood,   50
this notion of returning.

[1]The area of China formerly known as Canton, located in the south part of China at the mouth of the
Pearl River.
[2]Chinese immigrant workers were instrumental in building the transcontinental railroad at the end of
the nineteenth century.
[3]When news of the discovery of gold in California reached Guangzhou, thousands of Chinese came to
America and joined the Gold Rush. In 1852, about 25,000 Chinese arrived at San Francisco. The city was
sometimes called "Gold Mountain" by these immigrants.

It skipped two generations, lay fallow,
the garden an unmarked grave.
On a spring sweater day
it's as if we remember him.   55
I call to the children.
We can see the mountains
shimmering blue above the air.
If you look really hard
says my son the dreamer,   60
leaning out from the laundry's rigging,
the work shirts fluttering like sails,
you can see all the way to heaven.

[1988]

LI-YOUNG LEE ■ (1957—)

Li-Young Lee was born in Jakarta, Indonesia. His parents were Chinese, and his father, while living in China, was a personal physician to Mao Zedong. Lee's father relocated his family to Indonesia, and, later, after periods in Hong Kong, Macau, and Japan, to the United States, where the family settled in 1964.

Lee attended the universities of Pittsburgh and Arizona and the State University of New York at Brockport. He has been a teacher at Northwestern, the University of Iowa, and other schools. Lee's books of poetry include *Rose* (1986), *The City in Which I Love You* (1991), *Book of My Nights* (2001), and *Behind My Eyes* (2008). He is also the author of a memoir, *The Winged Seed: A Remembrance* (1995). He, his wife, and their two sons live in Chicago, Illinois.

Lee's poetry, it has been noted, highlights "his perceptions of the Chinese diaspora, his understanding and acceptance of his own father, and his identity as formed in relation to his native and adopted languages." Of his creative work in the English language, Lee said, "I'm highly aware that I'm a guest in the language. I'm wondering if that's not the truth for all of us, that somehow we're all guests in language, that once we start speaking any language somehow we bow to that language at the same time we bend that language to us."

For commentary, see Sam Hamill, "A Fool's Paradise," *American Poetry Review* 20:2 (March–April 1991), 33–40; and Zhou Xiaojing, "Inheritance and Invention in Li-Young Lee's Poetry," *MELUS* 21:1 (Spring 1996), 113–132.

The Gift

To pull the metal splinter from my palm
my father recited a story in a low voice.
I watched his lovely face and not the blade.
Before the story ended, he'd removed
the iron sliver I thought I'd die from.   5

I can't remember the tale,
but hear his voice still, a well
of dark water, a prayer.
And I recall his hands,
two measures of tenderness   10
he laid against my face,
the flames of discipline
he raised above my head.

Had you entered that afternoon
you would have thought you saw a man   15
planting something in a boy's palm,
a silver tear, a tiny flame.
Had you followed that boy
you would have arrived here,
where I bend over my wife's right hand.   20

Look how I shave her thumbnail down
so carefully she feels no pain.
Watch as I lift the splinter out.
I was seven when my father
took my hand like this,   25
and I did not hold that shard
between my fingers and think,
Metal that will bury me,
christen it Little Assassin,
Ore Going Deep for My Heart.   30
And I did not lift up my wound and cry,
Death visited here!
I did what a child does
when he's given something to keep.
I kissed my father.   35

[1986]

Mnemonic[1]

I was tired. So I lay down.
My lids grew heavy. So I slept.
Slender memory, stay with me.

I was cold once. So my father took off his blue sweater.
He wrapped me in it, and I never gave it back.   5
It is the sweater he wore to America,
this one, which I've grown into, whose sleeves are too long,
whose elbows have thinned, who outlives its rightful owner.
Flamboyant blue in daylight, poor blue by daylight,
it is black in the folds.   10

A serious man who devised complex systems of numbers and rhymes
to aid him in remembering, a man who forgot nothing, my father
would be ashamed of me.

[1]A device to aid the memory, especially a pattern of letters or associations that assists in remembering
something.

Not because I'm forgetful,
but because there is no order   15
to my memory, a heap
of details, uncatalogued, illogical.
For instance:
God was lonely. So he made me.
My father loved me. So he spanked me.   20
It hurt him to do so. He did it daily.

The earth is flat. Those who fall off don't return.
The earth is round. All things reveal themselves to men only gradually.

I won't last. Memory is sweet.
Even when it's painful, memory is sweet.   25

Once, I was cold. So my father took off his blue sweater.

[1986]

This Room and Everything in It

Lie still now
while I prepare for my future,
certain hard days ahead,
when I'll need what I know so clearly this moment.

I am making use   5
of the one thing I learned
of all the things my father tried to teach me:
the art of memory.

I am letting this room
and everything in it   10
stand for my ideas about love
and its difficulties.

I'll let your love-cries,
those spacious notes
of a moment ago,   15
stand for distance.

Your scent,
that scent
of spice and a wound,
I'll let stand for mystery.   20

Your sunken belly
is the daily cup

of milk I drank
as a boy before morning prayer.

The sun on the face 25
of the wall
is God, the face
I can't see, my soul,
and so on, each thing
standing for a separate idea, 30
and those ideas forming the constellation
of my greater idea.
And one day, when I need
to tell myself something intelligent
about love, 35

I'll close my eyes
and recall this room and everything in it:
My body is estrangement.
This desire, perfection.
Your closed eyes my extinction. 40
Now I've forgotten my
idea. The book
on the windowsill, riffled by wind...
the even-numbered pages are
the past, the odd- 45
numbered pages, the future.
The sun is
God, your body is milk...
useless, useless...
your cries are song, my body's not me... 50
no good...my idea
has evaporated...your hair is time, your thighs are song...
it had something to do
with death...it had something
to do with love. 55

[1990]

MARTIN ESPADA ■ (1957—)

Born in Brooklyn, New York, Martin Espada has held a variety of jobs, including bartender, bouncer, gas station attendant, salesman, clerk, attorney, and, currently, professor in the English department of the University of Massachusetts, Amherst. He is an editor, a translator, and, above all, a poet. Among his books of poetry are *Trumpets from the Islands of Their Eviction* (1987, expanded edition, 1994), *Rebellion Is the Circle of a Lover's Hands* (1990), *City of Coughing and Dead Radiators* (1993), *Imagine the Angels of Bread: Poems* (1996), and *A Mayan Astronomer in Hell's Kitchen: Poems* (2000). Espada has also published a volume, *Zapata's Disciple* (1998), that combines free-verse poems and essays. The best approach to Espada is through *Alabanza: New and Selected Poems, 1982–2002* (2003) and *The Lover of a Subversive Is Also a Subversive: Essays and Commentaries* (2010), a collection of essays on poetry and politics.

Espada's books, observed the critic David Charlton, with their focus on working-class and immigrant experience "have consistently contributed to unglamorous histories of the struggle against injustice and misfortune." A similar point was stated strongly in reviews of and commentaries on *Rebellion Is the Circle of a Lover's Hands*, from which the following poem, "Bully," is taken. One reviewer stated that the book is "continually informed by anger at social and economic injustices," adding, "this anger gives the book considerable moral urgency." Another remarked, "The poems in this collection tell their stories and flesh out their characters deftly, without shrillness or rhetoric, and vividly enough to invite the reader into a shared sense of loss."

For context and discussion, see the interview with Martin Espada included in *Giving Their Word: Conversations with Contemporary Poets*, ed. Steven Ratiner (2002).

Bully

Boston, Massachusetts, 1987

In the school auditorium,
the Theodore Roosevelt[1] statue
is nostalgic

---

[1]Politician and statesman (1858–1919) and the twenty-sixth president of the United States. In 1897, Roosevelt was appointed Assistant Secretary of the Navy by the newly elected President William McKinley. In 1898, Roosevelt made a concerted and successful effort to initiate war with Spain over Cuba. While motivated partly by humanitarian reasons, Roosevelt was also driven by an exaggerated conception of the glory of war. "No qualities called out by a purely peaceful life stand on a level with those stern and virile virtues which move the men of stout heart and strong hand who uphold the honor of their flag in battle," he wrote. He distinguished himself during the Spanish-American War, leading U.S. troops into battle in Cuba, and later became McKinley's vice president. When McKinley was assassinated in 1901, Roosevelt assumed the presidency.

for the Spanish-American war,[2]
each fist lonely for a saber   5
or the reins of anguish-eyed horses,
or a podium to clatter with speeches
glorying in the malaria of conquest.

But now the Roosevelt school
is pronounced *Hernández*.   10
Puerto Rico has invaded Roosevelt
with its army of Spanish-singing children
in the hallways,
brown children devouring
the stockpiles of the cafeteria,   15
children painting *Taíno* ancestors[3]
that leap naked across murals.

Roosevelt is surrounded
by all the faces
he ever shoved in eugenic[4] spite   20
and cursed as mongrels, skin of one race,
hair and cheekbones of another.

Once Marines tramped
from the newsreel of his imagination;
now children plot to spray graffiti   25
in parrot-brilliant colors
across the Victorian mustache
and monocle.[5]

[1990]

---

[2]See note 1.
[3]A native people from the Caribbean.
[4]The hereditary improvement of the human race by selective breeding. In this case, the belief that the
genes of one group of people are superior to another's.
[5]An eyepiece for one eye.

SHERMAN ALEXIE ▪ (1966–)

A Spokane/Coeur d'Alene Indian, Sherman Alexie was born on the Spokane Indian Reservation in Wellpinit, Washington. For his undergraduate work he attended Gonzaga University in Spokane, Washington, but later he transferred to Washington State University in Pullman, graduating in 1991 with a major in American Studies.

Alexie has written a number of novels and collections of stories: *The Lone Ranger and Tonto Fistfight in Heaven* (1993, stories), *Reservation Blues* (1994, novel), *Indian Killer* (1996, a murder mystery), *The Toughest Indian in the World* (2000, stories), and *Ten Little Indians* (2003, stories). But, as he noted in an interview, "My beginnings are as a poet. My first form of writing was poetry. While there's certainly a strong narrative drive in my poetry, it was always about the image, and about the connection, often, of very disparate, contradictory images." Alexie's books of poetry include *The Business of Fancydancing* (1992), *I Would Steal Horses* (1992), *First Indian on the Moon* (1993), *Old Shirts & New Skins* (1993), *Water Flowing Home* (1995), *The Summer of Black Widows* (1996), *The Man Who Loves Salmon* (1998), and *One Stick Song* (2000). For *War Dances* (2009), a book of stories, essays, call-and-response sequences, and poems, Alexie received the 2010 PEN/Faulkner Award for fiction—the first Native American author to win this award. The recipient of many other awards and honors, he lives with his wife and son in Seattle, Washington.

"I write about the kind of Indian I am," Alexie said, "kind of mixed up, kind of odd, not traditional. I'm a rez [reservation] kid who's gone urban." He commented elsewhere about the responsibilities of the Native American writer: "I want us to write about the way we live.... When I see words like *the Creator, Father Sky, Mother Earth, Four Legends*, I almost feel like we're colonizing ourselves. These words, this is how we're supposed to talk—what it means to be Indian in white America. But it's not who we really are; it's not what it means to be Navajo or Spokane or Coeur d'Alene."

For a profile of Alexie's life and literary career, see Lynn Cline, "About Sherman Alexie," *Ploughshares* 26:4 (Winter 2000/2001), 197–202. See also John Newton, "Sherman Alexie's Autoethnography," *Contemporary Literature* 42:2 (Summer 2001), 413–428; and Stephen F. Evans, "'Open Containers': Sherman Alexie's Drunken Indians," *The American Indian Quarterly* 25:1 (Winter 2001), 46–72. See also *Conversations with Sherman Alexie*, ed. Nancy J. Peterson (2009), a collection of interviews.

On the Amtrak from Boston to New York City

The white woman across the aisle from me says, "Look,
look at all the history, that house
on the hill there is over two hundred years old,"
as she points out the window past me

into what she has been taught. I have learned   5
little more about American history during my few days
back East than what I expected and far less
of what we should all know of the tribal stories

whose architecture is 15,000 years older
than the corners of the house that sits   10
museumed on the hill. "Walden Pond,"[1]
the woman on the train asks, "Did you see Walden Pond?"

and I don't have a cruel enough heart to break
her own by telling her there are five Walden Ponds
on my little reservation out West   15
and at least a hundred more surrounding Spokane,

the city I pretend to call my home. "Listen,"
I could have told her. "I don't give a shit
about Walden. I know the Indians were living stories
around that pond before Walden's grandparents were born   20

and before his grandparents' grandparents were born.
I'm tired of hearing about Don-fucking-Henley saving it, too,
because that's redundant. If Don Henley's[2] brothers and sisters
and mothers and fathers hadn't come here in the first place

then nothing would need to be saved."   25
But I didn't say a word to the woman about Walden
Pond because she smiled so much and seemed delighted
that I thought to bring her an orange juice

back from the food car. I respect elders
of every color. All I really did was eat   30
my tasteless sandwich, drink my Diet Pepsi
and nod my head whenever the woman pointed out

another little piece of her country's history
while I, as all Indians have done
since this war began, made plans   35
for what I would do and say the next time

somebody from the enemy thought I was one of their own.

[1993]

---

[1]A pond in Concord, Massachusetts, on the shore of which Henry David Thoreau (1817–62) lived from
July 4, 1845, to September 6, 1847, and about which he wrote in his famous book *Walden* (1854).
[2]Lead member of the rock band The Eagles, who was active in preserving the Walden Pond area from
building developers.

■■ GALLERY ■■

America Sings the Blues:
A Collection of Songs and Poems

Blues music, which emerged and developed during the late nineteenth and early twentieth centuries, embraces a range of styles and forms, including Delta blues (Mississippi and Louisiana), Texas blues, Piedmont blues (Georgia and the Carolinas), Chicago blues, and country blues, among others. It shaped and influenced rock and roll, rhythm and blues, and jazz, as well as religious and gospel music, and hip-hop and rap. Its roots are in the history and day-to-day experience of African Americans, reaching back to slavery (with its spirituals and work songs) and then emancipation in the 1860s and forward into the long, hard period of segregation. It is no accident that the blues came into prominence during the decades of the 1890s and 1990s—the period that one historian has termed "the nadir" of American race relations—when Jim Crow laws were introduced throughout the South and the horrific practice of lynching was widespread.

Focused on love, sex, grueling work, and death, the lyrics of blues songs are direct and vivid yet at the same time complex—simple-seeming things can indeed be complicated and subtle—and highly evocative. Often, a blues lyric expresses sorrow, anguish, or outright despair. But the blues are flexible and capacious; they can also be angry and defiant, and unabashedly paradoxical. In the blues one can locate humiliation and prideful boasting, beaten-down restraint and lusty exaggeration. One can even speak of some blues songs as happy/sad: the composer's (and the singer's) goal is to feel better, touched by joy and hope, by describing and working through wounded feelings and thereby gaining a measure of control over them.

American music's history includes many stellar composers and performers of the blues, who wrote and interpreted lyrics of stunning originality. Yet the blues are communal and collaborative. Key words, phrases, images, lines, and stanzas pass from one blues song to another, and from one generation to the next. It is perhaps misleading to refer to a "blues song" as such, since so many of these songs, in their music and in their lyrics, exist in multiple versions. The words are rarely exactly the same, and even when they are, their expression in performance depends crucially on the style, approach, tone, and phrasing of the person who sings them or plays them on a guitar. The great performers of the blues have maintained that they never sang a blues song the same way twice. For them, the same song was always different, a new turn, twist, or variation upon the original, and an original that itself was always a lot or a little in motion.

The blues were sung across the South before they were written down, transcribed, and recorded. W. C. Handy (included here), the author of the hit songs "Memphis Blues" (1912) and "St. Louis Blues" (1914), was a key figure in bringing the blues to the public's attention. His success led not only to an interest among white musicians and audiences in the blues, but also to an effort on the part of white musicians to learn and perform the blues themselves. These attempts were not always successful, and many white singers and bandleaders ended up doing little more than use the term "blues" in song titles or in parts of lyrics and in promotional materials.

Many white musicians, however, have deeply respected the blues and have honored such gifted African American pioneers and practitioners of the blues as W. C. Handy, Bessie Smith, Charley Patton, Son House, Robert Johnson, Blind Lemon Jefferson, Lead Belly, Muddy Waters, and Howlin' Wolf. This vast body of work, along with the blues-saturated achievements of the giants of jazz, including Louis Armstrong and Billie Holiday, inspired many of the best-known white performers in popular music and rock and roll, from Frank Sinatra and Elvis Presley to Mick Jagger and Keith Richards of The Rolling Stones. The impact of the blues has been so extensive, affecting painting and literature as well as music, that the blues may indeed be, as one scholar has said, "the most influential art form of the twentieth century."

Langston Hughes is often identified as the poet who introduced the blues into African American literature (his first book of poetry is titled *The Weary Blues*, 1926), but as a term, idea, inspiration, and feeling, the blues also appears in the poetry and prose of a number of other African American authors active in the first decades of the twentieth century—for

African American jazz band during World War I at Camp Upton, Yaphank,
Long Island, New York State.

instance, Paul Laurence Dunbar, Sterling Brown, and Zora Neale Hurston. For African American writers since World War II—for example, Ralph Ellison, James Baldwin, and Toni Morrison—the blues have proven a rich resource of formal and thematic elements.

What follows is a collection of blues and blues-influenced songs, by W. C. Handy, Bessie Smith, Robert Johnson, Johnny Cash, Merle Haggard, and Arrested Development, and blues poems, by W. H. Auden, Linda Pastan, Allen Ginsberg, Charles Wright, Marilyn Chin, and Sherman Alexie. As this range of selections bears witness, the blues have always been a treasure of African American culture but now have become central to multicultural American music and literature as a whole. It is all of America that's singing the blues.

W. C. HANDY ■ (1873–1958)

William Christopher Handy was born in 1873, in Florence, Alabama. The son and grandson of ministers, he attended Teachers' Agricultural and Mechanical College in Huntsville, Alabama, and then worked as a schoolteacher and bandmaster. Handy secured a place in the history of American music by combining the blues idiom with the popular form of ragtime. His musical structures helped to spur improvisation,

W. C. Handy, birthplace.
W. C. Handy was born in this cabin, in Florence, Alabama, on November 16, 1873.

which proved central to the development of jazz. Among his best-known works are "Memphis Blues" (1912) and "St. Louis Blues" (1914), "the first great blues pop song" (as one critic has described it), which Handy published himself; it was one of the first ventures of a publishing firm that he established and directed for decades. He also collected anthologies of blues, folk songs, and spirituals and encouraged the study of African American musicians. One commentator on "St. Louis Blues" has said that "it is emphatically a woman's lyric all the way." But there are many recordings of "St. Louis Blues" by male singers who have altered, shifted, and modified the lyrics to make them fit a male performer. Honored as "the father of the blues," W. C. Handy died in 1958.

St. Louis Blues

I hate to see that evening sun go down
I hate to see that evening sun go down
Cause, my baby, he's gone left this town

Feelin' tomorrow like I feel today
If I'm feelin' tomorrow like I feel today   5
I'll pack my truck and make my give-a-way

St. Louis woman with her diamond ring
Pulls that man around by her
If it wasn't for her and her
That man I love would have gone nowhere, nowhere   10

I got the St. Louis Blues
Blues as I can be
That man's got a heart like a rock cast in the sea
Or else he wouldn't have gone so far from me

I love my baby like a school boy loves his pie   15
Like a Kentucky colonel loves his mint'n rye
I love my man till the day I die

[1914]

BESSIE SMITH ■ (1894–1937)

Bessie Smith, the "Empress of the Blues," was born in 1895, in Chattanooga, Tennessee. She began her career as a singer while still a child, with the mentoring and support of Ma Rainey, a popular blues vocalist of the era. By her teens, Smith was touring with Ma Rainey's group, but it was not until the early 1920s that she gained national success. Her first hit song was "Downhearted Blues," in 1923, and she quickly became one of the best-known African American singers and entertainers in the United States. Her career faltered, however, as a result of serious injuries she suffered in a car accident and also from her alcoholism.

Smith died in 1937, a powerfully independent figure in the history of the blues and jazz, and one whose raw, aggressive approach to a song influenced Billie Holiday, Louis Armstrong, and countless other singers and musicians. As a literary scholar has pointed out, Smith also has been "identified by African American feminist critics as an important foremother for black women writers, who celebrate her independence and forthright attitudes about race and sexuality." Somewhere between 150 and 160 of Smith's recordings survive, including "Thinking Blues."

The "good book" in the fourth stanza is the Bible, and the reference is to Galatians 6:7: "Be not deceived; God is not mocked: for whatsoever a man soweth, that shall he also reap."

Thinking Blues

Did you ever sit thinking with a thousand things on your mind?
Did you ever sit thinking with a thousand things on your mind?
Thinking about someone who has treated you so nice and kind?

You'll get an old letter and you begin to read
You'll get an old letter and you begin to read   5
Got the blues so had tell that man of mine I wanna be

Don't you hear me baby, knocking on your door?
Don't you hear me baby, knocking on your door?
Have you got the nerve to drive me from your door?

Have you got the nerve to say that you don't want me no more?   10
Have you got the nerve to say that you don't want me no more?
The good book said you got to reap what you sow

Take me back baby, try me one more time
Take me back baby, try me one more time
That's the only way I can get these thinking blues off my mind   15

[1928]

ROBERT JOHNSON ■ (1911–1938)

The blues singer and guitarist Robert Johnson was born in 1911, the son of a Mississippi sharecropper. At a young age he learned to play the harmonica and the guitar, inspired by such Mississippi blues players as Son House and Charley Patton, whom Johnson knew personally and whose recordings he listened to. He traveled throughout the South and Midwest, and to New York, singing in venues of all kinds. He recorded twenty-nine songs in Texas, in 1936–37. The best of these, including "Me and the Devil Blues," "Hellhound on My Trail," and "Love in Vain," he wrote himself, and he sings and plays the guitar with raw immediacy and haunting power. So masterful is he as writer, singer, and guitarist that according to myth and legend he surely must have sold his soul to the devil in exchange for this musical prowess. "Walkin' Blues" is another of Johnson's compositions, though some scholars have suggested that he may have based it on, or adapted it from, one of Son House's songs. Johnson died in 1938, in mysterious circumstance (he may have been poisoned), in a town in Mississippi.

In "Walkin' Blues," "ride the blind" means taking an illegal ride on a train—the "blind" is the walkway between two of the train's cars. "Elgin movement": Elgin is the brand name of a watch or clock.

Walkin' Blues

I woke up this mornin', feelin' 'round for my shoes.
Know 'bout 'at I got these old walkin' blues.
Woke up this mornin', feelin' 'round all for my shoes.
But you know 'bout 'at I got these old walkin' blues.
Lord, I feel like blowin' my old lonesome horn.   5
Got up this mornin', my little Bernice was gone,
Lord, I feel like blow-ooowin' my lonesome horn.
Well, I got up this mornin', all I had was gone.
Well, ah leave this morn' if I have to ride the blind.
I feel mistreated and I don't mind dyin',   10
Leavin' this morn', ah, 'f I have to ride a blind.
Babe, I been mistreated, baby, and I don't mind dyin'
Well, some people tell me that the worried blues ain't bad.
Worst old feelin' I most ever had,
Some people tell me that these old worned, old blues ain't bad.   15
It's the worst old feelin' I most ever had.
She got a Elgin movement from her head down to her toes.
Break in on a dollar most any where she goes,
Ooooo-ooo, from her head down to her toes,
(spoken: 'Oh, honey')   20
Lord, she break in on a dollar most anywhere she goes.

[1936?]

W. H. A U D E N ■ (1907–1973)

One of the major poet-critics of the twentieth-century, Wystan
Hugh Auden was born in England in 1907 and educated at Oxford
University. His first book, *Poems*, was published in 1930, and it established him as an important figure in both literary and left-wing
political circles. In early 1939, Auden emigrated to the United States,
where in 1946 he became an American citizen. He is thus both an
English and an American writer. He lectured and taught widely in
colleges and universities in the United States, and in England as well,
holding an appointment as professor of poetry at Oxford from 1956
to 1961. Auden died in 1973. His *Collected Poems* was published three
years later. Auden's poem has been published both with and without
the title "Funeral Blues"; sometimes the poem is given the title of its
first line. The poem became all the more widely known because of its
significance in the film *Four Weddings and a Funeral* (1994); it is the
poem read by Matthew (John Hannah) at the funeral of his partner
Gareth (Simon Callow).

Funeral Blues

Stop all the clocks, cut off the telephone,
Prevent the dog from barking with a juicy bone,
Silence the pianos and with muffled drum
Bring out the coffin, let the mourners come.

Let aeroplanes circle moaning overhead   5
Scribbling on the sky the message He Is Dead,
Put crêpe bows round the white necks of the public doves,
Let the traffic policemen wear black cotton gloves.

He was my North, my South, my East and West,
My working week and my Sunday rest,   10
My noon, my midnight, my talk, my song;
I thought that love would last for ever: I was wrong.

The stars are not wanted now; put out every one,
Pack up the moon and dismantle the sun,
Pour away the ocean and sweep up the wood;   15
For nothing now can ever come to any good.

[1940]

JOHNNY CASH ■ (1932–2003)

One of the giants of country music, a singer and a songwriter who, in the words of one scholar, "always sought directness and simplicity" and composed "stark, austerely elegant music," Johnny Cash was born in Arkansas in 1932. After high school, he worked in an automobile factory in Detroit, Michigan, and later joined the U.S. Air Force. After completing military service, he settled in Memphis, Tennessee, and in 1955 made his debut as a singer with a recording for Sun Records. He was a popular performer during the late 1950s and 1960s, but he also suffered from drug addiction and other personal problems. In 1968, Cash married June Carter, a member of the Carter Family touring group, and he became a devout Christian. Cash received many honors, including eleven Grammy Awards. He was elected to the Rock and Roll Hall of Fame in 1992, and in 2001 he was awarded the National Medal of Arts. He died in 2003.

Folsom Prison is Folsom State prison, which opened in 1880, and which is one of the oldest prisons in California. San Antone: San Antonio, Texas. Reno: In northwest Nevada, it is known for its gambling casinos. Cash's song was released as a single in 1955. He performed it twice in concerts at Folsom State Prison. The first was in 1966, and

Folsom State Prison, cell door, 1960s. Photograph by Carol M. Highsmith.

the second, more famous, took place in the Folsom State Cafeteria, January 13, 1968, which was recorded as the album *At Folsom Prison*.

Folsom Prison Blues

I hear the train a comin', it's rollin' 'round the bend,
And I ain't seen the sunshine since I don't know when.
I'm stuck at Folsom Prison and time keeps draggin' on.
But that train keeps rollin' on down to San Antone.

When I was just a baby, my mama told me, "Son,   5
Always be a good boy; don't ever play with guns."

But I shot a man in Reno, just to watch him die.
When I hear that whistle blowin' I hang my head and cry

I bet there's rich folk eatin' in a fancy dining car.
They're prob'ly drinkin' coffee and smokin' big cigars,   10
But I know I had it comin', I know I can't be free,
But those people keep a movin', and that's what tortures me.

Well, if they free me from this prison, if that railroad train was mine,
I bet I'd move on over a little farther down the line,
Far from Folsom Prison, that's where I want to stay,   15
And I'd let that lonesome whistle blow my blues away.

[1955]

MERLE HAGGARD ▓ (1937—)

"He has written blues and folk songs," one music critic has said about Merle Haggard, "social commentaries and classic love songs, protest and anti-protest, gospel and ballads, prison and train songs, drinking songs, and updates of blue yodels." Another has compared him to the jazz and blues singer Billie Holiday for his ability to communicate the depths of "heartache and depression."

Haggard was born in Bakersfield, California, in 1937; his parents had moved west from Oklahoma, making their home in an old railroad car. He was a rebellious child and teenager, and even as he began in the 1950s to show talent as a singer, he was frequently in trouble with the law. Late in 1957, Haggard was arrested for robbery and sent to San Quentin prison; he was paroled in 1960 and turned his life around. During the early 1960s, reentering the country-music scene, he toured with his own band and gained renown as a singer, songwriter, and performer. One of his streaks, beginning in 1967, included thirty-seven consecutive top-ten hits, twenty-three of which reached number one. The recipient of many awards, Haggard was inducted into the Country Music Hall of Fame in 1994.

Working Man Blues

It's a big job just gettin' by with nine kids and a wife
I been a workin' man dang near all my life
I'll be working long as my two hands are fit to use
I'll drink my beer in a tavern,
Sing a little bit of these working man blues   5

I keep my nose on the grindstone, I work hard every day
Might get a little tired on the weekend, after I draw my pay
But I'll go back workin', come Monday morning I'm right back
    with the crew
I'll drink a little beer that evening,
Sing a little bit of these working man blues   10

Hey hey, the working man, the working man like me
I ain't never been on welfare, that's one place I won't be
Cause I'll be working long as my two hands are fit to use
I drink a little beer in a tavern
Sing a little bit of these working man blues   15

Sometimes I think about leaving, do a little bumming around
I wanna throw my bills out the window catch a train to another town
But I go back working I gotta buy my kids a brand new pair of shoes
Yeah drink a little beer in a tavern,
Cry a little bit of these working man blues   20

Hey hey, the working man, the working man like me
I ain't never been on welfare, that's one place I won't be
Cause I'll be working long as my two hands are fit to use
I drink a little beer in a tavern
Sing a little bit of these working man blues   25
Yeah drink a little beer in a tavern,
Cry a little bit of these working man blues

[1969]

Mini Blues

Like a dinghy
I always lag
behind, awash
in somebody else's wake.
Or I answer   5

the low call
of the foghorn,
only to find
that what it meant
was keep away   10

[1975]

ALLEN GINSBERG ■ (1926–1997)

Allen Ginsberg was born in Newark, New Jersey, in 1926, the son of
Russian Jewish immigrants. He attended Columbia University and became friends in New York City with the writers Jack Kerouac and William S. Burroughs. Ginsberg made his big impact on the literary scene
with the publication in 1956 of the fervent, fiery, bardic *Howl and
Other Poems*—a book that led to the arrest of its publisher, Lawrence
Ferlinghetti, because of the explicit sexuality and scandalous language it contained. The following poem, "Father Death Blues," was
composed while Ginsberg was in a plane flying over Lake Michigan.

Guru: In Hinduism and Buddhism, a spiritual teacher, especially
one who imparts initiation; Buddha: a title given to the founder
of Buddhism, Siddhartha Gautama (c. 563–c. 460 BCE); Dharma: In
Buddhism, the teaching or religion of the Buddha; Sangha: the
Buddhist community of monks, nuns, novices, and laity.

Father Death Blues

Hey Father Death, I'm flying home
Hey poor man, you're all alone
Hey old daddy, I know where I'm going

Father Death, Don't cry any more
Mama's there, underneath the floor   5
Brother Death, please mind the store

Old Aunty Death   Don't hide your bones
Old Uncle Death   I hear your groans
O Sister Death   how sweet your moans

O Children Deaths go breathe your breaths   10
Sobbing breasts'll ease your Deaths
Pain is gone, tears take the rest

Genius Death your art is done
Lover Death your body's gone
Father Death   I'm coming home   15

Guru Death your words are true
Teacher Death I do thank you
For inspiring me to sing this Blues

Buddha Death, I wake with you
Dharma Death, your mind is new   20
Sangha Death, we'll work it through

Suffering is what was born
Ignorance made me forlorn
Tearful truths I cannot scorn

Father Breath once more farewell   25
Birth you gave was no thing ill
My heart is still, as time will tell.

[1976]

CHARLES WRIGHT ▪ (1935–)

The poet and translator Charles Wright was born in Pickwick Dam,
Tennessee, in 1935, and educated at Davidson College and the
University of Iowa. He began writing poetry in the late 1950s while
he was serving in Verona, Italy, in the U.S. Army's Intelligence Unit.
Wright has taught at the University of California at Irvine, and at the
University of Virginia. His work as a poet has been collected in two
volumes, *Country Music: Selected Early Poems* (1982; 2nd ed., 1991)
and *Negative Blue: Selected Later Poems* (2000).

Laguna (Spanish for "lake" or "lagoon") Beach, located in Orange
County, California, is a beautiful resort area. The rich and famous often vacation there, and it is well known too for its theater, arts, and
literary events and activities.

Laguna Blues

It's Saturday afternoon at the edge of the world.
White pages lift in the wind and fall.
Dust threads, cut loose from the heart, float up and fall.
Something's off-key in my mind.
Whatever it is, it bothers me all the time.   5

It's hot, and the wind blows on what I have had to say
I'm dancing a little dance.
The crows pick up a thermal that angles away from the sea.

I'm singing a little song.
Whatever it is, it bothers me all the time.   10

It's Saturday afternoon and the crows glide down,
Black pages that lift and fall.
The castor beans and the pepper plant trundle their weary heads.
Something's off-key and unkind.
Whatever it is, it bothers me all the time.   15

[1981]

MARILYN CHIN ■ (1955—)

Born in Hong Kong in 1955 and raised in Portland, Oregon, Marilyn
Chin is the author of *Dwarf Bamboo* (1987), *The Phoenix Gone, The
Terrace Empty* (1994), and *Rhapsody in Plain Yellow* (2002). Her other
publications include, as coeditor, *Dissident Song: A Contemporary
Asian American Anthology* (1991) and, as co-translator, *The Selected
Poems of Ai Qing* (1985). The recipient of two National Endowment
for the Arts Writing Fellowships and other honors and awards, Chin
teaches in the MFA Program at San Diego State University.

Hirsute: hairy, shaggy, bushy. Taoists: the Chinese philosophy
of Taoism emphasizes inner contemplation and mystical union with
nature.

We Are Americans Now, We Live In the Tundra

Today in hazy San Francisco, I face seaward
Toward China, a giant begonia—

Pink, fragrant, bitten
By verdigris and insects. I singer her

A blues song; even a Chinese girl gets the blues,   5
Her reticence is black and blue.

Let's sing about the extinct
Bengal tigers, about giant Pandas—

"Ling Ling loves Xing Xing . . . yet,
We will not mate. We are   10

Not impotent, we are important.
We blame the environment, we blame the zoo!"

What shall we plant for the future?
Bamboo, sasagrass, coconut palms? No!

Legumes, wheat, maize, old swines   15
To milk the new.

We are Americans now, we live in the tundra
Of the logical, a sea of cities, a wood of cars.

Farewell my ancestors:
Hirsute Taoists, failed scholars, farewell   20

My wetnurse who feared and loathed the Catholics,
Who called out:

> Now that the half-men have occupied Canton
> Hide your daughters, lock your doors!

[1987]

SHERMAN ALEXIE ■ (1966—)

A Spokane/Coeur d'Alene Indian, Sherman Alexie was born in 1966
on the Spokane Indian Reservation in Wellpinit, Washington. He has
written a number of fictional works, including *The Lone Ranger and
Tonto Fistfight in Heaven* (1993, stories), *Reservation Blues* (1994,
novel), *Indian Killer* (1996, a murder mystery), and *The Toughest
Indian in the World* (2000, stories). But he has noted: "My beginnings
are as a poet. My first form of writing was poetry." His recent books
of poetry include *The Man Who Loves Salmon* (1998) and *One Stick
Song* (2000).

"The Indian Girl's Home"--a group of Indian girls and Indian police at Big Foot's village
on reservation, 1890. Photograph by John C. H. Grabill.

Reservation Blues

Dancing all alone, feeling nothing good
It's been so long since someone understood

All I've seen is, is why I weep
And all I had for dinner was some sleep

You know I'm lonely, I'm so lonely   5
My heart is empty and I've been so hungry
All I need is for my hunger to ease
Is anything that you can give me please

[chorus]
I ain't got nothing, I heard no good news
I fill my pockets with those reservation blues   10
Those old, those old rez blues, those old reservation blues
And if you ain't got choices
What else do you choose?

[repeat chorus twice]

And if you ain't got choices   15
Ain't got much to lose

[1995]

ARRESTED DEVELOPMENT

Arrested Development is an American hip-hop group that came into existence as an alternative to the gangsta rap that was very popular in the 1990s. It was founded by Speech (b. 1968, Todd Thomas) and Headliner (b. 1967, Timothy Barnwell), who had met as students at the Art Institute of Atlanta. "Tennessee" is the title of a single from their album *3 Years 5 Months & 2 Days in the Life of....* The single reached #1 on the Rhythm and Blues chart, and it won the Grammy Award for Best Rap Performance by a Duo or Group in 1993. Speech has said that he was led to write the song after meeting with his brother at his grandmother's funeral in Tennessee—his brother died not long afterwards. "The rural South is a place where a lot of the African traditions are still here in their rawest form from when our ancestors were here as slaves," Speech has said. About the name of the group, he explained: "We saw the state of the black community as being in a state of arrested development. So we wanted to constantly remind ourselves of what we wanted to get beyond." The song "Tennessee," which is a kind of 1990s blues, is a response to Speech's

own two losses, and also a message of (and a quest for) spiritual regeneration, hope, and renewal.

Dyersburg: Dyersburg is a city in, and the county seat of, Dyer
County, Tennessee, seventy-seven miles north-northeast of Memphis on
the Forked Deer River; Ripley is a city in Lauderdale County, Tennessee.

Tennessee

Lord I've really been real stressed
Down and out, losin ground
Although I am black and proud
Problems got me pessimistic
Brothers and sisters keep messin up   5
Why does it have to be so damn tuff?
I don't know where I can go
To let these ghosts out of my skull
My grandmas past, my brothers gone
I never at once felt so alone   10
I know you're supposed to be my steering wheel
Not just my spare tire (home)
But lord I ask you (home)
To be my guiding force and truth (home)
For some strange reason it had to be (home)   15
He guided me to Tennessee (home)

To be my guiding force and truth (home)
For some strange reason it had to be (home)
He guided me to Tennessee (home)

[Chorus]
Take me to another place   20
Take me to another land
Make me forget all that hurts me
Let me understand your plan

Lord it's obvious we got a relationship
Talkin to each other every night and day   25
Although you're superior over me
We talk to each other in a friendship way
Then outta nowhere you tell me to break
Outta the country and into more country
Past Dyersburg into Ripley   30
Where the ghost of childhood haunts me
Walk the roads my forefathers walked
Climbed the trees my forefathers hung from

Ask those trees for all their wisdom
They tell me my ears are so young (home)   35
Go back to from whence you came (home)
My family tree my family name (home)
For some strange reason it had to be (home)
He guided me to Tennessee (home)

[Chorus]
Take me to another place   40
Take me to another land
Make me forget all that hurts me
Let me understand your plan
Now I see the importance of history
Why people be in the mess that they be   45
Many journeys to freedom made in vain
By brothers on the corner playin ghetto games
I ask you lord why you enlightened me
Without the enlightment of all my folks
He said cuz I set myself on a quest for truth   50
And he was there to quench my thirst
But I am still thirsty...
The lord allowed me to drink some more
He said what I am searchin for are
The answers to all which are in front of me   55
The ultimate truth started to get blurry
For some strange reason it had to be
It was all a dream about Tennessee

[Chorus]
Take me to another place
Take me to another land   60
Make me forget all that hurts me
Let me understand your plan

[1992]

A Chronology of Works and Events
that Shaped American Literature
1860 to Present Day

1860	Abraham Lincoln elected 16th president (receives no electoral votes from the slave states)
1860	South Carolina secedes from the Union
1860	Ralph Waldo Emerson, *The Conduct of Life*; Nathaniel Hawthorne, *The Marble Faun*
1861	Vassar College, Poughkeepsie, New York, established for women
1861	Confederate States of America formed
1861	First federal income tax (3% on incomes over $800)
1861	Rebecca Harding Davis, "Life in the Iron-Mills"; Julia Ward Howe, "The Battle Hymn of the Republic"; Harriet Jacobs, *Incidents in the Life of a Slave Girl*
1861–65	Civil War
1863	First Union "conscription act," all men age 20 to 35 and all unmarried men to age 45 subject to military service
1863	Emancipation Proclamation grants freedom to slaves in southern states
1863	Abraham Lincoln, "The Gettysburg Address"
1865	Abraham Lincoln, "Second Inaugural Address"
1865	Abraham Lincoln assassinated
1865	Civil War casualties: North—362,000 dead, 278,000 wounded; South—261,000 dead, 194,000 wounded; total U.S. population in 1860—31,183,582
1865	Union Stockyards, for meat producing and meat packing, opens in Chicago
1865	Thirteenth Amendment abolishes slavery
1865	Walt Whitman, "When Lilacs Last in the Dooryard Bloom'd"; Mark Twain, "The Notorious Jumping Frog of Calaveras County"
1866	Ku Klux Klan organized, white supremacist organization
1867	First elevated railway begins operating in New York City
1867	United States purchases Alaska territory from Russia
1868	Louisa May Alcott, *Little Women*
1869	Transcontinental Railroad completed in Utah
1869	Bret Harte, "The Outcasts of Poker Flat"
1870	Great Atlantic and Pacific Tea Company (the A & P) begins chain of grocery stores
1870	John D. Rockefeller forms Standard Oil Company of Ohio

1870	Population, 38,155,505; native born, 32,675,877; foreign born, 5,479,628; white population, 33,242,349; "colored" (i.e., black) population, 4,835,562
1871	National Rifle Association formed
1871	Walt Whitman, *Democratic Vistas*
1872	Yellowstone National Park established
1874	First electric streetcar, New York City
1875	First Kentucky Derby, Churchill Downs race track
1876	Patent issued to Alexander Graham Bell for the telephone
1876	Centennial Exposition, Philadelphia, celebrates 100th anniversary of Declaration of Independence
1876	Mark Twain, *Tom Sawyer*
1877	Phonograph invented by Thomas Alva Edison
1877	Widespread strikes by railroad workers
1877	End of Reconstruction (reorganization and reestablishment of seceded southern states into the Union)
1878	Henry James, *The Europeans*
1879	Mary Baker Eddy founds Church of Christ, Scientist, of Boston
1879	Henry James, *Daisy Miller*
1881	Tuskegee Institute, Alabama, founded by Booker T. Washington
1881	Henry James, *The Portrait of a Lady*
1880	Population, 49,371,340
1881	Clara Barton establishes National Society of the Red Cross
1883	Brooklyn Bridge, spanning 1,595.5 feet, completed between lower Manhattan and Brooklyn
1883	Mark Twain, *Life on the Mississippi*; Emma Lazarus, "The New Colossus"
1884	Buffalo Bill Cody's first Wild West Show
1885	Washington Monument, height of 555 feet, 5 1/8 inches, dedicated, Washington, D. C.
1885	William Dean Howells, *The Rise of Silas Lapham*
1886	Statue of Liberty, gift of the French government, dedicated
1886	Rioting between anarchists and police in Haymarket Square, Chicago, eight policemen killed
1886	Sarah Orne Jewett, *A White Heron and Other Stories*
1888	George Eastman introduces Kodak hand-camera
1888–91	Ghost Dance, religious movement among Native Americans
1889	Hamlin Garland, "Under the Lion's Paw"
1890	U.S. troops attack Sioux Indians at Wounded Knee, South Dakota, hundreds of Sioux men, women, and children killed or injured
1890	23,000 children working in factories in the South
1890	Emily Dickinson, *Poems*; Jacob Riis, *How the Other Half Lives*
1891	First recorded use of the word "feminist"

1891	James A. Naismith, Springfield, Massachusetts, invents basketball
1891	First Boston marathon
1891	First International Copyright law involving the United States, gives protection to authors and prohibits cross-Atlantic pirating and reprinting of works
1891	Ambrose Bierce, *Tales of Soldiers and Civilians*; Hamlin Garland, *Main-Travelled Roads*; Mary Wilkins Freeman, "The Revolt of 'Mother'"
1892	Immigration station at Ellis Island, upper New York Bay; 446,000 immigrants arrive
1892	Charlotte Perkins Gilman, "The Yellow Wall-Paper"; Frances Ellen Watkins Harper, *Iola Leroy*
1893	World's Fair held in Chicago
1893	Henry James, *The Real Thing and Other Tales*; Stephen Crane, *Maggie*
1894	Strikes and protests across the nation by coal, railroad, and textile workers
1895	Stephen Crane, *The Red Badge of Courage*
1895	National Baptist Convention of the U.S.A. formed
1895	Sears, Roebuck Company opens mail-order business
1896	Supreme Court, Plessy v. Ferguson, rules "separate but equal" treatment of races is legal
1896	First public showing of a "moving picture," New York City
1896	Edward Arlington Robinson, "Richard Cory"
1898	Stephen Crane, "The Open Boat"
1897	Subway opens in Boston
1897	Paul Laurence Dunbar, "We Wear the Mask"
1898	Spanish–American War
1899	Charles Chesnutt, *The Conjure Woman* and *The Wife of His Youth*; Frank Norris, *McTeague*
1900	Population, 74,607,225; largest city, New York City, population of 3.4 million, followed by Chicago, 1.6 million
1900	Theodore Dreiser, *Sister Carrie*
1901	Booker T. Washington, *Up from Slavery*
1902	William James, *The Varieties of Religious Experience*
1903	First cross-country trip by automobile (52 days from San Francisco to New York City)
1903	Henry Ford establishes and becomes president of Ford Motor Company
1903	Wright Brothers fly airplane, in Kitty Hawk, North Carolina; first flight, covering 120 feet, lasts 12 seconds
1903	Henry James, *The Ambassadors*; W. E. B. Du Bois, *The Souls of Black Folk*; Jack London, *The Call of the Wild*
1904	Jack London, *The Sea-Wolf*
1905–14	10 million immigrants to the United States

1905	Eugene V. Debs founds Industrial Workers of the World, labor organization
1905	Edith Wharton, *The House of Mirth*
1906	Earthquake in San Francisco (population, 400,000) area, 3,000 killed, 28,000 buildings destroyed
1906	Upton Sinclair, *The Jungle*
1907	Financial panic, stock market falls and many banks fail
1907	Henry Adams, *The Education of Henry Adams;* William James, *Pragmatism: A New Name for Some Old Ways of Thinking*
1908	Ford introduces the Model T automobile, cost $850
1908	Jack London, "To Build a Fire"
1909	Sigmund Freud, founder of psychoanalysis, lectures in the United States
1909	Explorers reach the North Pole
1909–10	National Association for the Advancement of Colored People (NAACP) founded, New York City
1909	Ezra Pound, *Personae;* Gertrude Stein, *Three Lives*
1910	Population, 91,641,195; 4% of adults have graduated from college
1911	Harriet Monroe founds *Poetry: A Magazine of Verse*
1911	Edith Wharton, *Ethan Frome*
1912	Jim Thorpe, Native American athlete, wins pentathlon and decathlon at Olympics in Sweden
1913	Important exhibition of modern art (e.g., Pablo Picasso, Marcel Duchamp), New York Armory
1913	Ford Motor Company begins assembly-line production
1913	Willa Cather, *O Pioneers!;* Robert Frost, *A Boy's Will*
1914	Opening of Panama Canal, 40 miles in length, cost $365 million
1914–20	"Great Migration" of African Americans to the North
1914	Robert Frost, *North of Boston;* Amy Lowell, "The Captured Goddess"
1914–18	World War I
1915	Edgar Lee Masters, *Spoon River Anthology*
1916	H. D. (Hilda Doolittle), *Sea Garden;* Carl Sandburg, *Chicago Poems*
1916	First birth-control clinic opens, Brooklyn, New York
1916	Louis D. Brandeis, first Jew appointed to U.S. Supreme Court
1917	United States enters World War I
1917	First woman, Jeanette Rankin (Republican, California) elected to U.S. House of Representatives
1917	Abraham Cahan, *The Rise of David Levinsky;* T. S. Eliot, *Prufrock and Other Observations;* Susan Glaspell, *Trifles;* Edna St. Vincent Millay, *Renascence and Other Poems*
1918	Influenza epidemic kills 500,000 in the United States, 20 million deaths worldwide

1919	Sherwood Anderson, *Winesburg, Ohio*; Amy Lowell, *Pictures of the Floating World*; H. L. Mencken, *The American Language*
1920	Prohibition of the manufacture and sale of alcoholic beverages begins with ratification of Eighteenth Amendment
1920	Nineteenth Amendment gives right to vote to women
1920	Edith Wharton, *The Age of Innocence*; Sinclair Lewis, *Main Street*; Eugene O'Neill, *The Emperor Jones*; Ezra Pound, "Hugh Selwyn Mauberley"
1921	Nicola Sacco and Bartolomeo Vanzetti, anarchists, convicted of murder, believed by many to be innocent, leading to widespread protests; executed in 1927
1921	Langston Hughes, "The Negro Speaks of Rivers"; Edward Arlington Robinson, *Collected Poems*
1922	T. S. Eliot, *The Waste Land*; Sinclair Lewis, *Babbitt*; Eugene O'Neill, *The Hairy Ape*; Claude McKay, "America"
1923	Teapot Dome, political scandal affecting President Harding's and later President Coolidge's administrations
1923	E. E. Cummings, "Buffalo Bill's"; Wallace Stevens, *Harmonium*; Jean Toomer, *Cane*; William Carlos Williams, "The Red Wheelbarrow"
1925	Scopes Trial, Tennessee, about teaching of theory of evolution in public schools
1925	Countee Cullen, *Color*; Theodore Dreiser, *An American Tragedy*; F. Scott Fitzgerald, *The Great Gatsby*
1926	Book-of-the-Month Club begins
1926	Langston Hughes, *The Weary Blues*; Ernest Hemingway, *The Sun Also Rises*; Marianne Moore, "Poetry"
1927	First "talking" movie, *The Jazz Singer*
1927	Flight by Charles Lindbergh, New York to Paris, 3,600 miles, 33.5 hours
1927	Mississippi Valley floods, hundreds drown, 600,000 homeless
1927	Baseball star Babe Ruth hits 60 home runs
1927	Greyhound Bus begins service from Los Angeles to New York City, 3,400 hundred miles, 5 days and 14 hours
1928	Nella Larsen, *Quicksand*
1929	New York Stock Market crashes; Great Depression begins
1929	Ernest Hemingway, *A Farewell to Arms*; William Faulkner, *The Sound and the Fury*; Thomas Wolfe, *Look Homeward, Angel*
1930	William Faulkner, *As I Lay Dying*; Hart Crane, *The Bridge*; Katherine Anne Porter, *Flowering Judas and Other Stories*
1931	William Faulkner, "That Evening Sun"
1932	Franklin Delano Roosevelt elected 32nd president
1932	William Faulkner, *Light in August*
1933	Prohibition repealed

1933–38	New Deal legislation, social and economic policies and reforms launched during Roosevelt's administration
1933	Frances Perkins, secretary of labor, first woman member of presidential cabinet
1933	Gertrude Stein, *The Autobiography of Alice B. Toklas*; Zora Neale Hurston, "The Gilded Six-Bits"
1934	F. Scott Fitzgerald, *Tender Is the Night*
1935	Social Security Act, for care of elderly, poor, and disabled, passes
1935	Pan-American Airways begins trans-Pacific services, San Francisco to Manila (trans-Atlantic service begins 1939)
1935	Muriel Rukeyser, *Theory of Flight*
1936	Ernest Hemingway, "The Snows of Kilimanjaro" and "The Short Happy Life of Francis Macomber"
1937	African American boxer Joe Louis wins heavyweight championship
1937	Zora Neale Hurston, *Their Eyes Were Watching God*
1938	Thornton Wilder, *Our Town*
1939–45	World War II
1939	John Steinbeck, *The Grapes of Wrath*
1940	Population, 130,962,661, number of farms of 1,000 or more acres, 100,531, number of farms under 10 acres, 506,374
1940	Ernest Hemingway, *For Whom the Bell Tolls*; Carson McCullers, *The Heart Is a Lonely Hunter*; Richard Wright, *Native Son*
1941	Edna St. Vincent Millay, *Collected Sonnets*; Eudora Welty, *A Curtain of Green*
1941	Japanese forces attack Pearl Harbor, Hawaii
1943	T. S. Eliot, *Four Quartets*
1945	The United States drops atomic bombs on Hiroshima and Nagasaki, Japan
1945	U.S. armed forces total 7.2 million; 295,000 killed, 614,000 wounded in World War II
1945	United Nations founded
1945	Richard Wright, *Black Boy*; Tennessee Williams, *The Glass Menagerie*
1946	William Carlos Williams, *Paterson*; Robert Lowell, *Lord Weary's Castle*; Ann Petry, *The Street*; Robert Penn Warren, *All the King's Men*
1947	Jackie Robinson, first African American to play major league baseball, Brooklyn Dodgers
1947	Tennessee Williams, *A Streetcar Named Desire*
1948	Norman Mailer, *The Naked and the Dead*
1949	Arthur Miller, *Death of a Salesman*
1949	North Atlantic Treaty Organization (NATO), alliance between the United States and eleven western European nations
1949	Gwendolyn Brooks, *Annie Allen*
1950–53	Korean War; nearly 37,000 Americans killed

1950–54	Senator Joseph McCarthy investigates Communist subversion in United States
1950	Population, 149,895,183; 2,986,765 men and 2,229,525 women have completed four or more years of college
1950	Carl Sandburg, *Complete Poems*; William Faulkner, *Collected Stories*
1951	Marianne Moore, *Collected Poems*; J. D. Salinger, *The Catcher in the Rye*
1952	Ernest Hemingway, *The Old Man and the Sea*; Ralph Ellison, *Invisible Man*; Archibald MacLeish, *Collected Poems, 1917–1952*
1953	Arthur Miller, *The Crucible*; Conrad Aiken, *Collected Poems*; Saul Bellow, *The Adventures of Augie March*; James Baldwin, *Go Tell It on the Mountain*
1954	The U.S. Supreme Court in Brown v. Board of Education of Topeka, Kansas, declares segregated schools unconstitutional
1954	Sixty percent of American households own a TV set
1954	Survey reports that Americans' favorite meal is fruit cup, vegetable soup, steak and potatoes, peas, rolls and butter, pie à la mode
1954	Wallace Stevens, *Collected Poems*
1955	Rock 'n' roll music under attack for causing immorality and juvenile delinquency
1955	Montgomery, Alabama, bus boycott, begun by Rosa Parks, successfully protests the segregation of transportation system
1955	Tennessee Williams, *Cat on a Hot Tin Roof*
1956	Eugene O'Neill, *Long Day's Journey into Night*; Allen Ginsberg, *Howl and Other Poems*
1957	Office of Education reports that Soviet Union is far ahead of the United States in scientific and technical education
1957	Jack Kerouac, *On the Road*; Bernard Malamud, *The Assistant*
1958	Bernard Malamud, "The Mourners"; Vladimir Nabokov, *Lolita*
1959	Hawaii is 50th state admitted to the Union
1959	Lorraine Hansberry, *A Raisin in the Sun*; Robert Lowell, *Life Studies*; Grace Paley, *The Little Disturbances of Man*; Philip Roth, "Defender of the Faith"; Robert Duncan, *Selected Poems*
1960	John F. Kennedy elected 35th president
1960	Gwendolyn Brooks, "We Real Cool"; Robert Lowell, "For the Union Dead"; Randall Jarrell, *The Woman at the Washington Zoo: Poems and Translations*; Charles Olson, *The Maximus Poems*; John Updike, *Rabbit, Run*
1961	Peace Corps sends volunteer workers to developing countries
1961	James Baldwin, *Nobody Knows My Name*
1962	Supreme Court rules that school prayer is unconstitutional
1962	Cuban missile crisis

1962	Edward Albee, *Who's Afraid of Virginia Woolf?*; Robert Hayden, "Those Winter Sundays"; Sylvia Plath, "Daddy"; Anne Sexton, *All My Pretty Ones*
1963	Catholic Church begins use of English (rather than Latin) in services
1963	President John F. Kennedy assassinated
1963	Martin Luther King Jr., "I Have a Dream"; Thomas Pynchon, *V.*, John Crowe Ransom, *Selected Poems*
1964	Saul Bellow, *Herzog*; Amiri Baraka (LeRoi Jones), *Dutchman*
1965	Sylvia Plath, *Ariel*; A. R. Ammons, *Corsons Inlet*
1965	Voting Rights Act, civil rights legislation, requires federal supervision of state elections
1965	Medicare and Medicaid, government programs for health-care coverage
1965	*The Autobiography of Malcolm X*
1966	Truman Capote, *In Cold Blood*; Joyce Carol Oates, "Where Are You Going, Where Have You Been?"; Theodore Roethke, *Collected Poems*
1967	475,000 U.S. troops in Vietnam
1967	William Styron, *The Confessions of Nat Turner*
1968	Tet offensive in Vietnam
1968	Martin Luther King Jr. and presidential candidate Robert F. Kennedy assassinated
1968	Norman Mailer, *The Armies of the Night*; Louise Bogan, *The Blue Estuaries: Poems*, 1923–68
1969	Woodstock Music and Art Fair, Sullivan County, New York, 400,000 in attendance
1969	Stonewall riot in New York City marks beginning of gay liberation movement
1969	U.S. astronaut Neil Armstrong walks on the moon
1969	Yale, Colgate, and Bowdoin begin admitting women students
1969	John Berryman, *The Dream Songs*; Elizabeth Bishop, *Complete Poems*; Kurt Vonnegut, *Slaughterhouse Five, or The Children's Crusade*
1970	Four students killed in antiwar protest at Kent State University (Ohio)
1971	Voting age lowered to eighteen
1971	A. R. Ammons, *Collected Poems, 1951–1971*; Flannery O'Connor, *Complete Stories*; James Wright, *Collected Poems*
1972	First woman rabbi in the United States
1972	Frank O'Hara, *Collected Poems*
1973	Roe v. Wade, Supreme Court establishes women's right to an abortion within first trimester
1973	Vietnam War ends; military draft ends, all-volunteer armed forces begins
1973	Thomas Pynchon, *Gravity's Rainbow*; Adrienne Rich, *Diving into the Wreck: Poems, 1971–1972*; Alice Walker, "Everyday Use"
1973–74	Watergate scandal

1974	President Richard M. Nixon resigns
1974	Gary Snyder, *Turtle Island*
1975	John Ashbery, *Self-Portrait in a Convex Mirror*; E. L. Doctorow, *Ragtime*; Joy Harjo, *The Last Song*
1976	Elizabeth Bishop, *Geography III*; Maxine Hong Kingston, *The Woman Warrior*
1977	Toni Morrison, *Song of Solomon*; Howard Nemerov, *Collected Poems*; Leslie Marmon Silko, *Ceremony*; Allen Tate, *Collected Poems, 1919–1976*
1978	John Cheever, *Stories*; John Irving, *The World According to Garp*
1979	Three Mile Island nuclear plant, near Middletown, Pennsylvania, damaged in accident
1979	Iranians seize the American Embassy in Tehran, taking 52 people hostage; released in 1981
1979	Philip Roth, *The Ghost Writer*; Muriel Rukeyser, *Collected Poems*; John Updike, "Separating"
1980	Ronald Reagan elected 40th president in landslide victory
1980	40 percent of work force is female
1980	Study reports that half of all marriages end in divorce
1980	Toni Cade Bambara, *The Salt Eaters*; Sterling A. Brown, *Collected Poems*; Rita Dove, *The Yellow House on the Corner*; John Kennedy O'Toole, *A Confederacy of Dunces*
1981	Sandra Day O'Connor becomes first woman on U.S. Supreme Court
1981	Lorna Dee Cervantes, *Emplumada*; Sylvia Plath, *Collected Poems*
1982	Vietnam Veterans Memorial dedicated, Washington, D.C.
1982	Alice Walker, *The Color Purple*; Galway Kinnell, *Selected Poems*; James Merrill, *The Changing Light at Sandover*; Gloria Naylor, *The Women of Brewster Place*; Richard Rodriguez, *Hunger of Memory: The Education of Richard Rodriguez—An Autobiography*; Anne Tyler, *Dinner at the Homesick Restaurant*
1983	At four-year private college, average tuition is $7,475
1983	Rita Dove, *Museum*; Raymond Carver, "A Small, Good Thing"; Josephine Miles, *Collected Poems, 1930–1983*; Sharon Olds, *The Dead and the Living: Poems*; Cathy Song, *Picture Bride*; Robert Stone, *A Flag for Sunrise*
1984	Sandra Cisneros, *The House on Mango Street*; Louise Erdrich, "The Red Convertible"; David Leavitt, *Family Dancing: Stories*; David Mamet, *Glengarry Glen Ross*
1985	Louise Glück, *The Triumph of Achilles*; Jamaica Kincaid, *Annie John*
1986	Don DeLillo, *White Noise*
1986–89	Iran-Contra affair, scandal involving illegal covert actions by members of Reagan administration
1987	United States confirms 50,000 cases of AIDS

1987	Toni Morrison, *Beloved*; Philip Roth, *The Counterlife*; Richard Eberhart, *Collected Poems, 1930–1986*; August Wilson, *Fences*
1988	David Henry Hwang, *M. Butterfly*; Thomas McGrath, *Selected Poems, 1938–1988*; Richard Wilbur, *New and Collected Poems*
1989	Amy Tan, *The Joy Luck Club*
1990	U.S. census reports minority groups are 25% of population
1990	Frank Bidart, *In the Western Night: Collected Poems, 1965–1990*; Charles Johnson, *Middle Passage*
1991–92	UN force led by U.S. liberates Kuwait, defeats Iraq's army
1991	Collapse of communism in Eastern Europe and Soviet Union
1991	Amy Tan, *The Kitchen God's Wife*
1992	Bill Clinton elected 42nd president
1992	Cormac McCarthy, *All the Pretty Horses*; Mary Oliver, *New and Selected Poems*; Jane Smiley, *A Thousand Acres*
1993	Louise Glück, *The Wild Iris*; Tony Kushner, *Angels in America: Millenium Approaches*; Annie Proulx, *The Shipping News*
1993	Toni Morrison is the first African American writer to win the Nobel Prize for literature
1995	"Million Man March" of African Americans in Washington, D.C.
1995	Richard Ford, *Independence Day*; Li-Young Lee, *The Winged Seed: A Remembrance*; Terrence McNally, *Master Class*
1996	Robert Pinsky, *The Figured Wheel: New and Collected Poems, 1966–1996*
1998–99	Impeachment and acquittal of President Clinton
1999	David Ferry, *Of No Country I Know: New and Selected Poems and Translations*; Suzan-Lori Parks, *In the Blood*
2000	George W. Bush becomes 43rd president, in disputed election decided by U.S. Supreme Court
2000	Paul Auster, *The Book of Illusions*; Lucille Clifton, *Blessing the Boats: New and Selected Poems, 1988–2000*; Michael S. Harper, *Songlines in Michaeltree: New and Collected Poems*; Stanley Kunitz, *Collected Poems*
2001	Terrorist attacks destroy World Trade Center in New York City and damage Pentagon in Washington, D.C.
2001	David Auburn, *Proof*; Jonathan Franzen, *The Corrections*; Yusef Komunyakaa, *Pleasure Dome: New and Collected Poems*; Richard Russo, *Empire Falls*
2002	Sandra Cisneros, *Caramelo*
2003	United States invades Iraq, ends regime of Saddam Hussein
2004	Gay marriages begin in Massachusetts, the first state in the nation to legalize such unions; George W. Bush is reelected president
2004	Philip Roth, *The Plot Against America*; *The 9/11 Commission Report: Final Report of the National Commission on Terrorist Attacks upon the United States*, by the National Commission on Terrorist Attacks

2005	Hurricane Katrina, late August, causes catastrophic damage on the Gulf coast, more than 1,000 dead and millions homeless; eleven Asian countries devastated by tsunami in late December
2005	Zadie Smith, *On Beauty*; Joan Didion, *The Year of Magical Thinking*
2006	President Bush expresses regret for the U.S. abuse of prisoners at the Abu Ghraib prison, in Baghdad, Iraq
2006	Louise Glück, *Averno*
2007	The minimum wage increases to $5.85, up from $5.15, the first increase in 10 years
2007	Ha Jin, *A Free Life*; Alex Ross, *The Rest Is Noise: Listening to the Twentieth Century*
2008	Democratic senator Barack Obama wins the presidential election, the first African American to be elected president of the United States
2008	Tobias Wolff, *Our Story Begins: New and Selected Stories*
2009	In June speech in Cairo, Egypt, President Obama calls for "a new beginning between the United States and Muslims around the world"; in August, U.S. Senate approves nomination of Sonia Sotomayor to U.S. Supreme Court, first Hispanic Supreme Court justice and third woman to serve
2009	Lorrie Moore, *A Gate at the Stairs*
2010	World population: 6.8 billion; U.S. population: 310 million; in April, governor of Arizona, Jan Brewer (Republican), signs into law the country's most severe immigration bill, designed to identify and deport illegal immigrants
2010	Ann Beattie, *The New Yorker Stories*
2011	Tornadoes cause extensive damage throughout the South; many killed in the deadliest natural disaster in the U.S. since Hurricane Katrina.
2011	Osama bin Laden, leader of al-Qaeda, killed in Pakistan by U.S. forces.
2011	Jeffrey Eugenides, *The Marriage Plot*; Chad Harbach, *The Art of Fielding*
2012	President Barack Obama is reelected, defeating Republican candidate Mitt Romney.
2012	Junot Diaz, *This Is How You Lose Her*; Louise Glück, *Poems 1962–2012*
2013	Terrorists attack the Boston Marathon, detonating two bombs that kill three and injure hundreds of runners and spectators.

Text Credits

Williams, William Carlos, "The Dance" and "Landscape with the Fall of Icarus" from *The Collected Poems of William Carlos Williams 1939–1962, Volume II*. Copyright © 1944 by William Carlos Williams. Reprinted by permission of New Directions Publishing Corp.

Williams, William Carlos, "The Young Housewife," "Portrait of a Lady," "Spring and All," "To Elise," "The Red Wheelbarrow," "Death," and "This Is Just to Say" from *The Collected Poems 1909–1939, Volume I*. Copyright © 1938 by New Directions Publishing Corp. Reprinted by permission of New Directions Publishing Corp.

Wolfe, Thomas, "The Dark Messiah" from *You Can't Go Home Again* by Thomas Wolfe. Copyright 1940 by Maxwell Perkins, Executor, Estate of Thomas Wolfe. Copyright renewed © 1968 by Paul Gitlin, Administrator C.T.A. Estate of Thomas Wolfe. Reprinted by Permission of McIntosh and Otis, Inc.

Wright, C.D, "Tours" and "Personals" from *Steal Away: Selected and New Poems* by C.D. Wright. Copyright © 1982, 1991 by C.D. Wright. Reprinted by Permission of The Permissions Company, Inc. on behalf of Copper Canyon Press, www.coppercanyonpress.org.

Wright, Charles, "Laguna Blues" from *The World of the Ten Thousand Things: Poems 1980–1990* by Charles Wright. Copyright © 1990 by Charles Wright. Reprinted by permission of Farrar, Straus and Giroux, LLC.

Wright, James, "A Blessing," © 1961, from *Collected Poems* by James Wright. Copyright © 1971 by James Wright. Reprinted by permission of Wesleyan University Press.

Wright, James, "Autumn Begins in Martins Ferry, Ohio," © 1962, from *Collected Poems* by James Wright. Copyright © 1971 by James Wright. Reprinted by permission of Wesleyan University Press.

Wright, James, "To the Evening Star: Central Minnesota," © 1963, from *Collected Poems* by James Wright. Copyright © 1971 by James Wright. Reprinted by permission of Wesleyan University Press.

Wright, Richard, "Long Black Song" from *Uncle Tom's Children* by Richard Wright. Copyright 1936, 1937, 1938 by Richard Wright. Copyright © renewed 1964, 1965, 1966 by Ellen Wright. Reprinted by permission of HarperCollins Publishers.

Yamada, Misuye, "To the Lady" from *Camp Notes and Other Writings* by Misuye Yamada. Copyright © 1992 by Misuye Yamada. Reprinted by permission of Rutgers University Press.

Photo Credits

17: Pictorial Press Ltd/Alamy

42: Harry Mellon Rhoads/Denver Public Library

69: Bain News Service/Library of Congress Prints and Photographs Division

127: Bain News Service/Library of Congress Prints and Photographs Division

150: Bain News Service/Library of Congress Prints and Photographs Division

165: Frances Benjamin Johnston/Library of Congress Prints and Photographs Division

207: Udo J. Keppler/Library of Congress Prints and Photographs Division

223: Library of Congress Prints and Photographs Division

254: Bain News Service/Library of Congress Prints and Photographs Division

270: Lewis W. Hine/Library of Congress Prints and Photographs Division

299: Library of Congress Prints and Photographs Division

329: Marion Post Wolcott/Library of Congress Prints and Photographs Division

338: Arthur Rothstein/Corbis

363: Carl Van Vechten/Library of Congress Prints and Photographs Division

389: Carl Van Vechten/Library of Congress Prints and Photographs Division

421: Walter Albertin/Library of Congress Prints and Photographs Division

435: Carl Van Vechten/Library of Congress Prints and Photographs Division

472: akg-images/Newscom

482: Pictorial Press/Alamy

493: Carl Van Vechten/Library of Congress Prints and Photographs Division

501: Keystone Pictures USA/Alamy

572: Carl Van Vechten/Library of Congress Prints and Photographs Division

584: Carl Van Vechten/Library of Congress Prints and Photographs Division

594: Edric L. Eaton/Library of Congress Prints and Photographs Division

628: Carl Van Vechten/Library of Congress Prints and Photographs Division

645: Everett Collection/Alamy

674: Library of Congress Prints and Photographs Division

692: Jack Delano for OWI/Library of Congress Prints and Photographs Division

706: John Vachon for OWI/Library of Congress Prints and Photographs Division

748: Dorothea Lange for OWI/Library of Congress Prints and Photographs Division

749: Dorothea Lange for OWI/National Archives

781: AF archive/Alamy

864: Jack Delano/Library of Congress Prints and Photographs Division

1049: Everett Collection/Alamy

1153: Brian Harris/Alamy

1154: Carol M. Highsmith/Library of Congress Prints and Photographs Division

1156: epa european pressphoto agency b.v./Alamy

1159: Walker Evans/Everett Collection/Alamy

1161: AF archive/Alamy

1162: epa european pressphoto agency b.v./Alamy

1165: Krasilnikov Stanislav/ITAR-TASS Photo/Corbis

1169: Mick Stevens/The New Yorker Collection/www.cartoonbank.com

1173: El Chapulin/Alamy

1175: Mark Tansey/Peter Horree/Alamy

1176: akg-images/Newscom

1179: Courtesy of Vanderbilt University Special Collections and University Archives

1206: Carl Van Vechten/Library of Congress Prints and Photographs Division

1211: OWI/Library of Congress Prints and Photographs Division

1227: Library of Congress Prints and Photographs Division

1249: AP Images

1296: Library of Congress Prints and Photographs Division

1328: AF archive/Alamy

1354: Library of Congress Prints and Photographs Division

1381: Carol M. Highsmith/Library of Congress Prints and Photographs Division

1403: Library of Congress Prints and Photographs Division

1404: Library of Congress Prints and Photographs Division

1409: Carol M. Highsmith/Library of Congress Prints and Photographs Division

1415: John C.H. Grabill/Library of Congress Prints and Photographs Division

Index of Authors, Titles, and First Lines of Poems